Looking Out

Looking Out

The Growth of Global Financial Markets

U.S. investors have increasingly purchased foreign securities, and foreign investors have increasingly purchased U.S. securities. This table shows the extent of the increases of cross-border flows in selected years since 1982.

Year	U.S. Holdings of Foreign Stock (Billions of Dollars)	U.S. Holdings of Foreign Bonds (Billions of Dollars)
1982	$ 17.4	$ 61.1
1991	279.0	130.4
1998	1,407.1	450.9
1999	2,003.7	452.8
2000	1,852.9	468.0
2001	1,612.7	443.5
2002	1,345.1	410.0
2003	1,957.9	381.9
2004*	2,075.7	367.1

Year	Foreign Holdings of U.S. Stock (Billions of Dollars)	Foreign Holdings of U.S. Treasuries (Billions of Dollars)	Foreign Holdings of U.S. Corporate Bonds (Billions of Dollars)
1982	$ 88.3	$ 160.4	$ 68.3
1991	299.0	535.1	233.4
1998	1,250.3	1,622.2	607.8
1999	1,611.5	1,380.6	752.1
2000	1,643.2	1,471.4	920.6
2001	1,572.7	1,593.5	1,115.9
2002	1,260.8	1,883.6	1,266.9
2003	1,669.0	2,170.6	1,499.5
2004*	1,710.8	2,524.4	1,606.0

Note that domestic investors have a preference for foreign stocks over bonds while foreign investors prefer U.S. Treasuries, although the largest percent increase over the 1982–2003 period was in foreign ownership of U.S. stocks.

*As of June 30, 2004.

SOURCE: *Flow of Funds of the United States, Z1*, Board of Governors of the Federal Reserve System, various issues.

LOOKING OUT

Relevant international material that shows the interrelationships of global financial systems.

The Eurosystem: Europe's Central Bank
Chapter 4, p. 76

The Growth of Global Financial Markets
Chapter 15, p. 349

Capital Flows and the Mexican Peso Crisis
Chapter 27, p. 655

Cracking the Code

Measuring Unemployment

Statistics on the labor force, employment, and unemployment in the United States are gathered and published by the Bureau of Labor Statistics. Each month more than 65,000 households nationwide are surveyed. Based on their responses to a series of questions, individuals are classified as one of the following:

1. Unemployed (16 years or older, out of work, and actively looking for work)
2. Employed
3. Labor Force Participant (Employed plus Unemployed)
4. Not in the Labor Force (out of work and not actively looking for work; includes individuals who are under 16, retirees, disabled persons, and so-called discouraged workers who have lost their jobs and stopped looking for a job)

These data are then used to compute the unemployment rate, which is the percentage of the labor force unemployed:

unemployment rate = number of persons unemployed/labor force

To illustrate, in April 2004, 8.16 million people were unemployed, and the labor force totaled 146.741 million. Thus, the unemployment rate was 5.6 percent (8.16 million/146.741 million = 5.6 percent).

To appreciate the dynamics of the labor market and the relationship between the growth of the economy and unemployment, it is helpful to view the state of unemployment as a pool. Flowing into the pool are the new entrants to the labor force who have not yet found work and those who have recently lost or quit their jobs. Flowing out of the pool

CRACKING THE CODE

Shows students how to interpret the financial pages of daily newspapers.

The Stock Market
Chapter 16, p. 361

Foreign Exchange Spot and Forward Rate Quotations
Chapter 18, p. 419

Measuring Unemployment
Chapter 24, p. 587

Recap

Recap When net lenders lend directly to net borrowers, direct finance put their funds in financial intermediaries, which then lend to n nance occurs. Financial intermediaries acquire the funds of net on themselves. They use the funds to purchase the financial cla most important financial intermediaries are depository instituti deposits. Other financial intermediaries include life and casua pension funds, mutual funds, money market mutual funds, and fi

RECAP

Dispersed throughout each chapter to summarize analytical material the student should know before moving forward, and also to check if the student has mastered the preceding material.

Net Lenders and Net Borrowers
Chapter 1, p. 12

Carrying Costs
Chapter 18, p. 432

Open Market Operations and Real Balances
Chapter 21, p. 517

The **Financial System** and the **Economy**

PRINCIPLES OF MONEY & BANKING

Maureen **Burton**

California State Polytechnic University – Pomona

Ray **Lombra**

Pennsylvania State University – University Park

THOMSON

SOUTH-WESTERN

Australia · Canada · Mexico · Singapore · Spain · United Kingdom · United States

The Financial System and The Economy: Principles of Money and Banking, Fourth Edition

Maureen Burton and Ray Lombra

VP/Editorial Director:
Jack W. Calhoun

VP/Editor-in-Chief:
Dave Shaut

Sr. Acquisitions Editor:
Michael Worls

Sr. Developmental Editor:
Susanna C. Smart

Sr. Marketing Manager:
John Carey

Production Editor:
Stephanie Schempp

Production Technology Project Manager:
Peggy Buskey

Web Coordinator:
Karen Schaffer

Manufacturing Coordinator:
Sandee Milewski

Production House:
Pre-Press Company

Printer:
CTPS

Art Director:
Michelle Kunkler

Internal Designer:
Christy Carr Design

Cover Designer:
Christy Carr Design

Cover Images:
© mediacolor's/Alamy

Library of Congress Control Number:
2004113641

For more information about our products, contact us at:

Thomson Learning Academic
Resource Center
1-800-423-0563

Thomson Higher Education
5191 Natorp Boulevard
Mason, OH 45040 USA

Asia (including India)
Thomson Learning
5 Shenton Way
#01-01 UIC Building
Singapore 068808

Australia/New Zealand
Thomson Learning Australia
102 Dodds Street
Southbank, Victoria 3006
Australia

Canada
Thomson Nelson
1120 Birchmount Road
Toronto, Ontario
M1K 5G4
Canada

Latin America
Thomson Learning
Seneca, 53
Colonia Polanco
11560 Mexico
D.F.Mexico

UK/Europe/Middle East/Africa
Thomson Learning
High Holborn House
50/51 Bedford Row
London WC1R 4LR
United Kingdom

Spain (including Portugal)
Thomson Paraninfo
Calle Magallanes, 25
28015 Madrid, Spain

Burton, Maureen

California State Polytechnic University, Pomona

Maureen Burton received a BA from the University of Missouri at Columbia in 1971, an MA from California State University, Fullerton, in 1979, and a Ph.D. from the University of California at Riverside in 1986. All were in economics. She taught at Chaffey College from 1984 to 1987 and at Cal Poly Pomona since 1987 where she is a full professor. At Cal Poly Pomona, she has served as Coordinator of the Graduate Program and as Chair of the Economics Department. In addition to other publications, she co-authored an introductory text *Economics* (Harper Collins, 1987) with S. Craig Justice and *An Introduction to Financial Markets and Institutions*, (South-Western College Publishing, 2002) with Reynold Nesiba and Ray Lombra. Her main areas of research include monetary theory and financial markets.

Lombra, Raymond

Pennsylvania State University, University Park

Born in Hamden, Connecticut, Ray Lombra received a BA in Economics from Providence College in 1967 and an MA and Ph.D. from Penn State University in 1971. He served as a senior staff economist at the Board of Governors of the Federal Reserve System from 1971-1977 and specialized in financial markets analysis and the formulation and implementation of monetary policy. He joined the faculty of Penn State University in 1977, and has taught money and banking at the undergraduate level and monetary theory and policy at the graduate level for 28 years. He is a winner of the College distinguished teaching award for innovations and instruction and is the author and editor of 5 books and over 80 scholarly publications. Articles on monetary policy, the determination of interest rates, stock prices, and exchange rates, financial innovation, globalization, and expectations formation have appeared in leading journals, including the Quarterly Journal of Economics, the Journal of Money, Credit and Banking, the Journal of Monetary Economics, and the Review of Economics and Statistics.

Dedications

To my husband, Al Gagnon, as always,

and

To the new members of my family, Lance Christopher Paddock and Sara Brooke Zehntner

—Maureen Burton

Brief Contents

Contents

Chapter 4   The Overseer: The Federal Reserve System   63

Chapter 5   Financial Markets, Instruments, and Market Makers   87

Part 2 Financial Prices 107

Chapter 6   Interest Rates and Bond Prices   109

Chapter 7   The Structure of Interest Rates   133

Chapter 13   Financial Instability and Strains on the Financial System   281

Chapter 14   Regulation of the Banking System and the Financial Services Industry   305

Chapter 15   Securities Firms, Mutual Funds, and Financial Conglomerates   329

Chapter 19   The International Financial System 443

Part 5 Monetary Theory 467

Chapter 20   The Fed, Depository Institutions, and the Money 469

Chapter 21   The Demand for Real Money Balances and Market 499

Chapter 22   Financial Aspects of the Household, Business, Government, and Rest-of-the-World Sectors 527

Chapter 23   Aggregate Demand and Aggregate Supply   557

Part 6 Monetary Policy 579

Chapter 24   The Challenges of Monetary Policy   581

Chapter 25   The Process of Monetary Policy Formulation   603

Chapter 26   Policy Implementation 625

Chapter 27   Monetary Policy in a Globalized Financial System 645

Preface

INTRODUCTION TO THE TEXT

Financial markets and institutions have undergone significant changes in recent years. Technology, innovation, deregulation, competition, globalization, and financial crises have driven transformations. The explosion of international trade and capital flows has escalated the development of international currency markets. Financial institutions have entered nontraditional venues. Laws forbidding the mergers of banks, securities firms, and insurance companies have been overturned. Mega-mergers have occurred that change the scope, size, and activities of financial institutions. Changes in information and computer technologies have fostered the growth of new financial instruments and products, and the development of new and creative ways to hedge and manage risks in a globalized environment. Electronic transfers of funds have come to dominate both checks and currency as payment mechanisms, and e-cash for Internet payments is rapidly evolving. Anti-money laundering activities have become more important since the beginning of the War on Terror. Managers of financial institutions must now make decisions in this new and dynamic milieu where technological innovations are the driving force.

In the early 2000s, financial market participants face new challenges as they continue to adapt to the changing financial environment. The economy continues to recover from the last recession that began in early 2001 following the bursting of the stock market bubble. Stock prices increased over 20 percent in 2003 and continued to grow, albeit at a slower pace, in 2004. The War on Terror and wars in Afghanistan and Iraq continue to dominate the news along with record oil prices, record trade and government deficits, and a declining dollar.

Given this economic climate, the motivation in developing this text is twofold. First, to capture the ongoing changes in the financial system, particularly with regard to technology and globalization. Second, and most importantly, to present an analytical framework that enables students to understand and anticipate changes in the financial system and the accompanying changes in financial markets and institutions.

INTENDED AUDIENCE

The text is intended for an introductory undergraduate course in money and banking or financial markets analysis taught in either an economics or finance department. It may also be suitable for use in a financial markets course in an MBA Program.

CONTENTS OF THE TEXT

The Financial System and the Economy, 4th Edition, covers the traditional material found in a money and banking text and incorporates many of the recent changes and controversies within the financial services industry.

In addition, there are several unique features to this edition:

- Greater focus on technological change and its effects on the financial system.
- More thorough scrutiny of how the "modus operandi" of the Fed has dramatically changed , including the central bank's greater openness, its use of asymmetric risk management paradigms, policy regret, and other changes.
- Robust coverage of the securities industry, financial holding companies, equity and

debt markets, and the expansion of derivatives and securitizations to hedge risk.

- Greater detail in the analysis of the efficient market hypothesis.
- Continued focus on the globalization of financial markets.

This fourth edition continues to have a clear and engaging writing style and strong intuitive approach, avoiding the encyclopedic and seeking a balance between policy, theory, and institutions. Students find it easy to understand and enjoyable to read. The text makes use of many examples and analogies to illustrate how financial innovation, technological and structural change, and globalization affect the financial environment. Much attention is paid to how and why institutions evolve. Graphs and equations are used sparingly.

Financial markets are evolving at a rapid pace due to changes in technology, regulations, and globalization. We do not focus on "facts" regarding the current state of the financial system. Instead we emphasize the dynamics as to how the current state evolved and where it is likely head. We erect an analytical framework that allows students to unravel the dynamics and intricacies of the financial system.

The chapters contain many features that include examples, historical and international perspectives, and projections about the future that bring the material to life for students. Professors often view the examples that come along at the end of a lecture as a means to tie up the loose ends. We view the examples/illustrations as the nails in the wall on which we hang the analysis; our experience suggests it is the real-world dimension to the text and examples that stays with students well beyond the lecture and, indeed, the course.

A sample of topics covered in these features include recent mega-mergers among financial institutions, changes in the payments mechanism due to technology, the implicit guarantee of government-sponsored enterprise securities, buying and selling stocks over the Internet, purchasing power parity and interest rate parity, the causes of Asian financial crisis, Europe's new single currency, how price expectations are formed, the collapse of Barings Bank and Orange County, the current Federal Reserve Board, the use of intermediate targets since 1970, changes in how the discount rate is set, the flow of funds among sectors, and the bailout of Long Term Capital Management, among others.

The text also contains annotated Suggested Readings that give the students some idea about how the readings related to the material in the chapters. In addition, the Suggested Readings sections contain Internet addresses that pertain to the financial system.

Internet addresses also appear throughout the body of the text that send students to sites relevant to the topics being discussed. Some chapters have review and analytical questions and problems that direct the student to go to an Internet address to locate and analyze financial market data. Internet Applications and Interactive Quizzes can be found at the Web site for the text, http://burton.swlearning.com/.

ORGANIZATION OF THE TEXT

The Financial System and the Economy, 4th ed. is organized in six parts.

Part I consists of a five chapter introduction. The student is introduced to the economy, money and credit, financial intermediaries, the circular flow, the Federal Reserve System, and financial markets and products.

Part II consists of four chapters that focus on how interest rates and exchanges rates (financial prices) are determined and on the efficient market hypothesis.

Part III consists of six chapters on financial institutions and the forces that shape them. The roles of technology, competition, globalization, and regulations are emphasized in discussing how institutions evolve. The chapters on financial innovation, financial instability, and the securities industry have been updated.

Part IV (four chapters) focuses on financial markets including the stock market, the debt markets, the forward, futures, and options markets, and the international financial system.

Part V (four chapters) covers monetary theory including the money supply process, the demand and supply of money and credit, financial aspects of the behavior of households, firms, government, and the foreign sector, and the flow of funds among sectors. As a capstone, the aggregate demand and supply model is developed.

Part VI (four chapters) analyzes monetary policy in an increasingly globalized environment and focuses on the formulation of monetary policy by the Fed Open Market Committee and subsequent execution of the policy directive by the Trading Desk of the New York Fed. The growing need for greater international policy coordination are also addressed.

The Financial System and the Economy: Principles of Money and Banking is designed to be flexible. After completing Part I, the instructor can emphasize financial prices (Part II), financial institutions (Part III), financial markets (Part IV), monetary theory (Part V), or monetary policy (Part VI) depending on the focus of the class. In parts that are not being emphasized, chapters may be skipped.

PEDAGOGICAL FEATURES OF THE TEXT

In addition to presenting the material in a clear and concise manner, we have incorporated the following pedagogical tools to enhance the student's understanding.

- **Learning objectives** at the beginning of each chapter tell the student where the chapter is heading and what questions will be answered by studying the chapter.
- **RECAP** sections are dispersed throughout each chapter to summarize analytical material the student should know before moving forward, and also to check that the student has mastered the preceding material.
- Highlighted features include:
  - **A Closer Look** features that delve more deeply into the topic being discussed and provide enhancement material.
  - **Looking Out** boxes add relevant international material that shows how the interrelationships of global financial systems.
  - **Looking Back** features provide historical background of the foundations of current economic circumstances.
  - **Looking Forward** boxes make projections about possible future situations within the arena of the financial system and economies.
  - **Cracking the Code** features show students how to interpret the financial pages of daily newspapers, including stock, bond, Treasury bill, mutual fund, and foreign exchange quotes, and futures and options prices.
- **Key Terms** are bold-faced in the text where they are defined, listed at the end of each chapter, and also appear in the margins with definitions.
- **Summary of Major Points** are chapter summaries intended to reinforce the chapter content and aid in study for exams and quizzes, as well as provide another check for students to make sure they have not missed an important concept of the chapter.

- End-of-Chapter materials include:
  - **Review Questions, Analytical Questions**, and **Internet Questions** appear at the end of each chapter. Questions marked with an icon can be answered with a short answer or a single number. Instructors may choose to use these objective questions in larger sections.
  - Annotated **Suggested Readings** that direct the student to related material and include relevant information available on the Internet.

SUPPLEMENTS TO THE TEXT

The Financial System & the Economy offers a comprehensive and well-crafted supplements package for both students and instructors. Contact your Thomson/South-Western sales representative for more details, or visit the Burton Web site at http://burton. swlearning.com/.

- **Study Guide.** (ISBN: 0-324-28884-0) The study guide, revised by Christine Mooney of Queensborough Community College, provides chapter outlines and review questions to reinforce learning. These features include Highlights in Detail, Terms and Concepts with definitions, Fill-in questions by topic, True/False, Multiple Choice, and Essay Questions, and Problems, all with answers at the end of each chapter.
  Answers to True/False and Essay Questions, and Problems include detailed explanations.

- **Instructor's Manual.** (ISBN: 0-324-28882-4) This edition's Instructor's Manual, by Maureen Burton, includes chapter summaries, teaching tips, and solutions to all end-of-chapter questions.

- **Test Bank.** (ISBN: 0-324-28883-2) The test bank, revised by Ronnie J. Phillips of Colorado State University, contains multiple choice questions for each chapter.

- **ExamView Testing Software—Computerized Testing Software.** (ISBN: 0-324-28886-7) This testing software contains all of the questions in the printed test bank. ExamView is an easy-to-use test creation software compatible with Microsoft Windows. Instructors can add or edit questions, instructions, and answers; and select questions by previewing them on the screen, selecting them randomly, or selecting them by number. Instructors can also create and administer quizzes online, whether over the Internet, a local area network (LAN), or a wide area network (WAN).

- **Microsoft PowerPoint™ Slides.** The user-friendly slides, revised by Linda Ghent of Eastern Illinois University, serve as lecture enhancement for instructors. These consist of a set of lecture slides and a separate set of exhibits from the text, and are available to instructors only on the text web site at http://burton.swlearning.com/.

The Burton Interactive Study Center (http://burton.swlearning.com/)

The Web site designed to be used with this textbook provides a comprehensive chapter-by-chapter online study support that includes interactive quizzing, a glossary, updated and extended applications from the book, and numerous other features. Some of the highlights include:

- **Quizzes.** Interactive quizzes help students test their understanding of the chapter's concepts. Multiple-choice questions include detailed feedback for each answer. Students can email the results of a quiz to themselves and/or their instructor.

- **Key Terms Glossary.** A convenient, online glossary enables students to use the point-and-click flashcard functionality of the glossary to test themselves on key terminology.
- **Extensions of In-Text Web Features.** To streamline navigation, the Study Center links directly to Web sites highlighted in each chapter. These applications provide students with opportunities to interact with the material by performing real-world analyses. Their comments and answers to the questions posed in these features can be emailed to the instructor.

Burton Xtra! Web Site (http://burtonxtra.swlearning.com/)

By tapping into today's technology, this textbook can reach out to a variety of students with a variety of learning styles and can help instructors ensure that they address the needs of all students. The Burton Xtra! is available to be packaged with the textbook and provides access to a robust set of additional online learning tools. Burton Xtra! contains these key features:

- **E-Lectures.** Interactive E-Lectures. Difficult concepts from each chapter are explained and illustrated via Flash-animated tutorials.
- **Xtra! Quizzing.** In addition to the open-access chapter-by-chapter quizzes found at the Burton Product Support Web site (http://burton.swlearning.com), *Burton Xtra!* offers students the opportunity to practice for midterms and finals by taking more interactive quizzes.
- **e-con @pps Economic Applications.** EconNews Online, EconDebate Online, EconData Online, and EconLinks Online help to deepen students' understanding of theoretical concepts through hands-on exploration and analysis of the latest economic news stories, policy debates, and data.

None of these features requires detailed knowledge of the Internet. Nor are they required for a successful classroom experience if an instructor wants to assign only the materials contained within the textbook. The online enhancements simply offer optional paths for further study and exploration—new ways for students to use their individual learning styles and new ways for instructors to experiment with technology and a wider range of assignment materials.

ACKNOWLEDGEMENTS

Many people have made important contributions to this text. Special thanks go to Mike Worls and Susan Smart, editors at Thomson/South-Western who were always supportive, creative, and helpful, and to John Carey, who enthusiastically marketed our text. The technology team—Peggy Buskey and Karen Schaffer—also deserves thanks for its role in putting together the pieces of the Web site and Xtra! packages. The text's production editor, Stephanie Schempp, did a first rate job. All of our editors provided immediate answers, support, and assistance, and we are glad to have the opportunity to work with such professionals.

Other people also deserve special recognition. Dr. Bryan Taylor, President of Global Financial Data, in Los Angeles California, read much of the manuscript, answered numerous questions, provided much of the data, and gave invaluable criticisms and suggestions. Professor Emeritus George Galbreath and Professor James Sutton gave invaluable suggestions and support to the completion of this project. We are also grateful to our families and friends for their comfort, support, and understanding of our obsessive compulsive desires to create this text.

We are indebted to many current and former students who have assisted in myriad ways. Roberto Ayala, Adam DeAvilan, Benton Wolverton, provided valuable research assistance. Sara Crecelius provided invaluable research assistance for this edition.

We would also like to thank the following reviewers, whose comments on this and the previous edition are greatly appreciated:

Kathryn G. Marshall, *The Ohio State University*

Wm. Stewart Mounts, Jr., *Mercer University*

Christopher J. Niggle, *University of Redlands*

Jerome Picard, *Mount Saint Mary College*

Richard T. Selden, *University of Virginia*

William H. Wells, *Merrimack College*

Jon A. Hooks, *Albion College*

Gyan Pradhan, *Westminster College*

Matthew Rafferty, *Quinnipiac University*

Christopher A. Erickson, *New Mexico State University*

Gil Wolpe, *Mt. Ida College*

John Krieg, *Western Washington University*

CHAPTER ONE

Introduction and Overview

Learning Objectives

After reading this chapter, you should know:

The subject matter of economics and finance

The general role of the financial system in a modern economy

The major functions of financial markets and financial intermediaries

What saving is and its uses

How the financial system channels funds from lenders to borrowers

The role of the Federal Reserve and its regulatory and monetary policy responsibilities

What This Book Is About

Why have financial institutions and financial regulations changed so dramatically in the last 25 years? Why do banks and others pay so much attention to what the Federal Reserve is doing? What is meant by the "globalization" of financial markets? How have technological changes affected financial markets? What are the complex financial instruments known as *derivatives?* Why have there been so many mergers between financial institutions? Why does the international value of the dollar fluctuate so much? Why is the state of the federal government budget such a political and economic issue? Why does the economy experience periodic bouts of high unemployment and/or high inflation? Why do investors now have so many different ways to invest funds? Why do home buyers now have a choice among many types of fixed and variable interest rate mortgage loans?

We could go on, but you get the idea. This list of questions represents only a sample of the issues that motivate the discussions of theory, institutions, and policy found throughout the text. As the questions indicate, these matters affect many aspects of our lives every day.

This chapter begins your study of money and the financial system. It is designed to introduce the subject matter and provide an overview of the key concepts and relationships. Most of the details are ignored, and most terms are not rigorously defined and examined; this is an introduction! However, don't underestimate the importance of a good beginning.

Economic and Financial Analysis of an Ever-Changing System

Economics is the study of how a society decides what gets produced, how it gets produced, and who gets what. More specifically, given unlimited wants on the part of society, economics is concerned with the following processes:

1. How scarce resources (labor, capital, and natural resources) are allocated in the production process among competing uses.[1]

2. How income generated in the production and sale of goods and services is distributed among members of society.

3. How people allocate their income through spending, saving, borrowing, and lending decisions.

For methodological convenience, economics is traditionally divided into the study of the causes and consequences of individual decision-making units such as households and business firms in a particular market and the study of the causes and the effects resulting from the sum of decisions made by all firms or households in many markets. The former type of analysis is called **microeconomics**; the latter type, more aggregative analysis, is called **macroeconomics**.

Finance is, broadly speaking, the study of the financial or monetary aspects of the production, spending, borrowing, and lending decisions already mentioned. More to the point, finance deals with the raising and using of money by individuals, firms, governments, and foreign investors. We are familiar with our decisions to spend, borrow, lend, or save. Our everyday language includes such terms as *interest rates, checking accounts, debit cards, banks,* and *credit cards.* Finance in this context deals with how individuals manage money.

At a more aggregative, macro level, finance is concerned with how the financial system coordinates and channels the flow of funds from lenders to borrowers and vice versa, and how new funds may be created by financial intermediaries during the borrowing process. The channeling and coordination process and its effects on the cost and

Economics

The study of how society decides what gets produced and how, and who gets what.

Microeconomics

The branch of economics that studies the behavior of individual decision-making units such as households and business firms.

Macroeconomics

The branch of economics that studies the aggregate, or total, behavior of all households and firms.

Finance

The study of how the financial system coordinates and channels the flow of funds from lenders to borrowers—and vice versa—and how new funds are created by financial intermediaries during the borrowing process.

availability of funds in the economy link developments in the financial system to developments in the rest of the economy. This aspect of financial analysis is emphasized in this text.

As you will soon learn, the production and sale of goods and services within the economic system are intimately related to the deposits, stocks and bonds, and other financial instruments that are bought and sold in the financial system. Put more dramatically, what happens on Wall Street can have a profound effect on what happens on Main Street and vice versa.

Because the financial system is vital to a healthy economy, the government regulates and supervises its operation. Such regulatory policy is aimed at promoting a smooth-running, efficient financial system. By establishing and enforcing operating regulations for financial markets and institutions, regulators seek to promote competition and efficiency while preserving the safety and soundness of the system.

Complicating our analysis of the interaction between the financial system and the economy is the fact that the financial system is not stagnant. It continually evolves and changes, sometimes at a faster pace than at other times. For various reasons to be discussed in later chapters, the past several decades have seen rapid change, including the ongoing globalization of financial markets. The system is different from what it was 20 years ago, and it will be different 20 years hence. The major forces behind these changes are changes in government regulations, advances in computer technologies, and innovations in the ways people spend, save, and borrow funds.

In recent decades, firms and individuals have developed new ways to raise and use money. Today, many manifestations of these financial innovations are all around us. For example, most checking accounts now earn interest, and 24-hour automated teller machines (ATMs) are common. Debit cards and credit cards are widely accepted at grocery stores, gas stations, and department stores. Home equity lines of credit allow home owners to borrow against the equity in their homes by writing checks as the need arises. Investors have an increasing array of mutual funds and other domestic and global financial instruments to choose from. Stocks and bonds can be purchased for low fees over the Internet at a fraction of the brokerage fees charged by full service brokerage firms. None of these innovations were widely available 25 years ago. New ways for financial and nonfinancial firms to manage risks have been developed. Banks have merged with brokerage firms, insurance companies, and other firms that offer a whole host of financial and nonfinancial services. All this merger activity in the financial services industry has created new types of financial institutions that transcend national borders. Although still in an infantile stage in the United States, the use of smart cards and stored-value cards (as well as other ways to make electronic payments) is expected to explode in the very near future. These developments, most of which have been made possible because of changes in technology, have had or will have an impact on spending, saving, borrowing, and lending decisions. Not surprisingly then, we shall closely examine the causes and consequences of these changes in the financial system.

Deregulation
The removing or phasing out of existing regulations.

Because of these financial innovations and other factors, Congress and the regulatory authorities such as the Federal Reserve have had to reconsider the costs and benefits associated with certain regulations. From the early 1970s until the late 1980s, regulatory changes were mostly in the direction of **deregulation**, which is the removing or phasing out of some existing regulations. Some regulations were eliminated because many people felt that they had become increasingly ineffective as firms and households found ways to get around them. Other regulations were removed because they were believed to inhibit competition and weaken rather than strengthen the financial system. During the late 1980s and early 1990s, however, crises in various financial markets, sometimes requiring taxpayer bailouts, led to attempts at "re-regulation." By the mid-1990s, the recovery of the financial services industry and a booming economy led to the passage of major legislation that removed regulations which forbid interstate branching by banks. This, coupled with continuing advances in computer technologies, fostered dramatic changes in the financial system. In the early 2000s, major legislation took effect that further deregulated the activities of firms in the financial services industry. The new legislation allowed banking, investment, and insurance services to be offered by one giant financial supermarket that offered customers one-stop shopping for all their financial services needs. Such affiliations had not been allowed since the Great Depressions in the 1930s. Finally, as the financial system continues to evolve, we can expect that new and different ways of regulating will be introduced, analyzed, and tested, including the growth of international standards for financial institutions that participate in the global financial system. Nevertheless, the goals of ensuring the safety and soundness of the financial system while fostering efficiency and competition will remain the same.

Finance in Our Daily Lives

Money
Something acceptable and generally used as payment for goods and services.

Simply put, an individual's financial objective is to make payments when due and to manage funds efficiently until they are needed. To make payments we need **money**—that is, something that is acceptable in payment, whether it's for a cup of coffee or rent on a beach house.[2] Throughout this book keep in mind that only money can generally be used for payments.

In our daily lives, we receive income periodically (weekly, monthly, etc.), but our expenditures are more or less continuous, depending, of course, on our lifestyles. Given this lack of synchronization between the receipt of income and expenditures, we need to manage our money over, say, a month so that funds will be available when we make purchases of goods and services—called *consumption spending*. Income that is not spent on consumption is called **saving**. Part of household saving may be spent directly on investment goods, such as new houses.[3] With the remainder of saving, individuals will acquire financial assets, which also have to be managed.

Saving
Income not spent on consumption.

How might the funds not used for consumption or investment in new houses be managed? We could take currency (paper money), put it in an empty coffee can, and bury it in the backyard. We also could put the funds into a savings or money market account to earn some interest. Another alternative is to buy corporate bonds, shares of common stock, Treasury bills, or other financial assets. Which we buy depends on how we wish to balance the key financial characteristics of concern to savers: the expected return (gain) and the risk of loss associated with acquiring and holding a particular asset. Some assets, such as Treasury bills, are relatively riskless; if you own such bills, you can be pretty sure the government will pay the interest and principal you are due. Other assets, such as bonds issued by new corporations not yet earning significant profits, may offer a much higher return, but they also carry the risk that the firm will declare bankruptcy and you will get nothing! Moreover, if an unexpected need arises and you need to get back the funds you originally loaned, you want your funds to be invested in liquid assets that can be converted quickly to cash without substantial loss. Balancing such considerations is the essence of managing a portfolio—that is, a collection of financial assets—be it by an individual or by a financial institution.

What has just been described should not be unfamiliar to any student, but to facilitate clarity and effective communication, the terminology employed in this text must be distinguished from colloquial use. *Income* is the flow of revenue (receipts) we receive over time for our services. With this income we can buy and consume goods. If we have funds left over after consumption, we are saving, and we have to decide how to allocate those funds among the various types of financial assets available or to invest them in real assets

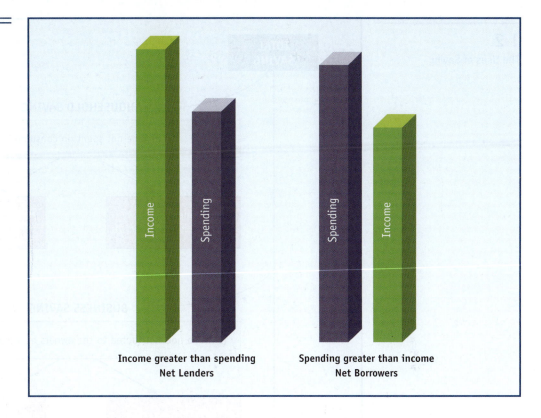

Income greater than spending
Net Lenders

Spending greater than income
Net Borrowers

Net Lenders
Spending units such as households and firms whose income
exceeds their spending.

Net Borrowers
Spending units such as households and firms whose spending
exceeds their income.

such as new houses. If, however, we spend more than we earn, we have a deficit and have
to decide how to finance it. When we spend less on consumption and investment goods
than our current income, we are **net lenders**. If the opposite is true, we have a deficit and
are **net borrowers**. Exhibit 1-1 portrays net lenders and net borrowers.

So far we have restricted our analysis to individuals and households, but business
firms may also spend more or less than their income. Business firms do not spend on
consumption, so all business income is saving except income distributed as dividends to
the owners of the firms. With their saving, business firms make investment expenditures
in capital and inventories or acquire financial assets. A firm's investment expenditures often exceed its available funds.[4] In this case, the firm incurs financial liabilities by issuing
financial claims against itself. Note that every financial instrument is an asset to the
owner (purchaser) of the instrument and a liability to the issuer. Exhibit 1-2 shows the
uses of saving for households and business firms.

The fact that some people or business firms are in deficit positions while others are
in surplus positions creates an opportunity or a need for a way to match them up. The financial system links up these net lenders and net borrowers. The government and foreign
sectors may also spend more or less than their current available funds and hence be net
borrowers or net lenders.

Recap   Economics studies how scarce resources are allocated among conflicting wants.
Finance studies how the financial system coordinates and channels the flows of funds
from net lenders to net borrowers. Net lenders spend less than their current income. Net
borrowers spend more than their current income. Household saving may be used for investment in new housing or to acquire financial assets. Business saving may be used for
investment in capital and inventories or to acquire financial assets. Financial instruments
are financial assets to the holder of the instrument and financial liabilities to the issuer.

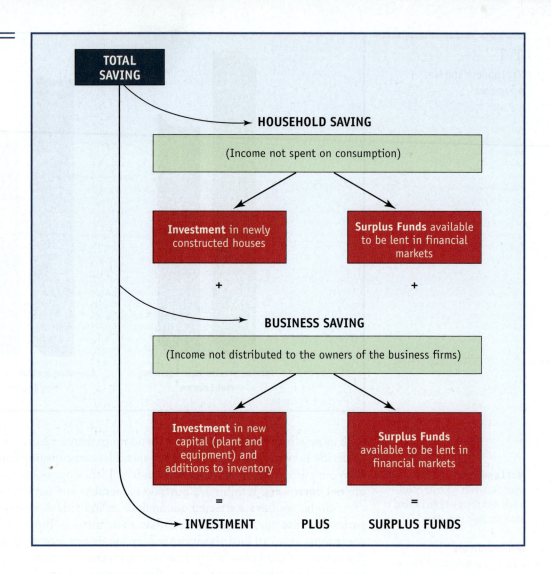

Introducing the Financial System

A well-organized, efficient, smoothly functioning financial system is an important component of a modern, highly specialized economy. The financial system provides a
mechanism whereby a firm or household that is a net lender may conveniently make
funds available to net borrowers who intend to spend more than their current income.
The key word here is *conveniently*.

The financial system is composed of financial markets and financial institutions.
Financial markets are the markets where net lenders can lend their funds directly to net
borrowers. An example is the market for corporate bonds. General Motors can sell bonds
to finance, say, the construction of a new plant in Mexico, and Emma from Kansas can
purchase some of the bonds with the income she does not spend on goods and services.
This is called **direct finance**. Purchasing stocks is another example of direct finance.
Financial institutions are firms that provide financial services to net lenders and net
borrowers. The most important financial institutions are **financial intermediaries**—various institutions such as banks, savings and loan associations, and credit unions—that

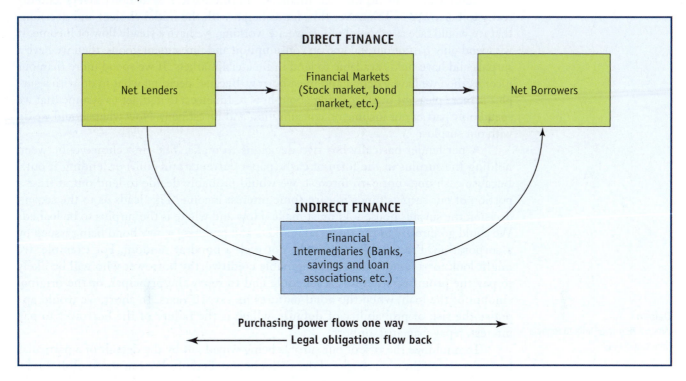

DIRECT FINANCE

Net Lenders → Financial Markets (Stock market, bond market, etc.) → Net Borrowers

INDIRECT FINANCE

Financial Intermediaries (Banks, savings and loan associations, etc.)

Purchasing power flows one way →
← Legal obligations flow back

Indirect Finance
When net borrowers borrow from financial intermediaries that have acquired the funds to lend from net lenders.

serve as go-betweens to link up net lenders and net borrowers. Here the linkage between saver and borrower is indirect. For example, a household might deposit some surplus funds in a savings account at a bank, and the bank, in turn, might make a loan to a borrower. This is called **indirect finance**. Even though the ultimate lender is the spending unit with surplus funds, the borrower owes repayment of the loan to the financial intermediary, and the financial intermediary owes repayment of the deposit to the lender. Other financial institutions, which are not financial intermediaries, merely link up (for a fee) the net lenders to purchase the stocks or bonds issued by net borrowers.

Exhibit 1-3 pulls together the discussion on this point. Net lenders can lend funds either directly in the financial markets or indirectly through financial intermediaries. If they lend funds in the financial markets, they acquire direct or primary financial claims against the income of the borrower. Net borrowers borrow funds by issuing these financial claims in the market. To the holder/purchaser, the claims are assets owned; but to the issuer, the claims are liabilities owed. For example, the General Motors bonds mentioned previously are assets to Emma and liabilities to General Motors.

If net lenders lend funds through financial intermediaries, they acquire indirect or secondary financial claims on those intermediaries, which, in turn, acquire direct claims on net borrowers. Putting funds into a savings account is a classic example of acquiring a secondary claim on a financial institution. The institution will, in turn, make loans directly to a net borrower. Through lending activities, some financial intermediaries may also create new funds (money), which meet the needs of a growing economy. In either case, whether funds flow directly from net lenders or indirectly from intermediaries, credit is extended.

More on Financial Intermediaries

One might ask, "Why do we need financial intermediaries? Why don't savers lend directly to borrowers?" To answer this, let us begin with the initial choices and decisions that we would face as a household. If we are working, we have a steady flow of income. If we spend only part of our income on consumption and investment goods, then we have a surplus and have funds available to lend in financial markets. If we spend more than our income, then we have a deficit and must borrow. Because deciding what to do with a surplus is more pleasant than worrying about how to finance a deficit, let us assume that we spend only part of our income on consumption and investment. Now what should we do with our surplus?

A net lender basically has two decisions to make. The first choice is between holding the surplus in the form of cash (paper currency and coin) or lending it out.[5] Because cash does not earn interest, we would probably decide to lend out at least a portion of our surplus funds to earn some interest income. This leads us to the second decision the surplus household must make: How and where is the surplus to be loaned? We could go directly to the financial markets and purchase a new bond being issued by a corporation. Presumably, we would not pick a bond at random. For example, we might look for a bond issued by a reputable creditworthy borrower who will be likely to pay the promised interest on schedule and to repay the principal, or the original amount of the loan, when the bond matures in, say, 10 years. In short, we would appraise the risk or probability of **default**, which is the failure of the borrower to pay interest, repay principal, or both.

Default
When a borrower fails to repay a financial claim.

To minimize the risk of our surplus being wiped out by the default of a particular borrower, we might want to spread our risks out and diversify. We can accomplish this by spreading our surplus over a number of net borrowers.[6] In nontechnical terms, we would avoid putting all our eggs into one basket. Moreover, most net lenders are not experts in appraising and diversifying risk and would have to hire a broker to advise us about the primary claims issued by net borrowers.

All of this would, of course, take time and effort. As a result, many prefer to rely on the expertise of others, such as financial intermediaries. Financial intermediaries acquire the funds of net lenders by offering claims on themselves. In other words, the net lender has really made a loan to the financial intermediary and therefore has a financial claim on the intermediary in the amount of the surplus funds. To determine its profit, the financial intermediary subtracts what it pays to net lenders for the use of the funds from what it earns on the loans and other investments it makes with those funds.

The financial intermediaries pool the funds they acquire from many individual net lenders and then use the funds to make loans to businesses and households, purchase bonds, and so forth. The intermediaries are actually lending out the surpluses they accept from individual net lenders while also appraising and diversifying the risk associated with lending directly to net borrowers. Because the intermediaries specialize in this kind of work, it is reasonable to presume that they know what they are doing and, on average, do a better job than individual net lenders could do. Put a bit more formally, financial intermediaries minimize the costs—called **transactions costs**—associated with borrowing and lending.

Transactions Costs
The costs associated with borrowing and lending or making other exchanges.

Another reason that net lenders often entrust their funds to financial intermediaries is that the secondary (indirect) claims offered by intermediaries are often more attractive to many lenders than the primary (direct) claims available in financial markets. In many cases, for example, the secondary claims of intermediaries are insured by an agency of the federal government such as the FDIC.[7] Therefore, the risk of default associated with holding a secondary claim is often less than with a primary claim.

In addition, secondary claims are attractive in that they are often more liquid than primary claims. **Liquidity** refers to the ease of exchanging a financial claim for cash without loss of value. Different types of claims possess varying degrees of liquidity. A claim easily exchanged for cash, such as a savings deposit, is highly liquid; exchanging a less-liquid claim involves more significant time, cost, and/or inconvenience. A rare oil painting is an example of a less-liquid asset.

Suppose you loaned funds directly to a small, obscure corporation and the loan's term of maturity (the time from when you gave the firm the funds until it must pay back the principal) was two years. You have a financial claim in the form of a loan contract, and the corporation has your surplus funds. What would happen if after one year you suddenly wanted the funds back for some emergency expenditure? You might ask the corporation to pay you back at once, before the due date of the loan. If this option is closed because the borrower is unwilling or unable to pay off the loan immediately, you might try to sell the claim on the borrower to someone else who is willing to hold it until maturity. Although there are organized markets for the buying and selling of certain types of existing financial claims, such markets do not exist for all types of claims. The hassle associated with unloading the loan contract in a time of crisis should be obvious. To avoid such inconvenience, many net lenders prefer to hold claims on financial intermediaries and let the "experts" worry about any problems.

Depository Institutions and Other Types of Intermediaries

The most familiar type and the largest group of financial intermediaries are **depository institutions** consisting of commercial banks, savings and loan associations, credit unions, and mutual savings banks. Not surprisingly, their principal source of funds is the deposits of individuals, business firms, and governments, both domestic and foreign. Depository institutions are particularly popular with net lenders because the secondary claims purchased by net lenders from depository institutions—that is, the deposits—are often insured and therefore relatively safe. **Checkable deposits**, which as the name implies are subject to withdrawal by writing a check, are now offered by all depository institutions. Such deposits are money per se because they can be used in their present form as a means of payment. Other claims on depository institutions, such as savings deposits, are also quite liquid.

Other types of intermediaries offer specialized secondary claims. For example, insurance companies offer financial protection against early death (life companies) or property losses (casualty companies), while pension plans provide financial resources for one's old age. All of these specialized intermediaries collect savings in the form of premium payments or contributions from those who participate in the plans. Each intermediary then uses the funds acquired to purchase a variety of primary claims from net borrowers. Investment-type intermediaries, such as mutual funds and money market funds, pool the surplus funds of many small savers and invest them in financial markets, thereby offering the small savers greater opportunities to diversify than they would otherwise realize. Exhibit 1-4 highlights the various types of intermediaries.

Although our analysis covers intermediation in general, we give particular attention to the role of depository institutions for several reasons. For one thing, depository institutions are by far the largest type of intermediary. They also are a central part of the process that determines the nation's money supply. Because one of our main objectives is to understand the nature and role of money in our economy, we will focus on the behavior of depository institutions and the process of intermediation in which they engage. By examining how money is provided, what it costs to obtain money when we need it, and

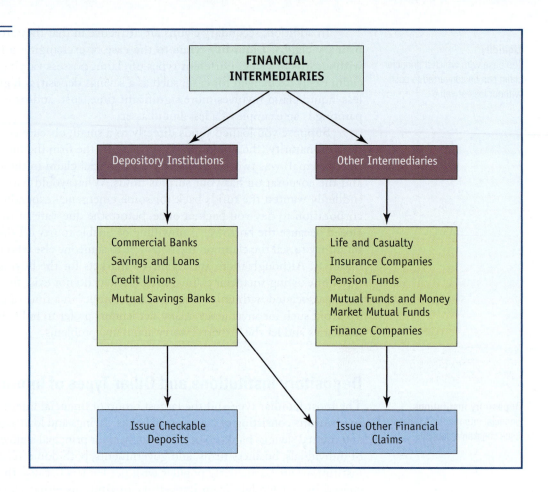

what we can earn when we have enough of it to lend out, we will learn much about how money and the financial system affect our economy.

Recap   When net lenders lend directly to net borrowers, direct finance occurs. When net lenders put their funds in financial intermediaries, which then lend to net borrowers, indirect finance occurs. Financial intermediaries acquire the funds of net lenders by issuing claims on themselves. They use the funds to purchase the financial claims of net borrowers. The most important financial intermediaries are depository institutions that issue checkable deposits. Other financial intermediaries include life and casualty insurance companies, pension funds, mutual funds, money market mutual funds, and finance companies.

The Federal Reserve System

Federal Reserve (Fed)
The central bank of the United States that regulates the banking system and determines monetary policy.

The way in which depository institutions serve as intermediaries and affect the money supply is greatly influenced by the **Federal Reserve**. Other financial markets and institutions are also greatly affected by the Federal Reserve. The Federal Reserve is a quasi-independent government agency that serves as our nation's central bank. Its influence begins with the depository institutions and their role in the money supply process and then spreads to other intermediaries and financial markets in general.

The Fed, as it is often called, has a profound influence on the behavior of banks through its regulatory policy and its ability to affect interest rates and the total volume of funds available for borrowing and lending. In recent years, depository institutions have experienced a declining share of the funds available for borrowing and lending, while other financial institutions and nonfinancial institutions have received an increasing share.[8] In addition, international financial flows (borrowing and lending that transcends national borders) have increased greatly. Because the Fed has more influence on domestic commercial banks and other depository institutions than on other financial institutions, there is concern that the Fed's ability to influence the economy through traditional avenues has actually declined. Nevertheless, the Fed continues to maintain a leading role in determining the overall health of the U.S. economy. The Fed's influence on banks spreads through a number of channels to other financial intermediaries and more generally to the transfer of funds from net lenders to net borrowers. By affecting interest rates and the volume of funds transferred from lenders to borrowers, the Fed can influence the aggregate, or total, demand for goods and services in the economy and, hence, the overall health of the economy. A general representation of this relationship is shown in Exhibit 1-5. The middle of this figure—the financial system and economic behavior of spending units—represents the essential anatomy or structure of the economy. The task before us is to learn how each part of the economy operates and how the collective activity of the parts is affected by the Fed's **monetary policy**—that is, the Fed's efforts to promote the overall health and stability of the economy.

Monetary Policy
The Fed's efforts to promote the overall health and stability of the economy.

In terms of Exhibit 1-3, the Fed monitors the performance of the financial system and the economy with an eye toward augmenting or reducing the supply of funds flowing from lenders through financial markets and financial intermediaries to borrowers. Any action the Fed undertakes sets off a chain of reactions as depicted in Exhibit 1-5.

For a brief history of the Federal Reserve, go to **http://www.minneapolisfed.org/ info/sys/history/**.

For more on monetary policy, see **http://www.minneapolisfed.org/info/policy/**.

As we begin to think about the Fed's conduct of monetary policy and its effects on the economy, an analogy might be helpful. Think of the U.S. economy as a human patient to be observed and hopefully understood. Just as a human body is made of many parts (arms, legs, torso), the U.S. economy is composed of many sectors (household, business, government, and foreign). Money and the acts of spending and saving and lending and borrowing are analogous to the blood and the circulatory system of the body. We want to study how the behavior of money and credit extension (borrowing and lending) affects the well-being of households, business firms, and, more generally, the overall

1-5

The Influence of the Fed's Monetary Policy

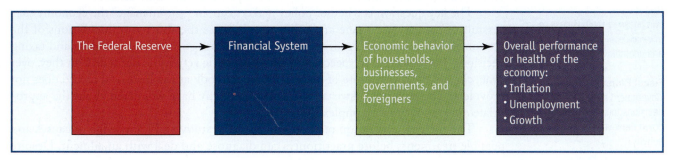

economy. By focusing on borrowing and lending money and on spending and saving, we shall see how the major sectors of the economy interact to produce goods and services and to generate income.

The health of the U.S. economy varies over time. At times the economy appears to be well and functioning normally; at other times, it appears listless and depressed; and at still other times, it seems hyperactive—characterized by erratic, unstable behavior. By studying how all the key parts of the economy fit together, we should be able to learn something about the illnesses that can strike this patient. What causes a particular type of illness (say, inflation or unemployment)? How is the illness diagnosed? What medicines or cures can be prescribed? If more than one treatment is possible, which will work best? Are any undesirable side effects associated with particular medications? Are the doctors who diagnose the problems and administer the treatment (the policy makers) ever guilty of malpractice?

Answers to all these questions will depend in part on "what makes the patient tick" and how we define "good health." A human patient's health is determined by the deviations, if any, from a well-established set of precise criteria involving temperature, reflexes, blood chemistry, appetite, and so forth. For the economy, however, we have no well-established, precise criteria that allow us to judge its health. Rather, loosely defined goals or objectives such as "full" employment or "low" inflation are used. If everyone agrees on these goals, including how to define and measure them, and the economy seems to be operating in the neighborhood of the goals, then we might say that the economy is in good health. If we are heading toward the goals, we would say that the economy's health is improving, but if the economy seems to be deviating from the goals, we would say that its health is not good and that prescriptive measures may be necessary to improve matters.

The Role of Policy: Changing Views

Good health for the economy, as with humans, has both short- and long-run dimensions. Over the long run, we and policy makers would like to have the economy grow such that the quality of life and standard of living for an increasing population can improve. In the short run, we would like to minimize the fluctuations or deviations from the long-run growth path. In economics these short-run fluctuations of the economy are part of what is appropriately called the **business cycle**. Exhibit 1-6 illustrates the various stages of the business cycle and shows how they are related to the longer-run growth of the economy. The economy, like most of us, has its ups and downs. During a recovery or **expansion**, economic activity, as measured by the total quantity of goods and services being bought and sold, increases and unemployment falls. During a **recession** or contraction, economic activity falls and unemployment rises. Just before the peak, all is bright and the economy/patient seems truly healthy. At the trough, all is bleak and the economy/patient appears quite ill. Over the longer run, we can calculate the average growth rate (trend), which smoothes out the expansions and contractions.

The key question is whether policy makers can, in fact, "manage" the economy successfully. Can they use monetary policy to minimize the short-run fluctuations of the economy over its long-run growth path? Can they use government spending and taxing decisions (**fiscal policy**) to speed up or slow economic activity as needed? Can they, over time, change the growth rate of output? Because a look at the historical record does not provide an encouraging answer to this question, many have wondered about the appropriate role of policy in a complex modern economy.

The medical profession requires considerable study and knowledge of causes and possible treatments before practitioners can diagnose and deal with an ailment. Despite

Business Cycle
Short-run fluctuations in economic activity as measured by the output of goods and services.

Expansion
The phase of the business cycle in which economic activity increases and unemployment falls.

Recession
The phase of the business cycle in which economic activity falls and unemployment rises.

Fiscal Policy
Government spending and taxing decisions to speed up or slow down the level of economic activity.

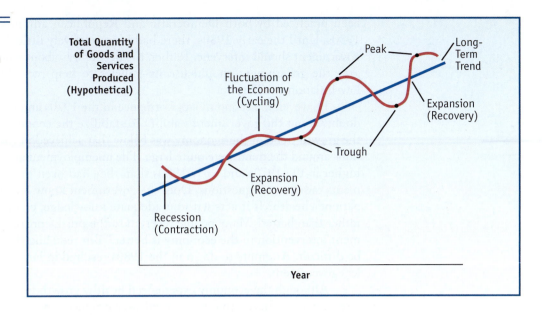

the best efforts of eminent researchers, we still do not know how to cure some diseases. So too in economics; cures for all the economic ills we may encounter are not known.

Why are the goals that policy makers are trying to achieve on behalf of society so elusive? The answers are complex and fall into three possible areas.[9] First, the diagnosticians may not understand all the causes of the problems. What this really means is that we do not fully understand how the economy functions. Second, policy makers may be reluctant to use the currently known medicines to treat the patient because they have undesirable side effects, which may, in fact, be worse than the disease. Third, the cure for the problem may not yet be known, so more research will be needed to find a useful therapeutic approach. Thus far we have assumed that the economy's illness can be cured only by the doctors and their medicines. But could the patient get better by itself?

Prior to the Great Depression of the 1930s, many economists tended to see the economy as inherently stable, having strong self-correcting tendencies. The prevailing belief was that the economy would never drift away from full-employment equilibrium for long; any disturbance or shock that pushed the economy away from full employment would automatically set in motion forces tending to move the economy back to full-employment equilibrium.[10] Thus, before the Depression, many economists felt that there was no need for corrective government action when the economy was disturbed because any movement away from equilibrium would be temporary and self-correcting. This view of the economy provided an economic rationale for the government to pursue a **laissez-faire**, hands-off policy.

Laissez-Faire
The view that government should pursue a hands-off policy with regard to the economy.

The Great Depression altered this view of the economy's internal dynamics. Between 1929 and 1933, the unemployment rate increased from about 3 percent to about 25 percent. The downturn was experienced worldwide and persisted until the start of World War II. Few could argue, in the face of such evidence, that the problem was correcting itself. The economist John Maynard Keynes and others suggested that once the economy's full-employment equilibrium was disturbed, its self-correcting powers were likely to be overwhelmed by other forces. The net result would be that the economy could operate below full employment for some time.

This new perspective gave the government an economic rationale for attempting to stabilize overall economic activity. A consensus formed that a highly developed market economy, if left to itself, would be unstable. As a result, "activist" stabilization policy has been practiced by both Democratic and Republican administrations since the mid-1930s. Until the early 1980s, there had been relatively little debate about whether the government should intervene. Rather, the debate was about when, how, and to what degree the government should use its policies to help reestablish a full-employment, low-inflation equilibrium.

However, the economy's performance in the 1970s and the early 1980s gave rise to doubts about the government's ability to stabilize the economy. As Exhibit 1-7 shows, the growth trend of the economy was below that achieved in the 1960s, and the fluctuations around the trend were quite large. The unemployment and inflation rates were both higher in the 1970s and early 1980s than they had been in the 1960s. These developments raised many questions. Does the government know how to proceed to restore the patient's health? If it acts without adequate knowledge, can policy make things worse rather than better? Many people reverted to the pre-Depression view that "less government intervention in the economy is better." But reducing the role of government may be difficult. Attempts to do so in the 1980s resulted in larger government deficits, not less government.

Although the economy experienced healthy growth from about 1983 until the late 1980s, many believed that this growth was produced by large government deficits and increases in military spending. Chronic trade deficits, problem loans to less-developed countries, troubles within the savings and loan industry, and the collapse of the junk bond market were of concern to many.

For more information about business cycle expansions and contractions, see **http://www.frbsf.org/education/activities/drecon/2002/0205.html**.

The recession of the early 1990s caused anxiety, not because of its depth or length, but because the recovery was so sluggish. Growth remained lethargic well into the first half of 1993, and in some regions beyond that. However, by early 1994, economic growth had accelerated and remained high throughout the remainder of the decade while inflation remained subdued. Toward the end of the 1990s, the long expansion resulted in an unemployment rate of 4 percent—the lowest rate in over 30 years. Surprisingly, there was little or no acceleration of inflation despite such low unemployment.

Stock and bond prices experienced extraordinary increases from the mid-1990s into early 2000, even though Alan Greenspan, the Fed chair, voiced concern in December 1996 that an "irrational exuberance" was taking over in these markets. Despite a moderate correction of stock prices in October 1997, the stock market again closed at a

---

1-7

Average Inflation, Unemployment, and Growth during Recent Decades

	Inflation	Unemployment	Growth (Output)
1960s	2.4%	4.75%	4.4%
1970s	7.0	6.25	3.2
1980s	5.5*	8.25	2.8
1990s	3.3	5.7**	3.7
2000–2004***	3.0	4.74	3.0

*Actually, if 1980 are not considered, inflation averaged just under 4 percent for the remainder of the 1980s.
**From mid-1997 through the rest of the decade, unemployment was below 5 percent.
***Annualized through first quarter 2004.
SOURCE: http://www.stls.frb.org/fred/

record high in July 1998. To some, the Asian Crisis of 1997 crisis meant good news for the U.S. economy, which was believed to be less likely to overheat. By late summer 1998, stock prices finally succumbed to international financial problems. Stock prices plummeted about 20 percent, and questions surfaced about whether the U.S. economy could withstand a global downturn. The Fed responded by lowering interest rates three times in the fall of 1998. The fiscal year ended on September 30, 1998, with a widely publicized federal government budget surplus of $70 billion—the first surplus since 1969. By the end of calendar year 1998, the lower interest rates had the desired effect, and the stock market strongly rebounded to new highs.

The economy continued to expand into the new millennium with the stock market reaching record highs in March 2000. However, there were clouds on the horizon that suggested the record long expansion could not last forever. From March 2000 on, the technology-dominated NASDAQ index of stock prices plummeted, losing over 50 percent of its value by December 31, 2000, and the DOW, the best-known index of stock prices, ended the year 2000 down for the first time since 1988. A contested presidential election gave the appearance of a divided nation. George W. Bush, the eventual winner, expressed concerns about the economy and further emphasized the need for a large income tax cut. Worries that the economy was heading steeply down caused the Fed to take action to lower interest rates in early January 2001 before the new president took office. Many factors continued to threaten the record expansion, including falling profits, a languishing stock market, escalating energy prices, announcements of significant layoffs, and drops in consumer confidence. The attack on the World Trade Center and the Pentagon in September 2001 resulted in further economic turmoil, and the government soon announced that a recession had actually begun in March 2001. All in all, the Fed took action to lower interest rates seven times in 2001 prior to September 11 and an additional six times between September 11, 2001, and June 2003. Although the recession officially ended in November 2001, the economy languished in a jobless recovery throughout 2003. A large tax cut and a weak economy caused tax revenues to decline while wars in Afghanistan and Iraq caused expenditures to balloon. The short-lived government surplus became a record government deficit. By early 2004, the expansion had picked up pace, and the Fed was hopeful that its aggressive monetary policy would continue the expansion and robust employment growth. The Fed reversed course and began increasing interest rates from 45-year lows in June 2004. Further increases followed as the economic expansion continued to pick up steam. One thing is clear: Monetary policymakers and those affected by changes in the financial environment—each one of us—will make better decisions if we understand as best we can the concepts of money and credit extension and their effects on the financial system and the economy.

Summary of Major Points

1. Economics is concerned with how, given people's unlimited wants, scarce resources are allocated among competing uses, how income is distributed, and how people allocate their incomes through spending, saving, borrowing, and lending decisions.

2. Finance focuses on the financial side of these decisions—that is, the raising and using of funds by households, firms, and governments.

3. The financial system coordinates and channels the flow of funds from lenders to borrowers and creates

new liquidity for an expanding economy. The characteristics of this process have changed over time as innovations and changes in regulations have occurred.

4. Spending units that spend less than their current income on consumption and investment are called *net lenders*. Spending units that spend more than their current income are called *net borrowers*.

5. In allocating funds among the various types of financial assets available, net lenders are concerned about the expected return, the risk of loss, and the liquidity associated with acquiring and holding a particular asset.

6. Direct finance involves lending directly to net borrowers. Indirect finance involves lending to a financial intermediary, a type of financial institution that borrows in order to relend. Financial intermediaries issue claims on themselves. The lenders receive financial claims on the financial intermediaries, and the borrowers receive funds from the financial intermediaries.

7. Financial intermediaries exist because they help to minimize the transactions costs associated with borrowing and lending. The financial services provided include appraising and diversifying risk, offering a menu of financial claims that are relatively safe and liquid, and pooling funds from individual net lenders.

8. The most important types of financial intermediaries are the depository institutions: commercial banks, savings and loan associations, mutual savings banks, and credit unions. These institutions are central to the process of determining the nation's money supply. Other types of financial intermediaries are life and casualty insurance companies, pension funds, mutual funds and money market mutual funds, and finance companies.

9. The Federal Reserve is a quasi-independent government agency that serves as our nation's central bank. Its regulatory policy is aimed at promoting a smooth-running, efficient, competitive financial system. The Fed's monetary policy, which influences interest rates and the volume of funds available for borrowing and lending (credit extension), is directed at enhancing the overall health and stability of the economy. Although the Fed works primarily through depository institutions, its influence spreads from depository institutions to the financial system.

10. Views on the appropriate role of policy in the economy—that is, how "activist" policy makers should be in trying to manage the economy—have varied over time. Throughout the 1980s, the economy experienced healthy growth that was accompanied by large trade and government deficits. After a recession in the early 1990s, economic growth resumed, and the economy achieved both low inflation and low unemployment with a record long expansion into the new millennium. A recession had actually begun in March 2001. Although the recession officially ended in November 2001, the recovery remained sluggish throughout 2003 despite aggressive expansionary monetary policy by the Fed. The recovery picked up steam in 2004.

Key Terms

Business Cycle, **14**
Checkable Deposits, **11**
Default, **10**
Depository Institutions, **11**
Deregulation, **5**
Direct Finance, **8**
Economics, **4**
Expansion, **14**
Federal Reserve, **12**

Finance, **4**
Financial Institutions, **8**
Financial Intermediaries, **8**
Financial Markets, **8**
Fiscal Policy, **14**
Indirect Finance, **9**
Laissez-Faire, **15**
Liquidity, **11**
Macroeconomics, **4**

Microeconomics, **4**
Monetary Policy, **13**
Money, **6**
Net Borrowers, **7**
Net Lenders, **7**
Recession, **14**
Saving, **6**
Transactions Costs, **10**

Review Questions

1. Provide a short discussion or definition of the following terms: *economics, finance, the financial system, net lenders, net borrowers, direct and indirect finance, financial markets, financial intermediaries, liquidity, business cycle, depository institutions,* and *monetary policy.*
2. Some people have money; some people need money. Explain how the financial system links these people together.
3. Discuss the statement: "Since I have high credit card limits, I have lots of money." Are credit cards money? Why or why not? (*Hint:* See Endnote 2.)
4. When are the surplus funds I have available to lend in financial markets equal to my saving?
5. Why do financial intermediaries exist? What services do they provide to the public? Are all financial institutions financial intermediaries?
6. What are transactions costs? Does financial intermediation increase or decrease transactions costs?
7. What is a depository institution? What is a checkable deposit? How does a depository institution differ from other intermediaries? Give three examples of depository institutions.
8. Why does the Fed monitor the economy? What actions can the Fed take to affect the overall health of the economy?
9. Why have views changed concerning the appropriate role of stabilization policies in managing the economy? Briefly discuss the historical evolution of these views.
10. What are the pros and cons of lending to my next door neighbor rather than putting my surplus funds in a bank?
11. Define *laissez-faire* and *fiscal policy.* Who determines fiscal policy? Who determines monetary policy?

Analytical Questions

Questions marked with an icon are objective in nature. They can be completed with a short answer or number.

12. Rank the following assets in terms of their liquidity, from least to most liquid: cash, savings deposits, gold, a house, a rare oil painting, a checkable deposit. Explain your rank order.
13. Is each of the following an example of direct or indirect financing?
    a. John purchases stock from the biotech firm that employs him.
    b. Mary purchases a newly issued government security.
    c. John places $3,000 in a savings account at the local savings and loan.
    d. John receives a loan from Mary.
    e. John receives a loan from Friendly Savings Bank.
14. Bill's income is $4,000. He spends $3,000 on consumption and $300 on an investment in a newly constructed house. He acquires $700 in financial assets. What is his saving? What is the amount of surplus funds he has available to lend?
15. A firm spends $100,000 on investment in plant and equipment. It has available funds of $30,000 and borrows the additional funds from a bank. Is the firm a net borrower or a net lender? What is the amount of the surplus or deficit?
16. Diane Weil earns wages of $45,000 and interest and dividend income of $5,000. She spends $8,000 as a down payment on a newly constructed mountain cabin and lends $4,000 in financial markets. Assuming that Diane spends the remainder of her income on consumption, what is her saving? Is she a net lender or net borrower? What is her consumption?
17. Tech Corp had gross sales of $9 million and total expenses of $8.5 million. Assume that Tech wants to undertake a capital investment of $1 million. What is the minimum amount of bonds it would have to issue to do so? Assume that Tech pays out $300,000 in dividends. Now what is the minimum amount it would have to borrow?
18. What are the phases of a business cycle? Draw a graph of a typical business cycle and label the various phases.
19. The *misery index* is defined as the sum of the unemployment and the inflation rates. Use Exhibit 1-7 to calculate the misery index for each decade since 1960.

Internet Exercise

Access the following Web site: **http://www.stats.bls.gov/**. List some key economic variables that are tracked on this Web page. What U.S. government agency is responsible for the data listed here?

Suggested Readings

If the material covered in the text is to come alive and make sense to you, we suggest you try to read *The Wall Street Journal* and *Business Week* regularly. In fact, hardly a day goes by without a report on an issue that is in some way relevant to our subject. You might also consult the *New York Times, Washington Post,* or *Los Angeles Times;* all have good financial sections. Or you can browse the financial sections of *USA Today* (**http://www.usatoday.com**) or CNN (**http://www.money.cnn.com**) on the World Wide Web.

Go to the library and thumb through the *Federal Reserve Bulletin.* A half-hour investment here will reveal the types of data collected and distributed by the Fed (contained in the second half of the *Bulletin*) and the range of issues the Fed concerns itself with (contained in the first half). A plethora of financial statistics can also be found in the Federal Reserve Bank Economic Database Web site (**http://www.research.stlouisfed.org/fred2/**).

A wealth of information about the current state of the economy and attempts at stabilization by the government can be found in *The Economic Report of the President.* It is published annually during the month of February by the U.S. Government Printing Office and is available at the reference desk of most libraries. It is also available on the Internet at **http://www.access.gpo.gov/eop/**.

The Statistical Abstract of the United States contains summary data on income, expenditures, wealth, prices, and the financial system (among other things). It is published annually during December by the Bureau of the Census, Department of Commerce. The *Survey of Current Business,* published monthly by the Bureau of Economic Analysis, Department of Commerce, contains current business and income statistics. The *Statistical Abstract* is also available at the following Bureau of the Census Web site: **http://www.census.gov/statab/www/**.

Endnotes

1 When economists use the term *capital* in this context, they mean machinery and equipment that are used to produce other goods and services. For example, a sewing machine that produces shirts is capital.

2 Credit cards are not money. When a credit card is used, the user is taking out a loan by authorizing the institution that issued the credit card to make a payment with money on his or her behalf. Ultimately, the individual must pay credit card balances with money.

3 As used here, *investment in houses* refers to expenditures for new residential construction, where a service is rendered over a period of time.

4 Firms also make investment expenditures to replace worn-out capital.

5 There is another option. If we owe back debts, we could employ surplus funds to pay off those debts.

6 If we have only a small amount of surplus funds available, it may be extremely difficult to diversify to a significant extent. As we shall see in later chapters, small investors can use mutual funds to accomplish this objective.

7 The Federal Deposit Insurance Corporation (FDIC) enables the public to feel confident that funds deposited in a bank or savings and loan, up to a limit (currently $100,000), are safe. If the institution fails, the FDIC will step in and pay off the depositors. When financial institutions were failing daily during the early years of the Great Depression in the 1930s, the government became convinced of the pressing need for such an agency. See **http://www.fdic.gov/**.

8 Examples of very large nonfinancial institutions that have entered the lending business include General Electric (GE), Sears, and General Motors (GM), all of which now issue credit cards.

9 The complex answers are tackled in Part Six of the text.

10 *Equilibrium* is a concept used by economists to help analyze the economy. It refers to a state of the economy from which there is no tendency to deviate—a state of rest. Of course, in reality, the economy is constantly being bombarded with disturbances and is hardly ever "at rest." The concept of equilibrium, then, is an analytical device that helps us sort out the influences of many different factors, which, in the real world, are often all changing at the same time.

If it waddles like a duck,

and quacks like a duck,

then it is a duck.

2

CHAPTER TWO

Principles of Money

Learning Objectives:

After reading this chapter, you should know:

How money is defined by its functions

How to apply the definition in measuring what money is and what it is not

Why the Federal Reserve publishes numerous measures of monetary aggregates including M1, M2, and M3

The meaning of domestic nonfinancial debt (DNFD)

The role of technology in the evolution of the payments system

How the existence of money facilitates the development of an economy

Conceptualization: A Key Building Block

As the week ends in the dormitory dining hall, Mary, the dining hall supervisor, calls Randy, the dishwasher, over and gives him his pay envelope. It should contain $50. Finding the envelope somewhat thicker than normal, Randy opens it and discovers five $10 tickets to the university's spring play next Saturday night. Tired and somewhat irritated, especially since he has already seen the performance, he tells Mary he wants money, not these tickets. Mary tries to persuade Randy to accept the tickets instead but fails and eventually produces a university check made out to Randy for $50.

A simple and, some might say, silly story. Yet it touches on most of the key issues addressed in this chapter: Why did Randy want money instead of the tickets? Why does he accept the check? Why aren't the tickets money? Why aren't they as good as money? Those of you who think the answers to such questions are obvious might be tempted to skip this chapter. Don't do it! As we shall see, the term *money* is used rather sloppily in everyday language. In this book, however, we need to be precise about how money is defined and how it is measured.

Defining Money

Unfortunately, students often treat definitions as something to be tolerated and memorized. No one would deny that memorization is part of the learning process, but we must store more in our minds than a collection of words. Definitions are part of a theoretical framework that facilitates our analysis and understanding. In the present context, understanding how money matters will be quite difficult unless we are clear on the definition of money and the measurement of what serves as money. Thus, defining money, the subject of this section, is of considerable importance.

A good definition enables us to separate the thing being defined from all other things. Economists define *money* in terms of its specific functions within the financial system, that is, by what it does. By specifying precisely what it does, we can distinguish money from everything else we observe in the financial system, even those things that at first glance appear quite similar. Of particular interest is what makes money unique: What does it do that other things do not?

The primary function of **money**, and the function that distinguishes it from all else in the financial system, is that it serves as a generally acceptable **means of payment**, or **medium of exchange**. As Chapter 1 stated, money is what we generally use to make payments and, hence, what is generally accepted as payment. The importance of money's function as a means of payment is so obvious that it is often overlooked.

Imagine a world without money where all goods were exchanged or traded by **barter**, that is, by trading goods for goods. If you worked in a computer factory, you might be paid in keyboards, which would be not only difficult to exchange for other goods and services but also rather cumbersome to carry around. To buy groceries, for example, you would have to persuade the grocer to accept your keyboards for payment. There would be no reason for the grocer to do so, unless she had a use for additional keyboards or knew someone else who did. Finding such a **double coincidence of wants**, the situation when the grocer has what you want (groceries) and you have what she wants (keyboards), would often be extremely difficult. Thus, exchange under a barter system is costly in terms of search time—the time spent looking for someone who has groceries and wants computer keyboards. In general, the considerable time and effort associated with barter make it a cumbersome and inefficient way to conduct transactions. It raises transactions costs, which are all costs involved with making exchanges. In turn, higher transactions costs hold down the volume of exchange in the economy. This is why barter economies tended to be mostly agricultural. With the volume of trade relatively low and exchanges costly to carry out, one

---

Money
Anything that functions as a means of payment (medium of exchange), unit of account, and store of value.

Means of Payment (Medium of Exchange)
Something generally acceptable for making payments.

Barter
Trade of goods for goods.

Double Coincidence of Wants
In barter, the situation in which each person involved in a potential exchange has what the other person wants.

could never be sure of finding a double coincidence of wants. As a result, almost everyone produced the food and other items they needed to survive so that very few exchanges would be necessary. If some individuals did decide to specialize and trade, they had an incentive to produce the goods that were easiest to trade rather than the goods that they were best at producing. For efficiency to occur, people should specialize in what they can most efficiently produce, which is exactly what "money" in an economy encourages.

Fortunately, all of this process is not necessary in a modern economy because we do have something that serves as a generally acceptable means of payment—money. As a result, people can exchange goods and services for money and vice versa. To illustrate, Randy, the dishwasher, planned to exchange a week's labor for $50 and the $50 for groceries. If Randy had accepted the tickets—a type of barter transaction—he could not have eaten until he found a grocer who wanted tickets to the play. If he failed to do so by curtain time on Saturday, Randy would find that the tickets had become worthless and hence he would go hungry for the next week. A monetary exchange eliminates the need for a double coincidence of wants and thus facilitates trade by reducing the transactions costs involved. Now is a good time to read the A Closer Look feature on money, exchange, and economic development on page 26.

Something that becomes generally acceptable as a means of payment in exchange for goods and services will necessarily also function as a **store of value**. To be acceptable, something must store value or, more specifically, purchasing power because people receive money and spend it at different points in time. In other words, there is a difference between the time pattern of people's receipts of money and the time pattern of their expenditures. If you are paid for your labor services today and do not need to purchase anything until tomorrow, you would presumably be unwilling to accept anything in payment that is likely to decline in value before you spend it. (Could Randy have sold the tickets to the play for $50 on Sunday, the day after the performance?) Conversely, people will accept something as a means of payment for goods and services when they believe that they can easily exchange it for something else of like value in the near future.

We now know that money functions as a means of payment and store of value and what these functions mean. For monetary exchange to proceed in an orderly fashion, however, there must be some method of specifying the amount of money required to pay for a given quantity of a particular good. In other words, there is a need for an accounting unit, commonly referred to as a *unit of account*. Because all domestic prices and financial records including debts in the United States are expressed in dollars, the dollar serves as our monetary **unit of account**—it is the standard measure of value. To appreciate why it is convenient to have a standardized unit of account, imagine the poor grocer and the grocer's customers who, in the absence of money and a unit of account, would have to remember that one computer keyboard equals 4 quarts of milk, 1 crate of oranges equals 3 pounds of cheese, and so forth. A unit of account facilitates actual transactions throughout the economy by making it possible to compare the relative values of different goods and services and to keep records about prices and debts.

In sum, money is whatever circulates in a modern economy as a generally acceptable means of payment. By necessity, money will also function as a store of value, and its unit of measurement will naturally become the unit of account and measure of value. The functions of money are portrayed in Exhibit 2-1.

The Monetary Aggregates and Domestic Nonfinancial Debt

Given our definition, measuring the quantity or stock of money in an economy should be straightforward: Add together those things functioning as a means of payment. In reality, as usual, measurement is not quite so simple. There are at least two difficulties.

Store of Value
Something that retains its value over time.

Unit of Account
A standardized accounting unit such as the dollar that provides a consistent measure of value.

Money, Exchange, and Economic Development

The body of the text describes how (1) the high transactions costs associated with barter tend to hold down the volume of exchange and (2) the low volume of exchange tends to "keep people on the farm." Most of us take for granted the existence of money; we have never experienced a barter system. How and why economies evolved from a primitive barter system to an advanced monetary system is a long story. The short, somewhat simplified version is that the high costs of barter exchange provided an economic incentive for people to devise a better system. Important in the early evolution of the system were the merchants who established trading posts or general stores. They purchased goods from farmers, often paying for the goods with a receipt that the farmer could later use at the store to purchase other items that the merchant had acquired from other farmers. The receipts were an early form of money, as were the gold and silver nuggets that also came to be exchanged for goods and services at the trading posts and elsewhere. Eventually, as governments developed and the benefits of standardizing the money within an economy became apparent, governments came to produce and certify coins and paper notes (currency) as money.

By eliminating the need for a double coincidence of wants, the existence of money dramatically reduces the costs of conducting trade, thereby encouraging a larger volume of exchange. With more opportunities for exchange, no longer do all of an economy's participants need to individually produce the same goods to survive and prosper; because exchanges are faster and easier, labor time is not wasted in the trading process. People can now more easily specialize in the production of goods to which they are relatively best suited, trade these goods for money, and use the money to purchase goods produced by others. The development of the financial system and the resulting division of labor (and other resources) into the production of an increasing variety of goods are key ingredients in the process of economic development. The accompanying schematic diagram ties these several thoughts together.

Transactions costs associated with barter

encourage

Development of money

facilitates

Exchange (trading)

facilitates

Specialization and division of labor

facilitates

Economic development

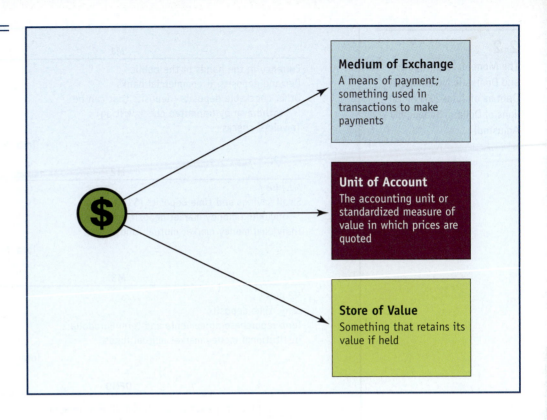

Medium of Exchange
A means of payment; something used in transactions to make payments

Unit of Account
The accounting unit or standardized measure of value in which prices are quoted

Store of Value
Something that retains its value if held

First, what functions as a means of payment in an economy will change over time, so what is considered money will need to be revised as the economy's financial system evolves. For example, once gold and silver coins were money. Now they are gone, having been replaced by paper currency, coins made out of nonprecious metals, and checkable deposits. Second, some things may be difficult to classify; that is, some financial claims are on the borderline between being and not being a means of payment. For example, **money market deposit accounts (MMDAs)** have limited check-writing privileges—up to three checks per month. First offered by banks in 1982, MMDAs earn higher interest than most checking accounts and generally require a higher minimum balance. Because of the limited check-writing privileges, MMDAs have some characteristics of checking accounts and, hence, are a borderline case.

Classification is not merely an esoteric or semantic issue. Historically, as we shall see in the next chapter, the Fed's policy actions have often been guided in part by what is happening to the money supply. Therefore, at any point in time, the Fed had to have as accurate a measurement of the quantity of money as possible. Today the Fed uses the monetary aggregates along with many other variables in the formulation and implementation of monetary policy. Given the existence of several financial claims that are close to being full-fledged means of payment and some controversy within the economics profession over the adequacy and narrowness of the means of payment definition, it should come as no surprise to learn that the following points apply:

1. Rather than relying on only one measure, the Fed hedges its bets by collecting, publishing, and monitoring data on several monetary measures.

2. The items included in the various measures have changed over time as the financial system and new means of payment have evolved and as the Fed has strived to improve its monetary measures.

Money Market Deposit Accounts (MMDAs)
Financial claims with limited check-writing privileges, offered by banks since 1982; they earn higher interest than fully checkable deposits and require a higher minimum balance.

M1	
Currency in the hands of the public	$ 676.7
Demand deposits at commercial banks	322.7
Other checkable deposits (deposits that can be withdrawn by unlimited check writing)	328.8
Travelers' checks	7.7
Total M1	**$ 1,335.9***

M2	
M1 plus	
Small savings and time deposits ($100,000), including money market deposit accounts	$ 4,203.1
Individual money market mutual funds	756.8
Total M2	**$ 6,295.6***

M3	
M2 plus	
Large time deposits	$ 988.2
Term repurchase agreements and term Eurodollars	898.2
Institutional money market mutual funds	1,112.9
Total M3	**$ 9,294.9***

DFND	
Federal: { Credit market debt of the U.S. government and state and local governments	$ 4,265.3
Nonfederal: { Corporate bonds / Mortgages / Consumer credit (including bank loans) / Other bank loans / Commercial paper / Other debt instruments	18,954.8
Total DNFD	**$ 23,220.1**

3. Because information about credit market activity can also provide useful information, the Fed further covers its bases by monitoring and publishing a broad measure of outstanding credit that measures unpaid loans and debts.

The Monetary Aggregates

Among the many jobs carried out by the Fed are the collection and regular publication of financial data. Currently, the Fed publishes data on several different monetary measures. These measures are referred to as **monetary aggregates**, or collections of monetary assets. Exhibit 2-2 shows the composition of **M1, M2,** and **M3,** the main monetary aggregates. The aggregates comprise several different types of financial assets. (Chapter 5 and the Glossary at the back of the book contain detailed descriptions of each item included in M2 and M3.) Some items clearly serve as a means of payment (currency and checkable deposits), some are clearly not means of payment ("large" time deposits), and some are in between (money market deposit accounts). Note that M2 consists of everything in M1 plus some other highly liquid assets, and M3 consists of everything in M2 plus some less-liquid assets. Thus, in general, as the aggregate gets bigger, it includes more less-liquid assets.

Monetary Aggregates
The measures of money—including M1, M2, and M3—monitored and tracked by the Fed.

M1
Currency in the hands of the public plus checkable deposits.

M2
Everything in M1 plus other highly liquid assets.

M3
Everything in M2 plus some less-liquid assets.

The measure that *currently* corresponds most closely to the definition of money is M1. It consists of currency held by the public and checkable deposits.[1] Checkable deposits are deposits that can be withdrawn by writing a check to a third party. They consist of

Demand Deposits
Non-interest-earning checking accounts issued by banks.

Checkable Deposits
Deposits that are subject to withdrawal by writing a check.

- **Demand deposits**, which are non-interest-earning checking accounts issued by banks.
- Other **checkable deposits**, which are interest-earning checking accounts issued by any of the depository institutions.

M1 contains the "monetary" assets that we *currently* use in transactions, and it is generally what we have in mind throughout the text when we refer to the *money supply*. All components of M1 are means of payment. This is not true of M2 and M3; for example, large time deposits, a component of M3, generally cannot be used to buy groceries. The accompanying A Closer Look feature discusses the relationships among money, near monies, and other financial claims.

Notice that the word *currently* has been italicized in the last two paragraphs. The reason, hinted at in the earlier part of this section, is that as financial regulations have changed and financial practices have evolved, the Fed has on a number of occasions refined and reconstructed the various monetary measures. For example, **negotiable orders of withdrawal (NOW) accounts**, which are essentially interest-bearing checking accounts, were not even in existence in 1970. "Born" in 1972 in Massachusetts and New Hampshire as the brainchild of some clever financial institution executives, these accounts were initially counted as part of M2. When their volume grew and they became legal nationwide, they were "promoted" to M1, having become a generally acceptable means of payment. Money market deposit accounts, on the other hand, are, as of this writing, included in M2. Because of the limitations on usage (only three checks per month), the Fed has concluded that depositors generally do not use these accounts as means of payment. Hence, MMDAs are included in M2—an aggregate containing M1 and other items that are so close to money that they are often referred to as **near monies**.

Negotiable Order of Withdrawal (NOW) Accounts
Interest-earning checking accounts.

The other near monies included in M2 are small time deposits, passbook savings deposits, and individual money market mutual funds. As previously mentioned, these assets are defined in more detail in Chapter 5 and in the Glossary. Even though they are not used to make transactions, they are all fairly liquid near monies because they can easily be converted to transactions money (checkable deposits or currency) without loss of value for the principal.

Near Monies
Highly liquid financial assets that can easily be converted to transactions money (M1) without loss of value.

The essential point to keep in mind as we end this section on measuring money is that measurement is not nearly so straightforward as one might have imagined. The difficulties and ambiguities, in turn, contribute to revisions in the various measures from time to time and lead the Fed to hedge its bets by monitoring several measures rather than relying on only one. Such flexibility is required by a dynamic financial system that is evolving through time as rules, regulations, and payment practices change.

Recap Money is anything that functions as a means of payment (medium of exchange), a unit of account, and a store of value. Money is acceptable in payment for goods and services. The Fed monitors several measures of money. M1 (transactions money) is currency in the hands of the public plus checkable deposits. M2 includes everything in M1 plus other highly liquid assets. M3 includes everything in M2 plus some less-liquid assets.

Money and Other Financial Claims

In Chapter 1 we saw that net lenders usually lend their surplus funds to net borrowers through the financial system (financial markets and financial intermediaries). Put another way, purchasing power is transferred from those who have it to those who need it. What is transferred, in fact, is current purchasing power, which is exchanged for another financial asset, or a future claim on money. In effect, net lenders "rent out" their surplus funds to net borrowers for a given period of time, much as a landlord rents out an apartment. In financial markets, the net lender acquires a financial asset, which is a claim on and liability of the borrower. The claim, an asset to the holder and a liability to the issuer, is really an IOU—a promise by the borrower to repay the original amount borrowed (the principal) plus "rent" (the interest) to the lender.

Financial claims, other than money, are issued by borrowers or financial intermediaries. The intermediaries issue claims on themselves and then, in turn, lend to borrowers. The financial system includes many different types of financial claims, reflecting the wide variety of borrowers and lenders and the tendency to tailor particular types of claims to the preferences and needs of the net lenders and net borrowers. Since the 1990s, the trend among net lenders has been to bypass depository institutions and to put a large share of their surplus funds into mutual funds, the most rapidly growing type of intermediary.[a]

Because all financial claims, whether they be bank deposits, stocks, or Treasury bills, are claims on money, they can in some sense be compared with one another as well as with money. Traditional standards of comparison include the risk and the liquidity of various claims.

Risk refers to the possibility or probability that the value of a claim will decline. One example of risk is the possibility that a borrower will default and fail to pay back all or part of the principal or the interest. This risk is similar to the risk that a renter will burn down the apartment building or fail to pay his rent and be difficult to evict. The higher the probability of receiving less money back than expected, the riskier the financial claim is relative to money.

The *liquidity* of a financial claim (or asset) is determined by how easy or difficult it is to convert the asset into money. The ease (or difficulty) is defined in terms of the cost and time associated with the conversion. If significant costs or considerable time is required to convert a particular type of asset to money, it is usually referred to as *illiquid.* As the costs and time required to exchange a particular asset approach zero, the liquidity increases, with money representing perfect liquidity.[b]

So what does all this have to do with the monetary aggregates? Some items included in M2, such as savings deposits, are very liquid and holding them exposes the owner to little risk, hence the term, *near monies.* Other items that are less liquid and/or entail more risk are included in M3 or DNFD. There is some logic to the system!

Domestic Nonfinancial Debt

Before we leave this section on money and the monetary aggregates, we need to introduce another aggregate that the Fed keeps track of along with M1, M2, and M3. This aggregate is **domestic nonfinancial debt (DNFD)**, which is a measure of outstanding loans and debts accumulated in the present and past years. Take a look at Exhibit 2-2 again for the components of DNFD.

Specifically, DNFD refers to total credit market debt owed by the domestic nonfinancial sector including the U.S. government, state and local governments, private nonfinancial firms, and households. Don't let the length of this definition confuse you. *Domestic* merely means U.S. entities excluding foreign entities. *Nonfinancial debt* excludes the debt of financial institutions—those institutions that borrow solely to relend. The debt of financial institutions is excluded to avoid double counting.

For example, suppose Friendly Savings and Loan borrows surplus funds from small passbook savers and relends those funds to Jorge and Maria to buy their first home. If the debt of the financial institution were counted, both Jorge and Maria's mortgage debt and Friendly's debt to the passbook savers would be included in the aggregate. This would be double counting, because the ultimate transaction went from the passbook savers to Jorge and Maria with the savings and loan in between. Furthermore, Friendly's financial debt to the passbook savers is offset by the financial claim (mortgage) Friendly holds against Jorge and Maria.

If all this sounds a bit confusing, think of DNFD as merely a measure of the unpaid claims lenders have against borrowers excluding the debt of financial intermediaries. DNFD is probably the best measure of outstanding nonfinancial credit that we have. When credit flows increase, DNFD (the aggregate amount of debt outstanding) goes up. Likewise, when credit flows decrease, DNFD declines. Exhibit 2-3 shows the relative size of the monetary aggregates and DNFD.

The Economy and the Aggregates

In the early and mid-1980s, M1 was the primary measure of money that the Fed watched. Targets were set for the growth rate of M1, and the Fed monitored these targets to provide a barometer of economic activity. If M1 growth was above the target rate, the Fed would take actions that resulted in a slowdown in the growth of M1. If M1 growth was below the target, the Fed would take actions that resulted in a speedup in the growth of M1. In either case, the goal was to nudge the economy in the desired direction.

During the late 1980s, M2 gained importance and prominence in the execution of monetary policy by the Fed. During this period, the relationship between changes in M2 and economic activity seemed more stable than that between changes in M1 and economic activity. Consequently, the Fed watched the growth rate of M2 for signals about how well the economy was doing and deemphasized the role of M1. In the early 1990s, the stable relationship between changes in M2 and changes in economic activity also seemed to break down. The growth rate of M2 moved in erratic and unpredictable ways. As a result, the Fed has also deemphasized the use of M2 as a policy indicator.

In the early 1990s, the Fed increasingly used changes in the growth rate of DNFD as an indicator of the direction of the economy. DNFD seemed, at least at that time, to have a quite stable relationship with changes in economic activity. If credit growth was increasing, then spending was likely to be going up. If credit extension was slowing, then the growth rate of economic activity was also likely to be slowing. Hence, the Fed was interested in monitoring changes in this broad aggregate. By the

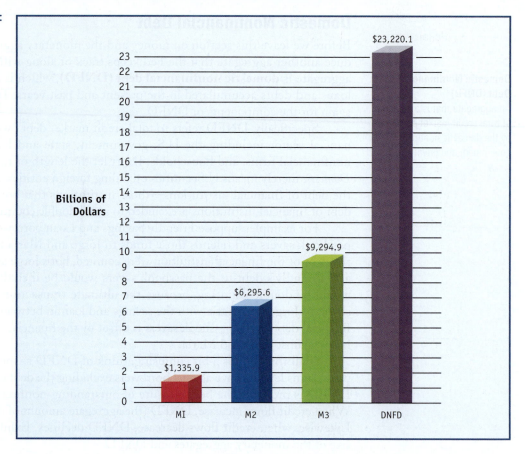

late 1990s and continuing into the early to mid-2000s, the Fed was using many other economic variables as barometers of economic conditions in addition to the monetary aggregates and DNFD. The monetary aggregates were increasingly de-emphasized in formulating policy and now are used primarily as informational variables along with many other variables.

For our purposes, then, it is probably best to think of M1 as a measure of transactions money and M2 as one of several broader measures of money or other indicators (including M3 and DNFD), which has been, at times, closely related to economic activity and hence was closely monitored by the Fed in its execution of monetary policy. If you are baffled by the reasons for the changes in the relationships between the aggregates and economic activity, don't be discouraged. By the time you have completed this text, we hope to have provided you with fairly good explanations of why these changes occur. Don't forget that the financial system of the economy in which we live is dynamic, innovative, and evolving. Exhibit 2-4 shows how the various aggregates have grown over time.

For current statistical data on the monetary aggregates, see **http://www.federalreserve.gov/releases/H6/**.

Recap   In addition to the monetary aggregates, the Fed monitors DNFD, a broad measure of credit. DNFD includes public and private debt but excludes the debt of financial institutions to avoid double counting. Sometimes a given aggregate has been more highly correlated with the level of economic activity than at other times.

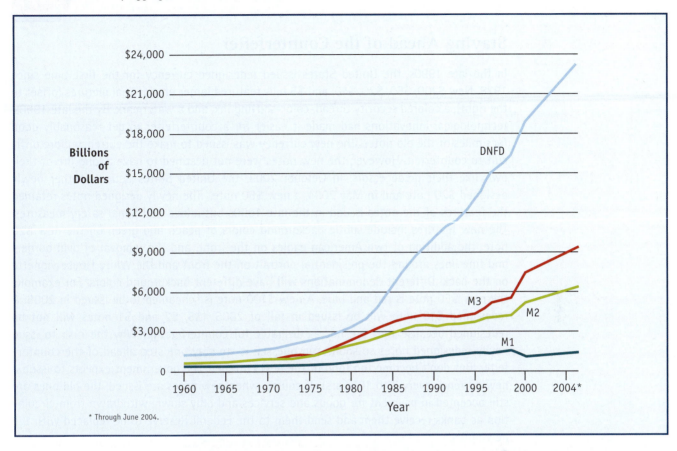

$24,000

$21,000

$18,000

**Billions
of
Dollars** $15,000

$12,000

$9,000

$6,000

$3,000

0

DNFD

M3

M2

M1

1960 1965 1970 1975 1980 1985 1990 1995 2000 2004*

Year

* Through June 2004.

The Ongoing Evolution of the Payments System: The Role of Computer and Telecommunications Technologies

Like the human race, the current financial system has evolved from a primitive state and will continue to evolve in the future. This tendency to change, which we have already seen in those things functioning as a means of payment, has been significantly influenced by the technology used to execute transactions. The **payments mechanism** is the means by which transactions are completed—that is, how money is transferred among transactors.

If someone now asked you what makes up the U.S. money supply, we hope you would answer "currency held by the public and checkable deposits, the primary components of M1." Checkable deposits are payable on demand to third parties. For example, if you write a check to your grocer, the first two parties are you and the depository institution; the grocer is the third party. The check in payment for goods purchased is an order for your bank to debit (subtract) a certain number of dollars from your checkable deposit account. The dollars are then credited (added) to the deposit account of the grocer, the third party. Thus, a checkable deposit is a means of payment, and the check is the method used to transfer ownership of the deposit between parties to a transaction. The point is that the check itself is not money; if it were, printing presses would work around the clock! The balances in checkable deposits are money.

In recent years, computer and telecommunications technologies have greatly altered the way in which payments are made. Technological innovations will eventually make checks much less important, or even obsolete, as a means of transferring

Payments Mechanism
The means by which transactions are consummated; that is, how money is transferred in an exchange.

Staying Ahead of the Counterfeiter

In the late 1990s, the United States issued redesigned currency for the first time since 1928. New $100, $50, $20, $10, and $5 bills featured larger presidential pictures (offset to the right), a colored security thread, color-shifting ink, and a watermark. By the late 1990s, technological innovations had made it easier for a counterfeiter to get reasonably good facsimiles of the old notes. The new currency was issued to make the currency more difficult to counterfeit. However, the new notes were not destined to have a long life of their own like their predecessors. In October 2003, the United States issued another newly designed $20 note and in May 2004, a new $50 note. The newly designed notes retained the features of the notes issued in the late 1990s but added additional safety measures. The new features include subtle background colors of peach and green on the new $20 note, the addition of two American eagles on the front, and the removal of oval borders and fine lines around the presidential portrait on the front and the White House vignette on the back. Different denominations will have different background colors. For example, the new $50 note is red and blue. A new $100 note is scheduled to be issued in 2005. A redesigned $10 note will be issued in fall of 2005. ($5, $2 and $1 notes will not be redesigned because they are not as desirable for counterfeiting.) Why the rush to issue newly redesigned notes so soon? You guessed it—to stay one step ahead of the counterfeiter. But don't become too fond of the new currency. The government expects to issue a new currency every 7 to 10 years! Of course, when new notes are issued, the old ones are still accepted in payment for goods and services and only slowly withdrawn from circulation as banks receive them and send them to the Federal Reserve to be replaced with the new notes.

Electronic Funds Transfer System
The transfer of funds to third parties in response to electronic instructions rather than a paper check.

Point-of-Sale Terminal
A computer terminal that uses a debit card to electronically transfer funds from a deposit account to the account of a third party.

Stored-Value Cards
Plastic cards that have a magnetic strip that is swiped through a card reader to make payments; they are usually single use.

purchasing power. Today we are making an increasingly larger percentage of payments through an **electronic funds transfer system**. In this system, payments are made to third parties in response to electronic instructions rather than instructions written on a paper check. Note that an electronic funds transfer system does not eliminate the need for deposit accounts; it is just a more efficient way of transferring funds from one deposit account to another. To pay your grocery bill, for instance, your account is debited by the amount of your bill, and the grocer's account is credited by the same amount at the time of the exchange. The whole system is computerized so that no written checks are necessary. All you need is an account number and a debit card that you present to the grocer. The grocer, in turn, enters the prices of your purchases into a computer terminal (called a **point-of-sale terminal**), and at the end of the month, you receive a statement giving your current balance and a record of all the charges and deposits to your account. This is just like a checking account statement, but you do not have to write all those checks.

Other forms of electronic funds transfer systems are stored-value cards and smart cards. **Stored-value cards** are plastic cards that have a certain amount of funds embedded on a magnetic strip. The owner of the stored-value card has somehow paid to have the funds transferred to the card. Stored-value cards look like credit cards and are swiped through a card reader when the owner wants to access the funds. As the funds are spent, the balance on the card is transferred electronically from the card to the card reader.

34   **Part One**   *Chapter Two*

Forget Your Checkbook

Bobbi doesn't own a computer, but she has not been left out of the telecommunications revolution—not as long as she has a telephone. Once a month Bobbi dials up her bank and pays all of her bills over the phone. She is hooked into an automated payments system that contains a list of the names, addresses, and account numbers of the bills she regularly pays. Each account is assigned a number, and by keying in certain numbers on her push-button phone, Bobbi tells the bank to make a payment, in a certain amount, on the due date of the bill. She never writes a check or pays for a stamp to mail a bill. Moreover, the amount of the bill does not come out of her account until the exact due date. Assuming that some of her bills have due dates in the middle or latter part of the month and that she has an interest-earning checking account, this practice saves her the interest that she would have lost if she paid all of her bills on the first day of each month.

Increasingly, consumers are being offered opportunities to pay bills over the phone. (In some locations, the first bill that consumers can pay like this is their phone bill!) Banks also offer customers the option of having monthly payments, such as house or car payments, automatically deducted from checking or savings accounts. These opportunities cut down on check writing, which, despite being popular with consumers, is a relatively inefficient (high cost) way of making payments in this computer age.

Despite the advantages of electronic or automatic payments, consumers in the United States have been slower than their European counterparts to give up checks for two reasons. First, checks leave a "paper trail," which many consumers still trust more than computers. Secondly, many consumers don't want to give up the "float." *Float* is the time between when a check is written to a third party until the check is actually deducted from the account. The third party first deposits the check in its bank, which then sends the check to the first party's bank for payment. When payment is made, the check is then deducted from the first party's account. Float can be a few days, and many consumers like the cushion, particularly if times have been hard and payday falls on a Monday. The consumer can safely buy groceries Friday night without the worry of bouncing a check!

Stored-value cards are popular on college campuses to pay for such things are photocopying in the library, meals in the dining hall, and parking fees. They are also used to prepay for toll roads and generally have a single use.

Smart cards are much more sophisticated than stored-value cards in that they have a microprocessor chip embedded in them that stores information and usually includes a "digital signature." The stored information leads to greater security for someone who accepts a smart card for a payment because the digital signature is verified. Each time the card is used, the amount of the payment is deducted electronically from the card and credited to the recipient of the payment by a point-of-sale terminal that is equipped to do so. At some point, the recipient transfers smart card payments from the point-of-sale terminal to its bank. If it is transferred immediately, the payment is completed in a matter of seconds. The microprocessor checks the authenticity of the transaction by examining the digital signature that is embedded in the chip. Although the validity is authenticated, the transaction is kept anonymous as if cash were used. Some smart cards are

Smart Cards
Plastic cards with a microprocessor chip that are used to make payments; the chip stores information that allows the payment to be validated.

Computer and Telecommunications Technologies and the International Financial System

In recent years, cross-border financial flows have exploded, financial markets around the world have become more integrated, and a dramatic increase in world trade has been facilitated. However, it is not the growth in world trade that has made the globalization of finance a reality. Rather, it was the development of electronic funds transfer systems to make payments that was the catalyst to the growth of the international financial system. The revolution in computer and telecommunications technologies has allowed funds to be transferred electronically around the globe almost instantaneously, 24 hours a day. Investors can now purchase a wide variety of foreign financial instruments much more easily than in the past. Funds can seek their highest return (wherever that may be) after adjustments have been made for differences in risk. In this way, economic efficiency is increased. Without the ability to electronically transfer funds, global financial markets would be much less interdependent than they are today.

issued by and accepted by a single institution only. Other smart cards are accepted by multiple institutions and multiple retailers. As such, smart cards offer the possibility of replacing cash and checks to make most payments because they may be more convenient and cheaper to use.

Currently, many employers, in cooperation with banks, pay salaries by automatically crediting their employees' bank accounts rather than by issuing the customary weekly or monthly check. Such automatic credits are also a form of an electronic funds transfer system.

One of the best known and most popular forms of electronic transfer of funds is **Automated Teller Machine (ATM)** the **automated teller machine (ATM).** Your depository institution most likely has ATMs, which permit you to make deposits and withdrawals, even late at night when the institution itself is closed. In all probability, your college has a few ATMs on campus. ATMs are also visible in grocery and convenience stores, at car washes, and at shopping malls. Recently, portable ATMs in vans have been established that can be moved to sporting event locations, concerts, and so on. As you may have guessed, the vans housing the ATMs have multiple security features that prevent theft. As the ownership of personal computers and modems has spread, it has become possible to conduct a large portion of one's financial transactions from home.

A final comment is in order. Basically, electronic funds transfer systems are nothing more than the application of computer and telecommunications technology to the entire area of financial transactions and services. The aim is to reduce the physical handling and labor costs associated with an ever-expanding volume of paper checks, deposit slips, and the like, as well as to provide increased convenience and service to the public. Transferring funds and making payments electronically is generally much cheaper than writing checks or using other paper instructions to transfer funds. The application of computer and telecommunications technologies thus greatly reduces the costs of making payments and improves the efficiency of the payments system. As questions regarding the privacy of financial records, security of the systems, and legal

Automated Teller Machine (ATM)
A machine that permits a depositor to make deposits and withdrawals to an account even when the financial institution is closed.

responsibilities are being resolved, new payments practices and electronic funds transfer systems are spreading rapidly. One thing is certain: In the future, more payments will be made electronically because they are cheaper and in most cases, more convenient. The result will be further evolution in how money is used and, perhaps, changes in what functions as money. From barter to Indian beads to gold and silver coins to checkable deposits to electronic money, the evolution of money and the payments mechanism goes hand in hand with the development of an economy and with computer and telecommunications technologies.

Summary of Major Points

1. The primary function of money, and the function that makes it unique, is that it serves as a generally acceptable means of payment.

2. Something that becomes a generally acceptable means of payment will, of necessity, function as a store of value.

3. The unit of account in the United States is the dollar. It serves as a common denominator or standardized unit of measure in which all prices and debts are quoted.

4. The high transactions costs associated with barter encourage the development of money. The existence of money facilitates trade, which, in turn, encourages specialization and division of labor. Thus, the development of the financial system contributes importantly to an economy's growth and development.

5. Measuring money is not easy. What functions as money will change over time as an economy's financial system evolves, and some financial claims may be difficult to classify.

6. The Fed monitors and publishes data on several monetary aggregates and refines and recomputes the various measures periodically.

7. M1 (currency plus checkable deposits) is the best measure of the money supply currently available for transactions purposes. In the late 1980s, the Fed used M2 (everything in M1 plus other highly liquid assets) to guide its execution of monetary policy. In recent years, the behavior of the aggregates has become a less reliable barometer of economic activity because of the less stable relationships between the aggregates and economic activity. The Fed has looked to other indicators to aid in the execution of policy and used the monetary aggregates as informational variables only.

8. Money represents current purchasing power—a claim on goods and services. Other financial claims represent future claims on money. Financial claims can be compared to each other and to money in terms of risk and liquidity.

9. The payments mechanism is the means used to transfer money among transactors. Checks, for example, transfer ownership of checkable deposits such as NOW accounts. Innovations now being adopted suggest that an increasingly larger percentage of payments is being made with electronic funds transfer systems. Such innovations include debit cards, stored-value cards, smart cards, point-of-sale terminals, and ATMs. Smart value cards have microprocessor chips that allow anonymous, secure payments to be made.

Key Terms

Automatic Teller Machine (ATM), **36**
Barter, **24**
Checkable Deposits, **29**
Demand Deposits, **29**
Domestic Nonfinancial Debt (DNFD), **31**
Double Coincidence of Wants, **24**
Electronic Funds Transfer System, **34**

Means of Payment (Medium of Exchange), **24**
Monetary Aggregates, **28**
Money, **24**
Money Market Deposit Accounts (MMDAs), **27**
M1, **28**
M2, **28**
M3, **28**
Near Monies, **29**

Negotiable Order of Withdrawal (NOW) Accounts, **29**
Payments Mechanism, **33**
Point-of-Sale Terminal, **34**
Smart Cards, **35**
Store of Value, **25**
Stored-Value Cards, **34**
Unit of Account, **25**

Review Questions

1. Discuss or define briefly the following terms and concepts: *means of payment, store of value, unit of account, barter, monetary aggregates, liquidity, nonfinancial debt, electronic funds transfer system*, and *risk*.

2. What are the functions of money? Which function do you think is most important?

3. Suppose we define *money* as that which serves as a store of value. Explain why this is a poor definition.

4. Suppose something is functioning as money within an economy. What could cause the population to lose confidence in the value of the means of payment? What do you think would happen as a result?

5. How does the Fed calculate M1, M2, M3, and DNFD? Are these aggregates all money? Why or why not? Which contains the most liquid assets? Which is smallest? Which is largest?

6. Why does the Fed have so many monetary measures? Which monetary aggregate is most closely associated with transactions balances?

7. What is the current role of the monetary aggregates in the formulation and implementation of monetary policy? How and why has that role changed over time?

8. Why is the debt of financial institutions excluded from DNFD?

9. What is the payments mechanism? What changes are occurring in this mechanism? Why are they occurring? How do smart cards differ from stored-value cards?

10. Zoto is a remote island that has experienced rapid development. In contrast, Zaha is an island where growth has been sluggish and the level of economic activity remains low. How could the existence of money have affected these two outcomes?

11. Is it necessary for the collection of assets called *money* to perform all of the functions described in the chapter? Why or why not?

12. In what ways is money similar to other financial assets? How can money be distinguished from other financial assets?

13. Your friend took a class in money and banking two years ago and recalls that currency in the hands of the public is in M1. Explain to your friend why currency in the hands of the public is also included in M2 and M3.

Analytical Questions

Question 15, marked with an icon, is objective in nature. It can be completed with a short answer or number.

14. Would each of the following assets be "good" money? Why or why not?
    a. Gold
    b. Dirt
    c. Corn
    d. Oil (often called liquid gold)

15. In which monetary aggregate(s) is each of the following assets included?
    a. Small savings and time deposits ($100,000)
    b. Money market deposit accounts
    c. Currency in the hands of the public
    d. Checkable deposits
    e. Individual money market mutual funds
    f. Institutional money market mutual funds
    g. Large time deposits
    h. Travelers' checks

Internet Exercises

1. Use the *Statistical Release H.6*, published by the Fed to report the most current measures of the money supply. You can employ the following root directory: **http://www.federalreserve.gov/releases/H6/**. How does the Fed differentiate among alternative measures of the money supply such as M1, M2, and M3? Which measure of the money supply is most liquid?

2. The following root directory from the Economic Bulletin Board provides historical estimates of the money supply: **http://www.federalreserve.gov/releases/H6/hist/**.

From the data, calculate and/or observe the approximate annual (seasonally adjusted) growth rates for M1 and M2 from 1970 until today. Verify that the growth rate of M1 increased from 1971 to 1985 while the growth rate of M2 registered a downward trend over the same time period. (*Hint:* To calculate the approximate annual growth rates for M1 or M2 for each year, subtract the January value from the December value and then divide the result by the January value.) What have been the relative growth rates of M1 and M2 in the last few years?

Suggested Readings

A beautiful book well worth the effort to locate is *Money: A History,* ed. Jonathan Williams (New York: St. Martin's Press, 1997).

For an extremely comprehensive look at money, see *A History of Money from Ancient Times to the Present Day,* 3rd. ed. Glyn Davies (Cardiff: University of Wales Press, 2002).

For an inclusive look at many of the topics discussed in this chapter including the face of U.S. currency, counterfeiting, new currency designs, and the history of money, go to **http://www. minneapolisfed.org/econed/curric/money.cfm**.

An interesting discussion that deals with many topics about our nation's coins and currency is found in the *Testimony of Louise L. Roseman,* director, Division of Reserve Bank Operations and Payment Systems before a subcommittee of the U.S. House of Representatives, March 28, 2000. The testimony includes a discussion of the introduction of the new currency, the new dollar coin, anticounterfeiting measures, and the advantages and disadvantages of high denomination banknotes. (Currently, the largest denomination U.S. note that is available is $100.) The testimony is available on the Internet at **http://www.federalreserve.gov/boarddocs/testimony/2000/**.

John Walter provides a noteworthy history of the evolution of the monetary aggregates, along with additional sources of data and further readings, in an article entitled "Monetary Aggregates." It can be found in *Macroeconomic Data: A User's Guide,* published by the Federal Reserve Bank of Richmond (1990): 36–44.

A useful Internet site is "Dollars and Cents: Fundamental Facts about U.S. Money"(2000). It can be obtained for free from the Federal Reserve Bank of Atlanta and is found on the Internet at **http://www.frbatlanta.org/publica/ brochure/fundfac/money. htm**. Another interesting site is **http://www.moneyfactory.com/**.

For additional information on the newly redesigned currency, see **http://www.moneyfactory.com/newmoney/**.

For a comprehensive discussion of all forms and aspects of "Electronic Money," see the article by the same name that is available on the Federal Reserve Bank of Chicago's Web site at **http://www.chicagofed.org/consumer_information/ electronic_money.cfm**

For an interesting discussion of many of the topics in this chapter, see the most recent Fed chairperson's "Monetary Policy Report to Congress" that is given in February and July of each year. The report and testimony of the chair is available on the Internet at **http://www.federalreserve.gov/**. The reports also appear in the March and August editions of the *Federal Reserve Bulletin.*

Endnotes

1 M1 also includes travelers' checks, which account for a relatively small portion. For simplicity we ignore travelers' checks.

A Closer Look, page 30

a Mutual funds are investment pools in which a large number of shareholders purchase securities such as stocks and bonds.

b During the middle of the nineteenth century, coal miners' wages in Staffordshire, England, were paid partly in beer! Commenting on this practice, Charles Fay, a historian, remarked: "This currency was very popular and highly liquid, but it was issued to excess and difficult to store" (*Life and Labour in the Nineteenth Century* [Cambridge: Cambridge University Press, 1920]: 197).

Looking Back, page 34

a Press Release for the U.S. Treasury, October 27, 1997.

b Press Release for the U.S. Treasury, May 9, 2000.

c **http://www.federalreserve.gov/boarddocs/testimony /2000/20000328.htm.**

Money is like muck—not good unless you spread it.

—Francis Bacon

3

The Role of Money and Credit

Learning Objectives:

After reading this chapter, you should know:

What the circular flow of income and expenditures is

What the interest rate is

How the supply of and demand for money—and/or credit flows—influence the interest rate

How, in general, changes in money and credit influence nominal GDP, real GDP, and prices

What the inflation rate is and how to calculate it

The Trees versus the Forest

A major objective of any science—be it physics, astronomy, or economics—is to find patterns where the untrained eye sees only disorder. To discover and understand these patterns, it is usually necessary to disregard inessential details. Such abstraction facilitates the identification of the fundamental and essential relationships linking the key elements of the process or phenomena being studied. In the study of money, credit, and the financial system, you may find the details of the analysis overwhelming. Unfortunately, they may obscure the broad fundamental patterns of order so important to an analytical foundation. The problem is akin to getting lost in a forest; by paying too much attention to the individual trees, you can become disoriented and lose your way.

Not that long ago, the role for money in the economy was more clear-cut than it is today, or so it seemed. During those simpler years, changes in the monetary aggregates were more closely correlated with the level of economic activity; hence, the monetary aggregates were useful in formulating monetary policy. Not so today. Financial innovation, technology, and the globalization of finance have blurred the relationships between the monetary aggregates and the level of economic activity. Nevertheless, changes in money and credit extension are important informational variables that the Fed monitors and that affect (or are affected by) changes in spending, saving, borrowing, and lending. The purpose of Chapters 1 and 2 was to introduce the roles of money, credit, and the financial system.

The general purpose of this chapter is to provide an analytical perspective on how money and interest rates fit into the overall economy. We begin with the circular flow of income and output in a simplified economy—an economy composed just of households that supply economic resources (factors of production) to firms that produce goods. The purpose of this section is to give you a broad overview of the theoretical role of money in the economy. The circular flow analysis and accompanying diagram should serve both as a road map through the economic "forest" and as an aerial photograph that reveals the patterns of order that link households, firms, financial markets, and financial intermediaries. We then move on to more specific ways in which changes in money and/or credit affect the level of economic activity today. We shall see that changes in the demand and supply of money affect interest rates. Changes in interest rates in turn affect changes in GDP and prices. Keep in mind that in a more sophisticated economy, money is just one of many financial instruments that net lenders may hold. As we saw in Chapter 2, money is unique, however, in that it is the only financial instrument that serves as a means of payment.

The Circular Flow of Income and Expenditures in a Simplified Economy

Circular Flow Diagram
A diagram that shows the real and financial flows between households and business firms.

In a simplified economy, firms and households meet in three markets: the product (output), factor (input), and financial markets.[1] The **circular flow diagram**, shown in Exhibit 3-1, pulls together the essential features of this simplified economy. It is designed to highlight the flows of income and expenditures, which link the various markets to the producing, spending, saving, borrowing, and lending behavior of firms and households.

In this simple circular flow diagram, real flows of products (outputs) and the services of the factors of production (inputs) go in one direction while money flows in payment for the products and the use of factors of production go in the opposite. Households supply labor and other factors of production to businesses. Money flows from businesses to households in payment for the services of labor and the other factors of production. The payments for factor services are household income. Households purchase consumer goods and services and new houses from businesses using part of the income they have received in payment for their factor services. Money flows from

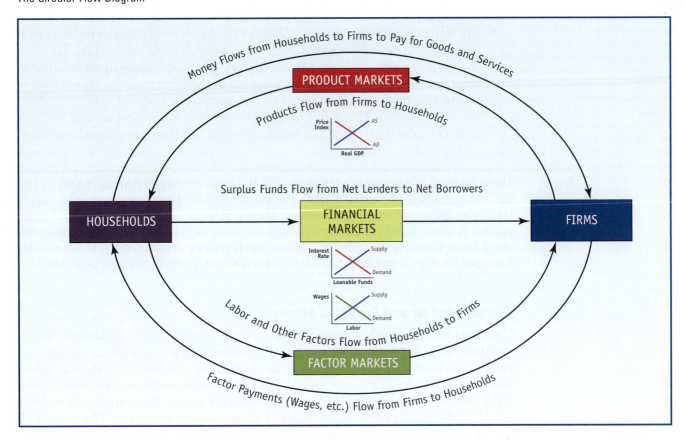

households back to firms to purchase goods and services. Usually, however, households do not spend all of the income they receive on goods and services. Instead, they are net lenders spending less than they receive on consumer and investment goods. The financial system links surplus households with net borrowers. The net borrowers are usually businesses that use the borrowed funds to purchase investment goods.

Funds flow from households (net lenders) to businesses (net borrowers) through the financial system either directly through financial markets or indirectly through financial intermediaries. Without developed financial markets, transferring the surpluses of net lenders to the net borrowers would be much more difficult. As we saw in Chapter 2, the transactions costs of such exchanges would slow down the volume of exchanges and, hence, slow economic growth.

Prices in the output, factor, and financial markets adjust to coordinate and balance the supplies and demands resulting from the plans of households and businesses to produce, spend, borrow, and lend. If a change occurs in one market, reflecting changes in the behavior of households or firms, repercussions will be felt throughout all markets in the form of price and quantity adjustments.

The roles, relationships, and interdependencies that Exhibit 3-1 depicts can be summarized as follows:

1. *The roles of firms:* Firms supply goods and services to the product (output) market, demand investment goods supplied by other firms, demand factor services in the factor (input) market, and demand funds (borrow) from the financial system.

2. *The roles of households:* Households demand goods and services in the product market, supply factor services in the factor market, and supply funds (lend) to the financial system.

3. *The roles of markets:*
   - The various markets coordinate and balance the supplies and demands resulting from the plans of firms and households to produce, spend, borrow, lend, and the like.
   - A change in supply or demand in one market, reflecting changes in the behavior of firms or households, will have repercussions in the other markets. This means, of course, that the financial system cannot be adequately analyzed in isolation from the other markets. Given this simplified overview, in the next section, we look more closely at the demand and supply of money in a more complicated economy.

Recap   The household and business sectors meet in the product (output) market, the factor (input) market, and the financial market. Households demand goods and services, supply labor and other inputs, and, in general, supply surplus funds (money or purchasing power). Businesses supply consumer goods and services, demand investment goods, demand factor inputs, and, in general, demand funds (money or purchasing). In the circular flow, real flows go in one direction while financial flows go in the opposite direction.

The Demand for and Supply of Money

Our closer look at the role of money in the economy begins with the demand for money and then moves on to the supply of money. To understand money's role in the financial system, it is helpful to view money as an asset, much as someone might view an apartment house. The rent for apartments and the quantity of apartment units constructed and rented are determined by the factors affecting the supply of apartments by builders as well as the factors affecting the demand for apartments by renters. The analysis of money proceeds in a similar fashion. The **interest rate** is the cost to borrowers of obtaining money and the return (or yield) on money to lenders. Thus, just as rent is the cost to apartment dwellers and the return to the owner, the interest rate is the rental rate when money is borrowed or loaned, and it is known as the *cost of credit*.[2] By identifying and analyzing the factors affecting the supply of and demand for money, we gain considerable knowledge of both the "rental rate," or interest rate, associated with borrowing or lending money and the quantity of money that is supplied and demanded.

Interest Rate
The cost to borrowers of obtaining money and the return (or yield) on money to lenders.

The Demand for Money

Quantity Demanded of Money
The specific amount of money that spending units wish to hold at a specific interest rate (price).

The **quantity demanded of money** is the specific amount of money that spending units wish to hold at a specific interest rate (price). If we hold other factors constant and allow only the interest rate to vary, we find there is an inverse relationship between the quantity demanded of money and the interest rate. Holding other factors constant is known as *invoking the ceteris paribus assumption*.[3] Thus, in this case, we conclude, ceteris paribus, that when the interest rate goes up, the quantity demanded of money goes down, and when the interest rate falls, the quantity demanded of money increases.

But why is this relationship between the quantity demanded of money and the interest rate inverse? The answer is quite simple if we consider that money (even in interest-earning checking accounts) generally earns less interest than nonmonetary assets (or near monies). Consequently, as the interest rate goes up, the opportunity cost of holding money goes up, and ceteris paribus, the quantity demanded of money goes down.[4] People conserve on their holdings of money balances and substitute holdings of other financial assets that pay a higher return. Thus, when the interest rate rises, "portfolio adjustments" decrease the holdings of money whose return has not increased or has increased less than that of nonmonetary assets.

Read the discussion of graphical analysis in the accompanying Cracking the Code feature, and then look at Exhibit 3-2 where we graph various interest rate–quantity demanded combinations to get a downward-sloping demand curve for money.

3-2
The Demand for Money

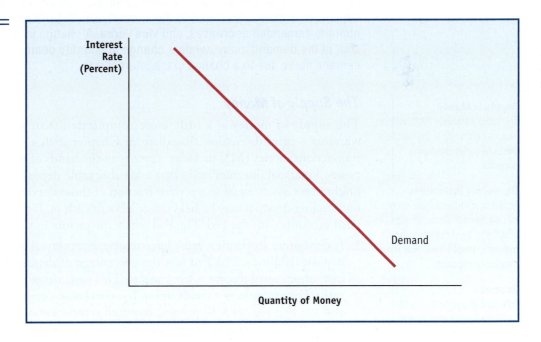

The quantity of money is measured on the horizontal axis, and the interest rate is measured on the vertical axis. Ceteris paribus, the quantity demanded of money is inversely related to the interest rate. As the interest rate falls, quantity demanded increases. As the interest rate rises, quantity demanded falls.

By the **demand for money**, we mean the entire set of interest rate–quantity demanded combinations—the entire downward-sloping demand curve. The demand for money by spending units is primarily determined by spending plans and by the need to pay for purchases. Spending plans and purchases, in turn, are influenced by income and generally go up when incomes go up. Thus, the demand for money to hold is positively or directly related to income. When our incomes go up, we hold more money for day-to-day transactions. (Melissa goes to the grocery store and takes her kids out for fast-food more often after she gets a raise.) In addition to income and spending plans, other factors also affect the demand for money. These other factors include changes in inflation, changes in computer and telecommunications technologies that affect how we make payments, and changes in the risk and liquidity of other financial instruments. We look at these other factors in Chapter 20.

In terms of Exhibit 3-2, when the demand for money changes, the entire demand curve shifts. For example, when the demand for money decreases, say, due to a decrease in incomes, the entire demand curve shifts to the left. Thus, we can see that changes in factors other than the interest rate affect the demand for money and cause the downward-sloping demand curve to shift. When the interest rate changes, we move along a single money demand curve, and there is a change in quantity demanded. Be certain you are clear about the difference between a *change in quantity demanded* and a *change in demand*. Exhibit 3-3 highlights the difference between a change in demand and a change in quantity demanded of money.

Recap The demand for money is the amount that will be demanded at various interest rates. The quantity demanded of money is the amount that will be demanded at a specific interest rate. Among other factors, the demand for money is directly related to income. When income increases, demand increases, and vice versa. Ceteris paribus, the quantity demanded is inversely related to the interest rate. When the interest rate increases, the quantity demanded decreases, and vice versa. A change in demand is represented by a shift of the demand curve, while a change in quantity demanded is a movement along a demand curve due to a change in the interest rate.

The Supply of Money

The **supply of money** is a little more complicated than the demand for money and warrants a brief discussion. Recall from Chapter 2 that our narrowest definition of transactions money (M1) includes currency in the hands of the public plus checkable deposits. Financial intermediaries that issue checkable deposits (**depository institutions**) hold reserve assets equal to a certain fraction of those deposits. The **reserves** against the outstanding deposits may be held either as vault cash or, for safety reasons, as reserve deposit accounts with the Fed. The Fed enters the picture in two places:

1. A depository institution must have reserve assets equal to a certain percentage of its deposit liabilities. The Fed sets the percentage of deposit liabilities that depository institutions must reserve assets equal to. This percentage is called the **required reserve ratio**. For example, if a credit union has checkable deposits in the amount of $1,000 and the Fed has set a 10 percent required reserve ratio, then the credit union must hold $100 in reserves either as cash in its vaults or as deposits with the Fed.

2. As we shall see in later chapters, the Fed influences the amount of cash assets outstanding and hence the amount available for reserves.[5]

Commercial banks (and other depository institutions) enter the picture by influencing the amount of checkable deposits. Banks issue checkable deposits when they receive

3-3

Changes in the Quantity Demanded of Money Versus Changes in the Demand for Money

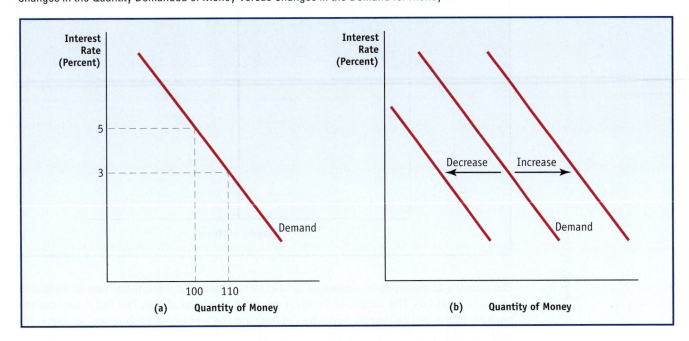

Graph (a) illustrates a change in the quantity demanded of money due to a change in the interest rate. If the interest rate falls from 5 to 3 percent, quantity demanded increases from 100 to 110 and vice versa. Graph (b) illustrates a change in the demand for money. A shift of the money demand curve means that the demand for money has changed. A shift to the right means that the demand for money has increased, and a shift to the left means that the demand for money has decreased. If spending and income increase, the curve shifts rightward and quantity demanded increases for every interest rate. Likewise, if income and spending plans decrease, the curve shifts leftward as demand decreases.

a deposit into a checking account or when they make a loan. The borrower signs the loan papers, and the intermediary (lender) credits the borrower's checking account with the amount of the loan, creating a checkable deposit or money.

Because the Fed, within some limits, controls the amount of funds available for reserves and sets the required reserve ratio, it exerts significant influence on the maximum amount of checkable deposits that depository institutions can create by making loans and, hence, has significant influence on the money supply. Exhibit 3-4 depicts the relationship between the **quantity supplied of money** and the interest rate as a vertical line (supply curve).[6]

Quantity Supplied of Money
The specific amount of money that will be supplied at a specific interest rate.

As in the case of demand, the quantity supplied of money is the specific amount that will be supplied at a specific interest rate. By the supply of money, we mean the entire set of interest rate–quantity supplied combinations—the entire vertical supply curve. By changing the quantity of reserves available to the banking system or the required reserve ratio, the Fed can change the supply of money. Changes in the supply of money, initiated by the Fed, are reflected by shifts of the vertical supply curve, as depicted in Exhibit 3-5. If the Fed speeds up the provision of reserves or reduces the required reserve ratio, the money supply curve shifts to the right, and the supply of money increases. Likewise, if the Fed slows down the provision of reserves or increases the required reserve ratio, the money supply curve shifts to the left, and the supply of money decreases.

3-4
The Supply of Money

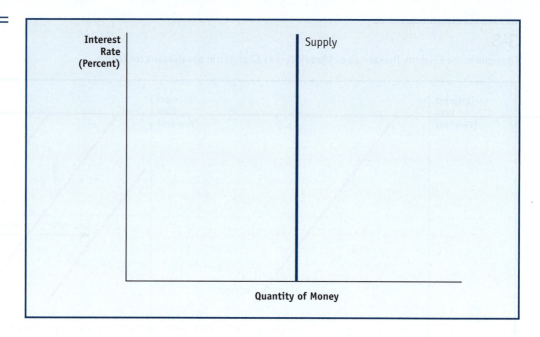

The quantity of money is measured on the horizontal axis, and the interest rate is measured on the vertical axis. The supply of money is depicted as a vertical line. The Fed influences the position of the vertical supply curve by determining the amount of cash assets available for reserves and by setting the required reserve ratio.

3-5
Changes in the Supply of Money

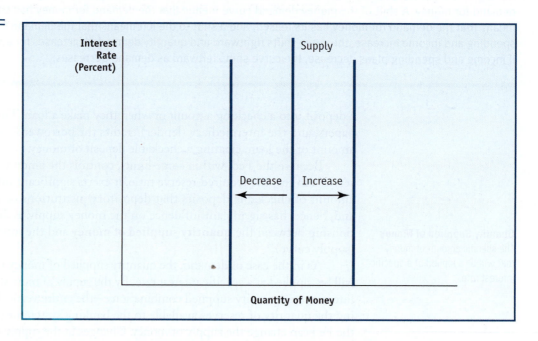

An increase in the supply of money is depicted by a rightward shift of the vertical supply curve. If the Fed speeds up the provision of reserves or reduces the required reserve ratio, the supply of money increases. A decrease in the supply of money is depicted by a leftward shift of the vertical supply curve. If the Fed slows down the provision of reserves or increases the required reserve ratio, the supply of money decreases.

Recap Depository institutions must hold reserve assets equal to a certain fraction of deposit liabilities—called the *required reserve ratio*—as set by the Fed. The Fed also influences the amount of cash assets outstanding and thus the amount available for reserves. These two factors give the Fed significant influence over the money supply.

Money and Interest Rates

Having previewed the factors that affect demand and supply, we are now in a position to see how the interaction between the supply of and demand for money determines its availability, or quantity, and its cost, or the interest rate. This is shown in Exhibit 3-6.[7] In this example, the market gravitates to i_e, or the equilibrium interest rate, where the quantity supplied of money equals the quantity demanded. If the interest rate is above i_e, there is an excess quantity supplied of money and, hence, downward pressure on the interest rate. If the rate is below equilibrium, there is an excess quantity demanded of money, and market forces will cause the interest rate to rise. Once the interest rate gravitates to i_e, the market will stay at the equilibrium rate until one of the curves shifts due to a change in either demand or supply.

Changes in the supply of or demand for money will affect the interest rate, just as changes in the supply of or demand for apartments will affect the rent of apartments. Ceteris paribus, if demand increases, the interest rate rises and vice versa. Exhibit 3-7 shows an increase in the demand for money due to increases in income or spending plans. This corresponds to a rightward shift of the demand curve. At the original interest rate, there is excess quantity demanded and upward pressure on the interest rate. The market gravitates to a new equilibrium at the higher interest rate, i_e'.

Likewise, if supply increases, ceteris paribus, the interest rate falls and vice versa. To illustrate, suppose that the Fed, through a stepped-up provision of reserves to depository institutions, succeeds in increasing the supply of money relative to the demand. As

3-6

Market Equilibrium

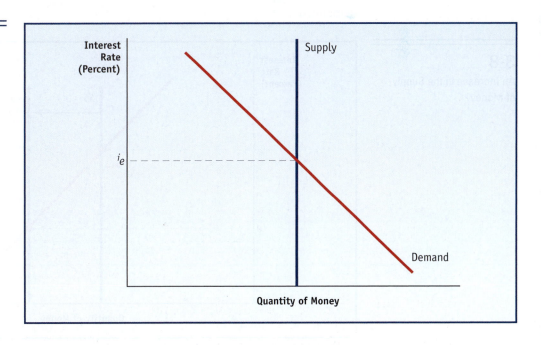

The market for money is in equilibrium when the quantity demanded is equal to the quantity supplied. This occurs at i_e where the demand and supply curves intersect.

An increase in the demand for money leads to an increase in the interest rate from i_e to i'_e.

Exhibit 3-8 shows, this corresponds to a shift of the supply curve to the right. At the original equilibrium interest rate (i_e), there is excess quantity supplied and, thus, downward pressure on the interest rate. The market gravitates to a new equilibrium at a lower interest rate (i'_e) where quantity demanded is equal to quantity supplied.[8] Note that the analogy continues to hold: We would expect that an increase in the supply of apartments, with no change in demand, would result in a fall in rents and an increase in quantity demanded.

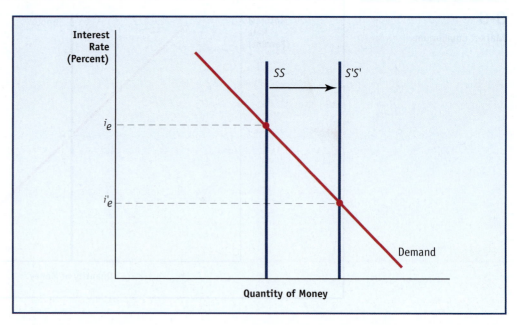

When the supply of money increases from SS to S'S', the equilibrium interest rate falls from i_e to i'_e.

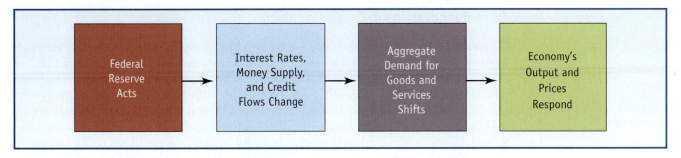

If the Fed wants to encourage an increase in economic activity, it will engage in actions that increase the money supply and credit flows and decrease interest rates. These changes will, in turn, tend to raise the demand for goods and services by households and firms. The response by producers (suppliers) of goods and services to the higher demand will probably include expansion of output and an increase in prices.

But what is the significance of the changes in interest rates caused by changes in the demand for or supply of money? Simply put, changes in the interest rate affect the aggregate (total) demand for goods and services. In the case of supply, if the supply of money increases, the fall in interest rates—reduction in the cost of borrowing—would probably encourage some spending units in the economy to borrow more money and use it to purchase more goods and services. Credit would increase, and, more specifically, the increase in the supply of money (or decrease in demand) would lead to an increase in the aggregate demand for goods and services. The increased demand for goods and services might lead to both an increase in the quantity of goods and services produced (supplied) in the future and an increase in the general level of prices.

Exhibit 3-9 shows how the general relationships discussed in this section are important for the economy as a whole. Remember, this is just a first approximation that does not include many details; we do not expect you to understand all specifics yet!

Recap   **The interest rate is determined by the supply of and demand for money. Equilibrium occurs at the interest rate where the quantity demanded of money is equal to the quantity supplied. Changes in the supply of or demand for money (shifts of the supply or demand curves) affect the interest rate. Ceteris paribus, if demand increases, the interest rate rises and vice versa. Ceteris paribus, if supply increases, the interest rate falls and vice versa.**

How Credit Matters: A First Approximation

So far we have been focusing on how the Fed influences spending via its influence on money or the monetary aggregates. This is all well and good in an economy where a large percentage of lending flows from commercial banks and other depository institutions such as savings and loans or credit unions. In such an economy, changes in the supply of money will be closely related to changes in the supply of **credit**—the flow of money from net lenders or financial intermediaries to net borrowers in a given time period.

It is fairly safe to say that this situation was typical of the U.S. economy until the late 1970s and early 1980s. Previously, when commercial banks' reserves increased—perhaps orchestrated by the Fed—the banks engaged in new lending, which caused both

Credit
The flow of money from net lenders or financial intermediaries to net borrowers in a given time period.

Recent Innovations in Credit Extension

General Electric, once known only for kitchen appliances, now offers the GE Rewards MasterCard. This card gives a rebate of up to 2 percent on credit card purchases. GE Vacations is the vacation service for GE Rewards, offering up to 4 percent back on vacation purchases made with the Rewards card. That's right—the GE card, like many, many others, pays you to use your credit card! Although GE is not a financial intermediary, its managers are interested in the credit extension business and have teamed up with other financial intermediaries to offer special deals. American Express allows college students, even without income, to get American Express cards that give discount certificates to fly on Continental Airlines. American Express offers other cash-back cards. AT&T and GM also offer credit cards that have special incentives. The GM credit card offers up to a 5 percent rebate on purchases of GM cars or trucks. An Exxon MasterCard features 3 percent rebates on Exxon gasoline purchases and 1 percent on other purchases. Shell offers a Shell MasterCard with a rebate of 5 percent on Shell gasoline purchases and 1 percent on other purchases. LL Bean offers a credit card that gives a 1 percent rebate on purchases but increases the rebate for purchases made from LL Bean.

Citibank has countered this competition with its own program that offers one advantage mile on American Airlines for every dollar in purchases on a Citibank credit card. Other bank cards offer airline miles that can be used on any airline, and a variety of bank cards offer other perks including cash back. Despite this, banks are facing a lot of competition in the credit card arena because consumers now have many alternatives to obtaining credit cards from depository institutions.

In recent years, business firms have also been able to bypass banks and other financial intermediaries and go directly to net lenders to borrow money. Small and medium-size businesses that previously relied on bank loans now have access to the commercial paper market where they can borrow directly from net lenders. (The commercial paper market is discussed in Chapter 5.)

As a result, the fraction of total credit extended by commercial banks is declining—down from almost 40 percent in the mid-1970s to less than 23 percent in mid-2004. The diminished role of banks in providing credit alters the ability of the Fed to use established methods to control the economy because the Fed works primarily through the banking system.

---

money and credit to go up. Increases in reserves, ceteris paribus, will almost invariably lead to decreases in the interest rate and increases in the supply of money and credit.

We will use DNFD as a measure of credit market debt or just "credit" outstanding and changes in DNFD to represent changes in outstanding credit.[9] Credit is borrowing power. Increases in credit cause spending (and incomes) to go up.

A word of caution is needed. Since the early 1990s, changes in money and credit flows have not been as closely related as they were in previous decades. Credit flows now come from the following three sources, with the last two gaining in relative importance:

1. Credit flows result from changes in credit extension by depository institutions—commercial banks, savings and loans, credit unions, and mutual savings banks. When these depository institutions make loans, they create money and extend credit.

2. Credit flows can also come from changes in lending at nondepository financial institutions and other nonfinancial institutions. For example, in a relatively recent development, many nonfinancial companies now offer credit cards. Originally, credit cards (MasterCards and VISAs) were primarily offered by banks and other depository institutions. In addition to these inroads by nonfinancial institutions into credit extension for consumers, corporations (both medium-size and large) have developed ways to bypass banks for their working capital and finance needs. Many avenues now exist for firms to borrow directly from lenders; this borrowing and lending then spurs economic activity. The accompanying A Closer Look feature on page 52 examines some of these dramatic changes in credit creation.

3. In addition to domestic sources, credit flows can come from abroad. In recent years, technological advances in computer technologies have reduced the costs of borrowing and lending across traditional national borders. A global financial system has emerged that has resulted in a massive increase in the flows of funds among countries.

But what does all this mean for the economy in general and the Fed in particular? Because the Fed's control over credit extension comes mainly from its influence on bank reserves and bank lending, to the extent that lending bypasses domestic depository institutions, the linkage between money and economic activity may be weakened. The commercial banking system, the primary avenue through which the Fed works, is playing a reduced role in credit extension—a development that undoubtedly is making the job of the Fed more difficult.

Recap   Changes in credit extension influence changes in spending and income. Historically, the commercial banking system has been the vehicle through which credit was extended and through which the Fed exerted its influence on the economy. There was a close relationship between the monetary aggregates and economic activity. By the mid-2000s, the commercial banks' share of total credit (lending) extended in the economy had declined significantly. This weakened the Fed's traditional avenues of control over the economy as well as the link between money and credit.

Money, Credit, and the Economy

Real Gross Domestic Product (Real GDP)
The real, or inflation-adjusted, quantity of final goods and services produced in an economy in a given time period.

Consumer Price Index (CPI)
A price index that measures the cost of a market basket of goods and services that a typical urban consumer purchases.

Inflation Rate
The rate of change in the Consumer Price Index, which measures the growth rate of the average level of prices paid by consumers.

The growth rate of economic activity is measured by the growth rate of **real gross domestic product (real GDP)**. Real GDP is the inflation-adjusted quantity of final goods and services produced in an economy in a given time period, usually a year.[10] It is fair to say that sometimes when the money supply and credit growth rates rise significantly, the general tendency is for the quantity of final goods and services produced and sold (real GDP) to also grow. Conversely, when the money supply and credit growth rates drop significantly, real GDP growth also tends to fall. There is a tendency for the money supply or the flow of credit to decline around the beginning of most recessions and to increase around the beginning of most expansions. Therefore, the obvious conclusion is that money and credit flows have a lot to do with fluctuations in economic activity.

There is also a relationship between the growth rate of money and credit and the rate of inflation. The **consumer price index (CPI)** is a price index that measures the cost of a market basket of goods and services that a typical urban consumer purchases. The rate of change of the CPI measures the **inflation rate**, which is essentially the growth rate in the average level of prices paid by consumers in the economy. The Cracking the Code feature on page 55 discusses how the inflation rate is calculated from the CPI.

Whenever aggregate (total) demand for goods and services increases, say as a result of a rise in the money supply or credit growth rates, there is a general tendency for output to rise fairly quickly and for prices to rise more gradually. Likewise, whenever aggregate demand decreases as a result of a fall in the money supply or credit growth rates, there is a tendency for output to fall fairly quickly and for prices to respond with a lag.[11] Put another way, the current inflation is heavily influenced by changes in money supply and credit growth that occurred some time in the past.

A final relationship that we want to introduce is between changes in the growth rates of the money supply and credit and changes in the growth rate of **nominal gross domestic product (nominal GDP)**. *Nominal GDP* is the quantity of final goods and services produced in an economy during a given time period and valued at today's prices. Not surprisingly, changes in money and credit are more closely correlated with changes in nominal GDP than with changes in real GDP. This is so because the growth rate of nominal GDP encompasses changes in both real GDP and prices.

We can summarize by the following general proposition: A sustained and significant rise in the money supply and credit growth rates will tend to raise aggregate demand for goods and services, increase output growth, and, with a lag, may at times tend to elevate the inflation rate.[12] Conversely, a sustained fall in money supply and credit growth rates will tend to lower aggregate demand, lower output growth, and, after a time, reduce the inflation rate. Exhibit 3-10 illustrates these relationships.

Tables showing recent changes in economic activity can be found at **http://www.bea.gov/**.

See the CPI and PPI at **http://www.bls.gov/ppi/** and **http://www.bls.gov/cpi/**.

For fun! Use the inflation calculator at **http://www.westegg.com/inflation.**

For economic statistics for the previous one-year period, see the links under "At a Glance Tables" at **http://www.bls.gov.**

Nominal Gross Domestic Product (Nominal GDP)
The quantity of final goods and services produced in an economy during a given time period and valued at today's prices.

Recap   Changes in the growth rates of money and credit are correlated with changes in nominal GDP, real GDP, and inflation. The strongest correlation is between changes in money and credit and changes in nominal GDP. Changes in inflation lag changes in money and credit. The correlations are far from perfect.

Are Money and Credit All That Matter?

The preceding discussion certainly suggests an important causal relationship that runs from changes in money and/or credit to key economic variables such as the inflation rate and real

3-10
Money, Output, and Inflation

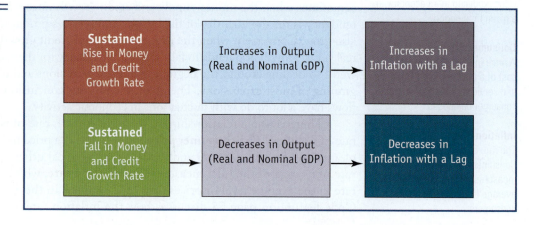

Cracking the Code

Calculating the Inflation Rate

The major price indexes in the United States—the Consumer Price Index (CPI) and the Producer Price Index (PPI)—are computed and published monthly by the government. A price index measures the changes in the costs of the items included in the index. The CPI is designed to measure changes in the cost of goods and services purchased by a typical urban consumer. The PPI measures the change in the cost of goods and services purchased by the typical producer. The inflation rate is generally measured by the percentage change in one of these price indexes. For example, the CPI rose from 179.9 in 2002 to 184 in 2003, an increase of 2.3 percent (184−179.9 = 4.1; 4.1/179.9 = .023 = 2.3 percent). Thus, the inflation rate during 2003 was 2.3 percent.

So far, so good. But where did the index number 184 come from, and what does it mean? The CPI is constructed by first selecting a group of goods and services—called the *market basket of goods and services*—representative of the purchases made by a typical urban household. Then, each month, the prices of the roughly 400 items included in this same market basket are surveyed. The hypothetical example in the following table illustrates how the resulting index and inflation rate are computed.

Year	Total Cost of Market Basket	Consumer Price Index	Annual Inflation Rate
1982–84	$500.00	100.0	
1990	653.5	130.7	—
1991	681.00	136.2	4.2%
1992	701.50	140.3	3.0
1993	722.50	144.5	3.0
1994	741.00	148.2	2.6
1995	762.00	152.4	2.8
1996	784.50	156.9	3.0
1997	802.5	160.5	2.3
1998	815.00	163.0	1.6
1999	833.00	166.6	2.2
2000	861.00	172.2	3.4
2001	885.50	177.1	2.8
2002	899.50	179.9	1.6
2003	920.00	184.0	2.3
2004	938.00	187.6*	—

*Through June 2004 only.
SOURCE: U.S. Department of Labor, Bureau of Labor Statistics, **http://www.bls.gov/cpi/home.htm**.

The years 1982–1984 are the base period years for computing the index in the sense that prices of the market basket in future years are compared to the prices of the same market basket in 1982–1984—that is, $500. More formally, the CPI in a given year is displayed in the following equation:

$$\text{CPI} = \frac{\text{(cost of the market basket in the given year)}}{\text{(cost of the market basket in the base period)}} \times 100$$

Accordingly, the CPI for 1982–1984 is 100, and for 2003, when the cost of the market basket rose to $920, the CPI is 184 [($920/$500) × 100 = 184]. Literally, the CPI of 184 for 2003 means that prices were 84 percent higher in 2003 than in the 1982–1984 time period.

A Brief History of U.S. Currency

Today currency in the United States is issued by the U.S. Treasury and circulated by the Fed. But this has not always been the case. During the colonial period, the British colonies were prohibited from printing or coining their own currency. Barter was commonplace, and other exchanges occurred using various "monies" such as wampum (beads made from seashells), tobacco, and gold or silver coins. To help finance the Revolutionary War, the Continental Congress issued a new kind of currency called the *Continental.*

The first privately owned bank in the United States, the Bank of North America, was chartered in Philadelphia in 1782. From the earliest years of banking until the Civil War, privately owned banks issued their own currency called *banknotes.* Banknotes were redeemable in gold, circulated as money, and dispersed when loans were made. However, because banks issued more notes than the amount of gold they held in reserve, note holders would become fearful that they would not be able to redeem their notes in gold. Note holders would rush to the banks to convert their notes to gold before the banks ran out. The result was that the banknotes often circulated at a discount well below their face value and banks often failed.

By the late 1830s, such problems and the widespread counterfeiting of banknotes led many states to require that banks post government bonds as collateral against the banknotes they issued. If a bank could not redeem its notes, the bonds would be sold, and the proceeds would go to the note holders. The period from the late 1830s until the Civil War became known as the *Wildcat Banking Era.* Banks that were unable to redeem their notes in gold would relocate to the woods where it was difficult for even a wildcat to find them.

During the Civil War, the government issued greenbacks to finance the war. By the end of the war, greenbacks (and closely related U.S. government notes) made up 75 percent of the money in circulation. Sundry banknotes issued by privately owned state-chartered banks made up the other 25 percent. In 1863 and 1864, Congress passed the National Banking Acts, which established a network of federally chartered national banks and created a uniform currency. The new currency was issued by the national banks and backed by government bonds. In addition, the acts levied a 10 percent tax on the banknotes issued by state-chartered banks. Subsequently, these banknotes disappeared, and the new uniform banknotes circulated at full value. The National Banking Acts were successful in providing a sound and stable national currency for the first time since the birth of the nation.

and nominal GDP growth. In the course of discussing the data, however, we emphasized that the correlations among money supply growth, credit flows, and these other variables are far from perfect. In addition, the correlations do not necessarily imply causation.[13] Simply put, this lack of perfect correlation means that changes in the growth rate of the money supply and/or credit are not the only factors that influence inflation and economic activity. Other factors, such as current fiscal policy and expectations about future monetary and fiscal policy and future inflation, can exert a powerful influence on prices and output, especially in the short run. In fact, some economists believe that the effects of movements in these other factors are as powerful as, or more powerful than, current and past movements in the money supply and/or credit flows in terms of their influence on the economy. Finally, as we have seen, the relationship between the monetary aggregates and credit flows may also change over time as commercial banks' share of total lending changes.

Money and Credit Flows: First Fiddle or Second Fiddle

Money has played an important historical role in economic systems; thus, economic literature may have given more attention to it than to the role of credit. Nevertheless, the historical and present economic roles and influence of both money and credit are not without controversy. Economists do not fully agree on the past or current role of money in the economy. In the 1970s, the economic profession was dominated by some economists who believed that money matters more than anything else in determining the overall health of the economy; they are appropriately called **monetarists**. Today monetarists may not believe that money matters more than anything else, but they still stress that monetary policy is the only game in town. Other economists focus on credit flows (loans) that trigger changes in spending, and still others believe that money and/or credit flows are only two among many factors affecting the economy. These economists carry various labels: nonmonetarist, Keynesian, neo-Keynesian, post-Keynesian, and so forth. As with music videos, there is often something to be gained by differentiating one's product from that of the competition!

> **Monetarists**
> Economists who stress the role of money in determining the overall health of the economy.

The controversy over the role of money and credit is somewhat like trying to determine whether the coach is the key to a team's success. Some will argue that the team won in spite of poor coaching, and others will attribute the team's triumphs to the insight and intelligence of the coach. It is difficult to resolve such debates. An important piece of evidence, however, is the team's record over a number of years. A team that continues to win year after year, even though its talent has varied noticeably, will convince even the skeptics that the coach played a key role in establishing the successful record.

Likewise, although not everyone agrees as to exactly how and to what degree money and credit matter, few dispute the contention that the weight of the historical evidence produced by economists indicates that changes in the growth rates of money and credit exert a powerful influence on spending, production, inflation, and unemployment. This is akin to the proposition first developed in Chapter 2 and reiterated in the circular flow diagram that a developed financial system with a mechanism for lending and borrowing (transferring purchasing power or money) is an important determinant of economic development.

Summary of Major Points

1. Firms and households meet in three separate markets—the output, input, and financial markets. Firms supply goods and services to the product market, demand investment goods supplied by other firms, demand factor services in the factor market, and demand funds (money or purchasing power) from the financial system. Households demand goods and services in the product market, supply factor services in the factor market, and supply funds (money or purchasing power) to the financial system. In the circular flow, real flows go in one direction while financial flows go in the opposite direction.

2. The interest rate is the cost to borrowers of obtaining money and the return (or yield) on money to lenders. It is the cost of credit. Ceteris paribus, the quantity demanded of money and the interest rate are inversely related.

3. The demand for money is determined by the spending plans of spending units, which are usually positively or directly related to income. The supply of money is strongly influenced by the Fed through its control over reserves and the required reserve ratio.

4. The interaction between the supply of and the demand for money determines the equilibrium quantity

of money and the equilibrium interest rate. In general, the initial effect of either an increase in the money supply or a decrease in money demand will be a fall in the interest rate, ceteris paribus. Conversely, the initial effect of either a decrease in the money supply or an increase in money demand will be a rise in the interest rate, ceteris paribus.

5. Credit flows (loan extensions) are also a key determinant of changes in spending and income. As depository institutions handle a declining share of credit, the relationship between the monetary aggregates and economic activity may be diminished.

6. Changes in the money supply, credit, and the interest rate will generally alter the aggregate (total) demand for goods and services in the economy. Changes in aggregate demand will, in turn, affect the overall level of output and prices. More specifically, a rise in the money supply and/or credit flows and the accompanying fall in the interest rate will generally raise aggregate demand and lead to an expansion of output and some rise in prices.

7. Historical data suggest that a sustained and significant rise in money supply or credit growth will tend to increase output growth and, with a lag, tend at times to raise the inflation rate. Likewise, a sustained and significant fall in money supply or credit growth will tend to decrease output growth and, with a lag, tend at times to lower the inflation rate.

8. The correlations among the rate of money supply growth, credit flows, and both inflation and output growth are far from perfect; this suggests that other factors, such as current fiscal policy and expectations about future monetary and fiscal policy, also influence inflation and economic activity. Put another way, money and credit flows are not "all that matter."

9. Controversy does exist within the economics profession about the specific role of money and credit: How much do they matter, and how precisely do they matter? However, few dispute the contention that the weight of the historical evidence indicates that money and credit flows exert a powerful, although changing, influence on the economy.

Key Terms

Circular Flow Diagram, **42**
Consumer Price Index (CPI), **53**
Credit, **51**
Demand for Money, **46**
Depository Institutions, **46**
Inflation Rate, **53**
Interest Rate, **44**
Monetarists, **57**

Nominal Gross Domestic Product (Nominal GDP), **54**
Quantity Demanded of Money, **44**
Quantity Supplied of Money, **47**
Real Gross Domestic Product (Real GDP), **53**
Required Reserve Ratio, **46**
Reserves, **46**
Supply of Money, **46**

Review Questions

1. Using Exhibit 3-1, explain why saving is equal to investment in a simplified economy with no government or foreign sector.

2. Briefly define *the interest rate, reserves, the required reserve ratio, the inflation rate*, and *nominal GDP*.

3. Discuss the similarities between how the price of compact discs is determined in the compact disc market and how the interest rate is determined in the market for money.

4. What is the difference between the demand for money and the quantity demanded of money?

5. What is the opportunity cost of holding money?

6. Chris and Harold Yoshida are a young couple with a growing income. What will happen to their demand for money over time?

7. In what form can a depository institution hold reserves? Who determines the amount of funds available for reserves? How does the Fed influence the amount of reserves a depository institution must hold?

8. What are the sources of credit? Explain the following statement: "The money supply is measured at a point in time, while the flow of credit is measured over time."

9. How does real GDP differ from nominal GDP?

10. Alarm clocks going off and sunrise are highly correlated. Does the sound of alarm clocks going off cause the sun to rise? Why or why not?

11. Explain the difference between money and credit. Give an example of each.

Analytical Questions

Questions marked with an icon are objective in nature. They can be completed with a short answer or number.

12. Draw a simple circular flow diagram between households and firms. Explain how "real" flows of products and the services of the factors of production go in one direction while "financial" flows of payments for products and the factor services go in the opposite direction.

13. Show on a graph how the interest rate and the quantity demanded of money are related. Do the same for the quantity supplied of money. When is the market in equilibrium?

14. Assume the market for money is originally in equilibrium. Explain what happens to demand, supply, quantity demanded, and/or quantity supplied, ceteris paribus, given each of the following events:
    a. The Fed lowers reserve requirements. *MS↑*
    b. Households increase their spending plans. *MD↑*
    c. Income falls due to a severe recession. *MD↓*
    d. The Fed steps up its provision of reserves to depository institutions. *MS↑*

15. Graph each case presented in question 14.

16. What are the effects of an increase in the supply of money on interest rates, prices, and output? What are the effects of a decrease in the supply of money on interest rates, prices, and output? Do these effects occur simultaneously?

17. Substituting the words *credit flows* for *supply of money*, answer question 16.

18. What happens to interest rates, prices, and output when the demand for money increases? What happens to the same variables when the demand for money decreases?

19. Substituting the words *credit flows* for *demand for money*, answer question 18.

20. Assume that the price of a market basket of goods and services is $2,000 in the base period, $2,060 one year later, and $2,100 two years later. What is the price index in the base period? After the first year? After the second year? What is the rate of inflation in the first year? In the second year?

21. Ceteris paribus, what happens to the demand for money if incomes go down? Ceteris paribus, what happens to the supply of money if reserves go up? In each case, does the interest rate change? Graph each case.

22. Use a graph to show what happens to the interest rate if the demand for money is increasing while the supply of money is decreasing.

23. Assume a price index increases from 145 to 150 to 155 over three consecutive years. Was the rate of inflation higher in the second or third year? What does it mean when a price index falls from 150 to 145?

(handwritten table)

Year	Market Basket	CPI	infl
B	2000	100	
1	2060	$\frac{2060}{2000} = 103$	3%
2	2100	$\frac{2100}{2000} = 105$	1.9%

Internet Exercises

1. Answer these questions by accessing the Gross Domestic Product (GDP) and Components Category at the following root directory: **http://www.research.stlouisfed.org/fred2/**. Look up the current real GDP numbers for the U.S. economy and compare them to the current-dollar GDP numbers over similar time periods. Why and how does the real GDP measure differ from the current-dollar GDP measure? (*Note:* In the body of the text, we refer to current-dollar GDP as *nominal GDP*.)

2. Obtain the current estimate of inflation as gauged by the Consumer Price Index (CPI) and the Producer Price Index (PPI) by going to the following Web sites: **http://www.research.stlouisfed.org/fred2/categories/9** and **http://www.research.stlouisfed.org/fred2/categories/31**. The CPI for urban consumers (CPI-U) is disaggregated by expenditure category. Name the explicit expenditure categories used by the Bureau of Labor Statistics.

3. Seasonally adjusted historical data on the CPI for urban consumers (CPI-U) are obtainable from the following Web site: **http://www.research.stlouisfed.org/fred2/series/CPIAUCSL/downloaddata**. Calculate a rough average annual inflation rate

for the most recent month. Next look at the CPI recorded over the mid-1970s, early 1980s, and early 1990s. Calculate some of the inflation rates when the changes in the CPI seem the largest. Compare these rates of inflation with the annual rates of growth of M2 over the same time periods. Use the following web site for calculating M2 growth rates during these periods: **http://www.research.stlouisfed.org/fred2/ data/M2SL.txt**. Is there any discernible relationship between the rate of growth of the money supply and the rate of inflation?

Suggested Readings

In this chapter, we have seen that changes in money (as measured by M2) were often highly correlated with changes in economic activity. That is why M2 has been used as a policy guide, particularly in the 1980s. However, a 1998 article concludes that "it would be unwise to place too much reliance on M2 in the formulation of monetary policy." The article, "Is It Time to Look at M2 Again?" can be found in the Federal Reserve Bank of San Francisco, *Economic Letter* 98-07 (March 6, 1998).

For an overview of statistics on inflation and consumer spending from the Bureau of Labor Statistics, see **http://www. bls.gov/bls/inflation.htm**

Visit the following web site for a brief history of money **http://www.kc.frb.org/Pubaffrs/moneystory.htm**.

For a more academic discussion "On the Evolution of Money and Its Implications for Price Stability," see Paul Dalziel's article by the same name in *Journal of Economic Surveys* 14:4 (September 2000): 373–393.

For an interesting article on the development of barter, metal coins, and paper money, see Robert Ferris, "Money: A Pictorial History," *Business Credit* 98 (June 1996): 20–31.

Two articles that discuss changes in how the CPI is calculated are Daniel Kadlec, "Measuring the New CPI," *Time* (March 9, 1998): 71; and Matthew D. Shapiro, "Alternative Strategies for Aggregating Prices in the CPI," *Federal Reserve Bank of St. Louis Review* 79 (May/June 1997): 113–125.

For an interesting discussion of many of the topics in this chapter, see the most recent Fed chairperson's "Monetary Policy Report to Congress" that is given in February and July of each year. The report and testimony of the chair is available on the Internet at **http://www.federalreserve.gov/**. The reports also appear in the March and August editions of the *Federal Reserve Bulletin*.

For recent Congressional testimony by Jeffrey Marquardt, associate director, Reserve Bank Operations and Payment Systems about the Fed's activities in currency design and coin distribution, see **http://www.federalreserve.gov/boarddocs/ testimony/2004/20040428/default.htm**.

Endnotes

1 In this very simple economy, the government and rest of the world sectors are left out.

2 The market in which money is borrowed and loaned is called the *credit market*. In Chapter 6, we look in depth at interest rate determination from the perspective of the credit market where the interest rate is determined by the supply of and demand for loanable funds.

3 In economics, we make the ceteris paribus assumption so that we can investigate the relationship between two variables without having changes in additional variables conceal the relationship.

4 The *opportunity cost* is the value of the next best alternative that is forgone.

5 From the discussion in Chapter 2, we now see that cash outside the Fed is either held by the public or deposited in a financial intermediary. If it is deposited, it serves as reserves for the financial intermediaries that issue checkable deposits, and it is considered a cash asset.

6 Some economists consider the money supply curve to be upward sloping instead of a vertical line. The reasoning is that when interest rates rise, depository institutions find innovative ways around reserve requirements in order to make more loans. The loans are more profitable because they are made at higher interest rates. In the process of making additional loans, more money is created.

7 As is commonly known, there are many interest rates in the economy, so speaking of "the interest rate" as if there were only one is an obvious simplification. Once the fundamentals have been developed, it will be much easier to extend our analysis to take into account the many different interest rates.

8 The ceteris paribus condition is very important here. For example, if the Fed takes actions that lead to increases in the money supply, then inflationary expectations may also increase. If inflationary expectations change, then the ceteris paribus condition is violated. In this case, increases in the money supply may lead to increases in interest rates because of the effect on inflationary expectations.

9 Recall that DNFD is a measure of private and government debt outstanding, net of the debt of financial intermediaries. It is a good measure of the outstanding credit that has been extended over a period of time in the economy.

10 Final goods and services are in the hands of the ultimate user as opposed to intermediate goods and services, which are inputs used to make final goods and services. Real GDP is discussed at length in most principles of economics text.

11 Although lagged changes in money and credit extension are most strongly correlated with price changes, this does not negate the fact that a weaker positive relationship exists between changes in money and credit and current price changes.

12 This proposition assumes the economy is not starting from a position of full employment. If the economy is at full employment and there is a sustained and significant rise in the money supply and credit growth rates, the increase in aggregate demand will most likely lead to inflation with no increase in output.

13 Events A and B are correlated if they occur together. Correlation does not mean that A caused B or vice versa.

4

CHAPTER FOUR

The Overseer: The Federal Reserve System

Learning Objectives

After reading this chapter, you should know:

How the Fed is organized

What the Federal Open Market Committee (FOMC) is

The most important functions of the Fed

The Fed's major policy tools

What a "lender of last resort" is

The controversy regarding Fed independence

Unraveling the Fed's Mystique

"Stock Market Surges Following Fed Testimony," "Interest Rates Rise in Anticipation of Tighter Fed Policy," "Fed Approves Mega Bank Merger," "Fed Actions Prevent Crisis after Bank Failure": Such headlines appear nearly every day in the nation's business and financial press. Yet despite its prominent role in the financial system and the economy and the efforts by the Fed to be more open in recent years, the Fed and its operations are not well understood by readers of these headlines (and perhaps even the headline writers). In part, the Fed's mystique reflects the fact that its organizational structure is somewhat complex and rather different from that of other governmental entities and that a considerable amount of puzzlement often surrounds its deliberations and actions.

To unravel this mystique, we begin our study of the Fed with an examination of its origin, role, organization, and policy tools. This first look includes an analysis of the administrative (power) structure where policy decisions are formulated and the various functions with which the Fed is charged. Many of the details regarding the formulation of policy and the precise linkages between policy actions and the economy will be examined in later chapters. For now, we want to focus on these questions: What is the Fed? Why does the Fed appear to have such great power and influence over the economy? Who does what within the Fed? Why do they do it?

Organizational Structure of the System

Several years ago, a weekly news magazine reported that respondents in a public opinion poll considered the chair of the Board of Governors of the Federal Reserve System to be the second most influential person in the United States, topped only by the president. This poll reflected the current importance of the Federal Reserve System and monetary policy in our lives. It was not always so.

The **Federal Reserve System** was created by Congress in 1913. Experience in the United States and abroad had finally convinced lawmakers that such an institution was needed to avoid the banking crises that had periodically plagued the economy, most recently in 1907. The main purpose of the **Federal Reserve Act** was simple. It created a central bank—a kind of bank for banks—that could lend funds to commercial banks during emergencies and thus provide these banks with the funds necessary to avoid insolvency and bankruptcy. An example of such an emergency is a major crop failure that makes it impossible for farmers to pay off their bank loans. The 1913 legislation referred to this role of the Fed as providing an "elastic currency," and it is today often referred to as "**the lender of last resort**" function.

Over time, the responsibilities of the Federal Reserve have been expanded. In the midst of the Great Depression, it was clear that the limited scope and powers of the Federal Reserve System were not up to handling the nearly 8,000 bank failures that occurred during the 1930–1933 period. In the **Banking Reform Acts of 1933 and 1935**, Congress provided many of the additional policy tools and regulations that the Fed needed.

The most significant change during this period involved the underlying role of the Federal Reserve—that is, the Fed's purpose and objectives. The Fed moved into a new era because of the economic crisis of the Great Depression, the changing view of the role of government policy after this collapse (discussed in Chapter 1), and the new legislation that broadened its powers. The Federal Reserve System became a full-fledged central bank. Now more than a bank for banks, it was charged with contributing to the attainment of the nation's economic and financial goals. More specifically, it was to regulate and supervise the operation of the financial system in order to (1) foster a smooth-running, efficient, competitive financial system and (2) promote the overall health and

Federal Reserve System
The central bank of the United States that regulates the banking system and determines monetary policy.

Federal Reserve Act
The 1913 congressional statute that created the Federal Reserve System.

Lender of Last Resort
The responsibility of the Fed to provide an elastic currency by lending to commercial banks during emergencies.

Banking Reform Acts of 1933 and 1935
Statutes passed by Congress in response to the collapse of the banking system between 1930 and 1933.

stability of the economy through its ability to influence the availability and cost of money and credit. Let us first identify the major parts of the Federal Reserve System and then discuss its functions.

For general information on the Fed, go to **http://www.federalreserve.gov** and **http://www.minneapolisfed.org/info/sys/**. For laws regulating the Fed, see **http://www.law.cornell.edu/uscode/12/ch3.html**.

The core of the Federal Reserve System is the **Board of Governors**, located in Washington, D.C. The board consists of seven members appointed by the president with the advice and consent of the U.S. Senate. The A Closer Look feature on page 66 presents brief biographical sketches of the present board members. The full term of a board member is 14 years, and the terms are arranged so that one term expires every two years. The long tenure and staggered terms were designed to insulate the board from day-to-day political pressures and encourage the members to exercise the same independent judgment that Supreme Court justices employ. In theory, a president would be able to appoint only two of the seven members on the board during a four-year term. In actuality, deaths and early resignations of board members have permitted recent presidents to name more than two new board members during a four-year term. We might also note that although board members cannot be reappointed if they serve a full term, they may be reappointed if the initial appointment was to fill an unexpired term due to an early resignation or death. Board members can be removed from office only under extraordinary circumstances. It has never happened.

The president, with the advice and consent of the Senate, appoints one of the seven board members to be the chair for four years and one to be vice chair. The choice of the board chair is crucial, for experience shows that he becomes the chief spokesperson for the Fed and thus a strong force in U.S. economic policy making.[1]

Federal Reserve Banks

The original Federal Reserve Act divided the nation into 12 districts. Each Federal Reserve Bank district is served by a **Reserve Bank** located in a large city in the district.

Thus, as shown in Exhibit 4-1, we have the Federal Reserve Bank of Boston, the Federal Reserve Bank of New York, and of Philadelphia, Richmond, Cleveland, Atlanta, Chicago, Dallas, Kansas City, St. Louis, Minneapolis, and San Francisco. The three largest are the Reserve Banks of New York, Chicago, and San Francisco, which account for more than 50 percent of Fed assets. The 12 Reserve Banks have a total of 26 branches, located in major cities in the respective district. For example, the St. Louis Fed has branches in Memphis, Tennessee, and Little Rock, Arkansas, and the Dallas Fed has branches in Houston, San Antonio, and El Paso, Texas. As we shall see in Chapter 11, all commercial banks that are federally chartered national banks must join the Federal Reserve System. State-chartered banks may join or not as they choose. The member banks within a Reserve Bank district (say, the Boston district) elect six of the nine directors of that Reserve Bank, and the Board of Governors appoints the other three. These directors, in turn, appoint the president and other officials of that Reserve Bank.

The reason the original Federal Reserve Act created 12 Reserve Banks and provided for the election of directors by member commercial banks was to decentralize policy-making authority.[2] Considerable antifederalist sentiment existed in Congress at the time. We will see later that, over time, the desire to decentralize authority has been stymied by the increased concentration of policy-making authority in Washington.

For a list of the 12 Federal Reserve Banks and Internet links to each, see **http://federalreserve.gov/otherfrb.htm**.

The Board of Governors

- Chair Alan Greenspan (b. 1926). Took office in June 2004 for a fifth four-year term as chair; originally appointed to the board to fill an unexpired term in August 1987; appointed to a full 14-year term in February 1992; term as a governor ends in January 2006. **Background:** Business economist; Chair and President of Townsend-Greenspan, an economic consulting firm, 1954–1974 and 1977–1987; Chair of the Council of Economic Advisers, 1974–1977; Chair of the National Commission on Social Security, 1981–1983; Ph.D. in economics from New York University, 1977.

- Roger W. Ferguson (b. 1951). Took office in November 1997 to fill an unexpired term ending in January 2000. Appointed to a full 14-year term in January 2000. Became Vice Chair in October 1999. His second term as Vice Chair ends October 2007 and as a governor in January 2014. **Background:** Business; Partner at McKinsey & Company, Inc., an international management consulting firm, 1984–1997; attorney for Davis Polk & Wardwell of New York City, 1981–1984; Ph.D. in economics from Harvard University, 1981.

- Edward M. Gramlich (b. 1939). Took office in November 1997 to fill an unexpired term ending in January 2008. **Background:** Academic; Professor of economics at the University of Michigan, 1976–1997; Senior Fellow at the Brookings Institution, 1973–1976; Director of Policy Research Division at the Office of Economic Opportunity, 1971–1973; Staff Member at the Federal Reserve Board, 1965–1970; Ph.D. in economics from Yale University, 1965.

- Susan Schmidt Bies (b. 1947). Took office in December 2001 to fill a full term ending in January 2012. **Background:** Academic and business; Assistant Professor of Economics, Wayne State University, 1977–1979; Associate Professor of Economics, Rhodes College, 1977–1979; various positions, First Tennessee National Corporation, 1979–2001; most recently, Executive Vice President for Risk Management and Auditor, 1995–2001; Ph.D. in economics from Northwestern University, 1972.

- Mark W. Olson (b. 1943). Took office in December 2001 to fill an unexpired term ending in January 2010. **Background:** Business; President and CEO of Security State Bank, Fergus Falls, Minnesota, 1976–1988; Partner with Ernst & Young and its predecessor, Arthur Young & Company, 1988–1999; Staff Director of the Securities Subcommittee of the Banking, Housing, and Urban Affairs Committee, U.S. Senate, 2000–2001; B.A. in economics from Saint Olaf College, 1965.

- Ben S. Bernanke (b. 1953). Took office in August 2002 to fill an unexpired term ending in January 2004. Appointed to a full 14-year term that begins February 2004 and expires January 2018. **Background:** Academics; Professor of Economics and Public Affairs, Princeton University, 1985 to 2002; Assistant and Associate Professor of Economics, Graduate School of Business at Stanford University, 1973 to 1985; Ph.D. in economics from Massachusetts Institute of Technology, 1979.

- Donald L. Kohn (b. 1942). Took office on August 2002 to fill a full term ending January 31, 2016. **Background:** Public service at the Fed; Staff Adviser to the Board for Monetary Policy, 2001 to 2002; Secretary of the Federal Open Market Committee, 1987 to 2002; Director of the Division of Monetary Affairs, 1987 to 2001, and Deputy Staff Director for Monetary and Financial Policy, 1983 to 1987; Associate Director, Federal Reserve Board's Division of Research and Statistics 1981 to 1983; Chief of Capital Markets, Federal Reserve Board's Division of Research and Statistics, 1978 to 1981; and Economist, Federal Reserve Board's Division of Research and Statistics, 1975 to 1978; Financial Economist, Federal Reserve Banks of Kansas City, 1970 to 1975; Ph.D. in economics from the University of Michigan, 1971.

4-1

The Federal Reserve System

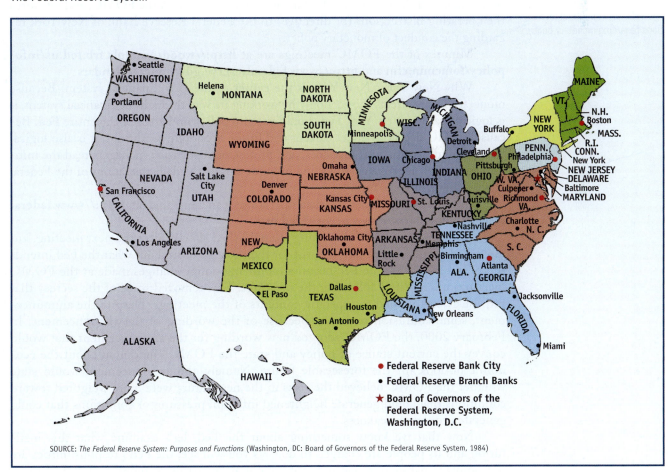

SOURCE: *The Federal Reserve System: Purposes and Functions* (Washington, DC: Board of Governors of the Federal Reserve System, 1984)

Federal Open Market Committee (FOMC)

Federal Open Market Committee (FOMC)

The principal policy-making body within the Federal Reserve System.

The **Federal Open Market Committee (FOMC)** is the principal policy-making body within the Federal Reserve System. The FOMC formulates monetary policy and oversees its implementation. The committee has 12 members including all seven members of the board and five of the 12 Federal Reserve Bank presidents. The president of the New York Federal Reserve Bank always sits on the FOMC and is a permanent voting member. This is so because the New York Fed, as we shall see, implements monetary policy in accord with the FOMC's instructions. The remaining four seats are filled by the other Reserve Bank presidents who serve one-year terms on a rotating basis. Although only five Reserve Bank presidents have voting rights on the FOMC at any one time, all 12 presidents and their senior advisers attend FOMC meetings and participate in the discussions. By law, the FOMC determines its own internal organization. By tradition, it elects the chair of the Federal Reserve Board as chair of the FOMC and the president of the New York Federal Reserve Bank as vice chair of the FOMC. With the board having seven of the 12 votes, you can see why most of the policy-making authority resides in Washington.

Policy Directive

A statement of the FOMC that indicates its policy consensus and sets forth operating instructions regarding monetary policy.

The FOMC meets in closed meetings in Washington eight times a year (about every six weeks or so). Included in the minutes of an FOMC meeting is the **policy directive**, which is usually a two- to four-paragraph statement.[3] This statement represents a digest of the meeting, indicates the policy consensus of the FOMC, and sets forth the operating instructions (or directive) to the Federal Reserve Bank of New York regarding the conduct of monetary policy.

Minutes of the FOMC meetings are at **http://woodrow.mpls.frb.fed.us/info/ policy/fomcmin.cfm** and **http://www.federalreserve.gov/fomc/#calendars**.

Why New York? New York is the center of the U.S. financial system. Because monetary policy affects the economy by working its way through the financial system, it is logical that the New York Fed should execute policy on behalf of the entire Fed. Because FOMC decisions affect current and future economic conditions, it is also logical that economists, financial investors, and professional portfolio managers read the minutes and policy directive carefully and monitor closely the daily operations of the Federal Reserve Bank of New York.

Information on open market operations can be found at **http://www.federal reserve.gov** or **http://www.newyorkfed.org**.

Minutes of an FOMC meeting are published shortly after the next meeting, but interested parties do not have to wait for their release to find out what the Fed intends to do. In early 1994, the Fed began announcing policy changes made at the FOMC meetings immediately following the meetings. This removed some of the secrecy that previously surrounded the specific contents of the meetings. Despite the announcement, some confusion remained because of the wording of the announcement. In February 2000, the FOMC adopted new wording for the announcement that would convey the current stance of policy and state the FOMC's judgment about the economic outlook for the foreseeable future. Namely, the announcement would state whether the FOMC believed the risks in the near future were more weighted toward conditions that could generate heightened inflation pressures or conditions that could generate economic weakness.

Now that we know something about the Fed, let's examine what this institution and its people are charged to do.[4] As you will see, the Fed's responsibilities are not simple in nature or scope and thus are not always easily accomplished. Before moving on, however, take a look at the outline of the Fed's organizational structure in Exhibit 4-2.

Board of Governors

Seven members appointed by the president of the United States and confirmed by the Senate for 14-year terms.

One of the seven governors is appointed chair by the president of the United States and confirmed by the Senate for a 4-year term.

The Board of Governors appoints three of the nine directors to each Reserve Bank.

Twelve Federal Reserve Banks

Each with nine directors who appoint the Reserve Bank president and other officers of the Reserve Banks.

Federal Open Market Committee (FOMC)

Seven members of the Board of Governors plus the president of the New York Fed and presidents of four other Reserve Banks.

Nearly 3,000 Member Commercial Banks

Elect six of the nine directors to each Reserve Bank.

Recap The Federal Reserve System was created in 1913. It consists of 12 Reserve Banks. The Fed is governed by the Board of Governors, whose seven members are appointed by the president to 14-year terms. The board chair is appointed for a four-year term. The FOMC is the major policy-making body. It includes the seven Fed governors plus five Reserve Bank presidents. The president of the New York Reserve Bank is a permanent member of the FOMC, and the other four slots rotate yearly among the remaining 11 Reserve Bank presidents.

The Fed's Functions

Over the 92-plus years since its inception, the Fed's powers and responsibilities have gradually expanded. In some cases, the Fed argued that it needed more powers to accomplish its existing responsibilities or that taking on additional responsibilities was a natural adjunct to what it was already doing. Congress often responded favorably to the Fed's arguments or simply let the Fed decide on its own whether it would be the best agency to handle a particular set of issues. The current list of Fed responsibilities is considerably longer and more encompassing than even the most farsighted legislator could have imagined in 1913. Fortunately, the list can be divided into four functional areas, depicted in Exhibit 4-3, and outlined in the following text.

Formulation and Implementation of Monetary Policy

Monetary Policy
The attempts by the Fed to stabilize the economy and to ensure sufficient money and credit for an expanding economy.

A primary responsibility of the Federal Reserve is the formulation and implementation of the nation's **monetary policy**. Broadly speaking, the conduct of monetary policy has two objectives: first, to ensure that sufficient money and credit are available to allow the economy to expand along its long-term potential growth trend under conditions of relatively

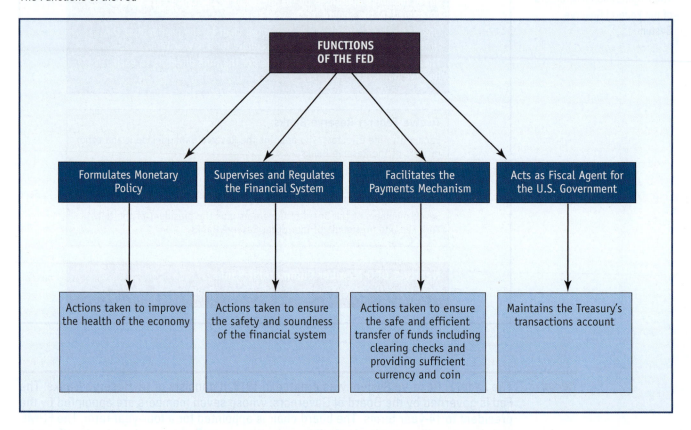

little or no inflation; second, in the shorter run, to minimize the fluctuations—recessions or inflationary booms—around the long-term trend.

In general, the Fed takes actions to affect the cost and availability of funds in the financial system.[5] More specifically, the Fed's actions have a direct effect on the ability of depository institutions to extend credit, on the nation's money supply, and on interest rates. Leaving many of the details for a later chapter, the key point here is that what the Fed does, or fails to do, has a pervasive effect on the environment in the financial system and the overall health and performance of the economy. For example, by taking actions that increase the availability of funds, the Fed may bring about an expansion of the money supply and a decline in interest rates, or it can do the reverse. Its decisions may, in turn, affect the spending, producing, borrowing, lending, pricing, and hiring decisions made in the rest of the economy.

Supervision and Regulation of the Financial System

The Fed, along with several other government agencies, is responsible for supervising and regulating the financial system.[6] In general, supervisory activities are directed at promoting the safety and soundness of depository institutions. From the Fed's perspective, this involves continuous oversight to ensure that banks are operated prudently and in accordance with statutes and regulations. Operationally, this means the Fed sends out teams of bank examiners (auditors) to assess the condition of individual institutions and to check compliance with existing regulations. On a more regular basis, banks must submit reports of their financial conditions and activities.

The promulgation of regulations is, of course, an activity that complements and defines the Fed's supervisory activities. Broadly speaking, regulation involves the formulation and issuance of specific rules that govern the structure and conduct of banking. The purpose of the rules is to establish a framework for bank behavior that fosters the maintenance of a safe and sound banking system and the fair and efficient delivery of services to bank customers. Operationally, the regulations (1) define which activities are permissible and which are not, (2) require banks to submit branch and merger applications to the Fed for approval, and (3) try to ensure that consumers are treated fairly when they engage in financial transactions. In later chapters, we shall see how the rules and regulations have changed over time and the implications of these changes.

Some specifics will illustrate the scope of the Fed's responsibilities and activities. The Fed is charged with ensuring that financial institutions comply with the Truth in Lending Act, the Fair Credit Billing Act, and the Equal Credit Opportunity Act. These statutes are designed to protect the customers of financial institutions from discrimination on the basis of race, sex, or age and from unfair or misleading lending practices. In addition, the Fed is responsible for ensuring compliance with the Community Reinvestment Act, which seeks to increase the availability of credit to economically disadvantaged areas and to ensure nondiscriminatory lending practices.[7] To carry out these responsibilities, the Fed monitors the advertising by institutions, investigates complaints from customers, reviews standard loan contracts used by institutions, and requires them to submit numerous reports summarizing their lending activities.

Another example of the Fed's supervisory and regulatory activities occurs when a bank encounters serious difficulties and is in danger of failing. The cause of the problems may be—and often is—related to fraudulent or misguided lending practices. Whatever the case, the Fed, along with the other relevant government agencies, tries to find an orderly solution that will preserve the public's confidence in the financial system. Often this involves finding a merger partner for the weak or failing institution, lending funds to the institution to give it time to work out its problems, and, in extreme cases, removing the bank's management. Perhaps you understand the quotation at the beginning of the chapter a bit better now.

Facilitation of the Payments Mechanism

Payments Mechanism
The ways in which funds are transferred to make payments.

The **payments mechanism** is at the heart of the nation's financial system. Many billions of dollars are transferred each day to pay for goods and services, settle debts, and acquire securities. Because any disruption of this mechanism could prove deleterious to the economy, the Fed is committed to the development and maintenance of safe and efficient means for transferring funds—that is, making payments.

Most obviously, the Fed facilitates the transfer of funds by providing currency and coin and clearing checks. As Exhibit 4-4 illustrates, the Fed plays a central role in the transfer of funds initiated by the writing of a check.[8] The task is enormous. The Fed clears millions of checks (or similar items) each business day. Now you can see why the Fed has encouraged the adoption of technological advances, such as the electronic funds transfer system discussed in Chapter 2, which can lower the cost and speed the transfer of funds.

In addition, starting October 28, 2004, banks are authorized to substitute an electronic image of a check for the actual paper check. Rather than physically transporting the original check, the electronic image can be sent almost instantaneously all over the country. This will allow checks to clear much faster and should reduce the costs of the check-clearing process.

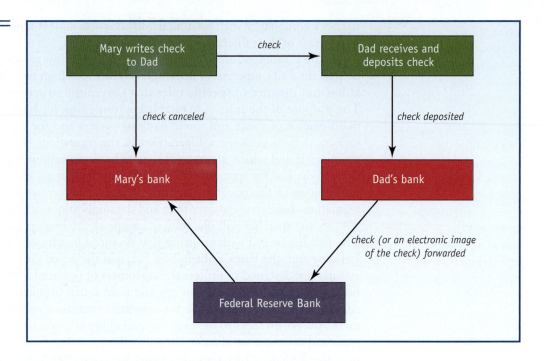

The arrows show the movement of a check through the system. The Fed plays two roles: (1) it forwards the check (or an electronic image of the check) from the bank receiving the check (Dad's bank) to the bank on which it is written (Mary's); (2) it transfers funds from the bank on which the check is written (drawn) to the bank receiving the deposit (Dad's). When the process is complete, Mary has less funds in her account and Dad has more funds in his.

Operation as Fiscal Agent for the Government

As chief banker for the U.S. government, the Fed furnishes banking services to the government in a manner similar to the way private banks furnish banking services to their customers. For example, the Fed maintains the Treasury's transactions account.[9] Government disbursements, such as funds for the purchase of a missile, are made out of this account, and payments to the government, such as taxes, are made into this account. The Fed also clears Treasury checks, issues and redeems government securities, and provides other financial services. It acts as the fiscal agent of the government in financial transactions with foreign governments and foreign central banks.

Now that we've explained the scope of Fed activities, we can focus on the major tools the Fed has at its disposal as it attempts to encourage and maintain a sound financial system and healthy economy.

Recap The major responsibilities of the Fed include setting monetary policy, regulating and supervising the financial system, facilitating the payments mechanism, and acting as fiscal agent for the U.S. government.

The Fed's Major Policy Tools

When someone is suffering from a back ailment, physicians usually have several therapeutic approaches available including rest, traction, braces, muscle relaxers, and surgery.

These "tools," which can be used in combination, are all designed to relieve pain and restore the patient's health. Because policy makers are similarly equipped and motivated, let's examine the Fed's major policy tools.

Open Market Operations

Open market operations represent the most important monetary policy tool at the Fed's disposal. These operations, which are executed by the Federal Reserve Bank of New York under the guidance and direction of the FOMC, involve the buying or selling of U.S. government securities by the Fed. When the Fed buys securities, reserves rise, and when the Fed sells securities, reserves fall. (Details of this concept are discussed in Chapter 20.) These operations are important because they have a direct effect on the reserves that are available to depository institutions. (Recall from Chapter 3 that depository institutions are required to hold reserve assets equal to a certain proportion of outstanding deposit liabilities.) Changes in reserves, in turn, affect the ability of depository institutions to make loans and to extend credit. When banks or other depository institutions make loans, they create checkable deposits. Thus, changes in reserves also affect the money supply. Consequently, when reserves change, the money supply and credit extension also change.

The Discount Rate and Discount Rate Policy

Because the Fed controls the amount of required reserve assets that depository institutions must hold, it also operates a lending facility called the *discount window* through which depository institutions caught short of reserves can borrow from the Fed. In January 2003 a new policy was implemented that established primary, secondary, and seasonal credit programs for discount window borrowing. Each program has its own interest rate, but the bulk of the borrowing and lending is in the primary credit program at the primary credit rate. Under the primary credit program, loans are made to depository institutions that are in a healthy and sound financial condition for a very short time (usually overnight). It is the **primary credit rate** that today is often referred to as the **discount rate**. Going along with the colloquial use, when we use the term *discount rate* throughout the text, we mean the *primary credit rate*. The primary credit (discount) rate is set one percent above another key short-term interest rate on which the Fed exerts a great deal of influence.[10]

The **secondary credit rate** is the rate charged for short-term loans to depository institutions that are having financial difficulties. The secondary credit rate is currently set one-half percent higher than the primary credit rate. *Seasonal credit* is extended to a small number of depository institutions that have recurring seasonal funding needs such as banks in agricultural or seasonal resort communities. The seasonal credit rate is an average of various market rates.

Prior to January 2003, the discount rate was set by the Board of Governors and in recent decades has been below other rates at which depository institutions could borrow reserves. The board usually approved requests for changes in the discount rate only after the broader monetary policy stance had been determined by the FOMC and was in the process of being implemented. Hence, changes in the discount rate often lagged changes in other interest rates, particularly short-term rates. Because the discount rate now automatically changes in response to changes in other short-term rates, changes in the discount rate no longer lag changes in other interest rates.

Changes in the discount rate can have several possible effects on depository institution behavior and the economy. Most obviously the cost of borrowing funds (reserves) from the Fed changes. If funds are withdrawn from a depository institution, not only do its deposits go down, but also it loses reserves equal to the full amount of the withdrawal.

Because depository institutions are required to hold reserve assets equal to a certain proportion of their deposit liabilities, the depository institution may be caught short of reserves and, as a last resort, may borrow the needed reserves from the Fed.

Increases in the discount rate raise the cost of borrowing, and decreases lower it. Holding other factors constant, we would expect an increase in the rate to lead to a drop in the volume of borrowing from the Fed and a decrease in the discount rate to lead to a rise in borrowing. Of course, in the real world, other factors are hardly ever constant, and decisions of whether to borrow from the Fed are based on several other considerations besides the discount rate.

The Fed views borrowing as a privilege accorded to depository institutions, not as a right. Because it is a privilege, the Fed urges these institutions to borrow only when other alternatives are not available. This sentiment is spelled out in the Fed's Regulation A, which sets out the Fed's discount policy, specifying the permissible size of loans, their frequency, and the reasons for which institutions may borrow. The rules make it clear that *under normal circumstances,* borrowing from the Fed is to be for short periods, preferably no more than a few days or weeks. Institutions that borrow frequently, say, for eight consecutive weeks or for 30 out of 35 weeks, can be examined by the Fed's team of auditors. The fact that the primary credit (discount) rate is now higher than other short-term rates also discourages borrowing. The Fed views the borrowing privilege as a means for banks and other depository institutions to deal with temporary liquidity needs caused, for example, by unexpected deposit outflows or an unexpected surge in loan demands. The key word is *temporary.* If an institution borrows persistently, the Fed begins to think that the institution's management is either consciously violating the provisions of Regulation A, cannot handle the liquidity pressures, or may have a chronic problem affecting its profitability and very existence. Perhaps its solvency, which is its ability to pay off or redeem its liabilities, is questionable. At this point, the Fed will step in. If the Fed believes that the borrowing privilege is being abused, it can deny the request to borrow.

We hope you noticed that the phrase "under normal circumstances" in the last paragraph was emphasized. The purpose was to stress how the Fed's discount policy usually works. Occasionally, "exceptional circumstances" such as a natural disaster, the shutdown of a large manufacturer in a small community, other developments over which an institution's management has no control, or poor management decisions may affect an individual institution and cause it to experience severe difficulties. Borrowers may not be repaying existing loans, depositors may be withdrawing large amounts of funds, and fears over the safety and solvency of the institution may be growing.

In such circumstances, the Fed stands ready to be a lender of last resort. More specifically, the Fed will consider lending funds to the institution for an extended period to help it adjust to its new circumstances, to provide time for management reform, or to work out a merger or orderly closing of the institution. Whatever the case may be, the Fed's main concern is to minimize the risk to the public interest and the financial system. Thus, the Fed's willingness to be a lender of last resort is closely related to its regulatory and supervisory responsibilities and its overall desire to preserve the public's confidence in the safety and soundness of the financial system, in general, and depository institutions, in particular.

Reserve Requirements

The major item on the liability side of depository institutions' balance sheets is deposits. The Fed requires depository institutions to hold **required reserves** equal to a proportion of checkable deposit liabilities. The Fed specifies the **required reserve ratio**, which is the

Required Reserves
The amount of reserve assets that the Fed requires depository institutions to hold against outstanding checkable deposit liabilities.

Required Reserve Ratio
The fraction of deposit liabilities that must be held as reserve assets.

fraction that must be held. Currently, the Fed is authorized to set the required reserve ratio anywhere between 8 and 14 percent. For example, if the required reserve ratio on checkable deposits is 10 percent, then for each $1.00 in checkable deposit liabilities outstanding, a depository must hold $.10 in reserve assets. During 2004, the required reserve ratio was 0 percent on the first $7 million of checkable deposits, 3 percent on checkable deposits of more than $7 million and less than $47.6 million, and 10 percent thereafter. For simplicity, we ignore the 0 and 3 percent requirements.[11]

In conjunction with its conduct of monetary policy, as noted above, the Fed—the Board of Governors to be precise—may vary the required reserve ratio. To illustrate, if the Fed wants to encourage bank lending, it could lower the required reserve ratio on checkable deposits from 10 percent to 8 percent. Then depository institutions would have to hold fewer reserve assets and would have additional funds to lend or to invest in other financial assets. This seemingly small change can have a powerful effect on the supply of money and the cost and availability of credit. The Fed does not change the required reserve ratio very often. When it does, the Fed is more likely to lower the ratio than to increase it. In December 1990 and again in December 1992, the required reserve ratio was lowered in an effort to stimulate the economy. At the present time, there are no reserve requirements on time and savings deposits although such requirements have often been imposed in the past. Rather than frequently changing the required reserve ratio, the Fed uses open market operations as its major instrument for implementing monetary policy.

In recent years, the amount of required reserves held by banks and other depository institutions has fallen dramatically because of the introduction and growth of sweep accounts. A **sweep account** is a financial innovation that allows depository institutions to shift customers' funds out of checkable accounts that are subject to reserve requirements and into highly liquid money market deposit accounts (MMDAs) that are not. For example, funds that were "swept" out of checkable deposits and into MMDAs totaled $5.3 billion in January 1994 when they were first tracked by the Fed. By August 2004, the cumulative funds in retail sweep accounts was over $641 billion. Some analysts have expressed concern that the reduction in required reserves because of the growth of sweep accounts will make it more difficult for the Fed to implement monetary policy. To date, the evidence does not seem to support this concern. Sweep accounts are discussed in more depth in later chapters.

Sweep Accounts
A financial innovation that allows depository institutions to shift customers' funds out of checkable accounts that are subject to reserve requirements and into highly liquid money market deposit accounts (MMDAs) that are not.

Recap   The Fed's main tools for implementing monetary policy are open market operations and setting the required reserve ratio and the discount rate. Open market operations are the most widely used tool.

Who Does What within the Fed

Having described the Fed's organizational structure, its functions, and the major tools available to Fed policy makers, we move on to identify the group within the Fed that has primary responsibility for each tool and function. Exhibit 4-5 shows the division of responsibility within the Fed. As you can see, the Board of Governors determines reserve requirements and the discount rate, and the FOMC directs open market operations.

Clearly, the board swings the most weight within the Federal Reserve System. The board even exercises general supervisory and budgetary control over the 12 Reserve Banks. Remember the golden rule: "He who has the gold rules!" The Reserve Banks deal directly with depository institutions. In dealing with these institutions, the Reserve Banks administer discount policy. In addition, they are an important part of the nation's check-clearing system and play an important educational role by providing financial

The Eurosystem: Europe's Central Bank

The European Union consists of 25 European countries that seek greater economic and monetary integration. Twelve of the 25 member countries have adopted a single currency called the *euro*. It replaced the national currencies such as the French franc, German mark, and Italian lira of the respective countries. The conversion began on January 1, 1999, and was completed on March 1, 2002.[a]

The Eurosystem is made up of the European Central Bank (ECB) and the national central banks of the 12 countries in the currency union. The ECB, which was created on June 1, 1998, has capital of 5 billion euro, which has been contributed on a pro rata basis by the national central banks. The Eurosystem formulates and implements monetary policy for the euro zone and is independent of control by any member country. In addition to directing monetary policy, the Eurosystem conducts foreign exchange operations and holds and manages the official foreign reserves of member countries. The ECB also operates a payment system called *TARGET*, which interlinks the national payment settlement systems of the countries in the European Union in order to promote smooth operation of the payments system.

The decision-making bodies of the Eurosystem consist of the Governing Council and the Executive Board. The Executive Board consists of the president, the vice president, and four other members, all appointed by the member countries. Minimum nonrenewable terms are eight years. The Governing Council consists of the Executive Board plus the governors of the national central banks of the member countries. A minimum renewable term for governors is for five years. The national central banks of the 12 countries in the currency union continue to perform many day-to-day monetary functions.

By law, the primary objective of the Eurosystem is to maintain price stability in the euro zone. The Eurosystem decides on quantitative definition of price stability, such as 2 percent inflation or less that is to be met over a medium time period. In addition, "two pillars" are used to achieve the goal. The first pillar is a quantitative reference value for the growth rate of a broad-based monetary aggregate, such as the M2 in the United States. The second pillar consists of a broad collection of indicators that policy makers consider to assess the outlook for price developments in the area as a whole. The former is similar to targeting a monetary aggregate to guide policy formulation. The latter is similar to using a more eclectic approach in policy formulation.

To achieve its goals, the Eurosystem uses tools similar to the Fed's, including open market operations, a lending facility like the discount window called a *standing facility*, and reserve requirements. The 12 national central banks hold the required reserves, carry out open market operations, and operate the standing facility. The Eurosystem must approve of the financial instruments that are allowed to be used in open market operations. The system also sets reserve requirements and interest rates on standing facility loans. It also takes actions that nudge interest rates and the monetary aggregates in one direction or the other as part of monetary policy. In many ways, the national central banks take on a role similar to the 12 Federal Reserve Banks, and the ECB takes on the role of the Board of Governors and the Fed Open Market Committee of the Federal Reserve System.

Board of Governors (7 Appointed Members)

- Sets reserve requirements and approves discount rates as a part of monetary policy
- Supervises and regulates member banks and bank holding companies
- Establishes and administers protective regulations in consumer finance
- Oversees Federal Reserve Banks

Federal Reserve Banks (Reserve Banks) (12 Districts)

- Lend funds to depository institutions (discount policy)
- Furnish currency
- Collect and clear checks and transfer funds for depository institutions
- Handle U.S. government debt and cash balances

Federal Open Market Committee (Board of Governors plus five Federal Reserve Bank Presidents)

- Directs open market operations (buying and selling of U.S. government securities), which are the primary instrument of monetary policy

SOURCE: http://www.federalreserve.gov/pf/pdf/frspf1.pdf.

institutions and the public with information on Fed policy and the workings of the financial system and the economy.

We can be even more specific about where the power to make policy within the Fed lies, thanks to an economist who has had a "lifelong interest in the relationship between political processes and macroeconomic outcomes, especially in the area of monetary policy."[12] According to Thomas Havrilesky, the chair of the Board of Governors has "power within the Fed's policy hierarchy because he molds the outcome of the meetings of the Board of Governors and the FOMC. The chairman plays a key role in shaping the FOMC policy directive. He expresses his own preferences and summarizes the sense of these meetings once deliberation and debate have been concluded."[13] Perhaps now you can see why this individual is such a powerful figure in U.S. policy circles.

The Federal Reserve System: An Independent Watchdog, Convenient Scapegoat, or Cunning Political Animal?

The Federal Reserve System is a quasi-government agency whose primary responsibility is to stabilize the economy. However, the Fed is just one of many government agencies that try to design policies to stabilize the economy. Others include the Council of Economic Advisers, the Treasury Department, and the Office of Management and Budget. Unlike the Fed, though, these agencies are under the direct control of the executive branch of government. Thus, the president can fire the chair of the council, the secretary of the treasury, and the budget director at any time.

As explained earlier, Congress established the Federal Reserve as an independent agency to shield it from the political process. The 14-year terms of the members of the board ensure that the members do not have to defend their actions to Congress, the president, or the public. In addition, the Fed does not depend on an appropriation from Congress for its funding. The Fed pays its own way from the interest income it earns on loans to depository institutions and its holdings of government securities. Finally, the Fed is exempt from many provisions of the **Freedom of Information Act (1966)** and "government in the sunshine" legislation, which call for government policy to be made in meetings open to the public. As a result, Fed policy makers usually meet in secret to formulate policy.

Freedom of Information Act (1966)

A 1966 law that requires more openness in government and more public access to government documents.

LOOKING BACK

Early Attempts at Establishing a Central Bank

The creation of the Fed in 1913 was not the first attempt to establish a central bank in the United States. Indeed, the first effort occurred back in 1791 when the Bank of the United States was given a 20-year charter with the government providing one-fifth of the start-up capital. The fledgling bank had elements of both a private and a central bank. Like other private banks, it made loans to businesses and individuals. Like a central bank, it issued banknotes backed by gold, attempted to control the issuance of state banknotes, acted as fiscal agent for the government, and was responsible for the aggregate quantity of money and credit supplied in the economy. However, the bank was not without its detractors who alleged that it represented big city "moneyed" interests. Fear and distrust, the unpopularity of centralized power, and questions about the bank's constitutionality all contributed to pressures to dissolve the bank. Its charter was allowed to run out in 1811.

The war of 1812 brought renewed pressures for a central bank that could oversee the financing of the war. Congress chartered the Second Bank of the United States in 1816. This bank also acted as fiscal agent for the U.S. government and issued banknotes redeemable in gold. Friction persisted between those who wanted a strong central bank (Federalists) and those who supported a more decentralized system (Anti-Federalists). After substantially reducing the bank's powers in the early 1830s, President Jackson vetoed the rechartering of the bank, and it went out of existence in 1836.

The National Banking Acts of 1863 and 1864 succeeded in establishing a uniform national currency, but the lack of a central bank meant that there was no easy way to regulate the amount of currency in circulation. Consequently, the country experienced periodic shortages that often led to financial crises. Such crises occurred in 1873, 1884, 1893, and 1907. Nevertheless, attempts at creating a central bank that could regulate the amount of currency in circulation were not successful until 1913 when the Fed was established.

Nevertheless, the Fed is not completely outside the government. It is firmly embedded in our political system. In the short run, however, the Federal Reserve does not take orders from anyone in the executive or legislative branch of government. Its decisions regarding monetary policy are, in theory, not constrained by the whims of the president or Congress or by any partisan politics. We say "in the short run" because in the long run Congress can pass laws that the Fed must obey. It could even abolish the Fed altogether. We think it fair to say that the Fed is aware of these possibilities and behaves accordingly.

Ever since the Fed was created, politicians and academics have argued about the desirability of its independence. The debate has largely focused on the degree to which the Fed should alter its policy in response to "suggestions" or directives from Congress or the president. Evidence suggests that since 1960, "outside forces" including Congress and the executive branch have become more aggressive in attempting to influence Fed actions. Obviously, the more responsive the Fed is to outside forces, the less independent it will be. Calls for reducing the Fed's independence in part reflect the frustration expressed by the president and some members of Congress in their often unsuccessful efforts to attain our economic goals. In the past decade, this frustration has led to several attempts not only to influence the Fed but also to make it more responsive to Congress. The Fed saw such moves as a serious threat to its independence and vigorously fought off overt efforts to clip its wings.

Those who support independence do so mainly on the grounds that anything less than independence will inject politics into monetary policy operations. This argument was put forth eloquently by Alan Greenspan, chair of the Board of Governors:

> We have to be sensitive to the appropriate degree of accountability accorded a central bank in a democratic society. If accountability is achieved by putting the conduct of monetary policy under the close influence of politicians subject to short-term election-cycle pressures, the resulting policy would likely prove disappointing over time. That is the conclusion of financial analysts, of economists, and of others who have studied the experiences of central banks around the globe, and of the legislators who built the Federal Reserve. The lure of short-run gains from running the economy can loom large in the context of an election cycle, but the process of reaching for such gains can have costly consequences for the nation's economic performance and standards of living over the longer term. The temptation is to step on the monetary accelerator, or at least to avoid the monetary brake, until after the next election. Giving in to such temptations is likely to impart an inflationary bias to the economy and could lead to instability, recession, and economic stagnation. Interest rates would be higher, and productivity and living standards lower, than if monetary policy were freer to approach the nation's economic goals with a longer term perspective.

> The recognition that monetary policies that are in the best long-run interest of the nation may not always be popular in the short run has led not only the United States but also most other developed nations to limit the degree of immediate control that legislatures and administrations have over their central banks. More and more countries have been taking actions to increase the amount of separation between monetary policy and the political sphere.[14]

Thus, proponents of continuing the Fed's independence argue that because politicians are interested in getting elected and reelected, they are short-run maximizers who do not take the long view. This could be disastrous if the long-run impacts of policy are different from its short-run impacts. For instance, to please the electorate, politicians might pursue an expansionary monetary policy that accelerates growth of economic activity, even though in the longer run this policy might increase inflation. Some have even suggested that the term of the Fed chair should be increased to further shield that individual from political influences.

On the other side of the debate, many people contend that the independence of the Fed is inconsistent with democracy. They argue that the president and Congress are held accountable for economic conditions. If unemployment is rising and inflation is rampant, the president and members of Congress will be driven from office at election time. Because the president and Congress are responsible for economic policy, they should have all the tools at their disposal. More generally, opponents of Fed independence argue that monetary policy, like other government policies, should be controlled by people directly responsible to the electorate.

Opponents of the Fed's independence would like to see reforms such as the following, which would reduce the autonomy of the Fed and make it more accountable:

1. *A change in the status of Reserve Bank presidents on the FOMC.* Proposals include removing the Reserve Bank presidents from the FOMC, making them nonvoting members, or changing the way Reserve Bank presidents are selected so that they will be more representative of the public at large. The concern is that the Reserve Bank presidents

Central Bank Independence and Macroeconomic Performance

Like the United States, most other industrialized nations have a central bank that directs monetary policy and supervises and regulates the banking system. Unlike the United States, which is divided into 12 Federal Reserve districts, most of these nations have highly centralized central banks.

Central banks vary in their degree of independence from government officials. As in the United States, almost all directors of foreign central banks are appointed by the government. Their terms, however, are often considerably shorter than the 14-year term of Fed governors. The shorter the term, the less independent the central bank is. In some countries, government officials actually sit on the governing board. In some, central banks are mandated by law to give credit to the government. In some, politicians can easily replace central bank governors. In others, it may not be so easy.

By considering these factors, researchers have judged the independence of various central banks. The less independent a bank is, the more vulnerable it is to political pressure. The most independent central banks include the European Central Bank, and the central banks of Switzerland, Canada, the Netherlands, and the United States. Countries with the least independent central banks include Portugal, Greece, and Spain.

But what does all that have to do with macroeconomic performance? Several researchers suggest that inflation rates are lowest in countries with the most independent central banks.[a] Apparently, the more independent the central bank, the less likely it is to expand (inflate) the economy in response to political pressure. Evidence also suggests that countries with the most independent central banks do not have higher long-run rates of unemployment. Thus, on both the inflation and the unemployment front, an independent central bank appears to enhance macroeconomic performance.

represent the interests of the banking community because they are chosen by the Reserve Bank directors, two-thirds of whom, in turn, are elected by the member banks.

2. *A broadening of the authority of the General Accounting Office (GAO) to audit the Fed.* At present, the GAO audits all aspects of the Federal Reserve with three exceptions: (1) deliberations and decisions regarding monetary policy, (2) transactions directed by the FOMC, and (3) transactions involving foreign exchange operations. Proposals would eliminate these exceptions.

In response to concerns about too much Fed autonomy and to facilitate the implementation of monetary policy, the Fed has become considerably more open in recent years. For example, even though it has no legislative requirement to do so, the FOMC releases edited minutes of its deliberations immediately after the next FOMC meeting, approximately six weeks later. As previously discussed, in early 1994, Chair Greenspan decided to announce several policy changes immediately after the FOMC meetings rather than waiting for the publication of minutes and the policy directive or for the policies to be implemented. This practice was formally adopted in February 1995. In 1993, the

Fed agreed to publish "edited" transcripts, not just minutes, of the FOMC meetings with a five-year delay.[15] Furthermore, in February 2000, the FOMC amended the language in the announcement to more clearly communicate the FOMC's judgment of the economic outlook in the foreseeable future. All of these actions confirm that the Fed is more open than in the past while maintaining that the present system gives it the proper degree of accountability necessary to carry out monetary policy.

Long-time observers of the political-economic wars believe that the debate over whether the Fed should be independent is more form than substance. For one thing, they point out, Congress finds the current system quite convenient. If the economy performs badly, Congress can engage in Fedbashing—blaming the Fed for what went wrong and telling the public that the Fed, insulated by its independence, would not respond to Congress's call to "do the right thing." In 1980, Edward Kane summarized this relationship as follows:

> Whenever monetary policies are popular, incumbents can claim their influence was crucial in their adoption. On the other hand, when monetary policies prove unpopular, they can blame everything on a stubborn Federal Reserve and claim further that things would have been worse if they had not pressed Fed officials at every opportunity.[16]

Kane's synopsis is as true today as it was in 1980. Scapegoats are convenient. If the Fed were directly and completely responsible to Congress, then who would Congress have to blame when things go wrong?

To sum up, the Fed's independence is in part an illusion. It can be maintained only if the Fed operates within politically acceptable bounds. If it pursues policies at considerable variance from what the president and Congress desire, Congress can change the law! Because changes have not occurred, we can infer that current arrangements are convenient and attractive. More specifically, political decision makers gain from having the public perceive the Fed as independent. This way the Fed can take the heat for unpopular policies, and the politicians can share the credit when things go right. At the same time, Congress and the president are probably confident that if push comes to shove, they can persuade the Fed to pursue policies conforming, at least broadly, to their wishes. This is part of what is popularly referred to as "the political economy of policy making."

In the next two chapters, we look at how interest rates are determined. It is time to move into the world of financial prices in which the Fed operates.

Summary of Major Points

1. The Federal Reserve System was established by an act of Congress in 1913. The original Federal Reserve Act was modified and strengthened in 1933 and 1935 following the economic and financial collapse during the Great Depression.

2. The Fed is charged with regulating and supervising the operation of the financial system to promote a smooth-running, efficient, competitive financial system and with promoting the overall health and stability of the economy through its ability to influence the availability and cost of money and credit.

3. The Board of Governors, located in Washington, D.C., is the core of the Federal Reserve System. It is composed of seven members appointed by the president, with the approval of the Senate, for 14-year terms. The terms are staggered so that one expires every two years. The president appoints one of the governors as chair for a four-year term.

4. The country is divided into 12 districts. Each district is served by a Reserve Bank located in a large city within the district. The framers of the original Federal Reserve Act hoped to decentralize policy-making

authority within the Fed through the creation of Reserve Banks.

5. The Federal Open Market Committee (FOMC) is the chief policy-making body within the Fed. It is composed of 12 members: the seven members of the Board of Governors and five of the 12 presidents of the Reserve Banks. The president of the New York Federal Reserve Bank is a permanent voting member, and the other four slots rotate yearly among the remaining 11 Reserve Bank presidents.

6. The Fed's functions can be classified into four main areas: formulating and implementing monetary policy; supervising and regulating the financial system; facilitating the payments mechanism; and acting as fiscal agent for the government.

7. The FOMC directs open market operations, the major tool for implementing monetary policy. These operations involve the buying or selling of government securities—actions that affect the volume of reserves in the banking system as well as interest rates. When the Fed buys securities, bank reserves increase. This, in turn, encourages bankers to expand loans and, hence, the money supply.

8. The FOMC meets eight times each year in closed meetings in Washington. Policy changes are announced immediately after the meetings. The minutes of the FOMC meetings are released to the public immediately after the next FOMC meeting. They contain the policy directive, which is the set of instructions regarding the conduct of open market operations that is issued to the New York Fed. The New York Fed, located at the center of the nation's financial markets, executes open market operations on behalf of the FOMC and the entire Federal Reserve System. The Fed announces FOMC decisions immediately following the meeting, including a statement about its judgment about the economic outlook in the foreseeable future.

9. In January 2003, the Fed established primary, secondary, and seasonal credit rates for discount window borrowing of reserves from the Fed. The primary credit rate is for short-term borrowing by healthy financial institutions. It is set higher than comparable short-term rates and is what we mean by the *discount rate* today. The secondary credit rate is one-half percent higher than the primary credit rate and is the rate charged for borrowing reserves by troubled depository institutions. Because the Fed views borrowing as a privilege rather than a right, institutions are encouraged to borrow only when absolutely necessary and only for short periods of time.

10. In exceptional circumstances, the Fed is prepared to serve as a lender of last resort. To preserve the public's confidence in the safety and soundness of the financial system, the Fed will lend for an extended period to an institution experiencing severe difficulties.

11. The Fed requires depository institutions to hold reserve assets equal to a proportion of each dollar of deposit liabilities. The Fed's required reserve ratio specifies the proportion.

12. There is an ongoing debate as to whether the Fed should continue to operate as an independent government agency. The Fed and others argue that independence is essential to the pursuit of economic stability. Opponents argue that such independence is inconsistent with our democratic form of government. Others observe that Congress and the president find the Fed a convenient scapegoat when the economy deteriorates. They further believe that the Fed is really not all that independent and that, at times, it does respond to political pressure. In recent years, the Fed has become more open.

Key Terms

Banking Reform Acts of 1933 and 1935, **64**

Board of Governors, **65**

Discount Rate, **73**

Federal Open Market Committee (FOMC), **68**

Federal Reserve Act, **64**

Federal Reserve System, **64**

Freedom of Information Act (1966), **77**

Lender of Last Resort, **64**

Monetary Policy, **69**

Open Market Operations, **73**

Payments Mechanism, **71**

Policy Directive, **68**

Primary Credit Rate, **73**

Required Reserve Ratio, **74**

Required Reserves, **74**

Reserve Bank, **65**

Secondary Credit Rate, **73**

Sweep Accounts, **75**

Review Questions

Questions marked with an icon are objective in nature. They can be completed with a short answer or number.

1. Discuss each of the four major functions of the Fed. Which do you believe requires Fed autonomy? Why?
2. List the major responsibilities of each of the following:
   a. the Board of Governors
   b. the 12 Reserve Banks
   c. the Federal Open Market Committee
3. Why was the Fed created? What effect should the existence of the Fed have on financial crises?
4. Why did Congress create 12 Federal Reserve Banks rather than one central bank?
5. What features of the Fed's structure serve to make it fairly autonomous? Is Congress able to wield any control over the Fed?
6. Why have the responsibilities of the Fed increased since its inception?
7. Discuss the major policy tools that the Fed can use to promote the overall health of the economy. What is the most widely used tool?
8. What are the primary and secondary credit rates? When do they change? How often does the Fed change the required reserve ratio? How often does the Fed engage in open market operations?
9. What are the arguments for increasing the autonomy of the Fed? The arguments for increasing the accountability of the Fed?
10. Suppose that the Fed were less independent. How could this affect monetary policy? Suppose that the Fed were more independent. How could this affect monetary policy?
11. Why is the president of the New York Fed a permanent member of the FOMC?
12. Is the Fed more accountable to Congress or to the president? Why? Who created the Fed? Who appoints the Fed chair?
13. How does each of the following affect the money supply?
    a. The Fed lowers the required reserve ratio.
    b. The Fed buys government securities.
14. What are sweep accounts? How do sweep accounts affect required reserves? Are balances in sweep accounts subject to reserve requirements?

Internet Exercises

1. This chapter has described the Federal Reserve System. Access the following Web site maintained by the Federal Reserve Bank of Minneapolis and answer the following questions: **http://www.minneapolisfed.org/info/sys/**.
   a. When and by whom was the Fed created?
   b. What is the Board of Governors of the Fed?
   c. Who are the current members of the Board of Governors?
2. The Federal Open Market Committee (FOMC) directs open market operations that involve the purchase or sale of government securities. Information on the FOMC can be found at the following Web site maintained by the Federal Reserve Bank of Minneapolis: **http://www.minneapolisfed.org/info/policy/fomc.cfm**. Access this site and answer the following questions:
   a. What is the current schedule of FOMC meeting dates?
   b. Who are the current members of the FOMC?

Suggested Readings

For an excellent monetary history and a summary of the events leading up to the legislation establishing the Federal Reserve, see Milton Friedman and Anna Jacobson Schwartz, *A Monetary History of the United States, 1867–1960* (Princeton, NJ: Princeton University Press, 1963).

The concern about political pressure on the central bank was well founded given the early history of banks in the United States. For a relevant discussion, see Bray Hammond, *Banks and Politics in America from the Revolution to the Civil War* (Princeton, NJ: Princeton University Press, 1957).

U.S. Monetary Policy and Financial Markets by Ann-Marie Meulendyke (1998) is a readable discussion of Fed procedures and the conduct of monetary policy. It can be obtained free of charge from the Public Information Dept., Federal Reserve Bank of New York, 33 Liberty Street, New York, NY 10045.

For an interesting history of the Fed, see James McAfee, "Historical Perspectives on Form and Function," *The Region,* Federal Reserve Bank of Minneapolis (September 2004). The article is available on the Internet at **http://www.minneapolisfed.org/pubs/region/04-09/McAfee.cfm**.

Fedpoints is a reference series explaining the structure and functions of the Federal Reserve System and other relevant economic concepts. It is available on the Internet at **http://www.newyorkfed.org/aboutthefed/fedpoints.html**.

For a discussion of The Federal Open Market Committee and the Formation of Monetary Policy, see the remarks by Fed Governor Mark W. Olson at the 26th conference of the American Council on Gift Annuities, Orlando, Florida May 5, 2004. It is available on the Internet at **http://www.federalreserve.gov/boarddocs/speeches/2004/20040505/default.htm**.

For two interesting articles on the Fed, see Thomas Cunningham, "Fed's Regional Structure Provides Unique Insight into the Economy," *EconSouth,* Federal Reserve Bank of Atlanta 2 (Quarter 2, 2000): 1; and Joel Hellier, "Independence of the Central Bank, Growth, and Coalitions in a Monetary Union," *Journal of Post Keynesian Economics* 22:2 (Winter 1999–2000): 285–312.

In the body of the chapter, we discussed that banks use sweep accounts to minimize the holdings of reserves. Payment of interest on reserves by the Fed would reduce the incentive to do so. See the "Testimony of Governor Laurence H. Meyer on the Payment of Interest on Reserves and Fed Surplus" before the Committee on Banking and Financial Services, U.S. House of Representatives, May 3, 2000. The testimony is available on the Internet at **http://www.federalreserve.gov/boarddocs/testimony/2000/20000503.htm**.

On May 6, 1997, the Bank of England gained substantially more independence in the conduct of monetary policy. An arti-cle that looks at the result of this increased independence is Mark M. Spiegel, "Central Bank Independence and Inflation Expectations: Evidence from the British Index-Linked Gilts," *Economic Review of the Federal Reserve Bank of San Francisco* 1 (1998): 3–14.

"The Independence of Central Banks" by Sun Bae Kim summarizes a study showing that countries with the most independent central banks have the lowest inflation rates. Furthermore, if the central bank has a reputation for controlling inflation, this can substitute for legal independence. The article can be found in the *Weekly Letter of the San Francisco Federal Reserve Bank* (December 13, 1991).

"An Independent Central Bank in a Democratic Country: The Federal Reserve Experience" by William McDonough offers a discussion of the historical development of central banking in the United States and of the need for the Fed to be somewhat independent of the day-to-day control of the government so that it will be less likely to succumb to short-term political pressures. The article can be found in the *Federal Reserve Bank of New York Quarterly Review* 19 (Spring 1994): 1–6.

Three additional articles devoted to the question of central bank autonomy can be found in "The Papers and Proceedings of the 107th Annual Meeting of the American Economic Association in Washington, D.C., January 6–8, 1995" as published in the *American Economic Review* (May 1995). These articles are "How Independent Should the Central Bank Be?" by Alberto Alesina and Roberta Gaiti; "Central-Bank Independence Revisited" by Stanley Fischer; and "Two Fallacies Concerning Central-Bank Independence" by Bennett T. McCallum.

Other articles dealing with central bank independence are Jakob de Haan, "Commitment Rather Than Independence: An Institutional Design for Reducing the Inflationary Bias of Monetary Policy: A Comment on Henriette M. Prast," *Kiklos* 51:1 (1998): 119–125; Richard W. Stevenson, "Divorcing Central Banks and Politics: Independence Helps Fight Inflation," *New York Times* (May 7, 1997): D6; and Susanne Lohmann, "Federalism and Central Bank Independence: The Politics and German Monetary Policy," *World Politics* 50:3 (1998): 401–406.

Endnotes

1 The Board has not yet had a female chair.

2 In addition, no two members of the Board of Governors may come from the same Reserve Bank district. This ensures that the board is not unduly influenced by any particular region of the country.

3 Excerpts from a policy directive are reprinted in Chapter 26.

4 In addition to the organizational structures mentioned in the body of the text, the Fed includes three advisory councils: the Consumer Advisory Council, the Federal Advisory Council, and the Thrift Institutions Advisory Council. Composed of representatives from each Federal Reserve

District, they meet several times a year with the Board of Governors to provide advice on issues relating to the Fed's responsibilities in the banking, consumer finance, and depository institutions areas. Federal Reserve insiders say that, as the name suggests, the advisory councils have no real power and serve mainly as a medium for public relations and the exchange of information.

5 The tools the Fed has available to affect the cost and availability of funds are discussed in the next section.

6 Many of the agencies that regulate the financial system are discussed in Chapter 14. Here, it is sufficient for you to know that the Fed has the broadest set of responsibilities, some of which overlap with the activities of other regulatory agencies.

7 The Community Reinvestment Act is discussed in greater detail in Chapter 14.

8 Other private institutions, known as *clearinghouses,* also help "clear" a substantial proportion of the checks written in the United States.

9 The transactions account of the government held at the Fed is similar to a checking account. However, the balance in the government's transactions account is not included in any monetary aggregate and therefore is not "money."

10 Depository institutions with excess reserves can lend them to other depository institutions that are short of required reserves. The fed funds rate is the interest rate for overnight borrowing and lending of reserves among depository institutions. The primary credit (discount) rate is currently set 1 percent over the fed funds rate, which is the rate for overnight borrowing of reserves among depository institutions. We discuss the fed funds rate in depth in later chapters.

11 The amount of checkable deposits against which the 3 and 0 percent applies is modified each year depending on the percentage change in checkable deposits. Because $45.4 million in deposits is a relatively small amount, we ignore the 3 and 0 percent requirements. The Fed may also set a required reserve ratio of up to 9 percent on nonpersonal time deposits. Currently the Fed does not impose reserve requirements on time deposits.

12 Thomas Havrilesky, *The Pressures on American Monetary Policy* (Boston: Kluwer Academic Publishers, 1993), preface.

13 Ibid., 4.

14 Statement by Alan Greenspan before the Committee on Banking, Finance, and Urban Affairs, U.S. House of Representatives (October 13, 1993).

15 The editing of the transcripts usually involves deleting a small amount of confidential material that pertains to foreign central banks or entities.

16 Edward Kane, "Politics and Fed Policymaking: The More Things Change the More They Remain the Same," *Journal of Monetary Economics* (April 1980): 199–211.

Looking Out, page 76

a On May 1, 2004, the EU was expanded from 15 to 25 countries. The original countries are Austria, Belgium, Denmark, Finland, France, Germany, Great Britain, Greece, Ireland, Italy, Luxembourg, the Netherlands, Portugal, Spain, and Sweden. The countries that joined in 2004 are Cyprus, the Czech Republic, Estonia, Hungary, Latvia, Lithuania, Malta, Poland, Slovakia, and Slovenia. Of the original 15, Denmark, Great Britain, and Sweden decided not to participate in the euro. The 10 additional countries may participate in the euro at a later date but do not at the present time.

Looking Out, page 80

a In addition to the Sun Bae Kim article in the Suggested Readings, see Alberto Alesina and Lawrence H. Summers, "Central Bank Independence and Macroeconomic Performance," *Journal of Money, Credit, and Banking* 25:2 (May 1993): 151–162. Note that some of the European central banks in these studies are now part of the Eurosystem. These studies predate the formation of the European Central Bank. However, they were used as resources in determining the structure that the new central bank should take with regard to central bank independence.

The worst form of inequality is to try to make unequal things equal.

—Aristotle

5

Financial Markets, Instruments, and Market Makers

Learning Objectives

After reading this chapter, you should know:

The various ways of classifying financial markets, including primary and secondary markets, money and capital markets, and spot and futures markets

The definitions and characteristics of the major financial market instruments

The functions of the key participants—the market makers

How the various sectors of financial markets are connected

Game Talk

To understand the role of financial markets and instruments in the financial system, we need to understand the jargon employed by insiders, or market participants, when they describe and discuss the "action" in financial markets. Trade jargon is not unique to these insiders, but it is pervasive in many aspects of life, including football. As the following example shows, even in this favorite American pastime the "players" need to understand the lingo.

> The time is Saturday afternoon during fall, and the place is the gridiron. When the quarterback reads a blitz (or red-dog) and man-to-man coverage, it is critical for him to call an automatic at the line of scrimmage and hit the flanker on a fly pattern. Of course, if the blitz does not materialize, the quarterback may find that he has thrown the pass into the teeth of zone coverage where the free safety can easily pick off the ball.

Such is the jargon of football. Much of this lingo is fully understood only by insiders—players, coaches, and football aficionados. Outsiders have difficulty understanding the game because they don't know the jargon, just as outsiders often have difficulty understanding financial market discussions. In this chapter, we will learn about financial markets and instruments (chiefly in the United States) and the language their participants use so that we too can understand what they are talking about.

Introducing Financial Markets

In general, a market for financial claims (instruments) can be viewed as the process or mechanism that connects the buyers and sellers of claims regardless of where they happen to be physically located. As you will see in this chapter, financial markets can be classified in many different ways. One of the most popular classifications divides the financial markets into individual submarkets according to the type of financial claim that is traded: stock market, corporate bond market, Treasury bill market, commercial paper market, and so forth. There is, however, at least one difficulty with this classification scheme; it suggests that the individual submarkets are separate, more or less unconnected compartments. A central message of this chapter is that the markets for the individual financial claims are connected and in many respects are more alike than different.

Another classification system, which recognizes that there are some similarities among the instruments, assigns the various financial markets to either the **money market** or the **capital market** based on the length of the term of the instruments traded there. The money market includes those markets where securities with original maturities of one year or less are traded. Examples of such securities include Treasury bills, commercial paper, and negotiable certificates of deposit (CDs). As you might guess, the capital market includes those markets where securities with original maturities of more than one year are traded. Examples here include corporate bonds, stocks, mortgages, and U.S. Treasury notes and bonds. Not surprisingly, some refer to the money market as the *short-term market* and the capital market as the *long-term market*.

Notice that together the money market and the capital market include all of the individual submarkets we identified in the first classification scheme. In this case, however, we are grouping instruments by their **term to maturity**, which is the length of time from when the instrument is initially issued until it matures. Put another way, the various markets may be separate institutionally, but we connect them analytically through the type of securities bought and sold by the participants in the markets.[1]

A third way to classify financial markets is to categorize them as the primary market and the secondary market. The **primary market** is the market in which a security is initially

Money Market
The market for financial assets with an original maturity of less than one year.

Capital Market
The market for financial assets with an original maturity of more than one year.

Term to Maturity
The length of time from the initial issue of a financial security until its maturity.

Primary Market
The market in which a security is initially sold for the first time.

sold for the first time. The security may be called a *financial instrument, claim,* or *IOU;* all of these terms are interchangeable. For example, if a firm needs to issue new bonds or stocks to finance investment in new equipment, the initial sale of these new securities occurs in the primary market. Thus, the primary market is where the public (individuals or financial institutions) buys newly issued bonds or stocks from the firms issuing them. Once a firm has issued bonds or stocks, further trading, say, a sale of bonds a month later by an initial purchaser, occurs in the **secondary market**. Most of the transactions in financial markets occur as portfolios are continually adjusted. It will be helpful to think of these financial transactions as occurring in the "used-car lots" of our financial system.[2]

Secondary Market
The market in which previously issued financial securities are sold.

The distinction between the primary and secondary markets is somewhat conceptual. In practice, the selling of new securities in primary markets by the firms issuing them and the trading of older securities in secondary markets occur simultaneously. An analogy may help. The market for autos is made up of the market for new autos and the market for used autos. However, if you go to a GM dealer looking for these subdivisions of the auto market, the only real distinction you will observe is that the used and new cars are located on different sides of the lot.

If this is so, why bother to distinguish analytically between primary and secondary markets? To understand why, we must first learn something about the quality of secondary markets. We assess the quality of a secondary market by the cost and inconvenience associated with trading existing securities. For example, in high-quality secondary markets, securities are traded at relatively low cost and little inconvenience. Such characteristics facilitate the sale and purchase of existing securities and thereby contribute to an efficient allocation of financial resources and a smoothly functioning savings-investment process.

To illustrate the point, imagine a financial system like those in many less-developed countries where formal secondary markets do not exist. Assume now that you want to sell a security you purchased several years ago when it was first issued, say, by LHT, Inc., an emerging high-tech firm. The absence of a secondary market means that you would first have to search for someone willing and able to purchase your LHT security and then negotiate a mutually acceptable price with that person. This process would obviously be quite time consuming and inconvenient, and the experience might discourage you from saving part of your income in this way in the future; that is, you would be less likely to buy LHT bonds in the future. If other people who own securities have similar experiences, LHT, Inc., and all firms like it will encounter some difficulty in financing future deficits, and the amount of borrowing and lending will be less than it otherwise would have been. Assuming that the deficits were to be used for planned additions to the firms' plant and equipment, the amount of investment will fall. Without this investment there will be less future growth of output and employment in the industry and the economy.

The message in this example is that the lack of a smoothly functioning secondary market will inhibit the financing of planned deficits in the primary market and thus have an adverse effect on investment and economic growth over time. In general, the strength and viability of primary markets are direct functions of the quality of secondary markets. Although the secondary market does not generate additional funds for the economy as a whole, its importance stems from the positive effect that a well-developed secondary market has on the primary market. Just as selling a used car does not add to the total number of vehicles on the road, the fact that there is a market for used cars improves the market for new cars.

Another way to classify financial markets is by whether the transactions they arrange occur instantly or in the future according to terms decided today; that is, by whether the markets are spot or futures and forward markets. In **spot markets**, financial instruments trade instantaneously, and the spot price is the price of a security or financial instrument for immediate delivery. We are all familiar with spot markets. For example, if

Spot Market
A market in which the trading of financial securities takes place instantaneously.

I decide to buy a share of IBM stock, I check with my broker and find out today's price for the stock. Or I may watch the financial news cable channel to check out the price of a bond for immediate delivery, say, one issued by LHT, Inc. I can also use my computer to check stock and bond prices online through my Internet account.

At other times, I may be interested in buying or selling financial instruments for delivery on some date in the future at a price determined today. In this case, I enter the **financial futures** or the **financial forward markets** where transactions are consummated today for the purchase or sale of financial instruments on a date in the future. Financial futures agreements trade U.S. government securities of several maturities, several stock market indexes, and foreign currencies on future specific dates. All quantities and futures dates are standardized. Financial forward agreements are transactions that are consummated today for the purchase or sale of financial instruments on a date in the future where the quantities and delivery dates are not standardized. Banks and other dealers and brokers customize financial forward agreements for their customers. Financial futures and forward markets are also called **derivative markets** because the value of the financial instruments (the futures and forward agreements) "derive" their values from the underlying instruments such as the government securities, the shares of stock, and so on that are traded on the future date. In recent years, other complex types of derivative instruments in addition to futures and forward agreements have also been created, and they are all part of the burgeoning derivative markets.

Financial futures and forward markets fulfill two basic functions. First, futures and forward markets may be used to reduce the risk associated with future price changes by "locking in" a future or forward price today. In recent years, financial futures and forward markets have experienced enormous growth. As financial prices have become more volatile, net lenders and net borrowers have turned to financial futures and forward markets to deal with the greater risk of unanticipated price changes. Second, financial futures and forward markets can also be used to speculate. **Speculation** in financial securities is the buying or selling of securities in the hope of profiting from future price changes. The many intricacies and nuances of financial futures and forward (derivative) markets are covered in detail in Chapter 18.

Having acquired an awareness of the various ways that financial markets can be classified, we move on to the noteworthy aspects of the major financial securities that are traded in U.S. financial markets.

Financial Futures Markets
Organized markets that trade financial futures agreements.

Financial Forward Markets
Markets that trade financial forward agreements usually arranged by banks or other brokers and dealers.

Derivative Markets
Financial futures markets where the value of the financial instruments (the futures and forward agreements) "derive" their values from the underlying instruments such as the government securities, the shares of stock, etc. that are traded on the future date; financial forward and futures markets, among others, are examples of derivative markets.

Speculation
The buying or selling of financial securities in the hopes of profiting from future price changes.

Recap   Financial markets can be classified as money or capital markets, as primary or secondary markets, or as spot or futures markets. Money markets trade financial instruments with an original maturity of one year or less. Capital markets trade financial instruments with an original maturity of more than one year. Primary markets trade newly issued financial instruments, and secondary markets trade previously issued financial instruments. In spot markets, the trading of financial instruments takes place instantaneously. In financial futures and forward markets, the terms of the trade including price are arranged today, but the transaction occurs at some date in the future. Financial futures agreements are standardized with regard to quantities and delivery dates. Financial forward agreements are customized with regard to delivery dates and quantities. Financial futures and forward markets are part of the growing derivative markets where the financial instruments derive their values from some underlying instrument.

Major Financial Market Instruments

Financial markets perform the important role of channeling funds from net lenders to net borrowers. Because the action in financial markets involves the trading of financial

5-1

The Principal Money Market
Instruments: Amount Out-
standing, End of Year (in
billions of dollars)

Type of Instrument	1960	1970	1980	1990	2000	2004[a]
Treasury bills	$37	$76	$200	$482.0	$ 647.0	$ 946.8
Negotiable CDs	0	45	260	546.9	1,052.6[b]	1,379.4[b]
Commercial paper[c]	5	35	99	558.0	1,602.0	1,314.2
Bankers' acceptances	1	4	32	52.0	9.0	4.4
Repurchase agreements and fed funds	1	22	102	324.0	1,197.0	1,585.1
Eurodollars	0.8	2.4	61.4	103.5	191.1	322.4

a As of June 30, 2004.
b Includes all large time deposits greater than $100,000.
c Includes commercial paper issued by financial and nonfinancial firms.
SOURCE: *Federal Reserve Flow of Funds Accounts, Z1* (September 16, 2004) at **http://www.federalreserve.gov/releases/Z1/**, the U.S. Treasury at **http://www.publicdebt.treas.gov/opd/opdhisms.htm**, and Table 4: the Federal Reserve Statistical Release, H6, Money Stock Measures, September 16, 2004, at **http://www.federalreserve.gov/releases/h6/hist/.**

instruments—in effect, IOUs issued by net borrowers—understanding the action requires us to be familiar with what is being traded. We first examine the instruments traded in the money market and then look at those traded in the capital market.

Money Market Instruments

The money market has undergone significant changes in the past 35 years, with new financial instruments being introduced and the amount outstanding of other instruments increasing at a far more rapid pace than the level of economic activity. In Chapter 12, we discuss the reasons for this growth and evolution when we look at the driving forces behind financial innovation. For now, we introduce and briefly describe each of the principal money market instruments. Exhibit 5-1 shows the dollar amount of the principal instruments outstanding at the end of 1960, 1970, 1980, 1990, 2000, and 2004. Exhibit 5-2 summarizes the typical maturities, major borrowers, and degree of secondary market activity for these instruments.

Instrument	Typical Maturities	Principal Borrowers	Secondary Market
Treasury bills	3 to 12 months	U.S. government	Very active
Negotiable CDs	1 to 6 months	Depository institutions	Modest activity
Commercial paper	1 to 270 days	Financial and business firms	Moderately active
Bankers' acceptances	90 days	Financial and business firms	Limited
Repurchase agreements	1 day, and 2 days to 3 months typical; 6 months less typical	Banks, securities dealers, other owners of securities, nonfinancial firms, governments	None, but very active primary market for short maturities
Fed funds	Chiefly 1 business day	Depository institutions	Active brokers' market
Eurodollars	Overnight, 1 week, 1 to 6 months, and longer	Banks	None

U.S. Treasury Bills

U.S. Treasury Bills (T-bills)
Short-term debt instruments of the U.S. government with typical maturities of 3 to 12 months.

U.S. Treasury bills (T-bills) are short-term debt instruments of the U.S. government with typical maturities of 3 to 12 months. They pay a set amount at maturity and have no explicit interest payments. In reality, they pay interest by initially selling at a discount—that is, at a price lower than the amount paid at maturity. For instance, in April 2004 you might pay $9,770 to buy a one-year Treasury bill that can be redeemed for $10,000 in April 2005; thus, the bill effectively pays $230 in interest ($10,000 − $9,770 = $230). The yield on such a bill is 2.35 percent or $230/$9,770 [(interest amount)/(purchase price)].

U.S. Treasury bills are the most liquid of all the money market instruments because they have an active secondary market and relatively short terms to maturity. They also are the safest of all money market instruments because there is no possibility that the government will fail to pay back the amount owed when the security matures. The federal government is always able to meet its financial commitments because of its ability to increase taxes or to issue currency in fulfillment of its scheduled payments. The Cracking the Code feature explains how to interpret the information about T-bills reported on the financial pages of major newspapers.

Information on T-bills can be found at **http://www.publicdebt.treas.gov**.

Negotiable Certificates of Deposit (CDs)

Negotiable Certificates of Deposit (CDs)
Certificates of deposit with a minimum denomination of $100,000 that can be traded in a secondary market, most with an original maturity of 1 to 12 months.

A certificate of deposit (CD) is a debt instrument sold by a depository institution that pays annual interest payments equal to a fixed percentage of the original purchase price. In addition, at maturity the original purchase price is also paid back. Most CDs have a maturity of 1 to 12 months. Prior to 1961, most CDs were not negotiable; that is, they could not be sold to someone else and could not be redeemed from the bank before maturity without paying a significant penalty. In 1961, with the goal of making CDs more liquid and more attractive to investors, Citibank introduced the first **negotiable certificates of deposit (CDs)**. Such negotiable CDs could be resold in a secondary market, which Citibank created. Negotiable CDs have a minimum denomination of $100,000, but in practice, the minimum denomination to trade in the secondary market is $2,000,000. Most large commercial banks and many large savings and loans now issue negotiable CDs. In addition, smaller banks are able to borrow in the market by using brokers.

Commercial Paper

Commercial Paper
Short-term debt instruments issued by corporations.

Commercial paper is a short-term debt instrument issued by corporations such as General Motors, AT&T, and other less well-known domestic and foreign enterprises. Most commercial paper is supported by a backup line of bank credit. Prior to the 1960s, corporations usually borrowed short-term funds from banks. Since then, corporations have come to depend on selling commercial paper to other financial intermediaries and other lenders for their immediate short-term borrowing needs. The growth of the commercial paper market since 1960 has been impressive and is partially due to the increase in commercial paper issued by nonfinancial firms. Initially, only large corporations had access to the commercial paper market, but in the late 1980s and early 1990s, medium and small firms found ways to enter this market. In addition, some financial intermediaries also get funds to invest and lend by issuing commercial paper.

Yields on financial and nonfinancial commercial paper can be seen at **http://www.economagic.com/fedbog.htm**.

Cracking the Code

Treasury Bills

Quotations for Treasury bills on May 11, 2004, are shown in the accompanying table found in *The Wall Street Journal,* May 12, 2004, under Treasury Bonds, Notes and Bills. When issued, all T-bills carry maturities of one year or less. As we saw in the body of this chapter, Treasury bills are issued at a discount from par—that is, at a price less than $100 per $100 of face, or par, value. The investor pays, say, $99, and at maturity receives $100. The interest received is, in effect, the difference between the face value and the price paid when the bill was purchased—that is, the discount.

Look at the highlighted bill quotation. The maturity date of the bill is Aug 12 04, which means August 12, 2004. Thus, as noted in the second column, there are 92 days to maturity, and, consequently, this is a 92-day Treasury bill that will mature in approximately three months. Dealers are bidding 1.03 percent for the issue and asking 1.02 percent. These bid and asked quotations are on what is called a *discount basis.* The discount is higher on the bid side than on the asked side, which means that the price at which dealers are offering to buy the T-bills is lower than the price at which they are selling the bills. The inverse relationship between yields and security prices (bills, notes, and bonds) will be discussed in Chapter 6.

The last column of the highlighted quotation indicates that the annualized yield to maturity (based on the asked price) on this bill is equal to 1.04 percent; this is what we mean when we refer to the *interest rate on the security.* The (−.02) in the next-to-last column means that the annualized yield to maturity decreased yesterday.

Maturity	Days to Mat.	Bid	Asked	Chg.	Ask Yld.
May 13 04	1	0.81	0.80	−0.01	0.81
May 20 04	8	0.84	0.83	0.02	0.84
May 27 04	15	0.83	0.82	...	0.83
June 03 04	22	0.86	0.85	...	0.86
June 10 04	39	0.87	0.86	−0.01	0.87
June 17 04	36	0.83	0.82	−0.04	0.83
June 24 04	43	0.83	0.82	−0.05	0.83
Jul 01 04	50	0.88	0.87	−0.02	0.88
Jul 08 04	57	0.89	0.88	−0.03	0.89
Jul 15 04	64	0.90	0.89	−0.04	0.90
Jul 22 04	71	0.93	0.92	−0.04	0.93
Jul 29 04	78	0.97	0.96	−0.03	0.98
Aug 05 04	85	1.00	0.99	−0.03	1.01
Aug 12 04	92	1.03	1.02	−0.02	1.04
Aug 19 04	99	1.03	1.02	−0.02	1.04
Aug 26 04	106	1.03	1.02	−0.04	1.04
Sep 02 04	113	1.07	1.06	−0.03	1.08
Sep 09 04	120	1.10	1.09	−0.01	1.11
Sep 16 04	127	1.13	1.12	−0.01	1.14
Sep 23 04	134	1.13	1.12	−0.02	1.14
Sep 30 04	141	1.15	1.14	−0.02	1.16
Oct 07 04	148	1.10	1.17	−0.02	1.19
Oct 14 04	155	1.19	1.18	0.01	1.20
Oct 21 04	162	1.22	1.21	−0.02	1.23
Oct 28 04	169	1.24	1.23	−0.01	1.25
Nov 04 04	176	1.28	1.27	−0.02	1.30
Nov 12 04	104	1.32	1.31	...	1.34

SOURCE: *The Wall Street Journal* (May 12, 2004): C15.

Bankers' Acceptances

Bankers' Acceptances
Money market instruments created in the course of international trade to guarantee bank drafts due on a future date.

Bankers' acceptances are money market instruments created in the course of financing international trade. Banks were first authorized to issue bankers' acceptances to finance the international and domestic trade of their customers by the Federal Reserve Act in 1913. Exhibit 5-3 depicts how bankers' acceptances work. A bankers' acceptance is a bank draft (a guarantee of payment similar to a check) issued by a firm and payable on some future date. For a fee, the bank on which the draft is drawn stamps it as "accepted," thereby guaranteeing that the draft will be paid even in the event of default by the firm. If the firm fails to deposit the funds into its account to cover the draft by the future due date, the bank's guarantee means that the bank is obligated to pay the draft. The bank's creditworthiness is substituted for that of the firm issuing the acceptance, making the

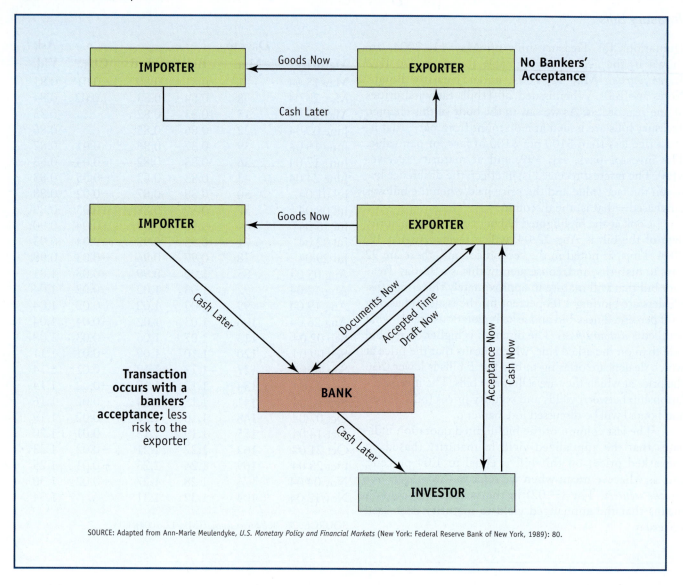

SOURCE: Adapted from Ann-Marie Meulendyke, *U.S. Monetary Policy and Financial Markets* (New York: Federal Reserve Bank of New York, 1989): 80.

draft more likely to be accepted when it is used to purchase goods abroad. The foreign exporter knows that even if the company purchasing the goods goes bankrupt, the bank draft will still be paid off. The party that accepts the draft (often another bank) can then resell the draft in a secondary market at a discount before the due date, or it can hold the draft in its portfolio as an investment. Bankers' acceptances that trade in secondary markets are similar to Treasury bills in that they are short-term and sell at a discount. The amount of bankers' acceptances outstanding increased by nearly 4,000 percent ($2 billion to $75 billion) between 1960 and 1984. Since 1984, however, the acceptance market has declined due to the growth of other financing alternatives and the increased trade in currencies other than the dollar. By June 2004, the amount of outstanding bankers' acceptances had fallen to $4.4 billion.

Repurchase Agreements

Repurchase Agreements
Short-term agreements in which the seller sells a government security to a buyer and simultaneously agrees to buy it back on a later date at a higher price.

Repurchase agreements are short-term agreements in which the seller sells a government security to a buyer and simultaneously agrees to buy the government security back on a later date at a higher price. In effect, the seller has borrowed funds for a short term, and the buyer ostensibly has made a secured loan for which the government security serves as collateral. If the seller (borrower) fails to pay back the loan, the buyer (lender) keeps the government security. For example, assume that a large corporation, such as IBM, finds it has excess funds in its checking account that it doesn't want to sit idly when they can earn interest. IBM uses these excess funds to buy a repurchase agreement from a bank. In the agreement, the bank sells government securities while agreeing to repurchase the government securities the next morning (or in a few days) at a higher price than the original selling price. The difference between the original selling price and the higher price for which the securities are bought back is, in reality, interest. The effect of this agreement is that IBM has made a secured loan to a bank and holds the government securities as collateral until the bank repurchases them when it pays off the loan. Repurchase agreements were created in 1969. Outstanding repurchase agreements are now an important source of funds to banks.

Federal (Fed) Funds

Federal (Fed) Funds
Loans of reserves (deposits at the Fed) between depository institutions, typically overnight.

Federal (Fed) funds are typically overnight loans between depository institutions of their deposits at the Fed. This is effectively the market for excess reserves. A depository institution might borrow in the federal funds market if it finds that its reserve assets do not meet the amount required by law. It can borrow reserve deposits from another depository institution that has excess reserve deposits and chooses to lend them to earn interest. The reserve deposit balances are transferred between the borrowing and lending institutions using the Fed's wire transfer system. In recent years, many large depository institutions have used this market as a permanent source of funds to lend, not just when there is a temporary shortage of required reserve assets. Financial market participants watch the federal funds rate closely to judge the tightness of credit in the financial system. When the fed funds rate is high relative to other short-term rates, it indicates that reserves are in short supply. When it is relatively low, the credit needs of depository institutions are also low.

Fed fund transactions are discussed at **http://www.newyorkfed.org**.

Eurodollars

Eurodollars
Dollar-denominated deposits held abroad.

Eurodollars are dollar-denominated deposits held in banks outside the United States. For example, if an American makes a deposit denominated in U.S. dollars in a bank in England or some other foreign country, that is a Eurodollar deposit.[3] Eurodollar deposits are not subject to domestic regulations and are not covered by deposit insurance. The Eurodollar market started in the 1950s when Soviet Bloc governments put dollar-denominated deposits into London banks. The funds were deposited in London because the governments were afraid that if the deposits were in the United States, they would be frozen in the event of a flare-up of Cold War tensions. Despite the easing of tensions, the Eurodollar market continues to thrive with Eurodollar deposits of U.S. addressees totaling over $320 billion in mid-2004.[4] Today many corporations and investors hold Eurodollar deposits in a foreign country if they have trade-related dollar transactions in that country. U.S. banks can also borrow Eurodollar deposits from foreign banks or their own foreign branches when they need funds to lend and invest. In recent years, borrowings of Eurodollars have become an important source of funds for domestically chartered banks.

Type of Instrument	1960	1970	1980	1990	2000	2004[a]
Corporate stock	$451	$906	$1,920	$3,530.0	$17,627	$15,982.7
Mortgages	142	297	965	3,804.0	6,886	9,884.0
Corporate and foreign bonds	75	167	319	1,704.0	4,991	6,728.6
U.S. government securities[b]	240	372	863	3,052.0	5,773	7,274.3
U.S. government agency securities	10	51	170	1,445.9	4,345	6,201.3
Municipal securities	71	144	337	983.0	1,481	1,977.2

a As of June 30, 2004.
b Includes Treasury bills, notes, and bonds held by the public and intragovernmental holdings such as by the Fed and the Social Security Administration.
SOURCE: *Federal Reserve Flow of Funds Accounts, Z1* (September 16, 2004); *Federal Reserve Bulletin,* various issues; *Banking and Monetary Statistics 1941–1970.*

Capital Market Instruments

The capital market is extremely important because it raises the funds needed by net borrowers to carry out their spending and investment plans. A smoothly functioning capital market influences how fast the economy grows. The principal capital market instruments introduced in this section are listed in Exhibit 5–4, with the amounts outstanding at the end of 1960, 1970, 1980, 1990, 2000, and 2004. Exhibit 5–5 describes the typical maturities, principal borrowers, and degree of secondary market activity for these instruments.

Stocks

Stocks
Equity claims that represent ownership of the net assets and income of a corporation.

Stocks are equity claims representing ownership of the net income and assets of a corporation. The income that stockholders receive for their ownership is called *dividends.* Preferred stock pays a fixed dividend, and in the event of bankruptcy of the

Instrument	Typical Maturities	Principal Borrowers	Secondary Market
Corporate stock	—	Corporations	Very active for large corporations
Mortgages	15 to 30 years	Home owners and other investors	Moderately active
Corporate bonds	2 to 30 years	Corporations	Active
U.S. government securities			
Notes	2 to 10 years	U.S. government	Very active
Bonds	30 years (currently)	U.S. government	Very active
U.S. government agency securities	Up to 30 years	U.S. government agency	Some activity
Municipals	2 to 30 years	State and local governments	Active

corporation, the owners of preferred stock are entitled to be paid first after the corporation's other creditors. Common stock pays a variable dividend, depending on the profits that are left over after preferred stockholders have been paid and retained earnings set aside.[5] The largest secondary market for outstanding shares of stock is the New York Stock Exchange. Several stock indexes measure the overall movement of common stock prices; the Dow Jones Industrial Average, perhaps the best known, is based on the prices of only 30 stocks. The Standard & Poor's 500 Stock Index is based on the prices of 500 stocks. The value of all outstanding stock was just over $20.1 trillion in early 2000, exceeding the value of any other type of security in the capital market. Note the dramatic increase in stock values between 1990 and early 2000—due to the very bullish stock market. In early 2000, the value of stocks began to fall in the deepest bear market in history, with the outstanding value of stocks falling from the $20.1 trillion high to less that $11 trillion by the end of the third quarter of 2002. After three successive years of decline, the stock market began to recover but by the end of the second quarter of 2004, still were still far below previous highs. The amount of new stock issues in any given year is typically quite small relative to the total value of shares outstanding. Chapter 16 has more on stocks.

Mortgages

Mortgages are loans to purchase single- or multiple-family residential housing, land, or other real structures, with the structure or land serving as collateral for the loan. In the event the borrower fails to make the scheduled payments, the lender can repossess the property. Mortgages are usually made for up to 30 years, and the repayment of the principal is generally spread out over the life of the loan. Some mortgages charge a fixed interest rate that remains the same over the life of the loan; others charge a variable interest rate that is adjusted periodically to reflect changing market conditions. Savings and loan associations and mutual savings banks are the primary lenders in the residential mortgage market, although commercial banks are now also active lenders in this market.

The federal government has played an important role in the mortgage market by creating two government-sponsored enterprises that sell bonds and use the proceeds to purchase mortgages. The two government-sponsored enterprises are the Federal National Mortgage Association (Fannie Mae) and the Federal Home Loan Mortgage Corporation (Freddie Mac). When the mortgages are purchased by these government-sponsored enterprises, new funds are provided to the mortgage market. The Government National Mortgage Association (Ginnie Mae), which is actually a U.S. government agency that is part of Housing and Urban Development (HUD), ensures the timely payment of principal and interest on mortgages, thus also facilitating greater lending in the mortgage market.

Corporate Bonds

Corporate bonds are long-term bonds issued by corporations usually (although not always) with excellent credit ratings. Maturities range from 2 to 30 years. The owner receives an interest payment twice a year and the principal at maturity. Because the outstanding amount of bonds for any given corporation is small, corporate bonds are not nearly as liquid as other securities such as U.S. government bonds. However, an active secondary market has been created by dealers who are willing to buy and sell corporate bonds. The principal buyers of corporate bonds are life insurance companies, pension funds, households, commercial banks, and foreign investors.

U.S. Government Securities

U.S. Government Securities
Long-term debt instruments of the U.S. government with original maturities of 2 to 30 years.

U.S. government securities are long-term debt instruments with maturities of 2 to up to 30 years issued by the U.S. Treasury to finance the deficits of the federal government. Notes have an original maturity of 2 to 10 years; bonds have an original maturity between 10 and 30 years. At the present time, the Treasury sells newly issued fixed rate 2-, 3-, 5-, and 10-year notes in regularly scheduled auctions. Sales of newly issued 30-year bonds were suspended in October 2001. Government notes and bonds pay semiannual dividends and return the principal at maturity. An active secondary market exists, although it is not as active as the secondary market for T-bills. Despite this, because of the ease with which they are traded, government securities are still the most liquid security traded in the capital market. In 1997, the U.S. government began issuing inflation-indexed securities with returns that were adjusted in response to changes in inflation. Inflation-indexed securities currently are issued with 5-, 10-, and 20-year maturities. (More on inflation-indexed government securities in Chapter 17). The principal holders of government securities are the Federal Reserve, financial intermediaries, securities dealers, households, and foreign investors.

U.S. Government Agency Securities

U.S. Government Agency Securities
Long-term bonds issued by various government agencies including those that support real estate lending and student loans.

U.S. government agency securities are long-term bonds issued by various government agencies including those that support commercial, residential, and agricultural real estate lending and student loans.[6] Some of these securities are guaranteed by the federal government, and some are not, even though all of the agencies are federally sponsored. Active secondary markets exist for most agency securities. Those that are guaranteed by the federal government function much like U.S. government bonds and tend to be held by the same parties that hold government securities.

State and Local Government Bonds (Municipals)

State and Local Government Bonds (Municipals)
Long-term instruments issued by state and local governments to finance expenditures on schools, roads, and so on.

State and local government bonds (municipals) are long-term instruments issued by state and local governments to finance expenditures on schools, roads, college dorms, and the like. An important attribute of municipals is that their interest payments are exempt from federal income taxes and from state taxes for investors living in the issuing state. Because of their tax status, state and local governments can issue debt at yields that are usually below those of taxable bonds of similar maturity. They carry some risk that the issuer will not be able to make scheduled interest or principal payments.[7] Payments are generally secured in one of two ways. **Revenue bonds** are used to finance specific projects, and the proceeds of those projects are used to pay off the bondholders. **General obligation bonds** are backed by the full faith and credit of the issuer; taxes can be raised to pay the interest and principal on general obligation bonds. Households in high tax brackets are the largest holders of state and local government bonds.

Revenue Bonds
Bonds used to finance specific projects with the proceeds of those projects being used to pay off the bondholders.

General Obligation Bonds
Bonds that are paid out of the general revenues and backed by the full faith and credit of the issuer.

Now would be a good time to read the accompanying A Closer Look feature, which describes some of the better-known interest rates for both money and capital market instruments.

In the next section, we discuss market makers. They are among the most important participants in financial markets because they facilitate the flow of funds from net lenders to net borrowers, and vice versa.

Recap   The major money market instruments are U.S. T-bills, negotiable CDs, commercial paper, bankers' acceptances, repurchase agreements, fed funds, and Eurodollars. The major capital market instruments are stocks, mortgages, corporate bonds, U.S. government securities, U.S. government agency securities, and municipals.

A Closer Look

Following the Financial News

The Wall Street Journal publishes the interest rates on many different financial instruments in its daily "Money Rates" column. The interest rates that are discussed most frequently in the media are listed here:

- *Prime rate:* The interest rate that serves as a basis for quoting rates to customers; an indicator of the cost to business of borrowing from banks.
- *Discount rate (primary):* The rate charged by the Federal Reserve Banks for lending reserve asset deposits to depository institutions that are financially sound.
- *Federal funds rate:* The interest rate charged on overnight loans in the federal funds market; a sensitive indicator of the cost to banks of borrowing funds.
- *Commercial paper rates:* The interest rates quoted on directly placed, dealer-placed, and euro commercial paper.
- *Treasury bill rate:* The interest rate on Treasury bills; an indicator of general levels of short-term interest rates.
- *Certificates of deposit:* The interest rates on one-month, three-month, and six-month certificates of deposit.
- *Bankers acceptances rates*: The interest rates on 30-, 60-, 90-, 120-, and 180-day bankers acceptances.
- *Eurodollar rates:* The interest rates on one-, two-, three-, four-, five-, and six-month Eurodollar deposits.
- *Foreign prime rates:* Prime rates of Canada, the European Central Bank, Japan, Switzerland, and Britain.
- *Overnight repurchase rate:* The overnight repurchase agreements rate.
- *Federal National Mortgage Association rate (Fannie Mae):* The interest rate on Fannie Mae mortgages; an indicator of the cost of financing conventional residential housing purchases.
- *Euro Interbank Offered Rates (EURIBOR):* The interbank rate for euro-dominated deposits among 57 euro zone banks.
- *London Interbank Offered Rate (LIBOR):* The interbank rate for dollar-denominated deposits in the London market among international banks; the interest rate that serves as a basis for quoting other international rates.

Although not included in "Money Rates," the rate on the 10-year U.S. government note is an important indicator of the level of long-term interest rates. Because of the length of time to maturity, small changes in interest rates cause much larger swings in longer-term note and bond prices. More on this in Chapter 6.

The Role of Market Makers

Market Maker
A dealer who links up buyers and sellers of financial securities and sometimes takes positions in the securities.

The participants in financial markets are the buyers, sellers, and **market makers**. The market makers function as coordinators who link up buyers and sellers of financial instruments. The link involves arranging and executing trades between buyers and sellers. Market makers may make markets in only one type of security, say, Treasury bills, or in several different types of securities, including stocks and corporate and government bonds. Who are these market makers? Where are they located? Why do they exist? What does "making a market" entail? These are some of the questions to which we now turn.

You probably have heard of large Wall Street firms such as Merrill Lynch, Smith Barney (part of Citigroup), Morgan Stanley, and Goldman Sachs—four leaders of finance. The main offices of these financial firms are in New York City, the financial capital of the United States. These offices are linked by telephone, telex, and the Internet to other major cities in the United States and the rest of the world where branch offices and regular customers are located. Like most enterprises, these firms are in business to earn profits. In this industry, profits are earned by providing financial services to the public. These services include giving advice to potential traders, conducting trades for the buyers and sellers of securities in the secondary market, and providing advice and marketing services to issuers of new securities in the primary market. The packaging and marketing of new stocks and bonds issued by a corporation are parts of what is often called *investment banking*—a function provided by most of the large market makers listed in the text. The term is potentially confusing for it suggests that these market-making firms are banks; in fact, they are not full-fledged banks, even though they provide some of the same services banks do. This is a good example of how market jargon can be misleading. In recent years, some large banks have merged with security firms that perform investment banking services. Despite the mergers, the banks and security firms still operate as separate entities (more on investment banking in Chapter 15).

Broker
A person who arranges trades between buyers and sellers.

Dealer
A person who arranges trades between buyers and sellers and who stands ready to be a principal in a transaction; a market maker.

To better understand the role of market makers, it will be helpful to distinguish between brokers and dealers. A **broker** simply arranges trades between buyers and sellers. A **dealer**, in addition to arranging trades between buyers and sellers, stands ready to be a principal in a transaction. More specifically, a dealer stands ready to purchase and hold securities sold by investors. The dealer carries an inventory of securities and then sells them to other investors. When we refer to *market makers* in this text, we will be referring to *dealers*, the market makers.

As a key player in financial markets, the market maker has an important role in our financial system. In particular, a market maker helps to maintain a smoothly functioning, orderly financial market. Market makers stand ready to buy and sell and adjust prices—literally making a market. Let us assume that there are 100,000 shares of a stock for sale at a particular price. If buyers take only 80,000 shares at that price, what happens to the remaining 20,000 shares? When such a short-term imbalance occurs, rather than making inconsistent changes in prices, the market maker takes a position (buys) and holds shares over a period of time to keep the price from falling erratically. Or the market maker may alter prices until all, or most, of the shares are sold. Thus, in the short run, market makers facilitate the ongoing shuffling and rearranging of portfolios by standing ready to increase or decrease their inventory position if there is not a buyer for every seller or a seller for every buyer. These actions enhance market efficiency and contribute to an orderly, smoothly functioning financial system.

Market makers also receive, process, interpret, and disseminate information to potential buyers and sellers. Such information includes the outlook for monetary and fiscal policy; newly published data on inflation, unemployment, and output; fresh assessments of international economic conditions; information on the profits of individual firms; and analyses of trends and market shares in various industries. As holders of outstanding securities and potential issuers of new securities digest all of this information, they may take actions that bring about a change in current interest rates and the prices of stocks and bonds.

To illustrate, assume that the political situation in the Middle East deteriorates, and experts believe a prolonged war, which would disrupt the flow of oil to the rest of the world, is likely. Analysts employed by the market makers would assess the probable impact on the price of oil, the effect on U.S. oil companies' profits, and so forth. Such information would be disseminated to and digested by financial investors and lead some of them to buy (demand) or sell (supply) particular securities.

In general, when something affects the supply of or demand for a good, the price of that good will be affected. In the financial markets, when something affects the supply of or demand for a security, its price will move to a new equilibrium and the market maker will facilitate the adjustment. As a quick perusal of the newspaper reveals, security prices change almost every day. Because of the activity of market makers, these changes usually occur in an orderly and efficient manner. In Chapters 16 and 17, we will learn how to read the information (crack the code) on prices of stocks and bonds as reported in major newspapers.

Why Market Makers Make Markets

The willingness of a market maker to make a market for any particular security will be a function of the expected profits and risks associated with buying, selling, and holding that type of security. The profits earned by a market maker flow mainly from the revenue generated by the price it charges for conducting a transaction, the number of transactions engaged in, and any capital gains or losses associated with the market maker's inventory of securities.[8] Generally, a market maker charges a brokerage fee or commission for each transaction. The fee may be per item, such as 10 cents per share of stock, or a specified percentage of the total value of the trade, such as 1 percent of the total proceeds from a sale of bonds. Market makers also collect a fee in some markets by buying a particular security at one price—the **bid price**—and selling the security at a slightly higher price— the "offer" or **asked price**. In this case, the revenue received by a market maker is a function of the spread between the bid and asked prices and the number of transactions in which the market maker and the public engage. Competition among market makers tends to minimize transactions costs to market participants.

To sum up, market makers play a key role in facilitating the buying and selling of securities by the public, as outlined in Exhibit 5-6. First, market makers assist in raising funds to finance deficits by marketing a borrower's new securities in the primary market. Second, they advise potential buyers and sellers of securities on the course of action likely to minimize costs and maximize returns. Third, they stand ready to buy or sell outstanding securities in the secondary market. To illustrate these various roles, Exhibit 5-7 on page 102 summarizes the trading of a bond issued by All Purpose Enterprise Inc. (APEI), a typical firm that wants to expand its scale of operations by building a new plant and acquiring additional inventories. Note the coordinating and connecting role played by Merrill Lynch and Smith Barney.

Market Making and Liquidity

The quality and cost of services provided by market makers affect the transactions costs associated with buying or selling various securities. The costs and convenience associated with trading particular securities, in turn, affect the liquidity of these securities. Because transactions costs and liquidity affect portfolio decisions, the market-making function influences the allocation of financial resources in our economy. Some markets, such as the T-bill market, are characterized by high-quality secondary markets. The large volume of outstanding securities encourages many firms to make markets in Treasury securities, and the volume of trading and competition among market makers produces a

Bid Price
The price at which a market maker is willing to buy securities.

Asked Price
The price at which a market maker is willing to sell securities.

5-6

Market Makers

5-7

The Marketing and
Subsequent Trading
of a Corporate Bond

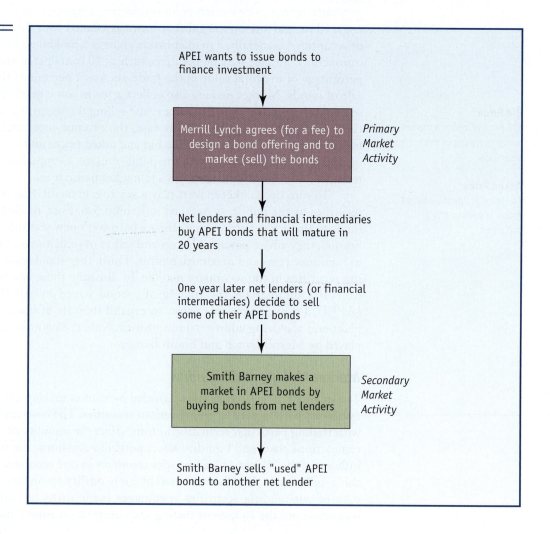

spread between the dealer bid and asked prices of only 0.1 to 0.2 percent—well below the spread of 0.3125 to 0.5 percent associated with transactions in less actively traded, longer-term government securities.[9]

Substitutability, Market Making, and Market Integration

Market makers play another important but less-obvious role in helping to integrate the various subsectors of financial markets. Market makers such as Merrill Lynch and Smith Barney make markets in numerous financial instruments. In general, the trading floor of the typical market maker is a busy place. On the floor of the trading room, the specialist in T-bills sits near the specialist in corporate bonds, who, in turn, is only 20 feet from the specialist in mortgage-backed securities. Assuming that these people talk to one another, the activity in one market is known to those operating in other markets. With each specialist disseminating information to customers via telephone and continually monitoring computer display terminals, a noticeable change in the T-bill market (say, a half percentage point decline in interest rates on T-bills) will quickly become known to buyers and sellers in other markets. Such information will, in turn, influence trading decisions in these other markets and thus affect interest rates on other securities.

This spillover from one submarket to another is important in understanding the ties that bind the various compartments of financial markets together. The key concept underlying these linkages is the notion of *substitutability*. Whether they be individuals allocating their own savings or bank managers, portfolio managers monitor the expected returns on the array of financial assets available in financial markets. They compare the returns on assets in their portfolios to others available in the market. For example, if a higher, more attractive return becomes available on a Treasury bond as compared to a municipal bond already in the manager's portfolio, the manager may decide to sell the municipal security and buy the Treasury bond. This exchange of a lower-yielding security for a higher-yielding one is the essence of substitution. Assuming that many portfolio managers undertake similar actions, the net effect is to increase the supply in the municipal securities market and the demand in the Treasury bond market. Our market makers then act in effect as auctioneers, responding to such changes in supply and demand by changing the prices at which they are willing to buy or sell securities.

So far we have restricted our discussion to domestic financial markets. Yet for almost every domestic financial market, a corresponding foreign market exists. For example, there are markets for Japanese government securities, Hong Kong stocks, Canadian mortgage-backed securities, and Greek bonds. The same factors that affect the viability of domestic markets affect the substitutability between and among domestic and foreign instruments. Most financial markets are becoming international in scope as improvements in communication technologies have made the world a smaller place. Foreign instruments are good substitutes for domestic instruments in such a world, and vice versa. The activities of the market makers are critical to "greasing the wheels" that allow for this market integration.

Leaving the details aside, we have come full circle from the beginning of the chapter: We have seen that the numerous instruments traded in financial markets can be classified in many different ways; we have also seen that the separate markets for the individual instruments are linked by the activities of market makers and the willingness of traders to substitute among the alternative instruments available.

Before ending this discussion, note one other aspect about market makers. The traders obtain details on current interest rates, securities prices, and other information. Among many bits of data watched closely by all market makers is information relating to the operations of the Federal Reserve. In fact, if you asked these analysts and traders which type of information is most important, they would probably answer "information on Federal Reserve policy." After studying Chapter 4, we are sure you will be able to see why.

Summary of Major Points

1. The markets for particular types of financial claims are connected, not separate, entities. The connectedness of the markets results from the buying and selling (trading) of securities by the participants in the markets—that is, the substitution among available alternative instruments.
2. The money market is where securities with original maturities of one year or less are traded. The capital market is where securities with original maturities of more than one year are traded.
3. Primary markets are where new securities, issued to finance current deficits, are bought and sold. Secondary markets are where outstanding securities (issued earlier) are bought and sold.
4. Secondary markets are important to the operation of an efficient financial system. Well-organized, smoothly functioning, high-quality secondary markets facilitate the trading of outstanding securities at relatively low cost and little inconvenience. This, in turn, facilitates the financing of planned deficits in primary markets.
5. The spot market is the market for the purchase or sale of securities for immediate delivery. In the futures and forward markets, contracts are entered into today to purchase or sell securities in the future at a price agreed upon today. Futures agreements are standardized as to quantities and delivery dates. Forward agreements are customized by banks and other brokers and dealers with regard to quantities and delivery dates to meet the needs of their customers. Futures and forward markets are used to either reduce risk or speculate. Futures and forward markets are part of the growing derivatives markets where the financial instruments derive their values from some underlying instrument.
6. The principal money market instruments are U.S. Treasury bills (T-bills), negotiable certificates of deposit (CDs), commercial paper, bankers' acceptances, repurchase agreements, federal (fed) funds, and Eurodollars. The major capital market instruments are stocks, mortgages, corporate bonds, U.S. government securities, U.S. government agency securities, and state and local government bonds.
7. Market makers are the specialists who function as coordinators in financial markets and link up buyers and sellers of securities. They serve three important functions: (1) they disseminate information about market conditions to buyers and sellers; (2) they connect the various markets by buying and selling in the market themselves; and (3) they provide financial services that determine the quality of primary and secondary markets. In turn, the quality of the primary and secondary markets affects the ease or difficulty associated with financing deficits, lending surpluses, and, more generally, shifting into and out of various financial instruments.
8. Most domestic financial markets have a comparable foreign market, such as a foreign stock market. Market makers have assisted in integrating domestic and foreign financial markets.

Key Terms

Review Questions

1. Distinguish between primary and secondary markets and between money and capital markets.
2. The secondary market for T-bills is active, and the secondary market for federal agency securities is limited. How does this affect the primary market for each security? Why are well-developed secondary markets important for the operation of an efficient financial system?
3. What is the difference between financial futures and financial forward markets? What are derivative markets? What are the ways derivatives can be used?
4. Discuss the major function of market makers in securities markets. What is the difference between a broker and a dealer?
5. If you call a local brokerage firm, you will find that the commission or brokerage fee charged for purchasing $10,000 of T-bills is less than the fee associated with purchasing $10,000 of, say, municipal bonds issued by the City of Cincinnati. Explain why.
6. Explain why it would be incorrect to view the various sectors of the financial markets as totally separate entities.
7. In Chapter 3, you saw that the Fed can change the amount of reserves available to depository institutions and the required reserve ratio. Why do market makers pay so much attention to what the Federal Reserve is doing?
8. Define *commercial paper, negotiable certificates of deposit, repurchase agreements, bankers' acceptances, federal funds,* and *Eurodollars.* In what ways are they similar, and in what ways are they different?
9. What are mortgages?
10. Define and contrast *stocks* and *bonds.* What are the advantages of owning preferred stock? What are the advantages of owning common stock?
11. What is the difference between a government security and a government agency security? Which asset would you prefer to own if safety and liquidity were important to you?
12. Would you rather own the stocks or bonds of a particular corporation if you believed that the corporation was going to earn exceptional profits next year?
13. Why are municipals attractive to individuals and corporations with high income or profits?
14. What are the fed funds rate, the Treasury bill rate, the discount rate, and the LIBOR?
15. Can the bid price ever be greater than the asked price?

Analytical Questions

Questions marked with an icon are objective in nature. They can be completed with a short answer or number.

16. Rank the following financial instruments in terms of their safety and liquidity:
    a. U.S. T-bills
    b. Large negotiable CDs
    c. Mortgages
    d. Government bonds
    e. Government agency securities
    f. Commercial paper
    g. Eurodollars
17. In June 2004, John pays $9,800 for a one-year T-bill that can be redeemed for $10,000. What is the effective interest? What is the yield?

Internet Exercises

1. The *Federal Reserve's Statistical Release H-15* reports yields on several financial instruments. Access the Web site http://www.federalreserve.gov/releases/H15/update/. Can you distinguish between the money market instruments and capital market instruments reported at this site?
2. From the bank rate monitor Web site http://www.bankrate.com/brml, access the consumer Mortgage Guide and find the local mortgage rates for 15-year fixed, 30-year fixed, and 1-year adjustable (ARM) loans in your hometown.
3. The New York Stock Exchange homepage at http://www.nyse.com describes trading activity on the exchange. What is today's value of the Dow Jones Industrial Average and the Standard and Poor's 500? What were the number of shares traded on the New York Stock Exchange today?

Suggested Readings

For one of the most comprehensive and readable surveys of money market instruments, see Timothy Q. Cook and Robert K. Laroche, eds., *Instruments of the Money Market*, (Federal Reserve Bank of Richmond, 1998). Although this publication is no longer in print, it remains popular and is available on the Internet at **http://www.rich.frb.org/pubs/instruments/**.

Two other older books that may be of interest are *The Money Market*, rev. ed. (Homewood, IL: Dow Jones-Irwin, 1990); and *Handbook of Securities of the United States Government and Federal Agencies, and Related Money Market Instruments* (First Boston Corporation, July 1990).

Additional Fed publications explaining fed funds, repurchase agreements, and government securities can be accessed on the Internet at **http://www.newyorkfed.org/publications/result.cfm**.

For a discussion of the commercial paper market, see Mitchell Post, "The Evolution of the U.S. Commercial Paper Market since 1980," *Federal Reserve Bulletin* (December 1992). For recent trends in the commercial paper market, see Pu Shen, "Why Has the Nonfinancial Commercial Paper Market Shrunk Recently?" *Economic Review*, Federal Reserve Bank of Kansas City 88:1 (First Quarter 2003): 55–76.

Some articles dealing with the stock market boom of the late 1990s follow: Nathan S. Balke and Mark E. Wohar, "Why Are Stock Prices So High? Dividend Growth or Discount Factor?" *Federal Reserve Bank of Dallas Working Paper No. 00-01* (January 2000); Simon Kwan, "Three Questions About 'New Economy' Stocks," *FRBSF Economic Letter*, Federal Reserve Bank of San Francisco, No. 2000-15 (May 12, 2000); William R. Nelson, "Why Does the Change in Shares Predict Stock Returns?" *Finance and Economics Discussion Series*, Board of Governors of the Federal Reserve System, No. 1999-06 (1999).

Endnotes

1 The nature of the connection leads some to distinguish among financial markets by whether the market facilitates the exchange of funds directly between net lenders and net borrowers or whether funds are channeled through financial intermediaries. In a *direct market*, funds are exchanged directly; that is, direct finance occurs. In an *indirect market*, funds flow through financial intermediaries, and indirect finance occurs. As discussed in Chapter 1, indirect finance occurs when financial intermediaries exchange their own liabilities or secondary claims with net lenders for funds and then provide such funds to net borrowers. In this latter transaction, financial intermediaries exchange the funds for direct claims on the net borrowers.

2 Note, however, that unlike used cars, securities usually do not fall in value through time.

3 Eurodollars must be distinguished from foreign deposits that are denominated in the currency of the host country. For example, a foreign deposit results when an American converts dollars to British pounds and deposits them in a bank in England with the deposit denominated in pounds.

4 *Federal Reserve Statistical Release H.6,* Board of Governors of the Federal Reserve System (September 16, 2004).

5 Note that the board of directors of a corporation may choose not to pay common stockholders dividends even if the corporation has profits left over after preferred shareholders have been paid. In this case, the income that stockholders receive will be in the form of capital gains if the stock appreciates because of the retained earnings.

6 The securities that are issued by Fannie Mae and Freddie Mac or that are insured by Ginnie Mae are called *government agency securities.* They are the agency securities that deal with residential lending and were discussed in the section on mortgages.

7 In mid-1995, investors in Orange County, California, found out firsthand about the risks of municipal bonds after the county declared bankruptcy in December 1994. The bankruptcy resulted from a $1.7 billion loss in the county's investment portfolio due to reckless risk taking in financial markets.

8 Market makers assume a large amount of risk when they take positions in long-term bonds. They bear the risk that bond prices will fall and the value of the bonds in their portfolios will decrease. As we will see in Chapter 6, small increases in long-term interest rates can lead to large decreases in long-term bond prices.

9 Spreads between dealer bid and asked prices for corporate bonds range up to 2 to 3 percent for securities with relatively low marketability.

Change must be measured from a known baseline.

—Evan Shute

6

Interest Rates and Bond Prices

Learning Objectives

After reading this chapter, you should know:

Why the interest rate represents the time value of money

What compounding and discounting are

Why interest rates and bond prices are inversely related

The major determinants of interest rates

The relationship between nominal and real interest rates

How interest rates fluctuate over the business cycle

The Present versus the Future

State University currently charges students $5,000 a year for tuition. Following the appointment of an innovative financial officer, it offers enrolling freshmen a new way to pay four years' tuition—pay $18,000 today rather than $5,000 per year for four years. Would you participate in the plan? Following her third box office smash, a Hollywood sensation has just signed a multipicture contract. As compensation, the star has been offered either $6,000,000 today or $7,500,000 in five years. You are her financial adviser; what should she do and why? You win a million-dollar lottery and learn that the million dollars will be paid out in equal installments of $50,000 per year over the next 20 years. Would you be willing to trade this stream of future income for one payment today? How large would that payment have to be?

The purpose of the first half of this chapter is to provide the analytical framework needed to understand and answer questions that involve comparing the present with the future, such as those just posed. As you will see, the framework developed and questions addressed, while important by themselves, are the keys to the second half of the chapter where we will examine the determinants of interest rates and the relationships among interest rates, bond prices, economic activity, and inflation. Even a casual reader of the financial pages of U.S. newspapers has seen headlines such as "Bond Prices Slump as Interest Rates Rise" or "Bond Market Rallies after Weak GDP Report" or "Inflation Fears Result in Lower Bond Prices." Understanding such headlines is the objective of the second part of the chapter.

The Time Value of Money

Interest rates have already popped up in numerous places in the text. In our earlier substantive discussion in Chapter 3, we emphasized that the interest rate is the cost of obtaining money to borrowers and the return (or yield) on money to lenders. Thus, just as rent is the cost to apartment dwellers and the return to the landlord, the interest rate is the rental rate paid by borrowers and received by lenders when money is "rented out."

Money represents purchasing power; a person who has money can purchase goods or services now. If someone does not have money now and wants to make purchases, she can rent purchasing power by borrowing. Likewise, if someone else has money now and is willing to postpone purchases to the future, he can rent out purchasing power. Note carefully the role played by the interest rate here. Presumably, the willingness to postpone purchases into the future is a function of the reward—that is, the interest rate. In particular, the higher the interest rate, ceteris paribus, the greater the reward and, hence, the greater the willingness to postpone purchases into the future and lend in the present. Similar reasoning applies on the borrowing side. We can think of someone who wants to purchase goods and services but is short of the necessary funds as having two options: (1) borrow now and purchase now or (2) save now and purchase later. Because the willingness to borrow depends on the cost, among other things, we can conclude that the higher the interest rate, ceteris paribus, the less attractive is option (1) and the more attractive is option (2).

The central point to remember from this discussion is the role that the interest rate plays in linking the present with the future. Lending in the present enables spending in the future the sum of what is lent plus the interest earned. Borrowing in the present enables spending in the present but requires paying back in the future what is borrowed plus interest. Because the interest rate is the return on lending and the cost of borrowing, it plays a pivotal role in spending, saving, borrowing, and lending decisions made in the present and bearing on the future. The concept we have been discussing is called the **time value of money.** Simply put, the interest rate represents

Time Value of Money
The terms on which one can trade off present purchasing power for future purchasing power; the interest rate.

the time value of money because it specifies the terms on which a person can trade off present purchasing power for future purchasing power. In the pages that follow, it should become crystal clear that this is one of the most important and fundamental concepts in economics and finance.

Compounding and Discounting

Compounding: Future Values

Compounding
A method used to determine the future value of a sum lent today.

Compounding is a method used to answer a simple question: What is the future value of money lent (or borrowed) today? As illustrated in Exhibit 6-1, the question is forward looking; we stand in the present (today) and ask a question about the future. To see how it works, a few examples will be helpful.

Suppose Joseph M. Student agrees to lend a friend $1,000 for one year. The friend gives Joe an IOU for $1,000 and agrees to repay the $1,000 plus interest in a year. The amount that is originally lent is called the **principal**—in this case, $1,000.

Principal
The original amount of funds lent.

If the agreed interest rate is 6 percent, the friend will pay a total of $1,060 ($1,000 + $60). In this example, the amount of interest is $60 ($1,000 × .06 = $60).

This general relationship can be expressed as

(A)   Amount repaid = principal + interest

The amount of interest can be expressed as

(B)   Interest = principal × interest rate

Substituting Equation (B) into Equation (A) yields

(C)   Amount repaid = principal + (principal × interest rate)

Because each term on the right-hand side of Equation (C) has a common factor, it can be rearranged and rewritten as

(D)   Amount repaid = principal × (1 + i)

where i is the interest rate. Using Equation (D) and our example, Joe's friend would repay

$$\$1,060 = \$1,000 \times 1.06$$

For later use, we will rewrite Equation (D) as

(6-1) $V_1 = V_0(1 + i)$

where V_1 = the funds to be received by the lender (paid by the borrower) at the end of year 1; note that this is a future value and V_0 = the funds lent (and borrowed) now; note that this is a *present value*.

6-1

Compounding: The Future Value of Money Lent Today

Imagine now that Joe's friend borrows for two years instead of one year and makes no payments to Joe until two years pass. Here is where compounding comes into play. Literally, *compounding* means to combine, add to, or increase. In the financial world, it refers to the increase in the value of funds that results from earning interest on interest. More specifically, interest earned after the first year is added to the original principal; the second year's interest calculation is based on this total. The funds to be received at the end of two years, V_2, consist of the original amount of funds lent out, V_0, plus the interest on the original amount, $i V_0$, plus the interest on the amount of funds owed at the end of the first year $[i(V_0 + iV_0)]$. In our example:

Principal	+	interest earned in first year	+	interest earned = in second year
$1,000	+	.06($1,000)	+	.06[$1,000 + .06($1,000)] =
$1,000	+	$60	+	$63.60 = $1,123.60

Note that the implication of the last term is that interest is earned on interest; this is compounding.[1] In the second year, Joe earns interest not only on the principal (.06 × $1,000) but also on the interest earned in the first year [.06 × .06($1,000)]. In effect, the interest earned in the first year is reinvested. Expressed symbolically:

(6-2) $$V_2 = V_0 + iV_0 + i(V_0 + iV_0)$$

Using some simple algebra, this equation can be reduced to[2]

(6-3) $$V_2 = V_0(1 + i)^2$$

Equation (6-3) can be generalized for any sum of money lent (invested) for any maturity of n years:

(6-4) $$V_n = V_0(1 + i)^n$$

The future value of a sum of money invested for n years, V_n, is equal to the original sum, V_0, compounded by the interest rate $(1 + i)^n$. In our last example, $V_0 = \$1,000$, $i = .06$, $n = 2$, and $V_2 = \$1,123.60$.

The formula in Equation (6-4) is actually quite easy to use. For example, most calculators have a y^x function, and $(1 + i)^n$ is a y^x calculation. Using $(1 + .11)$ for y and 10 for x, you should be able to verify that if Joe lends $1,000 for 10 years at an interest rate of 11 percent, he will receive $2,839.42 at maturity: $2,839.42 = \$1,000(1.11)^{10}$.

For information on estimating yields on Treasury securities, see **http://www. newyorkfed.org/publications/frame2.cfm?url=%2Faboutthefed%2Ffedpoint%2Ffed 07%2Ehtml**.

Discounting: Present Values

Compounding is forward looking. It addresses the question: What is the future value of money lent (or borrowed) today? As we shall see, understanding compounding is the key to really understanding what often seems to be a more difficult concept for students to grasp—**discounting.**

In effect, as shown in Exhibit 6-2, discounting is backward looking. It addresses this question: What is the **present value** of money to be received (or paid) in the future?

Perhaps the best way to learn how to answer this question and to see why such questions and answers are important is to address one of the examples mentioned at the beginning of the chapter. Remember the movie star? She has been signed to a multipicture

Discounting
A method used to determine the present value of a sum to be received in the future.

Present Value
The value today of funds to be received or paid on a future date.

6-2

Discounting: The Present
Value of Money to Be
Received in the Future

deal, and the studio has offered her either $6,000,000 today or $7,500,000 in five years. Which option should she select?

To calculate the answer, we can simply rearrange Equation (6-4). In the previous example, we knew the present value, V_0, the interest rate, i, and the number of years, n, and we wanted to solve for the future value, V_n. Now we want to solve for the present value, V_0, of a sum to be received in the future ($7,500,000), so we can compare it to another present value (the $6,000,000). Accordingly,

(6-5) $$V_0 = V_n/(1 + i)^n$$

Assuming that we know the interest rate—say, it's 6 percent—the present value of $7,500,000 to be available in five years is

$$\$7,500,000/(1 + .06)^5 = \$5,604,436.30$$

The present value of $6,000,000 received today for signing the multipicture contract is, obviously, $6,000,000. Given an interest rate of 6 percent, the present value of $7,500,000 to be received in five years is obviously less.[3] Accordingly, the movie star should take the $6,000,000 today. To see why more clearly, all you need to do is turn the discounting/present value problem into a compounding/future value problem; if the actress took the $6,000,000 today and invested it at 6 percent, she would have more than $7,500,000 in five years. To be exact, she would have $8,029,353.47 [$6,000,000(1 + .06)^5 = $8,029,353.47]!

To be sure you are completely with us, close the book and ask yourself what the present value of $7,500,000 in five years, given an interest rate of 6 percent, really represents. It is the sum you would need to invest today, given a 6 percent interest rate, to have $7,500,000 in five years; that is, to have $7,500,000 in five years given an interest rate of 6 percent, you would have to invest $5,604,436.30 today. To nail everything down, assume the interest rate is 4 percent instead of 6 percent. Would you still advise the movie star to take the $6,000,000 today, or does the change in the interest rate point to a different option? Why or why not? The explanation and calculation are in the endnote 4 on page 130; give the problem a try and then check your answer.[4]

Recap   Compounding is finding the future value of a present sum. Discounting is finding the present value of a future sum. The future value, V_n, of a sum, V_0, invested today for n years is $V_0(1 + i)^n$. The present value, V_0, of a sum, V_n, to be received in n years is $V_n/(1 + i)^n$.

Interest Rates, Bond Prices, and Present Values

In the previous example, you learned how to compute the present value of a single future payment. How does this help you to understand the relationship between bond prices and interest rates?

Although bonds issued by corporations and governments differ in a variety of ways, they generally share the following characteristics: They have an original maturity of more than 10 years, they have a face or **par value** (F) of $1,000 per bond, and the issuer (borrower) agrees to make equal periodic interest payments over the term to maturity of the instrument and to repay the face value at maturity. The periodic payments are called **coupon payments** (C) and are equal to the coupon rate on a bond multiplied by the face value of the bond. As you will see in a moment, the coupon rate, which usually appears on the bond itself, is not the same thing as the interest rate. The distinction between the coupon rate and the coupon payment and between the coupon rate and the interest rate is often a source of considerable confusion; bear with us and you can avoid the problem.

Given these characteristics, a bond represents a stream of future payments. To find its present value and thus the price it will trade at in financial markets, we need to compute the present value of each coupon payment and the present value of the final repayment of the face value on the maturity date. The appropriate formula is

(6-6) $$P = C_1/(1 + i)^1 + C_2/(1 + i)^2 + \ldots + C_n/(1 + i)^n + F/(1 + i)^n$$

where P = the price (present value) of the bond

C = the coupon payment on the bond (C_1 in year 1, C_2 in year 2, etc.)

F = the face or par value of the bond

i = the interest rate

n = the number of years to maturity (on a five-year bond, $n = 5$)

Notice that this formula is a descendant of Equation (6-5) with $P = V_0$ and $V_n = C$ or F. The only difference is that we use (6-6) to compute the present value of a number of future payments, such as occurs with a bond and (6-5) to compute the present value of a single future payment. To put some flesh on an otherwise bareboned formula, let's work through a few examples. Suppose Jane is about to buy a bond that will mature in one year, has a face value of $1,000, and carries a coupon payment of $60, and the prevailing interest rate in the market is 6 percent. What is Jane willing to pay for this bond? Using Equation (6-6),

$$P = \$60/(1 + .06)^1 + \$1,000/(1 + .06)^1 =$$
$$\$56.60 + \$943.40 = \$1,000$$

This tells Jane that the price of the bond or its present value is $1,000.[5] In other words, if the interest rate is 6 percent, the present value of receiving $1,060 in one year is $1,000, and this is what Jane (or anybody else) will pay for the bond. Because the coupon payment is $60, the coupon rate is 6 percent (6 percent = $60/$1,000). You might also note that when the price of a bond is equal to its par value ($1,000), the coupon rate is equal to the current interest rate.

Continuing with this example, Jane buys the bond for $1,000, and the next day the prevailing interest rate in the market rises to 8 percent. What effect does this have on the value (price) of Jane's bond? Remember that Jane's bond will pay her $1,060 in one year.[6] Imagine yourself with $1,000 to invest. How much would you pay for Jane's bond? Would you pay $1,000? We hope your answer is "no!" You could go out in the market and buy another bond yielding 8 percent for $1,000! Alternatively, you could buy Jane's bond. But you would do this if and only if it too was somehow made to yield 8 percent. How could this happen? The maturity of the bond (one year), the coupon payment ($60 per $1,000 of par value), and the par value ($1,000) are all fixed. They represent the contractual arrangements entered into by the bond issuer (borrower) at the time the bond was initially issued. What's left? The price of the bond! You and other investors would be willing to pay a price for the bond that, given the receipt of $1,060 at maturity, would represent a yield over the year of 8 percent. Using our Equation (6-5),

$$P = \$60/(1 + .08)^1 + \$1,000/(1 + .08)^1 =$$
$$\$55.55 \qquad + \$925.93 \qquad = \$981.48$$

The amount $981.48 is the present value of $1,060 to be received in one year if the interest rate we use to discount the future sum is 8 percent.

Put somewhat more intuitively, if you bought Jane's bond for $981.48, you would receive $60 of interest at maturity plus a capital gain of $18.52; the gain is equal to the par value you get back at maturity ($1,000) minus the price you pay at the time of purchase ($981.48). Together the interest and the capital gain ($60 + $18.52 = $78.52) give us an 8 percent yield over the year ($78.52/$981.48 = .08). Thus, in this example, you buy the bond at a price below its par value. This is called a **discount from par** and raises the yield on the bond, called the **yield to maturity,** from 6 percent to 8 percent. In sum, as the market interest rate rises, the price of existing bonds falls. The lower yield to maturity on existing bonds is unattractive to potential purchasers who can purchase newly issued bonds with higher yields to maturity. Therefore, the yield to maturity on previously issued bonds must somehow rise to remain competitive with the new higher level of prevailing interest rates. The yield on existing bonds rises when their prices fall. Hence, bond prices fall until the yield to maturity of the bond becomes equal to the current interest rate.

Suppose that instead of rising from 6 percent to 8 percent the day after Jane buys the bond, the interest rate in the market falls to 4 percent. You should now be able to do the arithmetic with the aid of Equation (6-6); the price (or present value) of Jane's bond will rise to $1,019.23. What does this represent? If any of us bought Jane's bond for $1,019.23, we would be paying a price above the par value. This is called a **premium above par**. At maturity we would get $60 minus a capital loss of $19.23; the loss is equal to what we pay at the time of purchase minus the par value we receive at maturity ($1,019.23 − $1,000 = $19.23). The $40.77 ($60 − $19.23 = $40.77) represents a 4 percent yield over the year ($40.77/$1,019.23 = .04). Thus, as the market interest rate falls, the prices of existing bonds rise. The reason is that the higher yield to maturity on existing bonds is attractive to potential investors, and as they buy existing bonds, the bond prices rise, reducing their yield to maturity.

In general, then, there is an inverse relationship between the price of outstanding bonds trading in the secondary market and the prevailing level of market interest rates. As a result, we can say that if bond prices are rising, then interest rates are falling, and vice versa. These are different ways of saying the same thing, and we need not resort to the formalities of discounting and present value analysis to see the bare essentials of this relationship. For practice, go to the "Credit Markets" section in the *The Wall Street Journal*, usually found about four pages from the back in the Money & Investing section, and read the article. You should now be able to follow the description of the happenings in the market.[7]

Fluctuations in Interest Rates and Managing a Bond Portfolio

In financial circles, one often hears conversation about the interest rate; people will ask, for example, "Do you think interest rates will rise or fall?" In such discussions, the reference to interest rates is, in fact, a reference to *yields to maturity*, or *yields*, for short.

Why would the manager of a bond portfolio for a large pension fund be concerned about the likely direction of interest rates? Simply put, if rates rise sharply, for example, the value of the manager's portfolio, which contains previously purchased bonds, would

Discount from Par
When a bond sells below its face value because interest rates have increased since the bond was originally issued.

Yield to Maturity
The return on a bond held to maturity, which includes both the interest return and any capital gain or loss.

Premium above Par
When a bond sells above its face value because interest rates have decreased since the bond was originally issued.

fall significantly. This year's bonus for skillful management could go right out the window. Conversely, if rates fall, the prices of previously purchased bonds increase, and capital gains are in the offing. Such possibilities are what motivate managers and their advisers to pay so much attention to the factors that determine interest rates. More specifically, a portfolio manager who believes the Fed is about to engage in actions that will raise interest rates is likely to sell a considerable amount of bonds now to avoid the capital losses on bonds held that will accompany any rise in market yields. Conversely, the expectation of a fall in interest rates would encourage purchases of bonds now in anticipation of the capital gains that will accompany such a fall.[8]

Positioning the pension fund to take advantage of any change in interest rates requires our portfolio manager to understand the major factors determining movements in interest rates. Accordingly, let's take a closer look at the determinants of interest rates. Note that it is the expectation of interest rate changes that motivates the portfolio manager into action. After interest rates have changed, it is too late to take advantage of potential capital gains or to avoid potential losses. Of course, it is not too late to try to avoid making the same mistake again and again.

Recap   The price of a bond is the discounted value of the future stream of income over the life of the bond. When the interest rate increases, the price of the bond decreases. When the interest rate decreases, the price of the bond increases.

The Determinants of Interest Rates

In previous chapters we emphasized the role of the financial system in coordinating and channeling the flow of funds from net lenders to net borrowers. The interest rate is of paramount importance in this process for the following reasons: (1) Because it is the reward for lending and the cost of borrowing, changes in the interest rate influence the amount of borrowing and lending, that is, the behavior of net borrowers and net lenders; and (2) conversely, the borrowing and lending behavior of net borrowers and net lenders influences the interest rate. In the market for loanable funds, as in other markets, supply and demand represent the key to determining interest rates. This means, of course, that any change in interest rates will be the result of changes in supply and/or demand.

Demand for Loanable Funds
The demand for borrowed funds by household, business, government, or foreign net borrowers.

The **demand for loanable funds** originates from the household, business, government, and foreign net borrowers who borrow because they are spending more than their current income. The downward-sloping demand curve indicates that net borrowers are willing to borrow more at lower interest rates, ceteris paribus.[9] Businesses borrow more at lower interest rates because more investment projects become profitable, ceteris paribus. Projects that would be unprofitable if the business had to pay 12 percent to borrow the funds become quite profitable if the funds can be had for only 2 percent. Consumers borrow more at lower interest rates, ceteris paribus, for such things as automobiles and other consumer durables.

Supply of Loanable Funds
The supply of borrowed funds originating from (1) household, business, government, and foreign net lenders or (2) the Fed through its provision of reserves.

The total **supply of loanable funds** originates from two basic sources: (1) the household, business, government, and foreign net lenders who are prepared to lend because they are spending less than their current income, and (2) the Fed, which, in its ongoing attempts to manage the economy's performance, supplies reserves to the financial system that lead to increases in the growth rate of money (and loans). We shall assume that the Fed's supply of funds is fixed at a particular amount for the time being. Adding the funds that net lenders are willing to supply to the Fed's supply of funds produces a supply curve for loanable funds that is upward sloping.

6-3
The Supply of and Demand for Funds

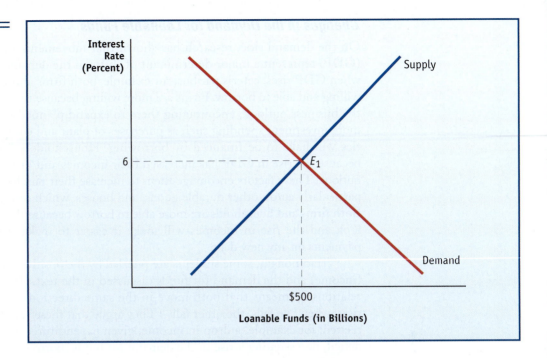

The interest rate is measured on the vertical axis, and the quantity of loanable funds is measured on the horizontal axis. At E_1, the quantity demanded is equal to the quantity supplied, and the market is in equilibrium. The supply of and demand for loanable funds determine the interest rate.

To illustrate how the behaviors of the Fed and net lenders interact, suppose that during the current period the Fed supplies reserves to the financial system leading to $300 billion of loanable funds being supplied to the market, and that this amount of funds will not increase or decrease as the interest rate changes. As for net lenders, suppose they are willing to lend $100 billion at a 4 percent interest rate, $200 billion at a 6 percent interest rate, and $300 billion at an 8 percent rate. Adding the fixed supply of loanable funds resulting from the Fed's supply of reserves to the interest-sensitive amount that will be supplied by net lenders, we get the total supply of funds of $400 billion at a 4 percent rate, $500 billion at a 6 percent rate, and $600 billion at an 8 percent rate. This is how the supply function shown in Exhibit 6-3 is calculated. Note that its upward slope reflects the changes in the quantity of funds supplied by net lenders at different interest rates, everything else remaining unchanged.

This indicates that net lenders are willing to supply more funds at higher interest rates, ceteris paribus. As Exhibit 6-3 shows, the quantity of funds supplied equals the quantity of funds demanded at point E_1. The equilibrium interest rate in the market for loanable funds is 6 percent, and the equilibrium quantity of funds borrowed and lent is $500 billion.

From the point of view of our portfolio manager, it is not sufficient to know the equilibrium or current interest rate. What is really of concern is the potential for future changes in interest rates and the capital gains (increases in bond prices) or capital losses (decreases in bond prices) that will accompany such changes. Because any change in interest rates will be the result of a change in either the supply of or demand for funds, let's take a close look at the major factors that can shift either of the curves.

Changes in the Demand for Loanable Funds

On the demand side, research has shown that movements in gross domestic product (GDP) represent a major determinant of shifts in the demand for funds. In particular, when GDP rises, ceteris paribus, for example, both firms and households become more willing and able to borrow. Firms are more willing because the rise in GDP has improved the business outlook, encouraging them to expand planned inventories and engage in more investment spending such as purchases of plant and equipment. These new activities will have to be financed by borrowing. Households are more willing to borrow because the rise in GDP has increased their incomes and/or improved the employment outlook. These factors encourage them to increase their purchases of goods and services, particularly autos, other durable goods, and houses, which often require some financing. Both firms and households are more able to borrow because the improved economic outlook and the rise in incomes will make it easier to make the interest and principal payments on any new debt.

Traditionally, some students are puzzled by the positive relationship between GDP (income) and the demand for funds discussed in the text. (Remember that a "positive" relationship means that both move in the same direction—when one rises, the other rises; when one falls, the other falls.) They argue that these variables should be negatively related; for example, a drop in income, given expenditures, will increase a household's deficit, necessitating a rise in the demand for funds (borrowing). The problem with this reasoning is that expenditures are assumed to remain constant. In fact, the drop in income will lead to a reduction in expenditures. More generally, historical experience shows that the willingness and ability to borrow and spend will fall when income falls.

Another factor that affects the demand for loanable funds is an increase in the anticipated productivity of capital investments. Anticipated increases in productivity lead to a greater demand for capital investment and, hence, increase the demand for loanable funds.

The effect of an increase in the demand for funds resulting from a rise in income or an anticipated increase in the productivity of capital investment is shown in Exhibit 6-4. The demand for funds shifts from DD to $D'D'$. Previously, the quantity of funds supplied was equal to the quantity of funds demanded at point E_1; the equilibrium

6-4

A Shift in the Demand for Funds

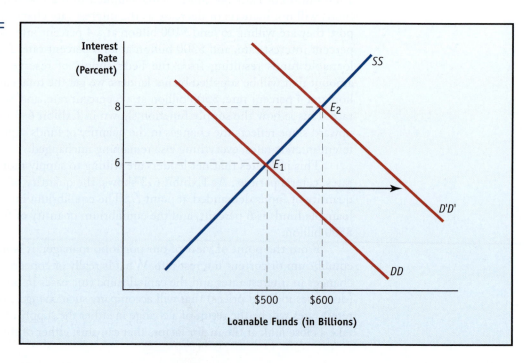

interest rate prevailing in the market was 6 percent, and the quantity of funds borrowed and lent was $500 billion. When the demand curve shifts to the right, ceteris paribus, a disequilibrium develops in the market. More specifically, at the prevailing 6 percent rate, the quantity of funds demanded exceeds the quantity supplied. Given this excess demand, the interest rate rises. The higher interest rate induces net lenders to increase the quantity of loanable funds they are willing to supply (a movement along the supply curve). Such changes in plans help to close the gap between quantity demanded and quantity supplied, and a new equilibrium is eventually established at point E_2 where the interest rate is 8 percent and the quantity of funds borrowed and lent is $600 billion. To sum up, we start with an equilibrium; demand increases, ceteris paribus, creating a disequilibrium; the interest rate goes up, and a new equilibrium is established.

Changes in the Supply of Funds

On the supply side, as you already know, one of the factors determining the supply of loanable funds is monetary policy. In particular, the Fed's ability to alter the growth rate of money in the economy means that it can have a direct effect on the cost and availability of funds. To illustrate, a Fed-engineered increase in the supply of funds, as shown in Exhibit 6-5, shifts the supply curve from SS to $S'S'$, ceteris paribus. This creates a disequilibrium: The quantity supplied of funds exceeds the quantity demanded of funds at the prevailing 6 percent interest rate. The excess quantity supplied puts downward pressure on interest rates. As interest rates fall, net borrowers and net lenders revise their borrowing and lending plans. For example, as the cost of borrowing falls, net borrowers will be induced to borrow a larger quantity (a movement along a demand curve). Such actions, which serve to narrow the gap between quantity supplied and quantity demanded, will continue until a new equilibrium is established at point E_2. The result is a fall in the interest rate from 6 percent to 4 percent and an increase in the quantity demanded from $500 billion to $550 billion. In sum, the money supply growth rate and the interest rate are inversely related, ceteris paribus. Holding other things constant, an increase in the money supply will lower the interest rate, and a decrease in the money supply will raise the interest rate via the effect of changes in the growth rate of the money supply on the supply of loanable funds.[10]

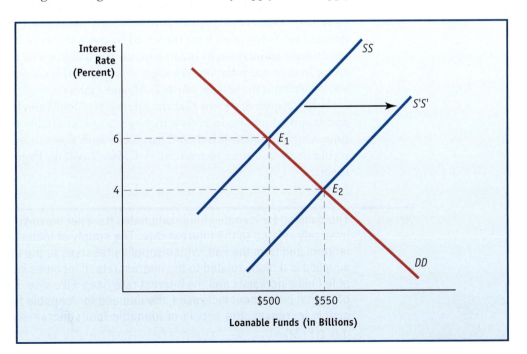

6-5

A Shift in the Supply of Funds

The graphical analysis illustrates the relationship between changes in the supply of loanable funds and interest rates. However, graphs by themselves explain little and prove nothing. If the illustration is really going to aid your understanding, you need to be able to breathe some life into the picture by knowing how and why the interest rate changes; that is, what is the mechanism or process that produces this result? The answer in this case is really quite simple. Visualize financial intermediaries in the economy, particularly depository institutions, as having more funds to lend as a result of the Fed's actions increasing the money supply.[11] In general, the intermediaries will use these funds to acquire interest-earning assets—securities and loans, in particular. If they demand more securities (bonds), this will raise the price and lower the yield to maturity on outstanding bonds, ceteris paribus. If the intermediaries want to extend loans, they will have to induce households and firms to borrow more than they are currently borrowing or planning to borrow. How can this be accomplished? If you said, "Lower the rates charged on loans," you are correct. Thus, the movement from E_1 to E_2 in Exhibit 6-5 is not a sterile hop to be memorized and reproduced in response to some exam question. It depicts a process and series of transactions, including the acquisition of securities, extension of loans, and accompanying changes in interest rates, that are at the heart of the operations of the financial system and its role in the economy.

The discussion of the determinants of interest rates, at least up to this point, can be summarized in a fashion that will prove quite convenient later on:[12]

$$(6\text{-}7) \qquad\qquad\qquad i = f(\overset{+}{Y}, \overset{-}{M})$$

Equation (6-7), which is really a sentence written in shorthand, says the interest rate is a positive function of income or GDP, Y, and a negative function of the money supply, M, ceteris paribus.[13] From the preceding discussion and accompanying graphical analysis, you should know that a rise in Y, holding other factors like M constant, will raise the demand for funds and, thus, the interest rate. Likewise, a rise in M, holding other factors like Y constant, will increase the supply of loanable funds and thus decrease the interest rate.

Of course, in the real world, other factors are not constant. Why is this important to keep in mind? Imagine that data released by the Fed indicate that both M and i are increasing. What could explain this seemingly paradoxical result? The answer is that the demand for funds must have increased by more than the increase in supply. This could result from an increase in income or, as you will learn in the next section, from an increase in expected inflation. We suggest graphing this case and others like it to make sure you understand the way in which Y, M, and i interact.

In Chapter 3, we saw that the interest rate could also be determined by the demand and supply of money. In reality, money is a stock variable that is measured at a point in time. Our loanable funds model here deals with flows of loanable funds over time. Now would be a good time to read the A Closer Look on Page 121 that reconciles the two theories.

Recap The demand for loanable funds originates from net borrowers. The quantity demanded is inversely related to the interest rate. The supply of loanable funds originates from net lenders and from the Fed, which supplies reserves to the banking system. The quantity supplied is directly related to the interest rate. If incomes increase, the demand for loanable funds increases and the interest rate rises. Likewise, if the anticipated productivity of capital investment increases, the demand for loanable funds increases. If the money supply increases, the supply of loanable funds increases and the interest rate falls: $i = f(\overset{+}{Y}, \overset{-}{M})$.

Interest Rates: Which Theory Is Correct? Reconciling Stocks and Flows

Liquidity preference is the name given to the theory based on the demand for and supply of money. It was developed by John Maynard Keynes in the 1930s. The supply of money is the stock of money, and the demand for money, or "preference for liquidity," is how much money spending units wish to hold. The supply of and demand for money are both measured at a point in time and refer to actual *stocks*. The stock of money is partially determined by the central bank through its control over the stock of reserves and reserve requirements. Also, remember from Chapter 3 that the demand for money is based on the spending plans of spending units. Demand is positively related to income, and quantity demanded is negatively or inversely related to the interest rate, ceteris paribus. The interest rate adjusts to equate the quantity supplied (stock) of money with the quantity demanded.

The loanable funds theory developed in this chapter is based on *flows* as opposed to stocks. Flows are measured through time, whereas stocks are measured at a point in time. Thus, if I offer you a job for $10,000, you will want to know whether this is per week, per month, or per year. Not so for stocks. If I give you a $10,000 savings account, there is no relevant time dimension. The loanable funds theory develops the argument that the interest rate is determined by the supply of and demand for loanable funds. The demand for loanable funds reflects borrowing plans by net borrowers while the supply of loanable funds reflects lending plans by net lenders. Ceteris paribus, the quantity demanded of loanable funds is inversely related to the interest rate while the quantity supplied of loanable funds is directly related to the interest rate. The interest rate adjusts to equate the quantity demanded of loanable funds with the quantity supplied.

To help you see that the theories complement each other, consider what happens when the Fed increases bank reserves. When reserves increase, banks create money by incurring deposit liabilities as they acquire loans as assets. In doing so, banks have simultaneously augmented the supply of loanable funds. According to liquidity preference, an increase in the supply of money, ceteris paribus, causes the interest rate to fall while according to the loanable funds theory, an increase in the supply of loanable funds has the same effect. Likewise, if the Fed decreases the supply of reserves, you should be able to verify that both the stock of money and the supply of loanable funds decrease, leading to a higher interest rate. Again both theories predict that the interest rate changes in the same direction.

Next consider what happens when the demand for loanable funds increases, reflecting an increased desire of people to borrow more at every interest rate. Because banks acquire loan assets when they create checkable deposits, which are also money, an increase in the demand for loanable funds corresponds to an increase in the demand for money. According to both theories, an increase in the interest rate results. Likewise, a decrease in the demand for loanable funds translates to a decrease in the demand for money and a lower interest rate.

From an intuitive standpoint, we can reconcile the two theories by recognizing that when there is a change in a stock measured at different times, a flow has occurred; that is, a flow over time results in a change in a stock. For example, if I have a gallon of milk in the morning, go to the refrigerator for a glass of milk repeatedly throughout the day, and have half a gallon left at the end of the day, then I can safely say that I consumed half a gallon of milk during the day. Consumption of milk over the course of the day represents a *flow*, but the amount of milk in the refrigerator at a point in time is a *stock*. The change in the stock of milk as measured at two different points in time depicts the flow. If I save $100 per year, at the end of the year, my stock of wealth will have increased by $100 (ignoring interest payments for the time being). Correspondingly, changes in the supply (flow) of loanable funds entail changes in the stock of money as measured at two different points in time. Likewise, changes in the demand (flow) of loanable funds entail changes in the demand for money. A theory stated in flows can always be reformulated in terms of stocks and vice versa.

Inflation and Interest Rates

If you lend a friend $100 today and she agrees to pay it back in one year with 5 percent interest ($100 × .05 = $5), you may consider yourself $5 richer and a shrewd financier. Your $100 will earn $5 of interest income for you. However, if during the year the inflation rate is 5 percent, the real value—purchasing power—of the funds lent plus interest will be exactly the same as the real value of your funds at the beginning of the year.[14] As a result, your real reward for lending would be zero. In fact, if the inflation rate is higher than 5 percent, your friend would be paying you back an amount of money one year from now that would buy fewer goods and services than the amount you lent would buy today. Your real reward would be negative. The shrewd financier in this case would be your friend, not you! You might, of course, still engage in this transaction if it is your absolute best opportunity. If you hold idle cash or money in a checking account earning low interest, you would lose even more in real terms. However, we hope you would be able to find a savings opportunity that paid you a positive real (inflation-adjusted) return.

This example suggests that lenders are concerned about two things: (1) nominal interest, or how many dollars they will receive in the future in return for lending now; and (2) inflation, or the real purchasing power the funds will be worth upon repayment. For example, a bond bearing even a relatively high interest rate may not be attractive to lenders if, due to price inflation, the money later repaid has less purchasing power than the money originally lent.

The implication of all this is that the market interest rate—called the **nominal interest rate**—is not an adequate measure of the real return on an interest-bearing financial asset unless there is assurance of price stability. Rather, the appropriate measure is the **real interest rate**, which is the return on the asset corrected for changes in the purchasing power of money. The real interest rate is the nominal interest rate minus the rate of inflation expected to prevail over the life of the asset. For example, if an investor expects inflation of 4 percent, an asset bearing 7 percent nominal interest will be expected to yield only approximately 3 percent in real terms. If inflation of 7 percent is expected, the investor would expect the asset bearing 7 percent nominal interest to yield nothing in real terms.

Money illusion is said to occur when investors react to nominal changes (caused by price changes) even though no changes in real interest rates or other real variables

Nominal Interest Rate
The market interest rate, or the real return plus the rate of inflation expected to prevail over the life of the asset.

Real Interest Rate
The interest rate corrected for changes in the purchasing power of money.

Money Illusion
When spending units react to nominal changes caused by changes in prices even though real variables such as interest rates have not changed.

have occurred. Financial investors who are not victims of money illusion will try to find an investment that pays the highest real return. Wise investors will concern themselves with the nominal market interest rate only insofar as it enters into their calculation of the real interest rate, which is the correct measure of the reward for lending and the cost of borrowing.

The discussion to this point can be summarized with the help of some simple definitions written in the form of identities that are true by definition:

$$(6\text{-}8) \qquad i = r + p^e$$

Inflation Premium
The amount of nominal interest added to the real interest rate to compensate the lender for the expected loss in purchasing power that will accompany any inflation.

Equation (6-8) says that the nominal interest rate has two parts: a real interest rate, r, and an inflation premium. The **inflation premium** is the amount of nominal interest that will compensate a lender for the expected loss of purchasing power accompanying any inflation. Accordingly, the inflation premium is equal to the expected inflation rate, p^e, and therefore, nominal interest rates rise or fall as expected inflation rises or falls, ceteris paribus. Rearranging Equation (6-8) produces

$$(6\text{-}9) \qquad r = i - p^e$$

One of the first economists to statistically analyze the relationship between inflation and nominal interest rates was Irving Fisher, a prominent economist of the early twentieth century. The available evidence, such as that shown in Exhibit 6-6, does show that nominal interest rates are highly correlated with inflation and inflationary expectations.

The reason for this correlation can be seen by using the equations just presented and the graphical analysis developed in the previous section. Suppose the commercial paper rate (remember this from Chapter 5?) is 5 percent and the current and expected rate of inflation is 3 percent. This means that the expected real interest rate is 2 percent. What happens if borrowers and lenders revise their expectation of future inflation upward to 6 percent? If the commercial paper rate remains at 5 percent, they will expect the real interest rate to be minus 1 percent. This is the real cost of borrowing funds. The fall in the expected real cost of borrowing will produce a rise in the nominal demand for funds. The rise in demand should, in turn, put upward pressure on the nominal commercial paper rate.

What about lenders of funds in the commercial paper market? Initially, they would have expected a real return of 2 percent (.05 − .03 = .02). If the lenders also revise their expectations of inflation upward to 6 percent, it seems reasonable to presume that an expected real return of minus 1 percent would make them less willing to lend and would thus reduce the nominal supply of funds available in the commercial paper market. The reduction in supply would also put upward pressure on the nominal commercial paper rate.

The combined effect of the increase in demand and reduction in supply, as shown in Exhibit 6-7, is a rise in the interest rate from 5 to 8 percent. With expected inflation rising from 3 to 6 percent, the inflation premium and, therefore, the nominal interest rate rises by 3 percent, from 5 to 8 percent. In this example, the increase in the interest rate is equal to the increase in inflationary expectations. In an imperfect world—the real world—this may not always be the case, but we can be pretty certain that the direction of the change in interest rates will match the direction of the change in inflationary expectations.

In sum, expectations of inflation affect portfolio choices that help determine the demand and supply of loanable funds. Because interest rates respond to changes in demand and supply, and expectations of inflation affect demand and supply, we can

6-6

Inflation and Interest Rates: The Data (1960–2004*)

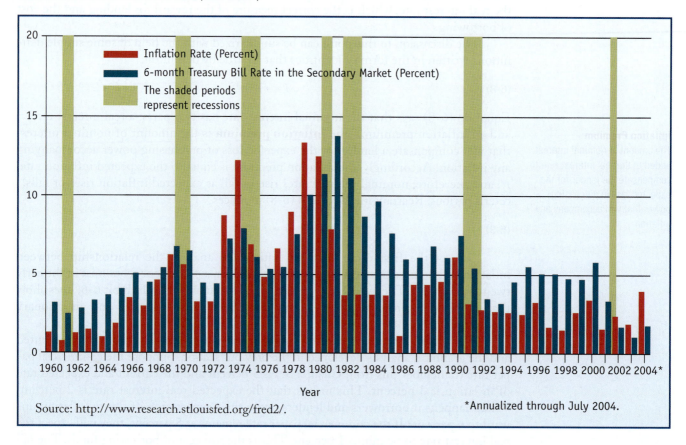

Source: http://www.research.stlouisfed.org/fred2/.

*Annualized through July 2004.

The inflation rate is measured as the percentage change in the consumer price index. The nominal interest rate is represented here by the six-month Treasury bill rate in the secondary market. When the inflation rate rises or falls, nominal interest rates also usually rise or fall. Note that the inflation rate was higher than the nominal interest rate during some years in the 1970s. What does this imply about the real rate of interest?

conclude that expectations of inflation affect interest rates. Given this relationship, we can rewrite Equation (6-7) as follows:

(6-10)
$$i = f(\overset{+}{Y}, \overset{-}{M}, \overset{+}{p^e})$$

The nominal interest rate is positively related to the expected inflation rate.

Recap   The nominal interest rate is the real interest rate plus the expected inflation rate. Money illusion occurs when investors react to nominal changes when no real changes have occurred. If expected inflation increases, the nominal interest rate will rise. Borrowers are then willing to pay an inflation premium, and lenders demand to be paid an inflation premium. Thus, nominal interest rates are correlated with expected inflation:

$$i = f(\overset{+}{Y}, \overset{-}{M}, \overset{+}{p^e})$$

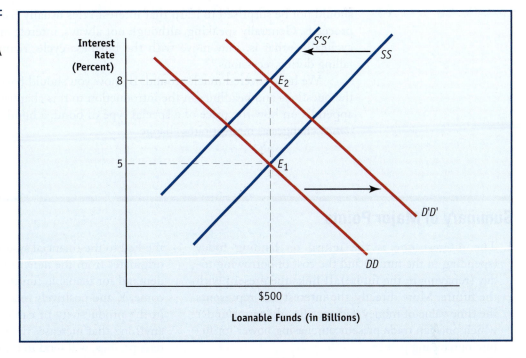

We begin, as in Exhibits 6-3, 6-4, and 6-5, with an initial equilibrium at point E_1 and a prevailing interest rate of 5 percent. If the expected inflation rate, p^e, is 3 percent, this nominal rate, i, implies a real rate, r, of 2 percent ($i = r + p^e$, or 5 percent-2 percent + 3 percent). Assume now that p^e rises to 6 percent, ceteris paribus. At a 5 percent nominal rate, lenders will now expect a lower real rate (−1 percent instead of +2 percent). Accordingly, they will be willing to lend less, shifting SS to $S'S'$. As for the borrowers, the rise in p^e means that the expected real cost of borrowing at a 5 percent nominal rate has fallen (from +2 percent to −1 percent). In response, they will want to borrow more, shifting DD to $D'D'$. The eventual result of the fall in supply and rise in demand is an increase in the nominal rate equal to the change in inflationary expectations.

The Cyclical Movement of Interest Rates

Suppose that, like Rip Van Winkle, you slept for a long time, and when you woke up, you read this chapter and Chapter 1. You would find yourself well rested and—believe it or not—quite able to explain how interest rates move over the business cycle and why they move as they do.

Recall from Chapter 1 that the stages of the business cycle are the recession, trough, expansion, and peak. The recession phase is usually characterized by falling GDP, a drop in the inflation rate (especially in the later stages of the phase), and, not surprisingly, given the Fed's desire to stabilize the economy, a rising money supply growth rate. Using Equation (6-10), we hope you would predict that such developments generally produce a decline in interest rates during recessions. Conversely, during the expansion phase of the cycle, income is rising, inflation usually reaccelerates (especially in the later stages of the phase), and the Fed may be trying to slow money supply growth to prevent an inflationary boom from developing. Again referring to Equation (6-10), you should not be surprised to learn that interest rates usually rise as an economic recovery proceeds. Generally speaking, although not always, interest rates tend to fluctuate procyclically—that is, they move with the business cycle, rising during expansions and falling during recessions.[15]

We have covered much ground. By now you should have a clear understanding of the questions and headlines in the introduction to this chapter. This chapter contains an appendix on how the price of a special type of bond, a bond with no maturity called a *consol*, changes as interest rates change.

Summary of Major Points

1. The interest rate is the return on lending today (spending in the future) and the cost of borrowing today (repaying in the future). It links the present with the future. More directly, the interest rate represents the time value of money and specifies the terms under which one can trade present purchasing power for future purchasing power.

2. Compounding answers this question: What is the future value of money lent today? Specifically, it is the increase in the future value of funds that results from earning interest on interest. Discounting answers this question: What is the present value of money to be received in the future? As long as the interest rate is positive, $1,000 received today is worth more than $1,000 to be received in the future. Discounting is the procedure used to compute the present value of funds to be received in the future. Here again the interest rate links the present with the future.

3. A bond represents a stream of future payments. The price of a bond will be equal to the present value of the discounted future stream of income. When the interest rate changes, the present value of the future payments will also change. More specifically, when interest rates rise, the prices of outstanding bonds fall. Likewise, when interest rates fall, the prices of outstanding bonds rise.

4. Ceteris paribus, the quantity demanded of loanable funds is inversely related to the interest rate. Ceteris paribus, the quantity supplied of loanable funds is directly related to the interest rate.

5. Changes in interest rates are the result of changes in the supply of funds and/or changes in the demand for funds. The supply of loanable funds results from the surpluses of net lenders and the provision of reserves by the Fed to the financial system. The demand for funds originates from the deficits run by net borrowers. The demand for loanable funds is positively related to income, Y, and positively related to anticipated increases in the productivity of capital investment. In general, anything that increases demand or reduces supply, ceteris paribus, will tend to raise interest rates. Anything that reduces demand or increases supply, ceteris paribus, will tend to lower interest rates. In summary,

$$i = f(\overset{+}{Y}, \overset{-}{M}).$$

6. The nominal interest rate, i, is composed of a real interest rate, r, and an inflation premium, reflecting the expected inflation rate, p^e: $i = r + p^e$. In general, the willingness to lend and the willingness to borrow depend on the real return to lending and the real cost of borrowing where $r = i - p^e$. In summary,

$$i = f(\overset{+}{Y}, \overset{-}{M}, \overset{+}{p^e}).$$

7. Interest rates tend to fluctuate procyclically. As a recession proceeds, income and GDP fall, tending to reduce the demand for funds, and the Fed's efforts to stabilize the economy generally result in a rising growth rate of the money supply. Conversely, as an expansion takes hold, GDP rises, tending to increase the demand for funds. Often inflation reaccelerates, and to prevent an inflationary boom from developing, the Fed will slow money supply growth. Reflecting such developments, interest rates will tend to rise.

8. A *consol* is a perpetual bond with no maturity date. The price of a consol is equal to the coupon payment divided by the nominal interest rate. (See Appendix 6A.)

Key Terms

Compounding, **111**
Consol, **126**
Coupon Payments, **114**
Demand for Loanable Funds, **116**
Discount from Par, **115**
Discounting, **112**

Inflation Premium, **123**
Money Illusion, **122**
Nominal Interest Rate, **122**
Par Value, **114**
Premium above Par, **115**
Present Value, **112**

Principal, **111**
Real Interest Rate, **122**
Supply of Loanable Funds, **116**
Time Value of Money, **110**
Yield to Maturity, **115**

Review Questions

1. Define the concepts of *compounding* and *discounting*. Use future values and present values to explain how these concepts are related.

2. Use the concept of present value to explain why a trip to Hawaii next year would mean more to most people than the same trip in the year 2015.

3. Under what conditions will a bond sell at a premium above par? At a discount from par?

4. During the Great Depression of the 1930s, nominal interest rates were close to zero. Explain how real interest rates could be very high even though nominal interest rates were very low. (*Hint:* Prices fell during parts of the Great Depression.)

5. Assume that after you graduate, you get a job as the chief financial officer of a small company. Explain why being able to forecast the direction of interest rate changes may be critical for your success in that position. Likewise, why are investment bankers concerned about future changes in the interest rate?

6. What factors affect the demand for loanable funds? The supply of loanable funds?

7. In general, discuss the movement of interest rates, the money supply, and prices over the business cycle.

8. A young couple is borrowing $100,000 to buy their first home. An older couple is living off the interest income from the $100,000 in financial assets they own. How does the interest rate affect each couple? If the interest rate increases, could that change the behavior of either couple? How and why?

Analytical Questions

Questions marked with an icon are objective in nature. They can be completed with a short answer or number.

9. What is the present value of each of the following income streams?
   a. $100 to be received at the end of each of the next three years
   b. $100 to be received at the end of each of the next three years plus an additional payment of $1,000 at the end of the third year

10. What is the price of a bond that pays the income stream in question 9 (b)?

11. Assume that a bond with five years to maturity, a par value of $1,000, and a $60 annual coupon payment costs $1,100 today. What is the coupon rate? What is the current yield?

12. The nominal interest rate is 12 percent, and anticipated inflation is 8 percent. What is the real interest rate?

13. Graph the demand and supply for loanable funds. If there is an increase in income, ceteris paribus, show what happens to the interest rate, the demand for loanable funds, and the quantity supplied of loanable

funds. If the Fed orchestrates a decrease in the money supply growth rate, ceteris paribus, show what happens to the interest rate, the supply of loanable funds, and the quantity demanded of loanable funds.

14. As an enrolling freshman, would you have been willing to pay $18,000 for four years' tuition rather than $5,000 per year for four years? (Assume you would be able to do so and that you have no fear of flunking out of college before you graduate.)

15. You win a million-dollar lottery to be paid out in 20 annual installments of $50,000 over the next 20 years. Assuming an interest rate of 6 percent, how large a payment would you accept today for this future stream of income?

16. Jake is given $10,000 in a CD that matures in 10 years. Assuming that interest payments are reinvested during the life of the CD, how much will the CD be worth at maturity if the interest rate is 5 percent? If the interest rate is 10 percent?

17. Henry and Sheree just had a baby. How much will they have to invest today for the baby to have $100,000 for college in 18 years if the interest rate is 5 percent? if the interest rate is 10 percent?

18. Use graphical analysis to show that if Y and M both increase, the interest rate may increase, decrease, or stay the same. In each case, what happens to the equilibrium quantity demanded and supplied?

19. Using Exhibit 6-6, determine in what years real interest rates were at their highest and lowest levels.

20. What is the price of a consol with a coupon payment of $200 per year if the interest rate is 10 percent? What is the interest rate on a consol if the coupon payment is $400 and the price of the consol is $8,000? (*See Appendix 6A.*)

21. I purchase a consol with a coupon payment of $100 when the interest rate is 10 percent. When I sell the consol, the interest rate has risen to 20 percent. What is the amount of my capital gain or loss? (*See Appendix 6A.*)

Internet Exercise

The realized real interest rate is the nominal interest rate minus actual inflation. Illustrate the relationship between actual inflation and nominal interest rates by accessing the following Web site for nominal interest rates: **http://research.stlouisfed.org/fred2/series/MPRIME/.** Use the prime rate as a measure of nominal interest rates. The actual inflation rate may be obtained from the following Web site: **http://research.stlouisfed.org/fred2/search/cpi/1**.

Suggested Readings

For a look at "International Linkages in Short- and Long-Term Interest Rates," see Guglielmo Maria Caporale and Geoffrey Williams' article by the same name, *Zagreb International Review of Economics and Business* 3:2 (November 2000): 39–61.

For an interesting book on an application of discounting, see Paul R. Portney and John P. Weyant, eds., *Discounting and Intergenerational Equity* (Washington, DC: Resources for the Future, 1999).

For a discussion of how policy makers may produce a permanent decrease in the real interest rate by accepting a permanent increase in the inflation rate, see Marco A. Espinosa-Vega, "Can Higher Inflation Reduce Real Interest Rates in the Long Run?" *Canadian Journal of Economics* 31:1 (1998): 92–103.

For a very readable article for students who would like more information about real interest rates, see Rosemary and Thomas J. Cunningham, "Recent Views of Viewing the Real Rate of Interest," *Economic Review of the Federal Reserve Bank of Atlanta* (July-August 1990): 28–37. Current abstracts of the *Economic Review* are available at the following Internet site: **http://www.frbatlanta.org/publica/pubs_pubrouter.cfm?pub_type=ECONOMIC%20REVIEW**.

For a sophisticated discussion about "The Cyclical Behavior of Interest Rates," see the article by the same name in the *Journal of Finance* 52 (September 1997): 1519–1542.

A classic work dealing with interest rate determination is Irving Fisher, *The Theory of Interest* (New York: Macmillan, 1930). A more recent article, "The Fisher Hypothesis Revisited: New Evidence," finds that nominal interest rates are directly related to expected inflation rates and government borrowing. It can be found in *Applied Economics* 29 (August 1997): 1055–1059.

For an interesting article on the relationship between interest rates and inflation, see Edward Renshaw, "Inflation and the

Search for a Neutral Rate of Return on T-Bills," *Challenge* (November-December 1994): 58–61.

For an analysis of the relationship between interest rates and bond prices, see Dale Bremmer, "The Relationship between Interest Rates and Bond Prices," *American Economist* 36 (Spring 1992): 85–86.

For a look at how long-term interest rates are determined in major industrialized countries, see "Determinants of the Expected Real Long-Term Interest Rates in the G7-Countries," by Klass H. W. Knot, in *Applied Economics* 30 (February 1998): 165–176.

Appendix 6A: The Inverse Relationship between Bond Prices and Interest Rates: The Case of Consols

The discussion in the text has developed the formal analytical link between changes in interest rates and changes in bond prices. Just in case you are not yet completely comfortable with the analysis, this appendix provides a simple, helpful example.

Consol

A perpetual bond with no maturity date; the issuer is never obliged to repay the principal but makes coupon payments each year, forever.

A type of bond called a **consol** has no maturity date. The issuer is not obligated to ever repay the principal but makes coupon payments each year forever. Thus, if I buy a consol today, I am entitled to receive the coupon payment forever but never to be repaid the principal. After some mathematical manipulation and simplification of Equation (6-6), found in endnote 16, such characteristics imply the following:[16]

$$i = C/P$$

The yield to maturity, or interest rate, i, on a consol is equal to the coupon payment, C, divided by the price of the bond, P. Suppose a new $1,000 face value consol is issued today and promises to pay $50 in interest each year. This is the coupon payment each year. Assuming the price of the new consol is $1,000, the $50 divided by the price shows that the consol yields 5 percent ($50/$1,000 = .05).

Now assume that a year later another $1,000 consol is issued by the same company. However, let's suppose the prevailing level of interest rates in the economy has risen so that the new consol will have to pay $60 a year in interest to be competitive. Clearly, the new consol is now a better investment than the one-year-old 5 percent consol.

Suppose now that some unforeseen financial problems lead the owner of the old 5 percent consol to sell it. Who would be willing to purchase the old 5 percent consol, given that they could instead purchase a new 6 percent consol? The answer is nobody, at least not yet. The older consol will have to yield 6 percent to be sold, and it will sell if it can somehow be made to yield 6 percent.

The older consol cannot change the fact that it pays $50 a year in interest. This is a contractual arrangement. However, the old consol can sell for a lower price. If the price drops to $833.33, then $50 a year interest would represent a yield of 6 percent ($50/$833.33 = .06). In fact, this is exactly what will happen. The owner of the old consol will offer the bond for sale at $1,000—the original price. Because no buyers appear, the market maker handling the transaction will lower the price. The price cutting will continue until buyers appear; this will occur when the price falls to $833.33 because at this point the yield on the old consol is competitive with the yield on new consols. Now close the book and work through the case where the interest rate on new bonds falls to 4 percent. What will happen to the price of the old consol and why?[17]

Endnotes

1 The simple interest rate in this example is 6 percent. If Joe took the interest earned on the loan after one year but left the principal, the total return over two years would be $120, or $60 each year. The average annual rate of return would be 6 percent [.06 = ($120/$1,000) ÷ 2]. If, as in the example, no interest payment is made after one year—the funds being, in effect, relent or reinvested—the total return is $123.60, and the compound annual return is 6.18 percent [.0618 = ($123.60/$1,000) ÷ 2]. The compound rate will always be higher than the simple rate due to the interest earned on interest.

2 For those who would like to work through all the steps, start with $V_2 = V_0 + iV_0 + i(V_0 + iV_0) = V_0 + iV_0 + iV_0 + i^2V_0 = V_0 + 2iV_0 + i^2V_0 = V_0(1 + 2i + i^2) = V_0(1 + i)(1 + i) = V_0(1 + i)^2$.

3 We are also assuming that she expects the interest rate to be 6 percent for the next five years.

4 The present value of $7,500,000 to be received in five years, assuming an interest rate of 4 percent, is $6,164,453.30. This is obviously more than $6,000,000. Put another way, if the actress took the $6,000,000 today and lent it at 4 percent for five years, she would have only $7,299,917.41 at the end of the period rather than $7,500,000. The $6,164,453.30 is what she would need to lend today at 4 percent for five years to have $7,500,000 at the end of the period. In sum, the actress should take the $7,500,000 in five years rather than the $6,000,000 today.

5 Are you puzzled by the fact that the price of the bond in the marketplace equals the present value of the bond? If so, think of what happens in any market when a product is selling for less or more than buyers and sellers think it's really worth. If it is selling for less, quantity demanded will be greater than quantity supplied, and the price will rise in response. If it is selling for more, quantity demanded will be less than quantity supplied, and the price will fall in response. Equilibrium is reached when the prevailing price in the market is such that quantity demanded equals quantity supplied. So too in financial markets.

6 Technically, the time to maturity is now one year less a day, but to simplify, we ignore the one day.

7 You should also be able to verify that the longer the term to maturity is, the greater will be the fluctuation in the price of the bond and, hence, the larger the premium above par or discount below par.

8 In Chapter 18, we will see that the managers could also use financial futures markets to reduce the risk of losses from changes in interest rates.

9 The federal government's demand for loanable funds is less sensitive to changes in the level of interest rates than are the other sectors. Namely, the federal government does not necessarily borrow less at higher interest rates than at lower interest rates. Ceteris paribus, as interest rates rise, the government may actually borrow more because of higher interest payments on the outstanding national debt.

10 Later in the text, we shall see that continuous increases in the growth rate of the money supply can lead to inflation, changes in inflationary expectations, and possible increases in interest rates.

11 We cover the specifics of this relationship in Chapter 20.

12 The effects of inflationary expectations on interest rates will be added shortly.

13 This equation is a reduced-form equation resulting from simultaneously solving a demand and supply equation for loanable funds.

14 The calculation is (funds received/price index) × 100. Assuming that the price index was 100 in the previous year, a 5 percent inflation rate produces a price index of 105 at the end of the year. Thus, the answer is ($105/105) × 100 = $100. The purchasing power or real value of $105 received one year from now, if the inflation rate over the year is 5 percent, is $100. This implies the real reward for lending is zero.

15 The correlation between the business cycle and interest rates is far from perfect. For example, during the expansion that began in the early 1990s and ended in the early 2000s, interest rates did not behave in the same manner described.

16 From Equation (6-6) the price of a consol is equal to $P = C/(1 + i)^1 + C/(1 + i)^2 + C/(1 + i)^3 + C/(1 + i)^4 + \ldots = C[1/(1 + i) + 1/(1 + i)^2 + 1/(1 + i)^3 + 1/(1 + i)^4 + \ldots] = C(1/i) = C/i$. Therefore, $i = C/P$.

17 The old consol represents a future stream of income of $50 per year forever. At an interest rate of 4 percent, the price rises to $1,250 ($50/.04 = $1,250), and the lucky owner makes a capital gain of $250.

Time gives good advice.

—Maltese proverb

7

The Structure of Interest Rates

Learning Objectives

After reading this chapter, you should know:

What a yield curve is

How expectations influence interest rates

What determines expectations

What determines credit ratings and how these ratings affect interest rates

Why interest rates on state and local (municipal) bonds are usually below the rates on other types of bonds

From One Interest Rate to Many

A familiar term we hope you have come to know and understand is the *interest rate*. Before you become too attached, however, the time has come to confess the obvious. Previous chapters have discussed in some detail what determines the interest rate as if there were just one interest rate. This simplification allowed us to abstract from many details and focus on the essential factors influencing interest rates in general. Of course, the real world is more complicated.

Numerous types of financial claims are traded in financial markets—Treasury bills, corporate bonds, municipal bonds, commercial paper, certificates of deposit, and Treasury notes and bonds, to name just a few. A glance at any newspaper reveals that the interest rates on the various types of financial claims differ. Lest you be overwhelmed by such differences, remember that our objective is to bring order to chaos. More specifically, we want (1) to understand the patterns and common threads that link the various interest rates together and (2) to identify the factors that explain the differences.

Simply put, interest rates generally move up and down together. All rates may not move the same amount; however, occasionally some rates may not even move in the same direction as the rest. As a result of such disparate movements, the spreads, or patterns of relationships, between rates can change. For example, the spread between Treasury bill rates and Treasury note rates may narrow while the spread between the rates on risky corporate bonds and the rates on those that are less risky may widen.

The purpose of this chapter is to study the factors that are primarily responsible for determining the relationships among interest rates. Financial analysts have isolated and identified four primary determinants of these relationships: (1) term to maturity, (2) credit risk, (3) liquidity, and (4) tax treatment.

Why is it important to know all of this, you ask? There are many possible responses, but this hypothetical example should suffice. Suppose you have $1 million available to purchase financial claims and you have narrowed your options to one-year Treasury notes yielding 3 percent, two-year Treasury notes yielding 4 percent, and two-year municipal notes yielding 2 percent. Which would you choose? More to the point, what would you need to know before you or any portfolio manager could make a rational decision? This chapter will provide answers to such questions.

The Role of Term to Maturity in Interest Rate Differentials

The U.S. Treasury issues different types of securities—bills, notes, and bonds—as it manages the nation's debt or finances a government budget deficit, if any. The major characteristic distinguishing one type of Treasury security from another is the term to maturity. For example, Treasury bills have short terms to maturity of one year or less, while **Treasury notes** and bonds have long terms to maturity of one year or more.[1] We are interested in discovering what determines the relationship between interest rates on Treasury securities of different maturities. For example, what is the relationship between the interest rate on a Treasury security with a short term to maturity and the interest rate on a Treasury security with a long term to maturity? The pattern of relationships among interest rates and the time to maturity are usually referred to in financial markets as the **term structure of interest rates**.

The Yield Curve

A common analytical construct used as a framework for addressing this question is a yield curve. Formally, a **yield curve** is a graphical representation of the relationship between interest rates (yields) on particular financial instruments (securities) and their

Treasury Notes
Securities issued by the U.S. government with an original maturity of 1 to 10 years.

Term Structure of Interest Rates
The relationship between yields and time to maturity.

Yield Curve
A graphical representation of the relationship between interest rates (yields) on particular securities and their terms to maturity.

Term to Maturity	January 16, 1981	January 29, 1993	July 17, 1998	June 1, 2003
3 months	15.19%	2.92%	5.01%	0.92%
1 year	13.91	3.41	5.36	1.01
2 year	13.15	4.24	5.46	1.23
5 year	12.69	6.08	5.47	2.27
10 year	12.53	6.46	5.49	3.33

SOURCE: *Federal Reserve Bulletin*, various issues (1981–2003).

terms to maturity. Put another way, a yield curve visually represents the term structure of interest rates—that is, it shows how interest rates vary with the term to maturity.

When constructing yield curves for the purpose of examining the role of term to maturity in explaining interest rate differentials, analysts traditionally focus on Treasury securities. By focusing on one particular type of security, we can control for factors other than term to maturity, such as friskiness and tax treatment, which could also affect the structure of yields.[2] In other words, focusing on Treasury securities permits us to isolate the effects of term to maturity. Although we use U.S. government securities, we could have used other types of assets to demonstrate yield curves. Other financial instruments (securities) that could be used include corporate bonds with the same default risk (and other non-maturity-related characteristics) or municipal bonds. Just be sure you understand that each individual asset is usually represented on a single yield curve, even though several yield curves may be drawn on one graph.

To construct yield curves, we begin with Exhibit 7-1. This table shows the interest rates on U.S. Treasury securities of different maturities prevailing on four different dates: January 16, 1981; January 29, 1993; July 17, 1998; and June 1, 2003. From this information, we can construct four different yield curves—one for each of the four dates. Term to maturity is always measured on the horizontal axis, while the return on an asset (yield to maturity) is measured on the vertical.

Using the data in Exhibit 7-1, the yield curves for the four dates are plotted in Exhibit 7-2. Notice that on January 16, 1981, the yield on three-month Treasury bills was 15.19 percent while the yield on 10-year Treasury bonds was 12.53 percent. Thus, the slope of the yield curve at that time was negative, meaning that yields declined as the

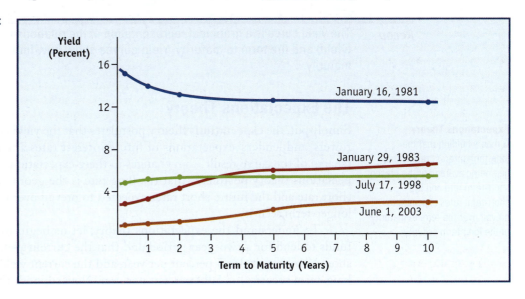

term to maturity increased. In contrast, on January 29, 1993, the yield curve had a positive slope, which means that yields rose with term to maturity. On this day, the yield on three-month Treasury bills was 2.92 percent while the yield on 10-year Treasury bonds was 6.46 percent. Thus, the slope of the yield curve changed over time. Notice also that all 1993 yields were below all 1981 yields. This indicates that the level of the yield curve as well as the direction of the slope changed.

Next look at the yield curve for July 17, 1998. On this day, the yields on three-month Treasury bills and 10-year Treasury bonds were 5.01 and 5.49 percent, respectively, resulting in a yield curve that was much flatter than the 1993 curve. Note also that short-term rates were higher in 1998 than in 1993 while the reverse was true of longer-term rates. Finally, look at the yield curve for June 1, 2003. On this date, the yields on three-month Treasury bills was less than 1 percent while the yield on the 10-year security was 3.33 percent. Although upward sloping (slightly), the yield curve was much lower than in the previous years reflecting the fact that in mid-2003, interest rates had fallen to 40-year lows. As you can see, there can be much variation in the shape and level among yield curves!

As mentioned earlier, the slope (shape) and position (level) of the yield curve are called the *term structure of interest rates*. We are interested in explaining what determines the term structure—that is, the shape of the yield curve and its level. Although much has been written to explain the term structure of interest rates, the conventional wisdom can be boiled down to expectations theory and some modifications of that theory. To simplify the explanation of the theory and the modifications, we shall assume that there are only two types of Treasury securities: T-bills with a short term to maturity (one year) and Treasury notes with a long term to maturity (two years). We shall develop our analysis in terms of the demand for and supply of these two securities.

In Chapter 6, we discussed interest rate determination in terms of the supply of and demand for loanable funds. By now you should be able to see that when we supply loanable funds, we demand financial securities, and when we demand loanable funds, we supply financial securities. Thus, developing our analysis of the expectations theory in terms of the demand for and supply of financial securities is consistent with our previous discussion.

For information on current daily yields and yield curves on government securities, go to **http://www.ustreas.gov/offices/domestic-finance/debt-management/interest-rate/yield.html**.

Recap   The yield curve is a graphical representation of the relationship between the interest rate (yield) and the term to maturity. Yield curves show how interest rates vary with term to maturity.

The Expectations Theory

Expectations Theory
A theory holding that the long-term interest rate is the geometric average of the present short-term rate and the short-term rates expected to prevail over the term to maturity of the long-term security.

Simply put, the **expectations theory** postulates that the yield curve is determined by borrowers' and lenders' expectations of future interest rates and that changes in the slope (shape) of the curve result from changes in these expectations. More specifically, the expectations theory postulates that the long rate is the geometric average of the current short rate and the future short rates expected to prevail over the term to maturity of the longer-term security.

To understand the expectations theory, let us begin by assuming that you have funds to lend for a two-year period and that the current yield, i_1, on a one-year bill (a short-term security) is 5 percent per year, and the current yield, i_2, on a two-year note (a long-term security) is 5.99 percent per year. Now suppose that you and everyone else with funds available to lend expect that the yield on short-term (one-year) securities, i_1^e, will be 7 percent one year from now. Assuming that you have no preference as to holding one-year or two-year securities—that is, you do not have a preference for either short- or long-term securities—which would you acquire now? If you are a wise investor, we predict you will acquire the security with the higher expected rate of return. Think of yourself as having two options: Option A is to buy short-term (one-year) securities today and short-term securities again one year from now; Option B is to buy long-term (two-year) securities now. Which of the options gives the higher expected rate of return?

The answer is derived in two simple steps: (1) calculate the expected return from acquiring the one-year bill now and the one-year bill one year from now; (2) compare it with the 5.99 percent return you would earn by acquiring the two-year note now.

To calculate the expected return of the one-year bill now and the one-year bill one year from now, we find the **geometric average** of the two rates. We use the geometric average instead of the simple arithmetic average to take into account the effects of compounding as discussed in Chapter 6. In other words, the use of the geometric average assumes that the interest earned the first year will earn interest during the second year. More precisely, using the geometric average, the long rate, i_2, can be calculated as follows:

Geometric Average
An average that takes into account the effects of compounding; used to calculate the long-term rate from the short-term rate and the short-term rates expected to prevail over the term to maturity of the long-term security.

(7-1)
$$(1 + i_2) = [(1 + i_1)(1 + i_1^e)]^{1/2}$$

Subtracting 1 from both sides of Equation 7-1 yields

(7-2)
$$i_2 = [(1 + i_1)(1 + i_1^e)]^{1/2} - 1$$

Returning to our numerical example, if we perform these calculations, we find that the expected return associated with Option A is 5.99 percent. More specifically, plugging the present one-year rate and expected one-year rate into Equations (7-1) and (7-2) yields

$$(1 + i_2) = [(1 + .05)(1 + .07)]^{1/2} = [(1.05)(1.07)]^{1/2} = (1.1235)^{1/2} = 1.0599$$

and

$$i_2 = 1.0599 - 1 = .0599 = 5.99 \text{ percent}$$

This is the geometric average of the short rate now, i_1, and the short rate expected to prevail one year from now, i_1^e. The expected return from Option B—acquiring the two-year note—is also 5.99 percent. Because both options provide the same expected return, you and other lenders (buyers of securities) will be indifferent between the two options and perhaps will purchase both short-term and long-term securities. More formally, because the long rate is, in fact, equal to the geometric average of the current short rate and the short rate expected to prevail one year in the future, we have an equilibrium configuration or term structure of interest rates. The associated yield curve is shown in Exhibit 7-3.

Our example does not prove the expectations theory postulated earlier; after all, we chose the numbers in the example. What happens when the numbers change?

To get the answer and in the process explain how the theory works, go back to our example and assume the one-year rate and two-year rate initially remain at 5 percent and 5.99 percent, respectively, but that expectations about future rates change such that the one-year rate expected to prevail one year from now rises from 7 to 9 percent. What would you and other potential purchasers of securities do, and how would those actions affect the term structure—that is, the slope and level of the yield curve in Exhibit 7-3?

You and other financial investors would presumably first recalculate the expected return from Option A (buy short-term securities now and again one year from now) and compare it to the expected return from Option B (buy long-term securities now). We use

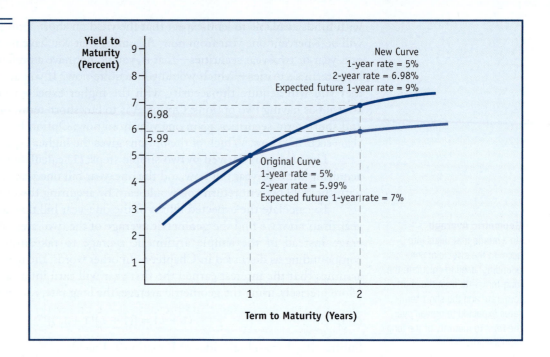

If the interest rate on a one-year security is 5 percent and the one-year rate expected to prevail one year from now is 7 percent, then the two-year rate is 5.99 percent. Because the future expected one-year rate is above the present one-year rate, the yield curve is upward sloping.

Equation (7-2) to calculate the geometric average—the expected return—of Option A. The calculation reveals that the expected return is 6.98 percent: $.0698 = [(1.05)(1.09)]^{1/2} - 1$. Because this is higher than the 5.99 percent return associated with Option B, you and others will want short-term securities. In fact, those who own long-term securities will want to sell them and buy short-term securities. What will happen as the demand for long-term securities falls in the market? We hope you said the price of these long-term securities will fall and, thus, ceteris paribus, their yields will rise.

How far will this portfolio reshuffling go? Or, to put it somewhat differently, how high will long rates rise? Given our theory, and assuming the short rate remains at 5 percent and the expected short rate remains at 9 percent, the long rate will have to rise to 6.98 percent.[3]

Why 6.98 percent? This is the only rate that will equate the expected returns from Options A and B and thus leave financial investors indifferent between them. If investors are indifferent, there is no tendency to change, and an equilibrium configuration or term structure of interest rates is realized. More formally, a 6.98 percent interest rate on the two-year note, i_2, will make it equal to the geometric average of the prevailing 5 percent one-year rate, i_1, and the 9 percent one-year rate expected to prevail one year from now, i_1^e. The relationship between long-term interest rates and short-term interest rates depends directly on interest rate expectations; as i_1^e changes, i_2 will change relative to i_1.[4]

In our example, the adjustment in the long (two-year) rate from 5.99 to 6.98 percent as a result of the change in interest rate expectations was developed from the demand side of the market for securities, that is, from the point of view of the lender. But do not forget that the securities market also has a supply side. The expectations of the borrower are also important. Suppose you need funds for two years and can either issue a security for two years with an interest rate of 5.99 percent or issue a one-year security at 5 percent now and another one-year security one year from now at an expected 9 percent rate. Which option would you choose? Again, if you are a wise borrower, we assume you will choose the option that minimizes the cost of borrowing and thus maximizes utility or profits. Accordingly, you would issue a two-year security with an annual interest rate of 5.99 percent rather than sell two consecutive one-year securities having an expected average annual interest rate of 6.98 percent.

When borrowers believe that the average of current and expected future interest rates on short-term securities exceeds the rate on long-term securities, they will increase their current supply of long-term securities, thus tending to raise the long-term interest rate. In other words, because borrowers will want to issue two-year notes, the supply of the notes will increase (causing their price to fall), ceteris paribus, and thus higher interest rates will have to be paid on them. The market will be in equilibrium when the quantity of notes supplied equals the quantity of notes demanded.[5]

Taken together, the effects of interest rate expectations of investors and borrowers on the demand for and supply of securities, respectively, will determine the term structure of interest rates. More specifically, if, as in our example, expectations about future interest rates change such that future rates are expected to be higher, the original yield curve in Exhibit 7-3 will turn into the new yield curve in Exhibit 7-4. As the demand for longs falls and the supply of longs rises, the price of longs will fall, and the long rate will rise relative to the short rate, resulting in a steepening of the yield curve.

The last few paragraphs have been jam-packed with information. Let's try to summarize and nail down some implications of the key points. First, the hypothetical yield curve accompanying our initial example, shown in Exhibit 7-3, is positively sloped—that is, yields rise with term to maturity. The explanation for the slope of the yield curve is directly related to the interest rate expected to prevail on short-term securities one year in the future—hence, the term *expectations theory*. More specifically, the positively sloped yield curve reflects expectations of a rise in the interest rate on short-term securities over the course of the year from the currently prevailing 5 percent to 7 percent.

7-4

New Hypothetical Yield Curve

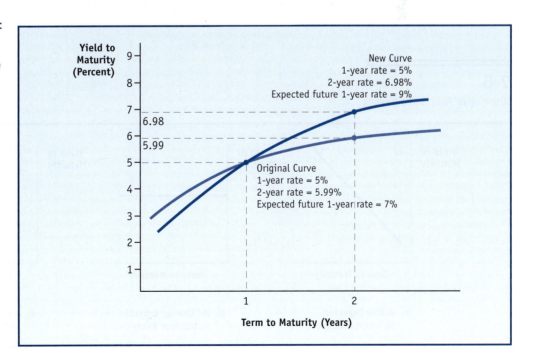

Second, the new hypothetical yield curve accompanying our second example where the expected future rate rose from 7 percent to 9 percent, is, as shown in Exhibit 7-4, even more positively sloped than the original curve. The explanation for the change in the slope is the change in future interest rate expectations. More specifically, the steeper slope reflects expectations of an even larger rise in the interest rate on short-term securities over the course of the year—that is, from the currently prevailing 5 percent to 9 percent rather than from 5 to 7 percent as in the previous example.

Third, the change in the slope of the yield curve, which accompanies a change in interest rate expectations, does not come about magically. Rather, it reflects changes in the supply of and demand for securities, which are induced by the change in interest rate expectations.

Fourth, assuming the expectations theory is basically correct, we can solve for the interest rate expected to prevail in the future by looking at the current structure of rates and doing some simple algebra. We start by squaring both sides of Equation (7-1):

$$(1 + i_2)^2 = \{[(1 + i_1)(1 + i_1^e)]^{1/2}\}^2 = (1 + i_1)(1 + i_1^e)$$

We then divide through by $(1 + i_1)$ to get

$$(1 + i_2)^2/(1 + i_1) = (1 + i_1^e)$$

Subtracting 1 from both sides of the equation, we arrive at Equation (7-3):

(7-3)
$$i_1^e = [(1 + i_2)^2/(1 + i_1)] - 1$$

Returning to our numerical example, if we know that the one-year rate is 5 percent and the two-year rate is 5.99 percent, as in our first example, we can plug the relevant numbers into Equation (7-3) and solve for i_1^e. Specifically,

$$i_1^e = [(1.0599)^2/(1.05)] - 1 = .07 = 7 \text{ percent}$$

If instead we observe in the market that the one-year rate is 5 percent and the two-year rate is 4.5 percent, we can use Equation (7-3) to find that the expected rate on a

7-5
Alternative Yield Curve Shapes

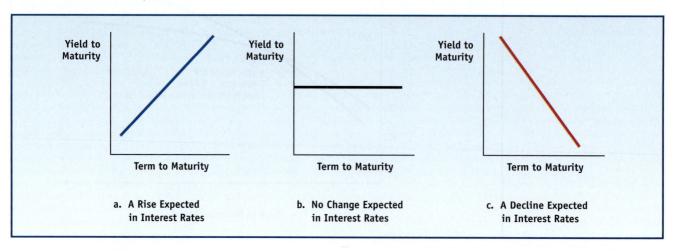

a. A Rise Expected in Interest Rates

b. No Change Expected in Interest Rates

c. A Decline Expected in Interest Rates

one-year security bought one year from now is approximately 4 percent: $i_1^e = [(1 + .045)^2/(1 + .05)] - 1 = .04$. Thus, based on the expectations theory, you can look at the yield curve and infer the market's expectation for the direction and level of future short-term interest rates.

Exhibit 7-5 shows the three most common shapes of the yield curve. Exhibit 7-5a shows a rising or positively sloped yield curve. When a rising yield curve is observed in the market, the implication under the expectations theory is that market participants expect future short-term interest rates, i_s^e, to rise above current short rates, i_s; that is, $i_s^e > i_s$. A horizontal or flat yield curve, as shown in Exhibit 7-5b, implies that interest rates are expected to remain constant, $i_s^e = i_s$. A declining or negatively sloped yield curve, as in Exhibit 7-5c, implies that interest rates are expected to decrease in the future, $i_s^e < i_s$.

You now know enough to say quite a lot about the actual data and yield curves in Exhibits 7-1 and 7-2. Referring to the yield curves shown in Exhibit 7-2, the expectations theory tells us that the shape of the January 16, 1981, curve indicates that investors expect future short-term rates to decline. Because, according to the expectations theory, the two-year rate is the average of the current one-year rate and the one-year rate expected one year from now, the one-year rate expected to prevail one year from now must be less than the current one-year rate. Using the data in the table in Exhibit 7-1, the expected one-year rate can be found by plugging the one- and two-year rates into Equation (7-3) and solving for the one-year expected rate. In this case, the one-year expected rate is 12.395 percent; since 12.395 percent: $.12395 = [(1 + .1315)^2/(1 + .1391)] - 1$.

According to the expectations theory, the shapes of the January 29, 1993, July 17, 1998 and June 1, 2003 curves indicate that, in all cases, investors expected future short-term rates to rise but by different amounts. See if you can figure out the one-year rate that was expected to prevail one year from each of the three dates.[6]

Now that you have the mechanics of yield curves and expectations nailed down, you are ready for the home stretch. For those who think they have already crossed the finish line, please note that the whole expectations theory is rather empty unless and until you can explain what determines future interest rate expectations and changes in those expectations. Otherwise you have a theory explaining the term structure via expectations that are left unexplained.

Recap   According to the expectations theory, the long-term rate is the geometric average of the short-term rate and the short-term rates expected to prevail over the term to maturity. Given the one-year rate and the two-year rate, we can solve for the expected one-year rate one year from now.

Determining Interest Rate Expectations

Naturally, then, the question is what determines interest rate expectations. The answer is much easier than you might think. In the last chapter, we examined the determinants of the interest rate and developed a general expression—Equation (6-10)—that brought together the most important supply and demand influences on the interest rate.[7] This expression is now Equation (7-4):

(7-4)
$$i = f(\overset{+}{Y}, \overset{-}{M}, \overset{+}{p}{}^e)$$

where Y = national income or gross domestic product

M = the money supply

p^e = inflationary expectations

The signs over the variables indicate that a rise in income or inflationary expectations will tend to raise the interest rate and that an increase in the money supply will tend to reduce the interest rate.

Now, assuming that we want to know what determines the expected short-term interest rate, i_s^e, how can Equation (7-4) be of help? The answer is straightforward; if the current short-term interest rate is determined by Y, M, and p^e, then the expected short-term interest rate must be determined by expectations about Y, M, and p^e. In other words,

$$(7\text{-}5) \qquad i_s^e = f(\overset{+}{Y^e}, \overset{-}{M^e}, \overset{+}{p^e})$$

the expected short-term interest rate, i_s^e, is a positive function of expectations about future income and inflation and a negative function of expectations about the future money supply.[8]

Tying the Determinants of Expectations to the Changing Shape and Level of Yield Curves

We have learned that a positively sloped yield curve reflects expectations of rising interest rates. Using Equation (7-5), we can be even more specific; a positively sloped yield curve reflects expectations of some combination of future increases in income and inflation and possibly some reduction in the future growth rate of the money supply—developments that would all tend to raise future short-term interest rates. Conversely, a negatively sloped yield curve usually reflects expectations of some combination of future declines in income and inflation and possibly some accompanying increase in the future growth rate of the money supply—developments that would all tend to lower short-term interest rates in the future.

Everything should now be coming together. To bring the picture into focus, ask yourself at what stage of the business cycle you would expect to observe a positively sloped yield curve. The answer is the stage when the future appears to hold some growth in income, a rise in prices, and perhaps slower growth of the money supply. This typically occurs at a business cycle trough and during the first half of a recovery. During the previous recession, real income fell, inflation decelerated, and the Fed probably responded with a more stimulative policy, resulting in a rise in the money supply growth rate. All of these developments contributed to a fall in the prevailing short-term interest rate and set in motion the forces of economic recovery. As the economy bottoms out and begins to recover, market participants expect future income and prices to rise as aggregate demand for goods and services increases, and they expect the Fed to be less stimulative so as to avoid an inflationary boom.[9] As a result, market participants expect future short-term interest rates to be higher than the prevailing level of short-term rates.

What about a negatively sloped yield curve? At what stage of the business cycle would market participants expect the future to bring a fall in income and inflation and Fed actions to increase the growth of the money supply? These developments usually occur around business cycle peaks including the late part of a recovery or expansion and the early part of a recession. Typically, income and prices have been rising quickly, and the Fed has moved to slow monetary growth—that is, "tighten" policy—to head off further surges in the inflation rate. As Equation (7-4) would lead one to predict, such developments have pushed up the prevailing level of short-term rates and set in motion forces that in the future are expected to lead to some slowdown in income, deceleration of inflation, and, after a time, a less restrictive monetary policy. Simply put then, future short-term rates are expected to be lower than the prevailing level of short-term rates; hence, we observe a negatively sloped yield curve.

Going back once again to Exhibit 7-2, we hope you are not surprised to learn that shapes of the yield curves somewhat coincide with what was going on in the economy at the time. For example, January 16, 1981, fell around a business cycle peak (the exact peak was July 1981).[10] January 29, 1993, fell during the lengthy beginning of a weak recovery. July 17, 1998, fell seven years into a long expansion that was characterized by relatively low inflation rates. Finally, June 1, 2003, came after two and one-half years of economic weakness, a recession, and a jobless recovery. The change in the shape of the yield curve among the four dates reflects changes in interest rate expectations. The changes in interest rate expectations, in turn, reflect expected changes in the performance of the economy (income and prices) and expected changes in the stance of monetary policy (specifically, the money supply growth rate). Such changes are typically observed as the economy moves from one stage of the business cycle to another.

Recap   Because $i = f(\overset{+}{Y}, \overset{-}{M}, \overset{+}{p}{}^e)$, then $i_s^e = f(\overset{+}{Y}{}^e, \overset{-}{M}{}^e, \overset{+}{p}{}^e)$. If Y^e, M^e, or p^e changes, then i_s^e changes. Changes in i_s^e cause the yield curve to shift.

Having identified and explained the major factors underlying the different shapes of the yield curves in Exhibit 7-2, we have one task left: to explain the different levels of the yield curves—that is, why all the rates prevailing in 1993, 1998, and 2003 were below the rates in 1981, why short-term rates were higher and long-term rates lower in 1998 than in 1993, and why all rates were significantly lower in 2003. We can address this issue in two parts:

1. In part, the difference in interest rates is due to the cyclical pattern of interest rates related to real economic activity and the supply of and demand for loanable funds. This part of the answer was discussed in Chapter 6. Expectations about the returns on financial securities and the returns to capital, the business outlook, and any other factors that influence the demand for and supply of funds will affect the level of the yield curve.

2. The second part of the answer is embedded in Equations (7-4) and (7-5). In 1993, inflationary pressures were lower than in the 1980s, and the economy was experiencing a mild recovery. In January 1981, the inflation rate was about 11 percent and was expected to fall to about 7 to 8 percent in coming years. Thus, in 1993 with the prevailing and expected inflation rates below those prevailing and expected in 1981, the inflation premiums embedded in both short- and long-term interest rates were considerably smaller than the inflation premiums embedded in short- and long-term rates in 1981. In 1993, Fed policy was keeping short-term rates abnormally low. Actual short-term rates were about equal to the inflation rate, yielding a real return of zero. The Fed adopted this strategy, which we will look at in more depth in a later chapter, to help the banking sector recover from massive losses experienced in the 1980s. But short-term interest rates could not remain so low forever, and the Fed increased them over the course of 1994. By 1998, actual inflation and inflationary expectations were even lower than in 1993. Hence, despite higher short-term rates, long-term rates fell to their lowest level in 30 years as the inflation premium plummeted. Finally, in 2003, the economy was struggling to pull itself out of a recession that had resulted from the bursting of the stock market bubble in early 2000, the terrorist attack on September 11, 2001, and the subsequent war against terror. Consequently, fears of deflation led to the lowest interest rates in 40 years with the Fed reiterating that it did not see interest rates rising in the near future.

Some Necessary Modifications to the Expectations Theory

The expectations theory of the term structure provides a powerful and widely accepted explanation for the relationship between long- and short-term interest rates. However, many researchers, taking note of several historical and institutional features of financial markets, have argued that the expectations theory needs to be modified somewhat to make it a more complete explanation of the term structure. First, it has been observed that over the last 50 years, yield curves have almost always been positively sloped. Taken literally, this would imply that financial market participants have almost always expected short-term interest rates to rise. Given the ups and downs in the economy and the accompanying fluctuations in the supply of and demand for funds, this implication is difficult to accept. Second, an assumption underlying the expectations theory is that lenders and borrowers have no preference between long- and short-term securities; they would just as soon lend or borrow for short terms to maturity as for long terms to maturity. The implication that long- and short-term securities are close substitutes for one another has been questioned in light of observations suggesting that (1) many lenders have a preference for liquidity and thus prefer to hold short-term financial claims, which are usually more liquid than long-term financial claims; (2) many borrowers would prefer to issue long-term claims, thereby avoiding the need to issue and reissue short-term claims; and (3) short- and long-term borrowers have different purposes, such as borrowing for inventory versus borrowing for capital expenditures.

The question then is how does the expectations theory need to be modified in view of these observations? There is little doubt that many borrowers and lenders have preferred maturities, or what have come to be called **preferred habitats,** and that this creates a degree of segmentation between the short-term and long-term markets. Nevertheless, abundant evidence exists to support the proposition that the short- and long-term markets are not watertight compartments. More specifically, research suggests that investors, for example, are willing to switch preferred habitats from short-term financial claims to longer-term claims if a bonus or "sweetener" is associated with doing so. This sweetener or bonus is referred to as a **liquidity premium;** in essence, it is the extra return required to induce lenders to lend long-term rather than short-term. In other words, it is the amount of interest that is required to induce lenders to abandon their preferred habitats. The size of the premium is presumed to rise with the term to maturity; the longer the term, the larger the premium must be to induce lenders to give up their preference for liquidity.[11]

How the existence of liquidity premiums modifies the expectations theory of the term structure and yield curves can be illustrated with the help of Exhibit 7-6. Suppose the current short rate and expected short rate are both 5 percent. The expectations approach suggests that the yield curve would be flat (curve A). However, the preceding discussion suggests that the issuers of long-term bonds have to offer an interest premium to get investors to buy bonds having long-term maturities. The size of the premiums is presumed to rise with the term to maturity. Curve B in Exhibit 7-6 shows the size of the liquidity premium at each maturity. Curve C represents the yield curve actually observed. The components of the total yield (curve C) are the interest rate expectations (curve A) and the liquidity premiums (curve B).

By way of contrast, note that the expectations approach would explain the shape of the yield curve depicted by curve C as indicating that market participants expect rates to rise over time.

So far this discussion has looked at the demand side of the market for securities. But let us not lose sight of the behavior of the suppliers of debt securities (borrowers) implied by this approach. Under normal circumstances, the demand for funds (supply of

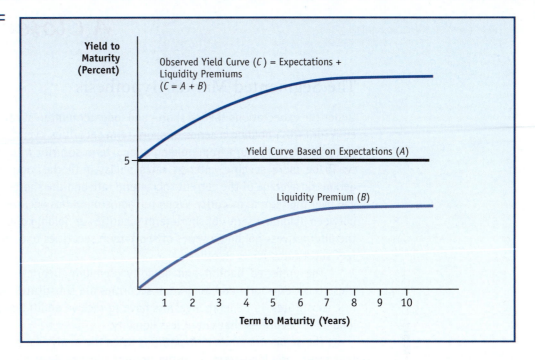

securities) is usually more fickle than the supply of funds. Changes in the demand for funds, which are driven by expectations, probably account for the largest part of the changes in interest rates. The existence of liquidity premiums means that borrowers are willing to pay them. But why would borrowers be willing to pay more to borrow for longer terms than they expect to pay by borrowing and reborrowing for short terms? Simply put, there is some chance that short rates will be higher in the future than the 5 percent expected rate assumed in our example. If higher-than-expected rates materialize, then borrowing and refinancing in the future would prove to be more expensive than borrowing for a longer term now. Also, the firm could suffer some difficulty in the future, which might reduce its credit rating and make it difficult to acquire funds later. By borrowing long-term, the adverse effects of such problems can be reduced.

In sum, the fact that yield curves have almost always been positively sloped over the past 50 years suggests that liquidity premiums do, in fact, exist. Theoretical considerations on both the supply and the demand side of the securities markets and a variety of empirical studies seem to support such a judgment. Consider again the relatively flat yield curve in July 1998 displayed in Exhibit 7-2. Given the modifications we have just made, it seems reasonable to modify our earlier conclusions based only on the expectations theory. When a liquidity premium is taken into account, it seems reasonable that the relatively flat yield curve of July 1998 may reflect constant or even slightly declining expected future interest rates.

Our discussion of the determinants of the relationship between short- and long-term interest rates (the term structure) can be easily summarized with the aid of Equation (7-6).

(7-6)
$$i_1 = f(\overset{+}{i_s}, \overset{+}{i_s^e}, \overset{+}{1})$$

The current long-term interest rate, i_1, is a function of the current short rate, i_s, the short rates expected in the future, i_s^e, and the liquidity premium, l. The nature of the relationship between the long rate and each of the determinants is indicated by the sign over each variable. Thus, we would expect long rates to rise if current short rates rise, if

The Segmented Market Hypothesis

Under the expectations theory, short- and long-term interest rates adjust until the expected return from holding a series of short-term securities over a certain term to maturity is just equal to the return from holding a long-term security with that same term to maturity. To be more specific, interest rates adjust until the long-term rate is equal to the geometric average of the current short-term rate and the short-term rates expected to prevail over the term to maturity. When full adjustment has occurred, an investor is indifferent between holding a series of short-term securities or holding one long-term security. Hence, the alternatives—holding a series of short-term securities or a long-term security—are perfect substitutes for each other.

The preferred habitat and liquidity premium theories modify this analysis. Under these theories, short- and long-term securities are substitutes for each other but not perfect substitutes. In general, investors have to receive additional compensation for holding long-term securities that entail less liquidity.

The *segmented market hypothesis* takes the analysis a step further by hypothesizing that short- and long-term securities are not substitutes at all, either perfect or imperfect. Rather, under the segmented market hypothesis, markets for short- and long-term securities are completely separate. Accordingly, interest rates are determined by supply and demand factors in each separate market.

The segmented market hypothesis received renewed interest in 2000 because of the federal government surplus and the behavior of long-term interest rates. After 30 years of deficits, the federal goverment budget balance went into a surplus position in the late 1990s. (As noted in Chapter 1, the surplus disappeared a few years later after the terrorist attack on September 11, 2001.) During 2000, long-term rates declined much more so than short- and mid-term rates. Analysts hypothesized that this was due to the federal government's use of the government surplus to buy back long-term government securities. As the supply of long-term securities declined, their prices rose and long-term interest rates fell. The federal government was not buying back short- and mid-term securities and hence their rates were not affected by the same supply factors. As a result, the yield curve beyond a 10-year term became inverted during this time period.

expectations about future short rates are revised upward, or if liquidity premiums rise. A Closer Look above discusses an alternative theory of how the shape and position of the yield curve is determined based on the segmented market hypothesis.

Recap   The expectations theory is modified by the fact that lenders may demand a liquidity premium to lend long-term and that borrowers may be willing to pay a liquidity premium to borrow long-term. Also borrowers and lenders may have preferred habitats (preferred maturities) that create a degree of segmentation between the short-term and long-term markets.

General Description	Standard & Poor's	Moody's	Fitch
Best quality	AAA	Aaa	AAA
High quality	AA	Aa	AA
Higher medium grade	A	A	A
Medium grade	BBB	Baa	BBB
Lower medium grade (speculative)	BB	Ba	BB
Not desirable investment (highly speculative)	B	B	B
Poor standing (high default risk)	CCC	Caa	CCC
Very high default risk	CC, C	Ca	C
(in default)	D	C	DDD, DD, D

The Role of Credit Risk and Taxes in Interest Rate Differentials

The previous section dealt with interest rates on securities that were alike in every respect except one—term to maturity. Now we will extend our discussion and examine the relationship among interest rates on securities that have the same term to maturity but have different credit risk or taxability.

Credit Risk

The term **credit risk** refers to the probability of a debtor not paying the principal and/or the interest due on an outstanding debt. In effect, credit risk is a measure of the creditworthiness of the issuer of a security. Treasury securities are considered to have the least credit risk because they are backed by the federal government. The basic idea here is that in the unlikely event the federal government collapses, we can be reasonably sure the rest of the economy will have collapsed as well. The reverse is not true because many individual firms can and do fail on a daily basis without the government collapsing. In contrast, corporate and municipal (state and local government) securities are viewed as being risky to some degree and are, therefore, analyzed and rated by firms that specialize in producing credit ratings. The three major credit-rating agencies, **Standard & Poor's, Moody's,** and **Fitch Investors Service,** evaluate a borrower's probability of default and assign the borrower to a particular risk class. With this information, a lender can determine to what degree a borrower will be able to meet debt obligations. Standard & Poor's, Moody's and Fitch distinguish among several general classes of risk. Exhibit 7-7 reproduces the various credit ratings with a brief description of each.

How are borrowers classified or rated? In the case of business firms, the credit-rating agencies examine the pattern of revenues and costs experienced by a firm, its degree of leverage (dependence on borrowed funds), its past history of debt redemption, and the volatility of the industry, among other things. A firm with a history of strong earnings, low leverage, and prompt debt redemption would get an Aaa rating from Moody and an AAA rating from Standard & Poor's or Fitch. A firm that has experienced net losses, has rising leverage, or has missed some loan payments would get a Baa or lower rating from Moody and a BBB or lower rating from Standard & Poor's and Fitch.

7-8

The Spread between Baa-Rated Municipal Bonds and Aaa-Rated Municipal Bonds, 1970–2004*

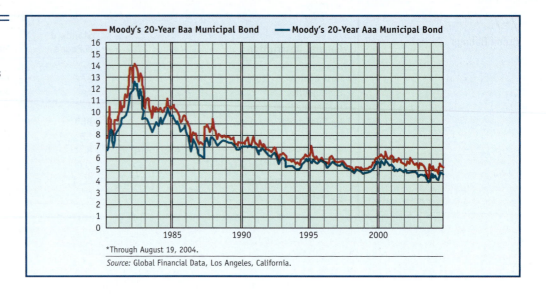

*Through August 19, 2004.

Source: Global Financial Data, Los Angeles, California.

The agencies also assign ratings to securities issued by state and local governments. Factors considered here include the tax base, the level of outstanding debt, the current and expected budget situation, and growth in spending.

To see how the credit ratings affect the spread between rates, let us make the reasonable assumption that most potential purchasers of securities would like to be compensated for risk taking. More formally, based on real-world observations, we can say that investors are risk averse and, thus, must be rewarded or compensated with extra interest for accepting more risk. The extra return or interest is called a **risk premium,** and its size increases with the riskiness of the borrower. To illustrate, the prevailing rate on securities issued by borrowers rated Aaa is less than the rate on securities issued by borrowers rated Aa, the second highest rating. The spread between the two rates $(i_{Aa} - i_{Aaa})$ is the premium necessary to induce investors to accept the extra risk associated with Aa-rated securities relative to Aaa-rated securities. Similarly, the rates on Baa-rated securities are higher than the rates on A-rated securities, and so on down the credit ratings shown in Exhibit 7-7.[12]

When we plot the spread between the interest rates on securities of the same maturity, but possessing different credit risks, as in Exhibit 7-8, which depicts the spread between Baa-rated and Aaa-rated municipal bonds, we find that the spread varies over time as the perceived credit risks among the securities change. For example, if a default occurs in a major market, many investors may perceive lower-rated bonds as relatively more risky and respond by selling lower-rated issues and purchasing higher-rated issues. This movement to higher-rated securities is usually referred to as a "flight to quality." Put another way, if investors perceive that relative risks have changed, they will demand different risk premiums, and thus the rate spread among securities will change.

Taxability

The last major factor influencing the structure of interest rates is the taxability of securities. As you may know, interest income earned from securities issued by state and local governments is exempt from federal income tax, while interest earned from corporate securities is taxed at the same rates as other ordinary income.[13]

The **marginal tax rate** is the rate paid on the last dollar of income the taxpayer earns. Because the United States has a progressive tax rate structure, higher rates apply to additional income earned beyond given tax rate brackets. Income under the bracket limits is taxed at lower rates. Interest income from bonds is additional income and is therefore taxed at the highest marginal rate that the taxpayer falls into. For bondholders who do not have much other income, interest income is taxed at a lower marginal rate than for bondholders whose other income puts them into a higher marginal tax bracket. This means, for example, that if you are in the 33 percent marginal federal income tax bracket, a 4 percent interest rate on a municipal bond is just as attractive as a 6 percent interest rate on, say, a taxable corporate bond; after taxes, both yield 4 percent.[14]

As we shall see, the tax-exempt status of municipal bonds makes them quite attractive to taxpayers in high marginal tax brackets. Financial intermediaries such as commercial banks and casualty insurance companies, which are subject to the 38 percent marginal corporate income tax rate, have traditionally been heavy purchasers of municipal securities.[15]

To see how the yields on municipals are related to the yields on other types of securities, the following simple equation is helpful.

(7-7) $$\text{after-tax yield} = i - it = i(1 - t)$$

where t = the marginal tax rate on interest income.

This says that the after-tax yield on a bond is equal to the interest rate earned, i, minus the portion that is taxed away, it; put another way, the after-tax yield is equal to the portion of the interest earned that is not taxed away: $i(1 - t)$.

Just as we care about our after-tax, take-home pay, rather than our before-tax gross pay, financial investors making portfolio decisions care about and, therefore, compare the after-tax returns on securities they might acquire. To see how this matters, suppose the rate on AAA-rated corporate bonds is 6 percent and the marginal tax rate of buyers is 33 percent, meaning that one-third of the interest income earned will be taxed away. If the only difference between the corporate bonds and AAA-rated municipal bonds is that the interest on corporate bonds is taxable while the interest on the municipal bonds is not ($t = 0$ percent), we would expect buyers to prefer the municipal securities to the corporate bonds as long as the rate on municipal bonds exceeds 4 percent. If the yield on municipal bonds equals 4 percent, investors in the 33 percent marginal tax bracket will be indifferent because the corporate bond yields 4 percent [6 percent − (.33 × 6 percent) = 4 percent] after taxes. What if the marginal tax rate of buyers of municipal securities is only 20 percent? What yield on municipal bonds would leave investors in the 20 percent tax bracket indifferent between our 6 percent corporate bond and a municipal bond? The answer is 4.8 percent.[16]

In general, we would expect the buying and selling by investors—more formally, the substitution among securities—to result in the yield on municipals being approximately equal to the yield on similarly rated taxable securities, such as corporate bonds, minus the portion of the yield that is taxed away. Close the book for a moment and see if you can explain why. Suppose, for example, that the interest rate on municipals is above the after-tax yield on corporates for the typical investor; municipals are obviously the more attractive security. The resulting purchase of municipals and sale of corporates will raise the prices and lower the yields on municipals and lower the prices and raise the yields on corporates. In this example, the effect of the substitution toward municipals and away from corporates will be to equalize the interest rate on municipal securities with the after-tax return on similarly rated corporate securities.

Average Marginal Tax Rate
The average of the marginal tax rates of all taxpayers.

We now know that the marginal tax rate that investors pay on interest income is the key to understanding the spread between the interest rates on tax-exempt municipal securities and the interest rates on taxable securities. We can also see that taxpayers, depending on their individual incomes, are in different marginal tax brackets, some high and some low. Thus, there is an **average marginal tax rate** somewhere between the high and the low marginal tax brackets. Because of substitution, the interest rate on municipal securities will gravitate to the rate that makes the "average" taxpayer (in the average marginal tax bracket) indifferent between municipals and similarly rated corporate securities.[17]

But why are those in high tax brackets, such as banks and rich individuals, especially attracted to municipals? Simply put, they are subject to a tax rate above the average marginal rate. To see precisely how this matters, assume that the average marginal tax rate is 20 percent, the rate on municipals is 4.8 percent, and the rate on corporates is 6 percent. The average investor—that is, the investor in the 20 percent marginal tax bracket—is indifferent between the two securities; both have an after-tax return of 4.8 percent. Not so the investor in a higher marginal tax bracket. Someone in the 33 percent marginal tax bracket, for example, would prefer the 4.8 percent return on the municipal security to the 4 percent after-tax return on the corporate security.

Recap   Other factors that affect the interest rates on different securities with the same maturity are credit risk and taxability of interest income. Taxpayers in marginal tax brackets above the average marginal tax bracket are particularly attracted to tax-exempt securities.

A final example shows how both credit risk and taxability play a part in determining yield to maturity. Under normal circumstances, yields on 20-year general obligation AAA-rated municipal bonds are less than 80 percent of yields on comparable Treasury securities. The yield spread mainly reflects the difference in the credit risk and the tax status accorded the earnings of the two assets. In December 1994, affluent Orange County, California, declared bankruptcy due to bond market losses in its investment pool. The bankruptcy created widespread uncertainty in the municipal bond market and the perception of greater risk. By year end, the municipal bond market had gone into a tailspin, and according to *Business Week*, "municipal bonds [were] trading at yields unusually close to those on Treasury bonds, so after-tax yields for many long-term muni buyers [were] roughly one-third higher."[18] Although the tax status had not changed, the relative credit risk had, causing the spread between the two categories of securities to narrow. Buyers of municipal bonds demanded a larger risk premium, and as the after-tax yields reflect, they received it.

To sum up, the yields on municipal securities are typically, but not always, well below the yields on other securities with similar credit ratings and similar terms to maturity. The interest rate differentials observed are a reflection of the different tax treatment accorded the interest earned on each type of security and the different credit risk.

Summary of Major Points

1. The yield curve is a graphical representation of the relationship between interest rates (yields) on a particular security and its term to maturity. It is a visual depiction of the term structure of interest rates. A unique yield curve exists for each type of financial asset, such as government securities and corporate bonds, among others.

2. The most widely accepted explanation for the shape (slope) and position (level) of the yield curve is the expectations theory.

3. The expectations theory postulates that the long-term rate is the geometric average of the current short-term rate and the short-term rates expected to prevail over the term to maturity of the long-term security. The geometric average is the appropriate average to use in explaining the expectations theory because it takes into account the effects of compounding. The interest earned during the first year earns interest during the second year.

4. According to the expectations theory, the slope of the yield curve depends on the interest rates expected to prevail on short-term securities in the future. More specifically, a positively sloped yield curve reflects expectations of a rise in future short-term rates, relative to current short-term rates; a negatively sloped yield curve reflects expectations of a fall in future short-term rates, relative to current short-term rates.

5. Expectations about future short-term rates depend on expectations about future income, the money supply, and inflation. As expectations about these variables change, expected short-term rates will change, resulting in a change in the slope and level of the yield curve.

6. The fact that yield curves have almost always been upward sloping and that some borrowers and lenders appear to have preferred habitats has led to the view that the expectations theory is an incomplete explanation of the term structure of interest rates. Accordingly, the expectations theory has been modified to include and take into account term or liquidity premiums—the sweetener or bonus (extra return) needed to induce investors to acquire longer-term financial claims. In general, long-term rates will be determined by current short-term rates, expected short-term rates, and liquidity premiums.

7. *Credit risk* refers to the probability of a debtor defaulting—that is, not paying the principal or interest due on an outstanding debt. Standard & Poor's, Moody's, and Fitch—the three major credit-rating agencies—evaluate a borrower's probability of default and assign the borrower a risk classification.

8. Because investors are risk averse, they must be offered the bonus of extra interest to accept more risk. The extra return or interest is called a *risk premium,* and its size increases with the riskiness of the borrower.

9. Financial investors care about the after-tax return on their investments. Because the interest earned on municipal securities is exempt from the federal income tax, the yields on municipal securities are typically well below the yields on other (taxable) securities with similar credit ratings and similar terms to maturity.

Key Terms

Average Marginal Tax Rate, **150**
Credit Risk, **147**
Expectations Theory, **136**
Fitch Investors Service **147**
Geometric Average, **137**
Liquidity Premium, **144**
Marginal Tax Rate, **149**

Moody's Investors Service, **147**
Preferred Habitats, **144**
Risk Premium, **148**
Standard & Poor's Investors Service, **147**
Term Structure of Interest Rates, **134**
Treasury Notes, **134**
Yield Curve, **134**

Review Questions

1. Discuss the factors that determine the shape and level of a yield curve. How do term to maturity, credit risk, and tax treatment affect the interest rate on a particular asset?

2. Explain why a yield curve can be negatively sloped. Would interest rates be abnormally high or low? What would be the overall expectation of the direction of future short-term interest rates?

3. According to the expectations theory, how is the long-term interest rate determined? Why is the geometric average used instead of the simpler arithmetic average?

4. BBB-rated corporate bonds are riskier than AAA-rated bonds. Explain where the two yield curves will lie relative to each other. What could cause the spread to widen?

5. What determines expectations? Are expectations about future prices independent of expectations about future money supply growth rates? Why or why not?

6. Could the yield curve for municipals ever lie above the yield curve for government securities? (*Hint:* Consider all tax rates.) What effect would an increase in marginal tax rates have on the position of the yield curve for municipals?

7. Use the liquidity premium to give an explanation for why yield curves have most often been upward sloping over the past 50 years. Could a yield curve be upward sloping even if short-term rates were expected to remain constant? If interest rates are expected to fall dramatically, under what conditions would the yield curve still be upward sloping?

8. Define *preferred habitats*. Explain how this modification affects the expectations theory. What could cause market segmentation based on preferred habitats to break down? How is the market segmentation hypothesis different from the expectations theory?

9. Discuss the following statements: Over a typical cycle, the movement of the yield curve is like the wagging of a dog's tail. The entire tail wags, but short-term rates wag more than long-term rates.

10. If yield curves became flatter (steeper), what does this say about expectations of future interest rates?

11. What would happen to the risk premium if the economy went into a strong expansion? A deep recession?

Analytical Questions

Questions marked with an icon are objective in nature. They can be completed with a short answer or number.

12. If the current short-term rate is 5 percent and the expected short-term rate is 8 percent, what is the long-term interest rate? (Use the expectations theory.)

13. If the current short-term rate is 5 percent and the current long-term rate is 4 percent, what is the expected short-term interest rate? (Use the expectations theory.)

14. Rework questions 12 and 13 assuming that there is no compounding. (*Hint:* Use the simple arithmetic average instead of the geometric average.)

15. Assume that current interest rates on government securities are as follows: one-year rate, 5 percent; two-year rate, 6 percent; three-year rate, 6.5 percent; four-year rate, 7 percent. Graph the yield curve.

16. Given the yield curve in question 15, what is the expected direction of future one-year rates? Under what circumstances would one-year rates be expected to decline?

17. If a taxpayer's marginal tax rate is 33 percent, what is the after-tax yield on a corporate bond that pays 5 percent interest? If the average marginal tax rate of all taxpayers is 50 percent, will the taxpayer with the 33 percent marginal tax rate prefer a corporate or a municipal security? Assume equivalent safety and maturity.

18. Gather data from *The Wall Street Journal* on interest rates for today's government securities of various maturities. Graph the yield curve. (*Hint:* Check your answer by looking at the yield curve for Treasury securities that the *Journal* publishes daily in its Part C.)

19. What would happen to interest rates, given each of the following scenarios?
   a. The government increases marginal tax rates.
   b. The tax exemption on municipals is eliminated.
   c. Corporate profits fall severely.
   d. The federal government guarantees that the interest and principal on corporate bonds will be paid.
   e. A broader secondary market for government agency securities develops.

20. Draw the yield curve assuming that future short-term rates are expected to remain constant and the liquidity premium is positive. Now assume that net lenders increase their preference for short-term securities. Show what happens to the yield curve.

Internet Exercises

1. Access the online financial dictionary at **http://www.investopedia.com/dictionary/** and define the following financial terms: *security, liquidity,* and *yield curve.*

2. Use the Internet site **http://research.stlouisfed.org/fred2/categories/22** to obtain January 2004 and January 2005 data on each of the following:
   a. The six-month Treasury constant maturity rate (a proxy for short-term interest rates)
   b. The three-year Treasury constant maturity rate (a proxy for medium-term interest rates)
   c. The seven-year Treasury constant maturity rate (a proxy for long-term interest rates)

   Graph two yield curves: one for January 2004 and one for January 2005. Compare the two curves.

3. Go to **www.stockcharts.com/charts/YieldCurve.html** and click on various points on the stock chart on the right. Do you see a correlation between the shape and level of the yield curve on the left and stock price levels on the left? Comment specifically about the yield curve on three different dates and its relation to stock price levels on each of those dates.

Suggested Readings

Read about "The Living Yield Curve" on the Internet at **http://www.smartmoney.com/onebond/index.cfm?story=yieldcurve**. This article analyzes normal, steep, inverted, and humped yield curves and allows you to compare yield curves on various dates.

For a readable survey article on the yield curve by Tao Wu, see, "What Makes the Yield Curve Move" in the *Federal Reserve Bank of San Francisco Economic Lettter,* Number 2003-15, June 6, 2003.

For a difficult and comprehensive book about the yield curve, see Moohrad Choudry, *Analysing and Interpreting the Yield Curve* (Hoboken, NJ: John Wiley & Sons, 2004).

For an article that looks at the relationship between the slope of the yield curve and economic activity and inflation, see Arturo Estrella, Anthony P. Rodrigues, and Sebastian Schich, "How Stable Is the Predictive Power of the Yield Curve: Evidence from Germany and the United States," *Staff Reports,* No. 113, Federal Reserve Bank of New York (September 2000).

For an article that looks at measuring the yield curve, see Brian Sack, "Using Treasury STRIPS to Measure the Yield Curve," *Finance and Economics Discussion Series No. 2000-42,* Board of Governors of the Federal Reserve System (2000).

"Admiring Those Shapely Curves: The Gap between Short-Term and Long-Term Interest Rates" is an article about how the shape of the yield curve can predict future economic growth. It is found in *The Economist* (April 4, 1998): 83.

Many of the conclusions arrived at in this chapter are discussed in Burton Malkiel, *The Term Structure of Interest Rates* (Princeton, NJ: Princeton University Press, 1966).

Endnotes

1 Recall from Chapter 5 that the U.S. Treasury suspended the issuance of 30 year bonds in October 2001. At the present time, the longest maturity of a newly issued fixed-rate Treasury security is 10 years. Treasury securities (bonds) with maturities greater than 10 years that were issued before October 2001 still trade in secondary markets and the Treasury now issues 20-year inflation-indexed bonds with rates that vary with inflation.

2 Later in the chapter, we modify the analysis to account for differences in liquidity between short- and long-term financial securities.

3 For simplicity, we are assuming that the short-term rate does not change. In reality, because the demand for short-term securities increases, their price would rise. The portfolio reshuffling would result in a fall in the short rate in addition to a rise in the long rate.

4 Equation (7-2) is easily generalized for a long-term security, with, say, 10 years to maturity. In this case, the 10-year rate would be the geometric average of the current short one-year rate and the one-year rates expected to prevail over the next nine years. Thus, $i_{10} = [(1 + i_1)(1 + i_1^e)(1 + i_2^e) \ldots (1 + i_9^e)]^{1/10} - 1$, where i_n^e is the expected one-year rate n years from now.

5 For simplicity, we are ignoring the fact that the supply of short-term securities will also be reduced, causing their price to rise and their yield to fall.

6 Using the expectations theory to solve for the expected future short-term rate on January 29, 1993, we get 5.08 percent: $[(1 + .0424)^2/(1 + .0341)] - 1 = .0508$. Solving for the expected future short-term rate on July 17, 1998, we get 5.556 percent: $[(1 + .0546)^2/(1 + .0536)] - 1 = .0556$. Solving for the expected future short-term rate on June 1, 2003, we get 1.45 percent because $[(1 + .0123)^2/(1 + .0101)] - 1 = .0145$.

7 Remember that this equation is a reduced-form equation derived from simultaneously solving a demand and supply equation for loanable funds.

8 An even deeper question is what determines Y^e, M^e, and p^e. A theory of how expectations are formed is covered in the next chapter.

9 In reality, the Fed may not put on the brakes until the economy is well into the recovery phase!

10 Note that negatively sloped yield curves have also been associated with abnormally high levels of interest rates when most market makers expect future interest rates to be lower. This was particularly true in 1981.

11 Of course, the lender who goes into the short-term market also faces the risk that interest rates could fall more than expected or rise less than expected. In this case, the lender would have been better off lending long. This is called the *reinvestment risk*. In general, it is believed that the liquidity premium outweighs the reinvestment risk.

12 For simplicity's sake, we have used Moody's ratings in this example. We could just as easily have used Standard & Poor's or Fitch's ratings.

13 In many states, interest on bonds issued by the investor's home state is also exempt from state income taxes. For example, California residents do not pay state income taxes on interest earned on bonds issued by California, but they do pay state income taxes on interest earned on bonds issued by Arizona. Although subject to federal income taxes, interest earned on federal government securities is exempt from state and local income taxes.

14 For simplicity, we are assuming equivalent safety and maturity.

15 Commercial banks often feel subtle pressure to purchase the securities issued by municipalities in the immediate geographical area. With the bank's deposits coming from the local citizens, such purchases are viewed as an investment in the community the bank serves, an investment that demonstrates the goodwill and intentions of the bank.

16 4.8 percent = 6 percent − (.20 × 6 percent).

17 Note that in actuality the yields on municipal securities are somewhat higher than one would expect after taking account of the average tax rate of all buyers. For the most part, the quality of the secondary market in municipal issues is not as good as the secondary market for Treasuries and many corporate issues. As a result, municipal securities possess somewhat less liquidity than other types of securities, and therefore the liquidity premium demanded by investors is larger on munici-pals than on other types of securities.

18 *Business Week* (December 26, 1994): 140.

8

CHAPTER EIGHT

Market Efficiency

Learning Objectives

After reading this chapter, you should know:

How prices of different financial instruments are related

How expectations are formed

The difference between rational expectations and adaptive expectations

What the efficient market hypothesis is and how it relates all financial prices

"Stock Prices Rise Over 28 Percent While Bond Prices Rise Over 9 Percent"

This was a typical newspaper headline reporting changes in financial prices during 2003. It is not always the case, however, that stock and bond prices move in these directions and by these magnitudes. For instance, in 2002, the headline would have read "Stock Prices Fall over 20 percent While Bond Prices Rise Over 15 percent." Other years are different—as different as day and night. The purpose of this chapter is simply to answer the question: Can these price movements among financial instruments be explained?

In Chapter 7, you learned how interest rates are determined. You saw that long-term interest rates are related to current short-term interest rates and to future short-term interest rates *expected* to prevail over the life of the long-term security. Interest rates change whenever short-term rates or *expected* short-term rates change. We also saw that present short-term rates are related to income, the money supply, and inflationary *expectations*. Ceteris paribus, a rise in income or inflationary expectations tends to raise the interest rate, and, ceteris paribus, an increase in the money supply tends to reduce the interest rate. However, if we do not assume that other factors are held constant, an increase in the money supply could increase interest rates through its effect on inflationary expectations.

We further concluded that if the current short-term interest rate is determined by national income, the money supply, and inflationary expectations, then expected short-term interest rates must be determined by *expectations* about these same variables. Thus, *expected* short-term interest rates are positively related to expectations about future income and inflation and negatively related to expectations about the future money supply, ceteris paribus.

In addition, you saw that when long-term interest rates change (either because present short-term or expected short-term rates change), bond prices change inversely. That is, when interest rates rise, ceteris paribus, bond prices fall, and vice versa. Recall from Chapter 7 that although we did not directly observe *expected* short-term rates, we were able to solve for them given current short-term and long-term rates.

It is clear that expectations are the key determinants of long-term interest rates and bond prices. Perhaps not as clear, however, is the difficulty in measuring expectations because they cannot be directly observed. Therefore, economists have spent a great deal of time and energy in developing various theories of how expectations are formed by market participants.

We divide this chapter into three parts:

- First, we identify the relationship between bond prices and the prices of other financial instruments such as stocks or mortgages. You shall see that prices of all financial instruments adjust so that expected rates of return on all financial instruments are equalized after adjustments for varying degrees of risk and liquidity have been made.[1] Again, expectations play a central role.

- Second, recognizing the important role of expectations, we develop the theories of adaptive and rational expectations.

- Third, we take the analysis of how market participants form expectations one step further by developing the efficient markets hypothesis that is based on the theory of rational expectations as applied to financial markets. We conclude that after full adjustment has occurred, prices of financial instruments are equal to their expected values, which equal the optimal forecasts of those variables given all available information.

Hopefully, the analysis will go a long way toward answering the question, Can these price movements among financial instruments be explained? found in the first paragraph of this section. We begin our discussion by relating expected rates of return to the prices of long-term financial instruments.

How Expected Rates of Return Affect the Prices of Stocks and Bonds

Stocks and bonds are two major, long-term financial instruments. Stocks represent ownership of part of the issuing firm whereas bonds represent debt of the issuer, whether it is a firm, government entity, or other net borrower. To streamline the analysis, we focus on how stock and bond prices are related while recognizing that the analysis could easily be extended to other long-term financial instruments such as mortgages.

A *portfolio* usually consists of many financial instruments including both stocks and bonds. Market participants hold combinations of various financial assets rather than one asset to take advantage of gains from diversification. **Diversification** is the allocation of surplus funds to a variety of financial instruments instead of holding just one asset. As a famous saying in the world of finance goes, "don't put all your eggs in one basket." Returns to holding two different assets may be positively or negatively correlated. Returns are positively (directly) correlated if they tend to move up or down together. For instance, if as the economy improves, two stocks also tend to improve, and vice versa, they are positively correlated. Note that the price of one stock may be increasing 6 percent while the other is increasing 2 percent but that they are still positively correlated even though the magnitude of the increase is different. To be positively correlated, the only thing that matters is that the change to each be in the same direction. Returns are negatively (inversely) correlated if the return on one increases while the return on the other tends to decrease. To be negatively correlated, the only thing that matters is that the change to each be in the opposite direction. Some financial instruments do better in recessions while most perform better in expansions. Returns on financial instruments that improve over the business cycle are negatively correlated with those that lose value. As long as returns among financial instruments are not perfectly correlated (that is, do not change by the same magnitude and direction all the time), then the risk or fluctuation of a combination or basket of assets with a given expected return will be less than the risk for any one asset with the same expected return. Thus, one can earn a higher return for any level of risk or be exposed to less risk for any given return by diversifying. Now would be a good time to read the A Closer Look on page 162 that looks more closely at the benefits of diversification.

Assuming that an individual opts for a portfolio of various financial instruments with different risks and returns, how would you go about managing such a portfolio? More specifically, how would you decide whether to purchase and hold stocks or bonds or some combination of both, and so on? We hope that you would compare the expected rates of return on the different types of financial assets, selecting those with the highest expected return consistent with the risk you are willing to take while realizing that by diversifying one can improve the expected performance or reduce the risk of your portfolio.

Stocks

The size of a shareholder's ownership position depends on the number of stock shares owned. For example, if 1,000 shares are outstanding, a stockholder who owns 100 shares in effect owns 10 percent of the firm. The value of each share—and, therefore, the value of the stockholder's holdings in the corporation—depends on the prevailing price of the firm's stock. If, for example, the stock's price is $50 per share, the total value of the stockholder's 100 shares is $5,000, and the total value of the firm is $50,000 ($50 × 1,000

Diversification
The allocation of surplus funds to more than one financial instrument in order to reduce risk.

The Benefits of Diversification

Assume there are two stocks with returns that are perfectly inversely (negatively) correlated. When the price of one increases by a certain percent, the price of the other decreases by the same percent. For example, SwimmingPools, Inc., pays a 16 percent return each year when temperatures are above average and zero percent in other years. SkiResorts, Inc., pays a 16 percent return each year when temperatures are below average and zero percent in other years. Assuming that half the time the temperatures are above average and half the time they are below average (a reasonable assumption given the nature of averages!), the expected return to holding either stock is 8 percent. If an investor chooses to hold one or the other, but not both, the expected return will be 8 percent, but the risk involves the fact that the return will fluctuate between either 0 or 16 percent. As the following table illustrates, smart investors will split their surplus funds equally between SwimmingPools and SkiResorts and earn an 8 percent return all of the time, thus eliminating all risk!

The expected return to owning a share of shock is the sum of each possible outcome multiplied by the probability of that outcome.

Stock	(a) Possible Outcomes	(b) Probability	(a) × (b)
SwimmingPools			
(above average temps)	16%	.50	8%
(below average temps)	0%	.50	0
Expected return to owners			8
Return fluctuates between 0% and 16%			
SkiResorts			
(above average temps)	0%	.50	0%
(below average temps)	16%	.50	8
Expected return to owners			8
Return fluctuates between 0% and 16%			

If an investor's surplus funds are split between SwimmingPools and SkiResorts, when temperatures are above average, half of the portfolio (the half invested in SwimmingPools) will earn 16 percent and half (the half invested in SkiResorts) will earn zero percent. As noted above, the expected return is the sum of the possible outcomes multiplied by their probabilities. In this case, the overall portfolio will earn 8 percent (.16 × .5 + 0 × .5 = .08). The reverse is true for below average temperatures with SkiResorts earning 16 percent and SwimmingPools earning zero percent. Again, the portfolio split between the two firms earns 8 percent. Thus, the risk or the fluctuation of returns between zero and 16 percent has virtually been eliminated by diversification, or owning both companies. The portfolio earns 8 percent when temperatures are above average and 8 percent when temperatures are below average. Risk has been eliminated because the returns to the two assets were perfectly inversely correlated. In the real world, few assets exhibit this property. However, it is also true that returns are usually not perfectly positively (directly) correlated, meaning that the prices of the two stocks usually do not always change by the exact same percent. If stock prices are perfectly correlated, risk is not reduced by diversification. In the case in which returns are correlated (either directly or inversely), but not perfectly so, risk can be reduced (although not eliminated as in the case of perfect inverse correlation) through diversification.

Thus, we can conclude the following:

- If returns to two assets held are perfectly negatively correlated, risk can be eliminated through diversification.
- If returns to two assets held are perfectly positively correlated, risk can *not* be reduced through diversification.
- If returns to two assets held are positively or negatively correlated, risk can be reduced for any given expected return but not eliminated through diversification.

shares). If the stock price rises to $60 per share, then the value of the stockholder's 100 shares increases to $6,000 and the value of the firm increases to $60,000. Likewise, given a fortuitous fall in the stock's price to $40 per share, the values of the stockholder's shares and the firm decrease to $4,000 and $40,000, respectively. The key question, then, is what determines the price per share.

Outstanding shares of stocks of publicly held companies are traded (bought and sold) on organized exchanges such as the New York Stock Exchange or by networks of brokers and dealers around the country. (More on this in Chapter 16.) Stock prices fluctuate daily, some going up, some going down, as financial investors buy and sell shares of various corporations. In part, those fluctuations occur because a share of stock represents a claim on the earnings of a firm. Tangible evidence of this sharing of earnings comes in the form of dividends, which are a distribution of profits to stockholders. If earnings prospects are improving, the share price and dividend paid per share may also be rising.[2] Financial investors will be attracted by the improved outlook (profitability) for the firm.

In general, as current and expected future earnings rise, stock prices also rise, and as current and prospective earnings decline, stock prices also decline. A growing economy means that sales, production, and incomes are expanding while a declining economy means the opposite. Because expected earnings also rise when the economy is expected to grow and tend to fall when the economy is expected to contract, there is often a positive correlation between the growth of real national income and stock prices.[3]

What is the expected return on stocks? Generally speaking, the expected return on a share of stock, say, over a year, is the expected dividend plus the expected change in the price of the stock, all divided by the share price at the time of purchase. For example, if you pay $50 a share, the expected dividend is $1 per share, and you expect the price to rise $3 over the year, the expected return is 8 percent [($1 + $3)/$50 = .08 = 8 percent].[4] An 8 percent expected return would also result if the expected dividend is $4 and the expected capital gain is $0 because [($4 + $0)/$50 = .08 = 8 percent]. Now would be a good time to look at Exhibit 8-1, which examines this relationship.

Bonds

With regard to bonds, the expected return to a newly issued bond is the current interest rate. Recall from Chapter 6 that bonds represent long-term debt and pay a fixed annual coupon payment.[5] The coupon payment is the product of the face value of the bond multiplied by the coupon rate. Bondholders are entitled to be paid the coupon payment

Expected Dividend	Expected Price Change [Capital Gain (+) or Loss (−)]	Expected Return
$3	−$2	($3 + (−$2))/$50 = 2 percent
$3	$0	($3 + $0)/$50 = 6 percent
$3	$2	($3 + $2)/$50 = 10 percent
$3	$4	($3 + $4)/$50 = 14 percent
$4	−$2	($4 + (−$2))/$50 = 4 percent
$4	$0	($4 + $0)/$50 = 8 percent
$4	$2	($4 + $2)/$50 = 12 percent
$4	$4	($4 + $4)/$50 = 16 percent

As the body of the text explains, the expected return of owning a share of stock for, say, one year is the expected dividend plus the expected capital gain or loss, divided by the share price at the time of purchase. Thus, when either factor changes, the expected return will change.

Assume that the stock originally costs $50 per share. The preceding table shows the rate of return for owning the stock given various expected dividends and expected price changes (the capital gains or losses).

If actual dividends or actual capital gains and losses turn out to be different from those expected, the actual return will be different from the expected. Needless to say, all investors hope that actual dividends and capital gains turn out to be higher than expected rather than the reverse.

before dividends are paid to stockholders. The coupon rate is the interest rate at the time the bond is originally issued and usually appears on the bond itself. The coupon rate is not the same thing as the current interest rate if interest rates have changed since the bond was issued.

For example, if the face value of a bond is $1,000 and the coupon rate is 6 percent, then the coupon payment is $60, since $60 divided by $1,000 is equal to 6 percent ($60/$1,000 = .06). This coupon payment does not change even if interest rates change after the bond has been issued. However, the bond's price will change whenever interest rates change or if the issuer's ability to make the agreed-upon interest or principal payments comes into question.

As portrayed in Exhibit 8-2, the expected return on previously issued bonds is the coupon rate plus the expected percentage change in the bond's price over the course of the year.

Let's assume that you purchase a $1,000 newly issued 30-year bond described above with a 6 percent coupon rate. One year after the bond is issued, interest rates fall to 4 percent. The price of the bond with 29 years to maturity would increase to $1,339.67

Expected Percentage Return on Bonds

= Coupon rate + Expected percentage change in the bond price

= (coupon payment/bond price at the beginning of the year) + (expected bond price at the end of the year − bond price at the beginning of the year)/bond price at the beginning of the year)

because the present value of the 29 coupon payments of $60 plus the present value of the repayment of the $1,000 principle at maturity would equal $1,339.67.[6] In other words, as you saw in Chapter 5, prices of previously issued bonds adjust so that they pay the new prevailing interest rate. The expected return on the bond is equal to the coupon rate (6 percent) plus the expected percentage capital gain from the change in interest rates. In our example, the new interest rate is 4 percent, and the expected percentage capital gain is 34 percent [($1,339.67 − $1,000)/$1,000 = .34 = 34 percent]. Thus, the expected return to owning the bond over the year is the coupon rate (6 percent) plus the expected percentage capital gain (34 percent), or 40 percent.

To see how bond prices fit into the picture, assume that the current interest rate on bonds is 6 percent and that the expected return on stocks is 8 percent, with the typical stock costing $50 and the expected dividend equal to $4. We also assume for simplicity that the expected capital gain is zero and that stocks and bonds have the same degree of liquidity.[7] Assuming that stocks are riskier than bonds and that the portfolio managers must be compensated 2 percent for the additional risks of owning stocks, when bonds pay a 6 percent return and stocks pay an 8 percent return, the typical portfolio manager is indifferent between stocks and bonds. He or she will presumably hold some of each because the risk-adjusted returns are equalized. Equation (8-1) depicts this situation:

(8-1)   Risk-adjusted return on stocks = risk-adjusted return on bonds
Nominal return on stocks − compensation for higher risk of owning stocks =
risk-adjusted return on bonds
(8 percent − 2 percent) = 6 percent

Now suppose that the Fed decides to pursue a more expansionary monetary policy. The initial result of this is a decline in the interest rate on bonds to 4 percent and a reduction in the risk-adjusted return on bonds from 6 percent to 4 percent.[8] The fall in the interest rate will tend to raise stock prices through two channels.

First, the expected return on bonds is now below the risk-adjusted expected return on stocks. Given the substitutability of stocks for bonds in investors' portfolios and the higher expected return on stocks, the demand for stocks will rise, tending to raise stock prices. Within the confines of our simple example, we can even say how high stock prices will rise: Stock prices will rise until the expected return on stocks is again 2 percent higher than the expected return on bonds (4 percent). This will occur when the price of our typical share of stock rises to $66.67. This is so because the $4 expected dividend divided by $66.67 equals 6 percent ($4/$66.67 = .06).

Second, the fall in the interest rate will be expected to raise the demand for goods and services and increase the sales and earnings of firms. With earnings expected to rise, dividends will also be expected to rise. This reinforces the first effect. For example, if the dividend is expected to rise to $5 per share, then financial investors will be willing to bid up the price per share even further to $83.33 because $5 divided by $83.33 is equal to 6 percent ($5/$83.33 = .06 = 6 percent).[9] Again, after stock prices have adjusted to the change in interest rates, the risk-adjusted return on stocks will be equal to the risk-adjusted return on bonds.[10]

Assuming that you and other portfolio managers would like to have owned the stock before all of this occurred, you can see now why actual and expected changes in the interest rate get so much attention in the stock market.

In the real world, many types of long-term financial instruments offer varying degrees of risk and liquidity. Because of the substitutability of various financial instruments, prices of financial instruments will adjust so that returns to owning different instruments are equalized after adjustments have been made for differences in risk and liquidity. In other words, in financial markets, risk- and liquidity-adjusted rates of return are equalized.

Recap

Prices of long-term financial instruments change as current and future expected earnings change. If interest rates fall, prices of previously issued bonds rise, and vice versa. If current and expected future earnings rise, ceteris paribus, stock prices also rise, and vice versa. In managing a portfolio, market participants compare expected rates of return and select those financial assets with the highest expected return consistent with varying degrees of risk and liquidity. As long as returns among various financial instruments are not perfectly correlated, diversification reduces risk for any given expected return. Stock and bond prices adjust until the portfolio manager is indifferent between stocks and bonds. If interest rates change, ceteris paribus, stock prices also change. When full adjustment has occurred, differences in returns on various financial instruments reflect differences in only risk and liquidity.

To reiterate, it is the expected return on bonds and the expected return on stocks that determine stock and bond prices. It should not surprise you that this is true of all financial instruments. Because expectations play such a central role, we turn now to a general theory of how price expectations are formed, which will then be applied to financial instruments.

The Formation of Price Expectations

The substantial research on the formation of price expectations suggests that the following factors are important in shaping the public's expectations of future prices as suggested in Equation (8-2):

(8-2) Price expectations = f(current and past prices, expected changes in national income, and expected changes in production costs)

This equation suggests that the formation of price expectations is both backward and forward looking. The idea that price expectations depend on the public's experience with prices, as reflected in current and past prices, is the backward-looking component. Expectations formed by looking back are typically called **adaptive expectations.** This experience is measured as a weighted average of past values because the recent past (say, the last one to two years) is likely to be more influential in forming expectations about the future than the more distant past. Thus, recent years are weighted more heavily than earlier years. For example, if the rate of inflation were 3 percent per year for 10 years and rose 4 percent in the most recent 2 years, then the public will probably expect inflation in the coming year to be closer to 4 percent than to 3 percent.

It is unreasonable to believe that the public will take only the past into consideration when anticipating future prices. Thus, expected changes in costs of production and in national income also contribute to the formation of price expectations. For example, will the price of oil rise or fall? If the public expects a large rise in the price of oil, government expenditures, or bank reserves in the coming year, expectations of inflation may be raised to, say, 5 percent. Expectations formed by looking both backward and forward using all available information, are typically called **rational expectations**. Exhibit 8-3 highlights the relationship between adaptive and rational expectations.

The **theory of rational expectations** states that expectations of financial prices will on average be equal to the optimal forecast. The **optimal forecast** is the best guess

Adaptive Expectations
Expectations formed by looking back at past values of a variable.

Rational Expectations
Expectations formed by looking both backward and forward.

Theory of Rational Expectations
The theory that expectations will on average be equal to the optimal forecast.

Optimal Forecast
The best guess possible arrived at by using all of the available information.

Adaptive Expectations	Rational Expectations
Expectations formed as a weighted average of past values	Expectations formed by looking at all available information
Usually more weight is given to more recent values of the variable	Looks at the past as well as all additional available information, such as information about expected changes in national income and costs
Backward looking	Backward and forward looking

possible, arrived at by using all available information both from the past and about the future. Even if a forecast is rational, there is no guarantee that the forecast will be accurate. All that is necessary is that, *on average*, the forecast be equal to the optimal forecast. There is an aspect of randomness in financial markets that, more often than not, makes the forecast either a little short or a little wide of the mark. Thus, the forecast error (the difference between the actual value and the forecast) will *on average* be zero. In any given time period, it is impossible to predict what the forecast error will be.

For a discussion of the development of the rational expectations theory, see **http://www.minneapolisfed.org/pubs/ar/ar1977.cfm?js=0**.

There is another reason besides randomness that the optimal forecast may deviate from what turns out to be the actual value of the forecasted variable: There may be one or more additional key factors that are relevant but not available at the time the optimal forecast is made. If the information is not available, then the forecast may be inaccurate. However, it is still rational because the decision maker makes use of all available information. This is different from the situation where market participants fail to use all available information because they are unaware of it or because it is too costly to do so. In this latter case, expectations formed in this manner are neither accurate nor rational.

The reasoning behind the rational expectations theory is that it is costly for market participants *not* to use all available information in forming price expectations. For example, if a producer ignores readily available information that interest rates are going up based on a change in Fed policy, then it may produce too much output, ignoring the effects that the interest rate hikes have on demand. Thus, the producer earns less profit than it otherwise would have. Or if a producer ignores the effect of higher oil prices on demand and costs, it may again produce more than the profit-maximizing output. In such cases, the errors are costly to management, employees, and stockholders and give a strong incentive to consider readily available information in the future.

An implication of rational expectations is that as new information becomes available, market participants should adjust expectations accordingly. The weight of current research on the formation of price expectations suggests that the public does not adjust its expectations instantaneously when new information becomes available. There are lags between the time that information becomes available and when it is fully incorporated into expectations. However, the evidence also suggests that as market participants (the public) have come to better understand the process of inflation, the lag in adjusting expectations has shortened considerably. Indeed, in recent years, the Fed has become more open about its policy stance partly because the Fed believes that its policy will be more effective if market participants better understand what the Fed is doing and what it perceives about the future direction of the economy.

Another implication of rational expectations is that if there is a change in the way a variable moves, the way in which expectations of the variable are formed will also change. An example will help to clarify. In the early 1980s, changes in the monetary aggregate M2 were highly correlated with changes in national income. Therefore, changes in M2 played a major role in forming expectations about changes in national income. Since the late 1980s, changes in national income have no longer been highly correlated with changes in M2. Therefore, changes in M2 will not be given a large weight in forming expectations about changes in national income.

Recap   Adaptive expectations are formed by looking at current and past prices. Rational expectations are formed by looking at past prices and at all currently available information about the economy that may affect prices. The theory of rational expectations is that expectations of financial prices will be equal to optional forecasts, which are the best guesses possible, arrived at by using all available information. Because of randomness in financial markets, the actual value of a financial variable is usually different from the optimal forecast. However, the forecast error (the difference between the actual value of the variable and the optimal forecast) will on average be zero.

The Efficient Markets Hypothesis: Rational Expectations Applied to Financial Markets

Efficient Markets Hypothesis
The hypothesis that when financial markets are in equilibrium, the prices of financial instruments reflect all readily available information.

The **efficient markets hypothesis** builds on the theory of rational expectations. Namely, when financial markets are in equilibrium, the prices of financial instruments reflect all readily available information. Financial markets are in equilibrium when the quantity demanded of any security is equal to the quantity supplied of that security. Returns reflect only differences in risk and liquidity. As in all markets, prices—in this case, prices of financial instruments—adjust to bring financial markets to equilibrium. In an efficient market, the optimal forecast of a security's price (made by using all available information) will be equal to the equilibrium price.

Let's assume that there is a financial instrument, say a share of stock, with an equilibrium return of 10 percent after adjusting for risk and liquidity. The stock clearly offers some combination of more risk and/or less liquidity than another financial asset whose equilibrium return is less than 10 percent. The dollar return in a given time period is equal to the price of the stock at the end of the time period minus the price at the beginning of the time period plus any dividend payment made during the time period. To express this return as a percentage, we need to divide the total return by the price at the beginning of the period, as in Equation (8-3), to get

(8-3) $$R = (P_{t+1} - P_t + D)/P_t$$

where
R = percentage return over the time period
P_{t+1} = price of the stock at the end of the time period
P_t = price of the stock at the beginning of the time period
D = dividend payments made during the time period

If at the beginning of the time period we know the price and dividend payment of the stock, then the only unknown variable is the price of the instrument at the end of the time period (P_{t+1}). The efficient markets hypothesis assumes that expectations of future prices of financial instruments are rational. This is equivalent to assuming that the expected or forecasted price of the stock at the end of the time period will be equal to the optimal forecast of that variable arrived at by using all available information. Thus, if expectations are rational, the expected return on the stock will be equal to the optimal forecast arrived at by plugging in the optimal forecast for P_{t+1} into Equation (8-3).

Returning to our example, let's assume that company A announces new profit numbers that raise the expected price of the instrument at the end of the time period. The question is how will today's price respond to the new higher expected price in the future. Assuming that the risk and liquidity of the financial asset have not changed and that the equilibrium return (based on that risk and liquidity) of A is 10 percent, the present price will adjust so that given the new expected price, the return will still be 10 percent. Thus, the conclusion is that current price will rise to a level where the optimal forecast of an instrument's return is equal to the instrument's equilibrium return.

For a historical development of the efficient markets hypothesis, see **http://www.investorhome.com/emh.htm**.

To clarify, let's assume that the original price and expected price of A was $100 and that the dividend was $10. Using Equation (8-3), the original return would be 10 percent, which we assumed, given the risk and liquidity of A, was also the equilibrium return. Let's assume that based on the new higher profit numbers, the expected price increases to $115.[11] The question is what will happen to the current price. Based upon our analysis, the current price should rise to a point where the expected return on A remains at its equilibrium return of 10 percent. In this case, we solve for the new current price based on an expected future price of $115 and a dividend of $10. Plugging the numbers into Equation (8-3), we get ($115 − P_t + $10)/$P_t$ =.10 or 10 percent. Solving for P_t, we get $113.63. Thus, the current price will immediately rise to $113.63, given the new higher expected price of $115. When the current price is $113.63, the expected return will be equal to 10 percent. At a price lower than $113.63, the expected return would be higher. For example, at the original price of $100, the expected return would be 25 percent (($115 − $100 + $10)/$100 = 25 percent). Funds would flow in this market by investors seeking the higher than equilibrium return of 15 percent based on risk and liquidity. As funds flowed in, the price of A would rise. Funds would keep flowing into the market, pushing the price up until the market returned to equilibrium. This occurs at a price of $113.63 because ($115 − $113.63 + $10)/$113.063 = 10 percent.

Two points are worth emphasizing. First, the equilibrium return is based on the risks and liquidity of this financial instrument relative to other financial instruments. Note that we are assuming that the risk and liquidity of A have not changed so that the equilibrium return to A relative to the risk and liquidity of other financial instruments is 10 percent. Second, *current* prices adjust whenever new information becomes available that changes current expectations about *future* prices.

The rationale behind the efficient markets hypothesis is straightforward. Namely, if current prices do not fully reflect any changes in expectations, then some market participants will earn less than what they otherwise would have. There will be unexploited opportunities to gain by purchasing those financial instruments that pay a return above equilibrium. The drive for profits ensures that all opportunities for profit will be exhausted and that prices of all financial instruments will adjust to the equilibrium return, which is the optimal forecast. Now would be a good time to read the A Closer Look on page 170 about the implications of the efficient markets hypothesis.

The efficient markets hypothesis holds that the prices of all financial instruments are based on the optimal forecast obtained by using all available information. A **stronger version of the efficient markets hypothesis** holds that the prices of all financial instruments reflect the true fundamental value of the instruments. Thus, not only do prices reflect all available information but also this information is accurate, complete, understood by all, and reflects the market fundamentals. **Market fundamentals** are factors that have a direct effect on future income streams of the instruments. These factors include

Stronger Version of the Efficient Markets Hypothesis
The theory that the prices of all financial instruments not only reflect the optimal forecast of the financial instrument but also the true fundamental value of the instrument.

Market Fundamentals
Factors that have a direct effect on future income streams of the instruments including the value of the assets and the expected income streams of those assets on which the financial instruments represent claims.

Implications of the Efficient Markets Hypothesis

The efficient markets hypothesis is attractive from an intuitive sense. However, for most investors who want to believe they can consistently get above average returns, it is unattractive. The implications are that a hot tip will not pan out unless it is based on information not readily available. Buying and selling stocks based on "insider" information (information available only to someone within the corporation), however, is illegal.

One implication of the efficient markets hypothesis is that prices of financial instruments reflect all readily available information. Thus, if information about an issuer is already expected, when an announcement of the information is made, the announcement will have little or no effect on the instrument's price. For example, if it is believed that the bankruptcy of a firm is eminent, prices of the stocks and bonds of the failing company will fall even before the actual bankruptcy is declared. Thus, prices of financial instruments change dramatically only when "unexpected information" becomes available.

Another implication of the efficient markets hypothesis is that it is impossible to beat the market (earn an above average return). This is so because current prices of financial instruments reflect the optimal forecast using all available information when markets are in equilibrium. If I read a favorable earnings report in the Sunday newspaper, by the time I buy the instrument on Monday morning, its price will already have adjusted so that I will not earn an above average return.

Whatever the available information, markets are always moving toward an equilibrium of sorts, which can mean moving toward or away from previous equilibriums as factors affecting supply and demand for securities or funds change. A market is really not efficient unless the available information is understood by significant participants. Inasmuch as there is a learning curve in understanding, adapting to, and using information that is not equally shared, understood, or held with great and unvarying confidence and that this information is subject to imminent change, volatility in the market is to be expected and may even be greater (1) the more information becomes available and (2) the faster it is disseminated.

The quality of information varies, and when traders are not sure of what they know or don't know, the market can be volatile even without any changes in the available information as confidence levels rise and fall. Add to this the rational or irrational emotions embodied in herd instinct, market momentum, market rotation, guru hypnosis, mythical mottos such as "buy on the rumor, sell on the fact," consensus forecasts, and so on. In areas of the market such as high-technology stocks in the late 1990s and early 2000s, it is unlikely that participants interpreted the available information the same way.

With increased individual control over pension plans and the rise of managed mutual funds, individuals are now participants in the stock and bond markets more so than in the past. Many make little use of information except for minimal asset allocation based on the reputation of a popular guru or fund manager. Fund managers consequently engage in highly competitive behavior to report good earnings results. Powerful mood swings of pessimism and optimism can by contagion sweep the markets and become part of the changing information that affects them.

For each person beating the average, someone is always being beaten by it. Whether someone can *consistently* beat the average is the question. John Maynard Keynes, the well-known economist, said that the true genius is the person who can accurately forecast what the average investor will believe about the direction of the economy or the future profitability of a corporation. In reality, forecasting what the average investor will believe is more important than forecasting what will actually happen.

One final note: When interest rates change, default risk also changes. For example, if the Fed takes action to increase interest rates, the economy slows and the risk of a default increases as the economy slows. Thus, the future income stream from the financial asset becomes less certain. This, in turn, affects the risk premium that the lender will require and hence the price of the financial instrument.

---

the value of the assets and the expected income streams of those assets on which the financial instruments represent claims. Thus, if markets are efficient, prices are correct in that they represent underlying fundamentals. In the less-stringent version of the hypothesis, the prices of all financial instruments do not necessarily represent the fundamental value of the instrument.

There have been extraordinary run-ups and collapses of stock or bond prices, known as bubbles, that do not seem to be related to market fundamentals. Such run-ups in stock prices have occurred in Japan in the late 1980s and more recently in the United States in the late 1990s. Some economists point out that such bubbles in financial markets can still be explained by rational expectations. It may be rational to buy a share of stock at a high price if it is thought that there will be other investors in the future who would be willing to pay inflated prices (prices that exceed those based on market fundamentals) for the stock. This phenomenon is sometimes called "the greater fool" theory. Subsequent collapses in stock prices occurred in Japan in the 1990s and in the United States in the early 2000s.

Other economists suspect that financial market prices may overreact before reaching equilibrium when there is a change in either supply or demand. That is, prices may rise or fall (overshoot or undershoot) more than market fundamentals would justify before settling down to the price based on fundamentals. In these cases, it may be possible for investors to earn above average returns or to experience above average losses.

Recap   The efficient markets hypothesis states that when financial markets are in equilibrium, the prices of all financial instruments reflect all readily available information. Prices of financial instruments are based on optimal forecasts. The rationale behind the hypothesis is that if prices do not reflect all available information, there will be unexploited profit opportunities. A stronger version of the efficient markets hypothesis holds that prices of financial instruments represent underlying or fundamental values of the assets and the expected income streams of those assets on which the financial instruments represent claims. Bubbles in financial markets where prices seem to exceed fundamental values can be rational if investors believe that other investors will buy the financial instrument at still higher prices. Some believe that financial prices overreact (overshoot or undershoot) in response to newly available information.

This completes our look at the efficient market hypothesis and financial prices. We return to stocks and bonds in Chapters 16 and 17. In the next chapter, we look at the determination of foreign exchange rates and their effects on the economy.

Summary of Major Points

1. Long-term interest rates are determined by current and expected short-term interest rates. Present short-term rates are determined by national income, the money supply, and inflationary expectations. Expected short-term rates are determined by expectations of those same variables.
2. If returns to various financial assets are not perfectly correlated, holding a portfolio of diversified assets reduces risk for any given expected return or increases expected return for any given level of risk. Thus, investors generally opt for a portfolio of various financial instruments with different risks and returns.
3. Prices of long-term financial instruments such as stocks and bonds change as current and future expected earnings change. If interest rates fall or rise, prices of previously issued bonds rise or fall, respectively. If current and expected future earnings rise, stock prices also rise, and vice versa. Thus, it is the expected return on bonds and the expected return on stocks that determine stock and bond prices.
4. Market participants compare expected rates of return for various financial instruments and select a combination of those with the highest expected return consistent with varying degrees of risk and liquidity. In equilibrium, differences in returns on various financial instruments reflect differences in risk and liquidity only.
5. Adaptive expectations are formed by looking at current and past prices. Rational expectations are formed by looking at past prices and all currently available information about the economy that may affect prices. The theory of rational expectations is that expectations will be equal to optimal forecasts or the best guesses possible based on all available information.
6. The efficient markets hypothesis says that when financial markets are in equilibrium, the prices of all financial instruments reflect all readily available information. The rationale behind the hypothesis is that if prices do not reflect all available information, there will be unexploited profit opportunities.
7. Market fundamentals are factors that have a direct effect on future incomes streams of financial instruments. A stronger version of the efficient market hypothesis holds that prices of all financial instruments reflect the true fundamental value of the instrument.
8. The efficient markets hypothesis does not imply that all participants in the market must know the optimal forecast; it is necessary for only few savvy investors to know the optimal forecast. These savy investors will then drive the price to the optimal forecast by exploiting opportunities for profit. The efficient markets hypothesis implies that it is impossible to maintain an above average return for a long period of time. Bubbles, investments based on insider information, and market overreaction to new information are exceptions to the efficient markets hypothesis.

Key Terms

Adaptive Expectations, **164**

Diversification, **159**

Efficient Markets Hypothesis, **166**

Market Fundamentals, **167**

Optimal Forecast, **164**

Rational Expectations, **164**

Stronger Version of the Efficient
Markets Hypothesis, **167**

Theory of Rational Expectations, **167**

Review Questions

1. Explain why stock and bond prices adjust until investors are indifferent between stocks and bonds, given varying degrees of risk and liquidity.
2. What is diversification? What is the expected return to a portfolio that is composed of a variety of financial assets?
3. If the returns to two different financial instruments are perfectly positively correlated, can holding a combination of the two reduce risk for any given return? Explain. If the returns to two different financial instruments are perfectly negatively correlated, can holding a combination of the two reduce risk for any given return? Explain.
4. When full adjustment has occurred, what do differences in returns on various financial instruments reflect?
5. If current and expected earnings rise, what happens to stock prices?
6. Interest rates are going up. What happens to the prices of previously issued bonds?
7. How do adaptive expectations differ from rational expectations?
8. Why is the actual value of a financial variable different from the optimal forecast of that variable? Assuming that expectations are rational, what, on average, will be the difference between the actual value and the optimal forecast?
9. What is the efficient markets hypothesis? How does it differ from the stronger version of the hypothesis?
10. What is the fundamental value of a financial instrument?
11. What is the rationale behind the efficient markets hypothesis?
12. Explain why the expected return on newly issued and previously issued bonds is the prevailing interest rate plus any expected capital gain or loss.
13. Must all market participants know the optimal forecast of a financial instrument for the price of the financial instrument to be driven to the optimal forecast?
14. What is a "bubble" in a financial market? Can financial prices ever overshoot or undershoot optimal values?
15. News comes out that leads investors to believe that there is more risk involved with owning financial instrument A. What will happen to its equilibrium return?

Analytical Questions

Questions marked with an icon are objective in nature. They can be completed with a short answer or number.

16. If the current price of a share of stock that pays a $1 dividend is $20 and if the expected capital gain is $2, what is the expected return? What is the return if there is an expected capital loss of $2?
17. Assume the equilibrium return on a financial instrument is 10 percent and the instrument pays no dividends or interest. If the current price is $100 and the expected future price one year from now just increased from $110 to $120, what will happen to the current price? What if the expected future price decreases from $110 to $100?
18. Assume that the equilibrium return on a financial instrument is 10 percent. If the current price is $100 and the instrument does not pay interest or dividend, what is the price expected one year from now when the market is in equilibrium? If the equilibrium return on the instrument increases to 15 percent because the instrument is perceived as more risky, what happens to the current price, assuming the expected price one year from now does not change?
19. Assume that HappyDays, Inc., pays an 8 percent return during expansions and a zero percent return during recessions with certainty. SadDays, Inc. pays a zero percent return in expansions and an 8 percent return in recessions with certainty. Show how the fluctuation in return is eliminated if an investor splits his or her surplus funds equally between HappyDays and SadDays.

Suggested Readings

For an interesting article about the efficient markets hypothesis, see Justin Fox, "Efficient Markets? Hah!" *Fortune* 139:4 (March 1, 1999).

For a history of the development of the efficient markets hypothesis, see **http://www.investorhome.com/emh.htm.**

Two interesting books that offer a contrary view are by Robert A. Haugen. They are *The Inefficient Stock Market: What Pays Off and Why*, 2nd ed. (Upper Saddle River, N.J.: (Pearson Edu-

cation, January 2002), and The *New Finance, Overreaction, Complexity*, and *Uniqueness*, 3rd ed. (Upper Saddle River, NJ: Prentice Hall, November 2003).

For a more thorough discussion of the benefits of diversification, see "Managing the Risks: The Importance of Diversification" at **http://www.ameritrade.com/educationv2/fhtml/learning/diversification.fhtml#meaning.**

Endnotes

1 Additional factors that can affect the prices of financial instruments are term to maturity, the taxability of earnings, and other supply and demand conditions affecting particular markets. For our purposes here, *term to maturity* is encompassed under risk with, ceteris paribus, longer-term instruments entailing more risk. Also by expected rates of return, we mean *after-tax returns*.

2 If a company pays out only a small portion of its earnings as dividends, then it has retained earnings, which it invests back into the company. Ceteris paribus, this usually leads to higher profits later. If the expected returns from retained earnings exceed the risk-adjusted returns that shareholders could expect to receive on alternative investments made with the dividends, a firm's stock price will rise, and the owner will earn a larger capital gain when the stock is sold. In the 1990s, the trend among many companies was against paying dividends so that profits could be plowed back into the corporation, thus "growing" the corporation. Due to changes in tax laws in the early 2000s that favored dividends over capital gains, the trend has been reversed.

3 Real national income is national income adjusted for changes in price or inflation. For our purposes, real national income is equivalent to real GDP.

4 The specifics of this relationship are flushed out in Equation (8-3) on page 166.

5 Coupon payments are usually made semiannually. We are assuming annual coupon payments here to simplify. The assumption does not substantively change the results.

6 Hopefully, you recall from Chapter 6 that after bonds are issued, the price of the bond is equal to the present value of the dividend payments and the repayment of principal at maturity. Thus, $1,339.67 is the present value of the 29 future dividend payments of $60, and the repayment of the $1,000 principle in 29 years. We are assuming that dividends are paid only once a year. If interest rates have fallen, the price of the bond increases. If this bond were a consol, the price of the bond would equal $1,500.

7 If both stocks and bonds have highly developed secondary markets, the assumption that they have the same degree of liquidity is not that unrealistic.

8 As previously noted, the decline in interest rates to 4 percent causes the prices of previously issued bonds to rise so that their risk-adjusted return equals 4 percent instead of 6 percent. Thus, the return on previously issued bonds will equal the return on newly issued bonds..

9 A more formal approach to this relationship between stock prices and interest rates uses the present value (discounting) analysis developed in Chapter 6. Within this framework, the share price is viewed as the discounted present value of a firm's expected earnings (or dividends). Accordingly, a fall in the interest rate and/or a rise in the stream of expected earnings increases the expected value of the firm—that is, the share price—in the market.

10 If the interest rate rises to 8 percent, then, in equilibrium, the risk-adjusted return on stocks will rise to 10 percent, assuming that the typical investor must be compensated 2 percent for the additional risk of owning stocks. The price of a typical share will initially fall to $40 because $4/$40 = .10 = 10 percent. Assuming the higher interest rate reduces demand and hence earnings, the dividend may be expected to fall to $3. If this is the case, the stock price falls further to $30 because $3/$30 = .10 = 10 percent.

11 For simplicity, we are assuming that despite the higher profit expectations, the dividend remains the same.

There are three main causes that dispose men to madness: love, ambition, and the study of foreign exchange.

—Walter Leaf, 1926

9

How Exchange Rates Are Determined

Learning Objectives

After reading this chapter, you should know:

What exchange rates are, and how they affect prices of imports and exports

How exchange rates are determined by supply and demand in the foreign exchange market

The factors that cause exchange rates to change

What the theories of purchasing power parity and interest rate parity are

The More Things Change, the More Things Stay the Same

Throughout the early and mid-1980s, typical headlines in *The Wall Street Journal* told of the strong dollar, its detrimental effects on U.S. jobs, and the eventual efforts to bring down the "overvalued" dollar. By the mid-1990s, the dollar had fallen to record lows against many currencies and was at less than half its mid-1980's value against the Japanese yen. Headlines such as "Dollar Rises in Foreign Exchange Market as U.S. Interest Rates Surge" were replaced with "Dollar Sinks to New Low against Yen." In the late 1990s, the dollar again strengthened against the yen and other major currencies, but not nearly to its mid-1980s level. In the early 2000s, the dollar was still riding high, particularly against the newly created European Union currency, the euro. The dollar reversed course in early 2002 and by late 2003, the trade-weighted dollar exchange rate had fallen almost 30 percent from its high in early 2002 and reached a historic low against the euro. In early 2004, a typical headline read "The Dollar Sinks Anew."

Just what does all of this mean to the average person? How do changes in the international value of the dollar affect job opportunities for recent college graduates and other workers? How are domestic interest rates linked with interest rates in the rest of the world? What happens to imports and exports when the value of the dollar changes? Perhaps most important, how are all of these questions and their answers related? Such questions about the dollar's value are often puzzling to the average person. Many diverse opinions exist about whether a strong dollar is good or bad for the economy even though the implications of a strong dollar are not often fully understood.

Thirty-five years ago, such questions and the interactions between the U.S. economy and the rest of the world were largely ignored by most bankers, stock market analysts, economists, accountants, corporate treasurers, policy makers—and textbook writers! The reasons were that trading of goods, services, financial securities, and currencies between the United States and other countries accounted for only a small portion of total transactions in the United States and that exchange rates between currencies were fixed by the central banks of the various countries and did not change on a day-to-day basis.

Today, the situation is much different for two simple reasons:

1. Cross-border trading of foreign currencies and financial instruments denominated in various currencies has increased much faster than the more visible explosion of international trade in goods and services.

2. The value of the dollar relative to other currencies changes daily.

Consequently, to ignore the globalization of financial markets in a study of the financial system would be a serious omission.

This chapter is included in this part of the text on financial prices because, as we shall see, exchange rates are merely prices (the price of one currency in terms of another) that are determined in a market (the foreign exchange market). As in all markets, prices (foreign exchange rates) are ultimately determined by the forces of supply and demand.

Defining Exchange Rates

The **exchange rate** is the number of units of **foreign currency (money)** that can be acquired with one unit of domestic money.[1] In other words, the exchange rate specifies the purchasing power of, say, the dollar in terms of how much it can buy of another currency. For example, if the yen/dollar exchange rate is 100 yen, this literally means that $1 will buy 100 yen.[2] If the exchange rate rises to 150 yen, meaning that $1 will now buy 150 yen, then the dollar is said to have **appreciated** relative to the yen. Because it will now buy more yen, the dollar's purchasing power has risen. It has grown stronger. On the other hand, if the yen/dollar exchange rate falls from 100 yen to 50 yen, the dollar is said

Exchange Rate
The number of units of foreign currency that can be acquired with one unit of domestic money.

Foreign Currency (Money)
Supplies of foreign exchange.

Appreciated
Description of a currency that has increased in value relative to another currency.

Cracking the Code

How Movements in the Exchange Rate Affect the Dollar Price of Foreign Goods

Suppose a Japanese auto costs 2,000,000 yen in Japan. Ignoring transportation costs and the like, what will it cost in the United States? The answer is that the price depends on the exchange rate between the yen and the dollar. The middle row in the following table lists the beginning situation: If the auto costs 2,000,000 yen and $1 buys 100 yen, then as Equation (9-1) indicates, the dollar price will be $20,000 (2,000,000/100).

The top row in the table shows that when the dollar appreciates from 100 yen to 150 yen, the dollar price of the Japanese auto falls to $13,333 (2,000,000/150). In contrast, as illustrated in the third row, a depreciation of the dollar results in a rise in the dollar price of the Japanese auto.

Yen Price of Japanese Auto	Exchange Rate	Dollar Price of Japanese Auto
(1)	(2)	(1)/(2)
2,000,000 yen	$1 = 150 yen	$13,333
2,000,000 yen	$1 = 100 yen	$20,000
2,000,000 yen	$1 = 50 yen	$40,000

Depreciated
Description of a currency that has decreased in value relative to another currency.

Foreign Exchange
Supplies of foreign currencies.

to have **depreciated** relative to the yen. Because it will now buy fewer yen, the dollar's purchasing power has fallen. It has grown weaker. Supplies of foreign currencies are called **foreign exchange**.

So what does all of this have to do with the price a U.S. importer will have to pay for Japanese autos? The following handy formula, linking prices and the exchange rate, provides the ingredients necessary to answer this question:

(9-1)   U.S. dollar price of foreign goods = foreign price of foreign goods/exchange rate

The accompanying Cracking the Code feature uses this formula and the hypothetical figures already mentioned to illustrate the key point of this discussion—the U.S. dollar price of a foreign good is inversely related to the exchange rate. More specifically, as the dollar appreciates, ceteris paribus, the price of foreign goods in the United States falls, even if the foreign price in yen is constant. Conversely, as the dollar depreciates, ceteris paribus, the price of foreign goods in the United States rises.

Needless to say, the importer and its customers (whether they realize it or not) are affected by changes in the exchange rate. More generally, the exchange rate links the domestic and foreign markets for goods, services, and securities. As a result, changes in the exchange rate will have repercussions in all the domestic and foreign markets, including markets for both inputs and outputs. Thus, if the dollar appreciates, ceteris paribus, U.S. imports (which are now relatively cheaper than before) increase, and U.S. exports to foreign countries (which are now relatively more expensive) decrease. As the dollar becomes stronger, ceteris paribus, we lose domestic jobs in both the industries in direct competition with the imports and the industries that end up exporting less. Hopefully, we have given you some insight into how these fluctuations affect the U.S. economy. Exhibit 9-1 shows the wide fluctuations in the value of the exchange rate since 1980.

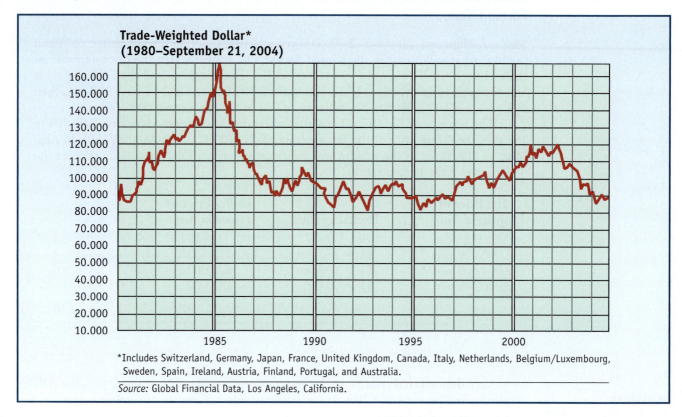

Trade-Weighted Dollar*
(1980–September 21, 2004)

*Includes Switzerland, Germany, Japan, France, United Kingdom, Canada, Italy, Netherlands, Belgium/Luxembourg, Sweden, Spain, Ireland, Austria, Finland, Portugal, and Australia.

Source: Global Financial Data, Los Angeles, California.

Foreign Exchange Market
The market for buying and selling the different currencies of the world.

To understand these various linkages and repercussions, we must first examine what determines the exchange rate. Simply put, the exchange rate, like all prices, is determined by supply and demand. The United States and the rest of the world trade goods, services, and securities. This trading gives rise to a supply of and demand for the various currencies that are traded in the so-called **foreign exchange market**. More specifically, the supply of dollar-denominated funds comes from the demand by U.S. residents for foreign goods, services, and financial claims during a specific time period; the demand for dollar-denominated funds comes from the demand by foreign residents for U.S. goods, services, and financial claims over a period of time. For simplicity, in the remainder of this chapter, we will follow common usage and use the word *dollars* to represent dollar-denominated funds.[3]

Recap The *exchange rate* refers to the number of units of foreign currency that can be acquired with one unit of domestic money. The U.S. dollar price of foreign goods is equal to the foreign price of foreign goods divided by the exchange rate.

Determining Exchange Rates

To understand how supply, demand, and exchange rates are related, it will be helpful to abstract from many of the complexities of the real world and to look at how the exchange rate between two currencies is determined. The general framework we develop is directly

Cracking the Code

Finding the Yen/Euro Exchange Rate

Because \$1 = 100 yen and \$1 = 1.1 euros, then 100 yen = 1.1 euros. If 100 yen = 1.1 euros, we can find how much 1 yen is worth by dividing both sides of the equation by 100:

$$100/100 \text{ yen} = 1.1/100 \text{ euros}$$
$$1 \text{ yen} = 0.011 \text{ euros}$$

This is the euros/yen exchange rate.

Likewise, we can find out how much 1 euro is worth by dividing both sides of the equation by 1.1:

$$1.1/1.1 \text{ euros} = 100/1.1 \text{ yen}$$
$$1 \text{ euro} = 90.9 \text{ yen}$$

applicable to the more complex relationships among all national currencies. For example, suppose we know the yen/dollar rate is 100 yen and the euro/dollar rate is 1.1 euros. Then, as demonstrated in the Cracking the Code feature above, it must follow that the euro/yen rate is .011 euros. This "transitivity" allows us to confine our analysis to two monies. We begin by considering how the exchange rate between the U.S. dollar and the Japanese yen is determined, recognizing that our analysis could easily be extended to relationships among more than two currencies. Now would be a good time to look at Exhibit 9-2 on page 180, which shows some of the basics of foreign exchange markets.

The Demand for Dollars in the Foreign Exchange Market

The demand for dollars in international financial markets originates from foreign purchases of U.S. goods, services, and securities. Drawing on Exhibit 9-2, we can write:

(9-2) Demand for dollars = f(foreign demand for U.S. goods, services, and securities)
$$\overset{+}{}$$

The plus (+) sign over the expression simply means that the foreign demand for U.S. goods, services, and securities and the demand for dollars are positively related; when the former rises, the latter will also rise. When foreign demand for U.S. goods, services, and securities falls, the demand for dollars falls.

Now consider what happens to the quantity demanded of dollars/month when the exchange rate changes.[4] (Note that the quantity demanded is the amount of dollars that will be demanded at a specific exchange rate.) The answer is that, ceteris paribus, the quantity demanded is inversely related to the exchange rate, as depicted in Equation (9-3):

(9-3) Quantity demanded of dollars/month =
$$\overset{-}{f}(\text{exchange rate})$$

When the exchange rate goes up, ceteris paribus, the quantity demanded of dollars/month goes down, and vice versa. To see how and why the exchange rate and the

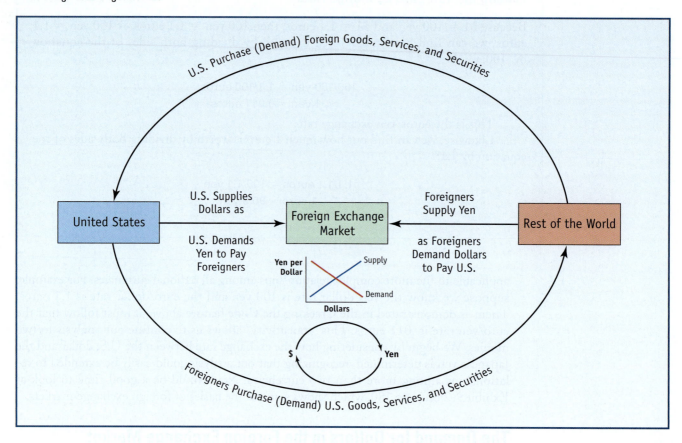

The foreign exchange market facilitates the trading of goods, services, and financial claims (securities) between countries. This global market is woven together by the market makers in foreign currencies—mostly, the foreign exchange departments of the largest commercial banks located in the world's major financial centers, such as New York, London, Frankfurt, and Tokyo. Without the ability to switch funds back and forth among the world's 100-odd currencies, Americans could neither dine in London, sell hot dogs to Japanese tourists, buy imported videocassette recorders, nor export computers. Furthermore, they could not buy and sell foreign exchange to speculate on future price (exchange rates) movements.

quantity demanded of dollars/month are inversely related as shown in this expression, we need to examine how the exchange rate and changes therein affect foreign demand for U.S. goods, services, and securities.

Focusing only on goods to simplify matters, the answer will depend on how the exchange rate affects the prices of U.S. goods in foreign markets—that is, the yen price of U.S. goods in Japan. The following formula provides the key to the entire question:

(9-4)   Yen (foreign) price of U.S. goods = dollar price of U.S. goods × exchange rate

For example, as in the Cracking the Code box on page 181, if an IBM computer costs $1,500 in the United States, and the yen/dollar exchange rate is 100 yen—meaning

The Cost of an IBM Computer in Japan

If an IBM computer costs $1,500 and the yen/dollar exchange rate is 100, then in Japan, assuming transportation costs are zero, the computer will cost 150,000 yen, calculated as follows:

Dollar price of U.S. goods × exchange rate = yen price of U.S. goods
1,500 × 100 = 150,000 yen

If the exchange rate appreciates to 150, then the computer will cost 225,000 yen:

1,500 × 150 yen = 225,000 yen

that $1 buys 100 yen or, equivalently, from a foreign perspective, it takes 100 yen to buy $1—the computer will cost 150,000 yen in Japan (1,500 × 100 yen = 150,000 yen).

If the dollar appreciates, from, say, 100 yen to 150 yen, this would raise the yen price of the IBM computer from 150,000 yen to 225,000 yen (1,500 × 150 yen). Following standard tenets of consumer demand theory, we can reasonably assume that foreigners, ceteris paribus, will respond to the price rise by reducing the quantity demanded of U.S. computers/month (and U.S. goods, more generally), thereby reducing the quantity demanded of dollars/month. Conversely, a depreciation of the dollar, from say, 100 yen to 50 yen, would lower the yen price of the IBM computer from 150,000 yen to 75,000 yen (1,500 × 50 yen). Again, it is reasonable to assume that foreigners, ceteris paribus, will respond to the fall in the yen price by raising the quantity demanded of U.S. computers/month (and U.S. goods, more generally), thereby raising the quantity demanded of dollars/month.[5]

To sum up to this point, the minus sign over the exchange rate in Equation (9-3) reflects the fact that, ceteris paribus, an appreciation of the dollar will raise the yen price of U.S. goods in Japan and thereby reduce the quantity demanded of U.S. goods and thus the quantity demanded of dollars/month. The reverse is also true.

Recap   The demand for dollars is directly related to foreign demand for U.S. goods, services, and securities. The quantity demanded of dollars/month is inversely related to the exchange rate, ceteris paribus. The foreign price of U.S. goods is equal to the dollar price of U.S. goods times the exchange rate. If the dollar appreciates, the foreign price of U.S. goods increases, ceteris paribus.

The Supply of Dollars in the Foreign Exchange Market

So much for the demand side—what about supply? In international financial markets, the supply of dollars originates from domestic purchases of foreign goods, services, and financial securities, as depicted in Equation (9-5):

$$+$$

(9-5)   Supply of dollars/month = f(U.S. demand for foreign goods, services, and securities)

As before, the plus sign over the expression means that U.S. demand for foreign goods, services, and securities and the supply of dollars in the foreign exchange market are positively related. When the former rises, the latter rises. This occurs because when U.S. demand for foreign goods, services, and securities rises, the demand for yen to pay for those foreign goods, services, and securities also rises. But how do U.S. residents get more yen? The short simple answer is by supplying more dollars! (Remember, dollars are being supplied to purchase yen to purchase foreign goods.) You should be able to explain why a drop in the U.S. demand for foreign goods (in this case, Japanese goods) will lead to a decrease in the supply of dollars.

The next step is to consider how the quantity supplied of dollars/month is affected by changes in the exchange rate. (Note that quantity supplied is the amount of dollars that will be supplied/month at a specific exchange rate.) The answer is that, ceteris paribus, the quantity supplied is directly related to the exchange rate, as shown in Equation (9-6):

$$\text{(9-6)} \qquad \text{Quantity supplied of dollars/month} = f(\overset{+}{\text{exchange rate}})$$

To see why the exchange rate and the quantity supplied of dollars/month are positively related, ceteris paribus, consider how changes in the exchange rate affect U.S. demand for foreign goods, services, and securities. Focusing again only on goods for simplicity, we can draw on the Cracking the Code feature on page 177 and the discussion of Equation (9-1). As you saw, the dollar price of foreign goods in the United States is equal to the yen price divided by the exchange rate. Thus, as shown in the feature, as the exchange rate rises, the dollar price of foreign goods falls. Accordingly, we would expect U.S. residents to increase the quantity demanded of foreign goods/month, which, in turn, will raise the quantity of dollars supplied/month to the foreign exchange market, ceteris paribus. Conversely, a fall in the exchange rate will raise the dollar price of foreign goods in the United States, thereby lowering the quantity demanded of foreign goods/month and, thus, the quantity supplied of dollars/month, ceteris paribus.[6]

We have established an inverse relationship between the quantity demanded of dollars/month and the exchange rate, ceteris paribus. In addition, given our assumptions, we have confirmed a direct relationship between the quantity supplied of dollars/month and the exchange rate, ceteris paribus. These relationships are graphed in Exhibit 9-3 on page 184, which depicts the determination of the equilibrium exchange rate. The foreign exchange market "clears" at the exchange rate where the demand and supply curves intersect. At this exchange rate, the quantity demanded of dollars/month is equal to the quantity supplied of dollars/month, and we have market equilibrium (at point *A*). At any other exchange rate, there is either a surplus or a shortage of dollars. Market forces generated by the surplus or shortage will cause changes in the exchange rate, which will continue until equilibrium is reached.

Recap   The supply of dollars is directly related to U.S. demand for foreign goods, services, and securities. The quantity supplied of dollars/month is directly related to the exchange rate, ceteris paribus. The exchange rate adjusts until the quantity demanded of dollars/month is just equal to the quantity supplied/month in international markets.

We have made a good start, but our ultimate objective is to understand the causes and consequences of changes in the exchange rate resulting from changes in supply or demand. Accordingly, we need to examine the factors that can cause the supply and demand curves for dollars in the foreign exchange market to shift.

Cracking the Code

The Foreign Exchange Market

Suppose that you need pounds for an upcoming trip to England. You call your local bank, say, in Nashville, Tennessee, and place a buy order for 1,000 pounds. Most likely, your local bank does not have a foreign exchange department, so it will call its correspondent bank that specializes in international transactions and place an order for pounds with Citibank's foreign exchange department.[a]

Most foreign currency transactions in the United States are executed by the foreign exchange departments of the largest banks, which are linked via modern telecommunications with foreign exchange dealers around the world. Accustomed to handling transactions from around the globe daily, they stand ready to buy or sell dollars and foreign currencies at the prevailing exchange rate. Acting as auctioneers, they (and other dealers nationwide and worldwide) are prepared to adjust the exchange rate up as buy orders for dollars rise relative to sell orders, or adjust the exchange rate down as buy orders for dollars fall relative to sell orders. Of course, this is just another way of saying that the exchange rate will change as supply and/or demand changes.

So how much will your 1,000 pounds cost? If you could "crack the code" in the relevant table in *The Wall Street Journal*, you could figure out the approximate cost. We have reproduced a portion of the foreign exchange table that appeared in the *Journal* on April 20, 2004. As noted at the top of the table, it shows the exchange rates as of 4 P.M. Eastern Time the preceding business day, Monday, April 19, 2004.

To find the exchange rate between the pound and the dollar on Wednesday look at the fourth column (Currency per U.S. $: Mon) in the highlighted row. The exchange rate was .5533, meaning $1 purchased .5533 pounds. Accordingly, 1,000 pounds would have cost $1,807.33 (1,000 pounds/.5533). By comparing the fourth column with the last column (Fri), we see that the dollar depreciated a bit on Monday as compared to the previous Friday. On Friday, $1 purchased .5566 pounds, slightly more than Monday. Accordingly, if you had bought the 1,000 pounds on Friday, you would have paid slightly less than on Monday ($1,769.22 = 1,000 pounds/.5566).

Note that the dollar exchange rate (the number of units of foreign currency $1 can buy), shown in the fourth and fifth columns, is simply the reciprocal of the pound exchange rate (the number of dollars that can be purchased with 1 pound or, equivalently, the number of dollars needed to purchase 1 pound), shown in the second and third columns (U.S. $ equiv.). Thus, on Friday, .5566 pounds to the dollar is the reciprocal of $1.7699 to the pound ($1.7699 = 1/.5566). Given this property, a depreciation of the dollar means $1 buys fewer pounds, or equivalently, it costs more ($1.8073) to buy 1 pound on Monday. It is crucial for you to see that these are two ways of saying the same thing.

Changes in the exchange rate have profound implications for any transactions between the two currencies. For example, suppose a hotel room in England costs 100 pounds on February 28, 2007, and is the same price one year later on February 28, 2008. If the pound/dollar exchange rate has changed from $1 = 2 pounds in 2007 to $1 = 1 pound in 2008, the traveler from the United States pays more for the room in 2008 (100 pounds/1 = $100 in 2008 compared to 100 pounds/2 = $50 in 2007).[b]

Exchange Rates

Monday April 19, 2004

The following New York foreign exchange selling rates apply to trading among banks in amounts of $1 million and more, as quoted at 4 P.M. Eastern time by Reuters and other sources. Retail transactions provide fewer units of foreign currency per dollar.

	Currency			
	U.S. $ equiv.		per U.S. $	
Country	Mon	Fri	Mon	Fri
England (Pound)	$1,807.33	$1,769.22	.5533	.5566

SOURCE: *The Wall Street Journal* (April 20, 2004): C10.

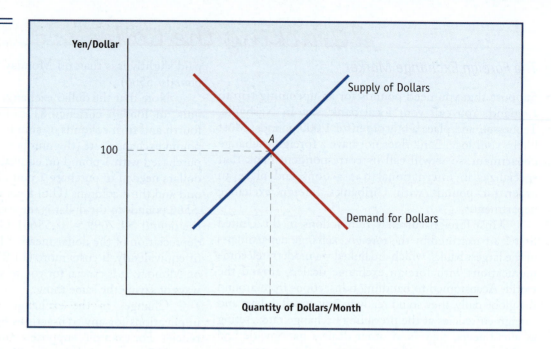

Yen/Dollar

Supply of Dollars

100

A

Demand for Dollars

Quantity of Dollars/Month

Changes in Supply and Demand and How They Affect the Exchange Rate

Starting with supply, let's first consider how and why changes in the supply of dollars in the foreign exchange market affect the exchange rate. The initial question that needs to be addressed is what factors, in addition to the exchange rate, could cause U.S. residents to alter their demand for foreign goods, services, and securities and thus their supply of dollars in the foreign exchange market. In other words, what factors could cause the supply curve of dollars to shift? Previous research suggests that the following factors play a major role:

1. *Changes in U.S. real income.* Changes in U.S. real income and changes in the supply of dollars are positively related. The reason is that as real income grows in the United States, households and firms have more funds to spend and save. Accordingly, they will demand more U.S. goods, services, and securities and more foreign goods, services, and securities. Thus, as U.S. real income grows, ceteris paribus, the supply of dollars will increase because Americans now have more income to spend on imports. Likewise, as U.S. real income falls, ceteris paribus, the supply of dollars will decrease.

2. *Changes in the dollar price of U.S. goods relative to the dollar price of foreign goods.* Simply put, if the prices of U.S. goods rise relative to the dollar prices of foreign goods, ceteris paribus, U.S. residents will demand more foreign goods and, therefore, supply more dollars in the foreign exchange market because foreign goods are now relatively cheaper than U.S. goods. Holding the exchange rate constant, what could cause such changes in relative prices? If you said a higher inflation rate in the United States than in Japan, you are right! Likewise, using similar reasoning, if the inflation rate in the United States falls relative to that in Japan, U.S. residents will supply fewer dollars in the foreign exchange market, ceteris paribus.

3. *Changes in foreign interest rates relative to U.S. interest rates.* As foreign interest rates rise relative to U.S. rates, ceteris paribus, foreign securities become relatively more attractive. Accordingly, U.S. residents will buy more foreign securities and, thus,

supply more dollars. Likewise, if foreign rates fall relative to U.S. rates, the supply of dollars decreases, ceteris paribus. To be more precise, U.S. residents will compare interest rates in the United States, i_{US}, with the expected return on foreign securities. As we shall see later in this chapter, the latter consists of the foreign interest rate, i_F, minus the expected appreciation (if any) in the value of the dollar.

For a graphical presentation of this analytical discussion of supply, see Exhibit 9-4. Study it carefully before moving on to the discussion of the demand for dollars.

Using the same logic and analytical framework we used for supply, we now ask what factors, in addition to the exchange rate, could cause foreigners to alter their demand for U.S. goods, services, and securities and thus their demand for dollars in the foreign exchange market. Remember that changes in the demand for dollars cause the demand curve for dollars to shift. We begin by identifying the major factors that can alter demand:

1. *Changes in foreign real income.* Ceteris paribus, changes in foreign real income and the demand for dollars are positively related. For example, if foreign real incomes rise, ceteris paribus, foreign firms and households will have more funds to spend and save. Accordingly, they will demand more of their own goods, services, and securities as well as more imported goods, services, and securities. Thus, as foreign real incomes grow, ceteris paribus, the demand for dollars, reflecting the increased supply of yen to execute transactions, will grow. Following similar reasoning, if foreign incomes fall, the demand for dollars will also fall, ceteris paribus.

9-4

Changes in the Exchange Rate: The Role of Changes in Supply

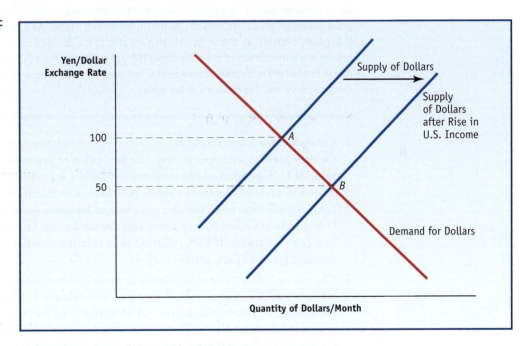

This exhibit begins with an initial equilibrium exchange rate of 100 yen. Assume that the equilibrium is now disturbed by a change in one of the factors that affect the supply of dollars, say, a rise in U.S. income, which increases the supply of dollars, as shown by the rightward shift of the supply curve. The new equilibrium at point *B* results in a depreciation of the dollar as the equilibrium exchange rate falls from 100 yen to 50 yen. Note that a rise in the prices of U.S. goods relative to the dollar prices of foreign goods, or a rise in foreign interest rates relative to U.S. interest rates, would have produced a similar increase in supply and depreciation of the exchange rate.

9-5

Changes in the Exchange
Rate: The Role of Changes in
Demand

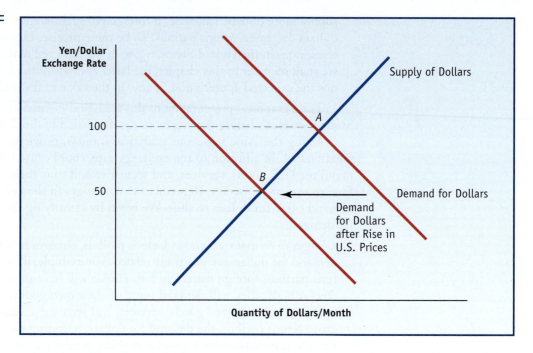

Assume that the initial equilibrium at point *A* is disturbed by a change in one of the factors that affect the demand for dollars. In particular, suppose that the yen price of U.S. goods rises relative to the yen price of foreign goods because of inflation in the United States. As a result, foreigners' demand for U.S. goods declines, as shown by the leftward shift of the demand curve. The new equilibrium (point *B*) results in a depreciation of the dollar from 100 yen to 50 yen. Note that a fall in foreign incomes or a rise in foreign interest rates relative to U.S. rates would have produced a similar leftward shift in the demand curve and depreciation of the dollar.

2. *Changes in the foreign (yen) price of foreign goods relative to the foreign price of U.S. goods.* Ceteris paribus, changes in, say, the yen price of Japanese goods relative to the yen price of U.S. goods and the demand for dollars are positively related. To see why, assume inflation accelerates in Japan but there is no inflation in the United States. The Japanese inflation will raise the yen price of Japanese goods relative to the yen price of U.S. goods. As a result, foreigners will demand more U.S. goods and, thus, more dollars, ceteris paribus. If U.S. inflation rises relative to inflation in Japan, foreigners will demand fewer dollars, ceteris paribus.

3. *Changes in U.S. interest rates relative to foreign interest rates.* A positive relationship also exists between changes in U.S. interest rates relative to foreign rates and the demand for dollars. For example, suppose that initially the interest rate on both foreign government bonds and U.S. Treasury bonds is 6 percent. Portfolio managers in Japan, noticing the identical rates and recognizing the benefits of diversification, hold some of both types of bonds in their portfolios. Now interest rates in the United States rise. As a result, the demand for U.S. securities and, thus, the demand for dollars rise, ceteris paribus. Likewise, if interest rates in Japan fall, the demand for dollars rises, ceteris paribus. More on this later in the chapter.

These points are illustrated graphically in Exhibit 9-5. Study this exhibit carefully before moving on. Make sure that you note the similarities between the factors that cause changes in the demand for dollars and the factors that cause changes in the supply of dollars.

Exchange Rates in the Long Run: The Theory of Purchasing Power Parity

We have covered some important material. Now is a good time to stop and see how to use this analysis. Suppose that the U.S. economy is expanding at a relatively slow pace, with real GDP growing at a 1 to 2 percent annual rate, compared to its potential growth trend of $2\frac{1}{2}$ to 3 percent. Against this background, the Federal Reserve decides that a rise in the aggregate demand for goods and services is in order. Accordingly, the Fed pursues a more stimulative monetary policy by taking action that causes interest rates to fall. The question we want to focus on in the present context is how the fall in U.S. interest rates will affect the exchange rate.

Believe it or not, the answer flows directly from the preceding discussion of changes in supply and demand. Ceteris paribus, the fall in U.S. interest rates relative to interest rates in Japan will lead to a depreciation of the dollar—that is, to a fall in the exchange rate. The reasoning is as follows: The fall in U.S. rates reduces the attractiveness of U.S. securities relative to foreign securities; as a result, foreigners will demand fewer U.S. securities and, thus, will demand fewer dollars in the foreign exchange market while U.S. residents will demand more foreign securities and, thus, will supply more dollars in the foreign exchange market. In sum, the dollar depreciates as a result of the reduction in the demand for and rise in the supply of dollars induced by the Fed's actions. Try sketching out this scenario graphically as in Exhibits 9-4 and 9-5. If the Fed's policy works, output will expand, income will grow, and demand for imports will rise, all of which will potentially further weaken the dollar, especially if the policy fuels the expectation of or actual inflation.

Taking our analysis one step further, consider the case in which the Fed policy and expanding economy causes an acceleration of the actual inflation rate in the United States. The theory of **purchasing power parity** asserts that in the long run, exchange rates adjust to different inflation rates among countries so that the *relative* purchasing power of various currencies is equalized. Thus, after full adjustment among all currencies, one currency, such as the dollar, will purchase the same market basket of goods and services in every country. In other words, while Paul is traveling in China, he can take the $1 he normally spends on a can of Coke in his college dormitory in Dayton, Ohio, convert the $1 to the Chinese currency, and purchase an identical can of Coke.

To help clarify this theory, assume that inflation is 5 percent in the United States and 3 percent in the European Union. After the inflation and at the original exchange rate, relative prices in the United States are roughly 2 percent higher than those in the European Union. As you saw earlier in the chapter, the European demand for the relatively more expensive U.S. exports will decline and the U.S. demand for relatively cheaper U.S. imports will increase. Thus, the demand for dollars will decrease and the supply of dollars will increase. As a result, the dollar will depreciate in terms of the euro. The question is how much the dollar will depreciate. According to the purchasing power parity theory, the dollar should then appreciate by 2 percent, thus exactly offsetting the higher U.S. inflation relative to the European Union (5 percent − 3 percent = 2 percent) and leaving the relative purchasing power between the dollar and the euro unchanged.

Purchasing Power Parity
The theory that in the long run, exchange rates adjust so that the relative purchasing power of various currencies is equalized.

The purchasing power parity theory is based on many, often unrealistic, assumptions. These assumptions include that all goods and services are identical and tradable, that there are no transportation costs and no barriers to trade such as tariffs, and that exchange rates are influenced only by relative inflation rates across the various countries. In reality, all goods such as Toyotas, Chevrolets, and BMWs are not identical and hence will not sell for the same prices. Furthermore, all goods are not tradable, and there are transportation costs and other barriers to trade. Try buying a fast-food imported hamburger or getting an imported haircut. Overall prices in one country may increase because of large price increases of nontradable goods such as housing, land, and nontradable services. In this case, a higher inflation in one country would not pass through to a depreciation of the currency.

In addition to the unrealistic assumptions, the purchasing power parity theory suffers from a lack of completeness because it neglects factors that can and do cause exchange rates to vary significantly over time. These factors include changes in productivity, economic growth, market structures, and technologies across countries, as well as shifts in factor supplies causing commodity price shocks. For example, countries with higher productivity growth or more competitive market structures, ceteris paribus, would experience relatively lower inflation and, hence, currency appreciation and vice versa. Finally, the purchasing power parity theory does not account for changes in tastes among countries. As preferences for another country's products increase, there is a tendency for that country's currency to appreciate. For example, if U.S. taste for French wine decreases (perhaps because of the development of the California wine industry), the supply of euros would decline, causing an appreciation of the dollar. Consequently, because of the unrealistic assumptions and the lack of completeness, a word of caution is needed. Although there is a tendency for currencies of countries with higher relative inflation to depreciate in the long run and vice versa, the trade-off is far from perfect as the purchasing power theory suggests.

Now would be a good time to read the accompanying A Closer Look that looks at the Big Mac Index, which attempts to test the purchasing power parity theory using McDonald's famous burger.

A Closer Look

The Big Mac Index and Purchasing Power Parity

Every year, *The Economist* news magazine publishes an interesting and fun Big Mac currency index based on the purchasing power parity theory. According to the theory, the dollar price of a Big Mac, the signature hamburger of the McDonald's chain, should be the same in all of the 120 countries around the world where the Big Mac is sold. The most recent table from the January 17, 2004 issue of *The Economist* is on page 189. To find the dollar price of a Big Mac, the price in the local currency is merely divided by the exchange rate. If the dollar price of a Big Mac is less than the $2.80 U.S. price, then the currency is thought to be undervalued relative to the U.S. dollar. Likewise, if the dollar price of a Big Mac is more, the currency is thought to be overvalued.

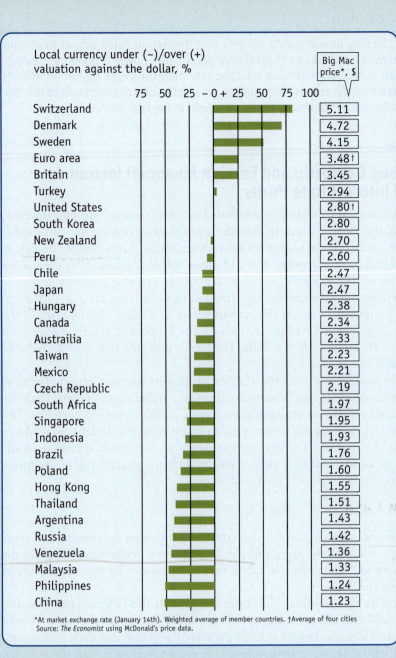

Local currency under (−)/over (+) valuation against the dollar, %

	Big Mac price*, $
Switzerland	5.11
Denmark	4.72
Sweden	4.15
Euro area	3.48†
Britain	3.45
Turkey	2.94
United States	2.80†
South Korea	2.80
New Zealand	2.70
Peru	2.60
Chile	2.47
Japan	2.47
Hungary	2.38
Canada	2.34
Austrailia	2.33
Taiwan	2.23
Mexico	2.21
Czech Republic	2.19
South Africa	1.97
Singapore	1.95
Indonesia	1.93
Brazil	1.76
Poland	1.60
Hong Kong	1.55
Thailand	1.51
Argentina	1.43
Russia	1.42
Venezuela	1.36
Malaysia	1.33
Philippines	1.24
China	1.23

*At market exchange rate (January 14th). Weighted average of member countries. †Average of four cities
Source: *The Economist* using McDonald's price data.

As the table shows, the dollar price of a Big Mac around the world varies from $1.23 in China to $5.11 in Switzerland. Hence, according to the Big Mac index, the currency in China is thought to be undervalued by 56 percent [$1.23 − $2.80)/$2.80 = −.56]. While the currencies of several Asian and other emerging economies appear to be undervalued, the currency of Switzerland is, according to the Big Mac index, overvalued by 83 percent (($5.11 − $2.80)/$2.80 = +.83). The theory of purchasing power parity does not seem to be able to explain these disparities.

The Big Mac index is also flawed by the unrealistic assumptions and the lack of completeness of the purchasing power parity theory. For example, not all Big Macs taste the same in all countries. Local customs and tastes dictate a large part of what the result is. In some countries, Big Macs are quite spicy. (In others, mayonnaise is served with McDonald's french fries.) Likewise, there can be large differences in local sales taxes, trade barriers on beef, and differences in local labor and rent costs. Thus, more factors, in addition to purchasing power parity, need to be considered in explaining exchange rate differentials and movements.

We have examined rather carefully the variety of domestic and foreign factors that, taken together, determine the exchange rate. We would be remiss if we failed to point out that changes in the factors that affect exchange rates are ongoing and therefore changes in exchange rates are ongoing. In other words, in reality, demands and supplies are changing all the time, so equilibrium is a constantly moving target. For example, changes in U.S. real incomes lead to changes in other countries' real incomes, which lead to changes in U.S. incomes, which lead to changes in . . . (and so on). The interrelationships and interactions are increasingly significant as the world's economies become more intertwined. In the next section, we look at how investors choose among financial instruments denominated in various currencies.

Recap The theory of purchasing power parity asserts that exchange rates adjust to varying rates of inflation across countries so that relative purchasing power among various currencies is equalized. Although there is a tendency for countries with higher inflation to see their currencies depreciate, the correlation is far from perfect because of the theory's limiting assumptions of the theory that do not hold in the real world.

Choosing among Domestic and Foreign Financial Instruments: The Theory of Interest Rate Parity

Read this

When comparing financial instruments denominated in the same currency, investors consider the return, the maturity, and the default risk. If instruments are denominated in different currencies, investors and borrowers must also consider the exchange rate risk, or the risk that the exchange rate between two currencies will change and alter the real return of the investment. For example, suppose that a U.S. investor converts dollars to Mexican pesos to make an investment denominated in pesos that earns a 10 percent nominal return. The investor expects the exchange rate to remain constant; but if the peso unexpectedly depreciates by 10 percent, the entire 10 percent return is wiped out when the pesos are converted back to dollars. Thus, exchange rate risk must be factored into any international investment.

In globalized financial markets, financial market players compare expected rates of return on instruments denominated in various currencies, including their own. To do so, they must convert all returns to an equivalent return in the domestic currency. The nominal rate of return in a domestic currency on an investment that is denominated in a foreign currency is the nominal foreign interest rate plus the expected change in the exchange rate less an adjustment for risk that results from the uncertainty of the future exchange rate. Equation (9-7) depicts such a situation:

(9-7)   *NOMINAL* $I_{US} = I_{FOR} + E$

where I_{US} is the nominal U.S. return on an investment in a foreign instrument that earns the nominal foreign interest rate, I_{FOR}, and E is the expected percentage change in the exchange rate plus an exchange rate risk factor that compensates for the uncertainty of the future exchange rate.

Lenders compare this nominal U.S. return, I_{US}, with the U.S. interest rate and choose the instrument that offers the highest return while borrowers choose to borrow in the market that offers the lowest rate as expressed in their domestic currencies. Because of market adjustments, if the nominal U.S. return is greater than the nominal foreign return plus the exchange rate adjustment, lenders will supply more funds in the U.S. market, and borrowers will borrow more funds in foreign markets. The theory of **interest rate parity** asserts that the adjustments will continue until the U.S. and foreign nominal interest rates are equal except for the expected exchange rate adjustment and an exchange rate risk factor. When interest rates have adjusted so that rates between countries differ only by the expected appreciation or depreciation of the currency, then interest rate parity has been reached and international financial markets are in equilibrium.

Interest Rate Parity
The theory that in equilibrium, interest rates adjust so that after adjustments have been made for expected inflation and exchange rate risk, returns are equalized across countries.

In reality, borrowers and lenders are making decisions based on the expected real return rather than nominal returns. The real interest rate (return) is the nominal return less expected inflation. At times, we may wish to express returns between nations in terms of real interest rates as opposed to nominal rates. To do so for the United States, we must subtract expected U.S. inflation from each nominal rate in Equation (9-7), as in Equation (9-8). In equilibrium, the real U.S. interest rate, R_{US}, will be:

(9-8)
$$R_{US} = I_{US} - P_{US} = I_{FOR} + E - P_{US}$$

where P_{US} is the expected U.S. inflation rate. Likewise, we can express the nominal foreign rate, I_{FOR}, in terms of the real foreign rate, R_{FOR}, plus the expected foreign inflation, P_{FOR}, to arrive at the equilibrium real U.S. interest rate in terms of the foreign real rate and domestic and foreign expected inflation. The results are summarized in Equation (9-9):

(9-9)
$$R_{US} = R_{FOR} + P_{FOR} + E - P_{US}$$

The degree of capital mobility is the ease with which funds can flow in and out of financial instruments denominated in different currencies. We can conclude that with greater capital mobility, the real U.S. and foreign interest rates will tend to be equalized after differences in expected inflation and expected changes in exchange rates and the uncertainty of these changes have been taken into account. As you shall see in Chapter 18, foreign exchange futures, forward, and swap agreements can be used to hedge or reduce interest rate risk. In the next section of this chapter, we look at the often mysterious concept of the balance of payments that keeps track of the financial flows among nations.

Recap   Financial market participants compare expected rates of return on instruments denominated in different currencies. The expected nominal rate of return on a foreign investment is the foreign interest rate plus the change in the exchange rate less an adjustment for risk from the uncertainty of the future exchange rate. The expected real return includes an adjustment factor for expected inflation in both countries. In equilibrium, interest rates adjust so that after adjustments have been made for expected inflation and exchange rate risk, returns are equalized across countries.

Balance of Payments
The record of transactions between the United States and its trading partners in the rest of the world over a particular period of time.

Credit
In the balance of payments, any item that results in a payment by foreigners to Americans.

Merchandise Exports
Foreign purchases of U.S. goods.

Debit
In the balance of payments, any transaction that results in a payment to foreigners by Americans.

Merchandise Imports
U.S. purchases of foreign goods.

Defining the Balance of Payments and Its Influence on the Exchange Rate, the Financial System, and the U.S. Economy

The supply and demand forces that determine the exchange rate are reflected in the **balance of payments.** Simply put, the balance of payments for the United States is the record of transactions between the United States and its trading partners in the rest of the world over a particular period of time, such as a year. It is a record of the international flow of funds for purchases and sales of goods, services, and securities.

The accounting procedure underlying the balance of payments is based on a standard double-entry bookkeeping scheme, such as that used by business firms or households to record receipts and payments. This means that receipts (sources of funds such as income or borrowing) will, by definition, equal payments (uses of funds). In the balance of payments, all transactions that result in payments by foreigners to Americans are recorded as receipts; they are **credit** or plus items. Examples of such transactions include foreign purchases of U.S. goods, called **merchandise exports;** foreign purchases of U.S. securities (in effect, exports of securities); and expenditures by foreign tourists in the United States (in effect, exports of services). All transactions resulting in payments by Americans to foreigners are recorded as payments; they are negative or **debit** items. Examples of such payments include U.S. purchases of foreign goods called **merchandise imports;** U.S. purchases of foreign securities (in effect, imports of securities); and expenditures by U.S. residents traveling abroad.

A Hypothetical and Simplified Balance of Payments for the U.S. Economy in the Year 2005 (in Billions of Dollars)

Account	Component	Receipts from Foreigners	Payments to Foreigners	Balance
		Use of $ by foreigners	Source of $ by foreigners	
Current	(2) Merchandise exports	+$400		(4) Balance of trade: (2) + (3) = −$200
	(3) Merchandise imports		−600	
	(5) Net exports of services	+$50		(6) Balance of goods and services: (4) + (5) = −$150 = net exports
	(7) Net unilateral transfers		−$30	(1) Balance on current account: (6) + (7) = −$180
Capital	(9) Capital inflows	+$280		(8) Balance on capital account: (9) + (10) = $180
	(10) Capital outflows		−$100	
Balance of Payments		Total uses +$730	Total sources −$730	(1) + (8) = 0

Over the years, government statisticians and analysts have found it useful to divide the balance of payments into several parts by grouping various types of receipts and payments into particular accounts. These accounts are discussed below and shown in Exhibit 9-6, which provides a simplified and hypothetical balance of payments for the United States. Note that for now we will ignore government transactions in foreign currencies—the so-called Official Reserve Account of the balance of payments. This complication will be taken up when we discuss international policy in Chapters 19 and 26. The balance of payments may seem imposing at first, but as we take a closer look at the various accounts, you will find that it is not so formidable.

The Current Account

The **current account** brings together transactions that involve currently produced goods and services. It is composed of exports and imports of goods and services and **net transfer payments** (also called *net unilateral transfers*). The difference between merchandise exports and imports, often referred to in news reports as the **trade balance,** is taken by many observers to be an important indicator of a country's ability to compete internationally in the production and sale of goods. When merchandise imports are greater than exports, as they have been in the United States for some years, a country has a **trade deficit,** suggesting some deterioration in international competitiveness. It could just as well suggest an improvement in the country's ability to attract foreign investment. The hypothetical figure in Exhibit 9-6 shows a U.S. trade deficit—indicated by (4) in the exhibit—of $200 billion. In contrast, if exports are greater than imports, as has been the case in Japan for some time, a country has a **trade surplus,** suggesting that it is competing successfully in the world economy or that its citizens are investing heavily abroad.

When net exports of services (5) involving tourism, transportation, insurance, and financial services are added to the trade balance (4), we get the **balance of goods and services** (6), which is often referred to as *net exports*. If net exports are negative, as they have been in the United States throughout the 1980s, 1990s, and 2000s, then we are buying more goods and services from foreigners than they are buying from the United States. Relatively speak-

Current Account
Transactions that involve currently produced goods and services, including the balance of goods and services.

Net Transfer Payments
In the current account, the difference between transfer payments received from and transfer payments made to foreigners.

Trade Balance
The difference between merchandise exports and imports.

Trade Deficit
Status when merchandise imports are greater than exports.

Trade Surplus
Status when merchandise exports are greater than imports.

Balance of Goods and Services
Net exports of services plus the trade balance.

ing, the result is that GDP and, thus, production and employment in the United States are lower than they would have been if net exports had been less negative, ceteris paribus.[7]

Net transfer payments are the difference between transfers received from foreigners and transfers made to foreigners, including payments such as U.S. government aid to foreigners, aid from foreign governments to the United States, and private charitable relief. Adding net unilateral transfers (7) to the balance of goods and services, or net exports (6), yields the **balance on current account** (1), which in our example is in deficit by $180 billion.

The Capital Account

The **capital account** summarizes the financial flow of funds and securities between the United States and the rest of the world. The globalization of the U.S. financial system—a fancy term to describe the tremendous growth of international lending and borrowing—is reflected in a surge of U.S. investment in international stocks, bonds, and mutual funds in the recent decades as well as the increased borrowing abroad by U.S. entities to fund the U.S. current account deficit.

Purchases of U.S. financial securities by foreigners and, more generally, borrowing from foreign sources by U.S. firms and residents result in **capital inflows** into the United States; these are receipt (credit or plus) items in the capital account, as shown in Exhibit 9-6. Purchases of foreign financial securities by U.S. residents and borrowing by foreigners from U.S. banks and other sources result in **capital outflows** from the United States; these are payment (debit or negative) items in the capital account. In our hypothetical example in Exhibit 9-6, the balance on capital account (8), which is equal to the difference between capital inflows and capital outflows, is in surplus by $180 billion—and the United States is experiencing a **net capital inflow.**

Recap The balance of payments for the United States is the record of transactions between the United States and its trading partners in the rest of the world over a particular time period. The balance of payments consists of the current account and the capital account. The current account brings together transactions involving currently produced goods and services. It includes the balance of goods and services and unilateral transfers. The capital account measures the flow of funds and securities between the United States and the rest of the world.

So much for the components of the balance of payments. What do they have to do with the exchange rate and U.S. markets? Believe it or not, the various tools of analysis necessary to answer this question have already been developed. All we need to do is to bring them together.

The Balance of Payments and the Exchange Rate

Take a careful look at the bottom line in Exhibit 9-6. Not surprisingly, it says that the balance of payments balances; the hypothetical $180 billion deficit in the current account (1) is exactly offset by a $180 billion surplus in the capital account (8).[8] Another way of saying the same thing is that the sum of all the items in the Payments by foreigners column is exactly equal to the sum of all items in the Receipts by foreigners column.

To see why this equality is not just the result of bookkeeping gimmickry and why it relates directly to the determination of the exchange rate and the role it plays in our economy, note that all items in the Receipts column represent foreign demands for U.S. goods, services, and securities—the very items that determine the demand for dollars in the foreign

The Causes and Consequences of Dollar Exchange Rate Movements since 1980

The internationalization or globalization of the U.S. economy became apparent to all during the first half of the 1980s. During 1979 and 1980, the international value of the dollar reached a record low. As can be seen in Exhibit 9-1, by early 1985, the dollar had appreciated by more than 60 percent from its low.

What caused this appreciation? Most experts agree that it was a combination of several factors. First, in late 1979 and early 1980, the Fed embarked on a program of monetary restraint to lower the high inflation rate in the United States. This had the effect of raising interest rates in the United States—in particular, real interest rates—relative to real interest rates in the rest of the world. Second, in 1981, Congress enacted a large tax cut. The tax cut, along with the failure to cut spending, led to a larger government deficit, which also tended to raise real interest rates in the United States.

The rise in real U.S. interest rates induced by the monetary and fiscal policy actions, in turn, increased foreign demand for U.S. securities and, thus, the demand for dollars, while reducing U.S. demand for foreign securities and, thus, the supply of dollars in the foreign exchange market. As a result, the rise in U.S. real interest rates relative to real rates in the rest of the world helped produce a substantial appreciation of the dollar.

What were the consequences of the dollar's appreciation? Simply put, the rise in the international value of the dollar had a dramatic effect on the U.S. economy. As one would predict, based on the discussion in this chapter, the appreciation tended to raise the prices of U.S. goods in foreign markets, discouraging exports, and tended to lower the prices of foreign goods in the United States, encouraging imports. The result was a substantial increase in the current account deficit. By 1985, the United States was buying $150 billion more goods and services from abroad than it was selling abroad. Naturally, this deterioration in U.S. international competitiveness reduced employment and output in the United States relative to what they would have been. [Actually, employment and output initially decreased, but by 1985 both were on the rise. In 1985, the current account deficit was rising, the budget deficit was rising, GDP was rising, and employment was rising!] The lower import prices encouraged by the appreciation also tended to dampen the inflation rate in the United States.

But the story does not end there! Beginning in early 1985, U.S. policy makers in coordination with major U.S. trading partners agreed to a concerted effort to lower the value of the dollar. Central banks would supply dollars and demand their own currencies. The pressure to intervene came from the realization that the U.S. economy was severely uncompetitive. The "overvalued" dollar was causing a record trade deficit, and U.S. jobs were being lost in domestic exporting industries and industries that suffered from competition from imports. The value of the dollar did fall consistently in the late 1980s due both to central bank intervention and to falling U.S. interest rates that reduced the demand for U.S. securities. The trade deficit also fell, but not as fast or as far as economists had expected, given the depreciation of the dollar. By the early 1990s, the dollar was about 50 percent lower than in 1985, but the trade deficit, although reduced, still persisted. In the short run, the percentage decrease in the demand for foreign products was less than the percentage decrease in the exchange rate, although this condition was not expected to persist in the long run.

In the early 1990s, the need to reduce the government budget deficit led to contractionary fiscal policy. At the same time, the Fed pursued a relatively easy monetary policy due to the weak economy and reduced fears of inflation. These policies produced lower interest rates and depreciation of the dollar. In mid-1993, despite these circumstances, the trade deficit began to widen. No doubt this was due to the mild recovery of the U.S. economy and the faltering of many foreign economies.

The demand for imports increased in the recovering domestic economy while the demand for exports decreased in the stumbling foreign economies. With U.S. interest rates at low levels relative to those of the rest of the world, particularly a united Germany, some economists wondered how far and for how long the dollar would fall.

By mid-1995, the dollar was again on the rise as U.S. interest rates had risen above foreign rates due to the strength of the U.S. economy and tightening actions taken by the Fed. The relatively higher U.S. interest rates led to increasing capital inflows. Continued strengthening of the U.S. economy raised expectations that the Fed would continue to take actions that would lead to increases in interest rates. Uncertainty abroad and the exceptionally strong performance of the U.S. economy led to further strengthening of the dollar.

During late 1997 and early 1998, the financial crisis in Asian economies caused the ongoing appreciation to escalate. A "flight to quality" in international financial markets triggered by the crisis in Asia often meant a flight into dollars and dollar-denominated financial instruments. Finally, in late fall 1998, the overvalued dollar did plummet as the Fed on two occasions took action that lowered interest rates.

By mid-1999, the dollar was again on the rise as an overheating U.S. economy continued to demonstrate incredible resilience. By late 2000, the dollar was stronger than it had been since 1986. The trade deficit was also very high, buoyed by a booming U.S. economy. As the economy began to slow in 2001, the Fed orchestrated numerous cuts in the interest rate, and the Bush administration had a significant tax cut passed by Congress. Ceteris paribus, the hope was that falling interest rates and a tax decrease would work together to offset the strong recessionary tendencies the economy was experiencing. The U.S. economy was experiencing expansionary monetary policy, which led to falling interest rates. The tax cut combined with increased government spending to fight a war in Iraq caused the budget surplus to reach a record deficit. Despite some wavering in mid-2001, the dollar ended the year about 5 percent higher than at the start. In early 2002, the dollar began to fall as the Fed suggested that U.S. interest rates would remain at 40-year lows for a considerable period of time. By early 2004, the dollar had fallen over 30 percent.

At the same time, the weaker dollar caused imports to be more expensive and should lead to a reduced trade deficit.[a] The low interest rates have indeed contributed to the declining dollar. To the extent that they will reduce the trade deficit in the mid-2000s remains to be seen.

For a discussion of U.S. foreign exchange intervention, see the New York Fed site at http://www.newyorkfed.org/aboutthefed/fedpoint/fed44.html.

For current information on international transactions, visit the Bureau of Economic Analysis at http://www.bea.doc.gov/bea/di/home/directinv.htm.

exchange market. Similarly, all items in the Payments column represent U.S. demands for foreign goods, services, and securities—the very items that determine the supply of dollars in the foreign exchange market. Assuming that the exchange rate is flexible and free to move in response to any change in demand or supply, the exchange rate will move to that rate where the quantity of dollars demanded/month is equal to the quantity of dollars supplied/month. Put in terms of Exhibit 9-6, the equilibrium exchange rate will change until the sum of all items in the Receipts column, which reflects the quantity of dollars demanded/month, is equal to the sum of all items in the Payments column, which reflects the quantity of dollars supplied/month. While the uses of funds are always equal to the sources (for every source, there is a use), the intended uses and sources may differ significantly, and these differences in plans and intentions move the exchange rate. While examining the factors determining exchange rates, you learned that a fall in U.S. interest rates relative to foreign rates would tend to decrease the foreign demand for U.S. securities and, thus, the demand for dollars. You also learned that a fall in U.S. rates relative to foreign rates would tend to increase the U.S. demand for foreign securities and, thus, the supply of dollars. In balance of payments terminology, the relatively lower U.S. interest rates would cause increased capital outflows and decreased capital inflows. The fall in the demand for dollars and the increase in the supply of dollars, in turn, would lead to a depreciation of the dollar.

If capital outflows rise and capital inflows fall, the capital account surplus in Exhibit 9-6 will fall. If nothing happens to the current account, the balance of payments will no longer balance. Obviously, something else must change. What happens is this: As the exchange rate depreciates, a number of adjustments in foreign demands and U.S. demands ensue. Among the most important is a decrease in the current account deficit, reflecting, in large part, a decrease in the trade deficit. To be more specific, the depreciation of the dollar will tend to decrease the yen (foreign) price of U.S. goods abroad, thus increasing U.S. exports. The depreciation will also tend to raise the dollar price of foreign goods in the United States, thus decreasing U.S. imports and the trade deficit. From a purely domestic perspective, the fall in U.S. interest rates pulls foreign funds from the U.S. financial system, leads to a depreciation of the dollar, and tends to increase foreign demand for U.S. output and, thus, increase U.S. employment relative to what it otherwise would have been.

For detailed information on the balance of payments, go to **http://www.new yorkfed.org/aboutthefed/fedpoint/fed40.html**.

Recap   The exchange rate adjusts until the quantity demanded of dollars/month is just equal to the quantity supplied/month in international financial markets. if the intended sources and uses of dollars differ, changes in the exchange rate will bring them into equality. We have now completed our four chapter discussion of financial prices. In Part III, we look at the major financial institutions in our economy.

Summary of Major Points

1. The exchange rate is the number of units of foreign money (currency) that can be acquired with one unit of domestic money. If the exchange rate rises, the dollar is said to have appreciated relative to other currencies. If the exchange rate falls, the dollar has depreciated.

2. The dollar price of foreign goods is equal to the foreign price of foreign goods divided by the exchange rate. The foreign price of U.S. goods is equal to the dollar price of U.S. goods multiplied by the exchange rate. Accordingly, a depreciation will lower the price of U.S. goods in foreign markets and raise the price of foreign goods in the United States. An appreciation will raise the price of U.S. goods in foreign markets and lower the price of foreign goods in the United States.

3. The exchange rate is a price—the price of one national currency in terms of another—and is determined by

supply and demand. The demand for dollars in the foreign exchange market reflects the demand by foreign residents for U.S. goods, services, and financial claims. The supply of dollars comes from the demand by U.S. residents for foreign goods, services, and financial claims.

4. The quantity demanded of dollars/month is inversely related to the exchange rate. The demand for dollars is positively related to changes in foreign income, to changes in the foreign price of foreign goods relative to the foreign price of U.S. goods, and to changes in U.S. interest rates relative to foreign interest rates. The quantity supplied of dollars/month is positively related to the exchange rate. The supply of dollars is positively related to changes in U.S. income, to changes in the dollar price of U.S. goods relative to the dollar price of foreign goods, and to changes in foreign interest rates relative to U.S. interest rates.

5. A depreciation of the dollar can result from one or more of the following: a fall in U.S. interest rates relative to foreign interest rates, a rise in U.S. income, a fall in foreign income, and/or more inflation in the United States than abroad. An appreciation of the dollar can result from one or more of the following: a rise in U.S. interest rates relative to foreign interest rates, a fall in U.S. income, a rise in foreign income, and/or less inflation in the United States than abroad.

6. If the exchange rate is flexible and thus free to move in response to any change in the demand for or supply of dollars, the exchange rate will move to that rate where the quantity of dollars demanded/month is equal to the quantity of dollars supplied/month. According to the purchasing power parity theory, exchange rates adjust in the long run so that the relative purchasing power of various currencies is equalized. The purchasing power parity theory is based on the assumption that goods are identical and tradable, and that there are no transportation costs or barriers to trade. Also, the theory ignores changes in tastes, productivity, economic growth, market structures, and technologies across countries. Thus there are many other factors that affect exchange rates. Thus, although there is a tendency for countries with relatively high inflation rates to experience currency depreciation, the correlation is far from perfect as the purchasing power parity theory implies.

7. The nominal rate of return on a foreign investment is the foreign interest rate plus the expected change in the exchange rate less an adjustment for risk from the uncertainty of the future exchange rate. The expected real return includes an adjustment factor for expected inflation in both countries. In equilibrium, when interest rate parity is achieved, interest rates adjust so that after adjustments have been made for expected inflation and exchange rate risk, returns are equalized across countries.

8. The balance of payments is the record of transactions between the United States and its trading partners in the rest of the world over a particular period of time. It keeps track of the flow of funds for the purchases of goods, services, and securities. Ignoring official government transactions, it is composed of the current account and the capital account. If something, such as a policy-induced rise in U.S. interest rates relative to foreign interest rates, results in capital inflows and a larger capital account surplus, it will also result in an appreciation of the dollar. In turn, the appreciation of the dollar will tend, among other adjustments, to reduce U.S. exports and to increase U.S. imports. These adjustments will tend to produce a larger current account deficit, which will rebalance the balance of payments.

Key Terms

Review Questions

1. Define *exchange rate, foreign currency,* and *foreign exchange market.*
2. Distinguish between a change in the quantity demanded of foreign exchange and a change in demand for foreign exchange. Do the same for the quantity supplied and the supply of foreign exchange.
3. Explain the relationship between the supply of dollars in the foreign exchange market and debit items in the balance of payments. Do the same for the demand for dollars in the foreign exchange market and credit items in the balance of payments.
4. Defend the following statement: The balance of payments always balances.
5. Explain how the trade balance, the balance of goods and services, and the balance of payments differ.
6. How is a surplus in the current account related to a deficit in the capital account? How is a deficit in the current account related to a surplus in the capital account?

7. If interest rates in the United States were lower than rates in the rest of the world, would the United States be more likely to be experiencing a net capital inflow or a net capital outflow? Ceteris paribus, would the current account be in surplus or deficit?
8. If the demand for U.S. exports falls, what will happen to the exchange rate? What will happen to the trade balance and the balance of goods and services?
9. What would happen to the exchange rate if foreigners decided to sell U.S. securities?
10. What is the difference between the trade balance and the current account balance?
11. What are the assumptions of the purchasing power parity theory? What are the reasons that the theory may not offer a complete explanation of exchange rate differentials?
12. What is interest rate parity?

Analytical Questions

Questions marked with an icon are objective in nature. They can be completed with a short answer or number.

13. If a hotel room in downtown Tokyo costs 20,000 yen per night and the yen/dollar exchange rate is 100, what is the dollar price of the hotel room? If the yen/dollar exchange rate increases to 150, what happens to the dollar price of the hotel room?
14. If a hotel room in downtown Los Angeles costs $100 per night and the yen/dollar exchange rate is 100, what is the yen price of the hotel room? If the yen/dollar exchange rate increases to 150, what happens to the yen price of the hotel room?
15. Assume that the dollar appreciates by 10 percent in terms of the Mexican peso. Explain what happens to the dollar price of tequila from Mexico after the appreciation. What happens if the dollar depreciates by 10 percent?
16. If a bottle of rare French wine sells for 40 euros in Paris and the exchange rate is 0.9 euros, how much will the bottle of wine sell for in New York City? (Ignore transportation costs, etc.)
17. Use graphs to show what happens to the demand for and supply of dollars in the foreign exchange market in the event of each of the following:

a. Domestic income rises.
b. Foreign income rises.
c. Domestic inflation rises relative to foreign inflation.
d. Domestic interest rates rise relative to foreign interest rates.
18. Use graphs to demonstrate that when both domestic and foreign incomes are rising, we cannot be sure of the direction of exchange rates.
19. If merchandise exports are $600 and merchandise imports are $500, what is the trade balance?
20. If there is a surplus of $100 in the capital account, no unilateral transfers, and a $50 deficit in the net exports of services, what is the trade balance?
21. If $1 = 150 yen and 1 yen = 75 British pounds, what is the pound/dollar exchange rate? What is the dollar/pound exchange rate?
22. If the yen/dollar exchange rate is 125, how much will 25,000 yen cost? If the exchange rate appreciates to 150, how much will the 25,000 yen cost?
23. If the yen/dollar exchange rate is 125, how many yen will $15,000 be worth? If the exchange rate depreciates to 100, how many yen will $15,000 be worth?

24. Explain how, according to the purchasing power parity theory, exchange rates will adjust if inflation in the United States is 3 percent and inflation in Japan is 1 percent.

25. If nominal interest rates fall by 2 percent in the United States, ceteris paribus, explain what will happen to exchange rates to achieve interest rate parity.

Internet Exercises

1. Go to **http://www.federalreserve.gov/releases/** for information on current exchange rates. Examine both the United Kingdom pound/dollar exchange rate and the China, P.R. yuan/dollar exchange rate. Access the historical data to determine whether the dollar has appreciated or depreciated since January 1995.

2. Monthly trade statistics may be accessed at the following site: **http://www.census. gov/foreign-trade/www/**. What is the current trade balance?

Suggested Readings

Although we ignored (for the time being) government transactions in foreign currencies, the *Federal Reserve Bulletin* includes a feature entitled "Treasury and Federal Reserve Foreign Exchange Operations" on a quarterly basis. This article provides an in-depth discussion of the reasons for recent movements in exchange rates. It is also available on the Internet at the Fed's site, **http://www.federalreserve.gov**.

For an interesting discussion about the relationship between the government and trade deficits, see the remarks by Governor Edward M. Gramlich, "Budget and Trade Deficits: Linked, Both Worrisome in the Long Run, but not Twins" at the Los Angeles Chapter of the National Association for Business Economics Luncheon, Los Angeles, California March 31, 2004. The remarks are available on the Internet at **http://www. federalreserve.gov/boarddocs/speeches/2004/200 40225/default.htm**

An article about the effects of a weak dollar on a college student traveling in Italy in 2004 is "Strategies for Coping with the Weak Dollar" by Beth J. Harpaz, the Associated Press, March 25, 2004. It is available on the Internet at **http:// www.msnbc.msn.com/id/4532426/**.

Are you interested in sampling Big Macs around the world? (We understand that local customs and tastes dictate the spices.) Refer to *The Economist*, which since 1986 has been tracing the dollar price of Big Macs around the world, as discussed in the body of the chapter. For the 2004 report, see "Big MacCurrencies," *The Economist* (January 17, 2004). Do you like Starbucks coffee? If so, see "Burgers or Beans?" page 67 of the same issue of *The Economist*, which looks at a Starbucks index for the dollar price of a Starbucks tall latte in some of the 32 countries in which it is now sold. Information about *The Economist* can be found on the Internet by accessing **http://www.economist.com**.

We also suggest three free publications from the New York Fed. They are *Basics of Foreign Trade and Exchange and Balance of Pay-*

ments (Fedpoints 40) and *All about the Foreign Exchange Market in the United States*. For those of you who prefer comic books, request *The Story of Foreign Trade and Exchange*. All are available by writing the Federal Reserve Bank of New York, Public Information Department, 33 Liberty Street, New York, NY 10045. You may order or browse Fedpoints and other New York Fed publications on the Internet at **http://www.newyorkfed.org/ aboutthefed/fedpoint/fed40.html**.

Another Fed publication available on the Internet is *Strong Dollar Weak Dollar, Foreign Exchange Rates and the U.S. Economy*, Federal Reserve Bank of Chicago. It is available at **http://www.chicagofed.org/publications/strongdollar /strongdollar.pdf**.

For a variety of articles on the international financial crisis of 1997 and 1998, see Clifford Krauss, "Argentine Leader Vows to Retain Currency Peg to Dollar," *New York Times* (September 14, 1998): C7; Peter Fritsch, "Brazil's Rate Boost Seems to Slow Dollar Flight," *The Wall Street Journal* (September 15, 1998): A17; Paul Krugman, "Saving Asia: It's Time to Get Radical," *Fortune* (September 7, 1998): 74–80; and Michael M. Weinstein, "Twisting Controls on Currency and Capital," *New York Times* (September 10, 1998): C11. A more academic and comprehensive article on international financial crises is Robert Z. Aliber, "Capital Flows, Exchange Rates, and the New International Financial Architecture: Six Financial Crises in Search of a Generic Explanation," *Open Economies Review* 11:0, Suppl. 1 (August 2000): 43–61.

For an interesting article on the euro and monetary policy, see David G. Mayes, "The Exchange Rate and Monetary Conditions in the Euro Area," *Review of World Economics* 136:2 (2000): 199–231.

For a look at the implications of the euro, see Robert A. Mundell, *The Euro as a Stabilizer in the International Economic System* (Norwell, MA: Kluwer Academic Press, 2000).

Endnotes

1 Remember our earlier warnings about market jargon? Well, the problem is acute in the international sphere. For example, note that the definition of foreign currency includes foreign coin, paper currency, and checkable deposits; in contrast, our definition of currency in the United States included paper currency and coin only (Chapter 2).

2 Exchange rates can also be expressed from the other direction. For example, if $1 will buy 100 yen, then 100 yen will buy $1 and 1 yen will buy $.01 [1/(100 yen) = $.01].

3 In Chapter 2, we defined the dollar as a unit of account by which exchange values of goods and services could be measured. In this chapter, we are talking about the flow of funds—that is, the supply and demand of dollar-denominated funds—not dollars. So, when we use the term *dollars*, we really mean *dollar-denominated funds*.

4 In Chapters 3 and 6, we saw that the interest rate can be determined by either a stock model (the supply of and demand for money) or a flow model (the supply of and demand for loanable funds/month). Exchange rate determination is an analogous situation in that the exchange rate can be explained using a stock model, dealing with the supply of and demand for foreign exchange at a particular moment, or a flow model, dealing with flows of foreign exchange over a particular time period. In this chapter, we have opted for the flow model, noting that just as with all stock and flow models, each can generally be converted into the other without loss of substance. We hope you recall that over time, flows generate changes in stocks and that by measuring stocks at two points in time, a flow over time can be determined. For simplicity, we arbitrarily picked one month as our time period. The quantity demanded of dollars/month is the amount of dollars that will be demanded at a specific exchange rate.

5 Actually, we are also assuming that the demand for computers, and U.S. products in general, is relatively elastic with regard to the exchange rate—that is, as the exchange rate changes, ceteris paribus, quantity demanded/month changes by a larger percentage than the exchange rate, causing total dollar expenditures to fall when the exchange rate increases and to increase when the exchange rate decreases. This is a reasonable assumption in the long run, although demand for U.S. products may be relatively inelastic in the short run.

6 We are also making the reasonable assumption that, ceteris paribus, the quantity demanded of foreign goods/month by U.S. residents changes by a larger percentage than the percentage change in the exchange rate. Thus, as the exchange rate appreciates, the quantity supplied of dollars/month also increases. And as the exchange rate depreciates, the quantity supplied of dollars/month also decreases. This assumption, which is reasonable in the long run, may not hold in the short run.

7 Don't let the terminology confuse you: *Less negative* refers to a smaller trade deficit of goods and services, meaning either more exports or fewer imports and, hence, ceteris paribus, more U.S. jobs and production in either the domestic exporting industries or those industries competing with imports. If the United States were running a trade surplus of goods and services, the greater the surplus, the greater would be the stimulus to U.S. GDP.

8 Remember that we are ignoring any official government transactions in foreign exchange markets until Chapter 19.

Cracking the Code, page 185

a A correspondent bank is merely a large bank, usually located in an important financial center, which provides the smaller bank with various services.

b The institutional details should be mentioned. First, the exchange rate quotations in the paper are for large, so-called wholesale transactions of $1 million or more among banks, as noted at the top of the table. The "retail" cost of purchasing marks for you or for us would be slightly higher than these quotes.

PART 3

Financial Institutions

Presume not that I am the thing I was.

—William Shakespeare

10

An Introduction to Financial Intermediaries and Risk

Learning Objectives

After reading this chapter, you should know:

The characteristics common to all types of financial intermediaries (FIs)

The services provided by FIs and the types of risks they must manage

The major types of depository institutions and other FIs

The principal assets and liabilities of the various FIs

The characteristics that distinguish one type of FI from another type

Are All Financial Intermediaries More or Less Alike?

It is the last day of the month. Sandi and Dave have both been paid by their employers, and it's now time to pay the family's bills and save something for their upcoming vacation. Sitting at the kitchen table, they write checks on their account at HLT National Bank to Prudential Insurance Company for the premium due on Sandi's life insurance policy, APEI Credit Union for the car loan payment, and the local savings and loan (S&L) association for the mortgage payment. When these and other bills are paid, a check for the surplus funds to be saved is sent to their money market mutual fund account at Merrill Lynch.

In this hypothetical series of transactions, Sandi and Dave dealt with five different financial intermediaries (FIs): a commercial bank, an insurance company, a credit union, an S&L, and a money market mutual fund. Why five instead of one? Can't one provide all of the relevant services? Put another way, how are these intermediaries similar to one another, and how do they differ? These are the questions to be addressed in this chapter. In essence, the chapter will examine the functioning and roles of those institutions that provide the public with a wide range of financial services and play a central role in coordinating and channeling the flow of funds in the economy.

Financial Innovation
The creation of new financial instruments, markets, and institutions in the financial services industry.

As we begin, we should emphasize that **financial innovation**, which is the creation of new financial instruments, markets, and institutions, has often been the key to growth and survival in the financial services industry.[1] This has been true during the past 40 years and is true at the present time. As in many other firms and industries, institutional details in the financial services industry are currently evolving at a rapid pace due to changes in technology and the globalization of finance. In a few years or sooner, Sandi and Dave may be paying their monthly bills as they sit in front of a computer terminal, and many of their payments may be made automatically from their checking account. After all, many households already do just that. Thus, we can provide you only a snapshot of the current state of affairs and point out how and why this snapshot differs from the picture of the financial landscape prevailing in the recent past. This will lay the groundwork for subsequent chapters in which we analyze the forces that have previously produced major changes in the financial system and are likely to remain influential in the future.

Common Characteristics

To the untrained eye, an insurance company and a commercial bank appear to be quite different institutions. However, the trained eye sees more. Both are FIs that link up net borrowers and net lenders and, in the process, provide the public with a wide range of financial services. Recall from Chapter 1 that a *net lender* is a spending unit such as a firm or household for which spending on consumption and investment is less than income. Likewise, a *net borrower* is a spending unit for which spending is greater than income. The linking or channeling function involves the acquisition of financial claims on net borrowers by the FIs and the acquisition of claims on the FIs by the net lender. (You might want to take a quick look at Exhibit 1-1 in Chapter 1.) The net borrowers sell financial claims against themselves, which the intermediaries purchase. The financial claims may be signed loan papers, equities, or securities. In this context, when we say FIs make loans to net borrowers, the FIs are purchasing financial claims, which are the signed loan papers, from the net borrowers. The intermediaries get the funds to lend by selling their own financial claims that the net lenders purchase. The financial claims against the FIs include checking, time, and saving deposits, among others. Even though funds flow ultimately from net lenders to net borrowers, the intermediaries do more than act as a go-between. The net lenders acquire claims against the FIs, which sell their own liabilities; thus, the FIs are in debt to the net lender.[2]

FIs as Firms

FIs are firms. We generally think of, say, manufacturing firms as acquiring inputs, including labor, capital, and natural resources, and using these inputs to produce outputs. In the case of FIs, their inputs, or sources of funds, are found on the liability side of their balance sheets. These funds are used to extend loans and acquire securities. Such financial claims appear on the asset side of the balance sheets and represent the outputs of the FIs. Banks, for example, incur deposit liabilities as a source of funds and use the funds to increase their asset holdings of loans and securities. Insurance companies receive premium payments from policyholders and provide benefits (protection) in return. The funds received are used to acquire assets—mainly loans and securities.

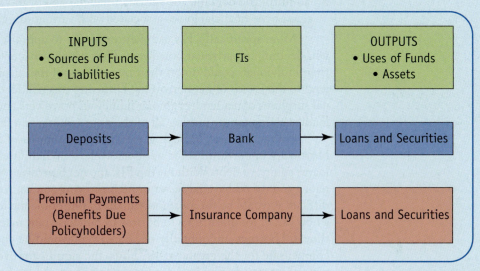

The characteristics common to intermediaries can be identified with the aid of the accompanying A Closer Look above, which conceptualizes the notion that FIs are firms producing services just as nonfinancial firms in the economy produce goods. Thus, we call these firms, collectively, the *financial services industry*. More specifically, in the process of acquiring and providing funds, FIs provide the public with a wide range of financial services. Two questions are pertinent: (1) Why do FIs do this? (2) What types of services are we talking about?

The answer to the first question is straightforward and represents a feature common to FIs and nonfinancial corporations. Intermediaries are by and large profit seeking.[3] In this context, this means that FIs provide financial services because doing so is profitable. By extension, it means that the quantity, quality, and type of financial services offered will expand or contract as the perceived profitability of this activity grows or shrinks.

To illustrate, banks "hire" funds from depositors. The interest a bank pays on its deposits is a cost of doing business, akin to the wages a manufacturing firm pays its workers. The bank then lends out the funds acquired to farmers, consumers, businesses, and governments. The interest earned on the loans represents revenue to the bank, akin to the revenue generated by a manufacturing firm's sales. Leaving some details aside, the difference between the interest earned and the interest paid is a primary determinant of the bank's profitability. If funds can be hired more cheaply by providing a new type of deposit service, FIs have an incentive to act accordingly. Similarly, if a particular type of lending turns out to be less profitable than expected, FIs have an incentive to lend less in this area or to attempt in some way to increase the expected revenue associated with such lending. As we shall see, the link between expected profitability and the specific services provided by FIs is a crucial part of the explanation of why FIs change over time.

With this point, we come to our second question about the types of services FIs provide. In general, FIs provide services to the public for the following purposes:

1. To reduce the risks and costs associated with borrowing, lending, and other financial transactions.

2. To fulfill the demand for various financial assets and services, including protection against the financial losses associated with various exigencies.

More specifically, FIs use their expertise to appraise the risk of default associated with lending to particular borrowers. They usually do a better job of assessing these risks than individuals could do on their own. FIs pool the surpluses of many net lenders and lend to thousands of net borrowers. Diffusing this risk, in effect, spreads out the individual surpluses of net lenders among numerous borrowers and further reduces risk. The net lenders are no longer putting all of their eggs in one or a few baskets.

On the flip side, by buying the financial liabilities of net borrowers, the FIs provide borrowing opportunities for net borrowers. The liabilities may be long- or short-term loans, equity, or debt. Without the FIs, the net borrowers would have to rely on direct finance and would have far fewer or no borrowing sources. If there were no FIs, think how difficult it would be for most individuals to find someone to lend them funds to purchase a new car, or for most firms to borrow to purchase new machinery and equipment. When they did borrow, undoubtedly net borrowers would be charged higher interest rates to compensate for the greater risks. Thus, the significant overall economic function of financial intermediation is to facilitate borrowing and lending that result in the allocation of resources to capital (plant, equipment, and the like) formation and other spending—the investment and spending processes.

In addition, FIs provide a menu of financial claims and depository services tailored to meet the needs of net lenders and, more generally, society at large. The menu includes (1) relatively safe and liquid claims, such as checking, time, and savings deposits at banks and other depository institutions, and (2) **contingent claims** on FIs, such as casualty and life insurance benefits, which offer the public some protection from the often catastrophic financial effects of theft, accidents, natural disasters, and death. Thus, the wide array of menu choices fulfills the demand for various financial assets by the net lenders.

With FIs playing such a vital role in the economy, it should not be surprising that they share another common feature. They are regulated by various levels and agencies of government. Government regulators establish and enforce operating regulations aimed at promoting a smooth-running, efficient financial system and protecting the public from fraud and other abusive practices. The regulators seek to promote competition in the market for financial services while preserving the public's confidence in the safety and soundness of the system.

By their nature, regulations represent an attempt to constrain or restrict an activity that might otherwise occur. In the financial system, regulations take on many forms. Entry into the industry is tightly controlled. For example, someone cannot just open a bank.

Contingent Claims
Claims such as casualty and life insurance benefits that offer the public protection from the often catastrophic financial effects of theft, accidents, natural disasters, and death.

A charter from the federal government or relevant state government is needed to engage in the business of banking. There are also restrictions on the particular types of assets and liabilities that specific FIs can acquire. S&Ls, for example, cannot acquire common stock. In the past, regulations limited the interest rates that FIs could pay to hire certain types of deposits and charge on certain types of loans. Last, although these regulations have been virtually eliminated, regulations have historically restricted the geographical areas in which some FIs can operate. Until the mid-1990s, for example, banks could not establish branches across state lines.

Such regulations, examined in detail in Chapter 14, have had at least three major effects:

1. For quite a while, they tended to reinforce and encourage specialization by FIs in particular financial services. For example, life insurance companies stuck pretty much to providing life insurance, and S&Ls stuck to purchasing mortgages. More directly, the regulations tended to limit competition among different types of FIs.

2. Such specialization helps to explain the different types and mix of assets and liabilities found on FIs' balance sheets.

3. Over time, FIs increasingly saw the benefits of diversifying. In other words, they saw that providing the public with a wider range of financial services could be profitable. Attempts to move in such a direction often involved innovations that got around some existing regulations, particularly restrictions that limited the range of services that FIs could provide and the competition among FIs in general. As you shall see in Chapters 11 and 14, legislation in late 1999 has also allowed commercial banks, securities firms, and insurance companies to affiliate under common ownership. Thus, one firm can offer its customers a complete range of financial services.

These more recent developments, which include the emergence of what have been called *financial supermarkets,* are discussed in this and the next chapters. As we shall see, Sandi and Dave, whom we met at the beginning of the chapter, may be dealing with far fewer than five FIs if they do business with one of these one-stop financial supermarkets that offers an array of financial services.

In addition to these regulatory effects, the 2000s continued the trend of increasing competition for FIs from nonfinancial institutions and from direct finance through the commercial paper market.[4] For example, many nonfinancial corporations such as General Motors, AT&T, Sears, and General Electric, to name only a few, now offer financial services and products such as consumer loans and credit cards. Whereas most firms used to rely on bank loans for the funds they needed to finance inventories and day-to-day expenses, firms of all sizes now have much greater access to borrow through the commercial paper market than in the past.[5]

Recap   FIs possess many common traits. In general, they are regulated, profit-seeking firms that provide the public with a wide range of financial services. These services help to reduce the risks associated with channeling funds from net lenders to net borrowers. The services provided include the appraisal and diversification of risk, the pooling of funds, and the provision of a menu of claims, including contingent claims, tailored to the needs of customers.

Types of Risks Faced by All FIs

To get a clearer picture of how the services that FIs provide reduce the risks associated with borrowing and lending, it is useful to visualize the various FIs as being exposed to and having to deal with several types of risks and uncertainties. FIs face each type of risk in varying degrees, depending on the composition of their assets and liabilities. Before turning to the composition of the balance sheets of the specific intermediaries, we first review the types of risks common to all intermediaries and net lenders and net borrowers in general.

Credit or Default Risk

If a stranger knocked on your door at 1 A.M. and asked to borrow $1,000, you would probably react quite negatively, regardless of the interest rate the stranger was willing to pay. Your reluctance is, of course, tied to the risk or likelihood that the borrower will default and not repay the loan. You don't know the person's financial history and current situation, and you are suspicious about why anyone would show up at this hour making such a request. How would one use a loan of $1,000 at 1 A.M.?

But every time an intermediary makes a loan or purchases a security issued by a borrower, it faces the same risk. Credit or **default risk** is the risk that the borrower will be unwilling or unable to live up to the terms of the liability it has sold. Perhaps the borrower is a firm that uses the funds for expansion, but the business it thought would boom turns out to be a bust because of some unanticipated complication or a general slowdown in the economy. Perhaps the borrower is morally unscrupulous and takes the money and runs. Thus, for whatever reason, when making a loan or buying a financial asset issued by a borrower, the intermediary, whether it be a bank, mutual fund, or insurance company, is exposed to the risk that the borrower will default.

We have already seen that a primary function of the management of an intermediary is to evaluate or assess the credit risk associated with purchasing the financial claims of net borrowers such as firms, individuals, and domestic and foreign governments. To do this, FIs employ experts in risk assessment who generally do a better job of assessing default risks than individuals could do on their own. Cynics say it is quite easy to get a loan as long as you can prove you don't really need the funds. In reality, managing credit risk does not mean denying loans to all borrowers who may default or failing to make any investments that could go sour. Maintaining and enhancing profitability in the financial services industry, as in other industries, entails taking some risks. The future is uncertain. Unforeseen events can turn an otherwise profitable endeavor into a losing and perhaps bankrupt situation. Thus, a "good" credit risk can become a "bad" investment. A fact of economic life is that despite good intentions, decent planning, and a successful track record, some borrowers will default. Conversely, some who have experienced financial difficulties in the past will "turn the corner" and become quite profitable.

Given this background, the task of financial managers is to lend and invest prudently. In general, this means gathering all relevant information on potential borrowers and using this information to avoid exposing the FI to excessive risk. The information should include balance sheets, income statements, credit checks, how funds are to be used, and so on. Recognize that the words *prudent* and *excessive* are somewhat nebulous. One cannot find a precise quantitative definition in the dictionary, so an FI's management team must establish guidelines that quantify the terms. This is what management is all about. Losses will occur. The trick is to cover the losses with profits on other loans and investments.

Interest Rate Risk

Another type of risk that must be managed is the **interest rate risk**. This is the risk that the interest rate will unexpectedly change so that the costs of an FI's liabilities exceed the

---

Default Risk
The risk that a borrower will be unwilling or unable to live up to the terms of the liability it has sold.

Interest Rate Risk
The risk that the interest rate will unexpectedly change so that the costs of an FI's liabilities exceed the earnings on its assets.

earnings on its assets. This risk emanates from the relationship between the interest rate (return) earned on assets and the cost of, or interest rate paid on, liabilities. An FI's profitability is directly related to the spread between these rates. FIs obviously strive for a large positive spread in which the return on assets significantly exceeds the cost of liabilities.

The potential problem is that a positive spread today can turn into a negative spread when the cost of liabilities exceeds the return on assets. For example, whenever intermediaries borrow short-term through passbook savings deposits or commercial paper and make long-term loans or purchase long-term fixed rate financial assets, such as bonds or mortgages, they are exposed to an interest rate risk. This risk has been a chronic problem for some intermediaries, particularly the S&L industry during the 1970s and 1980s when the financial system was deregulated and interest rates fluctuated over a fairly wide range. FIs have responded to this changing environment in a variety of ways, including using adjustable rate loans and financial futures, options, and swaps.[6] The latter three instruments, which will be analyzed in detail in Chapter 18, are now used extensively by FIs to hedge interest rate risk.[7]

In addition, as first discussed in Chapter 6, any intermediary that holds long-term bonds is subject to the risk that the value of these bonds will fall if interest rates rise. The value of other long-term fixed rate assets will also fall when rates rise.

Liquidity Risk

Liquidity Risk
The risk that an FI will be required to make a payment when the intermediary has only long-term assets that cannot be converted to liquid funds quickly without a capital loss.

Liquidity risk is the risk that will occur when an FI will be required to make a payment when the assets that the intermediary has available to make the payment are long-term and cannot be converted to liquid funds quickly without a capital loss. Such a situation could occur when depositors unexpectedly withdraw funds or when an insurance company incurs unexpectedly high claim losses as a result of an earthquake, fire, flood, or hurricane. All intermediaries may experience a sudden unexpected need for funds, but depository institutions are particularly vulnerable to a deposit run that can cause a financial crisis because their reserves are only a fraction of their liabilities and those liabilities are often payable on demand. In Chapter 4, you saw that the Fed stands ready to provide liquidity for depository institutions by acting as a lender of last resort. Intermediaries can reduce their liquidity risk by holding highly liquid assets that can be quickly converted into the funds needed to meet unexpected withdrawals or contingencies. They can also make other arrangements to mitigate this risk such as backup lines of credit to meet unexpected needs.

Exchange Rate Risk

Exchange Rate Risk
The risk that changes in the exchange rate will adversely affect the value of foreign exchange or foreign financial assets.

Last, financial markets have become increasingly international in scope. As a consequence, many large intermediaries as well as other large corporations maintain stocks of foreign exchange that are used in international transactions. In addition, some FIs may hold financial assets (investments) that are denominated in foreign currencies, such as foreign stocks or bonds. In either case, the FI is exposed to a risk that the dollar exchange rate between the two currencies will appreciate, causing the dollar value of the foreign currency or foreign financial assets to fall. Thus, an FI, like any holder of foreign exchange or foreign financial assets, is subject to an **exchange rate risk**—the risk that will occur when changes in the exchange rate will cause the dollar value of foreign currency or foreign financial assets to fall. For example, assume that an intermediary holds 10,000,000 yen or a financial asset valued at 10,000,000 yen. If the exchange rate is $1 = 100 yen, then 10,000,000 yen are worth $100,000. If the dollar exchange rate appreciates to $1 = 200$ yen, then the 10,000,000 yen are worth only \$50,000. In this case, the FI incurs a loss that is proportional to the amount of foreign currency or foreign financial assets that it holds and to the change in the exchange rate. As you shall see in Chapter 18, foreign exchange forward contracts, futures, options, and swaps can be used to mitigate this risk.

Recap All FIs face several risks in varying degrees. Default risk is the risk that the borrower will not pay the financial claim. Interest rate risk is the risk that will occur when changes in the interest rate will turn a profitable spread into a loss. Liquidity risk is the risk that funds will not be available when needed. Exchange rate risk occurs when changes in exchange rates will cause the FI to experience losses in the dollar value of foreign currency or foreign financial assets.

By now you should have a clearer picture of the similarities among FIs. We now turn to the differences among FIs, which are manifested in the composition of their balance sheets. An examination of FI balance sheets will not only highlight the differences among FIs but will also make clear why FIs are exposed to the sundry risks in varying degrees.

A Guide to FIs and Their Balance Sheets

Balance Sheet
An accounting statement that presents the monetary value of an economic unit's assets, liabilities, and net worth on a specific date.

Thus far we have stressed some of the features common to virtually all FIs and the risks that they must manage. In this section, we examine the balance sheets of the major FIs. A **balance sheet** is an accounting statement that presents the monetary value of an economic unit's assets, liabilities, and net worth at a specific point in time, such as the last day of a year. In this case, the economic unit is an FI; the assets are financial assets such as loans and securities while the liabilities are financial liabilities such as deposits and borrowed funds. The fundamental balance sheet identity is that assets equal liabilities plus net worth. If each dollar of assets is matched by a dollar of liabilities, net worth is zero. If the value of liabilities exceeds the value of assets, call the bankruptcy lawyer!

As we examine the balance sheets of the major FIs, it will be convenient and helpful to group FIs according to the nature of their liabilities or the major financial service they provide. Classifying "like with like" will facilitate the development of a lucid "snapshot" and help bring the relationship between past and current snapshots into clearer focus. We shall see that the nature of the liabilities sold by a particular type of FI bears a close relationship to the nature of the assets acquired. More specifically, the maturity, stability, riskiness, and liquidity of an FI's liabilities affect the maturity, liquidity, and safety of the assets it acquires. In other words, the structure of an FI's assets and liabilities affects the degree to which it manages each of the specific risks discussed in the preceding section.

Deposit-Type FIs

Thrifts
Depository institutions known as S&Ls, savings banks, and credit unions.

Depository institutions include commercial banks, S&Ls, savings banks, and credit unions. The savings and loan associations (S&Ls), savings banks, and credit unions are called **thrifts.** As the term *depository institution* implies, a large portion of the liabilities of these FIs are deposits. The depository institutions have issued the deposits in order to obtain funds (inputs) that can be used to make loans and other investments (outputs). Deposit-type FIs are also important in the nation's money supply process because many of their deposit liabilities are checkable deposits.[8] Let's take a closer look at the institutions within this category.

	Total	Percent of Total Assets
Total Assets[a]	**$7,946.5**	**100.0%**
Cash assets[b]	338.9	4.3
Bank credit	6,658.2	83.7
Loan and leases in bank credit[c]	4,731.8	59.5
Commercial and industrial	882.9	11.1
Real estate	2,446.9	30.8
Consumer	673.1	8.5
Security	235.5	3.0
Other	490.0	6.2
Securities in bank credit	1,926.4	24.2
Treasury, agency, and government-sponsored enterprises securities	1,186.3	14.9
Other securities	740.1	9.3
Interbank loans	352.4	4.4
Other assets	670.1	8.4
Total Liabilities	**7,283.4**	**91.7**
Deposits	5,164.6	65.0
Transaction	640.3	8.1
Large time	1,147.7	14.4
Other	3,376.6	42.5
Borrowings	1,583.0	19.9
From U.S. banks	441.1	5.6
Other	1,141.9	14.4
Net due to related foreign offices	30.6	.4
Other liabilities	505.1	6.4
Residual (Assets less liabilities)[d]		**663.5**

a Excludes unearned income, reserves for losses on loans and leases, and reserves for transfer risk. Loans are reported gross of these items.
b Includes vault cash, cash items in process of collection, balances due from depository institutions, and balances due from Federal Reserve Banks.
c Excludes federal funds sold to, reverse repurchase agreements with, and loans made to commercial banks in the United States. These items are included in interbank loans.
d This item in not intended as a measure of equity capital for use in capital adequacy analysis.

SOURCE: Board of Governors of the Federal Reserve, *Federal Reserve Statistical Release H.8*, Septembr 17, 2004. Available on the Internet at **http://www.federalreserve.gov/releases/h8/**.

Commercial Banks

The word *bank* is derived from the Italian word *banca*, which refers to the "table, counter, or place of business of a money changer." Although modern banks bear little physical resemblance to ancient moneychangers, their functions remain quite similar. In modern parlance, **commercial banks** are typically defined as institutions that issue deposit liabilities that are checkable and extend loans to commercial businesses. These two characteristics help to differentiate banks from other FIs; but, of course, banks do many other things too. For example, banks also issue time and savings deposits and offer many other types of loans including mortgages and consumer loans. They also provide electronic funds transfers, debit cards, international trade-related payments, credit cards, leasing, trust services, financial guarantees, and advisory and accounting services. Chapter 11 tells more about bank services. For now, Exhibit 10-1 presents aggregate balance sheet data for all banks in the United States.

Commercial Banks
Depository institutions that issue checkable, time, and savings deposit liabilities and, among other things, make loans to commercial businesses.

A bank's success depends on many factors, but especially important is its ability to attract funds by offering deposit liabilities. Deposits fall into three categories: transactions deposits, savings deposits, and time deposits. **Transactions deposits** can be exchanged for currency and are used in transactions to make payments to others by transferring the deposit claim by writing a check or making an electronic transfer. **Savings deposits** cannot be withdrawn by writing a check but are highly liquid. By custom, banks usually allow withdrawals on demand, although a waiting period could be required. **Time deposits** have a scheduled maturity, and if funds are withdrawn before that date, there is a penalty, usually the forfeiture of some interest that has already been earned. As you first saw in Chapter 2, another kind of account, a money market deposit account, has the characteristics of both transactions and savings deposits.[9] Because deposits are by far the main source of bank funds, banks continually strive to increase deposits. In addition, in recent decades, banks have developed other nondeposit sources of funds such as fed funds, repurchase agreements, and Eurodollar borrowings. A bank's success depends on local and regional factors, such as the population and economic vitality of the bank's service area, and its ability to attract deposits away from competing FIs or from banks in other geographical regions.[10]

Banking statistics for the latest quarter can be viewed at **http://www.fdic.gov/ bank/statistical/index.html**

Turning to the asset side of the balance sheet, a bank must decide how best to use its funds to meet its objectives. One obvious objective is to maximize profits. Stockholders will see to it that the bank's management does not lose sight of this goal. Banking can be a risky business, however, and the management and stockholders will also want to minimize the risks faced in the pursuit of profits. In particular, the bank will try to diversify its portfolio in a way that will ensure a considerable margin of liquidity and safety for the bank. Banks seek safety because they are highly leveraged institutions. That is, their assets are overwhelmingly supported by borrowed funds, which are either deposit or nondeposit liabilities. Banks hold a mix of loans (including business loans, consumer credit, and mortgages), government securities, municipal securities, corporate and foreign bonds, and other assets. Note that in late-2004, banks' holdings of real estate loans (primarily mortgages and home equity lines of credit) were more than two and three quarters times their holdings of commercial and industrial loans. This represents a dramatic change over the past 30 years because business loans were traditionally the lending venue for banks while mortgages were held by S&Ls. With the passage of legislation in 1999, banks may also underwrite and deal in municipal revenue bonds.[11]

In addition to these interest-earning assets, banks also hold reserve (cash) assets to help meet their liquidity and safety objectives. Another reason that banks hold reserve assets is that the Fed forces them to do so. As we first saw in Chapter 4, the Fed sets reserve ratios that require banks to possess reserve assets equal to a certain percentage of checkable deposit liabilities.

Banks' concerns about liquidity are generated in part by the nature of their sources of funds. For example, checkable deposits, which are obviously payable on demand, can and often do fluctuate widely. Nondeposit liabilities have the potential to fluctuate even more. For example, if a bank's solvency is questioned or if another depository institution offers more attractive rates, a bank can quickly lose some nondeposit funds such as fed funds, repurchase agreements, and Eurodollar borrowings that are usually placed for a relatively short time period.[12] When deposits and nondeposit liabilities fall, even the most solvent bank must have a cushion of liquidity to enable it to meet these withdrawals. Such liquidity needs can be satisfied by holding some highly liquid assets, such as Treasury bills and non-interest-bearing cash reserves.[13] If profits were all that mattered, a bank would never hold a Treasury bill yielding, say, 5 percent if another, equally safe asset such as a guaranteed student loan yielding, say, 6 percent were available.[14] However, the liquidity of Treasury bills in effect provides an implicit return to banks in addition to the explicit yield.

Guided by its liquidity, safety, and earnings objectives, a bank must make portfolio decisions regarding the optimal mix of loans, securities, and reserves that it will hold. Simply put, this means the bank must decide on the best way to use its funds.

The *capital base* is the value of the bank's assets less the value of its liabilities. In general, the smaller the capital base, the more vulnerable the bank is to adverse developments. Assume that some of a bank's larger loans go sour. The borrowers default and fail to pay the principal and interest due. These defaults will reduce the cushion provided by the bank's capital base and push the bank toward insolvency and bankruptcy. For example, suppose the bank's capital base amounts to 8.4 percent of assets. Thus, for every $1,000,000 in assets, the bank holds only $84,000 in capital. If loans are 65 percent of assets, then loans amount to $650,000 ($.65 \times \$1,000,000$). The bank's capital will be gone if 12.9 percent of its $650,000 loans go sour because $84,000 is 12.9 percent of $650,000 ($84,000 = $.129 \times \$650,000$). This is an equivalent way of saying that the bank has lost all of its capital.

We hope you can see why regulators are concerned that banks maintain adequate capital.

Savings Associations

Savings and Loan Associations (S&Ls)
Depository institutions established for the purpose of pooling the savings of local residents to finance the construction and purchase of homes; have offered checkable deposits since 1980.

Savings Banks
Depository institutions set up to help finance the construction and purchase of homes; located mainly on the East Coast.

Savings associations include S&L and savings banks. **Savings and loan associations (S&Ls)**, originally known as *building and loan associations*, were founded in the United States in the early 1830s. Their express purpose was to pool the savings of local residents to finance the construction and purchase of homes. **Savings banks** predate the S&Ls by about 20 years and are located mostly on the East Coast of the United States. Sixty percent are in New York and Massachusetts. Like S&Ls, savings banks were founded to encourage thrift and to help finance the construction and purchase of homes.[15]

Although the assets of S&Ls are much larger than those of savings banks, we have lumped S&Ls and savings banks together as savings associations because their assets and liabilities have a similar composition and because the institutions share other commonalities. Their combined balance sheet appears in Exhibit 10-2.

The major sources of funds for savings associations are time, savings, and checkable deposits. In the aggregate, these deposits accounted for about 60 percent of total liabilities on June 30, 2004. As in commercial banks, most deposits are insured for up to $100,000. Savings associations were first allowed to issue negotiable order of withdrawal (NOW) accounts (interest-earning checkable deposits) nationwide in 1980. Checkable deposits make up a growing source of funds for savings associations. They use the funds mainly to acquire mortgage loans, which comprised over 60 percent of total assets held in mid-2004. Treasury, agency, and government-sponsored enterprises securities made up about 15 percent of assets.

Although they still specialized in mortgage lending, savings associations diversified somewhat during the 1980s into other forms of lending that had previously been prohibited by regulations. Other regulatory changes allowed the institutions to offer time deposits with rates that went up and down with rates on money market instruments, such as Treasury bills.

Prior to the 1980s, savings associations were not only prohibited from offering checkable deposits but also not allowed to pay rates on time and savings deposits that exceed a ceiling rate or cap set by regulators. In this earlier environment, small savings deposits were the major source of funds for savings associations. Small savers found

10-2

Financial Assets and Liabilities of Savings Associations, June 30, 2004 (in Billions of Dollars)

	Total[a]	Percent of Total Assets[a]
Financial assets	**$1,597.8**	**100.0%**
Reserves at the Fed	6.3	.4
Checkable deposits and currency	28.2	1.8
Time and savings deposits	3.2	.2
Fed funds and repurchase agreements	26.3	1.6
Treasury, agency, and government-sponsored enterprises securities	232.1	14.5
Municipal securities	6.5	.4
Corporate and foreign bonds	59.9	3.7
Mortgages	966.5	60.5
Consumer credit	88.4	5.5
Corporate equities	27.9	1.7
Loans and advances	55.5	3.5
Miscellaneous	97.0	6.0
Liabilities	**$1,550.9**	**97.0%**
Deposits	955.9	59.8
Checkable	459.3	28.7
Small time and savings	205.6	12.9
Large time	290.8	18.2
Repurchase agreements	71.2	4.5
Corporate bonds	5.0	.3
Loans and advances	288.5	18.7
Miscellaneous	214.2	13.4
Net worth (capital)	**$46.9[b]**	

a Details may not sum to totals because of rounding.
b This item is not proposed as a measure of capital for use in capital adequacy analysis.

SOURCE: *Flow of Funds Accounts, Z1*, Second Quarter 2004, Board of Governor of the Federal Reserve System (September 16, 2004): 73. Available on the Internet at **http://www.federalreserve.gov/releases/Z1/**.

passbook savings accounts attractive relative to the alternatives then available to them. The accounts were liquid, safe, insured stores of value with fixed interest rates. In the new environment, savings associations have more flexibility and now offer the public more diverse types of liabilities. As a result, there is more competition among banks, S&Ls, and savings banks to attract checkable and flexible rate time deposits.

During the 1980s, the S&L industry experienced multiple strains (that came to be known as the *savings and loan crisis* or *debacle*). More than 500 institutions became insolvent and were seized by the regulators during the late 1980s at the taxpayers' expense.[16] The **Financial Institutions Reform, Recovery, and Enforcement Act (FIRREA) of 1989** attempted to resolve the crisis by creating a new federal regulatory structure, limiting the assets that S&Ls can acquire and requiring S&Ls to maintain adequate capital. The final cost to the taxpayers for the bailout is approximately $124 billion, which is much less than initial estimates.

Although heavily committed to the mortgage market, savings banks were somewhat more diversified than were the S&Ls during the 1980s. They held a substantial quantity of federal, municipal, and corporate securities. This diversification, plus higher reserve ratios, allowed the savings banks to avoid some of the strains experienced by the S&Ls.

Financial Institutions Reform, Recovery, and Enforcement Act (FIRREA) of 1989
An act that attempted to resolve the S&L crisis by creating a new regulatory structure, limiting the assets S&Ls can acquire, and requiring S&Ls to maintain adequate capital.

	Total[a]	Percent of Total Assets[a]
Financial assets	**$643.0**	**100.0%**
Checkable deposits and currency	39.8	6.2
Time and savings deposits	28.7	4.5
Fed funds and repurchase agreements	2.6	.4
Treasury, agency and government-sponsored enterprises securities	131.5	20.5
Mortgages	196.0	30.5
Consumer credit	212.9	33.1
Miscellaneous	31.4	4.9
Liabilities	**$585.7**	**91.1%**
Shares/deposits	566.5	88.1
Checkable	70.4	10.9
Small time and savings	439.6	68.4
Large Time	56.5	8.8
Miscellaneous	19.2	3.0
Net worth (capital)	**$57.3[b]**	

a Details may not sum to totals because of rounding.
b This item is not proposed as a measure of capital for use in capital adequacy analysis.

SOURCE: *Flow of Funds Accounts, Z1*, Second Quarter 2004, Board of Governor of the Federal Reserve System (September 16, 2004): 74. Available on the Internet at **http://www.federalreserve.gov/releases/Z1/**.

The changes in the structure of the assets and liabilities of savings associations over time suggest that FIs' areas of specialization are increasingly overlapping. Furthermore, recent legislation now allows banks and savings associations to merge. Reflecting this trend, the word *bank* is often used generically by the press and the public to refer to commercial banks, S&Ls, and savings banks.

Credit Unions

Credit Unions

Depository institutions that are cooperative, nonprofit, tax-exempt associations operated for the benefit of members who share a common bond.

Credit unions cater almost exclusively to small savers and borrowers. They are cooperative, nonprofit, tax-exempt associations operated solely for the benefit of members. By law members must share "a common bond" such as through an employer, a church, or a labor union. Not just anybody can join—deposit in or borrow from—a particular credit union. Although there are about 20,000 credit unions, most are small in size; 75 percent have total assets of $5 million or less. As in other depository institutions, deposits may be insured for up to $100,000. Exhibit 10-3 lists the major assets and liabilities of credit unions.

Credit unions get most of their funds from members' savings accounts. In addition, as with S&Ls, regulatory changes first permitted credit unions to offer checkable deposits in 1980. Interest-earning checking accounts at credit unions are called *share drafts*, and as Exhibit 10-3 shows, they are now a significant liability for credit unions. As of June 30, 2004, about 33 percent of the assets held by credit unions were in the form of consumer loans to members while about 30 percent were mortgages. Just over 20 percent of the assets held were Treasury, agency, and government-sponsored enterprises securities. The remaining assets were deposits at other FIs, fed funds, repurchase agreements, and miscellaneous items. Credit unions, which are exempt from most taxes, generally do not hold municipal securities. Municipals pay a lower rate of interest because their interest is exempt from federal taxation.

Although these proportions have been remarkably stable over time, the total funds acquired and loaned by credit unions have grown rapidly over the years. In 1970, for example, their assets totaled only $18 billion. The comparable mid-2004 figure was $643 billion. Credit union assets increased roughly thirty-fivefold while prices a little more than fivefold increase! Being nonprofit institutions, credit unions have often offered depositors slightly higher rates and loan applicants slightly lower rates than have competing FIs. This advantage, along with the convenient locations of many credit unions (close proximity to businesses or the company cafeteria, for example), helps to explain their growth.

Recap   The major sources of funds for commercial banks are checkable, savings, and time deposits plus nondeposit liabilities. Banks' major uses of funds are loans, government securities, and reserves. Because of legislation in 1999, banks have also been authorized to underwrite and deal in municipal revenue bonds. The major sources of funds for S&Ls are time, savings, and checkable deposits. The major use of funds is to make mortgage loans. Credit unions are tax-exempt and small in size but numerous. Their main sources of funds are share drafts and small savings accounts. They primarily make small personal and mortgage loans to their members and invest in government securities.

Contractual-Type FIs

As the name suggests, contractual-type FIs have liabilities that are defined by contract. In general, these contracts call for regular payments to be made to these FIs in exchange for future payments under specified conditions. Hence, as mentioned earlier, these claims are often referred to as *contingent claims*. More specifically, life and property and casualty insurance companies require premium payments in exchange for insurance coverage. Public and private pension funds require regular contributions, usually with each paycheck, in exchange for retirement benefits.

Life insurance companies offer the public protection against the financial costs, losses, and reductions in income associated with death, disability, old age, and various other health problems. Based on the principle of risk sharing, the public makes payments, generally called *premiums,* in exchange for this protection, and the companies lend out the funds collected to other households, businesses, and governments. The companies use the interest and dividend income received from the loans and the stocks and bonds, along with the premiums, to pay benefits to policyholders as they come due. The influx of premium payments is relatively steady and predictable, and statisticians (actuaries) can predict fairly well the proportion of policyholders likely to become disabled, die, or become ill in a given year, so life insurance companies have a reasonably predictable stream of benefit payments to policyholders distributed over time. This allows these institutions to use a fairly large portion of their funds to acquire longer-term assets or financial investments. Longer-term instruments generally provide higher yields than shorter-term assets but are not as liquid. Given the nature of the companies' liabilities, holding a large portion of liquid assets is not as essential for them as it is for banks, for example.

Exhibit 10-4 shows that on June 30, 2004, about 43 percent of life insurance companies' assets were corporate and foreign bonds, about 25 percent were equities, about 7 percent were mortgages, about 11 percent were Treasury, agency, and government-

Life Insurance Companies
Intermediaries that offer protection against the financial costs associated with events such as death and disability in exchange for premiums.

	Total[a]	Percent of Total Assets[a]
Financial assets	**$3,969.8**	**100.0%**
Checkable deposits, currency, and money market fund shares	189.6	4.8
Corporate and foreign bonds	1,701.2	42.9
Corporate equities	975.3	24.6
Treasury, agency, and government-sponsored enterprises securities	439.9	11.1
Mortgages	269.3	6.8
Policy loans	104.7	2.6
Mutual fund shares	95.0	2.4
Open market paper	57.2	1.4
Miscellaneous	110.2	2.8
Liabilities	**$3,724.1**	**96.3%**
Life insurance reserves	1,013.3	25.5
Pension fund reserves	1,800.9	45.4
Miscellaneous	909.9	22.9
Net worth (capital)	**245.7**	

a Details may not sum to totals because of rounding.

SOURCE: *Flow of Funds Accounts, Z1,* Second Quarter 2004, Board of Governor of the Federal Reserve System (September 16, 2004): 75. Available on the Internet at **http://www.federalreserve.gov/releases/Z1/**.

sponsored enterprise securities, and the remainder were miscellaneous items. The liabilities are the policy benefits (reserves) that are due and will be paid to policyholders in the future.

Pension funds are tax-exempt institutions set up to provide participants with retirement income that will supplement other sources of income, such as social security benefits. Some pension plans are run by private corporations, and others are associated with governmental units, including federal, state, and local governments. Like life insurance companies, pension funds have little need for a large amount of liquid assets. The number of people likely to retire each year is quite predictable. As a result, private pension funds and those associated with governments place 60 percent of their funds—acquired through contributions by employees and employers—into corporate equities, Treasury, agency, and government-sponsored enterprises securities, and corporate and foreign bonds. As Exhibit 10-5 shows, on June 30, 2004, of the approximate $7,341.4 billion of assets held by these funds, $3002.5 billion were in corporate equities, $671.3 billion were in Treasury, agency, and government-sponsored enterprises securities; and $730.5 billion were in corporate and foreign bonds. In fact, pension funds are the largest single class of investors in equities![17] The liabilities are the policy benefits that will be paid out to policyholders in the future.

In contrast to life insurance companies, which provide financial protection against some of the adverse developments that can affect individuals, **property and casualty companies** in exchange for premiums provide protection against the untoward effects of unexpected occurrences on property, particularly automobiles and homes. Two factors are relevant in trying to understand the composition of assets held by these FIs: (1) unlike pension funds, which are nontaxable, and life insurance companies, which are taxed at a

Pension Funds
Tax-exempt intermediaries set up to provide participants with income at retirement in exchange for premiums.

Property and Casualty Companies
Intermediaries that provide protection against the effects of unexpected occurrences on property.

10-5

Financial Assets and
Liabilities of Public and
Private Pension Funds,
June 30, 2004
(in Billions of Dollars)

	Total[a]	cf3 Percent of Total Assets[a]
Financial assets	**$7,341.4**	**100.0%**
Checkable deposits and currency	15.9	.2
Time and savings deposits	133.6	1.8
Repurchase agreements	67.0	.9
Money market mutual funds	76.2	1.0
Mutual funds	865.9	11.8
Corporate equities	3,002.5	40.9
Treasury, agency, and government-sponsored enterprises securities	671.3	9.1
Corporate and foreign bonds	730.5	10.0
Mortgages	66.1	.9
Commercial paper	87.2	1.2
Miscellaneous	1,624.8	22.1
Liabilities	**$7,310.9**	**.0**
Pension fund reserves	**$7,310.9**	**.0**

a Details may not sum to totals because of rounding.

SOURCE: *Flow of Funds Accounts, Z1,* Second Quarter 2004, Board of Governor of the Federal Reserve System (September 16, 2004): 76. Available on the Internet at **http://www.federalreserve.gov/releases/Z1/**.

very low rate, property and casualty companies are taxed at the full 38 percent corporate rate; and (2) compared to life insurance companies and pension funds, the stream of benefit payments made by these companies is less predictable. Accidents and natural disasters do not follow the more regular patterns of retirement and death. The great Mississippi flood of 1993, the Northridge earthquake in 1994, and Hurricane Opal in 1995 followed hurricane Andrew in 1992. Indeed, the attacks on the World Trade Center and the Pentagon on September 11, 2001, are expected to compose the largest loss for property and casualty companies in history, dwarfing all other single accidents or natural disasters. Tax considerations lead property and casualty companies to hold 21.5 percent of their assets, which totaled $1,116.2 billion on June 30, 2004, in the form of tax-exempt municipal securities, as seen in Exhibit 10-6. The need for liquidity helps to explain the 7.2 percent of assets held in the form of checkable deposits, currency, and repurchase agreements.

Investment-Type FIs

The major types of intermediaries in the investment category are mutual funds, also known as *investment companies,* and money market mutual funds. Generally speaking, **mutual funds** acquire and pool funds from the public, invest the funds in capital market instruments, and return the income received minus a management fee to the investors. Some funds invest in particular types of securities, such as corporate stocks and bonds, while others have broader asset portfolios that include stocks, bonds, mortgages, gold, and so on. In the 1990s, mutual funds experienced tremendous growth. Small depositors poured funds into mutual funds seeking higher returns than the low rates depository institutions were offering at the time. Mutual funds began expanding to offer other financial services previously provided by banks. Concern has been expressed regarding

Mutual Funds
Investment-type intermediaries that pool the funds of net lenders, purchase the long-term financial claims of net borrowers, and return the income received minus a fee to the net lenders.

10-6

Financial Assets and
Liabilities of Property and
Casualty Companies,
June 30, 2004
(in Billions of Dollars)

	Total[a]	Percent of Total Assets[a]
Financial assets	**$1,116.2**	**100.0%**
Checkable deposits, currency, and repurchase agreements	80.7	7.2
Corporate equities	190.5	17.1
Municipal securities	240.1	21.5
Treasury, agency, and Government-sponsored enterprises securities	192.9	17.3
Corporate and foreign bonds	234.4	21.0
Trade receivables	85.3	7.6
Miscellaneous	92.4	8.3
Liabilities	**$716.3**	**64.2**
Net worth	**$399.9**	

a Details may not sum to totals because of rounding.

SOURCE: *Flow of Funds Accounts, Z1,* Second Quarter 2004, Board of Governor of the Federal Reserve System (September 16, 2004): 75. Available on the Internet at **http://www.federalreserve.gov/releases/Z1/**.

the adequacy of the regulation of mutual funds, given their tremendous growth in the 1990s (more on this in Chapter 15) and revelations of unethical and illegal trading by some mutual funds in the early 2000s. As of June 30, 2004, assets of mutual funds totaled $4,969.7 billion.

Money market mutual funds, mentioned briefly in Chapter 2, are a good example of funds that limit the type of financial claims they purchase.[18] They acquire funds from individual investors and pool them to purchase money market instruments such as Treasury bills, bank CDs, and commercial paper. The interest earned, minus a management fee, is then paid to investors. Exhibit 10-7 shows the major assets and liabilities of mutual funds and money market mutual funds. As of June 30, 2004, assets of money market mutual funds totaled $1,912.3 billion.

Finance Company-Type FIs

Finance companies such as Household Finance Corporation, Beneficial Finance, Commercial Credit Corporation, and the General Motors Acceptance Corporation lend funds to households to finance the purchase of consumer durables such as automobiles, appliances, and furniture and to businesses to finance inventories and the purchase or leasing of equipment. In the past, finance companies often loaned to borrowers considered risky by other types of FIs, particularly depository institutions. Today finance companies lend to all types of borrowers. As Exhibit 10-8 shows, finance companies held assets totaling $1,385.6 billion on June 30, 2004. Their major sources of funds come from selling commercial paper and issuing long-term bonds.

Money Market Mutual Funds
Mutual funds that invest in money market instruments.

Finance Companies
Intermediaries that lend funds to households to finance consumer purchases and to firms to finance inventories.

Recap   Contractual-type intermediaries offer contingency claims in return for regular payments. They include life insurance companies, property and casualty companies, and pension funds. Investment-type intermediaries (mutual funds and money market mutual funds) pool funds from the public, invest the funds, and return the income received, less a management fee, to the investors. Finance company-type intermediaries lend to households to purchase consumer durables and to businesses to finance inventories.

10-7

Financial Assets and Liabilities of Mutual Funds and Money Market Mutual Funds, June 30, 2004 (in Billions of Dollars)

Mutual Funds	Total[a]	Percent of Total Assets[a]
Financial assets	**$4,969.7**	**100.0%**
Repurchase agreements	91.9	1.8
Corporate equities	3,319.2	66.8
Treasury, agency, and government-sponsored enterprises securities	609.1	12.3
Municipal bonds	288.8	5.8
Corporate and foreign bonds	583.8	11.7
Commercial paper	73.7	1.5
Miscellaneous	3.1	.06
Liabilities	**$4,969.7**	**100.0%**
Mutual fund shares	**$4,969.7**	**100.0%**

Money Market Mutual Funds	Total[a]	Percent of Total Assets[a]
Financial assets	**$1,912.3**	**100.0%**
Checkable deposits and currency	1.1	.05
Small time and savings deposits	162.2	8.5
Repurchase agreements	254.5	13.3
Foreign deposits	88.8	4.6
Treasury, agency, and Government-sponsored enterprises securities	378.1	19.8
Municipals	304.7	15.9
Commercial paper	404.8	21.2
Corporate and foreign bonds	183.8	9.6
Miscellaneous	134.4	7.0
Liabilities	**$1,912.3**	**100.0%**
Money market fund shares	**$1,912.3**	**100.0%**

a Details may not sum to totals because of rounding.

SOURCE: *Flow of Funds Accounts, Z1,* Second Quarter 2004, Board of Governor of the Federal Reserve System (September 16, 2004): 77. Available on the Internet at **http://www.federalreserve.gov/releases/Z1/**.

Pulling Things Together

FIs can be classified into four groups:

1. Deposit types (banks, S&Ls, savings banks, and credit unions)

2. Contractual types (insurance companies and pension plans)

3. Investment types (mutual funds and money market mutual funds)

4. Finance company types

As Exhibit 10-9 shows, contractual-type FIs are now by far the largest group of FIs in terms of total assets, while pension plans are the single largest type of contractual type FI. Banks are the largest FIs, with pension plans second. Each group can be distinguished from other groups by the financial services they specialize in and the composition of their balance sheets. Such factors also help to distinguish one member of a group from other members of the same group. More specifically, the composition of

10-8

Financial Assets and Liabilities of Finance Companies, June 30, 2004 (in Billions of Dollars)

	Total[a]	Percent of Total Assets[a]
Financial assets	**$1,385.6**	**100.0%**
Checkable deposits and currency	38.8	2.8
Mortgages	213.3	15.4
Consumer credit	324.7	23.4
Other Loans	471.3	34
Miscellaneous	337.6	24.4
Liabilities	**$1,502.7**	**108.5%**
Corporate bonds	768.9	55.5
Bank loans	52.6	3.8
Commercial paper	140.6	10.1
Miscellaneous	540.5	.39
Net worth (capital)	**117.1**	

a Details may not sum to totals because of rounding.

SOURCE: *Flow of Funds Accounts, Z1,* Second Quarter 2004, Board of Governor of the Federal Reserve System (September 16, 2004): 79. Available on the Internet at **http://www.federalreserve.gov/releases/Z1/**.

each FI's balance sheet depends mainly on (1) the range of financial services offered to the public; (2) any specialization in particular services offered to the public, perhaps as a result of custom; (3) the tax status of the institution; (4) the nature of the institution's liabilities; and (5) legal constraints or regulations governing the types of assets and liabilities that can be acquired.

Examples of these factors at work include the following:

1. S&Ls, reflecting custom and regulations, specialize in mortgage lending because they have a perceived competitive advantage and some tax advantages in that area.

2. Tax-exempt FIs, such as credit unions and pension funds, generally do not hold tax-exempt municipal securities, while institutions subject to the full corporate income tax, such as banks and property and casualty insurance companies, do hold such assets.

10-9

Total Financial Assets of Principal FIs (in Billions of Dollars)

	1970	1980	1990	2000	2004
Deposit-type:					
Commercial banks	$505	$1,481.7	$3,337.5	$6,468.7	$7,946.5[a]
Savings associations	252	792.4	1,323.0	1,217.7	1,597.8[b]
Credit unions	18	67.6	217.2	441.1	643.0[b]
Contractual-type:					
Life insurance companies	201	464.2	1,351.4	3,135.7	3,969.8[b]
Property and casualty companies	50	182.1	533.5	862.0	1,116.2[b]
Pension funds	170	786.8	2,767.7	7,511.9	7,341.4[b]
Investment-type:					
Mutual funds	47	69.7	661.3	4,576.5	4,969.7[b]
Money market mutual fund	—	76.4	493.3	1,812.1	1,912.3[b]
Finance company-type	64	196.9	547.0	851.2	1,385.6[b]

a As of September 8, 2004
b As of June 30, 2004

SOURCE: Figures for 1970 are from the *Annual Statistical Digest,* Federal Reserve Board, 1991, various pages. Figures for 1980, 1990, 2000, and 2004 are from the *Flow of Fund Accounts,* Z1, Board of Governors of the Federal Reserve System, various years.

3. FIs, such as life insurance companies, that have a relatively steady and predictable inflow of funds and a fairly predictable stream of liabilities (payment outflows) hold more long-term and less-liquid assets than do FIs, such as banks, which have a greater need for liquidity because a considerable portion of their liabilities (deposits) are payable on demand.

4. Banks do not hold corporate equities because regulations prohibit it.

In addition, the nature of an FI's assets and liabilities determines the degree to which it must manage specific risks. For example, an FI with a high percentage of long-term fixed rate assets must manage interest rate risks to a greater degree than an FI whose assets and liabilities do not have such a maturity configuration. Likewise, an FI with uncertain payment contingencies must manage the liquidity risk to a greater degree than an FI whose payments are more certain and stable.

Together, regulations and customs, or long-established practices existing from the time particular types of FIs began operating, can account for many of the differences among FIs. Nevertheless, while such distinguishing characteristics should not be ignored, it is equally important to keep sight of the "common threads" that bind all types of FIs together. Moreover, as this chapter has suggested, FIs are undergoing fundamental changes.

At the risk of oversimplification, we can say that banks are increasingly trying to enter the markets for financial services traditionally provided by other FIs, which are increasingly trying to enter the markets traditionally served by banks. This process of homogenization and the trend toward financial supermarkets mean that, as noted earlier, Sandi and Dave, whom we met at the beginning of the chapter (and the rest of us), no longer have to deal with five different types of FIs. One FI may provide the services previously supplied by many.

Although not all attempts at creating financial supermarkets have been successful, Merrill Lynch is a prime example of a supermarket that has prospered. It is the nation's largest brokerage firm, the second largest mutual fund company, the largest investment underwriter, and a major insurance broker. In addition, it manages retirement accounts, makes mortgages and other business loans, and manages a successful money market mutual fund. The trend toward supermarkets eroded the effectiveness of various regulations and thereby produced fundamental changes in regulations and traditional competitive positions. The tendency toward consolidation of financial services was given new impetus by the **Gramm Leach-Bliley Act (GLBA)**, which became effective in March 2000. It removed decades-old barriers between banking and other financial services by creating financial holding companies that linked commercial banks with securities firms, insurance firms, and merchant banks. (More on the GLBA in Chapters 11 and 14.)

Even though banks and other intermediaries have experienced tremendous growth, they are losing ground to other nonfinancial institutions and direct financing venues, which have grown even faster. As previously mentioned, many corporate borrowers, both large and small, now borrow by issuing commercial paper rather than obtaining bank loans; and many nonfinancial corporations such as Sears, AT&T, and General Motors now issue credit cards. In addition, more and more consumers bypass S&Ls to obtain mortgage loans directly from mortgage brokers.

Despite these ongoing developments, banks (and other depository institutions) probably are still the most important type of FIs because they have been central to the Fed's conduct of monetary policy and the determination of the money supply. They have also been at the forefront of innovation and deregulation. The next chapter focuses on banks and the banking industry.

Gramm Leach-Bliley Act (GLBA)
Legislation that removed decades-old barriers between banking and other financial services by creating financial holding companies that linked commercial banks with securities firms, insurance firms, and merchant banks; passed by Congress in November 1999 and became effective March 2000.

Summary of Major Points

1. In general, FIs are profit-seeking firms that link up net borrowers and net lenders and in the process provide the public a wide range of financial services. The linking or channeling function involves the acquisition of financial claims on borrowers by the FIs and the acquisition of claims on the FIs by lenders.

2. The quantity, quality, and type of financial services offered by FIs will vary with the perceived profitability of engaging in various activities.

3. FIs provide services to the public to reduce the risks and costs associated with borrowing and lending and other financial transactions. They also afford the public protection against the financial costs associated with various contingencies and fulfill the demand for various financial claims.

4. Most FIs are heavily regulated. Historically, regulations tended to encourage specialization by certain types of FIs—in particular, financial services—and thus limited competition among different types of FIs. More recently, FIs have come to appreciate the benefits of diversifying and providing the public a wider range of financial services. This trend has led to various, often successful, attempts to innovate around existing regulations, and competition has increased as a result. Recent changes in regulations have allowed banks, insurance companies, and securities firms to affiliate under common ownership.

5. All FIs are exposed to various risks in varying degrees. Credit or default risk is the risk that a borrower will not live up to the terms of the liability it has sold. Interest rate risk is the risk that unexpected changes in the interest rate will cause the value of fixed rate financial assets to fall or that the FI will experience a negative spread between assets and liabilities. Liquidity risk is the risk that the FI will not have funds available to make required payments and will be unable to convert long-term assets to liquid funds quickly without a capital loss. Exchange rate risk is the risk that changes in exchange rates will cause the FI to experience losses in the dollar value of foreign currency or foreign financial assets that the FI holds.

6. The differences among FIs manifest themselves in the financial services in which institutions specialize and in the composition of their balance sheets. The composition of a balance sheet depends mainly on the range of financial services offered; any specialization in particular services, perhaps as a result of custom; the tax status of the institution; the nature of the FI's liabilities; and legal constraints or regulations.

7. FIs can be grouped or classified according to the nature of their liabilities or the major activity (financial service) in which they engage. The major groups are deposit type, including banks, S&Ls, savings banks, and credit unions; contractual type, including insurance companies and pension plans; investment type, including mutual funds and money market mutual funds; and finance company type. The contractual-type group is the largest group, and commercial banks are the single largest FI.

8. The major sources of funds for commercial banks are checkable, savings, and time deposits plus nondeposit liabilities such as corporate bonds, fed funds, repurchase agreements, and Eurodollar borrowings. The major uses of funds for banks are loans, government securities, and reserves. The major sources of funds for S&Ls are time, savings, and checkable deposits. The major use of funds is to make mortgage loans. Credit unions are tax exempt, small in size, and numerous. Their main sources of funds are share drafts and small savings accounts. They primarily make small personal and mortgage loans to their members and invest in government securities. Savings banks, located mostly on the East Coast, lend heavily in the mortgage market.

9. Contractual-type intermediaries offer contingency claims in return for regular payments. They include life insurance companies, property and casualty companies, and pension funds. Investment-type intermediaries (mutual funds and money market mutual funds) pool funds from the public, invest the funds, and return the income received, less a management fee, to the investors. Finance company-type intermediaries lend to households to purchase consumer durables and to businesses to finance inventories.

Key Terms

Review Questions

1. List two services that FIs provide to the public. Why do intermediaries provide these services? What is a contingent financial claim? Give two examples.

2. "With financial intermediation, net lenders can earn a higher return on their surplus funds, and net borrowers can acquire funds at a lower cost." Explain how this seemingly contradictory statement can be true. (*Hint:* Consider a risk-free return.)

3. How are FIs like other firms? How are FIs similar to each other? How are they different?

4. If an FI has mainly long-term liabilities with few payment uncertainties, in what type of assets is it most likely to invest? Why?

5. What is a depository institution? What are the main types of depository institutions? What distinguishes them from other intermediaries?

6. Why do banks hold reserve assets?

7. Identify the major contractual-type FIs. What are their main sources of funds (liabilities) and their main uses of funds (assets)?

8. What are the main sources of funds (liabilities) and uses of funds (assets) for finance company-type FIs?

9. Why does A-1 Student Auto Insurance Company need to hold more liquid assets than Senior Life Insurance Company? How do depository institutions manage liquidity risk?

10. John, a recent college graduate, is buying his first house. From which FIs could he obtain a mortgage loan?

11. How do money market mutual funds differ from mutual funds? How are money market mutual funds similar to depository institutions? As an investor, Sam holds both mutual funds and money market mutual funds. Holding which asset entails greater interest rate risk for him? Why?

12. Would a property and casualty company hold municipal securities in its portfolio of assets? What about a credit union and a life insurance company? Why or why not?

13. How can diversification reduce credit or default risk? In the event of widespread economic collapse, will diversification always reduce this risk?

14. What are the major determinants of an FI's liability structure? Give examples of each.

15. What was the purpose of the Financial Institutions Reform, Recovery, and Enforcement Act (FIRREA) of 1989? Why was the act needed?

16. Which FIs have deposit insurance?

17. What is a mutual savings bank? (*Hint:* See Endnote 15.)

Analytical Questions

Questions marked with an icon are objective in nature. They can be completed with a short answer or number.

18. If a bank has assets of $100 million and liabilities of $95 million, what is its net worth? If 60 percent of its assets were loans, what percentage of the loans could go sour before the bank would lose all of its capital?

19. Make a chart listing the main sources of funds (liabilities) and main uses of funds (assets) in order of importance for the following depository institutions: commercial banks, S&Ls, mutual savings banks, and credit unions. Describe how the sources and uses of funds have changed through the years for the various depository institutions.

20. What type of risk does each of the following situations portray?

a. After the attack on the World Trade Center, several major insurance companies did not have sufficient cash assets available to meet casualty claims. *Liq*

For ex

b. ABC Bank, located along the U.S.–Mexican border, was holding a large quantity of Mexican pesos when the value of the peso collapsed.

c. Friendly S&L specializes in fixed rate mortgages. There is a sharp increase in short-term interest rates. *inte.*

d. A family needs funds immediately to meet a medical emergency. All of its assets are tied up in real estate. *liqu*

e. I am planning a trip to Europe next summer and have exactly $5,000. At the present exchange rates, I will have a great time. Is there any doubt?

f. Chad takes a loan for an expensive racing truck and then loses his job. *Default / Credit*

Internet Exercises

1. The FDIC maintains a Web page at **http://www.fdic.gov**. A useful link at this site provides quarterly banking statistics. Click on the "statistical" link under bank data. Access the latest balance sheet of all FDIC-insured depository institutions and answer the following:

a. What is the total number of commercial banks in the United States?

b. What is the amount of total assets that are owned by all FDIC-insured depository institutions in the United States?

c. What are the various components on the liability side of commercial banks' balance sheets?

2. Some interesting facts about the FDIC can be found at the following Web site: **http://www.fdic.gov/about/learn/learning/index.html**. Access this site and answer the following:

a. Whose deposits does the FDIC insure, and what does the federal deposit insurance cover?

b. What is the amount of FDIC insurance coverage? If you have deposits in several different FDIC-insured banks, will your deposits be added together for insurance purposes?

Suggested Readings

For a look at "How Low Interest Rates Impact Financial Institutions," see the article by the same name, by John V. Duca in *Southwest Economy*, Federal Reserve Bank of Dallas, November/December, 2003, issue 6: 8–12. The article is available on the Internet at http://www.dallasfed.org/research/swe/2003/swe0306b.html.

For a rather academic look at how some banking institutions compete, see William R. Emmons and Frank A. Schmid, "When For-Profits and Not-For-Profits Compete: Theory and Empirical Evidence from Retail Banking," Federal Reserve Bank of St. Louis, Working Papers, 2004-004A. February 2004. The article is available on the Internet at http://research.stlouisfed.org/wp/2004/2004-004.pdf.

For a look at some issues relating to pension funds, see Simon Kwan, "Underfunding of Private Pension Plans." *Economic Letter*, Number 2003-16, Federal Reserve Bank of San Francisco, June 13, 2003. It is available on the Internet at http://www.sf.frb.org/publications/economics/letter/2003/l2003-16.pdf.

For a look at how some nonfinancial firms also engage in financial intermediation, see Mitchell Merlin, "Trade Credit: Why Do Production Firms Act as Financial Intermediaries?" *Business Review*, Federal Reserve Bank of Philadelphia (3rd Quarter, 2003): 21–28. The article is available on the Internet at http://www.phil.frb.org/files/br/brq303mb.pdf.

The *Journal of Financial Intermediation* has numerous articles that deal with material in this chapter. It is available on the Internet at http://www.olin.wustl.edu/jfi/.

For a look at how technology is impacting financial intermediation, see "Earthquake on the Street," *Economist* (May 20, 2000).

For a look at "The Future of Financial Intermediation and Regulation: An Overview," see the article by Stephen Cecchetti, *Current Issues in Economics and Finance*, Federal Reserve Bank of New York, 5:8 (May 1999).

An interesting article that touches on the history of financial institutions is Eugene N. White, "Were Banks Special Intermediaries in Late Nineteenth Century America?" *Federal Reserve Bank of St. Louis Review* 80:3 (May/June 1998): 13–32.

Two rather fun books to read about FIs (and lots of other related subjects) are Tom Wolfe, *The Bonfire of the Vanities* (New York: Farrar, Strauss, & Giroux, 1987); and Martin Mayer, *The Money Bazaars* (New York: Mentor, 1984).

Endnotes

1 We look in depth at financial innovation in Chapter 12.

2 For the time being, we are ignoring the money creation process by depository institutions, which may also generate funds that are lent to net borrowers. This process will be covered in depth in Chapter 20.

3 The exceptions, such as credit unions, will be discussed later in the chapter.

4 In Chapter 5, we saw that commercial paper is short-term IOUs issued by creditworthy corporations to finance short-term borrowing needs.

5 The commercial paper may be issued through a broker who places it with a large corporation or other lender.

6 The interest rate on adjustable rate loans changes as market interest rates change. Thus, if interest rates go up, rates on adjustable rate loans also increase, and vice versa.

7 An FI can be exposed to losses if it has fixed-rate liabilities, such as fixed rate CDs, and variable rate assets, such as variable rate loans. In this case, if interest rates fall, the return on assets falls, while the cost of liabilities does not.

8 To clarify, banks attract deposits (inputs) in order to make loans and other investments (outputs). Because banks hold reserve assets equal to only a fraction of their deposit liabilities when banks make loans, they create checkable deposits that are part of the money supply process.

9 To refresh your memory, money market deposit accounts are individual accounts authorized by Congress in 1982 that offer limited check writing (say, up to three checks per month) and generally pay higher interest than other checkable deposits.

10 National factors, such as monetary policy, are also an important determinant of a bank's success.

11 The new legislation is the Gramm Leach-Bliley Act, which was passed in November 1999. This landmark legislation is further discussed in Chapters 11 and 14.

12 Small depositors do not have to worry about the solvency of their bank as long as it is a member of the Federal Deposit Insurance Corporation (FDIC). Currently, the deposits of all FDIC member banks are insured up to $100,000.

13 Banks may also hold liquid assets so that they will be able to accommodate unexpected loan demands from valued customers.

14 Don't forget that by holding long-term fixed-rate financial assets, banks are exposed to an interest rate risk. If the interest rate rises, the value of the asset falls. This risk is minimal for Treasury bills, which will mature relatively quickly.

15 The original savings banks were "mutuals," which meant that the depositors were really the owners of the institutions. They were actually benevolent philanthropic institutions set up to encourage the poor and the working class to save to relieve poverty and pauperism. The poor deposited whatever pennies they could, and the funds were managed by wealthy entrepreneurs. Today, roughly two-thirds of the savings banks retain this form of ownership, while one-third have sold stock and converted their ownership to stock savings banks.

16 We should also note that the bailout benefited the taxpayers by maintaining the solvency of the financial system.

17 It is worth noting that the often-heard calls to "tax corporations more" might, if implemented, have the effect of reducing corporate profits and, thus, dividends paid to shareholders, such as pension funds. The result would be smaller pensions for retirees. This is an example of the interdependencies we have been emphasizing.

18 In reality, money market mutual funds are a subcategory of the general category of mutual funds. However, when we refer merely to mutual funds, we mean those that invest in capital market instruments primarily as opposed to money market instruments.

A holding company is the people you give your money to while you're being searched.

—Will Rogers

11

Commercial Banking Structure, Regulation, and Performance

Learning Objectives

After reading this chapter, you should know:

Who regulates whom in the banking system and why

What a bank holding company is and why virtually all large banks are now organized as holding companies

What a financial holding company is

The reasons for the recent wave of bank mergers

The nature of the evolutionary changes of the banking system in recent years

The Biggest Intermediary in Town

The chief executive officer (CEO) convenes the regular Monday morning meeting of the managers of the bank's key divisions. As the division heads report, the managers learn that several large corporate customers are requesting short-term loans and that deposit growth has slowed in recent weeks. In response to this and other information, the CEO instructs the manager of the bank's liabilities to borrow more funds in the certificate of deposit (CD) market and directs the senior loan officer to pursue the corporate loan business aggressively by offering attractive terms on the requested loans. Because the slowdown in deposit growth appears to be related to increased competition from other financial intermediaries (FIs) in the area, particularly one large savings and loan (S&L), the managers endorse a major marketing plan designed to inform the public about several new services now available to depositors. The CEO also brings the committee members up-to-date on bank mergers among some key competitors. She also discusses several possible mergers upper management is considering. Although mergers are supposed to exploit economies of scale and make the bank more profitable, committee members silently worry that they may translate to a loss of jobs. Finally, "the chief" directs the members of the committee to be "on their toes." Bank regulators have arrived to conduct their periodic examination of the bank's books and operations.

This story depicts the start of a fairly normal week at a bank. We hope it conveys the flavor of the dynamic world of banking and helps to introduce the issues to be examined in this chapter. What risks must banks manage? What competition do banks face in the markets for loans and deposits? What new services are banks offering? Why have there been so many bank mergers in recent years? What is a financial holding company? Who are the regulators, and what are the auditors looking for?

As discussed in Chapter 10, banks are among the largest types of FIs and play an important role in transferring funds from lenders in our economy to borrowers. Banks borrow or hire funds from lenders and pay interest on the borrowed funds. They lend funds to borrowers and earn interest on the loaned funds. Ignoring some of the details for the moment, the excess of the interest earned on the loaned funds over the interest paid on the borrowed funds is the profit earned from financial intermediation.

As they "intermediate," commercial banks make a number of decisions. These decisions include (1) the interest rates they will pay to borrow or "hire" funds, (2) the types of deposits they will offer the public, (3) the interest rates they will charge to lend funds, (4) the types of loans they will make, and (5) the type of securities they will acquire. Each of these decisions affects the borrowers' demand for funds (borrowing) from banks and/or the lenders' supply of funds (lending) to banks. Ultimately, you need to know much about the macroeconomic and microeconomic aspects of banking. On the macro side, how does bank behavior affect interest rates, the money stock, the volume of credit extended by banks, and economic activity? On the micro side, how do banks make the pricing and quantity decisions just mentioned, how do regulations affect such behavior, and how has bank behavior changed over time? We begin by examining the banking regulations that have led to our current commercial banking system. We then look at how the system's structure has been changing in recent years. Finally, we discuss bank efforts to increase profits and look at how banks have performed in this area in recent years. Other issues are covered in succeeding chapters.

Again, we emphasize that banks, like many other firms and industries in our society, are continually changing and attempting to innovate. As a result, many institutional details will change somewhat as time passes. Nevertheless, we can look at how the banking system has evolved, provide a picture of the current system, and offer a glimpse at where the industry may be going.

The Banking Regulatory Structure

As you saw in Chapters 1 and 4, the primary reason the banking system is regulated is to preserve its safety and soundness and ensure the fair and efficient delivery of banking services to the public. From the regulator's perspective, continuous oversight is needed to ensure that banks are operated prudently and in accordance with standing statutes and regulations. Broadly speaking, *regulation* involves the formulation and issuance of specific rules to govern the structure and conduct of banks.

For the most part, the regulatory structure prevailing at the beginning of the 1970s was inherited from and the product of the 1930s. This structure was put in place as a result of events that occurred at the start of and during the Great Depression. In October 1929, prices on the New York Stock Exchange collapsed. The Dow Jones Industrial Index, a measure of stock market values, stood at 200 in January 1928, rose to 381 in September 1929, and then collapsed. Eventually, the Dow reached a low of 41 in July 1932. From 1929 through 1933, more than 8,000 banks failed, industrial production fell more than 50 percent, and the nation's unemployment rate rose from 3 percent to 25 percent. At the time, people believed that these events were intimately connected and that the Great Depression was caused and/or severely aggravated by serious defects in the structure and regulation of the financial system. More specifically, the failure of many financial institutions was alleged to be the result of (1) "excessive and destructive competition" among banks, which had led to the payment of unduly high interest rates on deposits, and (2) the granting of overly risky loans, particularly those extended to stock market speculators. Furthermore, it was believed that banks sought out such loans and the high yields they carried because of the high rates being paid on deposits. When the stock market crashed, the value of the speculators' portfolios collapsed, leading them to default on their bank loans. The banks, in turn, became insolvent (bankrupt) or were left so weakened that depositors rushed to withdraw their funds.

Given this diagnosis, the legislative and regulatory remedies established at the time are readily understandable.[1] Among the most widespread and ultimately pernicious "cures" was the establishment of maximum ceilings on the interest rates banks could pay on deposits. The ceilings, which were imposed under the **Glass-Steagall Act of 1933,** were popularly known as **Regulation Q.** Interest payments on demand deposits, which were the only type of checkable deposit in existence at the time, were prohibited, and interest payments on time and savings deposits were not to exceed the rate ceilings set by the relevant regulatory authority. The rationale for the ceilings was seductive and attractive: By holding down the rates on deposits (sources of bank funds), the rates on loans (uses of funds) could be held down. Banks would no longer need to seek out and grant high-risk, high-yield loans.

To further limit bank failures, the Glass-Steagall Act put deposit insurance into place with the creation of the **Federal Deposit Insurance Corporation (FDIC).** As noted in Chapter 10, the deposits of most banks and other depository institutions are now fully insured up to $100,000. The presence of deposit insurance eliminated bank runs or bank panics in which depositors, fearing that their bank would fail, "ran" to get their funds out.

In addition, the Glass-Steagall Act separated commercial banking from investment banking, which is the underwriting and marketing of primary corporate securities. Banks were no longer allowed to own or underwrite corporate securities. Thus, the assets commercial banks could hold were effectively limited to cash assets, government securities, and loans. The commercial bank's role was to accept deposits paying up to the Regulation Q interest rate ceilings and to make predominantly commercial loans.

Glass-Steagall Act of 1933
Banking legislation, enacted in response to the Great Depression, that established Regulation Q interest rate ceiling, separated commercial and investment banking, and created the FDIC.

Regulation Q
Interest rate ceilings on commercial bank deposits that were established during the Great Depression and phased out after 1980.

Federal Deposit Insurance Corporation (FDIC)
The federal agency that insures the deposits of banks and savings associations.

Looking Back

The Origins of the Dual Banking System

How did we end up with a dual banking system? Actually, it was not the intent of Congress. The National Currency Act of 1863 and the National Banking Act of 1864 established the Comptroller of the Currency, which chartered national banks for the first time. The banknotes issued by the national banks circulated at full value and were backed by government bonds.

Prior to this time, all banks had been chartered by the states. The state banks had issued their own banknotes, which, under normal circumstances, were redeemable at face value in the bank's geographic trade area. Outside the bank's geographic area, however, the notes were often redeemable at less than face value. The acts also imposed a 10 percent tax on banknotes issued by state banks. The purpose of the restrictive tax was to make state banknotes so undesirable that state banks would be driven out of business. If they were unable to issue notes, they could not make loans. A financial innovation—the acceptance of demand deposits—saved the state banks from extinction. State banks could stay in business without issuing their own banknotes. The innovation foiled the plans of Congress to drive state banks out of business.

Incidentally, if you have any old state banknotes or national banknotes lying around your house, you may want to check out how much they're worth. At a mid-1990s show in St. Louis, a $10 banknote from Platteville National Bank sold for $9,500.[a]

You have already seen that the Fed is the most important regulator of commercial banks that are members of the Fed. The Fed also sets reserve requirements and provides discount facilities for all depository institutions. Under the regulatory structure that prevailed from the 1930s until the early 1980s, the Fed shared regulatory responsibilities with two federal bodies—the **Comptroller of the Currency** and the FDIC—and with state banking departments. Prior to the 1980s, the scope of regulation included restrictions on entry, branching, types of assets and liabilities permitted, financial services that could be offered, and interest that could be paid on certain types of deposits and charged on certain types of loans. Today, banks have found ways around many of these regulations, many of which have been relaxed if not totally eliminated. Recently, other regulations dealing mainly with bank capital requirements and risk management have gained in importance. In Chapter 14, we look at major legislation in recent years that will drastically alter the structure of the banking system.

To aid in understanding this complex regulatory structure, it is useful to begin with the birth of a bank. Unfortunately (or should we say fortunately), none of us can just decide to open a bank tomorrow. Commercial banks in the United States are **chartered;** that is, they are given permission to engage in the business of commercial banking by either the federal government or one of the 50 state governments. When applying for a charter, the applicant must demonstrate a knowledge of the business of banking and have a substantial supply of capital funds.[2] If a bank's charter is granted by the federal government, the bank is called a **national bank.** The office of the Comptroller of the Currency is the federal government agency charged with chartering national banks. For example,

Comptroller of the Currency
The federal agency that charters national banks.

Chartered
Given permission to engage in the business of commercial banking. Banks must obtain a charter before opening.

National Bank
A bank that has received a charter from the Comptroller of the Currency.

Dual Banking System

The system whereby a bank may have either a national or a state charter.

Wells Fargo Bank of San Francisco is a federally chartered bank. A bank can also be chartered by a state banking authority. This system in which commercial banks are chartered and regulated by the federal government or a state government is usually referred to as the **dual banking system.** Think of it as a dual chartering system.

Banks that are federally chartered must belong to the Federal Reserve System and must subscribe to federal deposit insurance with the FDIC. The latter provides insurance for individual deposit accounts up to $100,000 per account and charges banks an insurance premium that varies with the reserves that the insurance fund has available. The premium is slightly more for high-risk banks. Thus, national banks are subject to the regulatory and supervisory authority of the Comptroller, the Fed, and the FDIC.

The FDIC site has general information about it, as well as related links. See **http://www.fdic.gov/**.

A state-chartered bank will be regulated by its state banking authority. If it chooses to join the Federal Reserve System, the state bank will also have to subscribe to federal deposit insurance because all Fed members must have it. Thus, in this case, the state-chartered bank will be subject to regulation by the Fed and the FDIC. Finally, state banks may also subscribe to FDIC insurance without joining the Fed.[3]

One of the interesting and probably unique features of the system is that those being regulated can choose the regulator. In effect, they can "vote with their feet." By this we mean that banks can apply for either a state or a federal charter or attempt to shift from one to the other.

The decisions banks have made on chartering are captured in Exhibit 11-1. Presumably, these decisions are based on expected profitability. The data in Exhibit 11-1 indicate that as of June 30, 2004, about 75 percent of the 7,691 banks had state charters while about 25 percent had national charters. The 7,691 banks had over 68,000 branches making the total number of banking offices almost 76,000. Most state-chartered banks do not belong to the Federal Reserve System, although larger state banks do tend to be Fed members.

Historically, most banks, especially smaller ones, found it more profitable to be state-chartered non-Fed members. State banking authorities were often viewed as being more friendly in regulating and supervising institutions and more lenient in allowing nonbanking activities than their federal counterparts. In addition, the reserve requirements, which specify that a bank must hold reserve assets equal to a portion of its deposit liabilities, were often lower for state-chartered/regulated banks than for national banks regulated by the Fed.

Lower reserve requirements meant more potential profits. Because a smaller amount of reserve assets were held, a larger proportion of deposit inflows could be used for loans and other interest-earning investments. (The required reserve ratio is now set

11-1

FDIC-Insured Banks, June 30, 2004

	Number of Banks	Deposits (in Billions of Dollars)	Assets (in Billions of Dollars)
Total domestic banks	7,691	$5,327	$8,049
National charter	1,959	2,984	4,597
State charter	5,732	2,343	3,452

SOURCE: Federal Deposit Insurance Corporation (http://www.fdic.gov).

by the Fed for all depository institutions and is the same for all depository institutions.) Larger banks, which usually were Fed members, often provided nonmembers with many of the services the Fed would normally have provided. Fed members also have to buy stock in the Fed equal to 3 percent of their assets. The stock pays dividends that are lower than what banks could earn by making loans.

Although not apparent in Exhibit 11-1, more than 97.5 percent of all banks have elected to be part of the FDIC. Apparently, banks feel it is important to offer depositors the safety and peace of mind federal deposit insurance engenders. For those who think this point is trivial, recall that in the midst of the Great Depression—between 1929 and 1933, to be exact—more than 8,000 banks failed in the United States. As those banks failed, depositors in other banks rushed to withdraw their funds out of fear that the problems would spread. Such a "run" on even a healthy, solvent bank can cause severe difficulties because the bank's asset portfolio may be illiquid with not enough cash or liquid assets on hand to pay off the many depositors making withdrawals. Limiting cash withdrawals (to, say, $25 a week) or closing the bank temporarily, as often occurred, reinforced the public's perception that this bank and perhaps all banks were in serious difficulty. As the epidemic spread, such illiquid banks were often forced out of business, and the entire financial system was threatened. In what must be judged one of the most successful pieces of legislation in history, Congress created the FDIC in 1933. This, by and large, halted the runs on solvent but illiquid banks and thus restored some stability to the banking and financial systems.[4] Deposit insurance was first made a "full faith and credit obligation" of the federal government in 1989. Prior to that year, the FDIC was on somewhat the same footing as private insurance companies in that the federal government was not required by law to pay off depositors if the FDIC ran out of funds in the face of widespread bank failures.

Clearly, having a dual banking system with a variety of regulatory authorities leads to a considerable overlap of responsibilities, with some institutions subject to regulation and supervision by as many as three regulatory authorities. In an attempt to minimize the overlap, primary regulatory responsibility for each category of banks has been assigned to one regulator, which then shares the resulting information. Regulatory responsibility has been distributed in the following manner: (1) the FDIC for state-chartered, insured banks that have not joined the Fed; (2) the Comptroller of the Currency for national banks, which also must be FDIC insured and Fed members; (3) the Fed for state-chartered, insured members of the Fed, and all bank and financial holding companies (more on them later); and (4) the states for state-chartered banks that do not subscribe to FDIC insurance or belong to the Fed. Exhibit 11-2 gives additional details for each category. The **Federal Financial Institutions Examinations Council (FFIEC),** which was created by Congress in 1979, prescribes uniform principles, standards, and report forms for the federal examination of financial institutions by the Fed, the FDIC, and the Office of the Comptroller of the Currency. The FFIEC also makes recommendations to promote uniformity in the supervision of financial institutions.[5]

Some people believe that the current set of regulations, supervisory authorities, and statutes of the dual chartering system provides an incentive for local banks with state charters to adapt and structure their services so as to fulfill the needs of the local community while guidelines for federally chartered banks may relate to national and international concerns. They also argue that the dual system fosters competition and innovation among banks. Opponents of the dual system argue that the overlapping of regulatory agencies breeds considerable confusion and leads to lax enforcement; they maintain that this system gives banks considerable freedom to escape proper supervision and regulation. By the early 2000s, many of these discussions had become irrelevant and obsolete because of ongoing changes in regulations, technological advances in the ways funds are transferred, and other financial innovations.

Federal Financial Institutions Examinations Council (FFIEC)
A federal agency that prescribes uniform principles, standards, and report forms for the federal examination of financial institutions by the Fed, the FDIC, and the Office of the Comptroller of the Currency and that makes recommendations to promote uniformity in the supervision of financial institutions.

- FDIC — Regulates state-chartered, insured non-Fed members and insured branches of foreign banks
- Comptroller of the Currency — Regulates national banks that are not bank holding companies and federally chartered branches of foreign banks
- Fed — Regulates state-chartered, insured members of the Fed, all bank holding companies, all financial holding companies, and branches of foreign banking organizations operating in the United States and their parent bank
- States — Regulate state-chartered, non-FDIC-insured banks that are not Fed members

SOURCE: Federal Deposit Insurance Corporation (http:///www.fdic.gov).

As Exhibit 11-3 shows, bank failures in the mid- and late 1980s were at the highest level since the inception of the FDIC in 1933. Between 1955 and 1981, bank failures averaged 5.3 per year. Between 1987 and 1990, they averaged a whopping 189 per year! Although still high in the early 1990s, by the end of the decade, bank failures had fallen dramatically, averaging around 5 per year between 1995 and mid-2004.

Even though bank failures fell to an insignificant level by the early 2000s and bank profits increased dramatically, the experience of the 1980s has left many industry observers nervous. In the aftermath, Congress has questioned the various agencies responsible for regulating banks, asking how so many banks could have failed if regulation and supervision were adequate.[6] In Chapter 14, we look at ways regulators have implemented new and existing regulations to ensure adequate banking supervision. We also look at suggestions for overhauling the federal regulatory structure of banking and other financial services in response to the ongoing changes that are occurring within the industry.

Recap   Federally chartered banks are called *national banks* and must belong to the Fed and subscribe to FDIC deposit insurance. State-chartered banks can, if they choose, belong to the Fed and/or subscribe to FDIC insurance. Nearly all banks subscribe to FDIC insurance. This dual banking system has allowed banks to choose their regulators. Seventy-five percent of banks have state charters while 25 percent have national charters. National banks tend to be much larger and have many more branches than state banks.

The Structure of the Commercial Banking System

In establishing the statutes and regulations that have contributed to the evolution of the structure of the commercial banking system, Congress and the regulatory agencies were guided by several considerations. It was assumed that a large number of small banks would encourage competition and efficiency, which would result in conduct or behavior by firms that was beneficial to the public and society at large. At the same time, the more competitive the market, the greater the risk of failure of an individual firm from the pressure of intense competition. Although the public would be provided with the largest quantity of financial services at the lowest prices, more banks could fail in a highly competitive environment.

In contrast, a structure characterized by a few large firms would result in limited competition, inefficiencies, and fewer benefits for the public in the form of lower prices and improved quality and quantity of financial services.[7] At the same time, fewer banks would

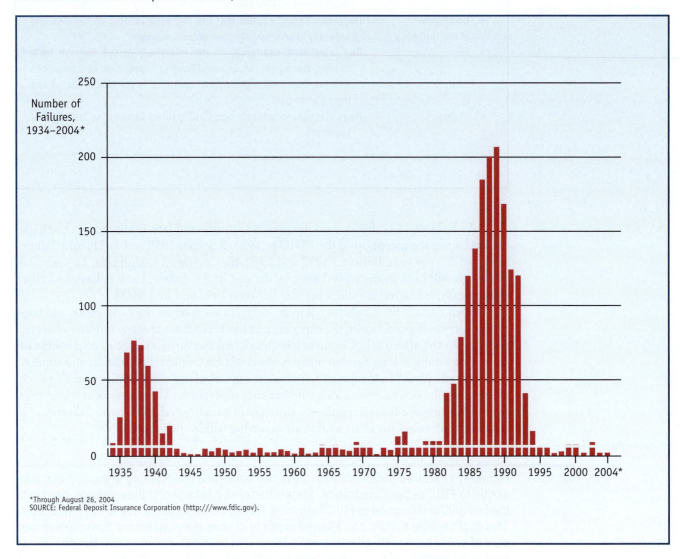

Number of Failures, 1934–2004*

*Through August 26, 2004
SOURCE: Federal Deposit Insurance Corporation (http:///www.fdic.gov).

fail in a noncompetitive market. (Because of a lack of competition, banks could charge higher prices for their services and earn higher profits.) Nevertheless, with only a few large banks, the failure of just one bank could have major ramifications throughout the economy. With many small banks, the failure of one would not be catastrophic. Presumably, regulators attempt to balance all of these considerations by encouraging bank behavior that is beneficial to society while ensuring the safety and soundness of the financial system.

Against this background, it should not be surprising that regulators were interested in monitoring and influencing, if not controlling, the structure of the market for banking services. In particular, regulators used their powers to control entry into the market, mergers among existing firms, and branching in an effort to maintain many small firms and a so-called competitive environment while protecting small banks from excessive competition. But, as you shall see, the regulators' attempts to maintain a competitive environment often resulted in a noncompetitive environment. Even though there were many banks, each bank was shielded from competition.

McFadden Act
The 1927 act by Congress that outlawed interstate branching and made national banks conform to the intrastate branching laws of the states in which they were located.

A local environment can become more competitive in several ways. One way, of course, occurs when a new institution secures a charter and sets up in competition with the local banks. Competition can also increase if existing banks located elsewhere in the state are allowed to open new branch offices in the area. Although not always the case, the vast majority of states allow statewide branching.

Historically, however, branching generally had to stop at the state line. The **McFadden Act,** passed by Congress in 1927, prohibited federally chartered national banks from branching across state lines. It also required national banks to abide by the branching laws of the state in which they were located. State banks that are Fed members can operate only in the state that grants them a charter. Generally, other state-chartered banks cannot open branches across state lines, although some states permitted entry by state-chartered banks that were not Fed members. Although it is now history, the McFadden Act is substantially responsible for the structure of the commercial banking system we have today.

Initially, state and federal restrictions on intrastate and interstate branching were motivated by a desire to prevent undue concentration and reduced competition in banking. For example, it was believed that with unrestricted statewide branching, a few large city banks would open branches across a state and drive the small community banks out of business. The result would be a worrisome concentration of economic and perhaps political power in a few large institutions and a reduction in the quality and quantity of financial services available in smaller communities.

This concern about "bigness" or "concentration" along with the fear that more competition in local banking markets might lead to more bank failures resulted in restrictions on entry and branching. This in turn led to a large number of small banks being located in relatively small communities. Despite the alleged competitiveness, many of these institutions have faced little or no competition because larger, and perhaps more efficient, banks were prohibited from entering the local market. Thus, entry and branching restrictions ultimately served to limit competition, not increase it. In part, this is why Congress decided in 1994 to allow interstate branching. The McFadden Act was effectively abrogated in September 1994, when President Bill Clinton signed the **Interstate Banking and Branching Efficiency Act (IBBEA).** The IBBEA has effectively allowed unimpeded nationwide branching since mid-1997.

Interstate Banking and Branching Efficiency Act (IBBEA)
Signed into law in September 1994, an act by Congress that effectively allows unimpeded nationwide branching.

Another reason for the enactment of the IBBEA was that Congress and the president were merely following the lead of the states. In 1985, the Supreme Court gave states the freedom to form regional banking pacts. Two years later, 45 of the 50 states allowed some form of interstate banking. More important, as you shall see in the next section, banks had, for all practical purposes, found ways to engage in interstate branching even before the law allowing branching was passed.

As Exhibit 11-4 shows, on June 30, 2004, there were 7,691 FDIC-insured banks in the United States. Of these, 50 percent had assets of less than $100 million each. Although $100 million might sound like a lot, it is small for a bank. At the same time, 95 percent of FDIC-insured banks had assets of less than $1 billion while 5 percent had assets of more than $1 billion.

A look at total banking assets for the industry reveals even more. The smallest 50 percent of all banks own less than 3 percent of total banking assets. The smallest 99 percent of banks had 26 percent of total assets. About 1 percent of all banks had assets of more than $10 billion, but they owned almost three-fourths of total banking assets! By any measure, it is clear that the industry is composed of a large number of very small banks and a small number of very large banks As you might guess, most of the industry giants have extensive branching networks and are located in states that had liberal branching laws long before the IBBEA.

11-4

Size Distribution of FDIC-Insured Banks as of June 30, 2004

Asset Size	Number of Institutions	Percent of Total	Cumulative Percent	Total Assets	Percent of Total*	Cumulative Percent*
<$100 million	3,819	50%	50%	$197.8	2.5%	2.5%
$100 million–$1 billion	3,444	45	95	923.6	11.5	14
$1–$10 billion	342	4	99	934.2	12	26
>$10 billion	86	1	100	5,992.8	74	100%
Total	7,691	100%	100%	$8,048.4	100%	100%

*Percents may not sum to 100% because of rounding.
SOURCE: Federal Deposit Insurance Corporation (http://www.fdic.gov).

But the numbers alone conceal additional relevant attributes of the banking structure—namely, that the numbers are changing dramatically as mergers occur and that virtually all of the large banks are organized as bank holding companies or as financial holding companies. To these subjects we now turn.

Recap The McFadden Act of 1927 outlawed interstate branching by national banks. The act required national banks to abide by the branching laws of the state in which they were located. In 1994, the Interstate Banking and Branching Efficiency Act (IBBEA) effectively allowed unimpeded nationwide branching as of June 1, 1997. Today, there are a large number of very small banks and a small number of very large banks.

Bank Holding Companies and Financial Holding Companies

When we hear the name Johnson & Johnson, many of us probably think of baby powder, shampoo, and Band-Aids. These are major products associated with the J&J brand name. In fact, however, J&J is a conglomerate, producing numerous other products through its many subsidiaries, including Tylenol, surgical instruments, sausage casings, toys, tranquilizers, and contraceptives. In other words, J&J is a company that owns and operates many firms that produce a wide variety of products.

Bank Holding Company
A corporation that owns several firms, at least one of which is a bank.

A **bank holding company** is a corporation that owns several firms, at least one of which is a bank. The remaining firms are engaged in activities that are closely related to banking. If the holding company owns one bank, it is called a *one-bank holding company*. If it owns more than one, it is called, not surprisingly, *a multi-bank holding company*.

Many banks organize themselves into holding companies because they expect this organizational form to be more profitable than a simple bank would be. More specifically, this corporate form allows banks to diversify into other product areas, thus providing the public with a wider array of financial services while reducing the risk associated with limiting operations to traditional banking services. In addition, prior to 1997, organizing as a bank holding company allowed banks to circumvent restrictions on branching and thus seek out sources and uses of funds in other geographical markets.

Thus, organizing as a bank holding company allowed banks to effectively circumvent prohibitions on intrastate and interstate branching, which have now been virtually

- Making, acquiring, brokering, and servicing loans
- Issuing and accepting letters of credit
- Appraising real estate and personal property
- Financing commercial real estate equity
- Providing check-guaranty services
- Performing collection agency services
- Providing credit bureau services
- Performing activities to transfer title to commodities underlying derivatives contracts instantaneously, on a pass-through basis
- Managing and servicing assets, providing collection activities
- Acquiring debt in default
- Operating real estate settlement services
- Leasing personal or real property
- Operating nonbank depository institutions
- Performing trust company functions
- Performing financial and investment advisory activities
- Providing feasibility studies
- Offering agency transactional services
- Performing investment transactions as principal including underwriting and dealing in government obligations, money market instruments, foreign exchange, forward contracts, options, futures, options on futures, swaps, and similar contracts
- Performing management consulting and counseling activities
- Providing courier services
- Printing and selling checks, deposit slips, etc.
- Providing insurance agency and underwriting activities
- Performing community development activities
- Issuing money orders, savings bonds, and traveler's checks
- Providing data processing
- Processing, storing, and transmitting nonfinancial data in connection with their financial data processing, storage, and transmission activities

SOURCE: Federal Reserve System, http://www.federalreserve.gov/regulations/default.htm.

eliminated, and to participate in activities that otherwise would have been barred. Such activities include data processing, leasing, investment counseling, and servicing out-of-state loans. For a summary list of activities that bank holding companies can engage in, see Exhibit 11-5.

Almost all large banks are owned by holding companies. The largest holding company is Citigroup, which resulted from the September 1998 merger of Citicorp and Travelers Group. Citigroup has almost $1,400 billion in assets and 100 million customers, and has a presence in more than 100 countries. Although the list is rapidly changing, the 25 largest bank holding companies appear next to a list of the 25 largest banks in Exhibit 11-6. You can observe for yourself how the two lists overlap and see the additional assets that the bank holding companies add to the largest banks.

Perhaps even more dramatic than the conversion of large banks to bank holding companies is the ongoing trend for bank holding companies to convert to **financial holding companies.** (Indeed, Citigroup mentioned earlier is also the largest financial holding company.) Under the Gramm-Leach-Bliley Act (GLBA) of 1999, bank holding companies, securities firms, insurance companies, and other financial institutions can

Financial Holding Companies
Holding companies that can engage in an even broader array of financial-related activities than bank holding companies, including securities underwriting and dealing, insurance agency and underwriting activities, and merchant banking activities; financial holding companies may engage in any other financial and non-financial activities as determined by the Fed.

Banks Ranked by Total Assets as of June 30, 2004.

Rank	Name	City	State	Total Assets(K)	Branches Domestic	Branches Foreign
1	BANK OF AMERICA, NATIONAL ASSOCIATION	CHARLOTTE	NC	706,888,184	4,665	36
2	JPMORGAN CHASE BANK	NEW YORK	NY	654,641,000	718	107
3	CITIBANK, N.A.	NEW YORK	NY	648,243,000	388	331
4	WACHOVIA BANK, NATIONAL ASSOCIATION	CHARLOTTE	NC	368,871,000	3,176	5
5	WELLS FARGO BANK, NATIONAL ASSOCIATION	SIOUX FALLS	SD	364,698,000	3,638	3
6	BANK ONE, NATIONAL ASSOCIATION	CHICAGO	IL	245,783,000	1,754	9
7	FLEET NATIONAL BANK	PROVIDENCE	RI	213,732,068	1,553	163
8	U.S. BANK NATIONAL ASSOCIATION	CINCINNATI	OH	189,736,629	2,637	1
9	SUNTRUST BANK	ATLANTA	GA	125,880,597	1,345	1
10	HSBC BANK USA	BUFFALO	NY	110,305,393	420	25
11	BANK OF NEW YORK, THE	NEW YORK	NY	94,536,383	346	10
12	STATE STREET BANK AND TRUST COMPANY	BOSTON	MA	90,895,554	2	11
13	BRANCH BANKING AND TRUST COMPANY	WINSTON-SALEM	NC	74,890,205	937	0
14	KEYBANK NATIONAL ASSOCIATION	CLEVELAND	OH	74,847,093	1,364	1
15	PNC BANK, NATIONAL ASSOCIATION	PITTSBURGH	PA	67,526,820	896	0
16	MERRILL LYNCH BANK USA	SALT LAKE CITY	UT	66,421,616	N.A.*	N.A.*
17	BANK ONE, NATIONAL ASSOCIATION	COLUMBUS	OH	64,770,000	393	0
18	LASALLE BANK NATIONAL ASSOCIATION	CHICAGO	IL	62,764,854	122	1
19	FIFTH THIRD BANK	CINCINNATI	OH	60,510,974	436	0
20	MBNA AMERICA BANK, NATIONAL ASSOCIATION	WILMINGTON	DE	57,380,041	2	1
21	COMERICA BANK	DETROIT	MI	54,646,420	382	1
22	CITIBANK (SOUTH DAKOTA), NATIONAL ASSOCIATION	SIOUX FALLS	SD	52,910,469	0	0
23	SOUTHTRUST BANK	BIRMINGHAM	AL	52,825,454	786	0
24	MANUFACTURERS AND TRADERS TRUST COMPANY	BUFFALO	NY	51,497,358	726	1
25	AMSOUTH BANK	BIRMINGHAM	AL	48,212,819	693	0

* Not available

Source: National Information Center, Federal Reserve System, http://www.ffiec.gov/nic.

affiliate under common ownership to form financial holding companies. A financial holding company can offer their customers a complete range of financial services, many of which were previously prohibited. These activities include:

- securities underwriting and dealing
- insurance agency and underwriting activities
- merchant banking activities
- any other activity that the Fed determines to be financial in nature or incidental to financial activities
- any nonfinancial activity that the Fed determines is complementary to the financial activity and does not pose a substantial risk to the safety or soundness of depository institutions or to the financial system

11-6b

The Giants: Bank Holding Companies

Bank Holding Companies Ranked by Total Assets as of June 30, 2004.

Rank	Name	City	State	Total Assets (K)
1	CITIGROUP INC.	NEW YORK	NY	1,396,568,000
2	BANK OF AMERICA CORPORATION	CHARLOTTE	NC	1,039,764,440
3	J.P. MORGAN CHASE & CO.	NEW YORK	NY	817,763,000
4	WELLS FARGO & COMPANY	SAN FRANCISCO	CA	420,305,000
5	WACHOVIA CORPORATION	CHARLOTTE	NC	418,441,000
6	TAUNUS CORPORATION	NEW YORK	NY	316,458,000
7	BANK ONE CORPORATION	CHICAGO	IL	299,303,000
8	HSBC NORTH AMERICA HOLDINGS INC.	PROSPECT HEIGHTS	IL	298,818,386
9	U.S. BANCORP	MINNEAPOLIS	MN	190,230,000
10	ABN AMRO NORTH AMERICA HOLDING COMPANY	CHICAGO	IL	131,361,819
11	SUNTRUST BANKS, INC.	ATLANTA	GA	128,135,048
12	NATIONAL CITY CORPORATION	CLEVELAND	OH	116,969,803
13	COUNTRYWIDE FINANCIAL CORPORATION	CALABASAS	CA	103,753,435
14	BANK OF NEW YORK COMPANY, INC., THE	NEW YORK	NY	97,575,127
15	BB&T CORPORATION	WINSTON-SALEM	NC	97,348,285
16	FIFTH THIRD BANCORP	CINCINNATI	OH	95,613,539
17	STATE STREET CORPORATION	BOSTON	MA	94,139,945
18	KEYCORP	CLEVELAND	OH	85,794,644
19	CITIZENS FINANCIAL GROUP, INC.	PROVIDENCE	RI	82,271,178
20	PNC FINANCIAL SERVICES GROUP, INC., THE	PITTSBURGH	PA	73,141,914
21	MBNA CORPORATION	WILMINGTON	DE	60,856,258
22	COMERICA INCORPORATED	DETROIT	MI	54,925,431
23	SOUTHTRUST CORPORATION	BIRMINGHAM	AL	53,031,918
24	M&T BANK CORPORATION	BUFFALO	NY	52,093,709
25	REGIONS FINANCIAL CORPORATION	BIRMINGHAM	AL	49,922,137

SOURCE: National Information Center, Federal Reserve System, http://www.ffiec.gov/nic/.

Merchant Banking

Direct equity investment (the purchasing of stock) in a start-up or growing company by a bank.

Merchant banking is the making of direct equity investments (purchasing stock) in start-up or growing nonfinancial businesses. Under GLBA, financial holding companies are able to own up to 100 percent of commercial, nonfinancial businesses as long as ownership is for investment purposes only, the financial holding company is not involved in the day-to-day management of the company, and the investment is for 10 years or less. Prior to the recent law, bank holding companies could own only 5 percent of a commercial company directly and up to 49 percent through certain subsidiaries.

To become a financial holding company, bank holding companies that meet certain criteria must file a declaration with the Federal Reserve.[8] The declaration must certify that, among other things, all of the bank holding company's depository institution subsidiaries are well capitalized and well managed.

As of March 11, 2000, the effective date of the GLBA, 117 institutions were certified as financial holding companies. As of January 2004, more than 625 financial holding companies had been formed.

To summarize, banks, under the holding company corporate umbrella, have been expanding the geographical areas they serve and the array of financial services they offer the public. Bank holding companies may also apply to become financial holding companies if they meet certain criteria. Under the financial holding company status, bank holding companies, insurance companies, and securities firms can affiliate under common ownership. In addition, financial holding companies can engage in an even broader array of financial and nonfinancial services than bank holding companies can. The expansion by banks into areas traditionally served by other more specialized FIs has been matched, as discussed in the last chapter, by other FIs and other nonfinancial institutions expanding into areas traditionally served mainly by banks, such as the checkable deposits offered by S&Ls and the credit cards offered by General Motors.

Ongoing Changes in the Structure of the Banking Industry

The breakdown of barriers to intra- and interstate branching and to certain activities has resulted in increased competition in the financial services industry and considerable erosion in the domain and effectiveness of many long-standing financial regulations. The changes in the structure of U.S. banking and banking laws have been revolutionary and have resulted in a drastic decline in the number of banks in the past few years. Between 1980 and mid-2004, more than 1,465 banks failed, about 9,800 mergers occurred, and about 4,700 new banks were started. The result was a net decline in the number of banks from more than 14,400 to less than 7,700 in late 2004. The movement toward integration and consolidation among financial institutions in the financial services industry is expected to continue.

A related trend is a significant increase in the share of total bank assets controlled by the largest banks. For example, in 1980, the 100 largest banking organizations (banks and bank holding companies) accounted for about one-half of total banking assets. By mid 2004, the largest 20 banks accounted for more than half of banking assets, the 3 largest banks controlled 25 percent, and the top 10 banks, about 45 percent. The increased concentration of banking assets in the largest banks has resulted from the removal of branching restrictions, particularly across state lines, and bank mergers. Despite the decline in the number of banks, the number of branches has actually increased since 1980.

In the 1990s, the pace and dollar volume of mergers increased significantly. Some of the largest mergers that took place during the early and mid-1990s include the Chase-Chemical Bank merger, the Wells Fargo-First Interstate merger, the Nations-Bank-Barnett merger, and the First Union-Core States merger. Although these mergers were the largest in history to that time, they are much smaller than the more recent mergers of Citicorp and Travelers, Wells Fargo and Norwest, Banc One and First Chicago, and NationsBank and BankAmerica. These mergers have set a new standard for sheer size in U.S. banking organizations. In early 2004, JP Morgan Chase and Bank One announced that they were merging, which caused many analysts to speculate that a new merger movement was about to begin. Recent mergers are occurring not only between banks but also, like the Citicorp-Travelers merger, between banks and other companies in the financial services industry.[9] Exhibit 11-7 shows how the number of banks has declined since the 1980s, largely due to bank mergers. The accompanying A Closer Look feature examines some of the recent megamergers.

Two things are certain: (1) The structure of the banking system is changing rapidly and looks far different than it looked 20 years ago and (2) profit-seeking banks will continue to adapt to changing regulations and the financial environment in which they operate in ways that will produce further structural changes.

11-7

The Declining Number of Banks

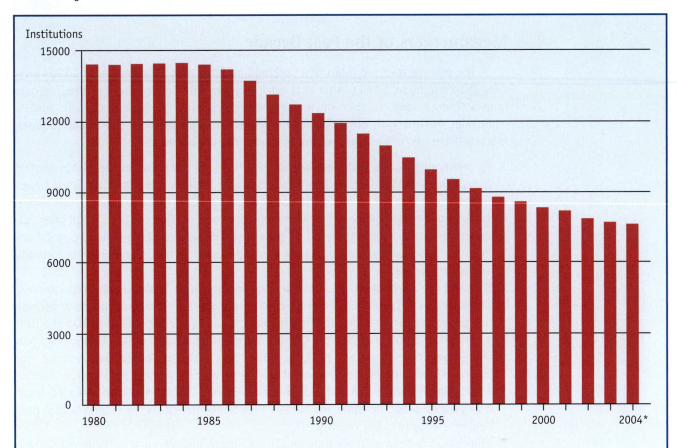

In the 1980s and early 1990s, some of the decline was due to bank failures. Since the mid-1990s, the decline was due to the record number of mergers among healthy institutions. The data also do not reveal that many of the mergers were between the largest banks.

*As of June 30, 2004.
SOURCE: Federal Deposit Insurance Corporation, http://www.fdic.gov.

Finally, as you have seen, banks, under the financial holding company status, can enter the securities, insurance, and merchant banking industries and engage in other financial and nonfinancial activities as determined by the Fed. Banks were officially barred from these activities between 1933 and 2000, although many had de facto found ways into some of these areas through nonbank subsidiaries. We expect the trend for extensive financial integration and concentration to continue in the financial services industry.

Megamergers of the Past Decade

The provisions of the Interstate Banking and Branching Efficiency Act of 1994 were fully phased in by mid-1997. After that time, mergers entered a new era as the size, geographical area, and number of mergers increased sharply. Moreover, bank holding companies merged with other financial services firms, producing mega-financial supermarkets. Here we review four mergers that occurred during the fall of 1998:

1. As mentioned in the text, the largest bank holding company resulted from another megamerger—that of Citicorp and Travelers Group. The new firm, Citigroup, is the largest financial services firm in the world with more than $950 billion in assets, outstanding stock valued at $82 billion, and 100 million customers in 100 countries. It can offer customers one-stop shopping for all of their financial service needs including retail and investment (securities) banking, credit cards, brokerage services, and property, casualty, and life insurance.

2. BankAmerica Corporation of San Francisco merged with NationsBank Corporation of Charlotte, North Carolina. The merger entailed a stock-for-stock swap valued at $60 billion between the two banks. The new megabank has assets in excess of $570 billion and a network of 3,800 branches in 27 states. Both NationsBank and BankAmerica had purchased securities firms in 1997. In 1991, San Francisco–based BankAmerica had purchased Security Pacific in what at that time was the largest bank merger ever. In 1997, NationsBank purchased Florida-based Barnett Bank and Missouri-based Boatman's Bancshares. The combined bank—called BankAmerica—is the second largest bank holding company in the country.

3. Ohio-based Banc One Corporation and First Chicago NBD Corporation swapped $30 billion of stock in order to merge. The result was the largest retail and commercial bank network in the Midwest. The new bank—called Bank One Corporation—has more than 2,000 branches and assets in excess of $275 billion.

4. Minneapolis-based Norwest Corporation merged with San Francisco–based Wells Fargo to become the nation's sixth largest bank with assets of more than $191 billion and operations in 21 states throughout the West and Midwest. The new bank, known as Wells Fargo, is the nation's leader in offering banking services over the Internet.

Although mergers continued at a rapid pace, the wave of megamergers subsided in late 1998 only to be revitalized in 2003 and 2004 with two of the largest mergers in history, which we review next.

1. On October 27, 2003, Bank of America, the third largest bank, announced that it was buying FleetBoston Financial Corporation, the nation's seventh largest bank, for about $47 billion. The new bank with about $950 billion in assets will be second largest U.S. bank behind Citigroup. The merger gives Bank of America a foothold in New England, something that it had lacked. The new bank will have about 180,000 employees and 5,700 branches.

2. On January 14, 2004, J.P. Morgan Chase, the nation's third largest bank, and Bank One Corporation, the nation's sixth largest bank, announced plans to merge in a $58 billion deal. The new bank will have more than $1.1 trillion in assets, 145,000 employees, and 2,300 branches, making it the second largest bank behind Citigroup, leapfrogging over the new bank created by the Bank of America–FleetBoston merger in October

2003. J.P. Morgan gains access to retail banking while Bank One gains access to investment banking.

These mergers resulted from the desire to slash costs (and often employees), boost stock prices, and offer customers more diversified services. The trend is from traditional local banks with limited services to multiregional and national banks offering customers in a wider geographical area a larger menu of services including bank accounts, loans, and investment and insurance services.

The Evolution of International Banking

The environment for banks has also changed dramatically in the international arena. A striking increase in international borrowing and lending by domestic banks began in the 1970s with the expansion of world trade that occurred shortly after the first OPEC oil crisis.[10] The amount of international lending as well as the number of participating banks increased. *Petrodollars,* as they came to be known, flowed into the OPEC nations in payment for oil. In turn, the OPEC nations deposited a large part of these funds in U.S. and European banks in exchange for deposit claims. Many U.S. banks began to loan funds denominated in dollars to less-developed countries. In the early 1980s, a crisis arose when the less-developed countries were unable to service their loans. As a result, many large banks had to write off or restructure those loans and incurred losses that took many years to be absorbed. Consequently, the 1990s and early 2000s have seen less emphasis on growth, more caution, and more emphasis on asset quality and rate of return.

In addition, many foreign banks had made significant inroads into U.S. markets by the 1980s. Many of these foreign banks got caught up in the same types of problem loans as domestic banks in the 1980s, however, and their growth slowed considerably. Nevertheless, foreign banks still have a major presence in the United States. On June 30, 2004, 231 foreign banks from more than 50 countries operated branches or offices in the United States. Branches of foreign banks controlled about 14 percent ($1,115 billion) of banking assets in the United States. In addition, foreign banks had a majority ownership interest in 66 U.S. commercial banks with about $356 billion in assets. Another 47 foreign banks operated agencies in the United States. An **agency of a foreign bank** is a more restrictive form of operation than a foreign branch in that the agency can raise funds only in the wholesale and money markets, whereas the branch of a foreign bank can accept retail deposits as well as borrow in the wholesale and money markets. An additional 134 foreign banks had representative offices in the United States.

In the 2000s, the banking system became truly international in scope. Advances in electronics and telecommunications allowed domestic and foreign banks to participate in worldwide transactions without leaving home. Now funds can be easily transmitted virtually anywhere in the world. Deregulation has also made it possible for U.S. banks to open offices and enter foreign markets more easily than before, and vice versa.

In this new environment, bankers have discovered that there is tremendous competition for international transactions involving the electronic transfer of funds—and, consequently, profit margins are declining. Scores of banks from around the world can bid on loans with the result that the interest rate, and hence the return, are driven to

Agency of a Foreign Bank
A U.S. office of a foreign bank that can borrow funds only in the wholesale and money markets and is not allowed to accept retail deposits.

rock-bottom levels. What appeared to be new lending opportunities have been somewhat disappointing because of the reduced profit margins. As a result, banks once again are looking to more traditional markets for expansion.

The time has come to round out our examination of commercial banking by focusing on the management of individual banks, with particular emphasis on the risks that banks face. In this way, you will gain a greater appreciation for what banks do and why.

Recap   Under the holding company corporate umbrella, banks have succeeded in expanding the geographical areas they serve and the array of financial services they offer the public. Barriers to interstate branching were removed in 1997 by the IBBEA. GLBA allowed banks, securities firms, and insurance companies to affiliate under common ownership and to provide their customers with an extensive array of financial services. Since the 1980s, the number of banks has declined because of bank failures and mergers. In the 1990s and early 2000s, many megamergers have occurred, and banking is becoming increasingly concentrated. Banking has become truly international in scope as well. Foreign banks own more than $1,115 billion of U.S. banking assets and have a majority ownership in U.S. banks with $356 billion in assets.

Bank Management: Managing Risk and Profits

After the ribbon is cut and the new bank or branch opens, the bank's managers swing into action. In essence, it is the bank's balance sheet—assets, liabilities, and capital— that is "managed." The management decisions involve what kinds of loans to make, what the prime rate should be, what interest rate to offer on one-year time deposits, and so forth. These decisions reflect an interaction between the bank's liquidity, safety, and earnings objectives and the economic and financial environment within which the bank operates.

To get a clearer picture of this interaction, it is useful to visualize bank management as having to face and deal with several types of risks and uncertainties including credit or default risk, interest rate risk, liquidity risk, and exchange rate risk. A primary function of a bank loan officer is to evaluate or assess the default risk associated with lending to particular borrowers, such as firms, individuals, and domestic and foreign governments. To do this, the loan officer gathers all of the relevant information about potential borrowers including balance sheets, income statements, credit checks, and how the funds are to be used.

In addition to developing reports that quantify risks, loan officers must also be aware that they are making decisions about whether to fund a loan under conditions of asymmetric information. **Asymmetric information** means that a potential borrower knows more about the risks and returns of an investment project than the bank loan officer. Thus, the borrower and the lender do not have equal, or symmetric, information. After all, don't many of those who apply for a loan obviously try to put their best foot forward and to conceal any blemishes? In addition, those with the most to hide and those willing to take the biggest risks are often the most likely to be less than forthright and/or to pursue a loan most diligently. If the bank funds these less-desirable loans, the result is an **adverse selection problem,** which increases the risk of default.

Moreover, after the loan is made, it may be difficult to guarantee that the loan is used only for the stated purpose, not for a more risky venture. This so-called **moral hazard problem** results from the fact that once borrowers get the funds, they may have an incentive to engage in a riskier venture.[11] This incentive occurs because higher-risk

Asymmetric Information
When a potential borrower knows more about the risks and returns of an investment project than the bank loan officer does.

Adverse Selection Problem
When the least-desirable borrowers pursue a loan most diligently.

Moral Hazard Problem
When the borrower has an incentive to use the proceeds of a loan for a riskier venture after the loan is funded.

ventures pay a higher return. After all, the borrowers are now risking the bank's funds. If the borrowers win, they keep the bigger profits; but if they lose, the bank bears the loss. Under these conditions, members of a bank's management team must be experts at assessing and evaluating risk. They must recognize that asymmetric information, adverse selection, and the incentive to engage in riskier ventures are usually facts of life.

Bank managers must also manage interest rate risk. As noted in Chapter 10, a positive spread today can turn into a negative spread later when the cost of liabilities exceeds the return on assets. An example will illustrate the point. Suppose that LHT National Bank is about to make a two-year loan to a local restaurant. The loan officer is satisfied that the credit risk is not excessive, and an interest rate of 7 percent is agreed upon. In effect, the bank, in view of the economic and financial outlook and its existing balance sheet, plans to finance the loan by issuing ("hiring") one-year time deposits paying 4 percent. The 3 percent spread will yield a handsome gross profit over the first year. What about the second year? As a great economic philosopher once said, "It all depends."

At the end of the first year, the time deposit matures, and LHT has to "rehire" the funds needed to continue financing the outstanding loan to the restaurant. If the funds can be rehired at 4 percent, the spread will not change. Suppose, however, that the overall level of interest rates has risen dramatically, perhaps due to restrictive policy actions being pursued by the Fed, and the bank must now pay 10 percent on one-year time deposits. The 3 percent positive spread (7 percent minus 4 percent) in the first year of the loan is exactly offset by a 3 percent negative spread (7 percent minus 10 percent) in the second year. When various administrative and processing costs are considered, the loan turns out to be quite unprofitable.

Banks can use financial futures, options, and swaps to manage interest rate risk. These three instruments are discussed in later chapters, particularly Chapter 18. **Adjustable (variable) rate loans** can also be used to hedge interest rate risk. The basic idea is quite simple. The loan contract specifies that the rate charged on a loan—be it a consumer loan, business loan, or mortgage loan—will be adjusted up or down, say, once a year, as the cost of funds rises or falls. The aim, of course, is to preserve a profitable spread and to shift the interest rate risk onto the borrower.

Going back to our example, suppose the loan contract with the restaurant calls for an adjustable rate of three percentage points above the bank's cost of funds instead of the fixed rate originally assumed. Such an arrangement produces the same 7 percent rate in the first year (4 percent plus 3 percent), but a 13 percent rate (10 percent plus 3 percent) in the second year. In effect, the bank has succeeded in shifting the interest rate risk to the borrower.[12] It is worthwhile emphasizing here that adjustable rate loans have become an important risk management tool. In the early 1990s, interest rates on liabilities fell faster than rates on assets, resulting in record bank profits. Imagine a positive spread becoming larger over time.[13]

Like other intermediaries, banks need to manage liquidity risk. As noted in Chapter 10, a fairly large proportion of bank liabilities are payable on demand. Checkable deposits and savings deposits are two prominent examples. Banks must be prepared to meet unexpected withdrawals by depositors and to accommodate unexpected loan demands by valued customers. The resulting need for liquidity can be satisfied by holding some highly liquid assets, such as Treasury bills or excess reserves, or by expanding particular types of liabilities as needs develop. One way to expand liabilities is to attract large negotiable CDs, possibly by offering higher rates than those offered by the competition. Other ways are to borrow more reserves from the Fed's discount facility or in the federal funds markets, or to increase borrowing in the repurchase agreements or overnight Eurodollar markets.

Adjustable (Variable) Rate Loan
When the interest rate on a loan is adjusted up or down as the cost of funds rises or falls.

Finally, because banking has become more international in scope, some banks maintain stocks of foreign exchange that are used in international transactions and to service customers who need to buy or sell foreign currencies. If the exchange rate between two currencies changes, the value of the stocks of foreign exchange will also change. Thus, a bank, like any holder of foreign exchange, is subject to an exchange rate risk. As you shall see in Chapter 18, banks and other holders of foreign exchange now use exchange rate forward, futures, option, and swap agreements to hedge this risk.

Perhaps the business of banking is beginning to sound somewhat more complex and challenging than you originally envisioned. But then again, most senior bank executives don't make six- and even seven-figure incomes just for showing up in gray pinstripe suits.

Bank Performance

As you have seen, banks are facing increasing competition from other FIs and other nonfinancial corporations in a global environment. They have confronted a volatile economic and regulatory environment. In the face of such challenges, bank profitability, which was low in the 1980s, improved significantly in the 1990s. For example, banks reported a record $15.9 billion in profits in April 1998—the fifth consecutive quarter in which a new record profit level was established. The strong profits were attributed to the strong economy that reflected favorably on bank assets, low interest rates, and growing sources of noninterest income.[14] Most analysts ascribed the better performance by banks to their more diversified portfolios and to their environment. The problem loans to less-developed countries such as Mexico, Brazil, and Argentina, which caused major loan losses for many large banks in the 1980s, were resolved. Banks have shored up capital due to new regulations. All of these factors led to record profit levels and high bank stock valuations.

Bank stocks performed below average in the late 1980s but did very well in the early 1990s and extremely well in the late 1990s, outperforming the S&P 500 index. In the early 2000s, banks stocks' declined as a result of the overall collapse of stock prices and the faltering economy. By early 2004, banks' stock prices were close to their 1998 peak as the banking system became more profitable in the recovering economy. Proceeding on the premise that the market value or price of a firm's stock—be it a bank or a manufacturing firm—is a function of current and expected earnings and the risk associated with the firm's operations, the better performance in the 1990s suggests that financial investors had gradually come to view bank stocks as much more attractive investments than they had been in the 1980s due to their record profit levels. Also, data from the FDIC shows that the number of problem banks has declined in recent years and that FDIC reserves for losses exceed by more than 20 percent the amount prescribed by law.[15]

The major challenge facing banks in this new millennium is competition from other intermediaries and other nonfinancial companies that have taken an increasing share of intermediation. These **nonbanks**, as they have come to be called, face less regulation and often lower costs. Costs may be lower because nonbanks are less regulated than banks are with regard to what they can do and where they can locate. In addition, nonbanks do not face reserve requirements; nor do they have to maintain full-service branches. As Exhibit 11-8 shows, despite the record profits, banks' share of total intermediation is declining. Banks must increasingly adapt to a changing industry to maintain profits as well as to maintain market share. It is no wonder that banks are merging with other financial services firms including savings and loans, securities firms, and insurance companies, as well as expanding into areas previously prohibited to banks.

In the next chapter we look at financial innovation.

Nonbanks
Other intermediaries and nonfinancial companies that have taken an increasing share of intermediation.

11-8
Commercial Banks' Declining
Share of Intermediation

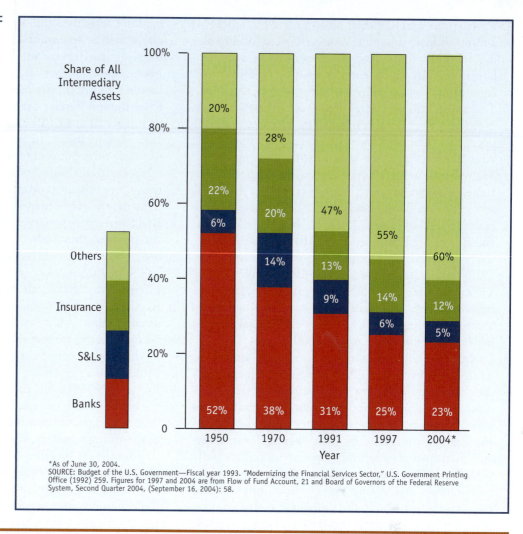

Share of All
Intermediary
Assets

Others

Insurance

S&Ls

Banks

	1950	1970	1991	1997	2004*
(top)	20%	28%	47%	55%	60%
	22%	20%	13%	14%	12%
	6%	14%	9%	6%	5%
Banks	52%	38%	31%	25%	23%

Year

*As of June 30, 2004.
SOURCE: Budget of the U.S. Government—Fiscal year 1993. "Modernizing the Financial Services Sector," U.S. Government Printing Office (1992) 259. Figures for 1997 and 2004 are from Flow of Fund Account, 21 and Board of Governors of the Federal Reserve System, Second Quarter 2004, (September 16, 2004): 58.

Recap Bank management must deal with the problems of asymmetric information, adverse selection, and moral hazard, as well as default risk, interest rate risk, liquidity risk, and exchange rate risk. Banks have made record profits since the 1990s after performing very poorly in the 1980s. Despite record profits, banks' share of intermediation continues to decline.

Summary of Major Points

1. Banking is a heavily regulated industry. Regulatory policy aims at promoting competition and efficiency while preserving the safety and soundness of institutions. The Glass-Steagall Act of 1933 was enacted in response to the financial collapse in the Great Depression. The law established interest rate ceilings that could be paid to depositors, separated investment and commercial banking, and created the FDIC.

2. Banks in the United States are chartered by either the federal government or one of the 50 state governments. Federally chartered banks are called *national banks* and must belong to the Fed and subscribe to

FDIC deposit insurance. State-chartered banks can, if they choose, belong to the Fed and/or subscribe to FDIC insurance. In fact, nearly all banks subscribe to FDIC insurance. Although only about 25 percent have federal charters and belong to the Fed, these banks tend to be the largest and have the most assets and banking offices.

3. The McFadden Act outlawed interstate branching by national banks. With regard to intrastate branching, the act required national banks to abide by the branching laws of the state in which they were located.

4. Restrictions were imposed on entry and branching as a result of fears that more competition in local banking markets might lead to more failures and that letting big city banks enter markets served by small community banks might result in concentration. These restrictions have resulted in a banking structure in which a large number of small banks control a small portion of total banking assets and a small number of large banks control the bulk of total banking assets. Many bank mergers have occurred in recent years—some of them between banks and other financial services firms. Banking is becoming more heavily concentrated. As of June 1, 1997, the Interstate Banking and Branching Efficiency Act (IBBEA) of 1994 effectively allowed unimpeded nationwide branching. With the passage of the Gramm-Leach-Bliley Act of 1999, banks, securities firms, and insurance companies have been able to affiliate under common ownership and to offer the public a vast array of financial services under one umbrella since early 2000.

5. Under the holding company corporate umbrella, banks have been expanding the geographical areas they serve and the array of financial services they offer the public. The expansion by banks into areas traditionally served by other more specialized FIs has been matched by other FIs and nonfinancial institutions expanding into areas traditionally served mainly by banks. The result has been more competition in the financial services industry and considerable erosion in the domain and effectiveness of many long-standing regulations. Under GLBA, bank holding companies can be certified as financial holding companies. In addition to banking, financial holding companies can engage in securities underwriting and dealings, insurance activities, merchant banking activities, and other financial and nonfinancial activities determined by the Fed.

6. Banking has become internationalized as U.S. banks have increased their participation in international lending and domestic banks have faced competition from foreign banks. Branches of foreign banks now own more than $1,115 billion, or about 14 percent, of U.S. banking assets. In addition, foreign banks have a majority ownership in 66 U.S. banks. Electronic and telecommunication advances have helped to increase the competitiveness of international lending, thereby reducing the profit margin.

7. Bank managers supervise a bank's balance sheet. In the process, they have to face and deal with default risk, interest rate risk, liquidity risk, and exchange rate risk. They must make decisions despite asymmetric information, adverse selection, and moral hazard.

8. Regulators periodically audit (examine) banks. Conducting more of a management appraisal than a financial audit, the examiners pay particular attention to the quality of a bank's assets and, thus, how the bank is managing risk.

9. In the early 1990s, the cost of liabilities fell faster than the earnings on bank assets, resulting in record profits. The record profits continued into the late 1990s due to the strong economy, low interest rates, and increases in noninterest income. Although bank stocks stumbled in the early 2000s, by early 2004, they were close to previous highs, and other indicators suggested that the banking system was healthy. Despite their success, banks' share of total intermediation is declining. This statistic is somewhat misleading because banks that are part of financial holding companies can affiliate with savings and loans, security firms, and insurance companies.

Key Terms

Review Questions

1. We have stressed that the goals of efficiency and competition may conflict with the goals of safety and soundness. Give an example of when this could occur.
2. What is meant by a *dual banking system?*
3. What is a bank *holding company?* Why have most large banks become bank holding companies? What is a *financial holding company?* What must a bank holding company do to become a financial holding company?
4. What are the two major provisions of the McFadden Act? What was the motivation behind its passage?
5. What is the IBBEA? What was the motivation behind its passage?
6. How did multibank holding companies "get around" the McFadden Act before the passage of the IBBEA? Defend the following statement: The IBBEA did nothing more than endorse what was happening in the marketplace.
7. Critique the following statement: Because there are more than 7,600 commercial banks in the United States, banking is obviously a highly competitive industry.
8. What is interest rate risk? Explain several ways that banks can reduce interest rate risk.
9. What is liquidity risk? Discuss ways in which banks deal with this risk. Does the development of nondeposit liabilities increase or decrease liquidity risk?
10. Identify two factors that have contributed to the growth of international banking. What factors contribute to reduced profit margins in this area?
11. What is adverse selection? What is moral hazard? How can a bank manager deal with these risks?
12. Discuss the factors that have contributed to the revolutionary changes in the structure of U.S. banking in recent years. Which factors are most important? Could regulators have prevented many of the changes?
13. Will the revolutionary changes in banking increase or decrease the competitiveness of the industry? Why?
14. Discuss the following statement: The breakdown of barriers to interstate and intrastate banking means that competition in banking is decreasing.
15. What is asymmetric information?
16. What is merchant banking?

Analytical Questions

Questions marked with an icon are objective in nature. They can be completed with a short answer or number.

17. On June 30, 2004, what percentage of bank assets did the smallest 50 percent of banks dddcontrol? What percentage of bank assets did the largest 1 percent of banks control?
18. Explain whether each of the following situations involves asymmetric information, adverse selection, or moral hazard:
    a. I am financing a new car. In applying for a loan, I withhold information about my student loan, and the loan does not show up on my credit report.
    b. Just before quitting my job, I obtain all the credit cards I can. I plan to run them up to the limit and declare bankruptcy.
    c. I take out a loan to manufacture a product. My costs end up being higher than expected, and there seems to be little market for my product. I am unable to repay the loan.
19. Use Exhibit 11-1 to calculate the following:
    a. What percentage of total assets do national banks own? What percentage of total deposits is in national banks?
    b. What percentage of total assets do state banks own? What percentage of total deposits is in state banks?

Internet Exercises

1. The U.S. commercial banking system is unique in the sense that it is a dual banking system with side-by-side federal and state-chartered commercial banks. Access the Internet site for the FDIC (**http://www.fdic.gov/**) and obtain data on the current status of commercial banks in the United States.

   a. What is the percentage of commercial banks that operate with a national charter? What percentage has a state charter?

   b. Classify the number of FDIC-insured commercial banks by asset size. What do you observe?

2. Browse the quarterly banking profile for the most recent quarter at the Internet site **http://www.fdic.gov/**. Locate information on the total deposits and income of banks with deposit insurance and the number of bank failures.

Suggested Readings

For a great book on banking consolidation, see Gary A. Dymski, *The Bank Merger Wave: The Economic Causes and Social Consequences of Financial Consolidation* (Armonk, NY: Sharpe, 1999). A recent article on the same subject is "Bank Consolidation: Regulators Always Have the Power to Pull the Plug" by Adam M. Zaretsky, *The Regional Economist,* Federal Reserve Bank of St. Louis (January 2004).

For an interesting discussion of "How Does the U.S. Banking System Compare with Foreign Banking Systems?" see *Ask Dr. Econ,* Federal Reserve Bank of San Francisco (April 2002). It is available on the Internet at **http://www.frbsf.org/education/ activities/drecon/2002/0204.html**.

For an in-depth look at "Changing Technology and the Payment System" with emphasis on the role of banks, see the article by the same name by Jamie B. Stewart, Jr., *Current Issues in Economics and Finance,* Federal Reserve, Bank of New York, 6:11 (October 2000).

For a current look at bank profitability and other issues, see Til Schuerman, "Why Were Banks Better Off in the 2001 Recession?" *Current Issues in Economics and Finance,* Federal Reserve Bank of New York, 10: (January 2004) and Alan Greenspan, "The State of the Banking Industry." Testimony Before the Committee on Banking, Housing, and Urban Affairs, U.S. Senate, April 20, 2004, **http://www.federalreserve.gov/ boarddocs/testimony/2004/20040420/default.htm**.

Another interesting article is Robert R. Bliss and Mark J. Flannery, "Market Discipline in the Goverance of U.S. Bank Holding Companies: Monitoring vs. Influencing," *Working Papers,* No. WP-00-3, Federal Reserve Bank of Chicago (March 2000).

For a fascinating article about the sometimes harrowing experiences of a bank examiner, see "Follow the Money," by David Fettig, ed., *The Region* 12:2 (June 1998): 16–21, published by the Federal Reserve Bank of Minneapolis.

For a discussion of the trends likely to influence banking, see Dev Strischek, "Commercial Lending and Lenders in the 21st Century," *Journal of Lending and Credit Risk Management* 80:12 (August 1998): 16–22.

For a glimpse into the future, see Robert T. Parry, "Financial Services in the New Century," *Federal Reserve Bank of San Francisco Economic Letter,* No. 98-15 (May 8, 1998).

For an interesting discussion of bank mergers, see Y. Amihud and G. Miller, eds., *Bank Mergers and Acquisitions* (Amsterdam: Kluwer Academic Press, 1998).

A collection of 124 articles in four volumes that looks at *The Regulation and Supervision of Banks,* is by Maximilian J. B. Hall, ed. (Northampton, MA: Edward Elgar, 2001). The series covers articles that span from 1973 to 1998.

For a look at "The Emerging Role of Banks in E-Commerce," see John Wenninger's article by the same name in *Current Issues in Economics and Finance,* Federal Reserve Bank of New York, 6:3 (March 2000).

Two books that look at banking systems abroad may be of interest. They are *Islamic Banking* by Mervyn K. Lewis and Latifa M. Algaoud (Northampton, MA: Edward Elgar, 2001), and *Banking and Financial Stability in Central Europe* by Karl Petrick and David M. A. Green (Northampton, MA: Edward Elgar, 2001).

Endnotes

1 Subsequent research has seriously questioned this analysis. For example, it appears that the banks that were paying the very highest rates on deposits prior to the Great Depression were not the most likely to fail.

2 In addition, the applicant must be free of a criminal record.

3 In 1989, the FDIC was also given the responsibility of insuring the deposits of savings associations (S&Ls and savings banks) that wished to join. At that time, the FDIC was divided into two parts. The Bank Insurance Fund insured commercial bank deposits of member banks, and the Savings Association Insurance Fund insured deposits of member savings associations.

4 The only time since the Great Depression when there were bank runs during 1985 when some state- (as opposed to federally) insured S&Ls in Maryland and Ohio experienced "runs." This, once again, illustrated the attractiveness of federal insurance to depositors.

5 The FFIEC also prescribes uniform principles, standards, and report forms for the federal examination of savings and loans and credit unions.

6 In addition to what appeared to be lax regulation, many banks had problems during years of prosperity because leveraging was high and bad loans had been made to developing countries.

7 Note that this argument is in sharp contrast to one of the reasons given for the recent wave of bank mergers. Presumably, because of technological changes in the 1990s, large banks now can be more efficient than small ones. A recent study suggests, however, that most economies of scale are exhausted by the time banks reach the size of $10 billion to $25 billion in assets, which is certainly small by today's standards.

8 Banks that are not bank holding companies may apply simultaneously to become bank holding companies and financial holding companies.

9 This merger actually occurred prior to the passage of the Gramm-Leach-Bliley Act. Because it involved the merger of a bank and an insurance company, it would not have been legal without the ultimate passage of the GLBA.

10 OPEC stands for the Organization of Petroleum Exporting Countries, a cartel dominated by the Middle Eastern oil-producing nations.

11 Deposit insurance causes a moral hazard problem in a macro sense. The presence of deposit insurance causes financial intermediaries to take more risks than they otherwise would because they know that if they lose, their depositors still get their funds back.

12 Note that even though the interest rate risk for the bank has been reduced, default risk has increased because the borrower is less certain of future payment obligations.

13 In a falling interest rate environment, a bank heavily into adjustable loans would be worse off than one that contracted at fixed rates on its assets.

14 In the early 1990s, profits rose mostly as a result of falling interest rates on liabilities, which lowered the cost of borrowing. The return on bank assets was also falling during the 1990s, but the cost of liabilities was falling faster, which resulted in increased profits.

15 The poor performance in the 1980s reflected troubled loans, which included loans to less-developed countries as well as energy and commercial real estate loans. Concerns about the safety of the financial services industry, given the general climate surrounding the savings and loan crisis, were also quite prevalent.

Looking Back page 232.

a "The Currency Dealer," *Greensheet Newsletter* (Torrance, CA: December 1995).

Necessity is the mother of invention.

12

CHAPTER TWELVE

Financial Innovation

Learning Objectives

After reading this chapter, you should know:

What financial innovation is and why it has occurred at a rapid pace since the mid-1960s

The major types of financial innovations since 1960

How regulations, increased competition, and volatile interest and inflation rates have triggered financial innovations

The role of computer and information technologies in fostering financial innovations and globalization

The direction of financial innovation in upcoming years

The Road from There to Here

Carol, a student at State University majoring in economics, is about to register for fall semester classes. She is interested in working overseas for a large financial institution, so she is attracted to a political science course (Pol Sci 505) that examines different political systems and how they influence the conduct of policy. The problem is that it is a graduate course, and undergraduates are not allowed to register for such courses. Undaunted, Carol meets with the instructor and convinces him that she is fully capable of handling the material. He tells her to register for Pol Sci 296, a listing usually reserved for special independent study courses, and to attend Pol Sci 505. In this way, Carol gets to take the course she desires and, in the process, evades the college regulation. We tell our students that if they can't find their way around most university rules, they aren't trying very hard.

In recent semesters, State University has been experimenting by offering several classes over the Internet. This year, it is starting a virtual university where students can earn a degree without ever coming to campus. This program will relieve the university's need for more classroom space and enable it to serve students who live in remote geographical areas and cannot come to campus. All in all, the university, driven to cut costs while serving more students, is finding creative ways to do so. Such adaptive or innovative behavior permeates many colleges today.

Innovation is also widespread in the economy at large. The driving force behind such behavior is reasonably straightforward: Participants in the economy (individuals and institutions) are simply trying to come as close as possible to achieving their objectives. The objective could be a well-rounded education likely to lead to a well-paying, interesting job in the case of a student, maximum return at the minimum risk for an investor, and maximum profitability in the case of a firm. This process, referred to as *maximization,* is nothing more than the attempt of economic units to do the best they can given their objectives and the circumstances they face. But what does "doing the best one can" mean in this context? Simply put, if the circumstances pose a barrier to achieving an objective, there is an obvious incentive to find a way to surmount, or otherwise avoid, the obstacle. As the quotation at the beginning of the chapter suggests, such incentives give birth to the innovation we subsequently observe.

In our discussion of the financial system, we have repeatedly emphasized that change is an enduring characteristic. The current system is different from what it was 10 years ago, and it will be different 10 years hence. Previous chapters have described some of the particularly noteworthy changes. Financial innovation is the creation of new financial instruments, markets, and institutions in the financial services industry. The major forces producing these changes include innovation in the ways people spend, save, and borrow funds in a globalized economy and innovation in the operations and scope of activities engaged in by financial intermediaries (FIs). In recent decades, computer and information technologies have played a major role in financial innovation. These advances have allowed for innovations in the way financial instruments are bought and sold, the creation of a variety of new financial instruments, and the globalization of financial markets that fulfill previously unmet services.

The purpose of this chapter is to develop a more complete understanding of the causes and consequences of the wave of financial innovation that has altered the U.S. financial system over the past 40 years. In Chapter 13, we look at the stresses and strains that the financial system faces and that are inherent in this dynamic environment.

Major Causes of Financial Innovation

The famous economist Joseph Schumpeter wrote extensively about the process of economic development, emphasizing the key role played by the entrepreneur/innovator.

The prototype is a creative, insightful individual or group of individuals willing to take a few risks in the pursuit of higher profits. The innovation may involve the development and adoption of a cheaper method of production or the introduction of an entirely new product. Holding other factors constant, lower production costs will, of course, raise profits. Similarly, if a new product catches on, sales and profits will increase.

Less dramatic but no less important examples of innovative activity include the application of newly developed or existing technology in a new field or product area and the discovery and adoption of new methods of operating that legally evade rules and regulations. In both cases, the innovation increases profits. As we shall see in a few moments, the adoption of new computer and information technologies and the avoidance of regulations have played key roles in the process of **financial innovation** since the 1960s. Two other factors have also been important in generating recent financial innovations: (1) FIs have faced increasing competition from other financial and nonfinancial institutions, causing them to innovate as part of a struggle to survive in a globalized environment and (2) as prices, inflation, interest rates, and exchange rates have become more volatile, innovations have been developed to deal with this instability. All told, these factors have caused the period since the mid-1960s to be an era of rapid financial innovation, with one innovation leading to another and resulting in a restructuring of the entire financial services sector.

Financial Innovation
The creation of new financial instruments, markets, and institutions in the financial services industry; new ways for people to spend, save, and borrow funds; changes in the operation and scope of activity by financial intermediaries.

The Analytic Foundations of Financial Innovation

Viewed analytically, the incentive for FIs to engage in innovative activity flows from a comparison of costs and benefits. More specifically, an FI, for example, compares the costs and revenues (benefits) associated with altering a prevailing portfolio practice. Adopting a new technology or developing a new product, such as a new type of time deposit, can be costly. If the end result is expected to be, say, a reduction in the costs of providing financial services or a rise in the revenue on earning assets—possible benefits of innovation that exceed the costs—then the FI has a clear profit incentive to innovate and alter prevailing practice.

On the cost side, one factor appears to have been particularly important. Since the 1970s, computer and telecommunications technologies have been increasingly available and powerful as well as less costly to adopt. As noted earlier when discussing electronic funds transfer systems, these advances have reduced the transactions costs associated with managing, moving, and monitoring funds. They have also allowed for the globalization of financial markets because funds can be transferred fairly instantaneously around the world.

Financial claims are particularly receptive to computer advances because these claims are quite fungible. **Fungibility** refers to the ease with which one item can be transformed into another. How does this characteristic fit in here? Think back to Carol and her professor at the beginning of the chapter. They innovated by essentially relabeling a course. This type of change is much easier and less costly than, say, turning an automobile plant into a computer factory. The situation is similar in the financial world where funds can be moved or transported and, in effect, relabeled relatively easily, making innovation less costly than it might be in other industries.

Fungibility
The ability to be easily converted from one type of instrument to another.

Technological advances have also allowed the risks associated with a particular financial asset to be *unbundled* or divided up into parts. These risks include credit risk, interest rate risk, exchange rate risk, and liquidity risk. Unbundling allows the specific risks of one financial asset to be borne by different investors. In this way, the investors most able and willing to bear certain risks can do so, making financial markets more efficient (more on this later).

Turning to the benefits side, the interaction between the prevailing economic environment and the structure of financial regulations initially played the major role. Recall from Chapter 11 that Regulation Q put interest rate ceilings on bank and savings and loan (S&L) deposits and that the activities of banks were fairly tightly controlled. If innovating around these controls could be extremely profitable, then substantial ingenuity would be expended to find ways around the restrictions. In the mid-1960s, such a situation developed when persistent inflation and rising interest rates occurred in a regulatory environment not designed to handle such events. The benefits of avoiding regulations greatly increased in an inflationary environment, and one of the first responses was to develop new products to avoid the binding effects of the regulations. A fatal flaw in the regulatory structure put in place during the Great Depression was that it failed to anticipate the sequence of events that would occur if market interest rates increased and remained above the Regulation Q ceilings for a significant period of time. We illustrate with the following scenarios.

Assume that you are a net lender with a savings deposit earning 5 percent, the ceiling rate, at HLT National Bank. Are you satisfied or not? The answer, once again, is "it depends." In particular, it depends on the rate you could earn on the next best option, say, on another highly liquid, safe financial claim that would be a substitute for the savings deposit, such as a Treasury bill (T-bill). Suppose the prevailing rate on T-bills in the Treasury securities market is 4 percent. Obviously, you can smile because your rate on the savings deposit is higher.

But suppose that the rate on bills is 8 percent. You would no longer be smiling. We would expect people to shift funds out of savings deposits and into T-bills. Such a removal of funds from banks and other intermediaries is called **disintermediation**.[1] The intermediaries are bypassed in the borrowing-lending process. The flaw in Regulation Q then was that there was no way to keep people from withdrawing their funds and seeking out better opportunities. As long as market interest rates are below Regulation Q ceilings, intermediaries subject to Regulation Q can effectively compete against open market instruments such as T-bills, commercial paper, and corporate bonds. However, if rates on instruments traded in the open market rise above ceiling limits, disintermediation follows as depositors take their funds out of intermediaries and invest them in open market instruments such as T-bills and commercial paper. The result is that banks are weakened as deposits flow out, subverting the good intentions of Regulation Q, which was supposed to strengthen the banks.

During the 1970s, disintermediation occurred at an alarming rate because market interest rates were substantially above Regulation Q limits. Savers with large balances had always been able to disintermediate and usually did so when market interest rates went above the Regulation Q limit. However, small savers with few alternatives were stuck earning the ceiling rate at depository institutions. Persistently high interest rates in the 1970s led to the development of money market mutual funds, which would change things. The ingenious entrepreneurs who devised these instruments gave small savers an alternative to deposits in banks or other depository institutions subject to Regulation Q limits.

As discussed in Chapter 5, money market mutual funds pool funds from small investors, say, $5,000 from five individuals, and acquire money market instruments, such as T-bills and commercial paper, that small savers on their own cannot afford because of the high minimum denominations. The money market mutual fund passes the higher interest earned, minus a management fee, on to the small investors. For example, suppose you have $5,000 in a bank savings deposit yielding the Regulation Q ceiling rate of 5 percent, and the rate on commercial paper is 10 percent. You would like to transfer your funds from the

Disintermediation
The removal of funds from a financial intermediary.

depository institution, but the minimum denomination on commercial paper is $25,000, so you don't have enough to acquire the market instrument. After the birth of money market mutual funds, you can transfer your $5,000 to a money market mutual fund that pools funds from several small depositors and buys higher-denomination instruments while keeping a management fee. The money market mutual fund is, of course, a financial innovation that created a new financial intermediary.

Now put yourself in the position of the bank's president. Profitable lending opportunities exist, but you are losing deposits through disintermediation and the transfer of funds to money market mutual funds.[2] You have an incentive to find a way to reverse the outflow of funds. A frontal attack is ruled out by Regulation Q. You cannot raise the explicit rate you pay on savings deposits. The breakthrough occurs when your bank and other FIs develop new liabilities, many of them created by taking existing bank liabilities from deposits subject to interest rate ceilings and other regulations and relabeling them as liabilities not subject to the regulations. Thus, the interaction between the prevailing economic environment and the structure of financial regulation, Regulation Q, in this case, produced rising benefits of innovation. The level of market interest rates coupled with relatively high inflation produced rising benefits if Regulation Q limits could be avoided. Or, put another way, as the changing environment made *not* complying with the regulations increasingly profitable, FIs and their customers were induced to alter prevailing practices. Eventually, Regulation Q ceiling limits were removed, but before that happened, additional factors came into play, spurring further innovation by banks and other FIs.

Since the mid-1970s, banks and other FIs have been challenged by a sharp rise in competition from other domestic and global financial and nonfinancial institutions. In any industry with increased competition, profit margins generally decline, and cost-saving technological advances become more important. In a more competitive environment, the benefits of developing a new set of financial products and services are greatly increased. As you saw in Chapters 10 and 11, all FIs are becoming less specialized and more alike as they offer new products and services. For example, banks, under the auspices of holding companies, now offer investment and financial advice, leasing, data processing, and tax planning. Look back at Exhibit 11-5 for a list of some activities now permitted for bank holding companies.[3] In recent years, the formation of financial holding companies has allowed banks to expand their wings into insurance, securities, merchant banking and other ancillary financial and nonfinancial activities that go far beyond the scope of those allowable under the bank holding company umbrella. Thus, the greater the competition, the greater the drive to innovate from both the costs and the benefits perspective.

Finally, the greater volatility of price indexes, stock values, interest rates, exchange rates, and the like increases the risks and hence the costs associated with intermediation. The increased risks make financial innovation to deal with this volatility more beneficial. New assets have been and are being developed to mitigate the risks associated with the volatility. Financial forward, futures, and options markets are financial innovations that attempt to hedge interest rate and exchange rate risks. These instruments, called *derivatives*, are discussed shortly and are also the subject of Chapter 18. FIs now use them and other instruments to unbundle risk into its various parts. This allows those most willing and able to bear some of the risks of intermediation to do so. In addition, they allow financial and nonfinancial institutions to exploit every opportunity for profit from minute price differentials.

To summarize, whenever the perceived benefits of innovation exceed the costs, an incentive exists to engage in innovation. The pace of innovation in the United States has

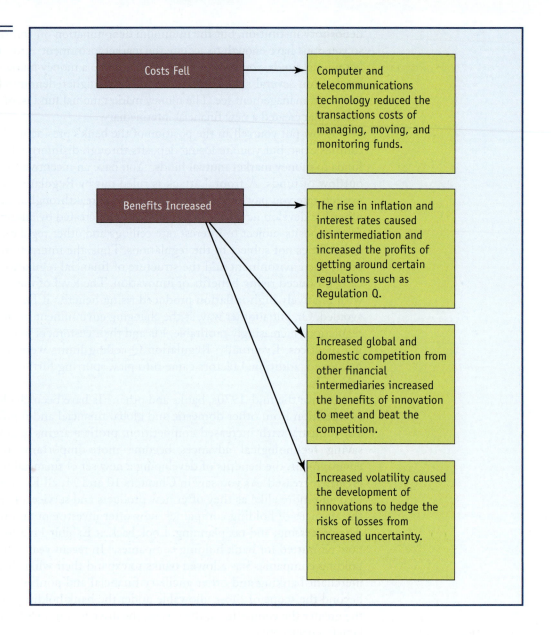

Costs Fell → Computer and telecommunications technology reduced the transactions costs of managing, moving, and monitoring funds.

Benefits Increased →

The rise in inflation and interest rates caused disintermediation and increased the profits of getting around certain regulations such as Regulation Q.

Increased global and domestic competition from other financial intermediaries increased the benefits of innovation to meet and beat the competition.

Increased volatility caused the development of innovations to hedge the risks of losses from increased uncertainty.

been rapid over the past 45 years as the costs of innovation fell and the benefits rose, as depicted in Exhibit 12-1. On the cost side, the malleability of financial claims and the application of emerging computer and telecommunications technology reduced the transactions costs associated with managing, moving, and monitoring funds. On the benefits side, three factors came into play:

1. The rise in inflation and interest rates increased the benefits in terms of higher profits associated with avoiding various regulations. For example, with market rates well in excess of Regulation Q ceiling rates on deposits, net lenders were induced to reduce their holdings of such deposits. The resulting disintermediation and its adverse effect on the profits of banks and other depository institutions prompted these FIs to find ways to pay implicit interest and to create "new" liabilities not subject to the regulation.

2. Additionally, increased domestic and global competition from other FIs increased the benefits of financial innovation to "meet and beat" this competition.

3. Price and interest rate volatility increased the risks of financial intermediation and hence increased the benefits of developing new instruments such as futures and options to deal with these risks.

The regulatory structure played a pivotal role in generating financial innovation, but as we have seen, on the cost side, advances in computer and telecommunication technologies that reduce the costs of transferring funds were also significant. In the near future, advances in computer and information technologies are expected to be the predominant factor in the development of innovations.

A final note: Perhaps you have noticed that the benefits and costs of financial innovations are often interdependent. For example, changes in computer and information technologies have not only reduced the costs of innovating but also led to increased price volatility and increased competition that increased the benefits of innovating.

Recap   Financial innovation will occur whenever the benefits are greater than the costs. Technological changes in computer and information technologies have dramatically reduced the costs of managing, moving, and monitoring funds. These have led to numerous innovations in the ways in which funds are invested and transferred. In the 1960s and 1970s, rising inflation and interest rates increased the benefits of innovating around some regulations. Increased competition among all FIs and greater price volatility also increased the benefits of innovating.

Early Financial Innovations

As discussed in earlier chapters, reserve requirements specify the reserve assets that banks and other depository institutions must hold as a proportion of their deposit liabilities. Even if there were no formal reserve requirements, banks would still hold some reserves in the interests of liquidity and safety. Doing so would simply reflect prudent management. However, if the reserve requirements set by the regulatory authorities force banks to hold more reserves than they otherwise would, this excess constitutes a tax or drain on bank earnings. That which must be held cannot be loaned! What cannot be loaned will not earn interest. Accordingly, the higher that the reserve requirements are relative to what banks would otherwise hold and the higher the interest rates are, the higher the forgone profits are.

Nondeposit Liabilities
Borrowed funds, such as Eurodollar borrowings, fed funds, and repurchase agreements, that are not deposits and are not subject to reserve requirements.

A way to reduce the burden of the Fed's reserve requirements was to relabel existing liabilities from deposits subject to reserve requirements to so-called **nondeposit liabilities** not subject to the requirements. In addition to being exempt from reserve requirements, nondeposit sources of funds offered another advantage: They were not subject to Regulation Q ceilings. Banks could pay whatever rate prevailed in the market rather than being limited to a maximum rate set by the regulators.

Major nondeposit liabilities include Eurodollar borrowings, fed funds, and repurchase agreements. Markets for nondeposit funds were small and relatively unimportant in the early 1970s but grew to be major sources of funds, especially for large banks.

Eurodollars are dollar-denominated deposits held abroad. U.S. banks sometimes borrow Eurodollar deposits to obtain additional funds. Eurodollar borrowings by U.S. banks provide an excellent example of a nondeposit source of funds that often represented a relabeling of liabilities to avoid Regulation Q (interest rate ceilings) and

Regulation D
A regulation that prescribed reserve requirements on some deposits.

Regulation D (reserve requirements). The result was a significant leak or hole in the regulatory dike and important shifts in the composition of bank liabilities (sources of funds) that spawned the growth of the Eurodollar and Eurocurrency markets.[4] The A Closer Look on page 266 looks at the development of the Eurodollar market.

The Development of the Eurodollar Market

In the 1970s, as we have seen, market interest rates frequently were above Regulation Q ceilings, causing disintermediation. Eventually, in 1980, Regulation Q was abolished on all but demand deposits. Corporations were still barred by regulation from holding negotiable orders of withdrawal (NOW) accounts and other interest-earning checkable deposits and, therefore, were left with their funds in short-term, no-interest demand deposits. Can you guess what happened? Corporate treasurers developed cash management techniques that would minimize their holdings of demand deposits. They moved liquid funds to money market instruments, such as commercial paper and T-bills. The banks responded with an all-out effort to maintain their liabilities and alleviate the disintermediation. They focused on getting corporations to convert what would otherwise be lost demand deposits into nondeposit liabilities. Even though the banks had to pay interest on the new liabilities, this was preferable to losing the liabilities altogether because if the liabilities were lost, the banks' ability to make loans would decrease. One of the ways banks converted demand deposits to nondeposit liabilities was through the use of Eurodollar deposits.

The following diagram shows how a demand deposits gets converted into a Eurodollar borrowing.

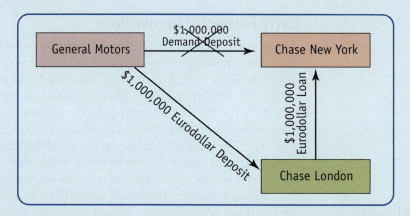

After its inception in the 1950s, the Eurodollar market was used to get around both Regulations Q and D. If market interest rates rose above the maximum rate that a bank—say, Chase—was allowed to offer on time deposits, disintermediation became a threat. Rather than sit idly by and watch its available funds dwindle and its ability to lend be constrained, the portfolio managers at Chase tried to persuade General Motors' financial officer to exchange the deposit at Chase New York for a deposit at the Chase branch in London. The deposit, which would be denominated in dollars and be free of reserve requirements and interest rate ceilings, would be known as a Eurodollar deposit.[a] The opportunity to evade some U.S. banking regulations by channeling funds through European banks encouraged the significant growth of the Eurodollar market.

As soon as General Motors deposited the funds in Chase's London branch, Chase's home office in New York would borrow the funds from its London branch. This is called a *Eurodollar borrowing*, a borrowing of dollar-denominated funds from Europe. As a nondeposit source of funds (liability), it is not subject to reserve requirements. Once Regulation

Q was abolished on all but demand deposits, the Eurodollar market became one of the vehicles that banks used to de facto pay interest on corporate demand deposits. Corporate demand deposits were simply converted into overnight Eurodollar deposits.

Returning to our example, as a net result of this series of transactions, Chase Bank in New York, in effect, relabeled its demand deposit liability (owed to General Motors) as a Eurodollar borrowing (owed to General Motors) from its London branch. In the process, Chase New York reduced the volume of required reserves it had to hold. Assuming the reserve requirement on demand deposits was 10 percent, Chase New York could now lend more even though its total liabilities had not changed. In addition, General Motors would earn and Chase would pay interest on the deposit.

In this example, General Motors converts a $1,000,000 demand deposit at Chase New York to a Eurodollar deposit at Chase London. Chase New York was holding $100,000 in required reserve assets against the $1,000,000 demand deposit. Chase New York borrows the Eurodollar deposit from Chase London. The Eurodollar deposit then becomes a $1,000,000 nondeposit liability, free of reserve requirements. General Motors earns interest on the deposit, and Chase New York has $100,000 in additional funds to lend.

One last point: Don't get the idea that the funds originally in Chase New York were withdrawn by General Motors, packed in a suitcase, flown to London, deposited, borrowed by Chase New York, and flown back to New York. We have traced out the relevant transactions in slow motion. In fact, the funds would never have left New York, and all the transactions could have occurred electronically within minutes using modern telecommunications technology.

As we first discussed in Chapter 5, fed funds are essentially reserves that banks trade among themselves for periods of one to several days. The interest rate determined in the market for fed funds is called the *fed funds rate*. Like other market interest rates, it is determined by the forces of supply and demand. The demanders are banks and other depository institutions that need reserves (funds) to meet their reserve requirements, to meet unexpected withdrawal demands, or to finance loans. The suppliers are banks and other depository institutions that have surplus funds and no other immediate use for them.

In the 1960s, the fed funds market for overnight borrowing and lending of reserves began to experience tremendous growth.[5] It also changed considerably. Rather than borrowing just to meet temporary shortfalls in reserves, larger commercial banks came to look to the fed funds market as a permanent source of funds. They borrowed large amounts each and every day and funded assets, including long-term assets, on a continuous basis with this source of funds. Small banks with fewer lending opportunities tended to be net lenders in this market.

Recall from Chapter 5 that an overnight repurchase agreement is an agreement in which a bank takes a government security from its asset portfolio and sells it with the simultaneous agreement to buy it back tomorrow at a price set today. The purchase price tomorrow is higher than the selling price today, with the difference being the interest that the lender receives from the bank. In reality, a repurchase agreement is a secured loan with the government security serving as collateral. Like fed funds, repurchase agreements became a significant new source of funds that large banks could access to get new funds to lend. These agreements were often "rolled over" on a daily basis, providing a "permanent" source of funds. As of June 30, 2004, the net amount of outstanding borrowings of fed funds and repurchase agreements by commercial banks exceeded $1,062 billion.

A more recent innovation, a **retail sweep account** also involves the relabeling of deposit liabilities to nondeposit liabilities. First appearing in 1994, these accounts "sweep" balances out of transactions accounts that are subject to reserve requirements and into other deposits (usually money market deposit accounts) that are not.[6] Required reserves fall by the amount of funds in sweep accounts multiplied by the required reserve ratio. Balances in sweep accounts grew from $5.3 billion in January 1994 to $641.9 billion in August 2004. In the aggregate, required reserves dropped from about $60 billion in 1994 to about $45 billion in August 2004. As required reserves fall, ceteris paribus, banks have more funds to lend.

Another innovation that did not involve relabeling deposit liabilities but was no less important was the creation of negotiable certificates of deposit (CDs). The creation of a secondary market for large certificates of deposit in 1961 made them "negotiable" CDs. Thus, a corporation with excess funds, perhaps not having to make payroll until next week, could invest the funds in a negotiable CD with the knowledge that if the funds were needed before the CD matured, the CD could be sold in the secondary market. Although they were subject to the same reserve requirements that other CDs were, CDs with maturities of 30 to 89 days were exempted from Regulation Q ceilings in 1970. Reserve requirements on all negotiable CDs were eliminated by the end of 1973. Negotiable CDs are a particularly important source of funds for banks because a bank can advertise and attract additional deposits of negotiable CDs to extend its lending. This advantage was particularly significant when restrictions on branching realistically restricted the growth of checkable deposits to a certain geographical area. A bank could attract CD deposits by advertising high rates.[7]

The financial regulations and structure that had been designed and erected during the Great Depression were increasingly ill-suited to the changing economic and technological environment of the 1970s. As innovations weakened the effectiveness of various regulations, regulators recognized the difficulty, if not the impossibility, of controlling financial flows and the market for financial services. Accordingly, they decided to **deregulate** by dismantling the regulations.[8] Landmark legislation enacted by Congress in 1980 and 1982 was the result.[9] These laws phased out Regulation Q, expanded the asset and liability powers of banks and thrifts, allowed thrift institutions to offer checkable deposits, and established reserve requirements that applied to and were the same for all depository institutions.

Two other laws in the mid- and late 1990s further deregulated financial markets by eliminating most restrictions on interstate banking and allowing banks to merge with securities and insurance firms, thus effectively repealing the Glass-Steagall Act.[10] We look in much greater detail at all of these laws in Chapter 14 on regulation of the financial services industry.

Innovation within the financial system has proceeded due to unprecedented competition among banks and other financial institutions in a globalized financial environment. Advances in computer and information technologies have made the increased competition possible and have transformed the financial system into a global system. With the new technologies, funds can be transferred instantaneously around the globe at a very low cost. Thus, globalization of finance due to technological advances would have proceeded even without the concomitant growth in world trade.

Recap A major form of innovation that got around Regulations Q and D was the relabeling of deposit liabilities as nondeposit liabilities. Examples include Eurodollar borrowings, fed funds, repurchase agreements, and retail sweep accounts. The creation of negotiable CDs was another innovation that allowed banks to attract additional funds. Because market participants had found ways around many regulations, Congress passed two major deregulation statutes in the early 1980s that phased out Regulation Q ceilings, expanded the asset and liability powers of banks and thrifts, allowed all thrifts to offer checkable deposits, and established the same reserve requirements for all depository institutions. Two other laws in the 1990s removed most restrictions on interstate banking and allowed banks to merge with securities firms and insurance companies.

Innovations in the Payments System

Innovations in the financial services industry have dramatically changed the nature of intermediation by creating new products, markets, and institutions. In recent years, these innovations have been made possible by advances in computer and information technologies. As Jamie B. Stewart, Jr. writes,

> I cannot recall a time of more fundamental and pervasive change in the financial services industry. Much of this change—and the pace at which it is taking place— is driven by extraordinary advances in computing and telecommunications technology. These advances in technology are not just evolutionary, they are revolutionary, and they are transforming virtually every aspect of commerce and banking.[11]

The payments mechanism is the means by which transactions are completed—that is, how money is transferred among transactors. The role of technology is perhaps nowhere more apparent or more important than in the innovations surrounding the payments system. Like the human race, the current payments mechanism has evolved from a primitive state and will continue to evolve in the future. This tendency to change, which we have already seen in those things functioning as a means of payment, is significantly influenced by the technology used to execute transactions.

Some of the more obvious innovations in the payments mechanism due to technological advances include such things as ATM machines, cash cards, debit cards, point-of-sale terminals, and home banking over the Internet. Other less-visible technology-related innovations include direct pay deposit and direct bill pay schemes. Electronic payments account for about 90 percent of the dollar value of all transactions! In this system, payments are made to third parties in response to electronic instructions rather than instructions written on a paper check or by using currency.

Note that an electronic funds transfer system does not eliminate the need for deposit accounts; it is just a more efficient way of transferring funds from one deposit account to another. To pay your grocery bill, for instance, your account is debited by the amount of your bill, and the grocer's account is credited by the same amount at the time of the exchange. The whole system is computerized so that no written checks are necessary. All you need is an account number and a debit card that you present to the grocer. The grocer, in turn, enters the prices of your purchases into a computer terminal (called a *point-of-sale terminal*), and at the end of the month, you receive a statement giving your current balance and a record of all the charges and deposits to your account. This is just like a checking account statement, but you do not have to write all of those checks.

Technological innovations will eventually make checks much less important, or even obsolete, as a means of transferring purchasing power. This is because checks are a much more costly way of making payments than via electronic impulses.

Currently, many employers, in cooperation with banks, pay salaries by automatically crediting them to their employees' bank accounts rather than by issuing the customary weekly or monthly check. Such automatic credits are also a form of an electronic funds

The Electronic Purse: An Innovation in the Making

Many banks have begun developing a new payments mechanism called the *electronic purse* or *stored-value card*. Prepaid cards for a single use have been available for many years. For example, some toll roads accept only a smart card in payment, college dorm cafeterias offer a prepaid smart card, libraries offer prepaid photocopy cards, and in many areas, phone companies sell prepaid calling cards.

The electronic purse will allow a single card the size of a credit card to be used in multiple locations to make many kinds of purchases. When making purchases, the card is passed through the merchant's point-of-sale terminal. Funds are deducted directly from the buyer's card and added to the point-of-sale terminal. Vendors can transfer the balances on their terminals to their bank accounts via a telephone transfer as frequently as they want. When the value on the card is spent, consumers can add additional funds to the card via a telephone transfer, an ATM machine, or a computer transfer. A personal identification number much like an ATM number can be used to validate that the card is being used by its owner.

The multiple-use smart card will have one or more computer chips embedded in it capable of storing and transferring information. The main benefit of the card to the consumer is convenience. Buying a cup of coffee, a newspaper, or a candy bar from a vending machine will no longer require fumbling for change. For merchants, the electronic card saves time and money in handling cash. Unlike checks, the card offers guaranteed payment and will most likely have lower transactions costs than those of credit cards or debit cards. For the issuer, there may be many benefits. For example, smart cards offer a potential source of fee income, and the issuer will earn interest on the unspent balances on the cards.

There are still many questions as to how smart cards will work. For instance, will transactions made on the cards be traceable? Such record keeping could help the police trace fraudulent use. Or should the use of the smart card be nontraceable like cash? Still other issues are whether the balances on smart cards will be covered by deposit insurance, whether nonbanks can issue the cards, and whether the cards will affect reserve management and the money supply. In the next few years, many of these questions will be resolved.

transfer system. More than 60 percent of workers (and 95 percent of federal government employees) now receive their pay in this manner. The vast majority of social security recipients receive their payments through direct deposit. Also, you can file your tax return electronically and receive a tax refund that is directly deposited into your checking account.

Your depository institution most likely has automatic teller machines (ATMs), which permit you to make deposits and withdrawals, even late at night when the institution itself is closed. In all probability, your college campus and your favorite grocery stores have a few ATMs. ATMs too are a form of an electronic funds transfer system. As the ownership of personal computers and modems spreads, it will be possible to conduct a large portion of one's financial transactions from home.

Basically, electronic funds transfer systems are nothing more than the application of computer and telecommunication technology to the entire area of financial transactions and services. Their aim is to reduce the physical handling and labor costs associated with an ever expanding volume of paper checks, deposit slips, and the like, as well as to provide increased convenience and service to the public. As questions regarding the privacy of financial records, security of the systems, and legal responsibilities are resolved, new payments practices and electronic funds transfer systems will spread. The result will be further evolution in how money is used and, perhaps, changes in what functions as money. The evolution of money and the payments mechanism go hand in hand with the development of an economy.

Derivatives and Other Recent Innovations
Forward, Futures, and Options Agreements

Advances in computer technologies have also allowed the unbundling of the risks inherent in financial products. The goal is to help firms and individuals manage risks and thus make the financial system more efficient. As you shall see in Chapter 18, forward, futures, and options agreements are routinely used to separate the total risk of a financial asset into subparts such as interest rate, credit, and exchange rate risk. Such **derivatives** derive their value from the underlying assets. The derivatives can be sold separately to the investors most willing and able to bear those risks.

There are many examples of risks that can be unbundled. For example, if a domestic firm issues foreign bonds, an exchange rate risk occurs because the bonds must be repaid in the foreign currency. The firm can use a foreign exchange forward agreement to hedge this risk. With the foreign exchange forward agreement, the firm locks in today the number of dollars that will be exchanged for the foreign currency at a later date. In this way, the firm unbundles the foreign exchange rate risk. In another example, the credit union that made two-year car loans funded by one-year deposits faces the risk that the interest rate will rise during the second year and the cost of the funds will exceed the rate on the car loans. The credit union can use futures or option contracts to hedge the interest rate risk. We cover in depth the mechanics of the forward, futures, and options markets in Chapter 18.

Swap Agreements

Swap agreements are another type of derivative. An **interest rate swap** is a financial innovation that can be used to reduce the risk of future interest rate changes over a long period of time, sometimes up to 15 years. Swaps involve two parties that trade interest payment streams to guarantee that their respective payment inflows will more closely match their outflows. Originating in 1982, they are a totally new instrument used mainly by entities such as commercial banks, savings and loans, other intermediaries, government agencies, and securities dealers to reduce interest rate risk. The use of swaps is growing fast, particularly at large banks. Interest rate swaps make markets more efficient and reduce risks, but they are often complex. Because of their complexity, we limit our discussion to a simple case.

Consider an example involving two commercial banks: Bank Two and Bank Three. Bank Two has long-term fixed-rate loans, such as mortgages, that it funds with floating or variable-rate money market accounts. The interest payments on money market accounts fluctuate with market interest rates, but the interest payments earned on the loans do not. The other bank—Bank Three—has made floating or variable-rate loans. The interest payments on these loans go up and down with an index of market interest rates,

Derivatives
Instruments such as forward, futures, options, swap, and other agreements that are routinely used to separate the total risk of a financial asset into subparts and that derive their value from the underlying assets.

Interest Rate Swaps
A financial innovation used to reduce the risk of future interest rate changes over a long period of time that involve two parties trading interest payment streams to guarantee that their respective payment inflows will more closely match their outflows.

such as rates on government bonds. The bank funds these loans with long-term fixed-rate deposits. The interest payments on these deposits do not change.

Both banks make a profit on the spread, or the difference between what the banks earn on their loans and what they pay depositors for the use of their deposits. But there is a problem: As the loans and deposits are now configured, both banks have some interest rate risk. In other words, both banks are in a position in which a change in interest rates can cause them to experience a loss. If interest rates go up, Bank Two (with fixed-rate loans and variable-rate deposits) may end up paying more for the use of its deposits than it is earning on its loans. If interest rates go down, Bank Three (with variable-rate loans and fixed-rate deposits) may end up paying more for the use of its deposits than it is earning on its loans.

All is not lost, however. These two intermediaries can get together through an interest rate swap arranged by another bank. Bank Two and Bank Three can trade the interest payments on their deposits (liabilities), but not the principal payments. After the swap, Bank Two will be funding fixed-rate assets with fixed-rate liability interest payments, and Bank Three will be funding variable-rate assets with variable-rate instruments. Both can hedge risk by engaging in the swap. The interest payments that Bank Two receives are fixed because it has fixed-rate loans. After the swap, the interest payments it makes to fund the loans will also be fixed. A rise in interest rates will no longer put Bank Two in a losing position. Bank Three's earnings on its loans will continue to move up and down with market interest rates, but the interest payments it makes to fund the loans will also be flexible. A fall in interest rates will no longer put Bank Three in a losing position. Exhibit 12-2 illustrates this example of an interest rate swap.

We have described a simple interest rate swap, but as noted previously, these instruments can be—and usually are—complex.

12-2

A Simple Interest Rate Swap

This Year	
Bank Two	*Bank Three*
Two-year loans earn 9% fixed	Two-year loans earn 8% variable
Deposits cost 5% variable	Deposits cost 6% fixed

Next Year Rates Go Up—No Swap	
Bank Two	*Bank Three*
Loans earn 9% fixed ☹	Loans earn 12% variable
Deposits cost 9% variable	Deposits cost 6% fixed ☺

Next Year Rates Go Down—No Swap	
Bank Two	*Bank Three*
Loans earn 9% fixed ☺	Loans earn 5% variable
Deposits cost 2% variable	Deposits cost 6% fixed ☹

Next Year Rates Go Up—They Swap	
Bank Two	*Bank Three*
Loans earn 9% fixed ☺	Loans earn 12% variable ☺
Deposits cost 6% fixed	Deposits cost 9% variable

Next Year Rates Go Down—They Swap	
Bank Two	*Bank Three*
Loans earn 9% fixed ☺	Loans earn 5% variable ☺
Deposits cost 6% fixed	Deposits cost 2% variable

The swap allows both banks to be happy all the time!

Currency Swaps

A financial innovation used to hedge exchange rate risk over a long period of time, whereby one party agrees to trade periodic payments in a given currency with another party who agrees to do the same in a different currency.

A **currency swap** is an innovation whereby one party agrees to trade periodic payments, over a specified period of time, in a given currency with another party who agrees to do the same in a different currency. Currency swaps can be used to hedge against foreign exchange rate risk over a multiyear period. Thus, through the use of currency swaps, foreign exchange risk can be reduced for a significant period of time in the future.

Like many financial innovations, currency swaps originally developed as a means to circumvent regulation. In the past, many countries employed capital controls that delayed or forbade the conversion of earnings by a foreign company in a local currency into the domestic currency of the foreign company. The plan was to encourage greater foreign investment by domestically based foreign subsidiaries. By delaying the conversion of foreign-denominated earnings into the parent-company's domestic currency, countries hoped that foreign subsidiaries would engage in increased investment. An example will make this clearer. Imagine a U.S. soft drink company with bottling and sales operations in China. If China delays the conversion of yuans into dollars, the bottling company will forgo interest earnings it could earn if it could convert yuans to dollars now. Thus, it makes sense for the soft drink company to borrow additional yuans, ask another Chinese company with U.S. subsidiaries to borrow dollars, and then the two companies can "swap" the proceeds from their respective loans. Each company gets immediate access to the currency that it wants and both innovate around the capital-control regulations. Like other regulations, currency controls have been greatly reduced or eliminated, but the innovation they spawned has not disappeared.

The examples of derivatives (including forwards, futures, options, and swaps) that we have just described are quite simple. Many derivatives in use today are far more complex and require the use of computers to evaluate the risk. Advances in the mathematical modeling of risk have made it possible to develop increasingly complex financial products and trading strategies. Indeed "financial engineers" have used financial and mathematical models to create innovative and exciting "hybrid" financial instruments that meet the needs of and give new opportunities to financial market participants. If used properly, these new products and strategies increase the efficiency of the financial system.

A new type of derivative, the credit derivative contract was first developed in the late 1990s and is used by banks and other lenders to unbundle credit risk. **Credit derivatives** transfer the risk to another party that the return in a credit transaction such as a loan falls below a certain rate. The party that accepts the risk receives a fee for doing so. Credit derivatives derive their value from the underlying debt instruments such as loans. For the purchaser (beneficiary), credit derivatives are like insurance to hedge default risk of the loans they hold. For the seller (guarantor), a risk is taken on return for a fee. Banks enter into both sides of these agreements either as guarantor (selling the insurance) or beneficiary (buying the protection) as a way of diversifying their credit risk more broadly than across their own portfolio of loans. As of September 30, 2003, the value of credit derivatives held by U.S. banks as guarantors was just under $350 billion, and the value held as beneficiaries was just over $400 billion. The 10 largest U.S. banks hold more than 95 percent of these credit derivatives.[12] Although this is a minuscule percent of the derivatives market, credit derivatives are expected to grow significantly in the years to come.

Credit Derivatives

Contracts that transfer the default risk of a loan or other debt instrument from the holder of the loan (beneficiary) to a guarantor who receives a fee for accepting the risk.

That risk-averse, profit-seeking financial market participants are resourceful and ingenious in dealing with risk is not surprising. When risks increase (as they do when markets become more volatile), market participants develop new ways to "handle" or manage the risk. Thus, we have witnessed the phenomenal growth of swaps and other derivatives. Financial and nonfinancial corporations must now be aware of and take every opportunity to reduce risks. If they fail to do so, they may find that they are not playing on a level field. Even the most skeptical of players may become convinced that they should be using the flashy new derivative instruments rather than be vulnerable to risk. If prices settle down (become less volatile), the growth of these markets may slow, but it is doubtful they will ever disappear. Once such markets are so highly developed, they will continue to be a means to capitalize on even small opportunities to reduce risk.

Recap

Derivatives such as forward, futures, option, and swap agreements have allowed the risks associated with intermediation to be unbundled. (Forwards, futures, and options are covered in depth in Chapter 18.) Interest rate swaps entail two parties trading interest payment streams to guarantee that the inflows of payments will more closely match the outflows. Currency swaps involve trading a set of payments in one currency for a set of payments in a different currency. They are used to reduce a firm's exposure to foreign exchange risk. Currency swaps can be done for multiple-year periods. Credit derivatives transfer the risk to another party that the return in a credit transaction falls below a certain rate. The party that accepts the risk does so for a fee.

Securitization

Securitization

The process whereby relatively illiquid financial assets are packaged together and sold off to individual investors.

Asset-Backed Securities

Securities that result from the process of securitization.

Another financial innovation resulting from the current financial environment is the spread of securitization to many loan markets. **Securitization** is the process whereby relatively illiquid financial assets are packaged together and sold off to individual investors. In essence, securitization turns relatively illiquid instruments into quite liquid investments called **asset-backed securities**. A market maker agrees to create a secondary market by buying and selling the securities. Securitization originated in the mortgage market in the early 1980s, when mortgage loans began to be packaged together and sold off as securities in the secondary market often with government insurance guaranteeing that the principal and interest would be repaid. Securitization became popular because it provides a way of protecting against interest rate risk in an environment of increased interest rate volatility.

Since the mid-1980s, securitization has spread from the mortgage market to other markets including credit card balances, vehicle loans and leases, accounts receivable, computer leases, home equity loans, student loans, railroad car leases, small business loans, and boat loans. Banks, finance companies, retailers, thrifts, and others issue asset-backed securities that provide them with new funds to lend. See the Looking Back feature for a discussion of the first securitization of small business loans.

Securitization has many advantages. Securitization offers reduced credit risk because of the pooling of assets. The securities are also available in small denominations for investors who are unwilling or unable to invest larger sums. The outstanding value of asset-backed securities increased from about $350 billion in 1991 to about $2.5 trillion in mid-2004. Securitization is an efficient way for borrowers and lenders to be brought together, and given its phenomenal growth since 1990, it now appears that securitization, which is a form of direct finance, will replace much of the lending that historically has gone through traditional intermediaries (indirect finance). We look at securitizations again in Chapter 15 when we discuss the role of government-sponsored enterprises that foster the growth of mortgage-backed and other asset-backed securities.

Collateralized Mortgage Obligations

Securitizations that redirect the cash flows (principal and interest) of mortgage-related products to various classes of bondholders, thus creating financial instruments with varying prepayment risks and varying returns.

The investor in mortgage-backed securities faces the risk that the mortgages will be prepaid before they mature because the property is sold or refinanced and that the return will fall short of expectations.[13] To reduce this risk, an innovation, **collateralized mortgage obligation**, has been developed. Collateralized mortgages redirect the cash

Securitization of Small Business Loans

In late 1993, small business loans were packaged into securities (securitization), and a secondary market for them was created. Indeed, a secondary market makes the securitization process much more successful because it increases the liquidity of the new securities. As is the case with all innovations and true to our quotation at the beginning of this chapter, "necessity" indeed "gave birth" to this innovation.

In the early 1990s, small businesses were particularly hard hit by a credit crunch due to new capital adequacy requirements imposed on depository institutions by the Financial Institutions Reform and Recovery Act (FIRREA) of 1989. Under the new laws, banks and savings and loans (S&Ls) were required to hold more capital in an attempt to shore up the financial system that was suffering severe strains due to the failure of the S&Ls. (We look in depth at the provisions of the FIRREA in Chapter 14.) The situation was particularly critical because small businesses did not have the same access to the commercial paper market as did medium-size and large firms. For a long time, securitization of the small business loan market had not seemed feasible because small business loans are particularly diverse and are often funded on a subjective basis. In other words, small business loans are by nature heterogeneous—a characteristic that did not make them good candidates for securitization.

Generally speaking, securitization develops most easily in markets in which financial assets are fairly homogeneous. For example, to be securitized and sold in a secondary market, mortgages are made to specific criteria regarding the income of the borrower and the loan-to-property value ratio. Under these circumstances, pools of mortgages are a fairly homogeneous lot. Vehicle loans, likewise, are made to certain income criteria with the vehicles serving as collateral. In the case of small business loans that are packaged and sold as securities, the backing includes accounts receivable, inventories, and equipment.

In early 1993, Fremont Financial Corporation of Santa Monica, California, sold $200 million of variable-rate certificates backed by a pool of loans to small and medium-size businesses. Merrill Lynch underwrote the offering, which quickly sold out, with the securities being bought by insurance companies, pension funds, and other large investors. An active secondary market exists for business loans with payments guaranteed by the Small Business Association of the federal government. The novelty of the Fremont offering is that there was no government guarantee.

In general, as more small business loans become securitized, the risks involved in lending to small businesses will be spread among many investors, fast-growing companies will be funded, and income will be generated for the innovators. As Fed Chair Alan Greenspan put it, a secondary market for business loans "would be a major contribution to the financial vitality of this country."[a]

Looking Forward

The Financial System of the Future

In this chapter, we have examined some of the ongoing changes in the financial system. We can still only guess what the future will bring. However, we believe that the following speculations are very interesting:

Although financial functions will be the same, they will be looked at differently in the twenty-first century. Thus, we will not refer to "loans," "borrowings," or "securities," but to "claims on wealth" or "financial claims." We will avoid the term *banks* because banks, certainly as we know them, will not exist. . . . A key to the system will be "wealth accounts" in which companies and individuals will hold their assets and liabilities. These accounts will contain today's relatively illiquid assets such as buildings and vehicles as well as what we know today as stocks, bonds, other securities, and new types of financial claims. These accounts would also contain all forms of liabilities. . . . There will be no special need for retail financial branches because everyone will have direct access to his or her financial suppliers through interactive TV and personal digital assistants. True interstate banking will have arrived at last! Or more accurately, true "global banking" will have arrived, as every household will be a "branch."[a]

flows (principal and interest) of mortgage-related products to various classes of bondholders, thus creating financial instruments with varying prepayment risks and varying returns. Those who are most risk adverse can choose an instrument whose the principal will soon be repaid. Those who are willing to bear more risk can choose an instrument whose principal will not be repaid until later. In exchange for more prepayment risk, the investor receives a higher return. Needless to say, such provisions make attractive choices available to a wider range of investors.

Recap Securitization has spread from the mortgage market to many markets including vehicle loans, credit card loans, student loans, and others. Collateralized mortgage obligations allow the prepayment risks of mortgage-backed securities to be distributed among various classes of bondholders.

Other Characteristics of the Financial System

Increased competition in the financial services industry has squeezed profit margins. Essentially, the average spread between the rate earned on assets and the average rate paid on liabilities has fallen for many FIs. In addition, banks have lost market share in the intermediation business. Investment bankers have developed new financial market instruments such as junk bonds and commercial paper for small and medium-size businesses that have taken away short-term and long-term loan business traditionally belonging to commercial banks. Banks have responded by increasingly entering markets that provide services such as data processing, accounting, and loan administration for fees. Fee income can reduce the erosion of bank profits caused by the declining bank market share and the declining spread in financial intermediation. In addition, many of the activities that generate fees, such as data processing, are also offered by nonbanks. By offering such services, banks can more effectively compete in the market for business loans. Thus, banks are becoming more like nonbanks, and vice versa.

Meanwhile, mergers are bringing about increased concentration in the financial services industry. Megamergers are creating institutions that can offer customers one-stop shopping for all their financial service needs including banking, credit cards, brokerage services, and property, casualty, and life insurance services. The enactment of legislation in 1999 allowed banks to enter the securities industry. This effectively ended the 65-year separation of investment and commercial banking instituted by the Glass-Steagall Act. In reality, banks have been effectively dismantling the provisions of Glass-Steagall for many years. With the new legislation, mergers under the bank holding company umbrella and the creation of financial holding companies have offered and will continue to effectively offer banks venues through which they can get into the securities industry. To date, the largest mergers have occurred among financial services firms within individual countries, although all industrialized countries have experienced financial consolidations. It is expected that financial service providers will continue to merge. Mergers have been made possible because of improvements in information technologies, financial deregulation, and globalization.

Information on the repeal of the Glass-Steagall Act of 1933 can be found at **http://www.captive.com/newsstand/articles/article_1.html**.

As financial firms try to cut costs, FIs have become increasingly automated. The resulting substitution of physical capital (such as automatic teller machines, debit cards, and point-of-sale terminals) for labor is having profound effects on the way transactions are conducted. Other automated payment systems include paying bills by automatic deductions from deposit accounts or other forms of automatic transfer and check cards. The National Automated Clearing House Association estimates that it is 10 times more expensive to issue and process a paper paycheck than to process a direct payment.[14] In addition to automation within the payments system, trading systems within the equity (stock) and bond markets have become increasingly automated. We look more closely at these in Chapters 16 and 17.

Geographical barriers to deposit taking, loan granting, and the provision of other financial services are fast eroding. Lenders advertise and solicit credit card accounts and make mortgage loans nationwide. Loans can be obtained over the Internet. This is very different from 30 years ago when lenders restricted mortgage lending to their immediate geographical area. Interstate branching is permitted nationwide, and some of the largest banks, operating through their holding company affiliates, provide many financial services nationwide and worldwide. Citigroup, the megacorporation created from the merger of Citicorp and Travelers, provides a vast array of financial services to more than 100 million customers nationwide and in more than 100 countries. The move to nationwide banking is being accompanied by an increasing level of international banking activity that complements the increased flows of funds among countries. The increased capital flows have also spawned new financial products. Small investors can now make liquid investments in global markets, including emerging economies, through what many would consider to be exotic mutual funds.

Finally, deregulation in the 1980s "let the genie out of the bottle" and taught us that once introduced, a financial innovation will not go away, even though the factors that caused its inception disappear. Two examples come to mind: (1) After the removal of Regulation Q, money market mutual funds did not disappear as many experts predicted and (2) when interest rates fell and became more stable in the early 1990s, the financial futures and options markets did not disappear but continued to grow and thrive in order to exploit every opportunity to hedge even the smallest risk. Exhibit 12-3 depicts recent changes in the financial system and indicates changes we believe will continue in the future.

Recap   Geographical barriers for many financial services have been reduced. FIs have become increasingly less specialized and more automated and have expanded the range of financial services they offer.

This completes our look at the causes and consequences of financial innovations in the past 40 years. In the next chapter, we look at the stresses and the strains intrinsic to the financial system. We shall see that financial innovations can both contribute to or alleviate financial instability.

12-3
Financial Market Changes in the 2000s

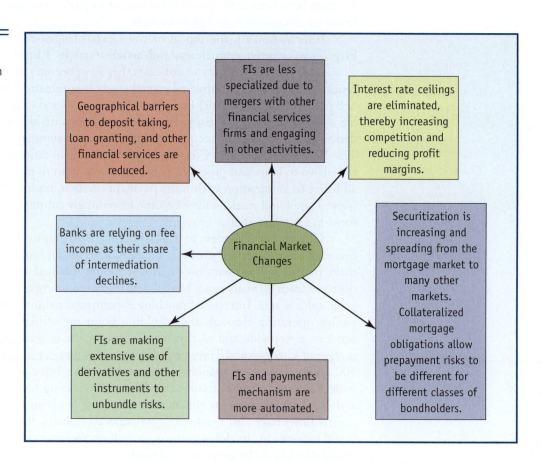

Summary of Major Points

1. Financial innovation is the creation of new financial instruments, markets, and institutions to increase profitability. Because financial claims are fungible and because other incentives have been present, during the last 40 years, a high level of financial innovation has occurred. This has happened because the benefits of innovating have exceeded the costs. Many of the innovations, particularly those in more recent years, have been due to advances in information and computer technologies.

2. In the 1970s, much innovation centered around evading regulations. Restrictions included setting reserve requirements (Regulation D) and interest rate ceilings (Regulation Q), limiting entry, separating commercial and investment banking, and specifying margin requirements.

3. In addition to information and computer technology advances, the incentives to innovate have included rising interest rates that led to disintermediation, volatile interest rates that increased interest rate risk, and increased competition.

4. The relabeling of deposit liabilities as nondeposit liabilities, which avoided both reserve requirements and interest rate ceilings, represented a major form of financial innovation. Included in this group of innovations are Eurodollar borrowings, fed funds, and repurchase agreements. In addition, the creation of a secondary market for CDs making them "negotiable" was also an important innovation. Retail sweep accounts represent a more recent innovation beginning in 1994 that reduces required reserves by sweeping deposit liabilities into nondeposit accounts overnight.

5. Beginning in 1980, the banking system was deregulated. Regulation Q interest rate ceilings were phased out and the asset and liability options for banks and thrifts were expanded. All depository institutions were allowed to offer interest-bearing checkable deposits, and reserve requirements are the same for all intermediaries. Two other laws in the 1990s eliminated barriers to interstate branching and allowed banks, securities firms, and insurance companies to merge.

6. The financial sector is becoming more competitive. Derivatives such as financial forwards, futures, options, and swaps are increasingly being used to hedge risk and to unbundle risks. Collateralized mortgage obligations reduce the prepayment risk of mortgage-backed securities by redirecting the cash flows of mortgage-related products to various classes of bondholders. Interest rate and currency swaps allow participants to hedge interest rate and exchange rate risks. Credit derivatives allow for the unbundling of credit risk.

7. Securitization is the process whereby relatively illiquid financial assets are packaged together and sold off to individual investors. Securitization is spreading from the mortgage market to many other markets including auto loans, credit card loans, small business loans, and student loans.

8. Geographical barriers for financial services are disappearing, and FIs are becoming less specialized and more concentrated. Profit margins from lending have been reduced. Financial transactions are becoming increasingly automated, and banks are expanding into other areas such as data processing and leasing. Mergers among large financial services firms are creating megafirms that offer one-stop shopping for all financial needs.

Key Terms

Asset-Backed Securities, 270
Collateralized Mortgage Obligations, 270
Credit Derivatives, 269
Currency Swap, 269

Deregulate, 264
Derivatives, 267
Disintermediation, 258
Financial Innovation, 257
Fungibility, 257

Interest Rate Swaps, 267
Nondeposit Liabilities, 261
Regulation D, 261
Retail Sweep Account, 264
Securitization, 270

Review Questions

1. Briefly discuss the incentives that have led to a rapid pace of financial innovation in the last 40 years.
2. What is *disintermediation*? When is it likely to occur? What factors can reduce it? If I take my funds out of my credit union and put them in a money market mutual fund, have I disintermediated? Why or why not?
3. Discuss the roles that technology and regulation play in aiding financial innovation. Will innovation always occur to exploit loopholes in regulations?
4. What are nondeposit liabilities? Give some examples. What are negotiable CDs? How do nondeposit liabilities differ from negotiable CDs? What are retail sweep accounts? What are *credit derivatives*?
5. What is Regulation Q? Regulation D? Discuss ways banks have found to get around both regulations.
6. What is securitization? How does it reduce interest rate risk? Name some types of liabilities that are now securitized.
7. Discuss some characteristics of the financial system of the early 2000s that make it different from earlier periods.
8. How have increased competition and price volatility affected financial innovation? What are some specific types of innovation that deal with these factors?
9. How do collateralized mortgage securities differ from mortgage-backed securities? Which has less risk?
10. Defend the following statement: Once an innovation appears, it will remain even after the impetus for its development disappears. Give an example.
11. Discuss how banks can reduce their reserve requirements.
12. Are financial claims more fungible today than in the past? Why?
13. Why didn't banks innovate to get around regulations in the 1940s and 1950s?
14. Explain why asset-backed securities are an example of direct finance. If a bank issues asset-backed securities, how does it get new funds to lend?

Analytical Questions

Questions marked with an icon are objective in nature. They can be completed with a short answer or number.

15. Treasury STRIPS are a type of government security that allows investors to register and trade ownership of the interest (coupon) payments and the principal amount of the security. The coupon and principal payments can each be sold separately at a discount so that no coupon payments are made until the STRIP matures. What risk is this innovation effectively allowing the investor to unbundle?

16. Explain the process by which a group of credit card balances could be securitized.

17. Assume a reserve requirement of 10 percent. If Chemical Bank is successful in getting Microsoft to convert a $2 million demand deposit to a Eurodollar deposit, how much can Chemical Bank lend out because of this transaction?

Internet Exercise

The Internet site **http://www.fdic.gov/regulations/laws/important/index.html** lists some important laws that have affected the banking industry in the United States.

- What is the Riegle-Neal Interstate Banking and Branching Efficiency Act of 1994?
- Which earlier banking act does Riegle-Neal effectively seek to repeal?

Suggested Readings

For an explanation of why securitizations have grown so much, see O. Emre Ergungor, "Securitization," *Economic Commentary*, Federal Reserve Bank of Cleveland (August 15, 2003).

For a discussion of *Financial Innovation and Effective Risk Management*, see the remarks by Fed Governor Susan Schmidt Bies to the Financial Services Institute 2004, Washington, D.C. (May 6, 2004). It is available on the internet at **http://www.federalreserve.gov/boarddocs/speeches/2004/200 40506/default.htm**.

Some recent innovative trends in banking are summarized in "Recent Developments in Business Lending by Commercial Banks," by William F. Bassett and Egon Zakrajsek, *Federal Reserve Bulletin* (December 2003): 477–492. The article is also available on the Internet at **http://www.federalreserve.gov/pubs/bulletin/2003/1203lead.pdf**.

For a look at financial innovation in Australia, see Colin Menzies, "A History of Financial Innovation," *Financial Review* (November 1, 2000).

For a look at financial innovation in the 1980s and 1990s, see Philip Molyneux and Nidal Shamroukh, *Financial Innovation* (New York: John Wiley, 1999).

For some differing views on the adoption of new technologies by banks, see Richard Beidl, "Battle for E-Mortgages," *Banking Strategies* (November/December 1999): 119–128; Thomas P. Johnson, Jr., "Putting Technology in Its Place," *Banking Strategies* (May/June 2001): 4; and Bob Gdovic, "Calling All Customers," *Bank Marketing* (May 2001): 32–36.

For an interesting article that touches on seveal topics in this chapter, see Roger W. Ferguson, Jr., "Understanding Financial Consolidation," March 9, 2001, at **http://www.federalreserve.gov/BoardDocs/Speeches/2001/20010309/default.htm**.

For an article that looks at securitization and monetary policy, see Arturo Estrella, "Securitization and the Efficacy of Monetary Policy," Federal Reserve Bank of New York Conference on Financial Innovation and Monetary Transmission, available on the Internet at **http://www.newyorkfed.org/research/economists/estrella/securitization.pdf**.

For a look at "The Emergence of Electronic Communications Networks in the U.S. Equity Markets," see James McAndrews and Chris Stefanadis's article by the same name in *Current Issues in Economics and Finance*, Federal Reserve Bank of New York, 6:12 (October 2000).

For a review of a study that forecasts what banks will look like in 2010, see "CFSI: A Glimpse of the Future," *The Banker* 148:866 (April 1998): 12. Another interesting article is Eric R. Hake, "Financial Innovation as Facilitator of Merger Activity," *Journal of Economic Issues* 32:1 (March 1998): 145–170.

For an interesting article on the role of banks in a new competitive environment, see "Delivering the Future," *Bank Management* (January/February 1995): 45–48. In Frank J. Fabozzi and Franco Modigliani, *Mortgage and Mortgage-Backed Securities Markets* (Boston: Harvard Business School Press Series in Financial Services Management, 1992), the authors present the economic forces that led to the development of secondary mortgage markets.

For an interesting analysis of the topic, see John Wenninger and David Laster, "The Electronic Purse," current issues, Federal Reserve Bank of New York (April 1995). This article is also available on the Internet at **http://www.newyorkfed.org/research/current_issues/ci1-1.html**.

For a discussion of privately issued currency, see Stacey L. Schreft, "Looking Forward: The Role for Government in Regulating Electronic Cash," *Economic Review of the Federal Reserve Bank of Kansas City* 82:4 (Fourth Quarter, 1997): 59–84. Another article, Kevin P. Sheehan, "Electronic Cash," *The FDIC Banking Review* 11:2 (1998), is also available on the Internet at **http://www.fdic.gov/bank/analytical/banking/1998summ/index.html**.

Endnotes

1 Actually, the removal of funds from depository institutions is only half of disintermediation; the other half is the disposal of primary securities by the intermediaries to obtain the funds to pay the depositors. Disintermediation upsets the process by which resources are allocated to capital formation.

2 Be sure you are clear that *disintermediation* means the removal of funds from FIs into open market instruments such as government securities, stocks, or bonds. When funds are removed from depository institutions and put into money market mutual funds, disintermediation has not occurred because money market mutual funds are intermediaries.

3 Despite their efforts, banks' share of total intermediation has been declining, and as in any business that is losing market share, attempts to stop the "bleeding" become more profitable.

4 Actually, the Russians were the pioneers of the Eurodollar. For political reasons, they preferred dollar-denominated deposits with London banks rather than U.S. banks.

5 The fed funds market was started in the 1920s by some New York banks that borrowed and loaned reserves overnight among themselves. The market died out in the 1930s when most banks had excess reserves. It started up again in the 1950s but was so small as to be insignificant. In the 1960s, the market began to grow, and by the early 1970s, many large banks were looking to the fed funds market as a permanent source of funds—not just as a way to meet temporary shortfalls in required reserves.

6 Wholesale sweep programs have been in existence since the 1970s. With wholesale sweep programs, the depository institution sweeps funds in a business's demand deposit into a money market instrument such as a repurchase agreement, Eurodollar deposit, or money market mutual fund. For wholesale sweep accounts, the deposits are swept into an account that may or may not be a liability of the depository institution. For retail sweep accounts, the swept funds stay on the books of the depository institution.

7 In the 1980s particularly, financially distressed banks have often offered higher rates on CDs to attract deposits.

8 In addition to the analytical factors, we should also mention that the general "political wind" had shifted in the late 1970s toward less regulation. We were deregulating airlines, trucking, and even monopolistic cable television operators. This also contributed to the impetus for financial deregulation in the 1980s.

9 The two laws were the Depository Institutions Deregulation and Monetary Control Act of 1980 and the Garn-St. Germain Act of 1982.

10 The laws are the Interstate Banking and Branching Efficiency Act of 1994 and the Gramm-Leach-Bliley Act of 1999.

11 Jamie B. Stewart, Jr., "Changing Technology and the Payment System," *Current Issues in Economics and Finance*, Federal Reserve Bank of New York, 6:11 (October 2000).

12 William F. Bassett and Egon Zakrajsek, "Recent Developments in Business Lending by Commercial Banks," *Federal Reserve Bulletin* (December 2003): 477–492.

13 If the mortgage is going to be securitized in the near future, interest rate risk is not as important to the lender because the lender will not be holding the mortgage for an extended period of time over which the interest rate could change significantly.

14 "Electronic Money," Federal Reserve Bank of Chicago, **http://www.chicagofed.org/ consumer_information/electronic_money.cfm**

A Closer Look, page 266

a Prior to the development of the Eurodollar market, a deposit made in a foreign bank was usually denominated in the currency of the host country. For example, an American would take dollars, convert them to British pounds sterling, and deposit them in a bank in London. When the funds were withdrawn, the pound sterling had to be exchanged for dollars.

Looking Back, page 275

a Kenneth H. Bacon and Eugene Carlson, "Market Is Seen in Small-Business Loans," *The Wall Street Journal* (October 18, 1993).

Looking Forward, page 276

a Charles S. Sanford, Jr., "Financial Markets in 2020," *Economic Review of the Federal Reserve Bank of Kansas City* (First Quarter 1994): 19–28.

The advantage of a bad memory is that one enjoys several times the same good thing for the first time.

—Friedrich Nietzsche

Get into a banker for enough money and you've got yourself a partner.

13

CHAPTER THIRTEEN

Financial Instability and Strains on the Financial System

Learning Objectives

After reading this chapter, you should know:

The ways in which financial intermediaries (FIs) deal with risk and why risk cannot be eliminated

The reasons that financial intermediation recurrently leads to financial crisis

What a debt deflation is and why it is so onerous

What the moral hazard problem is and how it may exacerbate financial crises

Other potential causes of future financial crises in a globalized financial system

Memory Is the Thing You Forget With[1]

In the 1920s, Charles Ponzi, a Boston financier (or slick con man), convinced people that he was able to make huge sums of money by arbitraging Spanish postage stamps—that is, by buying the stamps in a low-cost market (Spain) and selling them in a high-cost market (Boston). The large difference between the selling price and the buying price would result in a capital gain.

Unfortunately for investors, instead of making capital gains, Ponzi was using the money enticed from new investors to pay off the high profits early investors had anticipated. Inevitably, people lost faith in his capability to pay off their investments, and Ponzi's empire foundered and collapsed as he became unable to attract new investors. Later, Ponzi engaged in a land scheme—selling swampland in Florida—that also eventually collapsed.

Junk Bonds
Bonds rated below investment grade or too risky for investment; also called *high-yield bonds*.

In 1909 John Moody issued the first public rating for bonds considered "too risky for investment." He called that rating "below investment grade." These bonds are now called **junk bonds** or high yield bonds. During the Great Depression, many bonds originally recommended for investment were downgraded to "below investment grade." After the bonds had been issued, their ratings were lowered because the issuing corporations were not doing as well as expected. At the end of the Great Depression, 42 percent of all outstanding corporate bonds were rated as junk bonds. Even so, new issues of junk were nonexistent because widespread financial failures—the brute forces of events—had caused investors to grow weary of all but the top-rated grades. As a result, by 1977, only 3.7 percent of outstanding corporate debt carried the below investment grade rating.

But the market was ripe for change in the 1970s when Michael Milken joined the small, unknown brokerage house of Drexel Burnham Lambert. Under Milken's leadership, the house became a market maker for junk bonds. That is, Drexel began underwriting new issues of junk bonds and created a secondary market, standing ready to buy or sell as needed. The junk bond market grew rapidly throughout the 1980s as financial intermediaries (FIs) and individuals jumped on the bandwagon. By the end of 1989, more than 22 percent of outstanding U.S. corporate bonds were junk bonds. Furthermore, three-quarters of this debt had been issued below investment grade, and Drexel Burnham Lambert had grown to rival the largest investment banking firms on Wall Street. The junk bond market was headed for trouble, however, and two events would lead to its demise:

1. Campeau Corporation, a large issuer of junk bonds defaulted, causing panic and large sell-offs among junk bondholders.

2. Congress enacted a law forcing all U.S. thrift institutions—savings and loans, credit unions, and mutual savings banks—to sell off their junk bond holdings by mid-1994.

Faced with these events, the market collapsed, and Drexel Burnham Lambert declared bankruptcy. A liquidity crisis ensued and prices plummeted further. Milken, who was indicted on 98 counts of racketeering and tax and securities fraud, pleaded guilty to six charges. His sentence included a $600 million fine and 10 years in prison. He ended up serving a much shorter time in prison.

In the late 1990s, prices of Internet stocks increased exorbitantly in what came to be known as the "dotcom" bubble or fiasco, depending on how one looked at it. Small Internet companies launched initial public offerings (IPOs), selling newly issued shares of stock to the public. Investors fought to grab up stocks such as pets.com and etoys.com. Rumor had it that a company could just add "dotcom" to its name to see its stock soar. Companies without a product or any assets were snatched up in what was clearly a stock market frenzy. Technology became the latest hype, and the technology-laden NASDAQ composite stock index increased about 525 percent in the 5-year period from 1995 to

2000. The dotcom and other technology stocks were clearly in a stock market bubble. The bubble burst in early 2000, and the NASDAQ gave back about 90 percent of the previous 5-year gain over the next 2 ½ years. Internet companies failed, employees lost their jobs, and the paper wealth of investors in the dotcoms was destroyed. All of these factors contributed to the recession of the early 2000s. By mid 2004, the NASDAQ was yet to recover to its previous high.

How different were the financial institutions and individuals who participated in the junk bond market of the 1980s from those who fell victim to the Ponzi scheme in the 1920s or the dotcom bubble of the late 1990s?[2] Perhaps they were really not all that different in their desire for a big payoff, their willingness to take a risk, and their refusal to realistically evaluate that risk. Perhaps such behavior is part of human nature and hence endemic to financial institutions controlled by individuals.

In this chapter, we look at some of the reasons that certain strains have recurrently plagued our financial system. We look at the role of moral hazard in causing financial crises. Finally, we will examine some famous and some not-so-famous stresses that have led to financial crises.

Financial Intermediation, Risk, and Financial Crises

You have seen that FIs have developed numerous ways to manage risk. For example, diversification reduces the risks of insolvency from widespread defaults in one sector or region of the economy. By not putting all of their eggs in one basket, FIs are less likely to run into problems. Another factor that reduces credit risk is the use of experts to evaluate and access the creditworthiness of potential borrowers and potential investments. When all is said and done, there are few substitutes for painstaking credit analysis.

Interest rate risk can be reduced through the use of adjustable- (variable-) rate loans or the judicious use of forwards, futures, options, and swap agreements, and securitizations. Coping techniques have become more refined as interest rates have become more erratic. Forwards, futures, options, and swaps are also used to hedge exchange rate risk. In recent decades, foreign exchange rates have become more volatile, and finance has become more globalized. Both factors have caused this risk to increase significantly. Thus, we have seen the growing use of forwards, futures, and options agreements to hedge exchange rate risks. As noted in the last chapter, forwards, futures, and options are the subject of Chapter 18.

In addition to borrowing funds from the Fed, depository institutions can also rely on their ability to borrow nondeposit liabilities to meet liquidity needs. If liquidity is needed, funds can be purchased in the repurchase agreements, fed funds, or Eurodollar markets. Such ability to borrow reduces the liquidity risk. Depository institutions can also issue new negotiable certificates of deposit. In a liquidity squeeze, all FIs can sell any available liquid assets in secondary markets.

Even though strategies to reduce risks are significantly developed and appear comprehensive, risk is impossible to eliminate because the future is highly uncertain. Risk is simply an inherent part of life. If an FI makes loans or purchases financial assets that involve only little or no apparent risk, it is passing up opportunities for profit. A relationship between a borrower and an FI that is established today may continue far into the future. The future circumstances the borrower and the FI find themselves in may be far different from what they anticipated. What seems a sure bet today may turn out to be anything but that. Besides, if the entire economy collapses, even the most conservative FI is bound to see the value of its assets fall.

Risk is particularly acute and intensified in financial claims because payments from one party to another usually depend on a payment from a third party. For example, to make her house payment to the mortgage broker, Sally depends on receiving her paycheck from her employer. To pay the investor, the mortgage broker depends on getting the house payment from Sally, and so it goes. Financial claims are layered and depend on multiple parties fulfilling contracts or making payments that depend on still others fulfilling contracts. A default by one party sets off a chain reaction that can trigger multiple defaults. The more heavily spending units depend on payments from others, the greater the risk that a random default will lead to multiple defaults.

Because of its very nature, the financial system will be chronically plagued by various strains, some of which will lead to multiple defaults and a financial crisis. We define a **financial crisis** as a critical upset in a financial market(s) that is characterized by sharp declines in asset prices and the default of many financial and nonfinancial firms.

Financial crises have occurred in the distant past (the Ponzi scheme) as well as the recent past (the dotcom bubble). They will occur in the future. Like the business cycle, periods of severe strain are recurrent but not periodic. That is, they recur through time but not on a particular time schedule. Sometimes, long periods of time pass with no major strains. At other times, periods of stress occur very close together. Sometimes financial stresses are more severe than at other times. Sometimes strains are isolated in one market, and other times they spread throughout the entire system and beyond to the global economy. Exhibit 13-1 depicts the anatomy of a financial crisis.

Many interrelationships exist. For example, a general slump in the economy can create a financial crisis. One party defaults because of a downturn in the economy and sets off a chain reaction of defaults. The financial crisis worsens the already existing

Financial Crisis
A critical upset in a financial market(s) characterized by sharp declines in asset prices and the default of many financial and nonfinancial firms.

13-1
The Anatomy of a Financial Crisis

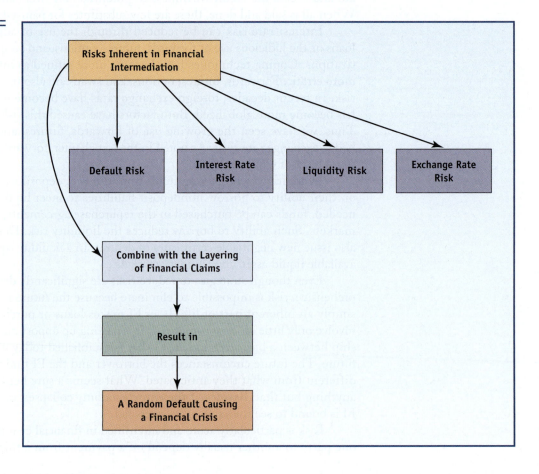

downturn and can result in a deep recession or depression. At other times, the causation may flow in the opposite direction. In this case, a financial crisis, such as a dramatic fall in stock prices or a random large bankruptcy that causes a chain reaction of defaults, leads to a general slump in business activity or a recession.

Many different factors may increase the probability of a financial crisis. First, for example, a sharp unexpected rise in interest rates increases the likelihood of multiple defaults. A sharp increase in interest rates raises the monthly payments of homeowners and other borrowers with variable-rate loans. Payments may be going up at the same time incomes and property and asset values are falling. (Remember the inverse relationship between interest rates and the value of long-term fixed-rate assets.) Moreover, for firms that rely on short-term borrowing, costs will increase and, hence, profits will fall. Eventually, declining profits could lead to losses, reduced borrowing, and insolvency.

Second, a fall in stock values can set off a chain of events that increases the likelihood of a financial crisis. A fall in stock prices makes it more difficult for firms or individuals to borrow. Lower stock values reduce the net worth of firms and stockholders. The value of possible collateral falls, the profit outlook dims, and potential borrowers appear less creditworthy. FIs may be hesitant to lend given the new circumstances and the less certain future.

Moreover, when interest rates are rising and stock values are falling, the most cautious borrowers will drop out of the market, postponing the investment or the large purchase until the future appears more certain. At such times, the adverse selection problem increases; that is, the pool of potential borrowers becomes more heavily weighted toward the less desirable borrowers—those who are more willing to take risks and have less secure financial positions.

Third, unanticipated declines in the overall level of prices can also intensify the risk of a financial crisis. Even though deflation sounds seductive to buyers who are thrilled at the thought of lower prices, deflation imposes many onerous burdens. One of these is debt deflation. A **debt deflation** is a real increase in debt burdens caused by falling incomes and prices.

For example, assume we are in a "typical" period of general deflation in which both prices and incomes are falling. If I have a $1,000 per month house payment on a house for which I paid $100,000 when I was making $40,000 and my income and the value of the house fall to $20,000 and $50,000, respectively, I am experiencing debt deflation. My income and the value of the house have been cut in half, but my house payment is still the same. In real terms, my house payment has doubled. Because my income and other prices have fallen, my real debt burden has increased, even though my nominal debt payment ($1,000 per month) has not changed. Individuals in such a situation cannot afford their house payments, so they try to sell—just as everyone in a similar situation also tries to sell. With the market glutted and prices falling, there probably are not many buyers, leading to further price declines and a downward spiral. Lenders move in and foreclose, individuals declare bankruptcy, and prices fall still further. Needless to say, the mood in the economy becomes highly pessimistic. This example is somewhat exaggerated, but you get the picture. For borrowers with adjustable- or variable-rate mortgages, the situation would probably not be so critical. In a deflation, interest rates and hence the monthly mortgage payments are probably also falling. In this case, the fall in the monthly payment would reflect the decline in the interest rate but not a decline in the principal, even though the real value of the property has fallen. For a borrower with a fixed-rate loan, the only way to lower the monthly payment is to specifically renegotiate the loan contract with the lender. This is sometimes done, although refinancing costs can be high, the property may no longer qualify because its value has fallen during the deflation, or the borrower may no longer qualify because her income has fallen. As a result, the

Debt Deflation
A real increase in debt burdens caused by falling incomes and prices and debt burdens that are denominated in dollars.

borrower gets squeezed between the constancy of her loan payment (the rock) and her falling income (a hard place). This unfortunate turn of events often leads to foreclosure in which the home is repossessed and possibly to bankruptcy.

Businesses are caught in a situation similar to that of individuals. Businesses can't repay debt on inventories as the value of inventories drops below the amount of debt contracted to purchase them, the value of finished goods drops below the amount of debt contracted to purchase raw materials, and so on. As businesses contract, employment and incomes decline, and the economy continues in a downward spiral.

If the frequency of foreclosures and bankruptcies accelerates, which it usually does in a deflation, a debt deflation is under way, and losses for bad debts mount at FIs, potentially leading to their collapse. Fortunately, periods of deflation were not "typical" during the middle and late twentieth century. Not since the Great Depression has the United States experienced widespread debt deflation in which thousands of banks failed in response to a scenario similar to the one just described. In response to the Great Depression, the government put in place safety nets such as the Federal Deposit Insurance Corporation (FDIC) and the Federal Savings and Loan Insurance Corporation (FSLIC).[3] Eventually, in a deflation, when prices fall to low levels, the seeds of recovery are planted as buyers scrape together enough funds to start buying again at the depressed prices. In reality this occurs when both input and output prices have adjusted to profitable terms of trade.

In the early years of the 2000s, the Fed feared the return of deflation. Because, as discussed, the costs of deflation are potentially so high, the Fed acted aggressively to ward off even the slim possibility of it. As the Fed implied, the costs of inflation and deflation are not symmetrical in that the effects of deflation are potentially more destructive to the economy than the effects of a comparable amount of inflation.[4] Thus, the Fed drove interest rates to 45-year lows and held them there until the fear of deflation abated.

Finally, in recent years, many financial crises have been global in nature with a crisis in one country quickly spreading to others in the region and beyond. The growth in world trade, the removal of barriers to capital flows, and the increase in capital flows among nations has increased the likelihood of a financial crisis in one country spreading to other interdependent economies. Technology has exacerbated the problem in that hybrid financial claims are much more fungible due to advances in computer and information technologies. The risks of financial intermediation are magnified in a world of sophisticated global electronic funds transfers. Funds can move in and out of markets instantaneously, causing widespread losses and gains in various markets. The Mexican peso crisis of 1994, the Asian crisis of 1997–1998, the 1998 crisis in Russia, and the 2001 crisis in Argentina are examples of financial crises in which the sudden and massive withdrawal of funds from the affected regions exacerbated the underlying causes of the crisis. Such fungibility of funds further contributes to financial instability. (We discuss the Asian financial crisis in more depth in Chapter 19.)

Consequently, because of the inherent risks of financial intermediation, a goal of regulators is to ensure the safety and soundness of the financial system. They do this in several ways including creating a safety net for depositors (and possibly other investors). At the same time, regulators from various countries and international financial organizations are working together to establish guidelines and criteria for countries that wish to participate in the international financial system. They hope to increase international financial stability and to reduce the incidence of international financial crises. A secondary effect of these efforts, both domestically and globally, however, may be to encourage behavior that actually makes the system more prone to financial crises. We now turn to the problem of moral hazard, which can result in excessive risk taking.

A financial crisis is a critical upset in a financial market and is characterized by sharp declines in asset prices and widespread defaults. Financial crises occur from time to time because of the inherent risks in financial intermediation and because financial claims are layered. A debt deflation is a real increase in debt burdens caused by falling prices and incomes, leading to a downward spiral of foreclosures and bankruptcies. Financial crises can be triggered by sharp increases in interest rates, falls in stock prices, or unanticipated decreases in the overall price level. A financial crisis in one economy can spill over to other economies. This effect is increased as economies become more interdependent due to the growth and fungibility of financial flows among countries.

The Problem of Moral Hazard in Financial Intermediation

The most severe financial crisis this country has ever experienced occurred during the Great Depression. During this period, which predated deposit insurance, more than one-third of the banks in the United States failed. To halt a series of bank runs in early 1933, President Franklin Roosevelt proclaimed a "bank holiday," shutting down all of the banks in the nation for one month. During this month, Congress passed the Glass-Steagall Act, which, among other reforms, established deposit insurance and created the Federal Deposit Insurance Corporation (FDIC). For the first time, small depositors did not have to worry about losing their deposits if their bank went belly-up. Soon deposit insurance became available for small depositors in almost all depository institutions.

Ever since the first deposit insurance statutes were enacted, there has been concern about the moral hazard problem that deposit insurance by its very nature causes.[5] In Chapter 11, we discussed moral hazard in terms of one borrower; that is, after getting the loan, a borrower may use the funds for a different, higher-risk project. In this chapter, the **moral hazard** problem refers to the reduction in market discipline experienced by FIs that stems from deposit insurance, a lender of last resort, and other practices of regulators.

Moral Hazard

The reduction in market discipline experienced by FIs that goes hand-in-hand with deposit insurance.

Increases in moral hazard go hand-in-hand with deposit insurance. For example, deposit insurance encourages banks (and other FIs) to make riskier loans because depositors do not keep as close tabs on how the bank is managing their funds as they would if their deposits were not insured. Insured banks take more risks because greater risks offer the possibility of higher returns, and after all, banks are highly leveraged—they are risking depositors' funds, as well as their own, and they get to keep all the winnings. Furthermore, loan officers do not have to lie awake at night worrying about losses when the funds (deposits) are insured. Well-managed banks are penalized because they have to help pay the losses incurred by poorly managed banks.

Even in light of all these concerns, until the 1980s, deposit insurance was widely viewed as an incredible achievement.[6] Despite the reduction in market discipline that resulted from it, the 1933 statute that established the FDIC was probably one of the most successful pieces of legislation of the twentieth century. Much of the FDIC's success is often attributed simply to knowledge of its existence. That is, there have been no significant general runs on FDIC-insured banks because depositors know their funds are safe, so a run would be a waste of time. For 50 years, the FDIC's losses were negligible, its reserves grew, and annually about two-thirds of all the insurance premiums paid in were refunded to the banks. As a result of the FDIC's success, Congress raised the insurance limit several times from the original $2,500 in 1934 to $100,000 per account at the present. We should note that the limit was raised to $100,000 in 1980 and that for a comparable amount of "real" or inflation-adjusted deposit insurance in 2004, the limit would be more than $200,000. Despite the moral hazard problem, along with other deposit insurance reforms, Congress has recently considered raising the limit further and indexing it to the rate of inflation. More on this in Chapter 14.

But behind closed doors, all was not well in the 1970s and 1980s.

During the 1970s, banks extended their lending to less-developed countries and to highly leveraged business ventures. They made more mortgages, which, because of the length of the loan commitments, also increased interest rate risk. Remember the inverse relationship between the interest rate and the value of long-term fixed-rate assets such as mortgages. In 2004, mortgages are now packaged together and sold off in secondary markets. These securitizations reduce interest rate risk because the loans are not held for extended periods of time. However, securitizations did not surface to a large extent until later. Also, in the 1970s and 1980s, variable rate loans that decrease interest rate risk were not as prevalent as they are today.

At the same time, the economy was becoming more volatile. These factors increased the fluctuations in the value of a bank's assets and, hence, increased risk. The fall in energy prices (particularly oil) caused many loans to go sour. Many large loans including some to less-developed countries could have been repaid had the price of oil stayed high. In addition, overbuilding of commercial real estate in the mid-1980s caused a sharp drop in prices, many foreclosures, and large loan losses for banks in the late 1980s. The overbuilding, low occupancy rates, and foreclosure problems of the commercial real estate market were still prevalent in certain regions of the country well into the mid-1990s.

As you saw in Chapter 11, beginning in the early 1980s, bank failures escalated. Between 1980 and 1994, 1,617 banks failed. Although it suspended premium rebates and sharply increased the premium, the FDIC's reserves, which peaked in 1987 at $18 billion, were depleted by the end of 1991. Many observers believed that excessive risk taking caused by the moral hazard problem was one reason that so many banks failed in the 1980s. Another factor that contributed to the problem was that bank regulators were hesitant to resolve insolvencies quickly, particularly when a large bank was involved. Regulators were also timid about imposing losses on uninsured depositors (those with account balances of more than $100,000) and other creditors. With the failure of Continental Illinois National Bank of Chicago in 1984, the doctrine of **"too big to fail"** became the official position of FDIC regulators.

"Too big to fail" means that the regulators will not allow a "big" bank to fail but instead will use the **purchase and assumption method** to resolve an insolvency. With the purchase and assumption method, a healthy institution is found to take over the assets and liabilities of the failed bank. The insurer, the FDIC in this case, pays the takeover institution the difference between the liabilities and the assets of the failed institution. The takeover bank benefits by ending up with a much larger portfolio. Neither the uninsured depositors (those with account balances higher than $100,000) nor the creditors lose. When the "too big to fail" doctrine is implemented, all deposits are "de facto" insured. With the **payoff method**, rather than finding a buyer for the troubled institution, the FDIC merely pays off insured depositors up to the $100,000 limit and closes down the bank. Thus, with the payoff method, creditors, stockholders, and uninsured depositors all lose. In Chapter 14, we shall see that a law passed in 1991 requires regulators to use the least-costly method to handle bank insolvencies in most circumstances. The exception applies to cases in which a bank's failure could threaten the safety and soundness of the entire financial system.

http://www.fdic.gov, the FDIC's home page, has numerous articles about deposit insurance including deposit insurance reform initiatives.

"Too Big to Fail"
The position adopted by FDIC regulators in 1984 whereby the failure of a large bank would be resolved using the purchase and assumption method rather than the payoff method.

Purchase and Assumption Method
The method of resolving a bank insolvency by finding a buyer for the institution.

Payoff Method
The method of resolving a bank insolvency by paying off the depositors and closing the institution.

http://www.ffiec.gov/, the home page of the Federal Financial Institutions Examination Council, has other relevant information about deposit insurance and risk.

In the early 2000s, banks, brokerage houses, insurance companies, and other financial services firms are consolidating into megafirms, the likes of which have never been seen before. A failure of a megafirm such as Citigroup, which was created from the merger of Citicorp and Travelers, would have catastrophic effects on the economy. In mid 2004, Citigroup had almost $1.4 trillion in assets! Failure of such a firm would quickly exhaust the resources of any safety net such as deposit insurance. (The FDIC currently has assets of around $45 billion.)[7] A moral hazard problem exists if market participants believe that the effects of such a failure would be so catastrophic that a taxpayer bailout would be inevitable. In this sense, despite the 1991 legislation, "too big to fail" may again become a reality. Given the correlation between risk and return, the incentive is to take on riskier ventures whenever moral hazard is increased. Note that a higher average expected return induces investors to accept more risk. But—investors beware—this does not imply that a higher return will be realized for any given investment. The A Closer Look on page 290 describes a private sector bailout of a firm, Long Term Capital Management. The Fed arranged the bailout to prevent large losses to banks that had loaned to the firm and the possible detrimental effects of the firm's failure on the economy.

As you saw in Chapter 11, the strains of the banking system were resolved in the 1990s as banks earned record profits. In a booming economy with low interest rates, their cost of funds fell faster than their earnings on assets. Banks also weathered the downturn in the early 2000s quite well despite the weakness in the economy. Regardless of the turnaround, industry experts believe that the present reforms do not sufficiently deal with the moral hazard problem inherent in deposit insurance.

In the mid 2000s, moral hazard is also a concern among those who are designing an international framework for financial stability. As financial flows across national borders increase, excessive risk taking may occur if financial participants think that international financial organizations such as the International Monetary Fund (IMF) will bail out a country in crisis by acting as a lender of last resort or encouraging policies that prevent currency devaluation. In any case, if investors' losses are reduced or eliminated, a moral hazard problem will exist that will encourage excessive risk taking. The Mexican peso crisis of 1994, the Asian crisis of 1997–1998, the 1998 crisis in Russia, and the crisis in Argentina in 2001 resulted in massive international financial support in an attempt to bail out the troubled economies. Indeed, investors did lose, but they would have lost more without the bailouts organized by the IMF.

Having considered the reasons that recurring financial crises plague the economy and some of the factors that increase the probability of a financial crisis, we now turn our attention to other areas of concern at the present time. Now would be a good time to read the accompanying A Closer Look on page 292 about the collapse of the savings and loan industry in the 1980s.

Recap   Moral hazard results from the reduction in market discipline caused by the presence of deposit insurance. Moral hazard led to excessive risk taking that contributed to record bank failures during the 1980s. The "too-big-to-fail" doctrine means that regulators will use the purchase and assumption method to resolve insolvencies instead of the payoff method. The existence of large megafirms could result in a moral hazard problem if market participants believe the firms are "too big to fail." The moral hazard problem may also exist in international markets if participants believe an international organization will bail out a country in crisis.

The Bailout of Long-Term Capital Management

One type of hedge fund is a nontraditional investment fund formed as a partnership of up to 99 investors. Partners in these hedge funds are wealthy individuals and institutions with a minimum net worth of $1 million. Minimum investments start at $1 million, and many have much higher minimum requirements to participate. These hedge funds attempt to earn high or maximum returns regardless of whether prices in broader financial markets are rising or falling. The funds trade securities and other creative financial instruments and try to outperform traditional investment funds by employing novel trading strategies. Because there are only 99 investors in this type of hedge fund, they are not regulated in the same way that traditional investment pools or mutual funds are.

Some of the strategies employed by these hedge funds include the following:

1. Selling borrowed securities (selling short) in the hope of profiting by buying the securities at a lower price on a future date.

2. Exploiting unusual price differences between related securities in anticipation of making a profit when the prices come into more traditional alignment.

3. Trading options and derivatives.

4. Borrowing to invest so that returns are increased.

We look at hedge funds in greater detail in Chapter 15.

One of the most famous (or should we say infamous?) of this type of hedge fund is Long-Term Capital Management (LTCM). It was founded in 1994 by John Meriwether, formerly of Salomon Brothers, and Robert Merton and Myron Scholes, who shared the 1997 Nobel Prize in economics for their work in modeling financial risk. LTCM required investors to make a minimum investment of $10 million for three years. LTCM made spectacular returns from the start by using trading strategies that suggested that prices of various securities should be related to one another based on risk, maturity, and liquidity. If rates got out of alignment, LTCM would, in effect, place bets that rates would return to the traditional or historical alignment. In reality, the fund was purchasing bonds it believed to be underpriced and selling short bonds it believed to be overpriced. Using such a strategy, LTCM made profits as long as the spread between the two types of bonds narrowed, regardless of the direction in which financial prices or interest rates moved. In addition, LTCM relied on short-term bank loans to increase the amount of investable funds.

The strategy worked extremely well until late summer 1998, when global financial turmoil caused rates to move in nontraditional ways. The prices of the securities that LTCM thought would rise relative to U.S. government securities did the opposite because of perceived increases in risk. The spread between the prices widened rather than narrowed as expected. There was a "flight to quality" as funds flowed into U.S. government securities and out of other securities. LTCM was particulary vulnerable because it had borrowed roughly 50 times its capital (investors' funds). When prices failed to move in the expected direction, the fund's capital base was swiftly depleted. With the value of LTCM's securities falling, banks suggested that the fund should liquidate its positions so that the bank loans could be repaid. Because of the high degree of leveraging, LTCM's losses quickly ate away its capital base.

To ward off the fund's certain bankruptcy, a consortium of 16 leading U.S. banks agreed to a $3.5 billion loan package to bail out LTCM on September 24, 1998. Thus, the securities whose prices had fallen did not have to be sold at a loss but could be held until their prices moved into more traditional alignment. In an extremely unusual and controversial move, the Fed arranged the bailout. LTCM had tried to arrange a deal on its own for more than a month but had failed. The Fed brokered the deal to prevent the liquidation of LTCM's $200 billion in securities and a probable frantic reaction in financial markets. The liquidation of LTCM's positions would have exacerbated the price falls and led to losses by the banks that had loaned to the hedge fund. There was also concern that if LTCM was forced to liquidate, a chain reaction could be set off. The dramatic drop in the prices of the securities that LTCM was liquidating could cause the crisis to spread to other hedge funds that employed similar strategies. In that event, other banks that had loaned to hedge funds could also experience losses.

The episode caused some analysts to call for the regulation of hedge funds. Others note that this is not a viable solution because hedge funds will merely go "offshore" where they can escape regulation. The problem seems to be not so much that the wealthy investors in hedge funds might lose but that the banks that loan to the funds to enable them to leverage their bets would also lose. Perhaps the solution would be for banks to be more judicious in lending to hedge funds and to more fully disclose their exposure to potential losses.

Other Areas of Concern

In addition to the standard risks experienced in the past, financial institutions in the mid-2000s face the potential for new stresses and strains. Some of these new situations result from the changing composition of balance sheets, some result from activities that never show up on financial statements, and others result from the overall growth of the financial system relative to the economy. We review a few of these areas briefly.

Growth of the Financial System and the Proliferation of Financial Claims

National wealth consists of real assets such as houses, roads, infrastructure, and factories, plus net financial claims owed to Americans by foreigners. Domestic financial assets are not a part of national wealth because what is a financial asset to one party is a financial liability to another. Thus, domestic financial assets and liabilities cancel each other out.

In recent years, new financial products, new markets, and new institutions have proliferated. Financial flows and instruments had grown faster than national wealth and national income. The financial system is relatively much larger than the real sector compared to their sizes a few decades ago. Derivatives allow new financial instruments to be created that base their claims on other financial assets, which base their claims on real assets. It is hoped that this potpourri of newly created instruments makes the financial system more efficient. However, the proliferation of financial instruments and the fungibility of financial claims in a global financial system augment the potential for new stresses and strains to the financial system. A crisis in one market quickly spreads to another through a contagion effect, and the unwinding of positions can take longer than in the past when the financial system was not so complex. Now would be a good time to read the accompanying A Closer Look on page 299 about the growth of Fannie Mae and Freddie Mac securities.

The Savings and Loan Debacle

Throughout most of the 1980s, the savings and loan (S&L) industry in the United States experienced severe strain. More than 1,500 institutions failed or went out of existence. Many others downsized, and the industry as a whole shrank considerably. Taxpayers spent billions of dollars to bail out the industry because the financial crisis threatened the health and stability of the entire economy. Today the industry is far different from what it was at the start of the 1980s. The public at large has been disillusioned, questioning the safety and soundness of S&Ls and the financial system as a whole. The honesty and integrity of S&L owners, regulators, and even some members of Congress have been doubted.

As in most crises, the seeds of the S&L debacle were planted long before the first sprouts of trouble appeared. In many ways, the roots of the crisis can be found in the way S&Ls do business. Unless interest rates remain fairly stable for long periods of time as they did from the early 1950s until the 1970s, it is risky to fund long-term loans or purchase long-term assets with short-term deposits. If interest rates rise, the cost of the funds borrowed over the short-term can increase above the amount long-term assets are earning. As you saw in Chapter 10, S&Ls were literally established for the express purpose of borrowing short from passbook savers and lending long in order to finance mortgage loans. That is, they were designed to engage in behavior that would be dangerous in an environment of volatile or rising interest rates.

From the early 1950s on, the U.S. economy experienced a slow upward drift in interest rates. Regulation Q, which put a ceiling on the interest rate that could be paid on deposits, applied to S&Ls as well as commercial banks. In fact, the ceiling for S&Ls was maintained at 0.5 percent above the ceiling for commercial banks. The express purpose of this differential was to encourage savers to deposit funds into S&Ls, which then could be used to make mortgage loans, thus encouraging home ownership. With Regulation Q in place, the cost of the funds borrowed mostly from passbook savers was maintained at or below the ceiling limits. Small savers, at least for a time, had few alternatives to passbook savings accounts in depository institutions. Consequently, disintermediation (the removal of funds from FIs) was relatively minor when interest rates on other financial assets such as Treasury bills or commercial paper went above the Regulation Q limits. The other financial assets were generally unavailable to small savers who did not have the minimum amounts required to purchase them. For example, $10,000 is the minimum amount needed to purchase a Treasury bill. By the 1970s, however, small savers did have money market mutual funds as an alternative to passbook accounts in depository institutions.[a] Still, the situation fermented for some time before the crisis occurred. By the late 1970s and early 1980s, events had begun to unfold that would result in total collapse of the industry and, as you shall see, a large taxpayer bailout.

To understand the burgeoning crisis, recall that nominal interest rates are approximately equal to real rates plus the expected inflation rate. In the late 1970s, high nominal rates reflected expectations about inflation and not high real rates. That is, the high nominal rates were the result of large inflation premiums. In fact, in the 1970s, real rates were often abnormally low and sometimes even negative despite the high nominal rates.

In late 1979, the Fed orchestrated a huge spike in already high nominal rates as part of a policy aimed at reducing inflation. Interest rates climbed far above the Regulation Q ceilings, which capped nominal rates while ignoring real rates. The spike in nominal rates caused severe disintermediation and/or the transfer of funds from S&Ls to money market mutual funds. Congress responded in 1982 by authorizing the S&Ls to offer money market deposit accounts that competed with money market mutual funds. Money market deposit accounts actually had an advantage over money market mutual funds because they were insured by the Federal Savings and Loan Insurance Corporation (FSLIC).[b] This legislative change slowed the disintermediation and the transfer of funds from the S&Ls to money market mutual funds, but it was probably too little too late. Also, it left the S&Ls with another problem. S&Ls had mostly long-term fixed-rate assets, primarily low-rate mortgages that were then funded by high-interest variable-rate accounts. Thus, the S&Ls were hit with a double whammy: their profits fell as their costs of funds increased faster than their earnings on assets, and the value of their assets also fell. Recall that when interest rates rise, the value of long-term bonds falls. Long-term fixed-rate mortgages are similar to long-term bonds in that when interest rates rise, the value of long-term fixed-rate mortgages goes down.

In 1981, economists estimated that the S&L industry had a substantial negative net worth that was far greater than the assets of the Federal Savings and Loan Insurance Corporation (FSLIC) that insured the deposits of the sickly S&Ls. Rather than confronting the problem head on in the early 1980s, which would have required injecting taxpayer funds into the system at that time, Congress responded with actions that would eventually make the situation much worse. Under the Garn–St. Germain Act, it expanded the lending powers of the S&Ls into product lines that paid a high return but were unfamiliar to S&L managers and entailed a lot of risk. Capital requirements—the cushion against losses—were also lowered so that the S&Ls could aggressively enter the new lending arenas. Rather than having to hold capital equivalent to 5 percent of assets, S&Ls were required to hold capital equal to only 3 percent of assets.

With expanded lending powers and lower capital requirements, the industry went for broke and made new high-earning investments in such ventures as junk bonds and commercial real estate. Guess what happened? The S&Ls ended up losing a lot more and literally went broke. In late 1986, Congress granted the FSLIC $10.8 billion funded by borrowing against future deposit insurance premiums to be paid by the thrifts themselves. In 1988, the Federal Home Loan Bank, the equivalent of the Fed for S&Ls at the time, liquidated more than 200 insolvent thrifts by selling the institutions to individuals and firms. In the liquidation process, the buyers were compensated for the negative net worth of the institutions with an array of future guarantees and obligations, including tax breaks. None of these compensations required congressional authorization or appropriation and have been subsequently viewed suspiciously.

Finally, in 1989, Congress responded with the Financial Institutions Reform, Recovery, and Enforcement Act (FIRREA), which attempted to resolve the problem of widespread failures within the industry and insufficient insurance funds to settle the crisis. Over the course of the next decade, the total cost to the taxpayers was approximately $124 billion, which was much less than initial estimates. At the time of the bailout, the costs had already been incurred. The bailout shifted the costs from the owners and depositors of the failed thrifts to the public (taxpayers) at large. We should also note that the bailout was to the benefit of taxpayers also. We look at the specifics of the FIRREA and other recent regulatory measures in Chapter 14.

What can we conclude about the causes of the crisis? It is difficult to apportion blame, and doing so would not be productive anyway. Undoubtedly, the inherent problem of lending long and borrowing short when interest rates were rising was a major factor. Another factor was the extension of lending powers to the thrifts in the early 1980s. These new powers that allowed for more risk taking also seem to have attracted some dishonest folk to the industry. Finally, regulators were slow to move in and shut down troubled thrifts, which caused eventual losses to be greater than they otherwise would have been. Congress was also slow to act. A lot of hard lessons were learned as taxpayer funds were diverted from potentially building better schools, roads, and infrastructure, among other more positive projects.

Off-Balance-Sheet Activities

Off-Balance-Sheet Activities
Activities such as standby lines of credit, overdraft protection, unused credit card balances, and other commitments for which a bank is liable but that do not show up on the balance sheet.

Standby Lines of Credit
Lines of credit (commitments) for which a bank is liable but that do not show up on the balance sheet.

Financial intermediaries now engage in new kinds of behavior, called *off-balance-sheet activities*, as they seek to obtain additional revenues and profits from areas outside traditional borrowing and lending. **Off-balance-sheet activities** include standby lines of credit, overdraft protection, unused credit card balances, and other commitments for which the FI is liable but that do not show up on the balance sheet. **Standby lines of credit** guarantee that the bank will lend funds to a borrower in the future as agreed upon today. One example of a standby line of credit is a letter given to an issuer of commercial paper that guarantees to pay off creditors on the due date if the issuer cannot. If a bank gives a standby line of credit for a fee to an issuer of commercial paper and the issuer defaults, the bank experiences a loss just as if it had made a bad loan. The only difference is that this exposure never shows up on the balance sheet, whereas the loan-loss exposure does. Unused loan commitments of banks and savings associations totaled about $6.2 trillion as of June 30, 2004. The increase since 1990 has been due almost exclusively to an increase in unused credit card balances, which tripled as a percentage of total assets. In the next chapter, we shall see that banks must now consider off-balance-sheet activities in calculating capital requirements.

Derivatives

Derivatives
Financial contracts whose values are derived from the values of other underlying assets; examples include financial futures and options.

A **derivative** is a financial contract whose is value derived from the value of some other underlying asset, such as foreign exchange, bonds, equities, commodities, or an index. A derivative's value fluctuates with the value of the underlying asset. Examples of derivatives include financial futures, options, and combinations thereof. Derivatives are used by banks and others, including virtually every large corporation in the United States, to hedge, speculate, or arbitrage price differences. The use of derivatives allows for the unbundling of specific risks of financial assets into parts so that those more willing and able to do so bear the unbundled risks. Thus, the use of derivatives in this manner makes the financial system more efficient. As of June 30, 2004, 637 banks held derivatives, with 96 percent of all derivative holdings by banks being held by just 7 banks and 99 percent held by the largest 25 banks. The value of the derivative contracts was about $81 trillion. Although this amount is extraordinarily high, it is not known what amount of these positions is offsetting to reduce risk or arbitraging to make a riskless profit. In these cases, there would be little or no risk.

The Implicit Fannie Mae and Freddie Mac Guarantee

As you shall see in more detail in Chapter 15, the Federal National Mortgage Association (Fannie Mae) and the Federal Home Loan Mortgage Corporation (Freddie Mac) provide loanable funds to the housing sector by selling their own securities and using the proceeds to purchase mortgages or mortgage-backed securities in the secondary market. Investors in the securities are paid from the mortgage payments of the mortgages or mortgage-backed securities that Fannie Mae and Freddie Mac have purchased. Fannie Mae and Freddie Mac are privately owned corporations whose stocks trade on the New York Stock Exchange.

Despite being privately owned and managed, Fannie Mae and Freddie Mac were chartered by the federal government, are exempt from state and local corporate taxes, and have a $2.25 billion line of credit with the U.S. Treasury. There is no explicit government that guarantee that the purchasers of Fannie Mae and Freddie Mac securities will be repaid. However, because of the close government ties, many investors in Fannie Mae and Freddie Mac securities believe that these securities have an implicit government guarantee, namely, that the government would bail out the corporations if they got in a jam, even if the government is not legally obliged to do so.

In the past decade, Fannie Mae and Freddie Mac have experienced astounding growth. In 2004, a significant majority of the homes sold in the United States were purchased with loans that Fannie Mae or Freddie Mac later bought. The high growth combined with the implicit guarantee has created concerns about the safety of Fannie Mae and Freddie Mac. In addition, Fannie Mae and Freddie Mac have loosened loan qualification requirements for the mortgages they purchase and are buying less-desirable, higher-risk, subprime loans. Such lending increases the possibilities that the companies could run into financial problems similar to the savings and loan industry in the 1980s. For example, if real estate prices fall, leading to massive defaults and foreclosures, Fannie Mae and Freddie Mac may not be able to pay the investors in their securities.

Others are concerned with the stupendous growth of Fannie Mae and Freddie Mac and its effect on competition. Competitors, such as commercial banks and mortgage brokers, and many financial services industry trade groups complain that these government-sponsored enterprises have an unfair advantage over their competitors because of their government ties that allow them to borrow at a lower cost. Furthermore, in 2003, Freddie Mac engaged in unethical accounting of practices designed to smooth out earnings to boost their stock prices. In late 2004, Fannie Mae was caught up in a similar accounting scandal. Allegedly Fannie Mae was manipulating earnings in order to meet Wall Street expectations and to justify million dollar bonuses for its top executives. Reforms have been and are being undertaken at both Freddie Mac and Fannie Mae to correct these abuses.

Needless to say, Fed Chairman Alan Greenspan and several Treasury officials have expressed concerns about the growth of Fannie Mae and Freddie Mac. If property values fall and massive defaults occur, would the government have to step in and bail them out? What would the effects of such a bailout be on the economy?

In recent years, derivatives have become even more complex. Powerful computers are often needed to assess the risks involved if one factor, say, an interest rate or exchange rate, changes by a small amount, perhaps only one-hundredth of 1 percent. Indeed, it is difficult, if not impossible, to understand all risks involved with extremely complex derivatives and all possible scenarios. Nevertheless, derivatives will undoubtedly become even more complex in the future.

Another problem is that even if they understand the risks, how can regulators be sure that institutions have proper oversight of their employees or operations to prevent the misuse of derivatives? Lax oversight could lead to large losses that catch management, regulators, and investors by surprise. The A Closer Look feature on page 301 gives an example of how derivatives brought down an otherwise healthy British investment bank and a wealthy southern California county.

For these reasons, some analysts worry that derivatives may be too risky for banks. They believe that bank participation in these markets should be limited or that the market should somehow be regulated. Others go so far as to suggest that Congress should ban the use of derivatives by banks altogether. This may be impossible because large banks could merely take this activity offshore beyond the venue of the regulators. The concern is that some participants do not know enough about how derivatives work and the risks involved. If rates move by a small amount in an unanticipated direction, large losses can occur if derivatives are used for speculation. As you shall see in Chapter 18, you cannot lose if derivatives are used only to hedge. When losses have occurred, it was often because of insufficient oversight, both internally by management and externally by regulators.

Could derivatives set off chain reactions in world financial markets that lead to financial instability? Do market participants, including banks, have enough knowledge about them to be heavily involved? Can firms sufficiently oversee derivative activity? Will regulators be able to properly regulate these markets? Risks from derivatives currently do not show up on balance sheets. Will regulators be able to ensure that such risks somehow are disclosed? These are questions to be answered in the near future.

The Eurodollar and Eurobond Markets

Other sources of concern are the Eurodollar and Eurobond markets. As you saw in Chapter 5, Eurodollars are dollar-denominated deposits held abroad. An example of a Eurodollar is a short-term deposit denominated in dollars and placed in a bank in England. The term of the deposit is often overnight. The Eurodollar market began in the 1950s in London but has spread around the world with the Caribbean being a particularly large haven for deposits. The Eurodollar market blossomed primarily as a result of banks' efforts to escape domestic regulation. Domestic banks could "suggest" Eurodollar deposits in a foreign subsidiary to their customers and then borrow funds from the foreign subsidiary. The depositors earned a higher rate of return than they could get on domestic deposits, and the banks had a source of funds that was not subject to domestic regulation (primarily Regulation Q and reserve requirements). Indeed, Eurodollar deposits have become an important source of funds for banks in the past 30 years.

Eurobond Market
The market for dollar-denominated bonds sold in a foreign country, often by corporations doing business in that country.

The **Eurobond market** is the market for dollar-denominated bonds sold in a foreign country, often by corporations doing business in that country. The Eurobond market has grown as a result of the effort to escape regulation and taxation and to tap into international sources of funds. New bond issues in the Eurobond market now exceed domestic bond issues.

The Collapse of a California County and a British Bank

What do Barings Bank of London and Orange County, California, have in common? Not much to the casual observer, but events in late 1994 and early 1995 put the two close together in the history books forever. Within the span of a few months, both institutions were brought to their knees by massive losses sustained in the derivatives market.

We begin in affluent Orange County, located just south of Los Angeles. Robert Citron, a Democrat, had served as county treasurer for more than 24 years in this traditionally Republican county. As such, he managed the county's investment pool. Starting in the late 1980s, the pool began to grow rapidly from less than $1 billion to more than $8 billion as many other municipalities outside the county and other public entities opted to join the pool. They were attracted by its high return and the impressive earnings record that Citron had amassed. He was considered brilliant for consistently earning an above-average return, and others sought to share his good fortunes.

But all was not well as wise investors should have suspected. After all, what is the probability of earning significantly above-average returns for several years in a row without taking more risks? Unfortunately, as Citron and the county found out all too late, the probability is not high. When all was said and done, Citron claimed to have had an "incomplete" understanding of the risks inherent in the financial instruments—or, as some would say, exotic derivatives—in which he was dealing. Having leveraged the $8 billion portfolio to $20 billion, he bet that interest rates would continue to fall in 1994. When the Fed began to raise rates in February, Citron failed to reverse his position. The pool owned securities whose value fell as rates rose. As rates continued upward, Citron faced reelection in June and denied to his constituency that the investment pool was in trouble. After his victory, he still tried to hold on, and by the time Wall Street refused to extend any more credit, the county was unable to come up with the funds needed to pay bondholders and was forced into bankruptcy. The portfolio was liquidated—that is, the securities whose value had fallen were sold—resulting in a $1.7 billion loss. Thus, the largest municipal bankruptcy in history had occurred in one of the country's wealthiest counties.[a]

Another unlikely candidate for bankruptcy was Barings, a prestigious British investment banking house that had been around for 233 years. Like Orange County, Barings was brought down by one individual. Nick Leeson was only 28 years old and by most accounts seemed to be on the fast track to success if not already there. He headed the futures trading department in Barings' Singapore branch. In 1994, his bonus topped $1 million—not bad for a kid who had grown up on the other side of the tracks. Who could guess that by late February 1995, he would be on the run and that Barings would be in bankruptcy? Here's how it happened.

Apparently, Leeson bought enough futures in a three-week period beginning in late January to have a $27 billion exposure. The transactions appeared normal because Barings had been taking large hedge positions for years in Nikkei Stock index futures—positions that were used to arbitrage even minute price differences between stocks traded in Singapore and Osaka, Japan. Around January 26, Leeson switched from a hedged position to a speculative position. No one knows for sure what his thinking was, but it is suspected that he thought that the Kobe earthquake would stimulate the Japanese economy and push up the Nikkei. As events unfolded, however, his strategy proved wrong, and he sold out and call options to raise cash for margin calls. In this situation, he was betting the Nikkei would settle into a narrow range. By February 20, his losses had accumulated to $700 million, and Barings put up more cash to cover his deficit. Barings believed that the margin call was for a corporate customer whose funds would be deposited in a few days. When Leeson couldn't produce the funds, he fled, leaving behind a note that said, "I'm sorry." By this time, the loss amounted to $900 million—more than all of Barings' capital. The Bank of England put Barings into bankruptcy. Less than a month had elapsed since the start of the fiasco. Leeson was eventually apprehended, extradited to Singapore, and sentenced to prison for three and a half years.

The Orange County and Barings examples are not unique.[b] As *Business Week* put it, "In the easy-money boom, too many securities executives lost the ability or will to scrutinize high-energy traders or guard against unethical salespeople. Too many bankers and CFOs [chief financial officers] neglected to ask whether they understood the complexity—or the downside—of the highly leveraged derivatives they were using to hedge financial risks."[c] In such a world, the value of derivative contracts can fluctuate wildly from even small changes in stock, bond, or currency prices. What should be done to protect investors and institutions? For now that remains an unanswered question. But one thing is certain: Both Barings' executives and the Board of Supervisors of Orange County regret not keeping a closer eye on the situation.

Concern has been expressed about the possibility of a liquidity crisis in the Eurodollar or Eurobond market. The ramifications of such a crisis are difficult to speculate about because the Fed is not involved with the Eurobond market and is, at most, indirectly involved only with Eurodollar deposits in subsidiaries of U.S. institutions. It has this responsibility only because it is possible that a liquidity crisis in the Eurodollar market could spread to domestic financial markets and that the Fed is responsible for maintaining the safety and soundness of the U.S. financial system. In reality, U.S. corporations and foreign subsidiaries of U.S. intermediaries are fully responsible for their liabilities, whatever denominations or maturities are involved.

Could a liquidity crisis in a foreign subsidiary of a U.S. institution threaten the domestic economy? Could a default crisis by a U.S. corporation in the Eurobond market spill over to U.S. financial markets? How much do we really know about the size and activities of these markets? Presumably not as much as we or the Fed would like to know. These questions will probably be answered one way or another in the not-too-distant future.

Recap The growth of the financial sector relative to the real sector, and the increased fungibility of financial claims may exacerbate financial crises in the future. Off-balance-sheet activities such as standby lines of credit and unused credit card balances increase potential losses for financial institutions but do not show up on financial statements. Derivatives are financial contracts whose values are derived from the values of underlying assets, such as foreign exchange, bonds, equities, and commodities. Large banks and other financial and nonfinancial institutions are heavily involved in derivatives, and without proper oversight and regulation, large losses could occur. Concern is also expressed about the liquidity of the Eurodollar and Eurobond markets and the possibility of a crisis spilling over into the domestic economy.

The Japanese Bubble Economy of the 1980s

During the mid-1980s, monetary and fiscal policies in Japan were expansionary, and the central bank took actions that steadily lowered interest rates. Despite the low rates, inflation in output markets was virtually nonexistent. In response to the low interest rates, stock prices that had been trending upward since 1984 continued to rally. The Japanese went on a domestic and international spending spree. In 1987–1989, the Nikkei Index of Japanese stocks, fueled by the spending splurge went up about 300 percent.

By the end of 1988, the stock market was in a full-fledged bubble, having gone through a period of excessive price increases accompanied by euphoric expectations. The bubble was not limited to asset prices but also encompassed the real estate market where prices more than doubled in four years. Record price increases in the stock and real estate markets continued in 1989 even though monetary policy turned contractionary in mid-1989. Interest rate increases set the stage for the bubble to burst.

Beginning in 1989, the "bubble economy" burst as the Bank of Japan increased interest rates from 2.5 percent to 6.2 percent. Real estate and stock prices in Japan fell more than 50 percent, and the economy moved into recession. The Nikkei Index, which stood at 38,915 on December 1989, fell to a low of 7,603 in early 2003, only to recover to 11,382.08 on June 18, 2004. Thus, in 2004, despite rising over 30 percent from its lows, the Nikkei was still less than one-third of its 1989 peak.

What have been the effects of the bursting of the bubble on the banking system and the economy? As you might guess, the banking system was in a crisis and the economy in a malaise for more than a decade. As of mid-2004, however, the economy was growing at a rapid pace and banks were recovering even though the ongoing battle against deflation brought on by the bursting of the bubble was still being fought.

In this chapter, we have come full circle from past stresses on the financial system and their resolution to the potential strains of the future. In Chapter 14, we look at the regulatory structure in place at the present time and possible areas of reform.

Summary of Major Points

1. FIs have developed numerous ways to reduce risk and deal with them. FIs use diversification and expert credit analysis to manage credit risk. They use adjustable rate loans, forwards, futures, options, swaps, and securitizations to manage interest rate risk. Liquidity risk is managed by the ability to borrow funds, and exchange rate risk is managed with forwards, futures, options, and swaps. Despite these measures and because of the uncertainty of the future and the inter- dependence of financial claims, financial crises will occur from time to time. A financial crisis is a severe upset in a financial market that is characterized by sharp declines in asset prices and the failure of many financial and nonfinancial firms.

2. Deflation can be worse than inflation because it increases the real value of debts that are denominated in dollars. A debt deflation occurs when prices and incomes fall, increasing the real value of debts and

resulting in foreclosures and bankruptcies. The last time the U.S. economy experienced depression was in the Great Depression, although Fed was concerned that the economy could slip into a deflation in the early 2000s.

3. *Moral hazard* refers to the reduction in market discipline that comes with the presence of a safety net to prevent losses. The presence of deposit insurance or the belief that regulators will take mitigating actions in the event of a financial crisis creates moral hazard. With moral hazard, banks and other intermediaries have an incentive to invest in riskier loans and investment. This gradual increase in riskier activities resulted in many bank failures in the 1980s. Megamergers in the financial services industry may also lead to a moral hazard problem if market participants believe that the resulting firms are "too big to fail." The moral hazard problem also exists in international financial markets if participants believe that an international organization such as the IMF will bail out a country in crisis, thus reducing losses from what they otherwise would be.

4. The financial sector has grown faster than the real sector, exposing the system to potential crisis because of its enormous size and the fungibility of financial claims. Off-balance-sheet activities such as standby lines of credit expose a financial institution to risks but do not show up on balance sheets. Derivatives are financial contracts whose values are derived from the values of other underlying assets, such as foreign exchange, bonds, equities, and commodities. Some large banks are heavily involved in derivatives, and concern has been expressed as to whether enough is known about the risks involved with this exposure. Concern is also expressed regarding the liquidity of Eurodollar and Eurobond deposits in foreign subsidiaries of U.S. financial institutions, particularly in light of how globalized financial markets have become.

Key Terms

Debt Deflation, **285**

Derivatives, **294**

Eurobond Market, **296**

Financial Crisis, **284**

Junk Bonds, **276**

Moral Hazard, **287**

Off-Balance-Sheet Activities, **294**

Payoff Method, **288**

Purchase and Assumption
 Method, **288**

Standby Lines of Credit, **294**

"Too Big to Fail," **288**

Review Questions

1. Discuss ways in which each of the following risks can be reduced: default risk, interest rate risk, liquidity risk, and exchange rate risk.

2. Why does financial intermediation inherently involve risk? Are FIs better at evaluating risks than you are? Why or why not?

3. What is a financial crisis? Why does an economic downturn often lead to a financial crisis? Explain why the reverse is also true.

4. Can sharp increases in interest rates increase the risk of a financial crisis? Explain.

5. What is a debt deflation and why is it so onerous for the economy?

6. Is a financial crisis more likely to be triggered by inflation or deflation? Explain.

7. What does "too big to fail" mean? What are the costs of such a policy? Under what circumstances would your funds be safer in a large bank that made risky loans rather than in a small conservative local bank?

8. What is moral hazard? Why does deposit insurance inherently involve moral hazard? What factors contribute to moral hazard on the international level?

9. Discuss the factors that contributed to the S&L debacle during the 1980s.

10. Define *derivatives*. Why can they be risky?

11. What are the Eurodollar and Eurobond markets? Does the United States regulate Eurodollar and Eurobond markets?

12. S&Ls had limited experience making commercial loans while commercial banks were extremely experienced. Explain how this difference could have exacerbated the adverse selection problem for the S&Ls in the 1980s.

13. Can derivatives cause massive losses if they are used only to hedge?

14. What caused the Japanese financial crisis of the 1990s? Compare and contrast the causes of the Japanese banking crisis with the causes of the U.S. S&L crisis in the 1980s.

15. What trading strategies did Long-Term Capital Management employ? Why did the Fed arrange a bailout?

16. What are Fannie Mae and Freddie Mac securities and why are they the subject of concern by regulators?

Analytical Question

The question marked with an icon is objective in nature. It can be completed with a short answer or number.

17. If all prices and my income fall by 25 percent, by what percent does the real value of my debt increase?

Internet Exercise

Legislation was passed by the U.S. House of Representatives in April 2003 and submitted to the U.S. Senate. Go to **http://www.fdic.gov/deposit/insurance/initiative/index.html** where the legislation can be found. Outline the proposed changes that the legislation would make.

Suggested Readings

An interesting book that looks at financial corruption and the ability of most Americans to invest their way to financial security is Roger Lowenstein, *Origins of the Crash* (East Rutherford, New Jersey: Penguin Books, 2004). For a look at the causes, consequences, and cures for instability in financial markets, see Colin Mayer, ed., *Financial Instability* (New York: Oxford University Press, 2001).

A paper that looks at many of the issues discussed in this chapter is "Financial Liberalization, Market Discipline and Bank Risk" by William C. Gruben, Jahyeong Koo, and Robert R. Moore, Federal Reserve Bank of Dallas, Center for Latin American Economics Working Paper (March 3, 2003). It is available on the Internet at **http://www.dallasfed.org/latin/papers/2003/lawp0303.pdf.**

For a look at "The Federal Reserve Responds to Crises: September 11th Was Not the First," see Christopher J. Neely, Federal Reserve Bank of St. Louis, Working Papers, 2003-034 (October 2003). It is available on the Internet at **http://research.stlouisfed.org/wp/2003/2003-034.pdf.**

For a look at "Sorting out Japan's Financial Crisis," see the article by the same name by Anil K. Kashyap, Federal Reserve Bank of Chicago, *Economic Perspectives*, 26:4 (Fourth Quarter 2002): 42–55.

For an article that looks at a model of domestic financial crises, see Martin H. Wolfson, "Neoliberalism and International Financial Instability," *Review of Radical Political Economics* 32:3 (September 1, 2000).

For an article that shows how confidence and decreases in financial instability are related, see Jenny Corbett and Janet Mitchell, "Banking Crises and Bank Rescues: The Effect of Reputation," *Journal of Money, Credit, and Banking* (August 2000).

For a look at "How the Asian Crisis Affected the World Economy: A General Perspective," see the article by the same name by Xinshen Diao, Wenli Li, and Erine Yeldal, *Economic Quarterly,* Federal Reserve Bank of Richmond, 86:2 (Spring 2000): 35–59. For a different perspective, see Joseph E. Medley, "The East Asian Economic Crisis: Surging U.S. Imperialism?" *Review of Radical Political Economics* 32:3 (September 1, 2000).

For a look at alternatives for a new financial architecture, see Kenneth Rogoff, "International Institutions for Reducing Global Financial Instability," *Journal of Economic Perspectives* 13:4 (Fall 1999): 21–42.

"The Cost of the Savings and Loan Crisis: Truth and Consequences" is discussed in an article by the same name by

Timothy Curry and Lunn Shibut, *FDIC Banking Review* 13:2 (December 2000).

An article that looks at the lender of last resort function from a global perspective is "The Free Market Is a Lie," *New Statesman* (October 9, 1998): 4.

In "Two Crises: Inflationary Inertia and Credibility," Sebastian Edwards looks at the role of government and the financial crisis in Mexico. The article can be found in *The Economic Journal* 108:448 (May 1998): 680–702.

For a look at the human costs of economic crisis in Russia, see "How Do They Survive," *The Economist* (October 3, 1998): 60–61. "Loss Adjusters" looks at the financial side of the Russian crisis. It can be found in *The Economist* (October 17, 1998): 881.

Three books on the S&L crisis are J. R. Barth, *The Great Savings and Loan Debacle* (Washington, DC: American Enterprise Institute, 1990); *The S&L Debate: Public Policy Lessons for Bank and Thrift Regulation* (New York: Oxford University Press, 1991); and Robert Emmet Long, ed., *Banking Scandals, The S&Ls and BCCI* (New York: H. W. Willson, 1993).

For interesting reading on financial instability, try Hyman Minsky, *Stabilizing the Unstable Economy* (New Haven, CT: Yale University Press, 1986).

Martin Wolfson, *Financial Crises: Understanding the Postwar U.S. Experience,* 2d ed. (Armonk, NY: M. E. Sharpe, 1994), gives a comprehensive history of financial crises through the mid-1980s.

Steven Fazzari and Dimitri B. Papadimitriou, eds., *Financial Conditions and Macroeconomic Performance: Essays in Honor of Hyman P. Minsky* (Armonk, NY: M. E. Sharpe, 1992), offers a unique view of financial instability.

Endnotes

1 The quote is from Alexander Chase.

2 There are some differences. The Ponzi scheme was pure fraud. Despite some illegal activities, the crisis in the junk bond and dotcom markets were not necessarily brought on by purely criminal activities.

3 Although not caused by debt deflation, the FSLIC failed during the 1980s savings and loan crisis, and taxpayers injected funds to save depositors from losses.

4 Fed Chair Greenspan develops this argument in his remarks "Risk and Uncertainty in Monetary Policy" at the Meetings of the American Economic Association, San Diego, California, January 3, 2004. The remarks are available on the Internet at **http://www.federalreserve.gov/boarddocs/speeches/2004/200 40103/default.htm**.

5 The moral hazard problem pertains to any depository institution that offers deposit insurance, including S&Ls. We focus here on commercial banks.

6 The inception of deposit insurance in the early 1930s resulted in federal examination of state banks that are not members of the Fed. This, in turn, caused a sharp decrease in some of the activities that contributed to the bank failures of the 1930s.

7 This includes the fund balances of the Bank Insurance Fund (BIF) and the Savings Association Insurance Fund (SAIF), both of which are part of the FDIC.

A Closer Look, page 292

a As you saw in Chapter 12, a person transferring funds from a depository institution to a money market mutual fund is not disintermediating but transferring funds from one type of intermediary to another.

b The FSLIC was dissolved in 1989 as part of the S&L bailout. Since that time, S&Ls have been able to obtain deposit insurance from the Savings Association Insurance Fund (SAIF), which is part of the FDIC.

a   If the county could have held on until mid-1995, when rates turned back down, the losses would have been much less.

b   In April 1994, Procter and Gamble sustained a $102 million after-tax loss in an interest rate swap. Also in April of that same year, Kidder Peabody found that one of its traders had parlayed a $210 million loss. After the loss, Kidder Peabody was sold to Paine Webber.

c   "The Lesson from Barings' Straits," *Business Week* (March 13, 1995): 30–32.

The dogmas of the quiet past are inadequate to the stormy present. As our case is new, so we must think anew and act anew. We must disenthrall ourselves, and then we shall save our country.

—Abraham Lincoln

The people's right to change what does not work is one of the greatest principles of our system of government.

—Richard Nixon

14

CHAPTER FOURTEEN

Regulation of the Banking System and the Financial Services Industry

Learning Objectives

After reading this chapter, you should know:

Why regulation is needed in the financial services industry

Who regulates whom in the banking system

Some of the major pieces of legislation important to the banking industry today

Regulatory challenges facing Congress and the regulators

The Role of Regulation

The ability of certain industries within a market economy to regulate themselves has been the subject of controversy for a long time. Some analysts believe that virtually no regulation is needed and that the market can handle practically every situation far better than a government regulatory agency. For example, they believe that airlines can regulate themselves better than a government regulatory agency can.[1] If an airline is unsafe, so the argument goes, it will experience more accidents than other airlines. As passengers became aware of this accident record, they will avoid flying on the unsafe airline, and it will be driven out of business. Likewise, the market can better regulate the financial services industry than any regulatory agency such as the Fed or the Office of Thrift Supervision can. According to this argument, a bank that takes too many risks will be driven out of business when cautious depositors become aware of the risks and withdraw their deposits or when the bank sustains losses and is unable to pay back depositors.

At the other extreme are those who believe that the economy needs a lot of regulation because the quest for profits is so strong that, without regulation, consumer welfare will frequently be jeopardized. For example, an airline may skimp on costly maintenance to keep its planes in the sky because planes on the ground do not generate profit. Or a financial intermediary (FI) might take a large risk because the potential payoff is so big. After all, the bulk of the funds that the intermediary is risking belongs to the depositors.[2] Although the unsafe airline may eventually be driven out of business in a market economy, that doesn't bring back the loved ones who were killed in a plane crash because the airline failed to take reasonable safety precautions. Likewise, depositors may feel some satisfaction when the depository institution that lost their life savings is driven out of business, but the institution's demise does not reduce their pecuniary losses.

In Chapter 11, we discussed the Glass-Steagall Act that was implemented in response to the financial collapse of the Great Depression. Glass-Steagall made the banking sector a highly regulated industry. Although the crisis in the Great Depression might suggest the need for some regulation, by the late 1970s sentiment in the United States had shifted to the belief that the economy had become a victim of overregulation. This change led to a deregulation movement that continues in varying degrees today. Industries such as the airlines, trucking, and financial services have been deregulated.

After deregulation, some industries experienced severe stresses and bankruptcies, particularly in the 1980s. The financial services sector in particular went through the collapse of the savings and loan (S&L) industry, the largest wave of bank failures, and the most serious strains since the Great Depression. Some blamed deregulation at least to some extent for these problems. Others argued, however, that the failures were the result of previous regulations that had protected inefficient operations and that the problems would be resolved in time. Indeed, as we have seen, by the late 1990s, the banking system had recovered and made record profits. Although the industry did not fare as well in the downturn of the early 2000s, by 2004, banking stocks were close to their previous highs, and the system was not threatened with significant failures.

The banking system, composed of depository institutions, is a major part of the financial services industry. In this chapter, we focus primarily on the regulatory structure of the banking system today and look at the major pieces of legislation that have created it. We begin with deregulation acts in 1980 and 1982 that removed many of the regulations imposed in the Great Depression. We look at the regulatory structure that was implemented in response to the financial crises of the 1980s and to new regulations that were designed in response to technological changes and the globalization of financial markets. We look at recent sweeping legislation that promises to overhaul the banking system and the financial services industry. Finally, because of the growing integration of banking and financial services firms, we summarize the major regulators of the financial services industry in general.

The Federal Aviation Administration is an example of a regulatory body. Visit it at **http://www2.faa.gov/**.

The How and Why of Financial Services Regulation

"Free to compete" means "free to fail." Because the failure of a significant number of FIs will undermine the public's confidence in the system, there is a potential conflict between the two objectives of regulation: competition and efficiency, on the one hand, and safety and soundness, on the other hand. The regulatory authorities attempt to balance these objectives, or at least so they tell us, by issuing regulations that govern banks and other financial intermediaries.

As you have seen, most, if not all, bank activities were regulated by various government regulators from the Great Depression in the 1930s until the 1980s. Given the despair and disruption accompanying the Great Depression, the financial regulators wrote regulations that limited "price" competition, restricted entry, controlled the various types of products and services that banks and other FIs could offer the public, and specified prudent capital positions for intermediaries. Specific regulations included Regulation Q interest rate ceilings, chartering and branching restrictions, assets and liabilities restrictions, and net worth requirements.

During the 1980s, banks and most other intermediaries were substantially deregulated. A series of financial crises followed that culminated in widespread insolvencies within the S&L industry and many bank failures.[3] The crises triggered attempts at reregulation and the thought that regulations needed to be overhauled.

Throughout this text, we have repeatedly emphasized the role of regulation in ensuring the safety and soundness of the financial system. Regulations were deemed necessary because of the nature of the financial system and the trade-off between high returns for net lenders versus safety and soundness. As you have seen, FIs can earn higher returns by assuming more risks. Indeed, some intermediaries offer higher returns for the acceptance of more risks. Historically, depository institutions within limits however, have offered a guaranteed, albeit lower, return.

When deciding how much risk to take on, an FI should evaluate the risks of an activity. Generally speaking, when the expected benefits outweigh the expected costs, the activity will, on average, be profitable to undertake. However, in the process of assessing the expected costs associated with various levels of risk, the intermediary considers only the costs to the stockholders, creditors, and depositors that would result from an investment or portfolio of investments going sour.[4] Because they are so highly leveraged, some FIs may fail to adequately consider how much risk they should take and may ignore the costs to the community at large that could result from the failure of the institution. The collapse of an FI not only affects those directly involved but also could impede the smooth functioning of a local community or the entire economy. The failure could lead to a bank run and a simultaneous financial collapse. Thus, we arrive at the crux of the problem: If left to decide the level of risk on their own, banks or other intermediaries will generally accept too much risk because they fail to consider the additional costs of failure that the community at large must bear. If banks and other intermediaries were left unregulated, the drive for profits might jeopardize the goals of safety and soundness for the system as a whole.

Prior to the 1980s, regulations encouraged specialization that resulted in the segmentation of the financial services industry. For many decades, the industry remained highly segmented. The limitations on portfolios were predicated on the alleged benefits of compartmentalizing FIs into various specialties. Insurance companies were to specialize in insurance and banks in banking and "never the twain shall meet." Thus, in the belief that competition needed to be limited among the compartments, the regulators effectively segmented the financial markets.

Slowly over time, however, barriers between intermediaries began to break down as financial institutions made inroads into each other's areas of specialty. The segmentation gave way as banks increasingly engaged in traditionally nonbanking activities, and nonbanks increasingly engaged in traditional banking activities. Finally, in 1999, landmark legislation underwrote the changes in the marketplace by allowing the full financial integration of banking, securities, and insurance firms as opposed to their segmentation into separate entities.

Historically, the regulatory structure was as segmented as the financial services industry. As the industry segmentation broke down, however, the regulatory segmentation failed to break down concurrently.[5] Who said government bureaucrats were flexible anyway? Today, however, although the historical segmentation of regulatory responsibilities persists, it has begun to change, albeit gradually.

Regulation can focus on either financial markets (products) or financial institutions. For example, stocks, bonds, and futures are financial products that are regulated, and banks, S&Ls, and insurance companies are financial institutions that are regulated. In addition, sometimes a particular financial product or institution may be regulated by more than one agency, and a single agency may regulate more than one financial product or institution. Given this background, now would be a good time to look at the accompanying A Closer Look feature, which surveys the many agencies currently regulating the financial services industry. Many of these nonbanking system regulators are covered in more depth in subsequent chapters.

A Closer Look

Regulators in the Financial Services Industry

- *Banks:* We have already discussed the dual banking system in which federal and state-chartered banks exist side by side. Federal banks are regulated by the Office of the Comptroller of the Currency, the FDIC, and the Fed. State banks are regulated by the state banking commissioner and possibly the Fed and/or the FDIC, depending on whether they choose to be members of the Fed and/or subscribe to deposit insurance. With regard to reserve requirements, all banks are regulated by the Fed.
Bank holding companies and financial holding companies are regulated by the Federal Reserve. However, unless the Fed suspects a problem, the Fed relies on the reports of a subsidiary's functional regulator such as the Securities and Exchange Commission or the state insurance commission.
- *Savings and loan associations:* S&Ls are regulated by the Office of Thrift Supervision (OTS) of the Treasury and, with regard to reserve requirements, the Fed. Those that subscribe to deposit insurance are also regulated by the FDIC.

- *Credit unions:* Federally chartered credit unions are regulated by the National Credit Union Administration while those with state charters are regulated by state banking commissioners. The National Credit Union Share Insurance Fund insures deposits in credit unions up to $100,000. Because they are nonprofit, tax-exempt institutions, credit unions have generally engaged in less risk taking than their for-profit competitors, and consequently they have experienced much milder strains. They have larger reserves and fewer losses. Unlike other depository institutions, credit unions do not pay an insurance premium but put up capital equal to 1 percent of their insured deposits with the insurance fund. If this reserve is ever depleted because of losses, credit unions are required to replenish it out of capital.
- *Finance companies:* Finance companies must obtain permission to open an office for business from the state in which they want to operate. Once that permission is obtained, there are virtually no restrictions on branching. The Federal Trade Commission (FTC) regulates finance companies with regard to consumer protection. However, there are no restrictions on the assets they hold or how they raise their funds other than those generally applying to the issuance of securities.
- *Financial futures:* Financial futures are regulated by the Commodity Futures Trading Commission and the National Futures Association. The latter was set up by the industry for self-regulation.
- *Financial options:* Financial options are regulated by the Securities and Exchange Commission (SEC), which was established in 1933. Options on futures are regulated by the Commodity Futures Trading Commission. The Options Clearing Corporation has been set up by the industry for self-regulation.
- *Mutual funds:* The SEC was given regulatory control over mutual funds by the Investment Company Act of 1940. Regulations include requirements to publicly disclose financial information and restrictions on how business can be solicited. Mutual funds experienced tremendous growth in the 1980s and early 1990s. Partially as a result, some people believe that additional regulation may be needed for two reasons: (1) Sales offices for mutual funds are now allowed to be located inside commercial banks, even though the funds are not sold directly by the bank. Apparently, a significant portion of customers erroneously believe that mutual funds purchased in a bank are insured by the bank. (2) Mutual funds have grown to be a significant portion of total intermediation while the regulatory structure has not grown at the same pace.
- *Insurance companies:* Insurance companies are regulated by the insurance commissioner of the state in which they do business.
- *Pension funds:* Pension funds are regulated by the Department of Labor. The Pension Benefit Guaranty Corporation provides insurance in the event that a pension plan is unable to pay the benefits defined in the pension agreement. The pension rights of more than 40 million Americans are protected by this insurance. In other words, if a plan cannot pay pension benefits because it invested the premiums poorly or because it was not funded properly to begin with, the Pension Benefit Guaranty Corporation will pay the benefits according to the contract and make up any payment deficiencies up to a limit.
- *Stocks and bonds:* Securities markets including brokers and dealers are overseen by the SEC. The SEC requires that companies fully disclose their financial condition before issuing bonds and while the bonds are outstanding. Likewise, issuers of new securities must register with the SEC and disclose all important financial information. If the equities are to be publicly traded, ongoing disclosure is required, and insider trading, which is trading of securities by those who have access to information about the companies involved before it is made public, is forbidden. Margin requirements specify the maximum

percent of borrowed funds that can be used in a stock purchase. The Fed sets margin requirements for the purchase of stocks and bonds.

- *Securities firms:* Securities firms are regulated by the SEC, the New York Stock Exchange (NYSE), and other exchanges. In addition, securities firms are self-regulated by the National Association of Securities Dealers. The Securities Investor Protection Corporation insures retail customers of securities brokerage firms for up to $500,000 of their portfolios in the event the brokerage firm becomes insolvent.
- U.S. government securities: U.S. government and U.S. government agency securities are regulated by the Fed and the SEC.

Noticeably absent from this list is a regulator of the money markets including the market for commercial paper, bankers' acceptances, and negotiable CDs, the mortgage-backed securities market, and the Eurodollar and Eurobond markets. Because the regulatory structure will continue to change as the financial services industry evolves, innovative regulations for new and existing markets and products may be just around the corner.

A final point needs to be reiterated. The regulatory structure of the financial services is in a process of ongoing change because of the continuing evolution of the industry resulting in new products and markets, technological changes in the delivery of financial services, and the globalization of financial markets. All of these changes leave many concerns about the adequacy of regulation.

The Federal Deposit Insurance Corporation (FDIC), which regulates banks and savings associations that purchase deposit insurance from it, is an exception to regulatory segmentation. Visit its site at **http://www.fdic.gov/**.

Recap   Regulation must balance the goals of competition and efficiency versus safety and soundness. FIs should balance the expected benefits and expected costs of assuming various levels of risk. Initially, regulation encouraged market segmentation and, hence, regulation was segmented. Although segmented markets are breaking down, regulations have been slower to change. Either financial products or financial institutions can be regulated. The regulatory structure is in the process of ongoing change because of the evolution of the financial services industry.

We now turn our attention to the most recent pieces of regulatory legislation, which govern the banking system in the early years of the new millennium.

Depository Institutions Deregulation and Monetary Control Act of 1980 and Garn–St. Germain Act of 1982: Deregulation in the Early 1980s

The burdens associated with complying with the regulations and the benefits associated with innovating around them produced numerous forms of adaptive behavior by banks and other FIs. For example, banks developed new types of liabilities to sidestep Regulation Q (interest rate ceilings that could be paid to depositors) and reserve requirements. These new types of liabilities included borrowings in the fed funds, negotiable CDs, repurchase agreements, and Eurodollar markets. Because these new types of liabilities were borrowings, not deposits, they were not subject to interest rate caps or reserve requirements. Banks also used the holding company corporate form to evade certain entry and branching restrictions and to engage in nonbanking activities. The financial regulations and structure that had been designed and erected during the Great Depression were increasingly ill-suited to the changing economic and technological environment of the 1970s. As innovations weakened the effectiveness of various regulations, regulators recognized the difficulty, if not the impossibility, of controlling financial flows and the market for financial services. Accordingly, Congress decided to **deregulate** by dismantling the regulations. Landmark legislation enacted in 1980 and 1982 was the result.[6]

The first legislation was the **Depository Institutions Deregulation and Monetary Control Act of 1980 (DIDMCA)**. Its numerous provisions reflect the compromises necessary to enact such an all-encompassing piece of legislation. As its title suggests, however, the major provisions of interest to us can be divided into two groups:

1. *Deregulation*
   a. The remaining Regulation Q ceilings were phased out over a six-year period that ended in 1986.
   b. Asset and liability powers of banks and thrifts were expanded:
      (1) *Assets:* S&Ls and savings banks were allowed to extend loans to businesses and offer more services to customers.
      (2) *Liabilities:* All depository intermediaries were permitted to offer NOW accounts (interest-bearing checkable deposits) to households.
      (3) State **usury ceilings** (maximum interest rates FIs are allowed to charge borrowers on certain types of loans) were suspended.

2. *Monetary control*
   a. All depository institutions were subject to reserve requirements (so-called **universal reserve requirements**).
   b. Reserve requirements were to be the same on particular types of deposits across institutions (so-called **uniform reserve requirements**); this provision was phased in over an eight-year period that ended in 1987.

In general, the deregulation provisions put some explicit price competition back into banking and permitted more competition among depository institutions. As a result, banks and thrifts would be more alike in terms of the products and services offered to the public. Congress hoped that the net result of more competition would be greater efficiency, an accompanying reduction in costs, and an improvement in the quantity and quality of financial services.

By mandating universal and uniform reserve requirements, the act strengthened the effectiveness of the regulatory process and expanded the powers of the Fed. Henceforth, when the Fed changed the amount of funds available for reserves, its control over the money supply and supply of loanable funds would be more direct. All in all, the DIDMCA was a landmark piece of legislation that brought many long overdue changes to the financial structure—changes that had been recommended by numerous federal studies over the previous 20 years.

Two years later, the **Garn–St. Germain Depository Institutions Act of 1982** was enacted. Like its 1980 predecessor, the 1982 act had many provisions. Chief among them were those that speeded up the pace of deregulation by allowing depository institutions to offer two types of deposit accounts designed to compete directly with money market mutual funds: (1) money market deposit accounts, which have no rate ceiling and permit six third-party payments transactions per month, and (2) Super NOW accounts, which also have no rate ceiling but are fully checkable.

Deregulate
To dismantle existing regulations.

Depository Institutions Deregulation and Monetary Control Act of 1980 (DIDMCA)
The statute that removed many of the regulations enacted during the Great Depression; phased out Regulation Q, established uniform and universal reserve requirements, increased the assets and liabilities that depository institutions could hold, authorized NOW accounts, and suspended usury ceilings.

Usury Ceilings
Maximum interest rates that FIs may charge on certain loans.

Universal Reserve Requirements
Reserve requirements to which all depository institutions are subject.

Uniform Reserve Requirements
Reserve requirements that apply to particular types of deposits and are the same across all depository institutions.

Garn–St. Germain Depository Institutions Act of 1982
A statute that, along with DIDMCA, deregulated depository institutions; authorized money market deposit accounts and Super NOW accounts.

Since this legislation was enacted, competition among FIs and between FIs and the open market has increased dramatically. For example, depository institutions now offer rates on all deposit liabilities that are closely correlated with market rates. Such dramatic changes in the competitive environment within which banks and other FIs operate have noticeable effects on the portfolio behavior and operations of depository institutions.

Recap   Because market participants had found ways around many regulations, Congress passed two major statutes that deregulated financial markets. The DIDMCA in 1980 phased out Regulation Q ceilings and expanded the asset and liability powers of banks and thrifts. It also established uniform and universal reserve requirements for all depository institutions. The Garn–St. Germain Act of 1982, among other things, authorized money market deposit accounts and Super NOW accounts.

Basel Accord—The Introduction of International Capital Standards

Bank capital is the difference between bank assets and liabilities. Until 1980, banks were pretty much free to establish their own capital requirements as the Fed and other regulators pursued different avenues of control such as reserve requirements, asset restrictions, chartering, and Regulation Q. Since the deregulation of these traditional avenues of regulation in the early 1980s, regulators have attempted not only to impose stricter capital requirements but also to use them as a primary vehicle of regulation.

Basel Accord
A 1988 agreement among 12 countries that established international capital standards for banks.

The trend toward stricter standards received further impetus in November 1988, when the United States and 11 other countries entered into the **Basel Accord**, which established uniform international capital standards for banks. The accord specified the amount of capital that banks must hold relative to assets. This standard was stricter than that imposed on U.S. banks at the time and involved risk-based capital standards for the first time. Thus, the amount of capital a bank was required to hold was based not only on total assets and liabilities but also on the measurable riskiness of those assets. Despite the regulators' efforts, many banks were holding less capital relative to assets than the new regulations required. Thus, as a result of the accord, many U.S. banks had to alter their behavior—to shore up bank capital relative to assets—in the early 1990s to meet the stricter standards. The accompanying A Closer Look feature explains the standards and gives an example of how they are implemented.

Looking Out

Basel Committee Announces 25 Core Principles for Effective Bank Supervision

The Asian meltdown of 1997–1998 demonstrated how crisis prone the international financial system can be as financial markets become more globalized. Long before this crisis, the Basel Committee on Banking Supervision had related concerns and was meeting on a regular basis at the Bank for International Settlements in Basel, Switzerland. The committee consists of central bank governors from the G-10 countries. Its goal is to improve banking supervision at the international level and enhance international financial stability.

In September 1997, the Basel Committee announced 25 core principles that the committee believes must be in place for a supervisory system to be effective. In addition to the G-10 nations, 15 other emerging economies participated in the discussions. Supervisory authorities throughout the world were asked to endorse the principles by October 1998. Endorsement includes a review of current supervisory arrangements and the changes that would have to be implemented for a country to be in compliance with the principles.

The core principles address "the preconditions for effective banking supervision, licensing and structure, prudential regulations and requirements, methods of ongoing banking supervision, information requirements, formal powers of supervisors and cross-border banking."[a] They are intended to serve as a reference for regulators to apply when supervising banks in their countries. In addition, the principles are designed to be verifiable by domestic and international regulators and the market. It is hoped that if countries strengthen areas where they fall short of the core principles, domestic and international financial stability will be improved.

A Closer Look

Bank Capital Standards under the Basel Accord (Basel I)

The Basel Accord established requirements for core capital and for total capital. *Core capital* is by definition the historical value of outstanding stock plus retained earnings. Total capital is core capital plus supplemental capital (loan-loss reserves plus subordinated debt). *Subordinated* debt is long-term debt that is paid off after depositors and other creditors have been paid in the event that the institution goes under. The amount of capital that must be held is based on the larger of two measures: one measure is based on risk-adjusted assets and the other on total assets.

The method based on risk-adjusted assets assigns different weights to different types of assets according to their risks. For instance, ordinary loans are counted at 100 percent of their value; mortgages are counted at 50 percent. Only half of the value of mortgages is counted because the property is held as collateral and repossessed in the event of default. Deposits between banks (interbank deposits) count at 20 percent, and T-bills and cash count at zero percent. In addition, off-balance-sheet activities that result in an obligation or potential obligation for the bank are also counted in risk-adjusted capital at their full value. For example, if a bank gives a standby letter of credit for $1,000, that letter of credit is counted at its full value ($1,000) in calculating risk-adjusted assets, even though it is not an asset. The reason for this is obvious. If the standby letter of credit is exercised, the bank stands to lose $1,000 just as if it had made a bad loan. For safety, a bank with off-balance-sheet activities that expose the bank to greater risk must maintain more capital. The risks of some activities such as futures, options, and swaps may be difficult to evaluate, however.

Once risk-adjusted assets have been determined, they are subject to two capital constraints: (1) core capital must be equal to at least 4 percent of risk-adjusted assets and (2) total capital must be equal to at least 8 percent of risk-adjusted assets. At the present time, risk-adjusted assets take into account only credit risk. They do not consider interest rate, liquidity, or exchange rate risks. Additional requirements that consider these risks may be implemented in the future.

In addition to the constraints based on risk-adjusted assets, banks are also subject to a leverage requirement stated in terms of total assets. In this case, all assets are weighted at 100 percent, and there is no accounting for off-balance-sheet activities. (The weight assigned to off-balance-sheet activities is zero.) According to the Basel Accord requirements, a bank must have core capital equal to at least 3 percent of total assets.

The use of international capital requirements has many desirable effects. All banks from the countries that abide by the standards are put on a more or less equal footing. The following table provides an example of how the standards are implemented under what has come to be known as Basel I.

Core Capital	$775,000		
Stock issued	500,000		
Retained earnings	275,000		
Total Capital	1,535,000		
Core capital	775,000		
Loan-loss reserves	260,000		
Subordinated debt	500,000		
Risk-Adjusted Assets			
Loans	$14,000,000 @	100%	$14,000,000
Mortgages	3,500,000 @	50%	1,750,000
Interbank deposits	2,000,000 @	20%	400,000
Government securities	3,000,000 @	0%	0
Reserves	1,800,000 @	0%	0
Standby letters and other lines of credit	3,000,000 @	100%	3,000,000
Total Risk-Adjusted Assets			19,150,000
Total Assets			
Loans	$14,000,000 @	100%	$14,000,000
Mortgages	3,500,000 @	100%	3,500,000
Interbank deposits	2,000,000 @	100%	2,000,000
Government securities	3,000,000 @	100%	3,000,000
Reserves	1,800,000 @	100%	1,800,000
Standby letters and other lines of Credit	3,000,000 @	0%	0
Total Assets			$24,300,000

Core capital must equal at least 4% of risk-adjusted assets: 4% × $19,150,000 = $766,000

Total capital must equal at least 8% of risk-adjusted assets: 8% × $19,150,000 = $1,532,000

Core capital must equal at least 3% of total assets: 3% × $24,300,000 = $729,000

As noted in the body of the text, very large complex banking institutions will be subject to additional capital requirements under Basel II.

The original Basel Accord, now known as *Basel I,* is believed to have achieved its primary goal of promoting financial stability by imposing risk-based international standards for banks. However, as some banking institutions have become more complex and as risk-management strategies have become more sophisticated, the need for additional standards for the largest and most complex banking institutions has been recognized. These institutions use instruments and procedures whose risk is not adequately measured under Basel I. Changes to the accord, known as *Basel II,* have been developed to which banks with assets of more than $250 billion or foreign exposure of $10 billion would be subject. The new framework maintains the minimum required 8 percent capital ratio but revises risk-weighted assets to include credit risk exposure, market risk exposure, and operational risk exposure. The revised standards are based on the best-practice risk-measurement and risk-management techniques that larger banks now use. Large banks which are subject to the new requirements, have been asked to develop plans by late 2004 to be implemented by 2007. Presently, about 10 large US banks are subject to the Basel II requirements. However, many banks in foreign countries must meet the new requirements. Other banks continue to abide by the Basel I requirements.

Financial Institutions Reform, Recovery, and Enforcement Act of 1989—Reregulation in Response to Financial Crisis (Bailing Out the Thrifts)

The **Financial Institutions Reform, Recovery, and Enforcement Act (FIRREA)** was signed into law in August 1989. The FIRREA was passed in response to the S&L crisis of the 1980s and was an attempt at reregulation following the deregulation and subsequent crises of the 1980s (see Chapter 13). The provisions of the FIRREA include the following:

1. An initial $50 billion was injected into the newly created Savings Association Insurance Fund (SAIF). The SAIF was established to provide insurance for the deposits of S&Ls, thereby replacing the Federal Savings and Loan Insurance Corporation (FSLIC). Additionally, the SAIF provided funding for government takeover of failed S&Ls. The original $50 billion was raised by selling bonds known as *bailout bonds,* and the money was used to compensate institutions that took over a failed S&L by making up the difference between the value of the assets and liabilities of the defunct institution. Administration of the SAIF was made the responsibility of the Federal Deposit Insurance Corporation (FDIC). The FSLIC was dissolved. It had virtually gone bankrupt because of the crisis of the 1980s and was unable to cover the losses of insured deposits.

2. Two new government agencies were created. The **Office of Thrift Supervision (OTS)** was established to oversee the S&L industry, replacing the **Federal Home Loan Bank Board**. The **Resolution Trust Corporation (RTC)** was set up as a temporary agency to dispose of the properties of the thrifts that failed between January 1, 1989, and July 1, 1995. The FDIC was put in charge of the RTC, and the board of the FDIC was expanded from three to five members with the addition of the director of the OTS and an additional appointment by the president of the United States.

For information about the Office of Thrift Supervision, visit **http://www.ots.treas.gov/**.

3. For the first time, deposit insurance was made a full-faith and credit obligation of the federal government rather than the FDIC. Until 1989, neither Congress nor the taxpayers were legally required to bail out an insolvent deposit insurance company,

Financial Institutions Reform, Recovery, and Enforcement Act (FIRREA)
Legislation passed in 1989 in response to the S&L crisis to bail out the failed thrifts and to establish new regulations for S&Ls.

Office of Thrift Supervision (OTS)
An agency created by the FIRREA to replace the Federal Home Loan Bank Board as the overseer of the S&L industry.

Federal Home Loan Bank Board
The regulatory body of the S&L industry until 1989.

Resolution Trust Corporation (RTC)
An agency created by the FIRREA to dispose of the properties of the failed S&Ls.

whether it be the FDIC or the FSLIC. In reality, the government was de facto required to bail out a failed deposit insurer, as it did with the FSLIC, but only because failing to do so might cause a systemwide collapse. Contrary to what most Americans thought, there was no legal responsibility for the bailout.

The new deposit insurance funds, the SAIF and the Bank Insurance Fund (BIF), both under the FDIC, were required to maintain reserves of at least 1.25 percent of insured deposits. Premiums paid are a percentage of total domestic deposits including deposits of more than $100,000. As of March 31, 2004, the BIF had assets of $34.2 billion, which amounted to 1.32 percent of insured banking deposits. The SAIF had assets of $12.4 billion, or 1.39 percent, of insured S&L deposits.

In the early and mid-1990s, the SAIF was seriously underfunded with reserves of only 0.38 percent of insured deposits. A special $2.1 billion assessment on insured institutions in 1996 and a substantial decline in thrift failures had returned the SAIF to a healthy position by the late 1990s.

4. New regulations restricted the investments of S&Ls by limiting commercial mortgage lending and by phasing out junk bond investments by 1994. Investments in junk bonds had first been authorized in 1982 by the Garn–St. Germain Act. In addition, S&Ls were required to hold at least 70 percent of their assets as mortgages or mortgage-backed securities. Commercial real estate loans were restricted to 400 percent of total capital.

5. Capital requirements were imposed on the S&Ls. The requirements were similar to those placed on banks under the Basel Accord. Risk-based capital standards were phased in, just as they had been for banks in participating countries (see the A Closer Look feature on pages 317–319). Core capital for S&Ls was to be 3 percent by 1995, and total capital was to be at least 8 percent of risk-adjusted assets by 1992. These new requirements more than doubled the amount of capital that had to be held under the previous standards. To demonstrate the extent to which the industry has recovered, as of June 30, 2004, the total capital-to-asset ratio of S&Ls was 10.94 percent, which is higher than it was in the 1940–1970 period when the ratio fluctuated around 7 percent.

Federal Deposit Insurance Corporation Improvement Act of 1991—Tightening Up Deposit Insurance

Moral Hazard Problem
The fact that the presence of deposit insurance causes financial intermediaries to take more risks than they otherwise would because they know that if they lose, their depositors still get their funds back.

Federal Deposit Insurance Corporation Improvement Act (FDICIA)
Legislation passed by Congress in 1991 to enact regulatory changes to ensure the safety and soundness of the banking and thrift industries.

Although it might seem that deposit insurance would solve the problem of excessive risk taking by protecting small depositors in the event of a depository institution's insolvency, deposit insurance actually increases the problem of excessive risk taking. Deposit insurance reduces market discipline because depositors no longer have to be concerned about the level of risk their bank engages in. This risk, known as the **moral hazard problem**, results from the fact that the presence of deposit insurance causes financial intermediaries to take more risks than they otherwise would because they know that if they lose, their depositors still get their funds back.[7] This encourages a financial institution to take on more risk because the greater the risk, the greater the possibility of higher returns. It's like going to Las Vegas to gamble with your neighbor's funds with the understanding that if you win, you get to keep the winnings and if you lose, your neighbor still gets paid back, but not by you.

In response to growing concern about this problem, Congress passed the **Federal Deposit Insurance Corporation Improvement Act (FDICIA)** in 1991. The FDICIA attempted to secure the safety and soundness of the banking and thrift industries (S&Ls,

savings banks, and credit unions) through regulatory changes and enacted several reforms including the following:

1. Insurance premiums were scaled to the risk exposure of the banks or thrifts. Now banks or thrifts that engage in high levels of risk or have low capital ratios are charged higher deposit insurance premiums. Thus, higher-risk institutions contribute more to deposit insurance funds than do lower-risk institutions. As noted earlier, because both funds are currently above the statutory reserves limit of 1.25 percent of insured deposits, healthy banks are not being charged premiums for deposit insurance. Higher-risk institutions are charged up to $0.27 per $100 in deposits, depending on their risk profile. Those with the most risk pay premiums at the higher end of the range. Approximately 92 percent of all insured institutions are in the lowest risk category and currently pay nothing for deposit insurance.

2. As of December 31, 1999, the FDICIA limited insurance coverage of regular accounts to a maximum of $100,000. On retirement accounts, the limit is $100,000 per depository institution.[8]

Payoff Method
The method of resolving a bank insolvency by paying off the depositors and closing the institution.

Purchase and Assumption Method
The method of resolving a bank insolvency by finding a buyer for the institution.

"Too Big to Fail"
The position adopted by FDIC regulators in 1984 whereby the failure of a large bank would be resolved using the purchase and assumption method rather than the payoff method.

3. The FDIC was also required to use the least costly method to resolve any insolvency. Prior to this time, an insolvency could be resolved by either the payoff method or the purchase and assumption method. Under the **payoff method,** depositors of a failed institution are paid off, the assets are liquidated, and the institution is closed. Depositors with balances of more than $100,000 lose the balances over $100,000. Under the **purchase and assumption method**, an insolvency is resolved by finding a buyer for the failed institution. In this case, all deposit liabilities (even those above the $100,000 limit) are assumed by the purchasing institution, and depositors do not lose anything. The payoff method is usually cheaper for the FDIC. Being required to use the least costly method to resolve insolvencies could prevent the FDIC from de facto insuring deposits more than $100,000 by using the purchase and assumption method to dispose of insolvent banks that are "too-big-to-fail." Under the **"too-big-to-fail"** practice, which was adopted by FDIC regulators in 1984, the failure of a large bank would be resolved using the purchase and assumption method rather than the payoff method. This clause of FDICIA formally ended this practice. Despite this provision, if the failure would result in a systemic risk (a risk to the entire financial system), the least costly method does not have to be used. An exception requires the approval of the Treasury in consultation with the president and the approval of two-thirds of the members of the Board of Governors of the Fed and the FDIC. Needless to say, an exception is unlikely to be granted unless the failure would cause serious adverse effects to the economy and the financial system.

4. The FDIC established a system that rated banks and savings institutions as well capitalized, adequately capitalized, and undercapitalized. The undercapitalized institutions were then categorized as undercapitalized, significantly undercapitalized, and critically undercapitalized. Institutions in each category are subject to appropriate treatment. The greater the degree of undercapitalization, the more severe the restrictions on the bank's operations. As of December 31, 2003, 98.9 percent of all banks were rated as well-capitalized.

5. The ability of foreign banks to use certain categories of deposits in the United States was limited. Foreign banks desiring to keep insured deposit accounts can do so only through insured U.S. subsidiary banks.

Thus, as a result of the Basel Accord, the FIRREA, and the FDICIA, banks and other depository institutions are now subject to both risk-based capital standards and risk-based insurance premiums. We turn now to the Community Reinvestment Act, which was actually passed in 1977 but was not really well known outside the banking industry until recent years.

The Basel Accord of 1988 established international capital standards for financial institutions. Twelve countries signed the original accord. Basel II revised capital standards for more complex banking institution. The FIRREA of 1989 bailed out the S&L industry, imposed new risk-based capital standards on S&Ls, and restricted the assets that S&Ls could hold. The FDICIA of 1991 imposed risk-based insurance premiums and eliminated the "too-big-to-fail" practice by requiring the FDIC to resolve insolvencies in the least costly way.

Community Reinvestment Act—Outlawing Discriminatory Lending Practices

Community Reinvestment Act
Legislation passed by Congress in 1977 to increase the availability of credit to economically disadvantaged areas and to correct alleged discriminatory lending practices.

Redlining
The practice of restricting the number or dollar amounts of loans in an area regardless of the creditworthiness of the borrower.

The original purpose of the **Community Reinvestment Act (CRA)** was to increase the availability of credit to economically disadvantaged areas and to correct alleged discriminatory lending practices. Minority borrowers and neighborhoods had long been the victims of redlining. **Redlining** refers to the practice of drawing a red line (or any colored line) around a certain area on a map and restricting the number or dollar amount of loans made in that area regardless of the creditworthiness of the borrower with respect to income or collateral.

The Community Reinvestment Act did not get much attention because it provided no means of enforcement for regulators to use. However, activist groups believed that many banks were not making significant efforts to comply with the law, and in recent years, many mainstream community groups have joined their calls for more stringent enforcement of the act.

During the late 1980s and the 1990s, a means of enforcing the act became available due to the wave of bank mergers and acquisitions that began in the late 1980s and accelerated in the late 1990s. In deciding whether to approve a bank merger or acquisition, the Fed now assesses how well the bank is meeting the CRA's lending criteria, and compliance statements are judged critically.[9]

In 1995, CRA regulations were revised to make them more objective and performance oriented as well as to reduce compliance and reporting costs for many banks. Under the new rules, banks are divided into three classifications: large retail, small retail, and wholesale or limited-purpose institutions. Large and small retail banks are evaluated principally on their performance in assessment areas, whereas wholesale and limited-purpose institutions are evaluated based on their nationwide performance as long as they have adequately addressed the needs of the assessment area. For large retail banks, current regulations establish performance goals for lending, investment, and service. Banks are classed as outstanding, satisfactory, needs to improve, or substantial noncompliance. Most banks have received satisfactory or better ratings. Now all federal agencies responsible for supervising depository institutions conduct CRA examination's and each institution's record is taken into account when considering an institution's application for deposit facilities. Bank performance in this area is often difficult to judge, however, because banks are required to practice nondiscriminatory lending while focusing on safety and soundness.

To the extent that the Community Reinvestment Act has forced financial institutions to recognize and respond to the changing demographics before they would otherwise have done so, the law has provided an important service to the industry and community. Many bankers now find that as they develop new markets, products, and services to meet the needs of the community that these new activities will be quite profitable.

Interstate Banking and Branching Efficiency Act of 1994— The Dawn of Nationwide Branching?

The **Interstate Banking and Branching Efficiency Act (IBBEA)** of 1994 eliminated most restrictions on interstate bank mergers and made interstate branching possible for the first time since the passage of the McFadden Act in 1927.[10] The law permits all bank holding companies to acquire banks anywhere in the nation as long as certain conditions are met. In addition, under the same conditions, banks in one state may merge with banks in another state, thus effectively branching. The conditions include meeting requirements for the safety and soundness of the institutions involved (they must be well capitalized and well managed) and making commitments to community reinvestment under the Community Reinvestment Act. Under no circumstances will banks be permitted to use a branch to generate deposits without considering community reinvestment needs. Prior to the law, some states had limited or put additional conditions on the acquisition of banks by out-of-state bank holding companies.

In addition, as of June 1, 1997, bank holding companies were permitted to convert their multiple banks in various states into branches of a single interstate bank. This reduced the costs of maintaining a separate board of directors for each bank and the costs of other duplicative overhead expenses. Whether significant savings will be realized remains to be seen.

We turn now to the final major piece of banking legislation in the twentieth century. With the passage of the Gramm-Leach-Bliley Act in 1999, the financial services industry of the twenty-first century is far different from that of the twentieth century.

The Gramm-Leach-Bliley Act (GLBA) of 1999—The Final Demise of Glass-Steagall

Until 1999, the most significant piece of banking legislation in the twentieth century had been the Glass-Steagall Act of 1933 that separated investment and commercial banking, created the FDIC, and limited the range of assets and liabilities that a commercial bank could hold and issue. After 67 years, this act was effectively repealed with the passage of the **Gramm-Leach-Bliley Act (GLBA)** in November 1999. The new landmark legislation became effective March 11, 2000, and significantly impacts the financial services industry. Rather than segmentation among financial service providers, the act allows for considerable financial integration in the financial services industry.

Major Provisions of the Gramm-Leach-Bliley Act

GLBA allows bank holding companies that meet certain criteria to be certified as **financial holding companies (FHCs)**. FHCs may engage in a broad array of financial and nonfinancial activities. To become an FHC, a bank holding company must file a declaration with the Fed that certifies that all of its depository institutions are well capitalized and well managed and have a "satisfactory" or better rating under the Community Reinvestment Act. A FHC may engage in the following activities:

1. Financially related activities including securities underwriting and dealing, insurance agency and underwriting activities, and merchant banking activities.

2. Other financial activities that the Fed determines to be financial in nature or incidental to financial activities.

Looking Back

A Time Line of Banking Legislation

During the twentieth century, the United States enacted a number of pieces of major banking legislation that shaped the industry and its evolution.

- *1913:* The Federal Reserve Act created the Federal Reserve System.
- *1927:* The McFadden Act prohibited interstate banking.
- *1933:* The Glass-Steagall Act established the FDIC as a temporary agency, separated commercial and investment banking, established Regulation Q interest rate ceilings, and set the interest rate ceiling on demand deposits at zero percent.
- *1935:* The Banking Act established the FDIC as a permanent agency.
- *1980:* The Depository Institutions Deregulation and Monetary Control Act (DIDMCA) authorized NOW accounts nationwide, thereby ending the monopoly of commercial banks on checkable deposits; phased out Regulation Q; established uniform and universal reserve requirements; granted new powers to thrifts; eliminated usury laws; and increased deposit insurance from $40,000 to $100,000 per account.
- *1982:* The Garn–St. Germain Act expanded the asset and liability powers of banks and thrifts; expanded the power of the FDIC to help troubled banks; and created money market deposit accounts and super NOW accounts
- *1989:* The Financial Institutions Recovery, Reform, and Enforcement Act (FIRREA) authorized a taxpayer bailout of the S&L industry; brought deposit insurance for thrifts under the FDIC; created the Resolution Trust Corporation, a temporary agency to dispose of the assets of failed institutions; and imposed new restrictions on S&Ls.
- *1991:* The Federal Deposit Insurance Corporation Improvement Act (FDICIA) abolished the "too-big-to-fail" policy; limited brokered deposits; established new capital requirements for banks; established risk-based insurance premiums; gave the FDIC new powers to borrow from the U.S. Treasury; restricted activities of foreign banks; and insured state banks.
- *1994:* The Interstate Banking and Branching Efficiency Act (IBBEA) as of June 1, 1997, allowed virtually unimpeded interstate branching by adequately capitalized and managed banks that meet CRA requirements.
- *1999:* The Gramm-Leach-Bliley Act (GLBA) allowed banks, insurance companies, securities firms, and other financial institutions to affiliate under common ownership and to offer a complete range of financial services that had been previously prohibited; created financial holding companies (FHCs) that could engage in financially related activities, other financial activities, and complementary nonfinancial activities; expanded allowable activities for banks and their subsidiaries; and repealed key provisions of the 1933 Glass-Steagall Act that separated commercial and investment banking.

3. Nonfinancial activities that the Fed determines are complementary to a financial activity and do not pose a substantial risk to the safety or soundness of depository institutions or the financial system.

The act also authorizes expanded powers for banks and their subsidiaries. Under the new law, banks are

1. Authorized to underwrite and market municipal revenue bonds.

2. Authorized to own or control a "financial subsidiary" that engages in activities that national banks are not permitted to directly engage in if prior approval of the Office of the Controller of the Currency is received. The activities of the financial subsidiary do not include insurance underwriting, real estate development or investment, or complementary activities.

Under the GLBA, the Fed is given the ultimate responsibility for supervising FHCs. This is similar to its ultimate regulatory responsibility for bank holding companies. However, under the law, the Fed is to rely on reports of examination prepared by the subsidiary's primary functional regulator as much as possible. For example, the primary banking regulator may be the FDIC, the Fed, or the Office of the Controller of the Currency; for securities activities, the primary regulator is the Securities Exchange Commission; and for insurance activities, the state insurance commissioner is the primary regulator. There are some exceptions: when the Fed believes that the activities of a subsidiary may pose a threat to an affiliated depository institution or if the subsidiary is in violation of any federal law that the Fed has jurisdiction to enforce.

As of March 2000, when the law became partially effective, 117 bank holding companies had been certified as FHCs. By January 2004, the number had increased to about 625. Full phase-in of the law became effective November 12, 2004, when financial subsidiaries of FHCs were allowed to engage in merchant banking activities.

Two important additional provisions of the GLBA protect consumers. The first requires that ATM operators post a notice of any fees that may be imposed and inform the consumer through an onscreen or paper message of the amount of the fee before the consumer is irrevocably committed to completing the transaction. The second includes a number of new requirements relating to the disclosure of financial information about consumers. Namely, financial institutions cannot sell information for marketing purpose and are required to disclose, prior to the opening of an account and at least annually thereafter, the institution's policies regarding the disclosure of nonpublic personal information to third parties.

Recap   The Community Reinvestment Act of 1977 was designed to eliminate discriminatory lending practices. The IBBEA of 1994 allowed unimpeded nationwide branching as of June 1, 1997. The GLBA of 1999 allowed for the certification of financial holding companies that could engage in banking, securities, and insurance activities. The GLBA effectively repealed the provisions of the Glass-Steagall Act, which separated commercial and investment banking.

To summarize, by the turn of the century, many regulatory changes had already occurred including the following: (1) scaling insurance premiums to the risk exposure of banks, (2) limiting foreign deposit coverage, (3) intervening early when a bank begins experiencing problems so that measures will be taken before bank capital is fully depleted, (4) ending the practice of "too big to fail," (5) increasing capital requirements, (6) expanding interstate banking, (7) allowing banks, securities firms, and insurance companies to affiliate under common ownership, and (8) authorizing FHCs to engage in many previously prohibited financial and nonfinancial services. We now focus on other concerns that still exist and possible areas of future reform that could alleviate these concerns.

Other Possible Areas of Reforms

Both the FIRREA and the FDICIA tightened regulations by requiring higher capital standards and risk-based deposit insurance premiums. This legislation has generally been praised as a much needed remedy to the moral hazard dangers of deposit insurance.

While believing that the current system is not fundamentally broken, the FDIC itself has suggested several reforms for deposit insurance that Congress has considered but not yet passed.

First, the FDIC recommends the merging of BIF and SAIF. It believes that a merged fund would be stronger than two separate funds. At the present time, institutions have an incentive to change their charter to qualify to purchase insurance from the fund with the lowest (or potentially lowest) premiums. The merged fund would save the resources that are being wasted in attempting to circumvent paying premiums from the higher priced fund.

Secondly, the FDIC has proposed increasing deposit insurance coverage levels and tying future increases to an inflation index. Thus, for example, if inflation was 2 percent, deposit insurance limits would increase by 2 percent automatically. This reform would stabilize the real amount of deposit insurance for consumers.

Thirdly, the FDIC recommends that it be given the authority to vary within limits the amount of reserves that the funds maintain. At the present time, reserves must be maintained at 1.25 percent of insured deposits and premiums are increased if reserves fall below this level. Reserves would most likely fall below 1.25 percent of insured deposits in an economic downturn when institutions were struggling (and failing). Raising deposit insurance rates at this time may exacerbate the situation. The FDIC would like the latitude to vary the reserve ratio within a specific range over the business cycle so that deposit insurance premiums are stabilized. The greater flexibility in setting the reserve ratio would reduce the pressure from higher premiums in stressful times.

Finally, under present law, when reserves of the fund are above 1.25 percent of insured deposits, the FDIC is prevented from charging any premiums to institutions that are both well-capitalized and well-managed. In 2004, 91 percent of BIF- and SAIF-insured institutions fall into this category and therefore pay no deposit insurance premiums. The FDIC believes that substantial and identifiable differences in risk exist among these institutions. The FDIC has proposed that it be given greater latitude in applying risk-based premiums.

Another suggested reform, although not endorsed by the FDIC is to privatize deposit insurance. Proponents argue that government-sponsored deposit insurance reduces the ability of banks to compete with other financial intermediaries by subjecting them to excessive regulations and imposing restrictions on the products they can offer. Opponents of this proposal suggest that a private system of deposit insurance might not be able to withstand a catastrophic wave of bank failures. For reasons we have suggested elsewhere, bank failures often occur in waves. In the event of a crisis, Congress may again have to step in but only after the system and the economy have suffered significant damage. Others argue that even with private deposit insurance, the government would still regulate banks in order to ensure the safety and soundness of the system. Moreover, the moral hazard problem would still exist with private deposit insurance. Any private insurance scheme would also need to set capital and management standards to reduce moral hazard.

Still another suggested reform, also contrary to the FFIC's suggestions, involves capping or limiting deposit insurance. Proponents contend that lowering the amount of a deposit that is insured to less than $100,000 would increase market discipline by causing depositors to monitor the activities of their banks more closely. After all, if deposits are insured, why worry about the health of the institution in which they are placed? Another suggestion is to limit systemwide coverage of deposits by an individual to $100,000, regardless of how many accounts the individual has. This could be implemented by using social security numbers to track accounts.

Finally in response to the existing regulatory potpourri and confusion, as well as the new risks and challenges that the financial services industry will face in the future, some people have suggested consolidating and streamlining the regulatory agencies. Most analysts believe that a complete regulatory overhaul is inevitable. Look again at the

A Closer Look feature on page 308. Current regulatory responsibility for the banking system (including banks and S&Ls) is distributed among four supervisory agencies: the FDIC, the Office of the Comptroller of the Currency, the OTS, and the Fed. Many analysts think that the present system causes duplication of regulatory functions and bureaucratic delays. They believe that multiple decentralized supervisory agencies result in costly systems that potentially decrease the effectiveness and efficiency of bank supervision. In response to these concerns, the Fed, the FDIC, and state banking departments are working together to make bank regulations more consistent and to make bank examinations more efficient and less burdensome.

At the present time, the impetus for major reform beyond the GLBA has declined due to the healthy profits that the banking system has earned in recent years. Congress rarely makes substantial changes without a crisis occurring first.

We would be remiss, however, if we did not discuss one final aspect of banking regulation. As we have seen, the Glass-Steagall Act separated commercial banking from investment banking. After 20 years of debate, Congress finally passed the Gramm-Leach-Bliley Act (GLBA) in late 1999 that repealed key provisions of Glass-Steagall and allowed full integration of banks and other firms that provided financial services as of March 2000. Nevertheless, even before the comprehensive GLBA was passed, banks had made substantial inroads into investment banking by the late 1990s because the regulatory barriers have been relaxed over time. For example, in 1986, a Fed ruling allowed bank holding companies (in certain cases) to obtain 10 percent of their revenues from securities that had been previously barred, including corporate debt and equities, commercial paper, municipal revenue bonds, mortgage-backed securities, and asset-backed securities. In February 1996, the Fed raised the limit to 25 percent, and as a result, most large bank holding companies not already in the securities industry are scrambling to get in. After all is said and done, the repeal of Glass-Steagall with the passage of the GLBA is similar to the passage of the IBBEA; that is, it underwrote what the regulators and markets had already accomplished. One thing we can be sure of is that the financial services industry and its regulation will continue to change in the twenty-first century.

Summary of Major Points

1. Because the failure of a depository institution has systemwide repercussions, Congress has enacted legislation to regulate the financial services industry with the goal of averting such a failure. A segmented financial services industry resulted in a segmented regulatory structure.

2. Regulation is by institution group or financial market (product). All depository institutions are regulated by the Fed with regard to reserve requirements. The FDIC also regulates banks and thrifts that opt for federal deposit insurance. Many other regulatory agencies regulate specific institutions. In addition, agencies such as the SEC regulate stocks and bonds. Other agencies regulate other financial products such as futures and options. Some product groups establish self-regulatory bodies. At the present time, no agency is in charge of regulating the money market. The regulatory structure is in an ongoing evolutionary process.

3. Beginning in 1980, the banking system was deregulated. The Depository Institutions Deregulation and Monetary Control Act (DIDMCA) of 1980 phased out Regulation Q interest rate ceilings and expanded the asset and liability options for banks and thrifts. All depository institutions were allowed to offer interest-bearing checkable deposits, and S&Ls and savings banks were allowed to make business loans. DIDMCA also expanded the powers of the Fed by authorizing uniform and universal reserve requirements.

4. The Garn–St. Germain Depository Institutions Act of 1982 allowed all depository institutions to offer money market deposit accounts, which had no interest rate ceilings, permitted limited check writing, and were fully insured up to $100,000. Also authorized were Super NOW accounts, which are checking accounts that pay a market interest rate.

5. The Basel Accord, an agreement among 12 countries, sets uniform international capital requirements for financial institutions as a primary vehicle of regulation. Requirements for core capital and total capital are

based on risk-adjusted assets and total assets. Core capital is the historical value of outstanding stock plus retained earnings. Risk-adjusted assets are calculated by assigning different weights to different types of assets, depending on risk. Basel II is revising the original capital requirements to more effectively regulate complex banking institutions.

6. The Financial Institutions Reform, Recovery, and Enforcement Act (FIRREA) of 1989 attempted to resolve the S&L deposit insurance crisis. It created the Office of Thrift Supervision and assimilated the defunct FSLIC into the FDIC. New regulations restricted the investments that S&Ls could make, and capital standards similar to those imposed on banks by the Basel Accord were adopted. Deposit insurance was made a full-faith and credit obligation of the U.S. government, and bonds, which would eventually be paid off by taxpayers, were sold to obtain the funds necessary to bail out the defunct S&Ls.

7. The Federal Deposit Insurance Corporation Improvement Act (FDICIA) of 1991 required higher deposit insurance premiums for banks and thrifts that undertake high levels of risk. The "too-big-to-fail" practice that had been in effect since 1984 was ended. Under the "too-big-to-fail" practice, the failure of large banks was resolved using the purchase and assumption method rather than the payoff method. Weak banks were categorized as either undercapitalized, significantly undercapitalized, or critically undercapitalized and subject to appropriate treatment.

8. The Community Reinvestment Act of 1977 gained prominence in the late 1980s as the Fed used compliance with this act as a criterion for approving or disapproving bank mergers. The regulations were further revised in 1995, and now all banking regulatory agencies examine all depository institutions for CRA compliance. CRA requires banks to lend in economically disadvantaged areas and to end the practice of redlining.

9. The Interstate Banking and Branching Efficiency Act (IBBEA) of 1994 allowed interstate branching by mergers of well-capitalized and well-managed institutions as of June 1, 1997. Under this law, bank holding companies can also convert separate banks into branches.

10. With the passage of the Gramm-Leach-Bliley Act (GLBA) in 1999, the final vestiges of the Glass-Steagall Act separating investment and commercial banking were removed. The stage is set for full financial integration of the banking, securities, and insurance industries. The GLBA allows for bank holding companies to be certified as financial holding companies (FHCs), which could engage in financially related activities, including securities underwriting and dealing as well as insurance and merchant banking activities. The GLBA also allows FHCs to engage in other financial activities and complementary nonfinancial activities. Banks had previously found ways into the securities industry through bank holding company subsidiaries. They have been able to do this because the Fed has relaxed or weakened many of the provisions of Glass-Steagall.

11. Despite the enactment of higher capital standards and risk-based insurance premiums, many believe that the reforms do not go far enough in dealing with the moral hazard problem. One recommendation is to privatize deposit insurance. Critics of this proposal contend that private deposit insurance might fail in the event of catastrophic bank failures and that regulators would still want to regulate banks to ensure the safety and soundness of the financial system. Others have suggested limiting deposit insurance or making it optional. The FDIC has recommended that BIF and SAIF be combined and that deposit insurance limits be indexed to inflation.

Key Terms

Review Questions

1. How is the failure of an FI different from the failure of a video rental store? What do these differences imply about the need for regulation?
2. Discuss the major provisions of the FIRREA and the FDICIA.
3. What is *redlining?* How is the Community Reinvestment Act supposed to affect it? What are the classifications for depository institutions and the ratings under the current regulations? Could my bank be violating the law if it fails to lend to businesses located in the deteriorating downtown area?
4. What is the Basel Accord? Why is it desirable to have uniform international capital standards for banks? What is the difference between Basel I and Basel II?
5. What is the intent of the 25 core principles for effective bank supervision?
6. Some contend that the passage of the IBBEA is having little effect on the banking industry. What is the basis of their argument? On what date were banks allowed to branch across state lines by merging with a bank in a different state?
7. Explain at least three suggestions for deposit insurance reform to deal with the moral hazard problem.
8. Would a wealthy individual with bank accounts of more than $100,000 prefer the FDIC to use the purchase and assumption method or the payoff method to liquidate failed banks? Why?
9. What is core capital? How do risk-adjusted assets differ from total assets?
10. Who regulates money markets? Who regulates capital markets?
11. What are the major provisions of the Depository Institutions Deregulation and Monetary Control Act of 1980? The Garn–St. Germain Depository Institutions Act of 1982? Which act expanded the powers of the Fed? How?
12. Explain the difference between risk-based capital standards and risk-based deposit insurance premiums.
13. What are the regulatory responsibilities of the Securities and Exchange Commission? What is insider trading? Who sets margin requirements?
14. Identify three self-regulating agencies and explain which industries they regulate. Speculate as to why an industry would self-regulate.
15. Explain the function of each of the following:
    a. National Credit Union Share Insurance Fund
    b. Pension Benefit Guaranty Corporation
    c. Securities Investor Protection Corporation
    d. FDIC
16. Explain the difference between the purchase and assumption method and the payoff method of resolving a bank insolvency. What does "too big to fail" mean?
17. What are the major provisions of the GLBA? What is an FHC? How does a bank holding company become an FHC? What conditions must be met to become an FHC?
18. Was investment banking effectively separated from commercial banking prior to the passage of GLBA? Explain.

Analytical Questions

Questions marked with an icon are objective in nature. They can be completed with a short answer or number.

19. Assume that a bank has core capital of $1,000,000 and total capital of $2,000,000. Its total risk-adjusted assets are $25,000,000 and total assets are $30,000,000. According to the Basel Accord (Basel I), does the bank have adequate capital?

20. Assume that a bank has the following:

Stock issued	$15,000,000
Retained earnings	2,750,000
Loan-loss reserves	2,600,000
Subordinated debt	5,000,000

What is its core capital? What is its total capital?

Internet Exercises

1. From the latest Quarterly Banking Profile, http://www2.fdic.gov/qbp/index.asp, access the latest balance sheet for FDIC-insured commercial banks and report the numbers for the total assets for all FDIC-insured commercial banks in the latest quarter. Compare this number to the assets figure for the same quarter of the previous year. Report the latest data on the equity capital (net worth) of all commercial banks.
2. Access the mission statements of the following regulatory agencies:
   a. OTS: http://www.ots.treas.gov.
   b. Office of the Comptroller of the Currency: http://www.occ.treas.gov/.
   c. FDIC: http://www.fdic.gov/.
   Do you believe that the present system involves multiplicity and duplication of regulatory functions?

Suggested Readings

For a discussion of recent recommendations for financial services regulation, see the Testimony of Governor Mark W. Olson (Financial Services Regulatory Relief Act of 2003) before the Subcommittee on Financial Institutions and Consumer Credit of the Committee on Financial Services, U.S. House of Representatives March 27, 2003. It is available on the Internet at http://www.federalreserve.gov/boarddocs/testimony/2003/20030327/default.htm.

For a discussion of Basel II, see L. Jacobo Rodriguez, "International Banking Regulation—Where's the Market Discipline in Basel II?"Cato Policy Analysis #No. 455 (October 15, 2002). It is available on the Internet at http://www.cato.org/pubs/pas/pa-455es.html.

For an excellent book on the material in this chapter, see Ken Spong, *Banking Regulation: Its Purposes, Implementation, and Effects,* 5th ed. (Kansas City: Federal Reserve Bank of Kansas City, 2000). The book is available online under banking system regulation and structure at http://www.newyorkfed.org/publications/frame2.cfm. Hard copies are also free for the asking from the Federal Reserve Bank of Kansas City.

For a look at "The Future of Financial Intermediation and Regulation," see the article by Stephen Cecchetti in *Current Issues in Economics and Finance,* Federal Reserve Bank of New York, 5:8 (May 1999).

For an analysis of the effects of IBBEA, see Ann B. Matasar and Joseph N. Heiney, "Lemonade or Lemon?: Riegel-Neal and the Consolidation of American Banking," *International Advances in Economic Research* 6:2 (May 2000): 249–258.

For an analysis of the success of the Community Reinvestment Act, see Robert B. Avery, Raphael W. Bostic, and Glenn B. Canner, "CRA Special Lending Programs," *Federal Reserve Bulletin* (November 2000): 711–731; also see "Does the Community Reinvestment Act Influence Lending? An Analysis of Changes in Bank Low-Income Mortgage Activity," *Working Paper No. WP-00-6,* Federal Reserve Bank of Chicago (May 2000).

A recent study of "Bank Merger Policy and the New CRA [Community Reinvestment Act] Data," by Anthony W. Cyrnak appeared in the *Federal Reserve Bulletin* (September 1998): 703–714. A related article, "New Information on Lending to Small Businesses and Small Farms: The 1996 CRA [Community Reinvestment Act] Data," appeared in the *Federal Reserve Bulletin* (January 1998): 1–21.

An article that concludes that bank regulation is needed to protect the payments system is Thomas M. Hoenig, "Bank Regulation: Asking the Right Questions," *Economic Review of the Federal Reserve Bank of Kansas City* 82:1 (First Quarter 1997): 5–10.

Two articles that deal with comprehensive regulatory reform are Gary H. Stern, "Market Discipline as Bank Regulator," and Roger W. Ferguson, Jr., "The Changing Banking Environment and Emerging Questions for Public Policy," in *The Region* 12:2 (June 1998): 2–3 and 34–39, respectively, published by the Federal Reserve Bank of Minneapolis.

An article that takes a novel approach to bank regulation is Charles Calomiris, "Could Banks Police Each Other?" *The Economist* (October 17, 1998): 94.

Matthew T. Billett looks at the topic of market discipline in "The Cost of Market versus Regulatory Discipline in Banking," *Journal of Financial Economics* 48:3 (June 1998): 333–358.

Gregory Elliehausen looks the labor costs of regulatory compliance in "The Cost of Bank Regulation: A Review of the Evidence," *Federal Reserve Bulletin* 84:4 (April 1998): 252–253

For an empirical study of banking regulations, see "The Efficiency of Financial Institutions: How Does Regulation Matter?" *Journal of Economics and Business* 50:2 (March–April 1998): 79–234.

An interesting article on the future is Charles S. Sanford, Jr., "Financial Markets in 2020," *Economic Review of the Federal Reserve Bank of Kansas City* (First Quarter 1994): 19–28.

Helen A. Garten offers a look at *Why Bank Regulation Failed: Designing a Bank Regulatory Strategy for the 1990s* (Westport, CT: Quorum Books, 1991).

For a look at how difficult true banking reform legislation is, see Sarkis Joseph Khoury, *U.S. Banking and Its Regulation in the Political Context* (Lanham, MD: University Press of America, 1998).

For an international perspective, see David Gowland, *The Regulation of Financial Markets in the 1990s: Issues and Problems in an Age of Innovation* (Brookfield, VT: Edward Elgar, 1990).

Reforming Financial Institutions and Markets in the United States, ed. George Kaufman (Hingham, MA: Kluwer Academic Publishers, 1994) is a collection of essays on the state of the financial system and rationales for reform.

Anthony Saunders and Ingo Walter, *Universal Banking in the United States* (New York: Oxford University Press, 1994), discuss the realities of expanded activities for U.S. banks.

For an engaging analysis of the present state of the financial system along with a blueprint for change, see *Transforming the U.S. Financial System*, ed. Gary Dymski, Gerald Epstein, and Robert Pollin (Armonk, NY: M. E. Sharpe, 1993).

A book that looks at banking and securities regulation in both the United States and the European Community is *International Financial Market Regulation*, ed. Benn Steil (New York: Wiley, 1994).

Endnotes

1 For the airline industry, the regulatory agency is the Federal Aviation Administration (FAA).

2 In a world with deposit insurance, the problem is even greater because the depositors will be paid off even if the venture fails.

3 Correlation does not imply causality, which means that deregulation did not necessarily cause the subsequent insolvencies.

4 Actually, as you have seen, in a world with deposit insurance, the intermediary may consider only the costs to the stockholders and creditors because large portions of the deposits are insured. In reality, bank managers may consider only the risk of losing their own jobs if investments go sour.

5 Perhaps the only exception to this is the creation of the SAIF under the auspices of the Federal Deposit Insurance Corporation (FDIC) in 1989.

6 In addition to the analytical factors, as noted earlier, the general "political wind" had shifted in the late 1970s toward less regulation.

7 In Chapter 11, we discussed moral hazard from a micro standpoint. In that case, borrowers had an incentive to use borrowed funds for a more risky venture once loan funds had been received.

8 This limit is rather easy for many families to circumvent. For example, a family of four can open 14 different accounts, each with $100,000 deposit insurance coverage, thus effectively giving them $1.4 million in deposit insurance at every institution. In case you are wondering how four people can have 14 accounts, it is by grouping them together in different ways. Thus, each can have an individual account; then there can be six accounts with two people on each account (such as father and mother, and mother and oldest child), three accounts with three people each, and one account with all four.

9 We shall also see that the Interstate Branching and Banking Efficiency Act of 1994 and the Gramm-Leach-Bliley Act of 1999 also emphasized compliance with the Community Reinvestment Act.

10 In Chapter 11, we saw that the McFadden Act outlawed interstate branching and made national banks conform to the intrastate branching laws of the states in which they were located.

Looking Out, page 312

a   Press Release, Bank for International Settlements (September 23, 1997).

15

Securities Firms, Mutual Funds, and Financial Conglomerates

Learning Objectives

After reading this chapter, you should know:

What securities firms are and what financial services they provide

What the various types of mutual funds are

What hedge funds and real estate investment trusts (REITs) are

What the role of government-sponsored enterprises (GSEs) is

What financial conglomerates are and why they have grown so much in recent years

The Boiler Room

Seth was a young, intelligent, upper-middle-class, frustrated college dropout who wanted to make a "quick, easy buck." In the fast-track economy of the 1990s, he saw many people had struck it rich in the stock market. From his apartment, Seth had been running a successful but illegal gambling operation that catered to college students who played cards between classes. His big chance came when a customer asked him to go to work for J.T. Marlin, a securities firm out on Long Island. He was told that like many other young stockbrokers in New York, he would be able to make $1 million within three years if he worked hard. Seth went for the bait.

He soon discovered that the securities he would be selling were bogus. The corporations issuing them had no assets or products, and the securities existed only on paper. Friends of Michael Brantley, the owner of J.T. Marlin, owned the fake corporations. The funds that were raised went to these friends, who then shared them with Brantley. In this way, the brokers working for J.T. Marlin could be paid commissions that exceeded the maximum allowed by securities regulations. Prices were pushed artificially high because of aggressive brokers who worked in a "boiler room" and created a false demand for the stock. Lies were told to potential investors about the prospects of the fake corporations, and unscrupulous brokers employed high-pressure sales techniques. Apparently not all of the brokers knew the depths of the scam and chose to look the other way as they made millions.

After all the shares of the spurious corporations had been sold, the brokers no longer pushed the stock and the stock's price fell through the floor. Investors were left with worthless securities. Many unsuspecting investors who hoped to make a killing in the market lost everything they had. Brantley, his friends, and the brokers who work for J.T. Marlin made a bundle.

Needless to say, the firm was violating many government regulations and committing many crimes. Regulators were hot on its trail. Eventually, J.T. Marlin was closed down and the owners hopefully brought to justice. For immunity and to save his father's career (his father was a judge), Seth Davis turned state evidence.[1]

You may recognize that interesting plot if you saw the hit movie *The Boiler Room*. It is far from realistic in that the overwhelming majority of securities firms operate above board, and regulators are keeping closer watch over the industry, particularly since the mutual fund scandal of the early 2000s. The movie does, however, capture some aspects of how securities firms operate, particularly in a booming economy. Brokers can be aggressive and investors can be naive. Sometimes, they do minimal research into the quality of the securities they purchase. Finally, financial prices can change dramatically based on rumors or whims.

In this chapter, we consider securities firms—investment banks, securities brokers, and dealers. As noted, not many securities firms are like J.T. Marlin in that they do not deal with phony securities or pay illegal commissions. Instead, securities firms are important in the marketing of newly issued and previously issued financial claims. They "grease the wheels" in the raising of funds for net borrowers and the transferring of debt and equity securities among investors.

We also look at mutual funds and government-sponsored enterprises (GSEs) in the chapter. Investment banks, brokers and dealers, mutual funds, and GSEs are the major financial institutions that make up the securities industry. These institutions play central roles in the financial system and help it function smoothly.

To conclude this section on financial institutions, we look at the emergence of financial conglomerates that meld together financial services once provided separately by several intermediaries and differing financial institutions. These new financial conglomerates offer a variety of financial services under one roof and operate on a nationwide and global basis. By proceeding this way, we hope to give you a more representative picture of the dynamic trends among major financial institutions and the key roles they play in the financial system. Keeping Seth in mind, we begin with a look at securities firms.

Securities Firms

Securities firms aid in the smooth functioning of the financial system. There are two main functions of securities firms: investment banking and buying and selling previously issued securities. Investment banking deals with the marketing of newly issued securities in the primary market. Brokers and dealers assist in the marketing of previously issued securities in the secondary market. Some securities firms provide both functions; others provide only one or the other.

During the 1990s, securities firms experienced tremendous growth as the average daily trading volume of U.S. securities increased 512 percent. In the bear market of the early 2000s, the industry shrank. Beginning in 2003, however, activity picked up and earnings for the industry in 2003 hit a record high. Households shifted their liquid financial assets away from bank deposits and into financial securities. In 1975, 55 percent of household financial assets were in bank deposits, 43 percent in stocks and bonds, and 2 percent in mutual funds. As of June 30, 2004, 28 percent of household financial assets were in bank deposits, 43 percent were in stocks and bonds, and 28 percent were in mutual funds and money market mutual funds.[2]

Investment Banks: The Primary Market

Investment Banks
Financial institutions that design, market, and underwrite new issuances of securities in the primary market.

We first discussed investment banks in Chapter 5. **Investment banks** are financial institutions that design, market, and underwrite new issuances of securities—stocks or bonds—in the primary market.[3] Merrill Lynch, Smith Barney (part of Citigroup), Morgan Stanley, and Goldman Sachs are some of the better-known investment banks. Their main offices tend to be in New York City, but they are electronically linked to branch offices in other major cities in the United States and around the world.

The design function of the investment bank is important because a corporation may need assistance in pricing the new financial instruments that it will issue in the open market. The corporation looks to the investment bank to provide advice about the design of the new offering. In return for their services, the investment bank is paid a fee. In addition to their primary market activity, many investment banks are also brokers and dealers in the secondary markets.

Responsibilities for New Offerings

Initial Public Offering (IPO)
An offering of stocks or bonds to the public by a company that has not previously sold securities to the public.

There are two types of new offerings. When a company has not previously sold financial stocks or bonds to the public, the offering is an **initial public offering (IPO)**. The investment bank will try to establish an appropriate price by looking at stock prices of other firms in the industry with comparable characteristics. Because no previously issued securities are being publicly traded, it is usually much more difficult to determine the price at which securities in an IPO should be offered. In the case of bonds, investment banks look to the market prices of existing bonds with comparable maturity, risk, and liquidity. The issuer's existing degree of leverage (reliance or borrowed funds) is also a determinant of how much can be raised and at what price in the bond market.

Seasoned Issuance
The offering of new securities by a corporation that has outstanding previously issued securities.

When stocks or bonds have been previously issued, the offering is called a **seasoned issuance.** The price of the new issue should be the same as the market price of the outstanding shares. However, the investment bank must still anticipate how the new issue will affect the market price of the outstanding shares. Likewise, with a seasoned issuance of bonds, the investment bank must anticipate how the greater degree of leverage will affect the price at which the new bonds can be sold.

Timing.   Timing is one of the most important factors affecting the selling price of new securities. For example, it may be a good time to sell newly issued shares if the corporation's outstanding stock were trading at relatively high prices, if favorable earnings reports have recently been issued, and if the economy is particularly strong. A relatively larger amount of funds can be raised by issuing fewer shares at a higher price than if the stock were trading at a lower price. Likewise, if long-term interest rates are relatively low and profit expectations are high, it may be a good time to issue bonds.

The Role of the Securities and Exchange Commission.   Once the amount, type, and pricing of securities have been established, the investment bank assists the corporation in filling out and filing the necessary documents with the **Securities and Exchange Commission (SEC)**. The SEC is a government regulatory agency that was created in 1934 to regulate the securities industry. Primary areas of regulation include setting "disclosure" requirements for new securities issues and monitoring illegal and fraudulent behavior in securities markets.

The SEC maintains active supervision of investment banks, particularly with regard to information that must be disclosed to potential investors. A corporation must go through the formal procedure of filing with the SEC if the securities issuance is higher than $1.5 million and if the term to maturity is more than 270 days. A **registration statement** must be filed with the SEC before the offering can be issued. This statement contains information about the offering, the company, and other disclosure information, including relevant information about management, what the funds will be used for, and the financial health of the corporation. Once the registration statement has been filed, the SEC has 20 days to respond. If the SEC does not object during the 20-day period, the securities can be sold to the public. The lack of an objection by the SEC in no way means that the new securities are of high quality or that the price is appropriate. It simply means that it appears that the proper information has been disclosed to potential investors. The **prospectus**, which is a subpart of the registration statement, *must* be given to investors before they purchase the securities. It contains all of the disclosures and pertinent information about the new offering that the SEC requires.

Credit Rating.   Investment banks also assist in obtaining a credit rating for the new bond issues from Standard & Poor's or Moody's Investors Services. A trustee is selected to monitor whether or not the corporation fulfills the terms of the offering as outlined in the **bond indenture**. The terms of the offering along with many other provisions are spelled out in the bond indenture before the bonds are issued. Investment banks may also assist in arranging that the issuance of new stock is listed (traded) on an exchange and or in the over-the-counter market.

Underwriting and Marketing.   Once the necessary steps to issue the new securities have been taken, the investment bank takes on the responsibility of underwriting and marketing the securities. In underwriting the security, the investment bank purchases the entire issuance at an agreed-upon price. It then assumes responsibility for marketing the newly issued securities. If the price at which the bank sells the securities is higher than the price it paid, the bank will earn a profit on the spread. If the securities sell for less than the agreed-upon price, the investment bank accepts the loss.

Sometimes one investment bank may be reluctant to take full responsibility for a new issuance. In this case, the bank may form a **syndicate** by asking other investment banks to underwrite part of the new offering. The syndicate is merely a group of investment banks, each of which underwrites a portion of a new securities offering. In a

Securities and Exchange Commission (SEC)
The government agency that regulates the securities industry and monitors illegal and fraudulent behavior in securities markets.

Registration Statement
A statement that must be filed with the SEC before a new securities offering can be issued.

Prospectus
A subpart of the registration statement that must be given to investors before they purchase the securities.

Bond Indenture
A document that outlines the terms of a bond issuance.

Syndicate
A group of investment banks, each of which underwrites a proportion of new securities offerings.

syndicate, each participating investment bank earns the profit—or assumes the loss—on the portion of the new offering it underwrites.

Investment Banks and the Functioning of the Primary Market

As a key player in financial markets, investment banks facilitate the smooth and orderly functioning of primary markets. They stand ready to buy and sell and to adjust prices—literally making a market. If there are 100,000 shares of a stock for sale at a particular price and if buyers take only 80,000 shares at that price, the investment bank that bought the securities may hold them for a time to keep the price from falling erratically. Or the investment bank may alter prices until all, or most, of the shares are sold. Thus, the investment bank enables the ongoing shuffling and rearranging of portfolios by standing ready to hold the securities if there is no immediate buyer. Although these actions can involve risk for the investment bank, they enhance market efficiency and contribute to an orderly, smoothly functioning financial system. The investment bank is rewarded with profits from fees for designing and assisting in the underwriting of the new securities and (as you saw earlier) from hopefully selling the securities at a higher price than what they paid for them.

Exhibit 15-1 shows U.S. corporate underwriting activity since 1985. Note that new debt issuances exceeded new equity issues in every year between 1985 and 2004 and by increasingly larger amounts. Outstanding debt does not grow as fast as the new issuances would suggest because some debt issues mature each year, while equity issues do not mature. However, in some cases, stocks are bought back and retired by the corporations that issued them. Note also the relatively large issuances of equity in the late 1990s when stock valuations were particularly high.

15-1
U.S. Corporate Underwriting Activity 1985–2004* (Billions of Dollars, Rounded)

Year	New Debt Issues	New Equity Issues	Total Underwritings
1985	$ 104.7	$ 33.3	$ 138.0
1986	227.7	57.1	284.8
1987	219.4	52.9	272.3
1988	237.2	37.3	274.5
1989	274.9	30.6	305.5
1990	288.4	23.9	312.3
1991	511.5	75.9	587.4
1992	753.8	101.8	855.7
1993	932.5	130.8	1,063.4
1994	639.5	76.9	716.4
1995	625.3	97.1	722.4
1996	827.0	151.9	979.0
1997	1,163.9	153.4	1,317.3
1998	1,715.6	152.7	1,868.3
1999	1,768.0	191.7	1,959.8
2000	1,646.6	204.5	1,851.0
2001	2,365.4	169.7	2,535.1
2002	2,427.2	154.0	2,581.1
2003	2,733.6	156.3	2,889.9
2004*	2,088.1	126.9	2,115.0

*Through September 30, 2004.
SOURCE: Thomson Financial

Private Placement

Private Placement
The sale of new securities to a limited number of large investors; because the number of investors is small, the underwriting process is avoided.

Investment banks also handle **private placement**. This is an alternative for a corporation issuing new securities that bypasses the process described previously and places the new securities offering privately. In a private placement, new securities are sold to a limited number of investors. Because the number of investors is small, they are of necessity very large investors such as commercial banks, insurance companies, pension plans, or mutual funds. Private placements occur more frequently with bonds than with stocks. **http://thomson.com/financial/fi_investbank.jsphttp** has information about capital markets around the world.

Recap Investment banks design, market, and underwrite the issuance of new securities (stocks and bonds) in the primary market. The securities may be an IPO or a seasoned offering. In addition to advising the issuer about market conditions and prospective prices, the investment bank also assists in filing the necessary forms with the SEC so that the new securities can be publicly sold. A registration statement must be filed with the SEC. Part of the registration statement is the prospectus that contains information and disclosures about the issuance. The prospectus is distributed to investors. The SEC is concerned that appropriate information is disclosed to the public, and approval by the SEC to sell the securities is in no way an endorsement of their quality or that the price is proper. Private placement of securities to a limited number of investors is an alternative to going through the underwriting process.

Brokers and Dealers: The Secondary Market

Broker
An individual who arranges trades between buyers and sellers of securities for a fee.

Dealer
An individual who arranges trade and stands ready to be a principal in a transaction.

Market Orders
Orders by an investor that direct the broker or dealer to purchase or sell securities at the present market price.

Limit Orders
Orders that instruct the broker or dealer to purchase securities at the market price up to a certain maximum or to sell the securities at the market price if it is above a certain minimum.

Bid Price
The price at which a dealer is willing to buy securities.

Asked Price
The price at which a dealer is willing to sell securities.

Short Sell
Investors' instructions to brokers or dealers to borrow shares of stocks and sell them today with the guarantee that the investors will replace the borrowed stocks by a date in the future.

Brokers and dealers make up brokerage firms, which are securities firms that also facilitate the smooth and orderly functions of secondary financial markets. **Brokers** arrange trades between buyers and sellers—that is, they arrange for a buyer to purchase securities from a seller. The broker charges a brokerage fee, or commission, for arranging the trade. **Dealers** are market makers who, in addition to arranging trades between buyers and sellers, stand ready to be a principal in a transaction and may maintain an inventory of securities. Dealers stand ready to purchase and hold previously issued securities sold by investors. Because the dealer carries an inventory of securities and then sells them to other investors. Because the dealer holds a stock of securities, there is the risk that the price of the securities will fall and the brokerage firm will experience a capital loss.

Types of Orders

Three types of orders may be placed with brokerage firms: market orders, limit orders, and short sells. **Market orders** direct the broker or dealer to purchase or sell the securities at the present market price. **Limit orders** instruct the broker or dealer either to purchase the securities at the market price up to a certain maximum if possible, or to sell the securities at the market price if it is above a certain minimum. Securities are bought at one price (the **bid price**) and sold at a higher price (the **asked price**).

A **short sell** instructs the broker or dealer to borrow shares of stocks and sell them today with the guarantee that the borrowed stocks will be replaced by a particular date in the future. The investor engages in a short sell if he or she believes that the stock's price is going to fall in the future and that the borrowed shares will be paid back with shares purchased in the future at the lower price. A high volume of short sells indicates that investors believe that the stock's price is going to fall. If the price does not fall, the buyer of the short sell must purchase the shares at a higher price and thus loses money. If many buyers of short sells are in this position, the market price is pushed even higher.

Margin Loans

Margin Loans
Loans to investors for which the proceeds are used to purchase securities.

Margin Requirement
The percentage of a stock purchase that can be borrowed.

Full-service brokerage firms not only arrange for the trading of securities but also give investment advice to potential investors. They may also make loans, called **margin loans**, to investors to help them purchase securities. In this case, investors do not have to put up funds equal to the full value of the purchase. Instead, they can purchase stocks on the margin by borrowing. The **margin requirement** is the percentage of a stock purchase that can be borrowed as opposed to being paid in readily available funds. The current margin requirement, which is set by the Fed, has been 50 percent since 1974 and applies only to initial purchases. Many individual brokerage firms set margin requirements higher than 50 percent and vary them depending on the stocks being traded and the trading behavior of individual customers.

Brokerage Fees

Until 1975, all brokerage firms charged investors virtually the same brokerage fees for executing trades of financial securities. Brokerage firms distinguished themselves among investors by engaging in nonprice competition. Some attempted to offer better and more attentive advice established through market research. Others had geographical advantages, name recognition, or other attributes that led to better customer relationships. All of this began to change when Congress passed the Securities Acts Amendment of 1975 that eliminated fixed commissions. Instead of engaging only in nonprice competition, brokerage firms could compete by offering lower fees.

Discount brokerage firms provide only limited or no investment advice, but their fees are much lower than those of full-service brokerage firms. In recent years, because of increased competition among brokerage firms and the emergence of discount brokers and online trading, brokerage fee revenues have fallen. In place of trading fees, brokerage firms are earning more from advising fees and from interest income on margin loans. The development of the Internet allows for the further evolution of securities marketing by allowing for online trading. The accompanying A Closer Look on page 342 explores the emergence of online trading.

National Association of Securities Dealers (NASD)
An association made up of members that self-regulate the securities industry.

Securities Industry Protection Corporation (SIPC)
A nonprofit membership corporation established by Congress that provides insurance to protect investors' securities from liquidation by the brokerage firm.

In addition to regulation by the SEC, the securities industry is also self-regulated by the **National Association of Securities Dealers (NASD)** and various securities exchanges such as the New York and American Stock Exchanges. Brokerage firms that are registered with the SEC must also purchase insurance for their customers from the **Securities Industry Protection Corporation (SIPC)**. SIPC is a nonprofit membership corporation that U.S. registered brokers and dealers are required by law to join. Congress established SIPC in 1970. Its purpose is to protect investors' securities from liquidation by the brokerage firm. Each investor is insured for $500,000. Note that this does not protect investors from losses because of falls in securities prices. It does protect the investor from losses resulting from the bankruptcy or insolvency of the brokerage firm.

The income of securities firms depends on the fees and commissions they generate in their day-to-day activities. In a booming economy, markets tend to be much more active and, hence, the income of securities firms increases. The reverse is true in downturns. As of June 30, 2004, the financial assets of security brokers and dealers were about $1,675 trillion, an increase from $83.3 billion in 1982.

Online Trading

What is online trading? In general, it means trading stocks, mutual funds, and money market shares via the Internet. Brokers and dealers, of course, use computers for most of their trading. However, online trading usually refers to an individual's use of computers for trading.

Online trading offers the public more control over trading and over their financial accounts. However, even more significantly, it offers lower fees for executing trades and hosting financial accounts. Online trading brokerage firms can do this because they use technology to automate these processes. This makes trading less costly and increases the volume that can be handled.

Before the Internet, only a few firms offered computerized trading, mainly through direct dialup connections. The customer base was very small. However, with the explosive growth of the Internet, the number of online trading brokerage firms and customers has shot upward. The number of online accounts increased from zero in 1994 to about 10 million in 2000. In 2004, it is estimated that 50 million people could have online accounts that will trade about $3 trillion worth of securities.

The rising popularity of online trading has brought about a new set of brokerage firms coming from three major sources. One source is discount brokerage firms seeking new ways to offer low-cost trading services. The second source is new companies created as online trading brokerage firms. The final source is existing full-service brokerage firms coming late into the online trading market; these firms have added online trading to their list of services to prevent the loss of customers to other online trading firms.

Even though many traditional full-service brokerage firms have added online trading to their list of services, they still have experienced a rapid decline in commission revenues. Consequently, these brokerage firms have concentrated on improving information services such as advising and consulting and offering other advanced trading services such as making margin loans to their customers.

Other types of online traders include people who do not work for brokerage firms but still trade for a living—commonly called *daytraders*—and people who have other jobs to earn a living and trade only as frequently as they wish. The latter group includes people with savings who want to earn extra money in addition to their primary income, often to build funds for retirement. Both types of online traders use the services of online trading brokerage firms.

Daytraders, however, typically use specialized online trading firms because they need more sophisticated services. The brokerage firms used by daytraders provide more sophisticated software and more real-time, direct, and detailed access to information and stock exchanges. This is often referred to as *direct access trading*. An example of this is NASDAQ Level II quotes. Typically, the general public and other online traders see only one price at a time listed for a particular security (for example, IBM stock). NASDAQ Level II, however, shows several prices and volumes for recent trades of a particular stock. This level of information is of little use to most non-daytraders, although it is sometimes offered to those with big accounts who engage in heavy trading.

Online brokerage firms engaged in price wars in the mid- to late 1990s. However, pricing has stabilized, and firms now compete more on features such as ease of use and quality of information. This competition has brought about two new services to the online trading market: (1) trading in foreign stock markets and (2) using remote handheld devices, such as cellular phones and two-way pagers, to get online information and to execute online trades.

The Securities and Exchange Commission has information about online trading available at **http://www.sec.gov/investor/online.shtml**.

Recap Brokerage firms are important financial institutions because they facilitate the smooth functioning of securities markets. Brokers arrange the trading of financial securities among corporations and investors in exchange for a brokerage fee. Dealers not only arrange trades but also buy and sell financial securities for their own portfolios in order to make a market. Market orders direct the broker or dealer to purchase or sell the securities at the present market price. Limit orders instruct the broker or dealer either to purchase the securities at the market price up to a certain maximum if possible or to sell the securities at the market price if it is above a certain minimum. A short sell instructs the broker or dealer to borrow shares of stocks and sell them today with the guarantee that the borrowed stocks will be replaced by a date in the future. The investor engages in a short sell if he or she believes that the stock's price is going to fall in the future and that the borrowed shares will be paid back with shares bought at a lower price.

Investment Companies
Companies that own and manage a large group of different securities for investors who have purchased shares of the companies.

Open-End
A mutual fund (type of investment company) that continually sells new shares to the public or buys outstanding shares from the public at a price equal to the net asset value.

Closed-End
Investment companies that sell a limited number of shares like other corporations but usually do not buy back outstanding shares.

Net Asset Value
The difference between the market value of the shares of stock that the mutual fund owns and the liabilities of the mutual fund.

Mutual Funds
Investment companies that pool funds from many small investors by selling shares.

Money Market Mutual Funds
Mutual funds that deal in money market instruments with an original maturity of one year or less.

Investment Companies

Unlike the securities firms just described, **investment companies** are financial intermediaries that raise funds from many small investors by selling shares in the company. The funds are then pooled together and used to purchase financial securities. Investment companies reduce risk for individual investors by purchasing hundreds or even thousands of different securities. This allows individual investors to diversify to a much greater extent than they would be able to by purchasing individual securities on their own. In addition, because large blocks of securities are bought and sold, the investment company can take advantage of volume discounts, and the transactions costs per share are less than had smaller amounts of securities been purchased or sold. Investors share in the gains and losses proportionate to the size of their investment.

Open-End and Closed-End Companies

Investment companies may be **open-end** or **closed-end**. An open-end fund continually sells new shares to the public or buys outstanding shares from the public at a price equal to the net asset value. The **net asset value** per share is found by subtracting the liabilities of the mutual fund from the market value of the securities that the fund owns and dividing the difference by the outstanding number of shares.

The vast majority of investment companies are open-end companies called **mutual funds**. Mutual funds that deal in money market instruments with an original maturity of one year or less are called **money market mutual funds**. They issue more shares as investors demand them. Because they buy and sell their own shares, mutual fund shares are not traded on organized exchanges. Mutual funds sell their own new shares to investors and stand ready to buy back outstanding shares.

Closed-end investment companies sell shares like other corporations, but usually do not buy back outstanding shares. Once the sale of a limited number of shares is completed, the fund is "closed" to new purchases, but the shares may be traded like shares of stock on organized exchanges. Because the price of a share of a closed-end fund is determined by supply and demand, it can differ from the net asset value.

Load and No-Load Companies

Load
A sales commission paid to a broker to purchase mutual funds.

No-Load
Mutual funds that are purchased directly from the mutual fund company and are not subject to a load.

Some investment companies require that a **load**, or sales commission, be paid to a broker to buy into a fund. **No-load** funds are purchased directly from the mutual fund company without a broker or a sales commission.

Both load and no-load companies deduct a percentage from the net asset value each year to administer the funds. The fees are usually in the range of 0.2 to 1.5 percent. Both types of funds may also deduct a fee called *12b-1* (named for the SEC regulation that authorizes the fee) for marketing and advertising expenses. By law, the load, administrative fees, and 12b-1 fees cannot exceed 8.5 percent of the investment for loaded funds. Finally, there can be a redemption fee, called a *back-end load*, to sell the investment company shares. An investor should know all of the fees before investing in a fund.

Growth of Investment Funds

Investment funds, particularly mutual funds, have experienced incredible growth since the late 1980s. One reason for this trend is legislation that gave individuals control over where their pension funds are invested, and many have chosen mutual funds. In July 2003, 53.3 million or 47.9 percent of U.S. households owned mutual funds. Exhibit 15-2 shows the growth of mutual funds, money market mutual funds, and closed-end investment funds from 1982 to 2004. Note that increases in mutual funds in each year in the late 1990s often exceeded the total amount outstanding prior to 1990. This was due not only to additional funds flowing into mutual funds but also to increases in market valuations due to the booming stock market. Also note that the dollar amounts invested in open-end mutual funds are much higher than those invested in closed-end investment companies.

Often many types of mutual funds are offered by a single investment company. Investors can own several different funds within the one investment company. They can choose the funds they prefer depending on their investment needs. Investors can also move funds in and out of various funds within one company at a relatively low cost. Some of the better-known and larger investment companies that you may have heard of are Fidelity, Vanguard, American Fund, Putnam, Janus, Franklin, and T. Rowe Price.

Exhibit 15-3 outlines various types of funds investors can select depending on their particular goals and risk tolerance.

Fund of Funds
A mutual fund that invests in a portfolio of other mutual funds rather than individual stocks and/or bonds.

Investment companies also create new funds that invest in several mutual funds. In reality, the investor purchases a **fund of funds**. For example, Vanguard's STAR fund invests in nine different Vanguard funds. In general, 60 to 70 percent of investments are held in stock funds, 20 to 30 percent in bond funds, and 10 to 20 percent in money market mutual funds. The advantages to investors are that funds of funds achieve much greater diversification than if they invested in only one mutual fund and they save the time and effort of investing in several different mutual funds on their own. A disadvantage is that costs can be high because both the individual funds and the fund of funds may charge fees. If investors pick different funds on their own, they can avoid the fund of funds fees.[4] In 2004, there were over 8,100 mutual funds. To put these numbers in

Year	Money Market Mutual Funds	Open-End Mutual Funds	Closed-End Investment Companies
1982	$ 219.9	$ 76.9	$ 7.5
1983	179.5	112.1	7.4
1984	232.2	135.6	6.4
1985	242.4	245.9	8.3
1986	290.6	426.5	14.5
1987	313.8	480.2	21.3
1988	335.0	500.5	43.2
1989	424.7	589.6	52.5
1990	498.3	608.4	52.9
1991	535.0	769.5	71.2
1992	539.5	992.5	93.5
1993	589.6	1,375.4	116.1
1994	602.9	1,477.3	117.8
1995	745.3	1,852.8	134.4
1996	891.1	2,342.4	144.7
1997	1,048.7	2,989.4	149.4
1998	1,334.2	3,613.1	151.0
1999	1,578.8	4,538.5	152.1
2000	1,812.1	4,435.3	141.9
2001	2,240.7	4,135.5	139.5
2002	2,223.9	3,638.4	150.8
2003	2,016.0	4,653.2	205.6
2004*	1,912.3	4,969.7	229.1

*As of June 30, 2004.
SOURCE: *Flow of Funds Account of the United States, Z.1*, Board of Governors of the Federal Reserve System, various issues.

perspective, note that stocks of only about 2,800 individual companies trade on the New York Stock Exchange.

Recap   Investment companies are financial intermediaries that pool the funds of many investors to invest in several hundred or even thousands of stocks. For any given investment, investment companies offer greater safety and more diversification than investing in one or a few stocks offers. Money market funds invest in financial instruments with an original maturity of one year or less. Some mutual funds invest in bonds or some combination of both stocks and bonds. An open-end fund continually sells new shares or buys shares from the public at the net asset value and is called a *mutual fund*. Closed-end investment companies sell a limited number of shares that may be traded on the open market and on organized exchanges. The value of open-end funds (mutual funds) greatly exceeds that of closed-end investment companies. The price of closed-end investment companies is determined by supply and demand and can differ from the net asset value. Mutual funds and closed-end investment companies can be either load or no-load funds and have experienced tremendous growth in recent years.

Hedge Fund
A nontraditional type of mutual fund formed as a partnership of up to either 99 or 499 wealthy investors with large minimum investments; attempts to earn maximum returns regardless of rising or falling financial prices.

Hedge Funds

Historically, a **hedge fund** was a nontraditional investment fund formed as a partnership of up to 99 "accredited" investors who invested in a variety of often risky

Stock Funds

- Aggressive growth funds seek capital appreciation by investing in small companies with potential for growth; such funds are risky but often pay high returns.
- Global equity funds invest in stocks from around the world, thereby achieving greater diversification than that achieved by investing in comparable stocks provided by one country; the downside is exposure to losses if exchange rates change adversely.
- Growth and income funds invest in companies that are expected to grow and that pay dividends.
- Income-equity funds invest in companies expected to pay high dividends.
- Index funds invest in a market basket of stocks that replicates the basket included in a stock market index such as the S&P 500; index funds attempt to match the performance of the index.
- Sector funds invest in stocks of particular industries such as biotechnology or health care; because diversification is less than that achieved in more broadly based funds, returns can be more volatile.
- Socially conscious funds invest in companies they believe to be ethically responsible; depending on the specific values and goals, these funds may avoid stocks of companies involved with cigarettes, alcohol, gambling, weapons, or nuclear power; they may also avoid stocks of a country whose leadership they believe is repressive.

Bond Funds

- Corporate bond funds invest only in corporate bonds.
- Global bond funds invest in bonds from around the world; the exchange rate risk can be high.
- Ginnie Mae funds invest in Ginnie Mae mortgage-backed securities.
- High-yield bond funds invest most of their portfolio in junk bonds; these funds offer the potential for high returns but also entail high risk.
- Long-term municipal bond funds invest in a broad base of municipal bonds; earnings are exempt from federal taxes.
- State municipal bond funds invest in municipal bonds from one state; earnings are exempt from federal taxes and from state taxes for investors living in the issuing state.
- U.S. government income funds invest in U.S. government bonds and government agency securities.

Stock and Bond Funds

- Balanced funds invest in some combination of stocks and bonds to preserve principal, generate income, and achieve long-term growth.
- Flexible portfolio funds can vary relative investments among stocks, bonds, and money market instruments depending on management.
- Income mixed funds invest in stocks and bonds to earn high dividend and interest income.
- Convertible securities funds invest in securities (such as preferred stock or bonds) that can be converted to common stock; such securities offer the potential to share in earnings if the company does very well by converting to common stock.

Cracking the Code

Investment Companies

Toward the back of the Money and Investing section of *The Wall Street Journal*, you can find quotations for open-end and closed-end mutual funds. The purpose of this Cracking the Code is to familiarize you with how to decipher those quotes.

FUND	NAV	NET CHG	YTD %RET	3-YR %RET
American Century 1st				
DivBnd..............10.07		+0.03	− 1.4	+ 5.6
EqIndex..............4.39		....	− 0.8	− 3.0
EqInc..................7.73		+0.01	− 0.2	+ 8.5
Growth..............17.65		−0.12	− 2.3	− 5.9
IncGro..............27.43		−0.01	− 0.6	− 0.8
IntlDisc r..........13.06		−0.19	− 3.4	+ 3.6
IntlGr................7.64		−0.03	− 3.8	− 5.2
LgCoVal.............. 5.76		+0.02	− 0.2	NS
Select................35.30		−0.03	− 1.4	− 5.0
SmCapVal............9.47		−0.02	+ 3.3	+ 12.6
StrConv..............5.40		−0.01	− 0.9	+ 3.1
StrMod................6.24		−0.01	− 1.4	+ 2.5
Ultra................27.70		−0.07	+ 0.7	− 2.5
Value..................7.62		+0.01	+ 1.7	+ 7.6

OPEN-END MUTUAL FUNDS

The following quotes are from *The Wall Street Journal* of May 17, 2004, and show a group of 14 different mutual funds offered by American Century 1st.[a] The funds differ by the amount of risk, and the name often describes the type of financial instruments in which the fund invests. Look at the highlighted row.

In the first column, *Growth* is the name of the fund within the group of American Century 1st Funds. As the name implies, this fund invests in growth stocks that are held in the hope of high potential appreciation as opposed to current income. The second column gives the net asset value (17.65) as of the previous trading day, which in this example is May 14, 2004. The third column gives the net change in the net asset value from the previous day (−0.12) while the fourth column gives the year-to-date percent return to the fund (−2.3). The fifth and final column gives the three-year percent return (−5.9) In this example, the net asset value is $17.65, down $0.12 from the previous day, the year-to-date percent return is negative 2.3 percent, and the three-year return is negative 5.9 percent.

Note that if you invest in the Growth fund of the American Century 1st Funds, you are investing in 1 of 14 funds offered by American Century 1st Funds, not in a fund of funds. An investor can invest in one or more of the funds to tailor the amount of overall risk to his or her specific needs. Some larger mutual fund companies offer far more than 14 different funds. For example, Fidelity Investments offers more than 80 different mutual funds.

CLOSED-END FUNDS

Below is a portion of the closed-end funds section of *The Wall Street Journal* of May 17, 2004.[b] This portion looks at U.S. government bond funds. Look at the highlighted row.

In the first column is the fund's name (MFS GvMkTr) followed by the fund's ticker symbol (MGF). The second column gives a one-letter abbreviation of the exchange (N) on which the fund is traded. The N stands for the New York Stock Exchange. The third column gives the net asset value ($7.27). The fourth column gives the closing market price of the fund ($6.34) of the previous trading day, which is May 14, 2004. Because this is a closed-end fund, the market or closing price can be more than or less than the net asset value. In this case, the net asset value ($7.27) is more than the market price of the fund ($6.34) and the fund is trading at a discount. The fifth column gives the change in price since the previous trading day, which in this case is 0.06, meaning that the $6.34 closing price on this trading day is $.06 higher than the previous trading day. The sixth column (916) gives the volume of trading in 100s, meaning that on May 14, 2004, a total of 91,600 shares of this mutual fund were traded. The seventh column gives the percentage premium or discount (above or below the net asset value) at which the fund is trading (($6.34 − $7.27)/$7.27 = −.128, or −12.8 percent). The final column gives the percentage 52-week market return (5.2 percent). For bond funds, the 52-week market return is based on the past 12-month income distributions as a percent of the current market price.

STOCK (SYM)	EXCH	NAV	CLOSE	NET CHG	VOL 100s	PREM /DISC	DIV	12 MO YIELD
U.S. Govt. Bond Funds								
ACM OppFd (AOF)	N	8.22	7.84	−0.05	315	−4.6	.72	7.9
ACM IncFd (ACG)	N	7.74	7.48	0.14	3998	−3.4	.81	9.4
MFS Govt Mkts (MGF) a	N	7.27	6.34	0.06	916	−12.8	.34	5.2
MS GvtIn (GVT)	N	9.57	8.60	0.01	248	−10.1	.38	4.6
♣ ScudderGvt (KGT) a	N	7.15	6.40	0.04	496	−10.5	.30	5.1
♣ WstAstClymrTreas (WIA) a	N	14.07	13.60	0.07	255	−3.3	.79	NS
WstAstClymrTreas2 (WIW) a	N	13.43	13.40	0.35	676	−0.2	.14	NS

securities. An accredited investor was one who had at least $1 million in investable assets. In April 1997, the SEC expanded the rules by allowing some hedge funds to raise money from 499 "qualified" investors. In this case, a *qualified investor* is an individual who has a minimum net worth of $5 million, or an institution such as a pension fund or mutual fund with at least $25 million in capital. Today, both types of hedge funds exist.[5]

For all hedge funds, a general partner usually organizes the fund and is responsible for making day-to-day trading decisions. Limited partners put up most of the funds but have limited or no say in the day-to-day decision making. Partners who buy into the hedge funds are wealthy individuals and institutions—minimum investments start around $250,000, and many hedge funds have much higher minimum requirements. Hedge funds may also limit withdrawals or require that funds be invested for a minimum time period, such as 10 years.

Because there are a limited number of wealthy investors, hedge funds are not regulated in the same way that traditional investment pools or mutual funds are. They are not required to file a registration statement and may engage in many trading strategies from which traditional mutual funds are barred. These strategies include borrowing funds to invest, purchasing many types of option and derivative instruments, short selling, and dealing in real estate and commodities.

Hedge funds attempt to earn high or maximum returns regardless of whether prices in broader financial markets are rising or falling. The funds trade securities and other creative financial instruments and try to outperform traditional investment funds by employing novel trading strategies.

In general, hedge funds use riskier investment strategies than traditional mutual funds, although some are less risky than others. As you have seen, the funds often rely on borrowed funds (leveraging) as well as the funds of the partners. This leverage increases the potential for profits but also magnifies the potential for losses. Short selling to take advantage of falling prices and the use of some risky financial instruments can also result in large losses if prices do not move in the anticipated direction. In general, hedge funds outperform other mutual funds when markets are falling.

Traditionally, hedge funds charge high fees and take a large percent of the profits. For example, some charge a 2 percent annual management fee and take 25 percent of the profits. The remainder of the profits is distributed to the partners based on their percentage of ownership in the fund.

Although the first hedge fund was established more than 50 years ago, the number and assets of hedge funds have grown tremendously since the mid-1990s. Domestic hedge funds now number more than 3,000. In late 2001, under the U.S. Patriot Act, hedge funds were required to meet new anti-money-laundering restrictions to prevent money-laundering activities from funding terrorists. Offshore hedge funds are located outside the United States, and they are difficult for most U.S. investors to invest in because of certain tax consequences. The number of partners in offshore hedge funds is unrestricted.

At the present time, hedge funds are becoming more accessible for investors because of the development of funds of hedge funds. A fund of hedge funds invests in multiple hedge funds, each usually employing a different investment strategy. Because of pooling, they have lower required minimums for participation and offer less risk due to diversification into many hedge funds.

To summarize, some of the strategies employed by hedge funds include the following:

1. Selling borrowed securities (short selling) in the hope of profiting by buying the securities at a lower price on a future date.

2. Exploiting unusual price differences between related securities in anticipation of making a profit when the prices come into more traditional alignment.

3. Trading options and other derivatives.

4. Borrowing to invest (leveraging) so that returns are increased.

Real Estate Investment Trusts

Real Estate Investment Trusts (REITs)
A special type of mutual fund that pools the funds of many small investors and uses them to buy or build income property or to make or purchase mortgage loans; pass-through institutions in which the rents from the income property and/or the interest income from the mortgages are passed through to shareholders.

A **real estate investment trust (REIT)** is a special type of mutual fund that pools the funds of many small investors and uses them to make investments. Whereas other mutual funds invest only in financial instruments, REITs may invest in real property as well. Their funds are used to buy or build income property or to make or purchase mortgage loans, unlike those of traditional mutual funds. Another difference is that to some extent, they also raise funds by taking out bank loans or issuing debt. REITs are pass-through enterprises in that rents from income property and/or interest income from the mortgages are passed through to shareholders. Shareholders are also entitled to any capital gains from the properties that the REITs own.

At least 75 percent of the assets of REITs must be either real property (generally commercial or industrial real estate) or mortgages. The majority of REITs invest in real property such as shopping malls, apartment complexes, hotels, golf courses, and other commercial buildings for income. REITs may either buy or provide the funding to build income property. The income from property provides a steady, dependable stream of income for investors. Some REITs either make or purchase mortgage loans on commercial property, and some do both.

REITs resulted from legislation passed by Congress in 1960. The intent of the legislation was to give small investors an opportunity to invest in commercial real estate. At that time, REITs could own income property but not manage it. REITs did not take off until 1986 when the restrictions on managing income property were removed. Now individual REITs have different characteristics and may be highly specialized, depending on the investment strategy and management style of the fund's manager. They are virtually diversified holdings of real estate investments that are professionally managed.

By law, REITs must return 95 percent of their earnings to shareholders each year. Therefore, if they want to expand, they must issue new equity or debt or take out bank loans. REITs are also attractive because most of their earnings (95 percent of which are passed through) are exempt from corporate federal and state income taxes, thereby avoiding double taxation and allowing for fairly predictable income streams.

Shares of REITs are traded on organized exchanges like shares of stock. Thus, they are liquid investments even though their equity is in real property and long-term mortgages. In recent years, the spreads between the bid and asked prices have narrowed significantly, signaling that the secondary markets are becoming more highly developed. Prices of REITs are determined by supply and demand. In this sense, they are like closed-end investment companies because the price can deviate from the underlying value of the assets owned.

Prices of REITs fell more than 20 percent in the 1998–1999 period as investors flocked to high-tech stocks that promised higher returns. Global financial crises in 1998 also contributed to the fall in prices. In the first half of 2000, funds flowed into REITs as prices increased more than 10 percent at the same time that prices of other securities were falling or earning far less. As of December 31, 2003, REITs controlled about $213 billion of the $4 trillion real estate market.

Recap A hedge fund is a type of mutual fund that has fewer than either 99 or 499 wealthy investors. The SEC does not regulate these funds. Hedge funds attempt to earn high returns for their investors regardless of whether financial prices are going up or down. Hedge funds engage in risky investment strategies. A REIT is a type of mutual fund that pools the funds of many small investors and uses them to buy or build income property or to make or purchases mortgages. These funds are pass-through institutions in that the rents from the income property and/or the interest income from the mortgages are passed through to shareholders. Whereas other mutual funds invest only in financial instruments, REITs may invest in real property as well as financial instruments. Shares of REITs are traded on organized exchanges. By law, REITs must return 95 percent of their income to shareholders each year. REITs allow for the integration of commercial real estate markets and capital markets.

Government-Sponsored Enterprises

Government-Sponsored Enterprises (GSEs)
Publicly held corporations that are chartered by Congress.

Government-sponsored enterprises (GSEs), as the name suggests, are corporations that are sponsored or chartered by Congress. Despite the federal charter, most GSEs are privately owned and privately managed. Some GSEs have issued shares of stock that are publicly held like shares in other corporations, and the stocks of these GSEs are traded on organized exchanges.

15-4

Financial Assets and Liabilities of Government-Sponsored Enterprises 1982–2004* (Billions of Dollars)

Year	Total Financial Assets	GSE Securities Outstanding	Total Liabilities†
1982	$254.8	$205.4	$249.1
1983	256.5	206.8	250.3
1984	297.7	237.2	291.0
1985	324.0	257.8	319.6
1986	346.4	273.0	342.8
1987	374.4	303.2	370.1
1988	421.7	348.1	416.1
1989	454.2	373.3	447.6
1990	477.6	393.7	469.1
1991	496.8	402.9	486.0
1992	552.3	443.1	538.7
1993	631.1	523.7	614.4
1994	781.8	700.6	761.7
1995	896.9	806.5	873.4
1996	988.6	896.9	964.1
1997	1,099.4	995.3	1,070.3
1998	1,403.8	1,273.6	1,368.1
1999	1,720,6	1,591.7	1,681.1
2000	1,969.4	1,825.8	1,922.5
2001	2,300.8	2,114.0	2,247.1
2002	2,543.3	2,339.9	2,475.6
2003	2,819.4	2,582.7	2,741.2
2004*	2,833.4	2,657.3	2,788.1

*As of June 30, 2004.
†Note that GSEs have other miscellaneous liabilities in addition to outstanding securities. The difference between total assets and total liabilities represents stockholder equity.

SOURCE: *Flow of Funds Accounts of the United States, Z1,* Board of Governors of the Federal Reserve System, Washington D.C., various issues.

GSEs issue short-term securities that sell at a discount, and long-term bonds that pay semiannual coupon payments. The majority of the issuances are long term. The proceeds are used to assist in some aspect of lending that the federal government has deemed desirable. GSEs operate mainly in the areas of housing, farm credit, and student loans. The securities that GSEs issue, called *government agency securities,* are considered government securities for SEC purposes.

In most instances, the federal government has no legal obligation to guarantee the timely payment of interest and principal of GSE securities. However, many market participants assume that the government does de facto guarantee the payments. The yield spread between government agency securities and U.S. government securities is due to differences in liquidity and risk. The yield spread can be significant because secondary markets do not have the breadth and depth of Treasuries. If market participants question the de facto government guarantee, the spread can also widen. Exhibit 15-4 shows the financial assets and liabilities of GSEs from 1982 to 2004. In recent years, GSEs have increased significantly in terms of their size and market share. This is particularly true with respect to lending in the housing sector.

The GSE Housing Market

Federal National Mortgage Association (Fannie Mae)
A GSE that issues bonds with no explicit government guarantee and uses the proceeds to purchase mortgages or mortgage-backed securities of banks.

Federal Home Loan Mortgage Corporation (Freddie Mac)
A GSE that issues bonds with no explicit government guarantee and uses the proceeds to purchase mortgages or mortgage-backed securities of thrifts.

Government National Mortgage Association (Ginnie Mae)
A government-owned enterprise that, for a fee, gives an explicit government guarantee that Ginnie Mae bonds issued by private financial institutions will be repaid.

The GSEs that pertain to the housing market are the **Federal National Mortgage Association (Fannie Mae)**, the **Federal Home Loan Mortgage Corporation (Freddie Mac)**, and the **Government National Mortgage Association (Ginnie Mae)**. Fannie Mae and Freddie Mac are exempt from state and local corporate income taxes and have a $2.25 billion line of credit with the U.S. Treasury. Fannie Mae and Freddie Mac provide loanable funds to the housing sector by selling their own securities and using the proceeds to purchase mortgages or mortgage-backed securities in the secondary mortgage market. The securities that Fannie Mae and Freddie Mac issue are backed by the principal and interest payments on the mortgages or mortgage-backed securities that Fannie Mae and Freddie Mac have purchased. However, there is no explicit government guarantee—Fannie Mae and Freddie Mac are privately owned and their stocks trade on the New York Stock Exchange. The difference between Fannie Mae and Freddie Mac is that Fannie Mae primarily buys the mortgages of banks while Freddie Mac primarily buys the mortgages of thrifts.

Congress created these GSEs in order to make housing more available by increasing the funds flowing into mortgages. The goal is to expand the opportunities for low- and moderate-income families to purchase houses. The Housing and Urban Development (HUD) Department regulates these GSEs with regard to meeting this goal and ensuring the financial safety and soundness of the corporations. In Chapter 13, we discussed recent issues involving potential stresses and strains associated with the rapid growth of Fannie Mae and Freddie Mac.

As part of HUD, Ginnie Mae is more accurately characterized as a government-owned enterprise. For a fee, Ginnie Mae guarantees that the mortgages purchased with bond proceeds will be repaid and, hence, the bonds will be repaid. Unlike Fannie Mae and Freddie Mac, Ginnie Mae does not issue bonds. Other financial institutions such as banks, savings associations, or mortgage brokers issue the bonds that are guaranteed by Ginnie Mae, referred to as *Ginnie Mae bonds.* The minimum denomination for Ginnie Mae Bonds is $25,000. Unlike Fannie Mae and Freddie Mac, Ginnie Mae securities are fully backed by the U.S. government and, thus, have no default risk.

Learn more about these GSEs at their Internet sites: **http://www.freddiemac.com**, **http://www.fanniemae.com** and **http://www.ginniemae.gov**. Other information on government-sponsored enterprises is available at the HUD Internet site at **http://www.HUD.gov**.

The GSE Farm Loan Market

Federal Farm Credit Banks Funding Corporation (FFCBFC)

A GSE that issues bonds and discount notes to make loans to farmers to increase the funds flowing into agriculture.

Farm Credit Financial Assistance Corporation (FACO)

A GSE that issues bonds to assist the FFCBFC, which was having financial problems at the time FACO was created.

Student Loan Marketing Association (Sallie Mae)

A GSE that issues securities purchase student loans to increase the funds flowing into student loans and make them more liquid.

Financing Corporation (FICO)

A GSE created in response to the S&L crisis that issued bonds to help shore up the FSLIC.

Resolution Trust Corporation (RTC)

A GSE created in 1989 in response to the savings and loan crisis that issued bonds and used the proceeds to dissolve or find buyers for the failed thrifts and their properties. The FTC went out of business on December 31, 1995, after completing its work.

The **Federal Farm Credit Banks Funding Corporation (FFCBFC)** issues bonds and discount notes and uses the proceeds to make loans to farmers in order to facilitate the funds flowing into agriculture. The bonds carry no explicit government guarantee that the principal and interest will be repaid. The FFCBFC ran into financial problems in the 1980s because many farmers defaulted on high-interest loans made in the late 1970s and early 1980s. Congress created the **Farm Credit Financial Assistance Corporation (FACO)** in 1987. FACO issues bonds and uses them to assist the FFCBFC. Unlike the bonds of the FFCBFC, FACO bonds do have an explicit government guarantee.

The GSE Student Loan Market

The **Student Loan Marketing Association (Sallie Mae)**, a publicly traded company, issues securities and uses the proceeds to purchase student loans. The securities are not backed by an explicit federal government guarantee. However, the federal government guarantees repayment of many of the student loans. The purpose of Sallie Mae is to increase the funds flowing into student loans and to make student loans more liquid. The company, which is the nation's largest supplier of student loans, owns or manages student loans for more than five million borrowers.

For more on Sallie Mae, go to **http://www.salliemae.com**.

Other GSEs

In 1987, Congress created a new GSE, the **Financing Corporation (FICO)**, in response to the savings and loan crisis. The savings and loan crisis is covered in detail in Chapter 13. FICO was to issue up to $10.825 billion in 30-year bonds to help shore up the insurance company (the FSLIC) that at the time insured deposits in the failed thrifts. FICO was capitalized by nonvoting stock purchased by the 12 regional Federal Home Loan Banks. It is to be dissolved by 2026 or earlier. FICO was not successful in bailing out the failed thrifts, so additional legislation and the creation of another GSE was needed.

In 1989, Congress created another GSE, the **Resolution Trust Corporation (RTC)**. The RTC was to dissolve or find buyers for the failed thrifts and liquidate the $450 billion of real estate properties owned by the thrifts being dissolved. Thirty-year bonds were issued to help finance the RTC, but the federal government did not explicitly guarantee the bonds. The RTC went out of business on December 31, 1995, after it had completed its work. By that time, it had resolved the insolvencies or closed more than 750 savings associations.

Recap   GSEs are privately owned government-sponsored enterprises that issue financial securities. The funds that are raised are used to provide funds to areas that the government deems desirable, including housing, farm credit, and student loans. The major GSEs that pertain to the housing market are Fannie Mae and Freddie Mac. The FFCBFC issues securities and uses the proceeds to make loans to farmers. Congress created FACO in 1987 because of financial troubles of the FFCBFC. Sallie Mae is a publicly traded company that issues securities and uses the proceeds to purchase student loans. FICO and the RTC were created in response to the Savings and Loan Crisis.

The Growth of Financial Conglomerates

Financial Conglomerates
Firms that own and operate several different types of financial intermediaries and financial institutions on a global basis.

Financial conglomerates are firms that own and operate several different types of financial intermediaries and financial institutions. As a rule, they operate on a global basis. Financial conglomerates usually result from the mergers of several firms. For example, one financial conglomerate may own a commercial bank, a savings institution, a mutual fund, a pension fund, a securities firm, and an insurance company. The alleged advantages of forming financial conglomerates include taking advantage of economies of scale, economies of scope, and diversification.

Economies of Scale
Gains from bigness that may result from several firms being able to streamline management and eliminate the duplication of effort that would result from several separate firms.

Economies of scale, which are gains from bigness, may result when separate firms owned by a conglomerate and offering the same product are able to streamline management and eliminate duplication of effort. The conglomerate may have fewer boards of directors than if there were many separate firms. They may also share a common technology infrastructure.

Economies of Scope
Advantages to firms being able to offer customers several financial services under one roof.

Economies of scope refer to the advantages of a conglomerate's ability to offer several financial services under one roof. This one-stop shopping is supposedly an advantage to financial services customers and, hence, gives financial conglomerates advantages over several separate firms providing the same set of services. In addition, the subsidiaries can share information about customers and seek new customers from other subsidiaries.

Diversification
The branching out of financial conglomerates into several product lines to reduce the dependence of the financial conglomerates on any single product line.

Diversification refers to the branching out of the financial conglomerate into several product lines. Diversification reduces the dependence of the financial conglomerate on one service. This, in turn, reduces the risk of failure for the financial conglomerate. If one division is performing poorly, the conglomerate can still be earning a profit if other divisions pick up the slack. For example, if the credit card division is losing money, it can be subsidized by the insurance division for a while. If credit cards were the dominant product line of a financial services institution, losses in this area could affect the solvency of the institution. This is not so in the case of a financial conglomerate.

Financial conglomerates have been emerging in the financial world since the early 1970s. Some of the first attempts were started by nonfinancial giants, such as Sears, that bought financial subsidiaries. Not all of the early attempts met with success, particularly when a nonfinancial firm was purchasing financial institutions. For example, in 1981, Sears purchased Dean Witter Stock Brokerage and Coldwell Banker Real Estate only to sell them in 1989 because of losses in these subsidiaries. Recently, Sears' sold its remaining financial services, mainly its credit card division, to Citigroup. And even more recently, Sears announced it would merge with K-Mart.

Regulations dating back to the Glass-Steagall Act during the Great Depression attempted to prevent different types of financial firms from merging and providing a vast array of financial services. However, by the mid-1990s, many institutions were already finding loopholes in existing regulations in order to form financial conglomerates, and impetus was building to do so. In November 1999, Congress passed the Gramm-Leach-Bliley Act (GLBA), also known as the *Financial Modernization Act*. The passage of this law gave new impetus to the formation of financial conglomerates. The law effectively repealed Glass-Steagall and allowed for the formation of financial holding companies (FHCs). FHCs may own securities firms, banks, and insurance companies. They may also engage in ancillary financial and complementary nonfinancial enterprises. By March 2000, the effective date of GLBA, there were already 111 FHCs, and by early 2004, the number of FHCs had increased to about 625.

Rather than maintaining the status quo of segmentation among financial service providers, the GLBA encourages considerable financial integration in the financial services industry and the formation of financial conglomerates. Many of these firms are transnational in that they offer a full range of financial services in many countries. Read

A Closer Look

Citigroup

In April 1998, Citicorp, the nation's second-largest bank holding company, announced that it would merge with Travelers Group, the parent company of Travelers Insurance and Salomon Smith Barney. Salomon Smith Barney (currently Smith Barney) was the nation's third-largest securities firm. Citigroup was on its way to becoming the quintessential financial conglomerate, operating globally and providing a vast array of financial services.

The rationale behind the merger was to take advantage of economies of scale and scope and diversification. Experts had forecasted that the merger would save at least $1 billion per year in expenses. Citigroup's first-year performance was disappointing due to losses related to the severe financial crises in Russia and Brazil and Citigroup stock suffered in the generalized bear market of the early 2000s. However, by mid-2004, Citigroup's 5.18 billion shares of stock were trading around $45 per share, and on an average day, 8 million shares changed hands. The price was up from around $30 per share in 1998.

The 1998 merger occurred before the passage of GLBA and, in its present configuration, Citigroup would not be a legal entity if GLBA had not passed. Indeed, the Fed approved the merger in September 1998 with the understanding that Citigroup would divest itself of several banned services—such as insurance underwriting—within five years if Glass-Steagall were not repealed. But GLBA passed and the merger was consummated in October 1998. At that time, Citigroup had more than $700 billion in assets, more than 100 million customers, and a presence in more than 100 countries.

Citibank, which is owned by Citicorp, is the nation's second-largest bank. In addition to Citibank, Citigroup has nonbank subsidiaries that provide services such as investment banking, credit cards, global asset management, trust services, buying and selling stocks, mutual funds, and bonds for customers; consumer finance; commercial lending; mortgage banking; data processing; leasing; securities advising and management; and insurance services.

On September 6, 2000, Citigroup announced the purchase of Associates First Capital Corporation, the largest U.S. consumer finance company, for about $31 billion in stock. The deal boosts Citigroup's consumer-oriented business lines. The purchase gives Citigroup about 2,000 retail locations in the United States and makes it the top U.S. provider of credit cards, home equity loans, and commercial leasing services. In addition, the acquisition strengthens Citigroup's international position. Associates First has 700,000 customers in Europe and is the fifth-largest consumer finance company in Japan. By late 2004, Citigroup had about $1,400 billion in assets, 275,000 employees and 200 million customer accounts in more than 100 countries on six continents. It is hoped that the description of Citigroup gives you a better understanding of financial conglomerates. As in this case, they often result from mergers and acquisition, operate on a global basis, and provide a vast array of consumer and business financial services.

Looking Out

The Growth of Global Financial Markets

U.S. investors have increasingly purchased foreign securities, and foreign investors have increasingly purchased U.S. securities. This table shows the extent of the increases of cross-border flows in selected years since 1982.

Year	U.S. Holdings of Foreign Stock (Billions of Dollars)	U.S. Holdings of Foreign Bonds (Billions of Dollars)
1982	$ 17.4	$ 61.1
1991	279.0	130.4
1998	1,407.1	450.9
1999	2,003.7	452.8
2000	1,852.9	468.0
2001	1,612.7	443.5
2002	1,345.1	410.0
2003	1,957.9	381.9
2004*	2,075.7	367.1

Year	Foreign Holdings of U.S. Stock (Billions of Dollars)	Foreign Holdings of U.S. Treasuries (Billions of Dollars)	Foreign Holdings of U.S. Corporate Bonds (Billions of Dollars)
1982	$ 88.3	$ 160.4	$ 68.3
1991	299.0	535.1	233.4
1998	1,250.3	1,622.2	607.8
1999	1,611.5	1,380.6	752.1
2000	1,643.2	1,471.4	920.6
2001	1,572.7	1,593.5	1,115.9
2002	1,260.8	1,883.6	1,266.9
2003	1,669.0	2,170.6	1,499.5
2004*	1,710.8	2,524.4	1,606.0

Note that domestic investors have a preference for foreign stocks over bonds while foreign investors prefer U.S. Treasuries, although the largest percent increase over the 1982–2003 period was in foreign ownership of U.S. stocks.

*As of June 30, 2004.

SOURCE: *Flow of Funds of the United States, Z1,* Board of Governors of the Federal Reserve System, various issues.

the accompanying A Closer Look feature on page 354 that discusses Citigroup, a financial conglomerate actually formed in 1998 before the passage of GLBA.

Since the 1990s, there have been three trends in financial markets: growth, consolidation, and globalization. These trends have been emphasized repeatedly throughout this text. We expect these trends to continue in the future and that financial markets and institutions will be most influenced by these factors as they evolve.

Recap   Financial conglomerates operate several different financial intermediaries and financial institutions that provide an array of financial services on a domestic and global basis. They result from consolidation in the financial services industry due to economies of scale, economies of scope, and diversification. Passage of the GLBA encouraged the formation of financial conglomerates.

This completes our look at financial institutions. You should have a better understanding of the evolution and current state of financial institutions. In the next section of the text, we move from a focus on financial institutions to a focus on financial markets and instruments, and we begin with a look at the stock market.

Summary of Major Points

1. Investment banks design, market, and underwrite the issuance of new securities in the primary market. The newly issued securities may be an IPO or a seasoned offering. In addition to advising the issuer about market conditions and prospective prices for the new securities, the investment bank also assists in filing the necessary reports with the SEC so that the new securities can be sold publicly. The securities may be stocks or bonds. A registration statement must be filed with the SEC. Part of the registration statement is the prospectus that will be distributed to investors. The SEC is concerned that appropriate information about the issuance is disclosed to the public.

2. Mutual funds pool the funds of many investors to invest in several hundred or even thousands of stocks or bonds. Mutual funds may offer greater safety and more diversification than investing in one or a few stocks. Mutual funds have experienced tremendous growth in recent years. Money market mutual funds invest in securities with an original maturity of one year or less.

3. An open-end fund continually sells new shares or buys outstanding shares from the public at the net asset value. Closed-end investment companies sell a limited number of shares that may be traded openly. The price is determined by supply and demand and can differ from the net asset value. The net asset value per share is the difference between the market value of the shares of stock that the fund owns and the fund's liabilities, all divided by the outstanding number of shares. Mutual funds can be either load or no-load funds.

4. Government-sponsored enterprises (GSEs) are corporations that are sponsored or chartered by Congress. Most GSEs are privately owned and privately managed. Some GSEs have issued shares of stock that are publicly held like other corporations. The stocks of these GSEs are traded on organized exchanges. GSEs issue short-term securities that sell at a discount and long-term bonds. The majority of the issuances are long term. The proceeds are used to assist in some aspect of lending that the federal government has deemed desirable. The major areas that GSEs operate in are housing and farm credit and student loans. The securities that GSEs issue are called *government agency securities.*

5. In most cases, the federal government has no legal obligation to guarantee the timely payment of interest and principal of GSE securities. However, many mar-

ket participants assume that the government does de facto guarantee the payments. The yield spread between government agency securities and U.S. government securities reflects differences in liquidity and risk. The yield spread can be significant because secondary markets do not have the breadth and depth of Treasuries.

6. Historically, a hedge fund is a type of mutual fund that has fewer 99 very wealthy investors. In 1997, the number of investors was expanded to 499 for some hedge funds. The SEC does not regulate hedge funds. Hedge funds attempt to earn high returns for their investors regardless of whether financial prices are going up or down. Sometimes, hedge funds engage in risky investment strategies. GSEs are privately owned government-sponsored enterprises that issue financial securities. The funds that are raised are used to provide funds to areas that the government deems desirable, including housing, farm credit, and student loans.

7. Real estate investment trusts (REITs) pool the funds of many small investors and use them to buy or build income property or to make or purchase mortgage loans. They are pass-through institutions in that the rents from the income property and/or the interest income from the mortgages are passed through to shareholders. At least 75 percent of the assets of REITs must be either real property (generally, commercial or industrial real estate) or mortgages. By law, REITs must return 95 percent of their earnings to shareholders each year. Shares of REITs are traded on organized exchanges like shares of stock.

8. Financial conglomerates are financial firms that provide an array of financial services that had been previously provided by several financial intermediaries and financial institutions. In theory, financial conglomerates offer economies of scale, economies of scope, and diversification. Changes in technology and regulations have given new impetus to the formation of financial conglomerates in recent years.

Key Terms

Asked Price, 334
Bid Price, 334
Bond Indenture, 332
Broker, 334
Closed-End, 337
Dealer, 334
Diversification, 347
Economies of Scale, 347
Economies of Scope, 347
Farm Credit Financial Assistance Corporation (FACO), 346
Federal Farm Credit Banks Funding Corporation (FFCBFC), 346
Federal Home Loan Mortgage Corporation (Freddie Mac), 345
Federal National Mortgage Association (Fannie Mae), 345
Financial Conglomerates, 347
Financing Corporation (FICO), 346

Fund of Funds, 338
Government National Mortgage Association (Ginnie Mae), 345
Government-Sponsored Enterprises (GSEs), 344
Hedge Fund, 339
Initial Public Offering (IPO), 331
Investment Banks, 331
Investment Companies, 337
Limit Orders, 334
Load, 336
Margin Loans, 335
Margin Requirement, 335
Market Orders, 334
Money Market Mutual Funds, 337
Mutual Funds, 337
National Association of Securities Dealers (NASD), 335
Net Asset Value, 337

No-Load, 338
Open-End, 337
Private Placement, 334
Prospectus, 332
Real Estate Investment Trust (REIT), 343
Registration Statement, 332
Resolution Trust Corporation (RTC), 346
Seasoned Issuance, 331
Securities and Exchange Commission (SEC), 332
Securities Industry Protection Corporation (SIPC), 335
Short Sell, 334
Student Loan Marketing Association (Sallie Mae), 346
Syndicate, 332

Review Questions

1. What are the functions of investment banks? Do they engage in primary or secondary market activity? What is a syndicate?
2. What is a prospectus? What are the differences among a prospectus, a registration statement, and a bond indenture?
3. What is the difference between a securities broker and a securities dealer? What roles do brokers and dealers play in the financial system?
4. How does a hedge fund differ from a traditional mutual fund? What are the two types of hedge funds and how are their requirements for participation different? What is the difference between a mutual fund and a money market mutual fund?
5. Are investment banks financial intermediaries? Explain why or why not.
6. The spread between the bid and asked price widens. What does this mean about the securities?
7. What is the difference between a load and a no-load mutual fund? Could a no-load fund ever result in higher total sales commissions and costs?
8. Miguel expects a stock's price to rise. Should he short sell the stock? Explain.
9. What is the difference between a market order and a limit order? What are the two types of limit orders?
10. What type of securities do GSEs sell? What is the purpose of GSEs? Does the federal government guarantee the securities of GSEs? Who owns the GSEs?
11. What are some of the factors for the growth of mutual funds in recent years?
12. List some reasons that Henry should consider purchasing a fund of funds. Are there any reasons he should not?
13. How do REITs differ from other mutual funds? Are all REITs pretty much the same? What are their differences?
14. What is a financial conglomerate? Discuss the factors that contribute to the formation of financial conglomerates.
15. How does diversification reduce the risk that a financial conglomerate will fail? What is the difference between economies of scale and economies of scope?

Analytical Questions

Questions marked with an icon are objective in nature. They can be completed with a short answer or number.

16. A mutual fund owns stocks with a market value of $1 billion and has liabilities of $1 million. What is the net asset value? If there are 2 million shares of stock outstanding, what is the net asset value per share?
17. What are some of the factors that determine the spread between the bid and asked price? If the bid-asked spread narrows, what does this mean?
18. What are the factors that determine the spread between agency securities and Treasuries? If agency and Treasury securities are perceived to have the same risk, why may there still be a positive spread between their prices?
19. Make a chart listing the similarities and differences among the following institutions: money market mutual funds, mutual funds, hedge funds, government-sponsored enterprises, and REITs.
20. Comment on the following: Frank calls his broker to complain that the stock the broker sold him has fallen in value and Frank has lost a lot of money. The broker says: "Look, I made money and the brokerage firm made money on the deal. Two out of three is not bad!"

Internet Exercises

1. Go to the Internet site for Ginnie Mae at **http://www.ginniemae.gov**. Click on "About Us." Summarize the material about Ginnie Mae.
2. Summarize the statements on the supervision and regulation of GSEs by Treasury Secretary John Snow on October 16th 2003. The testimony is available on the U.S. Treasury Web site at **http://www.treas.gov/press/releases/ js905.htm**.

Suggested Readings

For a look at government-sponsored enterprises from an educated point of view, see the "Testimony of Chairman Alan Greenspan, Government-sponsored enterprises" before the Committee on Banking, Housing, and Urban Affairs, U.S. Senate, February 24, 2004. The testimony is available on the Internet at **http://www.federalreserve.gov/boarddocs/ testimony/2004/20040224/default.htm**.

For a recent overview of some issues relating to mutual funds, see John B. Carlson, Eduard A. Peiz, and Erkin Y. Sahinoz, "Mutual Funds, Fee Transparency, and Competition," *Economic Commentary*, Federal Reserve Bank of Cleveland (March 1, 2004). The commentary is available on the Internet at **http:// www.clevelandfed.org/Research/Com2004/03-01.pdf**.

For an engaging article on "Why We Do What We Do: The Views of Bankers, Insurers, and Securities Firms on Specialization and Diversification," see the article by the same name by Tony Candito, Michael J. Castellano, Richard Heckinger, presenters, Darryll Hendricks, moderator, summary by Kevin J. Stiroh, *Economic Policy Review*, Federal Reserve Bank of New York, 6:4 (October 2000): 81–87.

For a discussion of many of the topics in this chapter, see Dimitri B. Papadimitriou, ed., *Modernizing Financial Systems* (London and Basingstroke: Macmillan/St. Martin's Press, 2000).

For a historical look at the securities industry at a time of dramatic change, see Alec Benn, *The Unseen Wall Street, 1969–1975* (Westport, CT: Greenwood Publishing Group, 2000).

For an analysis of mutual funds, see Peter Fortune, "Mutual Funds, Part I: Reshaping the American Financial System," *New England Economic Review*, Federal Reserve Bank of Boston (July 1997): 45–72; and Peter Fortune, "Mutual Funds, Part II: Funds Flows and Security Returns," *New England Economic Review* (January 1998): 3–22.

For a discussion of the size, number, behavior, regulation, and policy implications of hedge funds, see Barry Eichengreen and Donald Mathieson, "Hedge Funds: What Do We Really Know?" *Economic Issues*, International Monetary Fund, 19 (September 1999).

Endnotes

1 What the firm was doing would not have been illegal as long as there was no connection between the corporation issuing the stock and the securities firm. However, in reality, J.T. Marlin was undoubtedly committing many other acts of securities fraud.

2 In this case, household financial assets include only deposits, stocks and bonds, mortgages, and mutual funds and money market mutual finds. *Flow of Funds Accounts of the United States, Z1,* Board of Governors of the Federal Reserve System (September 16, 2004).

3 The Glass-Steagall Act of 1933 separated investment banking from commercial banking. As you have seen, this act was effectively repealed in 1999 with the passage of the Gramm-Leach-Bliley Act (GLBA). The passage of the GLBA is partially responsible for the emergence of financial conglomerates discussed later in this chapter.

4 With the Vanguard STAR Fund, Vanguard waives the fund of funds fee so that investors pay only the fees of the individual mutual funds.

5 As used here, *hedge fund* means any kind of private investment partnership. The most common meaning of *hedge* is to reduce risk. This can be misleading because hedge funds often engage in very risky activities.

6 The tax consequences include that net losses cannot be used to offset gains and that deferred interest payments are taxable in current years and investors are often not provided the information by the hedge fund that would allow them to make current tax payments and to avoid tax penalties. Offshore hedge funds are easily available to a small number of tax-exempt wealthy U.S. investors.

Cracking the Code, page 341

a Wall Street Journal (May 17, 2004): C16.

b Wall Street Journal (May 17, 2004): C14.

16

CHAPTER SIXTEEN

The Stock Market

Learning Objectives

After reading this chapter, you should know:

The major characteristics of the stock market

How the organized exchanges and over-the-counter markets function

What the various stock indexes are and what each measures

How the value of a share of stock is determined

Speculative Bubbles and Their Effects on the Economy

In the past, a text on the financial system and the economy would not routinely include a chapter on the stock market, nor would it include a chapter on the bond and mortgage markets (Chapter 17). Such chapters would more likely be found in a text dealing specifically with capital market assets. Texts on the financial system traditionally focused on the banking system. So why include such chapters here?

At this time, there are compelling reasons to include chapters on the stock, bond, and mortgage markets—reasons that relate to the recent price volatility of these assets and the changing structure of capital markets. Most of us are familiar with the record stock market boom of the late 1990s. Stock prices underwent dramatic increases despite some sharp sell-offs. Technological changes in the transfer of funds, increased globalization of financial markets, and other structural changes in the economy facilitated the flow of funds into equity investments around the world. Likewise, and depressingly so, most of us are familiar with the stock market collapse of the early 2000s when faltering economies, here at home and abroad, could not support the stratospheric prices of the late 1990s.

At the same time, more households than ever were and are investing in the stock market, whether directly through brokers, employers, or online or indirectly through savings or retirement plans.

When stock price movements are more pronounced, as in the late 1990s, stock markets have greater potential for speculative bubbles that cannot be sustained. A **speculative bubble** is an irrational increase in prices accompanied by euphoric expectations. As you saw in Chapter 13, when market participants realize that the speculative bubble cannot be maintained, they tend to liquidate their positions with the result that prices fall to lower levels than had the bubble not occurred in the first place. Such volatility in stock prices can cause financial instability as gains and losses are magnified. When the bubble bursts, as it did in the early 2000s, the resulting financial losses may spill over into the real sector, causing or contributing to unemployment and recession.

In Chapter 4, you saw that the Fed attempts to minimize fluctuations in output and prices around a long-term trend. In that chapter, we were concerned about output prices of goods and services. But, as the preceding discussion implies, the Fed must also be concerned about unstable stock prices. Volatile stock prices can affect employment, inflation, and the health and stability of the financial system. If a speculative bubble bursts and stock prices tumble, the real sector can be adversely affected for a considerable time. *The Economist* magazine aptly stated: "Just as champagne tastes wonderful until the bubbles go to your head, so financial bubbles tend to create nasty economic hangovers."[1]

The stock market rally of the late 1990s was interrupted briefly by a worldwide collapse of stock prices in October 1998. By early 1999, the market had fully recovered. In early 2000, the market reached a cyclical bull high and then turned down. An economic downturn began in early 2001 and was exacerbated by the attack on the World Trade Center and the Pentagon on September 11, 2001. The market experienced three down years (2000, 2001, and 2002) and the worst bear market in history. The market began a recovery in 2003 with stock prices in general increasing between 25 and 30 percent over the course of the year. The market was still recovering in early 2004, albeit at a slower somewhat stagnant pace. The accompanying A Closer Look feature on page 363 looks more closely at how volatile asset prices affect the economy.

In this chapter, we explore the anatomy of stock markets and their growth and changes in recent years. We will complete our discussion of capital markets with the next chapter on the bond and mortgage markets. This will lay the groundwork for our discussion of how policy makers should respond to price volatility in these capital markets in Part VI. For now, let's get down to the business of stocks.

Speculative Bubble
An irrational increase in stock prices accompanied by euphoric expectations.

How Volatile Asset Prices Affect the Economy

In March 2001, the U.S. economy entered into its first recession in more than 10 years. Many analysts attribute part of the downturn to the cataclysmic collapse of the overvalued stock markets that began in 2000.[a] Stock prices, led by dot.com[b] and technology stocks, experienced record increases in the late 1990s. Some analysts believed that stocks were overvalued as early as 1995. Between 1995 and 2000, stock prices more than doubled. By 2000, it was becoming clear that stock valuations were in a speculative bubble. Markets collapsed, with the dot.com and technology sectors experiencing the largest and earliest price declines. The Federal Reserve Board responded by lowering interest rates 11 times in 2001. As noted earlier, the market hit bottom by early 2003 and rebounded about 25 percent over the course of the next year as the economy continued to rebound. At the same time the lower interest rates also fueled the housing market and real estate prices were increasing to the extent that many analysts feared there was a bubble in the real estate market.

Given these trends, it seems apparent that asset prices are undergoing more pronounced fluctuations than in the past. Some of the reasons for this could be technological modifications in how funds are transferred and other structural changes in capital markets.[c] For example, technological improvements in electronic funds transfer systems and increased globalization of capital markets allow funds to flow more freely and quickly around the world, Other innovations have also made financial assets more liquid than in the past. At the same time, more households than ever before are investing in the capital markets, whether directly through a broker, their employer, or online, or indirectly through a savings or retirement plan.

Volatile asset prices can affect the real sector via several channels. One channel is the link between changes in asset prices and wealth. When asset prices increase, nominal wealth increases. The increases in wealth, in turn, can lead to spending increases in the goods and services markets and a willingness to take on more debt. Exclusive shops on Rodeo Drive in Beverly Hills had exceptional years in the late 1990s after the historic run-up of stock prices. Apparently investors spent some of their profits on high-end luxury items or increased their level of debt to purchase luxury items. The reaction of Sandi and Dave, who saw the value of their retirement funds increase dramatically, may be more mundane but no less significant. Because of their newfound wealth, Sandi and Dave felt they were in a position to finance the new car they hadn't planned to buy until two years down the road. These increases in spending and debt in response to gains in wealth speed up the level economic activity. If sustained, the increases in demand can also cause prices in the goods and services market to rise. Thus, inflation in asset markets may, after some time, spill over to cause inflation in the goods and services sector.

The flip side, of course, is that decreases in asset prices can trigger declines in spending and eventually price reductions in the goods and services markets. For example, if the value of J. P. Yuppie's stock portfolio falls from $100,000 to $50,000 when the market crashes, he experiences a drop in wealth and subsequently does not take the expensive vacation trip he had been planning. The reduced demand for vacation trips will slow economic activity and lead to prices being lower than they would otherwise have been. If asset prices are stable or change slowly, these spillovers do not affect spending, saving, borrowing, and lending decisions as dramatically as when asset prices are more unstable.

Volatile stock prices also affect the real sector through their effect on financial institutions and the financial system. The solvency of any institution that holds large amounts of stocks, bonds, and mortgages could be threatened if prices fall unexpectedly and significantly. Financial institutions, in particular, may see the value of their assets decline sharply while their liabilities, which are denominated in dollars, do not fall in value. Entire industries may be affected. For example, the U.S. savings and loan industry experienced enormous losses in the 1980s because of declines in the value of mortgages and other capital market assets. The value of mortgages can fall when declining real estate values cause some borrowers to default, or when rising interest rates decrease the value of outstanding mortgages. The resulting savings and loan crisis caused unemployment and bankruptcies in the industry and required a taxpayer bailout.

In other episodes, globalized financial markets have facilitated capital flows that ultimately contributed to speculative bubbles. The Mexican financial crisis of 1994–1995 and the Asian financial crisis of the late 1990s are examples of situations in which stocks, supported by large capital inflows, became overvalued. When exchange rates could not be maintained, what began as currency crises quickly spread to other markets. Stock, bond, and real estate prices plummeted, causing widespread bankruptcies of financial and nonfinancial firms. The financial systems and real sectors of the affected economies collapsed. Unprecedented international intervention was needed as domestic and international investors withdrew funds from the crippled regions. It became clear that investors were able to reverse capital flows just as quickly as J. P. Yuppie was able to cancel his vacation plans when the value of his stock fell.

The Anatomy of Stocks

Firms issue shares of stock when they need to raise long-term financial capital, usually for investment spending. If a corporation is publicly held, shares of stock are sold to the public. A share of stock represents equity in a corporation and entitles the owner to a share of the corporation's profits.[2] The stock may be **preferred stock** or **common stock**. Owners of preferred stock receive a fixed dividend to which they are entitled before owners of common stock can receive anything. The fixed dividend is similar to the interest payment that a bondholder receives. However, dividends must be paid to preferred stockholders only if the corporation earns a profit, whereas the corporation is liable for interest payments under all circumstances. In addition, interest payments to bondholders are tax write-offs for the corporation; dividend payments to preferred stockholders are not.

Common stockholders receive a variable dividend after preferred stockholders have been paid and retained earnings have been set aside. Retained earnings are profits not distributed to stockholders that are usually used to fund investment projects. In the 1990s, some "growth" companies such as Microsoft did not pay dividends. In this case, stockholders benefit from increases in the stock's price generated by putting the earnings back into the company or using the earnings to purchase back the company's own stock. In 2004, the trend of not paying dividends is changing due to legislation that reduces

Preferred Stock
Equity claims representing ownership of the net income and assets of a corporation.

Common Stock
Equity claims representing ownership of the net income and assets of a corporation.

taxation of most dividends received by households.[3] If a company buys back its own stock and does not resell it, the stock is retired. After shares of stock are retired, the remaining outstanding shares tend to appreciate in value. Common stockholders have voting rights within the firm, whereas preferred stockholders do not. Stockholders who own only a minuscule share of the outstanding stock of a firm do not usually exercise voting rights.

Investment bankers usually market new shares of stocks, or securities. One or more securities firms design and market the new securities offering. Sometimes, employees and individuals may purchase new shares of stocks directly from the company, thus bypassing investment banks. Stocks represent liquid claims because the shares can usually be sold relatively easily in secondary markets. Previously issued shares of stock are traded either on organized exchanges or over the counter. As you saw in Chapter 5, the marketing of newly issued shares represents primary market activity while the purchase or sale of previously issued securities represents secondary market activity. The Cracking the Code Box below deciphers the information about stock prices reported in major newspapers.

Cracking the Code

The Stock Market

Here is a section from a typical stock page of a major newspaper. To begin cracking the code, look at the following entry for Gap Inc., the popular clothing store.

52 Weeks

High	Low	Stock	Sym	Div	Yld.%	PE	Vol 100s	Close	Net Change
23.47	16.42	Gap Inc	GPS	.09	0.4	21	52403	22.51	0.11

SOURCE: *The Wall Street Journal* (May 21, 2004).

The name of the company is in the third column followed by the company ticker symbol and then the regular annual dividend paid by Gap, in this case, $0.09. The price of the stock at the close of the preceding day's trading was $22.51 (from the column labeled *Close*). The dividend is usually divided by the closing price to get the current yield (or return). The dividend of $.09 divided by the closing price $22.51 gives a current yield of .4 percent ($.09/$22.51 = .004%).

The column labeled *PE* indicates that the ratio of the price per share to the earnings per share of the company—that is, the price-to-earnings (P-E) ratio—is 21. The higher the earnings per share of the company (given the price of the stock), the lower the ratio. Stocks with low PE ratios compared to other firms in the industry are sometimes thought to be undervalued, and stocks with high PE ratios are thought to be overvalued.

The *Vol* column tells us the number of shares traded (in hundreds) on a given day. Thus, 52403 means that 5,240,300 shares of Gap were traded on this particular day. The price of the stock at the close was, as mentioned, $22.51. In the last column, the closing price per share was up 0.11 ($0.11) from the close of the previous day.

To the left of the company's name are two columns headed *High* and *Low*. These are the high and low prices of the stock for the last 52 weeks. Gap had traded at a low price of 16.42 ($16.42) and at a high price of 23.47 ($23.47). Those of you who bought at 16.42 ($16.42) can smile.

Famous Financial Quotations

"Stock prices could double, triple, or even quadruple tomorrow and still not be too high. Stocks are now, we believe, in the midst of a one-time-only rise to much higher ground—to the neighborhood of 36,000 for the Dow Jones Industrial Average."

> —James K. Glassman and Kevin A. Hasset, "Dow 36000,"
> *The Atlantic Online* (September 1999), http://www.theatlantic.com.

"In a [stock] market like this, every story is a positive one. Any news is good news. It's pretty much taken for granted now that the market is going to go up."

> —*The Wall Street Journal* (August 26, 1987),
> less than two months before the largest percentage
> drop in stock prices in history

Although there have been many stock market crashes, the most famous occurred in 1929 heralding the Great Depression. Although it was not known at the time, output had actually turned down before the market crashed. The market crash came at the end of a decade of rising stock prices and what many now realize was a speculative bubble. The following are some quotations from around that time:

"There will be no interruption of our permanent prosperity."
> —Myron E. Forbes, president, Pierce Arrow Motor Car Co. (January 12, 1928)

"I cannot help but raise a dissenting voice to statements that we are living in a fool's paradise, and that prosperity in this country must necessarily diminish and recede in the near future."
> —E. H. Simmons, president, New York Stock Exchange (January 12, 1928)

"Stock prices have reached what looks like a permanently high plateau. I do not feel that there will soon, if ever, be a fifty- or sixty-point break below present levels, such as Mr. Babson has predicted. I expect to see the stock market a great deal higher than it is today within the next few months."
> —Irving Fisher, one of the most prestigious economists of the day
> (October 16, 1929)

"I believe that the breaks of the last few days have driven stock prices down to hard rock. I believe that we will have a ragged market for a few weeks and then the beginning of a mild bull movement that will gain momentum next year."
> —Irving Fisher (October 22, 1929)

The value of corporate equities increased dramatically in the 1990s only to reverse course in the early 2000s. Exhibit 16-1 traces the outstanding value of corporate equities since 1982. On June 30, 2004, the outstanding value of domestic corporate equities was just under $16 trillion. This was up from $10.26 trillion just 8 years earlier and from $3.8 trillion 14 years earlier. However, the value of stocks in mid 2004 was about $3.5 trillion lower than the year-end peak of $19.5 trillion at the end of 1999. After the banner years of the 1990s, stocks did not fare as well in the early 2000s, when the value of outstanding corporate equities fell for three consecutive years to just under $11 trillion by the end of the third quarter 2002. As noted earlier, in early 2003, the market reversed course and closed the year up over 25 percent. Markets stalled somewhat in 2004 and whether or not a new bull market would start remains to be seen. Households, state and local governments, foreigners, and a variety of financial institutions hold domestically issued stocks. The major financial institutions that own shares of stocks are mutual funds, private and public pension funds, and insurance companies. In the mid 2004, foreigners owned about $1.7 trillion, or over 10 percent, of domestically issued stocks.

All companies that issue publicly traded shares of stock are regulated by the **Securities and Exchange Commission (SEC)**, which was created by the Securities and Exchange Act of 1934. The SEC has broad disclosure requirements to protect investors by requiring companies to file numerous reports detailing their financial condition, information about key personnel, and any changes that would be important to stockholders. The SEC also has extensive authority to regulate secondary market activities.

Securities and Exchange Commission (SEC)
A government agency created by the Securities and Exchange Act of 1934 that regulates disclosure rules for companies that issue publicly traded shares of stock.

16-1

The Value of Outstanding Shares of Domestically Issued Stock since 1982 (End of Year)

Year	Corporate Equities
1982	$1,562.5
1983	1,856.0
1984	1,789.2
1985	2,270.4
1986	2,682.6
1987	2,710.3
1988	3,076.3
1989	3,819.7
1990	3,542.6
1991	4,863.4
1992	5,430.9
1993	6,306.2
1994	6,333.3
1995	8,495.7
1996	10,255.8
1997	13,201.3
1998	15,427.8
1999	19,522.8
2000	17,627.0
2001	15,310.6
2002	11,870.9
2003	15,497.0
2004*	15,982.7

* As of June 30, 2004.
SOURCE: *Flow of Funds of the United States, Z1,* Board of Governors of the Federal Reserve System, various issues.

Stock Offerings

An **initial public offering (IPO)** is public offering of stock by a corporation for the first time. Many companies that have gone public in recent years are well known to college students. Some of them are Ben and Jerry's Ice Cream, California Pizza Kitchen, Martha Stewart Living Omnimedia, Guess?, and Krispy Kreme Doughnuts, as well as a rash of Internet start-up companies. Stock prices often move dramatically on the first day of trading. For example, on the first day of trading, California Pizza Kitchen's stock jumped 35 percent, Krispy Kreme Doughnuts stock's jumped 75 percent, and Red Hat Inc., an Internet company, saw its stock jump more than 80 percent. Price jumps among many of the Internet offerings did not last through a general downturn in Internet stocks in mid-2000. For example, Red Hat debuted in mid-1999 at $15 a share, rose to $151.31 by late 1999, fell to $3.81 a share by August 10, 2001, and was trading at $13.60 a share on October 7, 2004.

A **secondary stock offering** is an offering of newly issued shares by a firm that already has outstanding publicly held shares. To bring new shares to the market, a corporation must register the new issue with the SEC. Since 1982, the SEC has allowed corporations to register securities without immediately issuing them through a procedure called *shelf registration*. **Shelf registration** permits a company to register a number of securities and sell them over a two-year period rather than at the time the shares are registered. This avoids the costs in time and money of several registration processes and allows the firm to respond quickly to advantageous market conditions.

Recap   Stocks represent equity in a corporation. Preferred stockholders receive a fixed dividend, and common stockholders receive a variable or no dividend. Firms issue stock to raise funds for long-term investment spending. An IPO is a public offering of newly issued stocks by a corporation that has not previously sold stocks to the public. A secondary stock offering is an offering of newly issued stocks by a firm that has publicly held stocks outstanding. Shelf registration permits a company to register new shares of stocks at the present time but to issue the new shares over a two-year period.

The Stock Markets

When most people think about the stock market, they think of New York City's Wall Street, an actual street in South Manhattan that is home to New York's financial district and is also the nation's financial center. For financial market participants, however, Wall Street has a much broader connotation that includes many different organized stock exchanges and a nationwide network of brokers and dealers who buy and sell stock *over the counter*. In recent years, the volume and values of stocks traded—whether on exchanges or over the counter—have increased dramatically. Large institutional investors such as pension funds, insurance companies, and mutual funds have come to dominate the market. The institutional investors tend to trade large blocks of stocks (more than 10,000 shares of a given stock or trades with a market value higher than $200,000). Institutional investors, who owned only 7.2 percent of all equities in 1950, now own around a whopping 60 percent of the market valuation of all stock. The expanded use of computers to execute trades has accommodated the increased volume of trading and facilitated an increase in **program trading** by institutional investors. Program trading allows institutional investors to preprogram computers to buy or sell a large number (basket) of stocks. Although the volume of program trading fluctuates daily, in mid 2004, it was frequently over 50 percent of all trades.

Despite the increase in institutional trading, a higher percentage of households has a stake in the stock market than ever before, usually through retirement funds, direct ownership, or ownership of mutual funds. In 1989, only 31.6 percent of households owned stock in some form, but by 2003, that percentage had increased to more than 52 percent. As of June 30, 2004, households owned stocks and mutual funds valued over $9.5 trillion dollars As Exhibit 16-2 below shows, investing in the stock market has over time paid a higher total return than investing in the bond market or purchasing other financial assets. Other factors being equal, ownership of stocks entails a greater risk than ownership of bonds or other financial assets. Even though there is a higher expected return with stock ownership, there is no guarantee that any given investment will realize a higher return. Moreover, most financial assets issued by depository institutions offer the added advantage of deposit insurance. Stockholders own the excess, whether paid out in dividends or not, of what is left over after bondholders and other creditors have been paid fixed obligations. The residual may be huge, but then again it may fall short of expectations.

Investors do not have to put up funds equal to the full value of a stock purchase. Instead, they can purchase stocks on the margin ("buying on the margin") by borrowing. The **margin requirement** is the percentage of a stock purchase that can be borrowed as opposed to being paid in readily available funds. The current margin requirement, which is set by the Fed, has been 50 percent since 1974 and applies only to initial purchases. Buying on the margin allows an investor to amplify gains when the stock's price goes up because the investor has control, in essence, over a larger number of shares. It is thought that margin buying fuels speculation in stocks and can be particularly dangerous in a stock market bubble.

The New York Stock Exchange and the National Association of Securities Dealers require member firms to impose a minimum 25 percent **maintenance margin**

Margin Requirement
The percentage of invested funds that can be borrowed as opposed to being paid in readily available funds; currently margin requirements are set by the Fed at 50 percent.

Maintenance Margin Requirement
The minimum amount of equity the investor needs in his account relative to the market value of his stock.

16-2

The Returns to Stocks and Bonds over Time

Source: Global Financial Data, Los Angeles, California (http:\\www.globalfindata.com)

requirement on their customers. The maintenance margin requirement is the minimum amount of equity the investor needs in his or her account relative to the market value of the stock. The maintenance requirement comes into play if the stock has been purchased using borrowed funds and if the stock's value falls so that the investor has less equity than the amount required by the maintenance margin. Many individual brokerage firms set higher margin requirements and vary those requirements, depending on the stocks and trading behavior of individual customers. For example, assume that an investor purchases a share of stock for $100 with $50 or his or her own funds and borrows the rest from a broker. If the stock falls to $80, the owner has $30 equity in the stock, considering that there is a $50 loan. If there is a 25 percent maintenance margin requirement imposed by a broker or the exchange, the owner must have at least $20 (.25 × $80) equity in the stock. The owner has $30 equity, so all is well. If the stock falls to $60 per share, the owner's equity falls to $10 ($60 less the $50 loan). Because the owner is required to maintain a 25 percent margin, the owner is required to have $15 (.25 × $60) in equity. The owner has only $10 equity, so a margin call for $5 will be made to the owner. If the owner fails to provide the additional funds, the stock will be sold to pay off the loan. In a falling stock market, buying on the margin can present problems. As noted above, if the value of a stock falls to where the lender will put in a margin call that requires the investor to put up more funds, and if the investor fails to do so, the stock is sold at the low price so the lender can recoup part or all of its losses. The selling of the stock to recoup losses puts additional downward pressure on the flagging stock price.

In late 1999 and early 2000, margin credit grew much faster than the overall appreciation of the stock market. By early 2000, margin credit relative to the total value of stocks traded in the market reached a 29-year high. Raising margin requirements has also been proposed as a monetary policy tool to reduce speculative behavior that could fuel a stock market bubble, but the Fed did not choose to exercise this option in the bull market of the late 1990s.

U.S. markets in the mid- to late 1990s also experienced unprecedented capital inflows to purchase U.S. equities. The magnitude of these inflows is dramatic and is part of the ongoing globalization of financial markets. Exhibit 16-3 on page 367 shows the dollar value of net non-U.S. purchases of U.S. stocks since 1995.

Only life insurance companies and mutual funds purchased more U.S. equities than did non-U.S. purchasers. The inflows that many attributed to booming U.S. markets also contributed to those booming markets by increasing the demand for stocks. Without the inflow from abroad, demand for U.S. stocks would have been lower and equity prices not as high. Thus, it is difficult to say whether the inflows are the result of booming stock prices or if the inflows caused stock prices to boom. If foreigners sell U.S. equities or slow purchases, prices of U.S. equities will be lower than they otherwise would have been. Indeed, as Exhibit 16-3 shows, foreign purchases of U.S. equities slowed from $193.6 billion to $35.5 billion over the 2000 to 2003 period. In the first seven months of 2004, net foreign purchases of U.S. equities amounted to only $3.7 billion. It is difficult to say what the future trend will be.

The Major Domestic Exchanges

New York Stock Exchange (NYSE)
The world's largest market for trading stocks; trades the stocks of about 2,750 companies.

The New York Stock Exchange (NYSE)
The **New York Stock Exchange (NYSE)** located on Wall Street in New York City is the world's largest market for trading securities. In late 2004, the stocks of about 2,750 companies are traded on the NYSE and include 453 non-U.S. companies—up from only 95

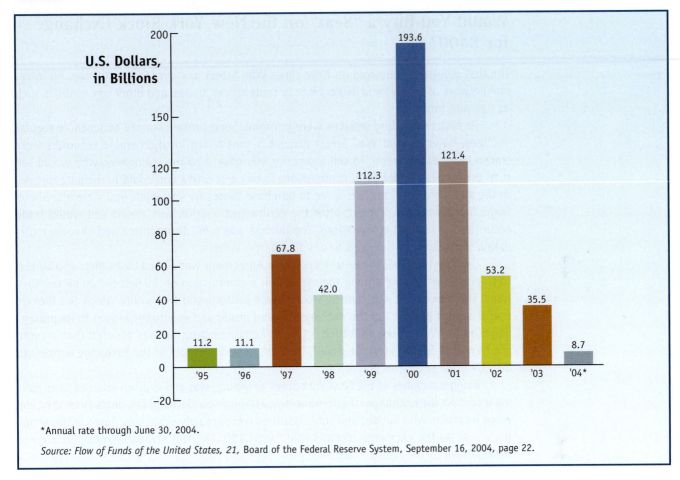

U.S. Dollars, in Billions

Year	Value
'95	11.2
'96	11.1
'97	67.8
'98	42.0
'99	112.3
'00	193.6
'01	121.4
'02	53.2
'03	35.5
'04*	8.7

*Annual rate through June 30, 2004.

Source: Flow of Funds of the United States, 21, Board of the Federal Reserve System, September 16, 2004, page 22.

foreign companies in 1990. To list its stock on the NYSE, the corporation must apply to the exchange and meet several criteria dealing with the size and number of shareholders. The NYSE seeks to enhance trading by ensuring that markets for any traded stock are sufficiently broad and deep. In the first nine months of 2004, 1,442.1 million shares worth $45.1 billion were traded on an average day. Exhibit 16-4 on page 368 lists the 10 largest companies whose stocks were traded on the NYSE.

The NYSE (known as the "Big Board") is a highly visible auction-type market where members, who act as agents for their customers, buy and sell shares of stock. Each member of the exchange has purchased a seat on it. The price of a seat is determined by supply and demand. In June 1999 the price of a seat reached a record high of $2.6 million. On September 16, 2004, a seat sold for $1.15 million. On June 30, 2004, the NYSE had 323 member firms that owned 1,366 seats. Mergers among large financial institutions represent one factor that has caused both the demand for seats on the NYSE and, hence, the price to fall since 1999. Another reason is the increased ability to trade stocks electronically over the Internet, thus bypassing an exchange.

The benefits of membership on the NYSE include participating directly in stock trading and charging commissions for trading stocks for customers. The customers may be financial or nonfinancial institutions or individual investors. The NYSE is

Looking Back

Would You Buy a "Seat" on the New York Stock Exchange for $400?

The first securities were sold on New York's Wall Street just over 200 years ago. An informal network of brokers and dealers met to trade stocks, bonds, and other commodities such as furs and tobacco.

At first the trading sessions were informal. Soon brokers started to schedule regular auctions, however, and Wall Street became a centralized location where securities were traded every day at noon. To sell a security, you gave it to the auctioneer, who would sell it to the highest bidder for a commission. To buy a security, you could participate directly in the auction or pay a broker a fee to purchase shares for you while you were elsewhere. Some individuals would meet after the centralized auction was closed and would trade securities for reduced commissions. The process was a bit disorganized and chaotic, motivating those who participated to design a better system.

On May 17, 1792, the Buttonwood Tree Agreement was signed by 24 men who agreed to trade securities only among themselves for a commission of .25 percent on all transactions. The agreement was named after a large buttonwood tree under which the brokers traded securities. In 1793 the exchange moved inside and eventually moved to its present home on 11 Wall Street. In March 1817, a formal constitution was adopted that created the New York Stock Exchange Board. The cost to be a member of the exchange entitled to directly trade securities was $400.

Being a member of the New York Stock Exchange was and is often referred to as having a *seat* on the exchange. The terminology, although outdated today, dates from the time when members who bought and sold securities were actually seated. As noted in the chapter, a seat on the exchange recently sold for $1,150,000, and invariably members are not sitting down as they make trades!

16-4

The Ten Largest Companies (Measured by Market Value) Traded on the Big Board, September 2004

Company Name	Symbol	SEPTEMBER 2004 Market Cap ($ bil.)	SEPTEMBER 2004 NYSE Average Daily Volume
General Electric Co.	GE	$354.5	17,169,046
Exxon Mobil Corp.	XOM	314.4	12,550,267
Pfizer Inc.	PFE	213.1	21,461,372
Citigroup Inc.	C	228.6	13,357,563
Wal-Mart Stores Inc.	WMT	225.7	9,876,872
American International Group Inc.	AIG	177.1	4,321,205
Bank of America Corp.	BAC	176.2	8,339,657
Johnson and Johnson	JNJ	167.2	5,341,172
International Business Machines Corp.	IBM	143.6	4,469,143
International Business Machines Corp.	IBM	149.8	5,267,720

SOURCE: http://www.nyse.com

self-regulated—meaning that every transaction is under constant surveillance by the exchange to ensure that trades are executed fairly.[4]

Each company whose stock is listed on the Big Board is assigned to a single post where a specialist in that stock manages the auction process. Members of the NYSE bring all large buy and sell orders to the floor either electronically or by broker on the floor of the exchange. Orders for a specific stock are funneled to the appropriate post. If the post is surrounded by more brokers looking to buy the stock than to sell at the existing price, the stock's price will rise. If the reverse is true, the price will fall. In this way, the forces of supply and demand determine prices.

When a new price is reached, a clerk records the information on a device that sends it out over the *ticker*. The ticker provides a constant stream of stock symbols and prices; each symbol consists of three or fewer letters and represents the stock of a particular corporation. The ticker continuously posts stock prices electronically on displays in brokerage houses and on computer screens around the world. For small orders of fewer than 3,000 shares, the process is a little different. The brokerage firm representing the buyer or seller of the stock routes the order to the **Designated Order Turnaround (DOT)** system. DOT is a computer system that sends buy or sell orders to the specialist's post where the transaction is automatically executed. The vast majority of trades are transacted through the DOT system.

To access closing prices, number and dollar value of shares traded as well as other information on NYSE-listed companies, search the exchanges' database at **http://www.nyse.com**.

On occasion, there have been large daily fluctuations in stock prices. During the week of October 12 to 16, 1987, the Dow Jones Industrial Average, an index of stock prices, fell 250 points. On Monday, October 19, 1987, it fell 508 points, or more than 20 percent. This was not only the largest point drop in history to that date but also by far the largest percentage drop. To give you some idea of its magnitude, the next largest percentage decline occurred on October 28, 1929, when the market fell 12.8 percent near the start of the Great Depression.[5] (More on the Dow later.)

In response to the October 1987 crash, certain reforms were instituted to limit such severe declines. In particular, **"circuit breakers"** were introduced to temporarily halt market trading if prices fall by a specified amount. During the halt, market makers have a chance to take positions and evaluate new information to provide support for the market. Bargains can be snatched up, stopping the free fall in prices. Originally, the new rules called for trading to be halted for half an hour if the market dropped 250 points from the previous day's close. If the market dropped 400 points, trading was to be halted for one hour.

The circuit breakers that halt all market trading were first tripped on October 24, 1997, as stocks fell in response to the Asian crisis. Shortly thereafter, the point ranges were broadened to 350 and 550 points. At the time, many analysts called for switching to a percentage change system from the point change system because trading halts based on percentage changes would be more meaningful. The Dow had increased so dramatically throughout the 1990s that a 350- or 550-point change was not nearly as significant as when the Dow was at lower levels.

In response, the NYSE adopted a threshold percentage rule that took effect on April 15, 1998. The point threshold is adjusted quarterly based on a percentage of the average closing level of the Dow Jones Industrial Average during the previous month, rounded to the nearest 50 points. The thresholds are as follows:

1. If the Dow declines 10 percent from the threshold before 2:00 P.M., the market will close for one hour; between 2:00 and 2:30 P.M., the market will close for 30 minutes; after 2:30 P.M., the 10 percent threshold is removed, and the market will continue trading.

Designated Order Turnaround (DOT)
A computer system used for trades of fewer than 3,000 shares on the NYSE.

Circuit Breakers
Reforms introduced in 1987 on the NYSE to temporarily halt market trading if prices change by a specified amount.

2. If the Dow declines 20 percent from the threshold before 1 P.M., the market will close for two hours; between 1 and 2 P.M., for one hour; after 2 P.M., for the day.

3. If the Dow declines 30 percent at any time, the market will close for the day.

For the fourth quarter 2004, the 10 percent threshold was a 1,000-point decline, the 20 percent decline was 2,050 points, and the 30 percent threshold was a 3,050-point decline.

Index-Arbitrage Trading
The purchasing (or selling) of a basket of stocks, usually through program trading, with the simultaneous selling (or purchasing) of a futures agreement in the same basket of securities in order to make a riskless profit (arbitrage) from the price differential between the basket of stocks and the futures agreement.

Circuit breakers also limit a form of program trading called **index-arbitrage trading**, which involves purchasing (or selling) a basket of stocks, usually through program trading, with the simultaneous selling (or purchasing) of a futures agreement in the same basket of securities. Index-arbitrage trading occurs when the price of the basket of stocks and the price of a futures agreement in those stocks diverge enough for someone to make a riskless profit (arbitrage) from buying in one market and selling in another. As you shall see in Chapter 18, spot prices and futures prices are highly correlated, and an arbitrageur can make a riskless profit if price differentials become out of alignment. A 50-point movement in the Dow originally triggered these limitations on index-arbitrage trading, which apply to both price advances and price declines. During the fourth quarter 2004, the point movement that would trigger the limitations on index-arbitrage trading was 200 points. Circuit breakers for index-arbitrage trading are triggered more frequently because of the smaller price change that is needed to trigger the circuit breaker than for those price changes that halt all market activity.

Other Exchanges

American Stock Exchange
A stock exchange located in New York City that trades the stock of more than 650 companies.

In addition to being the home of the Big Board, New York is the home of the **American Stock Exchange** on which the stocks of about 650 companies are traded.[6] The dollar value of stocks traded on the American Stock Exchange is small compared to that of the NYSE, and the criteria for the stock of a corporation to be traded are not so stringent. Regional exchanges that primarily trade stocks listed on the NYSE are located in Boston, Chicago, San Francisco, and Philadelphia. Stocks of a given company may be traded on more than one exchange, and specialists on the floor of each exchange watch prices on competing exchanges.

Many foreign countries also have stock exchanges with varying degrees of development and depth. Some European exchanges, such as the London Stock Exchange and Amsterdam Stock Exchange, predate those in the United States. The Nikkei Exchange in Tokyo, the London Stock Exchange, the DAX in Germany, and the Toronto Stock Exchange in Canada are among the busiest exchanges around the world. In September 2000, the Amsterdam, Brussels, and Paris stock exchanges merged to form the Euronext Exchange. More cross-border mergers are expected, particularly in European countries that participate in the Euro. In recent years, many emerging economies have developed stock exchanges concomitant with the globalization of finance and the increase in capital flows.

The American Stock Exchange provides a listing of current stock market performance at **http://www.amex.com**.

Recap The volume and value of stocks traded have increased dramatically. Program trading by institutional investors allows for the preprogramming of computers to buy or sell baskets of stocks. *Buying stocks on the margin* refers to putting up only a fraction of the stock's selling price and borrowing the rest. Currently, the margin requirement is 50 percent. Stocks may be traded in organized markets such as the NYSE, the American Stock Exchange, and other regional stock exchanges. Organized exchanges operate auction-type markets where a specialist trades large blocks of shares. The NYSE is by far the largest organized exchange. Each stock is traded at a specific post, which may trade up to several dozen stocks. Smaller trades are made on the NYSE via a computer system (the DOT system) that sends buy or sell orders to the specialist's post where the transaction is automatically executed.

The Over-the-Counter Market

Over-the-Counter Market
A network of securities dealers that trades stocks of more than 30,000 companies via telephone or computer.

National Association of Securities Dealers (NASD)
A privately owned organization that regulates the market participants in the over-the-counter market under the supervision of the SEC.

National Association of Securities Dealers Automated Quotation System (NASDAQ)
An association whose members trade stocks over an advanced computer system that provides immediate information about prices and the number of shares being traded.

The **over-the-counter market** is composed of thousands of securities dealers located all over the country. Transactions in the stocks of more than 30,000 companies are executed over the telephone or via computer. The dealers or brokerage firms that make a market in a particular security or securities buy and sell the securities at publicly quoted prices. The **National Association of Securities Dealers (NASD)** regulates the market participants in the over-the-counter market under the supervision of the SEC. The NASD is privately owned. Historically, the over-the-counter market dealt mainly with stocks of small companies. Today the over-the-counter market trades the stock of many larger firms, including such high-tech giants as Apple Computer and Microsoft.

About 3,300 of the larger 30,000 companies whose stocks are traded over the counter are also members of the **National Association of Securities Dealers Automated Quotation System (NASDAQ)**. Founded in 1971, NASDAQ is the world's first electronic stock market.[7] Stocks of NASDAQ members are traded on an advanced computer system that provides immediate information about prices and the number of shares being traded. To be listed on the NASDAQ, a company must meet several requirements including sales volume. More than 11,000 brokers and dealers in 790 firms participate in the NASDAQ market, and trading information is broadcast over more than 2 million computer terminals in 83 countries worldwide in 2004. The NASDAQ trades more shares per day than any other U.S. stock market. NASDAQ has also established a Pre-Market and an After Hours Market to trade listed stocks outside the regular trading session from 9:30 A.M. to 4 P.M. eastern time (ET). The session of the Pre-Market is from 8:00 A.M. to 9:30 A.M. ET, and of the After Hours Market is from 4:00 to 6:30 P.M. ET. The NASDAQ International Market session is from 3:30 A.M. to 9:00 A.M. ET. Trading in the pre- and after-hour markets usually offers less liquidity, inferior prices, and potentially more price volatility than trading during regular hours. These discrepancies may lessen as the Pre-Market and After-Hours Market become more developed.[8] In August, 2004, about 340 of the 3,300 NASDAQ companies are foreign companies, making the NASDAQ a leading U.S. market for non-U.S. corporations.

NASDAQ grew tremendously in the 1990s and 2000s to become a rival to the NYSE and bigger than all other domestic and foreign stock exchanges. Although the market capitalization of the stocks traded on the NYSE far exceeds that of stocks traded on the NASDAQ, the NASDAQ has been growing relatively faster in terms of the number of shares and dollar volume of trading.

Updated information about the stocks traded on the NASDAQ can be found on the Internet at **http://www.nasdaq.com**.

NASDAQ, however, is facing its own competition from another electronic stock exchange, ArcaEx, which is part of Archipelago, and other electronic trading networks. By April 2004, the fledgling ArcaEx, which began trading in March 2002, had managed to take about 20 percent of the trading volume of NASDAQ-listed stocks. ArcaEx was successful in luring customers from the NASDAQ by offering super-fast trades, user-friendly systems, and low trading fees. Instinet, although not an exchange, is a global electronic trading network with institutional clients, and has captured about 25 percent of the trading volume of NASDAQ-listed stocks. In response to these challenges, the NASDAQ has initiated huge price cuts for trades between its largest volume customers and is trying to regain its market niche. However this competition shakes out, it is clear that electronic trading is a supercompetitive business and that change can be expected to continue in the foreseeable future as technology continues to evolve.

For information about ArcaEx and Instinet on the Internet, go to **http://www.archipelago.com/** and **http://www.instinet.com/**, respectively.

Stock Market Indexes

A stock market index measures the overall performance of the stocks included in the index. An index can be used to evaluate how well a specific stock or mutual fund is performing relative to the stocks represented in the index. Almost 100 indexes monitor stock prices. The **Dow Jones Industrial Average (the Dow)** measures movements in the stock prices of 30 of the largest companies in the country. The Dow, first introduced in 1896, is the oldest index in use today and is probably the most famous. The stocks in an index may include all the stocks traded on a particular stock exchange, selectively picked stocks, or stocks that fall into a particular class based on the value of outstanding shares.

The following list describes the major stock indexes reported in the popular media. As a quick glance shows, other indexes are far more broadly based than the Dow. Over the long run, however, the movement of the Dow has closely paralleled other, more comprehensive indexes.

- *The Dow Jones Industrial Average* (the Dow or DJIA, for short) is an unweighted average of the sum of the daily closing prices of the stocks of 30 of the largest companies in the country, the "blue chips." The companies that make up the index are selected by Dow Jones & Company, which also publishes *The Wall Street Journal*. The companies are changed over time to reflect changes in corporate America. The 30 companies included in the index are listed in Exhibit 16-5 below. Note that the index is larger than the sum of the daily closing prices of the 30 stocks. The number that the sum is divided by is adjusted to account for the effect of stock splits and stock dividends. Also, when a company is dropped and a new company added, the average is adjusted so that the new index is comparable to earlier values.

- *The Dow Jones Transportation Average* is calculated using the prices of 20 airline, trucking, and railroad stocks.

Dow Jones Industrial Average (the Dow)
An index that measures movements in the stock prices of 30 of the largest companies traded on the NYSE.

16-5

The Companies That Make Up the Dow as of April 8, 2004

American International Group	Intel Corp.
Alcoa	J. P. Morgan Chase
American Express	Johnson & Johnson
Boeing	McDonald's
Caterpillar	Merck
Citigroup	Microsoft
Coca-Cola	Minn. Mining & Manufacturing
DuPont	Pfizer
Exxon Mobil	Philip Morris
General Electric	Procter & Gamble
General Motors	SBC Communications
Hewlett-Packard	United Technologies
Home Depot	Verizons Communications
Honeywell International	Wal-Mart
IBM	Walt Disney

SOURCE: http://www.nyse.com

- *The Dow Jones Utility Average* is calculated using the prices of 15 gas, electric, and power company stocks.
- *The Dow Jones 65 Composite Index* is calculated from all stocks in the Dow Jones Industrial, Transportation, and Utility Averages.
- *The Standard and Poor's 500* (the S&P 500 for short) is a weighted index of prices of 500 broad-based corporations. Stocks included in the index may be traded on the New York Stock Exchange (NYSE), the American Stock Exchange, or over the counter. They are selected by Standard and Poor's Corporation and changed over time as needed so that the index reflects general stock market conditions. As with other weighted indexes, the S&P 500 weights the stocks according to their relative values so that larger corporations contribute more to the index. Many analysts consider the S&P 500 to be a more meaningful index of overall stock market activity than the Dow.
- *The New York Composite Index* is a weighted average of the market value of all stocks traded on the NYSE. The index also reports four subgroup indexes representing industrial, transportation, utility, and finance stocks.
- *The Wilshire Equity Index Value* (the Wilshire 5000) is a weighted index of the value of all stocks listed on the NYSE, all stocks on the American Stock Exchange, and all over-the-counter stocks that are traded by NASDAQ members. As such, it includes virtually all companies in the United States and is the broadest measure of stock market activity. Today the Wilshire 5000 includes over 6,800 stocks. When the index was originally created, it included 5,000 stocks (hence the name).
- *The NASDAQ Composite Index,* as its name suggests, is a weighted index that measures changes in prices of all stock traded by the NASDAQ system.

Exhibit 16-6 on page 374 reports the value of the DJIA, the S&P 500, and the NASDAQ Composite from 1985 to October 11, 2004. Note the phenomenal increase in all of the indices. Exhibit 16-7 also on page 374 includes the daily averages of the stock market volume and the values traded from 1985 until June 1, 2004. Again, note the phenomenal increase in both volume and value of stocks traded. In the next section, we look at stock markets and mutual funds.

Recap   In addition to purchasing stocks from an organized exchange, investors may also purchase them over the counter. The over-the-counter market is an informal network of market makers who trade stocks via telephone or computer linkages. Stocks of more than 30,000 companies are traded over the counter. The NASD, a privately owned organization, regulates the over-the-counter market under the supervision of the SEC. Large companies may also be NASDAQ members. Stocks of NASDAQ members are traded on an advanced computer system that provides price quotes for NASDAQ members. Trading on the NASDAQ has grown faster than trading on the organized exchanges in recent years. However, NASDAQ has faced increased competition from other electronic trading firms in recent years.

The Stock Market and Mutual Funds

Mutual funds are companies that pool the funds of many investors and then invest in several hundred or even thousands of stocks. In addition, some mutual funds invest in bonds or some combination of both stocks and bonds. The small investor who buys into the fund can own a small piece of the large basket of stocks and/or bonds. As you saw in Chapter 15, any individual can tap into the higher returns of the stock market while minimizing the risk of doing so by purchasing shares of a mutual fund.

16-6

The Value of the DJIA, S&P 500, NYSE Composite, and NASDAQ since 1985

	Dow Jones Industrial	S&P 500	NASDAQ Composite
1985	1,546.67	211.28	324.93
1986	1,895.95	242.17	348.83
1987	1,938.83	247.08	330.47
1988	2,168.57	277.72	381.38
1989	2,753.20	353.40	454.82
1990	2,633.66	330.22	373.84
1991	3,168.83	417.09	586.34
1992	3,301.11	435.71	676.95
1993	3,754.09	466.45	776.80
1994	3,834.44	459.27	751.96
1995	5,117.12	615.93	1,052.13
1996	6,448.27	740.74	1,291.03
1997	7,908.25	970.43	1,570.35
1998	9,181.43	1,229.23	2,192.69
1999	11,497.12	1,469.25	4,069.31
2000	10,786.90	1,320.28	2,470.53
2001	10,021.50	1,148.08	1950.40
2002	8,341.63	879.82	1,335.52
2003	10,453.90	1,111.92	2,003.37
2004*	10,081.97	1,124.39	1,928.76

*As of October 11, 2004.
SOURCE: Global Financial Data, Los Angeles, California.

16-7

Daily Average of Stock Market Volume and Values Traded since 1985

	Stock Market Volume (Daily Average, Millions of Shares)		Value Traded (Daily Average, Billions of Dollars)	
	NYSE	NASDAQ	NYSE	NASDAQ
1985	109.2	82.1	$3.9	$0.9
1986	141.0	113.6	5.4	1.5
1987	188.9	149.8	7.4	2.0
1988	161.5	122.8	5.4	1.4
1989	165.5	133.1	6.1	1.7
1990	156.8	131.9	5.2	1.8
1991	178.9	163.3	6.0	2.7
1992	202.3	190.8	6.9	3.5
1993	264.5	263.0	9.0	5.3
1994	291.4	295.1	9.7	5.8
1995	346.1	401.4	12.2	9.5
1996	412.0	543.7	16.0	13.0
1997	526.9	647.8	22.8	17.7
1998	673.6	801.7	29.0	22.9
1999	808.9	1,081.8	35.5	43.7
2000	1,042.0	1,757.0	43.9	80.9
2001	1,240.0	1900.0	41.62	44.1
2002	1,441.0	1,753.0	40.79	28.8
2003	1,398.4	1,660.0	38.5	28.0
2004*	1,528.2	1,947.1	47.9	36.3

*As of June 1, 2004.
SOURCE: Securities Industry Association

For many investors, mutual funds may offer less risk and greater safety than individual stocks because of diversification. Because all securities do not perform equally well over the business cycle (returns are not perfectly correlated), diversification reduces risk. This greatly reduces the risk of investing in a single company that fails (putting all of your eggs in one basket). If a mutual fund has invested in 1,000 companies, the risk that all of them will go under at once is much less than the risk that any one of them will be forced into bankruptcy. If only one or a few of the companies perform poorly, the overall returns to the mutual fund are hardly affected. Mutual fund companies offer highly trained professional management to research the best investments. This not only saves the individual investor time and effort but also is intended to improve the performance (yield) of the portfolio. As you saw in Chapter 15, no-load mutual funds are bought directly from the mutual fund company and do not involve a brokerage commission.

Indexed Mutual Funds
A mutual fund that holds the same basket of securities that are represented in an index such as the S&P 500 or the Wilshire 5000 so that the investor receives roughly the same return as the index to which the fund is tied.

An **indexed mutual fund** holds the same basket of securities that are represented in an index such as the S&P 500 or the Wilshire 5000. The investor receives roughly the same return as that of the index to which the fund is tied. For example, if an index appreciates 10 percent, a mutual fund holding the same stocks as in the index also appreciates 10 percent. Indexed mutual funds usually have relatively low costs because little trading occurs. Management fees are low because the mutual fund's holdings do not have to be actively managed. For investors who are satisfied with the return of the overall market, these funds may be a good bet because of their low costs. Often actively managed funds earn lower returns that the indexed funds and involve significantly higher management fees and other costs.

Exchange-Traded Funds (ETFs)
A security created by a securities firm depositing into a fund that mirrors the holdings of stocks in an index.

In 1993, an alternative investment to indexed-mutual funds called *exchange-traded funds* was developed. **Exchange-traded funds (ETFs)** are shares of a security (such as shares of stock) that mirror the holdings and, hence, the performance of an index. ETFs result from the deposit by a securities firm of a large basket of stocks into a fund that make up (reflect) the holdings of the index. The securities firm than receives a block of ETFs shares against the basket of stock. The shares are then offered to individual investors. Because the shares mirror the holdings of stocks in an index, they offer approximately the same return (appreciation or depreciation) that the index does. However, they are like owning a share of stock rather than shares in a mutual fund. ETFs are traded on several exchanges and can be bought and sold through a broker anytime during the exchange hours at the prices they are trading at that moment. When mutual funds are traded, they are bought or sold at end-of-day prices. Unlike mutual funds, ETFs can be bought with borrowed funds (margin buying) and sold short. Limit orders can also be placed. The dollar value of ETFs, which go by names such as Diamonds, Ishares, Spiders, and Vipers, among others, has increased from their inception in 1993 to almost $150 billion in 2004. A disadvantage of ETFs is that a brokerage commission has to be paid to buy or sell them, which is avoided when no-load indexed mutual funds are bought directly. Both indexed mutual funds and ETFs may also have tax advantages for investors over other mutual fund investments.

Recap   Stock market indexes measure movements in stock prices. The Dow is an index of 30 of the largest companies in the country. The S&P 500 is a weighted average of 500 broad-based companies and is considered to be a more meaningful index than the Dow. Mutual funds are investment companies that pool the funds of many investors and purchase securities. They allow for much greater diversification than investors could achieve on their own. Mutual funds now offer indexed mutual funds that hold the same basket of stocks as represented in a stock index. ETFs are securities that mirror the holdings of stock in a market index.

The Valuation of Stocks

Should you buy a particular stock or not? It depends on whether you think it is your most profitable opportunity, given your tolerance for risk. At the present price at which it is trading, is the stock undervalued or overvalued? In this section, we will attempt to shed some light on these questions.

Given some of the material covered in Chapters 6 and 8, you will not be surprised to learn that the price of a share of stock in a firm should equal the present value of the expected future cash flows that the share will generate, where cash flows include both dividends and retained earnings. If we assume that the stock will be held indefinitely into the future (forever), then the current price of the stock will be equal to the present value of the expected cash flows, as portrayed in Equation 16-1.

(16-1) $$P = C1/(1 + d) + C2/(1 + d)^2 + C3/(1 + d)^3 \ldots$$

Where Cn is the expected cash flow in the nth year and d the discount factor (interest rate) applied to find the present value or price (P).

If we expect the firm to earn a constant cash flow, ($C1 = C2 = C3 = \ldots$), then Equation 16-1 simplifies to Equation 16-2.

(16-2) $$P = C/d$$

Assuming that we can estimate the expected cash flow (C) and the discount factor (d), we can solve for the current value of a share of the stock. If the stock is trading at a lower price, the savvy investor will buy; if it is trading at a higher price, the investor will sell. If there is agreement about expected cash flows, the stock's price should converge to the value based on that expectation. In the real world, there are often very divergent opinions about future cash flows. That is the reason some people are buying and others are selling at any given moment.

A question that remains is how the discount factor is determined. For any stock, there is a required return needed by investors who purchase the stock. This is the equilibrium return that is based on a risk-free return plus a risk premium associated with owning the stock, as discussed in Chapter 8. The risk-free return is usually measured by the long-term government bond rate.

The risk premium is composed of two parts:

- A **market risk premium** based on historical data that shows how much on average the ownership of stocks pays over the risk-free return.

- A **firm-specific risk premium** that is measured by a coefficient called **beta**, which measures the overall sensitivity or variability of the stock's return relative to changes in the entire stock market.[9] Changes in the S&P 500 can serve as a proxy for changes in the whole market. Thus, if on average when the S&P 500 increases (or decreases) 1 percent and a particular stock's price increases (or decreases) 2 percent, the beta for this stock is 2. This indicates that this stock is riskier than the average stock in the S&P 500 index because its value fluctuates more. On the other hand, if a 1 percent change in the S&P 500 generates a .5 percent change, beta is .5, and the stock varies less than the S&P 500.

The **capital asset pricing model** uses the preceding analysis to develop a model of the return needed to own a share of stock based on the market and firm-specific risks. According to the capital asset pricing model, the return needed is equal to the risk-free return plus beta multiplied by the market risk premium, as depicted in Equation 16-3.

(16-3) $$d = Rf + \beta(Rm)$$

Market Risk Premium
The risk based on historical data that shows how much on average the ownership of stocks pays over a risk-free return.

Firm-Specific Risk Premium
A risk measured by beta that shows the overall sensitivity of the stock's return relative to changes in the entire market.

Beta
A measure of the overall variability of a stock relative to changes in the entire stock market.

Capital Asset Pricing Model
A model that asserts that the value of a share of stock includes a risk-free return, a market risk premium, and a firm-specific risk premium that is based on beta.

where d is the discount factor, Rf is the risk-free return, β is beta for this particular stock, and Rm is the market risk premium with which investors must be compensated for owning stocks in general. The discount factor takes into account the risk-free return, the market risk premium, and the firm-specific variance of the return as measured by beta.

In the preceding example, if the risk-free return is 5.5 percent, the market risk factor based on historical data is 4 percent, and beta for this firm is 2, then d is equal to 13.5 percent $[5.5 + (2 \times 4)) = 5.5 + 8 = 13.5]$. 13.5 percent is the discount factor that we will plug into Equation 16-2 to find the present value of a share of the firm's stock. If the expected cash flow is \$10 per year, the price of the stock will be \$74.07, because \$10/.135 = \$74.07.

Note that the risk-free return and the market risk premium are the same for all firms while beta is usually different and dependent on the variability of a firm's returns.

The assumption of a constant expected cash flow is rather limiting because—we hope—cash flows will grow over time. If we assume that expected cash flows grow at a constant percent, g, then we can modify Equation 16-2 to take into account this common growth rate. This is done in Equation 16-4:

(16-4)
$$P = C/(d - g)$$

where P is the stock price, C is the expected cash flow today, d is the discount factor, and g is the constant growth rate of future expected cash flows.

Thus, modifying the example, if cash flows are expected to grow 5 percent annually $(g = .05)$, the new stock price will be \$117.65 because $(\$10/(.135 - .05) = \$117.65)$.

In Chapter 8, we considered the efficient markets theory, which laid much of the groundwork for this section. You saw that the prices of stocks and bonds adjust until the average investor is indifferent between stocks or bonds—in other words, until the risk-adjusted returns to owning stocks or bonds are equalized. In this section, we have expanded that analysis to consider a market risk of owning stocks versus bonds plus a firm-specific risk as measured by beta. The equilibrium return to owning stocks consists of a risk-free return, a risk premium for owning stock, and a firm-specific premium. Again, if the Fed takes action that causes interest rates to change, this changes the risk-free return of government bonds, and the financial prices of stocks and bonds adjust until the investor is again indifferent between stocks and bonds.

A point needs to be emphasized: Future cash flows are, of course, unknown. Therefore, it is the discounted value of expected cash flows that is used in stock valuation. You can see why cash flow and earnings reports get so much attention in the media. If earnings reports differ from what was forecasted, sharp price movements can occur immediately as investors take advantage of buying and selling opportunities. The A Closer Look feature on page 378 discusses some of the current issues with regard to the performance of U.S. stock markets in recent years.

Recap

The value of a stock is the discounted present value of the expected future stream of cash flows that the stock will generate. Investors require a return that is the sum of a risk-free return plus a risk premium to account for the fact that stocks are riskier than government securities. In addition to a market risk premium, there is a firm-specific risk premium based on beta that measures the variability of a stock's return relative to the entire market. If cash flows grow by a constant percent, g, the price of a share of stock will be equal to $C/(d - g)$, where C is the original cash flow, d is the discount factor based on the market and firm-specific risks, and g is the constant growth rate of the cash flow.

Can U.S. Stock Prices in the 1990s Be Justified?

As shown in Exhibit 16-6, U.S. stock markets reached levels that were unimaginable before the stock market boom began in the early 1990s. Some analysts believe that the market had been in an irrational bubble that could not be sustained and look to the downturn in the early 2000s to support their claim. Others believe that the record increases were justified. They say that increases in information technologies have transformed the way firms do business, have increased worker productivity, and have promised increased cash flows that justified the high prices.

Although a definitive answer has not been found, several theories have been put forth that attempt to explain the high stock valuations of the late 1990s. From the material in this chapter, we can see that the stratospheric stock prices could be justified under either or both of two conditions:

- first, if expected cash flows increased sufficiently to justify the high prices
- second, if the rate at which expected cash flows are discounted decreased enough to justify the high prices.

One theory holds that the high prices were justified if the growth rate of earnings increased from the 1.4 percent average over the past century to 2.4 percent in recent years and if the required rated of return fell from the 7.3 percent average over the last century to 6.6 percent.[a] This theory suggests that changes in stock market participation, consumer preferences, and earnings growth together could explain the higher prices. As noted elsewhere, a much larger percent of the population now participates in the market. Given increased life expectancies and uncertainty surrounding future social security payments, investors now have a longer time horizon for investments. Finally, given the growth of mutual funds, cash flows are less uncertain because of the greater extent of diversification that investing in mutual funds makes possible.

Another theory suggests that the high stock prices could be accounted for because of increases in productivity.[b] For example, productivity increased at an 8 percent annual rate in the 1960s, 2 percent in the 1970s, and 17 percent in the 1990s. Although many believe that the explosion of information technologies has increased worker productivity, these estimates seem unrealistic at best. They also raise another question. If volatile productivity growth can explain changes in stock prices, what are the factors that cause productivity growth to be so volatile?

A third theory is that a major technological innovation reduced the value of existing firms and caused a reduction in the stock market that continued until shares in new firms that make use of the technology make their way into the market.[c] The idea is that the information technology revolution began in the early 1970s with the invention of the microprocessor. However, older firms with existing technologies and capital were slow to adopt the changes and, hence, their values were reduced. The higher value of the new innovative firms was not reflected in stock markets because they did not offer tradable securities. Only after the new firms issued tradable stocks via IPOs would the value of new technologies be reflected in the market. To support the hypothesis, the authors show that most of the increased values in the stock market relative to gross domestic product since

1985 are the result of increases in the value of new firms. Firms that were in existence in early 1970s lost about half of their value in the early 1970s and have not fully recovered.

Finally, a fourth theory suggests that the run-up in stock prices was due to two factors:

- technological changes that were being assimilated into stock valuations
- Structural changes such as financial liberalization that allowed for more widespread participation in stock markets[d]

Both of these factors may help to explain the run-up in stock prices. In addition, there are learning curves for both the changes in technology and the increased participation that could help to explain market volatility.

In the bull market and new economy of the late 1990s, Internet stocks—referred to as *dot-coms*—experienced enormous gains. Some of these start-up companies had never made a profit, had never produced a product, and had virtually no real or financial assets. Then why were investors willing to pay such hefty prices? If you followed this chapter, you should be quick to answer, expected future cash flows. Of course, after spring 2000, when prices of many of the dot-coms collapsed, investors began to take a closer look and question whether or not the expected cash flows had been vastly overestimated. Perhaps some Internet stocks had been caught in a speculative bubble.

Other stocks that suffered significant losses at the time included media and telecommunications stocks. Indeed, the technology-laden NASDAQ index fell about 72 percent from February 2000 to February 2003 in the worst bear market in history.

We have completed our look at stocks. We hope you have a better understanding of these financial instruments. This chapter contains an appendix on how a firm that wishes to raise long-term financial capital chooses between issuing stocks or bonds. We will complete our discussion of capital markets with the next chapter on the debt markets. This will lay the groundwork for our discussion in Part VI on how policy makers should respond to price volatility in these capital markets.

Summary of Major Points

1. In recent decades, prices of stocks have become more volatile. The Fed is concerned about this because of the potential for stock price bubbles and crashes to cause unemployment or inflation, or to affect the solvency of financial institutions and the financial system.

2. Stocks represent ownership in a corporation. Preferred stock pays a fixed dividend, and common stock may pay a variable or no dividend. Under normal circumstances, publicly held stocks are liquid financial assets that may be traded in organized markets such as the NYSE, the American Stock Exchange, or regional stock exchanges. They may also be traded over the counter through computer networks and over the telephone lines.

3. Institutional investors in the stock market are primarily insurance companies, pension plans, and mutual funds. Program trading allows institutional investors to preprogram computers to buy or sell a market basket of stocks. *Buying on the margin* refers to buying stocks by using one's own funds and borrowed funds. At the present time, margin requirements for purchases are 50 percent. Exchanges set maintenance margins that must be maintained after the stock has

been purchased. Shelf registration allows a corporation to register stocks that it can issue over the next two years.

4. Organized exchanges operate auction-type markets on which a specialist trades large blocks of shares at a specific post. Smaller trades are made on the NYSE via the DOT system, which is a computer system that sends buy or sell orders to the specialist's post.

5. The over-the-counter market is an informal network of market makers who trade stocks of more than 30,000 companies via telephone or computer linkages. The NASD regulates the over-the-counter market under the supervision of the SEC. New issues of securities must be registered with the SEC. The NASDAQ is the world's first electronic stock market and trades the stocks of more than 3,300 of the larger 30,000 corporations that are in the over-the-counter market. The stocks are traded on an advanced computer system. In recent years, the trading volume on the NASDAQ has been growing faster than that on the NYSE. ArcaEx, a relatively new electronic exchange, and other online trading networks have taken a significant share of NASDAQ's trading volume.

6. Stock market indexes measure movements in stock prices. The Dow is an index of 30 of the largest companies in the country. The S&P 500 is a weighted average of 500 broad-based companies and is considered to be a more meaningful index than the Dow. Mutual funds are investment companies that pool the funds of many investors and purchase securities, allowing greater diversification for small investors. Indexed mutual funds hold the same basket of stocks as represented in a stock index. ETFs are securities that mirror the holdings of stock in a market index and offer the same advantages of investing in individual stocks.

7. The value of a share of stock is the discounted present value of the expected future cash flows that the stock will generate. Investors require a return that is the sum of a risk-free return plus a risk premium to account for the fact that stocks are riskier than government securities. In addition to a market risk premium, there is a firm-specific risk premium based on beta that measures the variability of this stock's return relative to the entire market. If cash flows grow by a constant percent, the price of a share of stock will be equal to $C/(d - g)$, where C is the original cash flow, d is the discount factor based on the market and firm-specific risks, and g is the constant growth rate of the cash flows.

8. If firms want to spend more than their receipts, they must decide between internal or external financing. If the firm uses external financing, it can issue new stocks or bonds. If a firm chooses external debt financing, it must also decide whether the debt will be long term or short term. Issuing stock dilutes the ownership of the firm. Issuing debt has tax advantages because interest payments are a tax write-off, whereas dividend payments are not. Issuing debt increases the firm's leverage ratio which makes the firm more vulnerable to a downturn in profits. (See *Appendix 16A*.)

Key Terms

Review Questions

1. How could a stock market crash affect the economy?
2. Assuming that other factors remain constant, is common or preferred stock riskier to hold?
3. Assuming that other factors remain constant, does holding common or preferred stock, pay a higher return?
4. To which market index would you refer to see how well the stock market is performing? Why? Why do you think the movements of the Dow and the S&P 500 are highly correlated?
5. Why are mutual funds generally perceived to be less risky than holding a market basket of individual stocks?
6. What are institutional investors, and what impact do they have on stock markets? What is program trading?
7. What is the over-the-counter market? Are only companies that are too small to be listed on an organized exchange traded over the counter?
8. Can a stock be listed on more than one exchange at the same time?
9. What are circuit breakers? How have the rules affecting them changed in recent years?
10. What is program trading? What is index-arbitrage trading?
11. Discuss the following statement: "Organized exchanges, like dinosaurs, will disappear."
12. In a paragraph, explain how inflation in stock markets can spill over to inflation in output markets. Do the same for deflation.
13. What is buying on the margin? Does it increase or decrease the risk of large losses? What about gains?
14. Can newly issued Microsoft stock be offered in an IPO? Explain. What is the difference between buying stock in a secondary public offering or in the secondary market?
15. What are the differences between indexed mutual funds and ETFs?
16. How does a firm choose between debt and equity financing? What are the advantages and disadvantages of each? (*See Appendix 16A.*)

Analytical Questions

Questions marked with an icon are objective in nature. They can be completed with a short answer or number.

17. If a share of stock pays a dividend of $3 and closes today at $36, what is the current yield?
18. What is the discount factor if beta is 1.2, the market risk premium is 5 percent, and the risk-free return is 4 percent?
19. If the expected cash flow is constant and equal to $10, what is the value of a share of stock with the discount factor in problem 18? If the cash flow is expected to grow 3 percent each year, what is the value?
20. If I bought $10,000 worth of stock by putting up 60 percent of the selling price and borrowing the rest, how much have I borrowed? If the stock falls to $3,000 and a margin call is put in for the difference between the value of the stock and the amount I have borrowed, how much will I have to put up?
21. New earnings figures suggest that cash flows will experience a $100 onetime increase because of a new product being brought online. If d is 15 percent and g is 3 percent, how much will the stock's value increase?
22. Jessie bought a share of stock for $100. She borrowed $50 from her broker. There is a 25 percent maintenance margin requirement established by the brokerage firm she does business with. The price of the stock falls to $80. Will her broker put in a margin call to her, asking her to put up more funds? If so, how much more? What if the price falls to $50? In each case, if so, how much more?

Internet Exercises

1. Go to the NASDAQ home page at (http://www.nasdaq.com) and click on the major indices to determine their latest performance. How do they compare?
2. Go to http://www.nasdaqnews.com/MarketData/News_mrktdata_home.htm and check on the percent of trades of NASDAQ listed stocks that occur on the NASDAQ. Compare this with the percent of trades on other exchanges.

3. What were the 10 most actively traded stocks on the American Stock Exchange today? What were the 10 most advanced? You can find this information by clicking on the appropriate link from the home page of the American Stock Exchange (http://www.amex.com/) in order to answer this question.

4. http://www.globalfindata.com contains financial data about the United States and global economies. From the home page, click on sample data. Under U.S. stock market indices, compare and contrast the performance of the New York Composite Index and the NASDAQ Composite Index over the last 10 years.

5. From http://www.globalfindata.com, click on sample data and look at graphs of world stock market indexes. What can you conclude about the performance of worldwide stock markets in the early and mid 2000s?

Suggested Readings

For an interesting look at the stock market in the 1990s, see Maggie Mahar, *Bull!: A History of the Boom, 1982–1999* (New York: Harper Business, 2004).

For a review of historical and recent market performances, see *Stock, Bonds, Bills, and Inflation Yearbook: 2004 Classic Edition* (Ibbotson Associates, March 2004).

For a look at "What Explains the Stock Market's Reaction to Federal Reserve Policy?" see the article by the same name by Ben S. Bernanke and Kenneth N. Kuttner, Board of Governors of the Federal Reserve, *Finance and Economics Discussion Series*, 2004-16 (March 2004). It is available on the Internet at http://www.federalreserve.gov/pubs/feds/2004/200416/200416pap.pdf.

"Should the Fed React to the Stock Market?" is the question posed in the article by the same name in the *Economic Letter*, Federal Reserve Bank of San Francisco, Number 2003-34 by Kevin J. Lansing (November 14, 2003).

For a sobering look at the stock market, see J. Patrick Raines and Charles G. Leathers, *Economists and the Stock Market: Speculative Theories of Stock Market Fluctuations* (Northampton, MA: Edward Elgar, 2000).

For a discussion of the linkages between asset prices and monetary policy, see "Manias and How to Prevent Them: An Interview with Charles Kindleberger" and "Market Volatility and Monetary Policy," by John Balder, Jr., both in *Challenge* (November–December 1997): 21–31 and 32–52, respectively. Also see "Monetary Policy and Asset Prices," by Andrew J. Filardo, *Economic Review of the Federal Reserve Bank of Kansas City* 85:3 (Third Quarter 2000): 11–38.

Technology has played a part in the formation of numerous stock market bubbles. For an in-depth look at technological innovation and stock market bubbles since the early 1900s, see Robert Shiller's *Irrational Exuberance* (Princeton, NJ: Princeton University Press, 2001).

For a historical look at a time when the New York Stock Exchange nearly collapsed, see Alec Benn, *The Unseen Wall Street, 1969–1975* (Westport, CT: Greenwood Publishing Group, 2000).

For a comprehensive view of the stock market and how it affects the economy, see John Charles Pool and Robert L. Frick, *Demystifying the Stock Market* (Winchester, VA: Durell Institute of Monetary Science at Shenandoah University, 1993).

One of the best resources for a layperson to learn about the stock market is William J. O'Neill, *How to Make Money in Stocks: A Winning System in Good Times or Bad*, 3rd ed. (New York: McGraw-Hill, 2002). Another good book is *One Up on Wall Street: How to Use What You Already Know to Make Money in the Market,* by Peter Lynch and John Rothchild, contrib. (New York: Simon and Schuster, 2000).

For a look at "Mutual Funds and the U.S. Equity Market," see the article by the same name by Eric M. Engen and Andreas Lehnert, *Federal Reserve Bulletin* (December 2000): 797–817.

For another point of view, see "The Long-Term Outlook for Stocks: Interview with Peter Diamond," *Challenge* 43:2 (March–April 2000): 6–16.

For an early 1998 article that predicted falling stock prices a few years before a significant downturn, see "Valuation Ratios and the Long-Run Stock Market Outlook," *Journal of Portfolio Management* 24 (Winter 1998): 11–26. Another article along the same line is Nathan S. Balke and Mark E. Wohar, "Why Are Stock Prices So High? Dividend Growth or Discount Factor?" *Working Paper No. 00-01*, Federal Reserve Bank of Dallas (January 2000).

Appendix 16A: The Choice between Stocks and Bonds

In the process of investing and operating on a day-to-day basis, firms experience periods when expenditures exceed receipts. As a result, a firm must make several portfolio decisions regarding the financing of excess spending. First, should the spending be financed internally or externally? **Internal financing** is simply the spending of money balances on hand or the liquidation of financial or real assets owned by the firm to finance the excess. Internal financing is the largest source of funds for business firms.

Internal Financing
Spending money balances on hand or liquidating financial or real assets to finance spending that exceeds current receipts.

External Financing
The financing of spending that exceeds current receipts by expanding either debt or equity.

As for **external financing**, there are two types: expanding equity or expanding debt. Thus, if a firm chooses external financing—perhaps because its financing needs exceed the internal funds available—it must then decide whether to issue new debt and/or equity.

External financing via equity involves issuing shares of common stock, thereby expanding the ownership in the firm. If the new shares are sold to existing shareholders, ownership is not diluted. Indeed, existing shareholders are sometimes given the first option to purchase the new shares. If the firm chooses external financing through borrowing, it must decide whether to issue long-term or short-term debt. For example, the firm must choose between loans or market instruments, such as commercial paper and corporate bonds. In general, each decision is guided primarily by the desire for profit maximization and the existing structure of financial liabilities. A firm will choose the option that minimizes the cost of funds.

For each firm, the prevailing financial environment, the stance of monetary policy, and so forth, will determine the overall cost of funds. The relative cost of alternative sources of financial capital and, therefore, the particular financing decision reached will be influenced by several considerations: (1) the particular type of expenditures being financed, (2) the current financial environment and expectations about the future environment, (3) the firm's financial structure, and (4) the tax laws. Traditionally, borrowing to finance inventories has taken the form of either short-term bank loans or the issuance of commercial paper. The usual maturity of the bank loans or commercial paper is one to six months, which is appropriate because inventories are typically not held for long periods of time. Fluctuations in inventory investment over the business cycle explain much of the variation in short-term debt accumulated by firms. The correlation is not perfect, however. For example, if many firms perceive prevailing long-term rates to be temporarily high relative to short-term rates, some firms will issue short-term debt to finance the initial phases of their investment spending on new capital. These firms expect that long-term interest rates will soon drop, at which point the firms will issue long-term debt to pay off the maturing short-term debt and finance subsequent phases of their investment spending. Thus, we see how current and expected financial environments play a role in firms' financing decisions.

From the mid-1970s until 1991, a substantial portion of externally financed investment spending, which by definition is the acquisition of capital (new plant and equipment), was financed by issuing long-term debt. Why long-term debt instead of equity? The answer is that U.S. tax laws tend to bias the financing decisions of business firms toward debt and away from equity. Interest paid on debt is a tax-deductible cost and thus is subtracted from gross revenues before the corporate income tax is computed. Dividends paid to equity holders, however, are not tax deductible. Dividends must be paid from after-tax earnings.[10] Thus, debt financing will initially be cheaper, on average, than equity financing, which may also entail higher flotation costs. Equity financing also dilutes the ownership of current shareholders.

Debt financing also has a downside. Increasing debt is believed to expose a firm to more risk and therefore weaken its financial structure. The exposure to more risk can ultimately raise the overall cost of capital because the suppliers of funds require higher returns to compensate them for the additional risk.

Leverage Ratio
The ratio of debt to equity on a firm's balance sheet.

The relationship among debt finance, risk, and the cost of capital is rooted in a common measure of the financial structure—the **leverage ratio**, or the ratio of debt to equity on a firm's balance sheet. Other things being equal, the higher the leverage ratio, the greater the risk to bondholders and stockholders. The reason is that if a highly leveraged firm experiences a substantial decline in earnings, it may default on its debt obligations and be forced into bankruptcy, possibly leaving its stockholders with nothing. A firm with a low leverage ratio could weather a decline in earnings by cutting dividends, which are residual claims, not contractual obligations. The leveraged firm does not have this option: It must pay its debt costs or fold. Hence, ceteris paribus, risk-averse investors will typically demand a higher yield on funds they lend to highly leveraged corporations. Firms that have considerable debt relative to equity will find the cost of debt financing (as well as equity financing) to be relatively high. As a result, they may decide to issue equity both to raise funds and to strengthen their balance sheets.

Another reason that firms issued new debt in the 1980s was to acquire the equities of other firms in whole or in part. Often referred to as *mergers and acquisitions*, this activity has sometimes been financed by the issuance of junk bonds that carry yields above those prevailing on higher-rated conventional corporate bonds. In this case, debt increases, but no new investment occurs. Whatever the benefits of this activity, the resulting expansion of debt relative to equities increases the leverage ratio of the corporate sector as a whole. This, in turn, generates concerns about increased risk—that is, the increased vulnerability of individual firms and the economy as a whole to adverse developments.

Starting in 1991 and lasting until early 1994, firms altered the trend of debt financing and issued new shares of stock instead. Because of lower interest rates on CDs, savers poured funds into mutual funds that soaked up the new stock issues. With stocks trading at high values, issuing relatively fewer shares could raise large amounts of funds. By mid-1994, the trend had reversed. From 1994 to the present, companies bought back record amounts of stock and stock buy backs remained brisk in 2004. Companies were using earnings to purchase their own stock rather than to pay dividends. In the bull market of the late 1990s, this activity was also pushing stock prices even higher.

Endnotes

1 "America Bubbles Over," *The Economist* (April 18–24, 1998): 67.

2 Corporations are legal entities that own the assets of the corporation. Stocks represent ownership of the legal entity rather than ownership of the assets directly.

3 Indeed in January 2003, Microsoft announced that it would begin paying dividends for the first time.

4 In September 2003, NYSE Chair Dick Grasso was forced to resign in a flack over his $140,000,000 multiyear compensation package. Many analysts thought the pay for an industry regulator who oversaw the NYSE was excessive.

5 Over time, movements in the Dow have been closely correlated with the overall movement of more broadly based stock market indexes.

6 As you shall see in Chapter 18, the American Stock Exchange also trades options.

7 The NASDAQ merged with the AMEX in March 1998. In June 2003, NASDAQ sold the AMEX to private investors undoing the merger.

8 The NYSE instituted a Pre-Market and After Hours Market in the second half of 2000.

9 The covariance between two variables is a measure of how the variables move together. The variance of a variable is a measure of how a variable moves relative to its mean. In reality, beta is the covariance between a specific stock's return and the market's return, all divided by the variance of the market's return.

10 Historically, dividends were subject to so-called double taxation. They were taxed as part of business income and taxed again as part of household income. Tax law changes in 2003 reduced taxes on dividend income that households receive.

A Closer Look, page 359

a The downward pressure on the U.S. economy was also greatly exacerbated by the attacks on the World Trade Center and the Pentagon on September 11, 2001, and the resulting economic turmoil.

b Dot.com stocks are those of Internet companies, many of which in the 1990s were small start-up companies that had never earned a profit.

c In Chapter 6, we saw that prices of long-term fixed rate debt instruments, including bonds and mortgages, fluctuate a great deal in response to small changes in interest rates. Money market assets are short term and do not experience such price volatility when interest rates change. In this and the next chapter, we are referring primarily to capital market assets.

A Closer Look, page 378

a John Heaton and Deborah Lucas, (1999), "Stock Prices and Fundamentals," http://www.kellogg.nwu.edu/faculty/heaton/research/macroa nnual.pdf

b Robert E. Hall, "The Stock Market and Capital Accumulation," http://www.stanford.edu/~rehall/384page2.html (2000).

c Bart Hobijn and Boyan Jovanovic; "The Information Technology Revolution and the Stock Market: Preliminary Evidence," Mimeo (New York University, 2000); and Boyan Jovanic and Peter L. Rousseau, "Vintage Organization Capital," Mimeo (New York University 2000).

d Joseh Zeira "Informational Overshooting, Booms and Crashes," *Journal of Monetary Economics* 43:1 (1999): 237–257 (1999).

17

CHAPTER SEVENTEEN

The Debt Markets

Learning Objectives

After reading this chapter, you should know:

The characteristics of the bond and mortgage markets and how the markets function

How corporate bond, government bond, and mortgage markets have changed in recent years

The characteristics and advantages of municipals

What government agency securities, mortgage-backed securities, and government-sponsored enterprises are

Bonds and Mortgages: The Major Debt Markets

Bonds (corporate and government) and mortgages are the major long-term financial instruments of the debt market. In Chapters 6 and 7, you saw that small changes in interest rates can cause large changes in the prices of these instruments. The longer the term to maturity, the greater the change in price for any change in the interest rate. In an era of volatile interest rates, price changes can be dramatic and bond and mortgage markets anything but dull. In recent years, there have been other noteworthy trends in both the bond and mortgage markets.

In this chapter we first explore the government and corporate bond markets. What are the characteristics that all bonds have in common? How do the federal government, government agencies, and government-sponsored enterprises affect the bond market? What are the advantages and disadvantages of bonds to firms and to investors? What is the international bond market?

In the second half of the chapter, we look at the mortgage market, which is the largest debt market in the United States.[1] Residential mortgages, which will be our focus, make up the largest segment of the market. How has the mortgage market changed in recent years? What are the roles of the government and government-sponsored enterprises in the mortgage market? What are the risks of investing in mortgages?

The Bond Market

Bonds issued by net borrowers are bought by and sold to net lenders in the bond market. The issuer may be the U.S. government, an agency of the government, a state or local government, a domestic or foreign corporation, or a foreign government. Bonds are debt instruments with an original maturity of more than 10 years that are issued by private and public entities. They normally pay a fixed interest rate, the **coupon rate,** which is stated on the face of the bond. The principal, also called the **par value** or face value of the bond, is repaid in full at maturity. The **coupon payments** are equal to the coupon rate multiplied by the face value of the bond and are usually made every six months.

As first discussed in Chapter 7, two major credit-rating agencies, **Standard & Poor's** and **Moody's Investors Service**, analyze and evaluate bonds and assign them to one of nine risk classes based on the probability that the issuer will fail to pay back the principal and interest in full when due. The credit-rating agencies examine the pattern of revenues and costs experienced by a firm, its degree of leverage (dependence on borrowed funds), its past history of debt redemption, and the volatility of the industry, among other things. A firm with a history of strong earnings, low leverage, and prompt debt redemption would get the highest rating from Moody's and Standard & Poor's. A firm that has experienced net losses, has rising leverage, or has missed some loan payments would be rated much lower.

Moody's and Standard & Poor's also assign ratings to municipal securities issued by state and local governments. Important factors in determining the rating include the tax base, the level of outstanding debt, the current and expected budget situation, and the growth in spending. Bond ratings are beneficial to lenders because they help the lender determine the risk involved in purchasing a specific bond. Bonds rated below investment grade are not recommended for investment and are often referred to as *high-yield* or *junk bonds*, depending on one's perspective. Of course, their high yield results from their riskiness. The accompanying A Closer Look on page 389 discusses some of the recent trends in the bond market.

Coupon Rate
The fixed interest rate stated on the face of a bond.

Par Value
The principal or face value of the bond, which is repaid in full at maturity.

Coupon Payments
The coupon rate on a bond multiplied by the face value of the bond.

Standard & Poor's Investors Service
A credit-rating agency that analyzes and evaluates bonds and assigns them to a particular risk class.

Moody's Investors Service
A credit-rating agency that analyzes and evaluates bonds and assigns them to a particular risk class.

Recent Trends in the Bond Market

In 2003 and 2004, interest rates fell to 45-year lows. As you saw in Chapter 5, interest rates and bond prices are inversely related. Therefore, it should be no surprise to money and banking students that bond markets have been profoundly affected by the low interest rate environment of recent years. Returns to bonds have been high as bond prices have rallied and holders of previously issued bonds made large capital gains.

Lower interest rates also stimulated borrowing, and new debt issues reached record levels in 2003, breaking the previous record set in 2002. New debt issues in U.S. government, agency, and corporate bond markets reached $6.92 trillion in 2003, up from the record $5.41 trillion in 2002. In addition, the mid-2000s bond market experienced several distinct trends.[a]

First, new issues of U.S. corporate bonds rose to $743.6 billion in 2003, up 13.9 percent from 2002. Part of the increase in corporate debt issues occurred late in the year in order to take advantage of the low interest rates. Corporate debt of nonfinancial firms has increased dramatically and, as a share of gross domestic product (GDP), is at an all-time high. Corporate debt relative to GDP (corporate debt/GDP) increased from just under 30 percent in 1960 to about 58 percent in 2003 with corporate debt increasing by 11 percent in 2003. In the 1996–2003 period, outstanding corporate bonds of the nonfinancial sector increased from approximately $2.07 trillion to approximately $2.87 trillion. Some analysts are concerned that the high level of debt could lead to problems for corporations in the future. High debt levels increase the vulnerability of a corporation because a decline in revenues or a spike in interest rates could call into question the corporation's ability to service its debt.

Second, after three years of surpluses and some paying down of the public sector debt in the late 1990s and early 2000s, the federal budget balance reversed course and went into a large deficit position. Falling tax revenues due to the faltering economy and collapses in asset prices that reduced capital gains taxes, combined with a tax cut and increases in government spending to fight the war on terror, caused this reversal. From the end of 1999 to 2001, federal debt owed to the public fell approximately $425 billion only to reverse course. The publicly held federal debt increased from $3,352.7 billion at the end of 2001 to $4,218.7 billion by mid 2004. Net issues of new government securities equaled more than $325 billion in 2003, compared to just over $160 billion in 2002. With an actual federal budget deficit of $413 billion in 2004 and deficits forecasted far out on the horizon, it is expected that new issues of government securities will continue to be very large. Long-term issuances of municipal securities were $135.1 billion in 2003, leading to a record total of $1.9 trillion of outstanding municipal securities.

Third, the issuance of long-term government agency securities also increased to a record $1.27 trillion in 2003, up 21.7 percent from 2002. The strong housing market fostered by low interest rates encouraged this new debt creation. At the end of 2003, outstanding agency securities totaled almost $2.7 trillion. About $1.19 trillion of the $1.27 trillion new issues of agency securities were associated with the housing market. In addition to this, in 2003, new issuances of private mortgage-backed securities increased more than 50 percent from 2002 to $466.9 billion. Other asset-backed securities including those backed by credit card balances, manufactured housing, student loans, automobile loans, equipment leases, and home equity lines of credit, among others, set a new record of $584.2 billion in 2003, up from the 2002 record level of $489.1 billion.

Finally, the inflows of capital to the United States from the rest of the world (foreign) sector to purchase long–term debt instruments continues to increase dramatically. Although the bulk of the inflow has been used to purchase government and agency securities, foreign holdings of U.S. corporate bonds has also increased. During 2003, foreigners purchased $287 billion in Treasury and agency securities, up from about $139 billion in 2002. By mid 2004, foreigners owned about $1.8 trillion of Treasuries and about $720 billion in agency securities.[b] In net, the value of domestic bonds purchased by foreigners grew consistently and far exceeded the value of foreign bonds purchased by U.S. residents. Foreign participation in the U.S. bond markets has contributed to their growth and kept interest rates lower than they would otherwise be. Although concerns have been raised about the impact of reversals in this trend of large capital inflows from abroad, so far there does not seem to be any reversal of the trend.

The Corporate Bond Market

Bond Indenture
A document stating the terms under which a bond is issued.

Trustee
An expert who interprets the provisions of a bond offering for investors and who sees that the terms and condition of the offering are fulfilled.

Debenture Bonds
Bonds with no specific collateral backing but with a general claim on the other unpledged assets of the issuer.

Subordinated Debenture Bonds
Bonds with no collateral backing but with a general claim after debenture bondholders have been paid.

Call Provisions
Provisions spelled out in a bond indenture that allow the issuer to buy back the bonds at a specified price.

Convertible Provisions
Provisions spelled out in a bond indenture that allow investors to convert the bonds to a specific number of shares of common stock.

As the name implies, corporations issue corporate bonds. Investment bankers such as Merrill Lynch, Smith Barney, and Bear Stearn design, market, and underwrite new corporate bond issues. The terms of the offering along with many other provisions are spelled out in the **bond indenture** when the bonds are issued. The indenture is made out to a **trustee** representing the investors who buy the bonds. The trustee usually works for a bond or trust company and is an expert in interpreting the provisions of the offering for the investor. The trustee also sees that the issuer fulfills the terms and conditions of the indenture.

Bonds may be backed by specific collateral such as real or personal property. The collateral can include plant, equipment, and financial assets that the issuing corporation owns. **Debenture bonds** are not backed by specific collateral but, in the event of a default, have a general claim on the issuer's otherwise unpledged assets. Finally, **subordinated debenture bonds** are not backed by collateral and have a general claim after debenture bondholders have been paid. Thus, in the event of a default, owners of subordinated debenture bonds are the last bondholders in line to receive any funds. As expected, other factors being equal, subordinated debenture bonds pay the highest return, followed by debenture bonds, and followed by bonds backed by collateral.

Some bonds also come with financial guarantees issued by insurance companies. The bond issuer pays a premium that guarantees the payment of interest and principal by the insurance company in the event the issuer defaults. In reality, the credit of the guarantor is substituted for the guarantee of the issuer. The bonds are issued at a lower interest rate than otherwise because of the guarantee. It is beneficial to the bond issuer to pay for the financial guarantee if the present value of the interest savings over the life of the bond is higher than the insurance premium.

Most corporate bonds are issued with **call provisions**. Call provisions allow the issuer to buy back the bonds before maturity at a specified price. Bonds tend to be called if interest rates have fallen since the bonds were initially issued. The issuer could issue new bonds at the lower rates to buy back the previously issued bonds. Other corporate bonds offer **convertible provisions** that allow investors to convert the bonds to a specific number of shares of common stock. Bonds that are callable offer higher coupon rates than comparable noncallable bonds, and bonds with convertible provisions offer lower comparable rates.

Some firms also issue **zero-coupon bonds**, which, as their name implies, do not have coupons and do not make coupon payments. Instead, the bonds are sold at a discount with the difference between the amount paid for the bond and the amount received at maturity being equal to the interest.[2] The advantage to the investor is that there is no risk that the interest earned over the life of the bond will have to be reinvested at a lower rate. A disadvantage to the investor is that the interest payments accrue over the life of the loan and taxes must be paid on the amount of the interest earned each year, even though the interest is not paid until the bond matures. An advantage for the corporation is that interest payments are written off on an annual basis, even though they are not paid until the bond matures.

A New York Fed publication on zero-coupon bonds (Fedpoint 42) is available on the Internet at **http://www.newyorkfed.org/aboutthefed/fedpoint/fed42.html**.

The secondary market in corporate bonds is a loosely connected array of brokers and dealers who buy, sell, and take positions in bonds in an over-the-counter market. In an over-the-counter market, brokers and dealers buy and sell bonds through computer links and over telephone lines. Although the bulk of bond trading takes place over the counter, some bonds are also bought and sold on organized exchanges such as the New York Stock Exchange.

Specific bonds trade with varying degrees of liquidity in the secondary market. Other factors being equal, the greater the expected liquidity, the lower the yield. Now would be a good time to read the Cracking the Code features on page 397, which explains how to interpret corporate bond prices and yields as reported in the financial pages of popular newspapers.

Recap   Bonds are debt instruments that may be issued by domestic or foreign governments and corporations. The terms of a corporate bond issue are spelled out by the bond indenture and interpreted by the trustee. Some bonds are backed by real or financial assets that the corporation owns. Debenture bondholders are entitled to be paid before subordinated debenture bondholders but after bondholders with bonds that are backed by specific collateral. Bonds with call provisions allow the issuer to buy back the bonds before maturity. Bonds with convertible provisions allow investors to convert the bonds to a prespecified number of shares of common stock. Zero-coupon bonds are sold at a discount. Secondary markets for bonds are primarily over-the-counter markets.

The Treasury Note and Bond Markets

As you saw in Chapter 5, government securities consist of Treasury bills, notes, and bonds. Bills have an original maturity of one year or less, notes have an original maturity of 2 to 10 years, and bonds have an original maturity more than 10 years. U.S. government (or Treasury) notes and bonds are issued in the primary market by the Bureau of the Public Debt in minimum amounts of $1,000. Historically Treasury notes and bonds were sold at a fixed coupon rate that did not change over the term of the security. Treasury bonds with maturities up to 30 years were sold in regularly scheduled competitive auctions. In October 2001, however, the Treasury suspended the issuance of new 30-year bonds. At the present time, the 10-year note is the newly issued fixed-rate government security with the longest maturity. However, there are longer maturity fixed-rate government bonds outstanding because through October 2001 the Treasury issued 30-year securities that would not mature until 2031. Treasury notes, like T-bills, are sold in other regularly scheduled auctions. The Treasury decides the maturity structure and the amount of the various offerings.

Information regarding Treasury securities and auctions can be found on the Treasury's Internet site at **http://www.treas.gov**.

Treasury notes and bonds are a full faith and credit obligation of the U.S. government. Consequently, investors view these Treasury securities as being free from default risk. The federal government, with its power to tax or issue currency, will definitely pay back the principal and interest as scheduled. Because they are so highly liquid and free of default risk, interest rates on Treasury securities serve as a benchmark to judge the riskiness and liquidity of other securities.

However, Treasury notes and bonds are not free of interest rate risk. If the interest rate goes up after the issuance of securities but before their maturity, the value of the notes and bonds will go down. If they are sold before maturity, the investor will receive less than the face value of the security and experience a capital loss.

The secondary market in Treasury notes and bonds is an over-the-counter market where a group of U.S. government securities dealers stands ready to buy and sell various issues of outstanding securities over the counter. Today Treasury securities are sold in secondary markets somewhere in the world 24 hours a day. An extensive and very active secondary market makes Treasury notes and bonds highly liquid. The dealers' profits stem from the spread between the bid (buying) and asked (selling) prices. In the low interest rate environment of the early 2000s, the Treasury has been buying back previously issued government securities to manage the maturity structure of the federal debt and to reduce government financing costs if outstanding debt can be replaced by debt issued at lower interest rates.

A desirable feature of Treasury bonds is that the interest earned on them is exempt from state income taxes. Not all states have state income taxes, so this feature is particularly beneficial in states with high income tax rates. The Cracking the Code feature on page 399 explains how to interpret the prices of Treasury bonds reported in major newspapers.

Treasury STRIPS
Fixed government securities that allow investors to register and trade ownership of the interest (coupon) payments and the principal separately.

Separate Trading of Registered Interest and Principal Securities, or **Treasury STRIPS** are fixed-rate government securities first offered in 1984 and sold through depository institutions and government securities dealers. All newly issued Treasury fixed-rate notes and bonds with maturities of 10 years or longer are eligible for the STRIPS program. STRIPS allow investors to register and trade ownership of the interest (coupon) payments and the principal amount of the security. The advantage of STRIPS is that the coupon and principal payments can be sold separately at a discount. STRIPS are sold in book entry form, meaning that the security is issued and accounted for electronically. The investor pays less today for the future payment than he or she will receive when the security matures. The interest the investor earns is the difference between what is paid today and what is received at maturity. Because the future payments are sold at a discount, the investor avoids the uncertainty that coupon payments may have to be reinvested at a lower interest rate because rates have fallen since the security was issued. The future payments of the STRIPS securities are direct obligations of the U.S. government.

The New York Fed describes the operation of the Treasury STRIPS program at **http://www.newyorkfed.org/aboutthefed/fedpoint/fed42.html**.

Inflation-Indexed Bonds
Bonds whose principal amounts are adjusted for inflation when coupon payments are made (usually every six months).

An inflation-indexed bond is a more recent hybrid, first offered for sale by the Treasury in January 1997. An **inflation-indexed bond** is one in which the principal amount is adjusted for inflation when an interest (coupon) payment is made, usually every six months. Although the interest rate does not change, the interest payments are based on the inflation-adjusted principal, and the inflation-adjusted principal is received at maturity. (In the event of deflation, the investor receives the original par value of the security.) Inflation-indexed bonds protect the investor from the ravages of inflation. Currently, five-year inflation-indexed securities are auctioned in April and October; 10-year inflation-indexed securities are auctioned in January, April, July, and October;

Cracking the Code

Corporate Bonds

The following table is a typical example of the way bond market information appears in *Barron's*, the weekly financial newspaper. The bonds under the subheading New York Exchange reports some of the more actively traded bonds of the approximately 2,000 bonds traded on the New York Stock Exchange. If we look at the AT&T (American Telephone and Telegraph) bonds, we see that a number of different types of bonds are outstanding. They were issued at different times to finance operations such as investment. Accordingly, all these issues are "used" (or "seasoned") bonds trading in the secondary market. We will focus on the highlighted bond.

New York Exchange

52-Weeks High	52-Weeks Low	Name and Coupon	Cur Yld	Sales $1,000	Weekly High	Weekly Low	Net Close	Net Chg
99 ½	85 ½	AES Cp 4 ½ 05	4.6	380	99	98 ½	98 ½	− ¼
94	43	AMR 9s16	11.9	958	76	72	75 ¾	+ 1 ¼
107 ¼	103 ⅜	AT&T 7s05	6.7	114	104 ³⁄₃₂	104	104	+ ⅜
111 ¼	106 ⅛	AT&T 7 ½ 06	7.0	297	107 ⅜	106 ¾	107	+ ⅝
113 ¾	106 ½	AT&T 7 ¾ 07	7.1	552	108 ⅝	107 ⅞	108 ½	+ 1
109 ⅝	98 ½	AT&T 6s09	6.0	774	100	99 ⅜	100	+ ½
109 ⅜	102 ¾	AT&T 8.35s25	9.0	180	104 ¼	102 ¾	104 ¼	+ 1 ¼
102 ⅝	**84 ½**	**AT&T 6 ½ 29**	**7.2**	**553**	**90 ⅛**	**88**	**90**	**+ 3**

SOURCE: *Barron's* (May 24, 2004): MW33.

First, in column 3, you see the issuing company's name—AT&T. Next to the name is 6½, the coupon yield. It appears on the face of the bond and indicates the amount of interest that AT&T will pay the holder annually; in this case, the 6½ percent (6.5 percent) indicates that $65 of interest will be paid annually (usually in semiannual installments) per $1,000 of face (or par) value of bonds held. The $65 is 6.5 percent of $1,000. Next is *29,* which means that the bond will mature in the year 2029. At that time, AT&T will give the holder of the bond the last interest payment and $1,000 of principal per $1,000 of face (or par) value. As the name suggests, the face value appears on the face of the bond.

The Weekly High, Low, Close and *Net Change* in the last four columns refer to the price of the bond during the week from May 17, 2004, through May 21, 2004. As you will see, the price code in the bond market is different from the price code in the stock market; this is part of a conscious plot to confuse "outsiders." To conserve space in the paper, bond prices are stated as percentages of 100, with 100 representing $1,000 face value. Hence, the closing price for the day was 90, which means $900. The weekly high was 90 ⅛, which means $901.25, and the weekly low was 88, which means $880. The closing price (90) was up 3 from the previous week's closing price. Thus, the previous week's closing price was 87, which means $870. Hence, the price of the bond has increased $30 during the past week. The first two columns give the high and low price that the stock traded at during the past 52 weeks. In this case, the high was 102 ⅝ ($1,026.25) and the low was 84½ ($845).

The fifth column labeled Sales $1,000 simply gives the volume of trading in thousand of dollars. In this case, the 553 means that $553,000 (553 × $1,000) worth of these bonds was traded during the past week. Not so simple is the current yield (Cur Yld) in the fourth column. This bond pays $65 annually to its holder. At the close on this day, someone could have bought the bond for $900. As a result, the current yield on the investment—that is, the bond purchased—would be approximately 7.2 percent ($65/$900 = .0722 = 7.22), which is approximately 7.2 percent). Thus, interest rates have increased since this bond was issued. Only if a bond is selling at 100, or at par value, will the coupon yield be equal to the current yield.

and 20-year inflation-indexed securities are issued in January and July. There are limits to the amounts that households can purchase annually.

Basic information about inflation-indexed bonds can be found at **http://www.publicdebt.treas.gov/sec/seciis.htm**.

Recap   Treasury securities are sold in competitive auctions. They are considered to be free of default risk, and their interest rate serves as a benchmark to judge the risk and liquidity of other financial assets. The secondary market for government securities is a highly developed over-the-counter market. STRIPS are government securities that allow the investor to register and trade ownership of the coupon payments and the principal separately. The principal of inflation-indexed bonds is adjusted for inflation every six months. Although the interest rate doesn't change, the coupon payment is based on the inflation-adjusted amount, and the investor receives the inflation-adjusted principal at maturity.

Municipal Bonds

Municipal Bonds (munis)
Bonds issued by state, county, and local governments to finance public projects such as schools, utilities, roads, and transportation ventures.

Municipal bonds (munis) are bonds issued by state, county, and local governments to finance public projects such as schools, utilities, roads, and transportation ventures. The interest on municipal securities is exempt from federal taxes as well as from state taxes for investors living in the issuing state. This allows the issuer to borrow at a lower rate than if investors had to pay taxes on the interest earned.

Municipal bonds are particularly attractive to taxpayers in high-income tax brackets. The interest rate on munis will gravitate to the rate at which the average investor is indifferent between purchasing munis or purchasing other bonds of comparable maturity, liquidity, and risk on which the interest income is not tax exempt.[3] This rate is depicted in Equation (17-1), where t is the average marginal tax rate, i_b is the rate on comparable bonds, and i_m is the rate on munis.

(17-1)
$$i_b(1 - t) = i_m$$

Taxpayers in a tax bracket higher than the average marginal bracket can earn a higher return by investing in munis. The cost to the state, county, or local government issuer is t percent less than it would be if the interest income were not tax exempt. Thus, if the comparable corporate rate is 8 percent, the average marginal tax bracket is 25 percent, and the muni rate is 6 percent, taxpayers in a tax bracket above 25 percent can earn a higher after-tax return by investing in munis. In addition, in this case, municipalities can borrow at a 2 percent lower rate than were the interest income not tax exempt.

General Obligation Bonds
Municipal bonds to be repaid out of general tax revenues.

Revenue Bonds
Municipal bonds to be repaid out of the revenues from a specific project that the bonds support.

As noted in Chapter 5, municipal bonds may be either *general obligation bonds* or *revenue bonds*. **General obligation bonds** are repaid out of general tax revenues. There has not been a default in the state-issued general obligation municipal bonds market in the last 100 years. This is not true for revenue munis issued by local and county governments. Repayment of **revenue bonds**, in contrast, is tied to the success of a specific project that the bonds support. That is, the bondholder is paid back out of the cash flows of a particular project. There have been defaults on revenue bonds when specific projects did not generate the forecasted revenues.

Government Agency Securities

As first discussed in Chapter 15, **government agency securities** are issued by private enterprises that were publicly chartered by Congress to reduce the cost of borrowing

Cracking the Code

Treasury Bonds

To understand how to read the accompanying table of developments that occurred in the government bond market on April 19, 2004 (taken from *The Wall Street Journal*), look at the highlighted line below. Under Rate (the first column) is 6.000. This is the coupon rate, and it indicates that the holder of this security receives $6 per year for each $100 (face or par value), usually paid in semiannual installments.

Rate	Maturity Mo/Yr	Bid	Asked	Chg	Ask Yld
6.000	Feb 26	109:10	109:11	−9	5.27

SOURCE: *Wall Street Journal* (April 20, 2004): C6.

The maturity date (second column) is Feb 26. This simply indicates that the security will mature in February of the year 2026.

The next two columns give the Bid and Asked prices. The bid price is the price the market maker (dealer) is willing to pay to acquire this security. Prices are quoted in 32nds. Thus, 109:10 bid means 109 10/32, or $109.3125 per each $100. Hence, for a $1,000 bond, you need only to move the decimal point to find that the bid rice is $1,093.125. The asked price is the price the dealer is asking when selling the security. In this case, the asked price is 109:11, which means 109 11/32, or $109.3438 per $100. For a $1,000 bond, the asked price is $1,093.438.

The column Chg shows that the bid for this particular government security decreased 9 on April 19, 2004, as compared with the close on the previous trading day. The change is also reported in 32nds, so the decrease is really 9/32, or $0.281 per $100, or $2.81 for a $1,000 dollar bond.

The last column gives the yield to maturity on an annual basis for this bond. It is 5.27 percent, which is the interest rate, or rate of return, on the bond. The yield to maturity takes into account the dollar return to the investor resulting from the coupon payment ($60 per year per $1,000 face value), the price appreciation or the depreciation between when the security is bought and when it matures, and the price paid.

In this case, there will be a depreciation at maturity; the security is selling at a premium: The market price of $1,093.44 exceeds the face value of $1,000.

Whenever the security sells at a premium, the yield to maturity is less than the coupon rate. Can you explain why the yield to maturity exceeds the coupon rate when the security sells at a discount (market price is less than the face value)?

to certain sectors of the economy. Government agency securities may be divided into two classes: government-sponsored enterprises and federally related institutions securities markets.

Areas where **government-sponsored enterprises (GSEs)** have been established include housing, farming, the savings and loan industry, and student loans. Among others, GSEs include the Federal Home Loan Banks, the Federal National Mortgage Association, the Federal Home Loan Mortgage Corporation, the Farm Credit System, and the Student Loan Marketing Association. All are privately owned and issue long-term securities (bonds) to assist in some aspect of lending,

Government-Sponsored Enterprises (GSEs)
Private enterprises that have been chartered by Congress to reduce the cost of borrowing in such sectors as housing, farming, the savings and loan industry, and student loans.

such as funding mortgage loans, student loans, and farm credit. In most cases, the federal government has no legal obligation to guarantee the timely payment of interest and principal. However, many market participants assume that the government does de facto guarantee the payments. We examine the GSEs that pertain to the mortgage market in more detail later in this chapter.

Government-sponsored enterprises have experienced tremendous growth in the 1990s and 2000s. Credit market debt outstanding, composed mostly of long-term securities, increased from about $525 billion at the end of 1993 to about $2.8 trillion in mid 2004. Thus, the outstanding GSEs securities increased more than 500 percent in just over 10 years.

In addition to government agency securities, the Federal Financing Bank, created in 1973, issues bonds to borrow for several federally related institutions. Among others, these institutions include the Commodity Credit Corporation, the General Services Administration, the Government National Mortgage Association, the Rural Telephone Bank, the Small Business Administration, and the Tennessee Valley Authority. The bonds issued by the Federal Financing Bank are backed by the full faith and credit of the U.S. government.

The yield spread between government agency securities and U.S. government securities reflects differences in liquidity and risk. The yield spread can be significant because secondary markets do not have the breadth and depth of Treasuries and, hence, agency securities are not as liquid as Treasuries.

Recap Municipal securities are bonds issued by state, county, and local governments. The interest income on municipal securities is exempt from federal taxes and from state income taxes for investors living in the state where the municipals were issued. Municipal securities may be either general obligation bonds or revenue bonds. Government agency securities are issued by government-sponsored enterprises and by the Federal Financing Bank.

Mortgage
A long-term debt instrument for which real estate is used as collateral and which results from loans made to individuals or businesses in order to purchase or refinance land, single- or multiple-family residential housing, commercial properties, and farms.

Collateral
The building (structure) or land that will be foreclosed on and repossessed if the borrower fails to make the scheduled payments.

Fixed-Rate Mortgages
Mortgages whose the interest rate remains the same over the life of the loan.

The Anatomy of Mortgages

A **mortgage** is a long-term debt instrument for which real estate is used as **collateral** to secure the loan in the event of a default by the borrower. If the borrower defaults, the property is usually sold to recoup some or all of the losses. Mortgages are assets to the holder (lender) and liabilities to the issuer (borrower) who signs the mortgage agreement. They are similar to bonds, with the caveat that the underlying real property or land serves as collateral.

Mortgages result from loans made to individuals or businesses to purchase land, single- or multiple-family residential housing, commercial properties, and farms. Mortgages may also be made to finance new commercial or residential construction. The building (structure) or land serves as collateral. The bulk of mortgages is made to individuals to purchase residential property. Thus, households are the major borrowers in this market. In mid 2004, single- and multifamily residential mortgages totaled about $8.1 trillion, or 82 percent of all mortgages, which were about $9.9 trillion. In general, borrowers put down a minimum of 5 to 20 percent to purchase a property and take out a mortgage loan for the balance of the purchase price.

Mortgages have either a fixed or a variable interest rate. With **fixed-rate mortgages**, the interest rate does not vary over the life of the loan. Lenders are exposed to an interest rate risk—the risk that nominal interest rates will rise, causing the value of

The International Bond Markets

As financial markets become more globalized, the international bond market plays an increasingly important role in the domestic bond market by augmenting the supply of funds available to the bond market and by increasing the array of bonds available to investors. The international bond market consists of primary and secondary markets for Eurobonds and foreign bonds. We review each here.

Eurobonds

Eurobonds are bonds denominated in a currency other than that of the country where they are marketed. For example, dollar-denominated bonds sold outside the United States are called *Eurobonds*. Like the term *Eurodollar*, the term *Eurobond* has come to mean any bond denominated in the currency of the country from which it was issued rather than that of the country where it is sold. The Eurobond market experienced tremendous growth in the 1980s, 1990s, and 2000s. No longer do domestic net borrowers have to look only to domestic net lenders or domestic financial intermediaries to obtain funds. Likewise, domestic net lenders have opportunities to supply funds denominated in dollars outside the United States. The Eurobond market has greatly expanded the borrowing sources for domestic borrowers. In addition, Eurobonds are less regulated than domestic bonds and offer some tax advantages.

Up to 1984, foreign purchasers of U.S. bonds were subject to a 30 percent withholding tax on all interest payments. Because of this, many Eurobonds were issued through subsidiaries of U.S. corporations in Netherlands Antilles. This location was picked because of a treaty between the United States and Netherlands Antilles that made non-U.S. investors exempt from the withholding tax. This effectively sidestepped the tax and allowed the bonds to be offered at a lower rate. To issue Eurobonds, however, corporations had to have or to establish a financial subsidiary in Netherlands Antilles. This was too costly for many firms. In July 1984, the U.S. government repealed the withholding tax and authorized U.S. corporations to sell bonds directly to non-U.S. investors without the withholding tax. This greatly increased the volume of bonds sold directly to non-U.S. investors.

Foreign Bonds

Unlike Eurobonds, foreign bonds are denominated in the currency of the country in which they are underwritten and sold to investors, although the issuer of the bonds is from a foreign country. An example is a bond issued by a French corporation, denominated in dollars (as opposed to euros), and marketed in the United States by U.S. investment bankers. Foreign bonds denominated in dollars and marketed in the United States are called *Yankee bonds*; foreign bonds denominated in Japanese yen and sold in Japan are called *Samurai bonds*; and foreign bonds denominated in British pound sterling and sold in Great Britain are called *Bulldogs*. Domestic corporations with overseas operations often issue foreign bonds in the countries where the overseas operations are located in order to finance those operations.

The Evolution of the Mortgage Market

Prior to the Great Depression, most mortgages were balloon mortgages on which only interest payments were made on a monthly basis and the entire principal was due at maturity. They required large down payments that averaged about 40 percent of the property value. At the end of the term (usually three to five years), the mortgage was usually renegotiated for a slightly lesser amount. Because of the economic havoc created by the Great Depression, many borrowers could not renegotiate the mortgages, and many lenders failed in the early 1930s. The widespread defaults caused the collapse of the mortgage market. The federal government stepped in and assisted homeowners by taking over the balloon payments and allowing borrowers to spread out the payment of both the principal and interest over a longer period of time. Thus, the first amortized mortgages were introduced. In addition, in 1934, the federal government established the FHA to insure the timely payment of principal and interest on long-term fixed-rate mortgages that met FHA's criteria. In 1944, VA-insured loans, similar to FHA loans, were established; they required no down payments for eligible veterans.

In the two decades after World War II, the mortgage market thrived and was dominated by savings and loan associations that held long-term mortgages funded with short-term deposits. By the late 1960s, an inflationary environment began to cause problems for savings and loans. The need to adjust asset maturities in the face of rising inflation and interest rates underscored the need for a secondary market. With a secondary market, the lender would not have to hold the mortgage until maturity but could sell it in the secondary market. Hence, the interest rate risk would be reduced. In 1968, the government established Ginnie Mae and rechartered Fannie Mae as a privately owned government-sponsored enterprise rather than as a government-owned enterprise. Advances in computer technologies and the emergence of mortgage-backed securities in 1970 fostered the growth of a secondary market.

By the 1980s, mortgage brokers and mortgage bankers were originating many mortgage loans that were then sold off in the secondary market to Fannie Mae, Freddie Mac, and other private issuers of mortgage-backed securities. Mortgage brokers and mortgage bankers originate mortgages but do not hold them as investments. Despite the collapse of the savings and loan industry in the 1980s, mortgage lending continued as other lenders including commercial banks stepped in to fill the void.

From 1982 until mid 2004, the dollar value of outstanding mortgages increased from $1,666.1 billion to $9,884.0 billion, an increase of more than 590 percent in nominal terms. During this same period, the consumer price index increased by about 95 percent, nominal GDP increased about 245 percent, and real GDP increased by about 106 percent. Thus, outstanding mortgages grew at a much faster rate than the overall level of prices and the levels of real and nominal economic activity.

Two other changes are noteworthy. First, in 1982, savings institutions held more than 35 percent of all outstanding mortgages. By mid 2004, savings institutions held only about 10 percent. Commercial banks that held approximately 18 percent of outstanding mortgages in 1982 experienced an increase in their share of all mortgages held to about 25 percent by mid 2004. Both institutions prefer to hold variable-rate mortgages because of the reduced interest rate risk.

Second, the largest holders today of mortgages are GSEs and GSE-backed mortgage pools. In 1982, they held 23 percent of all mortgages. By mid 2004, the percentage had increased to 40 percent. This does not include the mortgages that are federally insured by Ginnie Mae but held by private institutions. Except for insuring the timely payment of principal and interest on VA and FHA loans, the federal government did not play an important role in the mortgage market before 1970. With the creation of Ginnie Mae and Freddie Mac and the growth of Fannie Mae, the federal government has had a major impact on the industry since the early 1970s.[a]

In the mid-2000s, mortgage market activity consists of three distinct functions: originating, investing in, and servicing mortgages. Sometimes one institution performs all three activities. At other times, an institution may perform only one or two of them. For example, a mortgage broker may originate loans only while a bank may originate, invest in, and service the mortgages. A savings and loan may originate the loan, sell it in the secondary market but, continue to service the mortgage for a fee.

Variable-Rate Mortgages
Mortgages whose the interest rate is adjusted periodically to reflect changing market conditions.

fixed-rate mortgages to decline. In addition, if long-term fixed-rate mortgages are funded with short-term deposits, the lending institution can experience a negative cash flow if the costs of liabilities rise above the earnings on assets. As you saw in Chapter 5, with **variable-rate mortgages**, the interest rate is adjusted as other market interest rates change. If rates move up, the interest rate on the mortgages increases, and vice versa. Thus, variable-rate mortgages reduce the interest rate risk of holding long-term mortgages because in the event that interest rates rise, loan payments and interest rates on the mortgages also rise. The interest rate on some variable loans adjusts every month, and others adjust less frequently such as every 6 or 12 months. The rates adjust based on a mark-up or margin over some index that represents the cost of funds for the lender. The interest rates on newly issued variable mortgages is always lower than the comparable newly issued fixed rate mortgage to reward the borrower for accepting the added risk that the rate can go up.

Prepayment Risk
The risk that mortgages will be prepaid early and that the funds will have to be reinvested at a lower return.

An additional risk—the **prepayment risk**—is that mortgages will be prepaid early and that the funds will have to be reinvested at a lower return. This risk increases greatly when interest rates fall, particularly if rates stay low for a significant period of time as borrowers refinance their mortgages to take advantage of the lower rates. This risk is much lower for variable-rate loans than for fixed-rate loans because the interest rate on variable loans will fall along with other rates. Exhibit 17-1 on page 400 summarizes the risks of investing in mortgages.

Unlike a bond whose principal is repaid at maturity, the repayment of the principal on a mortgage is generally spread out over the life of the loan. Each month, a constant monthly payment is made that includes some part of the principal in addition to the interest payment. At the end of the loan, the mortgage has been fully repaid. This is known

Amortization
The paying off of the principal of a loan over the life of the loan.

as **amortization**.[4] Mortgages are usually made for up to 30 years, although in recent years, shorter term mortgages have increased because they result in tremendous interest savings over the life of the loan. In addition, hybrid 30-year mortgages that offer fixed rates for an initial time period, such as 1, 3, 5, 7, or 10 years, and variable rates thereafter have also been developed.

Residential mortgages may also be insured by an agency of the federal government. The insurance guarantees the repayment of the principal and interest in the event that the borrower defaults. This eliminates the credit or default risk for the lender. The two

Default Risk

The risk that the borrower will not make the principal and interest payments as scheduled.

- The longer the term to maturity, the greater the default risk because the more distant future becomes more uncertain.
- The lower the down payment, the greater the default risk. The borrower has less to lose by defaulting.
- If interest rates rise, the default risk on variable-rate loans increases because monthly payments rise and the borrower is less able to afford them.

Interest Rate Risk

The risk that interest rates rise and the value of long-term mortgages declines. If long-term mortgages are funded with short-term deposits, the spread between the earnings on assets and costs of liabilities narrows and may become negative.

- The longer the term to maturity, the greater the interest rate risk.
- Variable-rate loans reduce the interest rate risk.

Prepayment Risk

The risk that mortgages will be prepaid early and that the funds will have to be reinvested at a lower return.

- Prepayment risk increases greatly when interest rates fall, particularly if they stay low for a significant period of time.
- Prepayment risk is much less for variable-rate loans than for fixed-rate loans.

Federal Housing Administration (FHA)
A federal agency that for a .5 percent fee insures mortgage loans made by privately owned financial institutions up to a certain amount if the borrowers meet certain conditions defined by the FHA.

Veterans Administration (VA)
A federal agency that, among other things, insures mortgage loans made by privately owned financial institutions up to a certain amount if the borrowers meet certain conditions, including being military veterans.

Conventional Mortgages
Mortgages made by financial institutions and mortgage brokers without the federal insurance that the principal and interest will be repaid.

federal agencies that guarantee mortgages are the **Federal Housing Administration (FHA)** and the **Veterans Administration (VA)**. For a .5 percent fee, the FHA insures mortgage loans made by privately owned financial institutions up to a certain amount that varies by state and county, depending on average housing costs. In 2005, the typical figure was around $360,000. The loan limit is adjusted each year in response to changes in housing prices. FHA loans are designed to help low-income families purchase homes. Borrowers must meet certain conditions dealing with income and credit as defined by the FHA. With the government guarantee, the lender does not have to worry about the borrower defaulting. VA loans are similar to FHA loans but are designed to insure the principal and interest payments on loans made to veterans. The purpose is to help those who have served the country in the military to purchase homes. FHA and VA loans generally have small or no down payments.

Information about FHA loans is available at **http://www.hud.gov/buying/index.cfm**. Information about VA loans is available at **http://www.homeloans.va.gov/**.

Conventional mortgages have no federal insurance and are made by financial institutions and mortgage brokers. Conventional loans generally require a 5 to 20 percent down payment. Conventional mortgages may or may not require the borrower to purchase private insurance that would make the principal and interest payments in the event the borrower defaults. The borrower pays a higher interest rate to cover the cost of the insurance. Generally, when the down payment or equity in the property is less than 20 percent, lenders require borrowers to obtain private mortgage insurance. Private mortgage insurance is purchased from a privately owned insurance company.

Mortgage rates, the size of mortgage you can afford, and a payment calculator are available on the Internet at **http://www.mortgagequotes.lycos.com**. Another site with similar information is **http://www.mtgprofessor.com/**.

<table>
<tr><td>Recap</td><td>Mortgages are long-term debt instruments used to purchase residential, commercial, and farm properties. The underlying property serves as collateral. Fixed-rate mortgages carry the risk to the lender that nominal interest rates will rise and the value of the mortgages will fall. When the interest rate falls, borrowers will refinance at the lower rate, causing the lender to have to reinvest the funds at a lower rate. The interest rate on variable-rate mortgages is adjusted as market rates change. The principal of a mortgage is generally amortized over the life of the loan. The principal and interest payments may be insured by the FHA or VA, which are agencies of the federal government. Conventional loans have no federal insurance and are made by financial institutions and mortgage brokers. Lenders may require borrowers with conventional loans to obtain private mortgage insurance.</td></tr>
</table>

The Secondary Mortgage Market and Mortgage-Backed Securities

Federal National Mortgage Association (Fannie Mae)
A privately owned government-sponsored enterprise that sells securities and uses the proceeds to buy mortgages primarily from banks.

Government National Mortgage Association (Ginnie Mae)
A government-owned enterprise that guarantees the timely payment of interest and principal on bundles of at least $1 million of standardized mortgages.

Mortgage-Backed Securities
Securities backed by a pool of mortgages; they have a low default risk and provide a steady stream of income.

Secondary markets trade previously issued financial claims. Prior to 1970, only mortgages insured by the FHA or VA were sold in secondary markets, and these were sold directly to investors. The amount of market activity was very small. Congress had created the **Federal National Mortgage Association (Fannie Mae)** in 1938 but did not establish a secondary market for FHA and VA loans until 1972. Fannie Mae issued bonds and bought FHA- and VA-insured mortgages. Still the market did not grow to any significant extent and was even declining because of a decrease in VA loans.

In 1968, Congress created the **Government National Mortgage Association (GNMA, or Ginnie Mae)**. In 1970, Ginnie Mae began a program through which it guaranteed the timely payment of interest and principal on *bundles* of $1 million or more of standardized mortgages. Small denomination mortgages (mortgages up to the FHA and VA limits) were standardized with regard to the debt-to-income ratios of borrowers and the loan-to-value ratios of properties. The standardized mortgages were packaged together in a bundle to be resold in secondary markets. Thus, Ginnie Mae guaranteed (for a fee) that the mortgage bundles would be repaid. The guarantee was backed up by the full faith and credit of the U.S. government. Ginnie Mae fostered the creation of large secondary markets that increased the liquidity of previously illiquid mortgages.

The secondary market in mortgages created by the Ginnie Mae guarantee operates as follows: Private financial institutions such as banks or savings and loans gather or pool several Ginnie Mae federally guaranteed mortgages into a bundle of, say, $1 million. They then sell all or parts of the $1 million security, called a **mortgage-backed security**, to third-party investors such as pension funds, mutual funds, or individual investors. The principal and interest on the mortgage-backed security are paid from the payments that borrowers make on the original mortgages. If investors need their funds back before the security matures, they can sell them in a secondary market for mortgage-backed securities. The secondary market for mortgage-backed securities operates similar to the secondary market in corporate bonds.

Despite the lack of default risk because of the government guarantee, Ginnie Mae securities are subject to an interest rate risk. Namely, because they are long-term instruments, if the interest rate rises after the securities have been issued, the value of the securities will fall.

Find information on the operations of the GNMA (Ginnie Mae) at **http://www.ginniemae.gov**.

In 1970, Congress authorized Fannie Mae to purchase conventional (non-VA- or non-FHA-insured) mortgages. Congress also created the **Federal Home Loan Mortgage Corporation (Freddie Mac)** to lend further support to the VA, FHA, and conventional mortgage markets. Congress hoped to make housing more available by increasing the funds flowing into mortgages. The goal, which remains the same today, was to expand the opportunities for low- and moderate-income families to purchase homes. Although Fannie Mae purchased and held mortgages, it did not pool the mortgages to create a mortgage-backed security until 1981. Freddie Mac issued its first mortgage-backed security in 1971. It resulted from a pool of conventional mortgages. As you saw in Chapter 15, Fannie Mae primarily buys the mortgages of banks while Freddie Mac primarily buys the mortgages of thrifts.

Fannie Mae and Freddie Mac are government-sponsored enterprises (GSEs). They are exempt from state and local corporate income taxes and have a $2.25 billion line of credit with the U.S. Treasury. Fannie Mae and Freddie Mac provide loanable funds to the housing sector. They purchase conventional loans, package or pool the mortgages together, and issue mortgage-backed securities (also called *government agency securities*) using the pool of mortgages as collateral. The mortgages purchased by Fannie Mae and Freddie Mac may also be directly held by Fannie Mae and Freddie Mac as investments instead of being packaged and sold as mortgage-backed securities.

Investors who purchase Fannie Mae and Freddie Mac mortgage-backed securities can sell them in secondary markets if funds are needed before the securities mature. The secondary markets for mortgage-backed securities are created by market makers who buy and sell previously issued mortgage-backed securities. Some mortgage-backed securities are traded on organized exchanges.

In mid 2004, the amount outstanding of federally related mortgage-backed securities totaled more $3.5 trillion, up from $1.2 trillion in 1991 and $.18 trillion in 1982. Thus, these markets have experienced spectacular growth in the last two decades and, as discussed in Chapter 13, may pose potential risks to the financial system in the event of widespread defaults in the mortgage markets.

Information about Fannie Mae and Freddie Mac can be found on the Internet at **http://www.fanniemae.com** and **http://www.freddiemac.com**.

Collateralized Mortgage Obligations (CMOs)

As noted previously, investors in mortgage-backed securities face the risk that the mortgages will be prepaid before they mature because the property is sold or refinanced and that the return will fall short of expectations. To reduce this risk, collateralized mortgage obligations have been developed by Freddie Mac. **Collateralized mortgage obligations** redirect the cash flows (principal and interest) of mortgage-backed securities to various classes of bondholders, thus creating financial instruments with varying prepayment risks and varying returns. Those who are most risk adverse can choose an instrument whose principal will soon be repaid. Those who are willing to bear more risk can choose an instrument whose principal will not be repaid until later and, hence, is subject to a greater prepayment risk. In exchange for more prepayment risk, the investor receives a higher return. Needless to say, such provisions make attractive choices available to a wider range of investors.

Private Mortgage-Backed Securities

In 1984, some private groups started to issue their own mortgage-backed securities. The new securities did not rely on the backing of Ginnie Mae and were not issued by corporations such as Fannie Mae or Freddie Mac that had ties to the federal government. Such issuers of private mortgage-backed securities include, among others, commercial banks, mortgage bankers, and investment banking firms. Privately issued mortgage-backed securities may also be sold in secondary markets. Again, the secondary markets are created by market makers who trade the previously issued securities. In mid 2004, the total amount of outstanding debt issued by private mortgage pools exceeded $1.2 trillion, up from $11 billion in 1984 and $110 billion in 1991. Thus, like Fannie Mae and Freddie Mac securities, privately issued mortgage-backed securities have also exploded in recent years. Securities issued by private issuers are rated by the major credit-rating agencies. The credit rating may also be improved by obtaining insurance that guarantees the timely payments of principal and interest on the securities.

Recap   Fannie Mae and Freddie Mac are GSEs that issue mortgage-backed (agency) securities and use the proceeds to purchase mortgages. Ginnie Mae guarantees the timely payment of principal and interest on mortgage-backed securities put together by private lenders. Ginnie Mae securities have an explicit government guarantee. Other private groups issue mortgage-backed securities without government involvement. Secondary markets trade previously issued mortgage-backed securities. Collateralized mortgage obligations redirect the cash flows (principal and interest) of mortgage-backed securities to various classes of bondholders, thus creating financial instruments with varying prepayment risks and varying returns.

This completes our look at the bond and mortgage markets. This chapter contains two appendices on the pricing of bonds and mortgages. In the next chapter, we look at financial forwards, futures, and option agreements.

Summary of Major Points

1. Bonds are debt instruments issued by the U.S. government; an agency of the government; a state, county or local government; a domestic or foreign corporation, or a foreign government. The coupon payment is based on the par (face) value multiplied by the coupon rate. Bonds are rated by Moody's and Standard and Poor's with regard to creditworthiness.

2. The terms of a corporate bond issue are spelled out in the bond indenture. Some corporate bonds are backed by real or financial assets. Debenture bonds and subordinated debenture bonds are not. Most corporate bond issues have call provisions that allow the issuer to buy back the securities before maturity at a prespecified price. Corporations also issue zero-coupon bonds that do not pay interest but are sold at a discount. Secondary markets trade previously issued corporate bonds.

3. Treasury securities are considered to be free from default risk. The secondary market for government securities is the largest secondary market in the world. Treasury bonds are subject to an interest rate risk. In October 2001, the Treasury suspended new issues of

30-year securities. At the present time, the 10-year security is the longest maturity of newly issued fixed-rate securities.

4. STRIPS allow the coupon and principal payments of government securities to be sold separately at a discount. The principal amount of an indexed bond is adjusted for inflation when an interest (coupon) payment is made. The interest rate does not change, but the interest payments are based on the inflation-adjusted principal. The Treasury issues 5-, 10-, and 20-year inflation-indexed securities.

5. Municipal bonds are issued by state and local governments. Interest income on municipal securities is exempt from federal taxes and from state taxes for investors living in the issuing state. General obligation bonds are repaid out of general tax revenues. Revenue bonds are repaid from the revenues of a specific project that the bonds support. Government agency securities are issued by private enterprises that are publicly chartered by Congress to reduce the cost of borrowing in specific areas.

6. Bond markets have grown significantly, fueled by increases in nonfinancial corporate bonds and increases in bonds issued by the Treasury and government-sponsored enterprises. Foreign entities have made substantial net purchases of domestic bonds, increasing the supply of funds flowing into this market.

7. Mortgages are long-term debt instruments used to purchase residential, commercial, and farm properties. The underlying property serves as collateral that the debt will be repaid. The principal of the loan is generally amortized over its life.

8. The timely payment of the principal and interest on a mortgage may also be insured for a fee by an agency of the federal government. The purpose of FHA-insured loans is to help low-income families purchase homes. The purpose of VA loans is to help veterans purchase homes. Conventional mortgages are made by financial institutions without government insurance.

9. Mortgages have a default risk, an interest rate risk, and a prepayment risk. The prepayment risk is the risk that the borrower will repay the loan early and that the funds will have to be reinvested at a lower rate.

10. With fixed-rate mortgages, the interest rate remains the same over the life of the loan. With variable-interest rate mortgages, the interest rate fluctuates over the life of the loan according to the general level of interest rates.

11. In recent decades, the government has become much more active in the mortgage market by guaranteeing the repayment of Ginnie Mae mortgages and sponsoring Fannie Mae and Freddie Mac. Fannie Mae and Freddie Mac are privately owned, government-sponsored enterprises that issue mortgage-backed (agency) securities and use the proceeds to purchase mortgage loans. Private groups also issue mortgage-backed securities without an explicit or implicit government guarantee. Secondary markets exist that trade previously issued mortgage-backed securities.

12. The price of a bond is the present value of the future cash flows associated with the bond. The discount factor used to determine the price of a bond includes a risk-free rate and a risk premium. Treasury bonds are considered to pay a risk-free rate of return. The risk premium encompasses both economywide and firm- or industry-specific risks. Economywide factors include the stance of monetary policy, expected inflation, and the level of economic activity. The major firm or industry factors include the capital structure of the firm, the economic outlook for the firm, and the credit rating of the bond issuance. (*See Appendix 17A.*)

13. The price of a mortgage is the discounted value of the future stream of monthly payments over the life of the instrument. When the interest rate increases, the prices of long-term mortgage securities decrease, and vice versa. Prices of mortgage-backed securities are determined by the prices of the mortgages that make up the pool that backs the security. (*See Appendix 17B.*)

14. The discount factor used to determine the price of a mortgage or mortgage-back security includes a risk-free rate, a risk premium, and a premium for the higher servicing costs that mortgages entail. The risk premium includes the risk that the mortgage may be prepaid early when investment opportunities for the lender are less favorable. It also includes compensation for the lower liquidity of mortgages due to a less-developed secondary market. (*See Appendix 17B.*)

Key Terms

Review Questions

1. Define *par (face) value, coupon rate, coupon payment,* and *current yield.* What are *call provisions* and *convertible provisions*, and how do they affect the interest rates on newly issued securities?

2. What is a bond indenture? What is the role of the trustee?

3. What role do Moody's and Standard & Poor's Investors Services play in the bond market?

4. What is the difference between debenture bonds, subordinated debenture bonds, and bonds backed by specific collateral? What are zero-coupon bonds?

5. What are inflation-indexed bonds? How do they reduce the risk of holding long-term bonds? Does the interest rate on inflation-indexed bonds change after they have been issued?

6. Why are interest rates on Treasury securities used as benchmarks to judge the riskiness and liquidity of other securities?

7. What are the advantages of investing in STRIPS rather than Treasury securities that make regular coupon payments?

8. Are revenue bonds as safe as general obligation bonds?

9. What are the reasons for differences in interest rates between Treasury securities and government agency securities? Between Treasuries and municipals? When will a bond sell in the secondary market for its face value?

10. How is a mortgage similar to a bond? How is it different? What is the difference between a fixed-interest rate and variable-interest rate loan? What is amortization?

11. Explain the process by which a mortgage-backed security is created. What roles do Ginnie Mae, Fannie Mae, and Freddie Mac play?

12. If Sandi and Dave repay their mortgage early because they are refinancing or selling their home, what is the risk for the lender?

13. How can investing in a collateralized mortgage obligation entail less risk than investing in a mortgage-backed security? Can it ever entail more risk?

14. How would a fall in interest rates affect the value of previously issued mortgages?

15. What is the difference between the secondary market in mortgages and the secondary market in mortgage-backed securities?

16. Discuss what will happen to the discount factors used to determine prices of previously issued bonds sold in secondary markets, given the following scenarios (*see Appendix 17A*):
    a. A company's earnings report comes in much lower than expected.
    b. Your college is suffering from declining enrollments, particularly among students who want to live on campus. Revenue bonds have been issued to finance your college dorm.
    c. Fed policy turns expansionary.
    d. The performance of the economy is particularly strong.

17. What factors are important in determining the price of a previously issued bond? (*See Appendix 17A.*)

18. Discuss what would happen to the discount factor for mortgages under the following circumstances (*see Appendix 17B*):
    a. A recession is expected in the near future.
    b. The Fed has taken action to raise interest rates.
    c. International financial crises have caused an inflow of funds into the United States.
    d. The federal government is running a larger surplus than expected.

19. Technological advances have reduced the servicing costs on loans. What would happen to the discount factor applied to value mortgages and mortgage-backed securities and why? (*See Appendix 17B.*)

Analytical Questions

Questions marked with an icon are objective in nature. They can be completed with a short answer or number.

20. Can you explain why the bond in the Cracking the Code box on page 395 is selling at such a large premium above par?

21. A Treasury bond pays a 7.25 percent coupon yield. What is the coupon payment per $1,000 face value?

22. If the interest rate on a corporate bond is 10 percent, in equilibrium, what will be the rate on a muni with comparable risk, maturity, and liquidity if the average marginal tax rate is 20 percent?

23. Assume that the risk-free rate is 5 percent and the risk premium for investing in mortgages is 2 percent. Also assume that it costs approximately 1 percent to service a mortgage loan. What will the discount factor for mortgages be? (*See Appendix 17B.*)

24. Will the following events increase, decrease, or leave the mortgage rate unchanged? (See *Appendix 17B.*)
a. The Fed lowers the interest rate because of a slowdown in economic activity.
b. Technological changes reduce the costs of servicing mortgage loans.
c. The default rate on mortgages increases because of falling property values.

Internet Exercises

1. http://www.federalreserve.gov/releases/medterm contains information about 10-year medium-term corporate notes. In the most recent year for which there is data, what percent of newly issued notes were investment grade? How does the amount compare to the previous year? How many firms issued medium-term notes? Click on "Tables" at the bottom of the page. What are some of the trends in this market?

2. http://research.stlouisfed.org/fred2/categories/22/151 tracks 157 series of different interest rates. Compare and contrast trends in the 30-year conventional mortgage rate, the bank prime rate, the 10-year Treasury rate, the Aaa corporate bond rate, and the 10-year Treasury inflation-indexed rate.

3. Go to the Freddie Mac Internet site at http://www.freddiemac.com.
   a. Click on the "news and information" link. Scroll down to the Economic and Housing Outlook.
      • Summarize the most recent report.
      • How is the housing market faring?
      • What about interest rates and Fed policy?
      • Summarize any information about new or previously issued Freddie Mac securities.

4. Go to http://www.mtgprofessor.com. What is the monthly mortgage payment on a $500,000 mortgage amortized over 30 years? over 15 years? Assuming that the borrower has no other debts, what is the income needed to qualify for an 8 percent mortgage on a $200,000 house with 20 percent down? Next assume that the borrower has additional car, credit card, and student loan debt payments of $700 per month. What is the income needed to qualify now?

Suggested Readings

For a recent look at inflation-indexed debt, see Brian Sack and Robert Elsasser, "Treasury Inflation-Indexed Debt": A Review of the U.S. Experience," *Economic Policy Review*, Federal Reserve Bank of New York (May 2004): 47–63.

For a complete look at all aspects of the bond market, see Frank J. Fabozzi, *Bond Markets: Analysis and Strategies,* 5th ed. (Upper Saddle River, NJ: Prentice Hall, 2004).

For a more thorough discussion of inflation-indexed bonds, see Scott E. Hein and Jeffrey M. Mercer "Are TIPS Really Tax Disadvantaged? Rethinking the Tax Treatment of U.S. Treasury Inflation-Indexed Securities," *Working Paper,* Federal Reserve Bank of Atlanta, 2003–9 (July 2003); and Pu Shen, "Features and Risks of Treasury Inflation Protection Securities," *Economic Review of the Federal Reserve Bank of Kansas City* 83:1 (First Quarter 1998): 23–38.

For a discussion of high-yield (junk) bonds, see Glenn Yago, *Beyond Junk Bonds: Expanding High-Yield Markets* (New York: Oxford University Press, 2003).

For an article that gives some perspective on the international bond market, see Jane D'Arista, "Assessing International Banking and Bond Markets," *Capital Flows Monitor* (December 19, 2000).

"House Price Bubbles" are the subject of the *Federal Reserve Bank of San Francisco Economic Letter,* by John Krainer (March 7, 2003). It is available on the Internet at **http://www. frbsf.org/publications/economics/letter/2003/el2003-06.html**

Mortgage-backed securities are the subject of "Remarks by Chairman Alan Greenspan" before a conference on mortgage markets and economic activity sponsored by America's Community Bankers, Washington, D.C. (November 2, 1999). The remarks are available on the Fed's Internet site at **http:// www.federalreserve.gov/boarddocs/speeches/1999/19 991102.htm.** Another article on mortgage-backed securities is Wayne Passmore, "The GSE Implicit Subsidy and Value of Government Ambiguity" *Board of Governors of the Federal Reserve System, Finance and Economic Discussion Series,* 2003-64 (December 2003).

Other articles on mortgages are Paul S. Calem and Stanley D. Longhofer, "Anatomy of a Fair-Lending Exam: The Uses and Limitations of Statistics," *Finance and Economics Discussion Series No. 2000-15,* Board of Governors of the Federal Reserve System (2000); Joe Mattey, "B2B E-Commerce in Residential Mortgages," *FRBSF Economic Letter No. 2000-23,* Federal Reserve Bank of San Francisco (July 28, 2000); Stanley D. Longhofer and Paul S. Calem, "Mortgage Brokers and Fair Lending," *Economic Commentary,* Federal Reserve Bank of Cleveland (May 15, 1999); and Joe Mattey, "Mortgage Interest Rates, Valuation, and Prepayment Risk," *Economic Letter No. 98-30,* Federal Reserve Bank of San Francisco (October 9, 1998).

Appendix 17A: Factors That Affect Bond Prices

As you first saw in Chapter 6, the present value of the future income stream determines the price at which a bond currently trades and is determined by the current interest rate, not the coupon rate. When interest rates change, prices of previously issued bonds change.

To find its present value and, thus, the price at which the bond trades in financial markets, we need to compute the present value of each coupon payment and the present value of the final repayment of the face value on the maturity date. The appropriate discount factor is the current interest rate on a security of equal risk, liquidity, and maturity.

The formula for the price of a previously issued bond is depicted in Equation (17A-1):

(17A-1) $$P = C_1/(1 + i)^1 + C_2/(1 + i)^2 + \ldots + (C_n + i)^n + F/(1 + i)^n$$

where P = the price (present value) of the bond

C = the coupon payment on the bond (C_1 in year 1, C_2 in year 2, etc.)

F = the face or par value of the bond

i = the interest rate

n = the number of years to maturity (on a five-year bond, $n = 5$)

You can see that the price of a bond is equal to its par value only when the coupon rate is equal to the current interest rate.

The formula in Equation (17A-1) for determining bond prices is based on annual coupon payments. In reality, bonds usually make semiannual coupon payments.

When a bond pays semiannual coupon payments of $C/2$ (assuming that C is the annual coupon payment) and when this bond has n years to maturity, then $2 \times n$ payments (two payments per n year) will be made. The final payment at the end of n years will be equal to F. To find the present value (P) of the stream of income, we divide the interest rate (i) by 2, because two payments of $i/2$ over the course of the year will be equal to i. For example, if the coupon rate were 8 percent, then two semiannual payments of 4 percent would approximate an 8 percent annual return. The approximate discount factor for the final payment (F) is again $i/2$ because we are considering $2n$ periods.

Equation (17A-2) becomes

(17A-3) $P = C/2/(1 + i/2)^1 + C/2/(1 + i/2)^{2n} + \ldots + (C/2 + i/2)^n + F/(1 + i/2)^{2n}$

where $P =$ the price (present value) of the bond
$C/2 =$ the semiannual coupon payment on the bond
$F =$ the face or par value of the bond
$i =$ the interest rate
$2n =$ the number of six-month periods to maturity (on a bond with five years to maturity
$n = 10$)

Note that we used the word *approximate* because semiannual coupon payments of 4 percent would be more than an 8 percent annual return if the effects of compounding are taken into account. That is, because the coupon payment made in the first half of the year would earn interest during the second six-month period, the annual return would actually be more than 8 percent.

In the case of bonds, the expected future cash flows (the coupon payment and the repayment of the face value at maturity) are known with certainty unless the corporation or government entity runs into financial difficulties and cannot meet its obligations. That is, unless the issuer defaults, the interest payments and the principal payments are known in advance and there is no chance that they will be more or less. This is different from the case of stocks whose cash flow payments in the form of dividends are uncertain.

Because of the federal government's power to print money and to tax, Treasuries are considered to be default risk free, and the long-term government bond rate has been regarded as the risk-free rate. In the case of Treasuries, the current Treasury bond rate is the discount factor that is used to find the prices of bonds with equivalent maturities. Thus, to find the price an investor would be willing to pay for a stream of income from a Treasury that has 10 years to maturity, the appropriate discount factor to use is the 10-year Treasury bond rate.

Many factors affect the risk-free rate. One of the most important is the stance of monetary policy. If the Fed increases the supply of reserves, short-term interest rates fall, and the supply of credit is expanded; long-term interest rates will usually fall but by a smaller amount. Changes in inflationary expectations and the level of economic activity also affect long-term risk-free interest rates. If it is expected that inflation will increase in the coming years, then bond purchasers will require—and borrowers will be willing to pay—an inflation premium to compensate for the loss in purchasing power. Likewise, if income is increasing, this increases the demand for loanable funds and puts upward pressure on interest rates. In the real world, these factors are interrelated. For example, expansionary monetary policy may cause market participants to expect higher inflation. Rather than leading to lower interest rates, interest rates may rise despite the expansionary monetary policy. Likewise, a recession brought on by higher oil prices may lead to higher interest rates if the impact of the higher oil prices affects inflationary expectations more than the drop in income does. Other factors such as international capital flows and the amount of government borrowing also impact interest rates.

In the case of bonds that are not default risk free, investors require that a risk premium be added to the risk-free return. The sum of the risk-free return plus the risk premium will equal the appropriate discount factor to use in determining the price of a bond, as depicted in Equation (17A-2).

(17A-2)
$$d = R_F + R_P$$

where d is the discount factor, R_F is the risk-free rate, and R_P is the risk premium.

The question that remains is how the risk premium is determined. That is, what is the risk premium that investors require as compensation in order to purchase the bonds rather than Treasuries? A major factor that affects the ability of the bond issuer to make payments as prescribed is the level of economic activity. In a booming economy, sales, revenues, and cash flows all facilitate the timely payment of the corporation's obligations. Likewise, in a recession or depression, cash flows may fall short of what's needed to meet scheduled payments.

The capital structure of a firm is composed of debt and equity. Debt reflects borrowing, whereas equity reflects ownership in the form of stocks. The riskiness of a firm's capital structure is reflected by the firm's debt relative to its equity. Other things being equal, the higher the debt relative to equity, the greater the risk to bondholders and the higher the risk premium will be. The reason is that if a highly leveraged firm experiences a substantial decline in earnings, it may default on its debt obligations and be forced into

17A-1

Factors That Affect the Discount Factor for Bonds

Factors That Affect the Risk-Free Rate

- The stance of monetary policy
- Changes in inflationary expectations
- Changes in the level of economic activity
- Changes in capital inflows
- Changes in government borrowing

Factors That Affect the Risk Premium

- The credit rating of the bond as determined by Moody's and Standard & Poor's
- The economic outlook
- The capital structure of the firm
- Other firm-specific conditions
- Losses in international markets

bankruptcy. A firm with low debt relative to equity could weather a decline in earnings by cutting dividends to stockholders, which are residual claims, not contractual obligations. The highly leveraged firm does not have this option: It must pay its debt costs or fold. Therefore, firms that have considerable debt relative to equity will find the cost of debt financing relatively high.

Finally, there can be other firm- or industry-specific conditions that can affect the ability of a corporation to meet its debt obligations. To the extent that these factors exist, the risk premium is affected. Some of these factors are labor disputes, lawsuits such as those against the tobacco industry, losses in international markets, and oil shortages.

As you may have guessed, the credit rating of the issuing corporation will affect the risk premium because it should capture the firm, industry, and economic risk factors.

The factors that affect the risk-free return and the risk premium are summarized in Exhibit 17A-1 on page 409.

Present-value tables and financial calculators can be used to simplify the process of finding bond prices.

Recap   The price of a bond is the discounted value of the future stream of income over the life of the bond. The discount factor used to determine the price of a bond includes a risk-free rate and a risk premium. Treasury bonds are considered to pay a risk-free rate of return. The risk premium encompasses both economywide and firm- or industry-specific risks.

Appendix 17B: Determinants of the Price of Mortgages in Secondary Markets

A large and active secondary market exists for mortgages and mortgage-backed securities. In this appendix, we discuss how the price of a previously issued mortgage is determined. Because mortgage-backed securities are, as is obvious, backed by mortgages, we will also be able to conclude how the prices of mortgage-backed securities are determined in secondary markets.

Like bonds, the price of a previously issued mortgage is simply the present value of the future stream of income from the ownership of the security. This consists of the monthly payment stream that includes both an interest and principal payment as depicted in Equation (17B-1).

(17B-1) $$P_M = MP/(1 + d_M)^n$$

where

$\quad P_M =$ the price at which the security will trade in the secondary market
$\quad MP =$ the monthly payment (including both principal and interest)
$\quad d_M =$ the monthly discount factor required by lenders in this market
$\quad n =$ the number of months remaining on the loan

Once the mortgage has been made, the original interest rate becomes irrelevant. Only the remaining monthly payments and the current discount factor are relevant in determining the mortgage's present value and, hence, the price at which the mortgage will trade.

Note that in Equation (17B-1), because we are considering monthly payments instead of annual payments, d_M represents the monthly discount factor. To find the monthly discount factor, d_M, we merely divide the annualized discount factor, D_M, by 12. For example, a mortgage with five years remaining to maturity would have 60 more monthly payments, payment 1 through 60 spread over five years. If the annualized discount factor is 9 percent, the monthly discount factor is .75 percent (9/12). The payment at the end of the first remaining year is the 12th payment and the present value of this payment is $MP/(1 + .075)^{12}$. If annual payments (AP) were made instead of monthly payments, there would be five annual payments remaining, and the present value at the end of the first remaining year would be $AP/(1 + .09)^1$.

To find the price at which the mortgage will trade in financial markets, we need to compute the present value of each monthly payment remaining. The appropriate discount factor is the current interest rate on a security of equal risk, liquidity, servicing costs, and maturity. As noted before, servicing costs are the costs associated with collecting the monthly payments.

Because mortgages require the handling of monthly payments of principal and interest, mortgages have higher servicing costs than Treasury securities that make semi-annual coupon payments. Lenders in the mortgage market must be compensated for these higher costs.

As summarized in Equation (17B-2), the annualized discount factor that is used to determine the present value includes three components: a risk-free return, a risk premium, and a premium for the higher servicing costs that mortgages entail.

(17B-2)
$$D_M = r_F + r_P + r_{SC}$$

The risk-free return is composed of the return on a Treasury security of comparable maturity.[5] When the risk-free interest rate changes, the discount factor and, hence, the prices of previously issued mortgages also change.

The risk premium includes the return that the investor needs to be compensated for given the increased riskiness of owning mortgages. The risk premium includes compensation to the lender for the following possibilities:

- The borrower will default.
- The loan will be prepaid early when reinvestment possibilities for the lender are less favorable than when the mortgage was originally made.
- The lower liquidity of mortgages compared to Treasury securities will cause the lender to experience losses.

When the mortgage is federally insured, the risk premium will be lower than otherwise because the default risk is zero. In this case, the risk premium will include compensation for the prepayment risk and the lower liquidity of mortgages.

Treasury securities are considered to be default risk free, and the long-term government bond rate has been regarded as the risk-free interest rate. As noted earlier, the 10-year Treasury note rate has recently replaced the 30-year Treasury bond rate as the benchmark risk-free rate.

Many factors affect the risk free rate. One of the most important factors is the stance of monetary policy. If the Fed increases the supply of reserves, short-term interest rates fall and the supply of credit expands. Ceteris paribus, long-term interest rates will fall but usually not by as much as short-term rates. Changes in inflationary expectations and the level of economic activity also affect the long-term risk-free interest rate. If it is expected that inflation will increase in the coming years, lenders will require and borrowers will be willing to pay an inflation premium to compensate for the loss in purchasing power. Likewise, if income is increasing, this increases the demand for loanable funds and, ceteris paribus, puts upward pressure on interest rates.

In the real world, the factors that affect the risk-free interest rate are interrelated. For example, expansionary monetary policy may cause market participants to expect higher inflation. Rather than leading to lower interest rates, interest rates may rise de-

17B-1
Factors That Affect the Discount Factor for Mortgages

Factors That Affect the Risk-Free Rate

- The stance of monetary policy
- Changes in inflationary expectations
- Changes in the economic outlook and the level of economic activity
- Changes in government borrowing

Factors That Affect the Risk Premium

- Changes in the economic outlook and the level of economic activity (pertains to uninsured mortgages only)
- The prepayment risk that the mortgage will be prepaid early and that the lenders' reinvestment options will be less desirable than when the original mortgage was made (pertains to insured and uninsured mortgages)
- Changes in the relative liquidity of mortgages and mortgage-backed securities relative to Treasury securities

Factors That Affect Servicing Costs

- Any factors that affect the servicing costs of the loan such as changes in technology that reduce servicing costs

---

spite the expansionary monetary policy. Likewise, a recession brought on by higher oil prices may lead to higher interest rates if the impact of the higher oil prices affects inflationary expectations more than the drop in income. Other factors such as international capital flows and the amount of government borrowing also impact interest rates.

The risk premium with which investors need to be compensated in order to purchase the mortgages is affected by the borrower's ability to make the monthly payment. For insured mortgages, the risk premium is much lower than for uninsured mortgages. For uninsured mortgages, a major factor affecting the risk premium is the level of economic activity. In a booming economy, incomes and economic activity are increasing, thus reducing the number of defaults in the mortgage market. Likewise, in a booming economy, interest rates rise as does the prepayment risk. The reverse is true in downturns.

Changes in technology due to innovations reduce servicing costs. An example of such an innovation is the development of automatic payment deductions from a borrower's checking account. This saves the costs of sending out monthly statements and collecting and processing checks.

The factors that affect the discount factor are summarized in Exhibit 17B-1.

Note that as the economic outlook and the level of economic activity improve, the risk-free rate rises while the risk premium falls, and vice versa. Hopefully, you can explain why.

Recap   The price of a mortgage is the discounted value of the future stream of monthly payments over the remaining life of the loan. The price of a mortgage-backed security is based on the prices of the mortgages in the pool that backs the security. The discount factor includes a risk-free rate, a risk premium, and a premium for the higher servicing costs that mortgages entail. Treasury securities are considered to pay a risk-free rate of return. The risk premium encompasses economywide risks, the risk that the mortgage may be prepaid early when investment opportunities for the lender are less favorable, and a premium for the lower liquidity of mortgages. The premium for the higher servicing costs of mortgages is affected by changes in technology that reduce servicing costs.

Endnotes

1 Even though outstanding mortgages are the largest debt instrument the value of equities (stocks) has in recent years exceeded the value of mortgages by a substantial amount. The reason is that as new mortgages are issued, old mortgages continue to mature, whereas equities have no maturity date. For example, on June 30, 2004, the outstanding value of domestic equities was just under $16 trillion while the outstanding value of mortgages was about $9.9 trillion.

2 Zero-coupon bonds are similar to Treasury bills that are also sold at a discount.

3 As discussed in Chapter 7, the marginal tax rate is the tax rate on the last dollar of taxable income. Because the United States has a progressive income tax, the tax rate rises as income rises. Taxpayers, depending on their individual incomes, are in different marginal tax brackets, some high and some low. The average marginal tax rate is somewhere between the high and the low marginal tax brackets for all taxpayers. Because of substitution, the interest rate on municipal securities will gravitate to the rate that makes the average taxpayer (in the average marginal tax bracket) indifferent between municipals and similarly rated corporate securities.

4 The alternative to an amortized loan would be to make interest-only payments and to repay the principal in a balloon payment at the end of the loan. Although common prior to the Great Depression, this is unusual, but is becoming more common again today in the mortgage market.

5 The comparable maturity for a Treasury security and a mortgage are not the same as the terms to maturity. For example, because a 30-year mortgage payment includes both a principal and interest payment each month, the comparable term of the mortgage will actually be less than a 30-year Treasury that does not repay any of the principal until the end of 30 years.

A Closer Look, page 389

a *Research Quarterly*, The Bond Market Association, February 2004.

b *Flow of Funds Accounts of the United States, Z.1*, Board of Governors of the Federal Reserve System September 16, 2004: 22 and 67.

Looking Back, page 398

a *Flow of Funds Accounts of the United States, Z.1*, Board of Governors of the Federal Reserve System (September 16, 2004).

Never let the future disturb you. You will meet it, if you have to, with the same weapons of reason which today arm you against the present.

—Marcus Aurelius

18

Forward, Futures, and Options Agreements

Learning Objectives

After reading this chapter, you should know:

The difference between a forward contract and a futures contract

The scope and nature of organized financial futures and options markets

The relationship between spot and futures prices

The difference between put and call options

The reasons for the astounding growth of financial forward, futures, and options agreements in recent years

A Single Solution

It is 5:10 P.M. on Friday, the last day of a month in late 2005. The CEO's meeting with his staff has run later than usual, and a sense of uneasiness pervades the room. Doz-All, a newly emerging conglomerate, is involved in diversified financial and manufacturing areas. The mortgage banking division has committed to make $10 million in loans at 8 percent to be funded in 60 days; $25 million in bonds issued 10 years ago for start-up money is maturing in three months, and the company plans to pay off the existing bond-holders by issuing new bonds. The newly formed international division is converting $20 million to Japanese yen to invest in Japanese securities over the next few months. The stock adviser points out that although the corporation has a diversified portfolio, there is a general fear that the market may be heading down.

All of these situations expose the corporation to risks—the risks that interest rates (and hence bond prices), stock prices, or foreign exchange rates will move in an unexpected direction causing the corporation to experience a loss. The senior vice president appears tired. She cannot help but perceive that the risks associated with everyday business seem to have escalated in recent years.

In the past two decades, financial prices, such as interest rates, stock prices, and exchange rates, have become more volatile. This increased volatility has created greater risks.[1] The chief financial officer (CFO) is a young business school graduate whom senior management has come to rely on. He assures them that there are ways to deal with the increased risk, although doing so will cost money. In this case, however, his recommendations are the source of the tension felt in the room. To reduce Doz-All's risk exposure, the CFO is recommending that the corporation use the financial forward, futures, or options markets. In days long past, futures and options on agricultural products and commodities were considered to be highly risky, and forward agreements, which could be costly, had other drawbacks. Could the new financial forward, futures, and options markets that have emerged in the past 30 years actually be used to reduce or manage the risks inherent in everyday business?

In this chapter, we explore financial forward, futures, and options contracts. We shall see that risk-averse financial intermediaries and corporations increasingly use these markets in their everyday business for just this purpose—to reduce the risks associated with price fluctuations. The adage "necessity is the mother of invention" aptly applies because financial forward, futures, and options markets have experienced incredible growth in the past three decades in response to increased price volatility.

Forward Transactions

Financial Forward Transactions
Transactions in which the terms, including price, are completed today for a transaction that will occur in the future.

Financial forward transactions can be used to hedge the risks associated with price changes of any financial instrument. Although virtually all financial prices have become more volatile in recent decades, forward agreements are primarily and most widely used to deal with the risks created by price fluctuations in foreign exchange markets. Thus, foreign exchange forward markets are the focus of this section.

The exchange rate is the price of one currency in terms of another. As you have seen in earlier chapters, *exchange rate risk* is the risk that changes in the exchange rate will cause someone to experience unexpected losses. The more unpredictable and unstable that exchange rates are, the greater the exchange rate risk is. Exchange rates have become much more volatile since the major industrialized countries adopted the flexible exchange rate system in 1973.[2] Also, as international trade has increased and as financial markets have become more globalized, the demand for foreign financial instruments has soared. This has led to the increased trading of foreign currencies with more volatile prices and a dramatic increase in exchange rate risk for market participants. These participants have found ways to **hedge** this greater exchange rate risk through the development of forward markets.

In Chapter 9, we discussed how exchange rates are determined by supply and demand in the foreign exchange market. In that chapter, we were referring to *spot rates*—that is, the exchange rates of foreign currency for immediate delivery. In financial forward agreements, the terms (including prices and amounts) are completed today for a transaction that will occur on a specified date in the future. Financial intermediaries, acting as brokers or agents, can link up two parties in a forward transaction. As noted earlier, the most common type of *financial* forward agreement is the forward agreement in foreign currencies (foreign exchange). These agreements have been highly developed by large commercial banks to provide services to their customers who will need or receive foreign currencies on a future date. In this case, the bank is one of the two parties in the forward transaction. Commercial banks also sometimes hold large amounts of foreign currencies and hence can use forward markets to hedge their own exchange rate risk.

Large banks have many customers that operate on a global basis. These customers may know that they will receive and/or need foreign currencies on a future date. The foreign currencies are used by the bank's customers to purchase or to pay for goods, services, and financial instruments. For example, perhaps one U.S. company will be liquidating its holding of French stocks in six months to pay off a maturing domestic bond issue while another U.S. company plans to increase its investment in Europe. The first company will be receiving euros; the latter company will need euros. Another customer may be an importer, an exporter, or a securities firm that sells domestic and foreign financial instruments globally. Large banks buy and sell not only foreign exchange at spot rates for present delivery but also foreign exchange for future delivery at a **forward rate**. The forward rate for a foreign currency will gravitate toward the *expected* future spot exchange rate for that currency. The forward rate is affected by the same factors that affect spot rates as discussed in Chapter 9. These factors, which affect the supply and demand for foreign exchange, include expected inflation and interest rate differentials between the two countries, the economic outlook in both countries, and domestic and foreign monetary and fiscal policies. The forward rate can be used as a market-based forecast of the future spot rate.

Forward Rate
The price today for a delivery on
a future date.

A bank buys foreign exchange forward agreements from some customers and sells foreign exchange forward agreements to others. The bank engages in these forward agreements to earn profits and to provide a service to its customers who wish to hedge the exchange rate risk. The profit comes from buying the currency at one price, the bid price, and selling the currency at a slightly higher price, the asked price. Large banks have a long history of providing exchange facilities for foreign currencies as a service to their customers. These currency exchange facilities that facilitated trade predate flexible exchange rates. Forward agreements arranged by large banks were a natural outgrowth of this service under the post-1973 flexible exchange rate system.

A typical foreign exchange forward agreement works as follows: The forward agreement is a contract with a bank to purchase or sell on a future date a specific amount of foreign exchange at a forward rate (exchange rate) determined today.

For example, assume that a customer of Citibank is to receive 1 million euros in six months and another customer will need 1 million euros in six months. Both customers know the present spot rate but are worried that unknown future changes in the exchange rate could reduce their profits. Citibank can enter into a forward agreement with each that will hedge this risk. The agreements will also earn a small profit for Citibank. Just as in spot markets, Citibank buys forward contracts at one rate and sells forward contracts at a slightly higher rate. The difference between the bid and asked prices represents the profit margin on the transaction. If the forward rate for Citibank to buy euros from a customer with a delivery date in six months is 1 euro = $1.109, then 1 million euros can be sold to the bank by a customer for $1,109,000 (1,000,000 × 1 euro = 1,000,000 × $1.109). Thus, 1 euro = $1.109, which is the bid price.[3] A customer that will be receiving 1 million euros in six months may enter into this transaction to reduce the risk that the euro will depreciate and that she will receiver fewer than $1,109,000 in exchange for the 1 million euro. For example, if the euro depreciated to 1 euro = $1.108, then, without the forward agreement, the customer would be able to sell the euro for only $1,108,000 instead of $1,109,000.

Assume that the forward rate (exchange rate) for Citibank to sell euros with a delivery date in six months is 1 euro = $1.11. This is the forward asked price. A customer that will need 1 million euros in six months may enter into a forward agreement in order to reduce exchange rate risk. The 1 million euros will cost the customer $1,110,000 (1,000,000 × 1 euro = 1,000,000 × $1.11) in six months. A customer needing 1 million euros in six months may enter into this transaction to reduce the risk that the euro will appreciate and that he will have to pay more than $1,110,000 for 1 million euros. For example, without the forward agreement, if the euro appreciated to 1 euro = $1.112, then 1 million euros would cost the customer $1,112,000 instead of $1,110,000.

The profit to Citibank in the forward markets is, as noted previously, just as in spot markets: Citibank buys at one forward rate (the bid price) and sells at a slightly higher forward rate (the asked price). The bank makes a profit on the difference between the bid and asked prices multiplied by the number of euros bought and sold. In this case, the profit on the forward transactions in 1 million euros is $1,000 ($1,110,000 − $1,109,000). Exhibit 18-1 below highlights these relationships.

The one-, three-, and six-month forward rates for major foreign currencies such as the euro, the British pound, the Canadian dollar, the Japanese yen, and the Swiss franc are reported daily in *The Wall Street Journal* along with the spot exchange rates. The accompanying Cracking the Code feature on page 419 discusses how to read the spot and forward exchange rates reported by the *Journal* on April 20, 2004. Note that for both spot and forward rates, only one exchange rate is reported. This is the midrange rate between the bid and the asked prices.

If the bid and asked spot exchange rates six months from now are equal to the current forward rates, the customers both buying and selling forward agreements would be no better or no worse off financially. In addition, they may have slept more soundly at night because of the reduced exchange rate risk. In six months, the actual bid and asked spot exchange rates may be more or less than the forward rates today. In this case, one of the customers will be worse off and one will be better off than without the forward agreement, depending on how rates diverged from what was expected. However, both customers are willing to give up the opportunity to gain in exchange for reducing the risk of being worse off.

The problem is that today it is not known which one will lose and which one will gain without the forward agreement. Both customers can reduce the uncertainty of the

---

18-1

Citibank Engages in Forward Agreements

6-Month Forward Rates Today	
Bid (buy) Price	Asked (sell) Price
1 euro = $1.109	1 euro = $1.11
1,000,000 euros = $1,109,000	1,000,000 euros = $1,110,000

Profit to Citibank from buying and selling 1,000,000 euros at today's forward rates = $1,000 = ($1,110,000 − $1,109,000)

Foreign Exchange Spot and Forward Rate Quotations

The following foreign exchange quotations are from *The Wall Street Journal* on Tuesday, April 20, 2004. Spot rates are reported for about 55 countries, but forward rates are reported for only the major foreign currencies including the euro, the British pound, the Canadian dollar, the Japanese yen, and the Swiss franc. For both spot and forward exchange rates, the rate that is reported is the midrange rate between the bid and the asked prices. The name of the currency and the country it is from appear in column 1. Columns 2 and 3 give the midrange rates for the current and previous days in terms of U.S. dollar per unit of foreign currency. Columns 4 and 5 give the midrange rates in terms of foreign currency per U.S. dollar.

	U.S. $ Equiv		Currency Per U.S. $	
Country	Mon	Fri	Mon	Fri
U.K (Pound)	1.8075	1.7967	.5533	.5566
1-month forward	1.8029	1.7922	.5547	.5580
3-months forward	1.7932	1.7825	.5622	.5610
6-months forward	*1.7787*	*1.7681*	*.5622*	*.5656*

SOURCE: *Wall Street Journal* (April 20, 2004): C 10.

For example, the column for the six-month forward rate for the British pound is highlighted. On Monday, April 19, 2004, the midrange of the six-month forward bid and asked rates was 1 British pound = $1.7787. The pound had appreciated slightly from its rate of 1 British pound = $1.7681 the previous trading day, Friday, April 16, 2004. Columns 4 and 5 are merely the reciprocals of columns 2 and 3. Thus, on April 19, the forward rate was $1 = .5622 British pounds (1 British pound/1.7787 = $1.7787/1.7787 = $1). Likewise, on April 16, the forward rate was $1 = .5656 (1 British pound/1.7681 = $1.7681/1.7681 = $1). Note that $1 is worth less on April 19 than on April 16 and, hence, has depreciated slightly.

future exchange rate by engaging in a forward agreement with Citibank today. Thus, for reducing the possibility of a loss, they are both giving up the opportunity to gain. However, as noted earlier, the forward rate will converge to the market's general expectation of the future spot rate. Thus, market participants will give up the opportunity to gain only if there were unexpected changes in the future spot rate.

An example may help to clarify. As depicted in Exhibit 18-2 on page 420, assume the current bid and asked spot rates in six months are 1 euro = $1.099 and 1 euro = $1.1. This is different from the respective forward rates of 1 euro = $1.109 and 1 euro = $1.11 of six months previous. Without the forward agreement, Customer A receiving the 1 million euros would be able to exchange them for only $1,099,000, or $10,000 less than the $1,109,000 the euros could be exchanged for with the forward agreement. This customer would be better off with the forward agreement and worse off without it. Without the forward agreement, Customer B, needing or buying the 1 million euros, would pay only $1,100,000, or $10,000 less than the $1,110,000 the euro would cost if she entered into the forward agreement. This customer would be worse off with the forward agreement and better off without it. However, because the future rate is uncertain, with the forward agreement both have hedged the risk of being worse off.

	Current Spot Rates	Forward Rates Six Months Previous
Bid	1 euro = $1.099	1 euro = $1.109
Asked	1 euro = $1.100	1 euro = $1.110

No forward agreement (exchanges at current spot rates):
Customer A receives 1,000,000 euros and exchanges them for $1,099,000
Customer B needs 1,000,000 euros and pays $1,100,000 for them

With forward agreement entered into six months earlier:
Customer A receives 1,000,000 euros and exchanges them for $1,109,000
Customer B needs 1,000,000 euros and exchanges $1,110,000 for them

Reconciling
With no forward agreement, Customer A receives $10,000 less ($1,099,000 versus $1,109,000), and Customer B pays $10,000 less ($1,100,000 versus $1,110,000). Customer A is worse off and Customer B is better off.

With the forward agreement, Customer A receives $10,000 more ($1,109,000 versus $1,099,000), and Customer B pays $10,000 more ($1,110,000 versus $1,100,000). Customer A is better off and Customer B is worse off.

Any market participant that holds supplies of foreign currencies is exposed to exchange rate risk. This includes financial and nonfinancial firms that operate in many countries with many different currencies. Because the forward agreements arranged between banks and their customers are often not perfectly offsetting matches, the bank can be exposed to an exchange rate risk. For example, if one customer is to receive 1 million euros in six months and another needs 900,000 euros in six months, the bank can still arrange the forward agreements with both but is then subject to an exchange rate risk on the difference between what the receiving customer will receive and what the customer who needs euros will need. In this case, the amount of exposure to the bank is for 100,000 euros (1 million euros received less 900,000 euros needed). If the euro depreciates from 1 euro = $1.11 to 1 euro = $1.10, then 100,000 euros would fall in value $1,000 from $111,000 to $110,000. Likewise, if the euro had appreciated from 1 euro = $1.11 to 1 euro = $1.12, then 100,000 euros would increase in value $1,000 from $111,000 to $112,000.

Forward agreements can also be used to speculate about future exchange rates. The speculator may be a customer of the bank or the bank itself. If the speculator thought that the future spot price in six months would be lower than the current six-month forward rate, he would enter into a forward agreement to sell foreign exchange at the higher forward rate. If the speculator was correct, he could enter the spot market in six months and purchase the foreign exchange at a lower price than he sold it for in the forward market. Likewise, if the speculator thought that the future spot price of the currency would be higher than the current forward rate, he would enter into a forward agreement to buy the currency in six months. If correct, the speculator buys the currency in the forward market at a lower price than what it can be resold for in the spot market. Indeed, it is the buying and selling by speculators that causes the forward rate to converge to the market's expectation of future spot prices.

Limitations of Forward Agreements

As you have seen, forward transactions can reduce the risks of future price changes, which reduce profit. But, as with most things in life, appearances may not reveal the whole picture. The forward market in foreign currencies described previously works well because large banks have developed the market. For other financial instruments such as stocks and bonds, forward markets are not so highly developed. In this case, there are two general problems with arranging forward agreements:

1. Finding partners may be difficult; the transactions costs may be high and outweigh the possible gain. Finding partners who want the exact amount of the financial instrument on the exact date can be difficult at best.[4]

2. One party to the agreement may default, that is, not keep its part of the agreement. The party who is likely to default is the one that is worse off down the road by entering into the forward agreement earlier. Getting compliance may require legal action and may be costly if not impossible.[5]

Although volatile prices of financial instruments other than foreign exchange may lead to large losses that could be reduced with forward agreements, the forward markets are not highly developed. Consequently, the costs of finding a partner and then enforcing the forward contract may be prohibitively high. But all hope is not lost! To minimize the costs and risks involved with arranging forward transactions, standardized agreements called **futures contracts** have been developed for many types of financial instruments including stocks, government securities, and foreign currencies.

Futures Contracts
Standardized agreements in agricultural and commodity markets to trade a fixed amount of the product or commodity on specific dates in the future at a price determined today.

Recap

Forward contracts are agreements to buy or sell something at a price determined today for delivery on a later date. Forward agreements between individual market participants are arranged by intermediaries. In financial markets, forward contracts in the most widely traded currencies have been established by large commercial banks. In addition to buying and selling foreign currencies at spot prices, the banks also buy and sell the major currencies at forward rates. In this case, the bank is an actual partner in the transaction. When there are not exact offsetting transactions, the bank has some exposure to exchange rate risk. Foreign currency forward agreements can be used to hedge exchange rate risk or to speculate about future currency values. Forward markets are not highly developed for financial instruments other than foreign currencies.

Financial Futures

Because agricultural and commodity markets historically have experienced large price fluctuations, futures markets in these products evolved more than a century ago. In the case of agricultural products, demand is relatively stable, and price fluctuations are related to weather: bad weather greatly reduces supply and leads to higher prices, and vice versa. Prices of commodities such as oil, copper, and gold fluctuate because of large changes in supply or demand.

As noted earlier, prices of financial securities, stocks, and foreign currencies have become unstable during the past 30 years. Consequently, **financial futures markets**, which trade futures in financial instruments, appeared and are now used by most major financial institutions and other large corporations to manage the risk of losses because of price fluctuations of financial instruments.

Financial futures are contracts in which two parties agree to trade standardized quantities of financial instruments on standardized future dates, according to the terms (including the price) that are determined today. Financial futures can be used to reduce the risk associated with future price changes of financial instruments.

Futures contracts differ from forward agreements in that the amounts and delivery dates are standardized, whereas for forward agreements they are not. Forward agree-

Financial Futures Markets
Organized markets that trade financial futures including the Chicago Board of Trade, the Chicago Mercantile Exchange, and the London International Financial Futures Exchange.

Financial Futures
Standardized futures contracts that trade financial instruments on a future date according to terms (including the price) determined today.

ments for specific amounts and dates are negotiated with commercial banks and other financial intermediaries. Futures contracts with standardized amounts and dates are traded on the floors of organized exchanges for a small fee.

Financial futures markets trade a wide variety of contracts in underlying financial instruments such as government securities (Treasury bills, notes, and bonds), stock market indexes, Eurodollars, and numerous foreign currencies.[6] The contracts are traded on major exchanges around the world. For example, financial futures are traded on the Chicago Board of Trade, the Financial Instrument Exchange Division of the New York Cotton Exchange, the International Monetary Market of the Chicago Mercantile Exchange, the London International Financial Futures Exchange, the Sydney Futures Exchange, and the Singapore International Monetary Exchange. In early 2004, EUREX US became the first foreign-owned futures and options market to begin trading on U.S. soil. The purpose of EUREX is to provide more direct access to investment opportunities in U.S. Treasury futures for European customers. Futures markets for various currencies and U.S. government securities are available virtually 24 hours a day, somewhere in the world. Often these markets use electronic communication networks to provide information and execute trades. Thus, as you saw in Chapter 16, the floor of the exchange may soon be replaced by a system of electronic trading where futures trading can be executed 24 hours a day in "cyberspace" from a personal computer. The accompanying A Closer Look feature below lists information about the most actively traded financial futures.

A Closer Look

Futures, Exchanges That Trade Financial Futures, Minimum Amounts, and Open Interest

Consider for a moment the many types of futures markets that exist: grains and oil seeds (including corn, oats, soybeans, wheat, barley, flaxseed, and canola); livestock and meat (including cattle, hogs, and pork bellies); food and fibers (including cocoa, coffee, sugar, cotton, and orange juice); metals and petroleum (including copper, gold, platinum, palladium, silver, crude oil, heating oil, gasoline, natural gas, brent crude, and gas oil); interest rates (including 10-year agency and 10-year, 5-year, and 2-year U.S. Treasury notes, 30-day federal funds, Eurodollars, one-month LIBOR, Euroyen and Treasury bonds); currencies (including Australian dollars, British pounds, Canadian dollars, euros, Japanese yen, Mexican pesos, and Swiss francs); indexes (including Dow Jones Industrial and mini Dow Jones, Nasdaq 100, S&P Composite, and S&P Mini).[a]

Grain and commodities futures have been around for some 100 years. Financial futures including interest rate, currencies, and stock index futures are a relatively recent innovation (during the last 30 years) that has experienced tremendous growth.

The accompanying table shows some of the major financial futures, the contract size, the futures exchange, and the total open interest (number of outstanding contracts) as of May 21, 2004.

Type of Future	Contract Size	Exchange* at Which Trading Occurs	Open Interest May 21, 2004
Interest Rates			
10-year agency notes	$100,000	CBOT	50,718
10-year U.S. Treasury notes	$100,000	CBOT	1,323,506
5-year U.S. Treasury notes	$100,000	CBOT	1,070,881
2-year U.S. Treasury notes	$200,000	CBOT	198,614
30-day federal funds	$5 million	CBOT	503,197
Eurodollar	$1 million	CME	6,145,285
LIBOR—one month	$3 million	CME	604,925
Euroyen	100 million yen	CME	44,852
U.S. Treasury bonds	$100,000	CBOT	545,536
Currencies			
Australian dollar	$100,000 Australian	CME	39,118
British pound	£62,500 British	CME	44,513
Canadian dollar	$100,000 Canadian	CME	82,938
Euro	125,000 euro	CME	145,502
Japanese yen	12.5 million yen	CME	108,447
Mexican peso	500,000 pesos	CME	71,195
Swiss franc	125,000 S. francs	CME	36,766
Index Futures			
Dow Jones Industrial	$10 × DJIA	CBOT	45,925
Mini Dow Jones $5	$5 × Index	CBOT	56,768
Nasdaq 100	$100 × Index	CME	80,277
S&P Composite	$250 × Index	CME	586,543
S&P Mini	$50 × Index	CME	585,115

*Exchanges: CBOT (Chicago Board of Trade); CME (Chicago Mercantile Exchange).
SOURCE: *Barron's* (May 24, 2004): MW34.

Find information on the trading of futures and options at the Chicago Mercantile Exchange at **http://www.cme.com/**.

A futures contract trades a fixed amount of the instrument for delivery on specific dates in the future. For example, Treasury bond futures trade in contracts of $100,000 face value for delivery in March, June, September, and December over the course of the following year. There are four prices today for delivery of $100,000 of Treasury bonds on the four future dates. Likewise, Treasury bill futures, which trade in contract amounts of $1 million, are also available for delivery on the same dates at prices set today. Note that the futures contract can be bought or sold on any given day between now and the future delivery date. The predicament for the buyers and sellers is that the spot price on the delivery date may be different from the futures price agreed on today.

The seller of a September $1 million T-bill future has the right and obligation to deliver $1 million in T-bills in September for a price set today. The purchaser of the $1 million September T-bill future has the right and obligation to buy $1 million in T-bills in

September at a price set today. Hence, both parties know the terms of a transaction that will occur in September, a point in time in the future, and the risk to either party of a price change between now and then is eliminated. The buyer rarely takes physical possession of the securities on the delivery date. Likewise, the seller rarely delivers. If the price changes, the buyer or the seller merely settles up financially for any changes in value.[7]

If the price of T-bills rises between now and September, the seller has given up an opportunity to make a profit because she agreed to sell at the lower futures price established today. If the spot price falls in September, the buyer has given up the right to purchase the securities at the lower price in the spot market because he agreed to the higher futures price today. Without the futures contract, however, either party could lose if the price changes in an adverse direction.

Let's consider a simple numerical example. Assume that the futures price is $96,000 for the delivery of $100,000 of Treasury bonds next December. The seller agrees to deliver, and the buyer agrees to pay this much. (Make sure you are clear that December is the *delivery date* of the securities, not their *maturity date*, which may be several years hence.) When December actually arrives, if the spot price is $97,000, the seller still must make good on the contract for $96,000, even though he could sell them for $97,000 in the spot market. The buyer still pays $96,000 for the Treasury bond contract, even though she would have had to pay $97,000 for the same contract in the spot market. In this example, the seller is worse off by $1,000, and the buyer is better off by $1,000. (Remember that the securities are not usually physically delivered, but a financial settlement is made between the buyer and the seller.)

However, if the spot price is $95,000 when December arrives, the seller gets to sell at $96,000 even though he would get only $95,000 in the spot market. The buyer has to pay $96,000 even though she could have paid $95,000 to buy in the spot market. The seller is better off by $1,000, and the buyer is worse off by $1,000. Again, a financial settlement is usually made between the buyer and the seller.

The point is that at the time of the agreement, neither party knows what the spot price will be on the future date. Both were willing to accept the known outcome as opposed to an uncertain future spot price even though after the fact one could have been better off without the agreement. Because the contracts are standardized with respect to type (90-day T-bills, 10-year Treasury notes, and the like) and quantity ($1 million and $100,000 contract sizes), and because volume is large, brokerage fees for buying and selling futures are relatively small.

So far, we have been discussing futures in which the parties are hedging, or reducing, the risk of a price change in the future. Futures markets can also be used for speculation. Consider the case in which ABC Government Securities (a firm that specializes in trading government securities) believes that the spot price of T-bills is going to be much higher in September than today's futures price. If ABC holds this belief firmly, it can put its money behind the belief and buy a futures contract. If ABC is correct, it can resell the futures contract at the higher spot price on the delivery date. Contrarily, if the firm believes the price will be lower, it can sell a futures contract to make its profit.[8] Futures prices are reported daily in most major newspapers. Now would be a good time to read the accompanying Cracking the Code feature on page 425 on futures prices.

Because financial futures are written only in standardized contract amounts for delivery on a few specific dates, a perfect offsetting transaction between the buyer and seller, as in forward markets, is rarely made. For example, suppose a bank has loans that will be repaid next August and suspects that interest rates are heading down. The bank may have to reinvest the funds at a lower rate. The bank can buy a September T-bill futures contract today to hedge this risk. If interest rates do move down, the funds will be reinvested in August at a lower rate, but the reduction in earnings from the level the bank

Cracking the Code

Futures Prices

Toward the back of the Money and Investing section of *The Wall Street Journal,* you will find a table entitled "Futures Prices." Part of the Interest Rate Futures section of this table for Tuesday, June 1, 2004, is reproduced here. We can crack the code to futures prices by looking at the highlighted row starting on the left with July under "30 Day Federal Funds (CBT)."

30 Day Federal Funds (CBT)—$5,000,000; 100–daily average

	Open	High	Low	Settle	Chg	Lifetime High	Lifetime Low	Open Int
June	98.985	98.985	98.980	98.980	—	99.000	98.400	107,899
July	**98.77**	**98.77**	**98.76**	**98.77**	**−.01**	**98.98**	**98.18**	**198,990**
Aug	98.57	98.57	98.55	98.56	0.02	98.95	98.10	60,427

SOURCE: *Wall Street Journal* (June 2, 2004): C12.

The 98.77 in column 2 means that on June 1, the agreed-upon opening price for July delivery of Treasury bills was 98.77 percent of the face value of the contract. The low price for that day (column 4) was 98.76. The high for the day (column 3) was 98.77 percent, and the settle for the day (column 5) was 98.77. The −.01 in column 6 indicates that there was a negative .01 change from the previous day. To verify this, we would have to check the preceding day's newspaper to see whether the settle price was 98.78. Remember that 30-day federal funds sell at a discount, which is reflected in the price being less than 100 percent of the contract amount. For the fed funds contract, the contract amount (face value) is $5 million. The open interest is the number of contracts outstanding for the month of July—in this case, 198,990.

is currently receiving will be at least (partially) offset by the profit made on the September futures contract. (Recall that T-bills are sold at a discount, and, as with other securities, if interest rates go down, the price of the newly issued T-bills goes up.) Even though the standardized contracts do not provide an exact match (either by amount or by date), they do provide an offsetting transaction that reduces risk. Because a perfect match need not be found, the high transactions costs of finding a unique trading partner, as in forward agreements, are greatly reduced.

The futures price is set by bidding and offering in an auction-like setting on the floor of the exchange. Each financial instrument that is traded usually has its own **pit** (trading area on the floor) where authorized brokers gather to buy and sell for their customers. Bid and asked prices (to buy or sell) are called out until the brokers become aware of the prices in the market. The most favorable transactions (from the point of view of both the buyers and sellers) are consummated. Once an agreement is struck in the pit, the transaction becomes depersonalized, and the agents of the buyer and seller never meet again for that transaction. Instead, a **clearinghouse**, operated by the exchange, takes on the responsibility of enforcing the contract. Both the buyer and the seller rely on the clearinghouse to execute the transaction. Specifically, the seller looks to the clearinghouse to deliver, and the buyer looks to the clearinghouse to pay the amount due on the delivery date. In this way, the default risk associated with a forward transaction is greatly reduced because the clearinghouse of the exchange assumes the obligation.

Pit
The trading area on the floor of an organized exchange (such as the Chicago Board of Trade) where authorized brokers gather to buy and sell for their customers.

Clearinghouse
The part of an organized exchange that takes on the responsibility of enforcing a contract after the agreement is struck.

A Closer Look

LHT Inc. Enters the Futures Market

Let's consider an example in which financial futures are used to hedge. Assume that LHT Inc. issued bonds 10 years ago and that those bonds will mature in a year. When the bonds come due, LHT Inc. will not be in a position to pay off the debt. Instead, it will issue new bonds (borrow) to raise the funds to pay off the owners of the original bonds.[a] Let's further assume that LHT fears that interest rates could rise over the next year, causing the new bonds to be issued at a higher interest rate. If this scenario materializes, the firm will have to make higher interest payments on the new bonds, which will cut sharply into profits. But something as important as profits need not be left to the vicissitudes of unknown interest rates one year from now! LHT can protect itself against an undesirable increase in rates by selling a T-bill future today. The T-bill futures agreement will oblige LHT to deliver so many T-bills on a later date, say, in one year, at a price set today. If the interest rate does rise over the course of the year, as LHT expects, the spot price of the T-bills will fall. Remember the inverse relationship between the price of securities and the interest rate that we discussed in Chapter 6. LHT can buy the T-bills in the spot market at the lower price for delivery to the purchaser of the futures contract who pays the higher price agreed on earlier. If the interest rate does rise, the loss due to issuing new bonds at a higher interest rate is offset by the profit that LHT makes on the T-bill futures contract.

But what happens if LHT Inc. is wrong about the direction of the interest rate over the next year and the interest rate falls or, equivalently, the price of T-bills rises? LHT takes a loss on the T-bill future because it buys the T-bills in the spot market at the higher price to deliver to the buyer of the futures contract for the lower price previously agreed on. However, LHT is not really worse off. The loss in the futures market is offset by the savings on the new bonds the corporation issues at a lower rate because interest rates have fallen.

As you have seen, the securities usually are not actually delivered physically. Instead, the buyer or seller of the futures agreement merely pays any price difference between the spot price and the futures price. In this case, if the interest rate does go up, LHT receives a payment from the seller of the T-bill futures agreement that offsets the loss incurred by having to issue bonds at the higher interest rate. If the interest rate goes down, LHT makes a payment to the seller of the T-bill futures agreement but issues the new bonds at the lower interest rate.

LHT Inc. has successfully used the futures market to reduce the risk of losses if interest rates go up while sacrificing the possibility of gains if interest rates go down—a trade that the firm may be happy to make. Can you explain what happens if interest rates stay the same over the course of the next year? Think about it before checking the answer in endnote b.[b]

Performance Bond
A bond required by an organized exchange from both the buyer and the seller of a futures agreement to ensure that both parties abide by the agreement.

Margin Requirement
The amount that brokers must collect from their customers before they make any futures purchases or sales.

The futures contract is a standardized agreement to make a trade at a later date. In exchange for the small brokerage fee, the clearinghouse of the organized exchange guarantees that the terms will be met. To facilitate this guarantee, the exchange requires buyers and sellers of futures to put up a **performance bond**, called a **margin requirement**, set by the exchange. Brokers are required to collect margin requirements from their customers before they make any futures purchases or sales. Note that the performance bond or margin is required of both the seller and the buyer and that the brokerage fee plus the margin requirements are relatively small compared to the dollar value of the futures agreement. An example of how financial futures can be used to hedge interest rate risk is given in the accompanying A Closer Look feature on page 426.

In summary, financial futures markets have experienced spectacular growth in the past 30 years because the financial world has become a much more volatile place and financial futures can be used to reduce risks associated with this volatility. Because interest rate swings are larger, the prices of government securities (or the value of any fixed-rate instrument) oscillate more rapidly and over a broader range. Stock prices now fluctuate over a wider range, and flexible exchange rates have increased the movement of currency prices while foreign trade in goods, services, and securities has escalated sharply. Futures markets may be used to hedge all of these risks. We now turn to how the futures price is determined.

Recap   Financial futures are standardized contracts in which two parties agree to trade financial instruments at a future date according to terms, including the price, that are determined today. Financial futures are different from forward agreements because the quantities and delivery dates are standardized and, thus, the brokerage fees are relatively small. Financial futures markets exist for government securities, stock market indexes, Eurodollars, and foreign currencies. Both the buyer and the seller have obligations and rights. Financial futures can be used to hedge the risk of future changes in prices or to speculate. Organized exchanges trade the standardized contracts.

Determining the Futures Price

Financial futures are traded each day on exchanges around the world. The exchange delivers or accepts for delivery the futures contract at the specified future time and place at a price agreed on today. The buyer or seller merely accepts the risk of a price change of the contract and agrees to pay off any financial losses or to receive any financial gains. There are several different futures prices, depending on the expiration date of the futures contract. In this section, we pose the question, "How are those prices determined?" We hope that buzzers and alarms are going off in your head and that your immediate response is "supply and demand." Of course, you are right! But, in this case, it may prove beneficial to look a little more closely at what determines the supply and demand for financial futures and, hence, their prices.

Perhaps the first and most important thing to point out is that the futures price and the spot price are highly correlated—that is, they move up and down together. This is not accidental but due to actions of individuals called **arbitrageurs** who seek a riskless profit.

Arbitrageurs
Traders who make riskless profits by buying in one market and reselling in another market.

Consider what happens if a futures contract for Treasury bonds to be delivered in three months is much higher than the present spot price. An arbitrageur could purchase the Treasury bonds in the spot market while selling a futures contract. She could hold the bonds purchased in the spot market for delivery at the later date to fulfill the futures contract. Granted, she would incur some **carrying costs** in holding the Treasury bonds (or the gold or whatever), but as long as the futures price is higher than the current spot price plus the carrying costs, she would make a riskless profit. (Carrying costs generally consist of the interest costs for the use of the funds to purchase the securities, less the interest earned on the securities while the arbitrageur is holding them, plus other transactions costs of the exchange.) On the other hand, if the futures price were below the spot price plus carrying costs, arbitrageurs (who owned some of the securities) would buy futures, driving the futures price up, and sell in the spot market, driving the spot price down. Can you explain how a riskless profit would be made?[9]

When and if such an opportunity for riskless profit opens up, arbitrageurs move in, purchase in the spot market (driving up the price), and sell in the futures market (driving down the price), and vice versa. As the delivery date of the futures contract comes closer, the length of time in which funds are borrowed to establish the position is reduced. Therefore, as the delivery date nears, the carrying costs are reduced, and the futures price approaches the spot price. Arbitrage continues until the futures price is bid up (down) to the spot price plus carrying costs—a phenomenon called **convergence**. Thus, on the last day before the expiration date, the futures price is practically equal to the spot price because the carrying costs are negligible since only one day is left. Hence, because futures prices are highly correlated with spot prices and because convergence occurs, futures prices are ultimately determined by the spot prices of the underlying contract instruments. Now would be a good time to look at the accompanying A Closer Look feature on page 429, which discusses stock index futures and the October 1987 crash of the stock market.

Convergence
The phenomenon in which the futures price is bid up or down to the spot price plus carrying costs; the futures price approaches the spot price as the expiration date draws nearer.

Recap   The futures price is determined by supply and demand. If the futures price is higher than the spot price plus the carrying costs, an arbitrageur will sell a futures agreement and at the same time purchase securities in the spot market. The increased supply of futures will push the price down until the difference between the spot price and the futures price is equal to the carrying costs. If the futures price is lower than the spot price plus carrying costs, arbitrageurs (who own some of the underlying instruments) will buy futures and sell in the spot market. The futures price will go up, and the spot price will come down until the difference equals the carrying costs. As the delivery date nears, the spot and the futures prices converge.

Options

In the previous sections, we pointed out that business firms (financial and nonfinancial) or individuals can use the futures market to reduce the risk of price changes inherent in everyday business. Thus, if they need to buy or sell a financial instrument in the future, they can use the futures market to offset any possible loss due to an unanticipated price change between now and the day when they will be making the purchase or sale. An unattractive feature of the futures market, however, is that it also eliminates a possible gain from a price change.

For example, consider the case in which Michael needs to borrow $1 million in a month. He knows what the interest rate is today, but is concerned that it will be higher in a month. He can sell a T-bill future for $1 million that gives him the right and obligation to sell the T-bills in 30 days at a price determined today. If the interest rate goes up, he borrows at a higher rate, but the price of the T-bill futures contract falls and he makes a profit. This profit offsets the higher borrowing costs (and accomplishes his goal of reducing the risk of losses if the interest rate goes up). If the interest rate goes down, Michael gains by borrowing at a lower rate. However, he loses money on the T-bill

Stock Index Futures and the '87 Crash

A stock market index such as the Dow Jones Industrial Average is an index that measures price changes of a market basket of stocks included in the index. Stock index futures are contracts that give the purchaser (seller) the right and obligation to purchase (sell) a multiple of the value of the index on some specified date in the future at a price determined today. Stock index futures are available for several indexes of stock market activity, and the futures contract calls for the delivery of the cash value of a multiple of a particular stock index.

Perhaps the two most prominent stock index futures are the futures contracts for the S&P 500 and the NYSE Composite Indexes. In both cases, the contract size is $500 times the index on the delivery date. The financial futures contracts are available for the quarterly dates (during March, June, September, and December) over the next two years. For example, if Jamal purchases a December contract for the S&P 500, this gives him the right and obligation to receive on the delivery date $500 times the value of the S&P 500 stock index on that date. The price for the future delivery is negotiated today. Let's say Jamal negotiates a price today of $275,000, which he will pay on the delivery date. Consider the two cases for the delivery date on which the S&P Index is (1) 525 or (2) 575. If it is 525, the seller pays $262,500 (500 × $525) but receives $275,000 from Jamal. If it is 575, Jamal pays $275,000 but receives $287,500 (500 × $575). In the first case, the seller makes a profit. In the second case, Jamal makes a profit. If $500 times the value of the index is greater than the futures price, the buyer of the futures makes a profit. If it is less, the seller makes a profit.

As with all futures, the spot and futures prices move up and down together. In the case of stock index futures, arbitrage prevents the futures price from deviating a tremendous amount from the spot price. For instance, if the futures price is far higher than the spot price, an arbitrageur could make a riskless profit by buying a market basket of stocks that made up the index while selling a futures contract. As long as the futures price exceeds the spot price plus the cost of carrying the inventory of stocks, the arbitrageur could make a riskless profit. By doing so, however, she would be increasing the demand for stocks in the spot market (pushing up the index) and increasing the supply of futures contracts (pushing down their price). As in other futures markets, arbitrage would keep the spot and futures price in close alignment with one another.

But wouldn't it be difficult to recognize every opportunity for arbitrage and go into the spot market to purchase the market basket of stocks that make up the stock index? After all, in the case of the S&P 500, one would have to purchase (or sell) 500 different stocks. Not even the largest of most small investors can do this. As you saw in Chapter 16, however, the advent of sophisticated computer technology has allowed brokerage houses and institutional investors (such as mutual funds and pension plans) to program automatic purchases and sales of stock index market baskets into a computer. Sales or purchases can be triggered automatically when the stock index futures price gets out of alignment with the spot price. This program trading allows every opportunity for arbitrage to be exploited immediately. As advantageous as this may seem to the brokerage house that uses it, program trading can be controversial.

During the week of October 12–16, 1987, the Dow Jones Industrial Average fell 250 points, and on Monday, October 19, 1987, it plummeted 508 points, or more than 20 percent—the largest percentage drop in history and the largest point drop to that time. Could program trading have been the culprit in this major downturn?

Consider what would happen if a stock index futures suddenly fell steeply. Program trading would trigger spot market sales of the stocks that made up the index and purchases of index futures. A major fall in the futures price could bring about large sales (and plummeting prices) in the spot market for stock. *Stop orders* (or orders to automatically sell if the stock price falls to a certain level) would be triggered, which would cause further plummeting of spot prices and could reverse the trend of purchases in the futures market. Indeed, the October 1987 crash was triggered by program trading and stop orders.

To prevent a reoccurrence of the 1987 crash, many exchanges have put in circuit breaker restrictions that, among other things, limit computerized program trading if the index falls more than a certain amount on any day. They have been activated many times.

Other analysts are less concerned about program trading than about the cause of the fall in futures prices to begin with. If futures prices fall because of the expectation that spot prices will be falling, the arbitrage causing the present spot price to fall may simply be rational price adjustment in a declining market. By restricting computerized trading, we may be treating only the symptoms of a problem without treating the cause. Maybe the market, like a virus, should be allowed to run its course, or maybe a little preventive medication will stop a mild virus from turning into a severe infection. Opinions about the extent of intervention needed continue to differ.

futures (because lower interest rates cause the T-bill futures price to rise and he is locked into selling at the lower price). Therefore, to reduce the risk of losses from the interest rate rising, he forgoes the chance of a gain if the interest rate falls.

Could there be another way to get risk protection from a loss without giving up the possibility of a gain? If you said, "Surely there must be because markets are so quick to respond to changing needs and conditions," you are correct (or, as we shall see, almost correct). We now turn our attention to options to demonstrate how our friend Michael can use them to reduce the risk of an interest rate increase over the next month without forgoing a gain if rates fall.

Options are similar to futures in that they are used to reduce the risk of future price changes or to speculate. Options give the buyer the right but not the obligation to buy or sell an instrument in the future for a price determined today. The agreed-upon price is called the **strike price**. This right continues until an expiration date specified in the contract. Options exist for many agricultural products, commodities, individual stocks (such as AT&T, IBM, and EDS), and other financial instruments. In addition, options are also available on the major types of futures contracts, including stock index futures, currency futures, and interest rate futures. These options, called **options on futures**, give the buyer of the option the right (but not the obligation) to buy or sell a futures contract up to the expiration date of the option. As you have seen at the delivery date of a futures contract, the futures price converges to the spot price of the underlying financial instrument. Hence, on the delivery date, the investor should be indifferent between hedging with a futures contract or hedging with the underlying debt instrument. Option contracts are often written on futures contracts rather than on the underlying debt instruments themselves because the futures contracts are often more liquid than the underlying financial instruments. This is

Options
Standardized contracts that give the buyer the right but not the obligation to buy or sell an instrument in the future at a price determined today.

Strike Price
The agreed-upon price in an options contract.

Options on Futures
Options that give the buyer the right but not the obligation to buy or sell a futures contract up to the expiration date on the option.

Major Options, Exchanges, and Open Interest

Options are available for hundreds of individual domestic and foreign stocks, for many stock indexes (both broad based and sector indexes), and for foreign currencies. Most options must be exercised in less than one year. However, there are long-term options (both equity and index) whose specified time to exercise the option is more than one year. The American Stock Exchange, the Chicago Board Options Exchange, the Philadelphia Stock Exchange, and the Pacific Exchange are among the largest options exchanges in the United States. In addition, the International Securities Exchange, which is the first electronic options exchange, was launched in May 2000 and today rivals the options trading and products of the other exchanges.[a] *The Wall Street Journal* reports on the most actively traded equity options and the major stock index options. In addition to the options on individual stocks, stock indexes, and currencies discussed here, the Chicago Board Options Exchange also makes an option market for Treasury securities. These options can be used to hedge interest rate risk.

The following list shows the volume (contracts traded that day) and open interest (number of contracts outstanding) of call and put options at the largest exchanges as reported in *The Wall Street Journal* for June 1, 2004.

Exchange

American	Call Vol: 307,552	Open Interest: 52,593,865
	Put Vol: 235,332	Open Interest: 42,178,912
Chicago Board	Call Vol: 500,343	Open Interest: 70,414,522
	Put Vol: 467,935	Open Interest: 60,182,598
International Securities	Call Vol: 637,517	Open Interest: 62,239,191
	Put Vol: 420,782	Open Interest: 52,081,937
Philadelphia	Call Vol: 294,116	Open Interest: 50,757,183
	Put Vol: 147,342	Open Interest: 40,922,277
Pacific	Call Vol: 203,624	Open Interest: 64,265,242
	Put Vol: 106,304	Open Interest: 52,794,683

SOURCE: *The Wall Street Journal*, June 2, 2004, C15.

because the secondary markets for most financial instruments are not as highly developed as the futures markets. Financial options are available for specific dates in the future, often for the two closest months and then for March, June, September, and December for the next nine months. As in the case of futures, the clearinghouse of the exchange enforces the contract and, for a fee, takes on the default risk. Many of the similarities between futures and options stop here, however.

http://www.cbot.com provides information about options trading.

There are two kinds of options, and we will briefly outline each of them, focusing mainly on financial options. See the accompanying A Closer Look feature above for a list of the major U.S. options and the exchanges on which they are traded.

Put Options

Put Options

Options that give the buyer of the option the right but not the obligation to sell a standardized contract of a financial instrument at a strike price determined today.

Put options give the buyer of the option the right but not the obligation to sell a standardized contract of a financial instrument or a futures agreement at a strike price determined today. The seller has the obligation but not the right to buy the contract if the buyer exercises it before the expiration date.[10] Therefore, Michael, who has to borrow $1 million in the next month, can hedge the risk of a future interest rate increase by buying a put option on, say, a T-bill or Treasury bond contract. If the interest rate does go up, he exercises the option at a profit to offset the loss incurred by having to borrow at the higher rate. Like futures, financial options are written only in standardized contract amounts for delivery on a few specific dates, and a perfect offsetting transaction is rarely found. Nevertheless, risk is still reduced. Unlike futures, put options allow the risk of an interest rate increase to be hedged without losing the possibility of a gain if the interest rate goes down. If rates do fall, Michael simply does not exercise the option. He has used put options to reduce the risk of an interest rate increase when he has to borrow in the future. Put options could also be used to reduce the risk of a price decrease by anyone who has to sell a financial instrument in the future.

Call Options

Call Options

Options that give the buyer of the option the right but not the obligation to buy a standardized contract of a financial instrument at a strike price determined today.

Call options give the buyer the right but not the obligation to buy a financial instrument at a strike price determined today anytime before the expiration date. Note that the buyer has the right but not the obligation to buy. The buyer exercises the option (buys the instrument or futures contract at the strike price) only if it is in his or her interest to do so—that is, only if the price of the financial instrument is higher than the strike price. If the price of the financial instrument or futures contract falls, the buyer is not obliged to exercise the option and will let it expire. The option allows the buyer to limit the losses from a price increase without limiting his or her ability to take advantage of a price decrease.

Recap | Options give the buyer of the option the right but not the obligation to buy or sell an instrument in the future for a price determined today. Put options give the buyer the right but not the obligation to sell a standardized contract at a price determined today anytime before the expiration date on the option. A call option gives the buyer the right but not the obligation to buy a financial instrument at a price determined today anytime before the expiration date on the option.

The Option Premium

You might ask, however, why any individual or firm would hedge risk with futures that limit both losses and gains when they could use options that limit only losses. If you said, "Because futures must be cheaper," you may have a future as an economist! Futures cost very little—basically, only a small brokerage fee, which is low because the contracts are standardized and the volume in the market is very large. Both parties to the agreement have rights and obligations. With options, however, one party has rights with no obligations, and the other party has obligations with no rights. From the buyer's position, put or call options give the right but not the obligation to sell or buy the contract at the agreed-upon price if the buyer exercises the option. In addition to paying the exchange a brokerage fee, the party with the rights but no obligations (the buyer) pays an **option premium** to the party with the obligations but no rights (the seller).[11] The premium is the reward to the seller of either a put or a call option for accepting the risk of a loss with

Option Premium

The premium paid by the buyer of an option to compensate the seller for accepting the risk of a loss with no possibility of a gain.

Cracking the Code

Cracking the Code on Options

The following table is a typical example of the appearance of option market information in the newspaper. We have clipped a quote from *The Wall Street Journal* on April 20, 2004, from the "Futures Options Prices" table.

Interest Rate

T-Bonds (CBT)

$100,000; points and 64ths of 100%

Strike Price	Calls-Settle			Puts-Settle		
	May	Jun	Jly	May	June	Jly
106	2-06	2-52	2-35	0-04	0-50	1-59
107	1-16	2-08	2-00	0-14	1-06	2-24
108	**0-38**	**1-35**	**1-35**	**0-36**	**1-33**	**2-59**
109	0-13	1-04	1-10	1-11	2-02	3-34
110	0-04	0-45	0-54	2-02	2-43	4-13
111	0-02	0-28	0-38	3-00	3-26	4-61

SOURCE: *The Wall Street Journal* (April 20, 2004): C12.

We use the example of an option on an interest rate futures agreement because this is the preferred way of hedging. Using an option on a futures agreement is preferable to an option on the underlying asset because of the liquidity and homogeneity of the futures market. In this example, we are considering options on $100,000 of Treasury bond futures with a coupon rate of 8 percent and a 15-year maturity. In the T-bonds (CBT) section, we will consider the highlighted row that starts with the strike price of 108. The second, third, and fourth columns give the settle (final of the day) option premium for call options for May, June, and July, respectively. The last three columns give the settle option premium for put options on April 19, 2004, for May, June, and July.

Thus, on April 19, for a strike price of 108, or 108 percent of the face valued of the contract (in this example, $100,000), the option premium for a May call option was $593.75 (38/64% × $100,000). For a July put option, the premium (column 7) is $2,921.88 (2-59/64% × $100,000). If no price is given, the contract did not trade on this day.

To give some meaning to these numbers, let's assume that we purchased a June Treasury bond call option with a strike price of 108 for $593.75 on April 19, 2004. We pay a small brokerage fee (on April 19) for the right (but not the obligation) to purchase $100,000 face value in Treasury bonds (of 15-year maturity and 8 percent coupon rate) for $100,000 in June ($100,000 × 100% = $100,000). If the spot price of $100,000 in Treasury bonds in May is more than $108,000, we exercise the option. If the spot price is more than $108,000 plus the option premium of $593.75, we make money. If the spot price is less than $108,000, we do not exercise the option. In this case, we lose the option premium of $593.75! However, we can consider the $593.75 as an insurance premium insuring us against having to pay more than $108,000 for the Treasury bond futures in May.

no possibility of a gain. In the case of interest rate options, for the hedger to be better off, the loss from the interest rate increase that the hedger avoids must be larger than the put option premium. In addition to the option premium, the option still entails a small brokerage fee for arranging the trade.

So far, we have been discussing situations in which options are used to hedge. As you might have guessed, put and call options can also be used to speculate. Needless to say, speculation in this manner can be extremely costly because option premiums are often quite substantial (several thousands of dollars). If the option is not exercised, the buyer of the call or put option loses the option premium. Hedgers can think of the option premium as an insurance premium, limiting the amount of losses they will incur if a financial instrument must be purchased or sold at a later date. For speculators, the option premium is the amount that they are willing to bet when they believe that the price will change significantly from the strike price, thereby creating potential profit. As with hedgers, for the speculator to benefit from purchasing the option, the price must increase (in the case of call options) or decrease (in the case of put options) enough to more than cover the option premium. The downside to options, of course, is the option premium, which can be quite substantial, as compared to the usually small brokerage fee for buying or selling a futures contract. Economists are famous for saying "There is no such thing as a free lunch!" If options are used to exploit gains while limiting losses, this is certainly true.

In summary, someone who needs to buy a financial security or instrument in the future can hedge the risk of an inopportune price increase by paying an option premium to purchase a call option, which gives the buyer the right to purchase the instrument at a price agreed on today up to the expiration date of the option. On the other hand, someone who needs to sell a financial security or instrument in the future can hedge the risk of a price decrease by paying a premium to purchase a put option, which gives the buyer the right to sell the contract at a price agreed on today up to the expiration date. The sellers of the call or put options are not hedging but merely accepting risk for a price—in this case, the option premium. The buyer of a call or put option is hedging risk without giving up any potential for gains, as in the case of futures. Like futures, options can also be used to speculate about future price changes.

Like futures, option prices are quoted in many daily newspapers. The accompanying Cracking the Code feature on page 433 explains how to read option prices.

Determining the Option Premium

As in all unregulated markets, the price to buy either a call or a put option (the option premium) is determined by the forces of supply and demand.[12] Unlike futures markets in which both parties to the transaction can be hedgers, in the case of options, only one party to the transaction can be a hedger. For call and put options, the buyer can be a hedger. Both of these parties could also be speculators, but our point is that the seller of a call or put option can never be hedging. The seller is merely accepting risk for a premium—the option premium.

For any given options contract, the option premium will generally be higher when

1. The price of the contract instrument is more volatile.
2. The expiration date of the option is further into the future.
3. The strike price relative to the spot price for put options is higher or the strike price relative to the spot price for call options is lower.

First, volatility in the price of the contract instrument affects the option premium. If the price of Eurodollars fluctuates more than the price of T-bills (all other factors being equal), the option premium for the Eurodollar option will be higher than the option premium for the T-bill option.[13] Because of the greater volatility, the probability that the seller of the Eurodollar call or put option will lose is higher, and therefore the premium must be higher to compensate.

Second, time influences the option premium because the further into the future the expiration date is, the more time there is for the price to fluctuate and, hence, the more risk that the option will be exercised. Also, the further we look into the future, the more uncertain things become. Therefore, the further away the expiration date, the higher is the option premium.

Finally, the strike price also affects the premium. If the strike price for a call option is very low relative to the spot price, it is much more likely that the spot price will go above the strike price and that the option will be exercised. Hence, the lower the strike price for a call option, the higher the option premium will be. For a put option, the higher the strike price, the more likely it is that the spot price will be lower than the strike price and that the buyer will exercise the option. Therefore, the higher the strike price for a put option, the higher the option premium will be.

Recap The option premium is paid by the party who has rights but no obligations. The seller of the option receives the premium to compensate for accepting the risk of a loss with no possibility of gain. For any given options contract, the option premium will generally be higher when the price of the contract instrument is more volatile, the expiration date of the option is further in the future, or the strike price relative to the spot price for put options is higher or the strike price relative to the spot price for call options is lower.

One final note: We have looked at financial options and have seen that they can be used by business firms for managing risk due to price changes. Like forward and futures contracts, options can be used to reduce the risks of price changes in future time periods. All of the markets that we have been discussing—financial forward, futures, and options—are examples of derivatives. As you saw in Chapter 12, derivatives are financial contracts whose values are derived from the values of other underlying instruments, such as foreign exchange, bonds, equities, or an index. For example, the value of a financial futures contract in Treasury bonds derives its value from the underlying bonds. There are many kinds of derivatives, and those described in this chapter are relatively simple. This chapter contains one appendix that examines foreign exchange futures markets.

Summary of Major Points

1. In forward markets, the terms of a transaction (including the price) that will occur on a future date are arranged today. Forward transactions are used to reduce the risk that future price changes will eliminate profit. Forward agreements between individual parties are arranged by intermediaries. Forward agreements can have high transactions costs because they usually require the exact matching of two parties and because each party has a default risk in that the other party may not fulfill the agreement.

2. In financial markets, forward contracts in the most widely traded currencies have been established by large commercial banks. The bank is an actual participant in the agreement. In addition to buying and selling foreign currencies at spot prices, the banks also buy and sell the major currencies at forward rates. There does not have to be an exact matching of two parties. When there is not an exactly offsetting match, the bank has some exposure to exchange rate risk. Foreign currency forward agreements can be used to hedge exchange rate risk or to speculate about future currency values.

3. Financial futures are standardized contracts between two parties to buy or sell financial securities, such as government securities, stock indexes, Eurodollars, and numerous foreign currencies, on a future date at a price determined today. They are traded on major exchanges and are used to hedge interest rate risks, exchange rate risks, and the risk that stock prices will change. They can also be used to speculate about future price changes.

4. Because futures contracts are standardized, they have low transactions costs and high volume. They often do not provide an exact offsetting match with regard to the quality, the quantity, or the due date of the contract. The clearinghouse of the exchange enforces the contract and, for a fee, takes on the default risk. Both the buyer and the seller put up performance bonds. Arbitrageurs ensure that the futures price is equal to the spot price plus carrying costs. The futures price converges to the spot price on the delivery date.

5. Options are financial contracts that can also be used to hedge or speculate. They are available for many of the same financial instruments as futures. In addition, two kinds of options are offered for buying or selling futures contracts. A call option gives the buyer of the option the right but not the obligation to purchase the contract by the expiration date at a price determined today. A put option gives the buyer of the option the right but not the obligation to sell the contract by the expiration date at a price determined today. The buyer of a call or put option pays an option premium because she or he has rights but no obligations. The seller of the call or put option takes on the risk that the option will be exercised for a price, the option premium. Futures limit both gains and losses while options limit losses without limiting gains.

6. The option premium depends on the volatility of the financial instrument in the contract (such as T-bills), the difference between the strike price and the spot price, and the length of time until the expiration date on the option.

7. A foreign exchange futures market trades standardized contracts to buy or sell some amount of foreign exchange on a future date at a price determined today. These futures are widely used to hedge risks involving the delivery of one currency that must be converted to another currency at a later date. (*See Appendix 18A.*)

Key Terms

Review Questions

1. Define *financial futures, forward agreements,* and *options.* What are the advantages and disadvantages of each?

2. How do spot markets differ from forward markets? How do spot markets differ from futures markets?

3. A government report forecasts both higher inflation and higher interest rates in the future. Yvette needs to borrow money in six months. What can she, as a future borrower, do now to protect herself from the risk of an increase in the interest rate? What if she is the lender?

4. Why do both the buyer and the seller of futures contracts have to put up performance bonds? When does the seller profit? When does the buyer profit? How is the clearinghouse protected from losses?

5. Explain why the futures price is very close to the spot price on the day before the delivery date of a futures contract.

6. How do arbitrageurs and speculators differ?
7. Explain how arbitrage causes the futures and spot prices to converge.
8. Explain the difference between call and put options. Does the buyer or the seller of an option pay the option premium? Why does the seller of an option take on the risk?
9. What are options on futures?
10. Explain how an investor could use a stock index future to hedge the risk of a fall in stock prices.
11. Assume that an intermediary uses futures only to hedge risk but never to speculate. Is it as vulnerable to losses as an intermediary that uses futures to speculate? Explain.
12. What factors determine the size of the option premium?

Analytical Questions

Questions marked with an icon are objective in nature. They can be completed with a short answer or number.

13. Angela buys a Treasury bond futures agreement for $94,000. On the delivery date, the spot price is $95,000. Does she win or lose? By how much? If Angela bought the futures contract to hedge, can she lose? Explain. (*Hint:* What if she is willing to give up the opportunity for gain to reduce the risk of loss?)

14. IBM sells a Treasury bond futures agreement for $94,000. On the delivery date, the spot price is $95,000. IBM sold the futures agreement to speculate. Does IBM win or lose? Explain.

15. A firm buys a December $100,000 Treasury bond call option with a strike price of 110. If the spot price in December is $108,000, is the option exercised?

16. A firm buys a December $100,000 Treasury bond put option with a strike price of 110. If the spot price in December is $108,000, is the option exercised?

17. An investment firm buys a December $100,000 Treasury bond put option with a strike price of 105. If the spot price in December is $108,000, is the option exercised?

18. An investment firm buys a December $100,000 Treasury bond call option with a strike price of 105. If the spot price in December is $108,000, is the option exercised?

19. If the settle price for a T-bill futures contract is 96.75, what is the percent discount?

20. A brokerage house purchases an S&P 500 futures agreement for $300,000. On the delivery date, the S&P 500 Index is 575. Does the brokerage house make a profit? What if the S&P 500 is 625?

21. If I buy a T-bill future for $950,000 and interest rates go up between now and the delivery date, what will happen to the price of the T-bill future? Will I make money or lose money? Explain.

22. Assume that you will inherit a $1 million trust fund from your family when you turn 21 next year. Interest rates are high right now, and you fear they may be lower in a year. Explain in detail how you can use futures or options to alleviate your fears.

23. Ruben is exporting Colombian coffee to the United States. He will be paid $100,000 in six months, but he is concerned about how much of his domestic currency (Colombian pesos) he will receive for the $100,000. Explain in detail how he can reduce the risk that, in six months, the peso will depreciate in value against the dollar and he will receive fewer pesos than he anticipates. (*See Appendix 18A.*)

Internet Exercises

1. The Chicago Mercantile Exchange (CME) is the world's largest financial exchange where firms buy and sell derivative instruments. A glossary of financial instruments such as futures and options is available from the CME at **http://www.cme.com/ exchange/glossary.html**. Access this site, locate the glossary, and find the meaning of futures and options. From the information at this site, explain the difference between a call option and a put option.

2. Go to the Chicago Board of Trade Internet site at **http://www.cbot.com/**. Summarize the latest news about the exchange as reported on the *CBOT Today* link.

Suggested Readings

For a recent look at some of the material covered in this chapter, see Jeffery W. Gunther and Thomas Siems, "Debunking Derivatives Delirium," *Southwest Economy*, Federal Reserve Bank of Dallas, Issue 2 (March/April 2003). The article is available on the Internet at http://www.dallasfed.org/research/swe/2003/swe0302b.pdf.

For "An Option for Anticipating Fed Action," see the article by the same name by John B. Carlson, William R. Melick, and Erkin Y. Sahinoz, in *Economic Commentary*, Federal Reserve Bank of Cleveland (September 1, 2003). The article looks at how options on federal funds futures can be analyzed to gauge public expectations of future Fed actions. The article is available on the Internet at http://www.clevelandfed.org/research/Com2003/0901.pdf.

For a comprehensive analysis of futures markets, see A.B. Malliaris, *Foundations of Futures Markets: Selected Essays of A.G. Malliaris* (Northampton, MA: Edward Elgar, 2000).

For a collection of 70 articles written over the last 25 years on options, see *Options Markets*, George M. Constantinides and A.G. Malliaris, eds. (Northampton, MA: Edward Elgar, 2001).

An article that looks at how futures can be used to hedge risk or to speculate is Lorayne Fiorillo, "Back to the Futures: Ups and Downs Aside, Futures Investing Could Help You Diversify Your Portfolio," *Entrepreneur* (August 1998): 661.

For an article that looks at the recent performance of Asian futures exchanges after the Asian financial crisis, see Rachael Horsewood, "After the Crash, It's Back to the Futures," *Asiamoney* (March 1998): 15–17.

An article that discusses options and option pricing is John Krainer, "The Nobel Prize in Economics," *Federal Reserve Bank of San Francisco Economic Letter* 98-05 (February 13, 1998).

For a discussion of the risks that derivatives pose for banks, see Chapter 7 of Franklin R. Edwards, *The New Finance: Regulation and Financial Stability* (Washington, DC: The AEI Press, 1996): 120–147.

For a look into the future, see Asani Sarkar and Michelle Tozzi, "Electronic Trading on Futures Exchanges," *Current Issues in Economics and Finance* 1 (January 1998).

Two comprehensive and somewhat technical articles are "Money Market Futures" and "Options on Money Market Futures," both found in *Instruments of the Money Market*, 7th ed., Timothy Q. Cook and Robert K. LaRoche, eds. (Federal Reserve Bank of Richmond, 1993). Additional information on futures and other financial instruments may be found at http://www.e-analytics.com.

Appendix 18A: The Foreign Exchange Futures Market

In the body of this chapter, we discussed foreign exchange forward agreements that are offered by large banks to allow their customers to hedge exchange rate risk. In addition to these forward markets, large futures markets that trade foreign exchange futures contracts have also developed to hedge exchange rate risk. Both forward and futures agreements in foreign currencies facilitate cross-border trading in goods, services, and financial claims. Both achieve similar results. This appendix looks at foreign exchange futures contracts.

Foreign Exchange Futures Contract
A standardized contract to deliver a certain amount of a foreign currency on a date in the future at a price determined today.

A **foreign exchange futures contract** is a standardized contract to deliver a certain amount of a foreign currency on a date in the future at a price determined today. The agreed-upon price is the futures price. Like spot markets, foreign exchange futures markets have experienced remarkable growth due to the tremendous increase in trade and foreign investment, as well as the volatility of exchange rates. Foreign exchange futures markets have been organized since the mid-1970s and allow importers, exporters, and investors in foreign securities to hedge. Like other futures markets, they also provide the opportunity for speculation.

The foreign exchange markets, including both spot and futures markets, actually form the largest market in the world in terms of the volume of transactions. Spot markets do not have a single location, such as the New York Stock Exchange, but are located at large banks in the world's financial centers, in London, New York, Tokyo, and Frankfurt. Large banks in financial centers in other countries are usually linked to the major banks in one of the financial centers, which, in turn, are linked by telephone, telex or the Internet. Standardized futures contracts are traded on the Chicago Mercantile Exchange and require a relatively large minimum purchase. In reality, one worldwide foreign exchange market (either spot or futures) is open somewhere in the world 24 hours each day. Because supplies and demands change from day to day, exchange rates (both spot and futures prices) fluctuate day-to-day, hour-to-hour, and even minute-by-minute![14]

Foreign exchange futures markets, like all futures markets, offer the opportunity to hedge risk or to speculate. Importers and exporters often enter into agreements to deliver goods in the future for a price determined today. Because the price is agreed on today without knowing the future spot exchange rate, there is a risk that the exchange rate between the two currencies will change between now and the delivery date. Thus, there is a possibility that the anticipated profit could be eliminated or, worse yet, that a loss could occur. This risk is referred to as *exchange rate risk.*

To hedge, an importer can enter the foreign exchange futures market. An example will help to clarify. Assume that Jean is exporting computers to a firm (Choca Firm) in Switzerland that plans to resell them at a profit.[15] She agrees to deliver 500 computers in September, three months from now, at a price of $1,000 per computer, or $500,000. Choca Firm will have to come up with $500,000 in September to pay for the computers.[16] Checking the exchange rate today, Choca finds that the Swiss franc/dollar rate is 1.5025 Swiss francs. If the exchange rate stays the same (highly unlikely), Choca Firm would have to pay 751,250 Swiss francs (500,000 × 1.5025) in September for the $500,000. This is great because Choca is confident that it can resell the computers for 800,000 Swiss francs, making a nice profit. But what if the Swiss franc depreciates (or, in other words, if the dollar appreciates) between now and September? If the Swiss franc/dollar rate changes to 1.6 Swiss francs (a depreciation of the Swiss franc and appreciation of the dollar), Choca Firm will have to pay 800,000 Swiss francs (500,000 × 1.6) for the $500,000 and will lose all of its profit. Worse yet, if the dollar appreciates to 1.75 Swiss francs, the importer will have to come up with 875,000 Swiss francs (500,000 × 1.75), incurring a sizable loss! Thanks to organized futures markets, Choca can hedge this risk by buying a standardized foreign exchange futures contract in dollars.

For example, today a futures contract for delivery of dollars in September is selling for 1.508 Swiss francs. If Choca Firm purchases this contract, it knows that it will pay 1.508 Swiss francs for the delivery of $1 in September, or 754,000 (500,000 × 1.508) Swiss francs for $500,000, regardless of what the spot exchange rate is in September. For Choca Firm or any importer interested in importing computers rather than speculating on future spot exchange rates, this offers a simple way to reduce exchange rate risk.

Another use of foreign exchange futures markets is to hedge risk when foreign securities are purchased. For example, foreign purchasers of U.S. government securities know they will be delivered so many dollars in, say, 90 days when the security matures. Can you explain how selling a futures contract hedges the exchange rate risk in this case?[17] No wonder the growth of these markets has paralleled the growth of trade in goods, services, and financial securities.

Endnotes

1 For example, small changes in interest rates can lead to large changes in the prices or value of long-term fixed-rate assets such as bonds or mortgages.

2 With the fixed exchange rate system of the Bretton Woods Accord, under normal circumstances, there was no exchange rate risk. When situations were not normal—when there was a currency crisis—there could be substantial exchange rate risk if a country was seriously considering changing the value of its currency.

3 The exchange rate can also be expressed as $1 = .90 euro.

4 Note that in the case of foreign exchange forward markets, large banks are actually the partners to forward transactions—namely, the bank buys currency from one customer and resells all or part of it to another in two separate forward contracts between each customer and the bank. The point is that the transactions are not between the two customers.

5 The risk of default is greatly reduced when one of the partners to the forward transaction is a large bank as in the case of the foreign exchange forward markets.

6 As you saw in Chapter 5, Eurodollars are dollar-dominated deposits held abroad.

7 If the price of a futures contract changes, the buyer or seller merely settles up financially for any changes in value, usually by executing an opposing transaction. For example, if Suzanne purchases a futures contract, rather than taking delivery on the delivery date, she can sell a futures contract involving the same asset for the same delivery date. The sale effectively cancels out the purchase. Or if she had sold a futures contract, she can purchase a futures contract with the same delivery date, effectively canceling out the sale. Most futures contracts are settled in this manner: Purchases in the futures market are reversed by sales in the futures market; sales in the futures market are reversed by purchases in the futures market. This fact does not alter the analysis, however.

8 In case you want to check, the answer is that if ABC's guess is right, it can go into the spot market in September and purchase the T-bills at the lower price for immediate delivery to the buyer of the future. The difference between the futures price and what ABC pays in the spot market is its profit—ABC is good at counting this.

9 Likewise, forward prices cannot diverge from spot prices by more than the carrying costs.

10 In this chapter, we are limiting our discussion to American options, which can be exercised anytime before their expiration date. European options can be exercised only on the expiration date of the option.

11 Make sure you are clear that the buyer of a put option has the *right* but not the *obligation* to sell while the buyer of a call option has the *right* but not the *obligation* to buy.

12 The option still entails a small brokerage fee for arranging the option in addition to the option premium.

13 In this case, both Eurodollars and T-bills are available in $1 million contracts for delivery on the same dates.

14 The relationship between the spot and futures exchange rate is the same as the relationship between any spot and futures price.

15 Choca Firm previously specialized in Swiss chocolates but now is trying to diversify by importing computers.

16 In this example, we are assuming that the importer must exchange domestic currency for the foreign currency—that is, Choca Firm must pay for its imports with the currency of the exporting country. The situation could work in reverse. In that case, the exporter would be paid in the currency of the importing country and have to exchange it for the exporting country's currency. Either way, the risk is the same; the only difference is in who bears the risk.

17 For example, assume that a Japanese firm purchases a U.S. government T-bill for $9,900. The T-bill sells at a discount, and the Japanese firm knows it will receive $10,000 in three months. The yen/dollar exchange rate on the date of the purchase is 110. Thus, the Japanese firm pays 1,089,000 yen (110 yen × $9,900) for the T-bill. If the exchange rate is the same in three months, the T-bill will return 1,100,000 yen for a profit of 11,000 yen. It is highly unlikely, however, that the exchange rate will be the same, and if the yen depreciates, the Japanese firm could see its profit reduced or even incur a loss. To hedge this risk, the firm can sell a futures contract today that

agrees to deliver $10,000 three months from now at a yen price agreed on today. In this way, the firm will know exactly how many yen it will receive for the $10,000.

A Closer Look, page 422

a   Our list includes both financial and other futures because we believe you may find them interesting. Because these are information items only, we are not defining all of the terms.

A Closer Look, page 426

a   Borrowing to repay maturing debt is called *rolling over* and is actually quite common.

b   LHT Inc. buys T-bills in the spot market to deliver to the purchaser of the futures contract at the same price for which it sold the contract. Aside from a small brokerage fee to purchase the futures contract (that can be thought of as an insurance premium), LHT Inc. is no worse off.

A Closer Look, page 431

a   A wealth of information can be found at the Internet sites of the various exchanges that trade options. They are the American Stock Exchange, http://www.amex.com; the Chicago Board Options Exchange, http://www.cboe.com; the Philadelphia Stock Exchange, http://phlx.com; the Pacific Exchange, http://www.pacificex.com; and the International Securities Exchange, http://iscoptions.com.

19

CHAPTER NINETEEN

The International Financial System

Learning Objectives

After reading this chapter, you should know:

How and why the international financial system is changing

The role of the international financial system under the Bretton Woods Accord

How the present managed floating exchange rate system works

The role the dollar plays in the international financial system

The roles of the International Monetary Fund, the World Bank, and the Bank for International Settlements

A Dramatic Metamorphosis

International Financial System
The numerous rules, customs, instruments, facilities, markets, and organizations that enable international payments to be made and funds to flow across borders.

The **international financial system** consists of the numerous rules, customs, instruments, facilities, markets, and organizations that enable international payments to be made and funds to flow across borders. In recent years, the international financial system has experienced tremendous growth. New financial instruments have been created, and the volume of transactions has exploded. The dramatic metamorphosis of international financial markets is driven by technological changes, the growth in world trade, and the breakdown of barriers to financial (capital) flows.

From an economic standpoint, developments in the international financial system have made financial markets more efficient because funds (financial capital) can more easily flow around the world to wherever they will earn the highest return. Over time, as resources are allocated more efficiently, both developed and developing countries should experience increased economic growth. As a result, living standards around the world should rise more than they otherwise would have.

A more globalized environment can also entail costs. A disturbance in one financial market or in one country can have immediate effects on other countries and the entire international financial system. As Alan Greenspan puts it, "These global financial markets, engendered by the rapid proliferation of cross-border financial flows and products, have developed a capability of transmitting mistakes at a far faster pace throughout the financial system in ways that were unknown a generation ago."[1] An example is the Asian financial crisis of 1997–1998 that started in currency markets in Thailand and quickly spread to other countries in the region and beyond. This "contagion effect" was exacerbated by the increased integration of financial markets that has occurred in recent years.

The international financial system includes the international money and capital markets and the foreign exchange market. The international money market trades short-term claims with an original maturity of one year or less; the international capital market trades capital market instruments including stocks, bonds, mutual funds, and mortgages, with an original maturity of more than one year. In recent years, many new international financial products have been created to facilitate the increased financial flows. These include various types of mutual funds that allow investors to invest in developed and emerging economies.

A crucial part of the international financial system is the foreign exchange market, where foreign currencies are bought and sold in the course of trading goods, services, and financial claims (securities) among countries. As you have seen in earlier chapters, this global market is woven together by the dealers in foreign currencies—mostly, the foreign exchange departments of the largest commercial banks located in the world's major financial centers such as New York, London, Frankfurt, and Tokyo. In 2004, daily trading in the foreign exchange market exceeded $1.5 trillion.

In the post–World War II period, the international financial system has operated under two distinct exchange rate regimes. The specific exchange rate regime affects the trading of all international financial instruments. During the first regime from 1944 to 1973, major industrial countries maintained a system of fixed exchange rates, and currency values rarely changed. Under the second regime, which has been in effect since 1973, exchange rates fluctuate daily in response to changes in supply and demand (market forces). As we shall see, governments also intervene in this flexible exchange rate system.

So far in Part IV on financial markets, we have discussed many aspects of the international financial system. This chapter on the international financial system completes our coverage of financial markets by providing the international framework in which financial instruments trade. In this chapter, we examine the international exchange rate systems in effect since 1944. These exchange rate systems form the backbone in which the international financial system operates. We also discuss the unique role that the dollar plays in the international financial system. Finally, we look at the international organizations that seek to provide a framework for financial stability as the cross-border trading of all types of financial instruments continues to grow.

The International Financial System from 1944 to 1973

From the end of World War II until the early 1970s, the major economies of the world participated in a **fixed exchange rate system** with the U.S. dollar functioning as the **official reserve currency**. Other countries defined their currencies in terms of the U.S. dollar and agreed to buy or sell dollars to maintain the agreed-upon exchange rates.[2] The dollar, in turn, was defined in terms of gold. During the postwar period, 1 ounce of gold was set equal to $35, and the United States agreed to convert any unwanted dollars of foreign central banks into gold. In cases of fundamental imbalances, an orderly procedure was established to make adjustments in exchange rates and thereby avoid the disruptive changes that had occurred between World War I and World War II

This fixed exchange rate system was established by the **Bretton Woods Accord** of 1944, which was worked out by representatives from the major industrialized countries who met at Bretton Woods, New Hampshire, to design a new international financial system. Under the Bretton Woods Accord, if the trade deficit of a country other than the United States increased, that country effectively increased the supply of its currency in international markets. The increased supply put downward pressure on the exchange rate. To maintain the agreed-upon exchange rate, the country's central bank had to purchase the excess supply of its currency using dollars.

An example will help clarify. Assume that the exchange rate between the dollar and the British pound was set at $1 = 2 pounds, but supply and demand were causing the market value of the two currencies to gravitate to $1 = 3 pounds. Perhaps, ceteris paribus, Britain's trade deficit had increased significantly in recent months, causing Britain's balance of payments on current and capital accounts to move into a deficit position.[3] The smaller supply of dollars relative to pounds in international markets puts upward pressure on the exchange rate of the dollar while the larger relative supply of pounds puts downward pressure on the value of the pound. In such a case, the Bank of England, the central bank of Great Britain, would intervene in the market by buying pounds with dollars until the market value of the two currencies converged to the agreed-upon exchange rate. By changing the supply of dollars and pounds outstanding, the Bank of England could manipulate the market value of the dollar in terms of the pound. In this manner, the values of the dollar and the pound could be maintained at the agreed-upon exchange rate of $1 = 2 pounds.

Such government transactions in foreign currencies were measured in the **Official Reserve Account** of the balance of payments. We ignored this account in Chapter 9. You can now see that by supplying dollars and demanding pounds, the Bank of England would run a surplus in the Official Reserve Account that would just equal the deficit in the current and capital accounts of the balance of payments. Hence, under fixed exchange rates, it was (and always is) official government transactions in foreign exchange markets that brought the balance of payments into balance at the fixed exchange rate.

Because the Bank of England was maintaining the fixed exchange rate by buying pounds with dollars, Great Britain could continue to maintain the fixed rate only so long as it had or could acquire sufficient dollars to support the value of its currency as needed. If Great Britain (or another foreign country) ran a persistent deficit in its current and capital accounts, its central bank would eventually run out of dollars and have to

Fixed Exchange Rate System
An exchange rate system in which currency values do not fluctuate.

Official Reserve Currency
The currency used by other countries to define their own currency; the U.S. dollar was the official reserve currency under the Bretton Woods Accord.

Bretton Woods Accord
A 1944 agreement negotiated by the major industrialized countries that established fixed exchange rates with the U.S. dollar serving as the official reserve currency.

Official Reserve Account
The balance of payments account that records official government transactions in the foreign exchange market to bring the balance of payments into balance.

The Gold Standard

During the late nineteenth and early twentieth centuries, the United States, along with the other major world economies, was on a gold standard that lasted about 30 years. Under the gold standard, the amount of currency in circulation was backed by gold. Each country defined its currency in terms of gold and agreed to buy or sell unlimited quantities of gold at a preestablished price, called the *par value.*

A gold standard is a type of fixed exchange rate system. For example, if one ounce of gold in the United States is equal to $20 and one ounce of gold in England is equal to 5 British pounds, then the pound/dollar exchange rate is .25; that is, $1 equals .25 British pounds. The dollar and the pound will always trade in this fixed ratio as long as both countries redeem their currencies in gold at the par value.

A gold standard comes under strain if countries experience different growth rates. For instance, suppose that a gold standard was in existence and that the United States was growing faster than its neighbors. In that case, the United States would find that imports were increasing faster than exports. In the foreign exchange market, the quantity supplied of dollars would be greater than the quantity demanded. Foreigners would present the dollars to the U.S. Treasury to be redeemed for gold, and the United States would lose its gold supply. As the United States lost gold, its money supply would fall with resulting depressing effects on output, jobs, and so on.

If policy makers wanted to keep the U.S. economy growing faster than economies in the rest of the world, they would be under pressure to devalue the U.S. currency. A devaluation is an increase in the number of dollars that must be presented to the Treasury to receive an ounce of gold. Fear of devaluation would cause more of the currency to be presented for redemption. Holders of dollars would convert the dollars to gold, and if devaluation did occur, they would convert the gold back to more dollars than they started with! This would exacerbate the gold loss and result in periodic financial crises as gold redemptions were suspended and the par values among currencies had to be redefined. In fact, scenarios like this actually occurred and led to the end of the gold standard.

Devalue

Under a fixed exchange rate system, to decrease the value of a country's currency.

devalue, or decrease the value of, its currency in terms of the dollar in order to reflect the diminished value of the pound. Devaluation occurs when the monetary authorities reduce the value of a country's currency under a fixed exchange rate system. In terms of our analysis, the pound is devalued if the official rate is changed from $1 per 2 pounds to $1 per 4 pounds. At the original rate, each pound was worth $.50, but at the latter rate, after the devaluation, each pound is worth $.25. The need to devalue could be accelerated if speculators sensed an impending necessity to devalue and increased the supply of pounds from what it would be otherwise. The alternative to devaluing would be for Great Britain to run a severely contractionary policy designed to lower prices in pounds and make British goods more desirable. As exports increased and imports decreased, the value of the pound would be restored to the agreed-upon exchange rate.

As you have seen, in the decades immediately after World War II, the U.S. dollar served as the official reserve currency. Unlike Great Britain in our example, the United

States was eventually in the unique position of being able to run persistent balance of payments deficits on the current and capital accounts. Initially after World War II, the United States was running sizable trade surpluses financed by capital outflows under the Marshall Plan. Foreign central banks desired to accumulate stockpiles of dollars to function as international reserves. During this period, a "dollar shortage" occurred as countries scrambled for dollars not only for reserves but also to rebuild their economies.

Once foreign central banks had acquired sufficient reserves, the ability of the United States to run chronic deficits in the balance of payments on current and capital accounts was also limited. In this case, the dollar, ceteris paribus, would become overvalued in terms of one or more foreign currencies. Under the Bretton Woods Accord, the United States would lose gold as the unwanted dollars were presented for conversion. The United States would then pressure foreign central banks to **revalue**, or increase the value of, their currency in terms of the dollar.

Revaluation occurs when the monetary authorities increase the value of a country's currency under a fixed exchange rate system. For example, the pound is revalued if the official rate is changed from $1 = 2 pounds to $1 = 1 pound. In the original case, each pound was worth $.50 while in the latter case, each pound is worth $1. Ceteris paribus, the revaluation would in time reduce the U.S. balance of payments deficit on current and capital accounts and slow the flow of unwanted dollars abroad. In turn, the gold outflow would diminish.

A foreign central bank might be hesitant to revalue, however, because revaluation could adversely affect its country's economy. Among other things, revaluation could reduce net exports and have a negative impact on employment. Note that whether the United States was running a persistent surplus or a persistent deficit in its balance of payments on current and capital accounts, the foreign central bank had to change the value of its currency in terms of the U.S. dollar. The foreign central bank had to act because, under the Bretton Woods Accord, if the United States changed the value of the dollar, the change would affect the relationship between the dollar and all other currencies, even though the dollar might have been out of alignment with only one or a few of the foreign currencies. Consequently, foreign central banks would pressure the United States to correct the imbalance by reducing its deficit on the current and capital accounts. Note the irony of the situation and the potential for a stalemate in which each country is pressuring the other to take action.

A balance of payments deficit on current and capital accounts could also be caused by increases in the capital outflows of a country, ceteris paribus. If a country experienced a net capital outflow, this had the same effect as an increase in the trade deficit of the same magnitude. Ceteris paribus, an increased net capital outflow from the United States comes from an increase in direct foreign investment by U.S. individuals or firms. Likewise, if a country experienced an increased net capital inflow, this had the same effect on the balance of payments on current and capital accounts as an increase in the trade surplus. As you have seen, ceteris paribus, such capital flows resulted from changes in domestic interest rates relative to foreign rates.

During the 1960s and 1970s, some countries, including the United States, expanded their economies and their domestic money supplies relatively faster than others, such as Japan and Germany. The United States experienced inflationary pressures in the mid- to late 1960s as a result of monetary and fiscal policies associated with the Great Society's War on Poverty and the Vietnam War buildup. Consequently, some central banks outside the United States accumulated more dollars than they wished to hold as reserve assets. Rather than revaluing their currencies, they asked the United States to convert these unwanted dollars to gold.

As more and more central banks requested conversion, it became clear that the United States would not be able to continue to redeem the dollars in gold. In late 1971, the United States suspended the international conversion of dollars into gold. At the same time, the dollar was devalued by setting the value of 1 ounce of gold equal to $42 rather than the $35 that had been in effect since the inception of the Bretton Woods Accord. Hence, the "official value" of the dollar was reduced from $1 = 1/35 ounce of gold to $1 = 1/42 ounce of gold, even though the United States was no longer redeeming dollars with gold. In 1973, most countries abandoned fixed exchange rates altogether, and the value of the dollar began to float. The Jamaica Agreement of 1974 officially adopted floating exchange rates, underscoring what had unofficially been done in 1973.

A final comment is in order. During the Bretton Woods period, the amount of cross-border trading of financial assets such as stocks, bonds, and mortgages was much less than it is today. Under normal circumstances, exchange risk was minimal during this period, but many countries had capital controls that did not allow the purchase of foreign financial instruments. Also, technology was such that it did not foster cross-border financial flows.

Recap   The international financial system consists of the arrangements, rules, customs, instruments, facilities, and organizations that enable international payments to be made and funds to flow across borders. The international financial system includes the international money and capital markets and the foreign exchange market. The Bretton Woods Accord of 1944 established fixed exchange rates among major world currencies. The U.S. dollar, which was backed by gold, served as the official reserve currency, and other countries defined their currencies in terms of the dollar. If a country other than the United States had a deficit in its balance of payments, it used supplies of dollars to purchase its own currency to maintain fixed exchange rates. If a country other than the United States had a surplus in its balance of payments, it demanded dollars to maintain the value of its currency. The system broke down in late 1971 when the United States suspended the international conversion of dollars to gold. A flexible exchange rate system was adopted in 1973. In the Bretton Woods period, cross-border investment in financial instruments was much less than it is today.

The Managed Float Exchange Rate System since 1973

The demise of the Bretton Woods Accord initiated a new era in which the exchange rates of major industrialized countries are no longer fixed. Rather, these countries participate in a **floating (flexible) exchange rate system** in which exchange rates fluctuate by the minute and the hour as market forces change.

Floating (Flexible) Exchange Rate System
An exchange rate system in which currency values are determined by supply and demand and fluctuate in response to changes in supply and demand.

Like other major currencies, the exchange rate of the U.S. dollar is determined by demand and supply in international markets. The supply of dollars per month reflects the U.S. demand for foreign goods, services, and securities. Ceteris paribus, the quantity of dollars supplied is a positive function of the exchange rate. The demand for dollars reflects the foreign demand for U.S. goods, services, and securities. Ceteris paribus, the quantity demanded is a negative function of the exchange rate. The market gravitates to the equilibrium exchange rate where quantity demanded is equal to quantity supplied.

From an initial equilibrium, if U.S. incomes, U.S. inflation, or foreign interest rates rise, ceteris paribus, U.S. demand for foreign goods, services, and securities will increase, and so will the supply of dollars. The market will gravitate to a new equilibrium at a lower exchange rate that corresponds to a depreciation of the dollar.

Likewise, if foreign incomes, foreign inflation, or U.S. interest rates rise, ceteris paribus, foreign demand for U.S. goods, services, and securities will increase, and so will the demand for dollars. The market will gravitate to a new equilibrium at a higher exchange rate that corresponds to an appreciation of the dollar. Because we live in a very dynamic world, the factors that determine supply and demand are always changing. Hence, exchange rates change by the minute.

To summarize, factors such as domestic and foreign incomes, inflation rates, and interest rates affect exchange rates, and "flexible" exchange rates immediately adjust to changing market conditions and expectations. The A Closer Look feature on page 450 reviews the basics of exchange rate determination under flexible exchange rates as first presented in Chapter 9.

Our story does not end here, however. Market forces are not the only factor that affects exchange rates. In addition, central banks may intervene in the foreign exchange market by buying and selling currencies to influence exchange rates. Thus, the present international monetary system can be more correctly characterized as a **managed float exchange rate system** because exchange rates are allowed to fluctuate in accordance with supply and demand; but central banks may intervene if a currency is thought to be over or undervalued. This system is distinctly different from the fixed rate exchange system under the Bretton Woods Accord.

Interestingly, central banks have intervened more often under the managed float than under the previous fixed exchange rate system, which required them to intervene to maintain the agreed-upon exchange rate. Sometimes central banks have intervened more frequently than at other times. Often central banks of major countries have agreed to pursue similar exchange rate policies and have coordinated their interventions as part of the implementation of monetary policy. Central bank intervention is discussed more fully in Chapter 27.

One final point needs to be made. Under the managed float exchange rate system, many small countries peg the value of their currencies to the U.S. dollar or some other major currency or basket of currencies. By doing so, a small country reduces the risk that the value of its currency will fluctuate unpredictably. If the exchange rate of a small country fluctuates unpredictably, the value of real or financial assets denominated in that currency will also fluctuate unpredictably. By tying the value of its currency to the U.S. dollar or a basket of other major currencies, a small country can reduce this risk. A financial crisis can result, however, if the country cannot maintain the fixed exchange rate. Both the Mexican peso crisis of 1994 and the Asian crisis of 1997–1998 occurred when the affected countries were unable to maintain an exchange rate that they had fixed in terms of the dollar. In both cases, the eventual depreciation of the currencies triggered widespread losses, the failure of many financial and nonfinancial firms, and financial crises. Exhibit 19-1 on pages 452 and 453 gives the exchange rate arrangements for most countries in the world.

Managing Exchange Rate Risk under the Managed Float

Under flexible exchange rates, when market participants enter into contracts to receive or supply so much foreign currency on a future date, there is an exchange rate risk because the future spot exchange rate is unknown.[4] Market participants may be importers or exporters who will receive or who need so much foreign exchange on a future date, or they may be investors who have purchased or who plan to purchase foreign financial securities that will mature in the future. If the exchange rate changes unexpectedly between now and the future date, the anticipated profits of an exporter, importer, or investor could be reduced. Worse yet, a loss could be incurred. Thus, under flexible exchange rate systems, market participants are exposed to substantial exchange rate risk.

Managed Float Exchange Rate System
A system in which currency values fluctuate with changes in supply and demand but central banks may intervene if currency values are thought to be over- or undervalued.

The Foreign Exchange Market

In the accompanying graphs (a) and (b), the quantity of dollars is measured on the horizontal axis, and the exchange rate (euros per dollar) is measured on the vertical axis. The quantity supplied of dollars per month, reflecting U.S. demand for foreign goods, services, and securities, is, ceteris paribus, a positive function of the exchange rate while the

(a)

(b)

quantity demanded of dollars per month is a negative function of the exchange rate. In this case, quantity demanded is equal to quantity supplied at point A, producing an equilibrium exchange rate of two euros. Assume now that the initial equilibrium at point A in graph (a) is disturbed by one of the following developments: (1) the euro price of U.S. goods and services rises relative to the euro price of foreign goods and services because of inflation in the United States; (2) foreign interest rates rise relative to U.S. interest rates; or (3) foreign incomes fall relative to U.S. incomes. The result is a reduction in the demand for U.S. goods, services, and financial instruments by foreigners and thus a reduction in the demand for dollars—shown as a leftward shift of the demand function in graph (a). The new equilibrium at point B results in a depreciation of the dollar from two euros to one euro.

Next assume that the economy is again at the initial equilibrium exchange rate of $1 = 2 euros as in graph (b). The equilibrium is disturbed by one of the following developments: (1) a rise in U.S. income; (2) a rise in U.S. prices relative to the dollar prices of foreign goods; or (3) a rise in foreign interest rates relative to U.S. interest rates. As a result, U.S. demand for foreign goods, services, and securities increases, as does the supply of dollars—shown as a rightward shift of the supply function in graph (b). The new equilibrium at point B results in a depreciation of the dollar as the equilibrium exchange rate falls from 2 euros = 1 euro.

In recent years, international financial markets have developed hybrid instruments including foreign exchange forward, futures, options, and swap agreements to hedge exchange rate risk. These instruments, which are all forms of derivatives, can be used to reduce the risk of unforeseen price changes. In this case, the prices are exchange rates. Thus, these markets reduce exchange rate risk.

Forward, futures, options, and swap agreements effectively lock in today an exchange rate for a transaction that may or will occur in the future, thus reducing the risk that changes in the exchange rate will alter expected outcomes.

The development of foreign exchange forward, futures, options, and swap agreements coincides with the tremendous growth in trade and capital flows coupled with the increased volatility of exchange rates under the managed float exchange rate system. Because these instruments reduce exchange rate risks, they facilitate trade in goods, services, and financial claims.

The Role of the Dollar under the Managed Float

Under the Bretton Woods Accord, the dollar played a dominant role in the international financial system because it served as the official reserve currency. Under the managed float system, the dollar has continued to play an important role in the international financial system. Because of its relative stability, the dollar continues to serve as the major reserve currency.

In addition to serving as a reserve asset, the dollar is sometimes used as a medium of exchange and a unit of account in international markets. Exchanges between two currencies of small countries often take place through dollars rather than directly. For

Exchange Rate Arrangements and Anchors of Monetary Policy
(As of December 31, 2002)[1]

Exchange Rate Regime (Number of countries)	Monetary Policy Framework				Monetary aggregate target	Inflation targeting framework	Fund-supported or other monetary program	Other
	Exchange rate anchor							
Exchange arrangements with no separate legal tender (40)	**Another currency as legal tender**	**ECCU[2]**	**CFA Franc Zone**					**Euro Area[4,5]**
			WAEMU	**CAEMC**				Austria
	Ecuador*	Antigua & Barbuda	Benin*	Cameroon*				Belgium
	El Salvador[14]	Dominica	Burkina Faso*	C. African Rep.*				Finland
	Kiribati	Grenada	Côte d'Ivoire*	Chad*				France
	Marshall Islands Rep. of	St. Kitts & Nevis	Guinea-Bissau*	Congo. Rep.of*				Germany
	Micronesia. Fed. States of	St. Lucia	Mali*	Equatorial Guinea				Greece
	Palau	St. Vincent & the Grenadines	Niger*	Gabon*				Ireland
	Panama		Senegal*					Italy
	San Marino		Togo					Luxembourg
								Netherlands
								Portugal
								Spain
Currency board arrangements (8)	Argentina*							
	Bosnia and Herzegovina*							
	Brunei Darussalam							
	Bulgaria*							
	China. P.R. Hong Kong							
	Djibouti*							
	Estonia*							
	Lithuania*							
Other conventional fixed peg arrangements (including de facto peg arrangements under managed floating) (40)	**Against a single currency (30)**		**Against a composite (10)**		China, PR.: Mainland†[7]			
	Aruba	Namibia	Botswana[5]					
	Bahamas. The[6]	Nepal	Fiji					
	Babrain. Kingdom of	Netherlands Antilles	Kuwait					
	Bangladesh	Oman	Latvia*					
	Barabados	Qatar[7,8]	Libyan A.J.					
	Belize	Saudi Arabia[7,8]	Malta					
	Bhutan	Sudan[7]	Morocco					
	Cape Verde	Suriname[6,7]	Samoa					
	China, P.R. Mainland†[7]	Swaziland	Seychelles					
	Comoros[7]	Syrian Arab Republic[6]	Vanuatu					
	Iran[6,7]	Turkmenistan[7]						
	Jordan*[7]	United Arab Emirates[7,8]						
	Lebanon[7]	Zimbabwe[7]						
	Lesotho*							
	Macedonia, FYR*[7]							
	Malaysia							
	Maldives[7]							
Pegged exchange rates within horizontal bands (5)[10]	**Within a cooperative arrangement ERM II (1)**		**Other band arrangements (4)**			Hungary†		
	Denmark		Cyprus					
			Egypt[6]					
			Hungary†					
			Tonga					
Crawling pegs (4)	Bolivia*							
	Costa Rica[7]							
	Nicaragua*							
	Solomon Islands[7]							
Exchange rates within crawling bands (6)[11]	Belarus	Romania*[7]				Israel†		
	Honduras*	Uruguay*						
	Israel†	Venezuela, Rep. Bolivariana						

** ECCU: Eastern Caribbean Currency Union; WAEMU: West African Economic and Monetary Union; CAEMC: Central African Economic and Monetary Community

Exchange Rate Regimes and Anchors of Monetary Policy
(As of December 31, 2002)[1]

Exchange Rate Regime (Number of countries)	Monetary Policy Framework				
	Exchange rate anchor	Monetary aggregate target	Inflation targeting framework	Fund-supported or other monetary program	Other
Managed floating with no preannounced path for exchange rate (42)		Ghana* Guinea* Guyana* Indonesia* Jamaica*[7] Mauritius Mongolia* São Tomé and Príncipe* Slovenia Sir Lanka* Tunisia	Thailand*	Azerbaijan Cambodia[6] Croatia Ethiopia Iraq Kazakhstan Kenya Kyrgyz Republic Lao PDR[6] Mauritania Nigeria Pakistan Russian Federation Rwanda Trinidad & Tobago Ukraine Vietnam Yugoslavia. Fed Rep. of Zambia	Algeria[4] Angola[4] Burundi[4] Dominican Rep.[4,6] Eritrea[4] Guatemala[4] India[4] Myanmar[4,6,7] Paraguay[4] Singapore[4] Slovak Republic[4] Uzbekistan[4,6]
Independently floating (41)		Gambia, The* Malawi* Peru* Philippines* Sierra Leone* Turkey* Yemen*	Australia Brazil[13] Canada Chile[6] Colombia* Czech Rep. Iceland Korea Mexico New Zealand Norway Poland South Africa Sweden United Kingdom	Albania Armenia Congo. Dem. Rep. Georgia Madagascar Moldova Mozambique Tajikistan Tanzania Uganda	Afghanistan[6,12] Haiti[4] Japan[4] Liberia[4] Papua New Guinea[4] Somalia[6,12] Switzerland[4] United States[4]

Source: Staff Reports

Exchange Arrangements with No Separate Legal Tender: The currency of another country circulates as the sole legal tender or the member belongs to a monetary or currency union in which the same legal tender is shared by the members of the union.

Currency Board Arrangements: A monetary regime based on an explicit legislative commitment to exchange domestic currency for a specified foreign currency at a fixed exchange rate, combined with restrictions on the issuing authority to ensure the fulfillment of its legal obligation.

Other Conventional Fixed Peg Arrangements: The country pegs its currency (formally or de facto) at a fixed rate to a major currency or a basket of currencies where the exchange rate fluctuates within a narrow margin of less than ±1 percent around a central rate.

Pegged Exchange Rates Within Horizontal Bands: The value of the currency is maintained within margins of fluctuation around a formal or de facto fixed peg that are wider than at least ±1 percent around a central rate.

Crawling Pegs: The currency is adjusted periodically in small amounts at a fixed, preannounced rate or in response to changes in selective quantitative indicators.

Exchange Rates Within Crawling Bands: The currency is maintained within certain fluctuation margins around a central rate that is adjusted periodically at a fixed preannounced rate or in response to changes in selective quantitative indicators.

Managed Floating with No Preannounced Path for the Exchange Rate: The monetary authority influences the movements of the exchange rate through active intervention in the foreign exchange market without specifying, or precommitting to, a preannounced path for the exchange rate.

Independent Floating: The exchange rate is market determined, with any foreign exchange intervention aimed at moderating the rate of change and preventing undue fluctuations in the exchange rate, rather than at establishing a level for it.

Note: "Country" in this publication does not always refer to a territorial entity that is a state as understood by international law and practice; the term also covers the euro area and some nonsovereign territorial entities for which statistical data are provided internationally on a separate basis.
[1]A country with * indicates that the country has a Fund supported or other monetary program.
[2]A country with † indicates that the country has more than one nominal anchor that may may guide monetary policy. It should be noted, however, that it would not be possible, for practical purposes, to infer from this table which nominal anchor plays the principal role in conducting monetary policy.
[3]These countries have a currency arrangement.
[4]The country has no explicitly stated nominal anchor, but rather monitors various indicators in conducting monetary policy.
[5]Until they are withdrawn in February 2002, national currencies will retain their status as legal tender within their home territories.
[6]Member maintained exchange regimes involving more than one market. The regime shown is that maintained in the major market.
[7]The indicated country has a de facto regime which differs from its de jure regime.
[8]Exchange rates are determined on the basis of a fixed relationship to the SDR, within margins of up to ±7.25%. However, because of the maintenance of a relatively stable relationship with the U.S. dollar, these margins are not always observed.
[9]Comoros has the same arrangement with the French Treasury as do the CFA Franc Zone countries.
[10]The band width for these countries is: Cyprus (±2.25%), Denmark (±2.25%), Egypt (±3%), Hungary (±15%), and Tonga (±5%).
[11]The band for these countries is: Belarus (±5%), Honduras (±7%), Israel (±22%), Romania (unannounced), Uruguay (±3%), and República Bolivariana de Venezuela (±7.5%).
[12]There is no relevant information available for the country.
[13]Brazil maintains a Fund-supported program.
[14]For El Salvador, the printing of new colones, the domestic currency, is prohibited, but the existing stock of colones will continue to circulate, along with the U.S. dollar, as legal tender until all notes physically wear out.

example, Peru might convert its currency to dollars and use the dollars to purchase the currency of South Africa rather than using its own currency to purchase the currency of South Africa directly. Prices of standardized contracts of raw materials and commodities are often quoted in dollars. For example, the price of oil from the Middle East is quoted in dollars, and the dollar is also the medium of exchange through which oil is bought and sold around the world. The dollar is accepted for payments in many faraway places and has been widely used in countries experiencing political and economic unrest in the past, such as Russia, Ukraine, and Mexico.

The dollar also acts as a store of value. As you have seen, 50 to 60 percent of all U.S. currency and more than 70 percent of $100 bills are held abroad. The dollar is demanded as a store of value because of the political stability of the United States and the dollar's acceptance over time.

Although the dollar is no longer the official reserve asset, the demand for dollars to be used in international financial markets (either as reserves or for other uses) has continued to grow. Indeed, the demand for dollars has grown faster than domestic real incomes due to the increase in trade, capital flows, and real incomes around the world.

Despite its many roles, the dollar is less important in relative terms today than under the Bretton Woods Accord. Despite this, it has gained in relative importance, since 1993. Other currencies such as the euro, the Japanese yen, and the British pound are now also used as international reserves. In the coming years, it is expected that the euro may also gain in relative importance, and the trend may have already begun. Between the end of 1993 and the end of 1999, the percentage of official international reserve assets held in dollars or dollar-denominated assets increased from 56.6 percent to 67.7 percent. By the end of 2003, the U.S. dollar share hadslipped to 63.8 percent. At the end 1999, the newly created euro made up 12.6 percent of international reserves. By the end of 2003, this had increased to 19.7 percent. The Japanese yen and British pound sterling made up 4.8 percent and 4.4 percent, respectively, at the end of 2003.[5]

Within this changing environment, several international organizations are developing unique roles in the international financial system. These organizations include the International Monetary Fund, the World Bank, and the Bank for International Settlements. They seek to foster stability in the international financial system so that the benefits of trade and cross-border trading of financial instruments can be realized. Just as the financial system has evolved to deal with the growth in trade and capital flows, these organizations are redefining their roles in the increasingly globalized economy. It is to these organizations that we now turn.

Recap Since 1973, major industrialized countries have participated in a managed float exchange rate system. The value of a currency is determined by supply and demand, but governments intervene by buying and selling (demanding and supplying) currencies to affect currency values. Small countries often tie the value of their currencies to the dollar or some other major currency. Foreign exchange forward, futures, options, and swap agreements have been developed to allow market participants to hedge exchange rate risks. Under the managed float, the dollar is still the major international reserve asset although other currencies also serve as international reserves. In addition, the dollar is demanded in international financial markets because of its stability. It serves as a medium of exchange, a unit of account, and a store of value in some international markets.

The Path to a Single European Currency

In 1979, the European Monetary System was established to increase exchange rate stability among countries in Western Europe. Under the system, individual currencies had limited flexibility, and central banks intervened by buying and selling currencies if exchange rates moved outside a narrow band. If fundamental imbalances existed, exchange rates were changed to correct the imbalances. In that same year, the European Currency Unit (ECU) was created. The ECU was an accounting unit made up of a weighted basket of currencies. The weights were determined by the gross domestic product and other real and financial variables of the participating countries. It was hoped that the ECU would eventually lead to the creation of a single currency.

In the Maastricht Treaty of 1991, 15 European countries agreed to a plan to adopt a single European currency by no later than 1999.[a] During the phase-in period, the countries maintained exchange rates within a narrow range of the ECU.[b] As of January 1, 1999, 11 countries participated in the currency union. Exchange rates of the 11 participating countries were fixed and no longer fluctuated even within a narrow range. In addition, the newly established European Central Bank together with the national central banks formed the Eurosystem that took over the formulation of monetary policy. Although the new currency did not yet circulate, all newly issued stocks and government bonds, bank accounts, corporate books, credit card payments, and mortgages could be figured in euros.[c]

The euro did begin circulating on January 1, 2002. Europeans exchanged their own national currencies for euros. After March 1, 2002, the national currencies were no longer accepted as money.

To participate in the single currency, countries had to meet criteria including having annual budget deficits not greater than 3 percent of GDP and a government debt less than 60 percent of GDP or moving toward that goal. Of the 15 countries that signed the Maastricht Treaty, Great Britain, Denmark, and Sweden decided not to participate in the currency union. Greece did not meet the criteria to join on January 1, 1999. However, Greece became the twelfth country to participate in the currency union when it was able to join on January 1, 2001.

In giving up their national currencies, countries are surrendering the right to determine their own national interest rates, exchange rates, and monetary policies. In addition, they are giving up some control over the size of their budget deficits. For example, countries may not be able to run fiscal deficits as large as they would like or to lower interest rates as much as they would like in the face of unemployment, and they definitely will not be able to devalue national currencies!

Despite these potential disadvantages, the countries supported the common currency because it will lead to tremendous reductions in the transactions costs of making exchanges. Such reductions translate to higher economic growth. According to *Business Week,* "In one fell swoop, it [the euro] will create the world's second-largest economic zone. The potential benefits are limitless—and so are the risks."[d]

Major International Financial Organizations

As you have seen, the Bretton Woods Accord of 1944 established the fixed exchange rate system that remained in effect until the early 1970s. In addition, the meetings at Bretton Woods resulted in the creation of the **International Monetary Fund (IMF)** and the **World Bank**. Although the fixed rate exchange system has not survived, the IMF and World Bank did not meet a similar fate, as will be discussed in this chapter. Indeed, in recent years, both have gained in stature, and another international organization, the Bank for International Settlements (BIS), is also discussed. BIS predates the IMF and the World Bank and is the oldest major international financial institution in existence today.

Visit the sites of the World Bank, the International Monetary Fund, and the Bank for International Settlements at **http://www.worldbank.org, http://www.imf.org**, and **http://www.bis.org/index.htm**.

The International Monetary Fund (IMF)

The purposes of the International Monetary Fund are:

> to promote international monetary cooperation . . . ; to facilitate the expansion and balanced growth of international trade . . . ; to promote exchange stability . . . ; to assist in the establishment of a multilateral system of payments . . . ; to make its general resources temporarily available to its members experiencing balance of payments difficulties under adequate safeguards . . . ; and to shorten the duration and lessen the degree of disequilibrium in the international balances of payments of members. . . .[6]

As such, the IMF is a voluntary institution owned and directed by the countries that choose to join. The IMF is much like an overseer of the monetary and exchange rate policies of its members. Member countries agree to exchange their currencies freely with other foreign currencies, to keep the IMF informed of changes in financial and monetary policies that may affect other members, and to adjust these policies based on the recommendations of the IMF for the greater common good.

When joining the IMF, each country is assessed a quota (membership fee) based on its economic importance and the amount of its international trade. A country's voting rights in the organization are proportionate to the amount of its quota. At the IMF's inception, the total quota (subscription) was $8.8 billion of which the United States' share was 31 percent. Thus, the United States controlled 31 percent of the votes. Quotas are revised every five years to ensure that the IMF has adequate funds at its disposal. As of September 2004, 184 countries (including all major countries of the world) were members of the IMF, and the total subscription was roughly $311 billion. The amount of the subscription has grown as more countries have joined the IMF and larger quotas have been assessed. Over the years, the U.S. share has fallen to 17.43 percent. Therefore, the United States today controls 17.43 percent of the votes. The IMF is headquartered in Washington, D.C., and has approximately 2,700 employees from more than 141 countries. Other offices are in Paris, in Geneva, Switzerland, and at the United Nations in New York.

The IMF administers the pool of funds generated by the quotas to assist member countries that, because of deficits in their balance of payments, do not have enough foreign exchange to pay all of the claims that are being presented to them. Members can borrow from the pool of funds to resolve temporary imbalances. This influx of funds gives them time to change their economic policies so that balance of payment deficits are resolved in an orderly manner with minimal damages to themselves and to other countries. Members must request assistance and abide by IMF policy recommendations if receiving the funds. In addition to the pool of funds generated from the quotas, the IMF also has standby agreements to borrow supplemental funds, if needed, from the wealthiest members.

Special Drawing Rights (SDRs)
International reserve assets created by the IMF to supplement other international reserves.

In 1969, the IMF created **special drawing rights (SDRs)**, which are international reserve assets that supplement other international reserves. SDRs were created in response to a shortage in international reserves. At that time, the Bretton Woods Accord was still in effect, and the dollar was the official reserve asset. The value of the SDR is a weighted average of the U.S. dollar, the euro, Japanese yen, and British pound sterling, so it fluctuates daily. Today the outstanding value of SDRs fluctuates around $30 billion, depending on the value of the four currencies. The SDRs are equal to about 2 percent of nongold international reserves of the member countries. They are bookkeeping entries not backed by other reserve assets, and they provide the international financial system with additional liquidity. Central banks use SDRs, rather than other national currencies, to make payments to other member countries.

In the past, SDRs have been distributed to members of the IMF according to their quotas. Although only two distributions have been made since their inception, additional SDRs can be created and distributed if the IMF determines that there is a long-term global need for additional international reserves. The last distribution was in 1981. In September 1997, the IMF proposed an additional onetime allocation to spread the SDRs more equitably among members, of which 80 percent of IMF voting power must approve the allocation. As of September 2004, 77.3 percent of IMF voting power had approved the allocation. The United States, with just over 17 percent of the voting power, 77.3 had not yet voted for the amendment. Since the last allocation, 40 countries have joined the IMF and, hence, have never received an allocation.

The activities of the IMF can be divided into two distinct periods: the Bretton Woods era and the period since the managed float. During the Bretton Woods era, the IMF's activities centered on monitoring the fixed exchange rate system and assisting countries in maintaining it. The IMF would often make loans to countries to finance short-term deficits in their balance of payments so that the fixed exchange rates could be maintained. If long-term problems existed, the fixed exchange rates were adjusted to correct the imbalances. When making loans, the IMF often recommended that the recipient country change its domestic policies that had contributed to its balance of payments deficit. As already noted, loans were contingent on the borrower's acceptance of the IMF's recommendations.

When fixed exchange rates were abandoned in 1973, the IMF no longer had a fixed rate system to monitor, so its role changed. Now the IMF, in an advisory capacity, oversees economic policies that affect the balance of payments and exchange rates. In addition, the IMF provides information to members about countries that are experiencing balance of payments difficulties that could result in financial crises. Finally, the IMF continues to provide financial assistance to members that experience short-term balance of payments problems. As before, the financial assistance is contingent on the recipient's promise to reform its economic policies and adopt the IMF's recommendations. The IMF played a key role in resolving the international debt crisis that afflicted less-developed countries in the 1980s, the Mexican peso crisis of 1994–1995, and the Asian crisis of the late 1990s. Intervention by the IMF has also prevented many financial crises from occurring. For a discussion of the IMF's role in the Asian crisis of the late 1990s, see the accompanying A Closer Look feature on page 458.

In the 2000s, the growing economic integration of the world's goods, services, and capital markets has created new opportunities and challenges for the IMF. It is taking a leading role in defining and fostering a stable international financial system.

The Role of the IMF in the Asian Crisis

The IMF was created at the end of World War II to assist countries that were experiencing a financial crisis. The goal was to contain the crisis and prevent it from spreading to the global financial system.[a] The IMF assists countries that are experiencing a financial crisis by providing large-scale liquidity. In addition, the IMF can provide technical assistance to help policy makers find a resolution to the crisis.

The Asian crisis of 1997 arose out of a situation in which the currencies of Southeast Asia were pegged to the dollar and, thus, had appreciated along with the dollar. Given large current account deficits and relatively small supplies of international reserves, the currencies became overvalued. In addition, the countries were enjoying significant capital inflows and had large short-term loans denominated in U.S. dollars. If the currencies were devalued, more domestic currency would be required to pay back the dollar-denominated loans. The result would be many defaults and bankruptcies.

Throughout the crisis, the IMF played a significant role in helping the countries of Southeast Asia find a solution to their problems. Beginning in late 1997, the IMF recommended that the overvalued currencies be devalued. After the initial round of devaluations and the breaking of the dollar peg, the IMF called for the Asian nations to substantially increase their interest rates in an attempt to stop the continuing slide of currency values. In addition, the IMF made short-term loans to provide liquidity to the stricken economies. The goals of the rescue plans were to stabilize currency values, restore investor confidence, and reestablish the nations' access to international capital flows.

The IMF assistance did not come without strings attached. The IMF required the countries to pursue contractionary fiscal policies designed to cut consumption. The fall in consumption would lead to a decrease in imports and a reduction in the current account deficits. This policy recommendation was fairly typical for the IMF in such a situation.

In addition, the IMF required the governments to introduce structural changes into their financial systems, in particular, to improve the regulation and oversight of their banks. In the future, the countries were also to avoid becoming so dependent on short-term financing (especially from abroad) to prevent their financial systems from being so vulnerable to changes in market sentiment.

By mid-1998, some economies in Southeast Asia were on the road to recovery, although they were far from experiencing healthy growth. Without loans from the IMF, the crisis would have persisted. It is also highly likely that the countries would have defaulted on their short-term U.S. dollar loans.

Although the IMF had some success in alleviating the crisis, its policies have been criticized. Some critics complain that the rescue plans did not go far enough because they did not entail a restructuring of the short-term debt and left corporate sectors in very fragile financial positions. Without such a restructuring, the currencies continued to depreciate, and bankruptcies persisted longer than had a restructuring plan been part of the rescue package. At the other extreme, some critics argue that the crisis would have had a greater long-term, positive impact if it had been allowed to run its course without intervention from the IMF, although the short-term pain would have been greater. Still other critics argue that the crisis could have been prevented or at least mitigated if the IMF had warned the international financial community earlier about the problems of the troubled economies.[b]

Overall, the Asian crisis has caused the IMF to reconsider its role as an international financial organization, particularly as it relates to imposing structural reforms on its members and to fostering a stable international financial system.

The crisis also spawned the creation of the Financial Stability Forum to promote global financial stability.

The World Bank

Like the IMF, the World Bank was created in 1944 at Bretton Woods, is headquartered in Washington, D.C., and has 184 member countries as of 2004. The similarities stop there, however. The World Bank is an investment bank that issues bonds and uses the proceeds to make long-term, low-interest-rate loans to poor countries for economic development projects. The bonds have the highest credit rating because the World Bank's 184 member countries guarantee repayment.

The World Bank is really two organizations: the **International Bank for Reconstruction and Development (IBRD)** and the **International Development Association**. The latter makes interest-free loans with a maturity of 35–40 years to the world's poorest countries (in 2002, those having an annual per capita gross domestic product of less than $865). IBRD makes 12- to 15-year low-interest-rate loans to poor countries with annual per capita gross domestic product of less than $5,225 and more than $865. These countries may have private borrowing opportunities but at much higher rates of interest. The interest rate charged is slightly above the rate the bank pays to borrow when it issues the bonds.

Many of the loans financed by the World Bank are used to build infrastructure such as electric power plants and roads. The bank also finances projects to improve drinking water, waste disposal, health care, nutrition, family planning, education, and housing. In addition to loans, the bank also provides technical assistance. Many countries that borrowed from the World Bank in the past have developed sufficiently that they no longer need to do so. Thus, the bank can direct its aid to other poor countries.

The World Bank focuses on public projects rather than directly assisting private enterprises in developing countries. Another organization, the **International Finance Corporation**, seeks to mobilize funding for private enterprises. Although legally separate from the World Bank, the corporation is associated with it and is the organization through which the World Bank encourages small business development. The International Finance Corporation has also helped to establish stock markets in many developing countries, thus increasing their ability to attract international capital flows.

The Bank for International Settlements (BIS)

The **Bank for International Settlements (BIS)** is an independent international financial organization, headquartered in Basel, Switzerland, that was created in 1930, which was 14 years before the Bretton Woods Accord. As such, it is the world's oldest international financial organization. The purpose of the BIS was "to promote the cooperation of central banks and to provide additional facilities for international financial operations."[7] The BIS was originally established to monitor and administer the reparations that the countries defeated in World War I were required to pay to the victorious nations. In addition, the BIS was to provide specialized services to central banks and through them to the international financial system.

International Bank for Reconstruction and Development (IBRD)

A bank that makes 12- to 15-year loans to poor, but not the poorest, countries, charging an interest rate just above the rate at which the bank borrows.

International Development Association

An association that makes interest-free loans with a maturity of 35–40 years to the world's poorest countries.

International Finance Corporation

An organization that mobilizes funding for private enterprise projects in poor countries.

Bank for International Settlements (BIS)

An international financial organization that promotes international cooperation among central banks and provides facilities for international financial operations.

Since 1960, the BIS has become an important international monetary organization with expanding functions. The BIS acts as a trustee for many international financial agreements and monitors compliance with the agreements. It is very active in identifying, negotiating, and monitoring international standards for banking regulation and supervision. The BIS seeks to establish international reporting standards for financial institutions and to assist countries in developing safe and sound financial practices. It encourages cooperation among member and nonmember central banks.

At the present time, 55 countries are members of the BIS, and the bank's directors come from the central banks of 11 countries (Belgium, Canada, France, Germany, Italy, Japan, the Netherlands, Sweden, Switzerland, the United Kingdom, and the United States). Central bankers from Belgium, France, Germany, Italy, the United Kingdom, and the United States are permanent members of the board of directors. A country does not have to be a member of the BIS to have an account with the bank, and central banks of 140 countries have deposit accounts with the BIS totaling around 6 percent of world foreign exchange reserves as of March 31, 2004. The bank has 549 employees from 44 countries.

In addition to acting as a bank for central banks, the BIS is also a meeting place where central bankers consult on a monthly basis. Since the early 1960s, a group of 11 nations (Belgium, Canada, France, Germany, Italy, Japan, the Netherlands, Sweden, Switzerland, the United Kingdom, and the United States), widely known as the *G-10*, has held regular monthly meetings at the bank to discuss international financial matters including financial stability. As financial markets have become more globalized, these informal meetings have taken on more importance and led to greater international cooperation. In Chapter 14, we discussed the details of the Basel Accord of 1988 that established international standards for banking regulation among the 12 nations that signed the agreement. The agreement was negotiated at the BIS.

At the present time, the BIS is expanding its relationships with central banks in emerging economies and, thus, is increasing its stature in the international financial system.

The mission statement of the Bank for International Settlements, its latest annual reports, and more are available at **http://www.bis.org/index/htm**.

A Framework for International Financial Stability

Leaders from Canada, Germany, France, Italy, Japan, the United Kingdom, and the United States (known as the *G-7 countries*), have met annually since 1975 to discuss such common concerns including the international financial system. Discussions before and after meetings are sometimes broadened to include leaders from other countries, including but not limited to the leaders of the G-10 countries mentioned earlier who also meet annually. The financial crisis in Asia of the late 1990s revealed several deficiencies in the international financial system. As a result, the G-7 nations created the **Financial Stability Forum (FSF)** in early 1999 to promote international financial stability through the exchange of information and to foster cooperation in financial supervision and surveillance. The Financial Stability Forum consists of representatives of central banks, Treasury departments, and international financial institutions. Roger Ferguson, vice chair of the Fed, also chairs the FSF, which has offices at the BIS.

The G-7 leaders agree that as a prerequisite for participating in a stable international financial system, a country must have sound economic policies that foster noninflationary growth. Emerging countries that want to take advantage of increased international capital flows need support and encouragement to develop stable financial systems and markets that are appropriately supervised both internally and externally. Developing countries must establish banking systems that encourage the appropriate

Financial Stability Forum (FSF)
An organization of representatives of central banks, treasury departments, and international financial institutions created in 1999 to promote international financial stability through the exchange of information and to foster cooperation in international financial supervision and surveillance.

amount of risk taking. The system may include deposit insurance and a lender of last resort, but it should still allow private lenders to bear the costs of their decisions as well as to reap the rewards. If lenders know that national or international regulators will bail them out in the case of failure, they are likely to engage in too much risk taking. The case in which lenders are encouraged to take too many risks because they know they will be bailed out is an example of the moral hazard problem confronting institutions.

At the same time, the financial system should be strong enough that private failures rarely spill over to the entire financial system.

In addition to establishing healthy national financial systems, countries must also standardize the reporting of qualitative and quantitative information about their financial markets, institutions, laws, and regulations. Reporting of fiscal conditions should include information about international reserves, external debt (both short and long term), and the health of the banking sector. At the same time, financial and nonfinancial institutions should adopt international accounting standards that allow for effective international comparisons. International standards should be developed for auditing, disclosure, bankruptcy, corporate governance, and the valuation of stocks, bonds, and other assets.

Finally, organizations such as the IMF and BIS should work with the Financial Stability Forum to see that the international financial system is more transparent and that surveillance is more open.

More information about the Financial Stability Forum can be found at **http://www.fsforum.org/home/home.html.**

Between its inception and mid-2004, the FSF held 12 international meetings in various locations around the world in addition to a host of regional meetings. More meetings and much discussion will undoubtedly occur in the future if the full potentials of globalization are to be realized.

Recap   The IMF, the World Bank, and the BIS all have unique roles in the international financial system. The IMF promotes exchange rate stability, oversees the international financial system, and lends to member countries experiencing temporary balance of payments deficits. The World Bank promotes the economic development of the world's poorest countries by raising funds to make development loans. The BIS acts as a bank for central banks and seeks to establish and monitor international reporting and capital standards for financial institutions and to assist countries in developing safe and sound financial practices. The FSF, consisting of representatives of central banks, monetary authorities, and international financial institutions, meets regularly to exchange information and foster cooperation in financial surveillance and supervision in order to promote global financial stability.

Summary of Major Points

1. The international financial system consists of the arrangements, rules, customs, instruments, facilities, and organizations that enable international payments to be made and funds to flow across borders. The international financial system has experienced tremendous growth in recent years because of the increase in trade in goods, services, and financial instruments; technological advances; and the removal of barriers to capital flows. The international financial system is composed of the international money and capital markets and the foreign exchange market.

2. The Bretton Woods Accord of 1944 established fixed exchange rates between the U.S. dollar and other major currencies. Under the accord, foreign countries defined their currencies in terms of the U.S. dollar

and agreed to buy or sell dollars, the official reserve asset, to maintain the agreed-upon exchange rates. The dollar, in turn, was defined in terms of gold, and the United States agreed to convert any unwanted dollars of foreign central banks into gold.

3. Under fixed exchange rates, if a country other than the United States had a deficit in its balance of payments on current and capital accounts, it used supplies of dollars to purchase its own currency to maintain the exchange value. Likewise, if such a country had a surplus in its balance of payments on current and capital accounts, it demanded dollars to maintain or support the value of its currency. Persistent deficits and surpluses caused foreign countries to devalue or revalue their currencies, respectively.

4. The United States was in the unique position of being able to run persistent deficits in its balance of payments on current and capital accounts while foreign central banks were accumulating dollars to serve as international reserves. Once foreign central banks had acquired sufficient reserves, the ability of the United States to run deficits in its balance of payments on current and capital accounts was also limited. Eventually, the United States was unable to continue to convert dollars into gold, and the Bretton Woods system of fixed exchange rates collapsed in 1973. It was replaced by a system of flexible exchange rates. During the Bretton Woods period, trade in goods, services, and financial instruments was much less than it is today.

5. Under flexible exchange rates, the value of the dollar is determined by the demand for and supply of dollars, and the exchange rate will gravitate to the value at which quantity demanded is equal to quantity supplied. The demand for dollars is determined by foreign demand for U.S. goods, services, and financial instruments. The supply of dollars is determined by U.S. demand for foreign goods, services, and financial instruments. Ultimately, the demand for and supply of dollars are determined by domestic and foreign incomes, inflation rates, and interest rates.

6. Since 1973, the major industrialized countries have participated in a managed float exchange rate system. Under a managed float, market forces determine exchange rates, but governments may intervene by demanding or supplying currencies to affect exchange rates. Smaller countries often tie the value of their currencies to the dollar or some other major currency.

7. The dollar is very important in the international financial system because it serves as the major international reserve asset. Other currencies such as the euro, the Japanese yen, and the British pound also serve as international reserves. In addition, dollars are demanded in international financial markets to serve as a medium of exchange, a unit of account, and a store of value. Even though the dollar is no longer the official reserve currency, the international demand for dollars has increased because of the growth of trade in goods, services, and capital flows.

8. Foreign exchange forward, futures, options, and swap markets are used by market participants to hedge exchange rate risk. They effectively allow those who will need or will receive foreign exchange in the future to lock in an exchange rate today.

9. The IMF is an international organization owned and operated by its 184 member countries. The IMF promotes exchange rate stability, oversees the international financial system, and lends to member countries experiencing temporary balance of payments deficits. In addition to quotas from its members, the IMF also has lines of credit from the major industrial countries to lend, if needed, to member countries with balance of payments difficulties. SDRs are an international reserve asset created by the IMF to supplement the supply of international reserves.

10. The World Bank promotes the economic development of the world's poorest countries by raising funds to make development loans. A total of 184 countries belong to the World Bank. Whereas the World Bank funds public projects, the International Finance Corporation seeks to encourage private enterprise and development. The corporation is separate from the World Bank but works closely with it.

11. The BIS acts as a bank for central banks and seeks to establish and monitor international reporting and capital standards for financial institutions and to assist countries in developing safe and sound financial practices. The Financial Stability Forum, created after the Asian financial crisis, consists of representatives from central banks, Treasury departments, and international financial institutions. It meets regularly to establish and maintain a framework for international financial stability.

Key Terms

Bank for International Settlements (BIS), **459**

Bretton Woods Accord, **445**

Devalue, **445**

Financial Stability Forum (FSF), **460**

Fixed Exchange Rate System, **445**

Floating (Flexible) Exchange Rate System, **448**

Interest Rate Parity, **465**

International Bank for Reconstruction and Development, **459**

International Development Association, **459**

International Finance Corporation, **459**

International Financial System, **444**

International Monetary Fund (IMF), **456**

Managed Float Exchange Rate System, **449**

Official Reserve Account, **445**

Official Reserve Currency, **445**

Revalue, **447**

Special Drawing Rights (SDRs), **457**

World Bank, **456**

Review Questions

1. What is the international financial system, and how has it changed in recent years? What opportunities does the new system offer? What are the challenges?

2. Identify and explain three differences between the international monetary system under the Bretton Woods Accord and the managed float exchange rate system that replaced it.

3. Why did the Bretton Woods Accord break down?

4. What was the role of the dollar under the Bretton Woods Accord?

5. Why has the demand for dollars in international financial markets continued to grow, even though the dollar is no longer the official reserve currency?

6. When a country ran a deficit in its balance of payments under the Bretton Woods Accord, how was that deficit resolved?

7. Leticia is a small country that is experiencing a deficit in its current account in its balance of payments. The value of Leticia's currency is tied to the U.S. dollar, which has been appreciating. What options could the IMF recommend to correct the imbalance in Leticia's balance of payments?

8. Under flexible exchange rates, what happens if a country experiences a deficit in its balance of payments? How long can a deficit in the balance of payments persist?

9. Why and how do central banks intervene in foreign exchange markets under the managed float exchange rate system?

10. How do the roles of the IMF and the BIS differ? How are they similar? What is the primary function of the World Bank?

11. What is the difference between the types of projects financed by the World Bank and those funded by the International Finance Corporation?

12. What factors have contributed to the increase in capital flows among countries?

13. What is the contagion effect? Why is it more pronounced today than it was 20 years ago?

14. What were the causes of the Asian crisis? What did the IMF do to mitigate the Asian crisis?

15. Explain how foreign exchange futures contracts can be used to reduce exchange rate risk. Is there exchange rate risk under both fixed and flexible exchange rate systems? Explain.

16. Use Exhibit 19-1 to define *pegged exchange rates, currency board,* and *exchange agreements with no separate legal tender.* How many countries have currency boards?

17. What is the Financial Stability Forum? Why was it created?

Analytical Questions

Questions marked with an icon are objective in nature. They can be completed with a short answer or number.

19. The United States has capital inflows of $100 billion and capital outflows of $200 billion. What is the balance on the capital account?

20. Go to today's *Wall Street Journal* and find the yen/dollar exchange rate. Has the dollar appreciated or depreciated since October 22, 2004, when $1 equaled 107.27 yen?

21. Graphically demonstrate what would happen to the exchange rate in each of the following situations:
    a. The U.S. trade deficit increases, ceteris paribus.
    b. The U.S. trade deficit decreases, ceteris paribus.
    c. Capital outflows increase, ceteris paribus.
    d. Capital inflows increase, ceteris paribus.

Internet Exercises

1. From the home page for the International Monetary Fund, http://www.imf.org, provide some information on the organizational structure of the IMF. Where does it get its resources? Who can borrow money from the IMF? What are some criticisms being leveled at the IMF in the wake of the Asian crisis?

2. What are some of the differences and the similarities between the operations of the IMF and the World Bank? You may obtain answers to this question from the Web site of the IMF at http://www.imf.org.

3. Go to the web site for the Financial Stability Forum at http://www.fsforum.org/home/home.html. Summarize the press release from the most recent meetings.

Suggested Readings

Stanley Fischer, who served as deputy director of the IMF during the Asian crisis, gives an insightful look at many of the issues discussed in this chapter in *IMF: Essays from a Time of Crisis: The International Financial System, Stabilization, and Development* (Cambridge, MA: MIT Press, 2004).

For a book that looks at the somewhat controversial history of the Bank for International Settlements, see James C. Baker, *The Bank for International Settlements: Evolution and Evaluation* (Westport, CT: Quorum Books, 2002).

For a comprehensive and detailed look at some issues pertaining to global policymaking, see Claudio Borio and William R. White, "Whither Monetary and Financial Stability: The Implications of Evolving Policy Regimes," *Monetary Policy and Uncertainty, Adapting to a Changing Economy*, Proceeding, Federal Reserve Bank of Kansas City (2003): 131–211.

"Identifying the Role of Moral Hazard in International Financial Markets" is the subject of a paper by the same name by Steven B. Kamin, International Finance Discussion Papers, Board of Governors of the Federal Reserve, 2002-736 (September 2002). It is available on the Internet at http://www.federalreserve.gov/pubs/ifdp/2002/736/default.htm.

An article that looks at the role of the U.S. dollar in the global financial system is Stephan Schulmeister, "Globalization without Global Money: The Double Role of the Dollar as National Currency and World Currency," *Journal of Post Keynesian Economics* 22:3 (Spring 2000): 365–396.

For a discussion of "The IMF and Global Financial Crises" see Joseph Joyce's article by the same name in *Challenge* 43:4 (July–August 2000): 88–107. For another interesting article,

also in *Challenge,* see Jane D'Arista's "Reforming International Financial Architecture," 43:3 (May–June 2000): 44–82.

For a blending of theory and application to the changing international financial system, see Hans Visser, *A Guide to International Monetary Economics,* 2nd ed. (Northampton, MA: Edward Elgar, 2000).

For a look at "Liberalizing Capital Movements: Some Analytical Issues," see the article by the same name by Barry Eichengreen, Michael Mussa, Gjovanni Dell'Ariccia, Enrica Detragiache, Gian Maria Milesi-Ferretti, and Andrew Tweedie, *Economic Issues* 17, International Monetary Fund (1999).

For an in-depth look at the Asian crisis, see Uri Dadush, Dipak Dasgupta, and Marc Uzan, eds., *Private Capital Flows in the Age of Globalization: The Aftermath of the Asian Crisis* (Northampton, MA: Edward Elgar, 2000).

For a discussion of *European Monetary Integration,* see the book by the same name, Eric J. Pentecost and Andre Van Poeck, eds. (Northampton, MA: Edward Elgar, 2001). For a look at the euro as a global currency, see Pier Carlo Padoan, ed., *Monetary Union, Employment and Growth: The Impact of the Euro as a Global Currency* (Northampton, MA: Edward Elgar, 2001).

For a pessimistic view about the global financial system, see James L. Clayton, *The Global Debt Bomb* (Armonk, NY: M.E. Sharpe, 1999).

An article that touches on many of the issues of this chapter is Jane D'Arista, "Reforming International Financial Architecture," *Challenge* 43:3 (May–June, 2000): 44–82.

A book entitled *Maintaining Financial Stability in a Global Economy* contains a collection of articles resulting from a symposium sponsored by the Federal Reserve Bank of Kansas City at Jackson Hole, Wyoming, August 28–30, 1997. The 367-page book is available from the Federal Reserve Bank of Kansas City, and articles from the book are online at the Web site **http://www.kansascityfed.org/PUBLICAT/SYMPOS/1997/sym97prg.htm.**

For a comprehensive article on the IMF, see Jane Sneddon Little and Giovanni P. Olivei, "Rethinking the International Monetary System: An Overview," *New England Economic Review,* Federal Reserve Bank of Boston (November 1999): 3–24.

Another book that pertains to the material in this chapter is *Global Financial Crises: Lessons from Recent Events*, Joseph R. Bisignano, William C. Hunter, and George G. Kaufman, eds. (Norwell, MA: Kluwer Academic, 2000).

The annual report of the Bank for International Settlements can be found at **http://www.bis.org/index.htm**.

Endnotes

1   Remarks by Alan Greenspan before the 34th Annual Conference on Bank Structure and Competition at the Federal Reserve Bank of Chicago, May 7, 1998.

2   In this chapter, when we refer to *dollar* or *dollars*, we also mean *dollar-denominated deposits.*

3   Recall from Chapter 9 that the current account measures transactions that involve currently produced goods and services (exports and imports) and net transfer payments. The capital account measures the financial flows of funds and securities among countries.

4   We hope you recall that the spot exchange rate is the exchange rate of foreign currency for immediate delivery.

5   *Annual Report of the Executive Board for the Financial Year Ended April 30, 2004* (Washington, D.C.: International Monetary Fund): 102.

6   See the home page of the IMF at **http://www.IMF.org**.

7   From article 3 of the original statute creating the Bank for International Settlements.

Looking Out, page 455

a   The following countries signed the Maastricht Treaty: Austria, Belgium, Denmark, Finland, France, Germany, Great Britain, Greece, Ireland, Italy, Luxembourg, the Netherlands, Portugal, Spain, and Sweden.

b   A currency crisis in 1992 caused the bank to be widened from 2.5 percent to 15 percent.

c   Recall the discussion of the Eurosystem in Chapter 4.

d   "The Euro," *Business Week* (April 27, 1998): 90-94.

A Closer Look, page 458

a   A major rationale for intervening in financial crises was that an international financial crisis could lead to a military conflict. World leaders were painfully aware of the contribution of Germany's problems with hyperinflation in the 1920s to the rise of Hitler and subsequent world war.

b   Others believe that early warning systems may cause some crises to occur that otherwise would not.

PART 5

Monetary Theory

How do you make a million? You start with $900,000.

—Stephen Lewis to Morton Shulman

20

The Fed, Depository Institutions, and the Money Supply Process

Learning Objectives

After reading this chapter, you should know:

How the Fed can affect the supply of reserves in the banking system

How changes in the supply of reserves or reserve requirements affect the ability of depository institutions to expand loans and deposits

Why changes in loans and deposits are usually a multiple of any change in reserves

What the monetary base is

Why a change in the money supply is a multiple of changes in the monetary base

What affects the Fed's ability to control the money supply and credit

Where Money Comes From

Suppose that during one month, say, April, the Fed conducts a large open market operation; it sells government securities through its trading desk at the New York Fed. About a month later, in conjunction with its regular weekly release of pertinent financial data (usually on a Thursday afternoon), the Fed reports that the money stock fell during the month of May. The purpose of this chapter is to help you understand the relationship between these two events: the open market sale and the subsequent fall in the money stock.

Much of the groundwork for this chapter has already been laid. In Chapters 2 and 3, we examined the definition, measurement, and role of money in the economy; in Chapter 4, we introduced the Federal Reserve and the tools it uses in conducting the nation's monetary policy; and in Chapters 10 through 15, we examined various aspects of the behavior of financial intermediaries, with particular focus on depository institutions.

As you have seen, depository institutions include banks, savings and loan associations, credit unions, and mutual savings banks. They issue checkable deposits and hold reserve assets equal to a fraction of deposit liabilities. Taken together, depository institutions make up the banking system.

This chapter focuses on the ways in which the operations of the Fed affect the banking system and the ways that depository institutions, in turn, influence the supply of money and credit in the economy.

The Fed and Bank Reserves

Open Market Operations

Open Market Operations
The buying and selling of government securities by the Fed.

Open market operations refer to the buying and selling of government securities by the Fed. When the Fed engages in open market operations, a link is created between the Fed's actions and the nation's money supply. Open market operations affect the supply of reserves available to depository institutions. The volume of reserves has a direct effect on the banking system's ability to extend loans and thereby expand checkable deposits and the supply of money. In addition to their effect on the money supply, open market operations have an impact on the liquidity of the financial system, and more broadly, they affect the supply of credit in the economy. Look at Exhibit 20-1 below to make sure you are clear about these steps. We begin with the connection between open market operations and reserves.

The New York Federal Reserve Bank buys or sells U.S. government securities on behalf of the Fed and under the guidance and direction of the Federal Open Market

20-1

The Money Supply Process

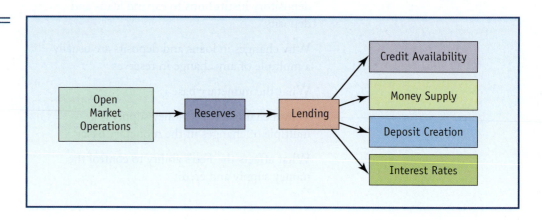

Committee (FOMC). Such day-to-day transactions are the most important monetary policy tool. In general, open market operations initially influence the financial system in two ways. First, they affect the amount of reserves in the banking system.[1] Second, they affect the level of interest rates, particularly short-term interest rates, such as the federal funds rate and Treasury bill rates. We use the word *affect* because, as you shall see, changes in other factors can have an impact on both reserves and interest rates. For now, we are going to focus on the effect of open market operations on reserves. There are two rules to remember:

1. When the Fed buys securities, reserves of depository institutions rise.

2. When the Fed sells securities, reserves of depository institutions fall.[2]

An excellent description of the Federal Reserve's open market operations and a discussion of how they enable the Fed to influence short-term interest rates can be found at **http://www.newyorkfed.org/publications/frame2.cfm?url=%2Faboutthefed%2F fedpoint%2Ffed48%2Ehtml.**

Because there is no reason for you to accept these propositions as true without proof and because so much depends on understanding these rules, we will trace out the mechanics of the relationship between open market operations and reserves of depository institutions.

Suppose that the Fed wants to add $1,000 to the supply of reserves in the banking system. The trading desk at the New York Fed, which is run by the manager of the Fed's portfolio of securities, will buy $1,000 of, say, Treasury bills (or Treasury bonds) from a group of dealers (market makers) with whom it does business regularly. The Fed pays for these securities by issuing checks to the sellers whom we shall treat as part of the public at large. The sellers, in turn, deposit their checks in, say, HLT National Bank. These checks are then cleared through the Fed's check-processing network (see Exhibit 4-4 to refresh your memory about this process). In this case, HLT sends the checks or as we saw in Chapter 4 electronic images of the checks to the Federal Reserve Bank in its district. The Fed then credits HLT's deposit balance at the Fed, which is a component of HLT's reserves. (Remember that reserves can be held in two forms, vault cash and deposits at the Fed.)

After the open market purchase, the Fed has $1,000 more in securities, and the dealers, who are the public, have $1,000 less in securities. In return for selling the securities to the Fed, the public gets checks worth $1,000 from the Fed, which for now we assume are deposited in HLT National. The deposits are an asset to the public and a liability to the bank. After HLT sends the check or electronic image of the check to the Fed for collection, the bank's deposit balance at the Fed—a component of its reserves—is credited with $1,000. In this case, reserves, deposits, and the money supply have all risen simultaneously by $1,000.

To generalize, when the Fed buys Treasury bills from the public, it pays with checks drawn on itself. In effect, the Fed "creates" the funds out of thin air! Using the power granted by Congress, the Fed pays for the securities with a stroke of its pen. The public exchanges these checks for deposits at depository institutions, which send the checks to the Fed for collection. The Fed, in turn, credits the reserve accounts of the depository institutions. For the depository institutions, both reserve assets and deposit liabilities have increased. Thus, through its purchase of securities, the Fed has augmented the supply of bank reserves. The rise in reserves enables HLT and other depository institutions to expand their lending, thereby increasing the supply of money and credit in the economy.

Simple T-accounts can be of considerable help in getting a feel for these transactions. We will use these simplified balance sheets to focus on changes in assets and corresponding changes in liabilities.[3] Exhibit 20-2 on page 472 shows T-accounts for the

20-2

The Effect of Open Market Operations on Reserves

FED		PUBLIC		HLT NATIONAL BANK	
Assets	**Liabilities**	**Assets**	**Liabilities**	**Assets**	**Liabilities**
(1) +$1,000 securities purchased from the public	(3) +$1,000 deposit due HLT	(1) −$1,000 securities sold to the Fed (2) +$1,000 deposits in the form of checks received from Fed and deposited in HLT		(3) +$1,000 reserves in the form of deposits at the Fed	(2) +$1,000 deposits by the public

Fed, the public, and HLT National. It traces the transactions and changes that occur as a result of the Fed's open market purchase. The Fed has experienced an equal change in assets and liabilities. Study this exhibit carefully, then close the book, and see if you can work through an open market sale of securities by the Fed and the fall in reserves that results.[4]

Discount Loans

As discussed in Chapter 4, the Fed controls the amount of required reserve assets that depository institutions must hold. Because of this, it also operates a lending facility called the *discount window* through which depository institutions caught short of reserves can borrow. Depository institutions are charged the discount rate to borrow reserves from the Fed through the discount window.

Like open market operations, changes in discount loans affect the volume of reserves in the banking system. When the Fed makes a discount loan to a depository institution, reserve assets increase by the full amount of the loan. When a discount loan is extended, the effect on reserves is the same as an open market purchase. Likewise, when a discount loan is paid off and borrowing from the Fed is reduced, the effect on reserves is the same as an open market sale. Exhibit 20-3 below illustrates the balance sheet effects of a discount loan to HLT Bank.

Although the Fed has complete control over the volume of open market operations, it cannot totally control the amount of borrowing from the discount window, which must be initiated by depository institutions. The Fed can discourage or encourage borrowing by raising or lowering the discount rate, and it can even refuse to make a discount loan. Fundamentally, however, decisions by banks to borrow or not to borrow from the discount window determine the volume of discount loans and, hence, the volume of reserves. Exhibit 20-4 on page 473 illustrates how open market operations and discount loans influence reserves.

20-3

The Effect of Discount Loans on the Monetary Base

FED		HLT NATIONAL BANK	
Assets	**Liabilities**	**Assets**	**Liabilities**
+$1,000 discount loans	+$1,000 deposits due HLT	+$1,000 reserves	+$1,000 discount loans

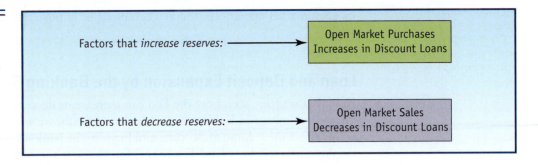

Factors that *increase reserves*: ⟶	**Open Market Purchases** **Increases in Discount Loans**
Factors that *decrease reserves*: ⟶	**Open Market Sales** **Decreases in Discount Loans**

Other Factors That Change Reserves

Offsetting Open Market Operations
Open market purchases or sales to offset changes in the monetary base caused by other factors.

Before moving on, we need to elaborate on two points. First, factors other than open market operations and discount loans can affect reserves. Second, the Fed can and does respond to changes in reserves caused by these other factors with **offsetting open market operations**. That is, if another factor causes an unexpected increase in reserves, the Fed can use an open market sale to decrease reserves. Likewise, if an unexpected decrease in reserves occurs, the Fed can use an open market purchase to increase reserves.

To clarify, let us consider an example of how one of the many factors affects the volume of reserves in the banking system and what the Fed can do about the effects. The federal government keeps most of its transactions balances in "tax and loan accounts" at various commercial banks throughout the country. Shortly before the federal government wants to make a payment, funds are transferred from the commercial banks to the government's account at the Fed. (Remember from Chapter 4 that the Fed is the fiscal agent for the U.S. government.) A check is then written by the government on the account at the Fed. Initially, reserves of commercial banks fall and the government's transactions account at the Fed increase. When the government actually spends the funds, reserves at commercial banks will again rise, as check's drawn on the government's account at the Fed are deposited into commercial banks. The net result of this series of transactions is that deposits and reserves in the banking system are lower than they otherwise would be during the period when the government's deposits are removed from the commercial banks and before they are re-deposited by the recipients of government checks.

Now suppose the Fed, given its current policy stance, does not want reserves and deposits to decrease. What can it do? The answer is that it can buy securities to offset the impact of the decline in reserves on the banking system. Likewise, if some other factor unexpectedly causes reserves to increase, the Fed can use an open market sale to offset the impact on the banking system.

In general, these offsetting open market purchases and sales are designed to counter movements in the reserves of depository institutions caused by other factors to maintain existing reserve conditions in the banking system. Because the Fed does not change its policy stance every day but other factors that affect reserves are always changing, the Fed conducts large amounts of day-to-day offsetting open market purchases and sales. In sum, even though a variety of factors including discount loans can affect the volume of reserves in the banking system, the Fed's powerful tool—open market operations—enables it to offset the impact of these other factors and thus greatly influence the reserves of depository institutions. The first appendix to this chapter looks in some detail at the other factors that influence reserves.

The rules we laid out at the beginning of this section should now be much clearer. Understand that in examining the first link in Exhibit 20-1, we have traced the transactions in slow motion. In practice, most of the transactions are conducted electronically and occur quickly. Regardless of timing, however, the essential point is that through its open market operations, the Fed can inject or remove reserves from the banking system.

Loan and Deposit Expansion by the Banking System

Now that we have seen how the Fed can increase or decrease reserves, we can examine the second linkage in Exhibit 20-1. More specifically, we want to see how changes in reserves affect the volume of deposits and loans in the banking system. To simplify, we will employ a balance sheet (and T-account) for a bank in our hypothetical banking system.[5]

Prototype Balance Sheet for a Bank

Assets	Liabilities
Reserves	Checkable deposits
Loans	

On the assets side are reserves and loans. For simplicity, we ignore other assets. On the liabilities side, we shall assume that there are only checkable deposits, the major component of the nation's money supply. Thus, we are ignoring other deposit and nondeposit liabilities and net worth. In addition, we focus only on changes in assets and liabilities resulting from various transactions.

Look at Exhibit 20-5 below, which begins where Exhibit 20-2 left off. HLT begins with the $1,000 of new **total reserves** and $1,000 of new deposit liabilities, which resulted from the open market purchase described in the previous section. Where do we go from here? HLT is not in business to hold idle funds as reserves; it uses funds deposited with it to acquire assets that earn interest income. If the Fed insists that HLT hold **required reserves** equal to 10 percent of its checkable deposit liabilities, the remaining 90 percent of reserves are **excess reserves**. In this example, required reserves are $100 (10% × $1,000) and excess reserves (total reserves minus required reserves) are $900 ($1,000 − $100).

Given their desire for profits, we assume that HLT and other depository institutions in our system will not wish to hold any excess reserves and will, therefore, use such funds to acquire assets. In our simple model, loans are the only assets that are acquired. Assuming that new loan customers are readily available, we are ready to consider the first stage of what will be a multistage process of loan and deposit expansion.

It just so happens that our old friend J.P. Young needs $900 to purchase a new stereo. Given the excess reserves it has on hand, HLT agrees to lend J.P. $900. He signs a

Total Reserves
Required reserves plus excess reserves.

Required Reserves
The amount of reserve assets that the Fed requires a depository institution to hold.

Excess Reserves
Reserves over and above those required by the Fed.

20-5
Loan and Deposit Expansion at HLT National Bank

HLT National Bank	
Assets	**Liabilities**
Total reserves $1,000	Checkable deposits $1,000

Beginning where Exhibit 21-2 left off, HLT has just seen both its total reserve assets and its checkable deposits increase by $1,000. Assuming the bank was loaned up to begin with, this represents an increase of $100 in required reserves and $900 in excess reserves. The bank can safely lend out its excess reserves. When a loan is made, the proceeds are disbursed by creating a checkable deposit. The bank's assets increase by the amount of the loan.

Assets		Liabilities	
Total reserves	$1,000	Checkable deposits	$1,000
Loan	900	New checkable deposits	900
Total assets	$1,900	Total checkable deposits	$1,900

loan contract, which HLT puts in its vault, and HLT credits $900 to J.P.'s deposit balance. The loan contract is an asset, and the deposit balance is a liability. Exhibit 20-5 also shows the T-account entries for HLT after this transaction.

Combining this stage with the initial situation, HLT's balance sheet shows a $900 rise in assets—the $900 loan is added to the original $1,000 in reserves. On the liability side there is also a $900 increase—the new $900 deposit in J.P.'s account is added to the original $1,000 deposit. Because deposits increase when the $900 loan is made, $900 of money has been "created."

Remember, however, that J.P. did not borrow the money to keep in his account. J.P. writes a check for $900 to pay I.M. Loud Inc. for the stereo equipment. We will assume that I.M. Loud Inc. does its banking at Second National Bank. Accordingly, I.M. Loud deposits the check received from J.P. in its deposit account at Second National. Second National credits I.M.'s account, and when the check is cleared, the Fed will debit (decrease) HLT's deposit account at the Fed by $900 and credit (add to) Second National's deposit account at the Fed by the same amount. HLT will, in turn, debit J.P.'s account for $900 for the check written to I.M. This series of transactions is shown in Exhibit 20-6 below.

So what is the net effect of those transactions on the supply of money and credit in the economy? When J.P. writes a check for $900 against his account at HLT, this reduces HLT's deposit liabilities and reserve assets by $900. (The $900 in reserve assets is credited to I.M. Loud's bank, Second National.) If we sum up the charges on HLT's balance sheet (bottom row), we see that the initial $1,000 deposit inflow is balanced by a $100 rise in reserves and a $900 rise in loans. HLT is now fully **loaned up**, which means that it has no excess reserves left to serve as a basis for lending. All of the $100 of reserves it holds is required reserves. HLT responded to the initial deposit inflow by expanding its loans and deposits by 90 percent of the inflow. Thus, HLT, and indeed any individual depository institution, can make additional loans and thereby "create" deposits equal to its excess reserves.

The process has not ended, however. Take a close look at Second National's balance sheet. It is clearly not loaned up. It has $810 of excess reserves. Just as HLT did, Second National will react to the deposit inflow ($900) by setting aside enough to meet the Fed's reserve requirement and lending out the rest. In this case, given our assumption of a 10 percent reserve requirement, it will keep $90 as required reserves and will have $810 of excess reserves. The excess reserves will serve as the basis of lending to, say, Jane Collins, who happens to need exactly $810 to pay her fees at State University. Jane gives a check to the university, which then deposits it in Third National Bank, as depicted in Exhibit 20-7 on page 476. As was the case before, the clearing of the check results in the Fed's crediting Third National's account at the Fed by the same amount. Second National will, in turn, debit Jane's account by the same $810, leaving it fully loaned up with the original gain of $900 in deposits on the liability side of its balance sheet and a rise of $90 in required reserves and $810 in loans on the asset side of its balance sheet. (Again, $810 in total reserve assets has been credited to Third National, State University's bank, because Jane's check is written to State.) If you are with us, you should now be able to describe what will happen in the next stage.

Loaned Up
Situation when a bank has no excess reserves left to serve as a basis for lending.

20-6

Transactions between HLT National Bank and Second National Bank

HLT National Bank				Second National Bank		
Assets		**Liabilities**		**Assets**		**Liabilities**
Total reserves	$ 100	Checkable deposits	$1,000	Total reserves $900		Checkable deposits $900
Loan	900					
Total	$1,000		$1,000	$900		$900

Second National Bank

Assets		Liabilities	
Total reserves	$900	Checkable deposits	$ 900
Loans	810	Checkable deposits	810
Total	$1,710		$1,710

The proceeds of the loan from Second National are spent and deposited in the university's account at Third National. Second National loses $810 in reserve assets, and the $810 deposit of the loan proceeds is extinguished. The resulting balance sheets of Second National and Third National are as follows:

Second National Bank				**Third National Bank**			
Assets		Liabilities		Assets		Liabilities	
Total reserves	$ 90	Checkable deposits	$900	Total reserves	$810	Checkable deposits	$810
Loans	810						
Total	$900		$900		$810		$810

We have shown that each individual bank was able to increase its earning assets by the amount of the excess reserves that resulted from a deposit inflow. Why, then, can't an individual bank (or other depository institution for that matter) expand deposits by more than its excess reserves (90 percent of the inflow)? In general, a bank cannot assume that new deposits created in conjunction with loans will be spent and redeposited in its coffers. Rather, it should expect to lose reserves equal to the loans extended and deposits created. If it loaned out, say, $1,000 (100 percent of the inflow) and subsequently lost $1,000 of reserves, it would find itself with the original $1,000 inflow of deposits on the liability side. If you think this is okay, you've forgotten one important factor—the Fed's reserve requirements. All depository institutions must have $100 of required reserves for each $1,000 of checkable deposits. To ensure that it meets the requirement, an individual institution will normally limit lending and deposit creation to its excess reserves.

As the loans of one depository institution increase, however, the use of the loan proceeds by the borrower leads to a deposit inflow at another institution. A deposit inflow increases total deposit liabilities and reserve assets. The depository institution will adjust to the inflow of reserves and deposits by expanding its loans and "creating" additional deposits. Subsequently, the individual institution will lose reserve assets and the additional deposit liabilities as the borrower uses the loan proceeds to pay for a purchase. However, one institution's loss is another's gain. Note that as this process occurs, the total volume of reserves in the banking system does not change. Instead, at each stages deposits rise and the composition of total reserves in the banking system changes: Required reserves rise and excess reserves fall.

The size of these changes can be stated precisely. As deposits flow through the banking system, the change in deposits at each depository institution can be represented as the change in required reserves plus the change in excess reserves. The change in required reserves is equal to 10 percent of the deposit inflow, and the change in excess reserve assets is equal to 90 percent of the deposit inflow. Hence, the change in loans and deposits created by each depository institution is equal to 90 percent of the inflow to that institution. In our example, the $1,000 increase in deposits at HLT is followed by a $900 increase in deposits at Second National, which is followed by an $810 increase in deposits at Third National. Taken together, that is, adding up the changes in all the individual balance sheets, the increase in total deposits in the banking system at each stage as loans are extended is 90 percent of the new deposits created at the previous stage. This means that, ultimately, the new deposits created at subsequent stages approach zero, and the process ends.[6]

Perhaps the most important aspect of the process to fix in your mind is that the total expansion of loans and deposits ($1,000 + $900 + $810 + . . .) is much greater than the initial injection of reserves into the banking system. In fact, the expansion of loans and deposits turns out to be a multiple of the initial injection of reserves. Some simple algebra presented in the next section will help confirm this point.

Recap   Open market purchases increase the supply of reserves while open market sales decrease the supply of reserves. When the Fed makes a discount loan, reserves increase. When a discount loan is paid off, reserves decrease. Depository institutions lend out excess reserves and in the process create money. Any one institution can safely lend only its excess reserves. When the proceeds of a loan are spent, however, deposits and reserves flow into another depository institution, which responds by expanding loans and creating additional deposits. Deposits and the money supply expand by a multiple of the injection of reserves.

The Simple Multiplier Model of the Money Supply Process

In our simple example, the process of creating money and credit from increases in reserves will end when all reserves in the banking system become required reserves—that is, when the banking system is fully loaned up. This situation is reached gradually as individual depository institutions create deposit liabilities and at the same time increase assets (loans in this case) in response to deposit inflows. When no excess reserves are left in the banking system, new loans cannot be made and new deposit creation ceases. The net result of the actions taken by individual depository institutions for the banking system and the economy as a whole can be illustrated with the aid of a simple model.

Required Reserve Ratio (r_D)
The fraction of deposits that depository institutions are required to hold as required reserves.

Required reserve assets, RR, are by definition equal to the **required reserve ratio, r_D,** multiplied by the amount of deposit liabilities, D:

(20-1)
$$RR = r_D \times D$$

Excess reserves, ER, are by definition equal to total reserves, TR, minus required reserves, RR.

(20-2)
$$ER = TR - RR$$

If total reserves equal required reserves, there are no excess reserves to serve as the basis of lending. As already discussed, this is the case when the banking system is fully loaned up. Therefore, when ER equals zero,

(20-3)
$$TR = RR = r_D \times D$$

Rearranging terms yields

$$(20\text{-}4) \qquad D = TR/r_D$$

or

$$D = 1/r_D \times TR$$

Simple Money Multiplier
The reciprocal of the required reserve ratio, $1/r_D$.

Total deposits are equal to the quantity of reserves multiplied by the reciprocal of the required reserve ratio. We shall refer to $1/r_D$ as the **simple money multiplier**.

For any change in reserves, TR, the change in deposits, D, is equal to the change in the multiplier multiplied by the change in reserves. Assuming excess reserves equal zero, we can rewrite Equation (20-4) as

$$(20\text{-}5) \qquad \Delta D = 1/r_D \times \Delta TR$$

Because we assumed that r_D was fixed at 10 percent (.1) in our example, the simple money multiplier is 1/.1, which is equal to 10. Therefore, the increase in deposits resulting from the $1,000 increase in reserves will be $10,000, assuming depository institutions hold no excess reserves. Although in our example reserves increased by $1,000, make sure you understand that the simple money multiplier works in both directions. If reserves decrease by $1,000, assuming depository institutions hold no excess reserves, there would be a corresponding decrease in deposits of $10,000.

Sometimes students come away from the preceding analysis feeling that they do not really understand how an injection of reserves into the banking system by the Fed leads to multiple increases in the money supply and credit. For those of you who fall into this category, we can illustrate this phenomenon without resorting to equations. Here is another way to understand this process.

Fractional Reserve Banking System
A banking system in which individual banks hold reserve assets equal to a fraction of deposit liabilities.

The simple multiplier process is a reflection of what is called the **fractional reserve banking system**. A depository institution must hold reserve assets equal to some fraction of deposit liabilities. The fraction it must hold is determined by the reserve requirements set by the Fed. If the reserve requirement is 100 percent, any increase in deposits would result in an identical dollar-for-dollar increase in required reserves. In this case, the simple money multiplier would equal 1. If the reserve requirement is less than 1, however, a given dollar increase in deposits will result in the need to hold required reserves equal to only some fraction of the increase in deposits. The remaining fraction of reserve assets is excess reserves and can serve as the basis of lending, which becomes new deposits as described before. In this latter case, the total change in deposits is greater than the amount of required reserves, and therefore, the multiplier is greater than 1. In general, the change in deposits and credit, which accompanies a given change in reserves, will be inversely related to reserve requirements. That is, for a given change in reserves, the smaller the required reserve ratio is, the larger the change in deposits and credit will be. Exhibit 20-8 on page 479 shows various combinations of required reserve ratios and the resulting simple money multiplier.

Details on reserve requirements and their role in monetary policy can be found at **http://www.ny.frb.org/aboutthefed/fedpoint/fed45.html**.

The whole process can be viewed as an inverted pyramid (∇). The original injection by the Fed leads to increased reserve assets and deposit liabilities and provides individual depository institutions with excess reserves. They adjust to this abundance of reserves by expanding loans and deposits. The deposits, when spent by loan recipients, flow to other depository institutions (higher up on the pyramid), which, in turn, expand loans and deposits. The process continues because profit-maximizing institutions are, in general, not interested in holding non-interest-earning excess reserves. As a result, the orig-

r_D	Simple Money Multiplier
.05	1/.05 = 20
.10	1/.10 = 10
.20	1/.20 = 5
.25	1/.25 = 4
.50	1/.50 = 2

inal injection of reserves—the foundation of the inverted pyramid—can support a multiple expansion in loans and deposits, as in Exhibit 20-9 below. The whole process is not unlike a family tree. A husband and wife have children, who in turn have children, and so forth.

Exhibit 20-10 on page 480 shows in tabular form the expansion of loans, deposits, and reserves for our example in which the injection of reserves is $1,000, the required reserve ratio is .1, and the multiplier is 10. Note that at each stage excess reserves decline and required reserves increase. At the final stage, excess reserves have fallen to zero, and required reserves are equal to the initial reserves supplied. Exhibit 20-11 on page 481 presents the same process and example in graphical form. At each stage, deposits expand by 90 percent of the deposit expansion at the previous stage. This process occurs because at each stage when the proceeds of a loan are spent and redeposited in another depository institution, required reserve assets equal to 10 percent of the new deposits must be held and 90 percent can serve as the basis of lending.[7] Again, the cumulative process continues until there are no excess reserves left to serve as the basis of lending—a point attained in our example when the total expansion of deposits has reached $10,000.

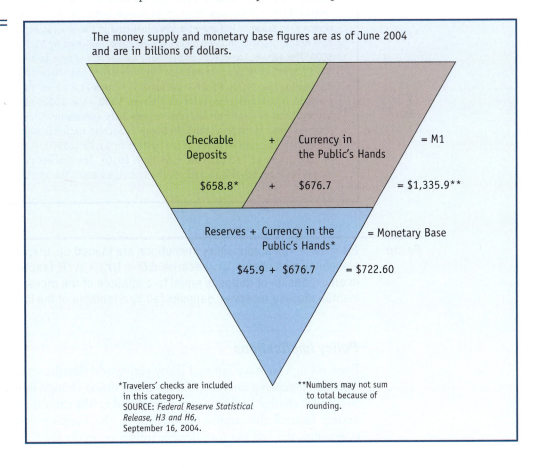

The money supply and monetary base figures are as of June 2004 and are in billions of dollars.

Checkable Deposits + Currency in the Public's Hands = M1

$658.8* + $676.7 = $1,335.9**

Reserves + Currency in the Public's Hands* = Monetary Base

$45.9 + $676.7 = $722.60

*Travelers' checks are included in this category.
SOURCE: *Federal Reserve Statistical Release, H3 and H6,* September 16, 2004.

**Numbers may not sum to total because of rounding.

20-10

The Multiple Expansion of Deposits and Loans in the Banking System with an Initial Increase in Reserves of $1,000 and a Multiplier of 10

	Total Deposits	Required Reserves	Excess Reserves	Total Reserves	Loans	Total Assets RR + ER + Loans TR + Loans
Initial reserves provided	$1,000	$100	$900	$1,000	—	$1,000
Expansion						
Stage 1	$1,900	$190	$810	$1,000	$ 900	$1,900
Stage 2	2,710	271	729	1,000	1,710	2,710
Stage 3	3,440	344	656	1,000	2,439	3,439
Stage 4	4,100	410	590	1,000	3,095	4,100
Stage 5	4,690	469	531	1,000	3,690	4,690
Stage 6	5,220	522	478	1,000	4,221	5,200
Stage 7	5,700	570	430	1,000	4,680	5,700
Stage 8	6,130	613	387	1,000	5,130	6,130
Stage 9	6,510	651	349	1,000	5,517	6,510
Stage 10	6,860	686	314	1,000	5,859	6,860
.	.	.	.	.	.	.
.	.	.	.	.	.	.
Stage 20	8,900	890	110	1,000	7,902	8,900
Final	$10,000	$1,000	$0	$1,000	$9,000	$10,000

SOURCE: Adopted from *Modern Money Mechanics* (Chicago: Federal Reserve Bank of Chicago, 1992).

Through a multistage, multiple expansion process, deposits grow to a total of 10 times the new reserves supplied to the banking system by the Fed through the open market purchase. The initial injection of reserves results in HLT National Bank and the banking system as a whole having an additional $1,000 of reserves, of which $100 represents required reserves and $900 represent excess reserves. In Stage 1, HLT makes a $900 loan and in the process expands deposits by a like amount. As a result, deposits in the banking system have now risen by $1,900—the initial $1,000 plus the $900. The deposits (proceeds of the loan) are spent and flow to another bank (Second National). The $900 inflow of deposits and reserves increases Second National's excess reserves by $810 and its required reserves by $90. For the banking system as a whole, the change in total reserves remains $1,000, but required reserves are now $190—the $100 held by HLT plus the $90 held by Second National—and excess reserves are $810 (remember that HLT lost its $900 of excess reserves when it made a loan). In Stage 2, Second National makes a loan for $810, raising the total expansion of loans in the system to $1,710 ($900 + $810) and the total expansion of deposits to $2,710 ($1,000 + $900 + $810). The process continues at each stage until excess reserves equal zero and required reserves equal the amount of initial reserves supplied.

Recap $ER = TR - RR$. If depository institutions are loaned up, then $TR = RR = r_D \times D$. The simple money multiplier is $1/r_D$ because $\Delta D = 1/r_D \times \Delta TR$. Fractional reserve banking results in an expansion of deposits equal to a multiple of the increase in reserves. If depository institutions lose reserves, deposits fall by a multiple of the loss.

Policy Implications

Even though we have ignored many real-world details, several policy implications flow from the preceding analysis. First, a given dollar change in reserves will lead to a larger (multiple) change in the money supply and credit extension. Because the Fed can ultimately control the supply of reserves in the banking system with its open market operations, the Fed has considerable influence on the lending activity of depository institutions and, therefore, the availability of funds in the financial system. Second, if the multiplier were really as simple as $1/r_D$, the Fed could actually control the money supply precisely. Simple arithmetic is all that would be required. If the Fed could control total reserves, TR, because it sets reserve requirements, r_D, it could make deposits, D, in Equation (20-3) or, more generally, the money supply do anything it wanted, assuming depository institutions wish to maintain zero excess reserves.

As the next section explains, however, the multiplier is actually more complicated than $1/r_D$ and is not under the Fed's complete control. Nevertheless, such complications should not obscure two features of monetary control: (1) the Fed's enormous influence on the value of borrowing and lending in the economy and (2) the cumulative process linking the Fed's actions to deposit creation and, hence, to the money supply. Simply put, whenever the Fed reports a large monthly decrease in the money supply, such as the one described at the beginning of the chapter, you can be reasonably sure that the decrease, to a large extent, is due to prior Fed actions, particularly open market sales.

Some Complicating Realities in the Multiplier Model

Let us take a look at the simplifying assumptions we made in developing our model of how money and credit are created and their implications. First, we assumed that depository institutions never hold any excess reserves. When deposits flow in and reserve assets increase, depository institutions continue to lend by creating new deposit liabilities until excess reserves equal zero. In fact, depository institutions do hold excess reserves, and the amount fluctuates over time. The excess reserves are a leakage from the flow of increases in deposits and credit extension. The effect of this leakage is similar to the effect of an

The Evolution of the Money Multiplier

Perhaps you had to study this chapter carefully to assimilate the material on the money multiplier. If so, you should not feel alone. Economists had grappled with ideas about how an increase in reserves led to a multiple increase in deposits and money for a long time before a clear, complete explanation emerged.

During the eighteenth century, writers such as John Law (1671–1729) and Alexander Hamilton (1755–1804) noticed that bank deposits were a multiple of the underlying cash base and inferred from this that banks create deposits. They did not see that the multiple resulted from the successive lending and redeposit of excess reserves. This idea was first put forth in 1826 by James Pennington (1777–1862), who recognized that a given increase in the reserve base causes deposits to multiply as the reserve increase shifts from bank to bank. It was left to Robert Torrens (1780–1864) to trace Pennington's notion of deposit expansion to its logical conclusion in 1837 (resulting in what we refer to as the *simple money multiplier* in this chapter). Thomas Joplin (1790–1847) clarified how expansion proceeds as one bank loses excess reserves to another, which then also expands. Alfred Marshall (1842–1924) provided the algebraic model for the simple multiplier that takes into account excess reserves—Equation (20-9) in this chapter. Finally, in 1921 Chester Phillips (1882–1976) "stated the theory with a power, precision, and completeness unmatched by his predecessors."[a]

Two steps remained to complete the analysis. First, the notion of a currency drain as deposits expand was developed by several economists between the 1930s and the 1950s. Finally, the work of James Meade, Milton Friedman, Anna Schwartz, and Phillip Cagan in the 1950s and early 1960s incorporated a currency drain into the money multiplier and fully explained the relationship between changes in the monetary base and changes in money. Thus, not until the early 1960s was the money multiplier fully expounded.

Don't you now think you mastered the material rather quickly?

increase in reserve requirements. The amount of loans and deposits created at each stage will be reduced by the volume of excess reserves held. The net effect will be to lower the simple money multiplier.

Second, we have ignored currency. If the stereo dealer (I.M. Loud) in our example exchanges J.P.'s $900 check for a $675 deposit at Second National and $225 of currency from the vault at Second National, the net change in the reserves of Second National is less than J.P.'s check. Second National has an increase in its reserve account at the Fed of $900, a reduction in vault cash of $225, and a net change in reserves of $675.[8] In other words, the stereo dealer exchanges the $900 check for a deposit equal to three-fourths of the amount of the check and currency equal to one-fourth of the amount. This reduces the flow of reserves and deposits from Second National to subsequent depository institutions by 25 percent and, hence, reduces the overall expansion of the money supply.[9]

Modifying the Multiplier Model

As a result of these implications, the actual multiplier is clearly not as simple as the one presented in Equation (20-4). We can develop a somewhat more realistic multiplier model by taking into account the factors already mentioned. Let us see what happens when we recognize that depository institutions hold excess reserves.

Now total reserves, TR, are equal to required reserves, RR, against checkable deposits, $r_D \times D$, plus excess reserves, ER.

(20-6)
$$TR = RR + ER$$

or

$$TR = (r_D \times D) + ER = r_D D + ER$$

Next assume that depository institutions hold excess reserve assets equal to a constant proportion of checkable deposit liabilities, D. For example, say they hold a few cents of excess reserve assets per dollar of deposits. Given this assumption, we can define ER as equal to eD, where e is the ratio of excess reserves held to checkable deposits, ER/D. More directly, e is the ratio of excess reserves depository institutions choose to maintain relative to the size of their deposit liabilities. Substituting this expression into Equation (20-6) yields

(20-7)
$$TR = r_D D + eD = (r_D + e)D$$

Solving this equation for D yields

(20-8)
$$D = 1/(r_D + e) \times TR$$

And in terms of changes in reserves and deposits, we have

(20-9)
$$\Delta D = 1/(r_D + e)\, \Delta TR$$

Equation (20-9) defines the new relationship between deposits and reserves. Two things are important to note about this relationship. First, the multiplier in Equation (20-9), $1/(r_D + e)$, is smaller than the simple multiplier, $1/r_D$, in Equation (20-5). For example, if r_D is .10 and e is .02, the multiplier is 8.33 [$1/(.10 + .02) = 8.33$], rather than 10 ($1/.10 = 10$). Second, the multiplier is not under the complete control of the Fed. Depository institutions can control the excess reserve ratio, e, which suggests that control by the Fed is not a matter of simple arithmetic.

In recent years, the excess reserves held by depository institutions have generally fluctuated between \$.75 billion and \$1.8 billion. (During this time, total reserves fluctuated between \$35 billion and \$65 billion.) The changes in excess reserves contribute to fluctuations in the multiplier and make it difficult to predict precisely. This difficulty is especially relevant in the short run (week to week and month to month). Over a longer period, say, three to six months, the fluctuations largely average out. That is, a large increase during one week is offset by a large decrease during another week. Hence, controlling the money supply is less difficult for the Fed over longer periods than over shorter periods.

Having shown that depository institutions can affect the multiplier through e, let us examine how the public can affect the money supply through its currency-holding behavior. Recall that the total money supply (M) is equal to checkable deposits, D, plus currency in the hands of the public, C. Let us assume that the public also desires to maintain its currency holdings as a constant proportion of its checkable deposits. Currency held by the public, C, is equal to cD where c is the desired ratio of currency to checkable deposits, C/D. Thus, we can write

(20-10) $$M = D + C = D + cD = (1 + c)D$$

Taking account of the public's desire to maintain its currency holdings equal to cD, we can see that open market purchases of securities by the Fed may result in an increase of both reserves and currency in the hands of the public. As members of the public sell securities, their checkable deposits increase, and they exchange some of those deposits for currency to maintain the desired currency-to-deposits ratio, c.

Monetary Base
Reserves plus currency in the hands of the public; denoted as *MB*.

We define the **monetary base**, MB, as the sum of reserves and currency in the hands of the public, $TR + C$. Although open market purchases initially show up as increases in reserves, which lead to new lending and deposit creation, the reserves become severely depleted as the newly created deposits are exchanged for currency to maintain the desired currency-to-deposits ratio.[10] Thus, when the Fed engages in open market operations, both reserves and currency in the hands of the public can change. In reality, open market operations change the monetary base. The multiplier is affected because some of the newly created deposits are exchanged for currency. Making the appropriate substitution for reserves from Equation (20-7) and substituting cD for C, as noted previously, we arrive at Equation (20-11):

(20-11) $$MB = TR + C$$

$$= (r_D + e)D + cD$$

$$= (r_D + e + c)D$$

Rearranging terms, we get

(20-12) $$D = [1/(r_D + e + c)]MB$$

Equation (20-12) shows the relationship between the monetary base and deposits. By combining Equations (20-10) and (20-12), we can derive the relationship between the monetary base and the money supply, M:

(20-13) $$M = D + C$$

$$= [1/(r_D + e + c)]\ MB + C$$

$$= [1/(r_D + e + c)]MB + cD$$

$$= [1/(r_D + e + c)]MB + c[1/(r_D + e + c)]MB$$

$$= [1/(r_D + e + c)]MB \times (1 + c)$$

$$= [(1 + c)/(r_D + e + c)]MB$$

In terms of changes in the monetary base and the money supply and assuming r_D, e, and c remain constant, we have

(20-14) $$[(1 + c)/(r_D + e + c)]\ \Delta MB = \Delta M$$

The Money Multiplier During the Great Depression

You might be interested to learn that between 1929 and 1933, bank holdings of excess reserves rose from $25 million to more than $2 billion and that the currency-to-deposits ratio increased from approximately 17 percent to 33 percent.[a] Why do you think these changes occurred? Borrowers were defaulting on loans as the Great Depression deepened, and depositors became wary of banks as thousands of them failed. Solvent banks found few attractive loan opportunities and tried to regain the public's confidence by staying liquid—that is, by holding excess reserve assets. People, however, had lost confidence in the banking system and responded by withdrawing funds, thus increasing their holdings of currency.

In this chapter, you have seen that the multiplier is equal to $(1 + c)/(r_D + e + c)$ and that the multiplier times the monetary base is equal to the money supply. Without knowing any of the facts, the multiplier tells us that if r_D and total reserves remain roughly unchanged, checkable deposits, and, therefore, the money supply, will decline as e rises. Although it is not as clear from the formula, the multiplier will also decline if c rises as the public withdraws deposits and reserves from the banking system.

Because these processes were not really understood in the 1930s, the money supply fell by about one-third between 1929 and 1933 due to the rise in both e and c and the resulting fall in the money multiplier. The drop in the money supply was hardly the type of anti-Depression policy one would have hoped for.

It is possible that the Fed could have moderated or reversed the decline in the money supply by sufficiently lowering r_D or raising total reserves. The Fed could have provided banks with additional reserves through open market purchases or by lending reserves to banks and serving as a lender of last resort. Thus, the Fed could have offset the drop in the multiplier by increasing the monetary base. A sufficient volume of such actions would have forestalled the decline in the money supply. That the Fed did not respond in this fashion is one of the reasons the Fed is often blamed for aggravating the Depression. In fact, it actually raised reserve requirements, believing this would help to restore the public's confidence in the banking system.

Of course, today our understanding of what determines the money supply and its importance in the economy is much greater than it was during the Great Depression. Thus, it is likely that such a rise in e and c today would produce a much more aggressive Fed reaction.

Money Multiplier
The multiple of the change in the monetary base by which the money supply will change.

Equation (20-14) defines the change in the money supply in terms of the monetary base and the expanded multiplier, which we will now refer to as simply the **money multiplier**. Taking account of another complication (the currency drain) has reduced the multiplier; if c is equal to .3, the multiplier is $(1 + .3)/(.1 + .02 + .3) = 3.1$ rather than the 8.33 in Equation (20-9). Because we are using $M1$ as our measure of the money supply, our money multiplier is actually the $M1$ multiplier. In Appendix B of this chapter, we develop the $M2$ multiplier. Exhibit 20-12 on page 486 presents the factors that cause the money multiplier to change.

An Increase in . . .	Caused by . . .	Results in . . .
c (the desired ratio of currency to checkable deposits)	The decision by the public to increase holdings of currency relative to deposits	
e (the ratio of excess reserves held to checkable deposits)	The decision by depository institutions to hold more excess reserves	A decrease in the money multiplier and a decrease in the money supply
r_D (the required reserve ratio)	The decision by the Fed to increase the required reserve ratio	

A Decrease in . . .	Caused by . . .	Results in . . .
c	The decision by the public to decrease holdings of curency relative to deposits	
e	The decision by depository institutions to hold fewer excess reserves	An increase in the money multiplier and an increase in the money supply
r_D	The decision by the Fed to decrease the required reserve ratio	

To summarize, the money multiplier in this more complete model is the multiple of the change in the monetary base by which the money supply will change. Thus, in our example, when the Fed uses open market purchases to increase the monetary base by $1,000, the money supply will increase by $3,100. The new money multiplier takes account of excess reserves and the currency drain. In the simple money multiplier case, the simple multiplier is the multiple by which a change in reserves leads to a change in deposits and loans without considering other factors.

Recap   The monetary base is reserves, *TR*, plus currency in the hands of the public, *C*. The money supply will be equal to the monetary base, *MB*, times the money multiplier. The actual money multiplier is more complicated than the simple money multiplier because depository institutions may hold excess reserves, *ER*, equal to some fraction of deposits and the public may withdraw cash as deposits expand to maintain a desired currency-to-deposits ratio, *C/D*. Taking both effects into account, the money multiplier is $(1 + c)/(r_D + e + c)$. $\Delta M = \Delta MB\,[(1 + c)/(r_D + e + c)]$.

The Fed's Control over the Money Supply

We could go on adding complications, but we hope you get the point. When the Fed engages in open market operations, reserves and the monetary base change. Compare Equations (20-5) and (20-14). In Equation (20-14) the multiplier is smaller, and the

Fed's control of the money supply is not so straightforward. The public, rather than the Fed, controls c, and depository institutions determine e.

Because c and e vary over time, the multiplier linking the monetary base and the money supply is not perfectly stable or predictable, especially in the short run. And what does that mean? It means that even if the Fed can control the monetary base, it may find controlling the money supply somewhat more difficult, especially in the short run. Over a longer period, fluctuations in the c and e ratios and, thus, the multiplier tend to offset one another. That is, a large increase is offset by a large decrease in some other period. Consequently, the Fed's ability to predict the money multiplier and, thus, control the money supply improves considerably over a longer time period.

The multiplier model presented in this chapter yields many insights into the money supply process, the interaction among depository institutions, and the effect of Fed actions. You should recognize, however, that it is really a "sausage grinder" model—the Fed increases the monetary base, you crank the handle, and loans, deposits, and currency held by the public come out at the other end. This model leaves out some of the points developed in earlier chapters. Nevertheless, when the Fed engages in open market operations, the effects ripple through the entire financial system including loans, deposits, credit availability, currency held by the public, and the monetary aggregates.

Remember that depository institutions are firms, and like all other firms, they are interested in maximizing profits. Given this objective, firms will consider the costs and revenues associated with alternative courses of action, such as lending versus not lending or borrowing reserves versus not borrowing reserves. The multiplier model simplifies away such notions. In particular, the cost of deposits and the return on loans—in other words, interest rates—were ignored. We simply assume that depository institutions always have customers ready, willing, and able to borrow.

The model also neglects to consider the creative ways that banks and other depository institutions develop to get around reserve requirements when the banking system is demanding more reserves than the Fed is willing to supply. The Eurodollar market is a prime example of a way that a bank can change a deposit liability with its corresponding reserve requirement into a nondeposit liability free of a reserve requirement. Credit extension can continue, even without the Fed feeding additional reserves into the system.

Also remember that the discount window can affect the supply of reserves and the monetary base as well. Acting as the lender of last resort through its discount facility, the Fed could supply depository institutions with all of the reserves they demand. In reality, the Fed can discourage discount window borrowing by raising the discount rate and making it uncomfortable for depository institutions to borrow from the discount window. Borrowing, after all, is a privilege, not a right, and should be exercised only to cover temporary shortfalls of reserves, never to extend new loans.

Given the preceding clarifications, some economists suggest that teaching this multiplier model should be done only from a historical perspective. They believe that in the complex financial system today, the model is merely a historical artifact with little relevance to the way depository institutions behave. We believe that if it is viewed with caution, the model gives some insight into the workings of the banking system.

In the next chapter, we look at the demand for money and credit. We also put demand and supply together to see how the public, the Fed, and the banking system jointly interact to determine a money market equilibrium. This chapter contains two appendices. The first is on other factors that affect the monetary base. The second develops the relationship between changes in the monetary base and changes in *M2* (the *M2* multiplier).

Summary of Major Points

1. The Fed's open market operations affect the amount of reserves in the banking system: When the Fed buys securities, reserves of depository institutions rise; when the Fed sells securities, reserves of depository institutions fall. Depository institutions must hold reserve assets, in the form of vault cash or deposits at the Fed, equal to a certain percentage of their deposit liabilities. The amounts that must be held are required reserves; any amounts held more than that are excess reserves. When the Fed makes a discount loan, reserves increase by the full amount of the loan. When a discount loan is paid off, reserves fall by the full amount of the loan.

2. For a depository institution, a deposit inflow increases total deposit liabilities and total reserve assets. Part of the reserves will be required and part will be excess. A depository institution can adjust to the inflow of reserves by expanding its loans and "creating" additional deposits equal to the amount of excess reserves that result from the deposit inflow.

3. As the proceeds of a loan are spent, the lending institution loses reserves. However, another depository institution gains reserves. The reserves lost by the lending institution flow to another as the funds are spent. The new depository institution gains deposit liabilities and reserve assets. This depository institution, too, can expand loans and create additional deposits in the amount of the excess reserves that flow to it.

4. Following an initial injection of reserves, the total volume of reserves in the banking system does not change. However, the composition of reserves changes; as deposits expand at each stage, required reserves rise and excess reserves fall.

5. The total expansion of loans and deposits is a multiple of the initial injection of reserves into the banking system. In the simplest model, which ignores excess reserves and currency, the multiplier is equal to $1/r_D$, that is, the reciprocal of the required reserve ratio. The simple multiplier is the multiple of the change in reserves by which deposits change. Thus, the lower the reserve requirements are, the larger the multiplier is. The higher reserve requirements are, the smaller the multiplier is.

6. The monetary base is reserves plus currency in the hands of the public. In a more elaborate model, excess reserves and currency drains are taken into account; the money multiplier is the multiple of the change in the monetary base by which the money supply will change. It is smaller than the simple multiplier and is influenced by the behavior of the Fed, depository institutions, and the public. This means that the money multiplier is not totally under the Fed's direct control and is not perfectly stable or predictable, especially in the short run.

7. Even if the Fed can control the monetary base, it may have difficulty controlling the money supply in the short run. Over a longer period (three to six months), the fluctuations in the multiplier tend to offset one another, and the Fed's ability to predict the multiplier and thus control the money supply improves considerably.

8. Other factors that affect bank reserves and the monetary base can be identified from the balance sheet of the Fed. The major assets of the Fed are gold, SDRs, other assets denominated in foreign currencies, discount loans, government securities, and float. The major liabilities of the Fed are Federal Reserve notes, bank deposits of reserves, and deposits of the U.S. Treasury. An increase in any of the assets of the Fed will increase the monetary base. An increase in any of the liabilities of the Fed will decrease the monetary base. The Fed exerts considerable influence on reserves and the monetary base through open market operations. (Appendix 20A)

9. The M2 multiplier tells us how much M2 will increase when the Fed increases the monetary base (MB). The M2 multiplier which is M2/MB is larger than the M1 multiplier because M2 contains small savings and time deposits, overnight repurchase agreements and Eurodollars, and individual money market mutual funds. (Appendix 20B)

Key Terms

Review Questions

1. Briefly explain why the Fed does not have precise control over the money supply.
2. If the public chooses to hold no currency, does the Fed control the money supply? If depository institutions choose to always loan up, does the Fed have precise control? If both of these situations occur, does the Fed have control?
3. In what form can a depository institution hold its required and excess reserves? What are the possible uses of currency outside the Fed?
4. If a depository institution has excess reserves, how much can it safely lend?
5. What are offsetting open market operations? When would the Fed use an offsetting open market purchase? An offsetting open market sale?
6. Explain how open market purchases and sales influence interest rates. To increase the money supply, should the Fed use an open market purchase or sale?
7. Comment on John D. Rockefeller's statement, "I believe that the power to make money is a gift from God." Do depository institutions really create money? Explain.
8. If the Fed lowers the discount rate, ceteris paribus, what will happen to the monetary base? Does the Fed have absolute control over the volume of discount loans?
9. If e increases given c and r_D, how can the Fed offset this change in e?
10. If discount loans increase, what happens to the monetary base?
11. What are the major assets and liabilities of the Fed? (*See Appendix 20A.*)

Analytical Questions

Questions marked with an icon are objective in nature. They can be completed with a short answer or number.

12. Assume that the Fed sets the required reserve ratio equal to 10 percent. If the banking system has $20 million in required reserve assets, what is the amount of checkable deposits outstanding?
13. If r_D = .25, what is the simple money multiplier? If reserves increase by $100, how much do deposits increase?
14. If c = .35, r_D = .10, and e = .10, what is the money multiplier? If a depository institution's excess reserves increase by $400, how much can it safely lend? Ceteris paribus, how much money will the banking system create?
15. If c = .25, r_D = .10, e = .05, and the Fed sells $100 in securities to the public, what happens to reserves, the monetary base, and the money supply after the change has worked its way through the entire banking system? Use T-accounts to explain your answer.
16. Using the same ratios as in question 15 and again using T-accounts, explain what happens to reserves, the monetary base, and the money supply if the Fed buys $100 in securities from the public.
17. In each of the following fictitious examples, tell whether the money multiplier will increase, decrease, or stay the same:
    a. Depositors become concerned about the safety of depository institutions, and there is no deposit insurance.
    b. Depository institutions do not see any creditworthy borrowers.
    c. The Fed lowers the required reserve ratio.
    d. Larger amounts of currency are demanded by the public to use in the "underground economy."[11]
    e. Depository institutions believe that overall default risk has decreased.
18. Assume that a depository institution has excess reserves of $100 and the required reserve ratio is 10 percent. What is the amount of checkable deposits at the depository institution resulting from new loans based on the excess reserves? Why is this amount different from the maximum amount of $1,000 in checkable deposits that can be generated by the banking system as a whole?
19. Suppose that you find $100 in the attic of an old house you have just purchased. You deposit the $100

in your checking account at Bank of America. Use a T-account to show what happens to the bank's assets and liabilities. What is the maximum amount that Bank of America can lend from this deposit given a required reserve ratio of 10 percent?

20. Suppose that you withdraw $1,000 in cash from your Bank of America checking account for a weekend trip to Las Vegas. Use a T-account to show the impact on the bank's assets and liabilities. Given a required reserve rate of 10 percent, what is the impact on bank lending?

21. By definition, narrow banking requires 100 percent reserve backing for checkable deposits. What is the money multiplier in this case?

22. If $M2$ is $4 trillion and the monetary base is $500 billion, what is the $M2$ multiplier? (*See Appendix 20B.*)

Internet Exercises

1. Access Fedpoint 32 from the New York Fed's Internet site at **http://www.newyorkfed.org/aboutthefed/fedpoint/fed32.html** and answer the following:
   a. What are open market operations?
   b. Who makes the decisions to conduct open market operations, and who executes these operations?

2. Access Fedpoint 18, **http://www.newyorkfed.org/aboutthefed/fedpoint/ fed18.html**, which pertains to the Fed's discount window. What is this window? From this Internet site, access the link to the discount rate (Fedpoint 30) and list some of its features.

3. Access Fedpoint 15, **http://www.newyorkfed.org/aboutthefed/fedpoint/fed15.html**, which describes federal funds. What role does the federal funds market play in the execution of monetary policy?

Suggested Readings

For a description of the money creation process using T-accounts and a discussion of the factors affecting reserves, see *Modern Money Mechanics,* rev. ed. (Federal Reserve Bank of Chicago, 1992).

For a discussion of a simulation model of the money creation process, see Norman E. Cameron, "Teaching Tools: Simulating Money Supply Creation in Class," *Economic Inquiry* 35 (July 1997): 686–693.

For a historic look at the role of money from the Fed's perspective, see "The Money Supply" on the Internet at **http://www.newyorkfed.org/publications/frame2.cfm?url=%2F aboutthefed%2Ffedpoint%2Ffed48%2Ehtml.**

Another valuable source for the material in this chapter is Tom Humphrey, "The Theory of Multiple Expansion of Deposits: What It Is and Whence It Came," *Economic Review of the Federal Reserve Bank of Richmond* (March–April 1987): 3–11.

Appendix 20A: Other Factors That Affect the Monetary Base

So far you have seen that the Fed, through open market operations, can change reserves and the monetary base. Although initially altering reserves, open market operations ultimately tend to change both reserves and currency held by the public. Although the Fed undoubtedly has enormous influence over reserve assets, other factors also affect them. This appendix identifies the various other factors that can affect reserves (and the monetary base) and shows how, despite these other factors, the Fed still exerts considerable influence over reserves, the monetary base, interest rates, and lending. The Fed monitors the net effect of movements in the other factors and uses open market operations to offset any net increase or decrease in the monetary base resulting from movements the Fed deems undesirable. Because the monetary base is the ultimate source of liquidity for the entire financial system, we frame our analysis in terms of it, rather than reserves, recognizing that reserves are merely the monetary base less currency in the hands of the public. Because the whole story flows from an examination and subsequently a rearrangement of the consolidated balance sheet for the entire Federal Reserve System—shown in Exhibit 20A-1 on page 492—we shall begin by describing the major items shown there.

Links to historical estimates of the U.S. monetary base, calculated on both a seasonally adjusted basis and a nonseasonally adjusted basis, can be found at **http://research.stlouisfed.org/fred2/categories/45**.

Major Assets of the Federal Reserve

The assets of the Federal Reserve are shown in the top portion of Exhibit 20-A1.

Gold and Special Drawing Rights (SDRs) Certificate Accounts and Other Assets Denominated in Foreign Currencies

The gold and special drawing rights (SDRs) certificate accounts and the other assets denominated in foreign currencies reflect the Fed's holdings of international reserves.[12] Changes in this account involve fairly complex transactions among the Fed, Treasury, International Monetary Fund (IMF), and foreign governments. Nevertheless, you simply need to recognize that acquisitions of gold, SDRs, or other assets denominated in foreign currencies will increase this asset account for the Fed and raise international reserves in the United States. Conversely, sales of gold, SDRs, or other assets denominated in foreign currencies will lower this asset account for the Fed and reduce international reserves.

Loans

As discussed in the body of this chapter, the various Federal Reserve Banks make discount loans to depository institutions via the discount window. Any changes in discount loans also change the volume of reserves and the monetary base.

Securities

The Fed acquires or sells government securities through its open market operations. The Fed can buy or sell securities in either of two ways. First, it can buy or sell securities outright. An outright trade, other things being equal, represents a permanent addition or subtraction of reserves from the banking system. Second, the Fed can buy or sell through repurchase agreements or reverse repurchase agreements. As discussed in Chapter 5, a **repurchase agreement** is an arrangement whereby the buyer, in this case the New York Fed, agrees to buy securities from the securities dealers with whom it regularly does business, and the dealers agree to repurchase the securities on a specific day in the near future. Most repurchase agreements are for one day, but from time to time, they run for more than one day. By using a repurchase agreement, the Fed can increase reserves temporarily, other things being equal, for a specific period of time.

Also, as discussed in Chapter 5, nonbank dealers are highly leveraged firms that generally borrow funds to finance their holdings or inventories of government securities. From the dealer's point of view, a repurchase agreement is a method by which the Fed finances the dealer's inventory of securities. Securities sold to the Fed under repurchase agreements will be available to the dealer to sell when the repurchase agreement matures.

The New York Fed can also execute a **reverse repurchase agreement**, which is the opposite of a repurchase agreement. In this case, the Fed agrees to a temporary sale of

Repurchase Agreement
An arrangement whereby the New York Fed agrees to buy securities from the securities dealers with whom it regularly does business and the dealers agree to repurchase the securities on a specific day in the near future.

Reverse Repurchase Agreement
An arrangement whereby the New York Fed agrees to sell securities to the securities dealers with whom it regularly does business and agrees to repurchase the securities on a specific day in the near future.

20A-1

The Fed's Balance Sheet as of July 21, 2004 (in Millions of Dollars)

	Assets
1 Gold certificate account	$11,045
2 Special drawing rights certificate account	2,200
3 Coin	725
4 Securities, repurchase agreements, and loans	718,032
Securities held outright	692,299
U.S. Treasury[a]	692,299
Bills[b]	255,248
Notes and bonds, nominal[b]	420,150
Notes and bonds, inflation-indexed[b]	14,862
Inflation compensation[c]	2,039
Federal agency[b]	0
Repurchase agreements[d]	25,500
Loans	233
5 Items in the process of collection	5,558
6 Bank premises	1,700
7 Other assets[e]	38,606
8 Total Assets	**777,861 ***

	Liabilities
9 Federal Reserve notes net if Federal Reserve Bank Holdings	699,168
10 Reverse repurchase agreements[f]	19,906
11 Total deposits	31,774
Depository institutions	19,906
U.S. Treasury—General account	26,508
Foreign—Official accounts	4,879
Other	99
12 Deferred credit items	5,862
13 Other liabilities and accrued dividends[g]	2,375
14 Total liabilities	**759,085 ***

	Capital Accounts
15 Capital paid in	9,245
16 Surplus	8,827
17 Other capital accounts	705
18 Total capital	**18,777**

* Note: Components may not sum to totals because of rounding.
[a] Includes securities lent to dealers, which are fully collateralized by other U.S. Treasury securities.
[b] Face value of the securities.
[c] Compensation that adjusts for the effect of inflation on the original face value of inflation-indexed securities.
[d] Cash value of agreements, which are collateralized by U.S. Treasury and federal agency securites.
[e] Includes assets denominated in foreign currencies, which are revalued daily at market exchange rates.
[f] Cash value of agreements, which are collateralized by U.S. Treasury securities.
[g] Includes exchange-translation account reflecting the daily revaluation at market exchange rates of foreign exchange commitments.
SOURCE: Federal Reserve Statistical Release, H.4.1, *Factors Affecting Reserve Balances* (July 22, 2004). Available on the Internet at
http://www.federalreserve.gov/releases/h41/Current/.

securities to dealers, which is matched by an agreement to repurchase the securities on a specific day in the near future. Again, most reverse repurchase agreements are for one day. Such transactions temporarily reduce reserves in the banking system. You will see in a few moments how repurchase agreements can come in handy.

Fedpoint 4 describes the repurchase and matched-sale transaction, initiated at the trading desk of the New York Fed, at **http://www.newyorkfed.org/ publications/ frame2.cfm?url=%2Faboutthefed%2Ffedpoint%2Ffed48%2Ehtml.**

Float (items in the process of collections)

Federal Reserve Float
The excess in reserves that results from a check being credited to one bank (or other depository institution) before it is debited from another.

Federal reserve float is an asset item arising from the accounting conventions underlying the Fed's check-clearing procedures. To review, suppose that you live in New York and send a check for $100 drawn on your account at a New York City bank or other depository institution to your mother, who lives in Chicago. She receives the check and deposits it in her bank account. Her bank credits her checkable deposit balance and sends the check or an electronic facsimile of the check to the Federal Reserve Bank of Chicago for collection. At this point, the check becomes a cash item in the process of collection for her bank. The Chicago Fed sends the check to the New York Fed, which returns the check to your bank. At that point, your deposit account is debited. For the two commercial banks (yours and hers), the Fed completes the transfer of funds arising from the check by increasing the deposit account of the Chicago bank at the Chicago Fed and lowering the deposit account of the New York bank at the New York Fed. Remember that deposit accounts at the Fed are part of reserves and the monetary base. When all of these transactions are completed, the total amount of deposits, reserves in the banking system, and the monetary base will, other things being equal, be as it was before. The only difference will be in the location of the deposits and reserves (commercial bank deposits at Federal Reserve Banks). Chicago will have gained and New York will have lost deposits and reserves.

Because it takes time to transfer the check physically, the Fed typically credits the Chicago commercial bank's account at the Chicago Fed before it debits the account of the New York bank at the New York Fed. Thus, for a short time (usually a day), the deposit and reserves in question appear on the balance sheets of both banks. As a result, the Fed is, in effect, providing credit to the banking system through this procedure.[13] In late 2004, the Fed authorized commercial banks to submit electronic image of checks rather than the actual paper check. As electronic technology is applied to the check-clearing process, the volume of float is likely to fall.[14]

Major Liabilities of the Federal Reserve

Now that we have sorted out the Fed's major asset accounts, let us briefly examine its major liability and capital accounts in Exhibit 20-A1.

Federal Reserve Notes

Federal Reserve notes are the paper money in circulation. These notes constitute about 90 percent of the currency in circulation in our economy. The other 10 percent of total currency in circulation consists mainly of coins minted by the Treasury. Federal Reserve notes may be either currency in the hands of the public or vault cash. If held as vault cash, they are part of reserves.

Bank Deposits

As you have already learned, banks may hold reserves in the form of vault cash or in the form of deposits at the Fed. Such deposits, which account for the majority of bank reserves, are assets for the institutions and liabilities for the Fed. These deposit balances are held at a bank's district Reserve Bank, and they rise or fall as the Fed credits or debits the bank's balance.

Deposits of the U.S. Treasury

Deposits of the U.S. Treasury are the Treasury's money account. The Treasury pays its bills by writing checks on its deposit balance at the Fed. When this happens, Treasury deposits decline. If tax receipts rise (as they do around major tax dates, such as April 15) or the Treasury issues and receives payment for securities to finance a deficit, the Treasury's deposits at the Fed rise. The level of Treasury deposits rises and falls with the ebb and flow of government receipts and expenditures.

The Monetary Base Equation

With all relevant items defined, we can develop a monetary base equation, which states the monetary base according to the factors that increase or decrease it. As mentioned earlier, we frame the analysis in terms of the monetary base because it is the foundation of liquidity for the economy. By subtracting currency held by the public from each side of the equation, we could express the equation in terms of reserves instead of the monetary base.

The first thing to notice about Exhibit 20-A1 is that the largest asset item is the securities account and the largest liability accounts are Federal Reserve notes and deposits (reserves) of depository institutions. The second thing to notice is that although the values of all items on the balance sheet change somewhat over time, the largest and therefore the most significant changes occur in the largest items.

To bring together all of the key items that affect the monetary base and thus derive the monetary base equation, we can rearrange the Fed's balance sheet. We know that total assets, TA, equal total liabilities and capital, TL:

$$(20A\text{-}1) \qquad\qquad TA = TL$$

On the liability side of the Fed's balance sheet, we have currency issued by the Fed, C^*, Treasury deposits, TD, depository institution deposits at the Fed, DF, and all other liabilities and capital, OL.

$$(20A\text{-}2) \qquad\qquad TL = C^* + TD + DF + OL$$

Note that in this case, C^* includes both currency in the hands of the public and vault cash. Because total reserves, TR, include vault cash, VC, plus deposits at the Fed, DF, while C is currency in the hands of the public, if we add DF to C^*, we get the monetary base, $TR + C$. Therefore, substituting $TR + C$ into Equation (20A-2) for $DF + C^*$, we get

$$(20A\text{-}3) \qquad\qquad TL = TR + C + TD + OL$$

Rearranging terms, we can express the monetary base—reserves, TR, plus currency in the hands of the public—in terms of the other items:

$$(20A\text{-}4) \qquad\qquad MB = TR + C = TL - TD - OL$$

Using Equation (20A-1), we can rewrite Equation (20A-4) substituting TA for TL:

$$(20A\text{-}5) \qquad\qquad MB = TR + C = TA - TD - OL$$

Total assets are equal to the gold and SDR account, reflecting international reserve holdings, IR, plus loans, L, plus government securities held, GS, plus float, F, plus other assets, OA:

$$(20A\text{-}6) \qquad\qquad TA = IR + L + GS + F + OA$$

The final step is to substitute Equation (20A-6) into Equation (20A-5), which gives us the monetary base equation:

$$(20A\text{-}7) \qquad MB = TR + C = IR + L + GS + F + OA - TD - OL$$

An increase in any of the items with a plus sign before it will raise the monetary base (and most likely reserves), and an increase in any of the items with a minus sign before it will lower the monetary base. Note that all items with a plus sign are from the asset side of the Fed's balance sheet and that the items with minus signs are from the liability side of the Fed's balance sheet.[15]

Appendix 20B: The M2 Multiplier

In the body of this chapter, we developed the money multiplier to calculate a change in the monetary base. In reality, because we were considering money to be currency, C, plus deposits, D, we were developing the multiplier for $M1$.[16] The $M1$ multiplier tells us how much $M1$ will increase when there is an increase in the monetary base; $M1$ will increase by the multiplier times the change in the monetary base.

In carrying out monetary policy, the Fed may be more interested in the behavior of $M2$ or another aggregate than in the behavior of $M1$. In this appendix, we develop the $M2$ multiplier, which tells us how much $M2$ will increase when the Fed increases the monetary base. In other words, $M2$ will increase by the $M2$ multiplier times the change in the monetary base. As we saw in Chapter 2, $M2$ is:

Currency in the hands of the public (C)
Checkable deposits (D)
Small savings and time deposits (D^*)

$$\left.\begin{array}{l}\text{Overnight repurchase agreements}\\\text{Overnight Eurodollars}\\\text{Money market deposit accounts}\\\text{Individual money market mutual funds}\end{array}\right\} = MI$$

To simplify, we will consolidate the last four items together as money market instruments, MI. Equation (20B-1) illustrates this relationship.

$$(20B\text{-}1) \qquad M2 = C + D + D^* + MI$$

We also assume that spending units have desired D^*/D and MI/D ratios, just as they have a desired C/D ratio. The $M2$ multiplier is the ratio of $M2$ to the monetary base, MB. With the use of Equations (20-2), (20-11), and (20B-1), we can derive the $M2$ multiplier:

$$(20B\text{-}2) \qquad M2/MB = (C + D + D^* + MI)/(RR + ER + C)$$

To express this multiplier in notation that is similar to the $M1$ multiplier developed in the chapter, we multiply Equation (20B-2) by $(1/D)/(1/D)$, which is equal to 1. The result is derived in Equation (20B-3).

$$(20B\text{-}3) \qquad M2/MB = (C/D + D/D + D^*/D + MI/D)/(RR/D + ER/D + C/D)$$

$$= (c + 1 + D^*/D + MI/D)/(r_D + e + c)$$

Rearranging the terms yields Equation (20B-4):

$$(20B\text{-}4) \qquad M2/MB = (1 + c + D^*/D + MI/D)/(r_D + e + c)$$

Multiplying both sides of Equation (20B-4) by the monetary base and expressing the result in terms of changes yields:

$$(20B\text{-}5) \qquad \Delta M2 = (1 + c + D^*/D + MI/D)/(r_D + e + c)\Delta MB$$

Equation (20B-5) defines the relationship between changes in the monetary base and changes in $M2$. Thus, the $M2$ multiplier is equal to $(1 + c + D^*/D + MI/D)/(r_D + e + c)$. It is similar to the $M1$ multiplier except that the numerator is larger by the magnitude $D^*/D + MI/D$. Therefore, the $M2$ multiplier is larger than the $M1$ multiplier, which is also apparent because $M2$ is larger than $M1$. As can be seen from Equation (20B-5), the $M2$ multiplier is positively related to both the D^*/D and MI/D ratios. Like the $M1$ multiplier, the $M2$ multiplier is inversely related to the required reserve ratio, r_D, the currency-to-deposits ratio, c, and the excess reserve ratio, e.

Endnotes

1 Shortly, you shall see that open market operations usually also affect currency in the hands of the public.

2 We should point out that when the Fed buys or sells "anything else" such as gold or foreign exchange, reserves also change. The buying and selling of securities is the primary tool used to change reserves.

3 The basic balance sheet identity is total assets equal total liabilities plus net worth. Expressed in terms of changes, this identity implies that the change in assets must equal the change in liabilities plus the change in net worth. In the examples in this chapter, we assume that the entity's net worth does not change. Thus, in each case, a change in assets must be matched by a corresponding change in liabilities. By dealing only with changes, we can ignore other details and concentrate instead on the essential transactions.

4 If you do it correctly, the entries should be identical to those in Exhibit 20-2 except that they all should carry opposite signs ($+$ changes to $-$, and $-$ changes to $+$).

5 Note that we could have used the balance sheet of any depository institution; we chose to use a bank in our example because banks make up the largest class of depository institutions.

6 To illustrate $.9 \times \$1,000 = \$900$; $.9 \times \$900 = \$810$; $.9 \times \$810 = \$729$; $.9 \times \$729 = \$656.10$; $.9 \times \$656.10 = \$590.49$; and so on.

7 In reality, the same expansion occurs whether the proceeds of a loan are spent and redeposited in another depository institution or in the same institution that made the loan.

8 Second National exchanges the \$900 check for an increase of \$900 in its reserve account at the Fed. However, the vault cash of Second National has gone down by \$225. If Second National replenishes its vault cash by drawing on its account at the Fed, its reserve account has a net change of \$675.

9 Other factors also complicate the simple multiplier. For example, until December 1990, depository institutions were required to hold reserves against some time and saving deposits. If State University decided to hold, say, one-fifth of the tuition payments it received from Jane and others in the form of large negotiable CDs rather than checkable deposits, then required reserves, checkable deposits, and $M1$ would initially fall. Reserve requirements were less on large negotiable CDs than on checkable deposits. The narrowly defined money aggregates fell as checkable deposits were exchanged for CDs, which are not included in $M1$. Total reserves in the system did not change although required reserves decreased. In late 1990 and early 1991, reserve requirements on virtually all time and savings deposits were eliminated. However, to the extent that checkable deposits are exchanged for time and savings deposits, as checkable deposits grow, the multiplier can still be affected.

10 The monetary base can also be defined as reserve deposits at the Fed, DF, plus currency outside the Fed, C^*. This is so because currency outside the Fed is either in the vaults of depository institutions, where it is part of reserves, or in the hands of the public. Thus, reserves include deposits at the Fed plus vault cash, VC, and vault cash plus currency in the hands of the public is currency outside the Fed. The following equation summarizes this relationship and illustrates the difference between C and C^*: $TR + C = DF + VC + C = DF + C^*$, and $VC + C = C^*$.

11 The underground economy consists of activities including cash transactions to avoid taxes and illegal activities that are not reported in the National Income and Product Accounts and, hence, do not show up in gross domestic product (GDP) and other measures of economic activity.

12 As you saw in Chapter 19, SDRs are international reserve assets created by the International Monetary Fund.

13 All of this is analogous to the way individuals use float. Many of us write checks and send them off to pay bills, even though at that specific moment we do not have enough funds in our accounts to cover the checks. Knowing that it takes time for a check to clear, we plan to add funds to our accounts in time to cover the checks.

14 On the Fed's balance sheet, float is actually the difference between a cash item in the process of collection (an asset) and a deferred-availability cash item (a liability). The asset item always exceeds the liability item because the Fed credits the deposit (reserve) account of the bank sending a check for collection to the Fed before it debits the deposit (reserve) account of the bank on which the check is drawn.

15 The plus items are sometimes called *factors supplying reserves* or *sources of reserves*, and the minus items are called *factors absorbing reserves* or *uses of reserves*. A table in the *Federal Reserve Bulletin* reports the data in this fashion.

16 For simplicity, we are following our convention of ignoring travelers' checks.

Looking Back, page 482

a Until 1980, banks were the only financial intermediaries that issued checkable deposits.

Looking Back, page 485

a The quotation is from Thomas M. Humphrey, "The Theory of Multiple Expansion of Deposits: What It Is and Whence It Came," *Economic Review of the Federal Reserve Bank of Richmond* (March–April 1987): 3–11. Much of the material presented in this feature is based on Humphrey's article.

Money is like muck—not good unless it be spread.

—Francis Bacon

21

The Demand for Real Money Balances and Market Equilibrium

Learning Objectives

After reading this chapter, you should know:

Why the demand for money is really a demand for real money balances

What transactions and precautionary demand for real balances are

How the demand for real balances is related to the level of real income and the interest rate

Other determinants of the demand for real money balances

How changes in the demand and/or supply of real balances affect the market equilibrium and the interest rate

The theories of monetarism and Keynes's speculative demand for money

Where Is All the Money?

In June 2004, $M1$ was $1,335.9 billion. Of this, roughly $676.7 billion was currency and the remainder was checkable deposits. This money was used to support a gross domestic product (GDP) of approximately $11.8 trillion, resulting in a velocity of about 8.8. Given that there were about 107 million households in this country at that time, the average holding of $M1$ per household was $12,845, and the average holding of currency per household was $6,325.

If you are from an average household, you probably find these figures relatively high. The authors and the people we know, who are mostly professors, students, government bureaucrats, and other professionals, just don't seem to hold that much in money balances. Although our evidence is hardly scientific, we have been asking our students, colleagues, and friends for many years and get answers that leave us in a quandary. So, you may wonder, where is all this money?

Possibly a little investigation can shed some light on the situation. Corporations, as we all know, are forbidden by law to hold interest-earning checkable deposits. We can speculate that a large portion of outstanding demand deposits, which totaled $322.7 billion in June 2004, are held by corporations. We also know that other checkable deposits, which totaled $328.8 billion, must be held by households. Thus, the average household balance held in interest-earning checking accounts amounted to $3,073. This figure certainly seems more realistic.

This explanation of where the outstanding checkable deposits are seems "somewhat reasonable," but what about those large outstanding holdings of currency? Where are they located? Part of the explanation is that most businesses (particularly the corner grocer, dry cleaner, and the like) need some currency. Additionally, estimates are that more than 50 percent and perhaps as much as 60 percent of U.S. currency in circulation is held outside the United States. Indeed, by early 2004, four countries have withdrawn their own national currencies from circulation and use the dollar exclusively in transactions. These four countries that have "dollarized" are Ecuador, Guatemala, El Salvador, and Panama. Moreover, many speculate that large amounts of currency are needed to support the illegal activities of the underground economy such as drug trafficking, and some currency, particularly coin is held by collectors. In addition, some otherwise legal activities are conducted with currency in order to evade taxes, which in itself, is illegal. Nevertheless, why the amount of currency outstanding per household has been growing consistently since 1960 remains a mystery.

In this chapter, we discuss the determinants of how much money households and firms want to hold at a given moment in time. Additionally, we analyze equilibrium in the market for money balances. Although we may be unable to resolve the enigma of the missing currency conclusively, we do explain a lot about the demand for money and equilibrium in the money market.

The Demand for Real Money Balances

Wealth may be held either in real assets, such as houses, gems, and rare oil paintings, or in financial assets, such as stocks, bonds, mutual funds, and money. From this perspective, money is viewed as just one of many real or financial assets in which households may hold their wealth. When relative rates of return on the various assets change, households adjust their portfolios toward those real or financial assets that offer a relatively higher return.[1] Therefore, as the returns on some assets rise, ceteris paribus, households will hold relatively more in those assets (either real or financial) that yield a higher return and less in the assets whose relative yield has decreased. Money, however, is exceptional among financial assets because it alone functions as a means of payment (medium of exchange), as well as a store of value. Therefore, we single money out for special attention.[2]

Monthly statistics on the U.S. money stock are available both seasonally adjusted (SA) and not seasonally adjusted (NSA). The data series, extending from 1959 to the last quarter of the current year, can be found at **http://research.stlouisfed.org/fred2/categories/24**.

Real Money Balances
The quantity of money expressed in real terms; the nominal money supply, *M*, divided by overall price level, *P*, or *M/P*.

The demand for money is actually a demand for **real money balances**, or the quantity of money expressed in real terms. Real money balances, or real balances for short, are adjusted for changes in purchasing power. We can define a real money balance as the nominal money supply, *M*, divided by the overall price level, *P*, as in Equation (21-1):

(21-1)   real money balances = *M/P*

P is a price index that measures changes in the overall price level. Examples of price indexes include the consumer price index (CPI) and the producer price index (PPI) introduced in Chapter 3.

To see why the demand for money is really a demand for real balances, consider the following example. What would happen if all prices including input prices and output prices quadrupled tomorrow? In nominal terms, everything would cost four times as much, but households and firms would be making four times as much money. Households and firms would demand to hold four times as much nominal money to make the same real transactions as before. The demand for nominal money balances would quadruple. Referring back to Equation (21-1), the numerator and the denominator both increase by a factor of 4, leaving the demand for real balances unchanged ($M'/P' = 4M/4P = M/P$).

Note that we are ignoring the effect of price changes on financial assets and liabilities. When the overall price level rises, net borrowers pay back their debts with "cheap" dollars, and the net lenders receive back less in real terms than they loaned. Because for every financial liability there is a corresponding financial asset, the benefit to the borrower that owes the financial liability offsets the loss to the lender that owns the financial asset.

Because the demand for money is a demand for real money balances, nominal money demand is proportional to the overall level of prices. If the price level increases by 10 percent, the nominal demand for money increases by 10 percent, and the demand for real balances remains unchanged. Likewise, if the price level decreases by 10 percent, nominal demand decreases by 10 percent, and the demand for real balances remains unchanged.[3] Sometimes we use the expression "the demand for money" for short to mean the demand for real money balances or just real balances. But don't be confused; the demand for money is always a demand for real balances because of the proportionality between nominal money demand and the overall price level. Having established this relationship, we turn our attention to the factors that motivate households and firms to hold real money balances.

Households' Demand for Real Money Balances

There are basically two motives behind households' demand to hold real money balances. First, households need money to consummate transactions. Someone who purchases real assets, nondurable goods and services, or financial assets must supply in exchange a means of payment that is generally acceptable to the seller. Money is the means of payment. Because financial transactions occur frequently (probably several times a day) and income is typically received less frequently (say, weekly or monthly), households hold an inventory of real balances to get from one income-receiving period to the next. We call this first motive for holding real money balances the **transactions motive**.

Transactions Motive
A motive for holding money based on the need to make payments.

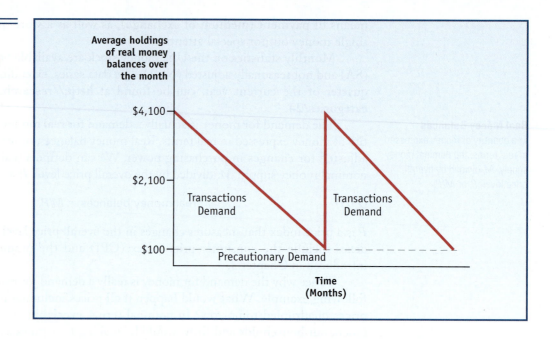

Exhibit 21-1 above illustrates the transactions motive for holding real money balances by showing a typical relationship among income receipts, financial transactions, and holdings of real money balances. The peaks in the holdings of real balances each month represent paydays, and the gradual decline in the holdings of real balances between paydays reflects spending on goods and services and other transactions. Note that the exhibit shows that the typical household has some real money balances left over at the end of each month. This reflects the second motive for holding real money balances, the **precautionary motive**. Households try to hold some real money balances—the most liquid asset there is—as a precaution against unforeseen developments.

The transactions and precautionary motives for holding real money balances are analogous to reasons that households keep an inventory of food on hand. In general, it is costly and inconvenient to run to the store every time we want to eat. Accordingly, the typical household buys groceries once a week and then uses them several times a day throughout the week. As in Exhibit 21-1, the inventory of food runs down and is replenished at the next shopping trip. Because we don't like an empty refrigerator, especially when guests drop in unexpectedly, most of us try to keep some food on hand as a precaution.[4]

In addition to fulfilling the transactions and precautionary motives, we can think of real money balances as yielding a stream of services to households and, in the case of interest-earning checkable deposits, some interest income. These are the **benefits of holding real money balances**. The stream of services that real balances yield is defined by the time and distress saved by having money on hand for immediate use. The value or benefits of such services can be seen by examining what would happen if a household held all its financial assets in the form of bonds instead of holding real money balances. When the household wanted to purchase goods or make a payment, it would first have to sell bonds and acquire money. More specifically, the household would have to call a brokerage firm, pay a brokerage fee, and wait for the money to actually arrive.[5] The benefits of holding real money balances are thus both monetary (saving the brokerage fee and earning interest on checkable deposits) and nonmonetary (the time and inconvenience of waiting for money to arrive when it is needed but is not there).

Precautionary Motive
A motive for holding money based on the desire to protect against unforeseen developments.

Benefits of Holding Real Money Balances
The stream of services that real balances yield defined as the time and distress saved by having money on hand for immediate use.

The **cost of holding real money balances** is the additional forgone interest that holding nonmonetary financial assets, such as stocks or bonds, would have yielded. When money does pay interest, as in the case of interest-earning checkable balances, the interest rate yield on real money balances is generally less than what could be earned on other less-liquid financial assets. These other assets must pay a higher return, ceteris paribus, to compensate for the loss in liquidity and greater risk.[6]

But how much money should a household hold given both the benefits and costs of holding real money balances? From an economist's point of view, the household should increase its holdings of real money balances as long as the benefits of doing so outweigh the costs. When we apply this rule to the transactions demand for real balances by households, two conclusions follow:

1. Ceteris paribus, the interest rate on nonmonetary assets and the quantity demanded of real money balances are inversely related; that is, as the interest rate increases, quantity demanded decreases, and vice versa. This relationship exists because if the interest rate on nonmonetary assets increases, the opportunity cost of holding real money balances also increases, and households will demand to hold less.

2. Ceteris paribus, the brokerage fee (the cost of transferring from nonmonetary to monetary assets) and the quantity demanded of real money balances is directly related. This relationship exists because if the brokerage fee increases, the household will make fewer calls to the broker and, hence, will hold a larger quantity of real money balances.

We leave the mechanics of demonstrating these particular results to the chapter appendix. Although the analysis is quite cumbersome, our abstract rules translate into behavior in the real world fairly easily. We now turn to the demand for real money balances by business firms.

Firms' Demand for Real Money Balances

Production, investment spending, and sales generate a variety of financial transactions. Over the past 30 years, universities have turned out large numbers of capable graduates trained in the intricacies of money and finance. In addition, the use of new technologies—computers, spreadsheet software, telecommunications—has become a routine necessity for firms. Cash management, in particular, and balance sheet management, more generally, have become highly sophisticated. As foreign activity by U.S. firms has increased, international financial transactions have expanded in size and importance. Nevertheless, the basic factors determining business holdings of real money balances can still be viewed in fairly straightforward terms.

Firms, like households, want (demand) real balances to consummate transactions, such as the regular, expected payments for factor services and tax payments. The payments to the factors include such things as wages, salaries, and rent. In addition, firms need money for transactions that cannot be perfectly anticipated. The timing of some transactions may be uncertain. A firm may not know when a certain delivery will be made or when it will have to pay for that delivery. Transactions balances are used to pay for normal day-to-day operations, even though the exact time of these payments may be difficult to predict.

Some transactions may be totally unexpected such as a bill for repairing equipment that broke down or expenses related to an unforeseen strike. Expenses, whether anticipated or not, must be paid. As a result, firms need some money and/or liquid assets such as Treasury bills (T-bills) as a precaution against these contingencies. Like households, firms have both transactions and precautionary motives for demanding real money balances.

Firms experience two flows of real money balances: expenditures that generate outflows of funds and receipts that generate inflows of funds. The basic problem is that these flows are not synchronized. Thus, when expenditures exceed receipts, a firm must have money either on hand or immediately accessible so that it can meet its financial obligations. Of course, if receipts exceed expenditures, the firm's financial manager must decide how much of the surplus to hold as real money balances and how much to use to acquire interest-bearing financial assets, such as T-bills and certificates of deposit (CDs).

The points just made are fairly obvious. But what determines the amount of real money balances that firms should hold? In essence, the basic framework is similar to that employed by households in deciding the size of real money balances to hold. That is, firms analyze the benefits and costs of holding real money balances.

For firms, the benefits of holding real money balances are the stream of services that money balances provide. Being able to make payments when they are due is a definite plus and a necessity if a firm is to retain its business reputation and integrity.[7] Indeed, a firm's long-run survival often depends on making payments in a timely fashion. The opportunity cost of holding real money balances is the forgone interest from retaining money in lieu of less-liquid, higher-earning assets. Real money balances held by firms (currency and demand deposits) do not, as of this writing, earn explicit interest. In any case, the relative interest rate differential between money and nonmonetary assets is the opportunity cost.

In deciding the optimum amount of money balances to hold, a cash manager will want to minimize money holdings subject to the constraint of having enough money on hand or accessible when needed. The cash manager will also attempt to maximize the return earned on the other financial assets held in place of money. In reality, firms, like households, will hold additional real money balances only if the benefits of doing so are greater than the costs, as depicted in Exhibit 21-2 below. We turn now to a discussion of interest rates, income, and real money balances.

21-2

How Households and Firms Decide What Amount of Real Balances to Hold

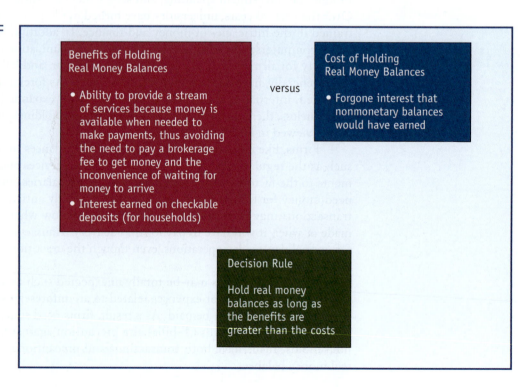

Benefits of Holding Real Money Balances

- Ability to provide a stream of services because money is available when needed to make payments, thus avoiding the need to pay a brokerage fee to get money and the inconvenience of waiting for money to arrive
- Interest earned on checkable deposits (for households)

versus

Cost of Holding Real Money Balances

- Forgone interest that nonmonetary balances would have earned

Decision Rule

Hold real money balances as long as the benefits are greater than the costs

Recap   The demand for money is a demand for real money balances (M/P). Real money balances are adjusted for changes in purchasing power. Households demand real money balances to fulfill the transactions and precautionary motives. The benefit of holding money balances is the stream of services that having money on hand provides. The cost is the forgone interest that holding nonmonetary financial assets would have yielded. Firms demand real balances to make transactions because inflows and outflows are not perfectly synchronized. Firms will minimize their holdings of money subject to the constraint of having money balances available when needed. Both households and firms will demand money balances as long as the benefits are greater than the costs.

The Interest Rate, Real Income, and Real Money Balances

The opportunity cost of holding currency or checkable deposits is the forgone interest that is given up when money balances are held. Currency and demand deposits earn no interest, and other checkable deposits earn less than various less-liquid financial assets. As the interest rate increases, ceteris paribus, the opportunity cost also increases.[8] Likewise, if rates fall, ceteris paribus, the opportunity cost falls.

At higher interest rates, spending units substitute into other less-liquid assets that yield a higher return.[9] In other words, at higher interest rates, households and firms will cut back on the quantity of real money balances they hold because there is a greater reward for doing so. Jose is not concerned about the idle $2,000 sitting in his checking account earning 2 percent if the rate on money market deposit accounts is 3 percent. If the rate on money market deposit accounts goes up to 10 percent, however, while the rate on checkable deposits increases to only 3 percent, he will try to hold a smaller average balance in his checking account.

In light of the preceding discussion, you can see the inverse relationship between the quantity demanded of real money balances and the interest rate on nonmonetary assets, ceteris paribus. This relationship is summarized in Equation (21-2). The negative sign over the interest rate specifies the inverse or negative relationship between the interest rate and the quantity demanded.

(21-2)   quantity demanded of real money balances = $f(\overset{-}{\text{interest rate}})$

In this analysis, we are following the convention of defining the quantity demanded as the amount of real balances that will be demanded as a function of a specific interest rate. If the interest rate increases, ceteris paribus, the quantity demanded of real money balances decreases, and vice versa. If any other factor affecting demand changes, the demand for real balances changes.[10] The demand for real balances is the quantity demanded at every interest rate.

Now is a good time to look at Exhibit 21-3 on page 506, which is a demand curve showing an inverse relationship between "the interest rate" and the quantity demanded of real money balances. Real money balances are measured on the horizontal axis, and the interest rate on nonmonetary financial assets is measured on the vertical axis. If the interest rate changes, ceteris paribus, we move along the demand curve as the quantity demanded of real money balances changes. Note that the demand curve is drawn holding other factors, including the price level, constant. For an alternative theory of why the quantity of real money balances demanded and the interest rate are inversely related, see the A Closer Look feature on page 506, which discusses Keynes's theory of liquidity preference.

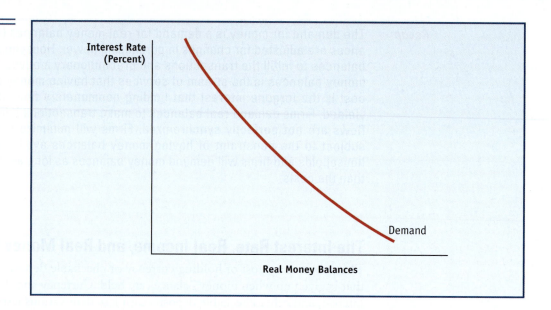

21-3
A Demand Curve for Real Money Balances

A Closer Look

Keynes's Speculative Demand for Money

So far, we have considered the quantity demanded of money to be inversely related to the interest rate, ceteris paribus, because money earns a lower rate of interest than nonmonetary financial assets. As the interest rate increases, the opportunity cost of holding money increases, and vice versa. Money is one of many financial assets that an individual may hold. As interest rates change, so do the relative rewards of holding various financial and real assets. Individuals adjust their portfolios to reflect these changes.

We would be remiss, however, if we did not introduce you to another theory that also results in an inverse relationship between the quantity demanded of money and the interest rate, ceteris paribus. This theory is known as *liquidity preference*. It involves the *speculative demand for money* and is attributable to John Maynard Keynes, perhaps the most influential economist of the twentieth century.

To simplify, Keynes assumed that individuals can hold their wealth in either bonds or money. Bonds earn the market rate of interest, and money earns no interest or less than the market rate of interest. Moreover, the price of bonds fluctuates when interest rates change. As you saw in Chapter 6, when interest rates rise, bond prices fall, and vice versa. Hence, when interest rates fall, individuals holding bonds experience capital gains, and when rates rise, individuals holding bonds experience capital losses. Consequently, from this analysis, Keynes concluded that if individuals expect interest rates to rise in the future, they are hesitant to buy bonds today because they will experience capital losses if their expectations are fulfilled and interest rates do rise. Hence, people prefer to hold money instead of bonds if they expect interest rates to rise. Likewise, individuals who expect interest rates to fall will prefer to buy bonds today so they will experience a capital gain if interest rates do indeed fall.

A caveat of this theory is that if interest rates are high, more and more individuals will come to believe that rates will be going down in the future and will therefore prefer to buy bonds today in the hope of a capital gain when interest rates do fall. Consequently, because individuals hold either bonds or money, when interest rates are high, the quantity demanded of money will be low. If interest rates are low, more and more individuals will believe rates will be rising in the future and will prefer to avoid holding bonds today out of fear of future capital losses. Hence, when interest rates are low, ceteris paribus, the quantity demanded of money will be high.

Keynes added one final twist. When interest rates are abnormally low, virtually everyone could come to believe that interest rates will be going up in the future. In this case, all individuals would prefer to hold money balances instead of bonds. This argument has a theoretically interesting implication for monetary policy. If the Fed increases the supply of reserves to the banking system, and the money supply, in turn, increases, individuals normally use part of the increase in money to buy bonds, thus increasing the demand for bonds. In the case of abnormally low rates, however, individuals fearing capital losses would choose to hold the increase in money instead of buying bonds. Without an increase in the demand for bonds to push up their prices, bond prices and, hence, interest rates would not change. Thus, the Fed would be unable to increase the quantity of real output demanded by lowering interest rates and increasing interest-sensitive spending. When the Fed increases the money supply, individuals would merely hold the increase as "idle" money balances. The economy, which would be flooded with liquidity, would be in what is known as a *liquidity trap*.

Although economists can describe a liquidity trap, they do not known whether the economy has ever actually been in one (Keynes couldn't find one). Nevertheless, this possibility was one reason that Keynes preferred an active fiscal policy—changing government spending or taxes—to a policy that worked solely through changing interest rates. If an economy is in a recession and a liquidity trap, monetary policy will be unable to lower interest rates and stimulate interest-sensitive demand. To see why, take a look at the accompanying graph. Note that the interest rate, which measures the overall level of rates, is measured on the vertical axis. In a liquidity trap, the demand for real money balances curve becomes horizontal.

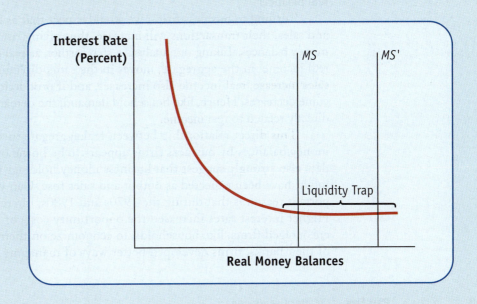

Later economists have questioned the validity of Keynes's speculative demand for money altogether. They point out that the theory implies that when interest rates are low, individuals prefer to hold money as opposed to bonds, waiting to buy until interest rates are up and bond prices are down. The problem is that the theory just does not seem realistic for the average person. How many "average people" do you know who hold money, say, in their checking accounts in lieu of bonds when interest rates are low because they fear a capital loss?[a] Apparently, many economists did not think they knew any. The point became somewhat moot because other economists showed that, ceteris paribus, there would still be an inverse relationship between the quantity demanded of money and the interest rate if money is viewed as one of many financial assets in which wealth can be held.

Real Income
Nominal income divided by a price index.

So far, we have considered the demand for real money balances for a given income. Now we want to look at what will happen to demand if income changes. We begin with households. As you first saw in Chapter 3, the amount of nominal money that a household demands at a point in time is directly related to its income. We can now extend that analysis to real money balances by recalling that real money balances are nominal money balances divided by a price index. Likewise, **real income** is nominal income divided by a price index. It is income adjusted for changes in prices. As real income increases, households on average are going to engage in more transactions and, hence, demand more real money balances. Households will also want to hold more real money balances to fulfill the precautionary motive. As real income decreases, the reverse is true. A high-income person is much more likely to carry around a few $100 bills in a purse or wallet for a "rainy day" than a poor person. Thus, like the transactions motive, precautionary demand for real money balances is also directly related to real income.

The relationship between the household demand for real money balances and real income is not strictly proportional. That is, a doubling of real income does not result in a doubling of the demand for real balances. From an intuitive standpoint, households are able to conserve on real money balances as income increases so that an increase in real income results in a less than proportional increase in the demand for real balances.[11]

Turning to business firms, we would expect that as businesses expand production and sales, their transactions will increase, thus giving rise to increased demand for real money balances. Taking our analysis a step further, as real output expands and contracts, real income, in the aggregate, moves in the same direction. That is, if production and sales increase, real income also increases, and if production and sales decrease, real income decreases. Hence, like household demand, the demand for real balances by firms is directly related to real income.

This direct relationship between real aggregate income and the demand for real money balances by business firms appears to be borne out by the data. However, the data also strongly suggest that business money holdings have generally risen less than might have been expected as output and sales rose. Can you guess why? The most important reason is that during the 1970s and 1980s, interest rates generally trended up. Higher interest rates increased the opportunity costs of holding money balances and encouraged firms, like households, to economize on their cash positions. With the aid of their banks, firms developed better ways of managing inflows and outflows so that the flows were better synchronized and the timing of cash payments was more certain. As a result, a portion of the funds that otherwise would have been held as money balances was used to expand operations, acquire other financial assets, pay off existing debts, and so forth. When interest rates fell in the 1990s, the innovations that firms had developed in response to the high-interest environment of the 1970s and 1980s did not disappear. Instead, firms continued to use these techniques to exploit even minute price differentials.

For data on money and income, visit **http://www.whitehouse.gov/fsbr/esbr.html**.

The desired accumulation of real money balances for both households and business firms is summarized in Equation (21-3). The plus sign over real income signifies the direct or positive relationship between real income and demand.

$$(21\text{-}3) \qquad \text{demand for real money balances} = f(\overset{+}{\text{real income}})$$

Exhibit 21-4 below shows various demand curves for real money balances. Real money balances are measured on the horizontal axis, and the interest rate is plotted on the vertical axis. Note that for every level of real income, there is a different demand curve, showing an inverse relationship between the quantity of real money balances demanded and the interest rate, ceteris paribus. If real income increases, the demand curve for real money balances shifts to the right and there is an increase in demand. If real income decreases, the demand curve shifts to the left and there is a decrease in demand.

21-4

The Demand for Real Money Balances

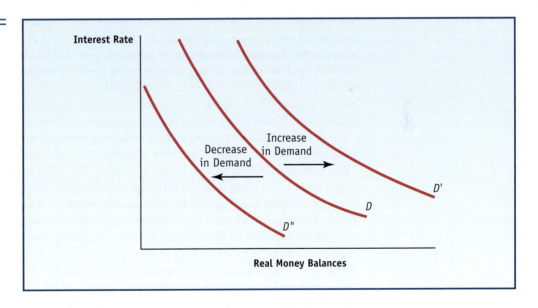

Each demand curve is drawn for a different level of real income. For simplicity, we are referring only to real income as a determinant of the position of the demand curve, recognizing that the level of production and sales is also a determinant. (Because production and sales are highly correlated with real income, this analysis is not significantly affected.) Because a direct relationship exists between the demand for real money balances and real income, if real income changes, the demand curve shifts. If the interest rate changes, ceteris paribus, there is a change in the quantity demanded of real money balances and a movement along a single curve.

The demand for real money balances by households and firms is directly related to real income. That is, increases in real income increase demand while decreases in real income decrease demand. Likewise, ceteris paribus, quantity demanded is inversely related to the interest rate. The interest rate is the opportunity cost associated with holding real money balances. Increases in the interest rate, ceteris paribus, decrease quantity demanded while decreases in the interest rate, ceteris paribus, increase quantity demanded.

Additional Factors Affecting the Demand for Real Money Balances

Although real income is the major factor that determines the demand for real money balances, demand can also be affected by other factors including the following:

1. Wealth
2. Payment technologies such as the introduction of ATM machines, debit cards, and credit cards
3. Expected inflation
4. The risk and liquidity of other financial assets

In turn, changes in these factors cause the demand curve for real money balances to shift.

As with real income, changes in wealth are directly related to changes in the demand for real money balances. As wealth increases, ceteris paribus, the demand for real balances also increases, and vice versa. At the same time, the widespread availability of ATM machines, allowing funds to be easily transferred between checking and savings balances, reduces the demand for real balances. Jose will hold fewer real balances if he can transfer funds from his savings account to his checking account 24 hours a day at an ATM machine. Likewise, the widespread availability of credit cards may reduce the need to hold money balances by firms and households and thereby reduce both the precautionary and transactions motives for holding real money balances from what they otherwise would be.

Inflation reduces the value and purchasing power of money. Assuming that a household starts out with a given amount of nominal money balances, if inflation occurs, the value of the real money balances falls. The larger the initial money balances are, the greater is the risk of incurring losses if inflation should occur. Expectations of higher inflation, therefore, reduce the demand for real money balances, ceteris paribus. Increased uncertainty about future inflation rates will also reduce the demand for real money balances.

If the liquidity of other financial assets increases, they are better substitutes for real money balances and can be held instead of real money balances. Thus, increases in the liquidity of other financial assets reduce the demand for real money balances. Therefore, when financial innovations increase the liquidity of other assets and create new highly liquid substitutes for money, the demand for real money balances decreases from what it otherwise would be.[12]

If the risk of holding other assets increases, the demand for real money balances increases, ceteris paribus. For example, if the stock and bond markets become more volatile, the demand for real money balances increases. Likewise, if the risk of holding money increases, the demand for other financial assets increases. Can you explain what happens if the risk of holding other financial assets decreases?

Exhibit 21-5 on page 511 summarizes the factors that affect the demand for money. Having completed our discussion of the demand for real money balances, we are ready to put demand and supply together. After all, it takes both to make a market.

An Increase in . . .	Will Cause the Demand for Money to . . .
Income	Increase
Wealth	Increase
Payment technologies	Decrease
Expected inflation	Decrease
Risk of other financial assets	Increase
Liquidity of other financial assets	Decrease

A Decrease in . . .	Will Cause the Demand for Money to . . .
Income	Decrease
Wealth	Decrease
Payment technologies	Increase
Expected inflation	Increase
Risk of other financial assets	Decrease
Liquidity of other financial assets	Increase

Looking Forward

Will Checks Go the Way of the Dinosaur?

Throughout this text, you have seen that it has become easier for consumers to make payments electronically, thus bypassing the use of checks or currency. For example, in Chapter 2, we described how point-of-sale terminals allow consumers to make purchases using debit cards and how consumers can pay some bills via phone transfers. In addition, a general-use prepaid card called an *electronic purse* is just around the corner and may replace currency in many uses. The electronic purse will most likely also reduce the use of checks.

In addition to these innovations, many banks now issue check cards. A check card allows users to pay for a purchase by making a withdrawal from their checking account without writing a check. Check cards look like ATM cards but have a credit card symbol (such as VISA) in a corner. Instead of writing a check to make a purchase, a check card can be presented anywhere the VISA credit card is accepted. But it is not a credit card because there is no borrowing. A personal identification number is needed for use.

A check cards has many advantages. It is convenient because it is similar to paying with a credit card. It is flexible in that it may be used in places that accept credit cards but won't take checks. It saves the time of writing a check and usually doesn't require additional identification as checks do. It allows the owner to get cash from a huge network of ATM machines around the world. Some check cards also offer other carrots such as travel insurance when tickets are purchased with the card, warranty services on goods purchased with the card, and so on. A monthly statement of every transaction makes record keeping easy. The costs vary from bank to bank, but most banks offer deals that for the majority of people are cheaper than using debit machines or paper checks.

What are the disadvantages? Identifying the disadvantages seems rather difficult at this time, which suggests that checks may indeed be going the way of the dinosaur.

Other factors that affect the demand for real balances include wealth, payment technologies, expected inflation, and/or the risk and liquidity of other financial assets. If wealth increases or the risk of other financial assets increases, the demand for real money balances increases. If payment technologies improve, if inflation is expected to increase, or if the liquidity of other financial assets increases, the demand for money decreases.

Equilibrium in the Market for Real Money Balances

In Chapters 4 and 20, you saw that the Fed, through the use of open market operations, exerts a great deal of influence over the supply of nominal money balances and interest rates. This implies that the Fed also exerts a great deal of influence over the supply of real money balances because real money balances are nominal balances divided by a price index. We can depict the supply of real money balances curve as a vertical line on the demand-supply plane.

So far in this chapter, you have seen that, ceteris paribus, the quantity demanded of real money balances is inversely related to the interest rate. By putting the supply and demand curves together as in Exhibit 21-6 below, we can describe how the interest rate is determined. Real money balances are measured on the horizontal axis, and the interest rate is on the vertical axis. Equilibrium occurs where the two curves intersect (point *A*) at an interest rate of 6 percent. At this rate, the quantity of real money balances demanded is equal to the quantity of real money balances supplied. If the interest rate is above 6 percent, quantity demanded is less than quantity supplied, and there is a surplus of real balances. Because of this surplus, the price of real money balances (the interest rate) will fall. If the interest rate is below 6 percent, quantity demanded is greater than quantity supplied, and there is a shortage of real money balances. Because of this shortage, the interest rate will rise. Thus, the interest rate is that rate at which the quantity demanded is equal to the quantity supplied and the market for real money balances is in equilibrium.

A couple of life's few absolutes are that the future is uncertain and that change is an inherent part of life. Consequently, either demand or supply will be constantly changing in the dynamic world in which we live. Let's observe how interest rates will change

21-6

Equilibrium in the Market
for Real Money Balances

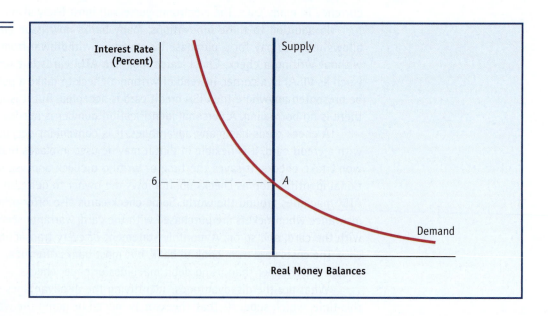

in response to changes in the demand for or supply of real money balances. We begin with changes in supply.

Open market operations lead to changes in reserves that change the nominal money supply. If prices remain constant when the nominal money supply changes, the supply of real money balances will also change. Is it reasonable, however, to assume that the price level will remain the same when the nominal supply of money increases? Recall from our discussion in Chapter 3 that changes in the money supply are correlated with changes in the price level. However, changes in the rate of inflation today are most highly correlated with changes in the money supply one to two years ago. The immediate response to an increase in the growth rate of the nominal money supply is a less than a proportional increase in the price level. For example, suppose that the nominal money supply increases at a faster rate. Then, because price changes usually lag, the supply of real balances also increases, as depicted in Exhibit 21-7 below. When the Fed increases the supply of reserves, ceteris paribus, the vertical supply curve of real money balances shifts to the right. When the Fed decreases the supply of reserves, ceteris paribus, the vertical supply curve shifts to the left. We should also note that as discussed in Chapter 20, other factors including changes in discount loans can and do change the supply of bank reserves, the monetary base, and the supply of real money balances.[13] If any of these factors change, ceteris paribus, the vertical supply curve of real money balances shifts.

Assume that economic activity seems sluggish, that growth has been disappointing, and that the Fed has become convinced of the need to do something to speed up the economy. It decides to use open market purchases to increase bank reserves. The supply of real balances increases, and, in turn, the supply curve shifts to the right. Assuming that the demand for real money balances does not initially change, the interest rate falls and

21-7

A Change in the Supply of Real Balances

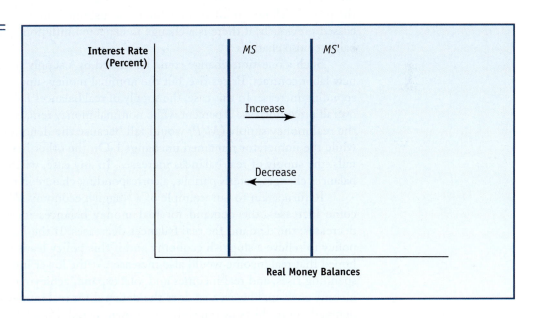

Assuming a given price level, when the money supply changes relative to that price level, the supply of real money balances also changes. If supply increases, the supply curve shifts to the right; if supply decreases, the curve shifts to the left. If the price level increases, however, the supply of real balances decreases, shifting the vertical supply curve to the left. If the price level decreases, the supply of real balances increases, shifting the vertical supply curve to the right.

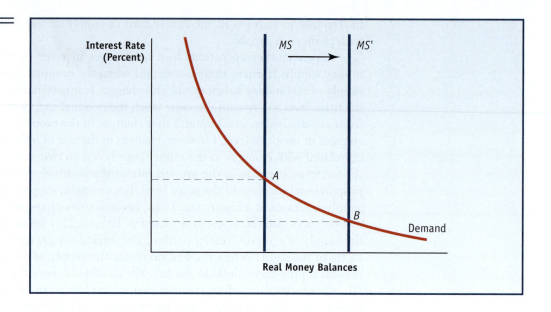

the market for real money balances moves to the intersection of the demand curve and the new supply curve (point B), as depicted in Exhibit 21-8 above.

A change in reserves or the monetary base is not, however, the only factor that can change the supply of real money balances. Another factor is the price level. If there is a one-time change in the price level for a given nominal money supply, the supply of real money balances also changes. Note that this discussion applies to a one-time change in the price level, not to inflation, which is a sustained increase in the price level. As discussed previously, if there is a change in expected inflation, the demand for real money balances also changes.

Such a one-time change could be caused by a supply shock, such as a drought or a new labor contract. Prices rise, but the nominal money supply does not undergo a corresponding increase. In this case, the supply of real balances falls. For example, assume that overall prices increase 2 percent while nominal money remains at $1 trillion. In this case, the real money supply (M/P) would fall because the denominator increased 2 percent while the numerator remained unchanged. On the other hand, if the overall price level falls, the supply of real balances increases. In any case, when the supply of real money balances changes, ceteris paribus, a corresponding change in the interest rate follows.

Return again to our example of a sluggish economy. We have seen that if real income increases, the demand for real money balances increases, and if real income decreases, the demand for real balances decreases. If the Fed engages in expansionary policy to relieve a sluggish economy and if this policy leads to lower interest rates, it is hoped that real income would also increase. At the lower interest rate, interest-sensitive spending rises, and real incomes and jobs expand, achieving the desired results. As real income goes up, however, so does the demand for real money balances, and, hence, the demand curve shifts to the right, as shown in Exhibit 21-9 on page 515. The market moves to a new equilibrium at the intersection of the new demand and supply curves (point C). The interest rate may end up higher or lower than the original rate, depending on the magnitude of the increase in demand for real balances due to the increase in real income. See if you can work through the analogous situation in which the Fed uses open market sales to reduce bank reserves in response to an economy that seems to be overheating. In this case, the interest rate initially rises, choking off interest-sensitive

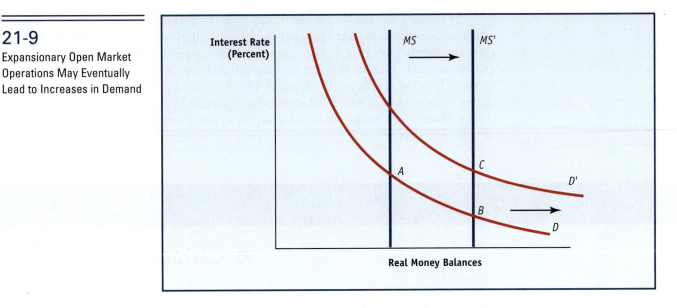

spending and resulting in a fall in real income. As real income falls, so does the demand for real money balances, and the demand curve shifts to the left. The interest rate may end up higher or lower than the original rate, depending on the magnitude of the decrease in the demand for real balances due to the decrease in income.

Look again at Exhibit 21-9, which depicts the situation in which real income and, hence, the demand for real money balances increase in response to lower interest rates. As you have seen, the demand for real balances can also increase for other reasons. For example, if wealth increases, if inflation is expected to subside, or if other financial assets become more risky and less liquid, the demand for real money balances increases. In this case, the demand for real balances curve shifts to the right. If the supply of real balances does not change, the interest rate rises. Such a situation is depicted in Exhibit 21-10 below. Likewise, if income decreases or other factors change (say, payment technologies improve), the demand curve shifts to the left and, ceteris paribus, the interest rate falls.

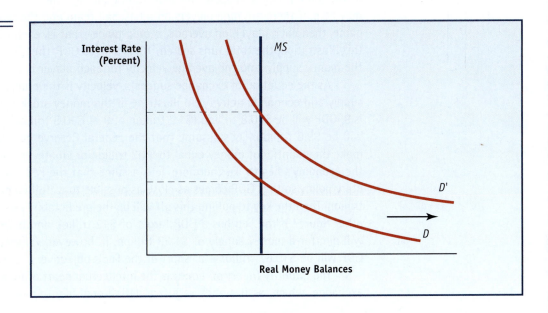

In any case, the market for real money balances always gravitates to the interest rate at which quantity demanded is equal to quantity supplied. When we observe interest rates constantly changing in our economy, they are responding to changes in supply and/or demand. That is, they are moving up or down in response to increases or decreases (shifts) in supply and/or demand. The A Closer Look feature below looks at the theory of monetarism, which is historically important in the development of monetary theory. Monetarism relates the nominal supply of money and changes therein to the level of economic activity.

A Closer Look

Monetarism

Monetarism is a school of thought in economics that, not surprisingly, emphasizes the importance of changes in the nominal money supply as a cause of fluctuations in prices, employment, and output. Leading monetarists include Milton Friedman (who received the Nobel Prize in economics in 1976), Karl Brunner, and Allan Meltzer. Monetarist analysis of the role of money usually begins with the *equation of exchange*, which can be written as

$$M \times V = \text{GDP} = P \times Y$$

This equation is really an identity—that is, it is true by definition. It says that the nation's nominal GDP (the overall price level, P, multiplied by the real level of output, Y) is equal to the money supply, M, multiplied by *velocity, V*, which is the number of times the money supply must "turn over" during a year to "mediate" all purchases of goods and services comprising GDP.[a] In effect, V is the average number of times the typical dollar component of the money supply is spent on final output through the economy in a year. An analogy may help. If there are nine players on a baseball team and the team scores 18 runs in one game, then each player, on average, scored twice—that is, each circled the bases twice. In this illustration, the total runs scored, 18, is akin to GDP, the nine players are analogous to the money supply, and the average velocity for each player is 2.

As the equation of exchange suggests, velocity is the crucial link between the money supply and economic activity. To illustrate, if the money stock is $1.2 trillion and velocity is 9, GDP will be $10.8 trillion ($1.2 trillion $\times$ 9 = $10.8 trillion); if velocity is 8, then GDP will be $9.6 trillion. Let's assume that the Federal Reserve can control M—that is, it can make the quantity of money equal to $1.2 trillion or whatever figure it believes is best for the economy's health. Furthermore, let's assume that the Fed would like to conduct monetary policy so that GDP comes as close as possible to a "full employment" figure, say, $12 trillion. Then the key to pulling this off will be the predictability of V. Will it be 8, 9, or some other figure? If the Fed has a GDP target of $12 trillion and believes velocity will be 9, it will aim for a money supply of $1.33 trillion. If, however, velocity turns out to be only 8, GDP will be $10.67 trillion—far short of the Fed's objective.

The *quantity theory of money* is the intellectual heart of monetarism. The equation of exchange, which, as it stands, is just a definitional identity, is transformed into a theory linking money and economic activity by first hypothesizing that V is reasonably predictable and then gathering evidence supporting this assertion. Why is this important? Let's take the simplest case. Suppose that V is stable (fixed). If policy makers could always count on V to be 9, they could be sure that a money supply of $1.2 trillion would produce GDP of $10.8 trillion. More generally, they would know that, for example, a $100 increase in the money supply would produce a $900 rise in GDP; that is, changes in the money supply would lead to proportional changes in GDP—this is in essence the quantity theory of money.

In many respects, the role of money within both monetarism and the quantity theory of money are not very different from that illustrated in Exhibit 3-6, Market Equilibrium. Monetarists tend to prefer the simpler and more direct quantity theory approach because they believe that the detailed linkages between money and economic activity are either relatively unimportant or, given the complexities and interdependencies characterizing the economy, too hard to figure out. Thus, it is argued, focusing on M and V is appropriate and sufficient for analyzing the general role of money in the economy.

As we have noted previously, major structural changes in financial markets have not only skewed the relationship between narrowly defined monetary aggregates and the level of economic activity but also made it difficult for a central bank to use monetary targeting in the execution of monetary policy, as the theory of monetarism suggests. Because credit now emanates from so many sources other than depository institutions such as mutual funds and finance companies, the degree of credit restraint in operation at any particular time is difficult to measure by a standard money supply aggregate, such as $M1$, $M2$, or $M3$, or a broader credit aggregate, such as domestic nonfinancial debt (DNFD).

Recap   Open market operations or a onetime change in the overall price level for a given nominal money supply causes the supply of real balances to change. The market for real balances always gravitates to the interest rate at which quantity demanded is equal to quantity supplied.

A Final Note

In this chapter, we extended the discussion introduced in Chapter 3 by developing a theory of interest rate determination based on the supply of and demand for real money balances. Real money balances are measured at a point in time and refer to actual stocks. The interest rate adjusts to equate the quantity supplied (stock) of real money balances with the quantity demanded.

In Chapter 6, we developed the loanable funds theory in which the interest rate is determined by the supply of and demand for loanable funds. The supply of and demand for loanable funds are measured through time and refer to actual flows. The interest rate adjusts to equate the quantity demanded of loanable funds with the quantity supplied. As in Chapter 6, we can reconcile the two theories by recognizing that when there is a change in a stock measured at different times, a flow has occurred. Correspondingly, changes in the flow of loanable funds entail changes in the stock of real money balances as measured at two different points in time. Make sure you are clear about the difference between stocks and flows and that interest rates equate both the supply of and demand for loanable funds and real money balances.

In this and the previous chapter, we have analyzed the supply of and demand for real money balances. This chapter has one appendix about the transactions demand for money by households. In the next chapter, we look at financial aspects of the household, business, government, and rest-of-the-world sectors in the hope of understanding how spending and financial decisions affect economic activity.

Summary of Major Points

1. The demand for money is really a demand for real money balances. Real money balances are the nominal supply of money divided by the price level. Changes in the overall price level lead to proportional changes in the demand for money and no change in the demand for real balances. Households demand real money balances to consummate transactions (transactions motive) and to fulfill the precautionary motive.

2. Holding real money balances involves both benefits and costs. The benefits are the interest payments that are earned on checkable deposits plus the stream of services that money balances provide. The costs are the forgone interest payments that holding nonmonetary financial assets would have yielded. Households and firms should adjust their holdings of real balances to the point where the marginal benefits of doing so are equal to the marginal costs.

3. Household demand for real balances is directly related to real income. Ceteris paribus, the quantity demanded of real balances is inversely related to the interest rate. A firm's demand for real money balances is directly related to its production and sales and its need to engage in transactions. Both are highly correlated with real income. The demand for real money balances is also affected by other factors including changes in wealth, payment technologies, expected inflation, the availability of near money substitutes, and the risk and liquidity of other financial assets.

4. The interest rate is determined by the demand for and supply of real money balances. If either demand or supply changes, the interest rate changes. The supply of real balances changes when the Fed uses open market operations to change the supply of reserves to depository institutions. Changes in the overall price level for a given nominal money supply also cause the

supply of real balances to change. If the Fed is successful in speeding up a sluggish economy by increasing the supply of real balances, the demand for real balances will also increase as real income increases.

5. Keynes's liquidity preference theory asserts that there is a speculative demand for money such that the quantity demanded of money is inversely related to the interest rate. The inverse relationship results because when interest rates are low, people will demand to hold money instead of bonds because they fear a capital loss when interest rates rise. Likewise when interest rates are high and bond prices low, people will hold bonds instead of money to take advantage of a capital gain when interest rates fall. When interest rates are abnormally low, the economy may be in a liquidity trap where the money demand curve becomes horizontal. In this case, increases in the supply of money do not cause the interest rate to fall, and monetary policy is less effective in affecting economic activity.

6. Monetarism is a theory that stresses the relationship between changes in nominal money and changes in GDP. Monetarists believe that the primary determinant of changes in GDP is changes in the supply of money because velocity is highly stable. More modern monetarists stress that although velocity may not be stable, it is sufficiently predictable.

7. The benefits of holding additional real money balances decline as additional calls are made to the broker each month. The cost of each call to the broker, however, is a constant amount per call. Calls to the broker should be made as long as the benefits of doing so are greater than the costs. The optimum number of calls determines the average daily holding of real balances and, hence, the transactions demand for real money balances by households. (*See Appendix 21A.*)

Key Terms

Review Questions

1. What is a real money balance? If the nominal money supply increases 20 percent while prices increase 20 percent, what happens to the demand for real money balances? What happens to the supply of real money balances?

2. If real income increases 20 percent, what happens to the demand for real money balances? Is the change in demand proportional to the change in real income?

3. What is the difference between a onetime increase in prices and inflation? How does a onetime increase in prices affect the demand for real money balances? How does expected inflation affect the demand for real balances? How does a onetime increase in prices affect the real money supply?

4. Why do firms want to hold real money balances? Why do households? What factors determine the quantity of real balances that each wants to hold?

5. What happens to the demand for real balances if interest rates on time deposits rise relative to interest rates on checkable deposits?

6. Correct the following statement: "When the interest rate increases, the demand for real money balances decreases."

7. In Chapter 3, our initial peek at the data showed that changes in money were more highly correlated with changes in nominal GDP than with changes in either real GDP or inflation. Does this finding support or refute monetarism? Explain.

8. Using the liquidity preference theory, explain why the quantity demanded of money is inversely related to the interest rate. What is a liquidity trap?

9. When is the market for real money balances in equilibrium? If the Fed engages in open market sales, what happens to the supply of real balances?

10. Explain the transactions and precautionary motives for demanding real money balances.

11. What are the benefits of holding real money balances? What are the costs? What is the optimum amount of real money balances that households and firms will demand?

Analytical Questions

Questions marked with an icon are objective in nature. They can be completed with a short answer or number.

12. Graph the supply and demand curves for real money balances. Explain what happens to the interest rate in each of the following situations:

  a. Credit cards become more widely used and accepted to make transactions.

  b. The economy is growing faster than the Fed thinks is desirable, and therefore the Fed sells bonds to the public.

  c. Many new near money substitutes are created.

  d. The overall price level falls while the nominal money supply remains constant.

  e. ATM machines become more accessible and more widely used.

  f. The secondary markets for negotiable CDs and junk bonds collapse.

  g. Inflation is expected to pick up in the coming year.

13. The graph in Exhibit 21-1 shows a typical household's real money holdings, assuming that real money balances are gradually depleted over the course of the month. Jacques gets paid on the first of each month but parties extensively over the next week and is broke for the remainder of the month. Graph Jacques's real money holdings over the course of a month.

14. Graphically show what happens to the interest rate if the Fed takes action that leads to a decrease in the supply of real money balances while the economy is in a liquidity trap.

15. What is the equation of exchange? If nominal GDP is $12 trillion and the money supply is $1.5 trillion, what is velocity? If the Fed increases the nominal money supply, what happens to nominal GDP? (*Hint:* First assume that velocity is constant and then relax this assumption.) Can we be sure of the direction of change in prices and real GDP?

16. Graphically show what happens to the real money supply if the price level rises while the nominal money supply remains constant. What happens to the real money supply if both the nominal money supply and the price level rise by the same percent?

17. If Sara earns $4,000 per month, the interest rate is 4 percent, and the cost of a call to the broker is $.75, what should be her transactions demand for real balances per month? (*See Appendix 21A.*)

18. Referring to question 17, if Sara's income increases to $6,000 per month, what happens to her demand for real money balances? (*See Appendix 21A.*)

Internet Exercise

Tabulate the relationship between interest rates and money (*M*1) growth for the years from 1962 to 1976. For data on interest rates, use the 3-month Treasury bill rate from the following Web site: **http://research.stlouisfed.org/fred2/categories/22**. For data on the rate of growth of *M*1, scroll down to the *M*1 (seasonally adjusted) link at **http://research.stlouisfed.org/fred2/categories/24** or check **http://www.federalreserve.gov/releases/h6/**. Verify that an increase in the rate of growth of the money supply during the mid-1960s and the 1970s did not lead to a decline in interest rates. Is this possible? Why? (*Hint:* See Exhibit 21-9 in the text for a possible explanation.)

Suggested Readings

For a fun and interesting article about the stone money of Yap, see Michael F. Bryan, "Island Money," *Economic Commentary,* Federal Reserve Bank of Cleveland (February 1, 2004). The article is available on the Internet at **http:// www.clevelandfed.org/Research/Com2004/0201.pdf**.

Electronic banking promises to revolutionize the demand for money in the next few years. For an interesting survey, see Chrisolav E. Anguelov, Marianne A. Hilgert, and Jeanne M. Hogarth, "U.S. Consumers and Electronic Banking, 1995–2003", Board of Governors of the Federal Reserve System, *Federal Reserve Bulletin* (Winter 2004): 1–18. The article is available on the Internet at **http://www.federalreserve.gov/pubs/bulletin/2004/winter04 _ca.pdf**.

For an interesting but highly technical discussion of some of the topics in this chapter, see Charles T. Carlstrom and Timothy S. Fuerst, "Money Growth Rules and Price Level Determinacy," *Working Paper 00–10,* Federal Reserve Bank of Cleveland (August 2000). The article is available on the Internet at **http://www.clevelandfed.org/**.

For an article that concludes that inflation around 2 percent is optimal, see Milton Marquis, "Inflation: The 2% Solution," *Economic Letter,* Federal Reserve Bank of San Francisco (February 2, 2001).

For an article that suggests that monetarism may be coming back into vogue due to the return of a more predictable relationship among money, output, and inflation, see "Follow the Money," *The Economist* (August 8, 1998): 64. Another article that looks at monetarism is Malcolm Wicks, "Beware the Monetarist Resurgence," *New Statesman* (August 28, 1998): 12.

For a look at two views of the quantity theory that the author concludes are similar, see Thomas M. Humphrey, "Fisher and Wicksell on the Quantity Theory," *Federal Reserve Bank of Richmond Economic Quarterly* 83 (Fall 1997): 71–90.

William J. Frazer, Jr., *The Legacy of Keynes and Friedman* (Westport, CT: Praeger, 1994) looks at the monetary theories of each economist.

Thomas Mayer, *Monetarism and Macroeconomic Policy* (Brookfield, VT: Edward Elgar, 1990), provides easy-to-read coverage of the topic.

For a history of the uses and abuses of money and debt, see G. Leigh Skene, *Cycles of Inflation and Deflation* (Westport, CT: Praeger, 1992).

For some engaging reading on monetarism, see Milton Friedman's classic article entitled "The Quantity Theory of Money: A Restatement," in *Studies in the Quantity Theory of Money* (Chicago: University of Chicago Press, 1956).

For an early discussion about the determination of velocity, see Irving Fisher, *The Purchasing Power of Money: Its Determination and Relation to Credit, Interest, and Crises* (New York: Macmillan, 1911).

For interesting reading that concludes that by the end of 1995, more than half of the U.S. currency was held abroad, see Richard D. Porter, "The Location of U.S. Currency: How Much Is Abroad?" *Federal Reserve Bulletin* 82 (October 1996): 883–903.

Appendix 21A: The Transactions Demand for Money by Households

You have seen that a household should demand real balances for transactions as long as the benefits of doing so are greater than the costs. A problem arises in that both the benefits and the costs increase as more real balances are held. The purpose of this appendix is to shed light on how this abstract rule can be translated into behavior in the real world. We use a numerical example to illustrate this procedure. Again, we are assuming that the household can hold money balances or bonds and that it must call its broker, pay a fee, and wait to liquidate the bonds when it needs funds.

Let's consider a simple example in which the household earns a fixed income of $4,000 per month and can make from zero to two calls to its broker each month, as shown in Exhibit 21A-1 on page 522. For simplicity, we will also assume that the price level is 1. If the household makes no calls, it puts $4,000 in its checking account and spends the funds evenly over the course of the month. On average, the household is holding half of its monthly income ($2,000) as nominal money balances. During the first 15 days of the month, the household is holding more than half of its income ($2,000), and during the last 15 days, it is holding less. Because the price level is 1, the household's **average daily holding of funds** ($2,000/1 = $2,000) is its demand for real money balances during the month.

Average Daily Holding of Funds

A household's demand for real money balances during the month; the amount of each withdrawal divided by two.

If the household makes one call to the broker during the month, initially half of its income ($2,000) is used to buy bonds, and the other half is spent evenly over the first 15 days of the month. On the sixteenth day, the household calls the broker to sell the bonds and receives back the half of its income ($2,000) originally invested in bonds. It then spends these funds ($2,000) over the last 15 days of the month. On average, the household holds one-fourth of its income ($1,000) as checkable funds. Because the price level is 1, this is its demand for real money balances ($1,000/1 = $1,000).

If the household makes two calls per month, it initially puts two-thirds of its income in bonds ($2,667) and spends the other one-third ($1,333) during the first third of the month. One-third of the way through the month, the household calls the broker to sell $1,333 worth of bonds for funds to spend during the middle third of the month. The household calls the broker a second time two-thirds of the way through the month for the remainder of the funds ($1,333). Because the household is removing one-third of its income each time it calls the broker and spending that amount equally over one-third of the month (approximately 10 days), its average holding of real money balances is half of each withdrawal, which is one-sixth of its income ($666.67). Because the price level is 1, the demand for real money balances is $666.67/1 = $666.67.

The Demand for Real Money Balances and Market Equilibrium **521**

Following the same methodology, if three calls per month are made, the demand for real money balances is $500/1 = $500. Having completed this rather mechanical exercise, let's now consider the benefits and the costs of making additional calls to the broker. We can make a few simplifying assumptions that will not change the conclusions:

1. We assume that the cost of a call to the broker (the brokerage fee, the time, and the inconvenience) is a constant amount per call regardless of how many calls are made.[14]

2. We assume that the benefit of an additional call to the broker is the additional interest that is earned on the larger amount of funds held in bonds during the month because of the call.

Armed with these two assumptions, we are now in a position to describe how many calls the household should make to the broker each month. Once we know this, we can determine the average daily balance and, hence, the real money balances that the household will demand each month for transactions. How so, you may ask? The number of calls determines how many time periods the month is divided into. If two calls are made, the month is divided into three time periods. If three calls are made, the month is divided into four time periods, and so on. The monthly income divided by the number of

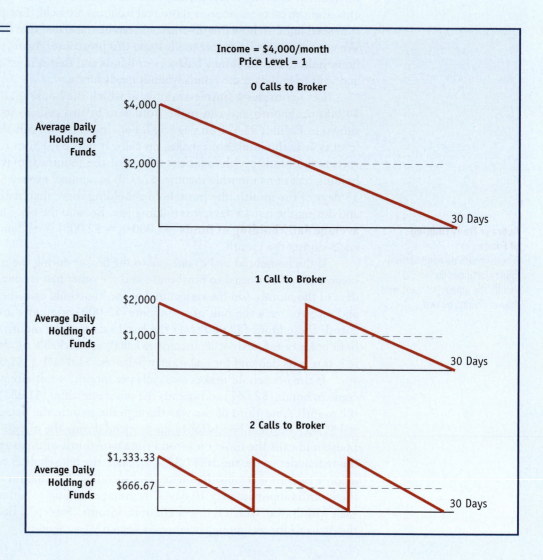

21A-1

The Number of Broker Calls Per Month and the Average Holdings of Real Balances (Transactions Demand for Real Balances)

time periods gives the amount of funds at the start of each time period. Because the funds are spent evenly over the period, one-half of this amount is the average holdings of funds. If we divide the average holdings of funds by the price level, we get the quantity of real money balances that the household will demand for transactions.

In our example, if the household makes one call to the broker, the demand for real money balances decreases by $1,000 from $2,000 to $1,000. The benefit of that first call is the interest earned on the $1,000 that is kept in bonds over the course of the month. If the household makes a second call, the demand for real money balances falls from $1,000 to $666.67, and the benefit of that second call is the interest that is earned on the additional $333.33 ($1000 − $666.67) that is held in bonds over the course of the month. If the household makes a third call to the broker, the demand for real money balances falls from $666.67 to $500, and the benefit of the third call is the additional interest earned on $166.67 ($666.67 − $500). We could keep going, but we hope you see the point. As additional calls to the broker are made, the benefit of each additional call, although positive, is decreasing. Total benefits are increasing but at a decreasing rate.

We now have all pieces in place to make a decision. Recalling that we assumed that the cost of calls to the broker is a constant amount per call regardless of how many calls are made, we can say that calls should be made as long as the marginal benefits (the interest earned on the additional funds kept in bonds) are greater than the cost of the additional call. Because marginal benefits decrease as additional calls to the broker are made and costs per call are constant, the household will be exploiting all opportunities to be better off if it makes all calls when the marginal benefits are greater than the marginal costs. Exhibit 21A-2 below shows the benefits and costs of additional calls. Assuming that the interest rate on bonds is 6 percent above the rate on money balances and the brokerage cost is $2.00 per call, one call should be made to the broker where the benefit is $5.00. If a second call is made, the benefit is $1.67 while the cost is $1.00. In this case, the quantity demanded of real money balances for transactions will be $1,000. In addition, the household will demand to hold a small amount of real money balances, say,

21A-2

Benefits and Costs of Additional Calls to the Broker

Call	(A) Transactions Money if Call Is Not Made	(B) Demand for Money if Call Is Made	(A) − (B)	Benefit: Interest on Additional Bonds Held
0	$2,000	—	—	
1	2,000	$1,000	$1,000	$5.00 ($1,000 × .005)
2	1,000	667	333	1.67 ($333 × .005)
3	667	500	167	.86 ($167 × .005)
4	500	400	100	.50 ($100 × .005)

Benefits: The benefit of a call to the broker is the interest that is earned on the additional funds held in bonds because of the call. To illustrate, we will assume the interest rate is 6 percent per year or approximately 1/2 percent per month.

Costs: Assume the cost per call is constant at $2.00 per call. Eventually, the cost of a additional call will be higher than the benefits, and the call should not be made. In this example, only one call to the broker should be made because the second call costs $2.00 and the benefits are only $1.67.

Call	(A) Transactions Demand for Money if Call Is Not Made	(B) Transactions Demand for Money if Call Is Made	(A) − (B)	Benefit: Interest Earned on Additional Bonds Held
0	$2,000	—	—	
1	2,000	$1,000	$1,000	$10.00 ($1,000 × .01)
2	1,000	667	333	3.33 ($333 × .01)
3	667	500	167	1.67 ($167 × .01)
4	500	400	100	1.00 ($100 × .01)

Costs: Assume that the cost per call is constant at $2.00 per call. In this case, the household should make two calls to the broker per month because the benefits of the second call ($3.33) outweigh the costs ($2.00). Hence, the quantity demanded of money for transactions is $667.

$100, to fulfill the precautionary motive. In this case, then, the total quantity demanded of real money balances is $1,100 ($1,000 + $100).

In this simple example, two factors can change the optimum number of calls to the broker per month: the cost per call and the interest rate. First, consider changes in the cost of brokerage calls.

Returning to Exhibit 21A-1, if the cost of brokerage calls falls to $1.00 per call, it is advantageous to make the second call, which has $1.67 in benefits. Again, the third call is not made. On the other hand, if the cost per call increases to $6.00, zero calls are made because the benefit of the first call is only $5.00. In this case, the household puts all of its income into its checking account and spends it evenly over the course of the month. Consequently, if the cost per call to the broker increases, households will make fewer calls. The average holdings of real money balances and, hence, demand will be greater. You should be able to analyze what will happen to the demand for real money balances if the cost per call to the broker decreases. Now would be a good time to look at Exhibit 21A-3 above, which illustrates what happens to the quantity demanded of real money balances if the interest rate per month increases from 1/2 percent to 1 percent. In this case, the benefits of each additional call double. If the cost per call is $2, the household makes two calls per month, and the quantity demanded of real money balances is $667. Hence, as the interest rate increases, the quantity demanded of real money balances for transactions decreases from $1,000 to $667.

Endnotes

1 The yield or return on real estate includes the value of the stream of services that the assets provide plus any capital gain.

2 The value of money itself is measured in terms of the unit of account, which is an abstract measure of the exchange value. Another unique feature of money is that it has a fixed price in terms of the unit of account. For example, the value of a NOW account (money) is measured in dollars, which is the unit of account.

3 In this example, we are considering a onetime increase in the price level as opposed to inflation, which is a sustained increase in the price level. As you shall see, changes in inflation affect the demand for money.

4 As for the role of risk, note that we generally choose not to store food that tends to spoil quickly because when we need it, it might not be edible. The poorer and more susceptible our refrigeration system is to breakdowns, the greater this risk. Likewise, the greater the probability of inflation, the greater is the risk that money held for transactions and as a precaution will lose value. The more prone the economy is to bouts of inflation, the greater is this risk and the fewer money balances we will hold. Instead, to hedge the risk of inflation, people might store value in the form of real assets.

5 The household could also hold savings or time deposits at banks or other financial intermediaries. In the case of savings accounts, the household members would have to make a trip to the bank to remove the funds or transfer them over the phone or from a home computer. The household would incur record keeping, time, and other transactions costs. In the case of time deposits, the same costs would be incurred, and the depositor might incur a penalty for removing the deposit before its maturity date.

6 Indeed, prior to the Depository Institutions Deregulation and Monetary Control Act of 1980 (DIDMCA), checkable balances paid no interest. Since that time, interest is allowed on nonbusiness checking accounts, but it is less than the market rate of interest on other less-liquid assets.

7 Some firms may also be able to take a discount if they pay within a certain time period. The discount often amounts to 1–2 percent of the invoice. This translates into an annual return of 12–24 percent on the funds used to make the payment.

8 In this discussion, as in our analysis in Chapter 7, we are referring to "the interest rate" as representative of the overall level of interest rates, assuming that rates move up and down together depending on risk, liquidity, maturity, and tax treatment.

9 Even if interest rates on checkable deposits and on other market instruments increase by the same percentage amount, the opportunity cost of holding funds in checkable deposits increases. For example, assume that the T-bill rate is 5 percent and the rate on checkable deposits is 2 percent. If rates rise by 10 percent, the T-bill rate rises to 5.5 percent and the rate on checkable deposits to 2.2 percent. After the increase, the opportunity cost of holding checkable deposits, assuming that T-bills are the next best alternative, is 3.3 percent (5.5 percent less 2.2 percent). Before the increase, the opportunity cost was 3 percent (5 percent less 2 percent).

10 In this section, you will see that income is one of these "other factors" that will cause demand to change. In the next section, we look at additional factors.

11 Note that earlier we saw that if prices double, the demand for nominal money will also double, but the demand for real money balances will not change.

12 These innovations include home equity lines of credit on homes, which make even real assets more liquid.

13 Recall from Chapter 20 that the Fed can use offsetting open market operations to offset the impact of these factors.

14 For example, if the cost per call is $2 and three calls are made, total cost is $6. If four calls are made, total cost is $8.

A Closer Look, page 506

a Keynes was also writing in the Great Depression, when a liquidity trap seemed particularly unlikely. If the Fed was successful in increasing the money supply, is it plausible that people would just hold this money and not spend it in the middle of a depression?

A Closer Look, page 516

a Consistent with general economic usage, we use the term *GDP* to refer to *nominal GDP*, which is equal to the total dollar value of all final goods and services produced by the economy during a year.

The farmer's way of saving money: to be owed by someone he trusted.

—Hugh MacLennan

CHAPTER TWENTY-TWO

Financial Aspects of the Household, Business, Government, and Rest-of-the-World Sectors

Learning Objectives

After reading this chapter, you should know:

How economic and financial conditions influence household spending, saving, borrowing, and lending

What determines the volume of investment spending in the economy

How firms finance current production and investment

How the government's spending, taxing, and borrowing affect the financial system and the economy

How the spending, saving, borrowing, and lending of the rest-of-the-world sector affect the domestic financial system and the economy

To Spend or Not to Spend

Reflecting the weak economy, sales of new cars have been disappointing, and inventories of unsold cars are piling up on dealer lots. Given this situation, General Motors (GM), among others, decides to take some bold action. The prevailing interest rate on consumer loans for new automobiles is 4.5 percent. Beginning next Monday and lasting for the next 30 days, buyers of new GM cars will be able to finance their purchases by borrowing funds from GM's finance company subsidiary at a zero percent interest rate, and the price of all cars purchased will be reduced by $1,000. Jan and Dave, who had been planning to buy a new car next year, believe this deal is too good to pass up and decide to buy now. Because they must come up with $2,000 as a down payment on the $20,000 auto they want to buy (borrowing the other $18,000 from GM), Jan and Dave withdraw the necessary funds from their savings deposit at HLT National Bank.

After discussion, study, and months of agonizing, it's time to act. The board of directors of All Purpose Enterprise Inc. (APEI), one of the 10 largest companies in the nation, decides to undertake three separate actions: (1) sell a subsidiary whose profitability has consistently trailed other parts of the firm, (2) construct a new plant in India, and (3) extend an offer to purchase a medium-size firm specializing in telecommunications. With the economic outlook expected to improve in the months ahead and interest rates incredibly low, APEI, in effect, decides to restructure itself. It expects to increase its earnings in an improving economic climate by redeploying its assets. Because these actions will, on balance, require APEI to raise $2 billion of new funds, the company hires Smith Barney (part of Citigroup) of New York, a preeminent investment banker, to manage the tender offer for the telecommunications firm, the finding of a buyer for the subsidiary, and the issuance of the new bonds and stock necessary to finance the actions undertaken.

Between 1969 and 1997, the federal government budget was in a deficit position. The booming economy of the 1990s caused the federal budget to move into a surplus position in 1998, and large surpluses were projected to loom on the foreseeable horizon. The best way to use the surpluses became a topic of discussion and, in 2001, the Bush administration proposed a tax cut both to stimulate the economy and to reduce the projected surpluses. The discussion about the surplus disappeared after the September 11, 2001, attacks on the World Trade Center and the Pentagon. Increased military spending, new tax cuts, and a weak economy were expected to eliminate the projected surpluses at least in the near term. Sure enough, after surpluses for four years, the surpluses evaporated, and the budget went into a deficit position in 2001, which escalated to a record $413 billion in 2004. Deficits also loomed over the foreseeable future.

In 2000, the dollar was worth around 108 yen but appreciated throughout 2001 to more than 130 yen. The dollar also appreciated with regard to the euro, and at the start of 2002, one dollar was worth more than 1.1 euro. The dollar reversed course in early 2002 with regard to both the yen and the euro. By mid-2004, one dollar was worth about 110 yen and .8 euro. Indeed, over the period from early 2002 to late 2004, the dollar fell about 33 percent against the currencies of its major trading partners.

Since 1982, the United States has run a continual deficit in the current account, dominated by a deficit in the balance of trade. The trade deficit with Japan and in the aggregate with the rest of the world has persisted regardless of whether the dollar was weak or strong. In the mid-2000s, a growing trade deficit with China received much media attention.

Although the preceding four scenarios seem unrelated, they are interdependent, and each affects the health of the economy and the functioning of the financial system. In this chapter, we look at the financial aspects of the spending, saving, borrowing, and lending behavior of the household, firm, government, and the rest-of-the-world sectors. It is this behavior that ultimately determines aggregate demand.

22-1
The Balance Sheet Entries of the Household Sector

Assets	Liabilities
Real estate	Real estate mortgages
Other real assets	Installment debt
Money	Other personal debt
Other financial assets	
	Net worth
Total assets	Total liabilities plus net worth

Like all balance sheets, the balance sheet for the entire household sector is arranged according to the fundamental identity that assets equal liabilities plus net worth. This means that the dollar value of the left column is identical to the dollar value of the right column. Other financial assets include time and savings deposits, stocks, bonds, mutual funds, money market mutual funds, and so forth. Not surprisingly, real estate holdings compose the largest portion of household assets, and mortgages on such real estate are the largest component of liabilities. Net worth measures the degree to which the value of assets exceeds the value of liabilities. Thus, net worth can be viewed as a measure of the financial health or wealth of households.

Household Behavior from a Financial Perspective

The collection of real assets (houses, autos, and the like), financial assets (money, stocks, bonds, savings accounts, and so on) and liabilities (mortgages, consumer loans, and the like) is called a **portfolio**. One's portfolio can be displayed on a balance sheet, which measures the monetary value of a household's assets, liabilities, and **net worth** on a specific date. A portfolio is a stock concept because it measures the value of assets and liabilities held at a particular point in time. Aggregating over all households gives a balance sheet for the household sector, which reflects assets, liabilities, and net worth. Exhibit 22-1 above shows the balance sheet entries of the household sector. Flows of spending, saving, borrowing, and lending that occur between given points in time cause balance sheet changes. The balance sheet transformations summarize the millions of spending, saving, borrowing, and lending decisions that households make in light of their objectives and constraints.

Consumption expenditures by households are by far the largest component of aggregate demand. In addition, when households spend money on investments such as houses, they also increase aggregate demand. Because household spending makes up more than 70 percent of aggregate demand, by its sheer size, household spending is extremely important in the macroeconomy. Our focus is on how and why the household spending flows, which are measured over an interval of time, change.

Research into consumer attitudes and behavior suggests that household portfolio decisions are guided by certain objectives, such as happiness, good health, and a high standard of living. Leaving happiness and good health for the psychologists and physicians, economists traditionally focus on living standards, arguing that as households strive for a better quantity and quality of life, they will develop desired portfolios. Operationally, they will then spend, save, lend, borrow, or work to move their actual portfolios toward their desired portfolios. The point is that household behavior is purposeful, not haphazard. The result is a process characterized by consideration of alternatives, calculation of costs and benefits, and careful planning. Let's take a closer look at the process of financial decision making and what lies behind it.

Portfolio
The collection of real and financial assets and liabilities.

Net Worth
The difference between assets and liabilities at a point in time.

Asset Accumulation: Spending and Saving

Real Assets
For households, durable goods and houses.

Households acquire **real assets** when they engage in consumption spending on durable goods or investment spending on newly constructed houses. If they have surplus funds left over to lend in financial markets, they acquire financial assets. In general, households desire real assets for the flow of services such assets provide. For example, a house (an investment good) provides shelter services over time. An auto provides transportation services, and a television provides entertainment services. Both the auto and the television are consumption goods. In addition, certain real assets such as houses and antiques may also be desired because of expected capital gains. The benefit or return associated with the acquisition of real assets is composed of the value of the flow of services together with any capital gain or loss. Such returns are analogous to and comparable with the returns on financial assets.

Financial Assets
Financial instruments such as stocks, bonds, and money, which serve as a store of value or purchasing power.

Financial assets, from the household perspective, serve as a store of value or purchasing power that can be used in the future, for example, to acquire real assets or pay for children's education. Financial assets, other than money, generally provide income to the holder in the form of interest and dividends and, sometimes, capital gains. This income supplements wages and salaries during the working years and supplements pensions during retirement. In fact, retirement constitutes a strong motive for households to be net lenders and thus accumulate financial assets during the working years. By doing so, households will be better able to maintain living standards in the retirement years.

Of course, retirement and future spending plans are not the only things that motivate the accumulation of financial assets. Equally important is the fact that we live in an uncertain world. Anyone can get laid off from a job, the refrigerator can break down, a medical emergency can occur, and so on. To cushion itself from the adverse effects of such happenings, a household will typically want to acquire some financial assets, especially liquid and safe assets, such as savings deposits, Treasury bills, and money market mutual fund shares. These near monies can be converted into money quickly at little cost and can involve little risk. The need for households to hold liquid assets for "a rainy day" has diminished somewhat in recent years as financial intermediaries have made so called lines of credit (including home equity lines of credit) increasingly available to consumers. In essence, a line of credit is a promise by, say, a bank, to lend you funds as you need them, up to the amount for which you have been approved. Thus, if you have a $10,000 line of credit, all or part of these funds is available to you if and when the need arises. Changes in the size and composition of financial assets over time also reflect capital gains or losses on assets owned and household decisions to spend, save, borrow, or lend.

Money is also one of many financial assets households may possess. As you saw in the last two chapters, money is unique among financial assets in serving as a means of payment. Because of its unique position, we devoted all of Chapter 21 to the demand for real money balances. For now, we are merely reminding you that money is one of an array of financial assets a household may hold and that the demand for real money balances is directly related to income while, ceteris paribus, the quantity demanded of real money balances is inversely related to the interest rate.

Liability Accumulation: Borrowing

Financial Liabilities
Debt incurred through borrowing.

Periodically, throughout its lifetime, a household will consider spending (consuming) more than its current income or portfolio of financial assets can finance at that time. This is where borrowing and the accumulation of debt, or **financial liabilities**, come in. By examining the motives for borrowing and what limits the ability and willingness of households to borrow, we can highlight the important interdependencies inherent in household portfolio decisions.

A decision to borrow today is really two decisions: a decision to borrow today and a decision to repay what is borrowed plus interest in the future. The borrower is willing to trade off or borrow against future purchasing power for current purchasing power. Why would a household want to do this? Visualize a student couple whose current income is low but whose future income is expected to be higher. They desire to consume more now. Borrowing and spending now will raise consumption relative to current income and lower consumption in the future relative to income as the debts accumulated now are paid off. In the process, borrowing facilitates the smoothing out of household spending and consumption over time. Of course, households may also borrow to acquire knowledge and skills (education), which will lead to a higher future income. Likewise, they may borrow to acquire real or financial assets that are expected to rise in value over time.

Sounds great—but one question still needs to be answered. Because borrowing facilitates the acquisition of real and financial assets, and we generally prefer more rather than less, why not borrow continually and without limit? The answer, of course, is that households will not be able to borrow an unlimited volume of funds at the prevailing interest rate. The impediment to continuous borrowing, a **borrowing constraint**, comes from both the lenders such as banks, for example, and the households themselves.

It is generally believed that as the ratio of debt or debt payments to income rises, the ability of a household to service or pay off additional debt is reduced. More specifically, the probability of default or delinquent payments on a loan rises. For this reason, financial intermediaries (FIs) are reluctant to grant new loans to heavily indebted borrowers. FIs require potential borrowers to fill out forms and undergo credit checks so that information on the household's balance sheet position and current and future income is available and can be used to gauge the riskiness of a potential loan. A household with little debt, a comfortable net worth position, and steadily growing income is obviously a more attractive borrower from a lender's perspective than a household with considerable debt, small net worth, and a highly volatile income stream

The considerations that influence a lender's willingness to lend also influence a household's willingness to borrow. After all, households understand that if they become overextended and default on a loan, their future ability to borrow and spend will be severely impaired. Even if we disregard any legal repercussions, such a credit history will clearly make future potential lenders more reluctant to lend.

To summarize, households accumulate assets and liabilities in the process of attempting to maximize their well-being. The decisions they make and actions they take are the product of their objectives and the economic and financial environment in which they operate. Assuming that the objectives remain relatively constant, it is changes in the economic and financial environment that will lead to more or less spending and/or saving and, thus, more or less accumulation of real and financial assets and liabilities. The process is depicted in Exhibit 22-2 on page 532.

Data on households' income, expenditures, and wealth can be found at **http://www.census.gov/prodwww/statistical-abstract-us.html**.

Check the data on consumer credit at **http://www.federalreserve.gov/releases/G19/**.

How Economic and Financial Conditions Influence Household Accumulation of Assets and Liabilities

Household spending must be financed, whether via income, existing holdings of money, or borrowing. In addition, other financial or real assets can be a source of funds for spending, but they must be liquidated. Accordingly, fluctuations in household income and net worth (wealth) are usually directly associated with household willingness and

Borrowing Constraint
The impediment to continuous borrowing that may come from the lender's unwillingness to keep lending or the borrower's unwillingness to keep borrowing.

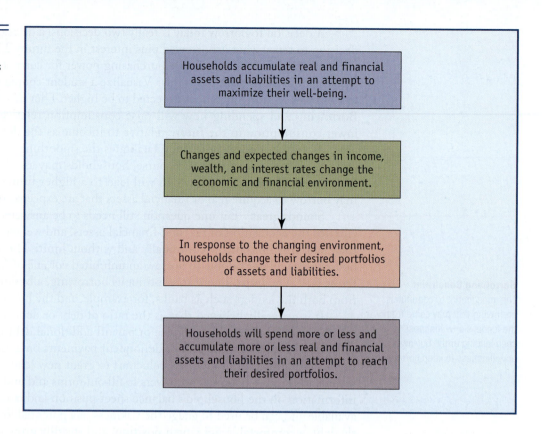

ability to spend and borrow. It is important to note that although these variables tend to move together, the relationship between the aggregate variables is quite complex with causation running in both directions. For example, while increases in household incomes surely encourage more consumption, it is also true that increases in aggregate consumption spending raise aggregate income.

Perhaps the most obvious financial determinant of spending and saving or borrowing and lending is the interest rate. Throughout this text, we have emphasized that the interest rate connects the present with the future. More specifically, it specifies the terms under which present purchasing power can be traded off for future purchasing power. To review, for the borrower who gets funds now and pays the principal plus interest in the future, the interest rate is the cost of borrowing and spending. For the lender who gives up funds now (forgoes some spending) and is paid the principal plus interest in the future, the interest rate is a reward for saving and lending. Thus, if interest rates rise as the result of the behavior of firms, government, or the rest-of-the-world sector, then both the cost of borrowing and the reward (return) for lending increase. Intuitively, we should expect households to respond by reducing their borrowing and spending on durables and housing and to increase their saving and, thus, their lending. In summary, changes (and expected changes) in income, wealth, and interest rates are the key forces driving household portfolio adjustments.

Recap   Households accumulate assets and liabilities in an attempt to maximize their well-being. Assets may be real or financial. Households compare relative returns on real and financial assets. Money is one financial asset that is demanded for the stream of services that it yields. Households also incur financial liabilities. Changes and expected changes in income, wealth, and interest rates cause households to alter the composition of their assets and liabilities through portfolio changes.

Financial Aspects of the Behavior of Nonfinancial Business Firms

Having devoted all of Part 3 to financial institutions, in this section we are restricting our analysis to nonfinancial firms. Business firms hold real assets such as plant and equipment and inventories. They also hold financial assets, including demand deposits and currency, as well as other highly liquid short-term financial assets such as money market mutual funds, negotiable certificates of deposit (CDs), foreign deposits, and trade credit. In addition, they hold time deposits, mutual funds, and other miscellaneous longer-term assets. Because business receipts and expenditures are not synchronized, firms use cash management techniques to move funds in and out of highly liquid short-term financial assets to minimize the costs of holding real money balances. We looked at the determinants of firms' demand for real money balances in Chapter 21. Taken together, these real and financial assets are what a firm owns.

Liabilities such as bonds outstanding, long-term mortgage loans owed, short-term debt including business loans from banks and other FIs, and commercial paper outstanding represent what the firm owes. The funds acquired through such borrowing are used to finance current operations and the acquisition of new capital. The difference between the value of assets and liabilities is a business's net worth or owners' equity. As with households, changes in balance sheets at different points in time are caused by flows. Aggregating over all business firms gives a balance sheet for the business sector that reflects assets, liabilities, and net worth. See Exhibit 22-3 below for the balance sheet entries of the business sector.

With this primer as background, it is natural to ask why firms wish to accumulate real assets. The simple answer is that real assets are used to produce goods and services and, therefore, earnings. Let's take a closer look at the key factors that underlie the accumulation of real assets.

For tables and graphs on corporate profits, see **http://www.whitehouse.gov/fsbr/output.html**.

The Accumulation of Real Assets by Firms: Capital and Inventories

A firm's most important real assets are its capital stock and inventories. We already know that capital is a key factor in the production process and that once existing factors are fully utilized, expanding production will require additional quantities of capital and/or other factors of production. If a firm is using only half of its existing capital, it would seem unlikely that investment spending would be high on the corporate priority list.

22-3

The Balance Sheet of the Business Sector

Assets	Liabilities
Real assets	**Equity**
Capital goods	Common stock
Inventories	
Financial assets	**Debt**
Currency, checkable Deposits	Long-term
Money market mutual funds	Short-term
Certificates of deposit (CDs)	
Mutual funds	
Trade credit	
Other financial assets	**Other financial liabilities**
Total assets	**Total liabilities plus net worth**

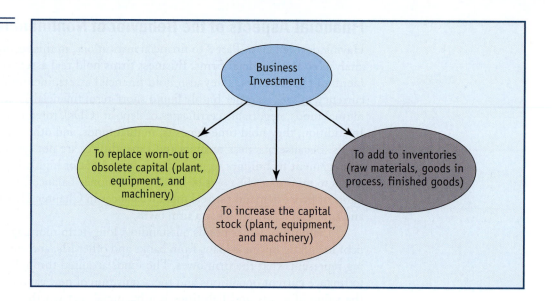

As depicted in Exhibit 22-4 above, business spending on new equipment, the construction of a new plant, and/or an increase in inventories is called **investment spending**. A firm's decision to invest, just like its decision to expand production, depends crucially on expected profits. If a firm finds that it can increase profits by expanding production, then output and sales rise. As production expands, capacity utilization increases, and at some point, the firm finds that it must undertake investment spending to expand further. If new equipment or a more modern plant can be expected to raise profits over time, a firm will invest. Depreciation is the amount of investment that would be required to replace the capital stock worn out in the current production process. As a firm's existing capital stock depreciates, the firm must decide whether to replace it. If a firm's investment spending on capital is only as large as depreciation, the capital stock does not increase. **Net investment**

increases the capital stock or inventories. Because the factors affecting replacement decisions are essentially the same as those affecting net investment, there is no real need for a separate analysis of investment spending that replenishes worn-out capital. Therefore, we shall focus on net investment, which is gross (total) investment minus depreciation.

From an economywide perspective, firms' decisions to invest play two key roles in the economy. First, investment spending is an important component of aggregate demand. Again, fluctuations in aggregate demand lead to changes in the overall price level and the level of real economic activity. Although investment spending is a much smaller component of aggregate demand than consumption, it is much more volatile than consumption spending. Hence, changes in investment spending are usually associated with fluctuations in business activity. Therefore, policy makers monitor investment spending closely because decisions to invest or not to invest have important effects on real GDP, unemployment, and prices. Second, increases in the capital stock raise the nation's productive capacity and enhance our standard of living and competitive position in the world economy.

To find information about specific companies, check Hoovers' list at **http://www. hoovers.com**.

Let's assume that a firm, which is currently using all of its existing capital, finds that it can increase profits by expanding production but must invest in new capital to do so. It begins by assessing the costs and revenues associated with various investment projects. Specifically, the firm will compare the rate of return on each project with the cost of financing that project. In making this comparison, both the rate of return and the cost of financing a project are typically expressed in annual percentage rates.

The cost side, specifically the cost of financial capital, can be kept fairly simple at this point. Suppose that the firm is considering a project that will cost $1 million. The firm can borrow the funds to finance the project, or it can use funds accumulated from past profits (retained earnings). If the firm borrows the $1 million, the cost of the funds will be the prevailing interest rate. If the firm uses funds from past profits, the cost of using the funds is measured by the return that the firm could earn if it loaned out the funds instead. Because the firm could lend out the funds at the prevailing interest rate, the interest rate is the cost of using the funds even though the firm is spending rather than lending them. This is an application of the notion of opportunity cost. The **opportunity cost** of holding or spending money is the return that one could have earned by using it in the next best alternative or opportunity. Whether the firm borrows or uses accumulated profits, the cost of funds is the prevailing interest rate. A final point should be noted: The interest rate that matters for investment decisions is the real interest rate, which is approximately the nominal interest rate minus the expected inflation rate. This is so because the real interest rate has been adjusted for expected inflation and represents the true opportunity cost of using funds. Another reason that the real interest rate is the relevant rate for investment decisions is that debts are denominated in dollars. If inflation is expected, a firm would be able to pay a higher nominal interest rate because the real value of its debt would be expected to fall. For example, if 5 percent inflation is expected, the firm would be willing to pay a 5 percent higher rate because the value of its outstanding debt would be falling by 5 percent in real terms. Also, if inflation does materialize, revenues coming into the firm would most likely increase.

As already discussed, whether a firm is willing to invest depends on a comparison of the cost of funds with the returns expected on the new capital goods. In general, the business outlook and the government's tax policy are important factors in the firm's assessment of the expected return on any particular investment project. The expected return is the present value of the future stream of returns likely to be associated with a particular project. The value of that stream is determined by the profits the project is expected to generate. Profits are a function of the productivity of the capital good, the price of the firm's output, the costs associated with operating and maintaining the capital good, and federal, state, and local taxes. If the business outlook is good, firms will expect demand for output to continue to grow, prices to rise, and, therefore, revenues to increase. On the other hand, if firms expect a long-lasting recession to begin shortly, the situation and outlook will not be conducive to investment: Lower expected future sales will mean lower future profits. Similarly, the future value of profits will also be lowered if the government is expected to raise corporate taxes.

In sum, the accumulation of capital by individual firms and, therefore, firms in the aggregate depends on the degree of capacity utilization, the business outlook, the government's tax policy, and the cost of financial capital (borrowing). Given firms' estimates of the returns on potential investment projects, the amount of investment spending on capital that will actually occur depends crucially on the prevailing financial environment including the level of interest rates and the stance of monetary policy.

Like sales, planned inventories fluctuate over the business cycle. In particular, as the economy expands, inventory investment picks up in anticipation of higher sales. As the economy contracts, inventory investment may slow down in anticipation of slower sales. Firms must also finance their inventory stocks. Accordingly, firms take account of the cost of financing and holding inventories. The interest rate accounts for a large portion of that cost. In general, the higher the interest rate, the smaller is the upward adjustment in the stock of desired inventories in response to a surge in sales. The lower the interest rate, the larger is the upward adjustment in response to a surge. In sum and ignoring the details, we can conclude that current and expected sales are the primary

Opportunity Cost
The return one could have earned by using funds in the next best alternative; for investment spending, the real interest rate.

determinant of the stock of planned inventories held by firms. Of course, the cost of financing inventories, the interest rate, also contributes to the decision.

Recap   Firms acquire real assets such as capital and additions to inventory. They also acquire financial assets (including money) and financial liabilities. Investment spending by the business sector is spending on capital or additions to inventories. The accumulation of capital depends on capacity utilization, the business outlook, the government's tax policy, and the cost of borrowing.

The Accumulation of Liabilities by Firms

In the process of investing and operating on a day-to-day basis, firms experience periods when expenditures exceed receipts. As a result, a firm must make several portfolio decisions, summarized in Exhibit 22-5 below, regarding the financing of excess spending. First, should the spending be financed internally or externally? **Internal financing** is simply the spending of money balances on hand or the liquidation of financial or real assets owned by the firm to finance the excess. Internal financing is the largest source of funds for business firms. As for **external financing**, there are two types: expanding equity and expanding debt. Thus, if a firm chooses external financing, perhaps because its financing needs exceed the internal funds available, it must then decide whether to issue new debt and/or equity.

External financing via equity involves issuing shares of common or preferred stock, thereby expanding the ownership in the firm. If the firm chooses external financing through borrowing, it faces a third decision of whether to issue long-term or short-term debt. For example, the firm must choose between loans or market instruments, such as commercial paper and corporate bonds. In general, each decision is guided primarily by the desire for profit maximization and the existing structure of financial liabilities. A firm will choose the option that minimizes the cost of funds.

For each firm, the overall cost of funds will be determined by the prevailing financial environment, the stance of monetary policy, and so forth. The relative cost of

Internal Financing
The spending of money balances on hand or the liquidation of financial or real assets to finance spending that exceeds current receipts.

External Financing
Financing spending that exceeds current receipts by expanding either debt or equity.

22-5
Business Finance

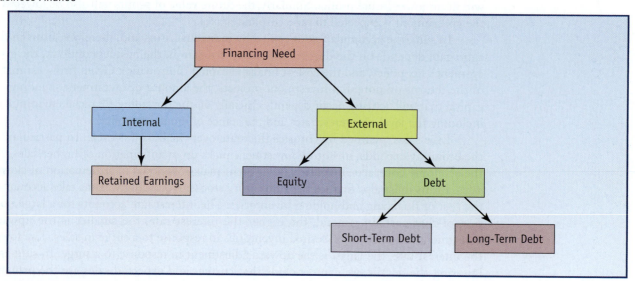

alternative sources of financial capital and, therefore, the particular financing decision reached will be influenced by several considerations: (1) the particular type of expenditures being financed, (2) the current financial environment and expectations about the future environment, (3) the firm's financial structure, and (4) the tax laws.

Traditionally, borrowing to finance inventories has taken the form of either short-term bank loans or the issuance of commercial paper. The usual maturity of the bank loans or commercial paper is one to six months, which is appropriate because inventories are typically not held for long periods of time. Fluctuations in inventory investment over the business cycle explain much of the variation in short-term debt accumulated by firms. The correlation is not perfect, however. For example, if many firms perceived prevailing long-term rates to be temporarily high relative to short-term rates, some firms will issue short-term debt to finance the initial phases of their investment spending on new capital. These firms expect that long-term interest rates will soon drop, at which point the firms will issue long-term debt to pay off the maturing short-term debt and finance subsequent phases of their investment spending. Thus, we see how current and expected financial environments play a role in firms' financing decisions.

The relationship among debt finance, risk, and the cost of capital is rooted in a common measure of the financial structure—the **leverage ratio**, or the ratio of debt to equity on a firm's balance sheet. Other things being equal, the higher the leverage ratio, the greater is the risk to bondholders and stockholders. The reason is that if a highly leveraged firm experiences a substantial decline in earnings, it could default on its debt obligations and be forced into bankruptcy, possibly leaving its stockholders with nothing. A firm with a low leverage ratio could weather a decline in earnings by cutting dividends, which are residual claims, not contractual obligations. The leveraged firm does not have this option: It must pay its debt costs or fold. Hence, ceteris paribus, risk-averse investors will typically demand a higher yield on funds they lend to highly leveraged corporations. Firms that have considerable debt relative to equity will find the cost of debt financing (as well as equity financing) to be relatively high. As a result, they may decide to issue equity both to raise funds and to strengthen their balance sheets.

From the mid-1970s until 1991, a substantial portion of externally financed investment spending, which by definition is the acquisition of capital (new plant and equipment), was financed by issuing long-term debt. Why long-term debt instead of equity? The answer is that U.S. tax laws tend to bias the financing decisions of business firms toward debt and away from equity. Interest paid on debt is a tax-deductible cost and, thus, is subtracted from gross revenues before the corporate income tax is computed. Dividends paid to equity holders, however, are not tax deductible. Dividends must be paid out of after-tax earnings. Thus, debt financing will initially be cheaper, on average, than equity financing, which may also entail higher flotation costs. Equity financing also dilutes the ownership of current shareholders.

Debt financing also has a downside. Increasing debt is believed to expose a firm to more risk and, therefore, to weaken the firm's financial structure. The exposure to more risk can ultimately raise the overall cost of capital as the suppliers of funds require higher returns to compensate them for the additional risk.

Starting in 1991 and lasting until early 1994, firms altered the trend of debt financing and issued new shares of stock instead. Because of lower interest rates on CDs, savers poured funds into mutual funds that soaked up the new stock issues. With stocks trading at high values, large amounts of funds could be raised by issuing relatively fewer shares. By mid-1994, the trend had reversed itself. Companies bought back record amounts of stocks, peaking at more than $200 billion in 1998. Since then, stock buybacks have continued and averaged between $40 and $50 billion per year between 2001 and 2004. Companies were using profits to purchase their own stock rather than pay dividends.

Leverage Ratio
The ratio of debt to equity on a firm's balance sheet.

In the bull market that lasted until early 2000, this activity was also pushing stock prices even higher. In addition, the capital gains of those who sold the stock back to the companies were subject to lower tax rates than dividends would have been. However, in 2004, taxes on dividends were significantly reduced, thus shifting household preferences toward dividends and away from capital gains.

Recap

Firms may use internal or external financing. Internal financing is the spending of money balances on hand. External financing involves expanding debt or equity financing. Firms choose the financing option that minimizes the cost of funds. The change in assets less the change in liabilities equals the change in net worth. Firms adjust their assets and liabilities in response to changes in expected profits, the business outlook, or interest rates.

Financial Aspects of Government Behavior

Government spending on goods and services is a component of aggregate demand, just as consumption and investment expenditures are. Note that it is government spending on goods and services, not government outlays, that affect aggregate demand. Government outlays include government purchases of goods and services plus transfers, such as social security and unemployment benefits, and interest on the public debt. Transfers merely shift purchasing power from one group to another. Unlike changes in government purchases of goods and services, they do not represent changes in the demand for output.

If government spending increases, ceteris paribus, aggregate demand increases, and the public benefits from the increased spending, whether it be for higher education, national defense, better roads, or the space station. If the economy is at less than full employment, then the increase in government spending may also lead to increases in income and employment as well as more consumption and investment spending. If the economy is at full employment and currently using all of its productive resources, then an increase in real government spending on goods and services will, of necessity, reduce real private spending or result in real borrowing from abroad.[1] The latter scenario may or may not lead to increased benefits for society as a whole.

If government spending decreases, ceteris paribus, aggregate demand decreases. Decreases in government spending usually also lead to decreases in income, increases in unemployment, and decreased benefits for society as a whole. If the economy is at full employment and currently using all of its productive resources, a decrease in real government spending on goods and services may result in increased real private spending or a reduction in real borrowing from abroad. The latter scenario may lead to increased benefits for society as a whole if the increased benefits of more real private spending or less borrowing from abroad outweigh the decreased benefits of less government spending.

Unfortunately, all increases in government spending must be financed either by tax increases or by the issuance of government securities, both of which can have a detrimental effect on the private sector. Ceteris paribus, increases in tax rates reduce disposable income. Because spending units have less income, consumption and investment spending decrease. Consumers and business firms are worse off, and aggregate demand is depressed from what it would be otherwise. If government securities are issued, you shall see that the economy can be adversely affected regardless of who purchases these securities. Interest rates may end up higher, and interest-sensitive spending on such things as investment in capital, inventories, and new houses may be negatively impacted. Likewise, the increased government spending may lead to higher inflation, which, if unanticipated, has detrimental effects on creditors and may debilitate the whole economy. Note that the real government expenditures on goods and services—rather than taxes—transfer goods from private to public use. Taxes in the aggregate merely influence whether the government allocates the goods with inflationary consequences.

Decreases in government spending can also be accompanied by decreases in taxes or a budget surplus that reduces the public debt. Both scenarios can have beneficial effects on the private sector. Ceteris paribus, decreases in tax rates increase disposable income. Because spending units have more income, consumption and investment spending increase. Consumers and business firms are better off, and aggregate demand is greater than it would be otherwise. If the government runs a surplus that reduces the public debt, interest rates may end up lower, and interest-sensitive spending on such things as investment in capital, inventories, and new houses may be favorably impacted. Likewise, the decreased government spending may lead to lower inflation, which can have beneficial effects on the aggregate economy.

Because the positive and negative impacts of increased or decreased government spending on the private sector are difficult to measure, judging whether the benefits outweigh the costs is a difficult task. In any case, before government spending is increased or decreased, the trick is to be sure that the benefits of that change are indeed greater than the costs.

The process of making decisions about government taxing and spending is complicated and frequently based on political rather than economic considerations. Taken together, individual policies aimed at many laudable objectives can add up to more government spending than either the president or Congress believes is economically sensible. Politicians are often reluctant to raise taxes or to cut spending on specific programs because both actions are likely to cost them votes. A moment's reflection on the implications of such behavior for the federal budget will help you understand why the government more often than not has run deficits since 1960, as shown in Exhibit 22-6 on page 540. The **public debt** is the total of all past deficits less past surpluses and is sometimes referred to as the *national debt*.

Public Debt
The sum of all past government deficits less past surpluses.

To obtain a relative gauge of the growth of the government sector, analysts find it useful to view government outlays and receipts in relation to the general economy as a whole. We have used this approach in Exhibit 22-7 on page 541, which shows federal outlays and receipts as a percentage of gross domestic product (GDP) since 1960.

Current information on federal, and state and local government finances can be found at **http://www.bea.doc.gov/bea/glance.htm.**

Borrowing directly connects government actions to the financial system. Building on discussions in previous chapters, you can see that the government sector is similar to the household and business sectors because if outlays exceed receipts, the resulting deficit must be financed by borrowing. Equation (22-1) ties government deficits to the government securities the Treasury must issue to finance the excess of outlays over receipts:

(22-1)   government outlays − government receipts
= new borrowing
= net new debt issued by the Treasury (bills, notes, and bonds)
= net government demand for loanable funds

Rolled Over
The result when the government borrows to pay off maturing debt.

Refunding
The refinancing of past government debt that is maturing.

In addition to borrowing to finance the current deficit, if some previously issued past debt is maturing and the government is not in a position to pay it off, that debt must be **rolled over**. That is, new borrowing called **refunding** must occur to refinance the part of the debt that is coming due. This type of new borrowing does not add to the public debt; only new borrowing to finance a current deficit increases the public debt.

22-6

The Difference between Federal Outlays and Federal Receipts, since 1960 (Billions of Dollars)

Fiscal Year	Receipts	Outlays	Surplus or Deficit (−)
1960	$ 92.5	$ 92.2	$ .3
1961	94.4	97.7	−3.3
1962	99.7	106.8	−7.1
1963	106.6	111.3	−4.8
1964	112.6	118.5	−5.9
1965	116.8	118.2	−1.4
1966	130.8	134.5	−3.7
1967	148.8	157.5	−8.6
1968	153.0	178.1	−25.2
1969	186.9	183.6	3.2
1970	192.8	195.6	−2.8
1971	187.1	210.2	−23.0
1972	207.3	230.7	−23.4
1973	230.8	245.7	−14.9
1974	263.2	269.4	−6.1
1975	279.1	332.3	−53.2
1976	298.1	371.8	−73.7
1977	355.6	409.2	−53.7
1978	399.6	458.7	−59.2
1979	463.3	503.5	−40.2
1980	517.1	590.9	−73.8
1981	599.3	678.2	−79.0
1982	617.8	745.8	−128.0
1983	600.6	808.4	−207.8
1984	666.5	851.8	−185.4
1985	734.1	946.4	−212.3
1986	769.1	990.3	−221.2
1987	854.1	1,003.9	−149.8
1988	909.0	1,064.1	−155.2
1989	990.7	1,143.2	−152.5
1990	1,031.3	1,252.7	−221.4
1991	1,054.3	1,323.8	−269.5
1992	1,198.5	1,479.4	−280.9
1993	1,275.1	1,525.8	−250.7
1994	1,374.4	1,561.4	−186.7
1995	1,463.2	1,637.1	−174.4
1996	1,587.6	1,698.1	−110.4
1997	1,723.4	1,752.2	−28.8
1998	1,721.8	1,652.5	69.2
1999	1,827.5	1,703.0	124.4
2000	2,025.0	1,788.0	236.9
2001	1,991.03	1,863.77	127.3
2002	1,853.23	2,010.07	−157.79
2003	1,782.32	2,157.64	−374.22
2004 estimate	1,798.09	2,318.83	−520.74
2005 estimate	2,036.27	2,399.84	−363.57
2006 estimate	2,505.67	2,473.30	−267.63
2007 estimate	2,350.80	2,592.07	−241.27
2008 estimate	2,485.32	2,724.28	−238.97
2009 estimate	2,616.40	2,853.47	−237.08

SOURCE: *The Budget of the United States Government, Fiscal Year 2005, Historical Tables* (Washington, DC: U.S. Government Printing Office); 22. Available on the Internet at **http://www.whitehouse.gov/omb/budget.**

Federal Outlays and Receipts as a Percentage of GDP, Fiscal Year Since 1960*

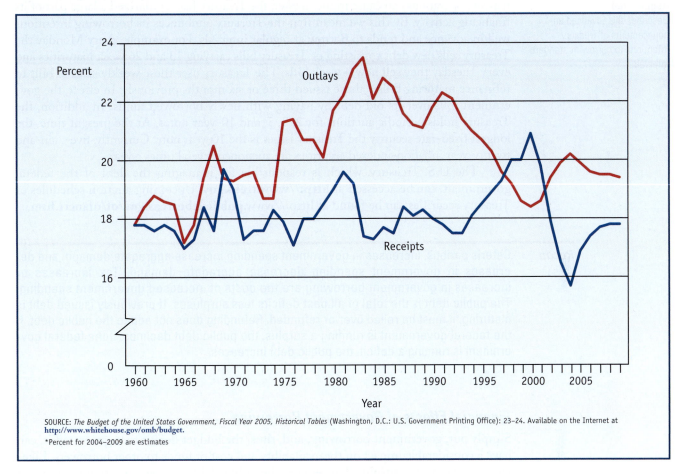

SOURCE: *The Budget of the United States Government, Fiscal Year 2005, Historical Tables* (Washington, D.C.: U.S. Government Printing Office): 23–24. Available on the Internet at **http://www.whitehouse.gov/omb/budget.**

*Percent for 2004–2009 are estimates

If the federal government is running a surplus, it can use the surplus to pay off maturing debt, thereby eliminating the need to roll over or refund the debt. When the government runs a surplus, the value of the public debt is reduced by the amount of the surplus. In terms of Equation (22-1), net borrowing, net new debt, and the government demand for funds are all negative when the government runs a surplus. In the early 2000s, there was much discussion in the popular media about how the burgeoning government surplus should be spent. We hope you see that if the government spends the surplus, there is no surplus. The only other possibly is for the public debt to be reduced by the amount of the surplus.

Reflecting the paucity of surpluses after World War II and the relatively larger deficits, federal government debt outstanding totaled about $7.4 trillion on September 30, 2004. As noted in Chapter 17, part of the public debt is held by government agencies such as the Fed and the Social Security Administration. Of the estimated $7.4 trillion public debt, only $4.3 trillion was held by the public. The rest was held by the government agencies. The U.S. Treasury is the department responsible for managing the debt of the federal government. The Treasury must decide what maturities of securities should be issued—that is, how many bills, notes, and bonds—and when they should be issued.

The Treasury is by far the largest single borrower in financial markets, and, as we have seen, it dominates the market for securities because of the large outstanding volume of securities as well as the large initial offerings. To minimize the disruptions that its financing operations can cause in the market, the Treasury has **regularized** a large part of its financing activity. By this we mean that the Treasury announces its borrowing intentions well in advance and tends to borrow at regular intervals. For example, every Monday the Treasury sells new debt consisting of Treasury bills carrying 13 and 26 week maturities and every Tuesday they sell new 4 week bills. The Treasury uses these weekly sales of bills to refinance maturing bills—those issued three or six months previously. In effect, the government rolls over its old debt by paying with newly borrowed funds. In addition, the Treasury holds periodic auctions for 2, 3, 5, and 10-year notes. At the present time, the longest fixed-rate security the Treasury issues is the 10-year note. Currently, five-, ten-and twenty-year inflation-indexed securities are auctioned several times a year.

The U.S. Treasury, which is responsible for managing the debt of the federal government, can be accessed at **http://www.treas.gov**. Upcoming auction schedules of Treasury securities can be found at **http://www.publicdebt.treas.gov/of/ofaucrt.htm**.

Recap   Ceteris paribus, increases in government spending increase aggregate demand, and decreases in government spending decrease aggregate demand. Tax increases or increases in government borrowing are the costs of increased government spending. The public debt is the total of all past deficits less surpluses. If previously issued debt is maturing, it must be rolled over or refunded. Refunding does not add to the public debt. If the federal government is running a surplus, the public debt declines; if the federal government is running a deficit, the public debt increases.

Financial Effects of Government Borrowing

Simply put, government borrowing, and, thus, the budget deficit that generated it, can have a considerable impact on the availability and cost of funds to other borrowers. Likewise, a government surplus that reduces the public debt can free up loanable funds for other borrowers. In either case, the changes in the spending plans of other borrowers will, in turn, affect the overall pace of economic activity and inflation.

A rise in government borrowing represents an increase in the government's demand for funds. Recall that a rise in the demand for funds will, ceteris paribus, raise the interest rate. Again, as in Chapter 7, we assume that the interest rate refers to the overall level of interest rates. In this case, the interest rate on government securities initially rises because of the increase in government borrowing. In turn, interest rates on other securities such as corporate bonds, municipal bonds, and perhaps even mortgages are also pulled up. As the yield on government securities rises, financial investors seeking higher returns will be attracted to these securities. Some will rearrange their portfolios by selling, say, corporate bonds and buying government bonds. This selling of corporate bonds will tend to raise the rate on corporate bonds (lower the price), and the purchase of government bonds will tend to lower the rate on government bonds (raise the price). This process of substitution binds together all of the interest rates in financial markets and generally causes all interest rates to move up and down together. Thus, we can refer to the overall level of interest rates or the interest rate as moving up and down.

Why are we interested in this financial effect of government borrowing? Simply put, the rise in interest rates generated by the government's deficit financing will, ceteris paribus, tend to reduce the funds flowing to private borrowers such as firms and households, as well as municipal and state governments. This phenomenon is known as **crowding out**, which means that the rise in rates could induce some who had planned to borrow and spend to cancel, postpone, or reduce their spending and borrowing plans. More specifically, the rise in interest rates will tend to lower investment spending by some firms relative to what it otherwise would have been because the firms find that the higher cost of financial capital now exceeds the expected return on some previously planned investment projects. Similarly, the rise in rates on mortgage and consumer loans will reduce spending by some households, particularly on consumer durables and housing, relative to what it otherwise would have been. The phrase "relative to what it otherwise would have been" is included to emphasize that consumption may increase even in the face of rising interest rates. However, the rise in rates will result in the increase in spending being smaller than it otherwise would have been.

A decrease in government borrowing represents a decrease in the government's demand for funds that will, ceteris paribus, tend to lower the interest rate. The interest rate on government securities falls because of the decrease in government borrowing. As the yield on government securities falls, financial investors seeking higher returns will be attracted to other securities. Some will rearrange their portfolios by selling, say, government securities and buying corporate bonds. This selling of government bonds will tend to raise the rate on government bonds (lower the price), and the purchase of corporate bonds will tend to lower the rate on corporate bonds (raise the price). As in the case of an increase in government borrowing, this process of substitution binds together all interest rates in financial markets and generally causes all interest rates to move up and down together.

From the preceding analysis, ceteris paribus, when the government deficit increased, the interest rate increased and when the government deficit fell, the interest rate decreased. A word of caution is in order: Interest rates and deficits do not always move up and down together. In the real world where thousands of factors are changing at once, the relationship between interest rates and deficits can be obscured by a variety of factors. For example, on the demand side, decreases in the demand for funds by households and firms may offset the increase in the demand for funds by government. Indeed, this is exactly what we expect could happen in a recession. A cyclical drop in production and employment during a recession can lead, ceteris paribus, to an increase in the federal budget deficit. Tax receipts fall as household and business income falls while government outlays rise mostly from increases in transfer payments such as unemployment compensation. The same cyclical drop in production that enlarges the deficit produces a reduction in household spending, particularly on housing and durable goods and in business investment spending. Because less spending typically means less borrowing, the increase in the government's demand for funds will offset a fall in demand by others, and interest rates can fall despite the rise in the budget deficit.

On the supply side, a fall in the total demand for funds, reflecting, say, a fall in the budget deficit, may not result in a decrease in interest rates if, at the same time, there is a decrease in the supply of funds. How could this occur? The supply of funds reflects the willingness of net lenders, both domestic and foreign, to supply funds and the Fed's provision of reserve assets to the economy.[2] Accordingly, if a fall in the government's deficit and, thus, its borrowing is accompanied by a decrease in the amount of funds supplied by the Fed, interest rates may not fall at all. Interest rates could even rise if the fall in the supply of funds generated by the decrease in reserves is relatively larger than the drop in demand.

Similarly, if foreign net lenders decide that U.S. financial claims are more attractive than foreign claims, there could be a rise in the foreign supply of funds. Large inflows of foreign funds into the United States during recent decades have played an important role in financing the U.S. government budget deficits. This inflow of funds from abroad have limited the rise in U.S. interest rates and the crowding out of consumption and investment spending that otherwise could have occurred.

Recap   Ceteris paribus, if the government deficit increases, the interest rate increases and may crowd out private spending. Ceteris paribus, if the government surplus increases, the interest rate decreases. However, other factors can often cause interest rates to move contrary to these predictions. During recessions, for example, even though the deficit is increasing, the interest rate may go down because of decreases in the demand for loanable funds by households or firms or increases in the supply of loanable funds orchestrated by the Fed. Likewise, both the interest rate and government surpluses may rise at the same time if the Fed is withdrawing funds from the U.S. economy. Inflows and outflows of foreign funds into the U.S. economy also affect the supply of loanable funds and the interest rate.

The Rest-of-the-World Sector and Its Effect on the Financial System

In Chapter 9, you saw that the exchange rate is the number of units of one currency that can be acquired with one unit of another. Like other prices, the exchange rate is determined by the forces of supply and demand. You saw that the demand for dollar-denominated funds is directly related to changes in foreign income and inversely related to changes in the foreign price of U.S. goods relative to the foreign price of foreign goods and to changes in foreign interest rates relative to U.S. interest rates. In turn, the supply of dollar-denominated funds is directly related to changes in U.S. income, to changes in the dollar price of U.S. goods relative to the dollar price of foreign goods, and to changes in foreign interest rates relative to U.S. interest rates. Hence, changes in the exchange rate can come about from changes in either the foreign or the domestic economy.

Let's consider how changes in the exchange rate will feed back into the domestic economy regardless of their source. Think about the relationship between the exchange rate and the balance of trade in goods. Ceteris paribus, as the dollar appreciates, exports become more expensive for foreigners, while imports become cheaper for domestic residents. Being rational, foreigners reduce their purchases of the now more costly exports while spending units in the domestic economy substitute into the now cheaper foreign goods. The result is that as the dollar appreciates, exports decrease while imports increase. Given that net exports are by definition equal to exports minus imports, as the dollar appreciates, net exports fall, and as the dollar depreciates, net exports rise. Consequently, ceteris paribus, the relationship between net exports and the exchange rate is inverse.

Net exports are also a component of aggregate demand along with consumption, investment, and government spending. Let's consider what happens to aggregate demand when the exchange rate changes. For example, if the dollar depreciates, then, ceteris paribus, net exports increase. Foreigners are purchasing more goods from the United States while domestic residents are purchasing fewer imports from abroad. In the United States, a depreciation in the dollar could mean more jobs and production and higher income than if the exchange rate remained unchanged. On the other hand, if the dollar appreciates, U.S. residents will, ceteris paribus, purchase relatively more goods from abroad; demand for domestic goods and services will be lower than it would be otherwise. This change could translate to fewer jobs, less production, and lower income in the United States. In other words, increases in the exchange rate, ceteris paribus, could lead to decreases in U.S. production, employment, and income while decreases in the exchange rate could lead to increases in U.S. production, employment, and income. So changes in the exchange rate are, ceteris paribus, inversely related to U.S. production and employment. Exchange rate changes feed back to the domestic economy via their effect on net exports, which are directly related to changes in aggregate demand.

Now we can begin to see the linkages among economies clearly. In addition to domestic factors, such as monetary or fiscal policy or changes in the behavior of households and firms, any factor that affects net exports also affects aggregate demand and hence domestic GDP and the domestic price level. For example, if foreign income (or the foreign price level relative to the U.S. price level or foreign interest rates relative to U.S. rates) changes, aggregate demand changes, causing domestic GDP and the price level to change. These changes then feed back to the foreign economy, which will, in turn, affect the domestic economy, and on it goes.

The rest-of-the-world sector clearly introduces additional complications that policy makers face in managing the domestic economy. Any policy action that affects the domestic economy will also affect the international economy, and the effects on the international economy will then feed back into the domestic economy. Likewise, developments in the international economy will affect the domestic economy. If a domestic economy is somewhat isolated from the rest of the world, this effect may be rather small; but as international trade and finance become more significant, as they have to the United States in the past 40 years, this effect also becomes more significant. Exhibit 22–8 on page 546 shows exports, imports, and the trade balance since 1960. Striving (and sometimes failing) to manage such effects to preserve the health and stability of the economy must necessarily involve international considerations—more on this in a later policy chapter. For now, we turn to the effects of foreign demand for U.S. securities on domestic financial markets.

A detailed analysis of the U.S. balance of payments can be found at **http://www.newyorkfed.org/aboutthefed/fedpoint/fed40.html**.

The Effects of International Events on the Interest Rate

Net Capital Inflow
Condition when the purchases of U.S. financial claims by foreigners exceed purchases of foreign financial claims by U.S. entities.

Net Capital Outflow
Condition when the purchases of foreign financial claims by U.S. entities exceed the purchases of U.S. financial claims by foreigners.

When purchases of U.S. financial claims by foreigners exceed purchases of foreign financial claims (securities) by U.S. residents, the United States experiences a **net capital inflow**. As a result, ceteris paribus, the supply of loanable funds is greater and the domestic interest rate is lower than they would be without the capital inflow. When net exports are positive (resulting in a surplus in the current account), there is a **net capital outflow**, and the supply of loanable funds is less and the domestic interest rate is higher than they would be otherwise. Thus, net capital flows affect domestic interest rates through their impact on the supply of loanable funds. Exhibit 22–9 on page 547 shows net capital flows since 1960.

In previous chapters, we considered the supply of loanable funds as consisting of the surplus funds generated by net lenders and increases in credit extension through financial intermediaries. Credit extension is often triggered by increases in reserve assets initiated by the Fed. We now are in a position to see that when foreigners purchase U.S. financial assets, they too are increasing the supply of loanable funds. Ceteris paribus, the inflow of funds from abroad leads to decreases in the interest rate. Likewise, decreases in foreign purchases of domestic financial assets lead to decreases in the supply of loanable funds and increases in the interest rate.

But, you may ask, why would foreigners want to increase or decrease their purchases of domestic financial assets? An obvious reason would be that U.S. interest rates had changed relative to the rest of the world, making U.S. securities more or less attractive relative to foreign securities. For example, if U.S. rates increase, ceteris paribus, funds will flow in from abroad to get the higher return. Note the paradox of the situation: The

22-8		(1) Exports	(2) Imports	(3) Net U.S. Exports of Goods and Services
Exports, Imports, and the Current Account Balance Since 1960 (Billions of Dollars)	1960	$27.0	$22.9	$0.4
	1961	27.6	22.7	4.9
	1962	29.1	25.0	4.1
	1963	31.1	26.2	4.9
	1964	35.0	28.1	6.9
	1965	37.2	31.5	5.6
	1966	40.9	37.1	3.9
	1967	43.5	39.9	3.6
	1968	47.9	46.6	1.4
	1969	51.9	50.5	1.4
	1970	59.7	55.8	4.0
	1971	63.0	62.4	0.6
	1972	70.9	74.2	−3.4
	1973	95.3	91.2	4.1
	1974	126.7	127.5	−0.8
	1975	138.7	122.7	16.0
	1976	149.5	151.1	−1.6
	1977	159.4	182.4	−23.1
	1978	186.9	212.3	−25.4
	1979	230.2	252.7	−22.5
	1980	280.8	293.8	−13.1
	1981	305.2	317.8	−12.5
	1982	283.2	303.2	−20.0
	1983	277.0	328.7	−51.7
	1984	302.4	405.1	−102.8
	1985	302.0	417.3	−115.2
	1986	320.6	453.3	−132.7
	1987	363.9	509.1	−145.2
	1988	444.1	554.5	−110.4
	1989	503.3	591.5	−88.2
	1990	552.4	630.3	−78.0
	1991	596.8	624.3	−27.5
	1992	635.3	668.6	−33.3
	1993	655.8	720.9	−65.1
	1994	720.9	814.5	−93.6
	1995	812.2	903.6	−91.4
	1996	868.6	964.8	−96.3
	1997	955.4	1,056.9	−101.6
	1998	955.9	1,115.9	−160.0
	1999	991.3	1,251.8	−260.5
	2000	1,096	1,475.8	−379.5
	2001	1,035.1	1,401.7	−366.6
	2002	1,006.8	1,433.1	−426.3
	2003	1,048.9	1,543.8	−494.9
	*2004	1,164.5	1,764.1	−599.6

*Annualized through second quarter 2004.
SOURCE: *Federal Reserve Statistical Release, Z.1, Flow of funds of the United States* (September 16, 2004: Current release and historical data). Available on the Internet at
http://www.federalreserve.gov/releases/z1/.

22-9

Net Financial Investment in the United States by the Rest-of-the-World Sector since 1960 (Billions of Dollars)

	Net Capital Infows*
1960	−1.8
1961	−2.8
1962	−2.3
1963	−4.1
1964	−5.9
1965	−4.8
1966	−3.3
1967	−2.1
1968	−.08
1969	1.6
1970	−1.6
1971	11.0
1972	8.3
1973	−3.9
1974	−.04
1975	−24.0
1976	−14.8
1977	18.4
1978	5.9
1979	−24.1
1980	−23.2
1981	−26.8
1982	−31.1
1983	22.5
1984	77.6
1985	101.7
1986	118.6
1987	169.7
1988	140.4
1989	49.9
1990	53.8
1991	41.9
1992	96.9
1993	81.4
1994	129.5
1995	86.6
1996	137.9
1997	219.6
1998	75.0
1999	231.7
2000	476.3
2001	415.0
2002	569.0
2003	542.7
**2004	585.9

*When net capital inflows is negative, the United States is experiencing a net capital outflow.
**Annualized through second quarter 2004.
SOURCE: *Federal Reserve Statistical Release, Z.1, Flow of funds of the United States* (September 16, 2004: current release and historical data). Available on the Internet at http://www.federalreserve.gov/releases/z1/.

capital inflow causes interest rates to be lower than they would be otherwise, but this occurs because interest rates are relatively high to begin. In addition, high U.S. interest rates relative to the rest of the world will increase the demand for dollar-denominated deposits and, hence, cause the dollar to appreciate relative to other currencies—and, as you have seen, changes in the exchange rate feed into net exports. It seems we have come full circle. Changes in the exchange rate affect net exports, which change aggregate demand. Changes in domestic interest rates affect capital flows, which also affect the exchange rate and, hence, net exports and aggregate demand. In the mid-2000s, U.S. financial instruments have been demanded by foreigners for reasons other than interest rate differentials. For example, despite low U.S. interest rates, the government of the Republic of China purchased large amounts of U.S. government securities to maintain the exchange rate between the Chinese yuan and the U.S. dollar. This strategy makes products from China more attractive in the United States.

A related question is why domestic interest rates would be high or low relative to the rest of the world. Perhaps the supply of and demand for loanable funds provide the answer. If the interest rate equates the quantity demanded of loanable funds with the quantity supplied, then any factor that affects either demand or supply will also affect the interest rate. On the demand side, changes in the spending plans of households, firms, or government will all affect the demand for loanable funds. On the supply side, changes in the surplus funds available from net lenders, credit extension by financial intermediaries, and capital flows from abroad will all change the supply of loanable funds. In addition, changes in domestic inflationary expectations relative to foreign inflationary expectations will also change the level of domestic rates relative to foreign rates.

To summarize, net exports affect the U.S. economy through their effect on aggregate demand. Output and prices are directly affected by changes in net exports. With regard to the financial side of the economy, ceteris paribus, net foreign demand for U.S. securities directly affects the supply of loanable funds and interest rates. If there is a net capital inflow, ceteris paribus, the exchange rate could be higher and net exports lower than they would be otherwise. Because of the large inflow of funds from abroad in recent years, we have focused on the net foreign demand for U.S. securities. Keep in mind that changes in the net domestic demand for foreign securities also affect the supply of loanable funds. Try working through the effects of an increase in foreign interest rates relative to U.S. rates. Can you explain what happens to the domestic supply of loanable funds and the interest rate?

In the final section of this chapter, we consider how all of the sectors discussed here are related through the flow of funds among sectors.

Flow of Funds
A social accounting system that divides the economy into a number of sectors and constructs a source and uses of funds statement for each sector.

Recap Net foreign demand for U.S. securities directly affects the supply of loanable funds and interest rates. If there is a net capital inflow, ceteris paribus, the exchange rate could be higher and net exports lower than they otherwise would be. Changes in the net domestic demand for foreign securities also affect the supply of loanable funds.

The Flow of Funds among Sectors

Sources and Uses of Funds Statement
A statement showing the sources and uses of funds for any sector.

The **flow of funds** is a social accounting system that divides the economy into a number of sectors and constructs a **sources and uses of funds statement** for each sector. The purpose of this section is to discuss the financial flows of funds among sectors and their relationship to the economy. We then construct a hypothetical sources and uses of funds table for the U.S. economy.

Sources of Funds
For any sector, income and borrowing.

As discussed earlier in the chapter, the four main sectors are the household, business, government, and rest-of-the-world sectors. For any sector, the **sources of funds** are

Uses of Funds

For any sector, current spending and changes in financial instruments held.

Surplus Sector

A sector whose combined surpluses of net lenders are greater than the combined deficits of net borrowers.

Deficit Sector

A sector whose combined deficits of net borrowers are greater than the combined surpluses of net lenders.

current income and borrowing. The **uses of funds** are current spending and changes in financial instruments held. Any sector is composed of both net lenders and net borrowers. For any sector, the combined surpluses of the lenders may be greater than the combined deficits of the borrowers. In this case, the sector would be a **surplus sector**. If the combined deficits of the borrowers are greater than the combined surpluses of the lenders, the sector is a **deficit sector**.

For *all* sectors combined, however, borrowing (issuing financial claims) must equal lending (acquiring financial assets). This is so because each financial claim, in turn, implies the existence of a complementary financial asset. In each individual sector, however, it is highly unlikely that the combined surpluses just equal the combined deficits. Thus, the economy is usually composed of surplus and deficit sectors. The combined surpluses of the surplus sectors equal the combined deficits of the deficit sectors for the economy as a whole. Exhibit 22-10 below flushes out these relationships.

Although the flow-of-funds accounts divide the economy into nine sectors, in Exhibit 22-11 on page 550 we simplify it as the household, business, government, and rest-of-the-world sectors as discussed. By adding a fifth sector, the financial sector, to the others, you can see how intermediation facilitates the flows of funds from the surplus to the deficit sectors, and vice versa. Note that for every use of funds, whether for acquiring financial assets or spending on goods and services, there must be a source, and every source is put to some use (if not spending on goods and services, then in acquiring financial instruments). Consequently, total sources and uses of funds are equal not only in each sector but also in the aggregate for the sectors taken together. Furthermore, the uses of funds by any one sector are the sources of funds for other sectors, and vice versa.

For example, the sources for households are income and debt; for business firms, net revenues and borrowings; and for the government, taxes or borrowing. Likewise, each sector has two major uses for funds. Households use funds for spending on consumption and investment as well as for acquiring financial assets; firms use funds for investment or for acquiring financial assets; the government uses funds for government expenditures or for acquiring financial assets; and the rest-of-the-world sector uses funds to purchase U.S. goods or services and to invest in U.S. securities.

Current flow of funds data can be found at the Fed's Internet site at **http://www.federalreserve.gov**.

22-10
Surplus and Deficit Sectors

If the combined surpluses of all spending units in the sector	>	The combined deficits of all spending units in the sector ⟷ Surplus sector
If the combined surpluses of all spending units in the sector	<	The combined deficits of all spending units in the sector ⟷ Deficit sector

For the economy as a whole

The combined surpluses of the surplus sectors	=	The combined deficits of the deficit sectors

For example, if the household and business sectors are deficit sectors and the government and the rest-of-the-world sectors are surplus sectors, the combined deficits of the household and business sectors must equal the combined surpluses of the government and rest-of-the-world sectors.

An analysis of flow of funds data can be found at the Financial Markets Center, **http://www.fmcenter.org.**

The numbers we use in Exhibit 22-11 are hypothetical but somewhat representative of the financial flows between sectors in 2004. As the exhibit data indicate, the surpluses of the rest-of-the-world and business sectors exactly offset the deficits of the household and government sectors.[3]

22-11

A Hypothetical Sources and Uses of Funds Statement for the U.S. Economy (in Billions of Dollars)

Sources of Funds	Uses of Funds
Households	
Disposable income: $8,500	Consumption spending on nondurables, durables, and services: $8,400
Net borrowing: $225	+
	Investment spending on real assets: $325
Deficit = $225	
Business Firms	
Net revenues: $1900	Net spending on real assets (plant and 1 equipment): $1,600
	+
	Net spending on real assets (inventories): $200
	Surplus $100
Government	
Tax receipts: $3,400	Government spending on goods and services: $1,650
	+
	Government spending on transfer payments: $1,915
	+
	Interest payments on the national debt: $360
Deficit = $525	
Rest-of-the-World	
Foreign purchases of U.S. goods and services: $1,000	U.S. purchases of foreign goods and services: $1,650
+	+
Net foreign purchase of U.S. financial assets: $850	Net U.S. purchases of foreign financial assets: $200
	Surplus = $650
Financial Intermediaries	
Net acquiring of financial assets: $2,738	Net incurring of financial liabilities: $2,738

The financial sector, composed of financial intermediaries, is included to show the extent of financial intermediation in the economy. Financial intermediaries acquire funds to lend by issuing claims on themselves. They use the funds to purchase financial instruments issued by net borrowers. As you may have guessed, the extent of financial intermediation in an economy has a direct relationship on the extent of economic development.

The format in Exhibit 22-11 allows you to analyze flows of funds among sectors, how those flows are intermediated, and how the Fed can monitor and influence them. During expansions, both income and interest rates normally rise along with the relative intentions to deficit spend. In recessions, the reverse happens. Nevertheless, no sector of the economy can run larger deficits unless other sectors accept larger surpluses.

Recap

If the combined surpluses of the net lenders are greater than the combined deficits of the net borrowers, the sector is a surplus sector. If the combined deficits of the net borrowers are greater than the combined surpluses of the net lenders, the sector is a deficit sector. For all sectors combined, the surpluses must equal the deficits. At the present time, the household and business sectors are deficit sectors and the government and the rest-of-the-world sectors are surplus sectors. The combined deficits of the household and business sectors must equal the combined surpluses of the government and rest-of-the-world sectors.

In this chapter, we have considered the financial aspects of the behavior of the household, business, government, and rest-of-the-world sectors and how they are interrelated. In the next chapter, we will pull together material from this and earlier chapters to take a closer look at aggregate demand and supply for the entire economy.

Summary of Major Points

1. Spending and saving decisions of households are based on their objectives and the economic and financial environment within which they operate. Assuming that the objectives remain relatively constant, it is changes in the economic and financial environment that lead to more or less spending and saving and, thus, more or less accumulation of assets and liabilities. Changes in income, wealth, and interest rates are the key forces driving household portfolio adjustments. Consumption spending by households is the largest component of aggregate demand.

2. Investment spending by individual firms and, therefore, firms in the aggregate depends on the degree of capacity utilization, the business outlook, the government's tax policy, and the cost of financial capital (borrowing). Given firms' estimates of the returns on potential investment projects, the amount of investment spending that will actually occur depends on the financial environment including the level of interest rates and the stance of monetary policy. Like consumption spending, investment spending is a component of aggregate demand. Investment spending is more volatile than consumption spending.

3. Firms also hold inventories of raw materials and finished goods to facilitate smooth and efficient production and to satisfy consumer demand. Accordingly, firms consider the interest rate, which is the cost of financing and holding inventories. In general, the higher the interest rate, the smaller will be the upward adjustment in the stock of desired inventories in response to a surge in sales, and vice versa.

4. Firms experience periods when expenditures exceed receipts. They must decide whether to finance the spending internally or externally. Assuming that a firm chooses external financing, it must then decide whether to issue new debt or equity. Debt financing offers tax advantages, but at the same time, financial leverage and its accompanying risks increase. Short-term borrowing is often used to finance inventories. Long-term borrowing is usually used to finance investment. If interest rates are expected to fall, short-term borrowing may sometimes be used for investment.

5. Politicians are sometimes reluctant to raise taxes or cut spending. Government outlays exceeded tax receipts between 1969 and 1997 and again from 2002 until the present. Increases or decreases in borrowing directly connect government actions to the financial system. If outlays exceed receipts, the resulting deficit must be financed by borrowing, which is carried out by the U.S. Treasury. Other maturing government debt must also be refunded.

6. Increases in the government deficit, ceteris paribus, push interest rates up by increasing the demand for loanable funds. Decreases in the government deficit or increases in the government surplus push interest rates down by decreasing the demand for loanable funds. Other factors operating on both the demand and the supply sides of the market for loanable funds may affect whether interest rates will indeed rise when the government deficit rises. Expectations about the government deficit affect the interest rate, particularly for long-term bonds, before the deficit changes. If the government deficit causes interest rates to rise, some private spending may be crowded out.

7. Net exports add to domestic demand. If net exports are positive, output and the price level could be higher than they would be otherwise. If net exports are negative, output and the price level could be lower than they would be otherwise. Net exports are inversely related to the exchange rate, ceteris paribus. If the exchange rate increases, ceteris paribus, net exports decrease, and vice versa. Therefore, if the exchange rate increases, income could decrease. Likewise, if the exchange rate decreases, income could increase.

8. Foreign demand for U.S. financial assets has a significant effect on the domestic supply of loanable funds. To the extent that foreigners demand U.S. securities, the supply of loanable funds is increased and interest rates are lower than they would be otherwise.

9. The flow of funds is a social accounting system that divides the economy into sectors and constructs a sources and uses of funds statement for each sector. For the economy as a whole, the combined surpluses of the surplus sectors must equal the combined deficits of the deficit sectors. When interest rates change, spending changes and some net lenders become net borrowers, and vice versa. Thus, when deficits and surpluses for individual spending units change in response to interest rate changes, the flow of funds among sectors is affected.

Key Terms

Borrowing Constraint, 531
Crowding Out, 543
Deficit Sector, 549
External Financing, 536
Financial Assets, 530
Financial Liabilities, 530
Flow of Funds, 548
Internal Financing, 536
Investment Spending, 534

Leverage Ratio, 537
Net Capital Inflow, 545
Net Capital Outflow, 545
Net Investment, 534
Net Worth, 529
Opportunity Cost, 535
Portfolio, 529
Public Debt, 539
Real Assets, 530

Refunding, 539
Regularized, 542
Rolled Over, 539
Sources and Uses of Funds
  Statement, 549
Sources of Funds, 549
Surplus Sector, 549
Uses of Funds, 549

Review Questions

1. Do assets equal liabilities for an individual household? for the household sector as a whole? for the economy as a whole? Explain.

2. Both changes in income and changes in the interest rate affect spending. Which has a greater effect? Explain.

3. Explain the effect that each of the following variables has on household and/or business spending or saving:
   a. Income
   b. Wealth
   c. The interest rate

d. Capacity utilization
e. Expectations
f. Monetary policy
g. Tax policy

4. Define the following terms: *depreciation, net investment,* and *investment spending.*
5. Is money a financial asset?
6. What are some of the factors that determine whether a firm chooses internal or external financing? How is the leverage ratio related to the borrowing constraint?
7. Do most college students face a borrowing constraint? Explain.
8. My income is going up, but interest rates are also higher. Will I buy a new car?
9. Would a firm ever use short-term debt to finance long-term capital expenditures? (*Hint:* Consider all possibilities for expected long-term rates.)
10. How should the government decide whether to increase or decrease its purchases of goods and services? How does this procedure compare with the political process that is used?
11. How will a reduction in a government deficit affect aggregate demand? Do changes in transfer payments affect aggregate demand?
12. How can government expenditures be financed?
13. Assume a constant supply of loanable funds. When government deficit spending leads to increases in the demand for loanable funds, do interest rates always rise? Explain. (*Hint:* Consider the role of expectations.)
14. If the economy is at full employment and the government increases its purchases of goods and

services, does this always lead to crowding out? Is crowding out good or bad for the economy?
15. Distinguish between the public debt and a deficit.
16. When the Treasury issues government securities, who buys the securities?
17. Will increased government spending always lead to crowding out if the economy is not at full employment? (Be sure to consider the case in which the increased spending involves transfer payments rather than the purchase of goods and services.)
18. Discuss the following statement: If the Treasury increases its borrowing today, interest rates will always go up.
19. Briefly discuss the long-term effects of government borrowing and the public debt.
20. What is the relationship between net exports and aggregate demand? between net exports and capital flows? If net exports increase, ceteris paribus, what happens to real GDP? If the domestic price level increases, ceteris paribus, what happens to net exports?
21. When the government balance is in surplus, does the government debt still have to be rolled over? Explain.
22. Why has the government regularized its borrowing?
23. What would happen to U.S. interest rates if, ceteris paribus, foreigners decided to sell some of the U.S. financial assets that they own?
24. Using the flow-of-funds framework, explain why the combined deficits of the deficit sectors must equal the combined surpluses of the surplus sectors.
25. If the household, business, and government sectors are all deficit sectors, what does this imply about the rest-of-the-world sector?

Analytical Questions

Questions marked with an icon are objective in nature. They can be completed with a short answer or number.

26. Assume that Rosemarie and Jack have the following assets at the end of the year:

House	$150,000
Stocks and bonds	10,000
Money	1,500
Furniture	3,500
Jewelry	2,000
Savings deposit	1,000
Car	10,000

What is the total of their real assets? What is the total of their financial assets? What are their total assets?

27. Assume that at the end of the year, Rosemarie and Jack have the following liabilities:

Mortgage loan	$120,000
Credit card debt	4,000
Car loan	6,000

What are their total liabilities? Assuming that the assets from question 26 and the preceding liabilities, what is their net worth?

Internet Exercises

1. Browse IBM's most recent annual report at the following site: **http://www.ibm.com/investor/financials/irfiar.phtml/**.
   a. What was the amount of IBM's total assets? Its total liabilities?
   b. How much was IBM's net worth (stockholders' equity)?
   c. What percentage of IBM's total assets was in cash and cash equivalents?

2. Fedpoint 40, which is available on the World Wide Web at **http://www.newyorkfed.org/aboutthefed/fedpoint/fed40.html**, contains information about the balance of payments accounting framework. Access this site, and answer the following:
   a. What are the subaccounts under the current account?
   b. What are the subaccounts under the capital account?

3. Access the Fed's statistical site at **http://research.stlouisfed.org/fred2/**. Obtain the statistics for the federal deficit from 1965 to 2004. Obtain data for the U.S. merchandise trade balance for the same period. Do you see any correlation between the federal deficit and the trade deficit over the entire period or within any subperiods of the entire period?

4. Go to the Internet site for the Flow of Funds of the United States at **http://www.federalreserve.gov/releases/Z1/**. Go to the *Debt Growth, Borrowing, and Debt Outstanding* tables for the current release. Compare the debt growth rates for the federal government, household, business, and foreign sectors. For each sector verify that, if a debt growth rate is negative, the total amount of borrowing is negative and the debt outstanding is falling for that sector. Likewise, verify that, if a debt growth rate is positive, borrowing is positive, and the debt outstanding is increasing.

Suggested Readings

For a look at "The Impact of Exchange Rate Movements on U.S. Foreign Debt," see the article by the same name by Cedric Tille, *Current Issues in Economics and Finance*, Federal Reserve Bank of New York, 9: (January 2003). The article is available on the Internet at **http://www.newyorkfed.org/research/current_issues/ci9-1.html**.

Every three years, the government surveys consumer finances. The latest survey (2004), as well as earlier surveys, are available on the Internet at **http://www.federalreserve.gov/pubs/oss/oss2/scfindex.html**.

For a look at the relationship between investing households and bankers, see John Hacket, "Luring Investors Back to the Market," *U.S. Banker* (June 2001): 28–34.

For insight into the relationship between households and firms, see Franklin Allen, "Financial Contagion," *Journal of Political Economy* 108:1 (February 2000).

A classic article on the flow of funds between sectors is Lawrence Ritter, "The Structure of the Flow-of-Funds Accounts," *Journal of Finance* 17: 2 (May 1963): 219–230.

The Federal Reserve System publishes quarterly the *Flow of Funds Account of the United States, Federal Reserve Statistical Release Z.1*. They make for interesting viewing because of the sometimes dramatic nature of changes in the flows of funds among sectors. They are available in hard copy from the Fed in March, June, September, and December each year and on the Internet at **http://www.federalreserve.gov**.

The Financial Market Center also puts out a quarterly publication, *Flow of Funds Review and Analysis*. It is available on the Internet at **http://www.fmcenter.org**.

Endnotes

1 As in previous chapters, the term *real* before a variable means that the variable has been adjusted for changes in the price level. In this case, the real amount of government spending (adjusted for price changes) has increased.

2 Recall from Equation (8-2) that $i = f(\bar{M}, \overset{+}{Y}, p^{+e})$, where i equals the interest rate, M equals the money supply, Y equals income, and p^e equals expected inflation. You can also think of the rise in government spending or cut in taxes, which necessitates more government borrowing, as raising Y and, thus, the demand for funds.

3 In the actual flow of funds, there is a rather large instrument discrepancy due to measurement errors.

One man's wage rise is another man's price increase.

—Harold Wilson

23

Aggregate Demand and Aggregate Supply

CHAPTER TWENTY-THREE

Learning Objectives

After reading this chapter, you should know:

The determinants of aggregate demand and aggregate supply

Why the aggregate demand curve is downward sloping and what causes it to shift

Why the short-run aggregate supply curve is upward sloping and the long-run aggregate supply curve is vertical

What causes the short-run and long-run aggregate supply curves to shift

How short-run and long-run aggregate supply are related

GDP Up 8 Percent: Does This Indicate an Economy in Good Health?

Over the four-year period 1979–1982, nominal GDP increased, on average, by about 8 percent per year. Over the four-year period 1997–2000, nominal GDP grew, on average, by about 6.7 percent per year. To the casual observer, these data might suggest that although the economy performed well in both periods, the performance was better in the first period. Nothing could be further from the truth!

The composition of the growth in nominal GDP was dramatically different across the two periods. From 1979 to 1982, prices rose about 8 percent per year, on average, while real GDP growth was essentially nil. In contrast, from 1997 to 2000, prices rose about 2.4 percent per year while real GDP rose about 4.6 percent per year. With inflation lower and real growth higher, the economy obviously performed considerably better over the 1997–2000 period. Armed with these facts, it is natural to ask what accounted for this improvement. Was it good luck, deft policy adjustments by the Fed, or clever fiscal decisions by Congress and the president?

To answer this and related questions, we shall build on material developed in the previous chapter on the behavior of households, firms, the government, and the foreign sector. You shall see, for example, that an increase in demand, regardless of the source, will initially tend to lead firms to raise some combination of production, employment, and prices (depending on the shape of aggregate supply). We will also show how changes in aggregate demand and/or supply combine to produce changes in the overall price level and real GDP—the two factors that make up nominal GDP. Within the context of this overall discussion, we emphasize why the short-run effects of changes in aggregate demand or supply on output, employment, and prices differ markedly from the long-run effects. As you shall see, this point is crucial in explaining fluctuations in the economy's performance and the role of policy makers in aggravating or moderating such fluctuations.

Aggregate Demand

As its name implies, *aggregate demand* is the quantity of real goods and services that will be demanded at various price levels over a specific time period such as a year. We can arrive at aggregate demand by summing the total demands of each sector in the economy at a myriad of price levels. These demands, which have been discussed in some detail in Chapter 22, flow from the various spending, saving, borrowing, and lending decisions made by the household, firm, government, and rest-of-the-world sectors. Equation (23-1) illustrates the various components of aggregate demand:

(23-1)   aggregate demand = consumption + investment + government + net exports

Consumption demand originates with the household sector and includes intended purchases of durable goods, nondurable goods, and services. Consumer spending, which has a relatively stable growth rate (or stable with respect to income), is directly related to income and inversely related to the interest rate, ceteris paribus.

Gross investment demand emanates from the business and household sectors and includes intended expenditures for replacement and new capital, increases in inventories, and additions to the stock of houses. Like consumption, gross investment is directly related to income and inversely related to the interest rate, ceteris paribus. Unlike consumption, investment demand is relatively volatile, and swings in investment spending have been associated with turns in the business cycle.

Government demand includes intended purchases of goods and services, such as roads, national defense, and education, at the federal, state, and local levels. Transfers, such as social security payments and unemployment benefits, are excluded from aggregate demand because transfers merely shift purchasing power from one group to another without adding to or subtracting from the level of aggregate demand. Ceteris paribus, increases in government purchases increase aggregate demand, and decreases in such purchases reduce it. As you have seen, a complex decision-making process involving Congress and the president determines government purchases of goods and services. In recent years, government purchases, including those by state and local governments, have accounted for about 17 to 19 percent of real GDP.

Net exports are the difference between exports and imports. Changes in net exports can be negative or positive. If the intended changes are positive, they add to aggregate demand; if negative, they reduce aggregate demand from what it otherwise would be. Ceteris paribus, net exports are inversely related to the exchange rate and to capital inflows.

Current statistics on GDP growth, personal income, aggregate demand, and the government's finances are available at **http://www.bea.doc.gov/bea/glance.htm**.

The Aggregate Demand Curve

Having defined our terms, we now turn to how the quantity demanded of real GDP (aggregate demand) is related to changes in the overall price level. Look at Exhibit 23-1 on page 560, which plots the relationship between the price level and aggregate demand using hypothetical figures. Real GDP is measured on the horizontal axis, and a price index, such as the GDP deflator, is measured on the vertical axis. The **GDP deflator** measures overall changes in the prices of everything in GDP. Like other demand curves, the **aggregate demand curve** is downward sloping, indicating that, ceteris paribus, an inverse relationship exists between the aggregate quantity of real goods and services demanded and the overall price level. Thus, points on the aggregate demand curve show the quantities of real GDP that will be demanded at various price levels, assuming that all other factors except the price level are held constant. These other factors include the nominal money supply, expectations about future economic conditions, interest rates, taxes, and government purchases, among others.

See price data and charts at **http://www.whitehouse.gov/fsbr/prices.html**.

Demand curves for individual products, such as hamburgers, baseballs, and dry cleaning, are downward sloping because of the *substitution effect.* As the price of hamburgers changes, ceteris paribus, hamburgers become either relatively cheaper or relatively more expensive than other goods and services. Ahmed and his friends substitute toward goods that are relatively cheaper and away from goods that are relatively more expensive. The result of such rational behavior is an inverse relationship between price and quantity demanded, ceteris paribus. For example, when the price of hamburgers goes up while the price of hot dogs remains unchanged, prudent shoppers substitute out of hamburgers and into hot dogs, which are now relatively cheaper.[1] The reverse happens when hamburger prices decline. Hamburgers are now relatively cheaper than hot dogs, and consumers find themselves enjoying more of the comparably cheaper burgers. Thus, when the price of hamburgers goes up, quantity demanded goes down, ceteris paribus, and when the price goes down, quantity demanded goes up.

The substitution effect cannot, however, explain why the aggregate demand curve is downward sloping. When aggregate demand is graphed, a price index—not a relative price—is measured on the vertical axis. When an individual price changes while other prices stay the same, a relative price change has occurred. When the price index moves up or down, overall prices change but relative prices remain unchanged. There is no substitution effect. Nevertheless, economists believe that the aggregate demand curve is indeed downward sloping and that an inverse relationship exists between the aggregate

GDP Deflator
A price index that measures the overall changes in the prices of everything in GDP.

Aggregate Demand Curve
A curve showing the inverse relationship between the overall price level and the aggregate quantity of real output that will be demanded at various price levels, ceteris paribus.

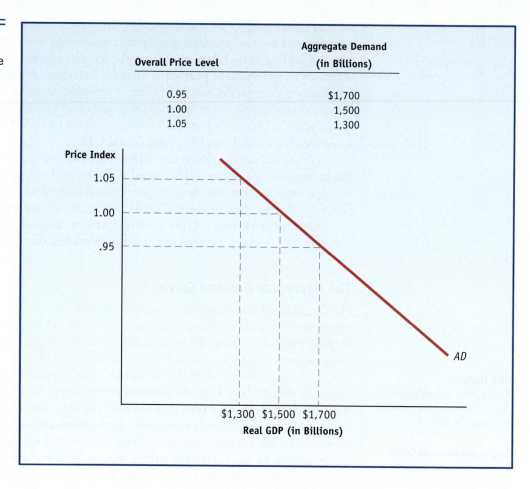

Overall Price Level	Aggregate Demand (in Billions)
0.95	$1,700
1.00	1,500
1.05	1,300

As the price level rises from 0.95 to 1.05, ceteris paribus, aggregate quantity demanded falls from $1,700 billion to $1,300 billion. The aggregate demand curve shows the relationship between total planned expenditures in the economy and the overall price level.

Wealth Effect or Real Balances Effect
The change in the supply of real money balances, which causes an increase or decrease in wealth, when the price level changes for a given supply of nominal money balances.

quantity of real GDP demanded and the overall price level, ceteris paribus. Exhibit 23-2 on page 561 summarizes three of the main reasons usually given for this inverse relationship. The next paragraphs examine each reason in more detail.

First, when the overall price level changes for a given nominal money supply, the supply of real money balances changes. (Remember that the nominal money supply was one of the factors we held constant when we drew our aggregate demand curve downward sloping.) For example, if the price level increases while the nominal money supply remains constant, the supply of real money balances decreases. When the supply decreases, ceteris paribus, spending units experience a loss in wealth because real balances are a component of wealth. At the higher price level, a smaller quantity of real GDP will be demanded because spending units are poorer. Likewise, if the price level decreases, the supply of real balances increases. Ceteris paribus, when the supply of real balances increases, spending units experience a gain in wealth and demand a larger quantity of real output. This effect, which leads to the inverse relationship between the price level and real GDP, ceteris paribus, is called the **wealth effect** or **real balances effect**. Consequently, with the money supply unchanged and prices down, people can and do demand (buy) more, ceteris paribus. The reverse is also true.

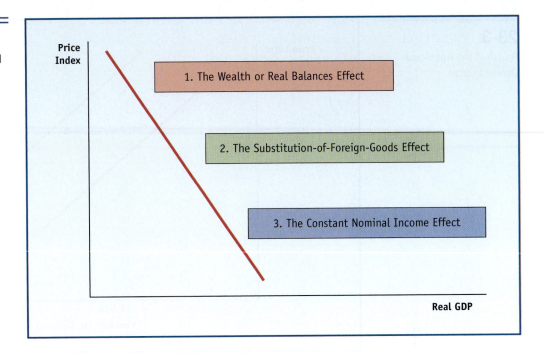

Second, when the overall price level changes, ceteris paribus, domestic goods and services become relatively cheaper or relatively more expensive than foreign goods, which can lead to changes in net exports. For example, if the U.S. price level rises relative to the foreign price level, U.S. goods are relatively more expensive than foreign goods. Purchasers substitute out of the relatively more expensive domestic goods and into the relatively cheaper foreign goods. Likewise, if the U.S. price level falls relative to the foreign price level, U.S. goods are relatively cheaper than foreign goods. Purchasers substitute out of the relatively more expensive foreign goods and into the relatively cheaper U.S. goods and services. As the price level rises, ceteris paribus, net exports fall, and as the price level falls, net exports rise. As the price level rises, the quantity demanded of real GDP falls because of the decline in net exports, and as the price level falls, quantity demanded increases. This effect, which, ceteris paribus, leads to the inverse relationship between the price level and the aggregate quantity of real GDP demanded, is called the **substitution-of-foreign-goods effect**.

Substitution-of-Foreign-Goods Effect

When changes in the domestic price level cause consumers to substitute into relatively cheaper foreign goods or out of relatively more expensive foreign goods.

Third, when we draw an aggregate demand curve, we consider what happens to the quantity demanded of real GDP as we vary the overall price level. Other factors, including nominal income, remain constant. By the equation of exchange, which we first discussed in Chapter 21, nominal income equals the overall price level multiplied by real GDP.[2] Hence, when the price level rises, the aggregate quantity demanded of real GDP must fall in accordance with the constant nominal income constraint. Simply put, less is demanded at higher prices because the funds run out sooner. We call this effect the **constant nominal income effect**.

Constant Nominal Income Effect

When changes in the price level necessarily cause the quantity demanded to change in the opposite direction to maintain constant nominal income.

Thus, the wealth effect, the substitution-of-foreign-goods effect, and the constant nominal income effect can explain why the aggregate demand curve is downward sloping. But what happens when aggregate demand changes? When aggregate demand changes, the entire set of relationships between the various price levels and the quantities demanded at those prices changes. Simply put, if aggregate demand changes, the entire aggregate demand curve shifts. For example, if aggregate demand increases, the aggregate demand curve shifts to the right, and if aggregate demand falls, the aggregate demand curve shifts to the left. The mechanics of such shifts are shown in Exhibit 23-3 above.

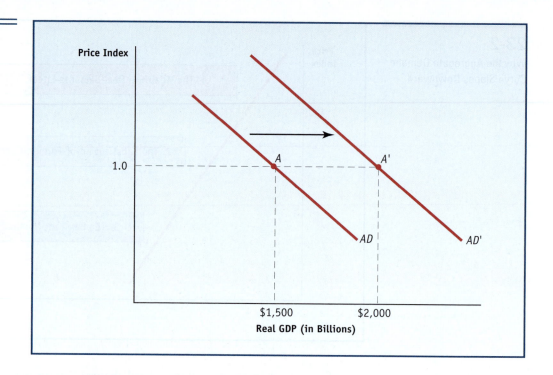

The first aggregate demand curve (*AD*) is identical to the one in Exhibit 23-1. If aggregate demand increases, the aggregate demand curve shifts to *AD'*. More specifically, the quantity demanded for goods and services at price level 1.0 rises from $1,500 billion to $2,000 billion, that is, from point *A* to point *A'*. The other points can be derived similarly.

To complete our discussion of aggregate demand, we need to address briefly one last but crucial question: What causes aggregate demand to change?

What Causes Aggregate Demand to Change?

Changes in aggregate demand are the key to understanding one side of the economy, so we turn now to identifying the primary causes of these changes.[3] As with any demand curve, the shape and position of the aggregate demand curve were initially determined by the factors we held constant, and it will change when and only when any of these factors changes.

From Equation (23-1), you can see that aggregate demand changes when any of its four components changes. If a component of aggregate demand increases while the others at least remain the same, aggregate demand is given a boost. If a component falls, aggregate demand also falls, and this decline may have undesirable ramifications for the economy as a whole.

A change in taxes, government spending, the money supply, interest rates, expected inflation, the economic outlook, and exchange rates can individually trigger changes in aggregate demand. We have already touched on the way that many of these catalysts activate fluctuations in the components of aggregate demand. For example, an increase in government spending, ceteris paribus, increases aggregate demand. Ceteris paribus, an increase in income tax rates decreases consumption expenditures, and an increase in corporate tax rates reduces the expected profitability of investment. Both would decrease aggregate demand. Changes in the money supply lead to changes in interest rates and liquidity within the entire financial system that affect consumption and investment spending. A change in expected inflation changes the demand for real money balances, ceteris paribus, and leads to changes in interest rates and stock prices. Moreover, a change in any of the factors usually affects the economic outlook, which then affects spending decisions.

To round out our picture of what causes changes in aggregate demand at this time, we can safely link changes in any of the factors to changes in government spending and taxing decisions and to changes in the money supply and interest rates as initiated by the Fed. That is, monetary and fiscal policies can and do cause aggregate demand to fluctuate. The linkages between fluctuations in demand in the United States and the various stabilization policies of the federal government and the Fed will be taken up in greater detail in the policy chapters in Part 6. It is important to note, however, that sustained changes in aggregate demand usually have been the result of monetary and fiscal policy actions in the United States and, on occasion, of monetary and fiscal policy actions abroad.

To summarize, the schematic diagram in Exhibit 23-4 brings together the essential parts of the story. Changes in U.S. monetary policy—and changes in fiscal policy—have a powerful impact on spending and, hence, on the components of aggregate demand through the effects on the financial system (interest rates and stock prices), international competitiveness (exchange rates), income, and expectations of future economic and financial developments.

Half of our demand and supply framework is now in place. To understand what happens to the price level and real output when aggregate demand shifts and how the price level and real GDP are ultimately determined, we need to develop the other half: a theory of aggregate supply.

Recap   *Aggregate demand* is the quantity of real goods and services that will be demanded at various price levels over a specific time period. There is an inverse relationship between the overall price level and the aggregate quantity of real output that will be demanded. The aggregate demand curve is downward sloping because of the wealth or real balances effect, the substitution-of-foreign-goods effect, and the constant nominal income effect. The components of aggregate demand are consumption, investment, government purchases of goods and services, and net exports. Aggregate demand changes when any of the four components changes. Catalysts that change aggregate demand include changes in taxes, government spending, the money supply, expected inflation, the economic outlook, and exchange rates.

Aggregate Supply

At the individual firm level, the concept of supply is fairly straightforward. It is the level of production of goods and services planned by the firm at various prices per unit of output over a specified time period such as a year. For example, at a price level of $10 per unit of output, the firm might plan to produce 1,000 units of output. At a price level of $11, ceteris paribus, the firm might plan to supply 1,010 units of output. Put another way, supply tells us the price a firm must receive to induce it to produce various levels of output during a specified time period.

So far so good. But what lies behind a firm's supply plans? Simply put, it is the price of output relative to the expected costs of production. If a firm is willing over time to produce 1,000 units of output per year at a price of $10 per unit, we can be sure this price covers the expected costs of production per unit.

What would lead our firm to alter its production? Again, the answer follows fairly directly. If the price of output falls relative to the expected price of inputs (which we will hold constant for now), the firm will ultimately reduce production because revenues are

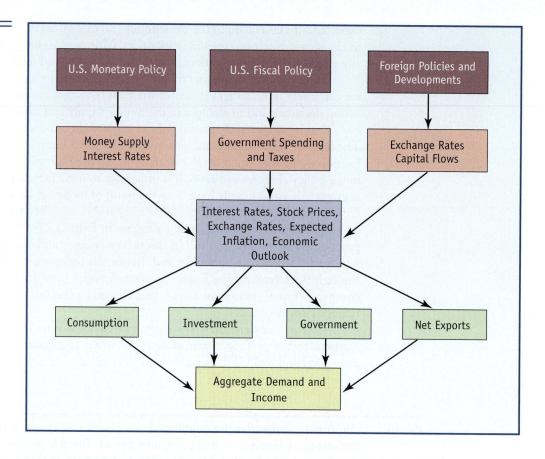

Policy actions in the United States and abroad are typically the source of major movements in aggregate demand. A policy action, such as a rise in the money supply engineered by the Fed, may lower interest rates in the United States. The resulting fall in the cost of financial capital will encourage consumption and investment spending, particularly the acquisition of real assets such as durable goods, houses, and plant and equipment. The increased spending will tend to increase production, sales, and profits, which will, in turn, tend to boost stock prices. On the international side, the fall in U.S. interest rates relative to foreign interest rates will tend to lower (or depreciate) the international value of the dollar. With import prices denominated in dollars rising and export prices denominated in foreign currencies falling, imports will tend to fall, and exports will tend to rise, boosting U.S. net exports. Thus, by affecting interest rates, exchange rates, stock prices, and, perhaps, expectations about future values of these magnitudes, policy alters aggregate demand in the United States.

falling relative to costs.[4] Conversely, if the price of output rises relative to the fixed price of inputs, the firm will increase production because revenues per unit of output will be rising relative to costs per unit. Make sure that you understand that the price of the firm's output is changing while input prices remain constant.

The central analytical point of our discussion thus far is the key role played by relative prices. More specifically, the price of the output relative to the expected price of inputs drives a firm's production decisions; anything that alters this relative price will alter the quantity produced by the firm. In our example, a rise in output prices led to a rise in production, ceteris paribus, and a fall in output prices led to a decline in production. Thus, we see that there is a direct relationship between output price and quantity supplied.

From the Individual Firm to the Aggregate

Aggregate Supply Curve
The curve graphically depicting the relationship between the overall price level and the aggregate quantity of real GDP that will be supplied at various price levels.

These "microfoundations" of supply by individual firms provide the basics of aggregate supply. The **aggregate supply curve** for the economy as a whole depicts the level of output that all firms and others will produce at various price levels over a specified time period, such as a year. The price level at the aggregate level is not the price of a particular unit of output but the average of all output prices as captured by a price index. The quantity is not the amount of a particular good but the real output for the entire economy. As with aggregate demand, the price index is the GDP deflator, and our measure of real output is real GDP.

To see how firms in general and, therefore, aggregate supply react to a change in the price level, let's work through an example. Suppose aggregate demand for goods and services increases unexpectedly. What will happen? The answer—which can initially be confusing and a bit frustrating—is that some combination of prices, output, and employment will rise in the short run. Given the same factors of production, state of technology, and full employment, however, only prices will rise in the long run.

We should note that over time our "givens" (the factors of production and technology) do not remain constant. In Chapter 24, we take up the dynamic nature of their long-run response. In this chapter, we restrict our analysis to the more static situation in which the givens remain constant.

What accounts for the different short- and long-run responses of the economy? The brief answer is the behavior of firms as reflected in aggregate supply. A somewhat more detailed answer is the dynamics of firms' behavior and the resulting adjustments in aggregate supply over time. Soon we shall visualize what lies behind major fluctuations in the economy. By doing so, you will gain some insight into the difficulties that policy makers face in achieving the nation's goals.

Short-Run Aggregate Supply

Long-Run Equilibrium
When all prices have adjusted to shifts in aggregate supply or demand and the flow of spending, saving, borrowing, and lending continues until something else changes.

Real Wage
The nominal wage divided by the overall price level.

Our analysis begins with the economy in **long-run equilibrium**. This term means that all prices (including wages) and quantities in the economy have fully adjusted to previous shifts in aggregate supply or demand, and the configuration of interest rates, exchange rates, expectations, and relative prices is producing a flow of spending, saving, borrowing, and lending that will continue unless and until something changes. Included in the relative prices that have adjusted is the **real wage**, which is the nominal wage deflated by the price level. An important characteristic of this analytical convention called *long-run equilibrium* is that expected values are equal to actual values. Sales are coming in as expected, so there are no unexpected changes in inventories. Actual inflation is equal to expected inflation, so there are no unexpected changes in real interest rates or real wages. Resources, including labor, are fully employed. There is no tendency for the real wage to fall because there are no involuntarily unemployed workers willing to accept jobs for slightly lower nominal wages and, thus, ready to bid the real wage down.

Seldom, if ever, is the economy precisely in such a state, but that's less of a problem than you might think. The concept and characteristics of equilibrium will enable us to isolate and trace the effects of major shocks to the economy.

With the economy in long-run equilibrium, suppose that the Fed moves unexpectedly to raise aggregate demand by increasing the reserves of depository institutions through substantial open market purchases. The resulting rise in the money supply and initial fall in interest rates stimulate nominal spending and sales. The question for us is this: What happens to aggregate supply? Or, more specifically: How do firms respond to the increase in aggregate demand?

The rise in firms' sales produces an unexpected decline in inventories and puts unexpected upward pressure on output prices. Holding the prices of inputs fixed for now, firms in the aggregate, just like the individual firm already discussed, respond to the decline in inventories and rise in output prices relative to input prices by expanding output. Because more output requires more inputs, employment of labor and other factors of production will also expand. Because we started at a position of full employment, however, firms in the aggregate find it impossible to hire more workers without increasing the nominal wage. So, rather than remaining fixed as we initially assumed, the nominal wage begins to rise, albeit at a slower rate than output prices. Employment temporarily goes above sustainable full employment.[5] Workers temporarily perceive the increase in nominal wages, even though it is less than the increase in prices, to be an increase in real wages and agree to supply more labor.[6] To sum up, the initial or short-run effect of a rise in demand will be an increase in the price level and an accompanying increase in output and employment. In other words, the quantity of goods and services supplied increases when the price level rises. The reason is that output prices are assumed to rise relative to input prices, providing the requisite incentive to raise production. Remember that a price index is measured on the vertical axis. When output prices rise, the overall price level rises. In this situation, however, we are assuming that, because input prices do not rise as quickly as output prices, relative prices are also changing.

What happens to the quantity of goods and services supplied in the short run if aggregate demand falls unexpectedly? The short answer is that there will be downward pressure on both the price level and the quantity of goods and services supplied. The reasoning parallels the preceding discussion: The unexpected fall in demand will produce an unexpected rise in firms' inventories and put downward pressure on output prices.[7] Firms respond to the rise in inventories and fall in output prices relative to input prices by reducing output. Reflecting the production cuts, employment of labor and other factors of production will fall. Thus, the initial or short-run effect of a fall in demand will be downward pressure on the price level and a reduction in output and employment. Here again, we see that the aggregate quantity of goods and services supplied will fall if the price level falls, reflecting a decline in output prices relative to input prices.

Short-Run Aggregate Supply Curve

A curve showing the direct relationship between the overall price level and the level of real output that will be supplied in response to changes in demand before full adjustment of relative prices has taken place.

The basic and essential features of short-run aggregate supply are nailed down graphically in Exhibit 23-5 on page 567, which depicts the **short-run aggregate supply curve**, showing the direct relationship, ceteris paribus, between the overall price level and the aggregate quantity of real GDP supplied. The short-run aggregate supply curve is positively sloped; the aggregate demand curve shifts along a given positively sloped short-run aggregate supply curve. By tracing the short-run response of firms and, thus, the economy to shifts in aggregate demand, we, in effect, trace the short-run aggregate supply curve. Again, hypothetical figures are used. Study the exhibit carefully before moving on.

Recap   Aggregate supply is the amount of output that firms will supply at various prices for the economy as a whole. In the short run, there is a direct relationship between the overall price level and the level of output supplied. If aggregate demand increases, firms will supply more output in response to higher output prices. In the short run, input prices are fixed, and firms respond to higher output prices by offering more for sale. If aggregate demand falls, there will be downward pressure on the price level and the aggregate quantity of real goods supplied. Because output prices fall relative to input prices, firms will produce less.

Long-Run Aggregate Supply

As discussed, it is entirely possible for the economy to move from one level of real output supplied (and demanded) to another in the short run. More generally, it is perfectly fea-

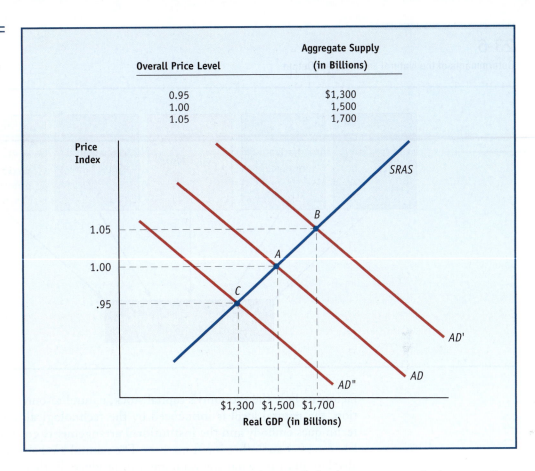

Overall Price Level	Aggregate Supply (in Billions)
0.95	$1,300
1.00	1,500
1.05	1,700

In the short run, shifts in aggregate demand generally lead to movements in the same direction in output, employment, and prices. Assume that the economy is in equilibrium at point A and aggregate demand increases (AD to AD'). With sales increasing, inventories falling, and output prices under upward pressure, firms respond by expanding output and employment. Input prices are assumed to be fixed or increasing relatively slower than output prices in the short run. Thus, output prices rise relative to input prices. The result for the economy as a whole is depicted by the movement from point A to point B. Output rises to $1,700 billion, and the price level increases to 1.05. Starting over again from point A, the result of a decline in aggregate demand (AD to AD") is that the economy moves from point A to point C; output and the price level fall.

sible for the economy to move from a position of long-run equilibrium (remember this is where we started our discussion of short-run aggregate supply) to a short-run equilibrium where the level of real output has changed.

The task before us is to explain (1) why at any particular time there is just one level of real output—called the **natural level of real output**—at which long-run equilibrium with a stable price level is possible; (2) why a short-run equilibrium, where the level of real output differs from the long-run natural level of real output, is a temporary, nonsustainable situation; and (3) how the economy moves back to long-run equilibrium. Put more simply, we want to understand what the natural level of output is and how and why the economy tends to move back toward this long-run norm whenever the level of output deviates from it.

An economy's natural level of real output is determined by the quantity and productivity of its factors of production. As summarized in Exhibit 23-6 on page 568, these

Natural Level of Real Output
The level of real output that is consistent with long-run equilibrium, given the quantity and productivity of the economy's factors of production.

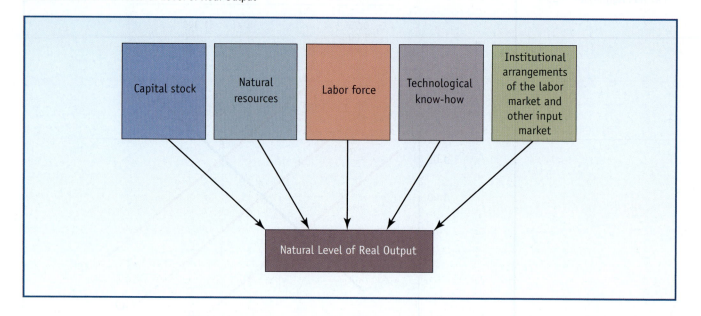

factors include the economy's capital stock, natural resources, and labor force. In addition, the natural level is influenced by the technological know-how that production techniques embody and the institutional arrangements governing the operation of the labor market and other input markets. The natural level should not be thought of as an absolute limit on what the economy can produce. Rather, it is the level to which the economy would move, given its factors of production and current technology.[8] As discussed previously, the actual level of real output can increase in the short run if, for example, firms respond to a rise in demand by operating overtime using standby plant capacity and employing more people than usual. More people than usual may accept jobs because they mistake an increase in nominal wages for an increase in the real wage. That is, they fail to recognize for a time that output prices are actually going up faster than the nominal wage. Similarly, the actual level of real output can fall for a time, as occurs in a recession when workers are laid off and some portion of plant capacity lies idle.

As we shall see, however, short-run equilibrium in which the actual level of output differs from the natural level of real output is not a long-run equilibrium and, thus, is not sustainable over time. When an economy is in long-run equilibrium, the prices of goods and services sold by firms will bear a consistent relationship to the prices of the inputs employed by firms. In particular, the prices of goods and services must be high enough to allow firms to cover their costs of production and earn a normal profit. Similarly, the prices of inputs—wages and salaries, in particular—must be high enough relative to the cost of living to make work worthwhile. The nominal cost of living can be measured by the prices of consumer goods, such as the consumer price index.

A helpful way to summarize the discussion to this point is to say that the economy is in long-run equilibrium when relative prices are correct—more specifically, when output prices are consistent and sustainable relative to input prices. As we pointed out at the beginning of the subsection on short-run aggregate real supply, the implication of saying that "relative prices are correct" is that all input and output prices in the economy have fully adjusted to previous shifts in aggregate supply or demand. The resulting configuration of interest rates, exchange rates, relative prices, and expectations is producing a flow of spending, saving, borrowing, lending, production, and employment that will continue unless and until something changes. A key characteristic of such a situation, which is crucial to everything that follows, is that actual values are equal to expected values. There are no surprises or unexpected developments. Actual sales are coming in as expected, and, thus, there are no unexpected changes in inventories or production.

Now suppose, for example, that output prices are expected to increase by 10 percent. With output prices expected to rise, input prices will rise proportionately in the long run to maintain the real incomes of the suppliers of the factors of production. With input prices rising in proportion to output prices, there will be no change in relative prices and, thus, no incentive for firms to produce more or for workers to work more. If output prices are expected to increase by 10 percent, the end result, depicted by the movement from point *A* to point *B* in Exhibit 23-7 below, will be a 10 percent increase in the price level from 1.00 to 1.10 with the economy continuing to operate at its natural level of real output. Actual prices will again be equal to expected prices, and, thus, there will be no unexpected changes in real wages or real interest rates; the economy will continue to operate at its natural level of real output, as shown in Exhibit 23-7.

In contrast, if actual values differ from expected values, adjustments in production, employment, spending, and so on, will occur. For example, if the actual price level turns out to be higher than expected, workers who bargained for and accepted a particular nominal wage rate based on an expected price level of 1.00 will, in time, come to realize that their real wages are lower than they anticipated. For example, if the price level turns out to be 1.05 rather than 1.00, workers will find that their real wages and real purchasing power are lower. Among other things, this will lead them to seek higher nominal

23-7

Long-Run Aggregate
Real Supply

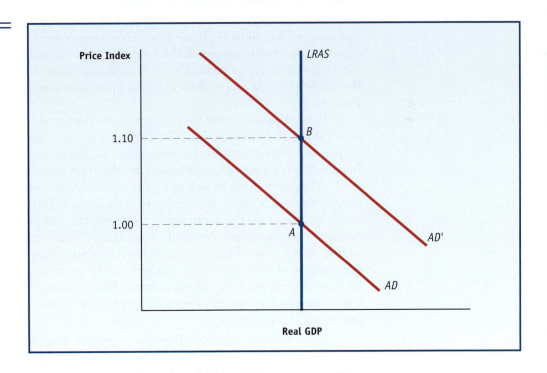

Suppose that the economy is in long-run equilibrium at point *A* with the actual price level of 1.0 equal to the expected price level and the economy operating at its natural level of real output. Now assume that firms and suppliers of factors of production expect aggregate demand to increase, and this in fact occurs (with *AD* shifting to *AD'*). The economy responds to the anticipated rise in demand by moving up a given vertical long-run aggregate supply curve to point *B*.

wages in an effort to restore their real wages and purchasing power. Any resulting wage increase will raise production costs, which, in turn, will affect employment, production, and output prices. By definition then, the situation when actual values differ from expected values cannot be a long-run equilibrium.

To sum up, we first discussed short-run aggregate supply in which input prices are initially assumed to be fixed or slower to change than output prices. In this situation, changes in output prices result in changes in relative prices and, thus, changes in production and employment. Second, we examined long-run aggregate supply in which input prices are not fixed and all input and output prices (and price expectations) have completely adjusted to various developments. The **long-run aggregate supply curve** is vertical at the natural level of real output, as shown in Exhibit 23-7. Along the long-run aggregate supply curve, there is no change in relative prices and the economy is operating at its natural level of real output, given the current technology and the quantity and productivity of the factors of production.[9] With these two building blocks in place, the final crucial question in our discussion of aggregate supply should be obvious: How is short-run aggregate supply related to long-run aggregate supply?

Long-Run Aggregate Supply Curve
The vertical curve through the natural rate of output to which the economy will return in the long run regardless of the price level.

Recap | In the long run when input prices are flexible and full adjustment has occurred, the economy will gravitate to the natural level of real output. The natural level of real output is determined by the quantity and productivity of the economy's factors of production.

The Relationship between the Short Run and the Long Run: Shifts in Short-Run Aggregate Supply

The task before us is, in effect, to integrate Exhibit 23-7 with Exhibit 23-5. More specifically, we need to show (1) how the short-run response of the economy to, say, a rise in aggregate demand compares to the long-run response and (2) how the different short- and long-run responses depend on changes in price expectations and associated shifts in short-run aggregate supply. Believe it or not, we have already developed the requisite analytical tools.

To begin, assume that the economy is in short- and long-run equilibrium at point A in Exhibit 23-8 on page 571. The actual price level is equal to 1.00, and the economy is operating at its natural level of real output: $1,500 billion in our hypothetical example. Because this is a long-run equilibrium, the actual price level is equal to the expected price level. All prices—input as well as output prices—have completely adjusted to previous developments. Therefore, the aggregate demand curve intersects the long-run aggregate supply curve and the short-run aggregate supply curve at point A. Note carefully that we assume that input prices, especially wage rates, reflect the price level expectations prevailing at the time. Thus, the short-run aggregate supply curve reflects price level expectations of 1.00 at point A, and because the actual price level is also equal to 1.00, we have a short- and long-run equilibrium. By definition, short-run aggregate supply always intersects the long-run aggregate supply curve at the expected price level governing the setting of input prices.

So far so good, but what happens to output, employment, and the price level if there is an unexpected rise in the money supply and aggregate demand increases unexpectedly from AD to AD'? In the short run, the economy will move to point B. Intuitively, the rise in demand results in an unanticipated fall in inventories and a rise in the level of output prices relative to the level of input prices, which are assumed to be fixed in the short run or to rise more slowly than output prices. Firms respond to the rise in output prices and fall in inventories by expanding production and employment. They quickly find that nominal wages, rather than remaining fixed as initially assumed, start

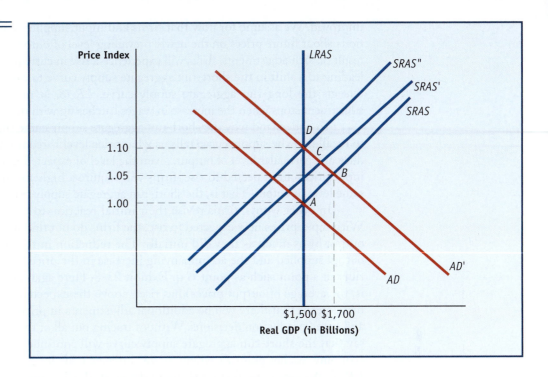

Initially, the economy is in long-run equilibrium at point A. The actual price level (1.00) is equal to the expected price level underlying the short-run aggregate supply curve, and the economy is operating at its natural level of real output ($1,500 billion). Subsequently, aggregate demand increases unexpectedly, shifting the aggregate demand curve from AD to AD'. In the short run, the economy will move to point B with output rising to $1,700 billion and the price level increasing to 1.05. Point B is not a long-run equilibrium, however, because the actual price level (1.05) is above the expected price level (1.00). As input suppliers respond to the unanticipated increase in prices (to 1.05), input prices increase, price expectations are revised upward to 1.05, and the short-run aggregate supply curve shifts from SRAS to SRAS". As SRAS shifts, firms revise their initial reaction to the rise in demand. The new equilibrium at point C is also not a long-run equilibrium because, here again, the actual price level has risen above the expected price level (1.05). This inequality induces another series of adjustments by input suppliers and firms, resulting in additional shifts of the short-run aggregate supply curve to the left. With no further shifts in aggregate demand, the economy will settle at a new long-run equilibrium at point D. In effect, the economy moves along the path A–B–C–D as successive shifts in short-run aggregate supply alter the initial, short-run effects of a rise in aggregate demand on the economy.

to rise, albeit at a slower rate than prices. The result in our hypothetical example is a rise in the price level to 1.05 and a rise in real output to $1,700 billion.

At point B, the economy is in a short-run equilibrium. This is not a long-run equilibrium, however, so it is not sustainable. The reason is that the actual price level (1.05) is above the expected price level (1.00). Accordingly, input suppliers, such as workers, have suffered a decline in real income relative to what they expected even though nominal wages may have risen. They will attempt to negotiate even higher wages and salaries as will other input suppliers. The decline in their real income is the result of the unexpected price level increase, which exceeds the increase in nominal wages. With employment up and, thus, unemployment down, labor markets and the markets for other inputs, more generally, have tightened up so that the bargaining position of workers and other input suppliers has improved. We assume for now that firms and input suppliers base their revised expectations about future prices on the newly prevailing level of output prices—that is, 1.05. As a result of such adjustments, firms will experience a rise in current and expected input prices, leading to a shift in the short-run aggregate supply curve to *SRAS'*. (Note that *SRAS'* intersects the long-run aggregate supply curve, *LRAS*, at price level 1.05.) Again, the adjustment stops when the increase in wages catches up with the increase in the price level.

To understand why the short-run aggregate supply curve shifts as it does, it is useful to recall that the supply curve tells us what price level is required to induce firms to produce any particular level of output, given the level of expected input prices. Accordingly, if input prices are expected to rise, firms will require a higher output price to produce the same level of output. That is, the short-run aggregate supply curve will shift to the left.

In other words, firms revise their initial reaction to the original rise in demand. With input prices now expected to rise, the firms do not find it profitable to expand their output by as much as they did initially. The reduction in the aggregate quantity of real output supplied and the accompanying increase in the price level produce a new equilibrium at a point such as point *C* in Exhibit 23-8. Here again, the actual price level (that is, the average of output prices) has risen above the expected price level (1.05). This, in turn, means that there will be additional adjustments in price expectations, input prices, and firms' production decisions. Without tracing out all of the intermediate steps, we can say that the short-run aggregate supply curve will continue to shift to the left until the economy reaches point *D*, where *SRAS"* intersects the long-run aggregate supply curve, *LRAS*. Assuming no further shifts in demand, this is a point of long-run equilibrium: The expected price level is equal to the actual price level (1.10), relative prices are correct in the sense that the level of output prices is consistent with the prevailing and expected level of input prices (input prices have caught up), and the economy is operating at its natural level of real output, given the quantity and productivity of its factors of production. The short-run aggregate supply curve shifts left until this equilibrium occurs.

So what is the end result of the rise in aggregate demand? In the short run, output, employment, and the price level rose. In the long run, output and employment were unaffected, returning to their natural levels, given the quantity and productivity of the factors of production. Prices, however, rose from 1.0 to 1.1. What explains the differing short- and long-run effects? In the short run, price expectations and, thus, expected input prices are assumed to be fixed or to change more slowly than output prices. As a result, the economy moves up along the short-run aggregate supply curve (from point *A* to point *B* in Exhibit 23-8) as demand increases. Over time, as actual prices rise, expectations and thus firms' production decisions and workers' decisions to supply labor adjust, resulting in successive shifts in short-run aggregate real supply. Reflecting these adjustments and assuming no further shifts in demand, the economy moves back to the natural rate of unemployment (from point *B* to point *D* in Exhibit 23-8).

What we have just described and analyzed is a case of **demand-pull inflation**. Demand increases and "pulls" up prices. Note that from a policy maker's perspective, the short-run outcome (point *B*) is fairly attractive. Output rises, unemployment drops, and the increase in prices is not dramatic. In the long run (point *D*), the situation is much less pleasant. The result of boosting demand with, say, monetary or fiscal policy is that prices have risen while employment and output have returned to the natural levels prevailing initially (at point *A*). If policy makers are nearsighted, they will tend to focus on (and value) the short-run effects of boosting demand on the economy, ignoring or downplaying the longer-run inflationary effects. More on this point will follow in the next chapter when we examine the effects of other economic scenarios and the Fed's response (monetary policy) from an aggregate demand and supply framework. Now would be a good time to read the accompanying A Closer Look on page 573 on the Phillips Curve.

Demand-Pull Inflation
Sustained increases in the overall price level due to high levels of demand.

The Phillips Curve

Our analysis so far suggests that there may be a trade-off between inflation and unemployment, which would imply that lower unemployment can be "bought" by the public's willingness to accept higher inflation. In 1957, A. W. Phillips noticed such a trade-off when analyzing British data for the 1861–1957 time period. Actually, Phillips's original work stressed the relationship between increases in the growth rate of wages and changes in the unemployment rate. When the unemployment rate was low, wages increased at a high rate. Likewise, when the unemployment rate was high, the rate of increase in wages was low or even negative.

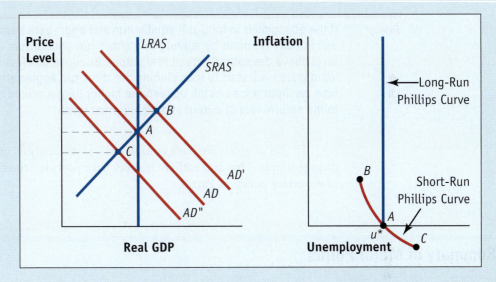

Phillips Curve
A curve suggesting a trade-off between unanticipated inflation and unemployment in the short run.

Later economists extended the analysis to suggest an inverse relationship between the rate of price changes (inflation) and changes in the unemployment rate. They could do so because of the strong correlation between changes in wages and changes in the overall price level. Thus, a low unemployment rate was associated with high inflation, and vice versa.

The concept was immediately embraced by economists and served as a springboard for much economic research over the next 20 years. But does the trade-off really exist? And, if so, can policy makers exploit it to achieve their goals?

Actually, we can use the analysis already developed to answer these questions. In the short run, a **Phillips curve** trade-off does exist. Starting from a point of long-run equilibrium, when there is an unanticipated increase in aggregate demand, the economy moves to a short-run equilibrium where the price level has risen, output has increased, and the unemployment rate has fallen. In the accompanying graphs, the economy moves from point A to B. The graph on the left is our familiar aggregate demand and aggregate supply model. In the graph on the right, the unemployment rate is measured on the horizontal axis, and the inflation rate is measured on the vertical axis; u^* is the unemployment rate that is expected when expected inflation is zero. This is the natural rate of unemployment. From the initial long-run equilibrium, if there is an unexpected decrease in aggregate demand, the price level falls, output falls, and the unemployment rate increases; the economy moves from point A to C in each graph.

Thus, in the short run, there is a trade-off, but only if the increase or decrease in demand is unexpected. Once expectations about the actual price level have been adjusted, there is no longer a trade-off as relative price adjustments bring the economy back to the natural level of output and the natural level of employment. Although a trade-off exists in the short run, in the long run the Phillips curve is vertical. The implication is again that myopic policy makers can buy "lower unemployment" in the short run by accepting more inflation, but not in the long run. As Robert Parry, formerly the chief executive officer of the Federal Reserve Bank of San Francisco put it, "A little inflation may get us more employment, but it would only be a temporary gain. The Fed simply doesn't have the power to push the economy beyond its capacity to produce goods and services for very long."[a]

Recap If the economy is in long-run equilibrium and aggregate demand increases, the economy will initially respond by moving to a short-run equilibrium at a higher price and output level above the natural rate of real output. Because this level of output is not sustainable, input prices will start to rise, shifting the short-run aggregate supply curve leftward. Over time, as input prices catch up with the higher output prices, the economy will move back to the natural rate of output at a higher price level.

In this chapter, we have completed a static analysis of aggregate demand and aggregate supply. This and earlier chapters have provided the framework for our discussion of monetary policy in Part 6.

Summary of Major Points

1. Aggregate demand is the sum of the quantities of goods and services demanded by each sector of the economy at various price levels. The aggregate demand curve shows the quantity of real GDP that people, businesses, and the government plan to purchase at various price levels. Ceteris paribus, quantity demanded is inversely related to the overall price level. The reasons for this inverse relationship include the wealth or real balances effect, the substitution-of-foreign-goods effect, and the constant nominal income effect.

2. The major causes of changes in aggregate demand (shifts of the aggregate demand curve) are changes in U.S. monetary and fiscal policies as reflected in changes in taxes and government expenditures or changes in interest rates and the money supply. Such policy changes have a powerful impact on spending plans through their effects on the financial system (stock and bond prices), our international competitiveness (exchange rates), and expectations of future economic and financial developments.

3. Firms' production decisions are guided by the price of their output relative to expected costs of production. A rise in output prices relative to input prices will lead firms to expand production, and a fall in output prices relative to input prices will lead firms to reduce production.

4. The short-run aggregate supply curve is positively sloped, ceteris paribus. It depicts the level of output firms will produce at various output price levels, assuming that input prices are constant or that changes in input prices lag changes in output prices. The assumption of constant or lagging input prices is what defines the short run and distinguishes the short run from the long run. Starting from a position of long-run equilibrium, an unexpected rise in demand will lead to a rise in output prices relative to input prices, an unexpected fall in inventories, and an accompanying increase in output and employment. In long-run equilibrium, expected values of sales, inventories, and prices are equal to actual values.

5. The long-run aggregate supply curve is vertical at the economy's natural level of real output. An economy's natural level of real output is determined by the quantity and productivity of its factors of production. What makes such a level of output "natural" is that it is sustainable in the sense that once output prices and input prices have fully adjusted to previous shifts in supply or demand, there is no tendency for the economy to move away from this equilibrium level of output and employment.

6. If something causes actual values to differ from expected values, an economy's long-run equilibrium is disturbed, and adjustments in production, employment, spending, and so on, will occur. More specifically, after a disturbance (such as an increase in aggregate demand), some initial adjustments occur, producing a short-run equilibrium. As time passes, additional adjustments occur, particularly in price expectations, in input prices, and in the short-run aggregate supply curve, causing the economy to move toward a new long-run equilibrium.

7. In the short run, an unexpected rise in aggregate demand will, ceteris paribus, lead to a rise in output and employment and some rise in output prices. Subsequently, there will be an increased demand for inputs that results in higher input prices. The short-run aggregate supply curve shifts to the left, and firms post higher prices and produce less. In the long run, when output prices and input prices have fully adjusted to the initiating increase in demand, the economy will return to its natural level of real output. This is a case of demand-pull inflation. In the long run, a rise in demand pulls up prices but does not affect output and employment.

Key Terms

Aggregate Demand Curve, **559**
Aggregate Supply Curve, **565**
Constant Nominal Income
  Effect, **561**
Demand-Pull Inflation, **572**
GDP Deflator, **559**
Long-Run Aggregate Supply Curve, **570**

Long-Run Equilibrium, **565**
Natural Level of Real Output, **567**
Phillips Curve, **573**
Real Balances Effect (Wealth Effect), **560**
Real Wage, **565**
Short-Run Aggregate Supply Curve, **566**
Substitution-of-Foreign-Goods Effect, **561**

Review Questions

1. Explain the difference between aggregate demand and the aggregate quantity demanded of real output. Ceteris paribus, how is quantity demanded related to the overall price level?

2. Explain the wealth effect, the substitution-of-foreign-goods effect, and the constant nominal income effect.

3. What are the major sources of changes in aggregate demand? What are the short-run and the long-run effects?

4. What does investment spending consist of? How is investment spending related to the interest rate? Which is more volatile, consumption or investment? Which makes up a larger component of GDP?

5. Explain why only government purchases of goods and services, not transfers, are a component of aggregate demand.

6. What are net exports? How are they related to the exchange rate?

7. If prices and wages always change by exactly the same percentage and are expected always to do so, how is the short-run aggregate supply curve shaped? Make an argument that in this case, there is no such thing as a short-run aggregate supply curve. What is the real wage?

8. What is the GDP deflator?

9. Can the natural level of real output ever change? If so, when? How is the natural level of real output related to the long-run aggregate supply curve?

10. How do price expectations affect the position of the short-run aggregate supply curve?

11. What causes the short-run aggregate supply curve to shift left? Right?

Analytical Questions

Questions marked with an icon are objective in nature. They can be completed with a short answer or number.

12. Graphically illustrate the difference between a change in aggregate demand and a change in the aggregate quantity demanded of real GDP. Illustrate an increase in aggregate demand and an increase in the quantity demanded of real GDP.

13. Use aggregate supply and aggregate demand curves to explain what will happen to prices, output, and employment, ceteris paribus, in each of the following situations:

  a. The government cuts spending.

  b. The Fed makes open market purchases.

  c. Corporate tax rates are increased.

  d. Interest rates abroad increase.

14. Why is the demand curve for wheat downward sloping? Why is the aggregate demand curve downward sloping? Explain why the reasons are different.

15. Draw a short-run aggregate supply curve. Why is the curve upward sloping? What causes the short-run aggregate supply curve to shift?

16. Use graphs to explain demand-pull inflation.

17. Assume that the economy is originally in long-run equilibrium and that there is a drop in demand. Use graphs to explain how and why the economy initially moves to a short-run equilibrium with unemployment. How does the economy return to long-run equilibrium?

18. Graph a Phillips curve. Explain why the long-run Phillips curve is vertical. Could there be more than one short-run Phillips curve? (*Hint:* Consider a change in price expectations.)

Internet Exercises

Access the World Wide Web site of the Federal Reserve Bank in Minneapolis at **http://www.minneapolisfed.org/research/data/district/usstates.cfm**, which sums up the "state of the economy." Check out your Federal Reserve district by clicking on the map of the United States provided at the site. Keeping this chapter in mind, comment on the following with regard to your Federal Reserve district:

  a. Its overall economic growth

  b. Manufacturing activity growth

  c. Inflationary pressures

  d. Retail spending

  e. Banking

Suggested Readings

Many principles of economics texts contain discussions of aggregate demand and aggregate supply. We recommend Chapters 33 of N. Gregory Mankiw, *Principles of Economics,* 3rd ed. (Cincinnati, OH: South-Western College Publishing, 2004).

Two recent books that look at how the economy functioned in the 1990s are Joseph E. Stiglitz, *The Roaring Nineties* (New York, NY: W.W. Norton, 2004) and Alan S. Blinder and Janet L. Yellen, *The Fabulous Decade* (New York, NY: Century Foundation, 2004).

For an interesting article that looks at how the economy functions, see Alan S. Blinder, "A Core of Macroeconomic Beliefs?" *Challenge* (July–August 1998): 26–44.

Robert Lesson looks at "The Political Economy of the Inflation-Unemployment Trade-off," *History of Political Economy* 29 (Spring 1997): 117–156.

For a discussion of many of the topics in this chapter, see Sandra E. Black and Lisa M. Lynch, *What's Driving the New Economy? The Benefits of Workplace Innovation*, Federal Reserve Bank of New York, Staff Reports No. 118 (March 2001).

For an interesting discussion of the Phillips curve, see Karl Whelan, *Real Wage Dynamics and the Phillips Curve*, Board of Governors of the Federal Reserve System, Finance and Economics Discussion Series, No. 2000-02 (2000).

For an interesting discussion of economic models versus recent economic performance, see Alan Greenspan, "Is There a New Economy?" *Vital Speeches of the Day* 64: 24 (October 1, 1998): 741–745.

E. P. Davis, *Debt, Financial Fragility, and Systemic Risk* (New York: Oxford University Press, 1993), looks at the financing behavior of households and businesses, which has generated high levels of debt since the 1970s, and its relationship to instability.

For a historical look at the inflation of the 1965–1979 era, see Thomas Mayer, *Monetary Policy and the Great Inflation in the United States* (Northampton, MA: Edward Elgar, 1999).

Endnotes

1 Note that nominal price of hot dogs has not initially changed even though their relative price has changed.

2 In Chapter 21, we introduced the equation of exchange, which can be written as $M \times V = \text{GDP} = P \times Y$. This equation says that the nation's nominal GDP (the overall price level, P, multiplied by the real level of output, Y) is equal to the money supply, M, multiplied by velocity, V.

3 Shortly, you shall see that aggregate supply is the other side.

4 When we invoke the ceteris paribus assumption, we hold all other factors, including input prices, constant and allow only output prices to vary.

5 Sustainable full employment is the level that can be maintained without upward or downward pressure on wages and prices.

6 If a large percentage of workers works under a contractual collective bargaining agreement that holds nominal wages constant over the course of the agreement, an unexpected rise in the price level will result in increases in nominal wages that lag increases in the price level.

7 In the post–World War II period, prices have been much less flexible downward than upward. That is, prices are much more likely to rise in response to increases in demand than to fall in response to decreases in demand.

8 As the factors of production and technology change over time, the natural level of real output will also change.

9 Note that the vertical long-run aggregate supply curve will shift if the quantity and productivity of the factors of production change—more on this in Chapter 24.

A Closer Look, page 573

a "Fed Official Defends Rise in Rates," *Orange County Register* (October 9, 1994): 5.

PART 6

Monetary Policy

Listen, there is no courage or any extra courage that I know of to find out the right thing to do. Now, it is not only necessary to do the right thing, but to do it in the right way and the only problem you have is what is the right thing to do and what is the right way to do it. That is the problem. But this economy of ours is not so simple that it obeys to the opinion of bias or the pronouncements of any particular individual.

—Dwight D. Eisenhower

24

The Challenges of Monetary Policy

Learning Objectives

After reading this chapter, you should know:

The goals of monetary policy, including economic growth, stable prices, full employment, and satisfactory external balance

How numerical goals are formulated and why they can differ in the short run and the long run

The monetary policy goals in terms of aggregate demand and aggregate supply

The monetary policy options available to respond to fluctuations in aggregate demand and aggregate supply

Can the Business Cycle Be Mitigated?

The Great Depression of the 1930s was by far the most severe downturn of the U.S. economy during the twentieth century. For more than a decade, output and employment remained considerably below the natural rate. Measured unemployment averaged more than 20 percent, and prices fell by more than 25 percent. During this painful period, macroeconomics underwent profound changes. Led by John Maynard Keynes, a school of thought was born that emphasized the need for government intervention to stabilize the level of economic activity. The problem according to Keynes was that only by accident would the level of aggregate demand be just sufficient to achieve full employment and stable prices. In the more likely situation, aggregate demand would be either too great or too little. Moreover, because relative price adjustments would occur only slowly, the economy could experience long bouts of either unemployment (too little demand) or inflation (too much demand).

The buildup for World War II in the early 1940s seemed to validate Keynesian theory. Almost overnight, the economy went to full employment, and measures were needed to "control" inflation. Based on such events, much of the academic community accepted Keynesian theory in the postwar period. During the 1960s, Keynesian policy prescriptions were put into practice by the government with some apparent success.[1] Although voices of dissent were always there, they became louder during and after the 1970s when the economy was plagued concurrently by high unemployment and high inflation, a condition that came to be known as **stagflation**. Economists struggled to understand the causes of and remedies for this dilemma, which Keynes believed could not happen.

Since the Great Depression, the U.S. economy has experienced 10 recessions. During these periods, output declined, unemployment increased, and the growth rate of prices generally fell. The economy also has experienced periodic bouts of rapid inflation. Some analysts believe that the government has been successful in reducing the length and magnitude of cyclical downturns and in lengthening cyclical expansions. A repetition of the Great Depression has been avoided, and the expansions of the 1980s and 1990s were of record length. The last recession in the early 2000s came on the heals of the longest expansion in history and still was relatively mild. Although researchers generally agree that the vast majority of these economic contractions and expansions resulted from fluctuations in aggregate demand, shocks to aggregate supply (shifts of the aggregate supply curve) have occasionally been responsible for both recessions and inflations. In these cases, analysis focusing only on aggregate demand may not be appropriate.

Since the early 1970s, international trade and finance have grown dramatically while barriers to capital flows have broken down. A flexible exchange rate system has replaced the fixed exchange rate system that was put into place in 1945. These factors have contributed to the increased volatility and relevance of exchange rates. The Fed has chosen on occasion to intervene in the foreign exchange market to smooth adjustments in the value of the dollar. Such intervention may interfere or conflict with the pursuit of other monetary policy goals. As you shall see, the Fed must be aware of the effects of its policies on the external balance of trade and capital flows.

At the same time, increased globalization means that the Fed must also respond to demand and supply shocks caused by events abroad. For example, on August 31, 1998, the Dow Jones Industrial Average fell 512 points, the largest point drop to that date. Most analysts attributed the drop to the financial and economic crisis in Russia, which followed on the heels of the Asian crisis. As you saw in Chapter 16, such a large drop in stock prices has the potential to destabilize the U.S. economy.

In this chapter, we look first at the macroeconomic goals and challenges of monetary policy. We then use an aggregate demand and supply framework to examine the specifics

Stagflation
A condition of concurrent high unemployment and high inflation.

of how to achieve these goals if the economy experiences either a recession or excessive inflation. As the preceding discussion implies, what "should" be done in response to fluctuations in aggregate demand or aggregate supply is often unclear and controversial.

The Goals of Monetary Policy

Macroeconomic policy consists of (1) monetary policy, which involves the Fed's use of its policy instruments to affect the cost and availability of funds in the economy, and (2) fiscal policy, which involves alterations in government spending or taxes proposed and enacted by Congress and the president. As illustrated in Exhibit 23-4, the changes in fiscal and monetary policies that lead to changes in aggregate demand interact, in turn, with aggregate supply to produce changes in prices, real output, and employment.

In conducting monetary policy, the Fed works through the financial system. Recall that the Fed's primary tools for influencing the financial system include control of the monetary base, the required reserve ratio, and the discount rate. Monetary policy, in turn, influences the borrowing, lending, spending, and saving behavior of the household, business, government, and rest-of-the-world sectors. As depicted in Exhibit 24-1 below, the specific goals of monetary policy are to design and implement policies that will achieve sustainable economic growth, full employment, stable prices, and a satisfactory external balance. In recent years, many members of the Federal Open Market Committee (FOMC) and other analysts have stressed that maintaining stable prices is the primary

24-1

The Goals of Monetary Policy

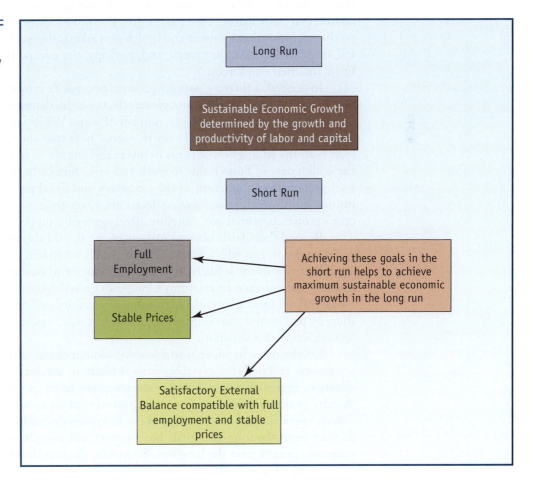

goal of the Fed. Others have contended that employment levels in the economy must not be ignored. Now let's take a closer look at the rationales underlying these goals.

Downloadable papers that describe the general purpose and goals of monetary policy can be found at **http://www.federalreserve.gov/pf/pf.htm**.

Economic Growth

The size of the "economic pie" divided up among a nation's citizens is determined by the quantity of goods and services produced. That is, the size is determined by real output or, specifically, real GDP. Simply put, if the size of a nation's economic pie and, thus, its potential standard of living are to rise over time, the productive capacity of the economy must expand. To use the terminology of Chapter 23, the natural level of real output (long-run aggregate supply) must increase.

Most economists agree that the growth of aggregate supply over time is determined primarily by the growth of capital, the labor force, and productivity. Thus, growth of the key inputs in the production process and technological improvements are the key to long-run growth of output. So far so good, but what determines the growth of capital, labor, and productivity?

The growth of the capital stock depends directly on the amount of investment spending undertaken by firms. By definition, the change in the capital stock is equal to net investment spending. The productivity of capital is thought to depend on the amount of resources devoted to research and development and on the resulting technological advances that lead to new and more productive plants and machines. Labor force growth flows from the growth of the population and from increases in the proportion of the population that participates in the labor force. The productivity of labor is thought to depend on the educational attainment and health of workers, the quantity and quality of the capital stock with which they work, and, perhaps, the competitive environment faced by firms and their employees.

In general, a thriving nation's productive capacity grows over time. Research shows that macroeconomic policy, through its effects on the determinants of economic growth, influences the pace of growth in a number of ways. While ignoring many of the detailed relationships and linkages, it is worth noting here that the government's tax policy affects both the willingness of firms to invest and engage in research and development and the willingness of households to work and save. Similarly, the level of interest rates resulting from the interaction of the monetary and fiscal policies pursued has a decisive influence on spending and saving decisions. Over time, such decisions affect an economy's growth potential and therefore affect aggregate supply.

Beyond these fairly obvious influences, we should also include the overall economic environment within which firms and households are making decisions. More specifically, a stable environment is likely to be more conducive to farsighted planning and decision making that enhance an economy's long-run growth potential. Such an environment is characterized by consistently high rates of capacity utilization and employment and, thus, by real output that is growing at a steady, sustainable pace. Exhibit 24-2 on page 585 depicts such a situation.

On the other hand, an unstable environment characterized by a series of inflationary booms and deflationary recessions is likely to inhibit long-run growth. In such a situation, aggregate demand almost always grows faster or slower than aggregate supply, thereby generating either inflationary pressures or an economic slowdown. Hence, the shorter-run stabilization objectives in the following discussion are not really separate and distinct from the long-run goals but support and complement the nation's pursuit of economic growth over the long run. Short-run fluctuations around the long-term trend influence the trend itself.

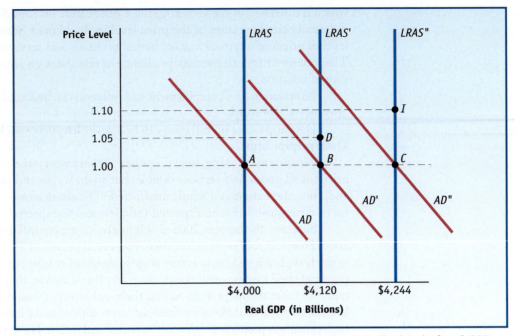

On the vertical axis is a price index, and on the horizontal axis is the level of real GDP. Assume that each year the nation's natural level of real output, as measured by long-run aggregate supply (*LRAS*), grows by 3 percent. Thus, in year 1, *LRAS* is $4,000 billion; in year 2, *LRAS* is $4,000 billion × 1.03 = $4,120 billion; and in year 3, *LRAS* is $4,120 × 1.03 = $4,244. If aggregate demand also grows by 3 percent per year, then the economy will follow the path *A–B–C* with 3 percent real GDP growth, a stable price level (1.00), and zero inflation. Alternatively, aggregate demand could grow faster than 3 percent, say, by 8 percent per year. Then, the economy would follow path *A–D–I* with prices rising 5 percent per year. Thus, in general, the growth in aggregate demand relative to aggregate supply determines the price-output performance of the economy.

Recap   The goals of monetary policy are sustainable economic growth, full employment, stable prices, and a satisfactory external balance. Sustainable economic growth is determined by the growth and productivity of the labor force and capital stock. Policies that achieve full employment and a noninflationary environment help to achieve maximum sustainable growth.

Stabilization of Unemployment, Inflation, and the External Balance

Discussions about the health of the economy usually focus on recent and expected movements in unemployment and inflation. Rarely do the evening news and political speeches fail to note what's happening on these fronts. One reason society is concerned about unemployment, as measured by the unemployment rate, is fairly obvious. We understand that if the nation is to reach its full economic potential, all individuals must have the opportunity to become productive, employed members of society. In the absence of this opportunity, poor families and individuals experience financial distress and hardships. From an economic standpoint, output that could have been produced last year by those who were unemployed is lost forever and can never be made up. Against this background, it is readily understandable why our nation's leaders operate with a clear mandate regarding unemployment. The Cracking the Code feature on page 587 explains how the official unemployment rate is measured.

What is less clear is why inflation generates so much concern. Simply stated, inflation is the rate of increase in the general price level. The consumer price index (CPI), which is discussed in the Cracking the Code feature on page 55 in Chapter 3, is the most frequently cited measure of the price level in the United States. It measures the average level of prices of a typical market basket of goods and services that consumers purchase. The month-to-month percentage change in this index gives us a somewhat reliable measure of inflation.

Information on unemployment and inflation can be found at **http://www.whitehouse.gov/news/fsbr.html**.

Data and tables on inflation can be seen at **http://www.clevelandfed.org/Research/Data/mcpipr.htm**.

Measurement aside, why do policy makers worry about inflation? After all, if the prices of all goods and services double, but so do wages and salaries, aren't all individuals and, thus, the nation as a whole unaffected? The short answer is no. To see why, it is useful to distinguish between expected inflation and unexpected inflation.

Suppose it's the year 2005 and households expect inflation to be about 3 percent in 2006. How will this expectation affect household behavior? First and foremost, the workers in the households will try to secure wage increases of at least 3 percent so that the purchasing power of their incomes will not decline. Ideally, of course, they would hope for a wage increase of more than 3 percent so that their real incomes would rise. Second, if they are net lenders, they will be looking for financial assets with nominal interest rates or nominal returns high enough to produce an adequate expected real return. For example, as discussed in Chapter 6, a nominal return of 7 percent, given expected inflation of 3 percent, is expected to produce a real return or real interest rate of about 4 percent. If inflation turns out to be close to 3 percent as expected, all is well. But what happens if prices actually rise by 5 percent?

First, the real wage of workers will fall because nominal wages will rise by a smaller percent than prices. The resulting change in output prices relative to input prices will, ceteris paribus, lead to an increase in firms' profits and encourage them to alter production and employment. As you saw in Chapter 23, the short-run aggregate supply curve slopes upward. That is, until expectations adjust to the unanticipated, higher price level, firms will offer more for sale than the natural level of real output. Second, the real return on financial assets acquired will be less than anticipated and perhaps even negative. In this case, the beneficiaries will be borrowers who find that the actual real cost of borrowing is well below what they expected. Beyond these types of redistribution, citizens living on fixed incomes, including many retirees, will find their purchasing power shrinking.

These simple examples illustrate a central reason why inflation, particularly unexpected inflation, is worrisome. Inflation redistributes income in arbitrary and unpredictable ways from workers to firms, from lenders to borrowers, and from those on fixed incomes to those with variable incomes that increase with inflation.

In addition, due to several features of the U.S. tax system, many firms and households will pay proportionately more taxes to the government in an inflationary environment. To illustrate, suppose that a household earns 4 percent interest on its surplus funds, the actual and expected inflation rate is zero, and the household is in the 25 percent tax rate bracket; then the household's after-tax real return is 3 percent, as Equation (24-1) shows:

$$
(24\text{-}1) \quad
\underset{.04}{\underset{\text{interest rate}}{\text{nominal}}}
\; - \;
\underset{0}{\underset{\text{inflation rate}}{\text{expected}}}
\; - \;
\underset{(.25 \times .04)}{\text{taxes}}
\; = \;
\underset{.03, \text{ or } 3\%}{\underset{\text{after-tax return}}{\text{real}}}
$$

Now suppose that, ceteris paribus, expected and actual inflation rises to 2 percent and the nominal interest rate rises from 4 to 6 percent to compensate lenders for the loss in purchasing power. The real after-tax return will again be the nominal rate minus the expected inflation rate and taxes. In this case, the real after-tax return equals 2.5 percent, as shown in Equation (24-2):

Cracking the Code

Measuring Unemployment

Statistics on the labor force, employment, and unemployment in the United States are gathered and published by the Bureau of Labor Statistics. Each month more than 65,000 households nationwide are surveyed. Based on their responses to a series of questions, individuals are classified as one of the following:

1. Unemployed (16 years or older, out of work, and actively looking for work)

2. Employed

3. Labor Force Participant (Employed plus Unemployed)

4. Not in the Labor Force (out of work and not actively looking for work; includes individuals who are under 16, retirees, disabled persons, and so-called discouraged workers who have lost their jobs and stopped looking for a job)

These data are then used to compute the unemployment rate, which is the percentage of the labor force unemployed:

$$\text{unemployment rate} = \text{number of persons unemployed/labor force}$$

To illustrate, in April 2004, 8.16 million people were unemployed, and the labor force totaled 146.741 million. Thus, the unemployment rate was 5.6 percent (8.16 million/146.741 million = 5.6 percent).

To appreciate the dynamics of the labor market and the relationship between the growth of the economy and unemployment, it is helpful to view the state of unemployment as a pool. Flowing into the pool are the new entrants to the labor force who have not yet found work and those who have recently lost or quit their jobs. Flowing out of the pool are those who have found jobs. If the inflow exceeds the outflow, the number in the pool rises. Conversely, if the outflow exceeds the inflow, the number in the pool falls. To understand the dynamics of unemployment, we must examine the causes and amounts of inflows relative to outflows. For example, from April 1999 to April 2004, the U.S. civilian labor force expanded by 7.6 million people, reflecting the ongoing growth of the population. Despite a recession in the early 2000s, the economy grew over this period, with real GDP increasing from about $9.315 trillion in the first quarter of 1999 to about $10.6 trillion in the first quarter of 2004. About 5.5 million new jobs were created, which fell short of the 7.6 million increase in the labor force. As a result, the number of people in the unemployment pool grew, and the unemployment rate increased from 4.3 percent to 5.6 percent.

During the 1991 recession, the labor force continued to grow, but job creation slowed dramatically as firms reacted to the fall in demand for their output and rising inventories by slashing production and laying off workers. The result was a large increase in the pool of unemployed people, and the unemployment rate rose sharply from 5.4 percent in 1990 to 7.4 percent in 1991. Clearly, economic growth and unemployment are tightly connected.

SOURCE: http://www.bls.gov/schedule/archives/empsit_nr.htm.

	nominal interest rate	−	expected inflation rate	−	taxes	=	real after-tax return
(24-2)	.06	−	.02	−	(.25 X .06)	=	.025, or 2.5%

Because nominal returns rather than real returns are taxed, inflation results in government taxes taking a larger portion of interest income than in a noninflationary environment. Inflation also reduces the real value of nominal money balances held. In this way, it acts as a tax on such holdings.

As for firms, standard accounting procedures base depreciation allowances on the historical cost of equipment and structures rather than on the replacement cost. In an inflationary environment, firms' depreciation allowances, which are deducted from revenues before taxable income is computed, are too small to replace the capital that wears out in the production process. More to the point, the too-small allowances result in taxes being proportionately higher than in a noninflationary environment. Again, as in the prior examples, inflation redistributes income and can distort economic decision making.

Returning to the uncertainty theme already discussed with regard to economic growth, we note that researchers have also found that as the inflation rate rises, the variability of inflation tends to increase and the relationship among relative prices tends to become more volatile and difficult to predict. Consequently, pricing, production, saving, and investment decisions have to be made in a more uncertain environment. Firms and households are likely to be much more cautious about making long-term commitments to spend, save, produce, or invest and focus instead on near-term opportunities. This perspective does not enhance long-run stability and growth and can aggravate short-run instabilities and cyclical fluctuations.

Inflation can also have an adverse effect on the nation's international competitiveness and, thus, its role in the world economy and in world affairs. For example, if the prices of U.S. goods rise relative to prices of competing goods in the rest of the world, ceteris paribus, the demand for U.S. products will fall with attendant effects on domestic production and employment. Although the resulting depreciation of the dollar will help to offset and reverse the negative effects on the trade balance over time, there is no assurance that this will occur quickly. In the meantime, U.S. firms will lose a portion of their share of world markets.

As the U.S. economy becomes more globalized, monetary policy makers must be aware of the international effects of policy. For example, if the Fed embarks on a program of monetary restraint to slow the growth rate of the U.S. economy, real interest rates could rise relative to foreign rates. A substantial appreciation of the dollar and augmented capital inflows can result. The dollar's appreciation may have a dramatic effect on the economy through its effect on net exports. Net exports fall as the foreign prices of U.S. goods increase and the domestic prices of foreign goods decrease. As a result, employment and output in the United States would be less than they would have been otherwise.

If monetary policy makers establish policy goals for inflation and growth that are widely divergent from those of other countries, substantial fluctuations in exchange rates can result. In addition to the price effects on net exports and the interest rate effects on capital flows, fluctuations in exchange rates greatly increase the exchange rate risks of international trade and finance. Central bank intervention may then be needed to stabilize exchange rates, but such intervention can dampen or conflict with the pursuit of other policy goals.

Deflation
A drop in the overall price level as measured by a price index.

Last, policy makers must also be on the alert for **deflation**, or a falling overall price level—something the U.S. economy has not experienced since the Great Depression. Deflation is often worse than inflation because it can lead to debt deflation, defaults, and bankruptcies. When inflation levels are very low, the potential that the economy could slip into a deflation increases. In the late 1990s and early 2000s, inflation rates fell to their lowest levels in 40 years. Because prices of many commodities also fell dramatically, some economists were concerned about actual deflationary pressures. They believe that the Fed must be more concerned about deflation than inflation because the effects are not symmetrical. As experienced during the Great Depression and more recently in the 1990s in Japan, deflation can be more deleterious to an economy than inflation, particularly if it leads to falls in asset prices and widespread bankruptcies. Because the effects of inflation and deflation on the economy may not be symmetrical, the Fed may be even more concerned about deflation than inflation.[2]

To summarize, monetary policy can cause dramatic changes in exchange rates and the balances on the current and capital accounts—that is, the external balance—which then feed back to the domestic economy. Exchange rate volatility can necessitate central bank intervention. The bottom line is that in designing and implementing monetary policy, monetary policy makers must seek to achieve an acceptable external balance compatible with the domestic goals of full employment and stable prices. In Chapter 27, we take a more in-depth look at the international effects of monetary policy. You shall see that this increasingly globalized environment will necessitate increased coordination among countries as they establish policy goals.

Monetary policy makers do not make policy decisions in a vacuum. They are not oblivious to the domestic and international environment, nor do they aim at abstract, long-run theoretical goals. Rather, they have specific numerical objectives in mind for unemployment and inflation when they make policy adjustments that are consistent with the economic environment. It is to these objectives that we now turn.

Recap   Full employment is necessary for a nation to reach its economic potential. A stable price level is desirable because unexpected inflation redistributes income in arbitrary and unpredictable ways and causes distortions in the U.S. tax system. Monetary policy can cause changes in exchange rates and the external balance that feed back to the domestic economy. Monetary policy makers must secure an external balance that is consistent with the domestic goals of full employment and stable prices.

The Source of Numerical Objectives for Unemployment and Inflation

Employment Act of 1946
The first statute that directed policy makers to pursue policies to achieve full employment and noninflationary growth.

Humphrey-Hawkins Full Employment and Balanced Growth Act of 1978
A statute that required policy makers to pursue policies to achieve full employment and noninflationary growth.

Natural Rate of Unemployment
The rate of unemployment consistent with stable prices; believed to be about 4.0 to 4.5 percent.

General guidelines for policy makers are contained in the **Employment Act of 1946** and the **Humphrey-Hawkins Full Employment and Balanced Growth Act of 1978**. Both statutes direct policy makers to pursue policies consistent with achieving full employment and noninflationary growth. Briefly, this legislation, in effect, leaves it to policy makers, their staffs, and the economics profession at large to determine, for example, what unemployment rate is consistent with full employment and nonaccelerating inflation.

In the early years of the twenty-first century, most estimates of sustainable employment imply an unemployment rate of about 4.0 to 4.5 percent. Also called the **natural rate of unemployment**, this rate is believed to be consistent with stable prices in the early 2000s. The natural rate of unemployment is the unemployment rate that corresponds to the natural rate of real output discussed in Chapter 23. Economists believe that a measured unemployment rate much below this level will trigger inflation as labor shortages appear in some markets driving up wages and prices. The natural rate can change over time for various reasons including the changing gender and age composition of the labor force and the changing safety net of benefits available to the unemployed.

In the late 1980s and early 1990s, the natural rate of unemployment was believed to be in the 5.5 to 6.0 percent range. Low unemployment in the mid-1990s with moderate inflation convinced many economists that the natural rate had fallen to the 5.0 to 5.5 range. In the late 1990s, unemployment continued to fall. By late 2000, actual unemployment had briefly fallen to 3.9 percent with no increase in actual inflation. Many economists believed that wage pressure would soon lead to price increases, but the inflation did not materialize. By the mid-2000s, it was thought that the natural rate of unemployment was in the 4.0 to 4.5 percent range.

On the inflation front, the problem is a bit more complicated. In the 1950s and 1960, inflation averaged 1 to 2 percent per year. In 1971, President Nixon imposed a 90-day freeze on wages and prices because the inflation rate had "surged" to 3.5 percent. An inflation rate of 2 to 3 percent, considered moderate today, was worrisome then to policy makers. In contrast, during President Reagan's administration, the inflation rate fell dramatically from the double-digit levels prevailing at the beginning of the 1980s to below 3 percent by 1986. President Reagan claimed "victory" over inflation as the inflation rate settled down in the 3 to 4 percent range. In 1994, even though inflation still hovered in the 3 to 4 percent range, the Fed raised interest rates several times out of fear that rapid economic growth would cause inflation to rise again.

Over time, policy makers desire price stability and often stress that this should be the primary objective of monetary policy. To some analysts, price stability means zero inflation while others associate it with inflation rates in the 1 to 2 percent range. Many economists prefer 1 to 2 percent inflation because they believe that when actual inflation is zero, the economy could easily slip into a deflationary period. At the same time, goals, such as for inflation, are not selected in a vacuum. In setting the inflation goal over the near term, such as the next year or two, policy makers consider recent experience and attempt to balance their desire to reduce inflation further with their desire to minimize the accompanying and possibly adverse near-term effects on unemployment and output growth. Thus, recent historical experience, judgments about what is feasible, and the political environment all play a role. Times change and so do economic goals.

In compliance with the Humphrey-Hawkins Act of 1978, the Fed must report its long-term goals to Congress in February and July of each year. See the latest Monetary Policy Testimony and Report to Congress by the chair of the Board of Governors of the Fed at **http://www.federalreserve.gov/boarddocs/hh/**.

In the long run, after all adjustments have been completed, the goals of stable prices and full employment are believed to be perfectly compatible. Thus, there is no need for trade-offs between goals. However, we all live and policy makers act in the short run. History, as well as theory, tells us that policy makers' attempts to lower inflation can reduce output growth and increase unemployment for a time while attempts to raise output growth and employment can aggravate inflation. In this context, concerns about the short-run versus the long-run effects of policy actions and the price versus the output effects of policy actions in the short run do arise.

Finally, based on our historical experience, economists estimate that the potential long-run growth rate for real GDP is around 2.5 to 3.0 percent per year over time. Growth beyond 3.0 percent per year does not seem to be sustainable over a long period. Sustainable growth in the 2.5 to 3.0 percent range is compatible with the other numerical goals for full employment and stable prices. If the economy grows at this sustainable rate, the vertical long-run aggregate supply curve shifts to the right by 2.5 to 3.0 percent per year.

In sum, the prevailing economic and political environment and the nation's historical experience all play a role in setting the priorities that guide policy actions. Because the policy makers and the environment can change over time, so can the weight given to each priority. We turn now to the aggregate demand and supply framework to look at policy alternatives.

Recap   General guidelines for numerical objectives are found in the Employment Act of 1946 and the Humphrey-Hawkins Full Employment and Balanced Growth Act of 1978. Full employment is believed to be about 4.0 to 4.5 percent measured unemployment in the mid-2000s. The goal for inflation depends on recent experience and the political and historical environment. Price stability does not necessarily mean zero inflation but low inflation in the 1 to 2 percent range. Sustainable growth is thought to be in the 2.5 to 3.0 percent range.

Changes in Aggregate Demand and Policy

From the perspective of an aggregate demand and aggregate supply framework, the obvious goals of monetary policy are to achieve successive long-run equilibriums with sustainable noninflationary growth. Such a situation occurs when the aggregate demand and long-run aggregate supply curves are both shifting to the right by the same relative magnitude. Look again at Exhibit 24-2 in which steady noninflationary growth is achieved because aggregate demand and long-run aggregate supply are both growing by 3 percent per year. Unfortunately, due to the extremely dynamic nature of the world, the economy may often fall short of achieving those goals. Consequently, policy makers may need to react to changes or to initiate changes that guide or sometimes push the economy in the right direction.

In Chapter 23, we discussed demand-pull inflation, which occurs when an excessive level of aggregate demand pulls up the overall price level. Ceteris paribus, starting from a long-run equilibrium position, an unexpected shift to the right in the aggregate demand curve—an increase in demand—initially leads to increases in both output and the price level. The economy moves to a new short-run equilibrium along an upward-sloping short-run aggregate supply curve. The output level is not sustainable, however, and price level adjustments bring the economy back to long-run equilibrium at full employment and a higher price level.

Look at Exhibit 24-3 below, which illustrates the adjustment of the economy in response to an increase in aggregate demand. Initially, the economy is in long-run equilibrium at point A. The actual price level (1.00) is equal to the expected price level underlying the short-run aggregate supply curve, and the economy is operating at its natural level of real output ($1,500 billion). Subsequently, aggregate demand increases unexpectedly, shifting the aggregate demand curve from AD to AD'. In the short run, the economy will move to point B with output rising to $1,700 billion and the price level increasing to 1.05.

24-3

An Unexpected Increase in Aggregate Demand with No Fed Response*

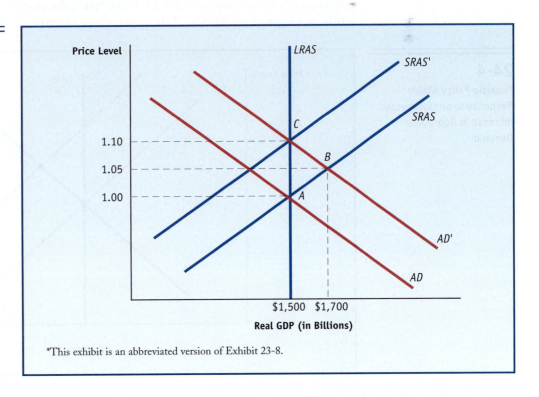

*This exhibit is an abbreviated version of Exhibit 23-8.

Point *B* is not a long-run equilibrium, however, because the actual price level (1.05) is above the expected price level (1.00). As input suppliers respond to the unanticipated increase in prices, the expected price level increases to 1.05 and input prices increase. The short-run aggregate supply curve eventually shifts from *SRAS* to *SRAS"*. With input prices and, thus, production costs rising, firms will require a higher output price than was initially the case to induce them to produce a particular level of output. When the adjustment is completed, the economy will settle at a new long-run equilibrium at point *C*. (See if you can explain why this is the case.) In effect, the economy moves along the path *A–B–C* as shifts in short-run aggregate supply alter the initial short-run effects of a rise in aggregate demand. In the end, the increase in aggregate demand results in a rise in the price level (1.00 to 1.10) and no change in real GDP.

Normally, we would hope that the Fed would not unexpectedly increase the growth rate of the money supply when the economy was in a long-run equilibrium with stable prices and full employment. As we have pointed out, however, myopic policy makers may have an incentive to do so because such policies can lead to short-run, unsustainable gains in employment. In an election year, some politicians may find it desirable to push the unemployment rate below its natural level despite the concurrent and subsequent increases in the price level. If no other action were taken, price increases would eventually move the economy to a new long-run equilibrium with a higher price level, as in Exhibit 24-3.

Unexpected increases in aggregate demand can also come from other sources such as swells in household, business, or government spending, and surges in net export demand. Regardless of the source, the Fed can use monetary policy and/or Congress can use fiscal policy to reduce the level of demand. For example, tighter monetary policy would reduce the growth rate of money and credit and at least temporarily raise short-term interest rates above what they would be otherwise. The appropriate fiscal policy would be to slow government spending or increase tax rates. In either case, the level of spending and, thus, aggregate demand would be reduced. The economy would then return to long-run equilibrium at a lower price level, perhaps more quickly than if the government did nothing. Exhibit 24-4 illustrates the path the economy would take to return to long-run equilibrium if the government intervenes.

24-4

Possible Policy Maker
Response to an Unexpected
Increase in Aggregate
Demand

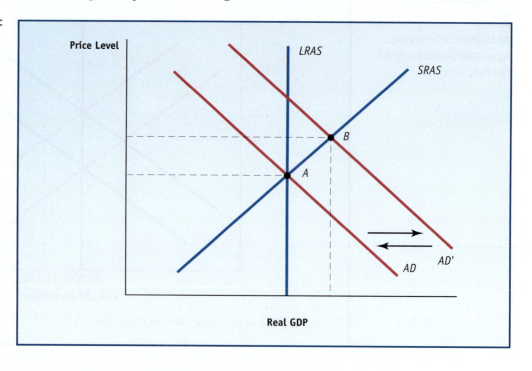

In response to an unanticipated increase in aggregate demand, the economy moves from long-run equilibrium at point A to point B, ceteris paribus. Output is above the sustainable full employment level, and the price level has risen. If policy makers respond by using fiscal or monetary policy to reduce the level of demand, the economy will move back to long-run equilibrium at a price level (point A) that is lower than it would have been if the government had failed to act.

Note the irony of this situation when the increase in aggregate demand is due to an increase in the money supply. After generating the increase in aggregate demand, the Fed engages in contractionary policy to bring the economy back to long-run equilibrium at the original point. We turn now to the equally sinister demand-induced recession.

Recap   Starting from full employment, an increase in aggregate demand initially leads to increases in both output and prices as the economy expands along the short-run aggregate supply curve. The higher level of output is not sustainable in the long run. Such unexpected increases in demand cause demand-pull inflation and can come from increases in spending in any sector. If policy makers do nothing, the economy returns to full employment at a higher price level. If policy makers engage in contractionary policies, the economy returns to full employment at the original price level.

Demand-Induced Recession

Whatever the source, the initial effect of an unexpected fall in aggregate demand is an unanticipated rise in inventories, ceteris paribus. In response, business firms cut production, employment, and prices. In the aggregate, output prices tend to fall relative to input prices, including wages, which do not fall immediately or fall slower than output prices in response to the reduction in demand. Exhibit 24-5 below illustrates the case of a demand-induced recession.

24-5

Demand-Induced Recession

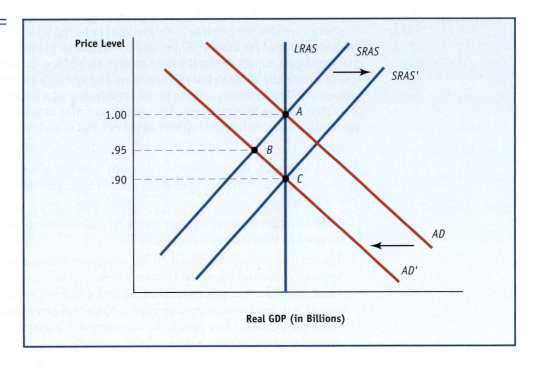

Initially, the economy is in long-run equilibrium at point A at the intersection of the aggregate demand and long-run aggregate supply curves. The short-run aggregate supply curve is in the initial position of *SRAS*. The economy moves along the short-run aggregate supply curve (from point A to point B in Exhibit 24-5) into a recession.[3]

Once in a recession, the economy can take two possible paths from this short-run equilibrium back to a long-run equilibrium. First, with the actual price level (0.95) below the expected price level, firms and workers presumably will adjust their price expectations downward. This, along with the decline in the employment of labor and other factors of production, leads to decreases in nominal wages and other input prices. The short-run aggregate supply curve shifts to the right, reflecting the fall in production costs, and the economy returns to a long-run equilibrium at the natural rate of output (point C). Thus, following this path, the end result of a fall in aggregate demand (10 percent in Exhibit 24-5) is a proportional fall in the price level (1.0 to 0.9) with no effects on real output or employment.

An important question about this first possible path is how long it will take. The answer is that it depends on how quickly input and output prices adjust downward. This adjustment, in turn, depends on how individuals (firm managers as well as workers) formulate and thus modify their price expectations. Suffice it to say that the adjustment of prices and price expectations in the United States during recessions has usually been a sluggish process. Accordingly, policy makers have found it economically and politically difficult to wait for the economy to take the B–C path back to long-run equilibrium.

Such considerations suggest a second possible route out of the recession. Aggregate demand can be boosted, for example, through expansionary monetary and fiscal policies such that aggregate demand rebounds (from AD' back to AD in Exhibit 24-5). The economy returns to the natural level of real output and the initial price level (point A). Again, the appropriate monetary policy would be to increase the growth rate of the monetary and credit aggregates and to lower interest rates from what they would be otherwise. Likewise, the appropriate fiscal policy would be to increase the growth of government spending and/or reduce tax rates.

Recap   Starting from full employment, an unexpected drop in aggregate demand causes a demand-induced recession. Output and prices fall as the economy moves down a short-run aggregate supply curve. If policy makers do nothing, the short-run aggregate supply curve eventually shifts to the right as firms and workers adjust their price expectations downward. The economy returns to full employment at a lower price level. Policy makers can also choose to boost demand through fiscal or monetary policy. In this case, the economy returns to full employment at the original price level.

Which route does the economy usually take out of a recession? In modern history, the second route, a policy-induced rebound in aggregate demand, has predominated for two reasons:

1. Recessions generate political pressures "to do something," and policy makers generally respond to such pressures eventually.

2. If firms and households, based on historical experience, expect policy makers to boost aggregate demand when the economy is in a recession, then the first route, a downward adjustment in price expectations and a rightward shift of short-run aggregate supply, will be slower to develop than if firms and households did not expect government intervention. As a result, the economy will stagnate, and the pressure on policy makers to boost aggregate demand will intensify.

Looking Back

How History Has Affected U.S. and German Policy Goals

A nation's priorities depend in an important way on its history. In the United States, for example, the trauma of the Great Depression contributed to a political environment in which policy makers tended to emphasize economic growth and employment objectives for many decades after World War II. In contrast, after World War I, Germany experienced hyperinflation that contributed to economic and political dislocations, including Hitler's rise to power. After World War II, memories of this past ordeal led the former West Germany to emphasize the price stability objective. Such tendencies, in turn, govern policy making in the sense that they condition the direction in which policy makers are generally prepared to err. Accordingly, and not surprisingly, the tendency for policy makers to err on the expansionary side in the United States and the tendency for German policy makers to err on the restrictive side have resulted in the U.S. inflation rate generally being above the German inflation rate in the post–World War II period.

In addition to a nation's long-run historical experience, recent history also influences the priorities assigned to the various policy objectives. For example, the significant acceleration in inflation in the United States during the late 1970s clearly influenced priorities and actions. More specifically, the appointment of Paul Volcker as chair of the Board of Governors of the Fed in 1979 and the two recessions the nation endured in 1980 and 1982 can be linked to some degree to a consensus that inflation had to be brought down even at the cost of a temporary rise in unemployment and a retardation of economic growth. In 1994, recognizing the difficulty of curbing inflation if inflationary expectations take hold, the Fed took actions that increased interest rates five times despite little concrete evidence that inflation was or would be much above 3 percent in the foreseeable future.

Similarly, after the unification of Germany in 1990, the price stability goal remained preeminent, and the German inflation rate remained below 4 percent. By 1995, German inflation was below 2 percent.[a]

Furthermore, when Germany joined the European Monetary Union and adopted the euro in 1999, it did so only on the condition that the primary goal of the Eurosystem (the central bank of the Euro Zone) be price stability.

Thus, in a very real sense, what firms and households believe policy makers will do has a direct influence on the economy's performance. More specifically, the beliefs of households and firms regarding the response of policy makers affect how prices and output adjust in the short run as well as the long run. What firms and households believe that policy makers will do is, in turn, heavily influenced by what policy makers have done in the past in similar situations. Given the short-run horizons of most policy makers, it should not be surprising that monetary and fiscal policies have, on average, been expansionary for most of the last 40 years.

A legacy of this interaction between policy makers and their constituents is that prices have risen more or less continuously since the end of World War II. However, the rate at which prices rise—that is, the inflation rate—has generally decelerated in recessions and accelerated in expansions. The expansion of the 1990s and the early 2000s is an exception; inflation rates fell for many years late into the expansion. For example, during 1998, more than six years into the expansion, the annualized rate of inflation fell to less than 1.5 percent.

Inflation and unemployment rates since the 1940s are available on the Internet at **http://research.stlouisfed.org/fred2/**.

So far, we have concentrated on developments that affect aggregate demand. To complete our examination, we need to analyze how developments that affect aggregate supply influence output, employment, and the overall price level in both the short and the long run.

Recap If firms and households based on historical experience expect policy makers to boost aggregate demand in recessions, then a downward adjustment in price expectations and a rightward shift of the short-run aggregate supply curve will take a long time to materialize. In general, inflation accelerates in expansions and decelerates in recessions. An exception is the expansion of the 1990s, which was not accompanied by an acceleration of inflation.

Changes in Aggregate Supply and Policy

Supply Shock
Any event that shifts the short-run aggregate supply curve.

A **supply shock** is any event that shifts the aggregate supply curve. An example of an adverse supply shock is a significant rise in the price of oil, a key input widely used in production. Major crop failures and natural disasters such as earthquakes or major floods are also examples of negative supply shocks. More generally, anything that destroys a significant portion of a nation's productive capacity or reduces the productivity of labor and capital is an adverse supply shock.

As in our analysis of the effects of shifts in aggregate demand, let's begin by assuming that the economy is in long-run equilibrium. Now suppose that an adverse supply shock occurs. For example, suppose, ceteris paribus, that the price of refined petroleum increases suddenly and substantially, as happened in 1974 when the price of refined petroleum increased by more than 70 percent, in 1980 when the price rose more than 50 percent, and in 2004 when the price again rose more than 70 percent.

Firms feel the effects of such a supply shock most immediately and directly. Simply put, input prices rise dramatically relative to what firms had expected. With costs of production higher, firms are unwilling to supply as high a level of output as before. More specifically, in the face of higher production costs, firms will, ceteris paribus, require a higher price level to produce the same level of output. Exhibit 24-6 on page 597 shows the resulting leftward shift in the short-run aggregate supply curve.

Cost-Push Inflation
Sustained increases in the overall price level, triggered by increases in input prices.

With firms posting higher output prices, ceteris paribus, the quantity of real output demanded falls, and firms cut their production and employment. In the short run, the economy moves from point *A* to point *B* and experiences rising prices and falling output and employment. Policy makers are on the spot because the economy is experiencing both a recession and inflation. Real output has fallen below its natural level and prices have risen. In contrast to demand-pull inflation, the economy has now experienced so-called **cost-push inflation** triggered by increases in input prices.[4]

Accommodation
When policy makers increase aggregate demand in response to an adverse supply shock.

The problem from the policy makers' perspective is that monetary and fiscal tools work mainly on the aggregate demand side while the more immediate problem confronting them emanates from the supply side. What can be done? First, policy makers can boost aggregate demand via fiscal or monetary policy. If they do, the economy moves from point *B* to *C* in Exhibit 24-6. Assuming that this so-called **accommodation** is done

24-6

An Adverse Supply Shock as a Cause of Cost-Push Inflation

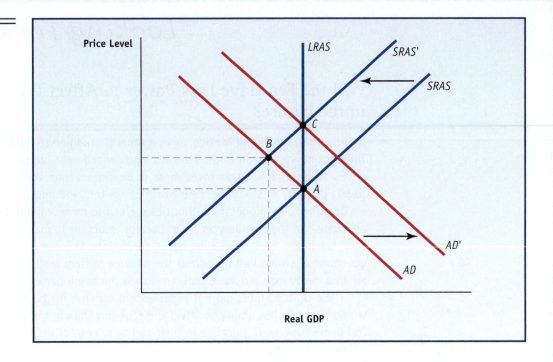

quickly, the recession will be shorter in duration and less severe, but the inflation problem will be magnified as prices rise further. Second, policy makers can literally do nothing. With the economy at point *B* and aggregate demand unchanged, the idle plants and unemployment in the economy will eventually put downward pressure on wages and overall prices. As this occurs, the short-run aggregate supply curve will begin to shift to the right toward its initial position. Given enough time, the economy could return to a position close to its initial long-run equilibrium (point *A*). We say *close* because if the price of a major input is permanently higher, the natural rate of output could presumably be reduced somewhat, but not permanently, as alternate inputs are developed or the output mix changes. However, because workers will be reluctant to accept lower wages in the face of higher heating and gasoline prices, the period of adjustment could be quite prolonged. It should not be surprising that policy makers have usually pursued an accommodating expansion in aggregate demand in response to an adverse supply shock.

Of course, supply shocks are not always adverse. In late 1985, the world petroleum market literally collapsed because of slow worldwide economic growth, weak demand, and the tendency for some OPEC members to cheat on their agreed-upon production quotas. With the price of crude petroleum falling from $24.09 in 1985 to $12.51 in 1986, countries such as the United States experienced a beneficial supply shock. The fall in production costs shifted the aggregate supply curve to the right, resulting in less inflation and more output growth than otherwise would have occurred. However, fortunes tend to reverse courses. In late-2004, increases in the price of oil to more than $55 a barrel caused many to be concerned that another cost-push inflation was on the horizon.

Recap   Adverse supply shocks shift the short-run aggregate supply curve to the left. Beneficial shocks shift it to the right. Adverse supply shocks cause rising prices and higher unemployment and are particularly difficult for policy makers to deal with. Given an adverse shock, an accommodating policy will increase employment but aggravate the inflation.

Will the Fed Have Less Power to Affect the Economy in the Future?

In the 1990s, Japan and Mexico, among others, struggled to fight the ravages of deflation. The banking systems in both countries experienced near collapse because of falling asset prices. As prices fell, banks owed more to depositors than the value of their assets. Loans to buy property or stocks became worthless as the land and stock prices fell and borrowers defaulted. The monetary authorities seemed to have only limited ability to counter the breakdown of the economy as banks became reluctant to make new loans. In Japan, reluctant taxpayers were forced to inject funds into the insolvent system. In Mexico, the government, which had privatized the banking system in the early 1990s, was forced to adopt a costly loan purchase program to aid the ailing banks.

The United States did not experience a collapse in the 1990s, but if it had, the Fed would have had less ability to affect the economy than in the past. The Fed and other central banks have seen a decline in their ability to control their domestic economies for the following reasons:

1. The banking system's share of intermediation is declining.

2. Control over banks is less stringent as banks find new ways to attract deposits that are not subject to reserve requirements.

3. Global forces are more important than ever before.

As a *Wall Street Journal* article puts it:

An even more pervasive myth is that central bankers have enormous powers to foster economic growth. Paul Volcker [chair of the Fed, 1979–1987] was wryly amused at magazine articles calling him the most powerful man on earth. He knew that global market forces were far more powerful than the Fed. But at least he had stronger controls in the early 1980s over the money supply than the Fed has today.[a]

We have considered increases and decreases in aggregate demand and aggregate supply. Whatever the case may be, the goals and policy responses brought together in this chapter suggest ways to achieve full employment and stable prices. The formulation and implementation of policies to achieve these goals are the subjects of the next two chapters.

Summary of Major Points

1. The goal of monetary policy is to influence the overall performance of the economy. The size of the "economic pie" in the long run is influenced by the growth of the labor force and the capital stock and by increases in the productivity of these inputs. Government policies affect growth through the mix of monetary and fiscal policies and resulting tax and interest rate structures, which affect incentives to invest, work, and save. In addition, to the extent that government policies encourage a stable environment, growth is also affected.

2. In addition to economic growth, full employment, price stability, and a satisfactory external balance are also goals of monetary policy. Over the short run, economic growth depends on the growth of aggregate demand relative to aggregate supply, which determines the resulting fluctuations in output, employment, and prices. An unstable short-run environment is believed to have an adverse effect on long-run growth, and a stable short-run environment is believed to have a beneficial effect on long-run growth.

3. Full employment is a goal because if a nation is to reach its full economic potential, individuals must have an opportunity to become productive members of society. Price stability is a goal because inflation tends to redistribute income in arbitrary and unpredictable ways, especially if the change is unexpected. Inflation also contributes to uncertainty and distortions in decision making. It can have an adverse effect on the nation's international competitiveness. When inflation rates are low, policy makers must also be on the lookout for deflation. Deflation is undesirable because it can cause a debt deflation, defaults, and bankruptcies. Monetary policy can cause dramatic changes in exchange rates and the balances in the current and capital accounts. Monetary policy must seek to achieve an acceptable external balance compatible with the goals of full employment and stable prices.

4. General guidelines for the macroeconomic goals are contained in the Employment Act of 1946 and the Humphrey-Hawkins Act of 1978. Specific guidelines and setting priorities are the result of historical experience, judgments about what is feasible, and the political environment.

5. In the short run, an unexpected increase in aggregate demand produces demand-pull inflation and unsustainable increases in output. If policy makers do nothing, the economy returns to long-run equilibrium at a higher price level. If the government uses appropriate monetary or fiscal policy, the economy returns to long-run equilibrium at a price level lower than it would otherwise have been.

6. In the short run, an unexpected fall in aggregate demand will produce a recession. There are two possible paths to recovery. First, as time goes on, price expectations will be revised downward, inflation will decrease, and the economy will recover as relative prices adjust. Alternatively, if policy makers and their constituents become impatient, demand can be boosted by expansionary monetary and fiscal policy. History shows that the second route has predominated.

7. Supply shocks cause a shift of the short-run aggregate supply curve. Adverse supply shocks pose a real dilemma for policy makers. Real output and employment fall while prices rise. An accommodating policy will moderate the recession but will aggravate the inflation. Cost-push inflation results when the overall price level increases due to increases in the cost of inputs.

Key Terms

Accommodation, **596**
Cost-Push Inflation, **596**
Deflation, **588**
Employment Act of 1946, **589**

Humphrey-Hawkins Full Employment and Balanced Growth Act of 1978, **589**

Natural Rate of Unemployment, **589**
Stagflation, **582**
Supply Shock, **596**

Review Questions

1. What are the goals of monetary policy?
2. How are the goals of full employment and stable prices related to the long-run goal of economic growth? How can policy makers affect long-run growth?
3. Why do policy makers have to be aware of the external balance?
4. Explain why the short-run goal for inflation is not always zero percent.
5. What is deflation, and why do policy makers have to be concerned about it?
6. Does the natural level of unemployment ever change? If it does, explain why.

7. Explain why the numerical objectives of policy change.
8. What is a supply shock? What is the appropriate policy response to a negative supply shock? What determines whether policy makers should act or do nothing in the face of adverse shocks to either aggregate demand or aggregate supply?
9. In the context of monetary policy, what is accommodation? If the Fed usually increases the money supply in response to decreases in aggregate demand, how will this affect the adjustment process?

10. Define both *cost-push* and *demand-pull inflation*.
11. How is the natural level of real output related to the natural rate of unemployment?
12. Can the economy experience a demand-pull inflation and a recession at the same time?
13. In the late 1990s, Congress and the president eliminated the federal deficit. What effect did this have on aggregate demand?
14. Can a person be employed but not be in the labor force? Can a person be unemployed but not be in the labor force?

Analytical Questions

Questions marked with an icon are objective in nature. They can be completed with a short answer or number.

15. Use aggregate supply and aggregate demand curves to analyze a supply shock.
16. Use aggregate supply and aggregate demand curves to illustrate demand-pull and cost-push inflation.
17. The nominal interest rate is 6 percent, expected inflation is 3 percent, and the tax rate is 20 percent. What is the real after-tax return? If the nominal interest rate and the expected inflation rate both decrease by 2 percent, what is the real after-tax return?
18. The nominal interest rate is 3 percent but people expect prices to fall by 4 percent. What is the real interest rate? If the tax rate is 20 percent, what is the real after-tax return?
19. Draw the long-run aggregate supply curves for successive long-run equilibriums with a potential growth rate of real GDP at 2.5 to 3.0 percent per year. What is the sustainable growth rate of output over time?
20. Graphically demonstrate the appropriate Fed policy in response to a severe unexpected drop in aggregate demand.

21. Graphically demonstrate how changes in aggregate demand cause inflation or deflation (falling prices) in the short run. Explain why only the price level changes in the long run. What happens to the price level over successive long runs?
22. In each of the following cases, explain whether the individual is in the labor force, not in the labor force, employed, or unemployed:
   a. A 14-year-old truant who is looking for work
   b. A person who has started her own business
   c. A college student
   d. My retired mother who does volunteer work at a hospital
   e. A discouraged aerospace worker who has given up looking for a job
   f. A recent college graduate who is actively seeking a job
23. Use aggregate demand and aggregate supply curves to show what will happen to output and the price level if government spending is reduced at the same time the Fed takes action to increase the money supply.

Internet Exercises

1. An extremely interesting article entitled, "Formulating a Consistent Approach to Monetary Policy" is obtainable from the following Web site: **http://minneapolisfed.org/pubs/ar/ar1995.cfm.** Read the introduction and answer the following:
   a. What is the principal long-run goal of monetary policy?
   b. How can monetary policy improve economic performance over the short run?
2. The chapter describes the natural rate of unemployment as the unemployment rate that is consistent with stable prices. Consider the behavior of unemployment, inflation, and the rate of growth of $M1$ from 1961 to 1971. Provide a "natural rate of unemployment" explanation for inflation in the late 1960s and the high unemployment rate of the early 1970s. Data on the unemployment rate, the money supply, and inflation rates may be accessed from the following Web site: **http://research.stlouisfed.org/fred2/.**

Suggested Readings

A highly recommended and comprehensive speech about monetary policy by Fed Chair Greenspan highlights the risk management aspects of monetary policy during Chair Greenspan's tenure. The speech is "Risk and Uncertainty in Monetary Policy," given before the American Economics Association, January 3, 2004, San Diego, California. It is available on the Internet at **http://www.federalreserve.gov/boarddocs/ speeches/2004/200 40103/default.htm**.

For a look at recent aspects of monetary policy, see Anthony M. Santomero, "Monetary Policy: Stability Through Change," *Business Review, Federal Reserve Bank of Philadelphia* Q1 (2004): 1–5. The article is available on the Internet at **http://www.phil.frb.org/files/br/brq104as.pdf**.

For a look at the systematic ways monetary policy affects the economy, see Michael Dotsey, "How the Fed Affects the Economy: A Look at Systematic Monetary Policy," *Business Review, Federal Reserve Bank of Philadelphia* Q1 (2004): 6–15. The article is available on the Internet at **http://www.phil.frb.org. files/br/brq104md.pdf**.

The Federal Reserve Bank of San Francisco maintains a very thorough Internet site on U.S. monetary policy at **http://www. frbsf.org/publications/federalreserve/monetary/**.

For an advanced look at monetary policy, see Carl E. Walsh, *Monetary Theory and Policy,* 2nd ed. (Cambridge, MA: MIT Press, March 2003).

For an article that discusses the challenges of monetary policy given ongoing changes in financial markets, see "Monetary Policy in a Changing World," by Thomas M. Hoenig, *Economic Review of the Federal Reserve Bank of Kansas City* 85:3 (Third Quarter 2000): 5–10. It may be viewed and/or ordered on the World Wide Web at **http://www.kc.frb.org/Publicat/ econrev/er00q3.htm#hoenig**.

Each year, the March and September issues of the *Federal Reserve Bulletin* contain the Fed's "Monetary Policy Report to the Congress," as mandated by the Humphrey-Hawkins Act of 1978. These reports make for interesting reading regarding monetary policy and the economic outlook. The Monetary Policy Testimony and the Report to Congress are available on the World Wide Web at **http://www.federalreserve.gov/ boarddocs/hh/**.

For a discussion of the challenges of monetary policy given structural changes in the economy, see Robert T. Parry, "Monetary Policy in a New Environment: The U.S. Experience," *Economic Letter,* Federal Reserve Bank of San Francisco, N. 200-31 (October 13, 2000).

For a discussion of Nobel laureate economist William Vickery's view that under normal conditions, inflation and unemployment are separable issues, see David Colander, "Macroeconomics: Was Vickery Ten Years Ahead?" *Challenge* (September–October 1998): 72–86.

Stephen G. Cecchitti, "Policy Rules and Targets: Framing the Central Banker's Problem," discusses many of the topics in this chapter. It can be found in the Federal Reserve Bank of New York, *Economic Policy Review* 4:2 (June 1998): 1–14.

Endnotes

1 Keynes viewed fluctuations as originating with aggregate demand, and, as you have seen, under normal circumstances both fiscal and monetary policies affect demand. Although we consider both policies to be Keynesian, Keynes's preference was for fiscal policy.

2 A fascinating speech by Fed Chair Greenspan that highlights the asymmetrical differences between inflation and deflation is "Risk and Uncertainty in Monetary Policy," before the American Economics Association, January 3, 2004, San Diego, California. It is available on the Internet at **http://www.federalreserve.gov/boarddocs/speeches/200420040103/default.htm**.

3 Technically speaking, *recession* is usually defined as a fall in real GDP lasting at least two consecutive calendar quarters. In actuality, the government maintains a Business Cycle Dating Committee to decide when the economy officially enters and leaves a recession.

4 We should note that a recession is not necessary to have cost-push inflation.

Looking Back, page 595

a In mid-1990, residents of the former East Germany turned in their ostmarks, the currency of East Germany, for deutsche marks, the currency of West Germany. In 2002, residents of a United Germany exchanged deutsche marks for euros.

Looking Forward, page 598

a George Melloan, "Don't Bank on the Fed to Ease Future Shocks," *The Wall Street Journal* (November 27, 1995): A17.

Comfort the afflicted and afflict the comfortable.

—Finley Peter Dunne

You must lose a fly to catch a trout.

—George Herbert

25

The Process of Monetary Policy Formulation

Learning Objectives

After reading this chapter, you should know:

The factors that guide the policy process

The various lags in the policy process

How and why the performance of the economy can differ from policy makers' objectives

What intermediate targets are and how they are related to the ultimate policy goals

How monetary policy is formulated by the Federal Open Market Committee (FOMC) and the major pitfalls of that process

Setting the Stage

It's the regular mid-month meeting of the Federal Open Market Committee (FOMC). The chair orders the huge doors to the Fed's impressive conference room closed and calls the meeting to order. In his opening remarks, he suggests that the ensuing discussion focus on policy actions that will raise the inflation rate and increase the cyclical fluctuation of the economy over the next 12 to 18 months.

We hope that the last sentence has startled you! Something is wrong. Policy makers and professors consistently tell us that policy actions are directed at reducing the inflation rate and decreasing cyclical fluctuations. If this is so, however, why did the United States experience two recessions at the beginning of the 1980s, a third recession at the beginning of the 1990s, and a fourth recession in the early 2000s? Why do the unemployment rate and/or the inflation rate periodically rise to unacceptable levels? Are maladies that strike the economy avoidable? Are they the result of bad luck or bad policy making? What role do economics and politics play?

In the last chapter, we discussed the major goals of monetary policy, which include sustainable economic growth, full employment, stable prices, and a satisfactory external balance. The Fed is charged with designing and implementing economic policies that will enhance the health and performance of the U.S. economy and achieve these goals. This chapter provides an overview of the monetary policy process with particular emphasis on what guides the plans of policy makers, how those plans get translated into actions, and how and why, despite good intentions, the performance of the economy can differ from policy makers' objectives. The discussion connects the world of theory to the real world in which policy is made. The approach is also general, leaving the specifics of policy to the next chapter.

The Policy Process

The essential elements of the policy process and the problems surrounding the conduct of monetary policy can be illustrated with the aid of Exhibit 25-1 on page 605 The policy goals, combined with the expected economic performance, guide policy actions, which then, in turn, alter spending, saving, borrowing, and lending decisions. Study this exhibit carefully because the rest of the chapter focuses in some detail on the elements and linkages it depicts.

At first glance, the challenges facing policy makers do not seem that imposing: Compare the expected performance of the economy to the goals. If the economy's performance is expected to be close to the goals, leave the policy unchanged; if the economy's performance is expected to fall well short of the goals, alter the policy accordingly. The reasoning is so simple and seemingly sensible that it leads one to wonder how policy and policy makers can ever go astray. Any policy maker, however, will tell you that making policy is both difficult and frustrating, laden with a never-ending series of problems and pitfalls. Obviously, we need to reflect a bit more deeply about the process depicted in Exhibit 25-1.

We begin with some specific questions about some basic generalities. How do policy makers figure out what the expected performance of the goal variables is likely to be? How do they decide what to do if they believe action is called for? Once they act, how do they know the actions taken are sufficient?

To begin, let's assume policy makers have already established goals and numerical objectives, as discussed in Chapter 24. The next step as depicted in Exhibit 25-1 is to determine the likely performance of the economy if policy remains unchanged. How do policy makers do this?

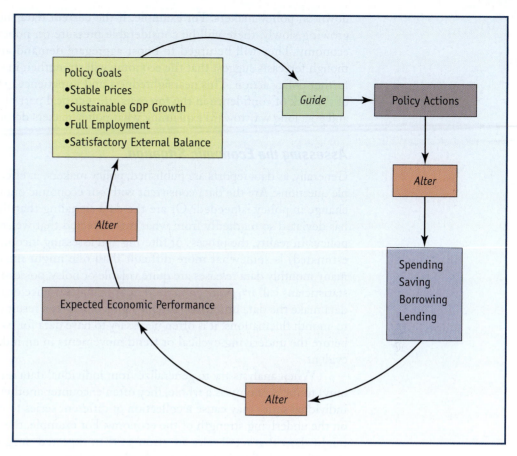

The basic approach is to use various statistical methods and models, judgment based on historical experience, and incoming data on the full range of factors comprising and determining aggregate demand and aggregate supply to develop a forecast for the variables of major concern such as real gross domestic product (GDP), inflation, the unemployment rate, and exchange rates. The data that are used include information about retail sales, industrial production, consumer confidence, business capital spending plans, wages, personal income, profits, and the external balance of payments. Assuming it is January, forecasts for key variables typically cover the first quarter of the year (January to March) and extend over a 12- to 18-month horizon. If the incoming data and the forecasts suggest the economy's performance is deviating significantly from the goals and priorities, the policy makers will consider a change in policy to move the economy's likely performance closer to the goals.

Current Conditions versus Forecasts

Two aspects of the forecasts and incoming data used by policy makers deserve special note. First, forecasting is an imperfect science, so forecasting errors can be fairly large. The greater the volatility in economic variables, the larger the errors tend to be. Because of the possibility of significant errors, policy makers typically do not give heavy weight to forecasts in policy discussions.

Second, there is a strong tendency to focus on incoming data and to use them to guide policy. These figures, which define "current economic conditions," attract considerable media attention and generate much of the political pressure that periodically bears down on policy makers. For example, if the current data suggest that the economy is growing slowly, there will be considerable pressure on policy makers to stimulate the economy. They will be urged to boost aggregate demand and economic growth even though forecasts suggest that the economy will strengthen in six to nine months without further policy action. This nearsightedness and impatience, which are partly a reflection of the lack of confidence in the forecasts, are a critical part of the policy-making process and go a long way toward explaining what policy makers do or fail to do.

Assessing the Economic Situation

Generally, as data reports are published, policy makers, in effect, ask themselves two simple questions: Are the data consistent with our economic outlook and desires, so that no change in policy is needed? Or are the data signaling that the economy's performance has deviated so markedly from what was expected that we should consider a change in policy? In reality, the process of filtering and assessing incoming data (much of which is estimated) is somewhat more difficult than one might imagine. The problem is that many monthly data releases are quite volatile or noisy, possessing a large element of what statisticians call *irregular variance*. The irregular variance or random fluctuations in the data make the data unreliable as policy indicators. As a result of potentially large month-to-month fluctuations, it is often necessary to have data for two to three months on hand before the underlying cyclical or trend movements in an individual data series become evident.

When analysts try to generalize from individual data series (or sectors of the economy) to the economy as a whole, they often encounter another problem. The noise in the individual series may cause a collection of different series to transmit conflicting signals on the underlying strength of the economy. For example, the data reported for February might show that retail sales are stronger than expected, suggesting that the rate of consumption spending is increasing. At the same time, new orders for capital goods and housing starts are weak, suggesting that the rate of business fixed investment and residential investment spending is slowing. Here again, if the economy is in fact deviating from its expected track, it will usually take several months of data releases covering the full spectrum of the economy's performance before the ambiguities in the monthly data are resolved. In sum, policy makers need time to recognize that a change in the economy's performance has occurred. This time between a significant and unexpected change in the economy's performance and policy makers' recognition of that change is called the **recognition lag** in the policy-making process.

Recognition Lag
The time it takes policy makers to recognize that a change in the economy's performance has occurred.

From Assessment to Action

As evidence begins to accumulate that the economy is deviating significantly from the desired path, a consensus develops among policy makers that policy needs to be altered. For example, if the economy is strengthening considerably and inflationary pressures are building, there is a need to reduce the growth of aggregate demand somewhat. At this point, the focus shifts from assessing the economy and considering whether anything needs to be done to deciding exactly what should be done. What policy tools should be used, how large or small should the policy adjustment be, and when should the policy change take place?[1]

Resolving these questions takes time, however. The net result is that policy actions can be paralyzed for a while and policy makers may do too little too late. In any event, the policy-making process includes a **policy lag**—the time between the point when the need for action is recognized and the point when an adjustment policy is decided upon and set in motion.

Policy Lag
The time between the point when the need for action is recognized and the point when an adjustment policy is decided on and set in motion.

From Action to Effect

When policy makers act, does the economy respond immediately? In general, the answer is no. The policy action will set in motion a series of adjustments in the economy that will gradually alter the performance of the economy relative to what it would have been in the absence of any new policy actions. To illustrate, suppose that the economy has been growing quickly with inflation accelerating, and the Fed decides to pursue a more restrictive monetary policy. To cut the growth in aggregate demand, the Fed takes actions that reduce the supply of funds, and interest rates rise. Will firms cut their investment spending right away? Not necessarily. If a new plant is half completed, capacity utilization in its existing plants is high, and the demand for a firm's products is expected to remain fairly strong for the foreseeable future, then the firm (and other firms like it) will continue spending on investment projects. Gradually, however, as the rise in interest rates and reduction in the availability of funds slow the growth of aggregate demand, sales and capacity utilization will fall, and expectations about the future will be modified. At this point, investment spending plans will be reevaluated and possibly postponed or canceled, leading to a further deceleration in the growth of aggregate demand.

On the aggregate supply side, the slowing of the growth in aggregate demand will be associated with a downward revision in price expectations and an adjustment of wages and other input prices. Here again, historical experience suggests that this process will be gradual rather than instantaneous.

The net result is an **impact lag** in monetary policy—that is, the time between when an action is taken and when that action has a significant impact on prices, employment, and output. How much time you ask? Available research suggests that significant effects generally begin to show up after six months to a year or more and continue accumulating for several years. However, some analysts suggest that one of the effects of the Fed's policy of increased openness in the last decade has been to shorten this lag. Exhibit 25-2 below brings together the various lags comprising the policy process.

Impact Lag
The time between when an action is taken and when that action has a significant impact on economic variables.

25-2

Lags in the Policy Process

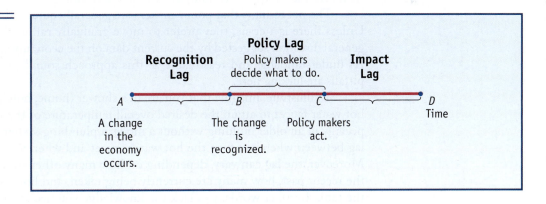

The economy begins to need corrective action at point *A*, but the need is not recognized until point *B* three months later. The time that elapses between point *A* and point *B* is called the *recognition lag*. Between point *B* and point *C*, policy makers think about what actions to take and reach a decision. The time that elapses between point *B* and point *C* is called the *policy lag*. Once action has been taken at point *C*, it takes time before the economy's performance is materially affected. The distance from point *C* to point *D* represents this *impact lag*.

Policy goals combined with expected economic performance guide policy actions. Policy makers tend to give more weight to incoming data about current economic conditions than to forecasts, which can be unreliable. The recognition lag is the time that it takes for policy makers to recognize that economic conditions have changed and that a policy change is necessary. The policy lag is the time between the recognition of the need for action and the implementation of the policy adjustment. The impact lag is the time that it takes for the policy action to have a significant impact on the economy.

Pitfalls in Policy Making

Despite good intentions, policy does not always produce an economic performance that closely coincides with the nation's economic objectives. There are no simple explanations for the periodic lack of correspondence between policy makers' plans and economic performance. As in all endeavors, honest mistakes can be made, analysis can be faulty, and unexpected events beyond the policy makers' control can occur. Against this background, let's briefly examine some of the most prominent problems affecting the successful conduct of policy.

Uncertainty and Lags

Our discussion of the impact lag for policy suggests that economic developments today are largely the result of policies pursued over the past several years. Logically, then, given such lags, policy makers can do little today to materially affect the current performance of the economy. What policy makers can do is affect the future performance of the economy. As we all know, however, the future cannot be known with certainty. Because economic forecasts, in particular, can be quite wide of the mark, policy makers cannot know for certain what, if anything, should be done today to improve the economy's future performance. To complicate matters further, the large month-to-month fluctuations in economic data that we discussed earlier prevent policy makers from knowing with certainty how the economy is currently performing.

The net result is that policy makers are generally quite cautious in adjusting policy. Unless there is a crisis, they prefer to move gradually rather than precipitously in the general direction suggested by the current data on the economy and the policy objectives. As understandable and reasonable as this approach sounds, some potentially serious pitfalls are lurking here.

To illustrate, imagine that you are in a shower (home, hotel, or dorm) adjusting the hot water faucet to attain the desired overall temperature of the water. The problem, especially in an older building without a modern plumbing system, is that there is often a lag between when you turn the hot water faucet and when the water becomes warmer. Moreover, the lag can vary, depending on how many other showers have been taken in the recent past, how many are currently being taken, and how much hot water is left in the tank. In other words, you lack the knowledge you need to fine-tune the hot water. When nothing happens after several gradual adjustments, you grow increasingly impatient and keep turning the knob. At some point, a rush of scalding water bursts out and you burn yourself. You never intended to burn yourself, but it happened anyway.

Policy makers have the same problem. They don't really intend, for example, to raise the inflation rate (and get burned), but it happens. The economy is performing sluggishly and policy makers want to increase economic growth. They increase aggregate demand (turn up the heat), but nothing seems to happen. They—and the nation—become increasingly impatient and undertake further demand-increasing policy actions.

Eventually, economic growth spurts ahead at an excessive pace, causing an unintended acceleration of inflation. Hopefully, increased knowledge will enable economic policy makers to take more precise actions, just as a modern plumbing system allows you to adjust the water temperature precisely.

In sum, the existence of lags in an uncertain world complicates policy makers' efforts to act appropriately in a timely fashion regardless of whether contractionary or inflationary forces are building in the economy. More specifically, acting or failing to act today may aggravate inflation and cyclical fluctuations later. The economy may be destabilized rather than stabilized. In the case of recession, the push to do something now to improve the current situation as soon as possible interacts with the difficulties associated with lags and uncertainty and may lead to higher inflation later. In the case of inflationary pressures, the pressure not to do something now may, as they say, let the horse out of the barn. When there is pressure "to do something now" or "not to do something now," consistent formulation and implementation of policies conducive to economic growth and stability become even more problematic.

Data Revisions and Policy Regret

Some economic data series such as exchange rates, stock prices, and nominal interest rates are directly observable and not subject to revision. Other data, such as those on employment and unemployment, nominal and real GDP, and inflation rates, are based on sample estimates that may be subject to numerous revisions as more accurate information becomes available. We have already noted that such incoming data are subject to a great deal of white noise or random fluctuation. Policy decisions are based on incoming data that are available when the decisions are made. Data used in policy actions, such as those on output or overall prices levels, are ofen subject to numerous revisions. **Policy regret** occurs if revised data estimates suggest that some other course of action should have and would have been taken if the revised data had been available. For example, the Fed generally considers how far actual output is from potential output and how far actual inflation is from the inflation rate associated with stable prices. If actual output and inflation are subject to revisions, policy makers may experience policy regret. Indeed, each additional revision may imply a different optimal policy strategy. In addition, some economic concepts such as potential output and the inflation rate associated with stable prices may also be subject to revision but, as noted earlier in this chapter, we are considering these numerical goals as already having been established. When revised data are used to evaluate past policy decisions, policy actions often appear to be overly accommodative or overly restrictive. In evaluating policy decisions, one must consider the data that were available when the decisions were made. If the data available at the time are used, policy decisions may seem more understandable. Because the Fed is aware of data revisions and the possibility of policy regret, the impetus would be to be more cautious in changing policy. Gradual change of policy reduces the effect of data uncertainty on policy recommendations. All policy actions are based on uncertain data and those that will be revised. However, some data are more uncertain than others. Some analysts suggest that the Fed could base policy actions on data that are less responsive to highly uncertain information or the Fed could respond to data that have been averaged over several time periods. Nevertheless, we hope that you can see how policy actions involve a great deal of skill and luck.

Policy Regret
A situation in which policy actions based on available data would not have been taken if more accurate data revisions had been available.

Globalization: A Financially and Economically Integrated World Economy

A new reality is having a profound influence on the conduct and effectiveness of domestic policies. Simply put, the economies of the world are becoming more interdependent.

What goes on in Tokyo, London, Hong Kong, Paris, and Frankfurt has an increasingly important effect on economic and financial conditions in the United States. Consequently, U.S. policy makers have somewhat less control over the performance of the U.S. economy than in previous eras when the U.S. economy was more isolated from international trade and finance. As a result, the Fed has reached out to other central banks on an informal basis to coordinate monetary policy on numerous occasions. For example, in September 2001, the central banks of Canada, England, and the European Monetary Union engaged in a coordinated interest rate cut shortly after the attacks on the World Trade Center and the Pentagon.

Such interdependencies have given rise to calls for increased cooperation and coordination among world policy makers. Although the difficulties some countries have in coordinating their domestic monetary and fiscal policies suggest that coordinating policies across countries will never be easy, the existence of globalization does highlight the new challenges and complexities facing policy makers.

Policy makers are attempting to meet the challenges of globalization through informal discussions among the major industrialized countries and through international organizations such as the International Monetary Fund and the Bank for International Settlements. These dialogues suggest that to achieve a stable international financial system, countries around the world must have healthy financial systems with noninflationary policies. In addition, countries must standardize the reporting of information about financial markets, institutions, laws, regulations, international reserves, external debt (both short and long term), and the health of the banking sector. Finally, the surveillance of international organizations that oversee the international financial system must be more transparent and open. In such an environment, the full benefits of globalization could be reached while minimizing the costs. For now, we turn to the specifics of how monetary policy is formulated.

Recap   The existence of lags in an uncertain world complicates policy makers' efforts to act appropriately in a timely fashion. In a recession, the push to do something now to improve the current situation as soon as possible interacts with the difficulties associated with lags and uncertainty and may lead to higher inflation later. Data revisions may result in policy regret. In the face of inflation, the pressure not to do something now may cause further instability later. Increased globalization suggests the need for increased global coordination of monetary policy.

Intermediate Targets

Intermediate Target
The use of a target midway between the policy instruments and the ultimate policy goals.

Given these complexities, uncertainties, and time lags, the Fed has long used an **intermediate target** approach to the formulation and implementation of policy rather than focusing on the ultimate goals. The basic idea, illustrated in Exhibit 25-3, is that the Fed selects a variable, such as a monetary aggregate or an interest rate, that is in some sense midway between its policy instruments and the ultimate or final goals or targets of policy.[2] The intermediate target is then used to guide day-to-day open market operations. The rationale is that if the Fed hits the intermediate target, it will come reasonably close to achieving its economic objectives.

How does the Fed select a particular intermediate target and a particular range of values for that variable? For example, the Fed could pick domestic nonfinancial debt (DNFD), the broadest measure of credit, as an intermediate target and choose a growth rate range of 4 to 8 percent. Or it could use an interest rate as an intermediate target and

25-3

The Use of an Intermediate
Target in Hitting the Final
Target

Why an intermediate target? Suppose you have a bow and arrow and desire to hit the center of a target that you can barely see way off in the distance. The bow is your instrument, and the target you really want to hit is your final target. The distance and poor visibility make it difficult, however, for you to hit the final target, so you select an intermediate target—a clearly visible target between you and the less-visible final target. You then align the intermediate target between you and the final target so that if you hit the center of the intermediate target, your arrow will continue on and strike the final target. In this way, you can hit the final target even though you can barely see it.

select a target range such as 3.5 to 4.5 percent for nominal short-term rates. In any case, the basic criteria for selecting an intermediate target variable are related to the characteristics of economic data and policy actions we discussed earlier.

First, the variable should be reliably and, thus, predictably related to the goal variables. If a variable were not so related, hitting the intermediate target range would not necessarily help to achieve the goals, and selecting a target range for the intermediate variable consistent with the economic objectives would be virtually impossible. To illustrate, a sailor traveling between point A and point B will often find it useful to guide the ship by initially aiming for a buoy firmly anchored midway between the two points. If the buoy were floating aimlessly instead of being anchored, it would not be a useful guide. Second, policy makers should be able to observe the intermediate target regularly. That is, the data about the target should be readily available. Third, the Fed should be able to hit the target range of the intermediate variable; that is, it should be able to control the intermediate variable with policy instruments with a reasonable degree of precision. Obviously, a variable that cannot be readily observed and controlled would be of little practical use to policy makers. Our intrepid sailor, for example, would find a navigation buoy of little use without a working compass and good visibility.

From the late 1970s until the early 1990s, the monetary aggregates and DNFD were monitored and used as intermediate targets to guide monetary policy because there was a stable relationship between changes in one or more of the aggregates and the level of economic activity. The Fed set growth target ranges for several aggregates to hedge its bets and to maintain as flexible a position as possible.

Despite setting target ranges for several aggregates, $M1$ was the most closely watched aggregate for use in policy formulation until the early 1980s. However, in the early 1980s, $M1$'s behavior became unstable and erratic, and the Fed de-emphasized its role as an intermediate target. In the mid-1980s, the Fed put more emphasis on changes in $M2$ and $M3$ because they seemed to have the strongest correlation with changes in economic activity. These relationships also became too unstable and unpredictable to be used in gauging policy. In the early 1990s, the strongest correlation seemed to be between changes in DNFD and changes in economic activity. However, the Fed's control over DNFD is far less precise than its control over the monetary aggregates because credit emanates from so many nonbanking sources. Hence, the ability to use DNFD in the implementation of monetary policy is severely limited.

The breakdown in the traditional relationships between monetary aggregates and economic activity caused an abandonment of the use of monetary aggregates as either targets or information variables in the early 1990s. In July 2000, the Fed even stopped providing projections about the growth rates of the monetary aggregates and DNFD.

Other models have fared no better in explaining the inflationary and growth processes. The result is that there is increasing reliance on a broad set of economic indicators to gauge monetary policy that is then implemented through changes in interest rates.

Consequently, since mid-1993, the Fed has emphasized interest rate targeting. Under such a regime, the Fed increases the interest rate target if it perceives a need to slow down the level of economic activity and decreases the target if it perceives a need to speed things up. The Fed carries out this procedure by announcing a target for the fed funds rate and using open market operations to hit the target. In this case, the fed funds rate is an **operating target** that is highly responsive to open market operations, the Fed's main policy tool. The Fed adjusts the fed funds rate with an eye toward raising or lowering other short- and long-term interest rates that are the intermediate target. Other short- and long-term interest rates adjust in response to changes in the fed funds rate. Note that the Fed has more direct control over the operating target than over the intermediate target. The accompanying A Closer Look feature on page 613 discusses the use of operating targets since 1970.

Why has the relationship between some monetary aggregates and economic activity failed to survive over time? Many analysts attribute the breakdown to technological changes in the payments systems and the electronic transfer of funds and to financial innovations that resulted in the creation of new financial instruments and markets. Some believe that the definitions of the aggregates need to be revised and refined to take account of these changes. In addition, deregulation is also believed to have weakened the

Operating Target
A target amenable to control by the policy tools and highly correlated with the intermediate target.

The Use of Operating Targets Since 1970

The ultimate goals of monetary policy are to affect the level of economic activity and the overall price level. As noted in the body of the text, monetary aggregates have historically been used as intermediate targets in the policy process because their behavior has often been related to both the ultimate policy goals and the policy tools that the Fed has available to influence those goals.

Until the 1980s, *M*1 had a stable and predictable relationship with nominal economic activity and, therefore, was the targeted aggregate. Even though control was imprecise in the short term, it was reasonably precise over a longer period, and changes in *M*1 were closely associated with changes in economic activity.

In the 1970s, the Fed sought to exploit the statistical regularity between changes in *M*1 and economic activity. It targeted the fed funds rate (the operating target) in an attempt to achieve the targeted growth rate range for *M*1 (the intermediate target). Under such a regime, if an increase in the demand for credit puts upward pressure on interest rates, including the fed funds rate, the Fed tends to be accommodating. That is, the Fed supplies reserves to the financial system to keep interest rates in their target range. Increases in the demand for credit were accommodated even though doing so led to an expansion of the money supply and caused the Fed to overshoot the *M*1 target range. When the Fed increased the interest rate target, the increase was usually not enough to choke off the demand for credit and keep the monetary aggregates in their target ranges. Consequently, because of the continual overshooting of the monetary aggregate target, this method was abandoned in late 1979.

In the early 1980s, the Fed focused on the level of nonborrowed reserves as the operating target. Nonborrowed reserves are total reserves less those reserves borrowed from the Fed at the discount window. The Fed was convinced that this method would give it more precision in hitting a monetary aggregate target and allow it to have greater direct control over inflation. If the demand for credit went up, the Fed would not increase the supply of nonborrowed reserves. As a result, the fed funds rate would go up. Note that, unlike today, the discount rate was set independently by the Board of Governors of the Fed while the fed funds rate was determined by market forces. In turn, when the fed funds rate increased because of market forces, borrowing reserves at the discount window was relatively cheaper, assuming that discount rate changes were fairly infrequent. The result was that there was more borrowing at the discount window and less borrowing in the fed funds market than there would have been otherwise.[a]

In the mid-1980s, the relationship between *M*1 and economic activity started to break down, and the Fed began placing greater emphasis on the other aggregates, particularly *M*2 and *M*3 as intermediate targets. In the mid-1980s and early 1990s, the Fed used the level of reserves borrowed at the discount window as the operating target. Under this procedure, the Fed picked a level of borrowed reserves that it believed corresponded to the desired growth range of a monetary aggregate. If the demand for credit increased, pushing up the fed funds rate, then the demand for borrowed reserves at the discount window increased. This is so because the fed funds rate had increased relative to the discount rate. To maintain the target range for borrowed reserves, the Fed would be forced to increase the supply of nonborrowed reserves. Consequently, this regime was more accommodating to increases in credit than the regime that targeted nonborrowed reserves. Beginning in the mid-1980s, depository institutions became increasingly reluctant to borrow reserves from the Fed, thus weakening the link between borrowing from the Fed and the fed funds rate. Also, the fed funds rate was often higher than the discount rate because some banks, particularly large ones, were using the fed funds market as a permanent source of funds to lend, not just when they were temporarily caught short of reserves.

In the early 1990s, the relationship between the aggregates $M2$ and $M3$ and the level of economic activity broke down because past relationships no longer held. In the early 1990s, DNFD, the broadest measure of credit, seemed to be the monetary aggregate that was most closely related to economic activity. Because DNFD includes credit extension from sources outside the banking system, however, it is not that amenable to control by the Fed.

In the early 2000s, the Fed stopped announcing target ranges for the monetary aggregates and DNFD. As stated in two monetary policy reports to the Congress in 2000:

> Given continued uncertainty about movements in the velocities of $M2$ and $M3$ (the ratios of nominal GDP to the aggregates), the Committee still has little confidence that money growth within any particular range selected for the year would be associated with the economic performance it expected or desired.[b]

> At its June meeting, the FOMC did not establish ranges for growth of money and debt in 2000 and 2001. Owing to uncertainties about the behavior of debt and money, these ranges for many years have not provided useful benchmarks for the conduct of monetary policy.[c]

As a consequence of all these changes, today the Fed uses the fed funds rate as the operating target and explicitly announces its short-term objective for that target after each FOMC meeting.

link between some monetary aggregates and economic activity by contributing to the decline in depository institutions' share of intermediation.

The Use of Interest Rates as Intermediate Targets

In the past, the use of interest rates as intermediate targets has been criticized for having either an inflationary or a recessionary bias. For example, let's assume that the Fed is targeting an interest rate at a given level and that aggregate demand increases. The increase in demand could emanate from the household, business, government, or foreign sector. In any case, the increase causes the demand for money and credit to increase also, as shown in Exhibit 25-4 on page 615. The demand curve shifts from D to D', creating upward pressure on the interest rate because the quantity demanded is greater than the quantity supplied at the targeted rate, i_T. To maintain the interest rate target, the Fed will merely accommodate the increases in demand by supplying more reserves, causing money and credit to expand. Down the road, such accommodation can lead to inflation. If inflation does increase, this will put upward pressure on nominal interest rates. To fight this pressure, the Fed must ease even more, creating more pressure, and the cycle accelerates.

Likewise, if there is a comparable drop-off in aggregate demand, the Fed will reduce the supply of money to prevent the interest rate from falling. In this case, the drop in demand is exacerbated by the Fed's action, and the downturn is greater than it would be otherwise.

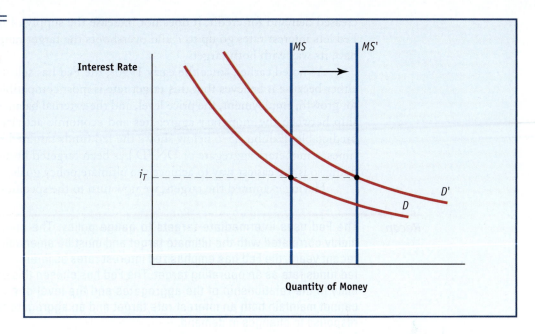

25-4

Maintaining an Interest Rate Target

One final point needs to be emphasized. At any time, the Fed can control either an interest rate target or an aggregate target, but not both. For example, assume that the Fed has both a monetary aggregate target (M_T) and an interest rate target (i_T) and that the demand for credit suddenly increases, as depicted in Exhibit 25-5 below. In such a situation, if the Fed is more concerned about maintaining the interest rate target in the face of the increased credit demand, it must use open market operations to increase the supply of reserves. When it does so, credit and, hence, the monetary aggregates are allowed to expand, and the Fed overshoots the monetary aggregate target range as the money supply increases to M'. Serious overshooting of the monetary target can also defeat the interest rate target as inflation sets in. If the Fed is more concerned about hitting the monetary aggregate target range, then, in the face of in-

25-5

Targeting Both an Interest Rate and an Aggregate????

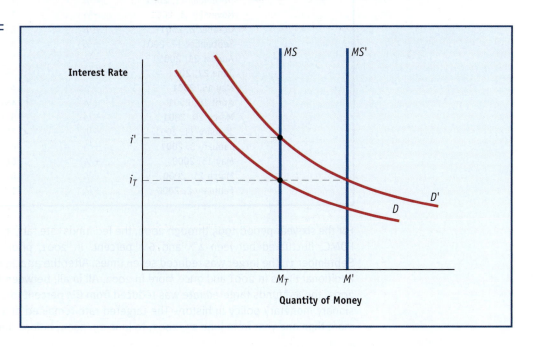

creased demand for credit, it does not increase the supply of reserves. In this case, the Fed lets interest rates go up to i' and overshoots the target range. Thus, the Fed cannot have its way with both targets.

As noted earlier, since the early 1990s, the Fed has selected an interest rate target either because it believes that this target rate is most compatible with the ultimate goals for growth, employment, the price level, and the external balance or because the relationship between the monetary aggregates and economic activity is no longer stable and predictable. Exhibit 25-6 below shows the fed funds targeted rate since 2000. At other times, a monetary aggregate or DNFD has been targeted because the Fed believes that doing so is the easiest way to achieve the ultimate policy goals.

Having examined the targets, we now turn to the specifics of how policy is framed.

Recap	The Fed uses intermediate targets to gauge policy. The intermediate target must be highly correlated with the ultimate target and must be amenable to control by the Fed. In recent years, the Fed has emphasized interest rates as intermediate targets and used the fed funds rate as an operating target. The Fed has chosen this path because of the instability in the relationship of the aggregates and the level of economic activity. The Fed cannot maintain both an interest rate target and an aggregate target at the same time in response to changes in demand.

25-6

Changes in the Fed Funds Targeted (2000–2004)

	Fed Funds Rate (Percent)	
Date of Change	**Change**	**New Level**
December 14, 2004	$+1/4\%$	$2 1/4\%$
November 10, 2004	$+1/4$	2
September 21, 2004	$+1/4$	$1 3/4$
August 10, 2004	$+1/4$	$1 1/2$
June 30, 2004	$+1/4$	$1 1/4$
June 25, 2003	$-1/4$	1
November 2002	$-1/2$	$1 1/4$
December 11, 2001	$-1/4$	$1 3/4$
November 6, 2001	$-1/2$	2
October 2, 2001	$-1/2$	$2 1/2$
September 17, 2001	$-1/2$	3
August 21, 2001	$-1/4$	$3 1/2$
June 27, 2001	$-1/4$	$3 3/4$
May 15, 2001	$-1/2$	4
April 18, 2001	$-1/2$	$4 1/2$
March 20, 2001	$-1/2$	5
January 31, 2001	$-1/2$	$5 1/2$
January 3, 2001	$-1/2$	6
May 16, 2000	$+1/2$	$6 1/2$
March 21, 2000	$+1/4$	6
February 2, 2000	$+1/4$	$5 3/4$

For the six-year period 1995 through 2000, the fed funds rate target, which is established by the FOMC, fluctuated between $4 3/4$ and $6 1/2$ percent. In 2001, prior to the Terrorist Attack on September 11, the target was reduced seven times. After the attack, the target was reduced four additional times in 2001 and once more in 2002. All in all, between May 15, 2000, and June 25, 2003, the fed funds targeted rate was reduced from $6 1/2$ percent to 1 percent in the most expansionary monetary policy in history. The targeted rate remained at 1 percent, a historic low, for more than one year from June 23, 2003, to June 25, 2004, before "measured" increases began.

Federal Open Market Committee Decisions

Economic Projections

Goals for nominal and real GDP, unemployment, and inflation over the next 12 to 18 months, set by the Fed at its February and July meetings each year.

Price Index for Personal Consumption Expenditures (PCE)

A price index that measures changes in overall prices that consumers pay; its changes are broader measures of consumer inflation than changes in the consumer price index (CPI) and are used by the Fed in economic projections of inflation.

Core PCE

The PCE excluding energy and food.

The FOMC establishes **economic projections** (goals) for nominal and real GDP, unemployment, and inflation at its meetings in February and July of each year. Prior to July 2004, the **price index for personal consumption expenditures (PCE)**, which is a broader measure than the consumer price index (CPI) of overall prices that consumers pay, was used in the projection for inflation. Beginning in July 2004, the price index for personal consumption expenditures, excluding food and energy (the **core PCE**) is used. The FOMC believes that the core PCE is a better indicator of underlying inflation. The projections are usually for 12 to 18 months. In compliance with the 1978 Humphrey- Hawkins Act, the chair of the Fed reports these long-term forecasts to Congress shortly after the meetings. Exhibit 25-7 below shows the forecasts presented to Congress in July 2004.

FOMC members believe that the forecasts are consistent with the long-term policy goals and are likely to emerge over the coming year. At the six other FOMC meetings over the course of the year (in addition to the February and July meetings), the long-term goals are reviewed and sometimes revised, but emphasis is on the short-term strategies.

Once the long-term policy stance is set, the focus of the FOMC shifts to the immediate period. In most periods, the policy discussions center on the fed funds rate itself, as well as other interest rates. As noted previously, interest rates have gained center stage as intermediate targets since the mid-1990s.

At the same time, in the late 1990s and early 2000s, policy has been somewhat eclectic, and "the process of probing a variety of data to ascertain underlying economic and financial conditions has become even more essential to formulating sound monetary policy."[3] As a result, the Fed now looks at many indicators.

Despite the independence, strong leadership, and eclectic nature of the Fed, an old controversy of how much discretion the Fed should have continually resurfaces at various times, sometimes more strongly than others. Now would be a good time to read the accompanying A Closer Look on Rules Versus Discretion on page 618 that weighs in on the controversy.

25-7

Economic Projections for 2004 and 2005

Board of Governors and Reserve Bank Presidents	
Indicator	**Central Tendency**
2004	
Change, fourth quarter to fourth quarter[a]	
Nominal GDP	$6\frac{1}{4}$ to $6\frac{3}{4}$
Real GDP	$4\frac{1}{2}$ to $4\frac{3}{4}$
PCE prices	$1\frac{3}{4}$ to 2
Average level, fourth quarter	
Civilian unemployment	$5\frac{1}{4}$ to $5\frac{1}{2}$
2005	
Change, fourth quarter to fourth quarter[a]	
Nominal GDP	$5\frac{1}{4}$ to 6
Real GDP	$3\frac{1}{2}$ to 4
PCE prices	$1\frac{1}{2}$ to 2
Average level, fourth quarter	
Civilian unemployment	5 to $5\frac{1}{4}$

[a] Change from average for fourth quarter of previous year to average for fourth quarter of year indicated.

SOURCE: *Monetary Report to the Congress* (July 2004). Available on the Internet at **http://www.federalreserve.gov/BoardDocs/HH2004/July/ful lreport.htm**.

A Closer Look

Monetary Rules Versus Discretionary Risk Management

Monetary policy could be implemented following a prescribed rule such as targeting a given inflation rate, a given money supply growth rate, a certain interest rate, or some other criteria. Regardless of how the economy functions, the central bank would follow the prescribed rule, which would be set by some governmental authority. On the other hand, the central bank could be autonomous and maintain a great deal of discretion in the formulation of policy.

In recent years, the Fed has been chaired by a strong leader who has aspired to an "eclectic" approach to monetary policy with a great deal of discretion. This discretion has focused on risk management where the risks range from "well-defined to the truly unknown."[a] Hence, the full range of outcomes and their probabilities are not known. Accordingly, monetary policy involves a great deal of judgment in evaluating the different risks and their probabilities. Consequently, discretion is a mainstay in policy formulation.

Some analysts have always questioned, however, the amount of freedom a central bank should have in deciding monetary policy. The controversy can be summarized by the following: Should the Fed be tied to a simple policy rule, or should it have a great deal of discretion in deciding policy actions?

Perhaps the best known advocate for rules is Nobel-laureate Milton Friedman, who suggested that the money supply should grow at a steady, publicly stated rate. The growth rate in the money supply over the long run would compensate for the growth in output and, therefore, stabilize the price level. This would reduce the uncertainty about what the Fed was up to. Advocates of such a rule argue that the effectiveness of discretionary policy is limited by data measurement errors, unknown and variable lags, changing relationships among variables, and political pressures to ease policy. Thus, to stabilize the economy, the best the Fed can do is to adopt to a rule to which it sticks, which removes the uncertainty surrounding what the Fed does.

In recent decades, others have pointed out that there is a time inconsistency problem in monetary policy. For example, a time inconsistency problem exists if you eat dessert today but intend to diet tomorrow but when tomorrow comes, you decide not to diet. Another example is smoking, where pleasure is in the present. In both examples, the cost of the action (or inaction) includes health problems, shortened lifespan, and so on, which are in the future. In monetary policy, an example of a time inconsistency problem is the benevolent Fed's stimulation of the economy today in a recession while anticipating that it will slow the economy tomorrow to prevent an inflationary boom. When tomorrow comes, what seemed optimal before now appears less than optimal, and policy ends up having an inflationary bias. Furthermore, without a rule, market participants are always guessing what the Fed's next move will be, increasing uncertainty and instability, which is the opposite of what the Fed is supposed to do.

On the other hand, a strong case for discretion was perhaps best made by Chair Greenspan:

Uncertainty is not just an important feature of the monetary policy landscape: it is the defining characteristic of that landscape. As a consequence, the conduct of monetary policy in the United States at its core involves crucial elements of risk management, a process that requires an understanding of the many sources of risk and uncertainty that policymakers face and the quantifying of those risks when possible. It also entails devising, in light of those risks, a strategy for policy directed at maximizing the probabilities of achieving over time our goal of price stability and the maximum sustainable economic growth that we associate with it. . . .

In implementing a risk-management approach to policy, we must confront the fact that only a limited number of risks can be quantified with any confidence. . . .As a result, risk management often involves significant judgment on the part of policy-makers, as we evaluate the risks of different events and the probability that our actions will alter those risks. For such judgment, we policymakers, rather than rely-ing solely on the specific linkages expressed in our formal models, have tended to draw from broader, though less mathematically precise, hypotheses of how the world works.

Some critics have argued that such an approach to policy is too undisciplined—judgmental, seemingly discretionary, and difficult to explain. The Federal Reserve should, some conclude, attempt to be more formal in its operations by tying its ac-tions solely to the prescriptions of a formal policy rules. That any approach along these lines would lead to an improvement in economic performance, however, is highly doubtful. Our problem is not the complexity of our models but the far greater complexity of a world economy whose underlying linkages appear to be in a continual state of flux. Rules by their nature are simple, and when significant and shifting uncertainties exist in the economic environment, they cannot substi-tute for risk-management paradigms, which are far better suited to policymaking. Were we to introduce an interest rate rule, how would we judge the meaning of a rule that posits a rate far above or below the current rate? Should policymakers adjust the current rate to that suggested by the rule? Should we conclude that this deviation is normal variance and disregard the signal? Or should we assume that the parameters of the rule are misspecified and adjust them to fit the current rate? Given errors in our underlying data, coupled with normal variance, we might not know the correct course of action for a considerable time. Partly for these reasons, the prescriptions of formal interest rate rules are best view only as helpful adjuncts to policy, as indeed many proponents of policy rules have suggested. In summary, then, monetary policy based on risk management appears to be the most useful regime by which to conduct policy. The increasingly intricate economic and finan-cial linkages in our global economy, in my judgment, compel such a conclusion.[b]

Perhaps the best solution would be something in the middle such as limited discre-tion but with an absolute inflation cap. Under such a rule, the Fed would have unlimited discretion as long as inflation or monetary growth is kept below a certain level. If it goes above this level, the Fed would have to follow the monetary rule of maximum inflation. In reality, as noted in Chapter 4, the Fed is probably constrained by what is politically accept-able. Recall that what Congress has created, Congress can uncreate, and if the Fed adopted a policy that was politically unacceptable, such as double-digit inflation, Congress could be quick to act. A popular suggestion and one followed by the Bank of England would be to announce an inflation target and implement policy so as to hit that target. With the Bank of England today operating via an explicit inflation target, policy makers' discretion is lim-ited. Not so for the Fed.

Given its assessment of current economic conditions and the economic outlook, the FOMC comes up with short-term (usually quarterly) policy goals consistent with its longer-range goals. Against this background, the FOMC issues a policy directive to the Trading Desk of the New York Fed that guides the conduct of open market operations until the next FOMC meeting in approximately six weeks.[4] The policy directive states a specific fed funds rate that the New York Fed is to target. In the next chapter, we look at the specifics of how the directive is implemented.

Recap   The Fed sets long-term growth ranges for nominal and real GDP and prices. The long-term policy goals reflect recent and prospective inflationary and unemployment outlooks. Given the long-range goals, the short-term specifications that guide monetary policy between FOMC meetings are set. In recent years, the Fed has looked to interest rates to guide policy.

Summary of Major Points

1. In general, a comparison between the expected performance of the economy and the economic goals guides policy actions. More specifically, given the goals and corresponding numerical objectives, policy makers establish priorities among the goals, develop the expected performance of the economy, and implement particular policy actions. If the economy's performance is expected to be close to the goals, policy is likely to remain unchanged. Conversely, if the economy's performance is expected to deviate markedly from the goals, policy will be altered.

2. Given the relatively large size of forecasting errors, policy makers tend to focus on incoming data and current conditions in considering policy adjustments.

3. The policy process involves three lags: the recognition lag, the policy lag, and the impact lag. The recognition lag is the length of time it takes for policy makers to recognize that an unexpected and significant change in the economy's performance has occurred. The policy lag is the time between the point when the need for action is recognized and when an adjustment policy is decided on and set in motion. The impact lag is the time between when an action is taken and when that action has a significant effect on prices, output, and employment.

4. The existence of lags in an uncertain world makes it difficult for policy makers to act appropriately in a timely fashion. Their actions today may increase price and cyclical fluctuations later, so they tend to be quite cautious in adjusting policy. Policy regret occurs when policy actions would not have been taken if data revisions had been available when the decisions were made. Policy regret can never be eliminated but can be reduced by basing policy actions on data that are less likely to be significantly revised or that are revised over several time periods.

5. The growing interdependence among the world's economies implies that U.S. policy makers have somewhat less control over the performance of the U.S. economy than previously, a factor that adds to the challenges and complexities facing policy makers.

6. Because of the complexities and lags involved with monetary policy, the Fed uses intermediate targets to policy. The basic idea is that the Fed selects a variable, such as a monetary aggregate or an interest rate, midway between its policy instruments and the ultimate or final goals or targets of policy. The intermediate target is then used to guide day-to-day open market operations. The rationale is that if the Fed hits the intermediate target, it will come reasonably close to achieving its economic objectives.

7. In past decades, at times one aggregate has been more closely related to the level of economic activity than at other times. Since the early 1990s, the monetary aggregates have been de-emphasized in favor of an interest rate target. The reason for this change is that the relationship between economic activity and the monetary aggregates had become unstable and difficult to predict since the early 1990s. The

Fed has opted for an eclectic approach of looking at a variety of indicators to gauge policy. The Fed can control either an interest rate target or an aggregate target but not both simultaneously.

8. The FOMC develops long-term policy goals and chooses among short-term policy options to achieve these goals. The major factors influencing the long-term policy decisions at any point in time include (1) recent and prospective inflationary pressures, (2) the current and prospective pace of economic expansion, especially with reference to the economy's growth potential and degree of capacity utilization, and (3) recent and prospective movements in the unemployment rate.

9. The major factors influencing the selection of the short-term specifications are current economic and financial conditions such as recent data on inflation, real growth, the exchange rate, and prevailing expectations, including those about policy.

10. The FOMC issues a directive to the Trading Desk of the New York Fed that guides the conduct of monetary policy until the next FOMC meeting.

Key Terms

Core PCE, **617**
Economic Projections, **617**
Impact Lag, **607**
Intermediate Target, **610**

Operating Target, **612**
Policy Lag, **606**
Policy Regret, **609**

Price Index for Personal Consumption Expenditures (PCE), **617**
Recognition Lag, **606**

Review Questions

1. What are the ultimate targets of monetary policy?
2. What is an intermediate target? Why does the Fed use intermediate targets instead of focusing on the ultimate targets? What is an operating target?
3. What is the recognition lag? The policy lag? The impact lag?
4. How would the recognition, policy, and impact lags differ with regard to monetary and fiscal policy? What role does uncertainty play?
5. Are current incoming economic data or forecasts more important in guiding monetary policy? Why?
6. When is it most difficult to interpret incoming data? (*Hint:* Consider the case in which retail sales are weak but new orders for capital goods are strong, etc.)
7. What is *policy regret?* What are some of the strategies that the Fed could use to minimize policy regret?
8. Why can short-term goals sometimes differ from long-term goals?

9. What is an irregular variance? How does it affect Fed behavior?
10. What are some common intermediate targets that the Fed has used to guide policy in recent years? Give two criteria for intermediate targets.
11. Why can't the Fed target both an interest rate and a monetary aggregate simultaneously?
12. Assume that the Fed is targeting the money supply and the demand for money falls. Explain why interest rates will fall.
13. Assume that the Fed is targeting an interest rate and the demand for money increases. Explain why the money supply will increase.
14. "The Fed should do everything it can to eliminate inflation." Do you agree? Explain.
15. Can using an interest rate as an intermediate target ever have an inflationary bias? Explain.

Analytical Questions

16. Find the minutes of the most recent FOMC meeting, either at the library in the *Federal Reserve Bulletin* or on the Internet at **www.federalreserve.gov**. (Because the FOMC meets about every six weeks, minutes appear in 8 of the 12 monthly issues of the *Federal Reserve Bulletin*.) Summarize the policy directive.

17. Assume that the Fed is targeting an interest rate and aggregate demand drops. Show graphically why the Fed will have to reduce the supply of money to maintain the interest rate target.

18. Use a graph to explain why the Fed cannot target both an interest rate and a monetary aggregate at the same time, assuming that there is a drop in aggregate demand.

Internet Exercises

1. Find out the unique responsibility of the New York Fed in conducting domestic and international monetary policy by accessing the following Web site: **http://www. newyorkfed.org/aboutthefed/fedpoint/fed13.html**.

2. Access the minutes of the most recent meeting of the FOMC from the following Internet site: **http://www.federalreserve.gov/fomc/#calendars**. Summarize the minutes, the policy directive, and the statement that was released to the public along with the policy directive.

Suggested Readings

The minutes of each FOMC meeting, including the directive, are published in the *Federal Reserve Bulletin* each month immediately after the minutes are released. They make extremely interesting reading. This information is also available on the Internet site of the Federal Reserve Board at **http://www.federalreserve.gov/**.

For an updated look at monetary policy, see "U.S. Monetary Policy: An Introduction, Parts 1, 2, 3, and 4," *Federal Reserve Bank of San Francisco, Economics Letters, Numbers 2004-01, 02, 03, and 04* (January 16, 23, 30, 2004, and February 6, 2004, respectively.

An article that looks at the "rules versus discretion" debate is Douglas Clement, "The Veil of Discretion: Does the Fed Have Too Much Freedom," *The Region,* Federal Reserve Bank of Minneapolis, 18:2 (June 2004): 10.

For a look at a risk management approach to policy, see "Monetary Policy Under Uncertainty," remarks by Chair Greenspan at a symposium sponsored by the Federal Reserve Bank of Kansas City, Jackson Hole, Wyoming (August 29, 2003). The remarks are available on the Internet at **http://www.kc.frb.org/Publicat/ sympos/2003/pdf/Greenspan.0902.2003.pdf**.

For a look at issues involving policy regret, see Sharon Kozicki, "How Do Data Revisions Affect the Evaluation and Conduct of Monetary Policy?" *Economic Review, Federal Reserve Bank of Kansas City* 89:1 (First Quarter 2004): 5–35.

Stephen G. Cecchitti, "Policy Rules and Targets: Framing the Central Banker's Problem," discusses many of the topics in this chapter. It can be found in the *Federal Reserve Bank of New York, Economic Policy Review* 4:2 (June 1998): 1–14. For a reliable reference *Guide to Economic Indicators*, see the Norman Frumkin's book by the same name (Armonk, NY: M.E. Sharpe, 2000).

For a look at the nature and consequences of uncertainty in monetary policy formation, see Jan Marc Berk's *The Preparation of Monetary Policy* (Norwell, MA: Kluwer Academic Press, 2000).

For a discussion that relates higher inflation in a country to a relatively larger financial sector, see Michael Frenkel, "Inflation and the Misallocation of Resources," *Economic Inquiry* 38:4 (October 2000): 616–628.

For a fascinating, in-depth description of an FOMC meeting, see Laurence H. Meyer, "Come with Me to the FOMC," *The*

Region (June 1998): 6–15, published by the Federal Reserve Bank of Minneapolis.

An easy-to-read and comprehensive book from which much of the material in this chapter is drawn is *U.S. Monetary Policy and Financial Markets* by Ann-Marie Meulendyke (1998). It can be obtained free for the asking from the Federal Reserve Bank of New York, 33 Liberty Street, New York, NY 10045.

Arturo Estrella and Frederic S. Mishkin ask, "Is There a Role for the Monetary Aggregates in the Conduct of Monetary Policy?" *Journal of Monetary Economics* 40:2 (October 1997): 279–304.

For an interesting article that deals with topics in the chapter, see Alan S. Blinder, "Distinguished Lecture on Economics in Government: What Central Bankers Could Learn from Academics—and Vice Versa," *Journal of Economic Perspectives* 11 (Spring 1997): 3–19.

For an article that looks at monetary policy in Canada, Sweden, the United Kingdom, and the United States, see George A. Kahn and Klara Parrish, "Conducting Monetary Policy with Inflation Targets," *Economic Review of the Federal Reserve Bank of Kansas City* (Third Quarter 1998): 5–32.

Endnotes

1   This aspect of the policy-making process, especially in the case of fiscal policy, can be agonizingly slow. It's one thing to decide to cut aggregate demand by reducing government spending and/or raising taxes. It's quite another to decide whose taxes to raise and exactly where spending should be cut. The latter inevitably involves political considerations.

2   Recall that the basic policy instruments that the Fed uses to manipulate the economy are open market operations, reserve requirements, and the discount rate, and that the major policy goals are full employment, stable prices, economic growth, and satisfactory external balance.

3   *Federal Reserve Bulletin* (September 1995): 853.

4   In the next chapter, you shall also see that the Fed, under the chair's leadership, can make an inter-meeting adjustment.

A Closer Look, page 613

a   Recall from Chapter 4 that, prior to January 2003, the discount rate was set by the Board of Governors and changed rather infrequently in response to requests from the Federal Reserve Banks. Changes in the discount rate usually lagged changes in other interest rates. At that time, the discount rate was often below other rates at which depository institutions could borrow reserves in the fed funds market. Since January 2003, the primary credit rate (the discount rate at which the most creditworthy institutions can borrow) is set 1 percent above the targeted fed funds rate. Hence, the discount rate is now above the fed funds rate and automatically changes whenever the fed funds target rate changes.

b   Monetary Policy Report to the Congress (February 17, 2000).

c   Monetary Policy Report to the Congress (July 20, 2000).

A Closer Look, page 618

a   "Risks and Uncertainty in Monetary Policy," Remarks by Chairman Alan Greenspan at the Meeting of the American Economic Association, San Diego, California, January 3, 2004. Available on the Internet at **http://www.federalreserve.gov/boarddocs/speeches/2004/200 40103/default.htm**.

b   "Monetary Policy under Uncertainty," Remarks by Chairman Alan Greenspan at a symposium sponsored by the Federal Reserve Bank of Kansas City, Jackson Hole, Wyoming, August 29, 2003. Available on the Internet at **http://www.federalreserve.gov/boarddocs/speeches/2003/20030829/default.htm**.

The eyes see only what the mind is prepared to comprehend.

—Robertson Davies

26

CHAPTER TWENTY-SIX

Policy Implementation

Learning Objectives

After reading this chapter, you should know:

What the contents and format of the policy directive are

How open market operations affect the fed funds rate

How the Trading Desk reacts to new information

How required reserves are calculated

The difference between temporary and outright open market transactions

A Morning at the New York Fed

System Open Market Account (SOMA)
The Fed's account of dollar-denominated Treasury securities, which are bought and sold by the Trading Desk to implement open market operations in accordance with policy directives.

Each morning, Dino Kos goes to work at the New York Fed with a specific job assignment—to implement the monetary policy of the United States. As manager of the Fed's **System Open Market Account (SOMA)**, which contains the Fed's dollar-denominated assets acquired through open market operations, he interprets and executes the policy directives of the Federal Open Market Committee (FOMC). Under his tutelage, the Fed operates a Trading Desk that buys and sells government securities from the SOMA to affect intermediate monetary policy targets and eventually the ultimate policy goals. Kos arrives at the office and immediately meets with his staff and is briefed on the opening level of interest rates that morning and any unusual events during the preceding night that may affect the supply of reserves to depository institutions. Late the previous afternoon, he has also consulted with his staff, securities dealers, and FOMC representatives. He decides the direction, if any, that interest rates should be nudged to fulfill the FOMC policy directive. Around 9:30 A.M., he issues buy or sell orders to a room of securities dealers who work for the New York Fed.[1]

The traders immediately call the primary securities dealers they work with and advise them that the Fed is either buying or selling. The **primary dealers** consist of 22 large banks and securities dealers with whom the Fed deals directly. Exhibit 26-1 below is a list of the primary dealers as of August 2, 2004. These dealers respond to the Fed's traders with offers to either sell or buy securities at various prices.

Primary Dealers
Large banks and securities dealers with whom the Fed directly engages in open market operations; at the present time, there are 22 primary dealers.

After a brief time, the Fed's traders gather in a room and announce their buy or sell offer prices. The manager tells the traders to discharge the most profitable transactions up to the amounts of the various Treasury securities that the Trading Desk is buying or selling. That is, if the Fed is buying, they execute the purchases up to the amount that the Fed wishes to buy at the lowest possible prices. If the Fed is selling on this day, they execute the transactions up to the amount that the Fed wishes to sell at the highest possible prices.

As the deals are consummated, reserves are either supplied or withdrawn from the banking system. In response to this change in reserves, it is hoped that interest rates move in the desired direction at approximately the desired magnitude. After lunch, Kos decides whether additional purchases or sales in the open market are needed. Did interest

26-1

Who Are the Primary Dealers? Primary Dealers as of August 2, 2004

Following is a list of the 22 primary dealers that buy and sell securities directly with the Fed in the execution of monetary policy. In recent years, the number of primary dealers has fallen due to mergers among large financial institutions.

ABN AMRO Bank, N.V., New York Branch	Dresdner Kleinwort Wasserstein Securities LLC.
BNP Paribas Securities Corp.	Goldman, Sachs & Co.
Banc of America Securities LLC	Greenwich Capital Markets, Inc.
Barclays Capital Inc.	HSBC Securities (USA) Inc.
Bear, Stearns & Co., Inc.	J. P. Morgan Securities, Inc.
CIBC World Markets Corp.	Lehman Brothers Inc.
Citigroup Global Markets Inc.	Merrill Lynch Government Securities Inc.
Countrywide Securities Corporation	Mizuho Securities USA Inc.
Credit Suisse First Boston LLC	Morgan Stanley & Co. Incorporated
Daiwa Securities America Inc.	Nomura Securities International, Inc.
Deutsche Bank Securities Inc.	UBS Securities LLC.

SOURCE: Federal Reserve Bank of New York, **http://www.newyorkfed.org/newsevents/markets/pridealers_current.html**.

rates overshoot or undershoot the desired target? In either case, an additional purchase or sale may be required, although usually it is not.

You may say what a simple story about an act with complex implications this is! Don't be fooled. Executing monetary policy is neither simple nor mundane. In a way, it is as much an art as a science, and the consequences are astronomical.

In the previous chapter, we looked at the difficulties in the policy process, focusing on how the FOMC makes decisions. In this chapter, we look at the intricacies of how those decisions are implemented by the Trading Desk of the New York Fed and how markets respond.

The FOMC Policy Directive

Once the long-term policy stance has been set, the focus of the FOMC shifts to the immediate period. The policy discussions center on the fed funds rate itself, as well as other interest rates. As noted previously, interest rates gained center stage as intermediate targets in the mid- and late 1990s and early 2000s. At the same time, policy has been somewhat eclectic, and "the process of probing a variety of data to ascertain underlying economic and financial conditions has become even more essential to formulating sound monetary policy."[2] As a result, the Fed now looks at many indicators.

Given its assessment of current economic conditions and the economic outlook, the FOMC comes up with short-term strategies consistent with its longer-range projections. Against this background, the FOMC issues a **policy directive** to the Trading Desk of the New York Fed that guides the conduct of open market operations until the next FOMC meeting approximately six weeks later. The directive is the link between the decisions formulating policy and the actions implementing policy. The policy directive and accompanying statement for the June 30, 2004 meeting of the FOMC is reproduced here.

Policy Directive
A statement issued by the FOMC to the Trading Desk of the New York Fed that directs monetary policy until the next FOMC meeting; in recent years, the policy directive has targeted a specific fed funds rate.

> The Federal Open Market Committee decided today to raise its target for the federal funds rate by 25 basis points to 1-1/4 percent.
> The Committee believes that, even after this action, the stance of monetary policy remains accommodative and, coupled with robust underlying growth in productivity, is providing ongoing support to economic activity. The evidence accumulated over the intermeeting period indicates that output is continuing to expand at a solid pace and labor market conditions have improved. Although incoming inflation data are somewhat elevated, a portion of the increase in recent months appears to have been due to transitory factors.
> The Committee perceives the upside and downside risks to the attainment of both sustainable growth and price stability for the next few quarters are roughly equal. With underlying inflation still expected to be relatively low, the Committee believes that policy accommodation can be removed at a pace that is likely to be measured. Nonetheless, the Committee will respond to changes in economic prospects as needed to fulfill its obligation to maintain price stability.
> Voting for the FOMC monetary policy action were: Alan Greenspan, Chairman; Timothy F. Geithner, Vice Chairman; Ben S. Bernanke; Susan S. Bies; Roger W. Ferguson, Jr.; Edward M. Gramlich; Thomas M. Hoenig; Donald L. Kohn; Cathy E. Minehan; Mark W. Olson; Sandra Pianalto; and William Poole.
> In a related action, the Board of Governors approved a 25 basis point increase in the discount rate to 2-1/4 percent. In taking this action, the Board approved the requests submitted by the Boards of Directors of the Federal Reserve Banks of Boston, New York, Philadelphia, Cleveland, Richmond, Atlanta, Chicago, St. Louis, Minneapolis, Kansas City, Dallas and San Francisco.[3]

The policy directive along with the statement is released to the public to communicate the FOMC's assessment of the risks to satisfactory economic performance in the foreseeable future. Note that each statement contains an evaluation of the risks with regard to sustainable economic growth and inflationary expectations (price stability). On June 30, 2004, the upside and downside risks were the same for both goals. This is often not the case. For example, on October 28, 2003, the part of the statement regarding the goals was as follows:

> The Committee perceives that the upside and downside risks to the attainment of sustainable growth for the next few quarters are roughly equal. In contrast, the probability, though minor, of an unwelcome fall in inflation exceeds that of a rise in inflation from its already low level. The Committee judges that, on balance, the risk of inflation becoming undesirably low remains the predominant concern for the foreseeable future. In these circumstances, the Committee believes that policy accommodation can be maintained for a considerable period.[4]

Thus, in October 2003, although the upside and downside risks to sustainable growth were roughly equal, in the FOMC's judgment, the probability of deflation, "an unwelcome fall in inflation" was greater than of inflation.

The preceding releases of information to the public are a relatively recent phenomenon for the Fed. In February 1995, the Fed formally adopted the practice begun in 1994 of announcing any changes in the targeted fed funds rate immediately following the FOMC meetings. By doing so, it eliminated questions and doubts about changes in policy. The announcements in 1994 occurred after a relatively long period of stable low interest rates. In these circumstances, a sudden shift to higher interest rates could have caught many market participants off guard and caused them to sustain real losses in the value of their portfolios. (Remember the inverse relationship between the interest rate and bond prices.) Thus, by announcing the increases, the Fed seems to have been attempting to give market participants a heads-up warning.

In December 1998, the FOMC also decided to announce any shift in its view of forthcoming developments in the economy. The shifts in perspective were communicated in a statement about the likelihood of future increases or decreases in the fed funds rate. The public was confused by how to interpret the statement about future assessment of the balance of risks and its policy leanings. In an effort for more openness, the Fed again modified its disclosure procedure in early 2000 to the format that is currently used. (Thus, the language in the previous examples represents the new format adopted in early 2000.) In addition, an individual roll call of FOMC members' votes was added instead of just the outcome of the voting being reported. These moves have reduced the uncertainty and guesswork about Fed policy and its direction at the time of the FOMC meetings. The accompanying A Closer Look on page 629 discusses why the Fed has become more open in recent years.

Testimony and speeches related to the Fed's public policy operations and links to the Humphrey-Hawkins testimony, testimony of other Fed officials, and texts of several speeches by Federal Reserve Board members are at **http://www.federalreserve.gov/newsevents.htm**.

New monthly data on economic growth and inflation, such as the unemployment rate, retail sales, industrial production, and the consumer and producer price indexes, are also released during the intermeeting period. The Fed, under the chair's leadership, can make an intermeeting adjustment. In recent years, intermeeting changes occurred in October 1998 in response to a financial crisis in Russia, twice in early 2001 in response to a weak economy, and once in September 2001 in response to the terrorist attacks on the World Trade Center and the Pentagon. Historically, an intermeeting change has been rare.

In the next section, we look at the specifics of how the directives are implemented.

A Closer Look

Why the Fed Has Become More Open

Throughout most of its history, the Fed has been a rather secretive organization surrounded by mystique. The Fed preferred to act covertly and to adjust policy gradually rather than abruptly with the belief that such behavior minimized market disruptions and reduced the chance of a major policy error. Accordingly, the Fed did not announce policy changes immediately following FOMC meetings and the public did not find out about changes until the release of the minutes after the next FOMC meeting more than six weeks later. Thus, the Fed was using open market operations to change policy without the public's knowledge. Because open market operations are a complex blend of offsetting operations and those reflecting a change in the stance of policy, it was difficult to distinguish between the two.

All of this has changed in recent years. As noted earlier, since 1994, the Fed has made public announcements about the fed funds rate target immediately following all FOMC meetings and has issued a public statement to communicate how they view economic pressures. This openness constitutes a significant departure from the Fed's traditional behavior.

Why has the Fed abandoned its recalcitrant secretive behavior in favor of public disclosure? The reason seems to be the Fed's belief that if it better communicates current and future policy moves, there will be less uncertainty. The less uncertainty means more control over future expectations and through this, more control over long-term rates. After all, these changes in long-term interest rates have the greatest impact on economic activity and it is long-term rate that the Fed is aiming to affect through changes in short-term rates.

A side effect of the new openness is that a smaller volume of open market operations is needed to hit a given targeted fed funds rate. The smaller volume results from the Fed's announcement of the new target directly and its effect on expectations of the short-term rate. The new expectations of market participants cause the rate to move in that direction before the Fed even intervenes.

A second side effect of the new openness seems to be a reduction in the long and variable lag for monetary policy to take effect in the economy. The conventional wisdom was that it took at least six months or more for an interest rate reduction to stimulate the economy. With the new openness of the Fed and the greater transparency, financial markets can more easily anticipate what the Fed will do and act accordingly and preemptively, thus reducing the lag.

Recap At each FOMC meeting, a policy directive is sent to the New York Fed that directs the stance of monetary policy. In recent years, the Fed has targeted the fed funds rate. Nevertheless, the Fed has taken an eclectic approach and looked at a wide range of data to gauge economic and financial conditions. The New York Fed implements the policy directive by using open market operations. In addition to the policy directive, the FOMC also issues a statement to the public stating the committee's expectation for the foreseeable future regarding the goals of price stability and sustainable economic growth.

The Reserves Market and Open Market Operations

To implement the policy directive, the Trading Desk of the New York Fed tries to manage reserve levels of depository institutions so that the fed funds rate will be equal to the targeted rate. To do this, the Trading Desk develops estimates of the likely demand and supply of total reserves. The demand for reserves consists of (1) the demand for required reserves plus (2) the demand for excess reserves. Depository institutions may demand excess reserves to avoid unintended shortages of required reserves. The supply of reserves has two major components: (1) borrowed reserves, which are reserves borrowed by depository institutions from the Fed's discount facility, and (2) nonborrowed reserves, which are reserves available in the open market. In equilibrium, the quantity demanded of reserves will equal the quantity supplied, making the market for reserves like any other market. Exhibit 26-2 below reviews the basic reserve components and determinants.

But how does this equilibrium come about? Suppose that under current market conditions including the current fed funds rate, the quantity demanded of reserves is greater than the quantity supplied. What will happen? Simply put, the excess quantity demanded would be reflected in the fed funds market where reserves are bought and sold among depository institutions. Given the excess of quantity demanded over quantity supplied, market forces will cause the fed funds rate to rise. Likewise, if the quantity supplied of reserves at the current fed funds rate is greater than the quantity demanded, the fed funds rate will fall.

In recent years, the Fed has implemented policy by focusing its open market operations with an eye toward achieving the targeted fed funds rate. Suppose the directive calls for "maintaining the federal funds rate at an average of around 3 percent." Immediately after the FOMC meeting, the Trading Desk derives the **reserve need**, which is the difference, if any, between actual reserves and those projected to be needed to keep the fed funds rate at the desired level. The reserve need must be met with open market opera-

Reserve Need
The projected amount of reserves to be supplied or withdrawn by open market operations to reach or keep the fed funds rate prescribed by the policy directive.

26-2 Total Reserves

tions in order to fulfill the policy directive. If the Trading Desk supplies more than the reserve need, the fed funds rate will fall. If the Trading Desk supplies less than the reserve need, the fed funds rate will rise. Note that the reserve need may be negative because reserves may need to be withdrawn by open market sales to meet the directive.

Operationally, the manager of the Trading Desk begins the initial period following the FOMC meeting with the understanding that he needs to supply the reserve need on average over the weeks until the next FOMC meeting by conducting open market operations designed to carry out the policy directive. In practice, the manager must also consider other factors that affect reserves. The overwhelming majority of open market operations is designed to offset unexpected swings in the supply of reserves caused by a variety of "other factors." If not offset, these variations in reserves would induce an undesired change in the fed funds rate. The other factors that can affect reserves include changes on the Fed's balance sheet in such items as the float, Treasury deposits, gold, currency holdings, and international reserves.

As the weeks between FOMC meetings pass, various pieces of information accumulate. Each day, the Fed updates its estimates of the supply of reserves, given yesterday's change, if any, in the Fed's portfolio and new information on the other factors affecting reserves. Using updated information, the manager revises his estimate of the reserves that need to be supplied or absorbed to maintain the desired reserve conditions that coincide with the targeted fed funds rate. Thus, in response to the incoming data, the reserve need may be revised.

Finally, we should note that in recent years, required reserves have declined substantially and are continuing to decline. This is due to the widespread growth of retail sweep accounts. A financial innovation that first appeared in 1994, **retail sweep accounts** "sweep" balances out of transactions accounts that are subject to reserve requirements and into other deposits (usually money market deposit accounts) that are not. **Wholesale sweep accounts** have been in existence since the 1970s. With wholesale sweep programs, the depository institutions sweeps funds out of a business's demand deposit into a money market instrument, such as a repurchase agreement, Eurodollar deposit, or money market mutual fund. For wholesale sweep accounts, the deposits are swept into an account that may or may not be a liability of the depository institution. For retail sweep accounts, the swept funds stay on the books of the depository institution. Required reserves fall by the amount of funds in sweep accounts multiplied by the required reserve ratio. Balances in retail sweep accounts grew from $5.3 billion in January 1994 to $641.9 billion in August 2004. In the aggregate, required reserves dropped about $15 billion between December 1993 and August 2004. Declines in required reserves are expected to taper off in future years, because all opportunities to reduce reserves will have been exploited. Depositors are not affected because the funds are swept back into the transactions account when they are needed. Banks benefit because of the resulting reduction in required reserves that do not earn interest and because of the ability to make more loans and other investments with the funds that otherwise would be held as required reserves.

The significant decline in required reserves in recent years due to sweep accounts has raised concern that the fed funds rate may become more volatile and may affect the implementation of monetary policy. This increased volatility would result from depository institutions attempting to manage reserve accounts at the Fed with very low balances. Although there is some evidence that the fed funds rate has become more volatile with the growth of retail sweep accounts, the increased volatility does not seem to be significant enough to cause major disruptions in the fed funds market or general instability in financial markets. So far, the implementation of monetary policy has not been affected.

Retail Sweep Accounts
Retail accounts, created in 1994, with balances that have been swept out of deposit accounts subject to reserve requirements and into savings accounts that are not.

Wholesale Sweep Accounts
Wholesale accounts, created in the 1970s, with balances that have been swept out of deposit accounts subject to reserve accounts and into money market instruments such as money market mutual funds, Eurodollar deposits, and repurchase agreements.

The Fed's Response to the Terrorist Attacks of September 11, 2001: America's Darkest Hour May be the Fed's Finest

The terrorist attack on the World Trade Center and the Pentagon on September 11, 2001, caused unfathomable despair and unparalleled loss of life and property. The attacks struck at the core of the U.S. financial system, destroying a part of the financial infrastructure, killing employees of major financial firms, and closing U.S. financial markets for one week. Communication networks were disrupted and backup systems in payment mechanisms were activated. Market participants had to conduct business from locations outside the nation's preeminent financial center. Uncertainties about payment flows disrupted the market for bank reserves. Depository institutions with excess reserves were not able to borrow through traditional venues. The result was a massive mushrooming of the effective demand for reserves. Float also increased considerably as air traffic came to a halt.

The Fed's first response to the attacks was to announce that it would supply all liquidity needed as a result of the disruption. The announcement was immediately followed by action. Increases in discount loans and open market operations supplied unprecedented liquidity to the financial system. Discount loans soared from around $200 million on September 11 to a record level of more than $45 billion on September 12. Reserve balances at Federal Reserve Banks jumped to more than $100 billion on September 12—an amount more than 10 times the normal level. Later in the week, open market operations were used to inject reserves as the record discount loans were repaid. Repurchase agreements (injecting reserves) peaked at $81 billion on September 14. The result of the Fed's swift action was a minimization of the fallout to the financial system from the attack and the avoidance of a financial crisis. By the end of September, reserve balances returned more or less to their pre-September 11 levels.

In addition, the Fed made an intermeeting in the fed funds rate on the morning of September 17, shortly before the reopening of U.S. stock markets. It also announced a corresponding decrease in the discount rate. The Fed coordinated the decrease in interest rates with other central banks, including the European Central Bank and those in Canada, England, and Sweden. The Fed also arranged currency swap agreements with the European Central Bank, the Bank of England, and the Bank of Canada. The currency swaps, which totaled $68 billion, aided foreign banks in the respective countries whose U.S. operations were disrupted by the terrorist attack.

Prior to the attack, the fed funds and discount rates had been lowered a full three percentage points in a series of seven cuts since the beginning of 2001. This was the most aggressive easing in 20 years. After the attack, the Fed followed with three more cuts in addition to the one on September 17.

What were the results of such dramatic actions? The Fed's swift action caused payment mechanisms to return to normal within a few short weeks. As a result, the U.S. financial system demonstrated profound resilience in response to the horrific events. By the first quarter of 2002, the economy had turned the corner, and moderate growth was returning much sooner than many analysts had expected. Many factors such as expansionary fiscal policy, continuing strength in consumer demand, automobile rebates, and declining inventories prompted the upturn. However, the Fed's lowering of interest rates also played a role in fostering the economic recovery. Looking back, few will say that the Fed was slow to respond to the crisis! Indeed, one of the saddest hours in U.S. history may prove to be one of the Fed's finest.

E-Money and Monetary Policy

There is some concern that the evolution of the payments system to an e-money system will reduce the ability of the Fed to execute monetary policy through traditional channels. Namely, the growth of e-money may supplant traditional payment mechanisms. E-money is privately created "money" that uses the Internet to execute payments. E-money bypasses both the use of currency and reserves. Depository institutions, other intermediaries, and nonfinancial firms may create e-money. E-money consists of credits similar to I.O.U.s that are used to make payments and are accepted in payment for goods and services. The firms that create e-money settle with each other rather than with the central bank. The concern is that if more payments are made in this way, the demand for currency and reserves will fall (and could theoretically fall to zero), thus reducing the ability of the Fed to control interest rates by changing the monetary base.

We are very far from the scenario in which the demand for reserves and currency becomes so insignificant that it interferes with the conduct of monetary policy. The demand for currency continues to increase, driven by both the growth of cash transactions in the United States and the international demand for dollars. This trend may slow in the future with the widespread adoption of smart cards to make payments.

The demand for reserve balances has rapidly decreased in recent years due to lower reserve requirements and the growth of retail sweep accounts. These developments do not seem to have reduced the Fed's ability to control interest rates.

Because a high proportion of e-money could displace traditional payment mechanisms in the future, however, the Fed's job in forecasting the demand for reserves and currency and thus implementing monetary policy may become more difficult. Consequently, e-money could have far-reaching implications for central banks.

In recent years, Congress has considered authorizing the Fed to pay interest on reserves. The Fed has long advocated this policy because it would make the banking system more efficient. At the present time, banks have an incentive to develop such mechanisms as sweep accounts to minimize their holdings of reserves. If interest were paid on reserves, this incentive would be gone. In reality, not being able to earn interest on required reserves represents a tax on banks and makes the banking system less efficient than it otherwise would be, because it uses resources to avoid the costly regulation. Congress has been hesitant to authorize this change because of the interest costs that the Fed would have to pay on reserve balances. Note that the Fed's earnings in the form of interest on the government securities that it holds and other fees that are now returned to the U.S. Treasury would be reduced. If adopted, however, this change would undoubtedly affect the amount of funds that is swept out of checkable deposits and into sweep accounts.

To summarize, if the fed funds rate rises above the targeted rate, the Trading Desk increases the amount of reserves available to depository institutions in order to bring the fed funds rate back to the targeted level. Likewise, if the fed funds rate falls below the targeted rate, the Trading Desk decreases the amount of reserves.

We are now in a position to look more closely at how required reserves are calculated.

Recap The Trading Desk derives the reserve need to fulfill the policy directive. The reserve need is based on the discrepancy between actual reserves and projections of the amount that will be needed to fulfill the policy directive. The reserve need must be met with open market purchases or sales. As new data come in about interest rates, the Trading Desk may adjust the reserve need. New data about the economy may also lead to changes in the stance of monetary policy, which will also change the reserve need. The growth of retail sweep accounts since 1994 has reduced the amount of required reserves and led to concerns about (1) increased volatility of the fed funds rate and (2) the Fed's ability to implement monetary policy using changes in the fed funds rate. So far, monetary policy does not seem to be affected.

How the Demand and Supply of Reserves Are Calculated

Computation Period
The period during which the actual amount of required reserve assets that must be held during the maintenance period is determined.

Maintenance Period
The period during which the actual amount of reserves held must at least equal the amount of required reserves, as determined during the computation period.

Banks are required to hold reserve assets during a two-week maintenance period that corresponds to the two-week computation period. During the **computation period**, the actual amount of required reserve assets that must be held during the maintenance period is determined. During the two-week **maintenance period**, the actual average amount of reserves held must at least equal the amount of required reserves.

The average daily amount of required reserve assets that must be held is equal to the required reserve ratio times the average daily amount of deposits subject to reserve requirements. At the present time, only checkable deposits are subject to reserve requirements. Required reserves against checkable deposits will equal the checkable deposit balances multiplied by the reserve requirement ratio on such deposits. During 2005, that ratio was zero percent on transaction deposits up to $7 million, 3 percent on transaction deposits between $7 and $47.6 million, and 10 percent on transaction deposits of more than $47.6 million. As first noted in Chapter 4, because $47.6 million is a relatively small amount of transactions deposits, we ignore the 0 and 3 percent requirements. By adding an allowance for excess reserves based on recent experience and any seasonal patterns, the staff of the New York Fed produces a path for the demand for total reserves including both required and excess reserves.

For example, if checkable deposits average $600 billion a day during the computation period, required reserve assets (deposits at the Fed plus vault cash) must average $60 billion a day during the maintenance period ($600 billion × 10 percent reserve requirement = $60 billion). If excess reserves have been averaging 1 percent of deposits, an additional $6 billion in excess reserves must be included in the path for total reserves that will be demanded ($600 billion × 1 percent excess reserves = $6 billion).

Contemporaneous Reserve Accounting
A reserve accounting system under which the maintenance period—when the reserve assets must be held—more or less corresponds to the computation period when the amount of required reserves is determined.

Between 1984 and July 30, 1998, a system called **contemporaneous reserve accounting** was used. Under such a system, the maintenance period, when the reserve assets must be held, more or less corresponds to the computation period. The two-week computation period starts two days before the two-week maintenance period. When one computation period ends, another immediately begins. The average daily balance of reserves held during the maintenance period must be equal to the average daily balance of reserves required during the computation period with the exception that average vault cash in a two-week computation period counts as reserves in the maintenance period ending two weeks later. Prior to 1992, the lag in counting vault cash toward required reserves was two weeks longer. When one maintenance period ends, another immediately begins. Part (a) of Exhibit 26-3 on page 635 illustrates how this reserve accounting method works in practice.

26-3

Reserve Computations Under Contemporaneous and Lagged Reserve Accounting[a]

(a) Reserve Computation and Maintenance Periods under Contemporaneous Reserve Accounting

Week 1	Week 2	Week 3	Week 4	Week 5
TWTFSSM	TWTFSSM	TWTFSSM	TWTFSSM	TWTFSSM

Two-Week Computation Period for Cash

Two-Week Computation Period for Checkable Deposits

TWTFSSM   TWTFSSM   TWTFSSM   TWTFSSM   TWTFSSM

Two-Week Maintenance Period

(b) Reserve Computation and Maintenance Periods under Lagged Reserve Accounting

TWTFSSM TWTFSSM TWTFSSM TWTFSSM TWTFSSM TWTFSSM TWTFSSM

Two-Week Computation Period for Cash and Checkable Deposits

Two-Week Maintenance Period

[a]Note: TWTFSSM = Tuesday, Wednesday, Thursday, Friday, Saturday, Sunday, and Monday

Lagged Reserve Accounting
A reserve accounting system under which the maintenance period—when the reserve assets must be held—follows some time after the computation period when the amount of required reserves is determined.

Beginning with the reserve maintenance period beginning on July 30, 1998, the system was changed from contemporaneous reserve accounting to **lagged reserve accounting**. Under this system, the reserve maintenance period for depository institutions begins 30 days after the beginning of the two-week reserve computation period. When one computation period ends, another immediately begins, and a corresponding maintenance period begins 30 days later. Thus, depository institutions know the exact amount of required reserves that will be needed in the maintenance period before the maintenance period begins because the required reserves in any maintenance period are based on a two-week computation period that started 30 days earlier. The change makes it easier for depository institutions to calculate their required reserve balances for the current maintenance period.

In addition, with this system the Trading Desk at the New York Fed can obtain more accurate information about required reserves, which is helpful in determining the overall demand for reserves by the banking system. Because the Fed currently implements monetary policy by targeting a fed funds rate, which is determined by the demand and supply of reserves, this change also makes the implementation of monetary policy easier. Part (b) of Exhibit 26-3 illustrates how this reserve accounting method works in practice.

The supply of total reserves can be determined by rearranging the Fed's balance sheet, which is displayed in Exhibit 26-4 on page 636. The major items on the Fed's balance sheet can be summarized as follows:

Assets

Government securities held
Gold and special drawing rights (SDRs) accounts, which reflect international reserve holdings
Discount loans
Float
Other assets

Liabilities

Reserve balances of depository institutions with the Fed
Currency outside the Fed
Treasury deposits
Other liabilities

	Assets
1 Gold certificate account	$11,045
2 Special drawing rights certificate account	2,200
3 Coin	725
4 Securities, repurchase agreements, and loans	718,032
Securities held outright	692,299
U.S. Treasury[a]	692,299
Bills[b]	255,248
Notes and bonds, nominal[b]	420,150
Notes and bonds, inflation-indexed[b]	14,862
Inflation compensation[c]	2,039
Federal agency[b]	0
Repurchase agreements[d]	25,500
Loans	233
5 Items in the process of collection	5,558
6 Bank premises	1,700
7 Other assets[e]	38,606
8 Total Assets	**777,861***

	Liabilities
9 Federal Reserve notes net if Federal Reserve Bank Holdings	699,168
10 Reverse repurchase agreements[f]	19,906
11 Total deposits	31,774
Depository institutions	19,906
U.S. Treasury—General account	26,508
Foreign—Official accounts	4,879
Other	99
12 Deferred credit items	5,862
13 Other liabilities and accrued dividends[g]	2,375
14 Total liabilities	**759,085***

	Capital Accounts
15 Capital paid in	9,245
16 Surplus	8,827
17 Other capital accounts	705
18 Total capital	**18,777**

*Note: Components may not sum to totals because of rounding.
[a] Includes securities lent to dealers, which are fully collateralized by other U.S. Treasury securities.
[b] Face value of the securities.
[c] Compensation that adjusts for the effect of inflation on the original face value of inflation-indexed securities.
[d] Cash value of agreements, which are collateralized by U.S. Treasury and federal agency securites.
[e] Includes assets denominated in foreign currencies, which are revalued daily at market exchange rates.
[f] Cash value of agreements, which are collateralized by U.S. Treasury securities.
[g] Includes exchange-translation account reflecting the daily revaluation at market exchange rates of foreign exchange commitments.
SOURCE: Federal Reserve Statistical Release, H.4.1, *Factors Affecting Reserve Balances* (July 22, 2004). Available on the Internet at http://www.federalreserve.gov/releases/h41/Current/.

Trading Desk Market Techniques

Each day, the Fed must decide whether to buy or sell securities outright or on a temporary basis. If bought or sold on a temporary basis, the transaction generally is reversed the next day or within two weeks. The manager deals with the various factors that affect reserves on a day-to-day basis, attempting to smooth out random factors that affect reserves while overall meeting the guidelines put forth by the FOMC in the policy directive.

Information on open market operations and their important role from a monetary policy perspective is at **http://www.newyorkfed.org/aboutthefed/fedpoint/fed32.html**.

Outright Transactions in the Market

In general, the manager uses **outright transactions** when he wants to provide or absorb reserves over relatively long time spans. Thus, outright transactions are typically used when projections show that a reserve need or reserve excess is likely to persist. Most outright transactions are technical operations designed to preserve existing reserve conditions against the background of the changing seasonal and secular (long-term) reserve needs of the economy. An example of a seasonal reserve need occurs every year between Thanksgiving and Christmas, when a rise in currency in circulation drains reserves from the banking system. Meanwhile, the requirements of a growing economy create an ongoing reserve need for more currency. Although most outright transactions are conducted to meet these seasonal and ongoing needs, in the past on rare occasions, the manager has used outright transactions to underscore the thrust of policy or to signal a change in policy.

The Trading Desk makes far more outright purchases than outright sales because of the growing demand for currency. Nevertheless, outright purchases in the open market, which supply reserves, typically account for no more than 10 percent of total Fed transactions. Even though outright purchases usually account for less than 10 percent of total Fed transactions at any time, the Fed's portfolio of securities consists mainly of those bought outright because the temporary purchases wash out over time.

The Trading Desk manager can buy Treasury bills (T-bills) and federal agency security issues in the secondary market. The Trading Desk has not added to its portfolio of agency securities since 1981, however. Consequently, the Fed's holdings of agency securities declined to zero in December 2003 because agency securities were not replaced as they matured. The Fed recently announced that it will continue this policy. Exhibit 26-5 below shows the SOMA's current holdings of securities.

By law, the manager is not allowed to add to the Fed's portfolio by purchasing new securities directly from the Treasury. He may, however, roll over maturing securities in whole or in part into new issues.

Traditionally, the largest portion of outright transactions in the secondary market is in T-bills. The huge size of the secondary market in T-bills and its considerable depth, breadth, and liquidity enable it to absorb large transactions smoothly. The desk also manages the composition of the portfolio with the main goal of ensuring that the portfolio has a high degree of liquidity in case liquidity is needed. Thus, a key objective of the FOMC is to maintain the average maturity of securities held in the SOMA at a relatively short length.

26-5

System Open Market Account (SOMA) Securities Holding as of July 21, 2004

Security Type	Total Par Value
U.S. Treasury Bills (T-Bills)	$255,247,686
U.S. Treasury Notes and Bonds (Notes/Bonds)	420,149,597
U.S. Treasury Inflation-Indexed Securities (TIIS)	14,862,483
Total SOMA Holdings	**$690,259,766**

SOURCE: Federal Reserve Bank of New York. Available on the Internet at **http://www.newyorkfed.org/markets/soma/sysopen_accholdings. html**.

Note that outright sales, even of T-bills, are relatively infrequent. As mentioned earlier, the growing demand for currency means that there will be more outright purchases than sales. Because sales are so rare, when they do occur, they tend to impart the kind of negative impact on market psychology the Trading Desk prefers to avoid when entering the market.

Temporary Transactions

The Trading Desk uses temporary transactions when it wants to supply or absorb reserves for relatively short periods, usually no longer than a few weeks. Typically, the need to conduct such transactions arises from swings in the various other factors affecting the supply of reserves, such as the float and Treasury balances. If the reserve need is for only a short period, the Trading Desk opts for temporary transactions because they are cheaper to execute than outright transactions. Two types of temporary transactions are used: repurchase agreements and reverse repurchase agreements.

When arranging repurchase agreements, the Trading Desk buys securities on a self-reversing, temporary basis. The seller, often a government securities dealer, agrees to buy the securities back from the Trading Desk on or before a specified date. Note that the term *repurchase agreement* has the opposite meaning to the Fed that it does to securities dealers. In Chapter 5, you saw that dealers use the term *repurchase agreements* to refer to the practice of borrowing money to finance their holdings of securities by selling the securities temporarily with an agreement to repurchase them at a later date.

To the Fed, the term refers to the temporary purchase of securities. Usually repurchase agreements are done overnight or for short periods of 2 to 14 days, although the Trading Desk can legally use repurchase agreements up to a maturity of 90 days. Because repurchase agreements provide reserves, they can be used to offset a temporary reserve drain arising from one or more of the other factors affecting reserves. If such drains were not fully offset, the supply of reserves would decline relative to the demand, reserve conditions would tighten, and the fed funds rate would rise. A repurchase agreement used to supply reserves on a temporary basis is called a **system repurchase agreement**. The securities that are purchased go into the Fed's system account.

Reverse repurchase agreements are arranged by the Trading Desk when the manager wants to drain reserves temporarily from the banking system. Technically, when initiating reverse repurchase agreements, the manager sells securities and simultaneously purchases the same securities for delivery the next day or perhaps several days later. Like their repurchase agreement counterpart, reverse repurchase agreements are most often used to maintain existing reserve conditions by offsetting other factors that have changed reserves. More specifically, they are usually used to offset temporary reserve excesses arising from the other factors, which, if not offset, would lead to an undesired, albeit temporary, easing in reserve conditions.

Note that the bulk of open market operations involve temporary transactions as opposed to outright purchases and sales. In the case of temporary transactions, government, agency securities, and mortgage-backed securities are used. Although the Trading Desk may enter the market several times in a day, in recent years it has normally entered the market only once per day, as described earlier.

Check out the Fed's temporary transactions, such as repurchase agreements and reverse repurchase agreements, at **http://www.newyorkfed.org/aboutthefed/fedpoint/fed04.html**.

The complexity of policy procedures, coupled with the political milieu within which policy makers operate and muddle, puts a considerable premium on understanding

System Repurchase Agreement

When the Trading Desk of the Fed buys securities on a self-reversing, temporary basis in order to supply reserves on a temporary basis.

Reverse Repurchase Agreements

The Fed's simultaneous sale and purchase of securities for delivery the next day or in a few days to withdraw reserves on a temporary basis.

26-6
A Guide to Open Market Operations

Fed Activity	Translation	Implication
1. No Fed buying or selling.	The Fed is not expected to intervene.	A reserve add or intervene drain is not required or (a) it can be accommodated later when more information is available or (b) market conditions begin to more clearly reflect or indicate the need.
2. The Fed uses reverse repurchase agreements.	The Trading Desk sells Treasury securities to primary dealers. Buyers agree to sell them back at a specified time, usually the next day, which temporarily absorbs reserves.	A reserve drain is required, which may mean that either (a) the drain is consistent with prevailing Fed policy and necessary to prevent undesired fed funds rate declines or (b) the Fed has tightened.
3. The Fed engages in system repurchase agreements.	The Trading Desk provides funds (reserves) in exchange for Treasury securities with an agreement that dealers will repurchase them, usually the next day, which temporarily increases reserves.	Reserves must be added, which may mean that either (a) the increase is consistent with prevailing policy and necessary to prevent undesired fed funds rate increases or (b) the Fed has eased.
4. The Fed makes outright sales.	A permanent transaction has occurred with no resale agreements. The Fed sells Treasury securities in the open market, absorbing reserves. Bills only are sold.	Reserves are drained out of the banking system. Such a move is usually not associated with a change in policy but is conducted seasonally and occasionally when underscoring a policy move toward restraint.
5. The Fed makes outright purchases.	The opposite of an outright sale has occurred. The Fed buys securities open market with no repurchase agreements on the part of the sellers, injecting reserves permanently.	Reserves are permanently added. The action is usually not associated with policy implications but is conducted seasonally to provide for economic growth. Can occasionally signal policy moves toward easing.

the relationship among the economic goals the Fed is loosely charged with achieving, the intermediate target approach embraced by the Fed, the economic analysis provided by the FOMC, the policy directive, incoming data, reserve projections, and, finally, open market operations. Exhibit 26-6 above provides a field guide to the Fed's open market operations. By understanding the process, market participants can minimize the risk of misinterpreting Fed actions and statements and thus be better positioned to anticipate and deal with Fed policy.

> **Recap** To change reserves, the manager of the Trading Desk may use open market purchases or sales, repurchase agreements, or reverse repurchase agreements. System repurchase agreements provide reserves for a few days. They are used to offset a temporary reserve drain. A reverse repurchase agreement is used to temporarily withdraw reserves from the system for a few days. If the change is thought to be permanent, outright purchases or sales are more likely to be used.

Our next and final chapter examines the global implications and linkages of monetary policy.

Summary of Major Points

1. The FOMC issues an operating directive to the Trading Desk of the New York Fed, which deals with how open market policy is to be implemented. In recent years, the policy directive has targeted a specific fed funds rate. Since 1994, the Fed has announced policy changes immediately following FOMC meetings.

2. The staff of the New York Fed estimates the amount of the reserve need to fulfill the policy directive. Given the directive, the manager of the open market Trading Desk then decides whether reserves should be added or removed from the system. The Trading Desk also makes other purchases or sales to neutralize or offset changes in other factors affecting reserves. In recent years, required reserves have declined because of the introduction of retail sweep accounts.

3. During a maintenance period, banks hold reserve assets that correspond to the amount of required reserves. The amount of required reserve is based on the amount of checkable deposits in a computation period multiplied by the required reserve ratio. Prior to 1998, a system of contemporaneous reserve accounting was used. Since July 1998, the reserve maintenance period begins 30 days after the beginning of the two-week reserve computation period (lagged reserve accounting). In the maintenance period, the average daily amount of reserves must equal the average daily amount of required reserves during the computation period.

4. The manager of the Trading Desk may use outright purchases or sales in the open market to change reserves. The transactions are usually in the secondary market in T-bills. In recent years, there have been far more outright purchases than sales because of the growing need for currency.

5. Alternatively, system repurchase agreements or reverse repurchase agreements may be used to change reserves. System repurchase agreements and reverse repurchase agreements are not restricted to government securities but may employ government agency securities or mortgage-backed securities. A repurchase agreement provides reserves until it matures in a few days. Repurchase agreements are used to offset a temporary reserve drain. A reverse repurchase transaction is used to temporarily withdraw reserves from the system. If the change is thought to be of a seasonal or secular (longer-term) nature, the manager is more likely to use outright purchases than if the need for reserves is thought to be temporary.

6. The seller of the repurchase agreement (usually a government securities dealer) agrees to buy the securities back from the Trading Desk on or before a specified date. In a reverse repurchase transaction, the manager of the Trading Desk sells securities and simultaneously purchases them back for delivery on a later date.

Key Terms

Computation Period, **634**

Contemporaneous Reserve
  Accounting, **634**

Lagged Reserve Accounting, **635**

Maintenance Period, **634**

Outright Transactions, **637**

Policy Directive, **627**

Primary Dealers, **626**

Reserve Need, **630**

Retail Sweep Accounts, **631**

Reverse Repurchase Agreements, **638**

System Open Market Account
  (SOMA), **626**

System Repurchase Agreement, **638**

Wholesale Sweep Accounts, **631**

Review Questions

1. What should the Trading Desk do if the fed funds rate falls below the targeted rate?
2. Explain what is meant by the *reserve need*.
3. For what purposes are system repurchase agreements and reverse repurchase agreements likely to be used?
4. For what purposes are outright purchases and sales likely to be used?
5. What is the computation period? What is the maintenance period?
6. When and why would the Fed accommodate a rise in reserve demand by supplying more reserves?
7. What characteristics of Treasury bills make them desirable for use in outright transactions by the Trading Desk?
8. The float increases unexpectedly. Will the Fed typically respond with outright purchases or temporary purchases?
9. Why have required reserves fallen in recent years? Will the trend continue?
10. Under lagged reserve accounting, how does the computation period correspond with the maintenance period? Under contemporaneous reserve accounting, how does the computation period correspond with the maintenance period? What are the advantages of a lagged reserve accounting period?
11. Why has the Fed become more open about monetary policy decisions in recent years?

Analytical Questions

Questions marked with an icon are objective in nature. They can be completed with a short answer or number.

12. Assume that checkable deposits are $500 billion, desired excess reserves are 1 percent of deposits, the required reserve ratio is 10 percent, and the amount of reserves is $50 billion. What is the reserve need to maintain the existing reserve conditions?
13. Describe what the Fed should do to meet the reserve need in question 12.
14. The Fed anticipates a seasonal reserve need of $10 billion over the next month. Is it more likely to use outright purchases or temporary transactions to meet this need? If the Fed supplies $20 billion in reserves, what will happen to the fed funds rate?
15. Explain the following statement: Even though outright purchases account for less than 10 percent of Fed transactions, the Fed's portfolio of securities consists mainly of securities bought outright.
16. Assume that the demand for required plus excess reserves is $50 billion, the level of discount borrowing is $100 million, and the actual level of nonborrowed reserves is $49 billion. What is the reserve need if the existing degree of pressure on reserve positions is to be maintained? What will happen if the Fed supplies less reserves than the reserve need?
17. What are the implications of the following Fed activities?
    a. The Fed sells securities using reverse repurchase agreements.
    b. The Fed buys securities using system repurchase agreements.
    c. The Fed makes outright purchases for the system account.

Internet Exercises

1. a. Access the following Web address: **http://www.newyorkfed.org/aboutthefed/ fedpoint/fed04.html**. Use the information to explain repurchase and reverse repurchase agreements.
   b. Access the following Web address: **http://www.newyorkfed.org/aboutthefed/ fedpoint/fed43.html**. Use the information to define *fedwire*.

c. Access the following Web address: **http://www.newyorkfed.org/aboutthefed/ fedpoint/fed27.html**. Discuss the content and function of the System Open Market Account.

d. Access the following Web site: **http://www.newyorkfed.org/aboutthefed/ fedpoint/fed13.html**. Discuss the function of the New York Fed.

2. In accordance with the provisions of the Humphrey-Hawkins Act of 1978, the Fed chair testifies before Congress twice a year, in February and July. Links to the most recent testimony can be found at **http://www.federalreserve.gov/boarddocs/hh/**. Access this address and answer the following:

a. According to the testimony, what was the overall performance of the U.S. economy in the most recent quarter?

b. What does the chair forecast about future economic growth?

c. What does the FOMC expect with regard to inflation?

d. What is the FOMC's current stance on monetary policy? What policy recommendations are made to support this stance?

Suggested Readings

For a discussion of "Declining Required Reserves, Funds Rate Volatility, and Open Market Operations," see the paper by the same name by Selva Demiralp and Dennis Farley, *Finance and Economics Discussion Series,* Board of Governors of the Federal Reserve System, 2003-27 (July 2003). The paper is available on the Internet at **http://www.federalreserve.gov/pubs/feds/ 2003/200327/200327abs.html**.

Each year, the March and September issues of the *Federal Reserve Bulletin* contain the Fed's "Monetary Policy Report to the Congress," as mandated by the Humphrey-Hawkins Act of 1978. These reports make for interesting reading regarding monetary policy and the economic outlook. The Monetary Policy Testimony and the Report to Congress are available on the Internet at **http://www.federalreserve.gov/**.

For an interesting discussion on monetary policy under different Fed chairs, see Cjristina D. Romer and David H. Romer, "Choosing the Federal Reserve Chair: Lessons from History," *Journal of Economic Perspectives* 18: (Winter 2004): 129–162.

For a discussion of Nobel laureate economist William Vickery's view that under normal conditions, inflation and unemployment are separable issues, see David Colander, "Macroeconomics: Was Vickery Ten Years Ahead?" *Challenge* (September–October 1998): 72–86.

For a discussion of the challenges of monetary policy given structural changes in the economy in the 1990s, see Robert T. Parry, "Monetary Policy in a New Environment: The U.S.

Experience," *Economic Letter,* Federal Reserve Bank of San Francisco, No. 200-31 (October 13, 2000).

"Open Market Operations in the 1990s," by Cheryl L. Edwards, contains a thorough and comprehensive overview. It can be found in the *Federal Review Bulletin* (November 1997): 859–874.

Chapters 6 and 7 of *U.S. Monetary Policy and Financial Markets* (1998), by Ann-Marie Meulendyke of the Federal Reserve Bank of New York, contain much valuable information on the execution of open market operations.

Canada, the United Kingdom, and New Zealand have conducted monetary policy without reserve requirements for several years. In the United States, required reserves have fallen significantly in recent years because of deposit sweeping. An article that looks at both issues is "Monetary Policy without Reserve Requirements: Case Studies and Options for the United States," by Gordon H. Sellon, Jr. and Stuart E. Weiner, in the *Economic Review of the Federal Reserve Bank of Kansas City* (Spring Quarter 1997): 5–30.

As mentioned in the chapter, the monthly *Federal Reserve Bulletin* contains the "Minutes of the FOMC Meetings" and the "Monetary Policy Report to Congress." In addition, the *Bulletin* contains many statements to Congress by the Fed chair and other Fed governors. This information may also be accessed on the World Wide Web site of the Federal Reserve Board: **http://www.federalreserve.gov**.

Endnotes

1 Since April 5, 1999, the Trading Desk has been entering the market during a 10-minute period around 9:30 A.M. Between 1997 and April 1999, the Trading Desk entered the market at 10:30 A.M. Prior to 1997, the Trading Desk entered the market at 11:30 A.M. The changes, which reflected the desire to enter the market at the most opportune time, were possible because of technological advances that led to the earlier receipt of critical data.

2 *Federal Reserve Bulletin* (September 1995): 853.

3 The Press Release is available on the Internet at http://www.federalreserve.gov/boarddocs/press/monetary/2004/20040630/default.htm.

4 The Press Release is available on the Internet at http://www.federalreserve.gov/boarddocs/press/monetary/2003/20031028/.

If countries don't discipline themselves, the world market will do it.

—Morris Offit, Offitbank

Monetary Policy in a Globalized Financial System

Learning Objectives

After reading this chapter, you should know:

How international trade and capital flows affect monetary policy in a globalized financial system

The limitations of domestic monetary policy under fixed and flexible exchange rate systems

Why monetary policy will most likely require increased global coordination in the future regardless of the exchange rate system

Monetary Policy and the Globalization of Finance

We have seen that one of the most important roles of the Fed is to formulate and implement the nation's monetary policy. The Fed attempts to ensure that sufficient money and credit are available to allow for a stable and healthy financial system. In this way, the economy can expand in accord with its long-run growth potential with little or no inflation and with minimum fluctuations in output and employment.

We have also seen that financial markets have experienced ongoing and dramatic changes. The financial system is experiencing a dramatic metamorphosis, driven by technological improvements in computers and telecommunications, the breakdown of barriers to capital flows, and an increasingly globalized environment. As a result, the international financial system has experienced inordinate growth, and economies have become much more interdependent in just a few short years. After international financial crises in Mexico, Asia, and Russia, most of us are keenly aware of just how interdependent the world's economies are and how events in one country can spill over to other countries, including the United States.

In this final chapter, we look at the policy implications of the continuing growth of international trade and the globalization of the financial system. We consider the effects of monetary policy under both fixed and flexible exchange rate systems. You shall see that the globalization of finance may, of necessity, change the modus operandi of the Fed even though the goals of monetary policy remain the same.

Monetary Policy under Fixed Exchange Rates from 1944 to 1973

As you saw in Chapter 19, from 1944 until 1973, the major economies of the world participated in the **Bretton Woods Accord**, a **fixed exchange rate system** with the U.S. dollar serving as the **official reserve asset**. Other countries defined their currencies in terms of the dollar and bought or sold dollars to maintain the fixed exchange rates. Supporters of the Bretton Woods Accord believed that the fixed exchange rate system offered several advantages.

One advantage was that under some conditions, inflation and unemployment could be self-correcting. If inflation or unemployment accelerated in one country relative to the rest of the world, market forces in international markets would come into play and cause the inflation and unemployment to be reduced.

Under a fixed exchange rate system, when a country experienced inflation higher than that of its trading partners, its balance of payments would go into a deficit position as net exports fell and capital outflows increased. Net exports would fall because the country's domestic prices were relatively higher than prices in the rest of the world leading to a decrease in exports and an increase in imports. If the inflation were due to increases in the money supply, lower interest rates initially could also lead to a net capital outflow as foreign financial securities became more attractive than domestic securities. The net capital outflow would further increase the deficit in the balance of payments. Under the Bretton Woods Accord, the inflation-ridden country would be forced to buy back its currency to maintain fixed exchange rates. The act of buying back its currency tended to reduce the country's domestic money supply and inflationary pressures, increase domestic interest rates, and improve the trade imbalance. Thus, inflation would be self-correcting.

Likewise, if unemployment in a country increased, income would fall, causing imports to decrease and, assuming that exports remained constant, net exports to increase. The balance of payments would move into a surplus position, and the country would experience an increase in international reserves. If policy makers allowed the increase in international reserves to also increase the domestic money supply, the level of economic activity would speed up and employment would increase. Note that if the increase in international reserves did not lead to expansion of the domestic money supply, employment would not rise.

Another advantage of a fixed exchange rate system was that it minimized **exchange rate risk**. This is the risk that changes in the exchange rate will cause the value of foreign currencies or foreign financial instruments to fall. Under a fixed rate system, such as the Bretton Woods Accord, currency values did not change under normal circumstances. Exchange rate risk was, therefore, very small and related only to the probability that the monetary authorities would redefine the currency in terms of the official reserve asset. Ceteris paribus, lower exchange rate risk is an advantage because it leads to increases in trade, capital flows, and economic efficiency. As you saw in Chapters 18 and 19, derivatives can be used to hedge exchange rate risk. Under a fixed exchange rate system, there is less need for derivatives because exchange rate risk is lower than under flexible exchange rates. Because derivatives involve some fees, the transactions costs of exchanging currencies are also reduced.

Despite these advantages, the Bretton Woods system also entailed some disadvantages. The ability of foreign countries to pursue their own monetary policies was limited because each country had to support its currency if market forces caused the currency's value to deviate from the agreed-upon exchange rate. For example, when a country wanted to pursue a more expansionary policy, its monetary authorities would increase the supply of reserves available to the banking system. Interest rates would fall and the monetary and credit aggregates would increase. This policy might result in a deficit in the balance of payments on current and capital accounts for two reasons. First, an increase in domestic income causes imports to increase. If the expansionary policy also causes domestic prices to increase, then exports decrease at the same time. Thus, net exports (exports minus imports) would decrease due to the rise in domestic income. Second, because of the falling interest rates, the country would also experience a capital outflow that would further contribute to the deficit in the balance of payments on current and capital accounts.

The central bank of the deficit country would then have to use its supplies of dollars to purchase its own currency to maintain the agreed-upon exchange rate. The act of buying back its currency would at least partially undo the stimulatory effects of the injection of reserves and would limit the monetary authorities' ability to pursue an expansionary policy. If the country ran out of dollars, it might have to devalue its currency. **Devaluation** entails discreet changes in the official exchange rate by the central bank but can destabilize financial markets and the domestic economy.

Likewise, if a country wished to pursue contractionary policies relative to those of the rest of the world, its balance of payments on current and capital accounts would move toward a surplus position. Net exports would increase as imports fell relative to exports. If prices also fell due to the contractionary policies, exports would increase. The higher interest rate would also lead to a capital inflow. Both factors would put upward pressure on the exchange rate. The ability of the monetary authorities to limit the growth of the money supply would be reduced by the necessity to supply the country's currency to maintain fixed exchange rates. The supplying of the currency would at least partially undo the contractionary effects. After a time, if the trade surplus and capital inflow persisted, the country would be under pressure to revalue its currency. In a **revaluation**, the monetary authorities increase the value of a currency relative to the official reserve asset. Again, financial markets and the economy would be destabilized. Although a country that is running a balance of your payments deficit and losing international reserves must at some point devalue, the situation is different for a balance of payments surplus. If a country is running chronic surpluses, it does not have to revalue. Because a country can always print more money, the country could keep supplying its own currency, although this is a highly unlikely scenario.

Exchange Rate Risk
The risk that changes in the exchange rate can adversely affect the value of foreign exchange or foreign financial instruments.

Devaluation
Under fixed exchange rates, a reduction in the value of a currency by the monetary authorities relative to the official reserve asset.

Revaluation
Under fixed exchange rates, an increase the value of a currency by the monetary authorities relative to the official reserve asset.

The Monetary Policy Report to the Congress always has a section on the external (rest-of-the-world) sector. The report is available at the Fed's Internet site at **http://www.federalreserve.gov/boarddocs/hh/**.

Check out foreign exchange rate data at **http://www.federalreserve.gov/releases/h10/Current/** or **http://research.stlouisfed.org/fred2/categories/15**.

As we noted earlier, under normal circumstances, exchange rate risk is lower with fixed exchange rates. When the situation is not normal, however, this advantage can turn into a major disadvantage. If a country is running a deficit in the balance of payments and devaluation seems likely, market participants will attempt to supply more of the currency to the central bank in exchange for dollars, the official reserve asset. By supplying more of the currency, however, market participants will further deplete the country's international reserves. Devaluation, which may have been only a possibility, would become a necessity. Thus, the expectation of devaluation may become a self-fulfilling prophecy.

For example, suppose that market participants expect the value of the peso to fall from $1 = 3.5 pesos to $1 = 7 pesos. Before the devaluation, an investor could exchange 350 pesos for $100 at the exchange rate of $1 = 3.5 pesos. If the investor is correct and the peso is devalued, the $100 will net 700 pesos after the devaluation. Note that the investor starts with 350 pesos and ends up with 700 pesos! As savvy investors exchange pesos for dollars, the country loses more of its international reserves, and the need to devalue becomes more imminent. In an attempt to stop the outflow of international reserves, policy makers may make the situation worse by denying that devaluation is a possibility. In this manner, the situation goes from bad to worse as devaluation is postponed until the problem becomes critical.

Another disadvantage of the Bretton Woods system was that it could be maintained only if all countries were willing and able to support their currencies and, if necessary, to periodically and orderly revalue or devalue them. As you have seen, foreign central banks had to adjust their currencies in terms of the dollar because the dollar was the official reserve asset. As long as foreign central banks were accumulating dollars to serve as international reserves, the United States could pursue expansionary domestic policies that resulted in balance of payment deficits on current and capital accounts. There was no need to worry about exchange rate pressures on its own or foreign currencies. Once foreign countries had acquired sufficient reserves, persistent U.S. deficits on current and capital accounts would result in the need for foreign countries to revalue their currencies. By the same token, persistent U.S. current and capital accounts surpluses would result in the need for foreign countries to devalue.

The need to periodically revalue or devalue was also related to the divergent domestic monetary and fiscal policies pursued by the Bretton Woods countries. Over time, if different countries pursued different policies, some countries would expand relatively faster than others, leading to exchange rate imbalances. For example, expansionary fiscal or monetary policy could cause one country to grow faster than another. Likewise, contractionary fiscal and monetary policy could cause a country to grow at a slower rate.

To the extent that countries experienced different growth rates, inflation rates, and interest rate structures, imbalances in the current and capital accounts would persist. If a country had more expansionary policies than the United States, it would experience chronic deficits in the current and capital accounts as well as the need to devalue. If a country had more contractionary policies, it would experience persistent surpluses and the need to revalue. If countries refused to make the necessary changes in their exchange rates, the system of fixed exchange rates established at Bretton Woods would break down.

As you saw in Chapter 19, the system did eventually break down when it became clear that the United States would not be able to continue to redeem dollars in gold. The breakdown occurred because U.S. policy makers were pursuing more expansionary policies than were some foreign economies, notably Germany and Japan. The result was an outflow of gold from the United States. With the suspension of the international conversion of dollars to gold in late 1971 and the official establishment of flexible exchange rates in 1974, the Bretton Woods fixed exchange rate system came to an end.

Recap

The Bretton Woods Accord of 1944 established fixed exchange rates among major world currencies with the U.S. dollar serving as the official reserve asset. Supporters of the system believed that inflation and unemployment would, under some circumstances, be self-correcting and that exchange rate risk would be reduced. The need to maintain fixed exchange rates limited the ability of a country to pursue its own monetary policy. If a country wished to pursue more expansionary policies, lower domestic interest rates and higher income could lead to a deficit in the balance of payments. The need to buy back one's own currency would thwart the expansionary policies.

Monetary Policy under Flexible Exchange Rates since 1974

Flexible Exchange Rate System
An exchange rate system in which the value of a currency is determined by supply and demand.

Under a **flexible exchange rate system**, market forces determine the value of a nation's currency. For the U.S. dollar, this means that the exchange rate is determined by the demand for and supply of dollars in international markets. The supply of dollars/month reflects U.S. demand for foreign goods, services, and securities. Ceteris paribus, quantity supplied is a positive function of the exchange rate. The demand for dollars reflects foreign demand for U.S. goods, services, and securities. Ceteris paribus, quantity demanded is a negative function of the exchange rate. The market, if left alone, will gravitate to the exchange rate where quantity demanded is equal to quantity supplied. As you saw in Chapters 9 and 19, factors such as domestic and foreign income, inflation rates, and interest rates affect exchange rates, and "flexible" exchange rates immediately adjust to changing market conditions and expectations.

With the enactment of a flexible exchange rate system in late 1974, countries in some ways gained more control over their own monetary policies. No longer would a monetary objective or policy be compromised by a country's need to maintain the agreed-upon exchange rate as it was under the Bretton Woods Accord. No longer would a country have to support its domestic currency if market forces were causing the currency to depreciate or appreciate. As discussed in Chapter 9, **depreciation** occurs when the value of a currency falls in terms of another currency under a flexible exchange rate system. **Appreciation** occurs when the value of a currency rises in terms of another currency.

Depreciation
A decrease in the value of a currency in terms of another currency under a flexible exchange rate system.

Appreciation
A rise in the value of a currency in terms of another currency under a flexible exchange rate system.

If monetary policy makers in a country are pursuing more expansionary policies than those of their neighbors, the balance of trade can move into a deficit position, with resulting deterioration in the balance of payments. Likewise, if a more contractionary policy is pursued, the balance of payments can move into a surplus position. Even though the country no longer has to defend its currency to maintain fixed exchange rates, it must consider other international ramifications of its monetary policy. Perhaps the most important effects are capital flows and the potential depreciation or appreciation of its currency. Depreciation and appreciation, in turn, can feed back to the domestic economy and cause changes in the growth rate of income through net exports.

If international trade and capital flows are small relative to the aggregate level of economic activity, monetary authorities may have greater latitude in the execution of policy. International trade and capital flows have increased significantly since 1970, however, so policy makers must consider how their policies will affect foreign countries and what the feedbacks to the domestic economy will be. For example, in mid 2004, U.S.

exports were about $1,188.2 billion while imports were roughly $1,816.0 billion in an economy where gross domestic product (GDP) was just over $11,803.5 billion. In 1960, exports were roughly $25.3 billion and imports $22.8 billion while gross national product (GNP) was $526.6 billion. Thus, in 1960, exports and imports were 4.8 and 4.3 percent of GNP, respectively ($25.3/$526.6 and $22.8/$526.6). By mid 2004, exports had grown to 11 percent of GDP ($1,188.2/$11,803.5), and imports had increased even more to 15.4 percent of GDP ($1,816.0/$11,803.5). In some ways, U.S. monetary authorities have always recognized that their monetary policies can affect interest rate, inflation, and growth in other countries. In recent decades, U.S. policy makers have also become increasingly aware that foreign events can at times influence the U.S. economy and, hence, the formulation and effects of policy.

Coincidentally with the growth in trade in the 1970s, governments began to remove barriers to international capital flows. The dismantling was virtually completed by the 1980s. In addition, major breakthroughs in telecommunications technologies and the electronic transfer of funds now allow funds to be transferred almost instantaneously anywhere in the world. These two factors have created a worldwide foreign exchange market where the buying and selling of different currencies take place and the "wheels are greased" for international trade and capital flows among nations. In 2004, the foreign exchange market traded more than $1.5 trillion every day—the equivalent of more than $250 per day per person in the world—making it the largest market in the world. Because enormous sums of funds flow with lightning speed, the ability for funds to find their highest return is greatly increased. From an economic standpoint, economic efficiency is enhanced when funds flow to the location with the highest risk-adjusted return.

Capital flows jeopardize or weaken the intended effects of monetary policy. To illustrate, we will consider the case of contractionary monetary policy in which the Fed raises interest rates to slow the level of economic activity. If U.S. interest rates move up relative to interest rates abroad, ceteris paribus, foreigners will demand more U.S. financial instruments, which will then pay a relatively higher return and less of their own financial instruments, which will then pay a relatively lower return. The demand for dollars increases and puts upward pressure on the exchange rate. Capital flows in from abroad as the dollar appreciates. The augmented supply of funds from abroad causes U.S. interest rates, although higher than before the Fed acted, to be lower than they otherwise would be. Thus, slowing the level of economic activity is more difficult because of the offsetting effect of capital flows on the supply of loanable funds.

In addition, because of the reduced demand for foreign financial instruments, ceteris paribus, there is also a tendency for prices of foreign financial instruments to fall and foreign interest rates to rise. Changes in the supply of and demand for financial instruments cause capital flows that will bring real interest rates between countries into closer alignment. Given a change in U.S. interest rates, freer capital movements will bring about immediate changes in the exchange rate and eventual interest rate adjustments in foreign economies.

Continuing with our example of contractionary U.S. policy, if the increase in the domestic interest rate causes the dollar to appreciate, the dollar price of foreign goods falls while the foreign price of U.S. goods rises. The result is a decrease in exports and an increase in imports. Thus, net exports will also fall in response to an appreciation of the exchange rate. This latter effect reinforces the contractionary effects of a rise in domestic interest rates.

At the same time that these forces are working to decrease net exports, two other effects are working in the opposite direction—to increase net exports. First, the increase in domestic interest rates could cause a reduction in domestic demand as the demand for

Dollarization and Currency Boards

Full Dollarization
Abandonment of a country's own currency to adopt another country's currency as its official currency.

Full dollarization occurs when a country abandons its own currency in order to adopt another country's currency as its official currency. The adopted currency becomes the medium of exchange and unit of account. The U.S. dollar is the currency that has been most widely adopted and used by other countries. Although the U.S. dollar is the most widely dollarized currency, the term *dollarization* is generic and, in many cases, has little to do with the United States or the U.S. dollar. For example, Greenland has adopted the Danish krone; Vatican City, the Italian lira; Tuvalu, the Australian dollar; and so on.

Since 1999, El Salvador, Ecuador, and Guatemala have dollarized by adopting the U.S. dollar and abolishing their domestic currencies. Argentina has seriously considered full dollarization. (Panama dollarized in the early twentieth century.) Full dollarization with the U.S. dollar is discussed as a way to help developing countries, particularly those in South and Latin America, to overcome monetary and exchange rate volatility and to stabilize prices.

There are both benefits and costs to full dollarization. On the benefits side, there can be no balance of payment crises or speculative attacks on the domestic currency if the currency does not exist. The increased stability should lead to increased capital inflows, lower interest rates, and greater investment and growth. Lower interest rates also reduce the government's cost of financing the public debt. Another possibility is increased trade and financial integration with the United States and reduced inflationary expectations.

The costs of full dollarization include the loss of the identity associated with one's national currency. Many of the European countries that participate in the euro had a difficult time giving up their domestic currencies. Seigniorage is a more direct cost. **Seigniorage** is the difference between the cost of producing and distributing currency and any revenues earned through the distribution. For example, the Fed issues currency by purchasing government securities that earn interest. The interest goes to the Fed and eventually to the government. On the other hand, the currency issued by the Fed does not pay interest. The amount of interest earned on the government securities less the cost of producing the Federal Reserve notes is seigniorage. If a country fully dollarizes with U.S. dollars, that country forgoes earning seigniorage and the United States earns additional seigniorage that is related to the amount of U.S. dollars circulating in the foreign country. If electronic payments reduce the use of currency in the future, the amount of seigniorage will be reduced.

Seigniorage
The difference between the cost of producing and distributing currency and any revenues earned.

Another cost of full dollarization is that the country that dollarizes loses the ability to pursue an autonomous monetary policy. Small countries that wish to become more integrated with larger economies to increase trade and attract capital inflows have limited ability to pursue an independent monetary policy anyway.

Currency Board
An organized body within a country with the sole responsibility and power to define the value of the country's currency.

A close alternative to full dollarization is the creation of a currency board. A **currency board** is an organized body within a country with the sole responsibility and power to defend the value of a country's currency. The currency board pegs or fixes the currency value to the value of the currency of the dominant trading partner. The country commits to a fixed exchange rate and the currency is fully convertible with the pegged currency. The government cannot print money unless it is backed by reserves of the currency to which it is pegged. Finally, the currency board has the power to force the government to eliminate a budget deficit that may be inflationary.

A currency board can achieve many of the benefits of full dollarization. Also, the value of the seigniorage from issuing one's own currency is not lost. The problem is that the currency board may not be perceived to be as permanent as full dollarization. Given the perception that the currency board could be abolished or modified, the full benefits of increased trade and investment and lower interest rates would not be realized. The currency could still be subject to speculative attacks if speculators sold the currency at the preset price, putting tremendous pressure on the currency board to devalue. In 1991, Argentina established a currency board that fixed the Argentina peso with the U.S. dollar and experienced a severe financial crisis in early 2002. Despite the presence of the currency board, there is less certainty with a currency board than with full dollarization. The increased uncertainty leads to higher interest rates, lower investment, and slower growth than what would be otherwise. Argentina, Bulgaria, Bosnia, and Hong Kong have had successful currency boards.

Finally, it should be noted that dollars already circulate and are widely used in many of the countries that could benefit from full dollarization. To the extent that the dollar displaces the national currency, seigniorage is already reduced.

interest-sensitive expenditures falls. The reduction in aggregate demand decreases the demand for imports, thereby increasing net exports from what they otherwise would be. Second, if the slowing of the economy causes domestic prices to fall relative to foreign prices, then, ceteris paribus, both foreign and domestic customers have an incentive to switch to domestically produced goods and services. These two effects work to increase net exports and to mitigate the decline in net exports that results from the appreciation of the dollar.

Nevertheless, in most cases, the decrease in net exports caused by the appreciation of the dollar will be larger than the increase in net exports resulting from these two additional factors. Hence, the total effect of contractionary monetary policy is to decrease net exports. Although that may not always be the case, we usually assume that higher U.S. interest rates lead to an appreciation of the domestic currency, capital inflows, a decrease in net exports, and a larger trade deficit (or smaller trade surplus). Exhibit 27-1 below provides a schematic diagram of the results of U.S. contractionary monetary policy under flexible exchange rates.

27-1   A Schematic View of the Results of U.S Contractionary Policy under Flexible Exchange Rates

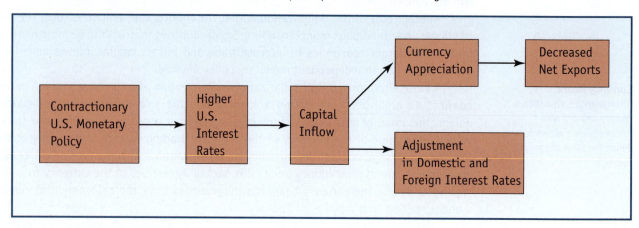

The impact of U.S. monetary policy also depends on the monetary and fiscal policies of other countries. If other central banks attempt to slow their economies when the U.S. monetary authorities are doing so, resulting effects on exchange rates depend on the relative magnitudes of the interest rate changes among the various countries. Thus, we can conclude that interest rates and exchange rates are determined jointly by the monetary and fiscal policies of the various interdependent countries and the resulting market forces.

In summary, the growth of trade and capital flows has occurred in a world that switched from fixed to flexible exchange rates. Because central banks are no longer necessarily committed to maintaining the value of their respective currencies, policy makers have more independence in formulating and executing monetary policy. A country's ability to run a monetary policy far different from that of its neighbors is limited by the increased interdependence of economies and the ease with which capital flows across borders. Capital flows and changes in the exchange rate offset the effects. The more important trade is to the domestic economy and the greater the ease with which capital flows between nations, the larger the effects. Thus, for the United States, external factors are likely to dampen the effects of any Fed actions that result in relative interest rate or income changes. In the near term, an increase in U.S. rates relative to foreign rates usually increases the exchange rate of the dollar and capital inflows, ceteris paribus. Similarly, a decrease in U.S. rates relative to foreign rates usually leads to decreases in the exchange rate of the dollar and capital outflows, ceteris paribus. Note that as a result of capital flows, these financial adjustments to U.S. monetary policy action will occur in advance of the slower response of output and prices.

Thus, the crux of the dilemma is that under fixed exchange rates, countries are limited in running their own monetary policies because of the need to maintain the value of their currency. Under flexible exchange rates, countries can also be limited. If a country tries to run a policy that is different from the rest of the world, capital and real flows will occur and will complicate the results and jeopardize that policy. What does all of this mean for the future? In a nutshell, it means that in all probability, nations will have to be more concerned about coordinating their monetary policies. The next section looks at the specifics.

Recap   Under flexible exchange rates, the value of a currency is determined by supply and demand. Flexible exchange rates free a country from the need to supply or demand dollars to maintain fixed exchange rates. In this way, flexible exchange rates allow policy makers more freedom in pursuing policies that diverge from those of other countries. At the same time, however, policy makers must also be concerned about the effects of their domestic policies on exchange rates and capital flows. Under flexible exchange rates, a country can pursue its own policy, but if it differs from policies in the rest of the world, changes in net exports and capital flows can mitigate the intended effects of the policy.

The Globalization of Monetary Policy

A new reality is having a profound influence on the conduct and effectiveness of domestic policies. Simply put, the economies of the world are becoming more interdependent. What goes on in Tokyo, London, Hong Kong, Paris, and Buenos Aires has an increasingly important effect on the financial system and the economy in the United States. Consequently, U.S. policy makers have somewhat less control over the performance of the U.S. economy than in previous eras when the U.S. economy was more isolated from international trade and finance. As Alan Greenspan said about the effects of the ongoing crises in Russia and Asia on the U.S. economy: "It is just not

Capital Flows and the Mexican Peso Crisis

The Mexican peso devaluation of late 1994 is a striking example of the implications of international capital flows and how quickly they can occur. The story begins in the early 1990s when large amounts of international financial capital poured into Mexico. Given its proximity and ties to the United States and the proposed North American Free Trade Agreement, Mexico appeared to be a safe haven. The market value of stocks traded on the Mexican stock exchange increased from $4 billion in 1985 to over $200 billion in 1993. In 1993, it was estimated that foreigners owned around 75 percent of the stocks traded on the exchange.[a] But the bubble could not last forever.

In the second half of 1994, Mexico began to experience capital outflows that resulted in a dramatic loss of international reserves, particularly the dollar. By December 20, 1994, Mexico found it necessary to devalue the peso by 15 percent from 3.50 to 4.00 pesos per dollar. Despite this move, the loss of international reserves continued, and three days later, when this exchange rate could not be maintained, the peso was allowed to float freely. The result was a 50 percent depreciation of the peso, massive capital outflows from Mexico, falling stock prices, skyrocketing interest rates, and an international financial crisis.

The capital outflow caused Mexico to lose most of its international reserves. Reserves fell from $17.1 billion on November 1, 1994, to $3.8 billion by January 30, 1995. There were fears that the government would default on the Tesobonos, which were dollar-indexed government bonds issued in pesos with maturities up to a year. Foreign investors, many of whom were in the United States, held half of the Tesobonos. President Bill Clinton authorized a $20 billion rescue package that would enable Mexico to redeem all maturing Tesobonos with U.S. dollars. (An additional rescue package later arranged by Clinton amounted to $30 billion.) As a result of the crisis, Mexico experienced a severe recession.

In addition to political instability in Mexico, many analysts believe that the crisis was caused by two international events. The first was the reversal of Japanese capital flows into Mexico in response to the domestic crisis in Japan. The second was the rise in U.S. interest rates orchestrated by the Fed starting in early 1994. Both caused capital flows out of Mexico and contributed to the subsequent crisis. Writing in the *Columbia Journal of World Business*, Michael Adler made three observations about the crisis:

Markets are extremely sensitive to uninsured risks and react quickly and massively when risks are perceived to rise.

Any rush to sell in one sector of the market produces liquidity shortages that cause selling pressures to cascade into other market sectors. [As a result of the Mexican peso crisis, other emerging markets and even other developed economies also experienced international capital outflows.]

Markets need some kind of insurance when governments, by suddenly changing the interest rate environment as the Federal Reserve did . . . can confront investors with the risk of ruin.[b]

As we noted in this chapter and in Chapter 19, the potential for crisis is augmented because capital flows are larger and more volatile than in the past.

The Eurosystem

One of the best examples of increased cooperation and coordination in the formulation of monetary policy is the Eurosystem. As you saw in Chapter 4, the Eurosystem consists of the European Central Bank and the central banks of the 12 countries that participate in the euro, Europe's single currency. As such, the Eurosystem implements and carries out monetary policies for the eurozone, with the primary goal of achieving price stability. To do this, the Eurosystem decides on a quantitative definition of price stability, such as 2 percent inflation or less.

In addition, "two pillars" are used to achieve the goal. The first pillar is a quantitative reference value for the growth rate of a broad-based monetary aggregate, such as *M*2 in the United States. The second pillar consists of a broad collection of indicators that policy makers use to assess the outlook for price developments in the area as a whole. The former is similar to targeting a monetary aggregate to guide policy formulation. The latter is similar to using a more eclectic approach in policy formulation.

To achieve its goals, the Eurosystem uses tools similar to the Fed's, including open market operations, a lending facility like the discount window called a *standing facility*, and reserve requirements. The 12 national central banks hold the required reserves, carry out open market operations, and operate the standing facility. The Eurosystem must approve of the financial instruments that are allowed to be used in open market operations. The system also sets reserve requirements and interest rates on standing facility loans. It also takes actions that nudge interest rates and the monetary aggregates in one direction or the other as part of monetary policy.

credible that the United States can remain an oasis of prosperity unaffected by a world that is experiencing greatly increased stress."[1]

Such observations have given rise to calls for cooperation and coordination among world policy makers. Although the difficulties some countries have in coordinating their domestic monetary and fiscal policies suggest that coordinating policies across countries will never be easy, the existence of globalization does highlight the new challenges and complexities facing policy makers.

As you first saw in Chapter 19, policy makers are attempting to meet the challenges of globalization through informal discussions among the major industrialized countries and through international organizations such as the International Monetary Fund and the Bank for International Settlements. The dialogues suggest that to achieve a stable international financial system, countries around the world must have healthy financial systems with noninflationary policies. In addition, countries must standardize the reporting of information about financial markets, institutions, laws, regulations, international reserves, external debt (both short and long term), and the health of the banking sector. Finally, the surveillance of international organizations that oversee the international financial system must be more transparent and open. In such an environment, the full benefits of globalization could be reached while minimizing the costs.

When considering the future, one must consider a wide range of possibilities. In the broadest sense, major world economies will either remain on a version of the present system of flexible exchange rates or return to a version of fixed exchange rates. In either case, the ramifications for monetary policy will be considerable.

A fixed exchange rate system can be sustained only if the growth and inflation rates of the participating countries are similar and only if devaluations and revaluations occur in an orderly manner. To maintain the system for any period of time, both the monetary policies and the fiscal policies of the participating countries must be coordinated. As you have seen, divergent monetary and fiscal policies will lead to different growth rates of income, different inflation rates, and different interest rate structures. If economies grow at different rates, changes in net exports and interest rates will cause exchange rate pressures.

If the participants' monetary and fiscal policies are similar, however, it is possible for them to reap large benefits from the increased trade and integration that fixed exchange rates could encourage. Increased trade would allow the countries to enjoy a higher standard of living, and capital flows would allow surplus funds to flow to their highest return. The downside is twofold: Countries that value their independence or have divergent goals with respect to unemployment and inflation would not do well under a fixed exchange rate system. In addition, countries may not have the political discipline to stick with fixed exchange rates if domestic problems become paramount.

Under flexible exchange rates, capital flows limit a country's ability to execute policies that deviate significantly from those of the rest of the world. Thus, incentive exists for nations to cooperate to find a workable policy acceptable to all. There is already a great deal of monetary policy coordination among developed countries. Some coordination is spearheaded by international organizations such as the International Monetary Fund, which was created at the Bretton Woods Conference, and the Bank for International Settlements in Basel, Switzerland. Informal groups of major trading partners meet regularly to discuss policy regimes and options and often communicate and work together to coordinate policies. One group, called the G-7 nations, includes the United States, the United Kingdom, France, Germany, Japan, Canada, and Italy. In a "managed" flexible exchange rate system, exchange rates are determined by the forces of supply and demand, with occasional central bank intervention. The central banks of the G-7 nations have frequently intervened by buying and selling in currency markets to affect exchange rates since 1971.[2] The accompanying A Closer Look feature on page 657 discusses some examples of coordinated intervention.

In the early twenty-first century, it is difficult to predict how the Fed will execute monetary policy. Its current intermediate targets may no longer be relevant or effectively related to the level of economic activity in a globalized financial system which the Fed must increasingly consider domestic exchange rates, capital flows, and foreign policies. Although the Fed's function will remain the same, it may have to work with new procedures and regulations, including some international regulations. International considerations will necessarily play a larger role. The Fed will have to design policies for a world with increasing trade and minimal barriers to international capital flows that can occur with great speed.

In conclusion, we can say that whether the world returns to fixed exchange rates or maintains the current flexible exchange rate regime, some policy coordination will be needed. Although flexible exchange rates increase the potential independence of monetary policy, the increasing openness of world trade and finance has heightened the interdependencies among nations. Flexible exchange rates allow a central bank to set its interest rates somewhat independently of other countries, but capital mobility means that a change in the interest rates relative to other countries is compensated for by changes in exchange rates and capital flows. Thus, a central bank's freedom to set

Foreign Exchange Market Intervention

On occasion, the U.S. Treasury and the Fed intervene in the foreign exchange market to restore orderly conditions or to influence exchange rates. Since the mid-1980s, intervention has often been coordinated with the governments and central banks of the other G-7 countries. Given the large volume of foreign currency transactions—averaging more than $1.5 trillion per day—intervention by the central bank to directly affect exchange rates would have to be on a very large scale, even for a central bank. Therefore, intervention affects the market primarily by influencing market sentiment, although on occasion several central banks will try to directly affect exchange rates through coordinated intervention.

An example of coordinated intervention occurred in 1985 when leaders of France, Germany, Japan, Great Britain, and the United States met and decided to intervene in foreign exchange markets to reduce the value of the dollar. At that time, U.S. interest rates were high relative to those in the rest of the world, causing large capital inflows and a strong dollar. The strong dollar fueled trade deficits that were having a negative impact on U.S. employment. The plan was named the *Plaza Accord* after the hotel where the meeting took place. Since then, these nations and others have met on a more or less regular basis in an attempt to coordinate economic policy and to open international markets.

Two more recent examples of coordinated intervention occurred in mid-1998 and mid-2000. The first involved intervention by the United States and Japan to boost the value of the Japanese yen. On June 17, 1998, the Fed bought about $2 billion worth of yen in the first intervention on behalf of the yen in six years. At that time, the value of the yen had been declining for three years, and the exchange rate was near an eight-year low. On June 16, 1998, the yen/dollar exchange rate was $1 = 142 yen. After the intervention on June 17, 1998, the yen appreciated to $1 = 137 yen. There were two major reasons for the intervention. First, the sagging yen put additional pressures on the struggling economies of Southeast Asia, which needed to sell their goods to Japan. The weak yen made goods from Southeast Asia more expensive in Japan. Second, there was fear that the weak yen would pressure China to devalue its currency. A Chinese devaluation could set off another round of devaluations and defaults throughout Southeast Asia, intensifying the Asian crisis just as the stricken economies were beginning to recover. A unique aspect of this episode is that China had asked the United States and Japan to intervene. The intervention was basically a failure, however, because by late August, the yen was trading at $1 = 145 yen. In the fall of 1998, the value of the yen in terms of the dollar did fall dramatically. However, the fall was not directly related to the intervention in June 1998.

The second example involved intervention by the G-7 major industrialized nations including the United States to boost the value of the euro. As noted in the body of the text, the G-7 nations include Canada, Germany, France, Italy, Japan, the United Kingdom, and the United States. The euro was launched on January 1, 1999, at a debut price of $1.17 against the dollar. By September 2000, the euro had fallen more than 28 percent to $.8439 against the dollar. Many analysts felt the euro was significantly undervalued but feared that a speculative attack on the euro would drive its value down even further. On September 22, 2000, the G-7 nations initiated a concerted intervention by buying euros in currency markets. The initial result was an increase in the value of the euro to more than $0.88 against the dollar. However, the increase was short lived. Within two weeks, the euro began a downward slide and by late October was trading at its all-time low. Several reasons were posited for the failure of the intervention. First, the European Central Bank followed the intervention with only a small increase in interest rates, and some felt that larger interest rate increases were necessary to support the currency. Second, with presidential elections in the United States in early November 2000, U.S. Treasury officials reiterated on several occasions that there was no change in the U.S. position on the strong dollar. Finally, others felt there were imbalances in the euro zone economies that would require structural changes in labor markets and tax laws before the euro would appreciate.

When central banks and governments decide to intervene in foreign exchange markets, they do so for three reasons:

1. To resolve a severe but temporary liquidity crisis and to stabilize international financial markets.
2. To signal that regulators believe exchange rates are deviating significantly from fundamental underlying values (that is, the dollar is overvalued or undervalued because of speculation in the market).
3. To signal a change in exchange rate policy or to clarify an existing policy.

When the Fed participates in an intervention, it does so by purchasing or selling dollars for other foreign currencies. Because the dollars go through the banking system, reserves are either augmented or decreased. They are augmented when the Fed buys foreign currencies with dollars. Reserves are decreased when the Fed buys dollars with foreign currencies that it has previously accumulated.

To limit the effects on reserves, the Fed can engage in *sterilization*. In this process, the full amount of the foreign exchange operation is offset by an open market operation so that the monetary base is unaffected by the foreign exchange operation. For example, suppose that the Fed in conjunction with Japan decides that the dollar is overvalued and the yen is undervalued. To prop up the value of the yen, the Fed sells dollars to purchase yen. If the transaction is unsterilized, the monetary base increases, and the domestic money supply and interest rates are affected. If the transaction is sterilized, the Fed uses open market sales to offset the increase in the monetary base. In general, in the United States, foreign exchange transactions are sterilized.

interest rates is only as great as its acceptance of the foreign exchange rate movements and the capital flows connected with a change in interest rates. Amid all of the uncertainties, one factor seems highly probable: Monetary policy in the future will most likely involve more global coordination and cooperation whether it be under fixed or flexible exchange rates.

Recap   The future will require countries to coordinate their monetary policies regardless of whether exchange rates are fixed or flexible as countries become more interdependent due to the growth of trade and capital flows.

Summary of Major Points

1. The Bretton Woods Accord of 1944 established fixed exchange rates between the U.S. dollar and other major currencies. Supporters of the fixed exchange rate system believed that under some circumstances, inflation and unemployment would be self-correcting.
2. The need to maintain the value of the currency under fixed exchange rates limited the ability of a country to pursue its own monetary policy independently of other participants in the agreement.
3. Because countries had divergent monetary and fiscal policies, exchange rate imbalances persisted. Eventually, the United States was unable to maintain the conversion of dollars into gold, and the Bretton Woods system of fixed exchange rates collapsed in 1971. It was replaced by a system of flexible exchange rates.
4. Under flexible exchange rates, the value of the dollar is determined by the demand and supply of dollars. Flexible exchange rates freed countries from the need to support their currencies to maintain fixed exchange rates. Each country in some ways gained greater latitude in adjusting its domestic monetary policy.
5. Even though countries do not have to support their currencies under flexible exchange rates, they must be aware of the effects that their monetary and fiscal policies have on the exchange rate, capital flows, and net exports. Monetary policy must be executed with an understanding of the international ramifications and the feedbacks to the domestic economy. This is particularly true if net exports are a relatively large component of aggregate demand and if capital flows are unrestricted.
6. Trade has increased because of the concerted efforts of developed nations since World War II. These efforts result from the recognition of the gains from trade to all trading partners. Capital flows have also increased because of the removal of capital barriers and because of technological advances that have increased the speed of such flows.
7. Under flexible exchange rates, there is an incentive for countries to work together to coordinate monetary policy. Indeed, there is already considerable monetary policy coordination, particularly among such groups as the G-7 countries. Regardless of whether exchange rates are fixed or flexible, monetary policy in the future will most likely entail increased global coordination as economies become more interdependent because of the growth in trade and capital flows.

Key Terms

Review Questions

1. Briefly explain the Bretton Woods exchange rate system. When was it created? When and why did the system collapse?
2. Under the Bretton Woods system, the U.S. dollar was the official reserve asset. How did this affect the U.S. balance of payments on current and capital accounts? Could the United States experience large balance of payments deficits on current and capital accounts indefinitely?
3. Assume that you work at the central bank of a small country that is considering an expansionary monetary policy to speed up the level of economic activity. Given fixed exchange rates, advise the president of your country what will happen to net exports if the country pursues a policy of monetary expansion. What action will the central bank have to take to support the agreed-upon exchange rate? How will that action affect the expansionary policy?
4. Argue that fixed exchange rates are preferable to flexible exchange rates. Then present the opposite argument.

5. For each of the following situations, assuming fixed exchange rates, tell what will happen to the balance of payments on current and capital accounts in the United States, ceteris paribus:
   a. Domestic income increases.
   b. Domestic interest rates fall.
   c. Foreign income increases.
   d. Foreign interest rates fall.
   e. Domestic inflation increases.
   f. Foreign inflation increases.

6. For each of the situations in question 5, tell what will happen to the exchange rate, assuming flexible exchange rates.

7. Explain whether you agree or disagree with the following statement: Flexible exchange rates allow nations to pursue their own monetary policies.

8. What are the advantages of fixed exchange rates? What are the disadvantages? Does it matter if the country is large or small?

9. Briefly explain how interest rates on instruments of comparable risk and maturity will tend to be equalized in a world without capital barriers.

10. Under a flexible exchange rate system, what effect does contractionary monetary policy have on the exchange rate?

11. Why is a country limited in executing its own monetary policy under a fixed exchange rate system? How is it limited under a flexible exchange rate system?

12. How can monetary policy coordination among countries increase the degree to which monetary policy can be used to pursue macroeconomic goals under fixed exchange rates? under flexible exchange rates?

13. Could high U.S. interest rates affect investment spending in foreign countries? Explain.

14. What is the Eurosystem? Briefly discuss how the Eurosystem conducts monetary policy.

15. What is full dollarization? How does it differ from a currency board? What is seigniorage?

Analytical Questions

Questions marked with an icon are objective in nature. They can be completed with a short answer or number.

16. Use graphs to demonstrate what will happen to the value of the dollar in terms of the Japanese yen in each of the following situations:
    a. U.S. income increases.
    b. Japanese income increases.
    c. U.S. interest rates fall.
    d. Japanese interest rates fall.
    e. U.S. inflation increases.
    f. Japanese inflation increases.

17. If the nominal U.S. interest rate is 10 percent and U.S. inflation is 6 percent, what is the real U.S. interest rate? What is the real U.S. rate in terms of foreign interest rates?

18. The Fed exchanges $1 million for 139 million yen. If the Fed sells $1 million worth of T-bills in the open market, what will happen to domestic interest rates and the money supply? If the Fed does not do the open market sale, what will happen to domestic interest rates and the money supply? In which case is the foreign exchange transaction sterilized?

Internet Exercises

1. A useful and interesting article, "Strong Dollar, Weak Dollar," which examines how the U.S. dollar's value relates to other currencies and how changes in its value affect international trade and the open economy, is available at the following site: **http://www.chicagofed.org/publications/**. Access the article and answer the following:
   a. What is meant by a "strong" dollar? Who gains from a strong dollar?
   b. Where are foreign exchange trades completed?
   c. During the 1980s, the value of the U.S. dollar was high relative to other currencies. What effect did this have on the U.S. economy?

Suggested Readings

For a survey that looks at international monetary policy coordination since the end of Bretton Woods, see "International Coordination of Macroeconomic Policies: Still Alive in the New Millennium?" by Laurence H. Meyer, Brian M. Doyle, Joseph E. Gagnon, and Dale W. Henderson, *International Finance Discussion Papers Number 723* (April 2002). The paper is available on the Internet at **http://www.federalreserve.gov/pubs/ifdp/2002/723/ifdp723.pdf**.

For a paper that shows that business cycles were more coordinated in the post-Bretton Woods era, see "International Business Cycles under Fixed and Flexible Exchange Rate Regimes" by Michael A. Kouparitsas, *Working 2003-28, Federal Reserve Bank of Chicago* (November 29, 2003). The paper is available on the Internet at **http://www.chicagofed.org/publications/workingpapers/papers/wp2003-28.pdf**.

For students interested in a "famous" fixed exchange rate system, the gold standard, see *The Key to the Gold Vault*, published by the New York Fed in 1991 (revised 2003). It is free for the asking from the Public Information Department, Federal Reserve Bank of New York, 33 Liberty Street, New York, NY 10045 and available on the Internet at **http://www.newyorkfed.org/education/addpub/goldvaul.pdf**.

Two interesting *Fedpoints* published by the Federal Reserve Bank of New York are "Federal Reserve in the International Arena" (June 2003) and "Balance of Payments" (June 2004). Both are available on the Internet at **http://www.newyorkfed.org/aboutthefed/fedpoints.html.**

An informative article about "Why Is Financial Stability a Goal of Public Policy?" by Andrew Crockett can be found in the *Economic Review of the Federal Reserve Bank of Kansas City* 82:4 (Fourth Quarter 1997): 5–22. In that same publication, another insightful article is Charles Morris and Klara Parrish, "Maintaining Financial Stability in a Global Economy: A Summary of the Bank's 1997 Symposium," 23–38.

For a discussion of "Short-Run Independence of Monetary Policy under Pegged Exchange Rates and Effects of Money on Exchange Rates and Interests," see the article by Lee E. Ohanian and Alan C. Stockman, *Journal of Money, Credit and Banking* 29:2 (November 1997): 783–806. Enrique G. Mendoze, "Comment on Short-Run Independence of Monetary Policy under Pegged Exchange Rates," can be found in the same issue, 807–810.

For a broad view of critical international financial events since World War II and their effects on U.S. monetary policy, see Paul Volcker and Toyoo Gyohten, *Changing Fortunes* (New York: Times Books, 1992).

For a look at how European central banks coordinated monetary policy and the effects on the Eurosystem, see Aerdt C. F. J. Houben, *The Evolution of Monetary Policy Strategies in Europe* (Norwell, MA: Kluwer Academic Publishers, 2000).

Endnotes

1   Speech by Alan Greenspan at the University of California, Berkeley (September 4, 1998).

2   Actually, the G-7 nations resulted from the 1986 expansion of a group of five (G-5) nations that had consulted since the flexible exchange rate system was put into place in the early 1970s. The G-5 nations were the United States, the United Kingdom, France, Japan, and West Germany.

Looking Out, page 654

a   Tom Petruno, "Global Money—Free Flows, Free Falls," *Los Angeles Times* (March 19, 1995): A11.

b   Michael Adler, "Mexico's Devaluation: The Beginning, Not the End, of Its Problems," *Columbia Journal of World Business* (Spring 1995): 112–120.

Glossary

A

Accommodation When policy makers increase aggregate demand in response to an adverse supply shock.

Adaptive Expectations Expectations formed by looking back at past values of a variable.

Adjustable (Variable) Rate Loan When the interest rate on a loan is adjusted up or down as the cost of funds rises or falls.

Adverse Selection Problem When the least-desirable borrowers pursue a loan most diligently.

Agency of a Foreign Bank A U.S. office of a foreign bank that can borrow funds only in the wholesale and money markets and is not allowed to accept retail deposits.

Aggregate Demand Curve A curve showing the inverse relationship between the overall price level and the aggregate quantity of real output that will be demanded at various price levels, ceteris paribus.

Aggregate Supply Curve A curve graphically depicting the relationship between the overall price level and the aggregate quantity of real GDP that will be supplied at various price levels, ceteris paribus.

American Stock Exchange A stock exchange located in New York City that trades the stock of more than 660 companies.

Amortization The paying off of the principal of a loan over the life of the loan.

Appreciated Description of a currency that has increased in value relative to another currency.

Appreciation A rise in the value of a currency in terms of another currency under a flexible exchange rate system.

Arbitrageurs Traders who make riskless profits by buying in one market and reselling in another market.

Asked Price The price at which a dealer (market maker) is willing to sell securities.

Asset-Backed Securities Securities that result from the process of securitization.

Asymmetric Information When a potential borrower knows more about the risks and returns of an investment project than the bank loan officer does.

Automated Teller Machine (ATM) A machine that permits a depositor to make deposits and withdrawals to an account even when the financial institution is closed.

Average Marginal Tax Rate The average of the marginal tax rates of all taxpayers.

B

Balance of Goods and Services Net exports of services plus the trade balance.

Balance of Payments The record of transactions between the United States and its trading partners in the rest of the world over a particular period of time.

Balance on Current Account The balance of goods and services plus net unilateral transfers.

Balance Sheet An accounting statement that presents the monetary value of an economic unit's assets, liabilities, and net worth on a specific date.

Bank for International Settlements (BIS) An international financial organization that promotes international cooperation among central banks and provides facilities for international financial operations.

Bank Holding Company A corporation that owns several firms, at least one of which is a bank.

Bankers' Acceptances Money market instruments created in the course of international trade to guarantee bank drafts due on a future date.

Banking Reform Acts of 1933 and 1935 Statutes passed by Congress in response to the collapse of the banking system between 1930 and 1933.

Barter Trade of goods for goods.

Basel Accord A 1988 agreement among 12 countries that established international capital standards for banks.

Benefits of Holding Real Money Balances The stream of services that real balances yield defined as the time and distress saved by having money on hand for immediate use

Beta A measure of the overall variability of a stock relative to changes in the entire stock market.

Bid Price The price at which a dealer (market Maker) is willing to buy securities.

Board of Governors The seven governors of the Fed appointed by the president with Senate approval for 14-year terms.

Bond Indenture A document that outlines the terms of a bond issuance; the bond indenture is interpreted and monitored for compliance by the trustee.

Borrowing Constraint The impediment to continuous borrowing that may come from the lender's unwillingness to keep lending or the borrower's unwillingness to keep borrowing.

Bretton Woods Accord A 1944 agreement negotiated by the major industrialized countries that established fixed exchange rates with the U.S. dollar serving as the official reserve currency.

Broker An individual who arranges trades between buyers and sellers of securities for a fee.

Business Cycle Short-run fluctuations in economic activity as measured by the output of goods and services.

C

Call Options Options that give the buyer of the option the right but not the obligation to buy a standardized contract of a financial instrument at a strike price determined today.

Call Provisions Provisions spelled out in a bond indenture that allow the issuer to buy back the bonds at a specified price; bonds tend to be called if interest rates had fallen after the bonds were initially issued.

Capital Account The financial flow of funds and securities between the United States and the world.

Capital Asset Pricing Model A model that asserts that the value of a share of stock includes a risk-free return, a market risk premium, and a firm specific risk premium that is based on beta.

Capital Inflows Purchases of U.S. financial securities by foreigners and borrowing from foreign sources by U.S. firms and residents.

Capital Market The market for financial assets with an original maturity of more than one year.

Capital Outflows Purchases of foreign financial securities by U.S. residents and borrowing by foreigners from U.S. banks and other domestic sources.

Carrying Costs Interest costs for funds used to purchase the security underlying a futures contract plus any transactions costs.

Chartered Given permission to engage in the business of commercial banking. Banks must obtain a charter before opening.

Checkable Deposits Deposits that are subject to withdrawal by writing a check.

Circular Flow Diagram A diagram that shows the real and financial flows between households and business firms.

Circuit Breakers Reforms introduced in 1987 on the NYSE to temporarily halt market trading if prices change by a specified amount.

Clearinghouse The part of an organized exchange that takes on the responsibility of enforcing a contract after the agreement is struck.

Closed-End Mutual funds that sell a limited number of shares like other corporations but usually do not buy back outstanding shares.

Collateral The building (structure) or land that will be foreclosed on and repossessed if the borrower fails to make the scheduled payments; the lender then sells the property to recoup some or all of the losses.

Collateralized Mortgage Obligations Securitizations that redirect the cash flows (principal and interest) of mortgage-related products to various classes of bondholders, thus creating financial instruments with varying prepayment risks and varying returns.

Commercial Banks Depository institutions that issue checkable, time, and savings deposit liabilities and, among other things, make loans to commercial businesses.

Commercial Paper Short-term debt instruments issued by corporations.

Common Stock Equity claims representing ownership of the net income and assets of a corporation. The owners receive a variable or no dividend after preferred stockholders have been paid and retained earnings have been put aside.

Community Reinvestment Act Legislation passed by Congress in 1977 to increase the availability of credit to economically disadvantaged areas and to correct alleged discriminatory lending practices.

Compounding A method used to determine the future value of a sum lent today.

Comptroller of the Currency The federal agency that charters national banks.

Computation Period The period during which the actual amount of required reserve assets that must be held during the maintenance period is determined.

Consol A perpetual bond with no maturity date; the issuer is never obliged to repay the principal but makes coupon payments each year, forever.

Constant Nominal Income Effect When changes in the price level necessarily cause the quantity demanded to change in the opposite direction to maintain constant nominal income.

Consumer Price Index (CPI) A price index that measures the cost of a market basket of goods and services that a typical urban consumer purchases.

Contemporaneous Reserve Accounting A reserve accounting system under which the maintenance period—when the reserve assets must be held—more or less corresponds to the computation period when the amount of required reserves is determined.

Contingent Claims Claims such as casualty and life insurance benefits that offer the public protection from the often catastrophic financial effects of theft, accidents, natural disasters, and death.

Conventional Mortgages Mortgages made by financial institutions and mortgage brokers without the federal insurance that the principal and interest will be repaid.

Convergence The phenomenon in which the futures price is bid up or down to the spot price plus carrying costs; the futures price approaches the spot price as the expiration date draws nearer.

Convertible Provisions Provisions spelled out in a bond indenture that allow investors to convert the bonds to a specific number of shares of common stock.

Core PCE The PCE excluding energy and food.

Corporate Bonds Long-term debt instruments issued by corporations.

Cost of Holding Real Money Balances The additional forgone interest that holding nonmonetary financial assets would have yielded.

Cost-Push Inflation Sustained increases in the overall price level, triggered by increases in input prices.

Coupon Payments The coupon rate on a bond multiplied by the face value of the bond; coupon payments are usually made every six months.

Coupon Rate The fixed interest rate stated on the face of a bond.

Credit The flow of money from net lenders or financial intermediaries to net borrowers in a given time period.

Credit Derivatives Contracts that transfer the default risk of a loan or other debt instrument from the holder of the loan (beneficiary) to a guarantor who receives a fee for accepting the risk.

Credit Risk The probability of a debtor not paying the principal and/or the interest due on an outstanding debt.

Credit Unions Depository institutions that are cooperative, nonprofit, tax-exempt associations operated for the benefit of members who share a common bond.

Crowding Out The reduction in private borrowing and spending due to higher interest rates that result from government deficit financing.

Currency Board An organized body within a country with the sole responsibility and power to define the value of the country's currency.

Currency Swaps A financial innovation used to hedge exchange rate risk over a long period of time, whereby one party agrees to trade periodic payments in a given currency with another party who agrees to do the same in a different currency.

Current Account Transactions that involve currently produced goods and services, including the balance of goods and services plus net unilateral transfers.

D

Dealer An individual (market maker) who arranges trade and stands ready to be a principal in a transaction; unlike brokers, dealers take positions and maintain inventories of securities.

Debenture Bonds Bonds with no specific collateral backing but with a general claim on the other unpledged assets of the issuer.

Debit In the balance of payments, any transaction that results in a payment to foreigners by Americans.

Debt Deflation A real increase in debt burdens caused by falling incomes and prices and debt burdens that are denominated in dollars.

Default When a borrower fails to repay a financial claim.

Default Risk The risk that a borrower will be unwilling or unable to live up to the terms of the liability it has sold.

Deficit Sector A sector whose combined deficits of net borrowers are greater than the combined surpluses of net borrow.

Deflation A drop in the overall price level as measured by a price index.

Demand Deposits Non-interest-earning checking accounts issued by banks.

Demand for Loanable Funds The demand for borrowed funds by household, business, government, or foreign net borrowers.

Demand for Money The entire set of interest rate–quantity demanded combinations as represented by a downward-sloping demand curve for money.

Demand-Pull Inflation Sustained increases in the overall price level due to high levels of demand.

Depository Institutions Financial intermediaries, such as commercial banks, savings and loans, credit unions, and mutual savings banks, that issue checkable deposits.

Depository Institutions Deregulation and Monetary Control Act of 1980 (DIDMCA) The statute that removed many of the regulations enacted during the Great

Depression; phased out Regulation Q, established uniform and universal reserve requirements, increased the assets and liabilities that depository institutions could hold, authorized NOW accounts, and suspended usury ceilings.

Depreciated Description of a currency that has decreased in value relative to another currency.

Depreciation Decrease in the value of a currency in terms of another currency under a flexible exchange rate system.

Deregulate The dismantling of existing regulations.

Deregulation The removing or phasing out of existing regulations

Derivatives Instruments such as forward, futures, options, swap, and other agreements that are routinely used to separate the total risk of a financial asset into subparts and that derive their value from the underlying assets.

Derivative Markets Financial futures markets where the value of the financial instruments (the futures and forward agreements) "derive" their values from the underlying instruments such as the government securities, the shares of stock, etc. that are traded on the future date; financial forward and futures markets, among others, are examples of derivative markets.

Deversification Designated Order Turnaround (DOT)(r) A computer system used for trades of fewer than 3,000 shares on the NYSE.

Devalue Under a fixed exchange rate system, to decrease the value of a country's currency.

Devaluation Under fixed exchange rates, reduction in the value of a currency by the monetary authorities relative to the official reserve asset.

Direct Finance When net lenders lend their funds directly to net borrowers.

Discount from Par When a bond sells below its face value because interest rates have increased since the bond was originally issued.

Discount Rate The rate that healthy depository institutions are charged for short-term borrowing of reserves from the Fed. Today the primary credit rate is referred to as the *discount rate*.

Discounting A method used to determine the present value of a sum to be received in the future.

Disintermediation The removal of funds from a financial intermediary.

Diversification The allocation, of surplus funds to more than one financial instrument in order to reduce risk; For financial institution, The branching out of financial conglomerates into several product lines to reduce the dependence on any single product line.

Domestic Nonfinancial Debt (DNFD) An aggregate that is a measure of total credit market debt owed by the domestic non-financial government and private sectors.

Double Coincidence of Wants In barter, the situation in which each person involved in a potential exchange has what the other person wants.

Dow Jones Industrial Average (the Dow) An index that measures movements in the stock prices of 30 of the largest companies traded on the NYSE.

Dual Banking System The system whereby a bank may have either a national or a state charter.

E

Economic Projections Goals for nominal and real GDP, unemploy-ment, and inflation over the next 12 to 18 months, set by the Fed at its February and July meetings each year.

Economics The study of how society decides what gets produced and how, and who gets what.

Economies of Scale Gains from bigness that may result from several firms being able to streamline management and eliminate the duplication of effort that would result from several separate firms.

Economies of Scope Advantages to firms being able to offer customers several financial services under one roof.

Efficient Markets Hypothesis The hypothesis that when financial markets are in equilibrium, the prices of financial instruments reflect all readily available information.

Electronic Funds Transfer System The transfer of funds to third parties in response to electronic instructions rather than a paper check.

Employment Act of 1946 The first statute that directed policy makers to pursue policies to achieve full employment and noninflationary growth.

Eurobond Market The market for dollar-denominated bonds sold in a foreign country, often by corporations doing business in that country.

Eurodollars Dollar-denominated deposits held abroad.

Excess Reserves Reserves over and above those required by the Fed.

Exchange Rate The number of units of foreign currency that can be acquired with one unit of domestic money.

Exchange Rate Risk The risk that changes in the exchange rate will adversely affect the value of foreign exchange or foreign financial assets.

Exchange-Traded Funds (ETFs) A security created by a securities firm that deposits a large basket of stocks into a fund. The basket of stocks in the fund mirrors the holdings of stocks in an index. Shares in an EFT are then issued against the basket of stocks, sold to individual investors, and traded like shares of stock on an exchange. The return on the ETFs mirror the return, on the index.

Expansion The phase of the business cycle in which economic activity increases and unemployment falls.

Expectations Theory A theory holding that the long-term interest rate is the geometric average of the present short-term rate and the short-term rates expected to prevail over the term to maturity of the long-term security.

External Financing Financing spending that exceeds current receipts by expanding either debt or equity.

F

Farm Credit Financial Assistance Corporation (FACO) A GSE that issues bonds with an explicit government guarantee and uses the proceeds to assist the FFCBFC, which was having financial problems at the time FACO was created in 1987.

Federal Deposit Insurance Corporation (FDIC) The federal agency that insures the deposits of banks and savings associations.

Federal Deposit Insurance Corporation Improvement Act (FDICIA) Legislation passed by Congress in 1991 to enact regulatory changes to ensure the safety and soundness of the banking and thrift industries.

Federal Farm Credit Banks Funding Corporation (FFCBFC) A GSE that issues bonds and discount notes with no explicit government guarantee and uses the proceeds to make loans to farmers to increase the funds flowing into agriculture.

Federal Financial Institutions Examinations Council (FFIEC) A federal agency that prescribes uniform principles, standards, and report forms for the federal examination of financial institutions by the Fed, the FDIC, and the Office of the Comptroller of the Currency and that makes recommendations to promote uniformity in the supervision of financial institutions.

Federal (Fed) Funds Loans of reserves (deposits at the Fed) between depository institutions, typically overnight.

Federal Home Loan Bank Board The regulatory body of the S&L industry until 1989.

Federal Home Loan Mortgage Corporation (Freddie Mac) A privately owned government sponsored enterprise that sells securities and uses the proceeds to buy mortgages or mortgage-backed securities primarily from thrifts with no explicit government guarantee.

Federal Housing Administration (FHA) A federal agency that for a .5 percent fee insures mortgage loans made by privately owned financial institutions up to a certain amount if the borrowers meet certain conditions defined by the FHA.

Federal National Mortgage Association (Fannie Mae) A privately owned government-sponsored enterprise that sells securities and uses the proceeds to buy mortgages or mortgage backed securities primarily from banks. With no explicit government guarantee.

Federal Open Market Committee (FOMC) The principal policy-making body within the Federal Reserve System.

Federal Reserve Act The 1913 congressional statute that created the Federal Reserve System.

Federal Reserve (Fed) System The central bank of the United States that regulates the banking system and determines monetary policy.

Finance The study of how the financial system coordinates and channels the flow of funds from lenders to borrowers—and vice versa— and how new funds are created by financial intermediaries during the borrowing process.

Finance Companies Intermediaries that lend funds to households to finance consumer purchases and to firms to finance inventories.

Financial Assets Financial instruments such as stocks, bonds, and money, which serve as a store of value or purchasing power.

Financial Conglomerates Firms that own and operate several different types of financial intermediaries and financial institutions on a global basis.

Financial Crisis A critical upset in a financial market(s) characterized by sharp declines in asset prices and the default of many financial and nonfinancial firms.

Financial Forward Markets Markets that trade financial forward agreements usually arranged by banks or other brokers and dealers.

Financial Forward Transactions Transactions in which the terms, including price, are completed today for a transaction that will occur in the future.

Financial Futures Standardized futures contracts that trade financial instruments on a future date according to terms (including the price) determined today.

Financial Futures Markets Organized markets that trade financial futures including the Chicago

Board of Trade, the Chicago Mercantile Exchange, and the London International Financial Futures Exchange.

Financial Holding Companies (FHC) Holding companies that can engage in an even broader array of financial-related activities than bank holding companies, including securities underwriting and dealing, insurance agency and underwriting activities, and merchant banking activities; financial holding companies may engage in any other financial and non-financial activities as determined by the Fed.

Financial Innovation The creation of new financial instruments, markets, and institutions in the financial services industry; new ways for people to spend, save, and borrow funds; changes in the operation and scope of activity by financial intermediaries.

Financial Institutions Firms that provide financial services to net lenders and net borrowers; the most important financial institutions are financial intermediaries.

Financial Institutions Reform, Recovery, and Enforcement Act (FIRREA) of 1989 Legislation to resolve the S&L crisis by creating a new regulatory structure, limiting the assets S&Ls can acquire, and requiring S&Ls to maintain adequate capital.

Financial Intermediaries Financial institutions that borrow from net lenders for the purpose of lending to net borrowers.

Financial Markets Markets in which spending units trade financial claims.

Financial Stability Forum (FSF) An organization of representatives of central banks, treasury departments, and international financial institutions created in 1999 to promote international financial stability

through the exchange of information and to foster cooperation in international financial supervision and surveillance.

Fiscal Policy Government spending and taxing decisions to speed up or slow down the level of economic activity.

Fixed Exchange Rate System System in effect when countries agree to buy or sell their currency to maintain fixed exchange rates with other currencies; an exchange rate system in which currency values do not fluctuate.

Fixed-Rate Mortgages Mortgages whose the interest rate remains the same over the life of the loan.

Floating (Flexible) Exchange Rate System An exchange rate system in which currency values are determined by supply and demand and fluctuate in response to changes in supply and demand.

Flow of Funds A social accounting system that divides the economy into a number of sectors including the household, business, government, rest-of-the-world, and financial sectors.

Foreign Currency (Money) Supplies of foreign exchange.

Foreign Exchange Supplies of foreign currencies.

Foreign Exchange Market The market for buying and selling the different currencies of the world.

Forward Rate The price today for a delivery on a future date.

Freedom of Information Act (1966) A 1966 law that requires more openness in government and more public access to government documents.

Full Dollarization Abandonment of a country's own currency to adopt another country's currency as its official currency.

Futures Contracts Standardized agreements in agricultural and commodity markets to trade a fixed amount of the instrument on specific dates in the future at a price determined today.

Fractional Reserve Banking System A banking system in which individual banks hold reserve assets equal to a fraction of deposit liabilities.

Freedom of Information Act (1966) A 1966 law that requires more openness in government and more public access to government documents.

Fund of Funds A mutual fund that invests in a portfolio of other mutual funds rather than individual stocks and/or bonds.

Fungibility The ability to be easily converted from one type of instrument to another.

G

Garn–St. Germain Depository Institutions Act of 1982 A statute that, along with DIDMCA, deregulated depository institutions; authorized money market deposit accounts and Super NOW accounts.

GDP Deflator A price index that measures the overall changes in the prices of everything in GDP.

General Obligation Bonds Municipal bonds to be repaid out of general tax revenues.

Geometric Average An average that takes into account the effects of compounding; used to calculate the long-term rate from the short-term rate and the short-term rates expected to prevail over the term to maturity of the long-term security.

Glass-Steagall Act of 1933 Banking legislation, enacted in response to the Great Depression, that established Regulation Q interest rate ceiling, separated commercial and investment banking, and created the FDIC.

Government Agency Securities Bonds issued by private enterprises that were publicly chartered by Congress to reduce the cost of borrowing to certain sectors of the economy, such as farming, housing, and student loans.

Government National Mortgage Association (Ginnie Mae) A government-owned enterprise that, for a fee, gives an explicit government guarantee that Ginnie Mae bonds issued by private financial institutions will be repaid.

Government-Sponsored Enterprises (GSEs) Private enterprises that have been chartered by Congress to reduce the cost of borrowing in such sectors as housing, farming, the savings and loan industry, and student loans.

Gramm-Leach-Bliley Act (GLBA) A 1999 act that repealed the provisions of the Glass-Steagall Act of 1933 that separated investment and commercial banking; allowed bank holding companies that became certified as financial holding companies (FHCs) to engage in securities, insurance, and merchant banking activities and other financial and nonfinancial activities.

H

Hedge An investment made to reduce risk.

Hedge Fund A nontraditional type of mutual fund formed as a partnership of up to either 99 or 499 wealthy investors with large minimum investments; attempts to earn maximum returns regardless of whether financial prices are rising or falling.

Humphrey-Hawkins Full Employment and Balanced Growth Act of 1978 A statute that required policy makers to pursue policies to achieve full employment and noninflationary growth.

I

Impact Lag The time between when an action is taken and when that action has a significant impact on economic variables.

Index-Arbitrage Trading The purchasing (or selling) of a basket of stocks, usually through program trading, with the simultaneous selling (or purchasing) of a futures agreement in the same basket of securities in order to make a riskless profit (arbitrage) from the price differential between the basket of stocks and the futures agreement.

Indexed Mutual Funds A mutual fund that holds the same basket of securities that are represented in an index such as the S&P 500 or the Wilshire 5000 so that the investor receives roughly the same return as the index to which the fund is tied.

Indirect Finance When net borrowers borrow from financial intermediaries that have acquired the funds to lend from net lenders.

Initial Public Offering (IPO) An offering of stocks or bonds to the public by a company that has not previously sold securities to the public.

Inflation-Indexed Bonds Bonds whose principal amounts are adjusted for inflation when coupon payments are made (usually every six months).

Inflation Premium The amount of nominal interest added to the real interest rate to compensate the lender for the expected loss in purchasing power that will accompany any inflation.

Inflation Rate The rate of change in the Consumer Price Index, which measures the growth rate of the average level of prices paid by consumers.

Interest Rate The cost to borrowers of obtaining money and the return (or yield) on money to lenders.

Interest Rate Parity The theory that in equilibrium, interest rates adjust so that after Full adjustments for expected inflation and exchange rate risk, returns are equalized across countries.

Interest Rate Risk The risk that the interest rate will unexpectedly change so that the costs of an FI's liabilities exceed the earnings on its assets; The risk that increases an interest rates value of long-term fixed rate assets to fall.

Interest Rate Swaps A financial innovation used to reduce the risk of future interest rate changes over a long period of time that involve two parties trading interest payment streams to guarantee that their respective payment inflows will more closely match their outflows.

Intermediate Target The use of a target midway between the policy instruments and the ultimate policy goals.

Internal Financing The spending of money balances on hand or the liquidation of financial or real assets to finance spending that exceeds current receipts.

International Bank for Reconstruction and Development (IBRD) A bank that makes 12- to 15-year loans to poor, but not the poorest, countries, charging an interest rate just above the rate at which the bank borrows.

International Development Association An association that makes interest-free loans with a maturity of 35–40 years to the world's poorest countries.

International Finance Corporation An organization that mobilizes funding for private enterprise projects in poor countries.

International Financial System The numerous rules, customs, instruments, facilities, markets, and organizations that enable international payments to be made and funds to flow across borders.

International Monetary Fund (IMF) An organization created in 1944 to oversee the monetary and exchange rate policies of its members who pay quotas that are used to assist countries with temporary imbalances in their balance of payments.

Interstate Banking and Branching Efficiency Act (IBBEA) Signed into law in September 1994, an act by Congress that effectively allows unimpeded nationwide branching by June 1, 1997.

Investment Banks Financial institutions that design, market, and underwrite new issuances of securities in the primary market.

Investment Companies Companies that own and manage a large group of different mutual funds.

Investment Spending For businesses, spending on new equipment and capital or net additions to inventories.

J

Junk Bonds Bonds rated below investment grade or too risky for investment; also called *high-yield bonds*.

L

Lagged Reserve Accounting A reserve accounting system under which the maintenance period—when the reserve assets must be held—follows some time after the computation period when the amount of required reserves is determined.

Laissez-Faire The view that government should pursue a hands-off policy with regard to the economy.

Lender of Last Resort The responsibility of the Fed to provide an elastic currency by lending to commercial banks during emergencies.

Leverage Ratio The ratio of debt to equity on a firm's balance sheet.

Life Insurance Companies Intermediaries that offer protection against the financial costs associated with events such as death and disability in exchange for premiums.

Limit Orders Orders that instruct the broker or dealer to purchase securities at the market price up to a certain maximum if possible or to sell the securities at the market price if it is above a certain minimum.

Liquidity The ease with which a financial claim can be converted to cash without loss of value.

Liquidity Premium The extra return required to induce lenders to lend long-term rather than short-term.

Liquidity Risk The risk that an FI will be required to make a payment when the intermediary has only long-term assets that cannot be converted to liquid funds quickly without a capital loss.

Load A sales commission paid to a broker to purchase mutual funds; by law the load cannot exceed 8.5 percent of the investment.

Loaned Up Situation when a bank has no excess reserves left to serve as a basis for lending.

Long-Run Aggregate Supply Curve The vertical curve through the natural rate of output to which the economy will return in the long run regardless of the price level.

Long-Run Equilibrium When all prices have adjusted to shifts in aggregate supply or demand and the flow of spending, saving, borrowing, and lending continues until something else changes

M

M1 Currency in the hands of the public plus checkable deposits.

M2 Everything in M1 plus other highly liquid assets.

M3 Everything in M2 plus some less liquid assets.

Macroeconomics The branch of economics that studies the aggregate, or total, behavior of all households and firms.

Maintenance Period The period during which the actual amount of reserves held must at least equal the amount of required reserves, as determined during the computation period.

Maintenance Margin Requirement The minimum amount of equity the investor needs in his account relative to the market value of his stock.

Managed Float Exchange Rate System A system in which currency values fluctuate with changes in supply and demand but central banks may intervene if currency values are thought to be over- or under-valued.

Margin Loans Loans to investors for which the proceeds are used to purchase securities.

Margin Requirement The percentage of a stock purchase that can be borrowed; currently the margin requirement that is set by the Fed is 50 percent.

Marginal Tax Rate The tax rate that is paid on the last dollar of income that the taxpayer earns.

Market Fundamentals Factors that have a direct effect on future income streams of the instruments including the value of the assets and the expected income streams of those assets on which the financial instruments represent claims.

Market Maker A dealer who links up buyers and sellers of financial securities and sometimes takes positions in the securities.

Market Orders Orders by an investor that direct the broker or dealer to purchase or sell securities at the present market price.

Market Risk Premium The risk based on historical data that shows how much on average the ownership of stocks pays over a risk-free return.

McFadden Act The 1927 act by Congress that outlawed interstate branching and made national banks conform to the intrastate branching laws of the states in which they were located.

Means of Payment (Medium of Exchange) Something generally acceptable for making payments.

Merchandise Exports Foreign purchases of U.S. goods.

Merchandise Imports U.S. purchases of foreign goods.

Merchant Banking Direct equity investment (the purchasing of stock) in a start-up or growing company by a bank.

Microeconomics The branch of economics that studies the behavior of individual decision-making units such as households and business firms.

Monetary Aggregates The measures of money— including M1, M2, and M3—monitored and tracked by the Fed.

Monetary Base Reserves plus currency in the hands of the public; denoted as *MB*.

Monetary Policy The attempts by the Fed to stabilize the economy and to ensure sufficient money and credit for an expanding economy; The Fed's efforts to promote the overall health and stability of the economy.

Monetarists Economists who stress the role of money in determining the overall health of the economy.

Money Anything that functions as a means of payment (medium of exchange), unit of account, and store of value.

Money Illusion When spending units react to nominal changes caused by changes in prices even though real variables such as interest rates have not changed.

Market Maker A dealer who links up buyers and sellers of financial securities and sometimes takes positions in the securities.

Money Market The market for financial assets with an original maturity of less than one year.

Money Market Deposit Accounts (MMDAs) Financial claims with limited check-writing privileges, offered by banks since 1982; they earn higher interest than fully checkable deposits and require a higher minimum balance.

Money Market Mutual Funds Mutual funds that invest in money market instruments.

Money Multiplier The multiple of the change in the monetary base by which the money supply will change.

Moody's Investors Service A credit-rating agency that analyzes and evaluates bonds and assigns them to a particular risk class based on the probability that the issuer will fail to pay back the principal and interest in full when due.

Moral Hazard The reduction in market discipline experienced by FIs that goes hand-in-hand with deposit insurance.

Moral Hazard Problem For an individual, when the borrower has an incentive to use the proceeds of a loan for a riskier venture after the loan is funded; For a financial intermediary, The fact that the presence of deposit insurance causes financial intermediaries to take more risks than they otherwise would because they know that if they lose, their depositors still get their funds back.

Mortgage A long-term debt instrument for which real estate is used as collateral and which results from loans made to individuals or businesses in order to purchase or refinance land, single- or multiple-family residential housing, commercial properties, and farms.

Mortgage-Backed Securities Securities backed by a pool of mortgages; they have a low default risk and provide a steady stream of income.

Mortgages Loans made to purchase singleor multiple-family residential housing, land, or other real structures, with the structure or land serving as collateral for the loan.

Municipal Bonds (munis) Bonds issued by state, county, and local governments to finance public projects such as schools, utilities, roads, and transportation ventures; the interest on municipal securities is exempt from federal taxes and from state taxes for investors living in the issuing state.

Mutual Funds Financial intermediaries that pool funds from many small investors by selling shares; the funds that are raised are used to purchase financial securities; the income and capital gains from the securities are passed through to the investors; investment-type intermediaries that pool the funds of net lenders, purchase the long-term financial claims of net borrowers, and return the income received minus a fee to the net lenders.

N

National Association of Securities Dealers (NASD) A privately owned organization that self-regulates the market participants in the over-the-counter market under the supervision of the SEC.

National Association of Securities Dealers Automated Quotation System (NASDAQ) An association whose members trade stocks over an advanced computer system that provides immediate information about prices and the number of shares being traded.

National Bank A bank that has received a charter from the Comptroller of the Currency.

Natural Level of Real Output The level of real output that is consistent with long-run equilibrium, given the quantity and productivity of the economy's factors of production.

Natural Rate of Unemployment The rate of unemployment consistent with stable prices; believed to be about 4.0 to 4.5 percent.

Near Monies Highly liquid financial assets that can easily be converted to transactions money (M1) without loss of value.

Negotiable Certificates of Deposit (CDs) Certificates of deposit with a minimum denomination of $100,000 that can be traded in a secondary market, most with an original maturity of 1 to 12 months.

Negotiable Order of Withdrawal (NOW) Accounts Interest-earning checking accounts.

Net Asset Value The difference between the market value of the shares of stock that the mutual fund owns and the liabilities of the mutual fund.

Net Borrowers Spending units such as households and firms whose spending exceeds their income.

Net Capital Inflow The Condition when the purchases of U.S. financial claims by foreigners exceed purchases of foreign financial claims by U.S. entities.

Net Capital Outflow The Condition when the purchases of foreign financial claims by U.S. entities exceed the purchases of U.S. financial claims by foreigners.

Net Investment Gross investment minus depreciation.

Net Lenders Spending units such as households and firms whose income exceeds their spending.

Net Worth The difference between assets and liabilities at a point in time.

New York Stock Exchange (NYSE) The world's largest secondary market for trading stocks; trades the stocks of about 2,825 companies.

No-Load Mutual funds that are purchased directly from the mutual fund company and are not subject to a load.

Nominal Gross Domestic Product (Nominal GDP) The quantity of final goods and services produced in an economy during a given time period and valued at today's prices.

Nominal Interest Rate The market interest rate, or the real return plus the rate of inflation expected to prevail over the life of the asset.

Nonbanks Other intermediaries and nonfinancial companies that have taken an increasing share of intermediation.

Nondeposit Liabilities Borrowed funds, such as Eurodollar borrowings, fed funds, and repurchase agreements, that are not deposits and are not subject to reserve requirements.

O

Off-Balance-Sheet Activities Activities such as standby lines of credit, overdraft protection, unused credit card balances, and other commitments for which a bank is liable but that do not show up on the balance sheet.

Office of Thrift Supervision (OTS) An agency created by the FIRREA to replace the Federal Home Loan Bank Board as the overseer of the S&L industry.

Official Reserve Account The balance of payments account that records official government transactions in the foreign exchange market to bring the balance of payments into balance.

Official Reserve Asset The asset (such as the dollar or gold) by which other countries define the value of their currency; used as international reserves.

Official Reserve Currency The currency used by other countries to define their own currency; the U.S. dollar was the official reserve currency under the Bretton Woods Accord.

Offsetting Open Market Operations Open market purchases or sales to offset changes in the monetary base caused by other factors.

Open-End A mutual fund that continually sells new shares to the public or buys outstanding shares from the public at a price equal to the net asset value.

Open Market Operations The buying and selling of government securities by the Fed to change the reserves of depository institutions.

Operating Target A target amenable to control by the policy tools and highly correlated with the intermediate target.

Opportunity Cost The return one could have earned by using funds in the next best alternative; for investment spending, the real interest rate.

Optimal Forecast The best guess possible arrived at by using all of the available information.

Options Standardized contracts that give the buyer the right but not the obligation to buy or sell an instrument in the future at a price determined today.

Option Premium The premium paid by the buyer of an option to compensate the seller for accepting the risk of a loss with no possibility of a gain.

Options on Futures Options that give the buyer the right but not the obligation to buy or sell a futures contract up to the expiration date on the option.

Outright Transactions Open market purchases that supply reserves or open market sales that withdraw reserves.

Over-the-Counter Market A network of securities dealers that trades stocks of more than 30,000 companies via telephone or computer.

P

Par Value The face value printed on a bond; the amount for which the bond originally sold and which is repaid in full at maturity.

Payments Mechanism The means by which transactions are consummated; that is, how money is transferred in an exchange. To Make payments period

Payoff Method The method of resolving a bank insolvency by paying off the depositors and closing the institution.

Pension Funds Tax-exempt intermediaries set up to provide participants with income at retirement in exchange for premiums.

Performance Bond A bond required by an organized exchange from both the buyer and the seller of a futures agreement to ensure that both parties abide by the agreement.

Pit The trading area on the floor of an organized exchange (such as the Chicago Board of Trade) where authorized brokers gather to buy and sell for their customers.

Point-of-Sale Terminal A computer terminal that uses a debit card to electronically transfer funds from a deposit account to the account of a third party.

Policy Directive A statement issued by the FOMC to the Trading

Desk of the New York Fed that directs monetary policy until the next FOMC meeting; in recent years, the policy directive has targeted a specific fed funds rate.

Policy Lag The time between the point when the need for action is recognized and the point when an adjustment policy is decided on and set in motion.

Policy Regret A situation in which policy actions based on available data would not have been taken if more accurate data revisions had been available.

Portfolio The collection of real and financial assets and liabilities.

Precautionary Motive A motive for holding money based on the desire to protect against unforeseen developments.

Preferred Habitats An expectations theory modification hypothesizing that many borrowers and lenders have preferred maturities, which creates a degree of market segmentation between the short-term and long-term markets.

Preferred Stock Equity claims representing ownership of the net income and assets of a corporation; The owners receive a fixed dividend before common stockholders are entitled to anything.

Premium above Par When a bond sells above its face value because interest rates have decreased since the bond was originally issued.

Prepayment Risk The risk that mortgages will be prepaid early and that the funds will have to be reinvested at a lower return.

Present Value The value today of funds to be received or paid on a future date.

Price Index for Personal Consumption Expenditures (PCE) A price index that measures changes in overall prices that consumers pay;

its changes are broader measures of consumer inflation than changes in the consumer price index (CPI) and are used by the Fed in economic projections of inflation.

Primary Credit Rate The rate for short-term borrowing of reserves by the healthiest depository institutions from the Fed, also known as the *discount rate*.

Primary Dealers Large banks and securities dealers with whom the Fed directly engages in open market operations; at the present time, there are 22 primary dealers.

Primary Market The market in which a security is initially sold for the first time.

Principal The original amount of funds lent.

Private Placement The sale of new securities to a limited number of large investors; because the number of investors is small, the underwriting process is avoided.

Program Trading The preprogramming of computers to buy or sell a large number (basket) of stocks usually by institutional investors.

Property and Casualty Companies Intermediaries that provide protection against the effects of unexpected occurrences on property.

Prospectus A subpart of the registration statement that must be given to investors before they purchase the securities; the prospectus contains a description of the securities and other disclosures.

Public Debt The sum of all past government deficits less past surpluses.

Purchase and Assumption Method The method of resolving a bank insolvency by finding a buyer for the institution.

Purchasing Power Parity The theory that in the long run, exchange rates adjust so that the relative purchasing power of various currencies is equalized.

Put Options Options that give the buyer of the option the right but not the obligation to sell a standardized contract of a financial instrument at a strike price determined today.

Q

Quantity Demanded of Money The specific amount of money that spending units wish to hold at a specific interest rate (price).

Quantity Supplied of Money The specific amount of money that will be supplied at a specific interest rate.

R

Rational Expectations Expectations formed by looking both backward and forward.

Real Assets For households, durable goods and houses.

Real Estate Investment Trusts (REITs) A special type of mutual fund that pools the funds of many small investors and uses them to buy or build income property or to make or purchase mortgage loans; pass-through institutions in which the rents from the income property and/or the interest income from the mortgages are passed through to shareholders.

Real Gross Domestic Product (Real GDP) The real, or inflation-adjusted, quantity of final goods and services produced in an economy in a given time period.

Real Income Nominal income divided by a price index.

Real Interest Rate The interest rate corrected for changes in the purchasing power of money.

Real Money Balances The quantity of money expressed in real terms; the nominal money supply, M, divided by overall price level, P, or M/P.

Real Wage The nominal wage divided by the overall price level.

Recession The phase of the business cycle in which economic activity falls and unemployment rises.

Recognition Lag The time it takes policy makers to recognize that a change in the economy's performance has occurred.

Redlining The practice of restricting the number or dollar amounts of loans in an area regardless of the creditworthiness of the borrower.

Refunding The refinancing of past government debt that is maturing.

Registration Statement A statement that must be filed with the SEC before a new securities offering can be issued; the statement contains information about the offering, the company, and other relevant disclosure information.

Regularized Describes the advanced announcements of Treasury intentions to borrow at standard intervals.

Regulation D A regulation that prescribed reserve requirements on some deposits.

Regulation Q Interest rate ceilings on deposits at commercial banks that were established during the Great Depression and phased out after 1980.

Repurchase Agreements Short-term agreements in which the seller sells a government security to a buyer and simultaneously agrees to buy it back on a later date at a higher price.

Required Reserves The amount of reserve assets that the Fed requires depository institutions to hold against outstanding checkable deposit liabilities.

Required Reserves The amount of reserve assets that the Fed requires a depository institution to hold.

Required Reserve Ratio (rD) The fraction of deposit liabilities that must be held by depository institutions as reserve assets.

Reserve Bank One of the 12 Federal Reserve Banks; each is located in a large city in its district

Reserve Need The projected amount of reserves to be supplied or withdrawn by open market operations to reach or keep the fed funds rate prescribed by the policy directive.

Reserves Assets that are held as either vault cash or reserve deposit accounts with the Fed.

Resolution Trust Corporation (RTC) A GSE created in 1989 in response to the savings and loan crisis that issued bonds and used the proceeds to dissolve or find buyers for the failed thrifts and their properties; The RTC went out of business on December 31, 1995, after completing its work

Retail Sweep Accounts A financial innovation that relabels deposit liabilities to nondeposit liabilities by "sweeping" balances out of transactions accounts that are subject to reserve requirements and into other accounts that are not.

Revalue Under a fixed exchange rate system, to increase the value of a country's currency.

Revenue Bonds Municipal bonds to be repaid out of the revenues from a specific project that the bonds financed.

Reverse Repurchase Agreements The Fed's simultaneous sale and purchase of securities for delivery the next day or in a few days to withdraw reserves on a temporary basis.

Revaluation Under fixed exchange rates, increase the value of a currency by the monetary authorities relative to the official reserve asset.

Risk Premium The extra return or interest that a lender is compensated with for accepting more risk.

Rolled Over The result when the government borrows to pay off maturing debt.

S

Saving Income not spent on consumption.

Savings and Loan Associations (S&Ls) Depository institutions established for the purpose of pooling the savings of local residents to finance the construction and purchase of homes; have offered checkable deposits since 1980.

Savings Associations S&Ls and savings banks.

Savings Banks Depository institutions set up to help finance the construction and purchase of homes; located mainly on the East Coast.

Savings Deposits Highly liquid deposits that can usually be withdrawn on demand but not by writing a check.

Seasoned Issuance The offering of new securities by a corporation that has outstanding previously issued securities.

Secondary Credit Rate The rate for short-term borrowing of reserves from the Fed by depository institutions experiencing financial difficulties.

Secondary Market The market in which previously issued financial securities are sold.

Secondary Stock Offering An offering of newly issued shares by a firm that already has outstanding publicly held shares.

Securities and Exchange Commission (SEC) A government agency created by the Securities and Exchange Act of 1934 that regulates disclosure rules for companies that issue publicly traded shares of stock; the SEC also regulates disclosure rules in secondary markets and monitors illegal and fraudulent behavior in securities markets.

Securities Industry Protection Corporation (SIPC) A nonprofit membership corporation established by Congress in 1970 that provides insurance up to $500,000 per investor to protect investors' securities from liquidation by the brokerage firm; U.S. registered brokers and dealers are required by law to join.

Securitization The process whereby relatively illiquid financial assets are packaged together and sold off to individual investors.

Seigniorage The difference between the cost of producing and distributing currency and any revenues earned.

Shelf Registration A procedure that permits a company to register a number of securities with the SEC and sell them over a two-year period rather than at the time of registration.

Short Sell Investors' instructions to brokers or dealers to borrow shares of stocks and sell them today with the guarantee that the investors will replace the borrowed stocks by a date in the future.

Short-Run Aggregate Supply Curve A curve showing the direct relationship between the overall price level and the level of real output that will be supplied in response to changes in demand before full adjustment of relative prices has taken place.

Simple Money Multiplier The reciprocal of the required reserve ratio, $1/rD$.

Smart Cards Plastic cards with a microprocessor chip that are used to make payments; the chip stores information that allows the payment to be validated.

Sources and Uses of Funds Statement A statement showing the sources and uses of funds for any sector.

Sources of Funds For any sector, income and borrowing.

Special Drawing Rights (SDRs) International reserve assets created by the IMF to supplement other international reserves.

Speculation The buying or selling of financial securities in the hopes of profiting from future price changes.

Speculative Bubble An irrational increase in stock prices accompanied by euphoric expectations.

Spot Market A market in which the trading of financial securities takes place instantaneously.

Stagflation A condition of concurrent high unemployment and high inflation.

Standard & Poor's, Moody's, and Fitch Investors Service The three major credit-rating agencies that evaluate a borrower's probability of default and assign the borrower to a particular risk class based on the probability that the issuer will fail tp pay back the principal and interest when due.

Standby Lines of Credit Lines of credit (commitments) for which a bank is liable but that do not show up on the balance sheet.

State and Local Government Bonds (Municipals) Long-term instruments issued by state and local governments to finance expenditures on schools, roads, and so on.

Stocks Equity claims that represent ownership of the net assets and income of a corporation.

Store of Value Something that retains its value over time.

Stored-Value Cards Plastic cards that have a magnetic strip that is swiped through a card reader to make payments; they are usually single use.

Strike Price The agreed-upon price in an options contract.

Stronger Version of the Efficient Markets Hypothesis The theory that the prices of all financial instruments not only reflect the optimal forecast of the financial instrument but also the true fundamental value of the instrument.

Student Loan Marketing Association (Sallie Mae) A GSE that issues securities with no explicit government guarantee and uses the proceeds to purchase student loans to increase the funds flowing into student loans and to make student loans more liquid.

Subordinated Debenture Bonds Bonds with no collateral backing but with a general claim after debenture bondholders have been paid.

Substitution-of-Foreign-Goods Effect When changes in the domestic price level cause consumers to substitute into relatively cheaper foreign goods or out of relatively more expensive foreign goods.

Supply of Loanable Funds The supply of borrowed funds originating from (1) household, business, government, and foreign net lenders or (2) the Fed through its provision of reserves.

Supply of Money The stock of money (M1), which includes currency in the hands of the public plus checkable deposits.

Supply Shock Any event that shifts the short-run aggregate supply curve.

Surplus Sector A sector whose combined surpluses of net lenders are greater than the combined deficits of net borrow.

Sweep Accounts A financial innovation that allows depository institutions to shift customers' funds out of checkable accounts that are subject to reserve requirements and into highly liquid money market deposit accounts (MMDAs) that are not.

Syndicate A group of investment banks, each of which underwrites a proportion of new securities offerings; reduces the risk to one investment bank of underwriting the entire new offering.

System Open Market Account (SOMA) The Fed's account of dollar-denominated Treasury securities, which are bought and sold by the Trading Desk to implement open market operations in accordance with policy directives.

System Repurchase Agreement When the Trading Desk of the Fed buys securities on a self-reversing, temporary basis in order to supply reserves on a temporary basis.

T

Term Structure of Interest Rates The relationship between yields and time to maturity.

Term to Maturity The length of time from the initial issue of a financial security until its maturity.

Theory of Rational Expectations The theory that expectations will on average be equal to the optimal forecast.

Thrifts Depository institutions known as S&Ls, savings banks, and credit unions.

Time Deposits Deposits that have a scheduled maturity and a penalty for early withdrawal.

Time Value of Money The terms on which one can trade off present purchasing power for future purchasing power; the interest rate.

"Too Big to Fail" The position adopted by FDIC regulators in 1984 whereby the failure of a large bank would be resolved using the purchase and assumption method rather than the payoff method.

Total Reserves Required reserves plus excess reserves.

Trade Balance The difference between merchandise exports and imports.

Trade Deficit Status when merchandise imports are greater than exports.

Trade Surplus Status when merchandise exports are greater than imports.

Transactions Costs The costs associated with borrowing and lending or making other exchanges.

Transactions Deposits Deposits that can be exchanged for currency and are used to make payments through writing a check or making an electronic transfer.

Transactions Motive A motive for holding money based on the need to make payments.

Treasury Notes Securities issued by the U.S. government with an original maturity of 1 to 10 years.

Treasury STRIPS Fixed government securities that allow investors to register and trade ownership of the interest (coupon) payments and the principal separately.

Trustee An expert (usually working for a bank or trust company) who interprets the provisions of a bond offering for investors and who sees that the terms and condition of the offering are fulfilled.

U

Uniform Reserve Requirements Reserve requirements that apply to particular types of deposits and are the same across all depository institutions.

Unit of Account A standardized accounting unit such as the dollar that provides a consistent measure of value.

U.S. Government Agency Securities Long-term bonds issued by various government agencies including those that support real estate lending and student loans.

U.S. Government Securities Long-term debt instruments of the U.S. government with original maturities of 2 to 30 years.

U.S. Treasury Bills (T-bills) Short-term debt instruments of the U.S. government with typical maturities of 3 to 12 months.

Uses of Funds For any sector, current spending and changes in financial instruments held.

Universal Reserve Requirements Reserve requirements to which all depository institutions are subject.

Usury Ceilings Maximum interest rates that FIs may charge on certain loans.

V

Variable-Rate Mortgages Mortgages who interest rate is adjusted periodically to reflect changing market conditions.

Veterans Administration (VA) A federal agency that, among other things, insures mortgage loans made by privately owned financial institutions up to a certain amount if the borrowers meet certain conditions, including being military veterans.

W

Wealth Effect or Real Balances Effect The change in the supply of real money balances, which causes an increase or decrease in wealth, when the price level changes for a given supply of nominal money balances.

Wholesale Sweep Accounts Wholesale accounts, created in the 1970s, with balances that have been swept out of deposit accounts subject to reserve accounts and into money market instruments such as money market mutual funds, Eurodollar deposits, and repurchase agreements.

World Bank An investment bank created in 1944 that issues bonds to make long-term loans at low interest rates to poor countries for economic development projects.

Y

Yield Curve A graphical representation of the relationship between interest rates (yields) on particular securities and their terms to maturity.

Yield to Maturity The return on a bond held to maturity, which includes both the interest return and any capital gain or loss.

Z

Zero-Coupon Bonds Corporate bonds sold at a discount with the difference between the amount paid for the bond and the amount received at maturity equal to the interest.

Index